A Companion to the
Philosophy of Mind

Blackwell Companions to Philosophy————

This benchmark student reference series offers a comprehensive survey of philosophy as a whole. Written by many of today's leading figures, each volume provides lucid and engaging coverage of the key figures, terms and movements of the main subdisciplines of philosophy. Each essay is fully cross-referenced and supported by a bibliography. Taken together, it provides the ideal basis for course use and an invaluable work of reference.

Already published:

Forthcoming:

*Blackwell
Companions to
Philosophy*

A Companion to the Philosophy of Mind

Edited by

SAMUEL GUTTENPLAN

Copyright © Blackwell Publishers Ltd, 1994, 1995
Editorial organization copyright © Samuel Guttenplan, 1994, 1995

The right of Samuel Guttenplan to be identified as author of this work has been
asserted in accordance with the Copyright, Designs and Patents Act 1988.

First published 1994
First published in paperback 1995
Reprinted 1996 (twice), 1997, 1998, 2000

Blackwell Publishers Ltd
108 Cowley Road
Oxford OX4 1JF
UK

Blackwell Publishers Inc.
350 Main Street
Malden, Massachusetts 02148
USA

British Library Cataloguing in Publication Data

A CIP catalogue record for this book is available from the British Library.

Library of Congress Cataloging-in-Publication Data
A Companion to the philosophy of mind / edited by Samuel Guttenplan.
     p.   cm.– (Blackwell companions to philosophy)
   Includes bibliographical references and index.
   ISBN 0–631–17953–4 — ISBN 0–631–19996–9 (Pbk)
   1. Philosophy of mind. I. Guttenplan, Samuel D. II. Series.
   BD418.3.C62   1993   93–39595
   128'.2–dc20   CIP

Typeset in 10.5 on 12.5pt Photina
By Acorn Bookwork, Salisbury, Wilts.
Printed and bound in Great Britain by MPG Books Ltd, Bodmin, Cornwall

This book is printed on acid-free paper

Contents

Contributors

Lynne Rudder Baker
*University of Massachusetts,
Amherst*

William Bechtel
University of Washington, St Louis

Ned Block
MIT

Michael E. Bratman
Stanford University

Malcolm Budd
University College London

Alex Byrne
MIT

Christopher Cherniak
University of Maryland

Noam Chomsky
MIT

Paul M. Churchland
University of California, San Diego

Andy Clark
University of Washington, St Louis

B. Jack Copeland
*University of Canterbury,
New Zealand*

Tim Crane
University College London

Donald Davidson
University of California, Berkeley

Lawrence H. Davis
University of Missouri – St Louis

Ronald de Sousa
University of Toronto

Daniel C. Dennett
Tufts University, Boston

Fred Dretske
Stanford University

Howard L. Fields
*University of California,
San Francisco*

Jerry A. Fodor
*Rutgers and City University of
New York*

Sebastian Gardner
*Birkbeck College, University of
London*

Jay L. Garfield
Hampshire College, Amherst

Alan Garnham
University of Sussex

Alvin I. Goldman
University of Arizona

Samuel Guttenplan
Birkbeck College, University of London

John Haldane
University of St Andrews

D. W. Hamlyn
Birkbeck College, University of London

William D. Hart
University of Illinois at Chicago

Christopher Hookway
University of Birmingham

Jim Hopkins
King's College London

Terence E. Horgan
University of Memphis

Annette Karmiloff-Smith
MRC Cognitive Development Unit and University College, London

Jaegwon Kim
Brown University

Kathleen Lennon
University of Hull

Ernie LePore
Rutgers University

David Lewis
Princeton University

William G. Lycan
University of North Carolina

Edwin McCann
University of Southern California

Colin McGinn
Rutgers University

Brian P. McLaughlin
Rutgers University

J. Christopher Maloney
University of Arizona

M. G. F. Martin
University College London

Kirstie Morrison
Wolfson College, Oxford

John Morton
MRC Cognitive Development Unit, London

Norton Nelkin
University of New Orleans

Brian O'Shaughnessy
King's College London

David Papineau
King's College London

Christopher Peacocke
University of Oxford

John Perry
Stanford University

Donald D. Price
Medical College of Virginia

Hilary Putnam
Harvard University

Georges Rey
University of Maryland

David M. Rosenthal
City University of New York

James Russell
University of Cambridge

Stephen Schiffer
City University of New York

Robert Schwartz
University of Wisconsin –
Milwaukee

John R. Searle
University of California, Berkeley

Gabriel Segal
King's College London

Sydney Shoemaker
Cornell University

Paul Smolensky
University of Colorado at Boulder
and *Johns Hopkins*

Robert Stalnaker
MIT

Dennis W. Stampe
University of Wisconsin – Madison

Stephen Stich
Rutgers University

Michael Tye
King's College London

Barbara Von Eckardt
University of Nebraska – Lincoln

Preface

Like most volumes in the Blackwell Companions to Philosophy series, this one contains alphabetically arranged entries covering its subject matter. However, there are differences between this Companion and the others, which it might be helpful to highlight.

1 *An Essay on Mind*, which forms Part I of this book, is intended to provide an alternative, non-alphabetic, way of navigating through the entries. No doubt the alphabetic arrangement will suit those who are familiar with philosophy of mind, but this will not be the position of all readers. The idea is for the reader to use the *Essay* to get his or her bearings in respect of some topic and then to pursue it in more depth by reading the entry which is cross-referenced in the *Essay*. SMALL CAPITAL LETTERS are used to indicate cross-references, as they are in individual entries throughout the *Companion*. The *Essay* is not a compendious survey of the whole of philosophy of mind as those areas which are extensively covered in the entries are touched on only lightly in it. Instead, it is a selective narrative which attempts to adumbrate a picture of the mind, and some of the philosophical problems it generates. It is my hope that it will tempt, rather than merely introduce, the reader into the subject.

2 There is a tendency to identify many viewpoints in the philosophy of mind by the authors with whom they are most closely associated. One often hears views described, for example, as 'Davidsonian', where this name conjures up a number of theses which together have been influential in the subject. It was this fact which led me to commission a number of 'self-profiles': straightforward accounts by certain well-known philosophers of their particular conception of the mind (or at least some of the central features of that conception).

3 Reflecting sometimes the lack of agreement, and sometimes the mere difference of approach which exists in respect of even basic notions in the philosophy of mind, I have in some cases commissioned two entries on the same topic, and these are always marked by (1) or (2) after the entry heading. Also, by commissioning longer entries than one finds in some of the other Companions, I have encouraged authors to go beyond introductory material. As a result, there is much contained in the volume which will be of interest to those who already work in the relevant fields.

4 Within philosophy, the philosophy of mind is easily the most active sub-discipline. It is virtually impossible to pick up a mainstream philosophy journal without finding one or more articles on some topic in philosophy of mind, and

there is a constant change in what are considered to be the most burning issues. To some extent this made the choice of entry headings difficult, and this was compounded by the fact that philosophy of mind has become inextricably linked to such related areas as computational modelling and cognitive psychology. However, I did not want to make this a Companion to all of these areas – to the whole of what is often called 'cognitive science'. So, whilst there are carefully selected entries on fields adjacent to the philosophy of mind, the focus of the book is definitely philosophical.

I cannot say that editing this Companion has been an easy task, but I have learned a great deal from it. And here I refer to what I have learned about the philosophy of mind and not to my now greater knowledge of the difficulties of working with sixty or so contributors. (Though that too is undoubtedly something that could be put to work in the philosophy of mind. *See* FOLK PSYCHOLOGY.) What I hope now is that others too will learn from it.

In compiling the original list of entries and in matching them to prospective authors. Ned Block gave me much helpful advice. Special thanks are due to Kirstie Morrison for the work she did in providing both philosophical commentary and editorial control over what turned out to be a typescript some twelve inches thick.

Samuel Guttenplan
Birkbeck College
London

PART I

AN ESSAY ON MIND

Preliminaries

Human beings *definitely* have minds. Other creatures on this planet or elsewhere *may* have minds. Inanimate objects such as rocks *do not* have minds. These claims will no doubt seem unexceptionable to all but the most perverse. Yet in attempting to understand them fully, the original intuitions on which they are based can get pushed and stretched to such an extent that, in the end and without any perversity, we can come to have doubts. It is as if our everyday and unexamined conception of the mind contains features that, when examined, undermine the very conception itself.

This observation may strike some as an unnecessarily pessimistic way to begin an introduction, but such a reaction ignores the central role that perplexity has always played in philosophy. In most disciplines, problems define at most the outer boundaries – the frontiers – of investigation, not the subject matter itself. For example, whilst the *research* programme of molecular biology is determined by what it is about biological structure and chemistry that we do *not* know, the subject itself – what someone would study in a textbook – is a growing compendium of what we have already found out. With philosophy, matters are, if anything, the reverse. Uninformed opinion sometimes mockingly implies there *isn't* any thing like philosophical knowledge, that philosophy makes no advances. This is not true. There has been over the centuries a considerable accretion of insight and analysis that could count as philosophical knowledge. However, in philosophy this accumulation serves at most as a background. The core of any philosophical subject matter – what is distinctive about it – is not what we know, but what continues to puzzle and perplex us. Indeed, it would not be an exaggeration to say that when someone speaks about 'The philosophy of X' for some specification of X, what is intended is a budget of unresolved questions – questions whose very form is sometimes a matter of intense debate. And even this way of putting it is not strong enough. For sometimes one finds not merely questions, but the dizzying prospect of paradox which threatens to overwhelm any attempt to think about some subject matter in a systematic way.

Nowhere is this shown more clearly than in the philosophy of mind. In trying to lay out our supposed wisdom about the mind, and, further, in trying to integrate that putative knowledge into our wider understanding of the world of nature, we end up with the fascinating, stubborn and even paradoxical problems that have come to define the subject matter of philosophy of mind. And, as was noted above, the very stubbornness of these problems has sometimes tempted philosophers into proposing radical solutions – solutions that challenge the original starting points of the investigation.

This Essay will outline the trajectory leading from our initial conception of the mind to the problems that can be uncovered in respect of that conception, and finally to the kinds of resolution that have been suggested for these problems. At numerous points, the outline can be filled in by consulting the entries that are highlighted in the text by small capital letters. Since there are problems enough in the philosophy of mind itself, I don't want to add to their number by making you wonder at each stage where we are headed. So, considering the mind to be something like a newly discovered territory, here is a brief account of what you will find in each of the three stages of this Essay.

Stage 1 Surface Exploration
Surveying a new territory – finding out what kinds of resources there are – we first have to make a sort of surface map and then try to bring some minimal order to what is there recorded. Thus, our first task will be to chart the mind and note the main features of its landscape.

Stage 2 Digging Deeper
Having a reasonably neat map of the terrain is only the first step, for surface features often have a deceptive appearance. In this second stage we shall begin to probe the surface landscape with various questions; this probing will reveal faults and fissures not evident, as it were, to the naked eye. The questions we shall ask are of the sort often labelled 'philosophical', but this does not mean that they are specialist in any way. Indeed, the fascinating thing is precisely that so many problems and puzzles begin to emerge when we ask certain obvious questions about the lay of the land characterized at stage 1.

Stage 3 Bedrock
The mysteries of what lies just under the surface of our initial map might well be thought work enough for philosophers of mind. But sometimes it is necessary to dig even deeper in order to understand the contours of the upper layers. In particular, it has seemed to many philosophers that we can never really be certain of what the mind is like without understanding how the whole of the structure sits on the relatively stable bedrock of the physical world. This is the world of material stuff, of atoms and molecules weaving their patterns in accordance with physical laws. We know that at the extreme limit of physical complexity are such things as biological organisms and the physiological structures that make them up. We know also, or at least strongly suspect, that certain of these physiological structures – brains and their attendant neuro-physiological mechanisms – are deeply implicated in the very possibility of a mental life. But how? How, if at all, does what was charted at stages 1 and 2 fit onto the bedrock of physical reality described by sciences such as physics, chemistry and biology? This will be the third and final stage of our investigation.

The metaphor that runs through this introduction is intended as more than a rhetorical flourish: it is extremely important that each of the stages be kept as separate as possible, and it may be easier to do this if we think of the mind as being subject to different layers of exploration. Stage 1 maps the surface, stage 2 explores just below the features of that surface, and stage 3 brings to bear a kind of geological knowledge on what we have already uncovered. Less metaphorically, the difficulties we will come across at stage 2 – certain philosophical problems of the mind – arise from the very conception of the mind with which we began. The difficulties considered in stage 3 – problems about how the mind is related to the world as described by science – have an origin outside that conception, though they are clearly not independent of it. As you will see, it is not always easy to keep these investigations separate – some ways of formulating various specific questions in these two areas can make them sound more or less the same. But it is worth trying, since not a little confusion can result from mixing them up.

Stage 1: Mapping out the territory

1.1 First Steps

The starting point for our map of the mind is description. With the minimum of theoretical (that is, philosophical) baggage, we need to describe those features of the mind that figure in the landscape we are trying to map. And, unlike any real charting of a territory, this task will not require field trips. Without going anywhere, each of us is perfectly well-placed to do the job, since we come equipped with (at least one of) the very things we aim to describe. Of course, it may well be that the proximity of the mind can be, in the end, a source of error. As you will come to appreciate, there can be two views here: one stresses that the mind is special precisely because it is knowable from the 'inside', whilst the other view, insisting that real knowledge must be observer-independent, demands that we study the mind from somewhere more object-ively 'outside'. Exactly what the 'inside/outside' metaphor comes to will be considered in later sections, but for the present we can proceed without worrying too much about this.

Ideally, I should like to ask my readers to think about how they would answer the following question: what things or phenomena count as mental, as showing the presence of minds? These answers would then serve as the starting point of our investigation. Though circumstances do not allow me to gather this information directly, I can do the next best thing. For, over the years, I have handed out a questionnaire to students before they have done any philosophy of mind, asking them to list the sorts of things that they would count as showing the presence of minds. Below is a lightly edited collation of their answers.

ability to learn	acting intentionally	agency
awareness	believing	building a house
ability to represent	choosing	ability to value
consciousness	deciding	desiring a holiday
dreaming	emotions	experiencing a pain
experiencing happiness	feelings	getting the point of a joke
having a point of view	having free will	hearing a violin
imagining	intending to write an essay	introspecting
loving	melancholy	painting a picture
perceiving	perceiving	pleasure

reasoning	reflecting on a problem	remembering
seeing a tree	self-consciousness	speaking
theorizing	the self	thinking
understanding language	understanding symbols	wanting
will power	anger	

No doubt one could think of ways in which this list could be altered. First, among other things, there might be felt to be a lot of unnecessary redundancy. For example, *seeing a tree* seems to be at the same level of generality as *hearing a violin*, and both would count as *perceiving* something. It is thus not clear why we need to have all three in the list. In defence of my editing let me say this: in response to my questionnaire, students tend to include items of radically different degrees of generality. This may itself provide important clues and, therefore, items should not be left out merely because of certain intuitions about what goes with what – at least not at this point.

Secondly, it should be remembered that the list I have given is a collation of the answers given by many different students, and you may not agree with a number of the choices. Most importantly, you might feel that some item does not belong on the list – is not genuinely of the mind. For example, it must be said that a number of students argue that actions should be counted as at most the *outcome* of what goes on in minds, and therefore as not deserving the same status as such things as feelings. To this I can only say that further discussion can show if this is a reasonable attitude. For there were many students convinced that human action was just as important to the characterization of the mind as other phenomena, and we must not begin our inquiry by closing off the possibility that they are right.

Let us call the subject matter that is defined by the above list the 'mental realm'. This somewhat grand-sounding title has a certain vagueness, but the items on the list are such a heterogeneous bunch that any less vague term would prejudice further discussion.

1.2 Order out of chaos

When discussing this list, it is possible to query various items and to see why they were chosen for inclusion. This interchange is important because it leads directly to the next task – putting the features into the order necessary for a map. Merely having a list of landmarks in the mental realm is not enough. A map must show the relationships among them.

The first thing to note about the list is that it contains broadly two sorts of item: (i) things people (or other possessors of minds) can be said to do or undergo which are naturally reported by verbs; and (ii) things that are, roughly, the products or outcomes of such activity and which are described by nouns. For example, *thinking of a number between 1 and 10* is certainly something done, whilst *the thought of a number between 1 and 10* could be considered the product or upshot of some such activity. We use a verb to describe the former and a noun phrase to describe the latter. (But don't think of 'product' in its most literal sense. Certainly, I do not want to be taken as saying that a thought is *manufactured* by thinking.)

Leaving 'products' on one side for the moment, it seems to me (and to the students with whom this was discussed) that there are three importantly different kinds of thing which minds get up to and which are represented in the list in more or less generality. With several specific examples of each, these main categories of the mental realm are given as follows:

Experiencing (having a pain, 'seeing' stars when you bump your head)

Attitudinizing (wanting a piece of chocolate cake, believing that the Earth is round)

Acting (signing a cheque, making a chair, reaching for a glass)

Each of these is an activity of mind, at least in the sense that the classificatory word is in each case a verb, though that alone does not tell us much. Moreover, there is bound to be some puzzlement about the second of these items. Experiencing and acting are themselves represented in the original list and I have simply drafted them in to be the names of general categories in the mental realm. But we do not ordinarily speak about 'attitudinizing' and this term requires, and will be given, further comment. However, everyone knows (sort of) what it is to want or believe something, so I shall let the examples serve for the moment, returning later to the mysterious 'attitudinizing'.

Insofar as each of the above is an activity, each of them will have a characteristic or associated 'product'. They are as follows:

Experiencing ---------> consciousness

Attitudinizing ------------> attitudes

Acting ---------------> actions

It might be thought odd that I have used the word 'consciousness' as the partner of the activity of experiencing rather than 'experience'. In fact, nothing much hangs on this, and my reason for having broken the symmetry is simply that 'experience' can be either a noun or a verb, whereas what was wanted was something more clearly a noun. Also, the point of the strange word 'attitudinizing' might now be clearer. Speaking of such things as beliefs and wants as attitudes is closer to ordinary usage. Nonetheless, to want something – to adopt that attitude – is a kind of doing; it is something we report with a verb. All I did was to make up the general verb which (interestingly) seems to be lacking in our language.

As you will come to see, these three pairs are particularly important to anyone trying to chart the mind's landscape. Like mountains, they constitute the most prominent features. Yet before using them as fixed points in our map-making activities, I should like to say something specific about each of them. Considering that they all figure, at least initially, in most people's inventory of the mental realm, they are surprisingly different from one another.

1.2.1 Experiencing and Consciousness

The laughter of the class, graduating from the first shrill bark of surprise into a deliberately aimed hooting, seemed to crowd against him, to crush the privacy that he so much desired, a privacy in which he could be alone with his pain, gauging its strength, estimating its duration, inspecting its anatomy. The pain extended a feeler into his head, and unfolded its wet wings along the walls of his thorax, so that he felt, in his sudden scarlet blindness, to be himself a large bird waking from sleep. The blackboard, milky slate smeared with the traces of last night's washing, clung to his consciousness like a membrane. The pain seemed to be displacing with its own hairy segments, his heart and lungs; as its grip swelled in his throat he felt he was holding his brain like a morsel on a platter high out of hungry reach. (From *The Centaur* by John Updike, pp. 3–4)

Perhaps the most persistent view that I have come across from students is that our ability to experience and, thereby, to be conscious or aware of certain things is a central activity of the mind. Indeed, some consider that the very essence of the mind lies here. But what sort of things figure in this awareness? Well, as the above quotation shows – graphically – there seems to be a special kind of awareness of the state of our bodies and of our perceptual interactions with the world. If you have been damaged or if certain bodily events are taking place, then this will usually result in a consciousness of pain or pleasure, pressure or fatigue, hunger or satiation, etc. Or, if you are seeing something there is often a particular consciousness of what it is like to have such a perception; the teacher described in the above passage sees the blackboard, and, in seeing it, experiences it in a particular way. Additionally there is a kind of experience that seems related to these but does not apparently depend on there being a particular kind of damage or event in the body, or a perception. Think of the moods and feelings that rise in us and accompany our other activities, often for no obvious reason. A sense of well-being, a lurking anxiety that all is not going well, these are just two of the many shades of experience that are like pains and bodily pleasure, but which do not seem to have a particular location in the way those do.

An important thing to notice about all of the above phenomena is that they count as experience of what goes on 'inside', even when, as in the case of perception, there is something external to our consciousness. Walking down a city street in the cool of March, you feel the wind in your face as it is funnelled through the gaps in the taller buildings, you have the experience of greys and browns of drab buildings and leafless trees, and you hear the hum of the traffic punctuated here and there by louder sounds of impatient drivers using their horns or trucks accelerating away from traffic lights. The wind, buildings, trees and traffic are 'outside' of us, but we nonetheless count our experience of them – what goes on when we perceive them – as 'inside'.

This whole show of experience – inside and outside, repeated in thousands of varying ways as we move from place to place – is what counts for many as the core of the mental realm. The view of some of my students tends to be: to have a mind is nothing other than to have what is often described as a 'stream of consciousness' – a kind of show that is going on most of the time. And the metaphor of a show is the one that crops up most often when I ask for a description of experience – a description of what it is like to be the possessor of a stream of consciousness. 'It is as if you were in a cinema watching a film from so close and with such involvement that you were only aware of *what* was happening and not *that* it was happening on a film in an auditorium.' Fine, I say to this recurrent sort of answer to my question, but it seems to require us to understand what it is to be *aware* of a film in some particularly close way, so it is not all that much help in telling someone what awareness itself is. Moreover, this account seems to apply best only to our perceptual experience, to the experience – itself inside – of what is happening outside. But what about such things as pains and other wholly inner sensations? The needed revision often runs as follows: 'Well, it's not exactly like the show in a cinema, but it does seem to involve witnessing various things – observing them, paying attention to them – even if sometimes from a very short metaphorical distance. When I have a pain, I direct my attention to it, just in the way that I direct my attention to my present experience of, say, colours in my visual field. This is sort of like a film or theatrical performance which I can witness and with respect to which I can differentially direct my attention from one character to another.' (*See* CONSCIOUSNESS.)

Does this sort of metaphorical description help? Perhaps it points you in the direction of what I mean to speak about under the heading of 'experience', but I doubt it is much more informative than that. Indeed, it raises more questions than it answers: for example, who or what does the directing of attention in this case? 'The self' comes the reply. But this reply also gets us into very deep waters. Is the self separate from experiential activity and its attendant consciousness or are they united rather as the dancer and the dance? Here we are beginning to see some of the problems that lie just beneath the surface of our conception of experience and consciousness, and for the present we shall leave well enough alone. In any case, perhaps there is not much more that one can do in directly characterizing experience than to reach for metaphors such as are found in Updike's wonderfully lurid description of a pain.

10

1.2.2 Attitudinizing and Attitudes

All this was lost on Alice, who was still looking intently along the road, shading her eyes with one hand. 'I see somebody now!' she exclaimed at last. 'But he's coming very slowly – and what curious attitudes he goes into!' (For the Messenger kept skipping up and down, and wriggling like an eel, as he came along, with his great hands spread out like fans on each side.)

'Not at all,' said the King. 'He's an Anglo-Saxon Messenger – and those are Anglo-Saxon Attitudes. He only does them when he's happy. (From *Through the Looking Glass* by Lewis Carroll, p. 175)

In the subtle shift of perspective in this passage – the shift from attitude as posture to attitude as a feature of a mind – Carroll has given us several important hints about mental attitudes. We are invited to imagine the Anglo-Saxon Messenger as taking up odd postures, setting his limbs in awkward or uncomfortable positions. However, in ways it is perhaps more tactful for me to leave unsaid, the Anglo-Saxons have the reputation of having odd (even sometimes uncomfortable) attitudes – beliefs and desires – in respect of a variety of subjects.

The appeal of this passage is that it effortlessly manages to shift our attention from a set of bizarre postures to a set of perhaps equally bizarre attitudes towards life. In using the two senses of 'attitude' in the same context, Carroll succeeds in getting us to pause over something that we don't usually bother much about – the aptness of the word in its 'posture' sense for characterizing such things as beliefs, desires and the like. A posture is something we manœuvre ourselves into and which is therefore observable in our behaviour. Similarly, we usually tell what someone believes or desires by things done and said – by behaviour; an attitude in this sense is a mental state which we often 'read' off from behaviour. Moreover, it is true of some attitudes, even in the posturing sense, that they are directed or indicative of something. When someone is said to adopt a menacing attitude towards another, what is in question is not merely how the first person is standing, though some such bodily position is being described. Rather what is special about a 'menacing attitude' is that it is a posture that is directed towards someone or something. And of course this is precisely what is typical of such things as beliefs and desires. They are not merely states of mind we discern through behaviour, they are states of mind that have a special kind of directedness. I don't just believe or desire – I believe that something is the case, or I desire someone or something.

The two crucial defining features that any case of attitudinizing displays are:

(a) A kind of behaviour that is typically characteristic of the particular attitude in question. (Imagine how you could tell the difference between someone who wanted something, believed something, intended something, etc.)

11

(b) A 'something' towards which the attitudinizing is directed, as when we say that:

Harry believes *that his telephone is out of order*, or
Jane desires *a new car*, or
Bill intends *to boil a kettle*.

Note that the items towards which the attitude is directed can be quite various: in the above three examples we have these three items:

that the telephone is out of order
a new car
to boil a kettle.

Focusing on the sentences we use to report attitudes and borrowing a term from grammar, we shall call the 'something' towards which attitudes are directed the *complement* of the attitude. That is, in the sentences given in (b) there are complement phrases which report the particular direction of the attitude. Note that the first of these has a declarative sentence as a complement. This is important because sentences like this are typically used to say, truly or falsely, how things are. One way to put this is to say that declarative sentences express PROPOSITIONS. Moreover, it seems possible (even if it might sound awkward in given cases) to report virtually all attitudes using complement phrases that contain whole sentences. We could have expressed the other examples in (b) as:

Jane desires that she has a new car.
Bill intends that he will make the kettle boil.

Because complements of belief reports typically contain a complete declarative sentence that expresses a proposition, and because the other attitudes can be twisted into this shape, philosophers have settled on the idea that the products of attitudinizing can all be called 'PROPOSITIONAL ATTITUDES'. So, the Anglo-Saxon messenger strikes odd postural and propositional attitudes.

Note, by the way, that one can also call the item to which an attitude is directed its *content*. The notion of a 'complement' seems to many to be too grammatical and too closely tied to the report of an attitude, whereas the word 'content' seems to capture something about the attitude itself. But for the present it won't matter much whether you think of the attitudes as having complements or contents.

It remains to be seen just how much trouble the propositional attitudes create for our understanding of the mental realm, but it is difficult to deny that they represent a large part of our everyday conception of that realm. And this comes as a bit of a surprise to those who are convinced that experience is the central feature of the mind. For, whatever else they are like, the propositional attitudes are not obviously items of experience. For example, suppose someone were to ask you, out of the blue, whether the present government will be returned to power at the next election. I have no doubt that your answer would be readily forthcoming and would begin like this: I believe that . . . But to get to this answer did you have to search the elusive stream of consciousness we just discussed? Does that stream contain a sort of banner on which is written 'the present government will not be returned to power at the next election'? Hardly. Of course, I don't doubt that images of governments – a sort of collage of images of politicians, government buildings, television coverage of elections and perhaps even images of words – might be prompted by the original question. Yet these do not constitute the belief itself. In fact, those not so wedded to the experiential picture of the mind as to rule out everything else tend to report that consciousness plays very little role in our ability to know and say what attitudes we have.

This last observation points the way down a number of difficult roads. If consciousness figures less (and sometimes not at all) in our apprehension of our beliefs, then how do we tell what we believe, want, intend, etc.? We certainly don't do it in the way we tell these things about other people, i.e. by looking at what they do and say. Moreover, what relation is there between the 'self' which made its appearance in our discussion of experience and the item that is the subject of attitude reports? In what way is the 'I' of 'I am in pain' related to the 'I' of 'I believe that it will snow'? These sorts of question are typical of the next stage of investigation. But our interest at present has only been in the kind of thing that comes under the headings 'attitudinizing' and 'attitude', and we have completed that task. The activity of attitudinizing results in our having attitudes towards the ways things are or might be; each attitude has its typical manifestation in behaviour; and all can be provided with propositional contents that are reported by complement sentences.

1.2.3 Acting and Actions

The astonishing thing about action is that it is possible at all. For, if a man is making a chair, you will find a physical causal explanation of the movement of each piece of wood from its initial to its final setting; everything that happens is in accordance with law; but you will look throughout this world or universe forever in vain for an analogous physical explanation of their coming together in the form they did, a form that mirrors human need and the human body itself. (Try it.) (From 'Observation and the Will' (*Journal of Philosophy*, 1963) by Brian O'Shaughnessy)

As I mentioned earlier, there is a strong tendency to overlook actions when thinking about what to count as items in the mental realm. Those who find themselves only reluctantly admitting attitudes into the fold, dig in their heels at what they regard as too physical a thing to count as anything mental. Such is the pull of the idea that the mental consists in the 'inner' – the show of

13

experience and consciousness – that actions can seem just too far removed from this centre to count as anything more than the mind's wake as it moves through the physical world. But this view is by no means universal, and one would do well to listen to those who oppose it.

The point of the above passage is to illustrate just how difficult it is to fit actions into the picture of the world encouraged by science. Thus, whilst each movement of the arms and hands, hammer and nails might well be explicable in terms of science, the fact that all these things come together as the making of a chair can seem quite mysterious. Discussion of how the mental realm fits in with the scientific picture of the world will only come in stage 3 of this introduction. But the situation described in the passage can be used to illustrate something more pertinent to our present concerns.

Begin by supposing that everything is as described in the passage except that the agent making the chair is invisible. To an unsuspecting witness the pieces of wood seem to rise up and be nailed and glued in place, and the chair just comes into being. This would of course be astonishing, but we can leave this on one side for the moment. What I want to ask is this: would the witness actually observe the action, the making of the chair? Clearly, by hypothesis, the agent goes unseen, but if you are one of those who think of the action as nothing but some sort of change in the physical world, you should be prepared to say that the action is seen, even if not the actor. Yet that is surely not how we would describe it. Why? Well, the very idea of an action – even of a purely 'physical' action – seems to require us to identify some sort of mental component. As the passage notes, were there not human desires and needs, as well as the further beliefs, desires and intentions to fulfil them, at work, then we would not have the faintest idea of what was going on. When we do see the actor, we see some or all of these attitudes *in* the transformation of the materials, and unless we can see the mind in the process unfolding before us, we simply don't count that process as an action; for all we know it might just be the accidental product of some strange cosmic wind.

The idea that an action is in this way at least partly a mental phenomenon is what one of my students had in mind with the comment: 'actions are the mind's purposes in movement'. But those who insist that actions are not themselves mental, still have something to say. Here is a typical rejoinder:

> What the example shows is that you couldn't imagine the pieces coming together unless there was some mind *orchestrating* the movements. But the action itself – the physical movement of the pieces – is not mental. What happens is that you see these movements – the action – and then *infer* that there are mental states directing them. In seeing the action, you don't literally *see* the mind.

This rejoinder throws up many intricate problems and these must await further discussion in stages 2 and 3. However, whatever we end up saying about an action such as making a chair, it must be pointed out that the class of things

14

called actions is much broader than we have so far allowed. Making a chair is what is called a 'physical action' – an action in which some change is effected in some physical object or event. Examples of this kind of action are what most people think of when they are asked to imagine an action taking place, and it is this kind of action that leads to the greatest disagreement in measuring the boundaries of the mental realm. However, there is another kind of action, which has been staring us in the face, the mental status of which must be beyond doubt. I have in mind here the very activities of experiencing and atti-tudinizing. Recall that I was careful to insist that the main categories of the mental realm had both an activity and a product sense: *experiencing* and con-sciousness, *attitudinizing* and attitudes, as well as acting and actions. But surely, for example, to direct one's attention to some item in the stream of con-sciousness – to experience it – is nothing short of an action, and a purely mental one at that. Moreover, once you begin to think about it, there seems to be a whole host of other things that we do which are 'in the mind' in this way. Think of your favourite colour! Work out (but don't say) the sum of 15 and 22! When you accede to these requests, you are certainly doing something – acting – only in neither case is there any ordinary change wrought in your physical environment. These episodes of thought and inference would thus seem to be the tip of a very large iceberg consisting of actions whose claims to belong in the mental realm are unimpeachable. (*See* ACTION.)

As with experience and attitudinizing, each case of an action comes with a subject (SELF), or, perhaps more appropriately in the case of action, an *agent*. Indeed, just as for particular items of consciousness or attitudes, it is simply impossible to have an action without an agent. The kind of impossibility here seems to be conceptual: we cannot conceive of an unowned pain, a subjectless belief, nor can we conceive of an action that lacks an agent. And now we have another element to add to the problem raised earlier: what relations obtain between the 'I' of 'I am in pain', and 'I believe that my keys are in the cookie jar' and the 'I' of 'I pruned the ceanothus too late in the year'? Clearly, there is an enormous pull in favour of saying that the items picked out by each pronoun are one and the same self. Indeed, this tends to be such a universally held view among my students that it takes them some time to see that there might be a problem – that the differences between experiencing, attitudinizing and acting might make it less than obvious why one and the same thing does all three.

1.3 Estimating Distances

As was mentioned earlier, experience, attitude and action are the three fixed points in the mental landscape. All that remains then before we are ready to produce a sketch-map of the terrain is some way to locate all the other items (from the first list) in respect of these landmarks. If this was more a real than a metaphorical map-making exercise, what would be required would be some way to estimate the distances and directions of each of these items from one or more of the fixed points. But, unlike the real case, there is more to it than mere spatial distance and direction. For as we have seen, the three categories are quite different from one another. Indeed they seem only to share this one feature: they are all reckoned to belong to the mental realm. So, it is no straightforward matter to decide how to locate the other items. For example, take the case of emotions such as anger. Should we show them to be closer to experience or to attitude? And what about acting? There is certainly a case for saying that emotions are expressed in action. Clearly, emotions share some features with each of experience, attitude and action. But which features? Before we can do any map-making we have to discuss the grounds on which we decide how near or how far to place an item with respect to our three fixed points.

Just to keep the metaphor going, you can think of the features or respects that distinguish the three main categories as like dimensions. Thus, there are a number of ways in which, for example, experience differs from attitude. To locate some particular item on the map what we have to do is to say it is *more* like experience in such-and-such a respect and less like it in another. It is the possibility of speaking this way that allows us to describe these respects as dimensions. But what are these respects and where do they come from? The list is as follows:

Observability,
Accessibility,
Expressibility,
Directionality,
Theoreticity.

As with everything discussed at this surface-mapping stage, they have their basis in the untutored judgments most people would volunteer. In that sense they come from the same source as the list with which we began. However, the fact that I have had to invent my own names for these dimensions does not mean that I am imposing my particular views on the shape of the final map. For, though the labels are mine, the conclusions reached about each of the dimensions is distilled from discussion with the students who supplied the data for the original questionnaire. So, I expect that the brief discussions below will both clarify the labels and strike familiar chords.

1.3.1 *Observability*

Confronted with a mind (someone else's), how easy is it to tell whether you are in the presence of experiencing, attitudinizing or acting? This is not meant to be a deep question. There is a long tradition in philosophy of considering how, if at all, we can justify our faith in the mindedness of others. This is not what we are up to here. Assume that others do have minds, that the extreme sceptical stance is inappropriate, and ask yourself this: how easy is it to tell just by looking that some mind is experiencing something, maintaining an attitude towards something, or acting? To many, at least part of the answer is straight-forward. Philosophical argument might well shake our convictions in respect of all three, but it is certainly easier to wreak sceptical havoc in respect of experi-encing than in respect of acting. The usual thought is that we can conceal what we experience, sometimes with no effort at all, but that what we do – our actions – are there for the looking. However, even in respect of this apparently obvious conclusion, one must be careful.

There are experiences that would be regarded as easily observable and actions that are not. It is natural to think that the victim of a serious accident can be seen to experience pain, whereas someone can do something completely away from even the possibility of prying eyes – something like adding up two numbers, as we say, 'in the head'. That is, there would seem to be cases where experiences are out in the open, and also cases of actions that are 'inside'. Moreover, the idea of observation that is in play here cries out for further elu-cidation. Still, let us agree that, though there is much more to it, the proper place for this is in our stage 2 investigations. For now we can say that 'in general and for the most part' experience comes at the low end of the observa-bility spectrum, while action lies at the other. A typical case of experiencing something – having an ache in a limb – is usually counted as fully discernible only to the subject of the experience, whereas a typical case of acting – signing a will – is rated as something anyone in the right place can witness.

But what about attitudes? How easy is it to see that someone wants an ice-cream or believes that it is about to rain? The temptation is to say: it all depends. If the circumstances are right, for example if there is enough beha-viour to go on, it would seem to be quite easy. The child irritably resisting his parents' best efforts to distract him from the ice-cream vendor can be clearly seen to want an ice-cream, whereas the academic comfortably engaged in reading a book might well believe that it is about to rain without giving our observational abilities any purchase at all. Still, if we abstract away from special cases and, as in respect of experiencing and acting, think only in general and for the most part, the attitudes seem to be somewhere in between the two extremes in respect of observability. It is easier to see what people do than what they believe, but it is also easier to see what they believe than what they experience. As before, there is a lot to be said about exactly what we think is going on when we are said to observe that someone wants or believes something, but discussion of this will come later.

1.3.2 Accessibility

How easy is it for you to tell of *yourself* that you are experiencing, wanting or doing something? That is, how accessible is your cwn portion of the mental realm? Do we always know what we are doing, or what we believe and want? No, but perhaps this is because we don't always attend to these things; the idea would be that if we did attend, we would know. Yet couldn't there be cases in which no amount of thinking about it would lead us to acknowledge particular

17

actions or beliefs and wants as our own? Indeed, aren't such cases perfectly familiar? Smith sets out to help Jones dig the garden; he believes that he is doing this from the goodness of his heart, and that is what he would avow after reflection. But, to those who know him, what he is doing seems more appropriately described as competitively displaying his horticultural superiority over Jones; the way in which he goes about 'helping' seems to give him away. Ask Smith what he is doing, believing and wanting and you get one answer. Ask his friends and you get another. Perhaps Smith could be brought to see himself in the way others do, but that is not really relevant. All that I want this example to remind us of is the perfectly ordinary fact that we don't always have instant accessibility to what we believe, want or are engaged in.

Experiencing, however, seems to be in stark contrast to these. Not only do we think that such things as pains and itches are highly accessible; we would find it difficult to imagine cases in which there was any attenuation of accessibility. Could you be in pain, for example, and not notice that you were? And here, by 'pain', I mean some fairly robust example of the kind, not a barely perceptible sensation which comes and goes too fleetingly to count as one thing or another. You could of course be stoical about it, not show others that you were in pain; you could even push it to the background so that it didn't interfere with your present activities. But could you have a pain and not notice it at all? This is a difficult question, a question whose very status has been debated. In particular, is it a question about how things are as a matter of fact in respect of pains, or is it somehow a more conceptual question: is the very concept of pain such that it is logically impossible to have an exemplar of it without noticing? (*See* INTROSPECTION.)

As in the case of observability, nothing we are engaged in just now requires us to deal with these worries. Whatever is to be said in the long run when we start to dig deeper, here it is enough to note what seems the unvarnished truth to most people (and, in particular, to the students who so forcefully expressed this view): we have a much greater degree of access to items of experience than we do to attitudes and actions.

How do attitudes and actions compare in respect of accessibility? There is a tendency to think that we know more about what we believe and want than about what we do. The reason most often given for this is that acting requires some cooperation on the part of the world: we have greater accessibility to what we intend to do (an attitude) than to what we are actually doing or achieving because we are only doing or achieving something if certain worldly events are actually taking place, and we may be in error about whether they are. Dreams illustrate the point nicely.

If, in a dream, you are about to sign a cheque then you seem to have the intentions, desires and beliefs appropriate to that commonplace action. But if you were actually signing a cheque, not only would there have to be this attitudinal background, your hand would have to hold the pen and move in some appropriate way. And it is precisely the latter that is missing in a dream. When you dream that yet another bill is overdue and, in a state of generalized anxiety, reach for your chequebook and write out a cheque hastily and without due care and attention to the balance remaining in your fragile account, you have a keen awareness of the attitudinal background – it seems wholly accessible to you. But, as you often come to realize on waking, one thing that didn't happen was that you signed a cheque.

Dreams are the extreme case here but there are less dramatic cases of actions being inaccessible in ways that the attitudes are not. So, summing up, we usually rank experiences at one extreme – immediate and full accessibility – whereas attitudes come somewhat further down the line with actions bringing up the rear.

1.3.3 Expressibility

It would seem equally easy to tell someone that you have a pain in your arm, that you believe right will triumph over wrong and that you are cooking your dinner. But many feel that this way of putting things misses an important feature of these categories. In particular, there is a prevalent idea that, though we can tell someone *that* we have a pain in the arm, we cannot express or communicate the experience itself. As one puts it colloquially, 'what it is like' to have a particular pain seems something that escapes even the most imaginative use of language. As we have found with the other dimensions, intuitions like this one raise more questions than they answer. For example, what exactly would it be like to express an experience if we could? What would constitute success in this apparently difficult task? If we don't know even that much, then perhaps our conviction that experiences cannot be expressed is less interesting than it seems. Still, we must not stop just yet at such deeper questions; there is a consensus that experiences are very low on the expressibility scale, and that is good enough for the present.

But what about attitudes and actions? Actions seem to be straightforwardly expressible: insofar as you know what you are doing, you just put it into words – you describe your action in some appropriate way chosen among all the ones available to you. In appropriate circumstances, you just say: 'I'm signing a cheque', 'paying the gas bill' or 'practising my signature on this already ruined cheque'. To be sure, there are cases where it is not quite that easy. I can imagine myself engaged in some intricate physical manœuvre which is necessary to the well-being of my bicycle, but which I cannot properly describe – it is just too complex, even though the aim of the action itself is simple. Of course, I could always just say: 'I am adjusting the brakes', or 'fixing my bicycle' and this might do. Telling someone what I am doing does not always require detailed description. In the end, then, there doesn't seem to be much of a problem about expression here.

With belief, want, and other attitudes, the problem comes down to getting hold of some appropriate sentence to use in the complement place in the attitude report. In most cases, this is straightforward. To be sure, there are times when you are not quite sure whether you believe something to be the case, or merely hope that it is. And there are also bound to be times when you, say, expect something to happen, but would be hard put to find the exact sentence that captures the content of your expectation. (I am assuming here that expectation is a specialized form of belief – belief about some future course of events.)

In sum, there are problems for both actions and attitudes in respect of expressiblity – problems that make them about equal in this dimension. But they are nowhere near as severe as the problems encountered in respect of one's experiences.

1.3.4 Directionality

An attitude is a mental item which can show itself in activities and behaviour. Of course, this is not invariably so; one can easily conceive of beliefs, desires and the like that happen never to leak out into the realm of action. Still, it is not unreasonable to think of the attitudes as having particular and typical kinds of manifestation in activity. A desire to buy a new coat, for example, will 'look' very different to observers from a belief that coats keep you warm in winter.

However, what is particularly characteristic of the attitudes is that they are attitudes *about* something – they are reported in sentences which contain complement clauses, or, using the other idiom, they have *contents*. Yet another way of putting this is to say that attitudes are never merely expressed in behaviour, they are also, and essentially, *directed* to, or at, something. For example, compare desire with, say, vanity. Both have a claim to be the kind of thing appropriate to the mind, but there is an important difference between them. A vain person, like a desirous one is disposed to act in various ways, but to understand the desire fully, we must know what it is a desire *for*. There is no counterpart to this directedness in the case of vanity.

On the face of it, directionality is virtually absent in those items that most naturally group themselves around the category of experience. Taking pain as the first example, imagine that you have overdone some exercise and that you are now suffering for it. You have various aches and pains and these seem to be located in various parts of your body. They are located – and they have specific characteristics, each different from one another – but they don't seem to be *about* anything; they lack directionality. Your aching thigh is not an ache *for* anything – it is not reported in a sentence containing a complement clause, and thus it does not have a content.

One must be careful here. The notion of content as just used is somewhat specialized. It is that item to which an attitude is directed. The content of the desire that you have a new coat is, roughly, the state of affairs of your having a new coat. If you had it badly enough, one could describe your state – somewhat fancifully – as an ache for a new coat. In a more general sense of the word 'content', of course it is true that a pain has a content. But this is not the sense of the word in question.

I said that directionality is virtually absent in typical cases of experiencing such as the pain case. Certainly, there is nothing that corresponds to the robust use of complement clauses with which we report beliefs. But why only

20

'virtually'? Well, it seems to many as if there is a kind of directionality in the pain case which it is easy to overlook. It is a lower grade of directionality than we have in connection with the attitudes, and it may in the end be nothing more than a phenomenon based on the attitudes, but it is worth remarking on. Certainly, pain is not usually a neutral item of experience: it is something unpleasant and which we seek to avoid. The directionality of an experience of pain may be no more than: 'would that it would go', but it is at least possible to see this as a primitive relation of the kind of directionality we have in full-fledged attitude cases. Of course, one might take the view that pains just happen to have (in us, and for the most part) a kind of *connection* to the attitudes. On this view, it is not the pain that has any kind of directionality, it is just that pains bring with them desires to get rid of the pain. The idea is that the desire, not the pain, is directed.

Somewhat differently from the pain case, think of what it would be like to be standing in front of a blue wall and looking directly at it. Your perception would be directed: it would be described as a perception of a blue wall. But that is not quite what is at issue. Try to forget about the fact that you perceive a blue wall (which is surely directional, like an attitude), and think instead of the conscious experience occasioned by the expanse of blue. This is something that happens when you perceive the blue wall, but is distinct from the latter. It is the experience found, as is said, by introspection in the stream of consciousness, and it can be separated from what causes it (the wall), or what it is about (the blueness of the wall). As the struggles of the last few sentences show, it is not an easy matter to use words to point in the right direction, but most people are, on reflection, only too eager to admit that there is such a thing as the what-it-is-like-to-see-blue sensation in their stream of consciousness when they direct their attention to a blue object.

Does the qualitative experience you have when you are perceiving a blue wall constitute a case of pure, non-directed experiencing? It certainly doesn't seem to have even the most primitive form of directionality. Unless the colour is particularly shocking, your experience of blueness does not come with the feeling: 'would that it would go away'. So perhaps the colour perception case is a better example than pain of non-directedness. Or perhaps the pain case really constitutes just as good an example, which only seems different because pain is hooked up *in us* to genuine attitudes such as the desire to get rid of the pain? Well, whether pain has a kind of primitive directionality, is not something we need to settle here. For whatever we end up saying, it seems at first that directionality is typical of, and central to, attitudinizing, and is only of marginal importance to experience.

What of the third category – acting? We have briefly discussed the question of the degree to which actions are mental items. Our discussion was admittedly inconclusive, but it was suggested that even a physical action could not be thought of simply as a sequence of physical movements: the mind is either actually present in the action or is intimately involved in it in some way. Thus, signing a cheque certainly involves various hand movements, but these are (at least) mind-directed. The movements have as their aim, for example, the payment of the electricity bill.

As always, there is much more to be said here. But for now, it is enough to note that, with respect to directionality, attitudes have it as a central feature, actions include elements which are directional, and items of consciousness have at most a minimal kind of directionality. (*See* INTENTIONALITY.)

1.3.5 Theoreticity

Is it possible to see electrons? Not an easy question, nor one we have to settle definitely here. But this much seems true: whether or not one can stretch the notion of 'seeing' sufficiently to allow it to be said that we see electrons, any seeing of them would be a wholly different kind of thing from our seeing of tables and chairs. Though not a precise business, it does seem that some items count as immediately or directly observable, whereas others are less directly observable (if observable at all). What have been called 'middle-sized dry goods' – taking tables and chairs to be representative – falls under the first heading, whereas electrons fall firmly under the second.

Recognizing that electrons are at best indirectly observable, the next question to ask is: do they really exist? Here again, brushing aside the deeper ruminations of certain philosophers, the answer is surely 'yes, there really are electrons'. But having admitted that electrons are only indirectly observable, what grounds do we have for saying that they exist? Undoubtedly, many people regard the best grounds for something's existence to be its direct observability, but there are other grounds. For instance, one could say this: the notion of an electron forms an essential part of a theory we have about the nature of matter – a theory that is by now established in the scientific community. Even though we may never be able (even in principle) to observe electrons directly, we are generally happy (give or take a few philosophical qualms) to say that they exist. They exist because they are integral to our well-established *theoretical* understanding of the universe.

Against this background, here are some things we can say about the feature of theoreticity: chairs and tables – things we regard as directly observable – have a *low* degree of theoreticity. We don't believe in the existence of these things on the basis of our theory of the universe – we just see them. On the other hand, electrons have a *high* degree of theoreticity: their very existence is bound up with our theoretical understanding of nature.

What about the items in the mental realm? There is generally a consensus for the view that, whatever else we say about other items, experiences have a very low degree of theoreticity. We do not regard a pain, a visual appearance, an experience of a sound, the changing coloured image which comes before our closed eyes just after we have seen a bright light, as things whose existence depends in any way on a theory we may have about how things work. Items of experience seem to be immediately apprehended. Indeed, there is a tendency, which has been encouraged, though not invented, by some philosophers, to consider items of experience as *more* directly observable than the middle-sized

22

dry goods that surround us. Introspection can seem a more direct and reliable guide to what exists than modes of 'extrospection' such as seeing, touching and hearing.

Allowing strength of opinion on this to be our guide, and leaving on one side any investigation of the basis of that opinion, we shall count experiencing as at the lowest end of the scale of theoreticity. But what about the other two categories: attitudes and acting? Here matters get more complicated. In discussing the accessibility of the attitudes, it was noted that, whilst we *sometimes* either make mistakes as to the direction of our attitudes, or, on occasion, just fail to register attitudes that others can more accurately gauge from our behaviour, we *often* have fairly immediate access to what we desire, intend, believe, etc. But one thing we also noticed was that, even when the access we have is fairly immediate, it doesn't appear to be like the access we have to such things as pain. For example, if asked whether next Sunday was the 15th, you would surely do some kind of ruminating before answering. However, compare this rumination with what you would go in for if I asked whether you could feel the pressure exerted by the chair you are now sitting on. Your answer in the second case seems something like a case of looking and discovering; that is why the expression 'intro*spection*' seems so apt. But this kind of introspection seems the wrong sort of method for discovering whether you believe next Sunday to be the 15th.

In cases of the attitudes and experiences of others, the contrast seems even more pronounced. You find out what someone's attitudes are by being sensitive to behaviour. Of course, you may be told point-blank what someone believes, but even this may not settle the issue. Perhaps they are not facing up to things, or are trying to see things in a better light. In cases more complicated than the one about Sunday the 15th, perhaps they are mistaken about what they believe. However, in the case of experience, it would seem that the verdict of the subject is both necessary to an accurate judgment, and final.

How can one explain this difference? One way is this: an experience is something that is directly observable – though only by the person whose experience it is – whilst an attitude is something not directly observable by either the subject or his friends. On this view, attitudes are items we attribute to ourselves and each other as part of trying to make sense of – to explain – behaviour. One way of putting this would be to say that attitudes are part of our *theory* of human nature. Clearly, a consequence of this view would be that attitudes are more theoretical in nature than experiences. Of course, this is not to say that they are just like electrons. After all, the explanatory theories of physics would seem to be quite different from the 'theories' with which we explain human activities. But the discussion of electrons was only meant to illustrate the notion of theoreticity.

Accepting then that attitudes come out as more theoretical than conscious experiences, what about actions? Do we directly observe actions, or do they have a somewhat more theoretical and less directly observable nature? Here the old wounds open up again. Those students who regarded actions as nothing much more than physical movements would see them as directly observable. Those who considered them to be 'purposes in movement' would demur, since a purpose is an attitude. And, of course, one must not forget actions that are generally classified as mental – actions such as thinking of a number between 1 and 10. Without even trying to sort all this out here, I shall take the easy way out by placing actions somewhere in between attitudes and experiences on the theoreticity scale. (*See* DENNETT.)

1.4 The Map of the Mind

With the help of the five dimensions it is now possible to construct a working map of the mental terrain. See figure 1.

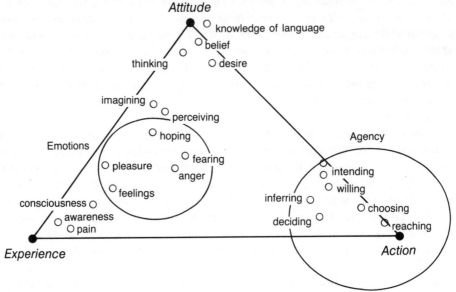

Figure 1.

The main categories are represented as three points equidistant from one another. Think of them as mountains (seen from above) whose summits mark boundaries derived by extrapolation from the five dimensions. Thus, for example, Experience is that peak at the summit of which one would put any feature of the mind that was wholly accessible, not observable, not expressible, not directional and not theoretical. Of course, no actual feature of the mind has this stark profile. Pain tends to be cited as the paradigm case of an experience but there are ways in which even it falls short of being what might be called a 'pure' experience. First, whilst pain is thought of as highly accessible to its sufferer, there is arguably room in our idea of the mind for pain that is not noticed at a given time. Secondly, we do think of pain as sometimes observable – think of the accident victim – even if it is in many cases difficult to discern from the

24

third-person perspective. Thirdly, it is not easy to express (describe) pain, but it is not impossible to go some way towards it: one need only think here (again) about Updike's description of the teacher in pain. Fourthly, as was noted, there is a kind of directionality that seems to accompany a painful experience – a sort of 'would that it would go away' content. Finally, it is possible to imagine cases in which pain was appealed to more on theoretical than observational grounds. Thus, a doctor might explain why you have a certain tiredness in your back by citing the fact that you have had a pain in your leg which caused you to walk and sit awkwardly. When you protest that you felt no such pain, the doctor might well say that the pain never expressed itself – that it remained, as is often said in medical circumstances, 'sub-clinical'. Given these considerations, pain must be placed short of the summit of Experience: its dimensional profile shows it to be some little way towards both Attitude and Action.

All the other features of the mental realm have been assigned places on the same basis: due account has been taken of their relative distances from the three summits. Of course, I don't want to insist that I have got these locations precisely right: figure 1 is only intended to be a sketch map – something we can use to orient ourselves. None the less, before we embark on the next stage of investigation, here are a few notes explaining some of the reasons for various placements.

(1) To keep the map uncluttered, I have left out some of the items that figured in the full list of items belonging to the mental realm, but it should be obvious where they would go. Thus, hope, fear, anger are placed more or less centrally and they mark out a region within which one could put any other EMOTIONS. This central location seems right because emotions look towards each of the peaks without being markedly closer to any one of them. Certainly, one can be, for example, angry *that such-and-such is the case* – anger is certainly something like an attitude with a content. Yet anger is often spoken of as a feeling, as something accessible in the stream of consciousness. And finally anger not only causes us to do various things, it is itself said to be *expressed* in action. Of course, differences will emerge as soon as one moves from anger to one or other of the emotions, so you should think of the central location labelled 'emotions' as a region within which more accurate placements can be made. Perhaps a 'calmer' emotion like regret will be closer to the attitudes than anger and further away from the other two fixed points, whilst love might be closer to experience and further away from attitude.

Note also that feelings are placed slightly closer to experience and further away from action than emotions. In some contexts, 'emotion' and 'feeling' are used interchangeably, but in others, feeling owes more to experience. Its location near the edge of the region is meant to cater for both of these possibilities.

(2) It may not be obvious why pleasure comes just within the emotion region, whilst PAIN is firmly outside and closer to Experience. After all, isn't it virtually a cliché to speak of 'pleasure and pain' as a contrasting *pair*? Yes, there is this

25

cliché, but there are also certain more pressing considerations which favour the placements in figure 1. In particular, the most common reference to pleasure is within what are clearly attitude-type contexts. Thus, one speaks of 'being pleased that' or 'taking pleasure in'. Pleasure here comes closer to an emotion than to any sort of bodily sensation: when, for example, it is appropriate to say that you are pleased to have gone to the dentist, it is unlikely that such pleasure would show itself in any particular part of your body, though of course any pain that the dentist caused certainly does show up in this way. This is not to deny that 'pleasure' can describe bodily sensations, nor that 'pain' can be used to describe a specially intense kind of sorrowful emotion. But the more typical uses of both justifies my having placed them as in figure 1.

(3) Why is consciousness not shown in exactly the same place as experience? Admittedly, I have at times used the two expressions interchangeably, but there is a reason – so far unremarked – that is responsible for this placement. One can use the word 'conscious' and its related forms of speech in two ways: either as a synonym for 'experience' or as qualifying such things as belief, decision and action. In this second sense, one says such things as: 'he consciously decided to . . .', or, 'she consciously believed that . . .', or, 'he consciously inferred that . . .'. Here the contrast is with cases in which decisions, beliefs and actions are somehow not directly available to the subject. Thus a conscious decision is one that has been reflected upon, taken after due deliberation, and to which the subject has the kind of access required for reporting the decision to others. It is not necessary for a decision to be conscious that it be experienced in the way that a pain is. In any case, it is not all that clear what such an experience would be like.

Sometimes this distinction is described as that between 'access' consciousness and 'PHENOMENAL' consciousness, and, without any particular commitment to this way of putting it, I wanted figure 1 to reflect something of the dual nature of the word. So, as would be expected of a notion that can figure in attitudes and actions, 'consciousness' is shown as some small distance towards each of them. (*See* CONSCIOUSNESS.)

(4) Reaching – stretching out one's hand and arm – is about as central a case of bodily action as one could have, and its location on the map reflects this. On the other hand, inferring – as in 'noticing that the shutters were closed, he inferred that they were not home' – is a clear example of an act that does not involve the body. For this reason it is placed further from action and closer to experience.

Intending, willing, choosing and deciding are intimately connected with actions of all sorts, and, according to some accounts, they are themselves forms of mental act. I have included these, and the more typical cases of action, within a region labelled 'agency' because, though I haven't discussed it at any length, these are the notions that together give us our idea of an agent – what we might call a 'self in action'.

(5) Speaking of which, notice that I have not been able to find a place for the self. But then again, it would have seemed odd if I had. For whatever it is, the self is not something you would expect to find along with the other items in figure 1. It is not as if you could say: let's put the self just here next to belief, or consciousness. Yet, as I suggested earlier, the self seems to accompany each and every item in the mental landscape. So, perhaps the best I can do here is to suggest that a full-scale map of mental features in the style of figure 1 – one in which everything is shown in great detail – would count, not as a mental map in general, but as of some one person in particular. The SELF thus would belong to the legend of each map – the bit that tells one whose specific territory the map depicts.

(6) Finally, as has been noted, we are not always the best judge of our attitudes, nor of our actions and decisions; our states of mind can be hidden from us. Sometimes this happens because the states of mind in question are as a matter of fact inaccessible to us and sometimes because we have in some sense made them so. Examples of the first sort usually involve a sort of knowledge that we have and use, but do not, and largely cannot, remark upon. For example, when we hear the sounds of our language, we are able to interpret them – indeed it is impossible not to – because of the vast number of things we know about the sounds, grammar and meanings of that language. Yet many skilled listeners (most of us in fact) are unable to describe these crucial bits of knowledge. They guide us though they remain in some way tacit. To mark this kind of circumstance, I put knowledge of language near the attitudes but on the other side from experience. (The whole idea of tacit knowledge, especially in connection with language, has been heatedly discussed by linguists and philosophers. (*See* CHOMSKY).)

The second way we can lose track of our own states of mind revolves around the notion of the UNCONSCIOUS, as this notion is used in psychoanalytic theory. The idea here is that some of our attitudes, decisions and actions are undertaken for reasons that we somehow manage to conceal from ourselves. Why we do this – and how – are questions that form the subject matter of PSYCHO-ANALYTIC EXPLANATIONS. Unconsciousness is a bit difficult to draw on the map. In one sense it is everywhere, since virtually any mental phenomena might be unconscious in the psychoanalytic sense. But if we think of it as a receptacle of such states – as *the* unconscious – then it would be better to include it in the legend along with the self. In any case, given the controversy which surrounds this notion, any placement should be thought of as provisional.

For more on specific items *see* BELIEF; DESIRE; IMAGINATION; INTENTION; MEMORY; PERCEPTION; THE WILL.

Stage 2: Digging Deeper

Natural historians of the seventeenth century were dismayed that the Earth had so many mountains and hills. They regarded these features as irregular, and hence as disfigurements of the landscape, some going so far as to think of mountains as God's particular way of telling us of our sinfulness. Leaving aside any aesthetic or theological speculation, it must be admitted that contours of the mental realm are far from regular – its landscape is just as lumpy, metaphorically speaking, as that of the Earth. The idea that the things of the mind are sufficiently uniform for us to separate them off from the rest of reality by some simple criterion is just not on. This is bound to be a disappointment to those who may have thought that the mind was a unified realm whose core is revealed in the so-called 'stream of consciousness'. Whether fortunately or not, this expectation cannot withstand the sheer force of the number and character of the items that queue up for inclusion in the mental order. If we take this variety seriously – and that is precisely what I have tried to do – then we must be satisfied with a more piecemeal approach to our deeper investigations in this stage.

That being said, however, I do not want to rush around the mental landscape taking soundings at every point. There are many interesting questions that could be asked about each and every one of the items in figure 1. In most cases our dicussion of them was cursory, and even basic things such as their location on the map could be profitably discussed further. But even though the mental order is lumpier than some might have hoped, I should like here to stick to the big picture as much as possible.

Throughout our investigations, there have been three constant landmarks towering above the landscape: Experience, Attitude and Action. These categories are the basis for the organization of the mental realm, and they are in large part responsible for its lumpiness. So, what I propose is that we confine our attention to these categories; that we set up our seismic apparatus so as to see what lies under them. Of course, in doing so we will have to make constant reference to those mental items that are typical of the categories – items such as pains, beliefs and specific types of action. But in every case our inquiry will be general. For example, we shall be interested in belief to the extent that it is representative of the category of attitudinizing; the more specific characteristics of belief – what distinguishes it from other attitudes – will not figure prominently. This way of proceeding should not lead us into error in regard to the attitudes, as long as we bear in mind that it is only a first step. The hope is that if we understand things that are typical of all the attitudes, we will be in a better position to understand their idiosyncrasies.

In every case, the procedure will be quite simple: certain questions – which are in no sense technical or specialist – will be asked about the assumptions that underpin each of the categories. What I shall try to show is just how difficult it is to answer them – how the most straightforward things we think about the mind just don't help. Or, worse still, how what we think actually makes answers more, rather than less, difficult. In short, my aim will be to reveal just how much trouble we can get into just by investigating the features of the mind's landscape.

2.1 Attitudes and Attitudinizing

2.1.1 Attitude Problems

I begin in the middle with the second of the categories – attitudinizing. This is not because of the well-known literary advice about where to begin a story. Rather, it is because attitudinizing looks both ways: many think that it has roots in experience – both of the bodily and perceptual variety – and it certainly seems to look towards actions in shaping and anticipating them. Besides, the attitudes have so far raised very few awkward questions, and it is now time to be awkward.

What is most striking about attitudinizing is the feature we have called directionality, and this will be the focus of our discussion. The idea that beliefs are directed, that they are reported by sentences that themselves contain sentence complements, that beliefs therefore have contents, these things are so familiar to us that it is easy to overlook just how special they are. When we say that Anne believes she left her coat in the hallway cupboard, we are, one would suppose, saying something true about Anne. Looked at from this perspective, there is a lot in common between our reporting that Anne has a belief and our reporting – truly – that she has a cold. In each case, there would seem to be state that Anne is in, albeit it is a mental state in the case of belief and a physical state in the case of the cold. However, from this perspective, we miss the crucial feature that differentiates the one state from the other.

A physical state of a person can be quite complex – it can take many words to describe it accurately. But no matter how complex it is, it never has the feature of directedness that goes with attitudinizing. Anne has a cold – certain unpleasant biological and chemical things are going on in her – but this state is not directed to anything, it is not about anything. Her physical state is somehow complete in itself and can be described without including reference to any other state of affairs. In contrast, Anne's belief is directed to another state of the world – her coat's being in the hallway cupboard. It is this latter state that forms the *content* of her attitude, and there is just no way of describing Anne's belief without referring to this content. (*See* PROPOSITIONAL ATTI-TUDES.)

29

In the literature the directedness characteristic of the attitudes, and the sentences we use to report them, is often called 'INTENTIONALITY'. However, in some of its forms ('intentional') this word can be misleading, so I prefer to use here the less common but more descriptive word 'directionality'. (Actually, there is a close connection between the attitude verb 'intend' and the idea of intentionality. But, even so, it can be confusing to speak of some belief being *intentional* when we usually reserve such a description for actions.) Also, 'the problems of intentionality' tends to be a label for difficulties that go well beyond any we shall discuss at stage 2, so it is as well to use the more restrictive name for the time being. (I shall later say something about the problems of intentionality in the wider sense.)

Whatever we call it, this remarkable feature of the attitudes is so familiar it is all too easy to be blasé about it, and to take for granted our command of the apparatus with which we report them. Anne's coat is there hanging in the hallway cupboard. This is as far from being a mental fact as anything can be; it is merely a state of the world at a given time. But Anne is in, or has, a special mental state – she has a belief – and the very description of this second state requires us to make reference to the first. What allows us to connect up these two claims in this way? Even if we are usually unreflective about it, what guides our ways of reporting beliefs and the other attitudes?

The first thought that someone might have here is tantalizingly simple. There is the coat hanging in the cupboard, and Anne is believingly related to this fact. That is, just as she might be owningly related to the house on 23 Elm Street, so is she believingly related to the coat's being in the cupboard. In the one case, she bears a complex physical, social and legal relation to a house, in the other a perhaps no less complex mental relation to something that is going on in the world. (*See* REPRESENTATION.)

Unfortunately, this simple account is beset with problems. The most obvious fault is that it signally fails to make room for false belief. Anne may truly *believe* her coat is in the cupboard but it may well not be – her belief may be false. In this perfectly ordinary case, it cannot be the relation between Anne and the coat's being in the cupboard that grounds our attribution of the belief to Anne, for there is no coat there and, hence, no such relation.

This is even more obvious in the case of desires. Suppose that you have a long train journey ahead of you and you absolutely must have a newspaper to make it pass more quickly. You see a shop and desire very much to acquire from it a copy of your usual daily. In the somewhat awkward idiom discussed earlier, we can say:

> You desire that you come to own one of the copies of the *Guardian* in the shop at the station.

But, sadly, there has been a run on *Guardians*, and there simply aren't any in that shop. So, you truly have the desire, but the desire can hardly be a relation between you and a newspaper in the shop which is (as you think) waiting there. There simply isn't any newspaper there answering to your desire.

In the face of these difficulties, it might be tempting to try to keep the spirit of the simple proposal by *retreating* a little. (Indeed, retreating is one of the main strategies for dealing with the problems of directionality.) We are prevented from seeing Anne as believingly related to the coat's being in the cupboard because it just isn't there. But why not still insist that she is believingly related to the coat (wherever it is), the cupboard and the relationship described by the words 'being in'. That is, why not invent a complex entity made up of these three items, which certainly exist in the world even if they do not exist together in the way envisaged by Anne? Thus, we can say what her belief state is directed at, without thereby guaranteeing that it is true. (Rather as we can say what an archer's target is without committing ourselves to whether the arrows hit the mark.)

The entity made up of the coat, the cupboard and the relationship is somewhat odd – it is a sort of abstract thing made up from concrete objects and relations – but that in itself is no special problem.[1] After all, one wouldn't expect mental attitudes to be completely straightforward. But oddness is only the beginning of the difficulties with this proposal. Consider for example this belief attribution:

Henrietta believes that Macbeth was not misled by a greedy wife.

---

[1] This entity is sometimes called a 'PROPOSITION', but – confusingly – it is not the only sort of item that claims this title. Some think that we can get away with simply saying that a proposition is whatever it is that serves as the content of a propositional attitude. The minimalism of this view has a lot to recommend it, but there are inevitably going to be questions about what kind of thing can serve that role. And the idea that a proposition is a sort of abstract confection with real objects sort of baked into it is one way of dealing with these questions. Though it does raise many more questions that are too technical to discuss here.

Another way in which to be less than minimalist about propositions is based on the idea of a *possible world*, and works as follows. Imagine all the different ways in which our world could be different – however slightly. Then call each of these ways a 'possible world'. Finally, say that a proposition is the group or set of possible worlds in which the relevant content sentence is true. Thus, there are many possible worlds in which Anne has a coat and it is in the cupboard, and many in which either the coat doesn't exist or it is not in the cupboard. The sentence: 'Anne's coat is in the cupboard' is of course true only in the first set of possible worlds, and we can define the proposition that the coat is there as that set. Anne can then be said to be related to this set of possible worlds so defined, though her belief will only be true if our own actual world happens to be in that set.

The possible-worlds treatments of propositions also raises many questions that won't be discussed here. However, I do not mean to suggest an aversion to this treatment just because the text employs the other. It is just that the confectionary sense of a proposition – sometimes called 'structured propositions' – lends itself to my particular account of attitude problems.

Are we saying that Henrietta is believingly related to Macbeth, his wife and an appropriate 'misleadingness' relationship? It certainly has seemed to many people as if one of the fascinating things about attitudes is that we can have them toward fictional characters and other non-existents (remember the desire for the newspaper). But doesn't this put a great deal of strain on the idea that belief consists in a relation to a complex of *existing* items?

Actually, whilst the answer to my last question is clearly 'yes', I don't think that worries about fictional entities constitute the main stumbling block to accepting the idea that attitudes are relations to things. Fiction creates havoc wherever it goes – whether in our accounts of language or in our accounts of attitude ascriptions. And it creates havoc for virtually every account in these areas. So, whilst it is worth mentioning, I shall put it on one side. There is a larger obstacle standing in the way of our present proposal regarding the world-directness of the attitudes, and we must deal with it before we can consider such relatively minor matters as so-called 'fictional' objects. (*See* STALNAKER.)

2.1.2 Deeper into Trouble in London and Paris

So far we have been trying to hang on to the idea that beliefs and other attitudes are directed at the things they most certainly seem to be about – the items referred to in the complement sentences of attitude ascriptions. However, we have seen that Anne cannot simply be related believingly to her coat's being in the cupboard because it might not be there. So we have retreated to the idea that she is believingly related to a made up, complex entity consisting of the coat, the cupboard and the feature of one thing's being contained in another. This seems to make room for falsity, since these items might not actually be in the relationship to each other that Anne thinks they are. But falsity (and fiction) are not the only problems. For the relation between the believer and the believed is much more elusive than we have so far noticed. For there is a kind of slack between believers and what beliefs are about which can make one despair of ever coming to understand the directionality of the attitudes. The following two examples will illustrate what I mean.

2.1.2.1 London Monique, on her first visit to London, takes a lightning tour from the top of a double-decker bus. Among the things pointed out to her is the British Museum. As a result of what she is told, and what she can see for herself, she comes to believe that the British Museum has two lions guarding its entrance.

On a later visit to London – this time in order to attend a literary party in a publishing house in Bloomsbury – she notices, as she arrives, that there is a large, sombre building with imposing columns opposite the offices she is to visit. She wonders whether this could be the British Museum (she knows it is in Bloomsbury), but, looking about in vain for the lions (there are none at the front entrance), she dismisses this possibility. But of course what she is looking at is simply the British Museum from another angle.

If we construe the belief formed on the sightseeing bus according to the proposal described earlier, we would say that Monique is believingly related to the 'triplex' entity consisting of:

the British Museum,
the two lions,
the relationship of guarding.

On the second visit, one would seem forced to say that she is believingly related to:

the British Museum (she is looking at it),
the two lions (she clearly remembers these),
the absence of the relationship of guarding (she can see that there are none flanking the entrance).

The first belief was attributed using the form of words:

Monique believes that there are two lions guarding the entrance of the British Museum,

and the second:

Monique believes that the building over there does not have two lions guarding the entrance.

However, in the example 'the building over there' in the second belief attribution is in fact none other than the British Museum, and this is what leads to trouble. What trouble? After all, the first part of the story describes in a coherent way the kind of mistake that we can all make, so it may seem that we have not uncovered any particularly shattering gap in our everyday understanding of the attitudes. But this is to forget how we got to the present position. Our question was: what counts as the content of a belief? The eventual answer was: it consists in an amalgam of those items to which the belief is directed: just describe that amalgam and you have the content of a belief attribution. What the above example apparently shows is that this cannot be right. In Monique's case, the key items that form the content of her two beliefs are the same – it is the British Museum and the lions that figure in both. There is as one might say just 'one reality' toward which Monique's beliefs are directed. But Monique has two beliefs about this reality which are simply not compatible. And it would be unfair to Monique to say that she believed both that the British Museum was guarded by lions and that it wasn't. Monique, we can assume, is much too rational for such an attribution to make any sense. Anyway, she would have to be quite mad to believe such an obvious contradiction. So, does she believe that the British Museum is guarded by lions? And if we say 'yes' (or 'no') to this, where does that leave our account of the directionality of the attitudes?

33

This first example seems to show that one can adopt two different (even incompatible) attitudes toward one and the same set of things, and this introduces a puzzling element of slack into the relationship between our attitudes and what they are about. It is as if our beliefs can slide about whilst still being apparently directed at the same things. (*See* INTENTIONALITY.) Before trying to alleviate this situation, let us consider the second example.

2.1.2.2 Paris   Richard hasn't been to Paris for years. When he was last there, he stumbled on a small brasserie near his hotel which he used to go to every day. In fact, it was in this brasserie that he first met the woman he would now describe as the love of his life. He was sitting at a table near the window, and all the other tables were fully occupied when she came in . . .

Now, all these years later, Richard is in Paris on business and he decides to see whether the brasserie is still there. Heading to the *quartier* of his former hotel, he has not reckoned on one thing: the tendency, in our times, for successful businesses to try repeating their success by forming chains of identical establishments. So, when he stumbles onto the second of the brasseries, he takes it for the one that was the object of his search. Indeed, so close is the resemblance between the two, and Richard's memory is very precise, that he finds the tables and chairs, the metal-covered *comptoir*, the curtains, the menus – everything seems to be just as it was before, give or take a new coat of paint.

On and before entering the brasserie, Richard had many beliefs and other attitudes which together contributed to what we would describe as his feeling of nostalgia. But for the purposes of the example, let us focus on some specific belief. Richard had believed that the chairs in that local brasserie were very comfortable. This belief has not changed in the intervening years, and, as he enters, one of the things he thinks is this: I hope they haven't changed the chairs. He is thus relieved to see the same (sort of) chairs set neatly around the tables. He now could correctly be described as believing that the chairs in the brasserie he used to go to every day have not changed, they are still comfortable. In short, he continues to believe what he had believed before.

But is what he believes true? This is not an easy question to answer. For the sake of definiteness, let us suppose that the brasserie he actually used to go to – the one he mistakenly thinks he is now in – has *changed* its chairs, and that they are no longer what Richard would describe as 'comfortable' if he were to come across them. In this case, there is some pressure for thinking that his present belief is false: the chairs in the brasserie *to which he used to go* are not comfortable. After all, Richard would be quite insistent that, whatever else was true, he had not changed his belief about the chairs, and *we* know – what Richard has yet to find out – that the chairs have changed. Yet, sitting there in the *new* brasserie entertaining the thought: these chairs are comfortable, one may be tempted to think that his belief is true. But it is certainly bizarre to describe one and the same belief as both true and false.

On the account of the directionality of beliefs within which we are working,

Richard's long-standing belief about the chairs was directed at an amalgam of these things:

the chairs in the original brasserie,
the property of being comfortable.

On the apparently reasonable assumption that Richard's belief hasn't changed, this belief continues to be directed at these things, only it is now false. However, it is difficult to ignore the fact that he is sitting there in a brasserie looking at some chairs and judging them to be comfortable. In this case, his belief seems to be directed at:

the chairs in the new brasserie,
the property of being comfortable,

and it is thus true. So, either he is thinking the same thing and, hence, thinking something false, or he has changed his mind (without realizing it!) and he is thinking something different and true. Neither seems very palatable, but the second alternative seems particularly bizarre.

2.1.2.3 The Moral The example involving Monique showed that there is one kind of looseness in the directedness of our beliefs: *we seem to be able to have quite different beliefs – even incompatible ones – about one and the same reality.* The case of Richard shows that this looseness can occur the other way around: *we apparently can have one and the same belief about two different realities.* Put together, these two examples put intolerable pressure on the idea that Monique or Richard can simply be described as being believingly related to features of the world. There are standards that must be met by anything we could regard as a genuine relationship, and these examples apparently show that the attitudes do not come up to scratch. (*See* BELIEF; THOUGHTS.)

Consider again the ownership relationship between Anne and her house. As was said, this is a complicated legal and social relationship – there may even be problems in telling whether it holds definitively. But this much is true: if Anne really does own a house, then she bears this relationship to it no matter how that house is described. And she bears this relationship to just that house and not to others merely because they resemble it.

Admittedly, the cases of Monique and Richard are those involving confusion and mistake, and you might think that they are therefore of less importance than I have made them out to be. But mistakes and confusion are just the things on which we must focus if we want to understand the attitudes. An attitude is a *state of mind* directed towards something or other, and it is therefore liable to go wrong. Indeed, where but in states of mind would you expect to find confusions and mistakes? But it is precisely the possibility of these confusions and mistakes that seems to undermine an account of the content of the attitudes that makes them relations to extra-mental reality.

At this point there are two ways to jump: either agree with the conclusion of the last paragraph when asked what we should make of the directionality of the attitudes. Or look for ways to get around the kinds of examples that created the problem in the first place. As one might guess the philosophical community has tended to go for the second option.

2.1.3 The Way Forward

Actually, though counting here is not a precise art, one can find at least four ways forward: three of them could be understood as ways to improve on the simple proposal of directionality that has led us into trouble, and the fourth as rather more thoroughgoing revision of that proposal. But one must be careful. As you will discern for yourself, these ways are not completely independent of one another. Each consists in a suggestion of how we might begin to cope with the puzzles about the directionality of belief described above, but there is nothing to prevent – and everything to encourage – taking to heart more than one suggestion at a time. For obviously if some combination of these strategies can convincingly describe the directionality of the atittudes whilst defusing the puzzling cases, then there is good reason to plump for it. I have chosen to describe them seriatum, since I want to highlight the essentials and not because I think that they are exclusive alternatives.

2.1.3.1 Language

Nothing could be more obvious than that attributing attitudes to someone involves careful choosing of one's words. To take an extreme example: a five-year-old looking westwards on a late March afternoon may well believe that the sun is setting. But it would be bizarre to say of him that he believes that the medium-size, fusion-powered star now visible on the western horizon is passing out of line of sight of the inhabitants of the British Isles. One feels he just doesn't believe *that*. And the reason? Clearly, it is partly a matter of language. The 'sophisticated' way of describing the setting sun uses words that stand for concepts unavailable to a five-year-old. Had we said simply: 'he believes that the sun is setting', this would have passed as reasonable.

Taking a lead from intuitions such as this, there has been an enormous effort to say just what about the choice of words (and/or concepts) governs our attitude attributions. The hope is that if we can get this right, then we can deal with the problems raised by examples such as those involving Monique and Richard. If there is something about the use of the phrases 'the British Museum' or 'the building over there with columns' that makes them function differently in sentences attributing beliefs, then perhaps we can avoid having to say that Anne is believingly related in different ways to the same reality. Maybe this will allow us to regard the apparent slack between Anne's state of mind and reality as due to the language we use to describe the beliefs and not to the beliefs themselves. (*See* THOUGHT AND LANGUAGE.)

The details of linguistic attempts to deal with the propositional attitudes are too complex to be described fully in this introduction. Indeed, there is a sense in which this approach takes the problem of the attitudes outside the scope of the philosophy of mind itself, and not merely beyond the reach of this survey. For the question of how it is that words connect their users with reality – and within what limits – falls squarely within the philosophy of language. Moreover, even a cursory look at the literature here will show just how complicated the story can get. It is enough to make one wonder how we ever do manage to say what people believe. However, for the sake of definiteness we ought to have at least a rough description of how things might go.

In their ordinary employment, phrases like 'the British Museum' and 'the brasserie I used to visit' refer to items in the world. That is, at least part of their linguistic function is, broadly, to bring reference to such items into our conversational exchanges. Yet, in sentences reporting what people believe, we get into trouble if we take these words simply to have that sort of function. Given this, one way to get out of trouble would be to say that, when these sorts of phrases (and indeed, words generally) occur in the context of propositional attitude reports, they change their function somewhat. Perhaps they cease to refer directly to items in the world and refer instead to how these items are thought of by the believer. Here is the proposal put more concretely.

Monique believes that the British Museum is guarded by lions. Think of the words 'Monique believes that' as having a strange effect on whatever it is that follows them. Thus, the underlined space in 'Monique believes that ___' is a linguistic context in which words do not function as they would outside such a context. To keep matters simple, let us just consider the phrase 'the British Musuem'. This is a name of that famous building, but in the above-mentioned context, this name does not simply refer to that building. Instead, it refers to Monique's way of thinking about that building – we could say that it refers to the way in which that building is *presented* to her. Thus, we should not think of the building itself as taking its place in the content of her belief. Instead, it is the 'mode of presentation' which is stuck into the propositional confection. Calling it 'the British Museum mode' (for want of a better way to describe it) here is the content of Monique's belief:

> the British Museum mode of thinking of the British Museum,
> the two lions,
> the relationship of guarding.

Now this will differ significantly from her second belief – the one we reported by the sentence, 'Monique believes the building over there is not guarded by lions' because the first element in the confection for this one will be:

> the building-over-there mode of thinking of the British Museum.

And we can say all of this even though the building her beliefs are about – the one presented by these two different modes – is one and the same.

Of course there are problems with this account, many of them. Just to

37

mention one troublesome area, there is the obvious difficulty we might have in spelling out what a mode of presentation is, and how it can happen that words sometimes refer to buildings and sometimes to modes of presenting them. Still, it is tempting to think that Monique's belief relationship to something or other is like ownership, i.e it is not the slack kind of relationship that it might appear to be. And it would therefore be nice if we could deal with the appearance of slack by attributing it to some more complicated way in which language functions in propositional attitude reports.

How does this kind of move fare in relation to Richard's encounter with the unsuspected change in brasserie? It must first be admitted that the kind of linguistic move described here was worked out with Monique-type cases in mind. But perhaps it could be adapted. For example, one might say that since his belief involves a relationship to the mode of presentation of the chairs rather than to the chairs themselves, his nostalgic belief is about the former brasserie even though he is no longer in that brasserie, and whatever truth there was in it stays the same. However, the troubles with this suggestion come thick and fast, and they point to certain deeper problems even in respect of Monique-type cases. For what they all stem from is this: we want beliefs to be about what is around us and to be made true or false by that reality. Indeed, this is surely a large part of what belief-talk is for. Yet, if we slip too deeply into the mode-of-presentation way of describing beliefs, we run the risk of making them completely unresponsive to reality. For example, by allowing Richard's belief to be tied to the original brasserie and to keep its truth value we risk cutting him off from his new surroundings. Admittedly, one nice feature about the present proposal is that it can explain why Richard would say such things as, 'Nothing much has changed in the old place.' This is because, so far as the content of his beliefs is concerned, nothing much has changed. And as I have emphasized all along, the attitudes are our main tool for explaining what people do and say. Still, we must be careful to preserve both our intuitions about the attitudes: they explain what we do *and* they do this by showing how the world seems to us to be. In other contexts, losing the world may be a good thing to do, but it makes little sense in the present one.

2.1.3.2 Styles of Believing An obvious thought to have, given the problems there are in coping with the two aspects of belief, is that there may well be *two* kinds of belief (and, as needed, two kinds of the other attitudes as well). One kind has Monique believingly related to the relevant items in the world. With respect to this kind, and appearances notwithstanding, Monique's beliefs just are about the British Museum; she just does believe of that famous landmark that it is both guarded by, and not guarded by, lions. In the trade, this kind of belief is called '*de re*' thereby indicating the connection between the believer and the relevant 'things' (Latin: '*res*') in the world.

The other kind, called '*de dicto*', is not only sensitive to the choice of words used in attributions, it goes so far as to have believers related not to the things of the world, but to the linguistic items (Latin: *'dicta'*) that figure in the attributions. With respect to this style of belief, Monique does believe that the British Museum is guarded by lions, but does not believe that the building over there is guarded by lions even though the building over there is none other than the British Museum.

It is sometimes difficult to get the hang of this, since it sounds so much like the way of putting matters that got us into trouble in the first place. What one has to do is to recognize that the *de dicto* style of belief has Monique believing a linguistic item: *the British Museum is guarded by lions*. And it not implausible to regard this linguistic item as quite different from the following one: *the building over there is not guarded by lions*.

The basic idea behind this strategy (though this is very rarely made explicit) is that by discerning two kinds of belief we can cope with the apparently puzzling cases in a divide-and-conquer way. The *de re* attribution shows Monique to have a problem: she has beliefs that make the British Museum a strange building indeed – one that both has and does not have lions guarding its entrance.

By itself this shouldn't be all that surprising. After all, the story I told is essentially one in which Monique is confused. So why shouldn't her confusion take this form? Still, as noted earlier, if this were *all* we could say about Monique's beliefs, things would not be very satisfactory. She is confused all right, but not as totally mad as this attribution makes her sound. And this is where the availability of the *de dicto* style comes in handy. It gives us the chance to add – almost as a qualification – that Monique is not as crazy as all that since she *de dicto* believes that the British Museum entrance is guarded by lions and that the building over there is not so guarded.[2] These latter claims might well make us less squeamish about the *de re* attribution because the two styles, taken together, seem to give us a reasonable handle on the nature and source of Monique's confusion.

---

[2] Philosophers who go in for the *de re/de dicto* distinction tend to try to convince us that there is an everyday linguistic device that does the work for us. Thus, the *de re* style is said to be captured by:

Monique believes *of* the British Museum that its entrance is guarded by lions,

and the *de dicto* by:

Monique believes *that* the British Museum entrance is guarded by lions.

However, most of those I have interrogated (before they were trained by philosophers) tend to use the 'believes of' and 'believes that' constructions interchangeably. Of course, the distinction made by philosophers is no less (or more) clear in virtue of the presence or absence of an ordinary language usage consistent with the distinction. It just would have been nice, for those who believe in it, if it were enshrined in ordinary language.

As will be obvious, the detailed working out of the *de dicto* style overlaps with the linguistic attempt to defuse the puzzles. For merely citing the *de dicto* style is not enough. We need to have an account of the *dicta* – an account that makes it plausible that Monique is related in various ways to the relevant bits of language and the world – and this is central to the linguistic approach.

Leaving aside the Byzantine details that have grown up around attempts to deal with the attitudes using linguistic resources, there are a number of more straightforward problems with this second, divide-and-conquer approach. Most of them begin with the obvious and simple question: what is the relationship between *de re* and *de dicto* belief? Note that this is not just an idle question – one that we would like to have answered but which can wait. Our original intuition about the directionality of the attitudes was that it was some kind of relationship between the attitude-taker and items in the world. We have been trying to see (in outline) how to spell this out whilst remaining faithful to our intuitions about how we actually use attitude-attributing sentences in particular cases. On the present approach, it would seem that all the world-directedness is handled by the *de re* style; the *de dicto* form helps us cope with those things we might say about believers when they are confused or ill-informed, though it does so at the cost of *not* being a relationship between believers and items in the world. But so far from helping, this bifurcation of tasks risks losing everything. For unless there is an intelligible relationship between the *de re* and the *de dicto*, each will end up a failure at giving an account of directionality – one because it ignores the attitude-taker and the other because it loses the world. We will have two wrong approaches instead of one.

Additionally, there is a real question about whether, on the present proposal, what we have are two different attitudes or merely two styles of attribution. If there is only one kind of belief but it can be attributed in two different ways, then our interest should be in the nature of this belief and not so much in the styles of attribution. And if the proposal is that there are really two kinds of belief (and two kinds, therefore, of each of the attitudes) where is the evidence for this?

The history of attempts to cope with the *de re/de dicto* distinction would require a book in itself. Indeed, the attempt to relate the two generated a thriving industry in philosophy – an industry whose output overlapped with the linguistic approach to the attitudes. Nor has production completely ceased, even though the main markets have moved elsewhere.

2.1.3.3 Styles of Content   The *de re/de dicto* distinction (and the use of philosophy of language to get clear about it) was historically connected with Monique's kind of problem. But what about Richard's predicament? Does the *de re/de dicto* distinction, problematic though it is, give us something to say in that case?

The origin of Richard's kind of trouble is a certain thought experiment suggested originally by Hilary Putnam, though it has gone through many variations since. In that experiment, you are asked to suppose that (a) there is a glass of water in front of you and that (b) you believe there to be a glass of water in front of you. Next you are invited to imagine that there is this other place called 'Twin Earth'. The name is appropriate because everything on Twin Earth is a molecule-by-molecule duplicate of things on our planet. In particular, there is a molecular duplicate of you, that duplicate is sitting in front of a glass and has a belief about its contents. Crucially, though, there is this one difference between Earth and Twin Earth: on Twin Earth the stuff in rivers, lakes and in the glass is not H_2O but something chemically called 'XYZ'. For reasons which are not really important to the present debate, we can take it that this means that there is no water on Twin Earth, though there is something very much like it which we could call 'twater' (twin water). Now, suppose that you are thirsty. Since you believe that there is water in the glass in front of you, you would probably reach out for the glass and drink it. Similarly, your Twin Earth counterpart would do the same. Why? Well, if you and the twin were molecularly identical, one would expect that your brains and nervous systems would support the same beliefs and other psychological states. (There will be further discussion of brains and beliefs in stage 3.) But your twin couldn't be described as having the belief that there is water in the glass in front of him, because, as we have assumed, there is no water on Twin Earth. There is only twater. Moreover, assuming that you don't know how to tell the difference (by looking) between water and twater, what do you suppose you would do if you (and your thirst) were miraculously transported to Twin Earth? You would reach for the glass.

What these things are held to show is that you and your twin's beliefs can be, in some respect, the same, even though the world they seem to be about is different. Or, in the case of transportation, your belief remains the same, but what it is about has changed. (The case of transportation is closest to the case of Richard in Paris.) One consequence that has been drawn from Twin Earth cases, is that there may well be two kinds of content. One kind is that you and your Twin Earth counterpart can share, even though there are differences in your respective worlds. This is called 'narrow' content. The other is that kind of content that shows your belief, which is after all about water, to be different from your twin's. This content is called 'wide' (sometimes 'broad') content. Applying these two kinds of content to Richard's case, we can say that when he walked into the new brasserie, he had a set of beliefs with narrow contents responsible for the things he did and said. In being narrow, these beliefs were not sensitive to the fact that Richard was not in the original brasserie. However, from another point of view, we could view his beliefs as having wide content – as being directed to real-world items and, hence, as sensitive to any swapping of such items. The narrow content of Richard's beliefs was not falsified by the surprising duplication of brasseries, but the wide content was. Insofar as Richard widely thought that the chairs in the old brasserie were still comfortable, his belief was false. (*See* EXTERNALISM/INTERNALISM/TWIN EARTH.)

Clearly, this proposal echoes some of those previously considered, especially the *de re/de dicto* distinction. But one should not assume that, for example,

41

narrow content and *de dicto* content are the same. The problems each were designed to deal with are quite different: narrow content is intended to help with Twin Earth kinds of duplication of reality; *de dicto* content is a way of dealing with the possibility of multiple beliefs about a single reality. One could look at it this way: narrow content comes from a kind of subtraction – take away from belief contents whatever it is that makes us think they connect directly to particular things. In contrast, *de dicto* content comes from a kind of addition – add to belief contents those elements that make them take on the way some particular person thinks of things. Of course, this subtracting and adding might get you to the same place – to a content which was expressible by *dicta* – but there is no guarantee of this.

Aside from the problems of understanding how the narrow/wide content distinction is related to the others, there is the even more vexed question of how these styles of content are related to each other and to our ordinary ways of speaking. For beliefs do seem to be about the world; hanging on to that idea in the face of certain problems is what we have been trying to do. Of course, it would be nice if we could simply say that narrow content, entertained in a particular environment, fixed wide content. That is, that what goes on in the relatively narrow confines of our minds serves to attach us to the wider world. But duplication cases like Richard's show that this just won't work; if it did, Richard wouldn't have been in his predicament in the first place. As with *de re/de dicto* styles of believing, there seems to be a danger that having two styles of content simply pushes our original problem under another part of the carpet. (*See* LANGUAGE OF THOUGHT; THOUGHTS.)

2.1.3.4 Troilism　The approaches considered so far have closely followed our talk about the attitudes in regarding them as essentially relations between attitude takers and some second item. We say:

Anne believes that her coat is in the hallway cupboard,

and this has set philosophers on the trail of that second item – the thing to which Anne is attitudinally related. Mesmerized by the language of attitude reports, they have assumed that whatever else they are, attitudes show themselves to be two-place relations. But some things work better in threes. Perhaps we could regard Anne's belief as really a three-place relation: one which holds between Anne, the set of items consisting of the coat, the cupboard and the relationship of being in, and a third element such as a sentence. In the problematic case of Monique in London, the proposal would come out roughly as follows:

Monique is believingly related in the *lions-guard-the-British-Museum* sort of way to the British Museum, the lions and the guarding relation.

But this is a different relationship from:

being believingly related in the *building-over-there-is-not-guarded-by* lions sort of way to the British Museum, the lions and the guarding relation.

This is a difficult proposal to come to grips with on first hearing, but the central idea is simple enough. By adding some third element to the belief relation, we give ourselves extra room to manœuvre – something we can use, in the appropriate circumstances, to get ourselves out of trouble. For example, we can use the above three-place belief relation to say that Monique's two beliefs really relate her to the same building, lions, etc., but that each of them does this in a slightly different way.

Of course, there is an obvious problem here: where does this third item come from? After all, the surface structure of attitude sentences reveals them to have just one thing in the 'that p' place, whereas the present proposal requires two. One serves to describe the reality to which Monique is fixed, and a second specifies the way in which she is fixed to it. To be sure, sometimes it may be possible to accomplish both of these jobs with a single sentence: just pick a content sentence that both shows what the world must be like for the belief to be true and displays the way in which the believer actually does her thinking about that world. But there are many times when we attribute beliefs without being all that careful. Indeed, there are times when we haven't a clue what sentence would faithfully reproduce the subject's point of view.

The idea that propositional attitude attributions make subtle use of two different content sentences has obvious connections with the proposals discussed earlier. One might even think that it was an amalgam of modes of presentation and styles of believing. Unfortunately, it is not that simple. There are currently a large number of different, incompatible and intricate suggestions for how to engage in this particular *menage à trois*, and any attempt to summarize them would be unfair.

2.1.3.5 Stepping Outside   I said earlier that retreat was the strategy most often used in trying to deal with the attitude problem. First, we retreated from regarding belief as a relation between a believer and some actual state of affairs, then we considered retreating from the idea that there was only one kind of belief (or style of belief attribution) and, most recently, we have seen that we may even have to retreat from the appearance that belief has of being a two-place relation. But I have saved the most dramatic retreat for last.

In one way or another all of the proposals so far considered begin with the idea that an attitude is a genuine state of a person, albeit a mental and relational one. There is something about Monique that is her mental state of believing and that state is somehow related to the British Museum, or her representation of it, or a sentence, or . . . whatever. But perhaps this is completely the wrong way to go about it. Maybe we are taking our talk about belief and the other attitudes too literally.

Look at it this way. We began with what is apparently a description of a person:

S believes that p,

(where S is a person and p is some belief complement). Then we searched around for something true of S – some state internal to the workings of S's mind – which made the above attribution correct, did so in a way which met various desiderata thrown up by the problem cases, and, most importantly, told us something sensible about the relation between S and the topic of the belief. (One must not forget this last thing since what started the discussion in the first place was the need to understand the directionality of the attitudes.) But perhaps we should be thinking of what goes on in attitude sentences in a completely different way.

Consider this sentence:

Henry weighed 80 kilograms.

In it, one seems to be claiming that there is some kind of relationship between Henry and a number of kilograms. After all, the sentence seems to have the same grammatical form as:

Henry sat in the armchair.

Yet there is clearly something misleading about this surface appearance. For you wouldn't expect to find the 80 kilograms that Henry weighed in the way you would expect to be able to find the armchair he sat on. The difference in the two cases is easily explained. Henry is a certain size. That is just one of his properties; it is not a relation between him and some other kind of object. But when we come to describe that property, we have a special way of doing it: we use a verb ('weighs') which relates Henry to a numerical scale, although the scale is used merely as an index of Henry's weight and not as something that can interact with him like an armchair.

The suggestion in the case of the attitudes is patterned on the case of weight: attitudes are seen as non-relational features or properties of individual human minds. However, when we come to describe these attitudes, we have devised a special scale for the job – a special way of indexing them. We use the sentences of our everyday language. Thus, going back to our first example: at a particular time, Anne is in a certain mental state. Call that state S. Now S is going to be very useful for our understanding of what Anne is likely to do and say, so it would be nice to have some revealing way of characterizing it. What we therefore do is to find some sentence ('The coat is in the hallway cupboard') in our language which, for example, is the likely kind of thing we might say if we were in a state like S. This sentence is then used in a verbal construction ('Anne believes that . . .') so as to provide us with a more useful description of S:

Anne believes that the coat is in the hallway cupboard.

Of course the sentence we choose has a meaning – it is about the way things are or might be – and it is because of its meaning that this sentence is a reasonable one to use in 'measuring' Anne's mental state. But in using it for indexing or measuring her state, we are not committed to regarding that state as intrinsically relational. There is no mysterious kind of thing to which Anne is believingly related just as there is no mysterious kind of thing called '80 kilograms' to which Henry is related merely because he is of a certain bulk.

Exactly how to choose our sentences to measure people's attitudes is something open to lots of different kinds of interpretation (*see* FOLK PSYCHOLOGY; BELIEF (2)). Above I suggested that we might choose sentences that reflect what we, the attributer, might actually say when in the same kind of mental state as the believer. But there are other possibilities. For example, the best sentence might simply be the one that the believer would assent to, if asked, though this tends to make it difficult for non-language users to so much as have attitudes.

As with the other proposed 'solutions' to the problem of directionality, this one has its drawbacks. Aside from the difficulty of giving an acceptable account of how to go about measuring attitudes with sentences, one is left with worries about these 'states' of believing (and desiring, hoping, etc.). Are they something over and above the patterns of action they are responsible for? Or do they just come into being when we measure them with sentences? Dealing with these sorts of worries would take us far beyond the task we have set ourselves in this stage.

2.1.4 Conclusion

We started with what seemed a straightforward question: how does the directionality of the attitudes work? In considering answers to it we have now gone inconclusively through a number of proposals: attitudes are relations to the world; to propositions; to modes of presentation; to things (*res*) and/or *dicta*, to wholly self-contained (narrow) contents and/or to wide contents; and, finally, we have even speculated that they might not be relations at all. Moreover, inconclusiveness here just reflects the state of play in the philosophical community: there just isn't a best theory of the directionality of the attitudes. (*See* BELIEF.)

And things get worse. The aim of stage 2 is to probe our conception of the mind – to ask questions about it and to see what assumptions lie below the surface. What we are not doing – yet – is to see how the mind fits into our wider understanding of the world, into the kind of understanding most often identified with scientific inquiry. But when philosophers talk about the 'problems of INTENTIONALITY', they tend to run together two things: what exactly is the directionality of the attitudes and how can anything *like that* exist in the world as described by science (*see* CONTENT). Of course, this is not necessarily a bad thing to do. After all, you've got to know what you are talking about before you see how it fits into your picture of the world's workings. Still, the running together of these questions can lead to confusion, and that is why I

45

have chosen to keep them in separate stages. What I have described here in stage 2 is how one of our most prominent ways of speaking about the mind – the attributing of attitudes – has a feature that is downright perplexing. When we dig just beneath beliefs, desires, etc. there is a labyrinth, and I have tried to supply a thread to guide you, though it is not enough of a guide to show you the way out. (*See also* CONCEPTS.)

2.2 Experience

2.2.1 An Experience

Before it was the usual practice to give injections, my dentist had a method intended to help alleviate the suffering. He would arrange that my right arm rested comfortably on the arm of the chair saying: 'If the pain is really bad, raise your arm and I'll stop drilling.' A fine promise. But, on more than one occasion, having suffered, as I thought bravely and for a long time, but needing a rest from the mounting agony, I would raise my arm only to be told: 'What I am doing to you just doesn't hurt. You are not in pain.'

In retrospect, even I can find the dentist's claim amusing because the thought behind it – if there was one – is so much at variance with both our ordinary conception of mental items such as pain and with the dentist's own affirmation of this conception. As noted in the first part of the *Essay*, bodily sensations are generally regarded both as highly *accessible* and as only poorly *observable*, where these terms are understood in the somewhat special ways outlined earlier. Thus, the pain I experienced in the dentist's chair was highly accessible (I was thoroughly and intimately aware of it) and only tenuously observable (the dentist and any other third parties cannot directly tell that I am in pain). In devising a system to signal him, the dentist apparently recognized these features of the situation. Yet, his later refusal to count my hand movement as a genuine indicator of pain contradicted that recognition. Perhaps because of his then advanced age and long experience with suffering, he was somehow more expert than most at telling whether someone was having pain. But however much of an expert he took himself to be, it does strike us as bizarre to regard his expertise as more reliable than his patient's, because we are so committed to the idea that our bodily sensations are accessible to us and not directly observable by others.

The above story brings out something else about the nature of experience. The dentist asked me to 'tell' him when I was in too much pain by raising my arm. Clearly, since I was unable to speak in those circumstances, some such relatively crude signalling device was necessary. But suppose that I could have spoken. Would this have allowed me to communicate my pain to him in any more adequate way? I think we would be tempted to answer 'no'. As was noted earlier, experiences such as pain tend to be very low on the expressibility scale: we can say that we have them and we can say a few things about them, but they have features that – as we commonly say – cannot be put into words.

In raising my arm, I was using a pre-arranged, uncomplicated signal to convey the idea *that* I was in pain. But I was not thereby making the pain itself – the content of my experience – available to the dentist. Nor would such conveyance seem easier, or even in principle possible, if I had been able to use the resources afforded me by the public language I shared with the dentist.

PAIN is often taken to be a good example of the category of experience. But when one realizes that this category includes the whole gamut of bodily sensations as well as the kind of thing that takes place when we perceive the outside world, or introspect our current mood or trains of thought, it may be unreasonable to use the example of pain in this way. For certainly there are differences between pain experiences and the others. Yet, pain has in common with these other experiences these features: high accessibility (to their subject), poor observability (by others) and poor expressibility (by the subject to others). And, since it is the conjunction of these three general features that makes so much trouble for our understanding of experience, we need not be worried here about specific differences within that category.

2.2.2 Knowledge

There are many different ways in which such trouble can be made to appear, but perhaps the most direct begins by a brief reflection on what it is to know something. Here is a truth – almost as a truism – about knowledge:

When you know something, there is something that you know.

This claim owes its obviousness to our understanding of what makes something a propositional attitude. For, though knowledge may be special in all sorts of ways, it is after all one among the attitudes, and as such it has content. A specification of a knowledge claim has the standard form 'x knows that p' where x is some knower and p is the knowledge content. So, of course when you know something, there is something – a content – that you know.

A second claim about knowledge would appear to follow directly on from this:

When you know something, you can say what you know.

Calling this the 'expressibility principle', you should be able to see why it might be thought to be a consequence of the claim about content. If the standard form of knowledge attribution is: 'x knows that p', then any such truth comes equipped with what is needed for expressing that knowledge. I know that Tower Bridge is in London, so I have available a form of words ('Tower Bridge is in London') with which I can express my knowledge to anyone who cares to listen.

There are many reasons one might have for resisting the idea that knowledge is essentially expressible, and some of them will emerge in the further discussion of experience. But there is one reason that is not particularly relevant

47

to our concerns, and it can be dealt with by a small qualification to the expressibility principle. There can be things that we know, but only in an implicit way. For example, I might be said to know all sorts of things about the grammar of English, though there would be no point in asking me what I know, since I might lack the requisite grammatical concepts to put my knowledge into words (*see* CHOMSKY). Usefully, such knowledge is called 'tacit' precisely because it is knowledge that we are unable to spell out. However, though it is clear that tacit knowledge, if there is any, makes trouble for the idea that we can always say what we know, this will not be relevant to the present argument. For it certainly seems plausible that when we know something in a completely explicit way – when we are non-tacitly aware of the content of our knowledge – then we ought to be able to say what we know.

2.2.3 The Problem

Against these background claims about knowledge, the path leading to trouble is uncomfortably straight. When someone has a pain, it certainly seems to be something known to the person whose experience it is. Equally, when I look out at an expanse of forest in the summer, the *experienced* quality of the shades of green, as well as that of the shapes of the trees, seems to be something in my CONSCIOUSNESS I not only know, but that I know in a way no one else does or can (*see* PERCEPTION and PERCEPTUAL CONTENT). Yet, the contents of my knowledge in these cases is not something that I can convey to someone else. I can of course say that I am in pain or that I am experiencing a complex range of shades of green. But neither of these would manage to convey the content of what I experience to someone else; neither would they make it apparent what it is like to have these experiences. So, it seems that I can know all sorts of things in respect of my conscious or experiential states that I cannot properly express. And this undermines the perfectly ordinary idea that if I know something, then I can say what it is that I know.

Initial reactions to this vary. I can even imagine someone thinking that there isn't much of a problem here – just a case of knowing something we are unable to find words to describe. Here we might be encouraged to think of times when something was so surprising, or passed by so quickly, that we struggled to find adequate descriptive language. And basically the thought here is that I was just wrong in suggesting that we can always say what we know. Perhaps, in spite of first impressions, the principle of expressibility is just not true of knowledge. Unfortunately, the tension between the expressibility of knowledge and the ineffability of experience will not go away so easily. Yet, if you are struggling to keep the tension in focus, perhaps the following example will help.

2.2.3.1 Simone's Story
Simone was born colour-blind. In her case, this meant that she could not distinguish any colour at all: her colour-discriminative abilities were no better than yours would be if you watched a black and white film and had to answer questions about the colours of the actors' clothes. However,

Simone did not accept her 'disability'. Instead, she set about trying to cope with the world of colour by other means. By laborious study, she came to understand the physical and psychophysical basis of ordinary colour perception. In time, and using devices to measure the wave-lengths of reflected and transmitted light, as well as allowing for the peculiarities of the way the human brain processes such input, she was able accurately to tell the colour – indeed even the shade of colour – of any object. Had you not been aware of the complex measuring devices, not to mention the theoretical reasoning that went into her judgments, you would not even suspect that her colour perception was inferior to yours.

That is the example. But dwell for a minute on the idea that, in spite of all her research and her uncanny accuracy in describing the colours of objects, there is still something *defective* about Simone's colour judgment. What makes it so natural for us to continue to think of Simone as colour-blind? I don't think it is difficult to offer some kind of answer here. She gets the colours of objects right, but she lacks something enjoyed by a non-colour-blind person – her perceptual experience is markedly different. Speculating a bit, we might imagine that her perceptual experience is something like that we would have if we were watching a black and white film. But whether or not this is exactly right, it seems clear that her inner world is markedly different from ours. And one way to summarize this difference is to say that we know something about, e.g. seeing the cloudless sky, that she doesn't.

Embellishing the story a little can make this point even more sharply. Suppose that Simone undergoes an operation which makes her experience exactly like ours. In this event, it is natural to imagine her saying something like this: 'I always knew that the sky was blue, but I never knew that blue was like *that*.' And this last word – the demonstrative 'that' – points directly at what we are trying to capture. The story of Simone seems to lead us inexorably to the idea of there being something it is like to perceive colours (and to have pains), and to the further idea that we *know* about this inner realm. We are led to these conclusions because – to repeat – it seems natural to think that Simone comes to know something about her experience of seeing *after* her operation that she didn't know *before*. (Remember that what Simone is said to know after her operation is not a fact about the sky, but one about her experience of it.)

The trouble is, though, that whatever it is that she knows remains strangely inexpressible. For, as we noted, there just doesn't seem to be a vocabulary suitable for giving any precise content to this knowledge. The best that I could imagine Simone as saying about her newly acquired knowledge is: 'I now know that blue is like *that*.' But this doesn't really convey the whole of what we usually expect from someone who is said to know something. Thus, consider how we manage with knowledge about our surroundings. I am just now sitting in my study, so I certainly know what it is like. And, given this, you would expect me to be able to tell you – to say things like: 'There is a desk in the middle, a pile of books on the floor', etc. But what would your reaction be

49

if, instead of these things, I said: 'Well, my study is like *that*'? I suppose that you would think that I either didn't know what I was talking about or that I was concealing certain things from you.

2.2.3.2 Introducing 'Qualia' It should be obvious that the problem we are having with our knowledge of experience is unlike cases in which we witness something so strange, or so terrifying, that we lack words to describe it. For it is possible to keep your attention fixed on what you are experiencing long enough to know (as we say) perfectly well what it is like. The trouble is that we just don't have words to express this knowledge. Of course we say all sorts of complicated metaphorical things about our states of mind: 'I felt as if I had been run over *slowly* by a 73 bus' (hangover), or 'I feel as if someone has tied a knot in my stomach and is *twisting* it' (anxiety). But our problem is not met by these sorts of description. What we lack are words for the simplest of experiences, such as the way it is with us when we see a perfectly ordinary shade of colour.

At this point you might be tempted by the thought that this lack is really quite superficial. After all, since we are mostly interested in telling each other what is going on in the world, it is perhaps not surprising that our language has developed without the necessary resources to describe our inner life. However, what is to stop us inventing some terms to fill this gap? Nothing – or so say those philosophers who have taken at least the first step in that direction.

Think of how things are when you look up at a cloudless sky. Asked, you will say that it is blue. But of course the colour word is used here to describe a feature or property *of the sky*, and no one would think otherwise. It is simply bizarre to say that your experience is blue. But then how can you even begin to describe how it is with you when you are seeing the blue sky? Here's how. Concentrate on the nature of your sky-directed experience, taking special care to keep fixed on what is happening to you, whilst ignoring as best you can how things are with the sky. There certainly seems to be something going on in your consciousness – something that has various properties. If you doubt this, just imaginatively compare how different these things would be if you were looking at the same sky, but that its colour began to change, having been made to glow red by the setting sun. No one could doubt your ability to distinguish the experiences of the two differently coloured expanses. And what else could explain this except that the experiences have different properties.

Now we of course don't have names for these properties – either the specific ones in the blue-sky case, or even their general category. But – at least in respect of the general category – why not just coin some suitable word? Why not follow the lead of some philosophers by suggesting we call the properties of experience (in general) 'QUALIA' (singular: 'quale')? The name seems apt since what we are dealing with are the *qualitative* aspects of experiences – the 'how it is to us' when we have them. Armed with this term, we can say this much about the blue-sky experience: it has qualia which distinguish it from, for example, the red-sky experience. We could also go on to invent terms for each of the specific qualia that mark our experience – we could say that the relevant quale of my experience when I look at the blue sky is 'bluish', though this latter term should not be confused with 'blue'. But what matters in making sense of such words as 'bluish' is that they pertain to qualia, so all the weight really hinges on the general term. For example, we can now (apparently) say what is defective about Simone's colour judgments before the operation: it is that she makes them without reference to the qualia of her experiences.

Does the coining of the term 'qualia' solve the problem with which we began? That is, can we now reconcile our knowledge of our experience with the demand that knowledge be expressible? This certainly would be a quick fix to the original problem – almost certainly too quick. Any new word only counts as a genuine extension to our language if we are fairly sure that we can understand what it is supposed to signify. And it is not clear that we have said enough to imbue 'qualia' with a meaning suitable to get over the expressibility problem. For the suspicion is that this new word doesn't do any more for us than the demonstrative 'that' as it occurred in Simone's original judgment: 'So *that* is what blue is like.' Indeed, I suspect that many of the proponents of this new word would be perfectly satisfied with this outcome. They never wanted to use the term to give a definitive answer to the expressibility problem. Far from it. What they wanted was some way to talk about that very problem. The word 'qualia' was invented as a way of answering those who take our lack of expressive means as indicating that there may not be anything it is like to have an experience. However, rather than spending any more time on qualia here, we should now review more complete responses to the expressibility problem. Considerations relevant to our understanding (or lack of it) of the word 'qualia' will be more intelligible against this background.

(Those familiar with some philosophical literature may think that 'qualia' is just another name for what used to be called 'sense data'. I don't think this would be quite right, but spelling this out is not appropriate here (*see* PERCEPTUAL CONTENT). Suffice it to say that those philosophers who have found it congenial to speak of sense-data have used them in projects different from our present descriptive one.)

2.2.4 *Grasping the Nettle*

I can imagine someone thinking that we have overlooked the best strategy for dealing with our present trouble in respect of knowledge of experience: what we should do is just brazen it out. If the accessibility and inexpressibility of our experiences do not fit with the idea that knowledge ought to be expressible, then why not just say – as far as experience is concerned – that the expressibility principle just doesn't apply? Why not just say that there is for each of us an inner realm to which we have a directness of access that is denied to anyone else and, further, that it is a mistake to regard the knowledge we have of this realm as expressible in the ordinary way? I can tell you that my study

51

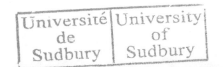

has a desk and books, but that is because the study and its contents are publicly observable – they are part of an 'outer' realm. However, when it comes to experience, the best I can do is to make a sort of gesture: I can tell you (as I did to the dentist) that I am in pain. I can tell you that my experience is of that special kind that I have when I see the blue sky or green leaves. And I can invent words like 'qualia' to make it seem easier to refer to these special features of my experience. What I cannot do is to be as fully informative about the inner realm as I am about the outer, but that is just how it is.

In essence, this suggested way with our problem comes under the heading 'grasping the nettle'. One admits that there are features of experience and knowledge that are in tension with one another, but then, rather than allowing this to bother us, we simply count the tension as itself a sign of the special nature of experience. The trouble is that grasping nettles – even philosophical ones – can be extremely painful. But before we see just how painful it is in the present case, I should like to point out something about the history of the view just canvassed.

As I have presented it, the view is a reaction to the apparent difficulties that we get into when we add our conception of knowledge to our conception of experience. However, the standard view of the history of these matters does not treat it as in any way a *reaction* to problems. Rather, in the works of Descartes (1596–1650), it is usually seen as the robust and confident statement of a conception of the mind that has been worked on – and over – during the past four hundred years. Indeed, it could be argued that Descartes himself only articulated what anyone would say about these matters; many regard the Cartesian view as the common-sense view. Moreover, the underlying tensions to be found in the conception have only been the centre of concerted philosophical attention in the past fifty years or so. Still, having admitted that my presentation is a-historical, I hope you will come to appreciate that it is none the worse for that. (*See* HISTORY.)

Grasping the nettle in the way described is tantamount to accepting that there is a sharp divide between our knowledge of the world – the external world of tables and chairs – and the inner world of our experiences which is commonly said to be known by INTROSPECTION. Of course, the spatial metaphor inherent in the words 'inner' and 'outer' is not mandatory. Less metaphorically, we could describe the Cartesian view as requiring us to recognize the divide as between *first-* and *third-person* knowledge – between what I know of myself, and what I can know of someone else. But whatever words we use, there is a high – and many think unacceptable – price to pay for maintaining this divide. (*See* SUBJECTIVITY.)

First of all, the existence of a sharp distinction between first- and third-person knowledge makes it difficult to understand how we can ever know that our friends and neighbours so much as have mental lives. For the Cartesian, each of the surveys of our feelings, perceptions, sensations and moods takes place in the privacy of our own minds and, though the 'qualia' we thereby come across can be as rich as anything, the attempts to convey these things –

to make them present in some way from the third-person perspective – never amounts to anything; all that we have as evidence of each others' mental lives are words issuing from our lips, and other bits of behaviour. But these words and behavioural manifestations could issue from creatures completely lacking in any inner life, so a complete scepticism about other minds is made possible by the Cartesian picture. And if we think that any view encouraging such scepticism is unacceptable, then this will be reason enough to look elsewhere to deal with the tension between knowledge and experience.

Of course, there are those who will not react to this kind of scepticism with horror: grasping the nettle a little harder (so to speak), they will insist that scepticism about other minds is perfectly reasonable – at least as a possibility. After all, no one has found a completely satisfying way of showing that philosophical scepticism in general is incoherent. The image of philosophers as people struggling to prove the reality of the kitchen table at which they are sitting is an enduring one. And philosophers know that these struggles can be interesting and helpful to our thinking, though they do not for a minute have any serious worries about resting their elbows on the table. So, why not admit that we might be unable to prove conclusively that the sceptic about other minds is wrong, whilst unconcernedly living and acting as if we had no doubt at all about the mental lives of other human creatures? What is to stop us saying that we can never *know* that those around us have minds, but that we can be pretty sure that they do – for practical purposes?

Leaving aside the issue of whether it is ultimately satisfying to deal with the sceptic by conceding even that much, there is a deeper problem which is easy to miss if you concentrate too hard on scepticism. In a nutshell, it is a question of the very coherence of the first-/third-person divide, and it is best approached by investigating the words that figure in our speaking about the mind. Take a specific example: Harry has a pain in his elbow, and he tells you this. Given the Cartesian picture, Harry has not thereby managed to convey fully what it is that he knows; full expressibility is denied to this sort of first-person knowledge. Yet Harry does use the word 'pain', so it is perfectly reasonable to ask what this word means both in his mouth and in his audience's ears. Here is one view: Harry uses the word 'pain' as the label of the experience he is presently undergoing. After all, he judges this experience to be sufficiently similar to other experiences he has previously labelled 'pains'. So, the word 'pain' has its meaning fixed by the inner landscape that Harry (and no one else) is in a position to survey.

This won't do. For how would *we* ever be in a position to understand what Harry said? If the meaning of Harry's remark depends on his own conceptualization of a realm completely unobservable by us, then he might as well have said something like this (with apologies to Lewis Carroll): 'My elbow feels uffish.' And actually the situation is even worse: for the conceptual location of pain depends upon the availability of general terms like 'feeling' of which pain is a sub-species. But the word 'feeling' too must get its meaning from Harry's inner survey, and it is thus no more available to third parties than 'pain'. So,

Harry's remark might have been: 'My elbow whiffles uffish' and this certainly leaves us in the dark about what is up with him. (Note that this line of reasoning would apply especially forcefully to the word 'qualia'. Indeed, the preceding sort of reasoning is what grounds some people's conviction that coining terms like 'qualia' does nothing to help us with the original problem.)

What can seem the natural move here is to admit that Harry's word 'pain' labels something unavailable to us, but to note that his use of the word goes with behaviour that *is* observable and is just like the behaviour we go in for when we have such experiences. Included here is behaviour such as uttering the sounds 'My elbow hurts.' Reasoning then by analogy with our own case, we say that Harry's behaviour shows him to mean pain by 'pain', since when we have pain, we behave in roughly the same way. But this won't do either. What we are asked to imagine is that the word 'pain' applies to me because of what I experience, but that it applies to others because they behave in roughly the ways I do when I feel myself to be in pain. Unfortunately, this appeal to analogy does not take seriously enough the confinement to our own case. For, given what has been described, it may be more sensible to say that the word 'pain' is systematically ambiguous than it is to say that it has the same meaning when I apply it to myself and when others apply it to themselves. This is because I never do manage to experience someone else's alleged pain – my analogical reasoning never gets a single confirmation. Even worse, it is not clear that I could now coherently say what constitutes a confirming instance. For, if I say that it is a case of someone else's having *just* what I have when I use the word 'pain', this never happens – one thinks indeed it *couldn't* happen. Yet, how could I even begin to say how someone's supposed inner life must differ from mine whilst remaining faithful to the idea that the word 'pain' is used in just the way I would use it? Given this problem, wouldn't it just be a lot more plausible to say that 'pain' means one thing for me and something else when used by others? The trouble is, this makes it wholly mysterious how we ever do manage to communicate with one another.

I have put this point in terms of words and communication, and there are those who might feel that such problems with language are relatively superficial. However, whilst the difficulty is easiest to explain as one about the use of words like 'pain', it is far more serious than that. For, given the Cartesian view, we seem unable even to *think* coherently about experience. If the concepts in terms of which we organize our thoughts about ourselves apply to a range of experiences that are only available from a first-person point of view, then there will be an unbridgeable divide between them and those concepts we use to think about others.

The trouble with scepticism seemed to be that it made knowledge of other minds impossible, though we imagined that we could at least formulate the hypothesis that others enjoy experience like ours. Now it should be apparent that there is a problem with the hypothesis even before we get to scepticism. If our conception of the mindedness of other people is determined by their patterns of action and speech, then of course we will often know that they have minds. But the hypothesis that is the subject of the sceptic's interest is not about publicly available behaviour. Yet how can we characterize the appropriate hypothesis? Is it that others can look inside themselves and see that things are like *this* (where we concentrate very hard on our stream of consciousness)? That can't be quite right. How can they find things to be 'like this' when what that is like is forever hidden from them? (Remember that the word 'this' refers to one's own conscious experience even though the aim is to give content to the thoughts of others about their experience.) How can I set out to imagine someone else enjoying my stream of consciousness?

To this you may be tempted to reply that I have overstated the case for the incoherence of the hypothesis: what is wanted is not that I imagine someone else enjoying *my* stream of consciousness, but just something *like* it. The trouble is, though, that on the Cartesian picture, the only experiences I ever come across are my own, and the concepts I use in framing my thoughts about that experience are forever bound to it. It is not easy to see what content I could give to the idea of someone enjoying what is not my experience but only very much like it, when the only idea of experience in play is my own. It is easy to miss this, since there is a tendency to think of cases where it makes perfect sense to make the first-/third-person shift. For example, though I have a particular kind of watch, there is no problem in imagining someone else having a watch of the same kind. But this is because the watch in question is in the public domain to begin with; anyone with the relevant discriminative abilities can frame a concept of that object and then use it to think about an object that would be *like* that one except in respect of ownership. But the Cartesian view makes it difficult to see how this sort of move is possible in respect of any given experience since ownership in this case is simply not detachable.

2.2.5 The No 'Know' View

Our discussion of the Cartesian attempt to grasp the nettle seems to lead to an impasse. But whether or not the case is proven, the time has surely come to see if there are less painful ways out of the original difficulty. Recall that all our trouble came from the fact that knowledge seems to be essentially expressible, whereas experience seems to be both known and inexpressible. I portrayed the Cartesian as someone prepared to say that we just have to live with the fact that knowledge of experience is an exception; someone prepared to say that there can be an inner realm of things which we can survey and thereby come to know about, though we cannot properly describe what we know. However, since there do seem to be reasons for thinking that we cannot really live with this picture, we ought to find something else to say about experience and knowledge. And a promising thing to do – almost as a reaction against the Cartesian picture – is to question the very idea of an inner realm known in this way.

The simplest expression of this questioning attitude consists in denying that the word 'know' is appropriate in the first-person case. Typically, when we know something, or are said to know it, we have had to do some looking around and checking. For example, I would now claim to know that there is a bird sitting on the branch I can see from my window. Of course, I could be wrong, and, if it was important, there are steps I could take to check this by, among other things, consulting with others. Putative knowledge is essentially fallible and it is also intersubjectively checkable. That is why the principle of expressibility seems so apt. However, none of these features seem to apply to what we have been calling 'knowledge' of our own experiences: it is not fallible in the way that my perceptually based knowledge is, and it is certainly not intersubjectively checkable. So, maybe the way forward is to deny that we have *knowledge* of an inner landscape of the kind suggested by the Cartesian. I shall call this the 'no-knowledge' view.

Here one must be very careful. It is all too easy to think that the suggestion just made is in effect a denial of the very existence of experience. To take our earlier example: when Harry says that his elbow hurts, the no-knowledge view will insist that Harry is not thereby attempting to express something he knows. And one might be tempted to think this was possible only on the assumption that Harry simply had no inner life – that there was nothing there to be the subject matter of any sort of knowledge. This temptation may even be further reinforced by remarks made by proponents of the view when they attempt to spell out just what it is that Harry is getting at. In particular, one suggestion has it that we should count Harry's words only as a piece of behaviour to be put alongside other things he might do in respect of his elbow, such as flinching when it is touched. When he says: 'my elbow hurts', he is in effect just saying 'Ouch!', though in a more complicated way. The one thing he is not doing is *describing* how things are with him, and this can lead one to think that the no-knowledge view is actually denying that there is any way things are with him. (*See* WITTGENSTEIN.)

A view that insists that mental concepts are in the end concepts that apply only to people's doings and sayings is usually labelled 'BEHAVIOURISM', and this view is beset with difficulties of its own. However, more important now is the simple fact that behaviourism is not really much of a help with our problem. We want to be able to say something about both experience and knowledge which makes it reasonable to regard experience as highly accessible without thereby threatening the expressibility of knowledge. A behaviourist interpretation of the no-knowledge view does not do this, since it just denies or ignores the thought that Harry has experiences that are highly accessible only to him. Of course, if the original problem proves completely intractable, someone might urge us to do the radical behaviourist thing, facing whatever further problems this leads to. However, for now it would be better to resist behaviourism and see if there is a way to understand the no-knowledge view which does help with the original difficulty. The no-knowledge view is after all the no-*knowledge* view, and, however tempting, this should not lead us too quickly to see it as the no-*experience* view.

As several of my earlier examples indicated, knowledge typically involves the application of our concepts to the objects and properties we come across. Thus, any knowledge I have of the bird sitting in the tree consists in my having concepts of such things as birds, trees and sittings, and my putting them together in appropriate ways in my thoughts. Note, by the way, that the objects and properties mentioned here are publicly available – one might say that they belong to no one and yet to everyone. However, on the Cartesian picture, the objects and properties that make up the inner landscape (experiences and their qualia) are quite different; they belong only to the person whose landscape it is. And this is what upsets the no-knowledge theorist. Such a theorist has nothing against experience or against the fact that experience is in some sense private. What he objects to is seeing the realm of experience as just like the realm of objects and properties that make up our public, intersubjectively available world.

Spelled out a bit more, the thought might be expressed this way: of course we all have mental lives and conscious experiences. And of course we inhabit a world consisting of objects and properties which we can come to know about and describe. But the conditions for our having concepts of, and describing, the external world are simply not met by experience. The Cartesian mistake consists in thinking that the 'inner world' is, for the purposes of knowledge and description, just like the external one. This mistake is signalled by the willingness to use the word 'knowledge' to describe our relationship to our experiences, but the mistake itself is not merely one about when to use this word. It is based on a deep misconception of the nature of experience. It assumes that our experiences are arrayed in something like a landscape even though none of the features of real landscapes apply.

The no-knowledge view is not an easy one to keep in focus. It has a tendency either to shift before your eyes into a kind of behaviourism or to disappear altogether. Returning to our example of Harry's pain, we certainly have a right to be told a convincing story about what Harry is up to when he says: 'My elbow hurts.' As I mentioned, if this is treated as nothing more than a complicated way for Harry to say 'Ouch!', then we are faced with a kind of behaviourism. Surely (many think) these sounds are not fully characterizable as a kind of ornate flinching. They say something about Harry's present experience – a kind of experience that explains why Harry made his remark and that, if Harry did flinch, would explain that as well. The no-knowledge theorist insists that we must not treat the phrase 'say something about Harry's experience' as just a paraphrase of 'tell us what Harry knows about himself'. For it is insisted that to do this invites the profoundly mistaken Cartesian view that Harry is the only possible *witness* to his 'private' pain, when the very idea of a witness only makes proper sense in respect of things that could be witnessed by others. Yet how else can we take Harry's remark? And, considering again the case of Simone after her operation, what could be more natural than to see her as saying: 'Now I know what it is like to see blue'?

Unless the no-knowledge theory can respond to these demands, it seems to be no more than a warning about how to use certain words. And the pressure on the no-knowledge theorist to let us use the word 'know' seems to many overwhelming. Yet there does seem to be something right about resisting the Cartesian picture and all the difficulties into which it tends to lead us. Given all of this, perhaps the way forward is to think of some way in which we can continue to allow that there is a special kind of knowledge which each of us has in relation to our experiences, but which is at the same time a kind of knowledge that steers clear of any commitment to the Cartesian picture. This is where the 'know-how' theory might come to the rescue.

2.2.6 The Know-how Theory

When we think of knowledge as essentially expressible, we surely have in mind knowledge having propositional content and characterized by the standard form: 'knows that p'. But there are other sorts. Thus, among his other accomplishments, Harry plays the piano rather well and it is natural to describe his talent by saying: he knows how to play the piano. But this attribution of knowledge does not require anyone (and this includes Harry) to be able to express what is known in some propositional form. The content of Harry's knowledge is not something like a proposition that is even a candidate for truth. Instead, it is an ability or capacity. (*See* LEWIS.)

Can the distinction between knowing that something is the case, and knowing how to do something help in our present predicament? Here is a suggestion. Suppose we agree that *knowledge that* is essentially expressible, and that Harry (in pain) and Simone have knowledge of their experiences. But we insist that, in the latter cases and appearances aside, there are no propositions that Harry and Simone know. Instead they each have a special kind of knowledge *how*. Consider Simone: before her operation, we felt that her vision was in some sense defective even though her judgments about the colours of things was spot on. After the operation, her judgments were no different, but it is natural to suppose that something had changed – that she had acquired some kind of perceptual knowledge. Well, why not say that what she had acquired was a kind of discriminatory knowledge – a knowledge of how to discriminate colours in a new way? The old way consisted in her appealing to measuring instruments and theories; the new way just involves looking.

Next consider Harry: he says that his elbow hurts, and it is natural to suppose that he is thereby expressing something he knows about himself. However, instead of telling the Cartesian story about Harry's inner landscape, why not just say that Harry's remark shows him to have a kind of discriminatory ability which is lacking in others? He can tell *just by paying attention* that his body is damaged in some way. Harry's specific ability is lacking in us because we have to examine him to see what the damage is – we cannot tell just by paying attention – though of course we each have an analogous discriminatory ability in respect of ourselves. And here the appeal to an analogy between Harry and ourselves is less fraught than it was in connection with the inner landscape view. For what is analogous is a perfectly accessible item: an ability to say – without instruments or detailed investigation – that one is damaged in a certain way.

The appeal of this know-how view is considerable. It allows us to say that the difference between the first- and third-person cases is one of knowledge: for Harry and Simone do know something. Yet we can say this without fear of contradicting the principle of expressibility of knowledge, since that principle only applies to propositional knowledge – knowledge *that*. Neither Harry nor Simone have that kind of knowledge about their states of mind. Additionally, this view gives us something to say about the accessibility and observability of our self-knowledge. For Harry and Simone not only know something – they know something we don't. That is, their abilities to tell what colour something is by looking, or to tell that they have suffered some kind of damage just by a sort of paying attention, are abilities special to them. To be sure, we can also tell what colour something is and whether their bodies are damaged, but not in the way they do. And it is the particular way – the particular ability – that is at issue here. So, we can say of this ability that it is highly accessible to those who possess it, but only low on the observability scale. Finally, as far as expressibility is concerned, it should come as no surprise to learn that it is virtually impossible to express what goes on when we exercise this kind of ability. No surprise, that is, just in the way that it is no surprise that Harry cannot describe his knowledge of piano-playing in any terms but these: 'I know how to do it.' Indeed, one could just about consider Simone's excited claim 'I never knew that blue was like that' as more or less equivalent to: 'I never knew how to tell by looking that something was blue. But now I do know how to do it.'

It is easy to get carried away by the know-how view, but all is not plain sailing. The main problem is that our abilities don't stand on their own: it is usual to ask for some kind of explanation of them. Thus, consider two abilities that Harry has: he can play the piano and he can hold forth about the kings and queens of England. The first of these is of course very complex and took years to develop, but it isn't unreasonable to say that it is partly a form of what is sometimes called 'hand–eye coordination'. Harry's eyes take in certain notes on the page and his hands, fingers and arms react to them as a result of the training he has received. Of course, if he is any good at the piano, he will also have the more conscious ability to control these reactions in ways that conform to his musical intentions. But for the moment let us think only of the more basic technical ability that consists in getting from the written to the played notes. How would we explain this? Clearly the answer to this would be enormously complicated (and is probably only known in outline), but whatever the details, we can with great plausibility say this much: our explanation will not have to appeal to anything that Harry explicitly knows or believes. And by 'explicit' I mean things to which Harry has conscious access. Thus, Harry doesn't consult some repository of consciously available information such as: if the black note is on the bottom line, then one must use the middle finger of the right hand. He will certainly know this sort of thing, but consciousness of this knowledge is not what guides his hands. If it did, it is unlikely that he would ever manage to move his fingers fast enough. (He might be guided by such things tacitly, but, whatever this means, we can leave it on one side for the moment for reasons that will become clear.)

Contrast piano playing with Harry's ability to tell you about the kings and queens of England. The obvious way to explain this ability is by appealing to a whole number of things Harry knows or believes, and to which he has conscious access. It is because he knows that Queen Victoria came to the throne in 1837 that he has the ability to say so. In a case like this, speaking about an ability is really only an indirect way of speaking about what someone knows in a fully propositional way. It is the knowledge of what is true that explains someone's ability to come out with it.

Given these two sorts of case, the obvious next question is which of them is the best model for cases of experiential know-how? That is, what explains the abilities Simone has with respect to the experience of seeing blue and Harry has with respect to his pain? Is it like the piano-playing case? Do they just come out with judgments about colours and pains as if they were producing these in unconscious response to something discerned – a sort of 'mind–mouth' coordinative ability? This seems absurd. What one would most naturally say is that the ability to say how things are (either with colour experiences or with one's body) is based on a prior awareness of the relevant experiences. It is because it is like *that* to see blue – and because Simone came to know this after her operation – that she has the ability to say of an object, without any use of instruments, that it is blue. And it is because Harry has an awareness of the pain that is undoubtedly connected with the damage to his body that he is able to make the discriminative judgments he does. In short, the more plausible model of our know-how in respect of experience is the one based on some kind of prior – and possibly propositional – knowledge. But, if this is the case, then we are back where we started: the know-how interpretation only hid from view the know-that problem.

Here I should insert a final note about the possibility of an explanation based on tacit knowledge, for it might seem as if this would be the best way to deal with our problem. This is because if tacit knowledge lies behind our abilities, then we would have a kind of knowledge that supported the know-how interpretation but avoided the expressibility problem (we already agreed that expressibility didn't apply to tacit knowledge). This move might seem especially appealing in view of the fact that many theorists of language (and piano playing) appeal to tacit knowledge to explain the relevant abilities. However, though all this is fine, it leaves out something crucial: we do want to preserve the special kind of access that we have to our experiences. But it is difficult to see how this can be preserved if we think that our experience of colour and bodily conditions is nothing other than a discriminative ability grounded in tacit knowledge. Just imagine being asked how it was that you could tell that the sky had changed colour towards sunset. This would be like asking Harry how he knew to begin the second bar with his right thumb. If, as we imagined, this was just a trained reaction on his part, he would simply say: 'don't know – just happened.' Though we could tell a story about his tacitly knowing a rule that connected the note and the hand movement, this would not be knowledge that Harry was aware of, and consulted, whilst he was playing. And could you really be satisfied saying that you had no idea why you said the two sky scenes differed – it just seemed right to say that they did?

2.2.7 Overall

That we know what we feel, that we know this in a way no one else can, and that we cannot fully convey what it is like to have these feelings – these things seem just obvious to many people. Unfortunately, when these are put together with equally obvious sounding claims about knowledge, the result is less than coherent. Moreover, as I have been labouring to show, it doesn't seem as if tinkering with our conception of knowledge or experience gets us very far in dealing with the threat of incoherence. So something has to give, something we think about the experiential aspects of the mental realm must be wrong. Or, at least, something we think must be re-interpreted in a fairly fundamental way. Radical solutions seem to be called for, and the philosophical community has not been slow in providing them. Here is a sample:

We don't really have experiences, we only *think* we do.

We don't really have experiences we only *say* we do.

We certainly do have experiences, and these are known only to us, but we don't know anything *else* including, among other things, about the existence of other people. (This position is best put in the first person: *I* know about *my* experiences and only about them, etc. It is called 'solipsism' and it is certainly a radical solution to the expressibility problem.)

We do have experiences but these are known as well, or better, to others – at least those who take an interest in the dispositions of our bodies. (On this view, maybe the dentist had a point after all.)

Most of these are not really motivated by local conceptual problems about experience that have been the subject matter of this part of stage 2. They arise more directly from the attempt to trace the foundations of experience and other mental items to the bedrock of the physical realm. This will be the subject matter of stage 3, but first we must consider the third of the categories, that of acting and actions. (*See also* DENNETT; IMAGERY; IMAGINATION.)

2.3 Acting and Actions

As was mentioned earlier, the mental status of actions is controversial: discussion following my informal questionnaires always shows up sharp disagreement about whether to count actions as mental phenomena. There are those who insist that they are no more than end-products of more genuinely mental items, and others who think that the credentials of actions to be included in the mental realm are just as impressive as those of the attitudes. The first group does not deny the important role that the mind plays in acting, but the point tends to be put this way: actions are the *outputs* of minds. As described earlier, they are the wake our minds leave as they travel through life, and for this reason they do not merit *equal* standing with the categories of experience and attitude. The opposing camp denies this second-class status for acting. On this view, when we see someone engaged in acting we are not merely seeing some sort of output, we are seeing the mind itself.

Disagreement about the status of acting suggests that there may be some fundamental difficulty in our thinking about actions, but it doesn't prove that there is. After all, supporters of one or the other position may just be wrong, and may change their minds when faced with a persuasive reason for doing so. Yet the aim here – as it was in respect of attitudes and experience – is to uncover any real difficulties infecting our understanding of actions. So, for the time being, I shall ignore the disagreement over status, and start from the beginning. What I intend to show is that there are several theses, each of which would be accepted as obviously true of actions, yet that when these are put together they yield unacceptable – even paradoxical – consequences. It will then be easy to see just how far the problem about status is a real reflection of the trouble with acting.

2.3.1 *Four Theses about Action*

The world contains lots of things – chairs, houses, people and the like. It also contains things that happen. Indeed, it would be impossible to explain what our world was like without saying both what things it contains and what happens in it. Can we sharpen or deepen our understanding by getting more specific – by replacing 'happening' with 'what takes place' or with 'event'? Perhaps, but any such improvements will not be necessary here. For the first thesis about action requires nothing more than the ordinary, if vague, word 'happen':

Thesis (I) Actions are things that happen.

Of course, there is a use of the word 'happen' that may seem less congenial to this thesis. For sometimes people speak of a happening as almost accidental. It might even be felt that this use *contrasts* with genuine acting, as in someone's saying: 'there was no action, it just happened'. Yet I suggest that even a moment's reflection will show that nothing in any of this undermines the truth of thesis (I). For, when it is claimed that there is a contrast between actions and happenings, the contrast is always between things done and things that *merely* (or *just*) happen. In order to make the contrast some such restriction is needed, and the felt need for this qualification actually supports thesis (I). The supposed contrast between actions and happenings is really a way of saying: look, actions are happenings alright, but they are not *just* happenings. And this shows the next thing we must do. We must supplement thesis (I) with some truth about actions that shows how it can be that the class of happenings is so much broader than that of actions – how it can be that there are plenty of happenings that are not actions. This supplement will take the form of a second thesis:

Thesis (II) Actions are those happenings involving agents: they are happenings that can be described as things done by agents.

This second thesis is a move in the right direction: it shows us how to draw the line between mere happenings and actions in the broadest sense, but it must be treated with caution. Here are two examples of happenings that count as actions in virtue of thesis (II).

(i) The tide scours a riverbed and deposits the silt outside the mouth of the river. In this case we say that the tide creates a harbour bar – this is something it does. We also say that it acts on the riverbed.

(ii) Harry puts on his left shoe. This is something that he did – it was an action on his part.

Now, clearly our interest is in actions of type (ii), but as stated thesis (II) seems promiscuous enough to allow in both of the above types of action. Of course it might be argued that tides only count as doing something – as agents – in a metaphorical sense. There is a sort of harmless, if not poetic, animism in thinking of tides in this way. And if this is right, then perhaps thesis (II) could be regarded after all as capturing just those cases that interest us: all we have to do is to insist that any metaphorical uses of agency don't count. However, whether we take this way out or not, we are going to have to say more about the kind of agency that does interest us, so it is perhaps just as well not to argue too much about thesis (II). If someone insists that type (i) cases are really (literally) cases of action, so be it. But even such a diehard would have to recognize that there is a world of difference between the kind of 'doing' brought about by tides and the kind that involves what we might call 'personal' agents. So, since there is this difference, and since our interest is wholly in personal (mostly human) agents, we might as well come clean and say:

Thesis (III) Personal actions are things done by agents who possess minds.

In being explicit in this way, we can from now on economize by using the simpler 'action' and 'agent' in place of having always to say 'personal action' and 'personal agent'. But of course there is much more to be said about what is involved in this kind of agency.

Theses (II) and (III) are unspecific about the relationship between agent and action; all they say is that a happening is an action if it 'involves' an agent, or if it is a 'thing done' by an agent. But neither of these will do. The problem is that there are many things that involve agents, or could be said to be done by them, that we would not ordinarily count as actions. One example should make the point clearly enough. Harry had a bad cold which left him with a rasping cough. On any of the occasions when he gives voice to his affliction, it makes perfect sense to ask: what did Harry just do? And for the answer to be: he coughed. Yet, even though coughing is something that involves Harry – is something that the agent Harry did – we would not count this among Harry's actions. To see this, think of a case in which Harry coughs, but this time because he wants to show his disbelief in what someone is saying. Both kinds of coughing are things Harry does, but only the editorial cough seems up to scratch as an action. And the difference between the cases is as plain as can be: some things we do are done deliberately or intentionally, some are not. Hence the next thesis is:

Thesis (IV) Things agents do count as actions if they are done intentionally.

There are lots of things to say about this thesis. On the one hand, it would be nice if we could spell out somewhat what is required for something to be done intentionally, and to show how the intentional is connected to the 'deliberate' and the 'voluntary'. More on all this shortly. But there is a more pressing need to say something to block what otherwise might be a devastating objection to thesis (IV), namely that it is false.

Consider again hapless Harry. He is being shown the porcelain collection of his neighbours and, when he reaches out in a suitably admiring way to grasp a figurine, he unbalances another (known to its owner as the 'Hunter and Dog') which smashes on the floor. No one thinks that Harry smashed the Hunter and Dog intentionally. Not even those who know he has always thought that porcelain figures were not much better than tacky souvenirs would think that. Even so, smashing the porcelain is surely not like his cold-induced cough; unlike the cough, the breaking was surely Harry's action. In sum, we seem to have a case of an action that is unintentional, thus contradicting thesis (IV).

One way to deal with this counterexample is to think about it a little more carefully. Contrast it with a case in which Harry smashes the Hunter and Dog, not by reaching for another piece of porcelain, but by a spasm that causes his arm to thrash out in the Hunter and Dog direction. Like Harry's coughing this kind of smashing is unintentional, but it seems quite different from the reaching case, and the difference is fairly clear. In reaching, Harry didn't smash the Hunter and Dog intentionally, but he did do something intentionally – he reached for the other piece. This was what brought about the destruction. As so often, what we intend and what we end up bringing about as a consequence, are two different things. But it is usual to regard something as a proper case of action as long as it can be described as intentional from some point of view. With this in mind, we might be able to repair the damage to thesis (IV) by changing it slightly:

Thesis IV (revised) Things agents do count as actions if they are done intentionally, or if what they bring about results from something done intentionally.

With thesis (IV) revised in this way, we are finally zeroing in on the essential features of those happenings that would be regarded as actions. Indeed, all that remains is to say what makes a doing intentional.

Note the heavy irony in my use of the phrase 'all that remains'. For one of the most complicated topics in the philosophical discussion of action consists precisely in saying what makes an act intentional. However, by sticking to the most general considerations, it should be possible to say something uncontroversial about all this. And given my ultimate aim of showing that our ordinary thought about action tends towards certain incoherencies, it is crucial that whatever is said be uncontroversially ordinary.

When Harry broke the Hunter and Dog, he reached for the neighbouring figurine intentionally. Another way to say almost the same thing is to say that he was minded to reach for the relevant object, and this quaint way of putting the matter can tell us quite a bit. For in saying this, we are indicating that there were features of Harry's mental condition directly implicated in the reaching – features that made the reaching intentional. Which features? Well, in the broadest sense, one could say that Harry believed certain things:

there was a reachable figurine in front of him,
it belonged to the collection of his friend,
his handling it in a respectful way would be appreciated,
etc.

and that he wanted certain things:

to put his hand on the reachable object,
to show interest in his friend's collection,
etc.

and finally that it was the combination of these beliefs and wants that constituted something we would call Harry's *reason* for reaching in the way he did (*see* REASONS AND CAUSES, RATIONALITY). Then all we have to add is that having some such reason is what makes it true that Harry was minded to reach, that his reaching was intentional. That much is surely uncontroversial, though things get sticky when we try to be more specific about the connection between having a reason and acting intentionally. Some are tempted to say that the reason brings about a further mental condition – Harry's having an INTENTION – and it is the presence of this that makes the reaching intentional.

Others say that there is no such further mental condition, and that having the appropriately active reason is itself what constitutes the intentionalness of the reaching. Moreover, there are long and contested stories told about the way reasons 'bring about' or show themselves to 'be active'. (Some discussion of this will figure in stage 3.) But since all we care about here is finding those features that determine which kind of happening is an action, it is perhaps forgivable if we pass over these disputes. For everyone accepts that if a happening can be traced back to a reason, and if that reason suffices to make the happening intentional, then we have a case of action.

Just before we move on, I should tie up one loose end. Earlier I said that being minded to do something would probably not be considered equivalent to doing that thing intentionally, and pointing out why this is so will remove a doubt about thesis (IV) that may have occurred to you. It has to do with the question of our awareness of our reasons. There are of course times when we ponder our next course of action, when we call to mind the beliefs and wants that finally figure in our reason for doing this or that. (Think here of deciding whether to make lunch now.) And there are other times when we act – and do so for a reason – but when the reason is not one we have contemplated in advance of acting. (Think here of suddenly squeezing the brakes on your bicycle when a pedestrian carelessly strays in your path.) It makes perfect sense to say that you were minded to make lunch, though it is doubtful that you were minded to bring your bicycle to a sudden stop. Yet both are clearly cases in which you acted intentionally, and both involve your having reasons. It is just that in the bicycle case, the reason you had to squeeze the brakes was not itself the subject of your deliberative awareness. Rather, it was something plausibly attributable to you on the basis of attitudes and propensities to act that were (one might say) silently at work as you were bicycling along. So, when thesis (IV) speaks of the actions as intentional and when we connect 'intentional' with the having of reasons, we are not thereby committing ourselves to any very fancy story about the explicitness or deliberative awareness of reasons.

2.3.2 Identity and Individuation

As preparation for taking our next step, here are a few words – and a picture – of where we have got to. Figure 2 is intended as a representation of the cumulative wisdom of the four theses about ACTION. As the concentric circles show, the successive restrictions we put on happenings have allowed us to narrow our focus until we can be fairly sure that the innermost circle contains actions. And being sure in this way that we have captured actions, we can now get to work on saying more precisely what they are. Since this last thought may come as something of a surprise to those who think we have been doing just that, let me amplify it a bit.

The contribution of theses (I)–(IV) was in helping us to locate actions by saying where to find them in our larger conception of the world. And what we have said in thesis (I) is that the place to look is at a certain range of

Figure 2.

happenings, namely those involving the mind in roughly the ways outlined by theses (II)–(IV). For example, we are now sure that Harry's reaching was an action because it was a happening suitably involving something we called a reason. However, though this helps us to recognize the reaching as an action, it doesn't tell us what a specific reaching is, and how it differs from, say, a grasping or pointing. One way to put this would be to say that the story so far helps us to *identify* actions, but not to *individuate* them. Here an analogy might help: you can identify something as a Beethoven symphony by saying who composed it, but this does not tell you what a specific Beethoven symphony is – what individuates it. It does not settle disputes about whether it is a pattern of printed notes in a score authorized by Beethoven, or is a performance according to that score, or is a pattern of imagined sound in Beethoven's mind, or . . . Similarly, in saying that actions are happenings located by means of agents' reasons, we have gone quite far in identifying those happenings that are actions without yet saying what the individual nature of an action is.

Of course, in saying what you need to be able to identify something as an action (or as a Beethoven symphony) you have to assume that your audience has some inkling of what specific thing you are talking about. How else could anyone understand the story about identification? So, perfectly reasonably, discussion of the identification of actions (or symphonies) has proceeded on the assumption that you have some grasp of the individual nature of an action (or symphony). The trouble is that in the case of actions (and here I think also in the case of symphonies) the inklings many people have are not sufficient to settle questions about individuation. For, as has been remarked, one gets nothing but dispute when trying to decide, for example, whether a specific act of reaching is a mental item or is merely the physical result of something mental. And yet this dispute can take place against the background of complete agreement in respect of theses (I)–(IV).

67

2.3.3 Once upon a Time

Where does this leave us? Well, the obvious thing to do is to set to work un-
covering theses that bear directly on the issue of individuation of action. In this
way, we might end up seeing what the real ground of disagreement is, and
whether it can be resolved. Of course, this route has risks. For my main goal is
to show that there are problems arising from uncontroversial thoughts that
people have about action. If I were to begin now suggesting theses likely to be
either technical, disputable (or both), this would ruin any chance of reaching
that goal. Fortunately, we are not going to have to run that risk. As thesis (I)
has it, actions are happenings. And though this perfectly ordinary thought is
hardly rich enough to take us all the way to an individuating conception of an
action, it will serve my nefarious purpose suprisingly well. For what I suggest is
that a little further reflection on thesis (I) will show just what a mess we get
into when we think about actions.

Bypassing all the complicated things we could say about happenings and
actions, the following certainly seems beyond dispute:

Thesis (V) When something happens, there is a time at which it happens.

This thesis is not meant to be particularly demanding. Certainly, it isn't meant
to suggest that we can always be very precise in our saying when something
happens. If you ask someone 'when was the Battle of Hastings?', you are most
likely to be told '1066'. Though historians can no doubt do better than this,
even they would be hard pressed to say exactly on which days and at what
hours it began and ended. All that is fine as far as thesis (V) is concerned:
battles are just too complicated to allow timing by stopwatches. Moreover, the
thesis does not even demand that we should always be able to *say* even
approximately when a happening takes place. There are things that go on in
the world when we are simply not around.

Nonetheless, even bearing in mind these qualifications, thesis (V) does assert
something substantial. It reveals our commitment to the idea that happenings
have locations in the temporal order – that it just wouldn't make sense to think
that there could be a happening that didn't take place during some more or less
determinate stretch of time. Moreover, if the happening is one we actually
witness, then, within relevant limits of precision, we ought to be able to say when
it began and when it ended. Finally, since actions fall into the class of happenings,
it should always make sense to ask the question: 'when did someone intentionally do such-and-such?' Moreover, since actions, unlike 'mere' happenings,
always involve an agent, this question should always be answerable. It just
doesn't make sense to think that someone could do something intentionally, but
that there would be no one around to count as a witness. Agents are witnesses.

Given all of this, what I propose is to consider some examples just to see how
we fare in placing human actions in the temporal order. Somewhat surprisingly, it turns out that we do not fare very well. Moreover, the problem is
deeper than it might at first seem – or so I shall argue.

2.3.4 *Moving, Breaking and Claudius*

2.3.4.1 *Moving* Just to get us off on the right track, I shall begin with an example that doesn't seem problematic. On the table in front of me is a bowl. By bringing my hand into contact with it, and exerting some small, even pressure, I have managed to displace it several inches to the left. What have I done? I have moved the bowl to the left. When did I begin to do this? At that very time when it began to make its way across the table. And when did I finish this act? When the bowl came to rest. Nothing seems difficult here: the happening that is my action can be located (within reasonable limits of precision) in the temporal order. My intentionally displacing the bowl would seem to coincide in time with the observable displacement of the bowl.

2.3.4.2 *Breaking* The second case raises more questions. Arm outstretched, I hold up a piece of chalk and then relax the grip of my fingers. The chalk falls to the floor and breaks. What I did – quite intentionally – was to break the chalk. When did this begin? Well, it is certainly tempting to think that I began the episode of breaking when I released my hold on the chalk. But when did I finish breaking it? At the moment when it began to slip through my fingers? This doesn't seem right, since the chalk is at that stage unbroken. At the moment when it hit the floor? This seems more like it, but there is a problem. For having released my grip, there is a sense in which I didn't do anything at all during the time it took to reach the floor; it is only a short time, but it is not unreasonable to think that I was *inactive* during it. So, it may seem odd to count that time as included in my action. Unlike the case in which I moved the bowl, the intended effect of my action seems not to coincide temporally with my being active. Still, since the time between my releasing my grip and the chalk's breaking is very small, we might get away with saying that I broke the chalk at 10 minutes past the hour, and leave it at that. After all, I did say earlier that a high order of precision in our timing of actions is not required by thesis (V).

Or we could take another tack – one less evasive. We could say that, strictly speaking, the action was nothing more nor less than the releasing of my grip. This happened at a particular moment in time, yet, as with many things we do, it had further consequences, among which was the breaking of the chalk. Knowing of this consequence, anyone who was a witness could *redescribe* the action – the releasing – as a breaking, even though the action itself ended before the breaking began. We go in for this kind of redescription all the time with particular concrete objects. Thus, we can describe one and the same object as 'the blue car in the drive' or as 'the car that stranded me on the motorway'. Same object but two different descriptions, though the second of these is only apt if certain facts about the car are known. (Before I set out for the motorway, it would not have been possible for me to describe it in terms of the stranding.) Similarly, the releasing of my grip – that very particular happening – can be described in many different ways, one of which becomes available only after the chalk reaches the floor and breaks. That particular releasing *was* a breaking. This is something we come to know after it happens, and all will be well so long as we don't allow ourselves to think about other releasings which could have taken place, but didn't. These other releasings might have misfired; one of them might have involved a carpet that cushioned the impact and the chalk might not have broken. But these other non-destructive releasings are not what took place.

Note that this way of dealing with the breaking was not apparently called for in the bowl-moving episode because the movement of the bowl and the action of moving the bowl were simultaneous. Of course, once we look at the bowl-moving case in this new way, we are committing ourselves to a distinction between some effect (the bowl's moving) and some action (moving the bowl), even though the effect and the action are simultaneous. Keep this in mind as it will be important later on.

2.3.4.3 Claudius   The following imagined case is meant to test the various suggestions made in respect of the chalk-breaking. Changing the well-known (though already fictional) story, consider the case of Claudius and the King. Claudius wants the King out of the way, but he wants to avoid any chance of being caught. So, he acquires a very slow-acting poison which he administers by pouring it into the ear of the sleeping King. Having administered the poison, he retires to his own castle and awaits the outcome. Sure enough, after a period of some six months, the King succumbs to the effects of the poison and dies. As he expected, Claudius appears to members of the court to be in the clear: he has been miles away from the King for most of the six months. Yet we who are in the know have no doubt in saying: Claudius killed the King. Yes, but when? Well, Claudius moved his fingers and hand in such a way as to empty the vial into the King's ear. Suppose this happened at 3 pm on the 5th of May 1360. It then seems perfectly plausible to regard this as what we might call the 'start time' of the deed. But a start time is not quite enough to get the happening properly settled into the temporal order. For we need to know when the killing ended, and many would be reluctant to say that Claudius killed the King on the 5th of May. After all, the King didn't die until the following November.

Someone might be tempted to say that the murder was a rather longish happening which began on the 5th of May and ended in November. The idea here would be that happenings can have parts and that the pouring was the first part and the dying the second. This would be like the move made earlier which treated the chalk-breaking as beginning with the releasing and ending with the breaking. However, though it just about sounded alright in that case, the length of time involved in the murder makes this suggestion much less appealing. What seemed odd before was that someone should describe me as engaged in breaking the chalk – being active in this way – when I was standing there inactive, having already made my contribution to the activity by releasing my grip. Whilst it is easy to think this was just picky in respect of the breaking, it is a serious difficulty in the case of the murder. Do we really want to say that what Claudius did happened from May to November? Suppose you see him sitting peacefully in his castle in September reading a book: do you want to be committed to saying that he is then both reading a book and murdering the King? And what if, as is possible, he had died before the King? Posthumous publication is one thing, but would we really countenance posthumous murdering (other than supernaturally)?

What about the second suggestion? Why not treat Claudius' activity as beginning and ending on the 5th of May when he poured the poison? The death was of course a consequence of this pouring, but is not itself *part* of the act. It is just that in November, when the King dies, we then have available a new way of describing the original pouring: we can now say it was a killing, indeed a murder.

As before this way of treating the matter makes more sense in connection with the chalk-breaking than it does in respect of the murder. For, whereas it may be just about acceptable to say that I broke the chalk when I released it, it seems odd to say that Claudius murdered the King on the 5th of May. This is because there seem to be so many things that must happen before the death occurs, and so many ways it could go other than as Claudius had hoped. Of course, we can stick to our guns here and say: 'Look, that very action – the pouring – had the death as a consequence. If the death had not occurred, then it would have been a different pouring of poison from the one that actually took place.' As long as you keep thinking of what Claudius did as a wholly specific thing which had the consequences it did have, then there is no harm in saying that he murdered the King on the 5th of May. It is just that this description of Claudius' act only becomes available in November.

It should be obvious that this kind of 'sticking to one's guns' brings with it a conception of action that goes beyond what is contained in theses (I)–(IV). We have now to think of each action as some kind of wholly particular thing which has its causes and consequences tied to it in some unbreakable way. If, even in thought, you change something about the consequences of an act, you are then barred from speaking about the very same action. For example, in connection with the present discussion, one might be tempted to appeal to a case of 'Claudius Interruptus': Claudius pours the poison in just the way that he did, but the King rolls over, or he later takes some substance which has the effect of an antidote, or his doctor figures out how to cure him. However, on the view we are considering, the very fact that the King does not die means that Claudius' act on 5th May is not the same act as the one which began our considerations – for that act resulted in the King's death.

Whether this conception of action is ultimately convincing enough to justify the claim that Claudius murdered the King on the 5th of May is, I would suggest, unclear. But remember that it or some other view is necessary to help us answer the question: when did Claudius murder the King? For no matter what deeper view we take of action, we are committed to the idea that actions have temporal locations, and we are certainly having trouble locating this dastardly deed. So, given that the view under consideration has less trouble-

71

some consequences than any other – for surely we do not want to say that the act took Claudius six months to complete – let us continue our discussion assuming that it is basically correct. It does commit us to saying some odd things, but maybe this is just the price to pay for having something to say about when the act took place.

2.3.4.4 *Moving Reconsidered*   We have settled for what can be called the 'act/effect' view. That is, it requires that we distinguish an agent's act from the effects that follow such acts *even when these effects are responsible for the descriptions we give of the original actions*. Thus, 'breaking the chalk' describes something that I did, but this is only appropriate because of the destructive effect of my loosening my grip. Indeed, according to the act/effect view, one should expect there to be lots of different descriptions of what will in fact be one and the same action: loosening my grip, releasing the chalk, breaking the chalk, making a mess on the floor, making a point to a lecture audience, etc. And since all of these descriptions point to the same bit of my activity (my loosening of my fingers), we might as well distinguish this activity by calling it my *basic* action. In the light of the distinctions between basic acts and descriptions, it is worth reconsidering our first example, the case of moving the bowl.

When we discussed this example, it seemed to cause us no trouble at all. And now we ought to be able to see why. The timing of my action in that case coincided perfectly with the effect it brought about: my moving the bowl (my basic action) and the bowl's moving (the effect of my act) took place simultaneously. So, of course we had no trouble in saying when I acted. Or so it can seem. What we have to do now is to see how, if at all, the act/effect view applies to basic actions. Don't be surprised about this. We have been assuming that we know when these take place – that we know when I move my hand whilst it contacts the rim of the bowl, that we know when I release the grip of my fingers on the chalk, and finally that we know when Claudius does what is appropriate to inverting the vial over the King's ear. But it is now important to see what is going on 'inside' basic actions. And for this purpose, the bowl-moving episode will serve as the example.

The first thing to do is to forget the bowl and its movement. We have agreed that this is an *effect* of what I did, and our sole interest now is in what I did. Well, the obvious thing to say here is that I moved my hand – that was my basic action. However, let us look at this more closely. Focus on the claim that I moved my hand. Can we see this – as per the act/effect view – as a complex consisting of some action and some effect? Admittedly it is a very small complex, but even so it does seem that there are two things discernible: one is that my hand moved and the other is that I moved it. And the first of these – the movement of my hand – could be seen as the effect of whatever it was that I did. On the act/effect view, it is perfectly reasonable to describe my action in terms of its effects, and in the present case we say 'I moved my hand' just because whatever it was that I did produced the hand movement as an effect. But what then did I do? And when? Neither of these questions is going to be easy to answer. In answering the first question, we need to find something that I did that can be described without mentioning its effect (the movement of my hand). But there doesn't seem to be any candidate description for this. Perhaps the best we can say is: I set myself to move my hand, and it was this that brought about the movement. And when did I do this? Well, precise temporal location isn't crucial, but, whenever it was, it certainly must have preceded the movement of my hand. Are these answers satisfactory?

Setting myself to move my hand at a time before it moves must be something that happens, as it were, 'inside' me; it would seem to be some kind of mental phenomenon (*see* THE WILL). We could even imagine a case where this mental activity took place without its bodily effect. For example, suppose that some demon psychologist gave you a drug which paralysed your hand and arm, but did so in such a way as to leave you ignorant of this fact. She then blindfolds you and asks you to move your hand as if you were pushing a bowl across a table. What do you think you would do? Well, as far as anyone watching you was concerned, you would *do* nothing. But how would it appear to you? Well, you would certainly be able to set yourself to move your hand, and, if the drug really did leave you ignorant of your state, it would appear to you as if you were doing that very thing.

Taking apart basic actions in this way seems to have at least this advantage: it allows us to locate the onset of an action in the temporal order. Setting yourself to move your hand – what has been called 'willing' your hand to move – begins in some small time interval before your hand actually moves. But when does it end? Does it continue even after the hand begins to move? Or are we to think of this act of will as somehow imparting its energy to the hand even though it ceases to work when the hand starts to move? It certainly doesn't feel that way in my own case: when I move my hand in the way required to move a bowl, it seems to me as if I am *guiding* my hand – as if my activity continues throughout. I can of course imagine what it would be like to have my hand move after just one, so to speak, push, but that is not how it seems in the normal case.

These questions are perhaps more difficult than the ones we asked of the chalk-breaking and of Claudius' felony. Moreover, even if we could answer them, we are still left with something very troubling. For, if we end up saying that an action is something like setting oneself to do something, or exercise of will, then, as was noted, this can take place without anyone seeing it. In the normal case, it will have effects on the body, and we will see these, but the act itself will escape the scrutiny of everyone but the agent. And do we really want to treat an action as subject to all the problems of the first-/third-person divide that were discussed in relation to experience?

2.3.5 *Conclusion*

We began with a few harmless theses about action and one thought about happenings in general. However, several straightforward examples later, we find ourselves in a bit of trouble. The theses told us that actions could be identified as happenings with the appropriate mental pedigrees, and, further, that as happenings, they ought to fit into the temporal order. But they don't fit – or at least not without great discomfort. And even stranger, we have found at least some reason to think that when we are genuinely active, the crucial ingredient in that activity is rather like an item of experience – something that raises the possibility that we will have some of the same problems with action as we did with pains.

This last result will no doubt appeal to those who insist that actions are mental phenomena. They might even take this as a victory over those who had maintained that actions were at most the visible signs of the mind. But things are not that simple. Recall that it was our need to assign a time to my breaking of the chalk that led to the doctrine of act/effect, and this doctrine seemed the only sensible thing to say about the case of Claudius and the King. For in that case the alternatives seemed to be: either say that the murder took six months or say that we cannot properly fit the murder into the temporal order. Admittedly, even the doctrine of act/effect has us saying that Claudius murdered the King six months before he died, but at least we saw the beginning of a more complex story about actions which might have made this palatable. Yet when we brought this apparently most plausible option to bear on the simplest of actions – the movings of our bodies which seem to be at the start of everything else we do – things seemed to dissolve in our hands. Instead of some well-behaved thing called a basic action, we ended up with an effect (a movement of the body) and a mental item (an exercise of will) neither of which meet all the criteria we expect in cases of action. The one is not really an action, just an effect, and the other is active, but it is not observable from an outsider's point of view except through its effects. In sum, it has turned out that when we try to say when actions happen, they tend to disappear from view. And even those who insist that actions are mental would not have been happy to think they were that elusive.

There are of course things we can do. But all of them involve a great deal more philosophy than one would have expected when we began. For example, we could just insist that an action is a *pair* consisting of an exercise of will and an effect on the body. Thus, we could simply refuse to count setting oneself to move a hand as an action unless it was successful – unless the hand moved. In this way, we could date the beginning of the action with the exercise of will and its end-point with the visible effect on the body. But we would then have to refuse to allow temporal assignment of this sort to any but basic actions, on pain of having to say that Claudius took six months over killing the King. Or we could bite the bullet and say that an action really doesn't belong in the physical realm, and that too much was being read into the idea that actions are happenings. Or, diametrically opposed to this, that much of the stuff about the mental pedigree of actions is misguided, and that actions are just bodily movements which are easily located in time.

These and many other options are all beyond my remit. For what they have in common is that they force us in one way or another to revise some of the things we ordinarily think true of actions, and my aim at stage 2 is restricted to investigating the consequences of ordinary thought. But just as something must be done about the attitudes and experience, it should be no less clear that this most important feature of the mind – its acting in and on the world – is a case for conceptual treatment.

Stage 3: Bedrock

3.1 Introduction

There is an enormous temptation to regard anything that happens as open to explanation in scientific terms. As with all temptations we can either steel ourselves to resist or give in. In the present case, I recommend giving in – though in a considered way – and I am supported in this recommendation by most writers in science, philosophy and related disciplines. Nonetheless, since so much of what goes on in contemporary philosophy of mind depends on it, I must say something about the background to this particular case of succumbing to temptation.

The present scientific picture of everyday changes and happenings is very impressive. Physical, chemical and biological phenomena which were once deeply mysterious are now routinely discussed and explained in an array of specialist journals and books. Indeed, the scientific enterprise has been so successful that it is now a commonplace to say that any one person cannot fully grasp the details of all its sub-disciplines. But in outline the picture is clear enough: the world seems to consist of such things as particles, atoms and molecules governed by laws, and it is this orderly and increasingly complex arrangement of energetic matter that gives shape to the world we experience. One science – physics – studies the configurations of energetic matter at the most basic level, and it is for this reason that the scientific world view is often called 'physicalism'. Other sciences – from chemistry through biology – attempt to unravel the laws that govern more complex configurations up to, and including, the organisms that have populated this planet.

Of course, many mysteries remain – there are many phenomena that are not explicable by the current physicalist picture of the world. And it this large reservoir of ignorance that might well encourage someone to reject the claim of this picture to any sort of comprehensiveness. This rejectionist line can seem particularly attractive, accustomed as we now are to be suspicious of scientific experts. Yet, in spite of its appeal, I would urge that taking the rejectionist line is much less rational than acquiescing in the scientific world-view. To understand why, some distinctions must be made between what actually comes with the scientific picture and what is inessential to it.

First of all, there is the distinction between the physicalist view of the world that goes with science, and the much more specific – and doubtful – view that all of science itself is essentially reducible to that part of itself known as physics (*see* REDUCTION). It is unfortunate that the commonly used word 'physicalism' hints at the latter idea – the idea that everything is reductively explicable by physics – but it isn't difficult to keep these things separate. Physics is the study of the laws governing such things as elementary particles and atoms, forces and fields. There may be every reason to think that the world is constructed out of such things, but one can think this without also thinking that such sciences as biology, zoology, chemistry, meteorology are themselves merely branches of physics – that there will be laws of *physics* that tell us everything about, for example, *biological* phenomena. All that the physicalist perspective requires is that whatever happens will be explicable by some branch of science or other; it does not require that all these specific scientific enterprises are themselves reducible to physics. How we should deal with the 'branches' of science will then be a further question, and not one on which we have now to take any stand. (Some prefer to speak of 'naturalism' or 'materialism' in place of physicalism here, but these labels can also be misleading. *See* PHYSICALISM; LEWIS.)

Talking in this general way about what some science may come to explain introduces a second distinction: that between the sciences we now have and the idea of science itself. At present we have a general idea of what physics, biology, chemistry and the other sciences say the world is like. But in adopting the physicalist or scientific perspective, we are not committing ourselves to believing that the present picture is correct. All we are claiming is that any phenomenon that is a genuine happening in this world is in principle explicable by a science, albeit by a science that might be quite different from any we now have at our disposal. Though it may be difficult to imagine, our present scientific perspective may be deeply misconceived. But all that the scientific or physicalist perspective requires is that the *methods* of science – not the laws or theories we now have – can in principle provide an explanation for whatever happens.

Finally, one must be careful not to misunderstand what it means to say that any happening must be explicable by science. For it should *not* be taken – as it so often is – to mean that what science has to say about a certain kind of happening is all that there is to say about it. The colours, shapes and images of a painting can be the subject of our aesthetic judgment, without this challenging, or being challenged, by the fact that science can explain everything about how the surface molecules and incident light produce (in us) the painting's appearance. Indeed, one may even find it possible to believe that there is a scientific explanation of the aesthetic judgments themselves, without this undermining their truth (or otherwise). In short, the universality of science should not be mistaken for a kind of tyranny.

Keeping in mind these three points, the thought that all phenomena (including the mental) must be in principle explicable by some science or other shouldn't be all that controversial. Whilst nothing I could say would constitute an air-tight argument in favour of it, I hope I have said enough to justify our proceeding as if the scientific perspective were true. To do the opposite would

77

certainly be rash, as we would have to believe *now* that some phenomena – say those of the mind – were not explicable by any present or future science. This last is certainly a possibility – one that we may want to return to when the going gets tough. But it is not sensible to start with it. (But *see* PHYSICALISM (2) for a less optimistic assessment.)

Why should the going get tough in respect of the scientific understanding of the mind? Answering this question will take a little time, but let us begin with the brighter side of the picture. The mental realm consists of a quite heterogeneous collection of things which share at least this feature: they are, in the broadest sense, things that happen. As you read this, as the light waves from the page strike your eye, you undergo various conscious experiences and, equally likely, you come to form beliefs and other attitudes, as well as going in for actions such as turning pages. The question of how to understand all this scientifically is thus no less pertinent here than it would be in respect of purely chemical, atomic or biological changes.

Put in this way, there seems to be no especially pressing reason for investigating the scientific basis of the mental. There are these phenomena – the mental – and we have just as much reason to expect that we will understand them in scientific terms as we have in regard to the weather or the behaviour of proteins. Of course, if some special need arises – as when a major mind-affecting drug is tested – then there is bound to be some more urgent interest in the various mental 'side-effects' that follow administration of the drug. But this kind of interest is much like the interest we all take in, say, seismology when earthquakes threaten large population centres; where human concerns figure prominently, the need to understand precisely why things happen – the need for scientific understanding – moves up the list of priorities.

The idea that the mental realm sits on the bedrock of the physical world as described by science, and that we shall gradually, and in our own good time, come to understand more about the contours of this fit, is by and large the common view in the scientific community (*see also* SEARLE). However, this relatively sanguine attitude about the relationship between the mental and physical is not typical of those in the philosophical community. Whereas the representative textbooks on neurophysiology tend to suggest that we will one day come to know more and more about the mind's relation to the brain, philosophical discussion of this issue shows no such equanimity (*see* PAIN). Indeed, it is only a mild exaggeration to say that what one finds instead is an urgent, even frenetic, search for some way to reconcile the mental and the physical; there is even a hint in some quarters of despair that the project will never get anywhere. Of course, even though I use terms such as 'frenetic' and 'despairing', I do not for a moment mean to suggest that the philosophical attitude is merely pathological – that, having opted for the idea that the physical is the bedrock reality of things that happen, philosophers have given in to a collective neurotic anxiety about the present impoverished state of our knowledge in that regard. On the contrary, it seems to me that the philosophical attitude is, if anything, more justified than that of the neurophysiologists, and thus the most immediate task is to show why.

One possible reason for the philosophical attitude arises from our ruminations in stage 2. The everyday notions of the mental are shot through with problems. The simplest of questions and assumptions lead to difficulties which can make us wonder whether we so much as have a coherent conception of the mental realm. The loose behaviour of the attitudes, the elusiveness of actions, the apparent incompatibilities of the first- and third-person perspectives, these problems are only samples, and yet they might easily provoke someone to worry about the possibility of ever having a proper science of the mental. After all, if we do not have a firm grasp of the mental happenings themselves how can we ever hope to understand their physical basis?

This last question seems calculated to invite the answer: 'we can't', but this would be too hasty. Granted that success in scientific understanding is made easier by our having a coherent grasp of the relevant phenomena, it does not follow that the lack of such a grasp renders the search for a physical basis impossible. For example, though the seventeenth-century account of what happened when things burned was largely incoherent, this did not prevent progress in the next century, and the eventual development of our now-accepted ideas about combustion and oxidation. So, whilst it would be nice if our conception of the mental was less problematic, this would not be a good enough reason for the widespread malaise in the philosophical community.

3.2 Reasons and Causes

The real reason for philosophical anxieties about the relations between the mental and the physical can be best brought out by backtracking a bit, i.e. by considering an issue which I touched on briefly in stage 2. I have in mind here the question of how acting is related to experiencing and attitudinizing. Consider the following mundane example.

> You are sitting on the sofa engrossed in reading. Whilst so doing you begin to be aware of rumblings in your stomach – they are almost audible – and a general feeling of emptiness. Could you be suffering from some sort of indigestion? You look at your watch and realize that you have lost track of time: it is now nearly 3 o'clock and you haven't had lunch. You decide that you are more likely to be suffering from *lack* of something to digest. Having been shopping the night before you know what is available, and you mentally run through the items. Believing that a sandwich would be the quickest thing to fix (though not necessarily the most tasty), you recognize that your desire for food *soon* is much stronger than for food *quality*. So, intent upon the idea of making a sandwich, you head to the kitchen and open the door of the refrigerator . . .

Clearly, as the dots show, the mental episodes reported in the example are followed by lots of activity. But for specificity let us focus on the action of reaching out and grasping the refrigerator door. This simple action is brought about in some way or other by the bodily feelings, beliefs, desires and intentions which you had in the minutes leading up to the action. It is clear enough that items of our first two categories – experiencing and attitudinizing – are in some way responsible for the eventual door-grasping behaviour. But in what way? That is, in what way is that amalgam of attitudes and experiences which could be called your 'mental condition' responsible for your subsequent action?

Two somewhat different sounding answers have been proposed. On the one hand, it would generally be held that your mental condition – or at least some element of it – was the *reason* for your opening the door. That is, if asked why you opened the door, you would make some more or less complicated reference to your beliefs, desires and feelings, saying that they provided your reason for so acting. On the other hand, it might be said (perhaps more naturally by an observer than by you) that your mental condition was the *cause* of your acting. Here the idea is that, just as we explain an earthquake by appeal to factors that cause it, so can we explain your fridge-directed behaviour by saying that your mental state caused it. And it is fair to say that these alternatives exhaust the field: the philosophical community seems agreed that minds rationalize – contain reasons for – actions, or they cause them.

Much effort has been expended in clarifying and defending these two possible explanatory stories. Attempts to understand what constitutes a reason for action began at least with Aristotle, and there is perhaps no more discussed notion in philosophy than that of a cause. However, for the present line of argument we do not need to spend a lot of time considering all of this background. For setting the stage to our problem, all we need to recognize is that these two answers are not necessarily incompatible: someone could hold (and many do) that a reason for an action can also be a cause of it.

Briefly, the story goes like this. A reason for an action is some set of attitudes and feelings which together show the action in a favourable light to the agent. Your mental condition in the above example made opening the refrigerator door an intelligible first step in the sequence of actions which followed. However, reasons tend to be a bit unspecific. Your reason for opening the door by grasping the handle would have equally made intelligible a whole host of slightly different movements. A reason doesn't explain precisely how our bodies move in acting on it. And this is where the idea of a cause comes in. For our original question was: what was the relationship between your mental condition and the *specific* action of opening the door that took place? A not implausible first reply is that your mental condition makes it *reasonable or rational* (from your point of view) for you to go in for some sort of refrigerator door-opening behaviour. But the full *explanation* of why you opened the door when and in the way you did must make reference to the cause of that very specific event. (*See* REASONS AND CAUSES.)

Bringing in causes helps, as they are the kinds of thing we appeal to when we want to explain why some specific thing happened. For example, suppose we are investigating the burning down of the house on 23 Elm Street. We know that faulty wiring can result in houses burning down. This is a general kind of truth which might well be in the background along with lots of other general truths (such as that gasoline and matches, when mixed with insurance policies, also bring about house burning). Knowing these sorts of thing helps, but in order to explain this particular burning down we must locate that actual state or event that preceded it and was, as one says, 'the' cause. Supposing it was in fact a loose wire in the kitchen wall that short-circuited the electrical supply, then the explanatory job is finished only if we can find evidence of this loose wire. If we can, we will have established a causal chain one could almost visualize: the loose wire in the wall touches another, there is no fuse to break the circuit, gradually heat builds up in the inner wall, combustion point is reached, the fire spreads in the wall, no one is home to notice the charring, the timber frames ignite . . . the house on Elm Street burns down.

Applying this to the refrigerator example, what we need is to find the cause for the quite specific door-reaching/grasping behaviour that took place. Now your mental condition functions to explain rationally why you went in for *the sort of behaviour* you did – it is (or contains) your reason for having so acted. But it doesn't by itself explain the particular door-grasping that occurred. So why not, as it were, kill two birds with one stone and recognize that the reason could itself also be the cause of the action? Philosophers have spent a lot of time considering what is involved in one thing's being the cause of something else, and at least the following three conditions are generally thought to be necessary:

1. A cause is some state, event or datable/placeable happening.
2. It precedes its effect.
3. It is such that if it hadn't happened then neither would the effect. (Since in a given case both the cause and effect have already happened, this last condition is 'counterfactual' – it says what would happen if things had been different. It thus places a very strong bond between cause and effect. Note too that some would argue that there must be laws of nature grounding these counterfactual claims. *See* ANOMALOUS MONISM; DAVIDSON.)

Unsurprisingly, these three conditions seem to be met by the very thing that is your reason for opening the fridge door. Your reason is part of your mental condition – a series of *states and events* which take place just *before* you open the door. This shows that conditions (1) and (2) apply. Moreover, it doesn't seem implausible to say that if you hadn't been in that condition you wouldn't have opened the refrigerator door. And this is a way of saying that condition (3) applies as well. So, the very thing that is a reason for an action also seems to have the characteristics necessary to make it a cause of an action. At least that will be the hypothesis which we shall adopt for our present expository purpose, and which we can represent by figure 3 below.

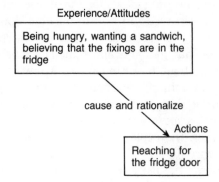

Figure 3.

3.3 Brains

Focus on the stage in our example where your arm is by your side but you are just about to reach for the handle on the fridge door. No one now knows everything about how our nervous systems work, but we do have some reasonable idea. Lots of electrochemical activity in the brain, channelled down appropriate neural pathways, causes the very complicated and yet delicately coordinated contracting and expanding of muscles in your arm. The precise nature of this contraction and expansion is continuously controlled by the brain's electrochemical activity, and this, in turn, is partly dependent on the neural activity in the optical system. To cut a long story short: your muscles – acting on the brain's electrochemical commands – extend your fingers to the fridge door handle, and all of this is achieved with the help of visual and other systems which monitor the position of your body and arm.

What is important is that what has just been imagined is a causal story, indeed it is what we might call a 'purely physical' causal story. Tracing backwards from contraction of your muscles which force your fingers around the handle to the neural excitation in your arm, and brain, and optic nerve, and so on, there is nothing here that anyone would regard as an activity of the mind. A textbook on the nervous system has no place in it for what would be a miraculous intervention of the mind in the causal chain just described. The physiologist doesn't even try to understand neural excitation and muscle contraction in any but chemical and physical terms. One would be stunned to read a paper in a journal of brain sciences which said: '. . . and just after this particular nerve sends its spiking pulse, the subject's thought intervenes to carry the message to the muscles in the arm.'

Have we any reason to believe that the neurophysiological story about your arm movements can be satisfactorily completed? After all, at present we know only a lot of general things about what goes on. I pointed out earlier that it may be an article of faith that all the happenings in this world are at bottom explicable in scientific terms. But I think that when it comes to that part of the world which is the human body, such faith couldn't be better grounded. For, unlike our picture of the sub-atomic basis of matter and energy, our *general* understanding of the biochemical basis of human biology is virtually complete. There are many details missing from the picture – and the details are crucial for such things as medical intervention – but there really do not seem to be the large scale mysteries in biology that there are in physics.

In respect of the hand poised for opening the fridge door, the picture shown in figure 4 seems to just about sum up the way things are expected to be,

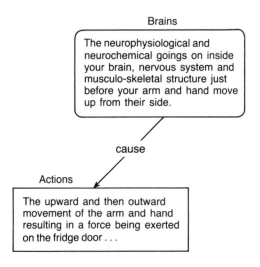

Brains

> The neurophysiological and neurochemical goings on inside your brain, nervous system and musculo-skeletal structure just before your arm and hand move up from their side.

cause

Actions

> The upward and then outward movement of the arm and hand resulting in a force being exerted on the fridge door . . .

Figure 4.

scientifically speaking. There are two things about the way the boxes are labelled in figure 4 which should be mentioned. Firstly, I use the label 'Brains' as a shorthand for the whole – and as yet unknown – physical story of what goes on. Clearly, where the mind is concerned, the brain itself will be particularly important, but I don't want you to think that I have forgotten about the rest of the nervous system, the muscles or the hormones. And there may well be other important elements to the story about the causation of action.

Secondly, anyone who followed my detailed story about actions in stage 2 will be somewhat surprised to see that the physical movement of the hand and arm is what gets the label 'action'. Given that discussion, it is far from obvious that the movement is itself an action; indeed, it may well be wrong to think this. Nonetheless, there is reason to think that an action such as reaching for the fridge door handle does include (or, less assertively, involves) such a movement, and that is the only thing intended by the label.

83

3.4 The Eternal Triangle

In matters of the heart, triangular relationships are celebrated for their difficulties. Two persons competing for the love of a third give the writers of soap
operas all they need to get going: only the details need to be filled in to generate endless different plots. What needs to be appreciated now is that putting
figures 3 and 4 together (figure 5 below) we get a triangular relationship
which, though hardly the matter of a soap opera, has at least at first glance
something of the same tensions – and leads to no fewer variations of plot.

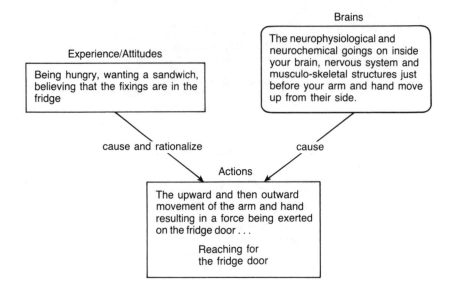

Figure 5.

In figure 5, the left-hand arrow represents the claims of the mind to be the
cause of what we do, whilst the right-hand arrow represents the claims of our
neurophysiological make-up. Now human relationships can be surprisingly
accommodating, but causal ones are not. It may really be possible for there to
be something like harmony in a love-triangle, but no such possibility exists in
respect of the causal claims shown in figure 5. Here is why.

Recall that among the very few things said about causality was this: some
event or state – call it A – is the cause of another (call it B) when it is true that
were A not to have happened then B wouldn't have happened either. This requirement can be true even though both A and B have in fact happened – remember that it is 'counterfactual'. The trouble is that the situation in figure 5
makes it impossible for this feature of causality to apply to either the left- *or*
right-hand side of the diagram. For example, suppose that it is really true that
you have some reason for an action which in fact causes it. Is it true that had

you not had this reason, this action would not have taken place? No, because so long as your neurophysiological state endowed you with the appropriate disposition, you would have acted, whether or not you had the supposed reason. Equally, it cannot be said of a case in which your neurophysiological state causes you to move in the active way that if you had not been in that state, you wouldn't have so acted. This is because figure 5 allows it to be *possible* for a reason to have brought about some action even in the absence of the neurophysiological state that in fact did cause it.

The problem here is known as that of *overdetermination*. It is arguably a feature of causality that effects cannot have two completely different causes competing for their attention. The counterfactual intimacy described above means that if there seem to be two completely independent causes, then one of them must give up its claim on the effect or, contrary to the original supposition, the causes are not fully independent. Here is a stark example to illustrate what I mean.

A house burns down, and the investigation unit of the Fire Department comes up with the view that it was caused by a short circuit in the kitchen wall. However, a neighbour has another idea. He believes that it was caused by a 'person or persons unknown' with a grudge to settle. Now, there seem to be three possibilities here: (i) the Fire Department are right about the short circuit; (ii) the neighbour is right about the grudge; or (iii) they are both right in that the grudge was settled by rigging the wiring so as to produce a short circuit. (They could of course all be wrong, but that is not worth considering here.) In possibility (iii), the causes are not independent – they are part of the same story – so this is not a relevant case of overdetermination. This is sometimes described by saying the causes are *overlapping*. Which leaves the other two. Is it reasonable to think that both (i) and (ii) obtain even when they do not overlap? That is, could the Fire Department and the neighbour both be right about the cause even though the grudge and the short circuit are both separate and independent causes of the fire? This would be a case of overdetermination, but can you really conceive of it whilst keeping your grip on the idea of a cause? I suspect not. How can the short circuit have been the cause if some second, and wholly independent, chain of events also brought about the fire? And how could the cause be the grudge if there was also a short circuit, which had nothing to do with the grudge, and which would have burned down the house anyway? Clearly, if we are careful about insisting on the non-overlapping condition, then overdetermination messes up the claims of both sides to be the rightful cause.

To be sure, there are cases where we might be tempted to think that we could rationally speak of overdetermination – cases where independent causes seem to be separately responsible for a single effect. For example, suppose that someone is very ill and suffers both a massive heart attack and respiratory failure – events that are followed by death. We may want to say that had the heart attack not killed the patient, then the respiratory failure would have – and vice versa – even though we would also insist that these do not overlap in the way the short circuit and grudge did in (iii) above. Is this a counterexample to the earlier claim about the incoherence of overdetermination? Not really. For even though the two conditions are different, there is nothing to prevent us seeing them as part of a larger condition which is itself the cause of death. Indeed, this is just how such cases are described when they occur: a doctor in such circumstances would cite the cause of death as 'a massive heart attack and respiratory failure'. Moreover, any attempt to press this verdict by asking which was really the cause of death would not unreasonably be resisted. For it would be downright misleading to single out one or other part of the larger circumstance as the real cause. What this shows is that, faced with a putative case of overdetermination, our intuitive understanding of causality forces us to see the competing events as parts of a single complex cause. In effect, the very idea we have of certain events as parts of larger ones is one we reach for naturally when overdetermination threatens. And this reaction shows just how deeply entrenched in our idea of causality is the rejection of genuine over-determination.

On the face of it, the situation in figure 5 is one where non-overlapping causes compete to bring about an effect. Since overdetermination is simply not reasonable, the situation in figure 5 is not a stable one – it is not a picture we can live with. But notice that this unstable situation arose from what seemed perfectly reasonable opinions about the causal prowess of both minds and brains. And it is this situation, arising as it does from these considerations, that grounds philosophical anxiety about the mental realm and its relationship to the bedrock of scientific description. When a philosopher thinks about how reasons cause actions and how our muscles are caused to move in response to brain events, these seem to lead inexorably to the precipice of over-determination. It will not help here to maintain the sanguine attitude that as we learn more about the brain, we will come to understand how the mind is related to it. For unless something is said *right now* about how to remove – at least in principle – the instability of figure 5, we aren't going to come to understand anything. Of course, there are many things we can say – and which have been said – about how to cope. Further, one of the conveniences of figure 5 (and this will make up for the initial embarrassment that it has caused us) is that it can help us organize the survey of these possibilities.

[Note: I have shown that the problems of overdetermination arise on the 'output' side: mind and brain both having causal claims on action. However, the whole triangle could have been based on the 'input' side: certain events producing beliefs and other attitudes via perception and, apparently at the same time, producing changes in the nervous system. This would have resulted in an inverted figure in which mind and brain occupy the bottom left and right vertices of the triangle respectively, with perceivable states of affairs at the apex (*see* PERCEPTION and PERCEPTUAL CONTENT). Of course, to see what the *problem* is we only need to look at one way in which overdetermination arises, and I think it is easier to see this in terms of the 'outputs' of minds and brains rather than in terms of their 'inputs'.]

3.5 Dualism

The triangular relationship is not stable, and we have to find acceptable ways to remove this instability. Of course, one way to go about it would be simply to eliminate or discount the claims of either Mind or Brain, though this rather drastic move will be considered only after we have discussed the gentler options. However, even before we get to them, I should like to say something about a view that is at the other end of the spectrum from the elimination strategy.

Descartes (1596–1650) held that mind and matter were distinct substances (*see* HISTORY), and one might wonder whether, if this sort of DUALISM can be defended, it would make a contribution to the present problem. Unfortunately, the answer here must be 'no'. For, whatever reasons one might have to share Descartes' view, the problem arises, not merely from the alleged independent existence of mind and matter, but from the fact that they both seem to make causal claims in respect of actions. If you are inclined to be a dualist, then you will be happy to drop the 'allegedly' in my last sentence. Mind and matter will be taken to be *in fact* independent existences. But this still leaves us in the dark about the rest of the picture. Indeed, insofar as we really do have distinct mental and material substances, overdetermination is, if anything, even more of a threat.

Descartes recognized that dualism alone was not a solution to the problem of seeing how the mental is related to the physical. Indeed, he thought that the mind brought about effects in the physical world; it acted on, and reacted to, things that were undeniably material. One could almost say that Descartes was the first to recognize the importance and difficulties of the triangular relationship, though not precisely in the form described above. He wondered how the mind could bring about effects in the physical world, since it was itself a substance not belonging to that world – his worries began with his dualism – whereas I am considering whether dualism can count as a way of dealing with the triangle. Still, both ways of approaching the matter lead to similar questions: are there mental causes of actions as well as material? If so, how does one deal with the threat of overdetermination? And, in any case, how can something mental cause something physical?

Descartes' answer to the third of these questions implied his answer to the others. What he claimed was that there is a little, very 'subtle' organ in the brain – the pineal gland – which is where mental states acquire the power to causally affect physical ones. This interactive view of the mental and the physical, if successful, would avoid the problem of overdetermination, since the mental would, in actual cases, provide links in a *single* causal chain leading to action. In effect, the mental and the physical would be overlapping causes rather like the unproblematic case of the grudge and short circuit in which the person with the grudge rigged the wiring in the house so that it would short and bring about the necessary heat in the wall to set off the fire.

Of course, as one is trained in philosophy to point out, in the case of mind and matter, Descartes' suggestion just doesn't work. For either the pineal gland is a mental or a material substance. If the former, then the problem of how the mental has physical effects is simply pushed that bit further back – to the relation between the pineal gland and whatever is the first physical waystation on the route to action. And if the pineal gland is material, as Descartes certainly thought it was, then the problem of causal interaction between the mental and physical doesn't go away – it simply takes place on the narrow stage of the pineal gland. Mere dualism of the mental and the physical will not make the problems go away, and Descartes' attempt to add a kind of interactionism to his dualism is usually counted a failure. Of course, this doesn't mean that dualism itself must be rejected. For all I have said, dualism might be true. But if it is, then it is difficult to see how to resolve the triangle. Indeed, since it is widely thought that such resolution cannot be achieved within the dualist framework, there is an urgent need to find some better way.

It should be noted here, if only for completeness, that an even more thoroughgoing dualism than Descartes' could provide a way to resolve the triangle. If one drops the idea that the mental and the physical interact, then one could convert the triangle into two stable pairwise relations in which the mental is partitioned from the material rather as in figure 6. However, this 'resolution' of the problem suffers from massive implausibility. For example, suppose you were hungry and, having thought about it, reached for the refrigerator handle. It would seem to you as if your thought processes eventuated in a movement of your arm, but, on the view being considered, this would be denied. Instead, it would be maintained that your thought processes eventuated in a mental action of some sort (note that I have carefully *not* labelled the arrows and bottom boxes), and that this action was accompanied by perceptions as of your arm moving. The whole of this train would be purely mental and it would be shadowed by, though would not causally interact with, a chain of purely physical events involving your brain, arm and the refrigerator. Such a parallelism would certainly avoid the problem of overdetermination, but almost no one finds the idea acceptable. Aside from anything else, it would require us to believe that there is a fortuitous synchronization of mental and physical chains of events which only appear to

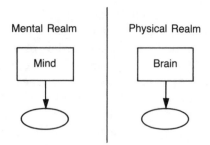

Figure 6.

be the result of interaction. (*See* HISTORY for a brief account of a philosopher – Leibniz – who did hold some such view.)

3.6 Coalescing

The problems would disappear at a stroke if some rationale could be found for seeing the mental and the physical as somehow combined or cooperating instead of competing. In particular, if we could coalesce two of the vertices of the triangle, then all would be well, since of course we would no longer have a triangle on our hands. Of course, though it is easy enough to suggest such a rearrangement, the real work lies in making any kind of coalescing plausible. And, as one might expect, there are a bewildering number of ways in which this has been attempted. However, within this mass of detail, one can discern two main approaches.

3.6.1 Mind into Action

BEHAVIOURISM counts as a manifestation of the coalescing strategy, insofar as it attempts to absorb the mind into the realm of action. As a simple illustration, consider the following behaviourist account of a belief. Begin by supposing it true that I believe my lawn needs watering – that I am in that mental state. Being in that state it is pretty likely that I would indulge in grass-watering activity, at least in the right, non-rainy, not-too-busy circumstances. Now it is this fact about what I am likely to do that behaviourists exploit. For they think it reasonable to *define* my mental state – my belief that the lawn needs watering – as *a tendency to water the grass in certain circumstances*. Continuing in this way, managing to define each and every mental item as nothing more than congeries of behavioural tendencies, they then insist that the mind need no longer be represented as an independent element in the triangle. It will have been, so to speak, superimposed onto action, and we will end up with figure 7: there will no longer be a need for any separate thing labelled 'Mind'. (*See also* DENNETT; LEWIS; QUINE; RYLE.)

Behaviourism that discerns the mind in action is at least concessive to the idea of the mental, since the mental is treated as genuinely present in patterns

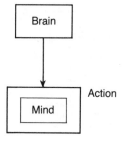

Figure 7.

of action. But there is a more ruthless kind of behaviourism which makes no such concession. Its adherents insist that there are brains and there is behaviour, but that mental states of any stripe are just surplus to requirements. As I have divided things up, concessive behaviourism counts as a coalescing strategy, since it is committed to seeing the mind as presented in complexes of actions and tendencies to act. The other sort – which could be called 'eliminative behaviourism' – will be discussed along with other radically eliminative strategies.

3.6.2 *Mind into Matter*

Behaviourism has fallen on hard times, in that few present writers actively pursue lines of thought that they would characterize as behaviourist. The example I used – counting my belief that the grass needs watering as a behavioural tendency – just totters on the edge of plausibility. For it certainly seems possible for someone to have such a belief without also having any specially devoted cluster of active tendencies that could be used to define it. But things really get difficult for the behaviourist with respect to experiences such as pain. It is not easy to accept that my tennis elbow consists in my complaining, tennis-avoiding and physiotherapist-visiting behaviour. What about the fact that it hurts?

The second coalescing strategy sets out from a different starting point: mental phenomena are superimposed, not on actions, but on the physical phenomena I have called 'brain'. This is shown in a general way by figure 8, but there are significant differences in the ways this superimposition is achieved, so I shall have to divide my survey of this strategy into sub-sections.

3.6.2.1 *Identity*   The IDENTITY THEORY takes the most direct route to the goal of coalescing the mental and the physical: mental phenomena are said *to be* physical phenomena – they are counted as one and the same. Stated in these bald terms, this view is unlikely to satisfy anyone, or even to be wholly intelligible. One needs to be told more specifically what is being identified with what, and, even more pressingly, why any kind of identity between the mind and material stuff is so much as reasonable. It is here that a certain philosophical view of science comes to the rescue.

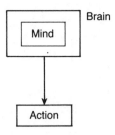

Figure 8.

Many philosophers have been attracted to the identity account of mind because of the way identity has figured in the evolution of scientific theories. For example, consider how we have come to understand a phenomenon such as lightning. Before the development of scientific theories of electricity, lightning must have seemed a very bizarre phenomenon indeed. But by the end of the nineteenth century, it could have been truly be said that we had come to know what lightning is, viz. the massive, sudden discharge of the collective electrical charge generated by the movement of many slightly charged water droplets or ice crystals that form the clouds. What had happened in the passage from ignorance to understanding could be put this way: there was this strange type of observed phenomenon (lightning) which was found to be one and the same with a type of electrical phenomenon (static discharge) that we had discovered in our search for a theory of the natural world. Note that one is not here saying that lightning is *caused* by electrical discharge. That would be to allow that they were in some sense different phenomena. Rather, the view is that lightning *just is* electrical discharge.

This sort of idea offers a promising way to deal with the problem of the mental and the physical: why not say that individual types of mental phenomena (such as beliefs or pains) are really types of state in the brain (perhaps certain patterns of neural firings)? On analogy with the lightning case, one would be thinking of scientific knowledge as providing insight into the nature of what are at first puzzling sorts of things. We are aware of such things as beliefs and pains, but we are as ignorant of their true nature as we once were of lightning. But if we can identify mental phenomena with the physical, we will both cease to be ignorant of their real nature and, treating mind and brain as one, we will overcome the difficulty posed by the triangle in figure 5.

The above is the merest sketch of one sort of identity theory. In particular, based as it is on the analogy with the scientific case, it features the identification of *types* of mental state with *types* of physical state. If we take, say, the pain resulting from a burn, as an example, then what the theory says is that whenever someone has that kind of pain, there will be some particular type of brain state or activity that is that pain.

Another way to look at it is to say that a type identity theory identifies one property with another, and that it does so partly on the basis of special sorts of laws of nature ('bridge' laws) connecting the two. Using the earlier example, it could be said that the property of the heavens known as *lightning* is one and the same as the property of *cloud-generated electrical discharge* because there is a universal law connecting the two as they occur in one and the same spatio-temporal location ('whenever and wherever you have the one, you have the other'). Similarly, one might hold that a burning pain is a property of a mind, and a configuration of neural activity is a property of a brain, though the discovery of a bridge law connecting them would imply that burning pain is nothing over and above some pattern of brain cell activity. (*See* CONCEPTS; LEWIS; PROPERTY.)

3.6.2.2 Aspects and Identity If it were true that a mental property was nothing over and above a physical one, then we could speak of the REDUCTION of the mental to the physical. This is moreover just what one would expect given the analogy between cases of scientific reduction and the type identity account of the mental. For, given our current state of knowledge, what one would say of lightning is that it has been reductively identified with electrical discharges.

But, to put it mildly, not everyone is happy with such talk in the case of the mind. There are a number of writers who think that mental phenomena are not reducible to the physical. In particular, it is argued that properties such as *believing that p*, or *having a pain* are just the wrong sort of thing to be identified with physical properties. For instance, some writers have suggested that there are a priori reasons why there could never be any bridge laws connecting mind and brain. This, it is argued, is because mental properties form a closely functioning network, not matched by any complex of properties in the physical realm. It is therefore wrong to think one could so much as imagine a law that singled out a mental property from this network and tied it to a physical one. The idea is that such a singling out would be tantamount to giving up the idea that the property was mental in the first place. (*See* DAVIDSON.)

Yet, in spite of their opposition to type identity, these writers are not in the least tempted by dualism: they do not think of the mental as a different *thing* from physical or material substance. What they want is some way to see the mental as physical, but to resist the idea that the mental is reducible to the physical on the model of, say, lightning and electrical discharge.

Given the thin line that is being trodden between dualism and reduction, it is a delicate matter to so much as label this position. One could describe it as a kind of dualism at the level of properties because mental properties are claimed to be irreducible to physical ones. But there are deep issues in ONTOLOGY which make talk of PROPERTIES suspect, at least to certain writers who are otherwise adherents of the view being discussed. Or one could eschew talk of properties and speak of a dualism of 'aspects': some phenomena have irreducibly both a mental and a physical aspect. Yet there is not all that much to be gained by using such a vague word: one suspects that an aspect is a property by another name or, if not, then it is very difficult to say exactly what it is. Finally, and least controversially, one could leave 'dualism' out of the characterization altogether by describing the view as 'ANOMALOUS MONISM'. This label – coined by DAVIDSON – has the virtue of emphasizing the coalescing credentials of the view – it is after all 'monism' – whilst at the same time signalling a refusal to countenance reduction. Describing the mental as anomalous in respect of the physical just is a way of denying reducibility.

Now it is one thing to argue about labels, it is another to justify the view itself. How can one be a monist – find that ontologically speaking there is only physical stuff – and yet insist that the mental is not reducible to, or is anomalous in respect of, that stuff? It is here that a second kind of identity theory comes into play, one made possible by the contrast between *types* and *tokens*.

To get hold of the TYPE/TOKEN distinction, think, for example, about the book you are now reading. On one way of understanding the expression 'the book' in my last sentence, it refers to that single work or type, the *Companion to the Philosophy of Mind*, first published in 1994 and edited by me with contributions from many different authors. But, given the right context, I could have used that same expression to refer, not to the one thing that Blackwells published under that title, but to the very object you are now holding. This object, one of thousands which were printed, is said to be a 'token' of the *Companion* (though in many ways it would do just as well to call it an 'instance' or an 'exemplar'). And just as one can think of types and tokens of books, one can also make the type/token distinction in regard to other items, e.g. mental (and physical) phenomena. The pain which, let us say, I now have in my elbow, is of a certain type. It is that intermittently sharp kind of pain one gets with so-called 'tennis elbow'. But I can also think of my pain as a token mental occurrence. For example, if you asked me why I just winced, I might say: 'I just felt a sharp jab in my elbow', and in this case, I would be speaking about that particular token of pain that caused me to wince. Similarly, there can be a certain type of brain state – say, a state consisting in the firing of C-fibres – which will have various tokens or instances at particular times.

As described earlier, the type theory sets out to identify types of pain with types of mental state. Suppose, for example, that it attempts to identify tennis-elbow pains with the rapid firing of certain neural C-fibres. As we saw earlier, this kind of identity supports the reduction of mental properties to physical ones: tennis-elbow pain is nothing over and above the firing of C-fibres. So if we are determined to deny reduction, we must be prepared to deny type identity. But one can still cleave to the idea that the world is at bottom physical by asserting token identity. Token identity theorists would expect there to be some particular token of a physical state that was my pain (when I winced), but they insist that this is the only kind of identity possible between the mental and the physical. So we end up with only one kind of thing – the physical – whilst still denying that mental states are reducible to physical states. Unfortunately, all is not plain sailing.

What does it really mean to say that the world is *at bottom* physical? The model provided by the case of lightning and electrical discharges shows one way to unpack this claim: all phenomena are reducible to the physical – for any real phenomenon we can always find out what type of physical thing it is. However, this straightforward reductionist response is not available to token identity theorists. Instead, they appeal to a notion of SUPERVENIENCE – a notion that signals a sort of dependency relation. As an example of this dependency consider the following case. Suppose that you judge a certain Corot painting of a landscape to be autumnal. This feature of the painting clearly depends upon the arrangement of pigments on the canvas, but one would not ordinarily say that this feature was reducible to the disposition of pigments, that 'autumnal-ness' in paintings *just is* that kind of arrangement. After all, another painting, which was physically quite different, could also be autumnal. The commonly used technical way of putting this is to say that autumnal-ness is 'multiply-realizable' – that there are many ways in which this property could be realized in different paintings. However, it is nonetheless true of the Corot painting that its being autumnal *supervenes* on the physical structure of the canvas. Or we could put it this way: if the Corot painting ceased to be autumnal – if this feature of the painting changed – then we would expect that some physical feature of the canvas would also have changed, perhaps because of ageing or destructive 'restoration'. Thus, being autumnal in the case of the particular Corot painting *depends* upon the physical arrangement of pigments on a specific canvas. And we can say this without committing ourselves to the idea that 'autumnal-ness' is a type of thing reducible to that particular physical arrangement.

Understood in this way, supervenience gives us a way of saying that mental phenomena depend on, in the sense that they are realized by, their physical embodiments without being reducible to them. Thus, the tennis-elbow pain I am now experiencing is a token physical state in my brain. And insofar as this sort of token identity holds for each mental phenomena, we can say that the mental supervenes on the physical. But there is no reason to believe that mental phenomena are themselves physical *types* of thing. Just as the property of being autumnal could have been realized physically in lots of different ways, so mental phenomena might well be realized by different types of physical states in different organisms. This means that the mental depends upon the physical without being reducible to it.

Substituting token for type identity and supervenience for reduction has an obvious appeal. It is the closest we can get to preserving something of the tri-angular relationship – keeping, that is, a certain distance between mind and brain – whilst avoiding overdetermination. (*See* figure 9 for the best I can do to represent anomalous monism. Mind lies outside brain – this indicates non-reducibility – though the projective lines show Mind's dependence or super-venience on the physical.) But there are deep problems with this view. In parti-cular, it has been argued that the price to be paid for avoiding over-

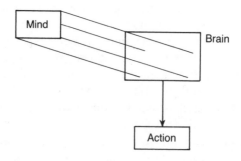

Figure 9.

determination, whilst maintaining only token identity, is a certain idleness for the mental. The details of this issue are complex and much discussed, but the basics are apparent enough even from Figure 9. In that figure, the arrow of causality connects physical phenomena to actions, whilst the mind, super-veniently out on its own, has no such direct causal link. But many think that we should only count something as genuinely real if it enters into causal rela-tions. Using the fashionable word, the mind in figure 9 seems to be EPIPHE-NOMENAL – sort of surplus to causal requirements – since what does the causal pulling and pushing are brain states.

There are no shortage of replies possible to this worry. One might try to find some special work for the mind by distinguishing between actions and move-ments of the body; actions would have a special explanatory (even if not causal) relation to the mind, though they too could be said to supervene on appropriate movements of the body. Or one might try to show that super-venience doesn't really render the mind idle. But these replies, and variations on them, go beyond the brief of this *Essay*. (*See* DAVIDSON; DENNETT; DRETSKE; FODOR; LEWIS; STALNAKER.)

3.6.2.3 Content and Identity Before considering certain other objections to identity theories, I must note something which, up to now, may have puzzled you. Mostly I have written in a general way about identifying the mental and the physical, though I have sometimes assumed that the identification would be between the mental and a more specific kind of physical item, namely brain states and processes. Indeed, my use of the label 'Brain' in figure 5 is explicitly non-committal as between brain phenomena narrowly conceived and more general physical happenings. It might at first seem that, if an identity theory is right, then mental states are bound to be states of the brain together with related parts of the central nervous system, so that it is just not necessary to be non-committal in this way. After all, since the brain is surely responsible for mentality, how could the physical embodiment of someone's mental state extend beyond the brain and body of that individual? How could mental phe-nomena either be or supervene on anything other than goings-on in the central nervous system?

Using pain and experiences generally as examples of the mental tempts us to think of the brain as the only possible physical foundation for mentality. But one must not forget about the attitudes. When we attribute to Anne the belief that her coat is in the hallway cupboard, we are characterizing Anne's state of mind and we are doing so by reference to how things are, or might be, in the world. In stage 2, we struggled with this feature of the attitudes without coming to any definite conclusion. But concerned as we are now with the rela-tion of the mental to the physical, this problem – the problem of directionality – reasserts itself in a slightly different way.

Suppose for the minute that some identity theory is right, though it doesn't matter for the present point whether it is of a type or token sort. Then when Anne has the belief that her coat is in the hallway cupboard, there is some physical state which is that belief. Suppose further that we accept the idea that this state (or event or process) is to be found somewhere in Anne's central nervous system. Call that item N. This means that we should accept that Anne's belief is N. But how can N – some neurophysiological state internal to Anne – be a belief about the coat's location, something wholly external to Anne? It is far from obvious how to answer that question.

A crucial feature of the attitudes is that they are directed to some actual or possible state of affairs. Understanding this is fraught with the difficulties grouped together in stage 2 under the label 'the problem of directionality'. The present worry extends beyond – though it includes – the problem of directionality. For what we are now wondering is how a 'mere' physical state internal to someone's nervous system can be about, or directed to, some feature of the world external to that individual. Philosophers tend to speak about the 'problem of intentionality', using this label to cover both the conceptual difficulties generated by the attitudes, and this issue of how to fit such directionality onto the bedrock of the physical world. It is also described as the problem of *naturalizing* intentionality.

One way in which an identity theory might try to cope is by denying the very thing we have been supposing, that is, by denying that the relevant physical state is in fact internal to the individual. In Anne's case, this would mean saying that her belief was one and the same with some physical state of the world which may well include N but which also takes in the state of affairs involving the coat, cupboard, etc. Of course, in doing this, one would be saying that Anne's mental state is somehow spread out so as to include much more than what is local to Anne. But this is not an easy consequence to accept, since many find it difficult to understand how Anne's mental states could be anything other than intrinsic to her, and thus located where and only where she is.

A second tack would be to insist that there is a wholly internal state corresponding to Anne's belief, and that the directionality of the belief is explicable by relations between this state and the state of affairs involving the coat. Thus, perhaps what makes some state of Anne's a belief about the whereabouts of her coat is that there is a *causal* relation between that state and the coat. One would here be trying to capture the directionality of the attitudes by citing causal relations between internal (presumbably, brain) states and actual and possible states of the world.

Naturalizing intentionality is a deeply perplexing problem. I have raised it in connection with identity theories, but it is by no means confined to them. Any coalescing strategy – any attempt to make out that the mental is superimposed on the physical – has to provide some account of how an attitude can be both a physicalistically respectable feature of an individual and yet have a content that extends beyond that individual. I shall return to this issue again in connection with the third attempt at coalescing, after first considering the sort of general criticism that has been levelled against identity theories. (*See* CONTENT; INTENTIONALITY; LANGUAGE OF THOUGHT.)

3.6.2.4 Against Identity   Independently of any doubts about this or that form of the identity account, there is a source of criticism that goes right to the core notion in all of them, viz. identity. Any claim of identity carries with it a logical commitment whose articulation is usually attributed to the seventeenth century German philosopher G. W. von Leibniz. Though it is not uncontroversial in certain philosophical circles, LEIBNIZ'S LAW seems to state a perfectly obvious truth about any kind of identity claim: if an identity is true – if, for example, one can truly claim of *a* and *b*, that *a* is identical to *b* – then anything true of *a* will be true of *b*. Moreover, it is a principle we use all the time. For example, suppose Smith, having had his bicycle stolen, is trying to find it in the police lost property office. There are a number of bicycles there of the same colour and make as his, and the police have given numbers to these recovered bicycles. Suppose Smith conjectures that his bicycle is number 234, i.e. it is one and the same as, or identical to, 234. If this conjecture is right, then, whether Smith can prove it or not, absolutely everything true of 234 must be true of Smith's bicycle. For instance, if it turned out that 234 was assembled in France, whereas Smith's had been assembled in Belgium, then this would be enough to falsify the identity claim that Smith made. For if 234 is Smith's bicycle, then we are only really talking about a single thing. And how can it possibly happen that one thing was both assembled in and not assembled in France?

Leibniz's Law, as in the above everyday example, gives us a certain leverage over claims to identity: it gives us a means of falsifying them. In the philosophy of mind, this kind of leverage has been employed often. It has been held that there are features of mental states not possessed by any brain states, and, of course, if this were true, we would have to give up on any account that identified these states. Typical of the features in question are these: mental states do not have spatial location in the way that brain states do; mental states such as pains can be sharp or burning, brain states are neither; one can conceive of mental states existing independently of brain states, but the same of course cannot be said of the brain states themselves. However, whether fortunately or not, none of these examples is uncontroversial, so identity theories are still very much a live option. Applying Leibniz's Law considerations to mental phenomena is just not as easy as applying them to stolen bicycles. (*See* IDENTITY THEORIES, LEWIS.)

3.6.3 Mind onto Matter

3.6.3.1 The Functionalist Idea   An identity theory answers the question 'What are mental phenomena?' essentially by telling us how they are constituted. Such a direct physicalist answer is one way to go about dealing with a 'What is . . . ?' question, but there are others. Moreover, thinking of things as physically constituted is sometimes a misleading way of trying to understanding them. In order to illustrate these points, consider this strange ad which once appeared in an Oxford newspaper:

Wanted: bicycle or similar.

What makes it strange is that a bicycle is an object with a certain basic shape and construction, and one most naturally answers the question:

What is a bicycle?

by giving some account of this physical embodiment. So, when someone speaks of wanting something 'similar' to a bicycle, it is difficult to understand this except as expressing a want for a bicycle. The natural way to take the word 'similar' in this context makes it redundant. (Of course, in some other sense of 'similar', everything is similar to everything else. Thus, my broken steam iron is similar to a bicycle: they are both manufactured objects. And yet one would hardly have thought that the need expressed in the ad would be satisfied by my old iron.)

In contrast to this case, suppose that the ad had said:

Wanted: word processor or similar.

There are lots of ways in which word processing can be achieved: dedicated machines, computers with word-processing programs, typewriters with memories, etc. Since these devices will look quite different from one another, the most straightforward way to say what a word processor is will not involve a description of a particular physical shape or construction. In answering the question:

What is a word processor?

what would be given would be some account of what the device *does*, rather than how it is physically embodied. For this reason, and unlike the bicycle case, a demand for a 'word processor or similar' wouldn't be strange. Any one of the physically different word-processing devices might satisfy the need.

As described earlier, the type identity theory treats mental phenomena as something like bicycles: understanding, for example, a pain or a belief involves understanding how each of them is embodied in some physical realm such as the central nervous system. (For the moment, leave token identity theories on one side.) But perhaps a better way to think of pains and beliefs is as we think of word processors: a pain or a belief is understood only when we know what each of them does. This idea – that we understand specific mental phenomena by describing what they do – is, in broad terms, at the heart of the view known as FUNCTIONALISM. And, in one or other of its versions, it is currently the most popular way to achieve coalescence between the mental and the physical.

Of course, it is not immediately obvious what it means to say that we understand a belief when we know what it does – what its work or function is. Certainly, it would be misleading to allow ourselves to be carried too far by the word processor analogy. Word processors have functions in a rather rich sense: they are designed to achieve certain purposes or goals. However, there are other senses of 'function' which, at least at first, are more plausible in helping us to understand the mental.

For example, consider my belief that Monday, 29 August 1994 (next Monday) is a Bank Holiday. Without claiming that this belief is somehow designed to achieve some goal or purpose, I can still describe it as having work to do, as having a functional role. For example, given that I have this belief, I am likely to go in for certain kinds of behaviour such as making sure I have enough cash to get through the weekend, making plans to leave town, etc. Also, there is a story to be told about the ways in which my seeing, hearing and remembering various things together account for the fact that I have this belief in the first place. If we describe how the belief affects my behaviour and other mental states as 'output' and the sources of its formation as 'input', then we can say that the functional role of the belief is some specific set of complex inputs and outputs. Indeed, we can go further: in response to the question 'What is SG's belief that the 29th is a Bank Holiday?', a complete answer will be: it is that feature of SG that comes about in virtue of such-and-such inputs and results in such-and-such outputs. Of course, there is a lot of complexity underlying this outline answer – filling in the detail of the 'such-and-suches' would be an enormous task. But this complexity should not prevent one seeing the core idea of functionalism: a mental phenomenon will be defined by its inputs and outputs, its functional role.

It is important to note that, in spite of talk about inputs and outputs, a functional account is not itself a behaviourist account. Behaviourists of the sort considered earlier aim to *define* such mental items as beliefs as patterns of behaviour, whether actual or potential. In contrast, a functionalist allows that beliefs and relevant behaviour exist independently of any behaviour. Indeed, given that mental states *cause* various patterns of behaviour, they cannot be defined in terms of them. Moreover, among the inputs and outputs that constitute the 'work' of a given belief – its functional role – there are bound to be other mental states. Thus, my belief about the Bank Holiday may well cause me to be mildly depressed, though this latter state of mind might never be expressed in behaviour which could be used to define it. Perhaps I am just so used to depression as to suffer a mild case of it without this in any way affecting my behaviour.

One reason for the popularity of functionalist accounts is that they seem to be untouched by various strong objections to type identity. Take pain as an example. On the identity theory a given type of pain will be identified with a given type of event in the central nervous system. Thus, burning pain might come out as the rapid firing of C-fibres in one area of the brain. But this would mean that a creature constructed differently from us – the proverbial Martian, to take one example – just couldn't have such pain. For if a type of pain is a type of neural event, then there can be no pain without neurons. Yet this seems hard to swallow. Surely we would want to allow that a Martian, though lacking neurons, could still experience pain. It is just that the physical basis for this pain would be different in his world. And this is precisely what the functional account allows. For the functionalist, pain of a certain sort is that phenomenon that comes about as the result of certain inputs and produces certain outputs. Any creature who possesses this pattern of outputs and inputs can be said to have a burning pain, whether or not that creature has neurons, silicon or something else in its physical make-up.

Burning pain, in being functionally characterized, is multiply-realizable, and most functionalists insist that mental phenomena supervene on the physical. These are of course features that functionalist accounts share with the token identity theory, and it is thus unsurprising to find that those newly introduced to these accounts tend to confuse them. The pictorial representation of token identity (figure 9) could serve as well as a representation of functionalism. However, what cannot be shown by such a simple sketch is the rationale for regarding the mental as projecting from the physical, and it is in this respect that certain token identity theories differ sharply from functionalist accounts.

DAVIDSON, and those prepared to count themselves as anomalous monists, accept both multiple realizability and token identity, whilst insisting that mental phenomena are not reducible to the physical. Indeed, these are the defining features of their view. But notice that nothing in any of this depends on seeing mental phenomena as functionally definable. In fact, one might have reasons to resist the idea that mental phenomena are somehow understood in terms of their location in a network of inputs and outputs without giving up any of the theses which define anomalous monism.

In contrast, the functionalist is someone driven by a particular conception of the mental – a conception that allows, and encourages, the token identity thesis and multiple realizability as ways of guaranteeing the physical credentials of the mind. However, it is perfectly conceivable that one could embrace the core functionalist idea without going the token identity route. There are two ways in which this could happen. On the one hand, one might be a *functional dualist*: someone who thinks that mental items are to be understood in terms of their characteristic work, without regarding the mind as in any way material. Of course, as was seen, dualism does not qualify as a way of defusing the overdetermination problem, but it is important in understanding functionalism to see that it can even make peace with dualism. This can happen simply because functionalism *per se* has no commitments to the material (or other) constitution of mind. On the other hand, one could be a functional reductionist: someone who thinks that the mental is type identical to the physical and, hence, to that extent, reducible. LEWIS among others holds this view, though it should be noted that he attempts to avoid the earlier-mentioned pitfall of type identity – multiple realizability – by confining identities to species or even individual members of a species.

3.6.3.2 Functionalism and the Computational Model of the Mind It is one thing to think that the core functionalist idea is attractive, it is another to describe it in the sort of detail necessary to establish its plausibility. Recall the earlier example: my belief that the 29th August 1994 is a Bank Holiday is functionally characterized when one can list all those states and events that cause me to have it and all those effects that it leads to. Yet even for such a mundane belief these inputs and outputs are going to be enormously complex – much too complex to think it a practical project to list them. So, what grounds the widespread conviction among philosophers of mind that functionalism of one sort or another has any chance of success? Is it simply the beauty of the core idea that blinds them to the fact that functionalism without the details is nothing more than gesture towards a defensible view?

It is all too easy to think that these questions point unflatteringly at a certain kind of philosophical gullibility. But underlying the large degree of 'hand-waving' towards details that one finds in treatments of functionalism, there is in fact a very solid foundation. For certain important results in the theory of computation (due to TURING) have shown that enormous complexity is no real obstacle to the project of functionalism. Indeed, what Turing showed was that *any* complex pattern of interrelation between inputs and outputs could be mimicked by very simple and orderly functional relations which have come to be called 'Turing machines' (*See* ARTIFICIAL INTELLIGENCE; COMPUTATIONAL MODELS). In essence, the work of Turing and others has made it possible to think functionalism is plausible – so far as complexity is concerned – without our having to work out a detailed functional account for any particular set of mental phenomena.

Any specific Turing machine is essentially a very simple sort of computer program – one which can transform certain inputs into some desired output. (In spite of the label, a Turing machine is not so much a physical device as it is a way of thinking about functional relationships based on analogy with an (imagined) physical device.) Thus, there are Turing machines that take any two numbers as input and produce their sum as output. One can think of these as just like a program for adding that one might load into a computer. Of course, the relationship between numbers and their sum is very straightforward. Yet, as was noted earlier, there are no patterned relationships between inputs and outputs so complex as to escape some Turing machine.

Insofar then as the core idea of functionalism is accepted, we can relegate the actual functional details to one or another way of employing the Turing result. Here there are a bewildering number of possibilities, which are best left to the more specific discussions of FUNCTIONALISM. Still, it might be helpful to at least outline the range of possibilities:

(1) The most direct use of the Turing result consists in treating such things as beliefs, desires, pains and other mental items as themselves states of a Turing machine appropriate to the mind being functionally characterized. Various features of the mental and Turing machine states have made this sort of 'machine functionalism' the least-preferred option.

(2) At the other extreme is the view that treats the commonsense conception of the mind as itself a causal/functional account which is underpinned by the

101

Turing result but which does not attempt to make any direct connections between Turing machines and mental items. Because this view insists that the commonsense account is already a functional characterization of the mental – an account which gives us the essential features of each mental item – it is sometimes called 'analytical functionalism'. (*See* LEWIS.)

(3) In between are a whole range of views that regard the commonsense conception as tied more or less loosely to some computational level of description, though not necessarily a level as basic as that conceived by Turing. Included here are views that employ the LANGUAGE OF THOUGHT hypothesis. Because this range of views makes the connection between the computational level and the commonsense conception a matter of empirical research, it is often described as 'psychofunctionalism'. This label hints that the final picture will be an empirical, though psychological, research result. (*See also* INNATE-NESS; MODULARITY OF MIND.)

Though the above only sketches the possibilities, it brings out something important about the connection between functionalism and detailed computational accounts: the fact that there is a certain slack between them. This slack accounts for the arguments one comes across over the claim that the 'mind is a computer program'. On the one hand, there are those who regard this claim as no more than a metaphor, and on the other, there are those who think it literally true. And it is not surprising that there should be this difference. For if you regard mental items as computational states, then the mind will count for you literally as a computer. But if you only think of the mental as loosely grounded on the possibility of a computational account of our neural workings, then the most you would allow is that the mind is like a computer program. However, in either case, there is something appealing about the idea. For it gives an interesting gloss to the functionalist idea that the mental is multiply-realizable. After all, we are all familiar with the fact that a computer program (the software) can run on all sorts of physically different machines (the hardware). On this conception – which is common though not mandatory for functionalists – the mind is like software and the brain is the hardware on which it is 'run' (for human beings at least).

3.6.3.3 Functionalism and Content   One of the problems discussed in connection with the identity theory was whether it could give a plausible account of mental states with contents – the propositional attitudes. The particular difficulty was this: if an attitude is identical to some wholly internal individual brain state, then how can that attitude have a content directed to something that is external to the thinker in space as well as time? And if the attitude is said to be identical to a physical state of the world which includes the brain state of the thinker but extends to those things that figure in the content, then we end up with very implausible identities. After all, it seems very odd to say that someone's thought is a physical state that includes items removed in space and time from the thinker.

This problem – the problem of intentionality – is one that arises in connection with any attempt to coalesce the mental and the physical. This is because, however such coalescence is achieved, one will end up by regarding some physical or functional type as the embodiment of an attitude. But then it will not be obvious how to accommodate the directedness of the attitude – its content. Physical states seem to differ from the attitudes precisely because they lack any sort of directedness, and functional states would seem to be no better off. Nonetheless, the problem of intentionality tends to be discussed mostly in the context of functionalist accounts, and this is probably because of the feeling that some kind of functionalism offers the best hope of a solution.

Recall that a functionalist would define, for example, Anne's belief about the whereabouts of her coat, by some complex of behavioural and mental inputs and outputs. Insofar as these are wholly realized in states internal to Anne's physical make-up, one might still try to explain the content of the belief by its location in the whole network (*see* CONCEPTUAL ROLE SEMANTICS). Or, if one is prepared to allow that items in the network have causal relationships to features of the world outside Anne, then there is the glimmer of hope that intentionality can be explicated in terms of that causal relation. Or if not a causal relation of the most direct sort, then perhaps some more complicated causal connection would do the trick. But many objections have been made to each of these attempts. (*See* CONTENT; FODOR; SEARLE.)

3.6.3.4 Functionalism and Consciousness Perhaps the most widely discussed problem for functionalist accounts of the mind is their apparent inability to give an intuitively acceptable account of conscious or experiential states. And though it is not necessarily the simplest way of putting it, a particularly striking way to outline the problem is in terms of the so-called 'inverted spectrum' first discussed by Locke. Imagine that you and I are looking at an expanse of blue. Both of us will say that what we see is blue and both of us will be able to match what we see with other samples of blue. Summing up a long story, it seems perfectly reasonable to assume that, insofar as we are both equipped with physiologically normal visual systems, our behaviours in respect of this expanse will be indistinguishable. We will be, or could be imagined to be, functionally identical at least in respect of our colour judgments and behaviours. Yet, as so many are willing to accept, none of this shows that what we experience – what it is like 'internally' for each of us to see blue – will match. For all I know, when you look at the blue expanse, what you experience is what I would if I were to look at something yellow. The matching of our behaviours only seems to show that we have, as it were, adapted to the use of public language and behaviour in a uniform way. If, as is imagined, our colour experiences are inverted with respect to one another, there is no way that this would show up, though it is no less a difference between us. If it is genuinely possible for there to be such spectrum inversion, then this would seem to show that functionalism is in trouble. For it can scarcely be true that our experiences of seeing blue consist in some complex pattern of inputs and outputs since these match, though our experiences do not.

There are many variations on this sort of example and many responses have been made to them by functionalists. Nonetheless, there is a widespread feeling that consciousness is just too elusive and subjective a phenomenon to be captured by functionalism. (*See* CONSCIOUSNESS; DENNETT; FUNCTIONALISM; INTROSPECTION; LEWIS; QUALIA; SEARLE; SUBJECTIVITY.)

3.7 Eliminating

As we saw at stage 2, the commonsense or 'folk psychological' conception of the mind is shot through with problems. In itself this is perhaps not enough of a reason to reject that conception, but when these difficulties are combined with those arising from attempts to reconcile the mental and the physical realms, one can understand why someone might be tempted by one or another rejectionist line. Dispensing with the commonsense conception – eliminating the 'Mind' box in figure 5 – would at a stroke save us from a host of philosophical problems intrinsic to that conception and would remove the threat of overdetermination. Eliminativism, as the view is described, has taken two forms, and, though one is more worked out and current than the other, both will be discussed.

3.7.1 Eliminative Behaviourism

The behaviourism discussed earlier aimed to superimpose the mind on action, attempting thereby to make the relation of the mental to the physical unproblematic. Crucially, this kind of behaviourism counts as an *account* of the mind, rather than as any sort of attempt to dispense with it. Conceding, for example, that there really are states of mind called 'beliefs', the aim would be to define these mental states in terms of what the believer does or is disposed to do. This concessive sort of behaviourism is largely the product of philosophical labour, whereas the more ruthless *eliminative* behaviourism can be found in the writings of certain psychologists during the period from about the early part of this century until about the mid-1960s. These psychologists, unhappy with what was they saw as the unscientific approach of psychology in the nineteenth century, insisted that only what was observable could be studied scientifically. Because they implicitly accepted the idea that the mind – as described in the philosophical and early psychological literature – was not observable, they adopted, as a methodological principle, the view that only behaviour measurable under experimental conditions was fit for psychological study. In some writers, this methodological principle became more than that: it became the view that there really was no such thing as the mind. (*See* PSYCHOLOGY AND PHILOSOPHY.)

Post-behaviourist, so-called 'cognitive' psychologists, count themselves no less scientific, but they have rejected methodological behaviourism in part because they have rejected the too simplistic idea that one can only scientifically study the directly observable (*see* COGNITIVE PSYCHOLOGY; DEVELOPMENTAL PSYCHOLOGY). In virtually every field of science, one deals both with observable behaviour and with the unobservable – but no less real – underlying causes of this behaviour. This is as true of the chemical behaviour of molecules as it is of the biological behaviour of genes, so why deny it in the case of the human mind? In finding no reason to cleave to the methodology of behaviourism, contemporary psychology offers no room for the more eliminative scepticism about the mind which characterized the writings of earlier psychologists such as B. F. Skinner.

3.7.2 *Eliminative Materialism*

The pull of rejectionism has never expressed itself in the philosophical literature by any straightforward advocacy of eliminative behaviourism. To be sure, there are deeply behaviourist leanings in many writers, but these are combined with a recognition that behaviour alone is not a sufficient base from which to mount the campaign. The aim being to eliminate the commonsense conception of the mind from serious scientific consideration, there is every reason to appeal both to behaviour and to those internal processes and events that cause, but are not themselves identifiable with, behaviour. (*See* QUINE.)

Because this sort of rejectionism is based more broadly on accounts of our physical constitution and functioning, it is generally called *eliminative materialism*. And interestingly (though also confusingly) its most recent manifestations are grounded in the computational model of the mind – a model which, as discussed earlier, also lies behind functionalism. Here in rough outline is how this has come about.

The core idea of functionalism does not *require* the computational model, though, as was pointed out, the availability of the computational account makes it easier to accept *as possible* the defining of functional relationships of great complexity. However, given this, it is possible to detach the idea that the mind is like a computer program from its typical functionalist setting. In particular, one might be tempted to argue as follows:

1. The brain is responsible for those phenomena we call 'mental'.
2. But the brain itself is a complex input/output device whose workings can be captured by some specific computational model.
3. There is no guarantee that the elements of this model will correspond to the commonsense or folk psychological categories we employ.
4. Given the problems that the commonsense conception engenders, and the fact that it has no real scientific credentials, there is reason to think that there will be no correspondence between computational and everyday categories.
5. The most plausible computational model of the brain is a CONNECTIONIST one. There is everything to suggest that attitude states and their contents –

105

or anything like them – will simply not figure as elements in the connectionist account.

Therefore, putting (4) and (5) together, we seem to have both philosophical and empirical reasons to think that our account of the brain – and thus the 'mind' – will simply have no need of the commonsense conception. Or, even more strongly, (4) and (5) might be taken as showing that all commonsense claims about beliefs, desires, intentions, and the rest are just false.

Fully understanding this argument requires a great deal more than can be provided here. Setting out the differences between connectionist and other computational models as well as giving the detailed arguments supporting (3), (4) and (5) would make this essay impossibly long. Added to this is the fact that the argument combines elements from several different eliminative materialist writers. (*See* FOLK PSYCHOLOGY, PSYCHOLOGY AND PHILOSOPHY.) The emphasis on connectionism is by no means uncontroversial: there are connectionists who are not eliminativists and there are non-connectionists who are. Additionally, there are those whose eliminativism comes, not from any interest in computational models, but more directly from physiological accounts of the brain. (Many of those who work in neurophysiology hold a position which flirts with eliminativism, though they call themselves 'reductionists'. The potential for confusion here is enormous, but as this *Essay* aims to sort out *philosophical* positions, terminology in the neurophysiological camp is not all that important.)

Evaluating eliminative materialism is not easy. Of course, in favour of this extreme position, it must be allowed that it gives a neat and direct answer to the problems posed by the triangle in figure 5. For if we needn't trouble ourselves about a box labelled 'Mind', then there is no threat of overdetermination. But, as has been pointed out in lots of different ways, the price paid for this kind of resolution is high: it requires the almost complete abandonment of our ordinary conception of ourselves. Some eliminative materialists point out that such a wholesale overturning of everyday conceptions is not unprecedented. After all, our ancestors are generally presumed to have thought of the natural world as animated by all sorts of spirits, and at some point this conception simply collapsed in the face of the growing body of scientific knowledge. Yet, in spite of this consideration, many have found the price to be paid for eliminativism just too high. For example, it has been argued that there is something self-defeating about it: if there are no such things as beliefs, then we cannot truly believe in eliminativism.

3.8 Conclusion

Eliminativism is the kind of view I had in mind in the opening paragraph of this essay when I suggested that difficulties both within our ordinary conception of the mind and in respect of the mind's relation to the physical realm can tempt us to take up extreme positions. And what could be more extreme than recommending the wholesale abandonment of the scheme by which we have up to now understood ourselves? Of course, there are many alternatives to this extreme position, the main outlines of which have been described. That none of them is wholly satisfactory would be something with which most philosophers of mind would readily agree. Yet as will be apparent from reading this *Companion*, philosophers have not been tempted by any sort of quietism – they have not thought that, given all the problems, it would be better to have no opinions at all.

PART II

A COMPANION TO THE PHILOSOPHY OF MIND, A–Z

A

action (1) In contrast to what merely happens to us, or to parts of us, actions are what we *do*. My moving my finger is an action, to be distinguished from the mere motion of that finger. My snoring likewise is not something I 'do' in the intended sense, though in another, broader sense, it *is* something I often 'do' while asleep.

The contrast has both metaphysical and moral import. With respect to my snoring, *I* am passive, and am not morally responsible (unless, for example, I should have taken steps earlier to prevent my snoring). But in cases of genuine action, *I* am the cause of what happens, and I may properly be held responsible (unless I have an adequate excuse or justification). When I move my finger, *I* am the cause of the finger's motion. When I say 'Good morning!' *I* am the cause of the sound. True, the immediate causes are muscle contractions in the one case and lung, lip and tongue motions in the other. But this is compatible with *me* being the cause – perhaps I cause these immediate causes, or perhaps it just is the case that some events can have both an agent and other events as their cause.

All this is suggestive, but not really adequate. We do not understand the intended force of 'I am the cause' any more than we understand the intended force of 'Snoring is not something I *do*'. If I trip and fall in your flower garden, 'I am the cause' of any resulting damage; but neither the damage nor my fall is my action.

We will consider four approaches to explaining what actions, as contrasted with 'mere' doings, *are*. But it will be convenient first to say something about how they are to be *individuated*.

INDIVIDUATION OF ACTIONS

If I say 'Good morning!' to you over the telephone, I have acted. But how many actions have I performed, and how are they related to one another and associated events? We may list several descriptions of what I have done:

(1) move my tongue and lips in certain ways, while exhaling;
(2) say 'Good morning';
(3) cause a certain sequence of modifications in the current flowing in our telephones;
(4) say 'Good morning!' to you;
(5) greet you.

This list – not exhaustive, by any means – is of *act types*. I have performed an action of each of these types. Moreover an asymmetric relation holds: I greeted you *by* saying 'Good morning!' to you, but not the converse, and similarly for the others on the list. But are these five distinct actions I performed, one of each type, or are the five descriptions all of a single action, which was of these five (and more) types (*see* TYPE/TOKEN)? Both positions, and a variety of intermediate positions, have been defended.

On the first view, a particular action (act *token*) just *is* the exemplification by an agent of an act *type* or *property* at a *time* (Goldman, 1970, p. 10). A difference in any of these three means a different action. Assuming for example that 'saying "Good morning!" to you' is an act property distinct from the act property 'saying "Good morning!"', my doing the one and my doing the other were two different actions I performed on this occasion. We can call this

111

the 'maximizing' view. On the second view, the 'minimizing view', particular actions are never more than movements of (parts of) the body; but these movements can be described in terms of their consequences and circumstances (Davidson, 1980, p. 58f). My saying 'Good morning!' just *was* my moving tongue, lips, and so on, in ways appropriate for producing a sound recognizable by other English-speakers as an utterance of 'Good morning'. This action had modification of the telephone current as an effect, and so it – the very same action – may be described as my causing those modifications. And because sound was produced at the other end, you were there to hear it, and the conventions of English are what they are, descriptions (4) and (5) apply also. But there was only one action.

One type of 'intermediate' view regards actions as events that can have 'smaller' actions and other events, especially their consequences, as *components* (*cf.* Ginet, 1990, pp. 49–50, for a similar view). My saying 'Good morning' to you consisted of the tongue and lip, etc., movements, *and also* the resulting sound, current modifications, sound at the other end, and impact on your auditory system. My greeting you was the same action, differently described. But my causing the current modifications did not include the sound at the other end nor the impact on you, and so was only a component, a proper part, of my greeting you.

Many variations of these three basic views have been developed and defended in the last two or three decades. Much of the debate has featured odd-sounding implications of one or another view, countered by attempts to down-play their significance. The maximizing view implies that every time we perform one action, we in fact perform indefinitely many. For besides the five so far mentioned, I made a sound, said something in English, used an electronic device, ... The minimizing view limits actions in time and space to movements of the body, even if the descriptions employed entail the occurrence of more remote effects of those movements. To use the standard

example, this means that I can shoot and even kill you before the bullet reaches your body. Intermediate views to the contrary treat these consequences as literally part of the action. But this means that my killing someone is still in progress so long as the victim clings to life – even if I myself die in the interim! None of the views seems to harmonize with all our intuitions, and it is unclear what might be compelling reason to favour one of the theoretical conceptions of events and event-language these views reflect (for general discussion, *see* Davis, 1979, ch. 2; Ginet, 1990, ch. 3). Our discussion, then, will be phrased neutrally as far as possible; but occasionally the minimizing view will be adopted for ease in exposition.

WHAT ACTIONS ARE

We return to the problem of distinguishing actions from other doings. Here are four general claims:

(1) Actions are doings having mentalistic explanations of a certain sort.
(2) Actions are doings that are intentional under some description.
(3) Actions are doings that begin with a certain kind of event.
(4) Actions are doings of which the doer has a certain kind of awareness.

These claims are not mutually incompatible; many theorists would assert all four. We will discuss them separately, however, as if each were offered as a complete account of being an action. We will also limit our attention to actions that involve bodily movements, excluding purely mental actions (e.g. mental arithmetic) and so-called 'negative actions' (e.g. refraining from nodding one's head).

(1) Actions as Doings having a Mentalistic Explanation

Coughing is sometimes like snoring and sometimes like saying 'Good morning!' – that is, sometimes a mere doing and sometimes an action. It is the latter when it is deliberate. And deliberate coughing can be explained by invoking an intention to cough, a desire to cough or some other 'pro-attitude' toward coughing, a reason for coughing or purpose in coughing, or something similarly mental. Especially if we think of actions as 'outputs' of the mental 'machine' (*see* FUNCTIONALISM), the availability of such a mentalistic explanation may well seem to be the crucial factor for status as an action.

Advocates of (1) differ on just what sort of mentalistic explainability is requisite, and how that explainability is itself to be understood. A popular view for example holds that actions are things the agent does for a reason and that doing something for a reason is doing it because the agent believes it will or may lead to something the agent wants (or has some other 'pro-attitude' toward). Many understand this 'because' as causal: my desire to attract your attention, say, together with my belief that coughing will have this effect, actually *causes* my coughing, and this is why my coughing is an action (*see* REASONS AND CAUSES). Others have offered non-causal interpretations of this 'because'. (*See* Davis, 1979, ch. 5, and Mele, forthcoming, for references and general discussion.)

The causal interpretations face the problem of *deviant causal chains*. Suppose, for example, I want and intend to get down on my knees to propose marriage. Contemplating my plan, I am so overcome with emotion that I suddenly feel weak and sink to my knees. Here, my sinking to my knees was *not* an action even though it was caused by my desire and intention to get down on my knees. The problem is that my sinking to my knees was not caused by the intention in the right way – and advocates of (1) have explored the possibility or impossibility of spelling out what this 'right way' is. One suggestion is that the intention must 'proximately' cause the doing for the latter to count as an action. In this example, an emotional state intervened. Difficulties in determining when an action begins (see below) may mean difficulties also in determining whether a cause of a putative action is really 'proximate'.

Another difficulty for (1) is the possibility of genuine actions that have no mentalistic explanation at all. For example, suppose at dinner you ask me to pass the salt, and I do. My passing the salt is a genuine action, but may have been a direct response to your request, with no role being played by any desire to pass the salt or anything similar. I have simply been trained to comply with such requests in ordinary circumstances – nor can this training be viewed, say, as my having come to have a 'standing pro-attitude' toward acts of compliance. It may even be denied that I had any relevant intention, though I did pass the salt intentionally (*see* below, and INTENTION). True, I had a reason for passing the salt: you asked for it. But even my auditory perception of your request is not the sort of reason proponents of (1) have in mind. Similarly, a purpose was served by my action of passing you the salt; but it is doubtful that it was *my* purpose.

Again, suppose while we are walking outside together I happen to look up at the sky. I may have had no reason whatsoever; I just did it, spontaneously. Still, it was something I *did*. I was the cause of my head's motion. If there were any moral issue, I could be held responsible, just as I can be judged (favourably, I trust) for passing the salt in the first example.

(2) Actions as Intentional Doings
The formulation 'Actions are doings that are intentional under some description' reflects the minimizing view of the individuation of actions. The idea is that for what I did to count as an action, there must be a description 'V-ing' of what I did, such that I V'd intentionally. Recall the five descriptions of my *one* action of greeting you by telephone. I presumably did not know or care about the modifications I was causing in the current. Still, since (on the minimizing view) my causing the modifications was the same event as my greeting you, and I greeted you intentionally, this event was an action. Or suppose I did not know it was you on the phone; I thought it was my spouse. Still, I said 'Good morning!'

113

intentionally, and that suffices for this event, however described, to be an action. My snoring and involuntary coughing, however, are not intentional under *any* description, and so are not actions.

The adequacy of (2) depends on what it is for an action to be intentional under some description. If it requires being caused by an intention, then (2) is just a version of (1) and subject to the same counterexamples. If it entails only that the agent have a certain kind of knowledge of what he or she is doing, then (2) is a version of (4), discussed below. Another possibility is that being intentional is a kind of goal-directedness in the action itself. Thus we noted that if I pass you the salt, I may have no purpose in passing you the salt. But I had a purpose in *moving my hand* as I did: to get the salt to a position within your reach. We may speculate about feedback mechanisms involving my eyes and hand which were 'set' to 'monitor' and 'guide' the motion of my hand to ensure that that purpose was accomplished. Perhaps this could be called 'intention *in* action', as opposed to an *antecedent* intention, which might be a cause of the whole action.

The adequacy of (2) given this last interpretation again depends on whether there are cases we would want to count as genuine actions despite absence of the goal-directedness described. To some extent this may be an empirical matter. Consider again the example of my spontaneously looking up while we are walking. Was the motion of my head goal-directed? Or did it result from muscle contractions not 'monitored' and 'guided' in any way? If the latter, my looking up was not done intentionally under any description – yet for all that, it was a voluntary movement, and it seems arbitary to exclude it from the class of actions.

Digression: When Do Actions Begin? On one important point the three theories of individuation presented earlier yield the same result, or are at least compatible with it. That is the question of when actions *begin*. Examining this question will prepare us for the question of what actions begin *with*, and to the suggestion (3), that they begin with a unique kind of event, from which their status as action derives.

Recall the three theories. Whether my killing someone ends when the victim dies or earlier, it begins when the act by which I do it – pulling the trigger, say – begins. I do not pull the trigger *and then* kill the victim, even if the two are entirely distinct actions, as on the maximizing view. On the minimizing view, there is only one action, so of course there is only one beginning point. And on intermediate views, my pulling the trigger is the first part of my action of killing; so again, there is just one beginning point.

When is that beginning point? The initially surprising answer is: before the trigger begins to move, even before the finger pulling the trigger begins to move. This is because I move that finger *by* contracting certain muscles; and those muscles begin to contract before the finger begins to move. I do not contract the muscles *and then* move my finger, so I must begin moving my finger when I begin contracting the muscles. Furthermore, the muscle contractions are caused by efferent neural impulses, whose role in the action seems comparable to that of the muscle contractions themselves. This suggests that the action does not begin any later than those impulses. (*Cf.* Hornsby, 1980, for similar argument. We are, of course, generally ignorant of these muscle contractions and neural impulses. It is unclear what relevance this might have. Note our similar ignorance of the tongue and lip movements and current modifications in descriptions (1) and (3) of our first example.)

In this connection we may note work by Libet (1985), which ostensibly determined moments by which agents judged that they had begun certain intentional limb movements. These moments preceded onset of actual motion of the limb by some tens of milliseconds, suggesting that English-speakers implicitly understand their own actions as beginning no later than certain neural impulses which precede the muscle contractions. (But this work and its interpretation are very controversial. *See* e.g. Dennett and Kinsbourne, 1992.)

(3) Actions as Doings Beginning with 'Act-beginners'

To say an action of moving a finger begins 'no later than' the efferent neural impulses that cause the muscle contractions that cause the finger's motion is still not to say when the action begins. Nor is it to say what it begins *with*. An 'act-beginner' in such a case would be an internal event which causes the neural impulses and is itself something the agent 'does', in the *broad* sense of 'doing'. Suggestion (3) is that there are such act-beginners, and it is in virtue of them that the doings they begin are actions. Alleged examples include events in which the agent:

(a) agent-causes some (presumably cerebral) event;
(b) wills to do something (e.g. move the finger); or
(c) tries to do something (e.g. move the finger).

Some versions of (3) treat act-beginners as themselves always actions – doings in the *narrow* sense – as well (e.g. Davis, 1979; Ginet, 1990). According to others, an action has been performed only if the act-beginner has had suitable consequences and/or has occurred in appropriate circumstances (e.g. Hornsby, 1980).

(a) 'Agent causation' is supposed to be a causal relation that holds *irreducibly* between an agent and certain events (*see* Chisholm, 1966; Taylor, 1966). *I* move my finger, and my doing so is an action, because I 'agent-cause' certain of the neural events that cause the muscle contractions that cause my finger's motion. If 'e' refers collectively to those neural events, then my agent-causing e is my doing, and this doing cannot be analysed, say, as the occurrence of another, earlier, event c which causes e. My action begins with my agent-causing e – and the time of my agent-causing e is precisely the same as the time of e itself.

(b) and (c) Many older accounts treated bodily actions such as moving a finger as things done by 'acts of will' or 'volitions'. Recently, a number of philosophers have spoken of 'tryings' or 'attempts' instead. I move my finger by trying to move it. Success is so much to be expected that I don't think of myself as 'trying' at all; I 'just' move the finger. Much is made, then, of cases like one described by William James: a blindfolded person is asked to move his anaesthetized arm, which is held down. The person is then 'astonished' to discover that his arm has not moved (James, 1950, II, p. 105). This is taken to show that the person tried to move the arm, in what he thought was a normal situation, implying that we also 'try' whenever we perform bodily actions. (*See* Hornsby, 1980, and Davis, 1979, for additional argument and references on the ubiquity of trying.) Finally, several recent theorists have revived the terms 'volition' and 'willing'. Ginet (1990) thinks volitions are mental actions, known to us by their 'actish phenomenal quality', and in every case having some 'exertion of the body' as their object. For Davis (1979), they are events of a kind characterized (in the spirit of functionalism) by their relations with their typical causes and effects; and their objects may extend beyond the body (e.g. a volition to tie one's shoe). Both authors use the terms 'volition' and 'willing' virtually interchangeably with 'trying' and 'attempt' (*See* THE WILL).

All three theories (a), (b) and (c), give us the same picture of bodily action involving act-beginners and the series of events they cause, culminating in motion of limbs or other parts of the body. Precisely where the action itself is located varies with one's theory of individuation. According to all, the action begins when the act-beginner begins. On intermediate views of act individuation, the action *consists* of the act-beginner *plus* the motion of, say, the finger, and all the events 'in between'. On the maximizing view, the actions are abstract entities distinct from these mereological sums, but having the same temporal limits. Most interesting is the minimizing view:

according to it, actions just *are* the agent-caused events, tryings, or willings with which they begin (so the term 'begin' is misleading). Moving one's finger, for example, is *entirely* something that takes place inside one's skin – presumably inside one's brain. The motion of the finger is just a consequence – though the act-beginner is describable as 'moving one's finger' only because it has this consequence.

(Different views are possible regarding the end-points of the act-beginners. We noted earlier that some actions seem to involve what could be called 'intention in action' – perhaps feedback mechanisms for ensuring that a goal, a certain end-state, is reached. Such mechanisms could be considered part of the act-beginner. This would mean that a trying, for example, lasts until the relevant body part's motion is completed. One says 'Good morning!' by *trying* to say it, and the trying lasts until the last syllable is pronounced.)

A main difficulty facing all these theories is the possibility that the act-beginners posited simply do not exist, or are not present in all cases we want to call cases of action. Many critics find the very idea of agent-caused events obscure, and the accounts of volitions and even tryings unconvincing. Perhaps there is no moment *at* which an action begins, even if there are moments (even prior to limb motion) *by* which it has begun. (Think of rivulets joining to form a stream and then a river: must there be a precise point at which the river begins?) There may be an intention, and then an action-in-progress, with nothing determinate marking the transition from the one to the other. If so, it may be actually misleading to posit act-beginners.

Or there might be act-beginners, but not for all actions. Consider what one does while driving – especially when, as we say, one's attention is elsewhere, perhaps on a conversation one is having simultaneously. A stop sign suddenly becomes visible, and one steps on the brake pedal. The stepping on the brake pedal here seems clearly to be an action, even intentional under that description; though like the earlier example

of passing the salt it is unclear what, if any, mentalistic explanation it can be given. Our new question is whether it began with an act-beginner, especially a trying or volition. How could we tell? Perhaps the physiology and psychology of this sort of leg-movement is so different from what happens in the self-conscious and isolated movements used most often as philosophers' examples, that there is no point to saying it begins with the 'same' sort of event, a trying, for example. Do we know enough to rule this possibility out?

(4) Actions as the Objects of Awareness of Agency

The last claim to be discussed is a suggestion based on features of our knowledge of our own action. A number of writers have stressed that this knowledge has at least two sources: perceptual (including kinaesthetic) and non-perceptual (Davis, 1979, pp. 15f, 61f; Ginet, 1990, p. 28). This is one of the lessons of the case described by William James: an agent deprived of perceptual information believes he has acted, entirely on the basis of some non-perceptual source. Normally, one knows by perception that one's arm, or whatever, is moving; but awareness that one is moving it, awareness of agency, is non-perceptual. (Awareness of *why* one is moving it, what one's reason or intention is, if any, is also non-perceptual, but presumably has a different etiology.) The view just discussed posits a kind of event, an act-beginner, as the source of this non-perceptual awareness, but we ended the discussion suggesting that there may not be a single kind of event playing this role in every case of action. It may turn out that there is no kind of event playing this role, or that there are a number of very different kinds of events playing it. But still, it may be that in each case of action there is non-perceptual awareness of acting. Or, rather, we can regard the class of doings that are actions as in effect *defined* by the doer's readiness – based on non-perceptual awareness – to claim the doing as his or her own, to express sentiments tantamount to '*I am the cause*'.

This suggestion may sound circular and vacuous. But it is not quite as empty as 'Actions are whatever a person believes are actions' would be. First, there is the requirement that the belief have a non-perceptual source. This rules out the possibility, for example, of someone's falling, or stumbling, being classed as an action. One knows of either only perceptually. Second, the 'persons' to which it is meant to apply are rational agents (like us) who have learned (like us) to act for reasons, etc., to be aware of their actions, to use this awareness purposively to modify their subsequent conduct, and so on. This ensures that their understanding of agency, their 'feel' for the distinction between what they *do* and what merely happens, will arise from their *being* agents, in line with the often-repeated claim that agency can be understood, the concept of action acquired, only 'from the inside'.

See also ACTION (2); BELIEF; DESIRE; *An Essay on Mind* section 2.3; INTENTIONALITY; PROPOSITIONAL ATTITUDES; THE WILL.

BIBLIOGRAPHY

Chisholm, R.C. 1966. Freedom and action. In *Freedom and Determinism*, ed. K. Lehrer. New York: Random House, pp. 11–44.

Davidson, D. 1980. *Essays on Actions and Events*. Oxford University Press.

Davis, L.H. 1979. *Theory of Action*. Englewood Cliffs, N.J.: Prentice-Hall.

Dennett, D.C., and Kinsbourne, M. 1992. Time and the observer: the where and when of consciousness in the brain. *Behavioral and Brain Sciences*, 15, 183–247.

Ginet, C. 1990. *On Action*. Cambridge University Press.

Goldman, A.I. 1970. *A Theory of Human Action*. Englewood Cliffs, N.J.: Prentice-Hall.

Hornsby, J. 1980. *Actions*. London: Routledge & Kegan Paul.

James, W. 1950. *Principles of Psychology*, 2 vols. Henry Holt, 1890; New York: Dover, 1950.

Libet, B. 1985. Unconscious cerebral initiative and the role of conscious will in voluntary action. *Behavioral and Brain Sciences*, 8, 529–66.

Mele, A.R. 1992. *Springs of Action*. Oxford University Press.

Mele, A.R. *forthcoming*. Recent work on intentional action. *American Philosophical Quarterly*.

Taylor, R. 1966. *Action and Purpose*. Englewood Cliffs, N.J.: Prentice-Hall.

LAWRENCE H. DAVIS

action (2)   A central question in the philosophy of action is what distinguishes a person's action from something that merely happens to him, such as sneezing or snoring. A popular answer to this question appeals to a causal theory of action (*see* REASONS AND CAUSES). Genuine actions or deeds, on this approach, are events with a distinctive internal cause, such as a desire, intention, or volition (*see* THE WILL). Sneezing, snoring, and stumbling over a rug are not actions because they are not caused by suitable desires or intentions.

Two problems face this kind of theory. First, many actions, especially automatic ones, do not seem to be preceded by any plan or intention to perform them. In playing a complex passage on the piano, it does not seem necessary for the performer to have a distinct intention or plan for each note played, at least if this means a conscious or introspectively available plan. In fact deliberate forethought may interfere with smooth performance. Second, there is the problem of 'deviant' or 'wayward' causal chains. To borrow an example from Davidson (1973), a climber might want to rid himself of the weight and danger of holding another man on a rope, and he might know that by loosening his hold on the rope he could rid himself of the weight and danger. This desire and belief might so unnerve him as to cause him to loosen his hold, and yet it might be that he never *chooses* to loosen his hold, nor is this something he intentionally or voluntarily *does*. Apparently, not every causal relation between seemingly appropriate mental events and behavioural upshots qualifies the latter as voluntary acts. The right sorts of causal relations would have to be specified if the causal theory is to succeed.

Despite these difficulties, the causal approach remains promising. Models of action in cognitive science may be able to explain what is common to automatic and deliberate action, and to identify the causal routes that are distinctive of action as opposed to mere happening. We shall consider a model due to Norman and Shallice (1986; *see also* Shallice, 1988, ch. 14), which postulates two complementary processes that operate in the selection and control of action. The first process is invoked to explain the ability of some action sequences to run off automatically without conscious control or the use of attentional resources. The second process allows for deliberate conscious control to initiate, guide, or modulate the course of action.

The first process is utilized in selecting and executing simple, well-learned, or habitual skills such as typing, or knotting a necktie. It is assumed that the motor control of well-learned movement is represented by means of a motor 'schema' or family of motor schemata (*see* Rumelhart and Norman, 1982). A motor schema is an organized unit of MENTAL REPRESENTA-TION, which has as its output the control of body movements. A set of such schemata operates as a motor 'program', understood as a flexible, interactive control structure capable of calling upon sub-programs and making local decisions as a result of current conditions. The basic framework in this approach is called an 'activation trigger schema' (ATS) system. Each schema has, at any time, an activation value that reflects the total amount of excitation it has received. The normal, resting value for a schema is zero. It can increase when the schema is activated, or decrease when the schema is inhibited. Various factors can influence the momentary activation value of a schema, including activation of a related schema (especially a 'parent' or 'source' schema), inhibition by rival schemata, and satisfaction of 'trigger conditions', which specify environmental circumstances that make the act in question feasible or appro-

priate. A schema is selected when its activation level exceeds a specified threshold. Once selected, it continues to operate (unless actively switched off) until it has satisfied its goal or completed its operations. The operation of a schema often consists in calling further ('child') schemata.

A concrete example can be given from the domain of typing (Rumelhart and Norman, 1982). A skilled typist will have a schema for a keypress action associated with each character on a standard keyboard. Each keypress schema specifies a target position, where position would be encoded in terms of finger and palm movements within a keyboard-centred coordinate system. A response sub-system feeds back information to the keypress system about the current location of the fingers. If a certain schema is highly activated, and if the current finger position is within some criterion distance of that schema's target position (thereby satisfying the trigger conditions), the actual keystroke is launched. Shortly after the launch, the keypress schema deactivates itself, resulting in a release of inhibition for all the succeeding keypress schemata. The system operates normally during the launch, and other keypress schemata may have their triggering conditions met and launch their own keystrokes before the earlier ones have been completed. People can type very fast; typing champions reach close to 200 words per minute (17 letters per second). This is possible, according to the Rumelhart–Norman model, because people carry out many actions at once. Responses are prepared and executed in parallel, so although the interval between two completed keystrokes may be, say, 60 milliseconds, each response takes much longer than that to complete.

Norman and Shallice call the foregoing a 'contention scheduling' mechanism. It permits simultaneous selection and execution of cooperative acts and prevents simultaneous performance of conflicting ones. This mechanism normally proceeds quite automatically. Some tasks, however, require deliberate attentional resources, viz., tasks that fall within the following categories: (1)

they involve planning or decision making, (2) they require troubleshooting, (3) they are ill-learned or contain novel action sequences, (4) they are judged to be dangerous or technically difficult, or (5) they require overcoming a strong habitual response or resisting temptation. Under any of these circumstances, use of an additional system is necessary: the 'supervisory attentional system' (SAS). SAS is a source of conscious control of the selection of schemata, which Norman and Shallice identify with the 'will'. SAS does not operate autonomously, however, but only via the contention scheduling mechanism, by applying extra, 'attentional' activation or inhibition to bias the selection of certain schemata. In other words, SAS does not directly control action selection, but only exerts itself indirectly through its effect on activation values. Thus, the basic mechanism of selection by activation values occurs in all voluntary behaviour, whether it is consciously willed or purely automatic.

Evidence for two levels of action control comes from clinical neuropsychology. It is well known that lesions confined to the prefrontal structures leave the execution of basic skills such as the use of objects, speaking, and writing unaffected, but can impair the performance of tasks involving novelty, error correction, or planning. Such lesions appear to involve damage to the SAS but not to the contention scheduling mechanism.

Let us return now to the problem of distinguishing action from mere undergoing of bodily movement. If the Norman–Shallice model is correct, voluntary action obviously cannot be identified with movement caused by 'will', or by conscious plans or intentions. Not only may an action sequence be run off without attention to each step, but an action may even be initiated without deliberate attention or awareness, as in beginning to drink from a glass while absorbed in conversation. The critical causal events distinctive of action, then, need not be conscious or deliberate. Just a sequence of schema activations and selections may constitute the necessary and sufficient causal elements to qualify a movement as a

voluntary action. Passive bodily happenings, such as accidentally loosening one's grip on the rope, would not be preceded by this sort of sequence.

Against this proposal it may be argued that an account of the ordinary concept of voluntary action should appeal to factors within the ken of ordinary people (cf. McCann, 1974, pp. 462–3). But the causal factors introduced here seem inaccessible to the ordinary person; they are apparently available only through scientific research. How can these factors, then, be the ones the ordinary person uses in distinguishing between voluntary action and bodily happening?

The second premise of this argument is questionable: the critical causal factors posited here may well be accessible to the ordinary person. Philosophers (e.g. Anscombe, 1957) speak of 'non-observational knowledge' of what one is doing, where the knowledge is not of a successfully executed movement but of an attempt to act. This may well consist in an awareness of the selection of an action schema, or a 'command' to the motor system. Cognitive theorists of motor action commonly postulate feedback processes by which information about the ongoing execution of motor programs is given to the controlling system (e.g. Wright, 1990). The philosopher's talk of 'non-observational knowledge' may be translatable into the cognitive theorist's language of 'feedback'. Is there empirical evidence of feedback from events of schema selection or action commands, as opposed to feedback from actual muscle movements? Yes there is. A study by McCloskey, Colebatch, Potter, and Burke (1983) found that normal subjects attend to different signals (feedback) when asked to judge the precise time of an internal 'command' to contract their hand muscles than when they are asked to judge the time of actual movements. Their subjective timing of movement commands was also studied in the absence of actual movements or local sensations from movements. (This was achieved by requiring subjects to attempt movements of the hand during local anaesthetic or blockade of the nerves to the forearm or hand). So there seem to be distinct signals from movement commands and from actual movements. The former may provide the sort of 'feeling of agency' characteristic of voluntary action, a feeling which is absent in cases of mere happening. A distinctive feeling would thus be associated with the normal selection or command of an action such as (voluntarily) loosening one's hold on a rope, a feeling that would be absent in a case of accidentally losing one's grip on the rope.

It may still be queried whether it is legitimate to appeal to the neural events in question in an account of the ordinary concept of action. Is it not necessary that the ordinary person be able to specify the events in detail, which obviously is not possible here? No. The situation may be compared to Putnam's (1975) treatment of natural kind concepts. Just as a specification of the detailed structure of water or gold may be relegated to the special sciences, so the special sciences, in this case psychology and neuroscience, are needed to spell out the detailed conditions distinctive of voluntary action. This fits an earlier suggestion of the present author that a solution to the problem of 'deviant causal chains' should be assigned to the scientific study of mind rather than to pure philosophy (Goldman, 1970, pp. 62–3. For doubts about this strategy, *see* Bishop, 1989.)

The approach developed here has much in common with certain conceptions of a volitional theory of action, in which a volition is not understood as a conscious occurrence but as a postulated cognitive-neurophysiological event. Our proposal is especially close to that of Davis (1979), who gives a functional characterization of a volition as 'an event which is normally a cause of the agent's belief that he is acting in a certain way, *and* which normally causes such doing-related events as make it true that he *is* acting in that way' (Davis, 1979, p. 16; cf. Ginet's account of volitions in Ginet, 1990). Hornsby's (1980) notion of a trying may also have kinship to the present conception, and perhaps Brand's (1984) quasi-technical notion of an intention as well.

It is fortunate that the present approach does not place much weight on conscious desires, intentions, or plans as the crucial causes of voluntary action, because some recent neurophysiological research points to the possible conclusion that conscious events have little causal role to play. Research conducted by Libet (1985) measured both cortical activity that initiates voluntary action and subjectively experienced onset of an intention to initiate it (Libet's 'W'). Libet found that the intention was experienced about 350 milliseconds *after* the cortical activity (though still 200 milliseconds before the motor performance), which invites the conclusion that the conscious experience itself plays no causal role. Libet's experiments are subject to rival interpretations, however, so no such conclusion should be drawn prematurely.

In addition to the problem of distinguishing action and happening, cognitive science may help resolve other problems and puzzles in the theory of action. Consider the much-debated puzzle of WEAKNESS OF WILL. So-called 'akratic' action is action wherein the agent intentionally does something that runs directly counter to his predominant desire, intention, or judgment (Davidson, 1970). How is such action possible?

A solution to the puzzle, at least a partial solution, may emerge from the same sort of psychological theory examined earlier. As we have seen, psychologists recognize that actions can be triggered quite independently of deliberate choice. Indeed, such actions can sometimes proceed contrary to choice or intention. One example is reading. When we see a billboard on a highway, we cannot help but read what it says, whether we want to or not. The forms on the sign proclaim that they are letters and words, and this is enough to initiate reading routines (La Berge, 1975). A striking demonstration of this phenomenon is the so-called 'Stroop effect' (Stroop, 1935). Subjects are shown a list of words printed in colour, and are asked to name the colours of the print. Quite diabolically, however, the words themselves are colour words, and they name colours distinct from those in which they are printed. For example, 'green' is printed in yellow, 'yellow' is printed in black, and so forth. Since the subjects are supposed to name the colours of the print, they should not read the words at all, which will only confuse them. But they cannot help reading the words and therefore find the task extremely difficult. This is an example of what philosophers call akratic action, since the subjects deliberately try not to read the words but do so anyway. If the psychologists are right, the phenomenon is explained by the presence of an automatic selection mechanism that can set actions in motion irrespective of, and even in opposition to, the decisions of the SAS, which embodies conscious, attentional motivation. This explanation might work for a wide range of so-called akratic actions.

See also ACTION (1); BELIEF; DESIRE; *An Essay on Mind* section 2.3; COGNITIVE PSYCHOLOGY; CONSCIOUSNESS; INTENTION; INTENTIONALITY; PROPOSITIONAL ATTITUDES; THE WILL.

BIBLIOGRAPHY

Anscombe, G.E.M. 1957. *Intention.* Oxford: Basil Blackwell.
Bishop, J. 1989. *Natural Agency: An Essay on the Causal Theory of Action.* Cambridge University Press.
Brand, M. 1984. *Intending and Acting: Toward a Naturalized Action Theory.* Cambridge, MA.: MIT Press.
Davidson, D. 1970. How is weakness of the will possible?. In *Moral Concepts,* ed. J. Feinberg. Oxford University Press, pp. 93–113.
Davidson, D. 1973. Freedom to act. In *Essays on Freedom of Action,* ed. T. Honderich. Routledge & Kegan Paul, pp. 137–56.
Davis, L.H. 1979. *Theory of Action.* Englewood Cliffs, N.J.: Prentice-Hall.
Ginet, C. 1990. *On Action.* Cambridge University Press.
Goldman, A.I. 1970. *A Theory of Human Action.* Englewood Cliffs, N.J.: Prentice-Hall.
Hornsby, J. 1980. *Actions.* London: Routledge & Kegan Paul.
La Berge, D. 1975. Acquisition of automatic processing in perceptual and associative learning. In *Attention and Performance,* vol. 5, ed. P. M. A. Rabbitt and S. Dormic. London: Academic Press.
Libet, B. 1985. Unconscious cerebral initiative and the role of conscious will in voluntary action. *Behavioral and Brain Sciences,* 8, 529–539.
McCann, H. 1974. Volition and basic action. *Philosophical Review,* 83, 451–73.
McCloskey, T.I., Colebatch, J.G., Potter, E.K., and Burke, D. 1983. Judgements about onset of rapid voluntary movements in man. *Journal of Neurophysiology,* 49, 851–863.
Norman, D.A., and Shallice, T. 1986. Attention to action; willed and automatic control of behavior. In *Consciousness and Self-Regulation: Advances in Research and Theory,* vol. 4, ed. R. J. Davidson, G. E. Schwartz, and D. Shapiro. New York: Plenum Press, pp. 1–18.
Putnam, H. 1975. The meaning of 'meaning'. In *Language, Mind and Knowledge,* Minnesota Studies in Philosophy of Science, vol. 7, ed. K. Gunderson. Minneapolis: University of Minnesota Press, pp. 131–93.
Rumelhart, B.E., and Norman, D.A. 1982. Simulating a skilled typist: a study of skilled cognitive-motor performance. *Cognitive Science,* 6, 1–36.
Shallice, T. 1988. *From Neuropsychology to Mental Structure.* Cambridge University Press.
Stroop, J.R. 1935. Studies of interference in serial verbal reactions. *Journal of Experimental Psychology,* 18, 643–62.
Wright, C.E. 1990. Controlling sequential motor activity. In *Visual Cognition and Action,* ed. D. N. Osherson, S. M. Kosslyn, and J. M. Hollerbach. Cambridge, MA.: MIT Press, pp. 285–316.

ALVIN I. GOLDMAN

agency A central task in the philosophy of action is that of spelling out the differences between events in general and those events that fall squarely into the category of human action. An earthquake is certainly something that happens, but it is not something done. Whereas when someone picks up a hammer and drives a nail into a piece of wood, this is both something that happens and something done or undertaken. In this second case, one has a clear case of agency – a case of an agent undertaking to bring about some change in the world. However, whilst it is easy enough to locate the notion of agency with respect to actions, it is not at all clear just what constitutes it, whether it is a special feature of the mind or is composed of such things as intentions, desires and beliefs.

See ACTION; DESIRE; INTENTION; THE SELF; THE WILL.

SAMUEL GUTTENPLAN

anomalous monism Monism is the view that there is only one kind of substance underlying all objects, changes and processes. It is generally used in contrast to DUALISM, though one can also think of it as denying what might be called 'pluralism' – a view often associated with Aristotle which claims that there are a number of substances (*see* HISTORY). Against the background of modern science, monism is usually understood to be a form of materialism or PHYSICALISM. That is, the fundamental properties of matter and energy as described by physics are counted the only properties there are.

The position in the philosophy of mind known as *anomalous monism* has its historical origins in Kant, but is universally identified with Donald DAVIDSON's views, and it was he who coined the term. Davidson has maintained that one can be a monist – indeed, a physicalist – about the fundamental nature of things and events, whilst also asserting that there can be no full REDUCTION of the mental to the physical. (This is sometimes expressed by saying that there can be an ONTOLOGICAL, though not a conceptual reduction.) To put it more concretely, Davidson thinks that complete knowledge of the brain and any related neurophysiological systems that support the mind's activities would not itself be knowledge of such things as belief, desire, experience and the rest of the mental. This is not because he thinks that the mind is somehow a separate kind of existence;

anomalous monism is after all monism. Rather, it is because the nature of mental phenomena rules out a priori that there will be law-like regularities connecting mental phenomena and physical events in the brain, and, without such laws, there is no real hope of explaining the mental via the physical structures of the brain.

See also SUPERVENIENCE.

SAMUEL GUTTENPLAN

artificial intelligence Marvin Minsky, founder of the MIT AI laboratory, has defined Artificial Intelligence as 'the science of making machines do things that would require intelligence if done by men' (1968, p. v). The field was given its name by John McCarthy, who in 1956 organized the conference that many AI researchers regard as marking the birth of their subject: the Dartmouth Summer Research Project on Artificial Intelligence. The last two words stuck.

One of the earliest lectures on computer intelligence – possibly the earliest – was given in 1947 by the British logician Alan TURING, then working at the National Physical Laboratory in London. The lecture was entitled 'Intelligent Machinery, A Heretical Theory'. (Turing's notes for the lecture are reproduced in Turing, 1959, pp. 128–34.) 'My contention is that machines can be constructed which will simulate the behaviour of the human mind very closely', said Turing with remarkable far-sightedness. At that time there were no more than two electronic computers in existence, the Colossus in Britain and the ENIAC in America, both of them extremely primitive. (The Manchester Mark I, the world's first stored-program general-purpose electronic computer, did not run its first program until June 1948.) In 1948 Turing circulated a startlingly original report on the prospects for machine intelligence. In it he anticipated many later developments, including CONNECTIONISM. In 1950 he published an article entitled 'Computing Machinery and Intelligence' in the philosophical journal *Mind* (he was by this time Deputy Director of the Computing Laboratory at Manchester). The article began 'I propose to consider the question "Can machines think?"'.

The first working AI program was a checkers (or draughts) program that incorporated a learning mechanism. The program rapidly picked up the skills of the game and was soon able to beat its creator, Arthur Samuel. This was the first heuristic program to be fully realized on a computer. (A heuristic program is one that follows 'rules of thumb', as opposed to following a rule that is guaranteed to lead to the desired result – in this case, that of winning the game.) Samuel gave a demonstration of the program on American TV in the early 1950s. Some years later, in 1956, came the most fecund of the early attempts at AI, the Logic Theorist, written by Allen Newell, Cliff Shaw and Herbert Simon. The Logic Theorist succeeded in proving 38 of the first 52 theorems presented in Whitehead and Russell's *Principia Mathematica*. In the case of one theorem, the machine's proof was shorter and neater than the one Whitehead and Russell gave.

I shall not here consider Turing's general question of whether a machine may properly be said to think or display intelligence (for a discussion see chapter 3 of Copeland, 1993). Assuming an affirmative answer to that general question, my concern here will be with the issue of whether the specific types of machines currently under investigation in AI are of the right sort to display general intelligence. With that topic in view I examine two of the fundamental assumptions of AI research: the symbol system hypothesis and the algorithmicity assumption. The symbol system hypothesis is associated more closely with the 'traditional' approach to AI than with the connectionist approach (which did not become widely pursued until the mid-1980s). The algorithmicity assumption is common to both approaches to AI. First articulated and explored within AI, this assumption has now become a foundational one in much of cognitive science and in much contemporary philosophy of mind.

THE SYMBOL SYSTEM HYPOTHESIS

From the most basic PC to the most advanced Cray, commercially available computers share the same basic principles of operation. All are symbol-processing engines. Information is stored in the computer's memory in the form of symbols, programs are internally stored lists of symbolically encoded instructions, and each step of a computation consists of a simple operation on a symbol string. These symbol strings that the computer stores and processes are rather like sentences of a language or code. Typically the code used is binary in nature, which is to say that it employs only two basic characters. Binary code is easier to implement electronically than a code like the one I am presently writing in, which of course employs over 26 characters. The symbol system hypothesis is the hypothesis that a symbol-processing system – that is, a computer – can be set up so as to exhibit general intelligence.

As I have said, there are at present two major approaches to AI, that of the traditionalists and that of the connectionists. Connectionists distance themselves from symbol-processing and are exploring an alternative approach to computation. Here is the recipe traditionalists propose for building a machine that is as intelligent as we are.

Use a language-like symbolic code to represent real-world objects, events, actions, relationships, etc.

Build up an adequate representation of the world and its workings (including human creations such as commerce) inside a computer. This 'knowledge base' will consist of vast, interconnected structures of symbols. It must include a representation of the machine itself and of its purposes and needs. Opinions differ as to whether programmers will have to 'hand craft' this gigantic structure or whether the machine can be programmed to learn much of it for itself.

Use suitable input devices to form symbolic representations (in the same code) of the flux of environmental stimuli impinging on the machine.

Arrange for complex sequences of the computer's hard-wired symbol-processing operations to be applied to the symbol structures produced by the input devices and to the symbol structures stored in the knowledge base. Further symbol structures result. Some of these are designated as output. The sequences of operations are selected by the computer by means of an algorithm. (This term is explained below.)

This output is a symbolic representation of appropriate behavioural responses (including verbal ones) to the input. A suitable robot body can be used to 'translate' the symbols into real behaviour.

The symbol system hypothesis is simply this: *the recipe will work*. According to the hypothesis any general-purpose computer with sufficient memory can, through further internal organization, acquire general intelligence. The nomenclature derives from Newell and Simon (1976). The symbol system hypothesis as here presented is the sufficiency-part of their physical symbol system hypothesis (the necessity-part being the claim that symbol-manipulation is necessary for general intelligent action). For ease I drop 'physical'.

This hypothesis is a bold empirical conjecture. At present no one knows whether it is true or false. Initially the impetus for advancing the hypothesis was provided by the success of programs like the Logic Theorist and Samuel's checkers player. In 1958, on the basis of their experience with the Logic Theorist, Simon and Newell wrote: 'Intuition, insight, and learning are no longer exclusive possessions of humans: any large high-speed computer can be programmed to exhibit them also . . . The simplest way [we] can summarise the situation is to say that there are now in the world machines that can think, that learn, and that create' (1958, pp. 6–8). Their enthu-

siasm led them to predict that by 1967 a digital computer would be able to beat any human at chess. A more recent prediction, by Doug Lenat and Ed Feigenbaum, is for a symbol-processing system with human-level breadth and depth of knowledge by the early years of next century (1991, p. 224). Artificial intelligence is 'within our grasp', declare Lenat and Feigenbaum (p. 188). Yet the truth of the matter is that after nearly half a century of grappling with some of the hardest problems known to science, AI has achieved only very modest results. The programs developed to date are like toys when matched against the overall goal of a machine that can operate at human levels of intelligence in the unruly complexity of the real world. At present the symbol system hypothesis has much the same standing as the hypothesis that there is intelligent life on other planets: people have strongly held opinions, both for and against, but as yet there is no firm evidence either way.

THE ALGORITHMICITY ASSUMPTION

First I will explain what an algorithm is. I'll call the steps of a procedure *moronic* if no insight, ingenuity or creativity is necessary in order to carry them out. A procedure for achieving some specified result is known as an algorithm when (1) every step of the procedure is moronic; (2) at the end of each step it is moronically clear what is to be done next (i.e. no insight, etc. is needed to tell); and (3) the procedure is guaranteed to lead to the specified result in a finite number of steps (assuming each step is carried out correctly). To give a simple example, if you've mixed up your keys and can't tell by sight which one fits your front door, the well-known expedient of trying them in succession is an algorithm for finding the right key: the procedure is sure to work eventually (assuming you haven't actually lost the key) and is certainly moronic. All (successful) computer programs are, of course, algorithms.

A system (real or abstract) is said to be *algorithmically calculable* if there is an algorithm – known or unknown – for calculating its behaviour. To put this more formally, the system is algorithmically calculable just in case there is an algorithmic procedure for deriving correct descriptions of the system's outputs from correct descriptions of the inputs it receives (and moreover a procedure that works for all possible inputs that will produce output).

ALGORITHMIC CALCULABILITY AND INTELLIGENCE

The types of machines used in AI are algorithmically calculable. Tautologically, a computer with a given set of programs is an algorithmically calculable system (provided it doesn't malfunction) because, of course, these programs are themselves algorithms for passing from input to output. Connectionist networks are also algorithmically calculable systems. In short, all current work in AI is based on the assumption that the way to build an artefact capable of general intelligent action is to build one or another type of algorithmically calculable system. The possibility that general intelligence may transcend algorithms is ignored.

As early as 1936 Turing mooted the possibility of our own cognitive processes being algorithmically calculable. Subsequently this has become an article of deepest faith among AI researchers, and has even acquired the status of something 'too obvious to mention'. For example, take the following famous argument due to Newell, which is intended to demonstrate that computer intelligence is achievable, at least in theory: 'A universal [symbol] system always contains the potential for being any other system, if so instructed. Thus, a universal system can become a generally intelligent system' (Newell, 1980, p. 170). What Newell means is that a universal symbol system (i.e. a general-purpose computer with no practical bound on the size of its memory) can be programmed to simulate any other algorithmically calculable system (this is known as the Church–Turing thesis or sometimes – less accurately – simply as Church's thesis). The assumption that a system exhibiting general intelligence will be algorithmically calculable is thought so obvious that Newell does not even mention it. Some of AI's most notable opponents also subscribe to the assumption that our cognitive processes are algorithmically calculable, for example John Searle. 'Can the operations of the brain be simulated on a digital computer? . . . [G]iven Church's thesis that anything that can be given a precise enough characterization as a set of steps can be simulated on a digital computer, it follows trivially that the question has an affirmative answer' (Searle, 1992, p. 200). In fact, this follows only given the premise that the brain is algorithmically calculable. The thought that it follows trivially from the Church–Turing thesis that our cognitive processes are algorithmically calculable is a modern fallacy; there is no reason to think that Turing himself saw the issue of the algorithmic calculability of cognition as being anything other than an empirical one.

THE ALGORITHMICITY ASSUMPTION STATED

There are two parts to what I am calling the algorithmicity assumption. AI as presently conceived is feasible only if both parts of the assumption are true.

(1) There exists, or can exist, some algorithmically calculable system exhibiting general intelligence.
(2) There is a *practicable* algorithm (known or unknown) for calculating the behaviour of the system.

By a *practicable* algorithm I mean one that can be implemented in a real machine in real time, as opposed to one that could be implemented only in an ideal world of unlimited resources – a world in which time is of no concern, in which issues of reliability and cumulative error can be ignored, and in which there are no bounds whatever on the capacity of the machine's memory devices.

The idealized computers invented by

Turing and now known as Turing machines are a rich source of examples of algorithms that can be run in an ideal world but not in the real world. A Turing machine is very simple: it consists only of a read/write head and a memory tape – a paper tape of unlimited length (Turing, 1936). In theory a Turing machine can be given an algorithm that will enable it to simulate a state-of-the-art Cray supercomputer. But it would take untold centuries for a Turing machine to simulate even a few hours of the Cray's operations, and the simulation might well demand more paper tape than our planet has to offer. (Turing's own formulation of the Church–Turing thesis was in terms of these idealized machines: a Turing machine can simulate any algorithmically calculable system (Turing, 1936).) Obviously, an algorithm for general intelligent action that could not be implemented on some real machine in the real world would be of no use to AI.

The remainder of this discussion focuses on the first part of the algorithmicity assumption. The mammalian brain is the best – indeed the only – example we have of a system capable of supporting general intelligent action. Is this system algorithmically calculable? In point of fact there is no reason – apart from a kind of wishful thinking – to believe that it is so. This is *terra incognita*, and for all we presently know many aspects of brain function may be non-computable. To pursue this point we need some terminology from computability theory.

A LITTLE LIGHT COMPUTABILITY THEORY

Let S be a set of sentences. For the moment it doesn't matter what these sentences are; I'm going to use S as the basis for a number of general definitions – general in the sense that they are applicable no matter what sentences S happens to contain. Call the language in which the sentences of S are written L. (So L might be English or the differential calculus or the first order predicate calculus, etc.) To say that S is *decidable* is to say that there is an algorithm for settling whether or not given sentences are members of S. The algorithm must give the right answer for each sentence of L. So for S to be decidable there must be an algorithm that can be applied to each sentence of L and that will deliver either the answer 'Yes, this sentence is in S' or 'No, this sentence is not in S' (and moreover the answers the algorithm gives must always be correct). S is said to be *undecidable* if there is no such algorithm. If there is such an algorithm it is called a *decision procedure* for S.

To give a straightforward example of a set that is decidable, let the only members of S be the sentences 'London is in England' and 'Paris is in France'. It is easy to compose a decision procedure for this two-membered set: given any English sentence, scan through it character by character and determine whether or not it is identical to either the first member of S or the second member of S. If it is identical to one of them then output 'This sentence is in S'; otherwise output 'This sentence is not in S'. This is called a *lookup* decision procedure (or *lookup* algorithm). The program contains a complete list of the members of S and tests sentences for membership of S simply by looking through the list.

Any finite set of sentences has a lookup decision procedure. In other words, every finite set of sentences is decidable. Lookup decision procedures become less practicable as the set in question gets larger. Indeed, it is easy to imagine lookup decision procedures that are completely impossible to implement in practice. Take a set containing N English sentences, where N is the number of atoms in the known universe. Since N is finite this set has a lookup decision procedure, but obviously it isn't one that any real computer could run. (Though a Turing machine could run it, since Turing machines have unbounded resources.) This is why lookup decision procedures for very large sets are of no relevance to AI.

Many sets have decision procedures that don't involve lookup. One example is the set of English sentences that are less than 100 characters long (to test whether a given English sentence is a member of the set just count the characters). However, some finite sets have no decision procedure apart from a lookup procedure. The sentences of this book form such a set. There is no rule for generating the sentences that an algorithm can exploit. I will describe such sets as 'undecidable save by lookup'. If the theory of cognition involves large sets that are undecidable save by lookup this could be very bad news for AI.

An *infinite* set is a set containing at least as many members as there are whole numbers. If an eternal being were to begin counting the members of an infinite set, one, two, three, four . . . then no matter how large a number the being gets up to, there will always be further members left to count. Infinite sets are not necessarily exotic things. An extremely humdrum infinite set can be constructed from nothing more than the sentence 'Fred is just an ordinary bloke' and the rule: if X is a member of the set then so is 'it is false that X'. Here are the first few of the set's infinitely many members.

Fred is just an ordinary bloke.

It is false that Fred is just an ordinary bloke.

It is false that it is false that Fred is just an ordinary bloke.

It is false that it is false that it is false that Fred is just an ordinary bloke.

Formal logic furnishes examples of both decidable and undecidable infinite sets. The set of valid sentences of truth-functional logic is infinite and decidable. Truth-functional logic is the branch of logic that focuses on the expressions 'if-then', 'and', 'it is false that' and 'either-or'. A *valid* sentence is a sentence that is true come what may, true in all circumstances. So an example of a valid sentence of truth-functional logic is 'either Fred is an ordinary bloke or it is false that Fred is an ordinary bloke'. The next step up from truth-functional logic is first-order quantifier logic. The quantifiers are

'some' and 'every'. In quantifier logic (but not truth-functional logic) it is possible to express such propositions as 'every cat has nine lives', 'some cats dribble', and 'some infinite sets are undecidable'. Logic books brim with examples of valid sentences of first-order quantifier logic: 'if it is false that everyone in the bar is drunk then someone in the bar is not drunk', 'either everyone loves Suzy or someone does not love Suzy', and so forth. The set of valid sentences of first-order quantifier logic is infinite and undecidable. (This was first proved by Church (1936).) Any attempt to write an algorithm that will test arbitrary sentences of first-order logic for validity is bound to be unsuccessful. Any procedure that anyone dreams up is bound to be unreliable, bound in the long run to give wrong answers or no answer at all at least as many times as it gives right ones. There simply is no decision procedure for the set of valid sentences of first-order quantifier logic.

However, this set is not completely intractable computationally. There is an algorithm (in fact many) meeting the following conditions.

(1) Whenever the algorithm is applied to a valid sentence of first-order quantifier logic it will (given enough time) deliver the result 'Yes, this sentence is valid'.
(2) Whenever the algorithm is applied to a sentence of first-order quantifier logic that is not valid it will either deliver the result 'No, this sentence is not valid' or will deliver no answer at all (i.e. will carry on computing 'forever' – in practice until someone turns it off or until it runs out of memory and crashes).

An algorithm that meets these two conditions is called a semi decision procedure. If there is a semi decision procedure for a set S then S is said to be *semidecidable*. Every answer that a semi decision procedure gives is correct, and every time the algorithm is applied to a sentence that *is* in the set it *gives* an answer, provided you wait long enough. When the algorithm is applied to a sentence that is *not* in the set it may give an answer (the right one) or it may never come to the end of its calculations.

Can you see why a semi decision procedure is not a decision procedure? The sticking point is the proviso that you wait long enough. If you're testing a sentence and no answer is forthcoming then no matter how long you wait you can never be sure whether the algorithm is just about to pronounce, perhaps positively, or whether the sentence is one of those invalid ones for which the algorithm never delivers a result.

Are there such things as *nonsemidecidable* sets – sets, that is, for which there is not even a semi decision procedure? Yes. Again formal logic furnishes an example. The set of valid sentences of *second-order* quantifier logic is known to be nonsemidecidable. First-order logic is all about saying that *things* have properties and bear relationships to other things: 'every thing has the property of being massive', 'some things have both the property of being a cat and the property of dribbling', 'there is some thing that stands in the relation of being-larger-than to every other thing'. The language of second-order logic allows us to quantify over not just things themselves but also over the properties that things have and the relationships that things bear to one another. In other words, in second-order logic we can write sentences containing such expressions as 'every property that' and 'there are some relationships that'. In second-order logic (but not first-order logic) it is possible to express such propositions as 'Jules and Jim have some properties in common', 'every thing has some properties', 'Napoleon has every property necessary to being a good general' and 'every constitutional relationship that holds between the US President and Senate also holds between the British Prime Minister and the House of Commons'. The set of valid sentences of second-order logic is as computationally intractable as they come. Any attempt to write an algorithm that will say 'Yes, that's a member' whenever it is applied to a member of the set (and never when it is applied to a non-member) is doomed. There

is no such algorithm: that is what it means to say that a set is nonsemidecidable. Turing proved the existence of non-semidecidable sets in his 1936 paper (although not by reference to second-order logic). Penrose (1989) contains interesting discussions of some of the issues that Turing's proof raises.

NONSEMIDECIDABILITY AND THE ALGORITHMICITY ASSUMPTION

There is an intimate connection between the concept of a system's being algorithmically calculable and the concept of a set's being semidecidable. Let the members of S be descriptions of the input/state/output behaviour of a system B. That is, each member of S is of the form 'If the system B is given input I while in internal state X then it goes into internal state Y and produces output O'. S contains all the sentences of this form that are true of B. If S is nonsemidecidable B is not algorithmically calculable; for if S is nonsemidecidable there can be no algorithm capable of computing a correct description of the ensuing output (if any) from each description of input into B.

If there were *no* nonsemidecidable sets then we could rest assured that *every possible* system is algorithmically calculable; and in particular we could be assured that any system capable of general intelligent action is algorithmically calculable. But thanks to Turing we know that there are nonsemidecidable sets; so we must accept that there is no a priori guarantee that intelligent systems are algorithmically calculable.

CAN A COMPUTER SIMULATE THE BRAIN?

In the particular case where the system B is the human brain I will call the set of descriptions of input/state/output behaviour β. The members of β are highly complicated sentences. Each records the total output (electrical and chemical) that the brain will produce in response to a particular total input received while the brain is in a particular (total) internal state.

Is β infinite? This is an empirical question and the answer is not yet known. It is certainly the case that the corresponding set for a Turing machine is infinite, since there are infinitely many possible inputs (infinitely many ways that the limitless tape can be inscribed with symbols before the machine is set in motion). Many believe there is a good *prima facie* case for thinking that β too is infinite. It is, of course, true that a brain can process only a finite number of finite inputs in its finite life. But it is not at all obvious that there are only a finite number of *potential* inputs from which the actual inputs that a given brain encounters are drawn. The potential inputs seem endless – in the same way that there are an endless number of English sentences. If the number of potential inputs is infinite then β is infinite, for β contains *all* input/state/output descriptions, potential as well as actual.

The same goes for states. Each brain can enter only a finite number of states in its life, yet the set of potential states from which this finite number is drawn may be infinite. For example, 'thinking that P' is an internal state, and there certainly seems to be no limit to the number of different things that a person might think. (Analogously the electrical potential of a cell membrane can take only a finite number of values in the course of the cell's finite life, yet there are an indefinite number of possible values lying between the maximum and minimum values for that membrane, from which the set of actual values is drawn.)

Nothing is known to indicate that β is either decidable or semidecidable. And if β is nonsemidecidable the brain is not algorithmically calculable. Even if β should turn out to be finite it may be undecidable save by lookup. The existence, in theory, of a lookup decision procedure could be of no conceivable relevance to AI, given the size of β (not to mention the sheer difficulty of listing the members of β). Ambitions to simulate the brain by computer depend for viability on there being a practicable algorithm that can generate members of β. One may hope that even if the brain should turn out not to be algorithmically calculable, it is

nevertheless 'recursively approximable' in the sense of Rose and Ullian (1963). A system is recursively approximable if and only if there is an algorithm that computes descriptions (not necessarily in real time) of the system's input/output behaviour in such a way that after a sufficiently large number of descriptions have been generated the proportion of the descriptions that are incorrect never exceeds a prescribed figure. However, this is at present no more than a hope. There are uncountably many functions that are not recursively approximable. One sometimes sees it claimed that any conceivable physical device or process can be approximated by a Turing machine to any required degree of fineness; but this is true only for devices and processes that are recursively approximable.

A MODEL FOR A NONCOMPUTATIONAL BRAIN

Readers who have studied the section on CONNECTIONISM may be interested to see a sketch of a type of artificial neural network that is not algorithmically calculable. In connectionist jargon, the *activation function* for a neural network is a description of what it takes to make the neurons in the network fire. For example, in a typical connectionist network a neuron fires if the weighted sum of its inputs exceeds its threshold. I will call a neural network *second-order* if the activation function for the network can be formulated only by means of second-order logic. That is, the activation function can be formulated only by means of quantifying over properties of neurons and/or relationships between neurons. An example of such an activation function is: a neuron n fires if all relationships of a particular sort holding between the neurons in some cluster of neurons containing n also hold between the neurons in some associated cluster. It remains to be seen whether 'global' activation functions such as this one are physically realizable in a way that is consistent with what is already known about neural tissue. (The function is 'global' in the sense that the neuron needs to know more than what is happening just on its own doorstep in order to be able to tell whether or not to fire – that is, the neuron needs non-local, or global, information. Certain types of second-order neural networks are not algorithmically calculable. For all that is presently known, significant portions of the brain may be like this.

CONCLUSION

AI researchers are fond of saying that they are looking for Maxwell's laws of thought. Last century James Clerk Maxwell reduced electrodynamics to a few elegant equations. The idea of doing the same for cognition is certainly appealing. Minsky speaks of the search for 'the three algorithms'. His metaphor is a child throwing three pebbles into a pond. The basic wavepattern produced by each pebble is very simple – concentric rings moving outwards – but the interaction of these three patterns produces a confusion of waves and ripples. The hope is – though it's fading – that the complexity of our cognitive life will similarly turn out to be the product of a small number of elegant algorithms.

Lack of success in the search for Maxwell's laws of thought is ushering in a new perspective. The mind is coming to be seen as a rag bag of large numbers of special-purpose algorithms, a motley assortment of *ad hoc* tools assembled by Mother Programmer, the greatest pragmatist in the universe. The latest generation of AI systems mirror this new image. For example, Lenat's CYC program contains around 30 different special-purpose inference mechanisms (Lenat and Guha, 1990).

AI is polarized around these two viewpoints – a small number of very powerful algorithms versus a large number of weaker, messier ones. Yet as we have seen there is a daunting third possibility. Algorithms may not be much of the story of intelligence at all – at best one of its minor characters, perhaps.

Traditional program-writing AI is, of course, irrevocably bound up with the assumption that intelligence is algor-ithmically calculable, and moreover calculable by means of practicable algorithms. Present forms of connectionism, too, are wedded to this assumption, in that all connectionist architectures currently under investigation are algorithmically calculable (indeed, investigation typically proceeds by means of computer simulation). I am certainly not denying the claim that a system capable of exhibiting general intelligence is algorithmically calculable; but I would stress that at the present moment there is precious little evidence either for or against this assumption, on which AI as we presently conceive it depends.

See also COGNITIVE PSYCHOLOGY; COMPUTATIONAL MODELS.

BIBLIOGRAPHY

Church, A. 1936. A Note on the Entscheidungsproblem. *The Journal of Symbolic Logic*, 1, 40–1.

Copeland, B.J. 1993. *Artificial Intelligence: A Philosophical Introduction*. Oxford: Basil Blackwell.

Lenat, D.B., Feigenbaum, E.A. 1991. On the thresholds of knowledge. *Artificial Intelligence*, 47, 185–250.

Lenat, D.B., Guha, R.V. 1990. *Building Large Knowledge-Based Systems: Representation and Inference in the CYC Project*. Reading, MA.: Addison-Wesley.

Minsky, M.L., ed. 1968. *Semantic Information Processing*. Cambridge, MA.: MIT Press.

Newell, A. 1980. Physical symbol systems. *Cognitive Science*, 4, 135–83.

Newell, A., Shaw, J.C., Simon, H.A. 1957. Empirical explorations with the logic theory machine: A case study in heuristics. In *Computers and Thought*, ed. E. A. Feigenbaum, J. Feldman. New York: McGraw-Hill, 1963, pp. 109–33.

Newell, A., Simon, A. 1976. Computer science as empirical inquiry: Symbols and search. In *Mind Design: Philosophy, Psychology, Artificial Intelligence*, ed. J. Haugeland. Cambridge, MA.: MIT Press, 1981, pp. 35–66.

Penrose, R. 1989. *The Emperor's New Mind*. Oxford University Press.

Rose, G.F., Ullian, J.S. 1963. Approximation of

functions on the integers. *Pacific Journal of Mathematics*, 13, 693–701.

Samuel, A.L. 1959. Some studies in machine learning using the game of checkers. In *Computers and Thought*, ed. E. A. Feigenbaum, J. Feldman. New York: McGraw-Hill, 1963, pp. 71–105.

Searle, J. 1992. *The Rediscovery of the Mind*. Cambridge, MA.: MIT Press.

Simon, H.A., Newell, A. 1958. Heuristic problem solving: the next advance in operations research. *Operations Research*, 6, 1–10.

Turing, A.M. 1936. On computable numbers, with an application to the Entscheidungsproblem. *Proceedings of the London Mathematical Society*, Series 2, 42 (1936–37), 230–265.

Turing, A.M. 1947. Lecture to the London mathematical society on 20 February 1947. In *A. M. Turing's ACE Report of 1946 and Other Papers*, ed. B. E. Carpenter, R. W. Doran. Cambridge, MA.: MIT Press, pp. 106–24.

Turing, A.M. 1948. Intelligent machinery. National Physical Laboratory Report. Reproduced in *Machine Intelligence 5*, ed. B. Meltzer, D. Michie. Edinburgh: Edinburgh University Press, 1969, pp. 3–23.

Turing, A.M. 1950. Computing machinery and intelligence. *Mind* 59, 433–60.

Turing, S. 1959. *Alan M. Turing*. Cambridge: W. Heffer.

B. JACK COPELAND

B

behaviourism Introductory texts in the philosophy of mind often begin with a discussion of behaviourism, presented as one of the few theories of mind that have been conclusively refuted. But matters are not that simple: behaviourism, in one form or another, is still alive and kicking.

'Behaviourism' covers a multitude of positions. Yet there is a common underlying thread. The behaviourist takes minds not to be inner psychic mechanisms merely contingently connected with their outer behavioural effects, but to be (at least to a significant extent) constituted by those outer effects. The behaviourist's motivation is often epistemological: on the picture of the mind as essentially inner, how can its outer effects provide us with the wide-ranging knowledge of others' minds we confidently take ourselves to possess?

As an imperfect but serviceable analogy, consider a clock. A clock has visible moving exterior parts – the hands. To the behaviourist about clocks, a clock is simply something with such time-indicating exterior parts. The inner workings of any clock are entirely irrelevant to its status as a clock, provided they produce (or at least don't interfere with) the movement of the hands. The anti-behaviourist, by contrast, thinks of a clock as an inner mechanism which, in favourable circumstances, can cause some exterior parts to move in a way which reliably indicates the time. But there is no a priori reason, according to the anti-behaviourist, why these favourable circumstances should be even possible. There may be clocks to which, given the laws of nature, hands cannot be attached. Moreover, such clocks need not be abnormal ones: they could even be paradigm examples of clocks.

Of course there are intermediate positions. One might hold that *typical* clocks must have, or be capable of having, time-indicating hands, while acknowledging that there could be *atypical* clocks of which this is not so. These atypical clocks would count as clocks in virtue of sharing inner mechanisms with typical clocks. Or one might, while insisting on the importance of the hands, impose some minimal constraints on the innards of a clock. For example, one might say that something could not be a clock unless the big hand and the little hand were controlled by the same mechanism; but beyond that, anything goes.

Suppose, to press the analogy still further, that we never open up any clocks to examine their inner parts. Clock anti-behaviourism would then seem to give us an epistemological problem: how do we know that there *are* any clocks?

Behaviourism flourished in the first half of the twentieth century. Philosophers from that period with behaviourist leanings include Carnap, Hempel, Russell, WITTGENSTEIN, and RYLE. Arranging some contemporary philosophers on a spectrum from the most behaviouristically inclined to the least finds QUINE at the behaviourist end, and SEARLE at the other. DAVIDSON, DENNETT and DUMMETT are closer to Quine than Searle, with FODOR, DRETSKE (and many others) closer to Searle than Quine. Armstrong and LEWIS are squarely in the middle.

PHYSICAL AND AGENTIAL BEHAVIOUR

Let us say that any instance of *physical behaviour* is a physical change to an agent's body (perhaps in relation to his environment), such as the rising of the agent's arm.

132

Let us say that any instance of *agential behaviour* is something an agent *does*, such as raising his arm. (For a related distinction, *see* Armstrong, 1968, p. 84.) We can similarly define *physical* behavioural dispositions and *agential* behavioural dispositions.

The relationship between physical behaviour and agential behaviour is controversial. On some views, all ACTIONS are *identical* to physical changes in the agent's body. (However, some kinds of physical behaviour, such as reflexes, are uncontroversially not kinds of agential behaviour.) On others, an agent's action must involve some physical change, but is not identical to it.

Both physical behaviour and agential behaviour could be understood in the widest sense. Anything a person can do – even calculating in his head, for instance – could be regarded as agential behaviour. Likewise, any physical change in a person's body – even the firing of a certain neuron, for instance – could be regarded as physical behaviour.

Of course, to claim that the mind is 'nothing over and above' such-and-such kinds of behaviour, construed as either physical or agential behaviour in the widest sense, is not necessarily to be a behaviourist. The theory that the mind is a series of volitional acts – a view close to Berkeley's – and the theory that the mind is a certain configuration of neural events, while both controversial, are not forms of behaviourism.

So either the behaviourist needs a less inclusive notion of behaviour or, at the very least, if he does allow some inner processes to count as behaviour, he must minimize their importance.

Waving to someone, or the consequent movement of one's arm, are more behaviouristically acceptable than calculating in the head, or the accompanying firing of neurons. If a philosophical theory of the mind emphasizes wavings or arm movements over silent cogitations and brain events, then it is, to that extent, behaviourist. Accordingly, 'physical behaviour' and 'agential behaviour' will henceforth be understood in a behaviouristically restricted way. Wavings or visible arm movements (together with, for example, blushing and standing still, which do not involve bodily movement) are included, inner goings-on are excluded. This is vague, but none the worse for that.

ELIMINATIVE, ANALYTIC, AND RYLEAN BEHAVIOURISM

Eliminative behaviourism is a forerunner of the contemporary doctrine of eliminative materialism (*see* ELIMINATIVISM). Eliminativists about the mental repudiate all or most of our commonsense psychological ontology: beliefs, conscious states, sensations, and so on. One argument for eliminativism, in contemporary dress, is this. First, 'FOLK PSYCHOLOGY', taken to be, *inter alia*, our tacit theory of the behaviour of others, suffers various deficiencies: widespread explanatory failings, for instance. Second, there are much better theories of behaviour which do not quantify over mental states. Therefore, in accordance with good scientific practice, folk psychology should be replaced by one of these superior theories. Eliminative behaviourism takes the replacement theory to be couched in t'e vocabulary of physical behaviour. (In fact, there are a number of choices for the vocabulary of physical behaviour: the austere terminology of kinematics is one, a certain rich fragment of English another. But at the least the vocabulary will not contain mentally loaded terms.)

Eliminative behaviourism is a dominant theme in the writings of Watson (1930) and Skinner (*see* the papers collected in Skinner et al., 1984): two central figures in the development of the now unpopular doctrine of *psychological behaviourism*. Psychological behaviourism is primarily a claim about the correct methodology of a scientific psychology, and arose in the early part of the twentieth century as a reaction to the 'introspective' psychology of Wundt, James and Titchener. According to the introspective school, the subject matter of psychology is CONSCIOUSNESS, and the proper methodology for its study is INTROSPECTION. Against this, Watson argued that a scientific psychology should just concern itself with what is 'objective', and 'observable', namely, according to him, behaviour.

There was more to psychological behaviourism than this, of course. Watson and Skinner both thought that the behaviour of an organism could be explained by its history of stimulation together with relatively simple processes of behavioural modification. Skinner's introduction of *operant conditioning* as one of these processes marked an improvement over the crude stimulus-response behaviourism of Watson.

Watson found it more acceptable than Skinner to go inside the organism to find stimuli and responses, but Watson gave these inner events no special status. Further, Watson took the brain to be just one inner part among others of equal importance: 'the behaviourist [places] no more emphasis on the brain and the spinal cord than upon the striped muscles of the body, the plain muscles of the stomach, [and] the glands' (1930, p. 49).

Both Watson and Skinner shared unclarities on two connected issues. They were unclear whether stimuli and responses can be described in mentally loaded terms, or whether only purely physical descriptions are allowed. They also vacillated between endorsing: (a) eliminativism about the mental; (b) the claim that mental states exist but are irrelevant to the scientific study of human beings; or (c) the claim that mental terminology can be translated into vocabulary of physical behaviour. But they both had a strong tendency towards eliminativism. Watson, for instance, took 'belief in the existence of consciousness' to go 'back to the ancient days of superstition and magic' (1930, p. 2). And Skinner has expressed similar sentiments (e.g. 1971, ch. 1). (For recent commentary on Skinner, *see* Skinner et al., 1984; Modgil and Modgil 1987.)

QUINE is another eliminative behaviourist, but for quite different reasons. His behaviourism appears to be motivated largely by his verificationism. He gives two reasons for eliminativism. The first is that belief and desire talk resists regimentation in first-order logic, which Quine takes to be the litmus test for complete intelligibility. The second is his argument for the thesis of the indeterminacy of translation, which purports to show that there is simply no 'fact of the matter' as to what someone's language means (Quine, 1960, ch. 2). Quine assumes a sufficiently intimate connection between language and belief for it to follow that there is also no 'fact of the matter' as to what someone believes.

Most behaviouristically inclined philosophers are not eliminativists. The most powerful and straightforward kind of (non-eliminative) behaviourism is:

analytic (or *logical*) *behaviourism*: statements containing mental vocabulary can be analysed into statements containing just the vocabulary of physical behaviour.

Skinner can be interpreted as a part-time analytic behaviourist (e.g. Skinner 1971, p. 24). And Hempel, stating a view common to many logical positivists, wrote:

All psychological statements which are meaningful, that is to say, which are in principle verifiable, are translatable into statements which do not involve psychological concepts, but only the concepts of physics. (1949, p. 18, italics omitted)

Hempel derived this strong thesis from two premises. First, he held (but later abandoned) the verificationist theory of meaning, namely that 'the meaning of a statement is established by its conditions of verification' (1949, p. 17, italics omitted). Second, he held that a person's physical behaviour was a large part of the evidence for ascribing to him particular mental states. Putting the two together, he concluded that statements about mental states were equivalent to statements (largely) about physical behaviour.

Largely, but not entirely. Hempel was not a thoroughgoing behaviourist in the sense of ignoring inner processes altogether. According to Hempel, the verification conditions (which amount to the meaning) of 'Paul has a toothache' include certain changes in Paul's blood pressure, his digestive processes and his central nervous system. But as gross bodily movements play a large role in the verification of psychological sentences, and hence play a large role in determining their meanings, Hempel's position is to a significant extent behaviourist.

We now briefly turn to Ryle's influential quasi-behaviourist polemic, *The Concept of Mind* (1949) (*see* RYLE). Somewhat confusingly, Ryle's position is often called analytic (or logical) behaviourism, but it is quite different, in content and motivation, from the positivist sort of behaviourism exemplified by Hempel.

Hempel's behaviourism is part of his PHYSICALISM. Ryle, in contrast, was no physicalist. He regarded the very question of whether the world is ultimately physical as conceptually confused. Accordingly, Ryle spoke of agential behavioural dispositions, and showed little inclination to analyse this away in terms of physical behavioural dispositions.

Further, it is arguable whether Ryle's primary intention was to offer *analyses* of statements apparently about inner mental occurrences in terms of agential behavioural dispositions. At any rate, he does not supply very many. Ryle was chiefly concerned to deflate the idea that there must be complex inner mental processes behind a person's public actions and to show how this dissolved the problem of other minds. In doing this, he often did not analyse the inner away, but merely derided it. 'Overt intelligent performances are not clues to the workings of minds, they are those workings. Boswell described Johnson's mind when he described how he wrote, talked, ate, fidgeted and fumed. His description was of course incomplete, since there were notoriously some thoughts which Johnson kept carefully to himself and there must have been many dreams, daydreams and silent babblings which only Johnson could have recorded and only a James Joyce would wish him to have recorded' (Ryle, 1949, pp. 58–9).

Ryle was indeed, as he reportedly said, 'only one arm and one leg a behaviourist'.

Physicalists such as Place, Smart, Armstrong, and Lewis, were able to find much to agree with in Ryle, despite his antipathy toward physicalism. They took Ryle to have in effect shown that physical behavioural dispositions were of great importance in understanding the nature of the mind.

Geach (1957, p. 8) raised an important difficulty for any behaviourist analysis of the propositional attitudes, whether in terms of agential or physical behavioural dispositions. Geach noted that what someone does, or is disposed to do, depends not only on the fact that he holds a *particular* belief, but also on his desires (and, it should be added, on his other *beliefs* as well). Therefore there can be no question of a *simple atomistic* behavioural analysis: one which matches each belief with a different kind of behaviour (whether specified in the language of agential or physical behaviour). A given belief may issue in practically any sort of behaviour, depending on the agent's other attitudes (*see* BELIEF; PROPOSITIONAL ATTITUDES.)

CONTEMPORARY BEHAVIOURISM

Geach's observation that belief types do not have characteristic behavioural expressions is now regarded as a datum of folk psychological explanation, and consequently few contemporary philosophers are tempted by any sort of (atomistic) analytic behaviourism. But the failure of this kind of behaviourist *analysis* does not imply the failure of behaviourism, construed as a metaphysical thesis about the nature of the mind. All it does imply is that the most direct route to behaviourism – namely a simple analysis pairing beliefs and behavioural dispositions – is a dead end. A convincing argument for behaviourism must proceed down a less obvious path.

Contemporary behaviourist views derive from three sources. The first is the analytic FUNCTIONALISM of Armstrong, Lewis and others (*see* LEWIS). According to this view, the meanings of mental terms are determined by their role in our commonsense theory of behaviour: folk psychology. This tacitly known theory is taken to consist of generalizations linking perceptual input, (physical) behavioural output, and mental states. Some of these generalizations will link beliefs to desires, thus incorporating Geach's insight that a belief does not have a fund of behaviour to call its own. However, if analytic functionalism is correct, then the analyses of mental terms will have a significant behavioural component.

Note that analytic functionalism, while not underwriting an *entailment* from having such-and-such physical behavioural dispositions to having a mental life, nonetheless does appear to solve the problem of other minds. According to analytic functionalism, one may reasonably conclude that a creature has a mind on the basis of its behaviour, just as one may reasonably conclude that a car has an engine on the basis of its motion.

The second source is opposition to the functionalist idea that an organism needs a certain kind of inner causal organization in order to be a genuine believer.

These two incompatible lines of thought have their roots in Ryle, although he would only have expressed agreement with the second. The third source of contemporary behaviourism is one on which Ryle's influence was at best indirect, although he would have found it perfectly congenial. That source is Wittgenstein's (1958) attack on the possibility of a 'private language', which some take to show that meaning and belief must be 'manifestable' in behaviour (*see* WITTGENSTEIN).

Roughly corresponding to these three sources are three behaviourist theses. The first is:

Behaviour-as-necessary: necessarily, anything that has no physical behavioural dispositions of a certain kind and complexity does not have a mental life.

This vague formulation should be taken to express the behaviourist thought that something like a stone could not possibly have a mental life, because it is *outwardly inert* (not because there is nothing sufficiently compli-

cated going on in the stone). It is a thesis which, incidentally, can with some safety be ascribed to Wittgenstein (1958, I, 281–4).

Analytic functionalism can evade the behaviour-as-necessary view to some extent, but not completely. Lewis's brand of analytic functionalism, for instance, has the consequence that anything which has no behavioural dispositions above a certain level of complexity either (a) has no mental life; or, (b) is an *atypical* member of its kind (Lewis, 1980). Therefore an extreme kind of permanent paralysis cannot be the typical condition of any population of thinking creatures: there cannot be a race of thinking stones.

A natural companion to the behaviour-as-necessary view, although logically independent of it, is:

Behaviour-as-sufficient: necessarily, anything that has physical behavioural dispositions of a certain kind and complexity has a mental life.

According to functionalism, whether of the analytic variety or not, minds must have some specific type of inner causal structure. Functionalism in general is therefore inconsistent with the behaviour-as-sufficient view. However, DENNETT – on whom Ryle had a direct influence – has been a longtime opponent of the idea that to have a mind is to have a specific type of inner causal structure. On the one hand, Dennett is unmoved by thought experiments – often involving Martian scientists controlling hollow anthropoid puppets – which purport to show that having a mind involves some restriction on inner causal order. (*See* p. 138 below.) On the other hand, Dennett is impressed, as was Hume, with the remarkable predictive power of everyday psychology. Adopting 'the intentional stance' (Dennett, 1971, 1981) – the predictive strategy of ascribing intentional states such as belief and desire to a system – is indispensable in many cases, its utility not diminished by any discoveries of bizarre inner causal organization.

Now if we can be assured that the assumption that a system has beliefs is not going to be defeated by future evidence – although specific belief attributions may well be – and that assumption is useful, why insist that there is some further question to be raised concerning whether the system *really has* beliefs?

Thus, according to Dennett, 'any object – whatever its innards – that is reliably and voluminously predictable from the intentional stance is in the fullest sense of the word a believer' (1988, p. 496).

The two behaviourist theses considered so far are certainly controversial, but both are weak forms of behaviourism. Even their conjunction does not imply that any two behavioural duplicates necessarily share the same mental states. That last claim is our third behaviourist thesis:

Supervenient behaviourism: psychological facts supervene on physical behavioural dispositions: necessarily, if x and y differ with respect to types of mental states, then they differ with respect to types of behavioural dispositions (*see* SUPERVENIENCE).

(Note that analytic behaviourism entails supervenient behaviourism, but not conversely.)

Supervenient behaviourism may be broadened to include the supervenience of linguistic meaning on behavioural dispositions, or narrowed to exclude, say, sensations. Supervenient behaviourism can accommodate the view that content is not entirely 'in the head' by taking the supervenience base to comprise physical behavioural dispositions together with facts about the subject's environment. (The possibility of this latter refinement will be taken for granted in what follows.)

Supervenient behavourism is quite compatible with eliminativism (according to which no x and y ever differ mentally!). And indeed Quine appears to need the former to derive the latter via the indeterminacy thesis (*see e.g.* van Cleve, 1992). However, some philosophers who repudiate eliminativism are at least attracted by supervenient behaviourism. More precisely, these philosophers hold a doctrine about the

mind which, together with assumptions they would probably accept, entails supervenient behaviourism. This doctrine may be explained as follows.

In the writings of DAVIDSON, and to some extent Dennett and Dummett, there is a strand of thought which amounts to a kind of third-person Cartesianism (*see* HISTORY). Where Cartesianism holds that someone has, under ideal conditions, complete and infallible access to *his own* mental life (*see* FIRST-PERSON AUTHORITY), the third-person version says that someone has, under ideal conditions, complete and infallible access to the mental life of *another*. Or, in its typical formulation, complete and infallible access to the PROPOSITIONAL ATTITUDES (and/or language) of another. Picturesquely: under ideal conditions a subject's belief-box and desire-box become transparent. This kind of claim is sometimes called *interpretivism* (Johnston, 1991).

We can dramatize interpretivism by introducing the familiar device of the *ideal interpreter*: an idealization of a human being, in ideal epistemic circumstances. The ideal interpreter is capable, according to interpretivism, of discovering exactly what a subject believes, desires (and/or means). The powers and data of the interpreter are a matter for dispute, but at least three points should be noted.

First, the interpreter's powers are not to be construed – on pain of triviality – to be just whatever powers are necessary in order to deliver the facts.

Second, the interpreter's official evidence does not include the contents of the subject's mental states, or the meaning of his utterances, for that is what the interpreter is supposed to be finding out.

Third, interpretivism does not offer a *reductive analysis* – at least of the attitudes; for the reference to our best *judgments* (captured in the heuristic device of the ideal interpreter) is supposed to be an ineliminable part of the story. Lewis (1974) makes use, in effect, of the ideal interpreter, but intends this to be a staging-post *en route* to a fully reductive account. That is not a version of interpretivism.

Bearing in mind the three points above, we could formulate interpretivism in the particular case of belief as the thesis that all biconditionals of the following form are a priori:

x believes that p if and only if, if there were an appropriately informed ideal interpreter, he would be disposed to attribute to x the belief that p.

Something like this seems to be clearly expressed by Davidson when he writes:

What a fully informed Interpreter could know about what a speaker means is all there is to learn; the same goes for what the speaker believes. (1986, p. 315)

Davidson is making a substantial claim, and so 'fully informed' should not be understood as 'fully informed about what a speaker means and believes'. He here has in mind his 'radical interpreter' (Davidson, 1973), starting the process of interpretation with no knowledge of the meaning of the subject's language or the content of his beliefs (although Davidson allows the interpreter's initial data to include intentional facts, namely what (uninterpreted) sentences the subject 'holds true').

Dennett comes to a similar conclusion:

[A]ll there is to being a true believer is being a system whose behaviour is reliably predictable via the intentional strategy, and hence all there is to really and truly believing that p (for any proposition p) is being an intentional system for which p occurs as a belief in the best (most predictive) interpretation. (1981, p. 29)

Now an interpretation requires a (hypothetical) interpreter, and so Dennett would appear to be saying that some ideal interpreter could deliver all and only the facts about what a subject believes. Moreover, as the failure of reductions in the philosophy of mind has been one of Dennett's major themes, he very likely thinks that this talk of interpretations and interpreters cannot be analysed away. But then Dennett is an interpretivist.

Interpretivism does not entail supervenient behaviourism. For it may be that the interpreter must take into account certain non-behavioural facts (e.g. facts about inner causal organization) when determining what someone believes. It seems likely, however, that Dennett's and Davidson's ideal interpreters would not ascribe different beliefs to two subjects unless they differed in their physical behavioural dispositions: their respective interpreters would judge any two behavioural duplicates alike. And as the ideal interpreter's word is gospel, this entails that no two subjects would differ in beliefs (or, we may assume, desires) unless they differed in physical behavioural dispositions. But this is supervenient behaviourism with respect to the propositional attitudes (and linguistic meaning, at least in the case of Davidson).

Dennett appears to arrive at interpretivism by an ambitious extension of his route to the behaviour-as-sufficient view. That is: why not take the ideal interpreter at his word, if we have no clear conception of how he can be mistaken? Davidson's reasons for interpretivism are less straightforward. The main ones emerge in the following passage, where Davidson argues for a behaviourist version of interpretivism from a Wittgensteinian premise about the 'publicity' of meaning:

As Ludwig Wittgenstein, not to mention Dewey, G.H. Mead, Quine, and many others have insisted, language is intrinsically social. This does not entail that truth and meaning can be defined in terms of observable behaviour, or that it is 'nothing but' observable behaviour; but it does imply that meaning is entirely determined by observable behaviour, even readily observable behaviour. That meanings are decipherable is not a matter of luck; public availability is a constitutive aspect of language. (Davidson, 1990, p. 314)

Dummett has expressed similar views (e.g. 1973, pp. 217–18).

Davidson's 'readily observable behaviour' is intended to be understood as 'behaviour observable *as physical behaviour'* (or, perhaps as: 'behaviour observable as *the holding true of sentences*'). For suppose that the relevant deliverances of observation include linguistic behaviour such as *saying that snow is white*. Then Davidson's claim that meaning is determined by *this* sort of behaviour is, while perhaps not entirely trivial, at least extremely weak. Alternatively, suppose that the deliverances of observation include psychological behaviour such as *intending to induce a certain belief in one's audience*, but exclude any kind of behaviour described in a way which presupposes linguistic meaning. Then Davidson's claim would certainly not be trivial, but would violate his well-known insistence that a speaker's propositional attitudes and the meaning of his language are settled together, neither one having priority over the other (e.g. Davidson, 1973).

It seems, then, that lying behind Davidson's argument is a controversial *epistemic* thesis: our warrant for saying that someone speaks a certain language, or has certain beliefs, is ultimately founded on behaviour, observed *as* physical behaviour (or, perhaps: observable *as* the holding true of sentences). But even if that is found acceptable, Davidson's apparent move from 'our judgements are *founded* on such-and-such data' to 'the truth of our judgements is *determined* by such-and-such data' is questionable. We have learnt much about the world that is not 'determined' by what we have learnt it from.

BEHAVIOURISM REFUTED?

To refute the view that a certain level of behavioural dispositions is *necessary* for a mental life, we need convincing cases of thinking stones, or utterly incurable paralytics, or disembodied minds. But these alleged possibilities are to some merely that.

To refute the view that a certain level of behavioural dispositions is *sufficient* for a mental life, we need convincing cases of rich behaviour with no accompanying mental states. The typical example is of a puppet controlled, via radio links, by other minds outside the puppet's hollow body (Peacocke, 1983, p. 205; Lycan, 1987, p. 5; *see also* Block, 1981). But one might wonder – and Dennett does – whether the dramatic devices are producing the anti-behaviourist intuition all by themselves. And how could the dramatic devices make a difference to the actual facts of the case? If the puppeteers were replaced by a machine (not designed by anyone, yet storing a vast number of input-output conditionals) which was reduced in size and placed in the puppet's head, do we still have a compelling counterexample to the behaviour-as-sufficient view? At least it is not so clear.

Such an example would work equally well against (the anti-eliminativist version of) the view that mental states supervene on behavioural dispositions. But supervenient behaviourism could be refuted by something less ambitious. The 'X-worlders' of Putnam (1965), who are in intense pain but do not betray this in their verbal or non-verbal behaviour, behaving just as pain-free human beings, would be the right sort of case. But even if Putnam has produced a counterexample for pain – which Dennett for one would doubtless deny – an 'X-worlder' story to refute supervenient behaviourism with respect to the attitudes or linguistic meaning will be less intuitively convincing. Behaviourist resistance is easier here for the reason that having a belief, or meaning a certain thing, lack distinctive phenomenologies.

There is a more sophisticated line of attack. As Quine has remarked, some have taken his thesis of the indeterminacy of translation as a *reductio* of his behaviourism (1990, p. 37). For this to be convincing, Quine's argument for the indeterminacy thesis has to be persuasive on its own terms, and that is a disputed matter.

If behaviourism is finally laid to rest to the satisfaction of most philosophers, it will probably not be by counterexample, or by a *reductio* from Quine's indeterminacy thesis. Rather, it will be because the behaviourist's worries about other minds, and the public availability of meaning, have been shown to be groundless, or not to require behaviourism for their solution. But we can be sure that this happy day will take some time to arrive.

See also CONTENT; DUALISM; *An Essay on Mind* sections 3.6. & 3.7. IDENTITY THEORY; INTENTIONALITY; THOUGHT; THOUGHT AND LANGUAGE.

BIBLIOGRAPHY

Armstrong, D.M. 1968. *A Materialist Theory of the Mind*. London: Routledge and Kegan Paul.

Block, N., ed. 1980. *Readings in Philosophy of Psychology*, vol. 1. Cambridge, MA: Harvard University Press.

Block, N. 1981. Psychologism and behaviourism. *Philosophical Review*, 90, 5–43.

Davidson, D. 1973. Radical interpretation. *Dialectica*, 27, 313–28. Reprinted in Davidson, *Inquiries into Truth and Interpretation*. Oxford University Press, 1984.

Davidson, D. 1986. A coherence theory of truth and knowledge. In *Truth and Interpretation: Perspectives on the Philosophy of Donald Davidson*, ed. E. LePore. Oxford: Basil Blackwell.

Davidson, D. 1990. The structure and content of truth. *Journal of Philosophy*, 87, 279-328.

Dennett, D.C. 1971. Intentional systems. *Journal of Philosophy*, 68, 87–106. Reprinted in Dennett, *Brainstorms*. Brighton: The Harvester Press.

Dennett, D.C. 1981. True believers. In *Scientific Explanation*, ed. A. F. Heath. Oxford University Press. Reprinted in Dennett, *The Intentional Stance*. Cambridge, MA: MIT Press, 1987; page references are to the latter.

Dennett, D.C. 1988. Précis of *The Intentional Stance*. *Behavioural and Brain Sciences*, 11, 495–504.

Dummett, M.A.E. 1973. The philosophical basis of intuitionistic logic. In *Logic Colloquium '73*, ed. H. E. Rose and J. C. Shepherdson. Reprinted in Dummett, *Truth and Other Enigmas*. London: Duckworth, 1978; page references are to the latter.

Geach, P.T. 1957. *Mental Acts: Their Content and their Objects*. London: Routledge & Kegan Paul.

Hempel, C.G. 1949. The logical analysis of psychology. In *Readings in Philosophical Analysis*, ed. H. Feigl and W. Sellars. New York: Appleton-Century-Crofts. Reprinted with revisions in Block 1980; page references are to the latter.

Johnston, M. 1991. The missing explanation argument and its impact on subjectivism. MS.

Lewis, D.K. 1974. Radical interpretation. *Synthese*, 23, 331–44. Reprinted with postscripts in Lewis, 1983.

Lewis, D.K. 1980. Mad pain and martian pain. In Block 1980. Reprinted with postscript in Lewis, 1983.

Lewis, D.K. 1983. *Philosophical Papers*, vol. 1. Oxford University Press.

Lycan, W.G. 1987. *Consciousness*. Cambridge, MA.: MIT Press.

Modgil, S., and Modgil, C., eds. 1987. *B. F. Skinner: Consensus and Controversy*. London: Falmer Press.

Peacocke, C. 1983. *Sense and Content*. Oxford University Press.

Putnam, H. 1965. Brains and behavior. In *Analytical Philosophy*, Vol 2, ed. R. J. Butler. Reprinted in Block, 1980.

Quine, W.V. 1960. *Word and Object*. Cambridge, MA.: MIT Press.

Quine, W.V. 1990. *Pursuit of Truth*. Cambridge, MA.: Harvard University Press.

Ryle, G. 1949. *The Concept of Mind*. New York: Barnes & Noble.

Skinner, B.F. 1971. *Beyond Freedom and Dignity*. New York: Alfred A. Knopf.

Skinner, B.F., et al. 1984. Skinner: canonical papers. *Behavioural and Brain Sciences*, 7, 473–701.

Van Cleve, J. 1992. Semantic supervenience and referential indeterminacy. *Journal of Philosophy*, 89, 344–61.

Watson, J.B. 1930. *Behaviorism*. University of Chicago Press.

Wittgenstein, L. 1958. *Philosophical Investigations* (2nd edn). Oxford: Basil Blackwell.

Thanks to David Lewis, Michael Thau and the editor for helpful comments.

ALEX BYRNE

belief (1): metaphysics of The two most important metaphysical theories of belief are what I shall call the 'propositional' and the 'sentential' theories. The German philosopher, Gottlob Frege, founded the propositional approach. The sentential view is developed most fully in the work of Jerry Fodor. I begin with the propositional theory.

PROPOSITIONAL THEORIES

According to Frege and his followers, propositions are abstract, non-mental entities which form the contents of beliefs (and certain other psychological attitudes, for example, desires). Belief consists in the mind standing in a special relation of direct apprehension to a proposition. So, if you and I both believe that unemployment is rising, say, we (or our minds) grasp (in the way distinctive of belief) the same abstract proposition. *What* we believe is the same, since there is a single proposition to which we are both here related.

Frege presented no doctrine about what direct apprehension comes to beyond saying that since its objects are both abstract and non-mental, it is different from either sense-perception or INTROSPECTION. He did, however, make a number of remarks about the character of abstract propositions. In Frege's view, propositions are structured entities, having as constituents the meanings or senses of the terms composing the sentences embedded in contexts of the form 'that p'. So, for example, according to Frege, the reason why

(1) Jones believes that the inventor of bifocals is a Philadelphian

may be true when

(2) Jones believes that the first U.S. Postmaster General is a Philadelphian

is false is that in the context of (1) and (2) 'the inventor of bifocals' and 'the first U.S. Postmaster General' do not denote a single person (even though in other contexts, of course, they do, namely Benjamin Franklin). Indeed they do not denote people at all. Instead they stand for their normal meanings or senses (which Frege termed 'individual concepts'). So, the proposition expressed by the 'that' clause in (1) has a

different component from the proposition expressed by the 'that' clause in (2). The propositions themselves must be distinct, then, and, as a result, belief in one can occur without belief in the other.

Critics of Frege's approach have sometimes argued that identifying propositions with the meanings or senses of sentences amounts to making propositions 'denizens of darkness', since the notion of meaning is itself radically unclear (*see* Quine, 1960). Some philosophers sympathetic to the general Fregean approach have responded to this charge by claiming that propositions are better identified with functions from possible worlds to truth values or equivalently with sets of possible worlds in which the value of the function is 'true' (Stalnaker, 1984). Propositions, conceived of in this way, do at least have the virtue of reasonably clear identity conditions. But these identity conditions themselves generate a serious problem for the abstract proposition theory; for the possible-worlds elucidation of propositions entails that, if the proposition that p is necessarily equivalent to the proposition that q, then the former proposition is identical with the latter. Hence, on the abstract proposition theory, if a person believes that p, he or she automatically believes that q. And this result seems unacceptable. Surely, for example, I can believe that all brothers are male siblings without believing that all ophthalmologists are eye doctors. The situation with mathematical beliefs is even more counterintuitive. It seems undeniable that I can believe that $7 + 5 = 12$ without possessing all true mathematical beliefs. But the proposition that $7 + 5 = 12$ is necessarily equivalent to every true mathematical proposition, so that really there is only one such proposition. Hence, in believing that $7 + 5 = 12$, I must also believe that $793 - 132 = 661$, that $18 \times 19 = 342$, and so on.

One standard reply to the problem mathematical beliefs present for the proposition theory is to argue that such beliefs really relate persons to contingent propositions about the link between overt, public mathematical sentences and the one necessary

141

proposition. Thus, to believe that $7 + 5 = 12$ is to believe the contingent proposition that '$7 + 5 = 12$' expresses the necessary proposition. Since this contingent proposition is not necessarily equivalent to the proposition that '$793 - 132 = 661$' expresses the necessary proposition, one can believe that $7 + 5 = 12$ without thereby automatically believing that $793 - 132 = 661$.

This reply faces a further objection, however. Suppose a Frenchman has a belief that he expresses by uttering the sentence 'Sept plus cinq fait douze'. If I have a belief that I express by uttering the sentence 'Seven plus five equals twelve', then, unless the contexts of utterance are atypical, it seems intuitively reasonable to say that we have the same mathematical belief. But according to the above reply, my belief must be different from that of the Frenchman.

It is worth noting that the original Fregean view that propositions are senses or meanings evidently handles the above problem of mathematical beliefs. But there remains another very significant objection (*see* Burge, 1978). This is simply that, contrary to what Frege supposed, synonyms are not always intersubstitutable *salva veritae* in belief contexts. Suppose, for example, that when asked about Jill and John's whereabouts, Paul says sincerely that they have gone to Paris for a dozen weeks. Suppose also that Paul is under the misapprehension that a dozen is 20 items, not 12, so that he expects Jill and John to return 20 weeks later. Then it seems reasonable to say both that

(3) Paul believes that Jill and John have gone to Paris for a dozen weeks

is true and that

(4) Paul believes that Jill and John have gone to Paris for 12 weeks

is false. However, (4) results from (3) by the substitution of terms that are ordinarily classified as having the same meaning.

One possible reply the Fregean might make to this problem is to argue that '12' and 'a dozen' do not really have exactly the same meaning. The difficulty now is that it is far from clear which expressions *do* have the same meaning. Moreover, for any two expressions that *are* synonymous, there might be someone who believes that they differ in meaning. So a case parallel to that in (3) and (4) could still be constructed.

SENTENTIAL THEORIES

Let us turn now to the sentential theory. According to sententialists, the objects of belief are sentences. Some sententialists maintain that public sentences are the objects of belief. Gilbert RYLE, for example, seems to have held that to believe that p is to be disposed to assent to some natural language sentence that means that p. And Donald DAVIDSON is usually read as accepting a version of the public sentence approach. The dominant version of the sentential theory, however, is the view that the objects of belief are private sentences. This view goes hand in hand with the computational conception of the mind (*see* COMPUTATIONAL MODELS; LANGUAGE OF THOUGHT).

Computers are symbol manipulators: they transform symbols in accordance with fixed syntactic rules and thereby process information. If the mind is a computer then its states must themselves be symbolic states in whatever inner language the mind employs (call it 'Mentalese'). So, belief must involve a relation to a string of symbols in Mentalese. This symbol string is a sentence of Mentalese which has, as its natural language counterpart, whatever sentence is used to specify the content of the belief in a public context. So, on the dominant version of the sentential theory, believing that nothing succeeds like excess, say, is a matter of the mind standing in a certain computational relation (distinctive of belief) to a sentence in Mentalese which means that nothing succeeds like excess. This sentence is physically realized in the brain by some neural state just as symbol strings in electronic computers are physically realized by charged states of grids or patterns of electrical pulses.

The sentential theory sketched above involves no explicit commitment to abstract propositions. But propositions can still enter in the analysis of what it is for a given sentence of Mentalese to mean that such and such is the case. Thus, it is a mistake to suppose that a sentential approach to belief *automatically* repudiates propositions.

There are four main considerations that proponents of the dominant version of the sentential theory usually adduce as motivating their view. To begin with, it is noted that the view that the mind is a computer is one that has considerable empirical support from COGNITIVE PSYCHOLOGY. The sentential theory, then, is an empirically plausible theory, one that supplies a mechanism for the relation that propositionalists take to obtain between minds and propositions. The mechanism is mediation by inner sentences.

Secondly, the sentential theory offers a straightforward explanation for the parallels that obtain between the objects or contents of speech acts and the objects or contents of belief. For example, I may say what I believe. Furthermore, the object of believing, like the object of saying, can have semantic properties. We may say, for example,

(5) What Jones believes is true

and

(6) What Jones believes entails what Smith believes.

One plausible hypothesis, then, is that the object of belief is the same sort of entity as what is uttered in speech acts (or what is written down).

The sentential theory also seems supported by the following argument. The ability to think certain thoughts appears intrinsically connected with the ability to think certain others. For example, the ability to think that John hits Mary goes hand in hand with the ability to think that Mary hits John, but not with the ability to think that London is overcrowded. Why is this? The ability to produce or understand certain sentences is intrinsically connected with the ability to produce or understand certain others. For example, there are no native speakers of English who know how to say 'John hits Mary' but who do not know how to say 'Mary hits John'. Similarly, there are no native speakers who understand the former sentence but not the latter. These facts are easily explained if sentences have a syntactic and semantic structure. But if sentences are taken to be atomic, these facts are a complete mystery. What is true for sentences is true also for thoughts. Thinking thoughts involves manipulating MENTAL REPRESENTATIONS. If mental representations with a propositional content have a semantic and syntactic structure like that of sentences, it is no *accident* that one who is able to think that John hits Mary is thereby also able to think that Mary hits John. Furthermore, it is no *accident* that one who can think these thoughts need not thereby be able to think thoughts having different components – for example, the thought that London is overcrowded. And what goes here for thought goes for belief and the other PROPOSITIONAL ATTITUDES.

Consider next the inference from

(7) Rufus believes that the round object ahead is brown

and

(8) The round object ahead is the coin Rupert dropped

to

(9) Rufus believes that the coin Rupert dropped is brown.

This inference is strictly parallel to the inference from

(10) Rufus uttered the sentence 'The round object ahead is brown'

and (8) to

(11) Rufus uttered the sentence 'The coin Rupert dropped is brown'.

If the immediate objects of belief are sentences, we should *expect* the former inference to be invalid just as the latter is.

Another motivating factor is the thought that, since the pattern of causal interactions among beliefs often mirrors various inferential relations among the sentences that are ordinarily used to specify the objects of beliefs, it is natural to suppose that these objects have logical form. For example, corresponding to the inference from

(12) All dogs make good pets

and

(13) All of Jane's animals are dogs

to

(14) All of Jane's animals make good pets

we have the fact that, if John believes that all dogs make good pets and he later comes to believe that all of Jane's animals are dogs, he will, in all likelihood, be caused to believe that all of Jane's animals make good pets. Generalizing, we can say that a belief of the form

(15) All Fs are Gs

together with a belief of the form

(16) All Gs are H,s

typically causes a belief of the form

(17) All Fs are Hs.

This generalization concerns belief alone. But there are also generalizations linking belief and desire. For example, a desire of the form

(18) Do A,

together with a belief of the form

(19) In order to do A, it is necessary to do B,

typically generates a desire of the form

(20) Do B.

Now these generalizations categorize beliefs and desires according to the logical form of their objects. They therefore require that the objects have logical forms. But the primary possessors of logical form are sentences. Hence, the (immediate) objects of beliefs and desires are themselves sentences.

Advocates of the propositional theory sometimes object to the sentential approach on the grounds that it is chauvinistic. Maybe *our* beliefs are represented in our heads in the form of sentences in a special mental language, but why should all beliefs necessarily be so represented in *all* possible creatures? For example, couldn't belief tokens take the form of graphs, maps, pictures, or indeed some other form dissimilar to any of our public forms of representation?

This objection is based on a misunderstanding. The sentential theory is not normally presented as an analysis of the essence of belief, of what is common to all actual and possible believers in virtue of which they have beliefs. So, it has nothing to say about the beliefs of angels, say, or other possible believers. Rather it is a theory of how belief is actually realized in us.

One great virtue of the sentential theory is that it provides a satisfying explanation of how it is possible to believe that p without believing that q even when 'p' and 'q' are synonymous. Consider, for example, the earlier case involving the sentences (3) and (4). Believing that Jill and John have gone to Paris for a dozen weeks requires Paul to token an inner sentence which means that they have gone to Paris for a dozen weeks. On the assumption that this sentence is not the same as the one that is tokened when it is believed that that Jill and John have gone to Paris for 12 weeks, there is no difficulty in explaining how (3) can be true when (4) is false. The beliefs are separable because they involve the same relation to different sentences with the same meaning. Just as writing down the sentence 'That is a vixen', for example, is quite distinct from writing down the sentence 'That is a female fox', notwithstanding their identity of meaning, so too the belief expressed in (3) is quite distinct from the belief expressed in (4).

So far I have focused exclusively on what are known as *de dicto* beliefs, that is, beliefs that are standardly attributed to people using predicates of the form, 'believes that *p*'. There is another important class of beliefs, however. These are standardly attributed using predicates of the form, 'believes of x that it is F'. Beliefs of this sort are called '*de re* beliefs'. Consider, for eample, my believing of the building I am facing that it is an imposing structure. This is a belief with respect to a particular building, however that building is described. Suppose, for example, the building is St Paul's Cathedral. Then, in believing *of* the building I am facing that it is an imposing structure I am thereby believing *of* St Paul's that it is an imposing structure. So, for a belief to be *de re* with respect to some object *O*, there must really be an object *O* which the belief is about. By contrast, if I simply believe *that* the building I am facing is imposing – this is the *de dicto* case – I need not believe *that* St Paul's is imposing. For I may not believe that the building I am facing *is* St Paul's. Moreover, it is not a condition of my having the belief that the building I am facing is imposing that there really be any building before me. I might, for example, be under the influence of some drug, which has caused me to hallucinate a large building.

De re beliefs, then, are beliefs held with respect to particular things or people, however described, that they have such and such properties. On the propositional theory, such beliefs are often taken to require that the given thing or person itself enter into the proposition believed. So, believing of Smith that he is dishonest is a matter of standing in the belief relation to the proposition that Smith is dishonest, where this proposition is a complex entity having the person, Smith, as one of its components.

The sentential theory can account for *de re* belief in a similar fashion. The assumption now is that the inner sentence is a singular one (consisting in the simplest case of a name concatenated with a predicate). This sentence has, as its meaning, a proposition which meets the above requirements (assuming a propositional approach to sentence meanings).

Of the two theories I have discussed, the sentential view probably has the wider support in philosophy today. However, as my earlier comments should have made clear, the two theories are not diametrically opposed to one another. For the sentential theory, unlike the propositional view, is not (in its standard form) an analysis of belief. Moreover, its advocates are not necessarily against the introduction of abstract propositions.

There is one further feature worth commenting upon that is common to both theories. This is their acceptance of the relational character of belief. The primary reason for taking belief to be relational is that existential generalization applies to its syntactic objects. For example,

(21) Jones believes that gorillas are more intelligent than chimpanzees

entails

(22) There is something Jones believes.

Not all philosophers accept that existential generalizations like this one should be taken at face value as indicating a metaphysical commitment to some entity which is the believed object. However, unless some strong arguments can be given which show that this case is anomalous, it is surely reasonable to classify it with other standard cases of existential generalization, and hence to grant that there really are objects to which we are related in belief.

See also BELIEF (2); DENNETT; DRETSKE; *An Essay on Mind* section 2.1; FODOR; INTENTIONALITY; RATIONALITY; THOUGHT; THOUGHT AND LANGUAGE.

BIBLIOGRAPHY

Burge, T. 1978. Belief and synonymy. *The Journal of Philosophy*, 75, 119–38.

Davidson, D. 1975. Thought and talk. In *Mind and Language*, ed. S. Guttenplan. Oxford University Press.

Fodor, J. 1978. Propositional attitudes. *The Monist*, 61, 501–23.

Fodor, J. 1978. *Psychosemantics*. Cambridge, MA.: MIT Press.

Fodor, J. 1990. *A Theory of Content and Other Essays*. Cambridge, MA.: MIT Press.

Frege, G. 1968. The thought: a logical inquiry. In *Essays on Frege*, ed. E. D. Klemke. Urbana, Ill.: University of Illinois Press.

Quine, W. 1960. *Word and Object*. Cambridge, MA.: MIT Press.

Ryle, G. 1949. *The Concept of Mind*. London: Hutchinson and Co.

Salmon, N. 1986. *Frege's Puzzle*. Cambridge, MA.: MIT Press.

Sellars, W. 1968. *Science and Metaphysics*. London. Routledge & Kegan Paul.

Stalnaker, R. 1984. *Inquiry*. Cambridge, MA.: MIT Press.

MICHAEL TYE

belief (2): epistemology of The general heading of 'The Epistemology of Beliefs' covers an array of closely interrelated questions. I shall discuss just three areas of interest. First, there is the question of how we actually go about ascribing beliefs in daily life. This question has a first- and a third-person angle: how do I ascribe beliefs to others? How do I ascribe beliefs to myself? What are the relations between the two? Second, there is a question concerning the extent to which our ordinary practices of ascribing beliefs are fallible, the extent to which they stand in need of ratification by something more – a scientific or philosophical theory of belief. Third, there is a question concerning the limits of our ability to know about beliefs. We seem to be very good at finding out about our own beliefs and those of other humans. But by what methods, and to what extent, can we know about the beliefs of non-humans such as animals, extra-terrestrials and robots? I shall discuss these issues in turn.

COMMONSENSE PSYCHOLOGY

As a lead into the topic I shall begin by elaborating a view that has been defended recently by a number of philosophers and psychologists (e.g. Churchland, 1981; Stich, 1983; Fodor, 1987, Wellman, 1990). The view concerns, in the first instance at least, the question of how we, as ordinary human beings, in fact go about ascribing beliefs to one another. The idea is that we do this on the basis of our knowledge of a common-sense theory of psychology (*see* FOLK PSYCHOLOGY). The theory is not held to consist in a collection of grandmotherly sayings, such as 'once bitten, twice shy'. Rather it consists in a body of generalizations relating psychological states to each other, to inputs from the environment, and to actions. Here is a sample from Churchland (1981, p. 71):

(1) (x)(p)(if x fears that p, then x desires that not-p)

(2) (x)(p)(if x hopes that p and x discovers that p, then x is pleased that p)

(3) (x)(p)(q) (if x believes that p and x believes that if p, then q, then, barring confusion, distraction etc. x believes that q)

(4) (x)(p)(q) (if x desires that p and x believes that if q then p, and x is able to bring it about that q, then, barring conflicting desires or preferred strategies, x brings it about that q)

All of these generalizations should be understood as containing *ceteris paribus* clauses. (1), for example, applies most of the time, but not invariably. Adventurous types often enjoy the adrenalin thrill produced by fear. This leads them, on occasion, to desire the very state of affairs that frightens them. Analogously with (3). A subject who believes that p and believes that if p, then q, would typically infer that q. But certain atypical circumstances may intervene: subjects may become confused, or distracted, or they may find the prospect of q so awful that they dare not allow themselves to believe it. The *ceteris paribus* nature of these generalizations is not usually considered to be problematic, since atypical circumstances are, of course, atypical, and the generalizations are applicable most of the time.

We apply this psychological theory to make inferences about people's beliefs, desires and so on. If, for example, we know that Diana believes that if she is to be at the airport at four, then she should get a taxi at half past two, and she believes that she is to be at the airport at four, then we will predict, using (3), that Diana will infer that she should get a taxi at half past two.

The Theory Theory, as it is called, is an empirical theory addressing the question of our actual knowledge of beliefs. Taken in its purest form it addresses both first- and third-personal knowledge: we know about our own beliefs and those of others in the same way, by application of commonsense psychological theory in both cases. However, it is not very plausible to hold that we always – or indeed usually – know our own beliefs by way of theoretical inference. I ask myself, do I believe that a certain student will get a First in her BA final exams? To answer this I do not, of course, theorize about myself and my beliefs: I reason about the student and her abilities. I decide that yes, she probably will achieve the desired result. And thereupon I know, immediately and without further reflection, that I believe that she will attain a First. A natural emendation to the pure Theory Theory would thus be to add to it the rider that, sometimes or often, we attribute beliefs to ourselves in this non-theoretical way.

Since it is an empirical theory concerning one of our cognitive abilities, the Theory Theory is open to psychological scrutiny. Various issues arise: we need to know the detailed contents of the hypothesized commonsense psychological theory, we need to know whether it is known consciously or unconsciously, and we need to know how it is acquired. I shall discuss one aspect of the last of these issues, since it has been the subject of interesting work in DEVELOPMENTAL PSYCHOLOGY. Suppose, then, that adult human beings are in the possession of a developed commonsense psychological theory, and can apply it with reasonable skill to the task of inferring the psychological states of others. How did this mature capacity evolve?

Research has revealed that three-year-old children are reasonably good at inferring the beliefs of others on the basis of actions, and at predicting actions on the basis of beliefs that others are known to possess. However, there is one area in which three-year-olds' psychological reasoning differs markedly from that of adults. Tests of the following sort, 'False Belief Tests', reveal largely consistent results. Three-year-old subjects are witness to the following scenario. A child, Billy, sees his mother place some biscuits in a biscuit tin. Billy then goes out to play, and, unseen by him, his mother removes the biscuits from the tin and places them in a jar, which is then hidden in a cupboard. When asked 'Where will Billy look for the biscuits?' the majority of three-year-olds answer that Billy will look in the jar in the cupboard – where the biscuits actually are, rather than where Billy saw them being placed. On being asked 'Where does Billy think the biscuits are?' they again tend to answer 'In the cupboard', rather than 'In the tin'. Three-year-olds thus appear to have some difficulty attributing false beliefs to others in cases in which it would be natural for adults to do so. However, it appears that three-year-olds are not lacking the idea of false beliefs in general, nor does it appear that they struggle with attributing false beliefs in other kinds of situation. For example, they have little trouble distinguishing between dreams and play, on the one hand, and true beliefs or claims on the other. By the age of four and a half years, most children pass the False Belief Tests fairly consistently. There is as yet no generally accepted theory of why three-year-olds fare so badly with the false belief tests, nor of what it reveals about their conception of beliefs. (*See* Wellman, 1990 and Perner, 1991 for detailed discussion.)

Recently some philosophers and psychologists have put forward what they take to be an alternative to the Theory Theory: the 'Simulation Theory' (e.g. Gordon, 1986;

Goldman, 1989; Heal, 1986). The basic idea of the Simulation Theory is that we understand the psychologies of others by using our own psychological processes to simulate those of others. The Simulation Theory builds upon the point, noted earlier, that we do not typically know about our own beliefs on the basis of theoretical inference. Rather, in the typical case, we know what we believe immediately and non-inferentially. Moreover, if we consider how we would act, or what we would believe, in some non-actual or future situation, it again appears that we do not proceed on the basis of theoretical inference. Rather, we imagine ourselves to be in the non-actual situation, and then indulge in a sort of 'pretend play' (Gordon, 1986): I imagine the sound of footsteps in the basement, I ask myself, in effect, 'What do I do now?' To answer the question I need to discover what I would believe, desire and so on, in such a situation. And to answer this, rather than theorize, I pretend to be (or play at being) in the situation, and I let my psychological processes run as normal: *footsteps in the basement: an intruder! How did he get in? It was a hot day, and I left the window open: he climbed in through the window.* I now know that I would believe that an intruder has climbed through the window. But I did not infer that I would believe this from general psychological principles. Rather, I let my belief-forming mechanisms run 'off line', within the scope of the pretence, and merely note the result. The Simulation Theory holds that the same method is applied to discovering the beliefs of others: one projects oneself into the other's situation and, once again, lets one's own psychological processes run off line, and notes the results. Of course, such projection usually requires imagining oneself not only in the other's spatio-temporal situation, but also in his psychological situation: that is to say, one adjusts for already known psychological differences.

The Simulation Theory thus addresses both first- and third-personal knowledge of beliefs, and offers an appealing account of the relationship between the two. While the Theory Theory must either hold that we know our own beliefs by theoretical inference, or allow for a sharp asymmetry between the two cases, the Simulation Theory argues that we know about the beliefs of others by a natural extension of our capacity to know about our own.

The Simulation Theory appears to face a challenge: How can one run the necessary simulations except on the basis of a psychological theory? After all, if one is to simulate some process, one generally needs to know how it works. And this would appear to require, precisely, a theory of the process. But this challenge, so put, misses the crucial point. As believers, we ourselves already have belief-forming processes to hand. And we can deploy these processes with the aim of discovering what beliefs they would produce in a given situation, without knowing how they work. We let the processes run, we then record the results. As Goldman (1989) points out, one can run a successful simulation without deploying a theory, providing (a) that the processes driving the simulation are the same as the actual psychological processes of the simulated agent and (b) the initial states of simulator and simulated are the same or relevantly similar. And that is surely fair enough.

However, the challenge does not end there. We need also to consider the vital element of making appropriate adjustments for differences between one's own psychological states and those of the other. My friend has been offered a job at a certain Philosophy Department. Will he take it? I cannot merely pretend that I have been offered the job, and run through the reasoning I would go through to see whether I would accept it. My friend and I differ in respect of certain potentially relevant desires and beliefs. The job is better paid than his present one. How relevant is this? I need to know how much he values money. Can I discover this by further simulation? Either I can or I cannot. If I cannot, then, it seems, I must do some research and make a theoretical inference. If I can, then surely a similar question will arise when I perform this further simulation: I will come to some psychological state of my own that I cannot assume to be shared by my friend. It is implausible that in every such case simulation alone will provide the answer.

The Simulation Theorist should probably concede that simulations need to be backed up by the independent means of discovering the psychological states of others. But they need not concede that these independent means take the form of a theory. Rather, they might suggest, we can get by with some rules of thumb, or straightforward inductive reasoning of a general kind.

A second and related difficulty with the Simulation Theory concerns our capacity to attribute beliefs that are too alien to be easily simulated: beliefs of small children, or psychotics, or bizarre beliefs deeply suppressed in the unconscious. The small child refuses to sleep in the dark: he is afraid the Wicked Witch will steal him away. No matter how many adjustments we make, it may be hard for mature adults to get their own psychological processes, even in pretend play, to mimic the production of such a belief. For the Theory Theory alien beliefs are not particularly problematic: so long as they fit into the basic generalizations of the theory, they will be inferrable from the evidence. Thus the Theory Theory can account better for our ability to discover more bizarre and alien beliefs than can the Simulation Theory.

The Theory Theory and the Simulation Theory are not the only proposals about knowledge of beliefs. A third view has its origins in the later philosophy of Ludwig WITTGENSTEIN. On this view both the Theory and Simulation Theories attribute too much psychologizing to our commonsense psychology. Knowledge of other minds is, according to this alternative picture, more observational in nature. Beliefs, desires, feelings are made manifest to us in the speech and other actions of those with whom we share a language and a way of life. When someone says 'It's going to rain' and takes his umbrella from his bag, it is immediately clear to us that he believes it is going to rain. In order to know this we neither theorize nor simulate: we just perceive. Of course this is not straightforward visual perception of the sort that we use to see the umbrella. But it is like visual perception in that it provides immediate and non-inferential awareness of its objects. We might call this the 'Observational Theory'.

The Observational Theory does not seem to accord very well with the fact that we frequently do have to indulge in a fair amount of psychologizing to find out what others believe. It is clear that any given action might be the upshot of any number of different psychological attitudes. This applies even in the simplest cases, like saying 'It's going to rain' and taking an umbrella from a bag. One might do this because one believes it's going to rain. But one might do it for any number of other reasons. For example: because one's friend is suspended from a dark balloon near a beehive, with the intention of stealing honey. The idea is to make the bees believe that it is going to rain, and therefore believe that the balloon is a dark cloud, and therefore pay no attention to it, and so fail to notice one's dangling friend. Given this sort of possibility, the observer would surely be rash immediately to judge that the agent believes that it is going to rain. Rather, they would need to determine – perhaps by theory, perhaps by simulation – which of the various clusters of mental states that might have led to the action, actually did so. This would involve bringing in further knowledge of the agent, the background circumstances and so on. It is hard to see how the sort of complex mental processes involved in this sort of psychological reflection could be assimilated to any kind of observation.

THE FALLIBILITY OF COMMONSENSE PSYCHOLOGY

Thus far I have considered three theories concerned with how we actually attribute beliefs to ourselves and to others. I now turn to the second area of enquiry mentioned above, the extent to which our lay practices of attributing beliefs are fallible and the extent to which they stand in need of correction or justification by other methods.

One extreme view holds that commonsense psychology is not merely fallible, but completely wrong. Thus Churchland (1981) holds that commonsense psychology is a terrible theory, riddled with explanatory gaps and failures. And Stich (1983) also finds commonsense psychology to be seriously flawed. Both conclude that the theory is a false one, and that therefore its basic explanatory apparatus of beliefs, desires and so on should be rejected from our ONTOLOGY. They conclude, then, that all belief ascriptions are false: there really are no such things as beliefs (see ELIMINATIVISM).

By contrast, FODOR (1987) argues that commonsense psychology is so successful that we would be well advised to take its explanatory apparatus most seriously. He points out that commonsense psychology is a far better predictor of people's actions than any other theory currently available. Fodor defends his claim by pointing to very simple, everyday cases. Suppose, for example, that I telephone Fodor at his office in New York and ask him if he would like to give a paper at King's College, London, on the 20th of June. Fodor accepts the invitation. I am immediately in a position to predict where Fodor will be on the 20th of June. This prediction is based on commonsense psychology: I hold that Fodor understood what I was asking him, that he was speaking sincerely, that he believed he would indeed come to London and so on. Of course the prediction is not infallible. Fodor might indeed not be in London on the relevant day. Perhaps he forgot that he had already agreed to be somewhere else. Or perhaps his flight will be cancelled. But the important point is that the prediction is very likely to be correct.

Predictions of the simple, everyday kind just illustrated are indeed very common, and do come out right most of the time. It can hardly be denied that the success of commonsense psychology provides good *prima facie* evidence that the theory is largely on the right track and that human beings really do have propositional attitudes of the kinds we commonly ascribe.

Ultimately one's opinion of the extent to which commonsense psychology is fallible will depend upon one's general ontological conception of belief. To illustrate this interplay between epistemology and ontology, I shall consider just one philosophical theory of belief, FUNCTIONALISM.

According to functionalism, psychological states are defined by their causal relations to each other, to inputs from the environment, and to behaviour. A psychological theory – for example, commonsense psychology, as illustrated by (1)–(4) above – specifies in general terms the relevant causal relations into which psychological states enter. Now, one can abstract from such a theory a specification of a pattern of causal interrelations among a network of states. For example (3) above tells us that if a subject believes that p, and believes that if p, then q, then (barring confusion etc.) he will believe that q. This specifies a pattern among three states, which we can describe abstractly as S1 and S2, which (barring S3 etc.) cause S4. One can imagine taking the whole psychological theory and abstracting a much larger pattern that exhausts the types of causal interaction among all psychological states: all explicit psychological terms are removed from the theory, and replaced by variable Ss. What remain specified are just the environmental inputs, the behavioural outputs and the causal interrelations among the intervening states. Functionalism holds that any network of states that fits this large causal pattern will automatically be a network of the psychological states described by the original theory. Thus being a given belief or desire just is being a state with a particular kind of causal role in relation to other, analogously defined states, inputs from the environment and behavioural outputs.

There are a number of different versions of functionalism that disagree over such matters as the kind of theory that defines the causal network (commonsense psychology, cognitive science, or something else) and the appropriate specifications of the inputs and outputs (e.g. are the inputs distal or proximal? Are the outputs bodily motions or impacts on the environment?). (For various versions of functionalism and critical discussion, see Block, 1980.)

If functionalism is true, then commonsense psychology is in principle open to validation or refutation by further enquiry. For functionalism imposes constraints on the causal structure of the aetiology of behaviour. A being might then act just as if it is the subject of a certain ensemble of propositional attitudes, without actually being so. For it may be that its behaviour is caused by some network of interrelated states that forms a quite different pattern from the one that would be required for it to have the desires, beliefs etc. that it outwardly appears to have. (*See* Block, 1981, for an example.) In such a case the being might have no psychological states at all, or quite different ones from those that would be ascribed, on the behavioural evidence, by commonsense psychology. It follows that to determine conclusively what beliefs someone has, one would need to investigate the causal structure of the aetiology of the behaviour, something that would presumably involve study of the brain.

THE LIMITS OF OUR KNOWLEDGE

I turn now to the third question I promised to address, and to a general epistemological problem about beliefs, one that seriously affects the project of giving a philosophical theory of belief. The problem concerns the beliefs (if any) of beings that are not human: gorillas, pigeons, sophisticated robots, silicon-based extra-terrestrials, etc. Which of these have beliefs? And what do they believe? Each of us has his or her own view of the matter. But what is striking is how little agreement there is and how little we know about how to resolve the questions. The problem seems to me to go very deep, for the following reason. Current psychological theories do not give us much

help. A fair amount is known about the behaviour of, for example, gorillas. But there is very little consensus as to the correct psychological explanation of the behaviour. The matter thus remains within the province of philosophy. But it seems impossible to arrive at a properly justified philosophical theory of belief without first having at least some idea about which non-human beings have beliefs.

Functionalists, for example, maintain that an appropriately programmed robot whose control centre is made of silicon chips would indeed have beliefs. Some physicalists argue against functionalism precisely on the grounds that such things would not have beliefs (*see* e.g. Searle, 1980). How is the issue to be resolved? This sort of impasse is typical: a given philosophical theory entails that a given type of being would (or wouldn't) have beliefs. Objectors then object that this consequence is unacceptable. Proponents of the theory bite the bullet and accept the consequence. Objectors deny the consequence and reject the theory.

The difficulty is deep because neither the theories of belief nor the intuitions about which beings have which beliefs have any independent justification. As matters currently stand, the theories get evaluated largely by how well they do at delimiting the range of possible believers. Since different theories make different predictions about the range of believers, we need some independent means of finding out about this range. But we have nothing to go on except our intuitions. And these are erratic and highly fallible. After all, why should we expect to have trustworthy intuitions about the beliefs of possums, extra-terrestrials or robots? We therefore need some independent way of evaluating the intuitions. But that, in turn, seems to require a theory of belief. We are therefore in an *aporia*: we can't trust our intuitions unless we have a theory by which to test them, but we have no way of testing a theory except by seeing how well it accords with our intuitions. Psychology and philosophy evidently have a long way to go.

151

See also ACTION; BELIEF (1); DAVIDSON; DENNETT; *An Essay on Mind* section 1.2.2: INTENTIONALITY; PROPOSITIONAL ATTITUDES; PSYCHOLOGY AND PHILOSOPHY; SEARLE.

BIBLIOGRAPHY

Block, N., ed. 1980. *Readings in Philosophy of Psychology*, vol. 1. Cambridge, MA.: Harvard University Press.

Block, N. 1981 Psychologism and behaviourism. *The Philosophical Review*, 90, 5–43.

Churchland, P. 1981. Eliminative materialism and propositional attitudes. *The Journal of Philosophy*, 78, 67–90.

Fodor, J. 1987. *Psychosemantics*. Cambridge, MA.: MIT Press.

Goldman, A. 1989. Interpretation psychologized. *Mind and Language*, 4, 161–85.

Gordon, R. 1986. Folk psychology as simulation. *Mind and Language*, 1, 158–171.

Heal, J. 1986. Replication and functionalism. In *Language, Mind and Logic*, ed. J. Butterfield. Cambridge University Press.

Perner, J. 1991. *Understanding the Representational Mind*. Cambridge, MA.: MIT Press.

Searle, J. 1980. Minds, brains and programmes. *Behavioral and Brain Sciences*, 3, 417–24.

Stich, S. 1983. *From Folk Psychology to Cognitive Science: The Case Against Belief*. Cambridge, MA.: MIT Press.

Wellman, H. 1990. *The Child's Theory of Mind*. Cambridge, MA.: MIT Press.

GABRIEL SEGAL

C

Cartesian *see* DUALISM; FIRST-PERSON AUTHORITY; HISTORY.

Chomsky, Noam What do I think is true of the mind, and what is the best way of studying it? These are the questions on which I have been asked to comment – with the understanding that the scope is so broad that only some general directions can be outlined, with no effort to motivate or to justify. More extensive discussion can be found in material cited at the end. In the interest of clarity, I will indicate some continuities, and some areas of controversy and disagreement, but without attempting any explanation or resolution.

Study of the mind is an inquiry into certain aspects of the natural world, including what have traditionally been called mental events, processes, and states. A 'naturalistic approach' would seek to investigate these aspects of the world as we do any others, attempting to construct intelligible explanatory theories and to move toward eventual integration with the core natural sciences. This 'methodological naturalism' is not to be confused with 'metaphysical naturalism' or other varieties (*See* NATURALISM). It should be uncontentious, though its reach remains to be determined.

Plainly, such an approach does not exclude other ways of trying to comprehend the world. Someone committed to it can consistently believe (I do) that we learn much more of human interest about how people think and feel and act by reading novels or studying history than from all of naturalistic psychology, and perhaps always will; similarly, the arts may offer appreciation of the heavens to which astrophysics cannot aspire. We are speaking here of theoretical understanding, a particular mode of comprehension. In this domain, any departure from a naturalistic approach carries a burden of justification. Perhaps one can be given, but I know of none.

Keeping to the search for theoretical understanding, are there alternatives to a naturalistic approach, perhaps with broader reach or deeper insight? In the case of language, there certainly are approaches that transcend the bounds of naturalistic inquiry outlined below; say, in sociolinguistics. But it is less clear that they are alternatives. The question is whether they presuppose (usually tacitly) an approach to language in these terms. I have argued elsewhere that they do, however vigorously the fact may be denied. Are there genuine alternatives? One naturally keeps an open mind. I will return to the question later, in connection with work in contemporary philosophy of language and mind that takes a different course.

There are, of course, important questions as to how naturalistic inquiry should proceed. These questions are most appropriately raised with regard to the advanced sciences, in which depth of understanding and range of success may provide guides to inquiry and analysis: physics, not psychology. In a naturalistic approach to humans, we may safely put such concerns aside, unless some reason is offered to show their unique relevance here. Again, I know of none.

Like other complex systems, the human brain can be profitably viewed as an array of interacting subcomponents, which can be studied at various levels: atoms, cells, cell assemblies, neural networks, computational-representational (C-R) systems, etc. We cannot know in advance which (if any) of these approaches will provide insight and understanding. In several domains, including language, the C-R approaches currently have the strongest claim to scientific status, at least on naturalistic grounds.

We might ask whether a study of the brain in such terms is improper or controversial. If not, we then ask whether the theories developed (say of language) are true. Does the brain in fact have the architecture, subsystems, states, properties, spelled out in such terms in some particular theory? As for the first query, it is hardly controversial to suppose that the brain, like other complex systems, has subsystems with states and properties. The properties attributed in C-R theories are by and large well understood. No general conceptual issues seem to arise, only questions of truth, the second query, which we may put aside here.

A related question is whether achievements, or promise, at other levels of inquiry eliminates the basis for recourse to C-R theories. In recent years, a great deal of interest has been aroused by neural net and connectionist models, and there has been much discussion of the implications of the possibility that, once developed, they might provide a preferable alternative (*see* CONNECTIONISM). These discussions appear to be naturalistic in temper, but that may be questioned. Suppose that someone were to propose that unstructured systems with unknown properties might some day make it possible to account for development of organisms without appeal to the complex constructions of the embryologist in terms of concentration of chemicals, the cell's internal program, production of proteins, and so on. Thoughts about the implications of this possibility would be unlikely to impress the biologist, even if such systems were argued to have some of the properties of cells, and to have successes in unrelated domains.

It is common to try to relieve uneasiness about C-R approaches by invoking computer models to show that we have robust, hard-headed instances of the kind (*see* COMPUTATIONAL MODELS): psychology then studies software problems. That is a dubious move. Artefacts pose all kinds of questions that do not arise in the case of natural objects. Whether some object is a key or a table or a computer depends on designer's intent, standard use, mode of interpretation, and so on. The same considerations arise when we ask whether the device is malfunctioning, following a rule, etc. There is no natural kind or normal case. The hardware–software distinction is a matter of interpretation, not simply of physical structure, though with further assumptions about intention, design, and use we could sharpen it. Such questions do not arise in the study of organic molecules, nematodes, the language faculty, or other natural objects, viewed (to the extent we can achieve this standpoint) as what they are, not in a highly intricate and shifting space of human interests and concerns. The belief that there was a problem to resolve, beyond the normal ones, reflects an unwarranted departure from naturalism; the solution offered carries us from a manageable frying pan to a fire that is out of control.

We naturally want to solve the 'unification problem', that is, to relate studies of the brain undertaken at various levels, much as nineteenth-century science looked forward to the integration of chemistry and physics that was finally achieved in the new quantum theory. Sometimes unification will be reductive, as when much of biology was incorporated within known biochemistry; sometimes it may require radical modification of the more 'fundamental' discipline, as when physics was 'expanded', enabling it to account for properties that had been discovered and explained, at another level, by chemists (*see* REDUCTION). We cannot know in advance what course unification will take, if it succeeds at all.

Take a specific current example. C-R studies of language give strong reasons to believe that linguistic expressions fall into many categories of 'well-formedness': non-deviant (though perhaps gibberish), and in violation of various conditions on rule systems that have been discovered. Recent studies of electrical activity of the brain (event-related potentials, ERPs) have succeeded in finding distinctive responses to several of these categories of expressions. These studies relate two levels of inquiry: electrical activity of the brain and C-R systems. In this case, the C-R theories have much stronger empirical support, and are far superior in explanatory power. The current significance of the ERP studies lies primarily in the correlations with the much richer and better-grounded C-R theories. Within the latter, the various categories have a place, and, accordingly, a wide range of empirical support, some of it indirect, by way of general principles confirmed elsewhere; in isolation from C-R theories, the ERP observations are curiosities, lacking a theoretical matrix. The situation could change, in which case the C-R theories would be confirmed, modified, or abandoned on the basis of studies of electrical activity. In naturalistic inquiry, the chips fall where they may, in terms of explanatory success.

The aspects of mind that have particularly concerned me are those involving language: its nature, development, and use. By 'language' I mean 'human language'. There is no more a study of 'language' for organisms generally than there is a study of 'locomotion', ranging from amoeba to eagle to science-fiction spaceship; or 'communication', ranging from cellular interaction to Shakespeare's sonnets to 'intelligent' extraterrestials. The human brain appears to have a subsystem dedicated to language. Most of our current understanding of this 'language faculty' derives from inquiry at the level of C-R systems, based on observation and study of perception, interpretation, and action. We may call this part of the study of mind, using the term only to refer to a domain of inquiry, with no metaphysical connotations, just as the study of chemical interactions in the nineteenth century, which could not be grounded in known 'physical mechanisms', entailed no metaphysical distinction between physics and chemistry.

Other components of the mind/brain, about which little is known, provide what we might call 'commonsense understanding' of the world and our place in it ('folk physics', 'FOLK PSYCHOLOGY', etc.).

Some components, perhaps different ones, make it possible for humans to conduct naturalistic inquiry, and sometimes to achieve remarkable insight: we may call them 'the science-forming faculty', to dignify ignorance with a title.

We hardly expect the constructions of the science-forming faculty to conform to common-sense understanding. The natural sciences have no place for such common-sense notions as *liquid*, *energy*, or *wave*, or the terms in which we describe a missile rising to the heavens and falling to the ground. No matter how much physics we know, we cannot help seeing the moon illusion or the setting of the sun, or sharing Newton's unshakeable belief in the 'mechanical philosophy' that he had refuted (with no little perplexity). It does not seem reasonable to expect folk psychology to fare differently from folk physics: say, to expect that *belief* and *desire*, or *language*, or *rule*, as the terms are commonly used and understood, will survive the transition to rational inquiry, if it can be made in these domains. Nor should we expect what may be discovered about language, perception, or thought to conform to folk psychology. That aside, in invoking folk psychology we have to be careful to observe the practice of serious ethnoscience, distinguishing parochial and culture-bound notions from the elements of 'folk theories' that are a common human endowment, grounded in our nature. Not an easy problem, and one that is, I think, too lightly dismissed.

Any organism has certain ways of perceiving and interpreting the world, a certain 'Umwelt' or 'cognitive space', determined in large part by its specific nature and general properties of biological systems. In Hume's terms, part of human knowledge derives 'from the original hand of nature' as 'a species of instinct'. Cognitive systems are grounded in biological endowment, shaped in limited ways by interactions with the environment (experience). In this regard, they are like other components of the body, which also may be profitably studied at various levels of abstraction from mechanisms.

155

Given an organism with its special cognitive systems, we can identify a category of 'problem situations' in which it might find itself: an array of circumstances that it perceives and interprets in a certain way by virtue of its nature and prior history, including (for humans) questions that are posed and background belief and understanding that are brought to bear on them. Sometimes the problem situation is contrived on the basis of theory-driven considerations and addressed with a degree of self-awareness – the activity that we call 'science'. Some problem situations fall within the animal's cognitive capacities, others not. Let us call these 'problems' and 'mysteries', respectively. The concepts are relative to an organism: what is a mystery for a rat might be only a problem for us, and conversely. For a rat, a 'prime number maze' (turn right at every prime choice point), or even far simpler ones, is a permanent mystery; the rat does not have the cognitive resources to deal with it, though a human might. A radial maze, in contrast, poses a problem that a rat might solve quite well. The distinctions need not be absolute, but they can hardly fail to be real.

If humans are part of the natural world, not angels, the same is true of them: there are problems that we might hope to solve, and mysteries that will be forever beyond our cognitive reach. We might think of the natural sciences as a kind of chance convergence between aspects of the natural world and properties of the human mind/brain, which has allowed some rays of light to penetrate the general obscurity; *chance* convergence in that natural processes and principles have not 'designed' us to deal with problems we face and can sometimes formulate. Since Charles Sanders Peirce, there have been proposals about evolutionary factors that allegedly guarantee that we can find the truth about the world, and there are much earlier beliefs about our unique access to the nature of our own minds and their products. But such speculations seem unpersuasive.

We might consider for a moment a traditional approach to problems of mind, one that may reflect 'commonsense understanding' to a considerable degree: metaphysical DUALISM. Take the Cartesian version. It offered a sketchy account of the physical world, basically in terms of a kind of 'contact mechanics'. Certain aspects of the world, it was then argued, do not fall under these principles. No artefact, for example, could exhibit the normal properties of language use: unbounded; not determined by external stimuli or internal state; not random but coherent and appropriate to situations, though not caused by them; evoking thoughts that the hearer might have expressed the same way – a collection of properties that we may call 'the creative aspect of language use'. Accordingly, some new principle must be invoked; for the Cartesians, a second substance whose essence is thought. We then have the problem of determining its nature, and we face the unification problem that arises throughout the natural sciences: showing how mind and body interact, in the traditional formulation. The approach is basically naturalistic, and the reasoning is unaffected when we move from the complex artefacts that fascinated the seventeenth-century imagination to those that excite many of the same questions and speculations today.

As is well known, this programme collapsed within a generation, when Newton demonstrated that the theory of the material world was fatally inadequate, unable to account for the most elementary properties of motion. Newton had nothing to say about the ghost in the machine. He exorcized the machine, not the ghost; the Cartesian theory of mind, such as it was, remained unaffected. Newton found that bodies had unexpected ghostly properties; their 'occult quality' of action at a distance transcends the common notion of body or material object. Like many other leading scientists of the day, Newton found these results disturbing, agreeing with the Cartesians that the idea of action at a distance through a vacuum is 'so great an Absurdity that I believe no Man who has in philosophical matters a competent Faculty of thinking, can ever fall into it', a reaction that is understandable, possibly even rooted in folk psychology. He concluded that we must accept that universal gravity exists, even if we cannot explain it in terms of the self-evident 'mechanical philosophy'. As many commentators have observed, this intellectual move 'set forth a new view of science', in which the goal is 'not to seek ultimate explanations', but to find the best theoretical account we can of the phenomena of experience and experiment (Cohen, 1987). Conformity to commonsense understanding is henceforth put aside, as a criterion for rational enquiry. (*See* Newton, 1693; Kuhn, 1959; Cohen, 1987.)

These moves also deprive us of any determinate notion of body or matter. The world is what it is, with whatever strange properties may be discovered, including those previously called 'mental'. Such notions as 'PHYSICALISM' or 'eliminative materialism' (*see* ELIMINATIVISM) lose any clear sense. Metaphysical dualism becomes unstateable, as does metaphysical naturalism, understood as the view that the study of mind must be 'continuous' with the physical. The mind/body distinction cannot be formulated in anything like the Cartesian manner; or any other, as far as I can see, except as a terminological device to distinguish various aspects of the natural world. The domain of the 'physical' is what we come more or less to understand, and hope to assimilate to the core natural sciences in some way, perhaps modifying them as inquiry proceeds. Ideas that yield understanding and insight are judged legitimate, part of the presumed truth about the world; our criteria of rationality and intelligibility may also change and develop, as understanding grows. If humans have 'ghostly properties' apart from those common to all of matter, that's a fact about the world, which we must try to comprehend in naturalistic terms, there being no other.

The natural conclusion from Newton's demolition of the commonsense theory of body is that human thought and action are properties of organized matter, like 'powers of attraction and repulsion', electrical charge, and so on. That conclusion was drawn most forcefully by De La Mettrie, a generation later by Joseph Priestley, though neither attempted to deal with the properties of mind identified by the Cartesians. (For De La Mettrie *see* Chomsky, 1966, ch. 1, and sources cited. Particularly Rosenfield, 1941. *See also* Wellman, 1992. For Priestley *see* Yolton, 1983.)

We now face a series of questions. What exactly are these properties of things in the world? How do they arise in the individual and the species? How are they put to use in action and interpretation? How can organized matter have these properties (the new version of the unification problem)?

On the last problem, progress has been slight. Matter and mind are not two categories of things, but they may pose entirely different kinds of quandaries for human intelligence, a fact that is interesting and important, if true, but in no way surprising to the naturalistic temper, which takes for granted that humans will face problems and mysteries, as determined by their special nature. It may be that central domains of the 'mental' are cognitively inaccessible to us, perhaps the creative aspect of language use, which lies as far beyond our understanding as it did to the Cartesians. If so, we shall have to learn about humans, as best we can, in other ways.

In some areas, there has been considerable progress. In the case of language, it has been possible, in the past generation, to formulate and study a number of traditional questions that had eluded serious inquiry, and more recently, to recast them significantly, leading to much new understanding of at least some central features of the mind and its functioning.

To say that someone has (speaks, knows, . . .) a language is to say that the person's language faculty has attained a certain state. The language, so construed, is a state of the language faculty. Adapting some traditional terms, we may call a theory of this state a 'grammar of the language', and a theory of the initial state, a 'universal grammar'. As in the case of other aspects of growth and development, the state attained and the course of development are internally directed in crucial respects; external conditions are far too impoverished to have more than a marginal impact on the highly articulated and intricate structures that arise as the language faculty develops to a 'steady state', apparently before puberty, afterwards undergoing only peripheral change in the normal case. To the extent that we can determine the properties of the state attained, we can ask questions about language use: how are expressions interpreted and produced? We can ask how properties of the initial state and external events interact to determine the course of language growth (what is called 'language learning', though 'language growth' might be less misleading). In all of these areas, there has been substantial progress – the normal use of language for expression of thought aside, a not inconsiderable gap.

The state attained consists of a cognitive system and performance systems. The cognitive system stores information that is accessed by the performance systems, which use it for articulation, interpretation, expression of thought, asking questions, referring, and so on. The cognitive system accounts for our infinite knowledge, for example, our knowledge about sound and meaning and their relations over an unbounded range. There is by now a large mass of reliable data about these matters from a great variety of typologically different languages, and non-trivial theories that go some distance in explaining the evidence.

It is natural to restrict the term 'language' to the state of the cognitive system of the language faculty. We say, then, that Smith has (knows, speaks, . . .) the language L if the cognitive component of Smith's language faculty is in state L. So regarded, we may think of the language as a way to speak and understand, a traditional conception. It is commonly assumed that the performance systems are fixed and invariant. The reasons are, basically, ignorance: that is the simplest assumption, and we have no evidence that it is false. The cognitive systems, however, do vary. English is not Japanese; the cognitive

systems have achieved different states – though not very different ones, it appears. A Martian scientist, observing humans from the standpoint that we adopt towards organisms other than ourselves, might not find the differences very impressive, compared with the overwhelming commonality.

The attained state of the cognitive system is a generative procedure that determines an infinite class of linguistic expressions, each a certain collection of phonetic, structural, and semantic properties. Particular 'signals' are manifestations of linguistic expressions (spoken, written, signed, whatever); speech acts are manifestations of linguistic expressions in a broader sense.

Note that the concept of language so developed is internalist, individualist, and INTENSIONAL, in the technical senses. It has to do with the internal state of the brain of a particular individual. Accordingly, Peter and Mary might in principle have different generative procedures that determine the same class of linguistic expressions, though the highly restrictive character of the initial state may rule out this possibility. If the case existed, the grammar of Peter's language would be different than the grammar of Mary's, though they could not be distinguished empirically solely on the basis of information concerning properties of expressions of Peter's and Mary's languages. Note that a naturalistic approach would never even consider the far more restrictive conditions of the familiar 'radical translation' paradigm, on which, a few words below. Similarly, Peter and Mary might, in principle, have visual systems that provide the same mapping of stimulus to percept, but in different ways, in which case the theoretical accounts of their visual systems would differ, though evidence for this would have to derive from sources beyond study of stimulus – percept pairing.

We may choose to ignore differences between states that are similar enough for the interests and purposes at hand, whether studying language, vision, or drosophila; from that we cannot conclude that there are 'shared languages' (or shared visual systems or drosophila-types). From the fact

158

that two people speak alike, we do not deduce the existence of a common shared language, any more than we deduce the existence of a common shared shape from the fact that they look alike.

A linguistic expression has two 'interface' aspects, each of which provides instructions to the performance systems. One interface includes information for the signalling apparatus: the vocal musculature and auditory system, among others. The second interface provides information relevant to the faculties of the mind/brain involved in thought and action. Not surprisingly, the first interface is much better understood. The second is harder to study, because the related systems are much more obscure, but there is, nevertheless, a great deal of relevant evidence and many interesting results and insights.

We may regard each interface as a symbolic system consisting of 'values', 'phonetic values' in one case, 'semantic values' in the other. Note that these are technical notions, to be divorced of connotations drawn from other domains of inquiry. The phonetic values are syntactic objects, elements of 'MENTAL REPRESENTATION' postulated in the (strictly naturalistic) study of states and properties of the language faculty of the brain (*see* SYNTAX/SEMANTICS). They are not vibrating air particles. Similarly, the semantic values are syntactic objects, not part of some extra-mental world. Internalist semantics seems much like the study of other parts of the biological world. We might well term it a form of syntax, that is, the study of elements of symbolic systems of the mind/brain. The same terminology remains appropriate if the theoretical apparatus is elaborated to include mental models, POSSIBLE WORLDS, discourse representations, and other systems of postulated entities that are still to be related in some manner to things in the world, or taken to be in the world – no simple matter, and perhaps even a misconceived project.

It is by virtue of the way the cognitive system is embedded in performance systems that the formal properties of expressions are interpreted as rhyme, entailment, and so on, not – say – as instructions for locomotion. We are studying a real object, the language faculty of the brain, which has assumed a particular state that provides instructions to performance systems that play a role in articulation, interpretation, expression of beliefs and desires, referring, telling stories, and so on. For such reasons, the topic is human language.

Pursuing the inquiry into language in these terms, we can account for many curious and complex properties of sound and meaning, and relations among expressions, in a wide variety of languages. Much of this appears to derive from our inner nature, determined by the initial state of our language faculty, hence unlearned and universal for human languages.

The inquiry seeks to attain both 'descriptive adequacy' and 'explanatory adequacy.' A proposed grammar of L is descriptively adequate insofar as it is correct, that is, is a true theory of L. A proposed version of universal grammar, call it UG, achieves descriptive adequacy insofar as it is a true theory of the initial state, of language in general. Insofar as UG is descriptively adequate, it provides an interesting kind of explanation for the facts described by the grammar of L. It provides the means for deriving the properties of the linguistic expressions of L from the properties of the fixed initial state of the language faculty, under the 'boundary conditions' set by experience.

We may put the point differently by thinking of UG as an 'acquisition device'. The initial state of the language faculty changes in early childhood, as a result of internally directed maturation and external inputs, until it assumes a (relatively) stable state: the language L. We may, then, think of the initial state as a procedure (algorithm, mapping), which takes as its input an array of data and yields as output the language L; the 'output' is of course internal, a state of the language faculty. With this perspective, the problem under investigation is sometimes called 'the logical problem of language acquisition'. A richer theory will be based on assumptions as to the right answer to the logical problem, seeking to fill in the details as to just how the processes take place, perhaps rejecting or modifying the assumptions. This is empirical inquiry; particular subparts claim no epistemological priority.

Many of the questions posed have a traditional flavour, though modern behavioural science and structuralist approaches largely avoided or denigrated them. It was evident to Wilhelm von Humboldt in the early nineteenth century that language crucially involves 'infinite use of finite means'. Otto Jespersen recognized that the central concern of the linguist must be free creation, the ability of each person to construct and understand 'free expressions', typically new, each a sound with a meaning. More deeply, the task is to discover how the structures that underlie this ability 'come into existence in the mind of a speaker' who, 'without any grammatical instruction, from innumerable sentences heard and understood . . . will abstract some notion of their structure which is definite enough to guide him in framing sentences of his own.' Though important and basically correct, these ideas had little impact, unlike the far narrower and more restricted Saussurean conceptions of the same period, which were enormously influential in many areas. The ideas could not receive clear expression until advances in the formal sciences provided the concept of generative (recursive) procedure. The modern study of these questions might be regarded as a confluence of traditional ideas that had been dismissed as senseless or unworkable, with new formal insights that made it possible to pursue them seriously. (*See* von Humboldt, 1836; *see* Chomsky, 1966 for discussion in the context relevant here. *See also* Jespersen, 1924.)

Traditional grammars do not describe the facts of language; rather, they provide hints to the reader who already has, somehow, the requisite 'notion of structure' and general conceptual resources, and can use the hints to determine the expressions of the language and what they mean. The same is true of dictionaries. Even the most elaborate do not go beyond hints as to what words mean, with examples to stimulate the conceptual resources of the mind. Traditional grammars and dictionaries, in short, presuppose 'the intelligence of the reader'; they tacitly assume that the basic resources are already in place.

For grammars, the enormity of the gap was not appreciated until serious attempts were made to formulate the generative procedures that determine sound and meaning. It quickly became evident that even short and simple expressions in well-studied languages have intricate properties that had passed completely unnoticed. The ensuing work sought to attain descriptive adequacy by filling these huge gaps – better, chasms – and to undertake the far more interesting project of explanatory adequacy for UG.

There is a tension between these two goals. To achieve descriptive adequacy, it is necessary to construct detailed and intricate rule systems to account for the phenomena. The rules for question-formation in English, for example, involve intricacies undreamt of in traditional accounts, and appear to be specific to the interrogative construction in English. The rules constructed to describe such newly discovered facts were language-particular and construction-particular, much like the hints called 'rules' in traditional grammar. But the empirical conditions of explanatory adequacy (language acquisition) require that the structure of language be largely predetermined. Therefore the rules must be largely universal and general in character.

To resolve the tension it is necessary to show that the apparent complexity is epiphenomenal (*see* EPIPHENOMENALISM), the result of interaction of fixed and probably quite abstract principles, which can vary slightly in the ways they apply, yielding apparent complexity and large phenomenal differences among languages that are basically cast to the same mould. The variations will be determined by experience; the basic principles are invariant, derived 'from the original hand of nature'. Efforts to pursue this path finally converged, about 1980, in a conception of language that departed radically from the 2500-year tradition of study of language. This 'principles-and-parameters' model proposed principles of a very general nature, along with certain options of variation (parameters), perhaps two-valued. The principles are language-independent and also construction-independent; in fact, it appears that traditional grammatical constructions (interrogative, passive, nominal phrase, etc.) are taxonomic artefacts, rather like 'terrestrial mammal' or 'household pet'. These categories, with their special and often intricate properties, result from the interaction of fixed general principles, with parameters set one or another way. Language acquisition is the process of determining the values of parameters. There are no 'rules of grammar' in the traditional sense: rather, language-invariant principles and values for parameters of variation, all indifferent to traditional grammatical constructions.

We may think of a language, then, more or less as a network that is not completely wired up at birth. It is associated with a switch-box, with a finite number of switches that can be set on or off. When they are set, the network functions; different settings may yield quite different phenomenal outputs. To the extent that the picture is spelled out, we can 'deduce' Hungarian or Yoruba by setting the switches one or another way. Elements of the picture seem reasonably clear, though a great deal is unknown, and clarification of principles regularly opens the doors to the discovery of new empirical phenomena, posing new challenges. Though much less is understood, something similar must also be true of the lexicon, with the links it provides to the space of humanly accessible concepts and signals.

Work of the past few years suggests further and, if successful, possibly quite far-reaching revisions of the general picture of language. The language L consists of a lexicon and a computational procedure that uses lexical materials to construct linguistic expressions with their sound and meaning. It may be that the computational procedure is fixed, identical for all languages; variation

is restricted to the lexicon. Furthermore, parameters seem to be of two types: either they hold of all lexical items, or of such formal elements as inflections; classes of substantive elements do not seem to be subject to parametric variation of this sort. Languages also of course differ in the sound–meaning linkage in the lexicon, and in the parts of the computation that are 'close to' phonetic form, hence detectable in the data. Differences of this kind are relatively superficial, sufficiently so, one would hope to show, to account for the observed process of precise acquisition on the basis of little usable evidence. The Martian observer might conclude that, superficial differences aside, there really is only one human language, basically 'built in', much as we assume to be the case, even without evidence or understanding, for other systems of the body.

It may be, furthermore, that many of the principles that seem fairly well established are themselves epiphenomenal, their consequences reducing to more general and abstract properties of the C-R system, properties that have a kind of 'least effort' flavour. This 'minimalist' program also seeks to reduce the descriptive technology to the level of virtual conceptual necessity, sharply restricting the devices available for description, which means that the complex phenomena of widely varied languages must be explained in terms of abstract principles of economy of derivation and representation. A linguistic expression of L, then, would be a formal object that satisfies the universal interface conditions in the optimal way, given the parameter values for L. Such a programme faces an extremely heavy empirical burden. If these directions prove correct, they should yield much deeper insight into the computational processes that underlie our linguistic abilities.

There are other empirical conditions to be met. It is well known that language is 'badly adapted to use'; of the class of 'free expressions' determined by the 'notion of structure' in our minds, only scattered fragments are readily usable. Even short and simple expressions often cannot be handled readily by our performance systems. Furthermore, usability cross-cuts deviance; some deviant expressions are perfectly comprehensible, while non-deviant ones often overload processing capacity. The unusability of language does not interfere with communication: speaker and hearer have similar languages and (perhaps identical) performance systems, so what one can produce, the other can interpret, over a large range. But a really far-reaching theory of language will want to provide an account of the 'usability' of various parts of the language and the categories of deviance, while explaining a broad range of properties of sound and meaning.

At this point we reach substantive questions that would carry us too far afield. Let me finish with some words about the limits of a naturalistic programme of the kind sketched, supposing it to be essentially 'on course'.

First, would it serve as a model for the study of other aspects of mind? Probably not, possible suggestiveness aside. As far as we know, there are no 'mechanisms of general intelligence', procedures of any generality that apply to various cognitive domains. Inquiry into particular skills, abilities, aspects of knowledge and belief, and so on, has regularly found that the subcomponents of the mind function quite differently. That is hardly a great surprise. It is pretty much what we find in the study of other complex systems: the visual cortex, the kidney, the circulatory system, and others. Each of these 'organs of the body' has its properties. They fall together, presumably, at the level of cellular biology, but no 'organ theory' deals with the properties of organs in general. The various faculties and cognitive systems of the mind can be thought of as organs of the body (in this case, of the brain) in much the same sense. There is little reason to suppose that an 'organ theory' exists for such mental organs, and to our (limited) knowledge, it does not.

Over a broad spectrum in psychology, philosophy, speculative neurophysiology, artificial intelligence, and cognitive science,

the opposite has long been assumed. But the belief in uniform mechanisms that apply in different cognitive domains seems groundless. If that turns out to be the case, there will be no serious field of 'cognitive science', dealing with the general properties of cognitive systems; and the study of language, however successful, will neither provide a useful model for other parts of the study of mind, nor draw from them significantly.

Note that, if true, this implies nothing about how language interacts with other mental faculties and systems; surely the interactions are dense and close, but that is another matter entirely.

In the philosophical literature, cognitive science is often construed as the study of how behaviour is caused by a complex of beliefs, desires, and so on (see REASONS AND CAUSES). The approach to the study of mind just outlined has nothing to say about these topics. I'm not sure that is a defect, since cognitive science in this sense does not really exist, and may not even be a reasonable goal. No principles are known, or even imagined, that go beyond low-level descriptive observations of limited credibility and scope. There are, furthermore, no strong grounds for believing that behaviour *is* caused, at least in any sense of 'cause' that we understand. I know of no good reason to suppose that the Cartesians were wrong in their basic descriptive observations about behaviour, in particular, about the creative aspect of language use; that is, behaviour that is appropriate and coherent but uncaused, the normal case, they argued. It could well be that we are approaching mysteries-for-humans, at this point.

It seems a reasonable guess that there is a crucial divide between causation of behaviour by situations and internal states, on the one hand, and appropriateness of behavior to situations, on the other; to adopt Cartesian rhetoric, between machines which are *compelled* to act in specific ways (irrelevant random elements apart), and humans who are only *incited and inclined* to do so. In the post-Newtonian era, the divide is not metaphysical, but mental–nonmental (in the naturalistic sense) – a fact about the special properties of one component of the world, the human mind, and its cognitive capacities. The divide might turn out to be unbridgeable for a human intelligence. We should not, I think, simply dismiss Descartes' speculation that we may not 'have intelligence enough' to comprehend the creative aspect of language use and other kinds of free choice and action, though 'we are so conscious of the liberty and indifference which exists in us that there is nothing that we comprehend more clearly and perfectly', and 'it would be absurd to doubt that of which we inwardly experience and perceive as existing within ourselves' just because it lies beyond our comprehension.

The 'internalist' approach to language also fails to provide an account of such notions as 'language of a community' or 'community norms' in the sense presupposed by virtually all work in philosophy of language and philosophical semantics. It gives us no notion of a common public language, which perhaps even exists 'independently of any particular speakers', who have a 'partial, and partially erroneous, grasp of the language' (Dummett, 1986). It has no place for a Platonistic notion of language, outside of the mind/brain and common to various speakers, to which each speaker stands in some cognitive relation, for which a place is often sought within theories of knowledge of a dubious character.

Again, I do not think these are defects of a naturalistic approach; rather of the notions that it does not expect to capture. We have beliefs about health, national rights, the plight of the average man, and so on. A person may know the construction business, or the secret of happiness. But we are not tempted to suppose that there are corresponding Platonic objects to which the person stands in some cognitive relation. The same is true of beliefs about language or knowledge of language (a locution of English that should not be taken too seriously, though having a language surely entails possession of rich and varied knowledge).

To ask whether Peter and Mary speak the same language is like asking whether Boston is near New York or whether John is almost home, except that the dimensionality of context-dependence provided by interest and circumstance is far more diverse and complex. In ordinary human life, we find all sorts of shifting communities and expectations, varying widely with individuals and groups, and no 'right answer' as to how they should be selected. People also enter into various and shifting authority and deference relations. The world is not divided into areas within which people are 'near one another', nor do such areas exist as idealizations. And human society is not divided into communities with languages and their norms. The problem is not one of vagueness; rather, of hopeless underspecification. As for Swedish-versus-Danish, norms and conventions, misuse of language, and other similar notions, they are fine for ordinary usage (as is 'near New York'), but they should not, I think, be expected to enter into attempts to reach theoretical understanding in anything like the ways that have been widely assumed. If so, a good deal of work has to be seriously reconsidered, it appears.

For similar reasons, such notions as 'competence in English' – which could hold, say, of Martians – also have no place in this approach. The question whether a Martian knows English, or whether bees have a language, is not meaningful within a naturalistic framework. The same is true of the question whether a robot is walking or reaching for a block on the table; or whether a computer (or its program) is doing long division, or playing chess, or understanding Chinese, or translating from English to German. These are questions of decision, not fact: how seriously do we choose to take a certain metaphor? Such questions are not settled empirically, any more than we can determine empirically whether an airplane can fly (say, if it can fool someone into thinking it is an eagle), or whether a submarine *really* sets sail but doesn't swim, or whether a camera sees what it films, or whether a high jumper is really flying, like a bird. In English, an airplane and an eagle fly, a high jumper doesn't. In Japanese, all do. In Hebrew, only an eagle does. No issues of fact arise.

In his classic 1950 paper that set off much of the inquiry and debate about whether machines can think, TURING recognized that the question, and others like it, may be 'too meaningless to deserve discussion', though in half a century, he speculated, conditions might have changed enough for us to choose to use such locutions, just as some languages use the metaphor of flying for airplanes and high jumpers. Turing seems to have agreed with WITTGENSTEIN as to the pointlessness of the debates that have raged in the years that followed, until today. In any event, the issues debated cannot be sensibly posed in the naturalistic framework sketched; again not a defect, but a merit, in my opinion. (*See* Turing, 1950.)

Another limitation of a naturalistic approach is that it has nothing to say about the problems raised within W. V. Quine's influential 'radical translation' paradigm, which underlies a good deal of the work of the past generation in philosophy of language and mind (Quine, 1960). The paradigm stipulates a certain epistemic situation for the person trying to communicate, the child acquiring a language, and the linguist studying it. Far-reaching conclusions are then reached about humans, their actions, thought, capacities, and so on. The force of the conclusions depends on the validity of the paradigm, that is, the initial stipulations. A number of questions arise. First, there are crucial differences among the cases grouped together. The epistemic situation of the infant equipped with the resources of the initial state of the faculties of mind cannot sensibly be compared with that of a scientist seeking to determine what these resources are; neither can be compared with the situation of a person in a communication situation whose mind has 'grown' the language L, or that of the linguist seeking to discover L and understand how it is used. More seriously, no stipulations or conditions comparable to those of the paradigm would be tolerated for a

moment in the study of the growth of an embryo to a chicken, or the development of the visual system, or the onset of puberty; or, in fact, in the study of any aspect of the natural world, apart from humans 'above the neck', metaphorically speaking. If so, then the failure of the naturalistic approach sketched earlier to deal with these questions is, again, exactly what we should want.

It is worth noting how radical is this departure from normal science. It seems fair to regard it as a new form of dualism, but one without the virtues of the earlier version. Cartesian dualism was a reasonable theoretical construction, which collapsed because of faulty assumptions about the material world. The new 'methodological/ epistemological dualism', in contrast, insists that the study of human thought and action be pursued in a manner that is completely unacceptable in the sciences. No justification has been given for these arbitrary demands, to my knowledge, though their historical antecedents are fairly clear; indeed the question is scarcely addressed. Not surprisingly, on adopting the framework we reach forms of sceptical doubt that were dismissed for good reason centuries ago.

It is sometimes argued that in the theory of meaning (a term used broadly enough to include much of the study of language) it is necessary to distinguish 'psychological hypotheses' from 'philosophical explanations'. Being limited to the former (or more broadly, to 'scientific hypotheses'), the naturalistic approach is therefore inadequate, it is argued. Suppose that naturalistic inquiry were to discover a C-R theory that spells out precisely what happens when sound waves hit the ear and are interpreted. Suppose this analysis is related to what cells of the body are doing, thus solving the unification problem. So far, we have a 'psychological hypothesis', but not a 'philosophical explanation', because the account does not tell us 'the form in which [the body of knowledge] is delivered' (Dummett, 1986). For the sciences, the account tells everything that can be asked about the form in which the body of knowledge is delivered; but for the theory of meaning (and, presumably, language and thought generally), some additional kind of explanation is required.

Suppose further that there is a Martian creature, exactly like us, except that it can become aware of the internal computations and can truly answer questions about them. The Martian understands the expressions (1) and (2) exactly as we do, with the same options for referential dependence of the pronoun *he* on the antecedent *the young man* – an option in (2) but not in (1):

(1) he thinks the young man is a genius –
(2) his mother thinks the young man is a genius.

By assumption, the Martian determines these options exactly as we do, but when asked, the Martian can state (correctly) the rules that guide its decisions, those of the C-R system postulated for humans. For the Martian, we would now understand the form in which the knowledge is delivered, and could properly attribute knowledge of the principles that determine referential dependence to the Martian. Actually, we would know nothing more of any relevance about the Martian than about the human; they differ only in that the Martian has awareness where the human has none. But we would have crossed the bridge to 'philosophical explanation'. As Quine, John Searle, and others put it, we would be allowed to say that the Martian is following rules or is guided by them, whereas the human, who is doing exactly the same thing, cannot be described in these terms. To avoid immediate counterintuitive consequences, Searle insists further on a property of 'access in principle' that remains obscure. (*See* Quine, 1972, and commentary by myself and Ned Block in Searle, 1990.)

Similarly, if experiment, analysis, and available theory convince us that Mary and Peter do long division exactly the same way, using the algorithm A, then a naturalistic approach will attribute A to both. If, furthermore, Mary is conscious of using A, but Peter not, the naturalistic approach will

state these facts. That is where the story will end – except, of course, to try to determine what is involved in conscious access and why Mary has it but not Peter: interesting questions, but irrelevant here. But on the non-naturalistic assumptions invoked in much of the literature, we must refrain from attributing A to Peter, unless (in some versions) 'access in principle' holds for Peter, in which case we may attribute A to him as well.

In the study of other parts of the natural world, we agree to be satisfied with post-Newtonian 'best theory' arguments; there is no privileged category of evidence that provides criteria for theoretical constructions. In the study of humans above the neck, however, naturalistic theory does not suffice: we must seek 'philosophical explanations', require that theoretical posits be specified in terms of categories of evidence selected by the philosopher (as in the radical translation paradigm), and rely crucially upon unformulated notions such as 'access in principle' that have no place in naturalistic inquiry.

However one evaluates these ideas, they clearly involve demands beyond naturalism, hence a form of methodological/epistemological dualism. In the absence of further justification, it seems to me fair to conclude, here too, that inability to provide 'philosophical explanations' or a concept of 'rule-following' that relies on access to consciousness (perhaps 'in principle') is a merit of a naturalistic approach, not a defect.

A standard paradigm in the study of language, given its classic form by Frege, holds that there is a 'store of thoughts' that is a common human possession and a common public language in which these thoughts are expressed (Frege, 1956). Furthermore, this language is based on a fundamental relation between words and things – reference or denotation – along with some mode of fixing reference (sense, meaning). The notion of a common public language has never been explained, and seems untenable. It is also far from clear why one should assume the existence of a common store of thoughts; the very existence of thoughts had been plausibly questioned, as a misreading of surface grammar, a century earlier.

The third component of the paradigm, a relation of reference, could in principle be accommodated within a naturalistic approach: a relation holding between certain terms of Mary's language and things in the world, or things as Mary conceives them to be, or natural kinds (understood as kinds of nature). But the existence of such relations is a matter of fact, not doctrine; and in fact it does not seem that terms of human language enter into such relations, as noted by P. F. Strawson years ago when he warned of 'the myth of the logically proper name' (Strawson, 1952), to which we may add related myths concerning indexicals and pronouns. True, people use expressions to refer to things and talk about them, but when we study these actions we typically find that the words and expressions provide rather intricate perspectives from which to view the world, perspectives that vary in determinate ways as interests and goals shift, but do not yield any notion of reference in the technical sense. Similarly, ordinary usage seems to have no such terms as 'reference', or 'meaning' understood as mode of fixing reference, in anything like the Fregean sense – which is why Frege had to invent technical concepts.

The fact that the philosophical theories depart from ordinary usage is not a criticism; so does rational inquiry generally, for good and understandable reasons. In this case, however, the theoretical systems that have been devised do not seem to apply to natural language. Study of reference and meaning in natural language, it seems, should follow a different course: asking how the representations at the interface enter into performance systems and relate to other systems of the mind/brain, much as we proceed in the study of articulation and perception. Similar questions arise more generally with regard to questions of INTENTIONALITY, and attempts to understand people and what they do, their thought and action.

Even if correct, such conclusions would not imply that the Fregean project is misguided insofar as it is concerned with a 'logically perfect language' designed for the formal sciences and perhaps the natural sciences as well. It could be argued that naturalistic inquiry seeks to construct a symbolic system with Fregean properties: a store of common thoughts; a common public symbolic system in which these are expressed, incorporating calculus, or formal arithmetic, or something else that is remote from natural language in its basic properties; and that the goal is for the terms of this system to denote in the technical sense, relating to what we take to be things in the world and the kinds of nature. If so, that is a fact about the science-forming faculty. But that would tell us nothing about language, or commonsense understanding ('folk science') generally. Theories of language and thought will have this naturalistic goal as well, but, obviously, we cannot impute properties of the theory to its subject matter.

The technical concepts 'broad content' (see EXTERNALISM/INTERNALISM) and 'perceptual content', which have played a leading role in recent thinking, also have no obvious place here. That too could turn out to be a merit. Insofar as these concepts rely on notions of community and norm, they suffer from serious problems; irremediable ones, I believe. Insofar as they are based on a relation of reference that holds between expressions of natural language and things (natural kinds, etc.), or perhaps between the terms of a 'language of thought' and things, that seems problematic. It is also not clear that these technical notions have counterparts in folk psychology, but if they did, it would not be of much significance for theoretical inquiry into language, meaning, and thought. No doubt it is by virtue of facts of the world that statements and beliefs are true, desires fulfilled, and so on. But we seem far short of any framework of theoretical understanding in which such facts can be accommodated and interpreted.

This only skims the surface of very large topics. I do not want to leave the impression that I think a naturalistic approach along the lines sketched deals with classic questions of language and thought. It definitely does not. For one thing, it omits entirely the creative aspect of language use, the best evidence for the existence of other minds, for the Cartesians. It does not reach as far as the study of groups and institutions in which people take part, though I see no issues here, apart from choice of topic of inquiry. The relevant question is whether there is a more promising path towards theoretical understanding of the range of questions that do seem amenable to naturalistic inquiry in the sense of this discussion. Not to my knowledge, at least.

See also COGNITIVE PSYCHOLOGY; CONTENT; DENNETT; DRETSKE; FODOR; LANGUAGE OF THOUGHT; LEWIS; QUINE; RATIONALITY; SEARLE.

BIBLIOGRAPHY

Chomsky, N. 1966. *Cartesian Linguistics*. New York: Harper & Row.
—— 1965. *Aspects of the Theory of Syntax*. Cambridge, MA: MIT Press.
—— 1968. *Language and Mind*. New York: Harcourt Brace Jovanovich. Enlarged edition 1972.
—— 1975. *Reflections on Language*. New York: Pantheon.
—— 1980. *Rules and Representations*. New York: Columbia University Press.
—— 1986. *Knowledge of Language*. New York: Praeger.
—— 1988. *Language and Problems of Knowledge*. Cambridge, MA: MIT Press.
—— 1992. Language and interpretation: Philosophical reflections and empirical inquiry. In *Inference, Explanation and Other Philosophical Frustrations*, ed. J. Earman. Berkeley: University of California Press.
—— 1993. Explaining language use. *Philosophical Topics*.
Cohen, B.I. 1987. The Newtonian scientific revolution and its intellectual significance: A tercentenary celebration of Isaac Newton's *Principia*. *Bulletin*, The American Academy of Arts and Sciences, *XLI: 3*.
De La Mettrie, J.O. 1966. *L'Homme Machine*. In my *Cartesian Linguistics*, ch. 1.
Dummett, M. 1986. Comments on Davidson and Hacking. In *Truth and Interpretation*, ed. E. Lepore. Oxford: Basil Blackwell.
—— 1991. *The Logical Basis of Metaphysics*. Cambridge, MA: Harvard University Press.
Frege, G. 1956. On sense and reference. In *Philosophical Writings of Gottlob Frege*, ed. and trans. M. Black and P. T. Geach. Oxford: Basil Blackwell.
Jespersen, O. 1924. *Philosophy of Grammar*. London: George Allen & Unwin, 1924.
Kuhn, T. 1959. *The Copernican Revolution*. New York: Vintage.
Newton, I. 1693. Letter cited by J. Yolton in *Thinking Matter*. Minnesota: University of Minnesota Press.
Quine, W.V.O. 1960. *Word and Object*. Cambridge, MA: MIT Press.
—— 1972. Methodological reflections on current linguistic theory. In *Semantics of Natural Language*, ed. D. Davidson and G. Harman. New York: Humanities Press.
Rosenfield, L.C. 1941. *From Beast-Machine to Man Machine*. Oxford University Press.
Searle, J. 1990. Consciousness, explanatory inversion, and cognitive science. *Behavioral and Brain Sciences*. 13(4).
Strawson, P.F. 1952. *Introduction to Logical Theory*. London: Methuen.
Turing, A.M. 1950. Computing machinery and intelligence. *Mind*, LIX, 236.
Von Humboldt, W. 1836. *Uber die Verschiedenheit des Menschlichen Sprachbaues*.
Wellman, K. 1992. *De la Mettrie: Medicine, Philosophy, and Enlightenment*. Duke.
Yolton, J. 1983. *Thinking Matter*. Minnesota: University of Minnesota Press.

NOAM CHOMSKY

cogito *see* HISTORY.

cognitive psychology The Oxford English Dictionary gives the everyday meaning of *cognition* as 'the action or faculty of knowing'. The philosophical meaning is the same, but with the qualification that it is to be 'taken in its widest sense, including sensation, perception, conception, etc., as distinguished from feeling and volition'. Given the historical link between psychology and philosophy, it is not surprising that 'cognitive' in 'cognitive psychology' has something like this broader sense, rather than the everyday one. Nevertheless, the semantics of 'cognitive psychology', like that of many adjective-noun combinations, is not entirely transparent. Cognitive psychology is a branch of psychology, and its subject matter approximates to the psychological study of cognition. Nevertheless, for reasons that are largely historical, its scope is not exactly what one would predict.

THE SCOPE OF COGNITIVE PSYCHOLOGY

The table of contents of a student textbook on cognitive psychology provides a good indication of the topics studied by cognitive psychologists. There are many such texts, but their authors are agreed on the broad divisions of the subject. For example, all the following were covered in four popular texts: sensory memory, pattern recognition, attention, MEMORY proper, learning, MENTAL REPRESENTATIONS (including schemata, IMAGERY, cognitive maps, CONCEPTS), organization of knowledge, language, thinking, reasoning, problem solving, decision making. More recent books are also likely to discuss the relation between cognition and EMOTION, reflecting a new-found interest in cognitive theories of emotion on the part of cognitive psychologists.

Cognition, Action and Emotion

It should come as no surprise to philosophers that the traditional three-fold distinction between cognition, conation, and affection, alluded to in the OED definition, is not important in contemporary psychology. Cognitive psychology is not defined by its contrast with conative and affective psychology. Indeed, psychologists who study ACTION and those who study emotion recognize that both have strong cognitive components. The study of action is fragmented. Skilled performance is studied in a different framework from decision making, for example. Decision making itself stands in an uncomfortable relation to the rest of cognitive psychology. In the 1950s and 1960s it was studied primarily by economists and mathematical psychologists. Since that time, its cognitive aspects have been

increasingly recognized, though its proper integration into cognitive psychology remains a distant prospect. Ironically, work on other aspects of reasoning has begun to suggest a strong link to practical reasoning. For example, 85 per cent of university students routinely fail to solve the abstract version of the notorious Wason selection task (figure 1). Problems with parallel structure, but with concrete content, can be much easier. Manktelow and Over (1991) and others have argued that the facilitatory effect of such content is explained by the fact that it elicits practical, rather than theoretical, reasoning skills.

The study of emotions in psychology is less fragmented, though nevertheless riddled with controversy. One major point of disagreement is whether there are any basic emotions. One view is that six basic emotions can be identified from facial expressions: happiness, surprise, sadness, anger, disgust, fear (e.g. Ekman, 1982, though Ekman's own views have changed since 1982). However, even if there are a small number of biologically based emotions, the other emotions are more complex, and have interpretative components that are cognitive in nature.

HISTORICAL CONSIDERATIONS

The many idiosyncrasies of contemporary cognitive psychology are largely the product of a complex set of historical processes. Its boundaries have been determined partly by the development of psychology since it became an independent empirical science in the 1870s. For example, low-level perceptual processes, corresponding roughly to 'sensation' in the OED definition, have from the early days of psychology been studied separately from cognition. Given what has been learned about these processes, the detailed links that have been made with the underlying physiology, and the tendency towards specialization that occurs as science advances, it is both unlikely and undesirable that the study of low-level perception will be reintegrated with cognitive psychology.

168

Figure 1. *The Wason Selection Task.*
(a) *Abstract Version.* Each of the four cards below has a letter on one side and a number on the other side. Which cards need to be turned over to see if the following statement is true of the cards? If a card has a vowel on one side it has an even number on the other side.

| E | K | 2 | 7 |

(b) *Practical Reasoning Version* (Manktelow and Over, 1991). Imagine that you are a boy who has been given a rule by your mother about keeping the house tidy while she is at work. The rule is: if you tidy your room you may go out to play. You have not been seeing eye to eye with your mother lately because you think that sometimes she makes rules like this but doesn't keep to them. So you decide to record on cards what she does on the first few days after she introduces the rule. You record on one side of each card whether you tidied up your room or not, and on the other side whether your mother let you go out to play or not. Which cards would show whether the mother had broken the rule?

| I tidied my room | I did not tidy my room | Mother let me go out to play | Mother did not let me go out to play |

Cognitive Psychology and Social and Developmental Psychology

A more problematic set of divisions within psychology, from the point of view of the integrity of cognitive psychology, recognizes DEVELOPMENTAL PSYCHOLOGY and social psychology as distinct branches of the discipline, even though there are cognitive components to social behaviour, and even though one of the central concerns of developmental psychology is cognitive development. For example, common-sense suggests that language use is primarily a social behaviour. However, cognitive psychologists believe that many, if not all, aspects of language processing are best studied away from the complexities of social interaction, and that they are best explained in terms of structures and processes in the mind of an individual language user.

The gulf between social psychology and cognitive psychology is wider than that between developmental psychology and cognitive psychology. Part of the reason has been the antagonism between some members of the social and cognitive psychological communities. Some social psychologists argue that laboratory testing not only changes the

behaviour it is supposed to be investigating, but that it makes it impossible to draw useful conclusions about that behaviour. Some cognitive psychologists argue that the alternative methods of study suggested by social psychologists are not rigorous enough to produce scientific knowledge. Other cognitive psychologists, particularly in memory research, have themselves identified problems with laboratory-based studies, but argue for rigorous experimental studies in *ecologically valid* settings. However, general considerations about scientific method provide no support for the idea that phenomena are best studied in their natural settings.

The call for ecologically valid empirical methods should not be confused with arguments for what is known as 'ecological psychology'. Ecological psychology, which takes a variety of forms, claims that environmental factors should play a greater role in theories of human behaviour. Ecological psychology is antipathetic to those types of cognitive psychology that place too much emphasis on what happens in the mind. However, there need be no real disagreement between the two approaches, provided that cognitive psychologists are

169

sensitive to the richness of environmental variations, which must be mentally represented if they are to influence behaviour.

Returning to social psychology, there is, within that subdiscipline, a strong experimental tradition. Indeed, there have been bitter methodological divisions *within* social psychology. Furthermore, there is a flourishing tradition of *cognitive social psychology*, which emphasizes the role of individuals' mental processes in social behaviour. Nevertheless, even though cognitive psychology and cognitive social psychology are both responses to criticisms of behaviourism, there is little interaction between cognitive psychologists and cognitive social psychologists, and cognitive social psychology is not regarded as part of cognitive psychology.

The link between developmental psychology and cognitive psychology is closer. Developmental psychology was for a long time dominated by the ideas of Jean Piaget, whose primary concern was a theory of cognitive development (his own term was 'genetic epistemology'). Furthermore, like modern-day cognitive psychologists, Piaget was interested in the mental representations and processes that underlie cognitive skills. However, Piaget's genetic epistemology never coexisted happily with cognitive psychology, though Piaget's idea that reasoning is based on an internalized version of predicate calculus has influenced research into adult thinking and reasoning. One reason for the lack of a closer interaction between genetic epistemology and cognitive psychology was that, as cognitive psychology began to attain prominence, developmental psychologists were starting to question Piaget's ideas. Many of his empirical claims about the abilities, or more accurately the inabilities, of children of various ages were discovered to be contaminated by his unorthodox, and in retrospect unsatisfactory, empirical methods. And many of his theoretical ideas were seen to be vague, or uninterpretable, or inconsistent. Despite the welcome turning-away from what was often an uncritical acceptance of everything Piaget said, developmental psychology has retained a strong cognitive component. However, if anything it has been more strongly influenced by ideas from the philosophy of mind than by ideas from cognitive psychology. This is particularly true in work on children's theory of mind, which rose to prominence in the late 1980s. One reason why work in the philosophy of mind is important in this field is that it is often hard to determine, or even to decide how one might determine, what a child believes or how a child conceptualizes the world, for example. In the face of these difficulties, philosophical analysis is sometimes useful.

Information Theory and Human Experimental Psychology

From the 1920s to the beginning of the 1950s, BEHAVIOURISM was the dominant tradition in Anglo-Saxon psychology, and the primary focus of research was on laws of learning. These laws were assumed to apply to all 'organisms', and so were studied in rats and pigeons, which are easy to keep in the laboratory. By the beginning of the 1950s, however, ideas from the nascent study of complex computing machines began to influence psychologists. In particular, Claude Shannon's information theory suggested to Colin Cherry and Donald Broadbent new ways of thinking about information encoding and selective attention. The same theory suggested to George Miller new ideas about constraints on short-term memory, and about how language allows communication between one person and another. Behaviourists also realized the importance of language – which they termed 'verbal behaviour' – as an aspect of human behaviour that presented a challenge to the generality of the laws of learning. Skinner, the most influential behaviourist of the period, devoted a book (called *Verbal Behavior*, 1957) to an attempted demonstration of how behaviourist principles could be extended to language.

The use of information theory, together with other influences, led to a substantial body of research, which was originally dubbed 'human experimental psychology'.

For reasons to be described below, people whose primary interest was in the processes of language understanding were shortly diverted in another direction. Meanwhile, work on sensory memory, pattern recognition, memory and attention continued apace. It was this work that formed the basis of Ulric Neisser's (1967) book *Cognitive Psychology*, which popularized the term as an alternative to 'human experimental psychology', and which bears much of the responsibility for its current ubiquity.

COGNITIVE PSYCHOLOGY AND GENERATIVE GRAMMAR

George Miller, under the influence of the linguist Noam CHOMSKY, had become dissatisfied with the application of information theory to language processing. Chomsky, in addition to introducing new methods for describing regularities in the syntactic systems of natural languages, proposed a cognitive interpretation of linguistic theory. Rules discovered by linguists were held to be in the minds of language users, and used to understand and produce utterances and texts. Miller proposed a psychological theory, the Derivational Theory of Complexity, which suggested one way in which Chomsky's rules might be used in comprehension.

Although Chomsky is recognized as one of the main forces in the overthrow of behaviourism and in the initiation of the 'cognitive era' – his review of Skinner's *Verbal Behavior* had a huge rhetorical impact – the relation between psycholinguistics and cognitive psychology has always been an uneasy one. Indeed the term 'psycholinguistics' is often taken to refer primarily to psychological work on language that is influenced by ideas from linguistic theory. Mainstream cognitive psychologists, for example when they write textbooks, often prefer the term 'psychology of language'. The difference is not, however, merely in a name. In a discussion of the psychology of language one is likely to encounter notions such as *semantic network* and *spreading activation* that are common in other areas of cognitive psychology. There may be an active hostility toward, and often an insensitivity to, the issues that interest linguistic theorists. Furthermore, a discussion of the psychology of language is likely to emphasize commonalities between language processing and other cognitive processes. Psycholinguists are more likely to endorse FODOR's modularity hypothesis, and to see language processing as drawing on a special and encapsulated set of linguistic knowledge.

THE INFLUENCE OF ARTIFICIAL INTELLIGENCE

Information theory was the first set of ideas from computer science to have an impact on what was to become cognitive psychology. ARTIFICIAL INTELLIGENCE (AI) has had a more profound, and more complex, relation with the discipline. One strand of this relationship can be traced back to the first main wave of AI research, Newell, Shaw and Simon's studies of heuristic problem-solving techniques, which were intended to suggest models of human abilities. Newell et al.'s (1957) first important program, the Logic Theorem Machine (LT), scored a remarkable success when it produced a proof of a theorem in Whitehead and Russell's *Principia Mathematica* that was shorter and more elegant than the original. Principles embodied in LT and in Newell et al.'s chess playing programs were generalized in the General Problem Solver (GPS) and in later production system-based models of human problem solving (Newell and Simon, 1972). GPS's lack of success (in solving problems, rather than in elucidating principles) was attributed to the later recognized importance of domain-specific knowledge in problem solving, an idea that is readily incorporated within the production system framework, in particular in expert systems.

Within cognitive psychology Newell and Simon's work has had its greatest impact in research on problem solving. Newell (1990) subsequently proposed that the theory of

171

problem solving can be generalized to a unified theory of cognition. In particular he argued for two ideas. First, almost any cognitive 'task', and also its subtasks, can be thought of as a heuristically guided search through a space of possibilities (as problem solving can). This idea is supported by work in AI where, for example, parsing has been conceptualized as a search through the set of possible analyses for sentences for the analysis of the sentence currently being processed. Newell's second idea is that, when an impasse is reached in searching for a solution, weaker but more generally applicable techniques should be used to resolve it. Once the impasse has been resolved, the solution (in the form of a production rule), but not the details of how the solution was discovered, can be stored in long-term memory. Thus Soar, as Newell calls his 'architecture for cognition', contains both a problem-solving and a learning mechanism.

COGNITIVE PSYCHOLOGY AND COGNITIVE SCIENCE

In the late 1970s the relation between cognitive psychology and AI was further complicated by the emergence of cognitive science. Cognitive science is an interdisciplinary approach to cognition that draws primarily on ideas from cognitive psychology, artificial intelligence, linguistics and logic. It attempts to wed the concern for formal, well-specified, testable theories from the last three of these disciplines with the attention to properly psychological methods and psychological data that characterizes cognitive psychology. For many, language is the central concern of cognitive science, particularly those of its adherents who accept Fodor's notion of a LANGUAGE (or languages) OF THOUGHT – a language-like representational system (or systems) for encoding and utilizing information in the mind. However, the paradigmatically successful piece of research in cognitive science remains David Marr's (1982) study of visual processing. Indeed, so important is this work, that it has been claimed for AI and for connectionism (see below) as well as for cognitive science. One of the most important aspects of Marr's work is his identification of three levels at which a cognitive system must be analysed. First, a task analysis leads to a computational theory of what the system does, and why it does it. Second, details of the algorithm and (system of) representation used to make the computations specified by the computational theory must be determined. Third, the neural implementation has to be specified – details of the machinery on which the computations are carried out. Neurophysiologists, AI researchers and cognitive psychologists all, according to Marr, tend to be guilty of ignoring the all important level of computional theory.

In vision, unlike in some other branches of cognitive psychology, there is a real possibility, as Marr showed, of integrating detailed information about the underlying neurophysiology into a broadly psychological theory (though Marr's greatest success in this respect was at the lowest levels of visual processing which, at least arguably, lie outside the domain of cognitive psychology). In the psychology of language, for example, almost nothing is known about neural mechanisms at the level of individual cells. However, much is known about the neuropsychology (as opposed to neurophysiology) of language. Traditional neuropsychology focuses on brain lesions, and tends to describe the cognitive impairments they produce in relatively unsophisticated terms. Modern cognitive approaches sometimes eschew information about lesion sites altogether, but take a more analytic approach to patterns of deficit, and in particular focus on double dissociations, in which each member of a pair of cognitive functions is, in different patients, destroyed while the other is preserved. Cognitive neuropsychology has been particularly important in informing models of word identification, and it may yet prove the downfall of the connectionist models (see below) that have proved so successful in explaining word identification in normal adults.

COGNITIVE PSYCHOLOGY AND CONNECTIONISM

CONNECTIONISM is another development of the 1980s whose relation to cognitive psychology remains problematic. Connectionist theories model the learning and performance of psychological tasks (not necessarily cognitive) in terms of interactions between a large number of simple interconnected neuron-like units that exchange activation until they settle into a stable state, which is interpreted as a response to the current state of the world. Learning in connectionist systems is a process of making very many small adjustments to the strengths of the interconnections between the units, using a technique called *back propagation*. The adjustments are made on the basis of the difference between the system's actual response to an input and the correct response. There are connectionist models of processes, such as word identification, that are traditionally studied in cognitive psychology, though some would argue that, with its emphasis on COMPUTATIONAL MODELS, connectionism is cognitive science (or even AI). Indeed connectionism has been described as challenging the traditional symbolic paradigm of AI.

Connectionist models respond to statistical regularities in the world. They may appear to follow rules, but because they are basically associationist, it has been argued that they cannot operate successfully in complex domains, such as natural language syntax, where the descriptive power of (at least) a phrase-structure grammar is needed. On this view, connectionist systems cope well with, for example, mappings between the spellings and sounds of English words because those mappings are just sets of statistical regularities. They have problems, for example, in parsing English sentences because sentence structure is described by rules, not statistical regularities.

Even if cognitive science has not resulted in the interdisciplinary research teams that were once envisaged, much of the best work in cognitive psychology draws on ideas from related disciplines in modelling the mental mechanisms, representations and processes that underlie our cognitive abilities. And there is a trend toward better formulated theories, though this is partly a reflection of the maturity of the discipline. The tendency remains, however, for cognitive psychologists to be relatively weak on theory and over-zealous on data collection. There is, for example, almost nobody who could reasonably be described as a theoretical cognitive psychologist. Before the advent of connectionism, many theories in cognitive psychology were presented in the form of box diagrams, in which neither the contents of the boxes nor the nature of the interconnections was well-specified. Furthermore, theoretical ideas that have been borrowed from other disciplines have often proved problematic. Notoriously, the concept of a *schema* (originally borrowed by AI from psychology!) has been used to 'explain' the fact that structured knowledge in long-term memory is vitally important in many cognitive tasks. Unfortunately, the notion of a schema is so vague that it imposes almost no constraints on how knowledge is organized. Furthermore, many researchers have failed to distinguish between describing the structure of particular bits of information in memory, and contributing to a theory of how knowledge is organized.

The lack of theoretical sophistication, together with the fact that some – though a diminishing proportion – of findings in cognitive psychology are obvious or commonsensical, has led to its positive achievements being underestimated in neighbouring disciplines. The best cognitive psychologists have an eye for a good problem and for a good experimental paradigm, even if there are, often lengthy, disputes about how data should be interpreted. However, one of the problems with good paradigms in cognitive psychology is that once they are discovered they are overworked, with rapidly diminishing returns.

THE METHODOLOGY OF COGNITIVE PSYCHOLOGY

Most cognitive psychologists prefer to investigate cognitive processes using tightly controlled experiments rather than, say, naturalistic observational studies. Depending on the aspect of cognition under investigation, subjects will be set a task to perform, their responses will be recorded (classified as right or wrong, if appropriate), and perhaps timed. More controversially, the subjects might be asked to 'think aloud' as they perform the task. The methodology of cognitive psychology can be illustrated with two pieces of work widely regarded as important within the discipline. However, it should be borne in mind that these studies are only illustrative, and that the amount of research carried out in cognitive psychology is enormous.

In the first piece of work, Roger Shepard (Shepard and Metzler, 1971) showed pairs of pictures of simple 3-D objects to people and asked them to judge whether the objects were identical or mirror images. He found that the time to make the judgment was directly proportional to the angle through which one of the images had to be rotated so that it could be superimposed (in the case of identical objects) on the other. This finding has obvious implications for the kinds of representations and processes used by subjects to perform such tasks. However, the exact sense in which people perform 'mental rotations' remains unclear. In the second piece of work, Anne Treisman (Treisman and Gelade, 1980) asked subjects to find specified items in two-dimensional displays containing up to 30 items. If they had to pick out a blue letter from green letters or an 'S' from 'T's, the time was approximately constant, no matter how many items were in the display. However, if the subjects had to pick out a blue 'S' from a mixed display of green 'S's and green and blue 'T's, the time taken increased in an approximately linear manner with the number of other items in the display. These results suggest that the simple discriminations can be carried out by processes that work on the whole display at once, no matter how many items are in it, whereas the more complicated discriminations have to be carried out by examining each item in turn.

Although the mechanics of these experiments is easy to grasp, the point of them may not be, without the requisite background knowledge. Philosophers (and linguists) often misunderstand what cognitive psychologists are trying to do. Some of the reasons why can be illustrated using a different example: pronoun interpretation. Philosophers find little of interest in a 'text' such as:

John went into the room. He sat down.

In their study of pronouns they focus on cases in which there are known difficulties in providing a systematic account of meaning, such as the infamous 'donkey sentences', for example:

Every farmer who owns a donkey beats it.

Such sentences may be very rare, and they may, for all philosophers know, be very difficult to understand. All that is important is that clever people who think about them for long enough can agree on what their meaning should be. Philosophers can ignore sentences of the first kind, because they can see how to assign them meaning systematically. However, even if psychologists can also think of a mechanism that can assign meanings to such sentences, they have to determine whether it is psychologically plausible, and whether it is compatible with what is known, empirically, about how pronouns are interpreted. Furthermore, philosophers may dismiss as ill-formed 'texts' such as:

Young Toby fights every playtime, but they never lead to injuries.

Psychologists, on the other hand, have to ask if they cause comprehension problems; if, for example, they are more difficult to understand than corresponding well-formed texts:

Young Toby gets into fights every play-time, but they never lead to injuries

or what judgments unsophisticated subjects make about them. There has been, since the advent of cognitive science in the late 1970s, a narrowing of the gap between the interests of formal semanticists and cognitive psychologists. A comparison of the concerns of Hans Kamp's (1981) discourse representation theory, or Jon Barwise and John Perry's (1983) situation semantics, and the mental models theory of text comprehension (Garnham, 1987; Johnson-Laird, 1983) makes this point. Nevertheless, psychological concerns and philosophical ones do not always coincide, and without an understanding of why this lack of coincidence arises, philosophers and psychologists are likely to dismiss each other's work unnecessarily and to the detriment of progress in understanding cognition.

PHILOSOPHY OF COGNITIVE PSYCHOLOGY

Some philosophers may be cognitive scientists, others concern themselves with the philosophy of cognitive psychology and cognitive science. Indeed, since the inauguration of cognitive science these disciplines have attracted much attention from certain philosophers of mind. The attitudes of these philosophers and their reception by psychologists vary considerably. Many cognitive psychologists have little interest in philosophical issues. Cognitive scientists are, in general, more receptive.

Fodor, because of his early involvement in sentence processing research, is taken seriously by many psycholinguists. His modularity thesis is directly relevant to questions about the interplay of different types of knowledge in language understanding. His innateness hypothesis, however, is generally regarded as unhelpful, and his prescription that cognitive psychology is primarily about PROPOSITIONAL ATTITUDES is widely ignored. DENNETT's recent work on CONSCIOUSNESS treats a topic that is highly controversial, but his detailed discussion of psychological research

findings has enhanced his credibility among psychologists. In general, however, psychologists are happy to get on with their work without philosophers telling them about their 'mistakes'.

Connectionism has provoked a somewhat different reaction among philosophers. Some – mainly those who, for other reasons, were disenchanted with traditional AI research – have welcomed this new approach to understanding brain and behaviour. They have used the success, apparent or otherwise, of connectionist research, to bolster their arguments for a particular approach to explaining behaviour. Whether this *neuro-philosophy* will eventually be widely accepted is a difficult question. One of its main dangers is succumbing to a form of reductionism that most cognitive scientists, and many philosophers of mind, find incoherent.

See also INNATENESS; MODULARITY; PSYCHOLOGY AND PHILOSOPHY.

BIBLIOGRAPHY

Barwise, J., and Perry, J. 1983. *Situations and Attitudes*. Cambridge, MA: MIT Press/Bradford Books.

Ekman, P. 1982. Emotion in the Human Face. Cambridge University Press.

Garnham, A. 1987. *Mental Models as Representations of Discourse and Text*. Chichester, Sussex: Ellis Horwood.

Johnson-Laird, P.N. 1983. *Mental Models: Towards a Cognitive Science of Language, Inference, and Consciousness*. Cambridge University Press.

Kamp, H. 1981. A theory of truth and semantic representation. In *Formal Methods in the Study of Language*, ed. J. Groenendijk, T. Janssen, and M. Stokof. Amsterdam: Mathematical Centre Tracts, pp. 255–78.

Marr, D. 1982. *Vision: A Computational Investigation into the Human Representation and Processing of Visual Information*. San Francisco: Freeman.

Manktelow, K.I., and Over, D.E. 1991. Social roles and utilities in reasoning with deontic conditionals. *Cognition*, 39, 85–105.

Neisser, U. 1967. *Cognitive Psychology*. New York: Appleton-Century-Crofts.

Newell, A. 1990. *Unified Theories of Cognition: The 1987 William James Lectures.* Cambridge, MA.: Harvard University Press.

Newell, A., Shaw, J.C., and Simon, H.A. 1957. Empirical explorations with the Logic Theory Machine: A case study in heuristics. *Proceedings of the Western Joint Computer Conference,* 15, 218–239.

Newell, A., and Simon, H.A. 1972. *Human Problem Solving.* Englewood Cliffs, N.J.: Prentice-Hall.

Shepard, R.N., and Metzler, J. 1971. Mental rotation of three-dimensional objects. *Science,* 171, 701–703.

Skinner, B.F. 1957. *Verbal Behavior.* New York: Appleton-Century-Crofts.

Treisman, A., and Gelade, G. 1980. A feature-integration theory of attention. *Cognitive Psychology,* 12, 97–136.

ALAN GARNHAM

computational models of mind The hypothesis driving most of modern cognitive science is simple enough to state: *the mind is a computer.* What are the consequences for the philosophy of mind? This question acquires heightened interest and complexity from new forms of computation employed in recent cognitive theory.

Cognitive science has traditionally been based upon *symbolic computation*: systems of rules for manipulating structures built up of tokens of different symbol types. (This classical kind of computation is a direct outgrowth of mathematical logic; *see* ARTIFICIAL INTELLIGENCE; TURING). Since the mid-1980s, however, cognitive theory has increasingly employed *connectionist computation*: the spread of numerical activation across interconnected networks of abstract processing units (*see* CONNECTIONISM). Symbolic and connectionist computation respectively constitute computational accounts of idealized mental and neuronal processes; thus the interaction of these two forms of computation in contemporary cognitive theory provides, at the very least, food for thought concerning the mind–body problem.

How can the mind perform in accordance with epistemic constraints? How can it possess unbounded competence, in reasoning, arithmetic, grammar? How can abstract mental elements arise from a physical substrate, and interact causally with the physical world? Approaches to answering these fundamental questions can be derived from the hypothesis that the mind/brain is a computer: for computers are well understood, physically realized abstract systems that can be endowed with unbounded competence, and whose function can respect epistemic constraints. The answers to the fundamental questions differ, however, depending on the *kind* of computer the mind/brain is alleged to be: a symbolic computer, a connectionist computer, or some mixture of the two.

(1) VARIETIES OF COMPUTATION: ALTERNATIVE COMPUTATIONAL ABSTRACTIONS

Different types of computation provide different kinds of computational abstractions to serve the role of mentalist theoretical constructs. These abstractions, which will be denoted 'α', can be considered in light of the following criteria for assessing their adequacy in meeting the needs of cognitive theory.

Desiderata for Mentalist Abstracta α

(1) *Computational sufficiency:* α must be part of a system with sufficient computational power to compute classes of functions possessing the basic characteristics of cognitive functions. Frequently attested such characteristics include: unbounded competence or 'productivity'; recursion; systematicity; Turing Universality; structure-sensitivity; concept and language learnability; statistical sensitivity.

(2) *Empirical adequacy:* α must enable the construction of accounts of human competence and performance which explain the empirical facts of human cognition acknowledged by COGNITIVE PSYCHOLOGY, linguistics (*see* CHOMSKY), etc.

(3) *Physical [neural] realizability*: α must be realizable in a physical [neural] system

These criteria together pose *the central paradox of cognition*. On the one hand, especially in higher cognitive domains like reasoning and language, cognition seems essentially a matter of structure processing. On the other hand, in perceptual domains, and in the details and variance of human performance, cognition seems very much a matter of statistical processing; and the underlying neural mechanisms seem thoroughly engaged in numerical processing. Thus these criteria seem on the one hand to demand computational abstractions α which provide symbolic structure processing, and on the other, abstractions α which provide numerical and statistical processing. And, indeed, contemporary cognitive theory relies on two types of computation, one addressing the structural, the other the numerical/statistical, side of the central paradox.

Symbolic Computation and the Classical Computational Theory of Mind

In symbolic computation, the abstractions provided are symbols (α_{sym}) and rules (α_{rul}). According to the classical computational theory of mind, MENTAL REPRESENTATIONS are symbol structures, and mental processes consist in the manipulation of these representations according to symbolic algorithms, based on symbolic rules.

The symbolic computational abstractions $\alpha_{sym\&rul}$ fare admirably with respect to the structural side of the criteria of computational sufficiency and empirical adequacy. Physical computers demonstrate the physical realizability of symbolic computation. But the statistical side of computational sufficiency and empirical adequacy are essentially ignored by pure symbolic computation, and little if any insight has arisen from the symbolic theory concerning whether, and how, it can be effectively neurally realized.

Local Connectionist Computation

'Local connectionist models' are connectionist networks in which each unit corresponds to a symbol or symbol structure (perhaps an entire proposition). Typically, the connections in such networks, and the computations performed in each connectionist unit, are carefully hand-constructed to implement specific symbolic rules.

The abstractions provided by this computational framework are the individual unit's activity ($\alpha_{ind.act}$) and the individual connection ($\alpha_{ind.cnx}$). These function very much like the symbol and rule of symbolic computation. Indeed, this kind of connectionism has strong affinities to traditional symbolic computation. It is the kind of network proposed by McCulloch and Pitts (1943; reprinted in Boden, 1990) which historically contributed to the development of symbolic computation; it is intimately related to contemporary research in the design of algorithms with 'fine-grained parallelism'. It offers some of the same kinds of computational sufficiency as symbolic computation, but with significant limitations. These networks often employ units which are discrete-state machines, with discrete messages passed along connections. However, genuine numerical processing can also be used; certain kinds of statistical inference can then be performed.

Neural realizability has been a main driving force in much of this research, through Jerome Feldman's '100 step rule': these networks are typically designed to perform their computations in roughly the same number of steps or 'cycles' available to neurons – 100. The plausibility of these networks as simplified neural models depends on the hypothesis that symbols and rules are more or less localized to individual neurons and synapses (*see* Feldman's article in Nadel et al., 1989, which includes references on local connectionist models).

PDP Connectionist Computation and an Eliminativist Theory

A different style of connectionist modelling is the 'parallel distributed processing (PDP)' approach. Here, the computational abstractions offered to replace symbols and rules are patterns of numerical activity over groups of units ($\alpha_{pat.act}$), and patterns of weights over groups of connections ($\alpha_{pat.cnx}$). Crucially, a given unit or connection participates in many such patterns, which may be simultaneously present (multiple patterns being superimposed upon each other).

Whereas local connectionist models typically rely explicitly on symbolic rules and representations which are *implemented* in individual units and connections, PDP cognitive models typically strive to *eliminate* such symbolic elements. As a result, such models usually do not provide much (if anything) in the way of structure-sensitive processing. Rather than implementing explicitly stated rules through hand-designed connections and units, PDP modellers typically put the necessary knowledge into the connection weights by training the network, using a PDP learning procedure, on examples of the desired performance. The resulting weights generally constitute some sort of complex statistical analysis of the training data. PDP algorithms are heavily numerical.

The strengths and weaknesses of the abstractions $\alpha_{pat.act\&cnx}$ of PDP computation are almost exactly the mirror image of those of symbolic computation. Computational and empirical sufficiency is greatest with respect to the statistical, and weakest with respect to the structural, side of the central paradox. With respect to most of the specific criteria listed in 'computational sufficiency', PDP computation (in the basic form considered now) is quite limited. On the other hand, while much remains in obscurity with regard to the neural realizability of PDP models, this form of computation has for the first time provided a bridge for fruitful interaction between computational cognitive modelling and neuroscience.

An Integrated Connectionist/Symbolic Cognitive Architecture

The complementary strengths and weaknesses of symbolic and PDP connectionist computation have increasingly led cognitive scientists to attempt to combine the two computational frameworks. Most often this takes the form of 'hybrid architectures' in which the overall computational system has two separate components, one symbolic, the other connectionist. The relation between these components is that of being two parts of a common whole.

In an alternative, more integrative, approach, a symbolic and a PDP connectionist component are each two *descriptions* of a single, unitary, computational system; the symbolic and the connectionist are related as higher- and lower-level descriptions of a common system (*see* SUPERVENIENCE). This is achieved by structuring PDP networks so that the computational abstractions $\alpha_{pat.act\&cnx}$ which they provide – activation and connection *patterns* – are simultaneously describable as the computational abstractions $\alpha_{sym\&rul}$ of symbolic computation – symbol structures and rules.

This 'integrated connectionist/symbolic (ICS)' computational framework is presented in Smolensky, Legendre, and Miyata (1994). The structuring of PDP computation which enables the higher-level structure of activation and connection patterns to be analysable as symbol structures and rules is achieved by applying the mathematics of tensor calculus. The distributed pattern of activity **s** realizing a symbol structure is a superposition (sum) of distributed patterns c_i, each of which realizes one of the symbolic constituents of the structure: $s = \Sigma_i c_i$. The pattern c_i which realizes each constituent has the following structure: it is a distributed pattern f_i encoding a symbolic part multiplied by another distributed pattern r_i encoding the role played by the part in the structure as a whole. The multiplication used is the tensor product $\otimes$; $c_i = f_i \otimes r_i$ [Given two activity patterns $f = (0.2, -0.3)$ and $r = (0.1, 0.5)$, their tensor product is simply $f \otimes r = (0.02, 0.05, -0.03, -0.15)$: the elements of the pattern $f \otimes r$ are all numerical products of one element of f and one element of r.]

Such 'tensor product representations' enable distributed patterns of activity to realize much of symbolic representation, including recursion. These representations can be processed by simple connectionist networks, 'tensor networks', in which the connections have a higher-level tensorial

Representation	Processing	Combined
α_{sym} = symbol structure	α_{rul} = symbolic rule	$\alpha_{sym\&rul}$
$\alpha_{pat.act}$ = pattern of activity	$\alpha_{pat.cnx}$ = pattern of connection weights	$\alpha_{pat.act\&cnx}$
$\alpha_{ind.act}$ = individual unit activity	$\alpha_{ind.cnx}$ = individual connection weight	$\alpha_{ind.act\&cnx}$

Table 1. Summary of Computational Abstractions

structure which comports with that of the representations. These networks can provably compute specific symbolic functions, including recursive functions. Since it will be referred to several times below, a tensor network which computes a symbolic function f will be denoted N_f. Such a network can be described at multiple computational levels (cf. §2). At the lowest level, it is a set of units and connections, and processing is simple spread of activation. The distributed activity and connections are globally structured in such a way that they can be given a formal higher-level description using tensor calculus. The elements of this description, in turn, can be precisely redescribed as symbols and rules. The function f computed (but, as discussed shortly, not the means of computing it) can be given a formal symbolic specification.

Connectionist computation is *not* used in ICS merely to implement symbolic computation (cf. §3). For example, ICS provides a new formalism for grammar, 'Harmonic Grammar', according to which the linguistic structures of a language that are grammatical are exactly those that optimally satisfy a set of conflicting parallel soft constraints of varying strength: these soft constraints constitute the grammar. The strengths of constraints may be numerical, or the constraints may simply be ranked by strength, each constraint stronger than all weaker constraints combined. This latter grammar formalism, Optimality Theory, developed by Prince and Smolensky (1994), turns out to significantly strengthen the theory of the phonological component of grammar: it becomes possible to eliminate delicately ordered sequences of symbolic rewrite-rules in favour of parallel soft con-

straints of great generality. These constraints often turn out to be universal (applying in all languages): languages differ principally in the relative strengths they assign the constraints. By formally realizing aspects of symbolic computation in lower-level PDP connectionist computation, ICS leads to new grammatical theories which strengthen the theory of universal grammar, enhancing the explanatory adequacy of linguistic theory.

In addition to this evidence for its empirical adequacy, a number of formal results argue the computational adequacy of the ICS framework. ICS unifies the computational abstractions of symbolic and PDP computation, summarized in Table 1, in order to confront effectively both the structural and the numerical/statistical sides of the central paradox of cognition.

Other important abstractions α which can be treated computationally but which are not discussed here include propositions and goals/desires (*see* PROPOSITIONAL ATTITUDES) and images (*see* IMAGERY).

(2) VARIETIES OF COMPUTATIONALISM: ALTERNATIVE ROLES FOR COMPUTATIONAL ABSTRACTIONS

Having distinguished several different types of computational abstractions α which are made available by various kinds of computation, we now turn to consideration of various roles a given computational abstraction α may play in a theory of mind.

Computation is a complex notion, and different aspects of it can figure in formulating the hypothesis *cognition is computation*. Elaborating on a notion of computational *level* articulated by Marr (1982), we can

179

Computational Level l		Computationalist Hypothesis at level l concerning abstractions α (and cognitive process P)
Description	Function	$CH_{fun}(\alpha)$: P can be described as instantiating a function f, mapping inputs to outputs, specifiable in terms of α
Explanation	Proof	$CH_{prf}(\alpha)$: That P instantiates f can be explained by proofs based on properties of P stated in terms of α
Causation	Algorithm	$CH_{alg}(\alpha)$: P can be described via an algorithm A, stated in terms of α, which computes f
Realization	Implementation	$CH_{imp}(\alpha)$: The spatiotemporal structure of A, stated over α, corresponds to that of its physical realization

Table 2. Summary of Computationalist Hypotheses

distinguish different members of a family of computationalist hypotheses, summarized in table 2. Each computationalist hypothesis $CH_l(\alpha)$ asserts that some cognitive process P can be given a computational account at level l in terms of a class of abstract elements α. We focus on $\alpha = \alpha_{sym\&rul}$, and abbreviate $CH_l(\alpha_{sym\&rul})$ by CH_l.

CH_{fun}: Description of cognitive behaviour via function specification
The weakest hypothesis, $CH_{fun}(\alpha)$, asserts only that the cognitive process P can be analysed (using α) as a function mapping certain inputs to certain outputs. If the abstract elements α in question are $\alpha_{sym\&rul}$, as we assume for the rest of §2, then $CH_{fun}(\alpha_{sym\&rul}) = CH_{fun}$ claims that P is a process which takes symbol structures as inputs, that P produces symbol structures as outputs, and that the function f from input structure to output structure that P instantiates can be specified, somehow, using symbol manipulation rules.

For example, CH_{fun} holds of the following inference process P (*see* RATIONALITY): an input is a REPRESENTATION (as formulae) of a set of propositions, and an output is a corresponding representation of a specified set of propositions which follow from the input propositions, according to some criteria specified over the formulae.

To suggest how CH_{fun} might fail, consider a perceptual process P, where the inputs are sensory stimuli and the output is a percept. Such inputs and outputs might well fail to be satisfactorily analysed as structures of discrete symbols, in which case the corresponding function f could not possibly be specified via symbol manipulation rules. (Certain 'cognitive linguistic' theories claim that for linguistic processes, input and/or output representations must be analysed as non-discrete structures: something more like images.)

CH_{prf}: Explanation of cognitive behaviour via proof
Whereas CH_{fun} makes the purely descriptive claim that P instantiates a function f specified using symbols and rules, CH_{prf} further claims that some properties p of P can be characterized using symbols and rules such that it can be proved from p that the output resulting from a given input i is indeed $f(i)$: these properties provide some explanation of how it is that P instantiates f.

The network N_f introduced in §1 illustrates one way CH_{prf} can hold. P is realized in a connectionist network whose connection weights possess tensor-algebraic structure capturable in some mathematical property p; and from p it follows that when an input activity pattern is given to the network which is tensor-product realization of a symbol structure i, then an output pattern is produced which realizes $f(i)$ (where f is a symbolically specified function). The property p explains how P instantiates f.

CH_{prf} might fail, even when CH_{fun} holds (this is a kind of EPIPHENOMENALISM with respect to $\alpha_{sym\&rul}$). Suppose a connectionist network has been trained on appropriately encoded examples of input/output pairs of a symbolically specified function f, and that the net eventually learns f (i.e. CH_{fun} holds). Typically, (a) no analysis of the connection weights can identify any properties from which it may be proved that the net computes f; and (b) it cannot be proved that f is guaranteed to be learned by the connectionist learning algorithm. Then there is no evidence that the special situation CH_{prf} demands actually holds.

CH_{alg}: Abstract causal account of cognitive processing via algorithms

In classical symbolic cognitive theory, CH_{prf} is typically known to hold because in fact a stronger hypothesis, CH_{alg} holds: a symbolic *algorithm* characterizes P, and this algorithm A can be proved to compute f.

For example, suppose P can be characterized as following the steps of some theorem-proving algorithm A: then it can be proved that the function f which P instantiates maps input propositions to valid consequences. Or suppose P follows the steps of a rewrite-rule grammar for a language L: by sequentially rewriting strings of sym-bols, the rules provably generate all and only the strings ('sentences') of L, so P provably instantiates a function f which (say) takes as input a phrase category label and generates as output an example string of that category. Such examples could be multiplied almost without bound, since traditional symbolic cognitive science has for decades been successfully producing symbolic algorithms A for computing interesting cognitive functions f; each of these provides a process for which CH_{alg} holds. (*See* Newell and Simon, 1976, reprinted in Boden, 1990.)

CH_{alg} can fail even though CH_{fun} holds. The network N_f takes an input activity pattern which realizes a symbol structure i and, in one step, directly computes the output activity pattern which realizes the structure $f(i)$. 'In one step' means that the input activity flows from the input units through a single set of connections to the output units, which immediately then contain the output activation pattern. There is no symbolic algorithm which describes how N_f computes its output structure from its input structure. There exists a traditional symbolic algorithm for computing f which sequentially performs primitive symbolic operations such as extracting elements from lists or trees, comparing tokens to see if they are of the same type, and concatenating smaller lists or trees together to form larger structures. But such algorithms do *not* describe how N_f performs its computation: CH_{alg} fails. That f is computed by N_f is not a mystery, however: this is provable from the structure of N_f's connection weights, as discussed above: CH_{prf} holds.

CH_{imp}: Physical realization of cognitive systems via implementation

The distinction between the algorithmic level and the implementation level can be stated in terms of the properties of P available at each level of description. The level of physical implementation involves properties such as the actual time required to compute output from input; the actual physical location of computational elements; the actual material of which the computing device is constructed, and the physical states and causal processes which realize the computational states and processes. The algorithmic level provides a more abstract causal account of P: instead of actual time to compute the output, we have the number of primitive steps of computation required; instead of the actual physical location of computational elements (e.g. symbols), we have 'locations' in an abstract data structure; instead of physical causation leading from one physical state to the next, we have abstract causation in which primitive steps in an algorithm lead – by unexplained means – from one computational state to the next.

When $CH_{alg}(\alpha)$ holds, the stronger hypothesis $CH_{imp}(\alpha)$ can be formulated: the abstract causal structure of the algorithm A corresponds to the *physical* causal structure of the device realizing the process P. This means that there is a direct one-to-one correspondence between primitive steps in an algorithm and physical events, between abstract locations and physical locations, etc.

Traditional electronic computers running a program for a symbolic algorithm provide an example in which CH_{imp} holds: at any given moment during computation, it can be said of each symbol and each rule in the algorithm exactly which physical location in the computer's memory 'holds' the symbol – exactly what part of the physical state of the hardware physically realizes the symbol or rule.

To illustrate a case when CH_{imp} fails, but CH_{alg} holds, consider a direct physical implementation of 'Tensor Product Production System' (Dolan and Smolensky, 1989), a connectionist network which realizes a symbolic algorithm in which production rules are sequentially applied to manipulate a working memory storing triples of symbols. The reason CH_{imp} fails is that the symbols in working memory are all superimposed on top of each other, so that a given connectionist processing unit participates in the representation of many symbols. There is no one-to-one correspondence between abstract locations of symbols in structures and physical locations in the device. (While $CH_{imp}(\alpha_{sym\&rul})$ fails, CH_{imp} $(\alpha_{ind.act\&cnx})$ holds, as we now discuss.)

(3) IMPLICATIONS FOR THE PHILOSOPHY OF MIND

Table 3 summarizes the consequences of the various computational theories from §1 for the various computationalist hypotheses CH_l from §2: shown are the abstractions α for which each CH_l holds in each theory.

Symbolic and Local Connectionist Theory: The Success of Symbolic Computationalism
Commitment to CH_{alg} – the existence of algorithms stated as rules for manipulating symbol structures – is the heart of the symbolic theory of mind. In philosophical terms, the symbolic story is that elements of a LANGUAGE OF THOUGHT – symbolic constituents of beliefs, desires, and the like – have causal roles in the functioning of the mind: there is a causal story to be told, an algorithm, about how these symbolic constituents 'push each other around', through the mediation of rules. For instance, if the rules are taken to be valid rules of inference, then their operation on symbolic belief structures will be truth-preserving. If the rules are ones for generating grammatical sentences, or for arithmetic manipulation of numerals, then their operation will provide unbounded grammatical or arithmetic competence. In many parts of cognitive science outside philosophy – notably artificial intelligence, psychological modelling, and computational linguistics – the main theoretical activity of symbolic theory has been the development of rule-based symbol-processing algorithms to compute cognitive functions.

With the validity of CH_{alg} in this theory comes the validity of the weaker hypotheses

Level	Symbolic	Local Connectionist	PDP Connectionist	Integrated (ICS)
CH_{fun}	$\alpha_{sym\&rul}$	$\alpha_{sym\&rul}, \alpha_{ind.act\&cnx}$	Input/output: $\alpha_{pat.act}$ Function: –	$\alpha_{sym\&rul}, \alpha_{pat.act\&cnx}$
CH_{prf}	$\alpha_{sym\&rul}$	$\alpha_{sym\&rul}, \alpha_{ind.act\&cnx}$	–	$\alpha_{sym\&rul}, \alpha_{pat.act\&cnx}$
CH_{alg}	$\alpha_{sym\&rul}$	$\alpha_{sym\&rul}, \alpha_{ind.act\&cnx}$	$\alpha_{ind.act\&cnx}$	$\alpha_{ind.act\&cnx}$
CH_{imp}	–	$\alpha_{sym\&rul}, \alpha_{ind.act\&cnx}$	$\alpha_{ind.act\&cnx}$	$\alpha_{ind.act\&cnx}$

Table 3. Summary of Computational Theories and Computationalism

CH_{fun} and CH_{prf}: from the existence of (provably correct) symbolic algorithms come the existence of proofs that the computational system actually computes the cognitive function $f(CH_{prf})$ as well as a symbolic way of specifying f directly via the algorithm, if no more perspicuous specification can be given.

That symbolic computation can be physically realized is important, but a commitment to CH_{imp} is not part of the symbolic theory of mind: there is no claim that the brain, like a traditional computer, will have separate locations for each symbol and rule. More than an absence of commitment, in fact, the symbolic theory is essentially silent on the matter of its physical realization in the human case.

Local connectionist theory, like symbolic theory, entails that CH_{alg} holds, provided we admit the corresponding parallel algorithms into the class of symbolic algorithms. Since individual units and connections correspond quite directly to symbol structures and rules, these parallel algorithms provide a new sort of rule-based symbol manipulation. As in symbolic theory, CH_{fun} and CH_{prf} typically also hold. In addition, under the typical assumption that a unit corresponds to a physical neuron (or small distinct group of neurons), CH_{imp} also holds. Thus every computationalist hypothesis holds of $\alpha_{sym\&rul}$, as well as $\alpha_{ind.act\&cnx}$.

PDP Connectionist Theory: The Failure of Symbolic Computationalism

At its most eliminativist, the PDP connectionist theory of mind denies that *any* of the computationalist hypotheses are valid with respect to the abstractions $\alpha_{sym\&rul}$. Even the inputs and outputs of cognitive functions, the extreme position would claim, must be treated as graded, non-discrete, patterns of activity: even the weakest hypothesis, CH_{fun}, fails with respect to discrete symbolic structures.

With respect to non-symbolic computational abstractions, however, certain of the computationalist hypotheses hold in the PDP theory, although the story is more complicated than for the symbolic view.

Semantically interpretable inputs and outputs of cognitive functions are defined over distributed patterns of activity ($\alpha_{pat.act}$). A typical PDP network does not allow a semantic characterization of the function f computed: $CH_{fun}(\alpha_{pat.act})$ fails. Except for the simplest (feedforward) networks, the function f cannot even be specified in terms of individual unit activities: $CH_{fun}(\alpha_{ind.act})$ fails. The failure of $CH_{fun}(\alpha)$ entails the failure of $CH_{prf}(\alpha)$. PDP networks are algorithms defined over individual activities and connections $\alpha_{ind.act\&cnx}$, a lower level of description than the pattern level $\alpha_{pat.act}$ where semantic interpretation occurs: $CH_{alg}(\alpha_{ind.act\&cnx})$ holds. The most straightforward neural realization of a PDP network identifies each unit with a neuron and each connection with a synapse; in this case, $CH_{imp}(\alpha_{ind.act\&cnx})$ also holds. The same is true under the more typical assumption that each connectionist unit corresponds to a (distinct) group of neurons.

The failure of PDP theory to satisfy $CH_{prf}(\alpha)$ for any kind of abstraction α can be viewed as a failure of that theory to offer strong *explanations* of cognitive behaviour.

ICS Theory: A New Explanatory Strategy

In the ICS theory, networks such as N_f provide a story intermediate between the symbolic and the eliminativist PDP. With respect to $\alpha_{sym\&rul}$, CH_{fun} and CH_{prf} both hold: the inputs, outputs, and function f computed all have a symbolic characterization, and proofs that the network computes f rely crucially on symbolic abstractions. However, CH_{alg} (and CH_{imp}) fail: at the level of algorithm (or implementation), symbolic abstractions do not figure. Instead, the story is the same as for PDP theory: $CH_{alg}(\alpha)$ (and $CH_{imp}(\alpha)$) hold for $\alpha = \alpha_{ind.act\&cnx}$. And, because of the tensor-algebraic structure of activity and connection patterns in ICS, $CH_{fun}(\alpha)$ and $CH_{prf}(\alpha)$ hold not just of $\alpha = \alpha_{sym\&rul}$, but also of $\alpha = \alpha_{pat.act\&cnx}$: symbols and rules are realized as distributed patterns of activity and connections.

While both the symbolic and ICS stories explain how cognitive functions get computed, they differ crucially. The symbolic story derives its explanation from the causal roles of symbols and rules, captured in algorithms: $CH_{alg}(\alpha_{sym\&rul})$ *holds*. In the ICS story, however, $CH_{alg}(\alpha_{sym\&rul})$ *fails*: it is not in virtue of *algorithmic* or causal structure that symbolic functions get computed. Rather, it is a more abstract tensorial structure present in the network which enables proofs and explanations of how f gets computed. This structure resides in the global properties of activity patterns and connections, not in the spatio-temporal interactions which are manifest in algorithms.

In other words, in ICS, symbols and rules have crucial *explanatory* roles, but no *causal* roles. There is no magic here: symbols and rules are realized in lower-level activities and connections which themselves have causal roles: $CH_{alg}(\alpha_{ind.act\&cnx})$ holds. But these lower-level processing algorithms cannot be 'pulled up' to the higher level: symbols and rules have no causal roles *in their own right* – in stark contrast to the symbolic theory.

Other Issues

Besides computationalism, several other issues are at stake in the question of which kinds of computational abstractions provide appropriate models for the mind/brain.

One is the problem of the semantic relation between internal mental representations and their external referents (*see* CONTENT; INTENTIONALITY). If mental representations are built of continuous connectionist activity or connection patterns rather than discrete symbols or rules, then the relevant referents ought to be continuous properties quite different from traditional discrete propositions (*see* Haugeland's chapter in Ramsey et al., 1991). The functional roles in the overall computational system of connectionist as opposed to symbolic representations seem quite different (*see* FUNCTIONALISM). If representations are constructed through connectionist learning, then their functional roles may need to be understood through their adaptational roles (i.e. in evolutionary terms).

A number of questions concerning cognition can be phrased: how can we explain the goodness of fit between adaptive, intelligent agents and their environments? The intricate structure of the linguistic environment of the child is remarkably matched by ultimate adult linguistic competence; the rational adult's behaviour is remarkably attuned to the truth-relations between propositions about the environment. Traditional symbolic cognitive theory has been focused on those environmental regularities that are heavily structural. PDP theory redirects attention to environmental regularities that are statistical, and contributes to understanding how adaptive agents can become successfully attuned to such regularities. ICS theory, in turn, challenges us to address new regularities where structure and statistics, discrete and continuous, merge.

Finally, discussions of the mind–body problem, especially those concerning various IDENTITY THEORIES, often presuppose a high degree of discord between the natural kinds of mentalist psychology and those of neuroscience. This presumption may be quite mistaken. Computational cognitive theory proposes to analyse both the mind and the brain as kinds of computers. Contemporary research such as the ICS work discussed above suggests that there may well be a natural fit between the computational abstractions characterizing mentalist psychology and their counterparts in neuroscience.

See also COGNITIVE PSYCHOLOGY; MODULARITY.

BIBLIOGRAPHY

Boden, M.A., ed. 1990. *The Philosophy of Artificial Intelligence*. Oxford University Press.

Clark, A., ed. 1992. Special issue: Philosophical issues in connectionist modeling *Connection Science*, 4, 171–381.

Cummins, R. 1989. *Meaning and Mental Representation*. Cambridge, MA: MIT Press/Bradford Books.

Dolan, C.P. and Smolensky, P. 1989. Tensor product production system: a modular architecture and representation. *Connection Science*, 1, 53–68.

Horgan, T., and Tienson, J. 1991. *Connection-ism and the Philosophy of Mind*. Dordrecht: Kluwer Academic Publishers.

Kirsh, D., ed. 1991. Special volume: Foundations of artificial intelligence. *Artificial Intelligence*, 47, 1–346.

Legendre, G., Miyata, Y., and Smolensky, P. 1994. *Principles for an Integrated Connectionist/Symbolic Theory of Higher Cognition*. Hillsdale, New Jersey: Lawrence Erlbaum Associates.

Marr, D. 1982. *Vision*. San Francisco, Calif.: Freeman.

Nadel, L., Cooper, L.A., Culicover, P., and Harnish, R.M., eds. 1989. *Neural Connections, Mental Computation*. Cambridge, MA.: MIT Press/Bradford Books.

Partridge, D. and Wilks, Y., eds. 1990. *The Foundations of Artificial Intelligence: A Sourcebook*. Cambridge University Press.

Prince, A., and Smolensky, P. 1994. *Optimality Theory: Constraint interaction in generative grammar*. Cambridge, MA.: MIT Press/Linguistic Inquiry Monograph Series.

Pylyshyn, Z. 1984. *Computation and Cognition: Toward a Foundation for Cognitive Science*. Cambridge, MA.: MIT Press/Bradford Books.

Ramsey, W., Stich, S.P., and Rumelhart, D.E. 1991. *Philosophy and Connectionist Theory*. Hillsdale, New Jersey: Lawrence Erlbaum Associates.

Smolensky, P. 1994. Constituent structure and explanation in an integrated connectionist/symbolic cognitive architecture. In *The Philosophy of Psychology: Debates on Psychological Explanation*, ed. C. G. Macdonald and G. Macdonald. Oxford: Basil Blackwell.

Smolensky, P., Legendre, G., and Miyata, Y. 1994. *Principles for an Integrated Connectionist/Symbolic Theory of Higher Cognition*. Cambridge, MA: MIT Press.

PAUL SMOLENSKY

concepts The notion of a *concept*, like the related notion of *meaning*, lies at the heart of some of the most difficult and unresolved issues in philosophy and psychology. The word 'concept' itself is applied to a bewildering assortment of phenomena commonly thought to be constituents of THOUGHT. These include internal MENTAL REPRES-ENTATIONS, IMAGES, words, stereotypes, senses, PROPERTIES, reasoning and discrimination abilities, mathematical functions. Given the lack of anything like a settled theory in this area, it would be a mistake to fasten readily on any one of these phenomena as the unproblematic referent of the term. One does better to survey the geography of the area and gain some idea of how these phenomena might fit together, leaving aside for the nonce just which of them deserve to be called 'concepts' as ordinarily understood.

There is a specific role that concepts are arguably intended to play that may serve as a point of departure. Suppose one person thinks that capitalists exploit workers, and another that they don't. Call the *thing* that they disagree about 'a proposition', e.g. [Capitalists exploit workers]. It is in some sense shared by them as the object of their disagreement, and it is expressed by the sentence that follows the verb 'thinks that' (mental verbs that take such sentence complements as direct objects are called verbs of 'PROPOSITIONAL ATTITUDE'. We won't be concerned here with whether propositions are ultimate objects, or whether talk of them can be reduced to talk of properties or predicates). Concepts are the *constituents* of such propositions, just as the words 'capitalists', 'exploit' and 'workers' are constituents of the sentence. Thus, these people could have these beliefs only if they had, *inter alia*, the concepts [capitalist], [exploit], [workers] (I shall designate concepts by enclosing in square brackets the words that express them).

Propositional attitudes, and thus concepts, are constitutive of the familiar form of explanation (so-called 'intentional explanation') by which we ordinarily explain the behaviour and states of people, many animals, and perhaps some machines (*see* INTENTIONALITY, REASONS AND CAUSES). In the above example, the different thoughts that people have about capitalism might explain their different voting behaviour. By and large, philosophers and psychologists such as Fodor (1975, 1991) or Peacocke (1992), interested in intentional explanation take themselves to be committed to the existence of concepts; whereas those wary of this form of explanation, e.g. Quine (1960), tend to be sceptical of them.

Just which sentential constituents express concepts is a matter of some debate. The central cases that are discussed tend to be the concepts expressed by *predicates* or *general terms*, such as 'is a capitalist' or 'x exploits y', terms true of potentially many different individual things. But there are presumably concepts associated with logical words ('and', 'some', 'possibly'). And some philosophers have argued for the importance of *individual concepts*, or concepts of individual things, e.g. [Rome], [25], both in psychology, and in logic and mathematics.

Since concepts as constituents of thought are shareable, both by different people, and by the same person at different times, they need to be distinguished from the *particular* ideas, images, sensations that, consciously or unconsciously, pass through our minds at a particular time. Just what kind of shareable object a concept might be is a matter of considerable difference between theorists. In much of the psychological literature, where the concern is often with an agent's system of *internal representation*, concepts are regarded as internal representation *types* that have individual ideas as their specific *token see* TYPE/TOKEN (in the way that the type word 'cat', can have many different inscriptions as tokens). But many philosophers take the view that these internal representation types would no more be identical to concepts than are the type words in a natural language. One person might express the concept [city] by the word 'city', another by the word 'ville'; still another perhaps by a mental image of bustling boulevards; but, for all that, they might have the same concept [city]: one could believe and another doubt that cities are healthy places to live. Moreover, different people could employ the same representation to express different concepts: one person might use an image of Paris to express [Paris], another to express [France].

Now it might be supposed that the common object of people's thoughts are simply the *referents* of their terms, that is, the objects *in the world* picked out by the terms or internal representations, for example, in the case of 'city', all the particular cities in the world (this is a view defended by some proponents of theories of 'direct reference'). There are a number of difficulties with this view. At least in the case of *general* terms (or predicates), there are standardly at least *three* different candidates for their referents: (1) the *extension*, or set of *actual* objects that satisfy the predicate (e.g. the particular cities: New York, Paris, . . .); (2) the *intension*, or function from POSSIBLE WORLDS to sets of *possible* objects that satisfy the predicate in a world (e.g. [city] would be the function that takes us in the real world to the set containing New York, Paris, etc., and in another world to a set of *possible* cities, e.g. North Polis); and (3) the causally efficacious *property* (e.g. cityhood) that all the (possible) objects have in common. Extensional logicians like Quine (1960), eschewing all talk of non-actual worlds or ontologically suspicious 'properties', prefer the first option; modal logicians and formal semanticists like Montague (1974), interested in accounting for the semantics of natural languages, tend to prefer the second; and many philosophers of mind like Dretske (1987), Millikan (1984) and Fodor (1991), interested in causal interactions between animals and the world, tend to prefer the third.

Moreover, in addition to the *referent* of a general term, many (following Frege, 1966) have argued that there exists its '*sense*', or 'mode of presentation' (sometimes 'intension' is used here as well). After all, 'is an equiangular triangle' and 'is an equilateral trilateral' pick out the same things not only in the actual world, but in all possible worlds, and so refer – insofar as they are taken to refer to any of these things at all – to the same extension, same intension and (arguably from a causal point of view) the same property; but they differ in the way these referents are presented to the mind: it's one thing to think of something as an equilateral triangle, another to think of it as an equilateral trilateral (which is why the

186

proof that they're necessarily coextensive is interesting). For some (e.g. Peacocke, 1992) concepts might be senses so understood. But we then need a theory of senses. Some philosophers look to an *ability* and/or a *rule* that prescribes a particular *inferential* (or 'conceptual') *role* that a representation plays in an agent's thought, from stimulation through intervening states to behaviour: e.g. stimuli and inferences that lead to the application of a term, and from it to the application of other terms and action (*see* CONCEPTUAL ROLE SEMANTICS). Thus, the counting of angles might lead to 'triangle' and back again; or the sight of crowds might lead to 'crowded', which might in turn lead to 'ten or more' and perhaps certain (dispositions to) behaviour, e.g. to say 'Ten's a crowd', and these patterns of cause and effect (or causal roles) might be taken to be constitutive of the concepts [triangle] or [crowd].

In respecting all of the above distinctions, it is important to be especially careful with the peculiar idiom 'concept of x', as in 'the child's' or the 'ancient Greek's concept of causality', an idiom that figures prominently in DEVELOPMENTAL PSYCHOLOGY and studies in the history of science. This could mean merely the concept [causality], which the child has (as do most adults); or it could mean the child's *ability* to deploy the concept in reasoning and discrimination; or it could mean any of the extension, intension, or rule that children associate with the English word 'causality' and its related forms; or it could mean (as in fact it very often does mean) the representation and/or standard beliefs (what I prefer to call the *conception*) that children associate with the extension, intension, rule or ability [causality]. Which of these candidates is intended would all depend upon what entity one thinks of as the concept and what a mere accompaniment of it. What can't be seriously intended is the suggestion that a child has a concept [causality] that is *both* identical to but different from the adult's.

But choosing what one thinks of as a concept and what a mere accompaniment depends upon one's theory of concepts and of what explanatory role they are being asked to play, to which issues we now turn.

THEORIES ABOUT CONCEPTS

The Classical View

Historically, a great deal has been asked of concepts. As shareable constituents of the objects of attitudes, they presumably figure in cognitive generalizations and explanations of animals' capacities and behaviour. They are also presumed to serve as the meanings of linguistic items, underwriting relations of translation, definition, synonymy, antinomy, and semantic implication (*see* Katz, 1972). Much work in the semantics of natural languages (e.g. Jackendoff, 1983) takes itself to be addressing conceptual structure.

Concepts have also been thought to be the proper objects of 'philosophical analysis', the activity practised by Socrates and twentieth-century 'analytic' philosophers when they ask about the nature of justice, knowledge or piety, and expect to discover answers by means of a priori reflection alone (*see* e.g. Chisholm, 1957).

The expectation that one sort of thing could serve all these tasks went hand in hand with what has come to be called the 'Classical View' of concepts, according to which they have an 'analysis' consisting of conditions that are individually necessary and jointly sufficient for their satisfaction, which are known to any competent user of them. The standard example is the especially simple one of [bachelor], which seems to be identical to [eligible unmarried male]. A more interesting, but problematic one has been [knowledge], whose analysis was traditionally thought to be [justified true belief].

This Classical View seems to offer an illuminating answer to a certain form of metaphysical question: in virtue of what is something the kind of thing it is – e.g. in virtue of what is a bachelor a bachelor? – and it does so in a way that supports counterfactuals: it tells us what *would* satisfy the concept in situations other than the actual ones (although all actual bachelors might turn out to be freckled, it's *possible* that there might be unfreckled ones, since the analysis doesn't exclude that). The View also seems to offer an answer to an *epistemological* question of how people seem to know a priori (or independently of experience) about the nature of many things, e.g. that bachelors are unmarried: it is constitutive of the competency (or possession) conditions of a concept that they know its analysis, at least on reflection.

Empiricism and Verificationism
The Classical View, however, has always had to face the difficulty of *primitive* concepts: it's all well and good to claim that competence consists in some sort of mastery of a definition, but what about the primitive concepts in which a process of definition must ultimately end? Here the British Empiricism of the seventeenth century began to offer a solution: all the primitives were *sensory*. Indeed, they expanded the Classical View to include the claim, now often taken uncritically for granted in discussions of that view, that all concepts are 'derived from experience': 'every idea is derived from a corresponding impression'. In the work of Locke, Berkeley and Hume this was often thought to mean that concepts were somehow *composed* of introspectible mental items – 'images', 'impressions' – that were ultimately decomposable into basic sensory parts. Thus, Hume analysed the concept of [material object] as involving certain regularities in our sensory experience, and [cause] as involving spatiotemporal contiguity and constant conjunction.

Berkeley noticed a problem with this approach that every generation has had to rediscover: if a concept is a sensory impression, like an image, then how does one distinguish a general concept [triangle] from a more particular one – say, [isoceles triangle] – that would serve in imagining the general one. More recently, Wittgenstein (1953) called attention to the multiple ambiguity of images. And, in any case, images seem quite hopeless for capturing the concepts associated with logical terms (what is the image for negation or possibility?). Whatever the role of such representations, full conceptual competence must involve something more.

Indeed, in addition to images and impressions and other sensory items, a full account of concepts needs to consider issues of logical structure. This is precisely what the Logical Positivists did, focusing on logically structured sentences instead of sensations and images, transforming the empiricist claim into the famous 'Verifiability Theory of Meaning': the meaning of a sentence is the means by which it is confirmed or refuted, ultimately by sensory experience; the meaning or concept associated with a predicate is the means by which people confirm or refute whether something satisfies it.

This once-popular position has come under much attack in philosophy in the last fifty years. In the first place, few, if any, successful 'reductions' of ordinary concepts (like [material object], [cause]) to purely sensory concepts have ever been achieved (*see* e.g. Ayer, 1934 for some proposals, and Quine 1953, and Chisholm 1957 for criticism). Our concept of material object and causation seem to go far beyond mere sensory experience, just as our concepts in a highly theoretical science seem to go far beyond the often only meagre evidence we can adduce for them.

Moreover, there seemed to be a pattern to the failures. Taking a page from Pierre Duhem, Quine (1951) pointed out that 'our beliefs confront the tribunal of experience only as a corporate body': litmus paper turning red confirms that a solution is acidic only in conjunction with a great deal of background chemical and physical theory, indeed, many have argued, only in conjunction with the *whole* of a person's system of beliefs (a view called 'confirmation holism'). Hence, if a concept is to be analysed as its verification conditions, its meaning would be similarly holistic ('meaning HOLISM'). Given that no two person's beliefs are likely to be precisely the same, this has the consequence that no two people ever share precisely the same concepts – and no one could, strictly speaking, remember the same thing over any amount of time that included a change of belief! 'Sameness of concept' for Quine becomes by and large an 'indeterminate' issue. The best one might hope for is a *similarity* of inferential role between symbols in different theories or symbol systems, a conclusion enthusiastically endorsed by such diverse writers as Kuhn (1962), Harman (1972) and Block (1986).

Fodor and LePore (1992) have recently argued that the arguments for meaning holism are, however, less than compelling, and that there are important theoretical reasons for holding out for an entirely *atomistic* account of concepts. On this view, concepts have no 'analyses' whatsoever: they are simply ways in which people are directly related to individual properties in the world, ways which might obtain for someone for one concept but not for any other one: in principle, someone might have the concept [bachelor] and no other concepts at all, much less any 'analysis' of it. Such a view goes hand in hand with Fodor's rejection of not only verificationist, but *any* empiricist account of concept learning and construction: indeed, given the failure of empiricist constructions, Fodor (1975, 1979) notoriously argues that concepts are not constructed or 'derived from experience' at all, but are (nearly enough) all *innate* (*see* INNATENESS).

Non-classical Approaches: Prototypes

WITTGENSTEIN (1953) raised a different issue of whether a concept actually *need* have any Classical analysis at all. Certainly, people are seldom very good at producing adequate definitions of terms that they are nonetheless competent to use. Wittgenstein proposed that, rather than classical definitions that isolated what, for example, all games had in common, the different uses of the word 'game' involved a set of overlapping and criss-crossing 'family resemblances'. This speculation was taken seriously by Rosch (1973) and Smith and Medin (1981) as a testable psychological hypothesis. They showed that people respond differently (in terms of response time and other measures) to questions about whether, for example, penguins as opposed to robins are birds, in a fashion that suggested that concept membership was a matter not of possessing a Classical analysis; but of 'distance' from a 'prototype' or typical 'exemplar'. Thus, a robin satisfies many more of the features of a typical bird than does a penguin and so is a 'better' member of the category; and a malicious lie is a better case of a lie than a well-intentioned one.

It has not always been clear precisely what sort of thing a prototype or examplar might be. One needs to resist a strong temptation to import into the mind or brain procedures, such as comparing one *actual* bird, or even a picture of one, with another, that make sense only outside of it. Presumably it is some sort of list of selected properties, perhaps accompanied by a mental image, and a metric for determining the distance of a candidate from that list. Some writers have proposed exploiting the resources of 'fuzzy set theory' to capture the intended structure, whereby membership in a category is not understood as an all-or-none affair, but a matter of degree: everything satisfies every concept to *some* degree, however small.

But prototypicality, which presumably involves distances among a complex cluster of diverse properties, must be distinguished from both *vagueness* and *guessing*. It is a commonplace that nearly every concept that applies to things in space and time is to some extent 'vague' in that there are always 'hard cases' in which it is not clear whether or not the concept applies. There are, for example, plenty of people for whom it seems to be indeterminate whether or not they are bald, but *this* is no objection to the Classical View that [bald] is analysable as [lacking cranial hair], since, whatever vagueness is involved in applying [bald] might well be involved in applying that analysis.

Guessing, like prototypicality and vagueness, also comes in degrees. Unlike them, however, it is not a metaphysical issue of the actual conditions something must satisfy in order to satisfy the concept, but rather an epistemological one concerning the belief or epistemic probability that something satisfies the conditions, *given certain evidence*. The sight of someone with a toupé may mean that there is a 90% probability that he's actually 50% bald, or a 40% probability that he's actually 95% bald. The question of whether [bald] is Classical or prototypical is untouched by this issue as well.

This distinction between the metaphysical question about how things are and the epistemic one about evidence is, however, particularly difficult to enforce with regard to concepts (ordinary English can often encourage running the two questions together: the metaphysical question can be phrased 'What *determines* what's what?' and can then be confused with the epistemological one 'How does someone determine what's what?'). As Rey (1983, 1985) pointed out, concepts are too often expected to answer both sorts of question, and we shouldn't suppose without argument that they can perform both sorts of work. For example, what metaphysically determines whether something is male or female is presumably facts about its reproductive capacities or genes; but neither of these are the way we standardly guess a person's gender, which usually involves accidental features of name, hair and dress. Indeed, in view of the aforementioned confirmation holism, epistemic procedures may well involve almost anything whatsoever, since there may be no limit to the ingenuity of a person in exploiting roundabout evidence and inferences – or just relying on what other people say. But surely the fact that people may exploit anything in finding out what's what doesn't entail that just anything is part of a concept's proper analysis. In any case, the fact that people may be slower to agree that penguins rather than robins are birds is no reflection upon the status of penguins as bona fide birds even in the minds of the subjects of these experiments. Most people, after all, know that the stereotypes they have of things are not entirely reliable and

can be transcended on a little reflection. Indeed, there is no reason to suppose that the Classical analyses of a concept need be employed in 'on-line' reasoning except in the unusually demanding tasks of 'philosophical analysis'.

The empiricist tradition, particularly in its verificationist mood, made a point, however, of connecting the metaphysical with the epistemic: the defining conditions for a concept were to be stated in terms of experiential evidence. If that tradition is to avoid the move from confirmation to meaning holism, it would need to distinguish among the ways in which concepts are related to experience those ways that are due to the genuine analysis of the concept and those that are due merely to beliefs an agent may have involving it. The aforementioned 'inferential role' accounts of concepts hope to begin to do this, distinguishing inferences from 'bachelor' to 'unmarried' from 'bachelor' to 'freckled'. Those interested in defining concepts in terms of their roles in theories are presumably making just such an appeal.

However, Quine's (1953) famous attack on the analytic/synthetic distinction has seemed to many to show that no such distinction among inferences can generally be drawn (*see* QUINE). He argued that the notions of analyticity, meaning, synonymy and possibility form a vicious circle of notions insusceptible to empirical test. Quite apart from this issue, moreover, there is the difficulty of drawing a principled limit to how deviant people can be about the inferences they draw with concepts they seem nonetheless entirely competent to use: some creationists believe that people aren't animals, idealists that material objects are ideas, and nominalists that numbers are numerals. These all seem like possible cognitive states, and so present a *prima facie* difficulty for a theory of concepts that claims their identity involves specific connections to other concepts or experiences.

Non-classical: Causal Approaches
The work of Kripke (1972), Putnam (1975) and Burge (1979) suggests another strat-

egy. They argue that the meanings of words, particularly of proper names and natural kind terms, don't involve definitions known to users of them, but rather causal relations with their actual referents and/or the social community in which the term is used. (Whether there nevertheless *exist* definitions that users may not know is an issue neither they nor many others address.) PUTNAM (1975), in particular, imagined there to be a planet, TWIN-EARTH, exactly like the earth in every way except for having in place of H_2O, a different, but superficially similar chemical XYZ. He argued that the word 'water' in Twin-Earthling's mouths would mean something different from what it means in ours, and that they would have a different concept [twater] from the concept [water] that we on earth normally employ, despite the fact that everything about the organization of the brains of Twin-Earthlings would be (*ex hypothesi*) indistinguishable from that of our own.

While these intuitions provide an interesting challenge to the Classical View, they sacrifice its account of conceptual competence. If competence doesn't consist in a grasp of a definition, what makes it true on this view that someone has one concept rather than another? What makes it true that a child or an adult has the concept [cause], or [knowledge], if she can't define it? Merely causally interacting in a certain community and environment can't be enough, since surely not *every* sentient being in New York City has all the concepts of a Columbia University physicist.

So a number of writers have proposed varieties of counterfactual causal links: x has the concept y iff some state of x did/would causally co-vary with y (i.e. x did/would discriminate instances of y) under certain (ideal, normal, evolutionarily significant) conditions, as a matter of nomological necessity. Thus, someone has the concept [horse] iff she could under certain conditions tell the horses from the non-horses. This is the idea behind 'informational' (or 'covariational') theories of the sort proposed by Dretske (1980), Millikan

(1984) and Fodor (1991). In a way, it is simply a development of an idea that empiricists often implicitly presumed (and that was explicit in the work of B. F. Skinner) for the sensory primitives: someone had the concept [red] iff she could discriminate red things. Informational theories simply extend this idea to non-sensory terms as well.

Unfortunately, this solution doesn't seem quite adequate. There is first of all the substantial difficulty of specifying the appropriate conditions for the covariation in a non-circular fashion. Many suspect that this will fall afoul of 'Brentano's Thesis' of 'the irreducibility of the intentional': spelling out the appropriate conditions would involve mentioning other intentional/semantic/conceptual conditions, such as that the agent is *paying attention*, doesn't *believe* her perceptual experience is misleading, *wants* to notice what's going on, etc. This potential circle is particularly troubling for those concerned with 'naturalizing' talk of concepts, i.e. of fitting it into theories of the rest of nature (biology, physics).

But there are also a number of more specific problems that have been widely discussed, but not decisively solved in the literature: *transitivity, disjunction, coextensivity* and *co-instantiation*. Transitivity is the problem that, whereas covariation (and other causal 'information') is a transitive notion, conceptual representation is not (if A covaries with B and B with C, then A covaries with C; but 'A' doesn't thereby express both [B] and [C]). For example, the symbol 'smoke' might covary under the appropriate conditions with smoke, and smoke, itself, might covary with fire; and so 'smoke' would covary with fire as well; but 'smoke' means [smoke] and not [fire].

Disjunction is the problem of distinguishing the *misapplication* of a concept [A] to Bs, from the *correct* application of the disjunctive concept [A or B]: e.g., a representation that covaries with horses and is *misapplied* to cows on a dark night is a representation that could be taken to covary with *horses or cows on dark nights*

(Fodor (1991) discusses these latter problems in detail; *see also* the related problem of determining which arithmetic function someone is computing, discussed in Kripke, 1982).

We already noticed the problem of necessary coextensiveness in the case of triangles versus trilaterals: covariation of a symbolic state with one would necessarily be covariation with the other. The problem of coinstantiated concepts is different. Quine (1960, ch. 2) first raised it with his famous discussion of translating a foreign sentence 'Gavagai', tokens of which he assumes covary with the presence of rabbits. The problem is that whenever there is a rabbit present there are both *undetached rabbit parts* and *time slices of rabbits*. The respective concepts in each of these cases are not even coextensive (rabbits aren't parts or slices of rabbits) much less identical. Yet because of their necessary coinstantiation, any state that covaried with one would covary with the other. So something else is needed to pin particular concepts down.

TENTATIVE CONCLUSION

It is tempting to return to some feature of the Classical View and select some feature of inferential role that would disambiguate these cases: patterns of inference would certainly seem to be what distinguish [smoke] from [fire], [horse] from [horse or cow on a dark night], [triangle] from [trilateral], [rabbit] from [undetached rabbit parts]. Another possibility, explored most extensively by Millikan (1984) and Dretske (1987), has been to appeal to the teleological functions related to a discrimination ability (perhaps there is or was a biological advantage to discriminating rabbits rather than their undetached parts) that might play a role in explaining why a trait was selected. Probably the best hope is in some subtle amalgamation of the various views that have been sketched here – for example, of both a type-representation, inferential role, and some covariational view. These are the issues of continuing research.

We might summarize the present situation with regard to candidates for 'concepts' that have been discussed here as follows: there is the *token representation* in the mind or brain of an agent, *types* of which are shared by different agents. These representations could be *words, images, definitions,* or '*prototypes*' that play specific *inferential roles* in an agent's cognitive system and stand in certain *causal* and *covariant relations* to phenomena in the world. By virtue of these facts, such representations become associated with an *extension* in this world, possibly an *intension* that determines an extension in all possible worlds, and possibly a *property* that all objects in all such extensions have in common. Which of these (italicized) entities one selects to be concepts depends on the explanatory work one wants concepts to perform. Unfortunately, there is as yet little agreement on precisely what that work might be.

See also BELIEF; CONTENT; DRETSKE; FODOR; HISTORY; RATIONALITY.

BIBLIOGRAPHY

Ayer, A.J. 1934 *Language, Truth and Logic.* New York: Dover.

Block, N. 1986. Advertisement for a semantics for psychology. In *Studies in the Philosophy of Mind,* ed. P. French, T. Vehling and H. Wettstein. Minneapolis: University of Minnesota Press.

Burge, T. 1979. Individualism and the mental. In *Studies in Metaphysics,* ed. P. French, T. Vehling and H. Wettstein. Minneapolis: University of Minnesota Press.

Carnap, R. 1969. *The Logical Structure of the World and Pseudo-problems in Philosophy.* Berkeley: University of California Press.

Chisholm, R. 1957. *Perceiving: a Philosophical Study.* Ithaca: Cornell University.

Dretske, F. 1980. *Knowledge and the Flow of Information.* Cambridge MA.: MIT Press.

Dretske, F. 1987. *Explaining Behavior.* Cambridge MA.: MIT Press.

Fodor, J. 1975., *The Language of Thought.* New York: Crowell.

Fodor, J. 1979. 'The present status of the innateness controversy.' In *Representations;*

Essays on the Foundations of Cognitive Science. Cambridge MA.: MIT Press.

Fodor, J. 1991. *A Theory of Content.* Cambridge MA.: MIT Press.

Frege, G. 1966. *Translations from the Philosophical Writings of Gottlob Frege,* trans. P. Geach and M. Black. Oxford: Blackwell.

Harman, G. 1972. *Thought.* Princeton University Press.

Jackendoff, R. 1983. *Semantics and Cognition.* Cambridge MA.: MIT Press.

Katz, J. 1972. *Semantic Theory.* New York: Harper and Row.

Kripke, S. 1980. *Naming and Necessity.* Cambridge MA.: Harvard University Press.

Kripke, S. 1982. *Wittgenstein on Rules and Private Language.* Cambridge MA.: Harvard University Press.

Kuhn, T. 1962. *The Structure of Scientific Revolutions.* Chicago: University of Chicago Press.

Millikan, R. 1984. *Language, Thought and Other Biological Categories.* Cambridge MA.: MIT Press.

Montague, R. 1974. *Formal Philosophy.* New Haven: Yale Univeristy Press.

Peacocke, C. 1992. *Concepts.* Cambridge MA.: MIT Press.

Putnam, H. 1975. The meaning of 'meaning'. In *Language, Mind and Knowledge.* ed. K. Gunderson. Minneapolis: University of Minnesota Press.

Quine, W.V. 1953. Two dogmas of empiricism. In *From a Logical Point of View and other Essays.* Cambridge MA.: Harvard University Press.

Quine, W.V. 1960. *Word and Object.* Cambridge MA.: MIT Press.

Rey, G. 1985. Concepts and conceptions. *Cognition,* 19, 297–303.

Rey, G. 1983. Concepts and stereotypes. *Cognition,* 15, 237–62.

Rosch, E. 1973. On the internal structure of perceptual and semantic categories. In *Cognitive Development and Acquisition of Language.* ed. T. E. Moore. New York: Academic Press.

Smith, E., and Medin, D. 1981. *Categories and Concepts.* Cambridge MA.: Harvard University Press.

Wittgenstein, L. 1953. *Philosophical Investigations.* New York: Macmillan.

GEORGES REY

conceptual role semantics Conceptual (sometimes computational, cognitive, causal or functional) role semantics (CRS) entered philosophy through the philosophy of language, not the philosophy of mind. The core idea behind CRS in the philosophy of language is that the way linguistic expressions are related to one another determines what the expressions in a language mean. These relations constitute the role of an expression in a language. This core idea goes back in philosophy at least as far as Wilfrid Sellars. Its most vigorous defenders at present in the philosophy of mind are Ned Block, Michael Devitt, Gilbert Harman, Brian Loar, and William Lycan.

There is a considerable affinity between CRS and structuralist semiotics that has been influential in linguistics. According to the latter, languages are to be viewed as systems of differences; the basic idea is that the semantic force (or 'value') of an utterance is determined by its position in the space of possibilities that one's language offers (Saussure, 1983). CRS also has affinities with what the ARTIFICIAL INTELLIGENCE researchers call 'procedural semantics'. The essential idea here is that providing a compiler for a language is equivalent to specifying a semantic theory for that language; semantics consists of procedures that a computer is instructed to execute by a program (Woods, 1981).

POSITIVE REASONS FOR CRS

Frege-Problems
In order to get a grip on this idea it's useful to keep in mind that traditionally the meaning of an expression was thought to involve some symbol–world relation. So, the expression 'the World Trade Towers' differs in meaning from the expression 'the Empire State Building' because the former is *about* the World Trade Towers, whereas the latter is *not.* CRS got its footing in the philosophy of language because of a perceived deficiency in this idea that meaning is somehow determined by word–world relations. Meaning, according to this criticism, can't simply be a word–world relation because, in

the classic example, 'Hesperus' and 'Phosphorus' are both attached to the same non-linguistic thing, viz., to Venus. Yet someone can, without self-contradiction, assert that the Hesperus shines, while denying that the Phosphorus shines. According to CRS, 'Hesperus' and 'Phosphorus' mean different things, despite their both being attached to Venus, because they have different roles in the (English) language.

CRS and Logical Connectives

On a more constructive side, practically everyone believes that CRS is most plausible for an account of the meaning of the logical constants. Indeed, beginning as early as with the logician Gentzen some philosophers and logicians have characterized a logical constant as an expression whose meaning is fixed by the ordered pair of the set of inferences you can validly infer from, and the set of inferences you can validly infer to, a sentence dominated by it. For example, consider what would be involved for a symbol '#' in a language to express the material conditional: the '#' in 'Bob is a man # Bob is human' expresses the material conditional only if when (tokenings of) this sentence interacts appropriately with (tokenings of) 'Bob is a man', the result is a tendency to token 'Bob is human' (*ceteris paribus*); or only if when it interacts with 'Bob is not human', the result is a tendency not to token 'Bob is a man' but rather a tendency to token 'Bob is not a man'. And so on. Plainly, talk of tendency to token here requires that it is tokens of datable, placeable inscriptions, sounds, etc., that have conceptual roles. (*See* Field, 1977, and Harman, 1987 for further discussion.)

The Language of Thought

What has any of this to do with the philosophy of mind? Philosophers of mind are interested in the nature of thought. Thoughts have contents (meanings) in much the same way that linguistic expressions do. My thought that the World Trade Towers were bombed differs in content (meaning) from my thought that the Empire State Building was bombed. The former is

true and the latter false; the former is about the World Trade Towers and the latter is not. Since, as many philosophers maintain, it is the content (or the meaning) of a thought that determines what that thought is about, its INTENTIONALITY, it is natural to think that content (or meaning) involves some symbol–world relation, where the symbols here are expressions in, if you like, a LANGUAGE OF THOUGHT – say, mentalese. But now notice how the same problems that apparently threaten the classical referential model of meaning for natural language expressions, also apparently threaten a classical referential story about the content of thoughts.

If you think that there is *no* apparent contradiction in believing that Hesperus shines without believing that Phosphorus shines; or in believing that water quenches thirst, without believing that H_2O quenches thirst, or in my believing that I'm thirsty without my believing that Ernie Lepore is thirsty, say, because I simply forgot that I'm Ernie Lepore or am deluded in thinking that I'm David Hume, then the content of these thoughts cannot be determined solely by the relationship between these thoughts and what they are about in the non-linguistic world. Each pair of thoughts is about exactly the same thing, and apparently no mind–world relation will distinguish them. And thus entered CRS into the philosophy of mind: it is the way mentalese expressions are related to *one another* that fixes what they mean. These relations constitute the role of a mentalese expression.

CRS as Semantics versus CRS as Metaphysics

In describing the relations between expressions, we say (depict systematically) what each expression means. In this sense, a CRS is in much the same business as any other semantic theory. It aims to assign to each meaningful expression in a language L – spoken, written or thought – a meaning, viz., for CRS theorists, a conceptual role. However, some CRS theorists defend not a semantic thesis about what expressions of a language – mental or public – mean, but instead a thesis about the *nature* of meaning. For these philosophers, CRS theorists are in much the same business as are those philosophers who are either intention-based Griceans or information-based semanticists. Griceans tell us that at least public linguistic expressions have their meaning in virtue of the intentions with which they are spoken (H. P. Grice, Jonathan Bennett, and, at one time, Brian Loar and Stephen Schiffer). Information-based semanticists tell us that expressions have their meanings in virtue of certain causal or nomological relations that obtain between tokens of expressions and features of the non-linguistic world (Jerry FODOR, Fred DRETSKE, Ruth Millikan). Some CRS theorists intend to answer the non-semantical metaphysical question, *In virtue of* what does, say, an expression *e* of language L mean *m*? The following, though not equivalent, are sometimes used interchangeably with this 'in virtue of' question: what *determines* that expression *e* in language L means *m*?; what is the meaning *m* of expression *e* *constituted by*?; what is it metaphysically *dependent upon*?; what does e's meaning *supervene on*? Any philosopher who asks these questions probably supposes that semantic facts cannot be brute, primitive, facts, but must somehow be explicable in terms of more basic facts.

As a metaphysician, a CRS theorist might hold that the meaning of a thought is a function from possible worlds to truth values (*à la* Montague), or that the meaning of a thought is its truth condition (*à la* DAVIDSON), or a structured interpreted tree (*à la* Katz), but that it's in virtue of *e*'s having a certain conceptual role that a thought has the semantic properties it does. Semantic theories do not, normally, wear their metaphysical commitments on their sleeves.

Methodological Solipsism

A more sophisticated reason, squarely in the philosophy of mind, for adopting CRS other than the Frege-problem derives from Jerry Fodor's worries about methodological solipsism. In a series of highly influential papers in the 1970s, Hilary Putnam, David Kaplan, Saul Kripke, and Tyler Burge, each drew attention to the ways in which the meanings of many terms depend crucially upon the environment of the speaker. Putnam, for example, asks us to imagine two planets, Earth and TWIN EARTH, and two of their residents, say, Harry and Twin-Harry. Twin Earth is almost a physical replica of Earth. The only difference is that on Twin Earth the clear liquid the twin-people drink, that fills their oceans, and that they call 'water', is composed not of H_2O molecules but of XYZ molecules. According to Putnam, the expression 'water' on Earth refers to the stuff composed of H_2O and not composed of XYZ. It is exactly the reverse for the same expression on Twin Earth. Thus, two subjects can be molecule for molecule alike inside their heads and still have intuitively different beliefs. Harry's belief that water is wet is about H_2O, while Twin-Harry's belief 'that water is wet' is about XYZ, and their truth and referential conditions differ accordingly.

What such examples are suppose to show is that the contents of thoughts, in the referential sense, do not *per se* figure in the explanation of brute physical behaviour, since people who are brain state type-identical will behave alike regardless of what their beliefs are about. Methodological solipsism is Fodor's idea that psychologists, in explaining behaviour, must rely only on what is in the head. So, if semantics is to help in explaining behaviour, it would seem that purely referential theories are insufficient for this task. The mind (and its components) has no way of recognizing the reference or truth conditions of the representations it operates on.

Enter CRS, the referential theories' solipsistically motivated rival. Since, according to CRS, the meaning of a thought is determined by the thought's role in a system of states, to specify a thought is not to specify its truth or referential conditions, but to specify its role. Harry's and Twin-Harry's thoughts, though different in truth and referential conditions, share the same conceptual role, and it is by virtue of this commonality that they behave type-identically.

If Harry and Twin-Harry each has a belief that he would express by 'water quenches thirst', CRS can explain and predict their dipping their cups into H_2O and XYZ respectively. Thus CRS, it would seem (though not to Fodor, who rejects CRS for both external and internal problems – see below), is better suited to predicting and explaining what someone decides or does, so long as it ignores information about the external world.

But, if, as Fodor contends, thoughts have recombinable linguistic ingredients, then, of course, for a CRS theorist, questions arise about the role of expressions in this language of thought as well as in the public language we speak and write. And, accordingly, CRS theorists divide not only over their aims, but also about CRS's proper domain. Two options avail themselves. Some hold that public meaning is somehow derivative (or inherited) from an internal mental language (mentalese), and that a mentalese expression has autonomous meaning (partly) in virtue of its conceptual role (Block, 1986). So, for example, the inscriptions on this page require for their understanding translation, or at least transliteration, into the language of thought; representations in the brain require no such translation or transliteration. Others hold that the language of thought just is public language internalized and that it is expressions of public language that have autonomous (or primary) meaning in virtue of their conceptual role (Sellars, 1963; Harman, 1987; Devitt, 1981). On this option, English is the language of thought for English speakers.

What are Conceptual Roles?
After one decides upon the aims and the proper province of CRS, the crucial question remains of exactly which relations among expressions – public or mental – constitute their conceptual roles. Because most CRS theorists leave the notion of a role in CRS as a blank cheque, the options are open-ended. The conceptual role of a (mental or public) expression might be its causal associations: any disposition to token (for example, utter

or think) one expression e when tokening another e', or a an ordered n-tuple $<e'\ e''$, $...>$, or vice versa, can count as the conceptual role of e. A more common option is to characterize conceptual role not causally, but inferentially (these need not be incompatible, contingent upon one's attitude about the naturalization of inference): the conceptual role of an expression e in L might consist of the set of actual and potential inferences to e or the set of actual or potential inferences from e, or, as is more common, the ordered pair consisting of these two sets. Or, if it is sentences which have non-derived inferential roles, what would it mean to talk of the inferential role of words? Some have found it natural to think of the inferential role of a word as represented by the set of inferential roles of the sentences in which the word appears (Block, 1986).

No matter how broadly inferential role is characterized, even if it is unpacked causally, some philosophers argue it is a mistake to identify conceptual role with inferential role. They want to include non-inferential components, for example,sensory input and behavioural output, as contributing to the conceptual role of an expression. Sellars speaks of 'language entry and exit rules' in his specification of conceptual role. Harman distinguishes between purely inferential accounts of conceptual role (which he dubs solipsistic CRS) and a broader notion of conceptual role (which he dubs non-solipsistic CRS). Obviously, these non-solipsistic CRS theorists do not respect Fodor's methodological solipsism.

Unlike most semanticists, the majority of CRS theorists argue not for specific semantic theories, but for a whole class of them. Sellars, Harman, and Block provide only frameworks for a future CRS, and some arguments why this framework is the only adequate one. A 'possible' exception is Field, who has developed a more detailed account in terms of subjective probability.

Field characterizes conceptual role in terms of a subjective probability function defined over all the sentences of a person's language. It specifies a person's commitments concerning how he will change degrees of belief when he acquires new information. The probability function, by specifying inductive and deductive relations, characterizes the conceptual roles of expressions. A and B are said to have the same conceptual role if, and only if, $P(A/C) = P(B/C)$, for all sentences C in the language. On this account 'Tully orates' and 'Cicero orates' may have different conceptual roles for a person, since there may be an S for which $P(\text{'Tully orates'}/S) \neq P(\text{'Cicero orates'}/S)$. The conceptual role of non-sentential expressions is specified in terms of the conceptual roles of all the sentences in which it appears. There may be a simple characterization of the conceptual roles of some expressions. For example, the role of negation is specified by the probability laws involving negation.

Field's account is but a 'possible' exception because Field writes that he is giving a notion of sameness of meaning, not meaning itself. And also, since his account is based on subjective probabilities, whatever criterion of sameness of meaning he comes up with is *intra*personal, not *inter*personal. He does not think it makes sense to compare different individuals' conceptual roles.

REASONS AGAINST CRS

Whatever version of CRS one adopts, one must meet a couple of principled objections, both external and internal.

Epistemological and Ontological Problems with CRS

External criticisms of CRS impugn its consequences for epistemology and ontology, rather that its actual coherence. Regardless of how one characterizes conceptual role, if the meaning of an expression is (or supervenes upon) its role in a language or a mind, this invites the inference that expressions that belong to different languages – public or mentalese – are *ipso facto* different in meaning. Once you start to identify the meaning of an expression e with its con-

ceptual role in a language L, it's hard to avoid (short of question begging) proceeding to identify the meaning of e with its whole role in L, and having gone that far it's hard to avoid the conclusion that if languages differ at all with respect to the propositions they express, they differ completely with respect to all the propositions they endorse (Fodor and Lepore, 1992). And if languages differ at all in respect of the propositions they can express, then they differ entirely in respect of the propositions they can express. For example, Field's characterization of conceptual role is holistic. In characterizing the conceptual role of a sentence one must simultaneously characterize the conceptual roles of all other sentences. Any change in the probability function – even just extending its domain to a new vocabulary – results in a change in conceptual role for every sentence (because two people will seldom assign the same conceptual role to expressions).

Ultimately, it looks as if the CRS theorist must wind up endorsing a number of relativistic, idealistic and solipsistic consequences: that no two people ever share a belief; that there is no such relation as translation; that no two people ever mean the same thing by what they say: that no two time slices of the same person ever mean the same thing by what they say; that no one can ever change his mind; and that no two statements or beliefs can ever be contradicted (to say nothing of refuted). A number of philosophers, linguists and AI theorists are prepared to bite these big bullets.

CRS and Truth/Reference

Independently of these external problems, there are also internal questions about whether CRS can capture key aspects of meaning. If you believe, as do many philosophers, that meaning determines truth and reference conditions, then meaning can't be conceptual role alone (Field 1977; Lepore and Loewer, 1987; Lycan 1984). If someone knows the meaning of a sentence and is omniscient regarding physical facts (that is, is omniscient about all the non-semantic/

non-intentional facts), then he knows whether the sentence is true. But Twin Earth cases show that conceptual role does not satisfy this condition. One can know the conceptual role of 'this is water' and also know just which things are H_2O and which are XYZ without thereby knowing whether 'this is water' is true in a given context, because conceptual role does not distinguish water from XYZ.

Dual Aspect Semantics

A number of philosophers have responded to this argument not by rejecting CRS *in toto* but by constructing two-factor (also called two-tiered and dual-aspect) semantic theories (Block, 1986; Field, 1977; Lycan, 1984). According to these accounts, a theory of meaning for a language L consists of two distinct components. One component, usually, a theory of truth, is intended to provide an account of the relations between language and the world: truth, reference, satisfaction, etc. The other, usually CRS, is supposed to provide an account of understanding and cognitive significance, that is, whatever is entirely 'in the head' (what Block calls 'narrow meaning').

Gilbert Harman, as mentioned above, advocates a semantic theory with only a single factor, viz., conceptual role. Yet he tries to avoid the criticism that an adequate semantic theory must not ignore truth and referential conditions by having his notion of conceptual role 'reach out into the world of referents'. Block speaks of Harman's conceptual roles as 'long-armed', extending into the world, in opposition to the 'short-armed', stopping at the skin, conceptual roles of two-factor theorists like himself (Block, 1986, p. 636). Block argues that Harman's non-solipsistic CRS is equivalent to the two-factor account he endorses; that difference between Harman's non-solipsistic account and Block's two-factor account 'is merely verbal'. Loar (1981) criticizes Harman's non-solipsistic account by arguing that it is *ad hoc*.

The two-factor approach can be regarded as making a conjunctive claim for each sentence: what its conceptual role is and what its (say) truth conditions are. Two-factor theories of meaning incur the obligation of saying which conceptual roles pair up with which contextually determined aspects of meaning, which truth conditions, to constitute specific meanings. I know of no reason to think that this obligation can be met (*see* Fodor and Lepore, 1992, p. 170). Still, it would seem that two-factor theories are prey to the one external objection above. On the two-factor view, if two sentences differ in their conceptual roles, then they differ in the propositions they each express. Since conceptual role is holistic (on the two-factor view), it follows that if two sentences differ in conceptual roles in different languages, then no two sentences in the two languages will ever express the same proposition.

CRS and Compositionality

Another internal problem is the following (Fodor and Lepore, 1992): you can't identify meanings with conceptual roles *tout court*, since unlike meanings conceptual roles *tout court* aren't *compositional*. That is, the meanings of syntactically complex expression (for example, mental sentences) are a function of their syntactic structures and the meanings of their lexical constituents. Some inferences, for example, the inference from 'that's a rattling snake' to 'that's rattling', is compositional in the sense that it follows just from the linguistic principles which connect the meanings of syntactically complex English expressions with the meanings of their syntactic constituents. However, the thought 'that's a rattling snake' licenses the inference 'that's dangerous'. Intuitively, that it does depends *not* just on the meaning of 'rattling' and 'snake' but also on a (presumed) fact about the world; viz., the fact that rattling snakes are dangerous. So, this inference is non-compositional (as are, by parity of argument, all other synthetic inferences). In short, it appears that some, but not all, of the inferential potential of 'that's a rattling snake' (some of its role in one's language or belief system), is determined by the respective inferential potential of 'rattling' and 'snake,' the rest being determined by one's 'real world' beliefs about rattling snakes. How bad is this?

Productivity is the thesis that every language, natural or mental, can express an open-ended set of propositions. And systematicity the thesis that every language, natural or mental, that can express the proposition that P will also be able to express many propositions that are semantically close to P. If, for example, a language can express the proposition that aRb, then it can express the proposition that bRa; if it can express the proposition that P → Q, then it can express the proposition that Q → P, and so forth (*see* Fodor and Lepore, 1992, ch. 6). If compositionality is the only available explanation of productivity, and these are both pervasive features of natural languages and of the mental life, then you cannot identify meaning with conceptual role (Fodor and Lepore, 1992, pp. 175–6). You still might identify meanings with conceptual roles in (non-structural) *analytic* inferences; viz., inferences that you must accept if you mean F by (the expression) 'F'. The contrast between *structural* and *non-structural* analyticities is illustrated by the following examples respectively: 'rattling snake' → 'rattling' and 'rattling snake' → 'rattling reptile'. The former inference is guaranteed by the linguistic principles that effect the construction 'rattling snake' alone, whereas the latter turns on the lexical inventory of its premise as opposed to its linguistic structure.

Let's suppose that just these inferences are meaning determinate; the others semantically irrelevant. So, for example, though the inference from 'that's a rattling snake' to 'that's dangerous' is not meaning determinate, the non-structural inference from 'that's a snake' to 'that's a reptile' is meaning determinate, that is, is analytic, is definitional.

In the context of characterizing the nature of meaning, it may be question begging to invoke the notion of an 'analytic' inference. But also, obviously, the cost of identifying meanings with roles in these so-called analytic inferences is to buy into the analytic/synthetic distinction. So the cost of CRS is buying into the analytic/synthetic distinction. But many philosophers, if not most, think that there is no notion of analyticity that a CRS theorist, *qua* CRS theorist, can legitimately invoke to preserve compositionality. If, then, you believe that compositionality is non-negotiable, it follows that either the analytic/synthetic distinction is in fact principled, contrary to what Quine is thought to have established, or CRS is internally flawed.

In conclusion: there is ample reason for more attention to detailed versions of CRS; however, before evaluating the prospects of these prospective CRS theories, some serious objections require response.

See also CONCEPTS; CONTENT; FUNCTIONALISM; THOUGHT; THOUGHT AND LANGUAGE.

BIBLIOGRAPHY

Block, N. 1986. Advertisement for a semantics for psychology. In *Midwest Studies in Philosophy*, vol. 10, Minneapolis: University of Minnesota Press.

de Saussure, F. 1983. *Course in General Linguistics*. ed. C. Bally and A. Sechehaye, tr. and annotated by R. Harris. London: Duckworth.

Devitt, M. 1981. *Designation*. New York: Columbia University Press.

Field, H. 1977. Logic, meaning and conceptual role. *Journal of Philosophy*, 69, 379–408.

Fodor, J., and Lepore, E. 1992. *Holism: A shopper's guide*. Oxford: Basil Blackwell.

Harman, G. 1987. (Non-solipsistic) conceptual role semantics. In *New Directions in Semantics*, ed. Lepore, E. London: Academic Press.

Lepore, E., and Loewer, B. 1987. Dual aspect semantics. In *New Directions in Semantics*, ed. E. Lepore. London: Academic Press.

Loar, B. 1981. *Mind and Meaning*. Cambridge University Press.

Lycan, W. 1984. *Logical Form in Natural Language*. Cambridge, MA. MIT Press.

Putnam, H. 1975. The meaning of 'meaning'. In *Mind, Language and Reality*. ed. H. Putnam. Cambridge University Press.

Sellars, W. 1963. Some reflections on language games. In *Science, Perception, and Reality*. London: Routledge & Kegan Paul. An article based on Sellar's reading of Wittgenstein's *Philosophical Investigations*.

Woods, W. 1981. Procedural semantics as a theory of meaning. In *Elements of Discourse Understanding*, ed. A. Joshi, B. Webber and I. Say, Cambridge University Press.

What preceded benefited from suggestions by Johannes Brandl, Jerry Fodor and Sam Guttenplan.

ERNIE LEPORE

connectionism Theorists seeking to account for the mind's activities have long sought analogues to the mind. In modern cognitive science, these analogues have provided the bases for simulation or modelling of cognitive performance (*see* COGNITIVE PSYCHOLOGY). Simulation is one way of testing theories of the mind: if a simulation performs in a manner comparable to the mind, that offers support for the theory underlying that simulation. The analogue upon which the simulation is based, however, also serves a heuristic function, suggesting ways in which the mind might operate.

In cognitive science, two analogues have provided the basis for most of the simulation activity. On the one hand, the digital computer can be used to manipulate symbols; insofar as it became possible to program the symbol processing computer to execute tasks that seemed to require intelligence, the symbol processing computer became a plausible analogue to the mind and numerous cognitive science theorists have been attracted to the proposal that the mind itself is a symbol processing device (*see* COMPUTATIONAL MODELS). The other analogue was the brain. As techniques for analysing the anatomy and physiology of the brain were developed in the first half of the twentieth century, the view that the brain consisted of a network of simple electrical processing units which stimulated and inhibited each other became popular. Researchers such as McCulloch and Pitts (1943) began to analyse how networks built out of such pro-

cessing units could perform computations such as those of sentential logic. Other researchers, such as Rosenblat (1962) and Selfridge (1959), explored the usefulness of networks in more perceptually oriented tasks.

The second approach came to be known as *connectionism*, although some theorists, often those coming from the neurosciences, prefer the term *neural networks* and others prefer the term *parallel distributed processing*. While at the outset connectionism was a serious competitor to the symbol processing approach to simulating cognition, by the time cognitive science began to take shape as a multidisciplinary research cluster in the 1970s, the connectionist approach had lost much of its appeal. In part this was due to the success of symbol processing approaches in developing plausible models of performance on higher cognitive tasks (Newell and Simon, 1972; J. R. Anderson, 1976). In part it was due to the apparent limitations of networks; Minsky and Papert's (1969) mathematical analysis of Rosenblat's perceptrons, for example, was often taken as showing the inherent limitations of network approaches. As a result, use of networks to simulate cognitive activities did not expand during the 1970s, while simulations within the symbol processing tradition mushroomed. There were, however, some extremely important theorists who persevered during this time: J. A. Anderson (1972), Grossberg (1982), and Kohonen (1972). Interest in connectionism was rekindled in the 1980s (two influential publications were Hinton and Anderson, 1981 and McClelland and Rumelhart, 1981). In part this new interest stemmed from growing frustration with the dominant symbol processing approach. It was further due to advances in network design, some stemming from the influential physicist John Hopfield (1982, 1984), others from psychologists David Rumelhart, Jay McClelland, and their colleagues (*see* Rumelhart, Hinton, and Williams, 1986). The latter collaborators, then both at the University of California San Diego, developed an influential research group (the PDP Research Group); publication of their two-volume work, *Parallel Distributed Processing: Explorations in the Microstructure of Cognition*, was one of the galvanizing developments in the emergence of the new connectionist movement. By 1990 connectionism had once again emerged as a credible competitor to the symbol processing approach to simulating cognition.

THE MECHANICS OF CONNECTIONIST MODELS

To see how connectionist networks operate, let us begin with a relatively simple network which nonetheless simulates an interesting cognitive task: generating the proper phonemic representation of the past tense of English verbs. This task is challenging since, although most verbs form their past tense in a regular manner by adding either /ed/ (*add→added*), /d/ (*play→played*), or /t/ (*walk→walked*), some verbs form their past tense in an irregular fashion (*is→was*). Rumelhart and McClelland (1986) simulated this task with a network of only two layers, an input layer and an output layer, with connections going from each input unit to each output unit. While their network exhibited some significant features of the pattern exhibited by humans learning the English past tense, it was severely criticized by Pinker and Prince (1988). (*See* Bechtel and Abrahamsen, 1991, for discussion and evaluation of that controversy.)

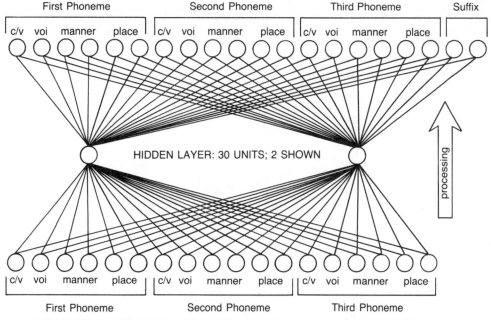

Figure 1. Three-layer feedforward network used in Plunkett and Marchman's (1991) simulation of learning the past tense of English verbs. The input units encode representations of the three phonemes of the present tense of the artificial words used in this simulation, while the output units encode the three phonemes employed in the past tense form and the suffix (/d/, /ed/, or /t/) used on regular verbs. Each input is connected to each of the 30 hidden units and so spreads activation to those units in proportion to its activation and the weight on the connection. Likewise, all hidden units are connected to every output unit.

201

Subsequently, Plunkett and Marchman (1991) developed an alternative simulation that addressed many of the objections to the earlier work and provides a clear example of how multi-layer feedforward networks operate. They developed an artificial vocabulary of 500 three-phoneme words. Most of the vocabulary items formed their past tense in one of the three regular ways. Some, however, were assigned irregular forms (either arbitrary mappings such as found in the English *go→went*, identity mappings as in *hit→hit*, and vowel change mappings as in *run→ran*.

In the network simulation each phoneme is represented on 6 of the 18 input units; these units encode whether each phoneme is a vowel or consonant, is voiced or unvoiced, as well as the manner and place of articulation (figure 1). From these input units activation is passed along weighted connections to 30 hidden units, and from them to 20 output units. On the output units the network generates a representation of the past tense of the verb supplied on the input units; 18 of the output units serve

the same function as they do on the input layer, while the remaining two units encode the possible regular endings.

The ability of the network to determine the correct past tense is governed by the weights on the connections. These weights determine how much a unit on one layer excites or inhibits a unit on a subsequent layer. For example, the input from a given input unit to a hidden unit is obtained by multiplying the activation of the input unit by the weight of the connection leading to the hidden unit; the corresponding values from all the input units are summed to determine the netinput to the hidden unit (figure 2). The hidden unit's activation is then determined from the netinput by using the logistic activation function. The process is repeated to determine the activations of the output units.

One of the attractions of connectionist networks is that there are procedures that a network can use for determining the appropriate weights on the various connections in it so that these connections do not have to be hand set. These procedures are known

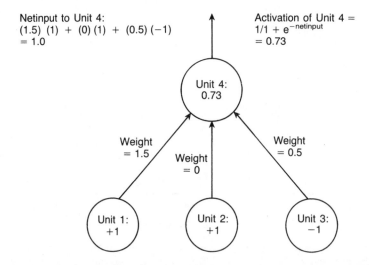

Netinput to Unit 4:
(1.5) (1) + (0) (1) + (0.5) (−1)
= 1.0

Activation of Unit 4 =
$1/1 + e^{-netinput}$
= 0.73

Unit 4:
0.73

Weight
= 1.5

Weight
= 0

Weight
= 0.5

Unit 1:
+1

Unit 2:
+1

Unit 3:
−1

Figure 2. An illustration of processing in a connectionist network. The activation levels of the four units are shown beneath their labels. The weights on the three connections leading to Unit 4 are also shown. The netinput to Unit 4 is determined by multiplying the activation of each feeding unit by the weight on the connection and summing across the three feeding units. The activation of Unit 4 is then determined according to the logistic activation function.

as *learning rules*; a general principle applied to learning rules is that they must invoke only information locally available at the units so that application of a learning rule does not require an external homunculus overseeing the behaviour of the network. Plunkett and Marchman employed one of the most commonly used learning rules, backpropagation (Rumelhart, et al., 1986). To apply this rule, the network starts with a set of random weight assignments, is supplied with the phonemic representation of a verb on its input layer, and is allowed to compute the values for the various output units. The activation generated on a given output unit is compared with the target activation for that unit: the difference constitutes a measure of error. The derivative of the error with respect to the activation of the unit is then used to guide changing the weights on the connections feeding into that unit so as to generate weights that will reduce the error in the future; this procedure is recursively applied to connections at lower levels in the network.

Plunkett and Marchman demonstrated not only that their network could learn to generate the proper past tense for the words in their vocabulary, but also that the learning showed some important similarities to the way children learn the English past tense. The network was initially trained on a set that included a large number of irregular words. Then additional words, including a smaller percentage of irregulars, was gradually added to the training set. Like children, the network first learned the correct form of the irregulars in its corpus, but subsequently tended to overgeneralize the regular form and applied it to some of the irregular forms (thus producing, using an English example, *comed* instead of *came*), before learning the correct past-tense of all verbs in its corpus.

A network such as this is considered *feedforward* because connections carry activations in only one direction, from the layer of input units to the layer of output units. Connectionists have also explored a variety of network designs. An important kind of design employs inhibitions (connections with negative weights) between units in a layer so that, while processing cycles between units of the layer, one unit or group of units becomes active and suppresses the activation of all the other units (Kohonen, 1988). Another strategy is to permit activations to flow in both directions between layers, allowing units in later units that become active to further excite those input units that have excited them (McClelland and Rumelhart, 1981). An additional strategy is to do away with the notion of layers and allow connections in both directions between units (Hopfield, 1982; Ackley, Hinton, and Sejnowski, 1985).

As exciting as some of these alternative designs are, feedforward networks continue to be the most widely used, perhaps because it is far more easy for researchers to keep track of and interpret processing in them. However, researchers also recognize that in order for connectionist networks to simulate interesting cognitive tasks, more structured networks are required. Some interesting variations in the standard feedforward network have appeared in recent years (these are described more fully in Bechtel, 1993). One strategy has been to modularize networks by allowing, for example, different networks (often with different numbers of layers and units) to process the same input (*see* MODULARITY). In this design, a further network serves as a gating network, determining which network is permitted to respond to a given input. Jacobs, Jordan, Nowlan, and Hinton (1991) have shown that the gating network can be trained by similar algorithms as used for the other networks to select the network that has given the best answers to particular classes of input. The result is a set of expert networks, each trained to respond to particular input sets. By allowing separate experts to handle different tasks, modularization overcomes one of the most severe problems confronting standard feedforward networks, that later learning can cause *catastrophic interference* with material learned earlier (McCloskey and Cohen, 1989).

Another limitation of feedforward networks is that all information to which the network is to respond must be presented at once on the input units; the network has no memory of what has been recently processed. This makes it very difficult for a network to process serially encoded information such as that of natural language. Elman (1990), adapting a design of Jordan (1986), has proposed an alternative approach. In what he calls *recurrent networks*, the activations produced on hidden units on previous cycles of processing are copied back onto a set of special input units called *context units*. These are fed into the network along with new input patterns on subsequent cycles of processing. Elman has shown that such networks can become sensitive to such things as syntactical dependencies in language. The recurrent network design has been employed in a more elaborate network by St. John and McClelland (1990) which has demonstrated remarkable abilities to arrive at semantic interpretations of a significant variety of active and passive English sentences.

CONNECTIONIST COGNITIVE ARCHITECTURES: PRO AND CON

On the basis of this brief overview, let us turn now to the usefulness of connectionist networks for simulating human performance. Perhaps the first thing to note about connectionist systems is that they point to a very different conception of cognition than do symbolic simulations. The symbol strings that are stored and manipulated in symbolic simulations are often propositions and the rules for manipulating are inspired by symbolic logic. The result is that symbolic simulations have proven quite useful in modelling cognitive performance that seems to involve logical or quasi-logical reasoning. Connectionist simulations, on the other hand, operate on very different principles. In feedforward networks, the connections allow the network to respond to patterns activated on the input units by activating patterns on the output units. Networks can be trained so that a variety of different patterns all result in activation of the same output pattern, while other collections of

patterns generate different output patterns. As a result, such networks can readily be interpreted as performing activities of pattern recognition and categorization. These networks, in fact, exhibit some rather useful properties for pattern recognition; for example, patterns similar to but not identical to those on which the network was trained will generally result in generation of output patterns similar to those used in training.

For many cognitive scientists, and especially for philosophers (*see* Rosenberg, 1990), however, the term *cognition* refers not to such basic processes as pattern recognition, but to processes involving reasoning (*see* RATIONALITY). So far, connectionist networks have proved less adept at modelling reasoning tasks (except for ones involving satisfaction of multiple soft-constraints, which is a strength of connectionist systems). Thus, one might be inclined to dismiss connectionism as irrelevant to cognition proper. In the face of this sort of objection, two sorts of responses can be advanced. First, it appears possible to train connectionist networks to use their pattern recognition capacities to carry out logical operations and even construct natural deductions (Bechtel and Abrahamsen, 1991; *see also* Touretzky, 1990), thereby showing how to ground symbol processing on connectionist pattern recognition. Second, one might construe it as an advance to refocus attention in cognitive science away from reasoning to these more basic cognitive processes that have been overlooked. Two of the most important aspects of our lives are our ability to navigate our world and to identify objects in it. This requires recognizing patterns in our environment and inaugurating patterns of response. These are abilities we share with many other creatures. But these are precisely the abilities that have been most troubling for investigators interested in robotics. In part, the difficulty in accounting for these processes may be that they require pattern recognition and this process needs to be taken more seriously.

The idea that pattern recognition and categorization are basic to cognition has been advanced by a number of theorists. Margolis (1987) argues that thinking is simply a process of pattern recognition; sequential thinking involves recognizing one pattern and using that recognition as part of the input for recognizing another pattern. Dreyfus and Dreyfus (1986) contend that skilled or expert performance in a domain such as chess rests on 'holistic discrimination and association'; one recognizes a situation to be like a previous situation and applies similar strategies to the new situation as worked in the old one. Paul Churchland (1989), drawing on the notion of *prototype* which has become central in recent psychological research on categorization, argues that the most basic form of cognitive life consists in activating perceptual prototypes and transforming them into motor prototypes.

Van Gelder (1992) has challenged this proposal to reinterpret cognition in terms of pattern recognition. Claiming that what is central to pattern recognition or categorization is putting items into similarity classes to which like responses can be given, van Gelder argues that in at least two domains, motor control and language comprehension, what is required of a cognitive system is continuously varying responses, not discrete responses, and the capacity to recognize new inputs as distinctive, not instances of previously encountered categories. Each time we reach for an object, we typically must reach to a new location, and each sentence we hear is generally different than those encountered previously. There is some irony in van Gelder's objection: in order to get networks to give categorical responses, special strategies need to be employed; otherwise, networks tend to give similar but slightly varying responses to new inputs that are similar to previous inputs. Moreover, research since Rosch (1975; *see* Barsalou, 1992, for a review) shows that people readily make prototypicality judgments when assigning items to categories, suggesting that categorization is not an all-or-nothing matter. Perhaps, then, van Gelder is employing a common but inappropriate concept of categorization.

However, the broader thrust of van Gelder's complaint is clearly correct: categorization cannot be all there is to cognition. Processing novel sentences is not simply a matter of responding as one did to the most similar sentence in the training set. At minimum, the cognizer must be sensitive to the grammatical structure of sentences and the constraints these place on interpretation. One way more complex processing is achieved in connectionist networks is to employ multiple layers of units so that each layer can recategorize the outputs of categorization by lower layers. This allows connectionist networks to accomplish more than simple association. But is it enough?

Fodor and Pylyshyn (1988; *see also* Fodor and McLaughlin, 1990) argue that it is not. They appeal to properties of language such as productivity (the fact that additional sentences can always be added to the corpus of a language) and systematicity (the fact that for any sentence of a language there are systematically related expressions that are also sentences of the language) and argue that these are also characteristics of thought (*see* FODOR). Thus, focusing on systematicity, they argue that any cognitive system that can comprehend a sentence such as

Joan loves the florist

can also understand the systematically related sentence

The florist loves Joan.

They argue that classical symbol systems, like languages, naturally exhibit systematicity since they employ operations upon symbolic representations which are built up via a compositional syntax that supports compositional semantics. Connectionist architectures do not employ symbolic representations with a compositional syntax (although they can be used to implement such systems) and hence are themselves inadequate as cognitive models.

Fodor and Pylyshyn's critique has provided a host of responses by advocates of connectionism. One is to deny that most thought, especially infra-human thought, is systematic (Bechtel, 1990; Dennett, 1991; Groschke and Koppelberg, 1991). While this might reduce the challenge facing connectionists, since it allows that much cognition might have a different character than Fodor and Pylyshyn assume, connectionists must still explain how adult human cognition, at least, often does manifest systematicity. Some connectionists have attempted to demonstrate ways in which connectionist networks, without employing explicitly syntactically compositional representations such as those found in natural language, can employ functionally compositional representations, that is, representations from which component structure can be extracted but is not present on the surface (van Gelder, 1990). Two of the best known examples of this approach are the tensor product networks of Smolensky (1990) and the RAAM (recursive auto-associative memory) networks of Pollack (1988). The claim of those pursuing these models is that while connectionists may have to employ structured internal representations, the structuring principles might be fundamentally different from those employed in natural language or symbolic models of cognition. Yet a different strategy is to argue that the systematicity that does appear in human cognition is due to the fact that humans have learned natural languages, which themselves employ a compositional syntax and semantics (Clark, 1989; Bechtel and Abrahamsen, 1991; Dennett, 1991; see Clark and Karmiloff-Smith (1993) for a critical response). On this view, networks must become sensitive to the structure of language so as to be able to extract information from linguistic inputs and produce linguistic outputs, but this does not entail building up an internal replica of the linguistic structure for use in internal processing. Simulations such as those of St. John and McClelland (1990) are suggestive as to how this might be accomplished.

It is unclear as yet whether any of these approaches are sufficient to account for the kind of cognition found in adult humans. It may be that ultimately some version of the classical symbolic approach will be required. Some connectionists are disposed to such a possibility and are developing hybrid models that employ both connectionist principles and symbolic processing principles (Dyer, 1991; Sun, 1991). Even if a hybrid approach is required, though, the connectionist elements in such models serve to extend the conception of cognition beyond the traditional perspective of logical reasoning. In helping create this expansion of our understanding of the cognitive, connectionism has thus made a contribution to cognitive science.

PHILOSOPHICAL IMPLICATIONS OF CONNECTIONISM

Insofar as it expands or transforms our understanding of cognition, connectionism will necessarily have implications for philosophy of mind. Two areas in particular on which it is likely to have impact are the analysis of the mind as a representational system and the analysis of intentional idioms (see CONTENT; INTENTIONALITY; REPRESENTATION).

Fodor (1980) distinguishes the computational theory of mind from the representational theory of mind. The representational theory holds that systems have mental states by virtue of encoding representations and standing in particular relations to them. The computational theory adds that cognitive activity consists of formal operations performed on these representations. Fodor and Pylyshyn's arguments against connectionism noted above fault it for failing to endorse the computational theory (connectionist processing does not respect the formal, compositional structure of representations). But Fodor and Pylyshyn construe connectionist models as nonetheless representational and so potentially conforming to the representational theory of mind. This is because connectionists routinely interpret the activations of units or groups of units as representing contents. This is most obviously the case for input and output units; in order to supply a cognitive interpretation of a network's activity, a theorist must treat the input as a representation of a problem and the output as representing the answer. Connectionists also tend to interpret the activations of units within a network. Sometimes this is done unit by unit: a given unit is found to be activated by inputs with certain features and so is interpreted as representing those features. Other times a more holistic analysis is used: a cluster analysis may reveal that similar patterns of activation are generated by common features in the input. This is interpreted as showing that the network has differentiated inputs with those features from inputs with different features. This suggests that connectionist systems can indeed be understood as embodying the representational theory of mind: each layer of units in a network generates a different representation of the input information until the output pattern is produced.

Even if connectionist networks exemplify the representational theory of mind, they are significantly different from more traditional exemplars of the representational theory. First, it is not clear that we can always give an interpretation of what units in a connectionist network are representing in natural language terms. Even when it appears that we can do so, there seems to be considerable noise in the representation so that the units or patterns do not seem to be picking out precisely what we designate in natural languages. Second, the representations that are constructed are not discrete but distributed or superimposed (van Gelder, 1991). That is, the same units and same connections subserve many different representational roles rather than employing one representation per role. This distinguishes connectionist representations from those humans have previously designed. Third, it needs to be emphasized that the patterns of activations on hidden units in connectionist systems are the product of the learning the system has undergone. The interpretations assigned to these units are not arbitrary, as they often seem to be in symbolic systems, but are analyses of how the network has solved the problem it was

confronting. Especially in cases in which the network is connected to real sensory inputs, and not supplied inputs by the modeller, the intentionality of these representations is genuine, not merely a product of the theorist's interpretation.

The intentional representations found within connectionist networks are typically not representations of propositions. When philosophers focus on the intentional states of cognitive systems, however, they tend to focus on states characterized in terms of PROPOSITIONAL ATTITUDES (e.g. the belief that the storm will soon cease). Propositional attitudes comprise the core of what philosophers call 'FOLK PSYCHOLOGY', since it is in terms of propositional attitudes that ordinary people typically characterize their own and other peoples' mental states. A number of philosophers attracted to connectionism have argued that connectionism, if correct, would show that folk psychology is wrong (this claim is often referred to as 'ELIMINATIVISM'). The reason for this is that, due to the distributed and superpositional nature of connectionist representations, connectionist models do not seem to have internal states that could be discretely identified as particular intentional states (Churchland, 1989). Ramsey, Stich, and Garon (1991), for example, argue that in a network they trained to report the truth values of 16 propositions there are not functionally discrete, semantically interpretable states that can play distinct causal roles. Whereas according to folk psychology we may claim that a person did something for one reason and not another, we cannot do so with a connectionist network since all units and connections are always involved. Thus, they claim that if connectionism is true, folk psychology must be false and should be eliminated.

Not all philosophers have concurred with this judgment of the relation of connectionism to folk psychology. Lycan (1991), for example, argues that even if connectionist networks only employ units representing microfeatures of what is represented at the propositional attitude level, propositional representations and consequently propositional attitudes may supervene upon these. Even though the presence or absence of a representation of a proposition about which we may have a belief may not directly figure in the causal machinery of the system, the differences between a system on which that propositional representation supervenes and one on which it does not will suffice to make the relatively imprecise causal claims we commonly make in the folk idiom. Another approach, largely compatible with Lycan's, is inspired by DENNETT's (1978) reasons for instrumentalism about intentional attitudes. While Dennett acknowledges that intentional attitudes provide important information about cognitive systems, they do not pick out internal states of those systems. This permits one to advance a realist interpretation of intentional attitudes as long as such attitudes are assigned to cognitive agents, not their sub-personal operations. The internal operations must make the whole system adhere to the folk psychological characterization, but the folk vocabulary need not refer to discrete internal states. On this construal as well, connectionism offers no threat to folk psychology (Bechtel and Abrahamsen, 1993).

Whether or not connectionism undercuts folk psychology, however, it clearly challenges any philosophical view that assumes that cognition is primarily a matter of storing propositions and processing them according to rules of logic. If, for example, an epistemology construed knowledge as involving the internal representation of a proposition and the justificatory argument for its truth, that epistemology would not be compatible with connectionism. However, if all that is required is the capacity to produce a proposition and, if required, to identify evidence for it, then a linguistically trained connectionist network is subject to epistemological analysis. However, connectionism might also have further implications for epistemology. It might, for instance, inspire us to consider evidential relations less strong than logical argument and the possibility that knowledge might be exhibited in abilities to act (what Ryle referred to as *knowing*

how) as well as in propositions that can be recited. Thus, connectionism might also broaden our perspective not just in our theories of mind, but also in our theories in domains such as epistemology.

BIBLIOGRAPHY

Ackley, D.H., Hinton, G.E., and Sejnowski, T.J. 1985. A learning algorithm for Boltzmann machines. *Cognitive Science*, 9, 147–69.

Anderson, J.A. 1972. A simple neural network generating an interactive memory. *Mathematical Biosciences*, 14, 197–220.

Anderson, J.R. 1976. *Language, Memory, and Thought*. Hillsdale, NJ: Lawrence Erlbaum.

Barsalou, L.W. 1992. *Cognitive Psychology: An Overview for Cognitive Science*. Hillsdale, NJ: Lawrence Erlbaum.

Bechtel, W. 1990. Multiple levels of inquiry in cognitive science. *Psychological Research*, 52, 271–81.

Bechtel, W. 1993. Currents in connectionism. *Minds and Machines* 3.

Bechtel, W., and Abrahamsen, A. 1991. *Connectionism and the Mind. An Introduction to Parallel Processing in Networks*. Oxford: Basil Blackwell.

Bechtel, W., and Abrahamsen, A. 1993. Connectionism and the future of folk psychology. *Minds: Natural and Artificial*, ed. R. Burton. Albany, NY: SUNY Press.

Churchland, P.M. 1989. *A Neurocomputational Perspective. The Nature of Mind and the Structure of Science*. Cambridge, MA: MIT Press.

Clark, A. 1989. *Microcognition: Philosophy, Cognitive Science, and Parallel Distributed Processing*. Cambridge, MA: MIT Press.

Clark, A., and Karmiloff-Smith, A. 1993. The cognizer's innards: A philosophical and developmental perspective on human thought. *Mind and Language*, 6, 487–579.

Dennett, D.C. 1978. *Brainstorms*. Cambridge, MA: MIT Press.

Dennett, D.C. 1991. Mother nature versus the walking encyclopedia. In *Philosophy and Connectionist Theory*, ed. W. Ramsey, S. P. Stich, and D. E. Rumelhart. Hillsdale, NJ: Lawrence Erlbaum.

Dreyfus, H.L., and Dreyfus, S.E. 1986. *Mind over Machine: The Power of Human Intuition and Expertise in the Era of the Computer*. New York: Harper & Row.

Dyer, M. 1991. Symbolic neuroengineering for natural language processing: A multilevel research approach. In *Advances in Connectionist and Neural Computational Theory*, ed. J. Barnden and J. Pollack. Norwood, NJ: Ablex.

Elman, J.L. 1990. Finding structure in time. *Cognitive Science*, 14, 179–212.

Fodor, J.A. 1980. Methodological solipsism considered as a research tradition in cognitive psychology. *Behavioral and Brain Sciences*, 3, 63–73.

Fodor, J.A., and McLaughlin, B.P. 1990. Connectionism and the problem of systematicity: Why Smolensky's solution doesn't work. *Cognition*, 35, 183–204.

Fodor, J.A., and Pylyshyn, Z.W. 1988. Connectionism and cognitive architecture: A critical analysis. *Cognition*, 28, 3–71.

Groschke, T., and Koppelberg, D. 1991. The concept of representation and the representation of concepts in connectionist models. In *Philosophy and Connectionist Theory*, ed. W. Ramsey, S. P. Stich, and D. E. Rumelhart. Hillsdale, NJ: Lawrence Erlbaum.

Grossberg, S. 1982. *Studies of Mind and Belief*. Dordrecht: Reidel.

Hinton, G.E., and Anderson, J.A. 1981. *Parallel Models of Associative Memory*. Hillsdale, NJ: Erlbaum.

Hopfield, J.J. 1982. Neural networks and physical systems with emergent collective computational abilities. *Proceedings of the National Academy of Sciences*, 79, 2554–8.

Hopfield, J.J. 1984. Neurons with graded response have collective computational properties like those of two state-neurons. *Proceedings of the National Academy of Sciences*, 81, 3088–92.

Jacobs, R.A., Jordan, M.I., Nowlan, S.J. and Hinton, G.E. 1991. Adaptive mixtures of local experts. *Neural Computation*, 3, 79–87.

Jordan, M. 1986. Attractor dynamics and parallelism in a connectionist sequential machine. *Proceedings of the Eighth Annual Conference of the Cognitive Science Society*. Hillsdale, NJ: Lawrence Erlbaum.

Kohonen, T. 1972. Correlation matrix memories. *IEEE Transactions on Computers C-21* 353–9.

Kohonen, T. 1988. *Self Organization and Associative Memory*. New York: Springer-Verlag.

Lycan, W.G. 1991. Homuncular functionalism meets PDP. In *Philosophy and Connectionist Theory*, ed. W. Ramsey, S. P. Stich, and D. E. Rumelhart. Hillsdale, NJ: Lawrence Erlbaum.

Margolis, H. 1987. *Patterns, Thinking, and Cognition*. University of Chicago Press.

McClelland, J.L., and Rumelhart, D.E. 1981. An interactive activation model of context effects in letter perception: Part I. An account of basic findings. *Psychological Review*, 88, 375–407.

McClelland, J.L. Rumelhart, D.E., and the PDP Research Group 1986. *Parallel Distributed Processing: Explorations in the Microstructure of Cognition, Vol. 2: Psychological and Biological Models*. Cambridge, MA.: MIT Press.

McCloskey, M., and Cohen, N.J. 1989. Catastrophic interference in connectionist networks: The sequential learning problem. In *The Psychology of Learning and Motivation*, vol. 24, ed. G. H. Bower. New York: Academic Press.

McCulloch, W.S., and Pitts, W.H. 1943. A logical calculus of the ideas immanent in nervous activity. *Bulletin of Mathematical Biophysics*, 5, 115–33.

Minsky, M.A., and Papert, S. 1969. *Perceptions*. Cambridge, MA: MIT Press.

Newell, A., and Simon, H.A. 1972. *Human Problem Solving*. Englewood Cliffs, NJ: Prentice Hall.

Pinker, S., and Prince, A. 1988. On language and connectionism: Analysis of a parallel distributed processing model of language acquisition. *Cognition*, 28, 73–193.

Plunkett, K., and Marchman, V. 1991 U-shaped learning and frequency effects in a multi-layered perception: Implications for child language acquisition. *Cognition*, 38, 1–60.

Pollack, J. 1988. Recursive auto-associative memory: Devising compositional distributed representations. *Proceedings of the 10th Annual Conference of the Cognitive Science Society*. Hillsdale, NJ.: Erlbaum.

Ramsey, W., Stich, S.P., and Garon, J. 1991. Connectionism, eliminativism, and the future of folk psychology. *Philosophy and Connectionist Theory*, ed. W. Ramsey, S. P. Stich, and D. E. Rumelhart. Hillsdale, NJ: Lawrence Erlbaum.

Rosenberg, J.F. 1990. Treating connectionism

properly: Reflections on Smolensky. *Psychological Research*, 52, 163–74.

Rosenblat, F. 1962. *Principles of Neurodynamics: Perceptrons and the Theory of Brain Mechanisms*. Washington, DC: Spartan Books.

Rosch, E. 1975. Cognitive representation of semantic categories. *Journal of Experimental Psychology: General*, 104, 192–233.

Rumelhart, D.E., and McClelland, J.L. 1986. On learning the past tense of English verbs. In *Parallel distributed processing: Explorations in the microstructure of cognition, Vol. 2: Psychological and Biological Models*, ed. J. L. McClelland, D. E. Rumelhart and the PDP Research Group. Cambridge, MA.: MIT Press.

Rumelhart, D.E., McClelland, J.L., and the PDP Research Group 1986. *Parallel Distributed Processing: Explorations in the Microstructure of Cognition, Vol. 1: Foundations*. Cambridge, MA.: MIT Press.

Rumelhart, D.E., Smolensky, P., McClelland, J.L., and Hinton, G.E. 1986. Schemas and sequential thought processes in PDP models. In *Parallel distributed processing: Explorations in the microstructure of cognition, Vol. 2: Psychological and Biological Models*, ed. J. L. McClelland, D. E. Rumelhart, and the PDP Research Group. Cambridge, MA.: MIT Press.

Selfridge, O.G. 1959. Pandemonium: A paradigm for learning. *Symposium on the Mechanization of Thought Processes*. London: HMSO.

Smolensky, P. 1990. Tensor product variable binding and the representation of symbolic structures in connectionist systems. *Artificial Intelligence*, 46, 159–216.

St. John, M.F., and McClelland, J.L. 1990. Learning and applying contextual constraints in sentence comprehension. *Artificial Intelligence*, 46, 217–57.

Sun, R. 1991 Connectionist models of rule-based reasoning. *Proceedings of the 13th Annual Conference of the Cognitive Science Society*. Hillsdale, NJ: Erlbaum.

Touretzky, D.S. 1990. BoltzCONS: Dynamic symbol structures in a connectionist network. *Artificial Intelligence*, 46, 5–46.

van Gelder, T. 1990. Compositionality: A connectionist variation on a classical theme. *Cognitive Science*, 14, 355–84.

van Gelder, T. 1991. What is the 'D' in 'PDP'? A survey of the concept of distribution, In *Philosophy and Connectionist Theory*, ed. W. Ramsey, S. P. Stich, and D. E. Rumelhart. Hillsdale, NJ: Lawrence Erlbaum.

van Gelder, T. 1992. Is cognition categorization?

WILLIAM BECHTEL

consciousness T. H. Huxley (1866) said 'How it is that anything so remarkable as a state of consciousness comes about as a result of irritating nervous tissue, is just as unaccountable as the appearance of Djin when Aladdin rubbed his lamp.' This is the famous 'explanatory gap'. We have no conception of our physical or functional nature that allows us to understand how it could explain our subjective experience. This fact (in a form expressed by Nagel, 1974; the term 'explanatory gap' comes from Levine, 1983) has dominated the last 20 years of discussion of consciousness. Francis Crick and Christoff Koch (1990) have famously hypothesized that the neural basis of consciousness is to be found in certain phase-locked 40 Hz neural oscillations. But how does a 40 Hz neural oscillation explain *what it's like* (in Nagel's memorable phrase) to be us? What is so special about a 40 Hz oscillation as opposed to some other physical state? And why couldn't there be creatures with brains just like ours in their physical and functional properties, including their 40 Hz oscillation patterns, whose owners' experiences were very unlike ours, or who had no subjective experiences at all? One doesn't have to suppose that there really *could be* creatures with brains just like ours who have different experiences or no experiences to demand an account of *why not?* But no one has a clue about how to answer these questions. This is the heart of the mind–body problem.

Consciousness in the sense discussed is phenomenal consciousness. 'What's *that?*', you ask. There is no non-circular definition to be offered; the best that can be done is the offering of synonyms, examples and one or another type of pointing to the phenomenon (Goldman, forthcoming). For example,

I used as synonyms 'subjective experience' and 'what it is like to be us'. In explaining phenomenal consciousness, one can also appeal to conscious properties or qualities, e.g. the ways things seem to us or immediate phenomenological qualities. Or one can appeal to examples: the ways things look or sound, the way pain feels and more generally the experiential properties of sensations, feelings and perceptual experiences. I would also add that thoughts, wants and emotions often have characteristic conscious aspects, and that a difference in representational content can make a phenomenal difference. Seeing something as a cloud differs from seeing it as a part of a painted backdrop (*see* PERCEPTUAL CONTENT). What it is like to hear Bulgarian spoken depends on whether one understands the language.

We gain some perspective on the explanatory gap if we contrast the issue of the physical/functional basis of consciousness with the issue of the physical/functional basis of thought. In the case of thought, we do have some theoretical proposals about what thought is, or at least what human thought is, in scientific terms. Cognitive scientists have had some success in explaining some features of our thought processes in terms of the notions of representation and computation (*see* Block, 1990). There are many disagreements among cognitive scientists: especially notable is the disagreement between connectionists and classical 'LANGUAGE OF THOUGHT' theorists (*see* COGNITIVE PSYCHOLOGY; CONNECTIONISM). However, the notable fact is that in the case of thought, we actually have more than one substantive research programme, and their proponents are busy fighting it out, comparing which research programme handles which phenomena best. But in the case of consciousness, we have nothing – zilch – worthy of being called a research programme, nor are there any substantive proposals about how to go about starting one. (*See* Baars, 1988, for an indication of how what passes for a research programme about phenomenal consciousness is just more cognitive psychology – actually a

theory of a different notion of consciousness, access-consciousness, to be described below.) Researchers are *stumped*. There have been many tantalizing discoveries recently about neuropsychological syndromes in which consciousness seems to be in some way missing or defective (*see* Young, 1994; Baars, 1988), but no one has yet come up with a theoretical perspective that uses these data to narrow the explanatory gap, even a little bit.

PERSPECTIVES ON THE EXPLANATORY GAP

Needless to say, there are many different attitudes towards this problem, but five of them stand out. First, we might mention ELIMINATIVISM, the view that consciousness as understood above simply does not exist (Churchland, 1983; Dennett, 1988; Rey, 1983). So there is nothing for there to be an explanatory gap about. Second, we have various forms of reductionism, notably FUNCTIONALISM and PHYSICALISM. According to these views, there is such a thing as consciousness, but there is no singular explanatory gap, that is, there are no mysteries concerning the physical basis of consciousness that differ in kind from run of the mill unsolved scientific problems about the physical/functional basis of liquidity, inheritance or computation. On this view, there is an explanatory gap, but it is unremarkable. A third view is what Flanagan (1992) calls the new mysterianism. Its most extreme form is *transcendentalism* (White, 1991), the view that consciousness is simply not a natural phenomenon and is not explainable in terms of science at all. A less extreme form of new mysterianism is that of McGinn (1991), which concedes that consciousness is a natural phenomenon but emphasizes *our* problem in understanding the physical basis of consciousness. McGinn argues that there are physical properties of our brains that do in fact explain consciousness, but though this explanation might be available to some other type of being, it is cognitively closed off to us. A fourth view that has no well-known name (*see* Nagel, 1974; Flanagan, 1992; Searle, 1992), holds that though there may be important differences between a naturalistic explanation of consciousness and naturalistic explanations of other phenomena, there is no convincing reason to regard consciousness as non-natural or unexplainable in naturalistic terms (*see* NATURALISM). This view is suggested by Nagel's remark that we are like the person ignorant of relativity theory who is told that matter is a form of energy but who does not have the concepts to appreciate how there could be chains of reference-links leading from a single phenomenon to both 'matter' and 'energy'. The explanatory gap exists – and we cannot conceive of how to close it – because we lack the scientific concepts. But future theory may provide those concepts. A fifth view could be described as deflationist about the explanatory gap. The gap is unclosable, but not because we cannot find the right physical concepts. Rather, it is unclosable because reductive explanation requires an a priori analysis of the phenomenon to be explained, and no such analysis can be given of our concepts of conscious experience. (*See* QUALIA for more on this view.)

Dennett (1988) argues for eliminativism. He uses a thought experiment about two coffee tasters, Chase and Sanborn. Both liked Maxwell House coffee when they started, and both dislike it now. But they tell very different stories about what happened. Chase says that he has become more sophisticated; he used to like the taste of Maxwell House, but he no longer does. Sanborn is equally certain that he can remember what the coffee used to taste like, but he still thinks that that original taste is a great taste: the source of *his* change, he says, is a change in his perceptual apparatus, perhaps his taste buds. He no longer *gets* that nice old taste when he drinks Maxwell House. Dennett points out that either Chase or Sanborn (or both) might be wrong because of changes in their *memories* of the tastes. For example, perhaps Maxwell House coffee still tastes exactly the same to Sanborn as it always did, but his memory of what it used to taste like has slowly, imper-

ceptibly changed over time. So Sanborn's current dislike of Maxwell House could be traced to a memory change plus a change in his standards with no change at all in his perceptual machinery. Further, Dennett points out, their reports are consistent with a variety of combinations of partial or total changes in memory, aesthetic standards and perceptual machinery.

It is not easy to see how this example is supposed to support eliminativism, but I would reconstruct the main argument as follows:

(1) Suppose phenomenal consciousness exists, that is, there are real phenomenally conscious properties.
(2) Then there can be a fact of the matter as to whether Chase and Sanborn are right.
(3) But if there are real phenomenally conscious properties, they are transparent.
(4) However, only an expert, say a neurophysiologist who can examine the brains of Chase and Sanborn, could tell whether their memories, aesthetic standards and current conscious qualities on drinking Maxwell House have changed.
(5) The fact that we cannot rely on the testimony of Chase and Sanborn themselves shows that phenomenally conscious qualities are not transparent.
(6) From (3) and (5) we can deduce that there are no real phenomenally conscious qualities.

Once we actually set out the argument, it is easy to see what is wrong with it: for (3) and (5) to both be true, there must be an equivocation on 'transparent'. The fact that it is possible that the stories Chase and Sanborn believe are wrong shows only that their memories could be wrong, and that an expert might be able to tell them that. But no advocate of transparency of phenomenal consciousness ought to suppose that *memories* of conscious states are literally *incorrigible*. There are a variety of ways of understanding 'transparent' in which it plausibly applies to phenomenally conscious qualities of my states *when I am having those states*, and these senses would make (3) true without making (5) true. (*See* Flanagan, 1992, for reconstructions and rebuttals of other arguments for eliminativism.)

OTHER CONCEPTS OF CONSCIOUSNESS

Thus far I have been talking about phenomenal consciousness. But there are other concepts of consciousness – cognitive or intentional or functional concepts of consciousness – that are often not distinguished from it, and it is common for deflationists or reductionists about phenomenal consciousness to tacitly slide from phenomenal consciousness to one or another of these cognitive or intentional or functional concepts (*see* Dennett, 1991, and my review, Block, 1993). I will mention three such concepts of consciousness: self-consciousness, monitoring-consciousness and access-consciousness.

(1) *Self-consciousness* is the possession of the concept of the SELF and the ability to use this concept in thinking about oneself. There is reason to think that animals or babies can have phenomenally conscious states without employing any concept of the self. To suppose that phenomenal consciousness requires the concept of the self is to place an implausible intellectual condition on phenomenal consciousness. Perhaps phenomenally conscious states have a *non-conceptual* content that could be described as 'experienced as mine', but there is no reason to think that this representational aspect of the state exhausts its phenomenal properties. After all, if both my experience as of blue and my experience as of red are experienced as mine, we still need to explain the difference between the two experiences; the fact, if it is a fact, that they are both experienced as mine will not distinguish them. (The 'as of' terminology is intended to preclude cases in which red things don't look red.)

(2) *Monitoring-consciousness* takes many forms. (The source of these ideas in the philosophical literature is Armstrong, 1968, 1980; *see also* Lycan, 1987; Rosenthal, 1986; Carruthers, 1989.) One form is 'internal scanning', but it would be a mistake to conflate internal scanning with phenomenal consciousness. As Rey (1983) notes, ordinary laptop computers are capable of internal scanning, but it would be silly to think of one's laptop as conscious. Rey favours supposing that internal scanning is sufficient for consciousness, if there is such a thing, and so he concludes that consciousness is a concept that both includes and precludes laptop computers being conscious, and hence that the concept of consciousness is incoherent. But even if we acknowledge 'internal scanning consciousness', we should drop the idea that internal scanning is sufficient for *phenomenal* consciousness, and so we get no incoherence.

Another form of monitoring consciousness is that of accompaniment by a higher-order thought. That is, a conscious state is one that is accompanied by a thought (grounded non-inferentially and non-observationally) to the effect that one is in that state. I favour a liberal terminological policy, and so I have no objection to this idea as a concept of consciousness. But I do object to the idea (Rosenthal, 1986) that phenomenal consciousness should be identified with higher-order-thought consciousness. One way to see what is wrong with that view is to note that even if I were to come to know about states of my liver non-inferentially and non-observationally – as some people just know what time it is – that wouldn't make the states of my liver phenomenally conscious (*see* Dretske, 1993). Another objection is that phenomenal consciousness does not require the intellectual apparatus that is required for higher-order thought. Thus, the identification of phenomenal consciousness with higher-order thought shares the over-intellectualism of the identification of phenomenal consciousness with self-consciousness. Dogs and babies may have phenomenally conscious pains without thoughts to the effect that they have those pains.

A distinction is often made between *state consciousness*, or intransitive consciousness – and *consciousness of*, or transitive consciousness (Rosenthal, 1986). For example, if I say I'm nauseous, I ascribe a kind of intransitive consciousness to myself, and if I say I am now seeing something as a mosquito, I ascribe transitive consciousness. The higher-order thought view purposely collapses these notions. According to the higher-order thought view, a conscious state (intransitive consciousness) of mine is simply a state that I am conscious of (transitive consciousness), and consciousness of is simply a matter of accompaniment by a thought to the effect that I am in that state. So what it is for a state of mine to be conscious (intransitively) is for it to be accompanied by a thought that I am in that state (*see* Rosenthal, 1986; Carruthers, 1989).

This intentional conflation has an element of plausibility to it, which can be seen by comparing two dogs, one of which has a perceptual state whereas the other has a similar perceptual state plus a representation of it. Surely the latter dog has a conscious state even if the former dog does not! Quite so, because consciousness *of* brings consciousness with it. But it is the *converse* that is problematic. State consciousness makes less in the way of intellectual demands than consciousness of, and so the first dog could be conscious without being conscious of anything.

(3) *Access-consciousness* does not make the intellectual demands of self-consciousness or higher-order-thought consciousness, and for that reason, reductionists about phenomenal consciousness would do better to identify phenomenal consciousness with access-consciousness. A state is access-conscious if, in virtue of one's having the state, a representation of its content is (a) inferentially promiscuous, i.e. freely available as a premise in reasoning, and (b) poised for rational control of action and (c) poised for rational control of speech. One can speak of both states and their contents as access-conscious. My claims about access-consciousness have been criticized in Flanagan (1992, p. 145–6), in Searle (1990; 1992, p. 84), and improvements suggested in Davies and Humphreys (1993b). There are three main differences

between access-consciousness and phenomenal consciousness that ought to be acknowledged by those of us who are realists about a non-intentional, non-functional, non-cognitive notion of consciousness. First, it is in virtue of its phenomenal content (or the phenomenal aspect of its content) that a state is phenomenally conscious, whereas it is in virtue of its representational content or the representational aspect of its content that a state is access-conscious. Second, access-consciousness is a functional notion, but phenomenal consciousness is not. If you are a functionalist about phenomenal consciousness, it would be very natural to identify it with access-consciousness. Note that I deny that the concept of phenomenal consciousness is functional, but I acknowledge the empirical possibility that the scientific essence of phenomenal consciousness is something to do with information processing (*see* Loar, 1990). Third, access-consciousness applies to state tokens, or rather tokens at times, but phenomenal consciousness is best thought of as a feature of state types. Let me explain. The following inscription, 'teeth', that you just read contains five letter tokens, but of only three letter types. There is a token of the type *dog* in my office, but the type *dog* itself is an abstract object that doesn't exist anywhere in space-time. Here is why access is a matter of tokens at times: a single token state might be access-conscious at one time but not another, because of changes in information flow in the system, just as my keys are accessible at some times but not others (when I lose them). (And any actually accessible token might not have been accessible.) But a token of a phenomenal type is necessarily phenomenally conscious – it can't become non-phenomenally conscious without disappearing altogether. In other words, access-consciousness – but not phenomenal consciousness – is a functional notion – and a single token can change function (both actually and counterfactually).

A good way to see the distinction is to note cases of one without the other. Consider a robot with a computer brain that is behaviourally and computationally identical to ours. The question arises as to whether what it is like to be that robot is different from what it is like to be us, or, indeed, whether there is anything at all that it is like to be that robot. If there is nothing it is like to be that robot, the robot is a zombie. If zombies are conceptually possible, they certainly illustrate access-consciousness without phenomenal consciousness. But there is widespread opposition to the conceptual coherence of zombies (*see* Shoemaker, 1975, 1981; Dennett, 1991). So for illustrating access-consciousness without phenomenal consciousness, I would rather rely on a very limited sort of partial zombie.

Consider blindsight, a neurological syndrome in which subjects seem to have 'blind' areas in their visual fields. If the experimenter flashes a stimulus to one of those blind areas, the patient claims to see nothing at all. But if the experimenter insists that the subject guess, and the experimenter supplies a few alternatives, the blindsight patients are able to 'guess' reliably about certain features of the stimulus, features having to do with motion, location, direction, and they are able to discriminate some simple forms (Weiskrantz, 1986; Young, 1994). Consider a blindsight patient who 'guesses' that there is an 'X' rather than an 'O' in his blind field. The patient has no access-consciousness of the stimulus (because, until he hears his own guess, he cannot use the information freely in reasoning or in rational control of action), and it is plausible that he has no phenomenal consciousness of it either. Now imagine something that does not exist, what we might call *super-blindsight*. A real blindsight patient can only guess when given a choice among a small set of alternatives ('X'/'O', horizontal/vertical, etc.). But suppose (apparently contrary to fact) that a blindsight patient could be trained to prompt himself at will, guessing what is in the blind field without being told to guess. Visual information from the blind field simply pops into his thoughts the way that solutions to problems sometimes pop into ours or (to use an example given earlier) the way some people just know what time it is without any special perceptual experience. The super-blindsight patient says there is something it is like to see an 'X' in his sighted field, but not in his blind field, and we believe him. This would be a case of access-consciousness without phenomenal consciousness, a sort of partial zombie.

Here is an example of the converse of the zombie cases, namely phenomenal consciousness without access-consciousness. It appears that some areas of the brain specialize in reasoning and rational control of action, whereas other areas subserve sensation. If a person's brain has the former areas destroyed, he is unable to use the deliverances of the senses to rationally control action, to reason or to report sensibly, but he can still have experiences. Such a person has phenomenal consciousness without access-consciousness.

Here is a different sort of example. Suppose that you are engaged in intense thought when suddenly at midnight you realize that there is now and has been for some time a deafening pounding noise going on. You were aware of the noise all along, but only at midnight were you consciously aware of it. That is, you were phenomenally conscious of the noise all along, but only at midnight did you become access-conscious of it. The period before midnight illustrates phenomenal consciousness without access-consciousness. 'Conscious' and 'aware' are roughly synonymous, so it is natural to use one for the period before midnight, and both for the period after midnight when there are two kinds of consciousness present.

Another illustration of phenomenal consciousness without access-consciousness derives from a famous experiment by George Sperling. Sperling (1960) flashed arrays of letters (e.g. 3-by-3) to subjects for 50 milliseconds. Subjects typically said that they could see all of the letters, but typically could report only about half of them. Were the subjects right in saying that they could see all of the letters? Sperling tried signalling the subjects with a tone. A high tone meant that the subject was to report the top row, a

215

medium tone indicated the middle row, etc. If the tone was given immediately after the stimulus, the subjects could usually get all the letters in the row, no matter which row, but once they had named those letters they could get no others. The experiment is taken by psychologists to indicate some sort of raw visual storage, the 'visual icon'. But I have a different interest, the question of what it is like to be a subject in this experiment. My own experience is that I see all or almost all the letters – other subjects report the same thing (Baars, 1988, p. 15). And I would say I see them as 'N', 'J', 'B', etc., as specific letters, not just as blurry or vague or non-specific letters. I (and others) cannot report much more than a single row. So subjects are phenomenally conscious of all (or almost all) the letters at once, but not access-conscious of all of them at once. In sum, one can be phenomenally conscious of more than one is access-conscious of.

The two cases I've mentioned of phenomenal consciousness without access-consciousness are also counterexamples to the higher-order thought theory of phenomenal consciousness. If the subject has no access to the phenomenal state, he can't think about it either. Before midnight, I have a phenomenally conscious state caused by the noise but no thought to the effect that I am in such a state. And in the Sperling experiment, I am phenomenally conscious of all or almost all the letters, but since I can't access all the letters at once, I can't represent them all at once (except as letters).

Akins (1993) has argued against the distinction between a phenomenal and a representational aspect of experience. She keys her discussion to Nagel's (1974) claim that we cannot know what it is like to be a bat, challenging the reader to imagine that what it is like to be a bat is just what it is like to be us – only all those experiences represent totally different things. Correctly, she says that you cannot imagine that. That is because, as I mentioned earlier, representational differences of a certain sort make a phenomenal difference. What it is like to hear a sound as coming from the left is different from what it is like to hear a sound as

coming from the right. And what it is like to hear Bulgarian depends on whether one speaks the language (see Goldman, 1993; Davies, forthcoming; Peacocke, 1992; Tye, forthcoming a). But from the fact that some representational differences make a phenomenal difference, one should not conclude that there is no distinction between the representational and the phenomenal. Note, for example, that representational differences of the sort that obtain between me and my twin on Putnam's TWIN EARTH needn't make a phenomenal difference. Further, there are phenomenal states that aren't at all representational, orgasm for example. Further, two distinct phenomenal contents can overlap representationally, for example a visual and a kinaesthetic representation of one's hand moving. Note that the point is *not* just that there is a representational overlap without a corresponding phenomenal overlap (as is said, for example, in Pendlebury, 1992). That would be compatible with the following story: phenomenal content is just one kind of representational content, but these experiences overlap in non-phenomenal representational content. The point, rather, is that the phenomenal qualities are themselves representational; the *as of motion* is part of the two phenomenal contents, two phenomenal contents that themselves overlap representationally, but the two phenomenal contents represent the same thing via different phenomenal qualities.

IS 'CONSCIOUSNESS' AMBIGUOUS?

I have distinguished a number of different concepts of consciousness, phenomenal consciousness, self-consciousness, monitoring consciousness and access-consciousness. Am I saying that the word 'conscious' is ambiguous? I don't think that the different concepts of consciousness I have mentioned indicate a straightforward ambiguity; for example, you won't find a straightforward distinction among any of these concepts in a dictionary. (Though some dictionaries mention self-consciousness separately.) I would rather say that 'conscious' (together with 'aware', 'experience' and other words similarly used) *should* be ambiguous. An analogy: Kuhn (1964) points out that Aristotle failed to distinguish between average velocity and instantaneous velocity, and made a crucial mistake because of this conflation. There is no ambiguity in 'velocity' or 'speed' in ordinary English, but the seeds are there, and a distinction is needed for some purposes. My own view on the empirical linguistic question as to what 'consciousness' means is that it is a cluster concept. Consider the concept of a religion, a cluster concept that involves belief in a supreme being, a moral code, rituals, sacred objects, a special plane of experience, etc. There can be (and often are) religions that lack any one or two of these (*see* Alston, 1967). The cluster in the case of 'consciousness' involves phenomenal consciousness, access-consciousness, self-consciousness, monitoring-consciousness, and perhaps other elements. The problem is that these elements are so different from one another that failure to distinguish among the different elements can lead to serious confusion. An undifferentiated 'conscious' works well for most purposes, but for serious thinking we need conceptual clarification. (Of recent books on consciousness, the ones I've noticed that distinguish phenomenal consciousness from other notions are Lycan, 1987; Flanagan, 1992; and Davies and Humphreys, 1993a.)

CONFLATIONS

There are two notable sorts of trouble writers get into by not making these distinctions. One is to be found in Jaynes (1976) and Dennett (1986, 1991). These authors allege that consciousness is a cultural construction – Jaynes even gives its invention a date: between the events reported in the Oddysey and the Iliad. They seem to be talking about phenomenal consciousness, but if one accepts a notion of phenomenal consciousness as distinct from the cognitive and functional notions I have described, the idea that consciousness was invented by the ancient Greeks is ludicrous. If there is such

a thing as phenomenal consciousness as distinct from the cognitive and functional notions I have described, surely it is a basic biological feature of us. The same is true for access-consciousness, which is the best guess as to what Dennett is usually talking about. Obviously, our ability to access information from our senses is genetically programmed. And I would say the same for most forms of monitoring. What Jaynes and Dennett ought to be saying is that there is no such thing as phenomenal consciousness as distinct from the other consciousnesses. They ought to be reductionists or eliminativists about consciousness. The conflation is especially silly in Jaynes, where it is obvious that 'consciousness' in the sense in which it is supposed to have been invented by the Greeks is something like a *theory* of consciousness in roughly the phenomenal sense. (*See* Dennett, 1986, for a defence of Jaynes.)

Another type of problem has nothing to do with reductionism or eliminativism. Consider, for example, Searle's (1992) reasoning about a function of consciousness. Searle mentions Penfield's description of petit mal epilepsy patients who are 'totally unconscious', but nonetheless continue their activities of walking or driving home or playing a piano piece, but in an inflexible and uncreative way. Searle says that the lack of consciousness explains the lack of flexibility and creativity, and so one of the functions of consciousness is to add powers of flexibility and creativity. Searle is talking about the function of *phenomenal consciousness*, but he gives no reason to think that the petit mal patients lack *that* kind of consciousness. The patients don't cope with new situations very well, but they show every sign of normal sensation. For example, Searle describes the epileptic walker as threading his way through the crowd. Isn't there something it is like for him to see, say, a red sign, which he knows to turn right at? What is most obviously deficient in these patients is not phenomenal consciousness, but cognitive and functional consciousnesses. Penfield (1975) does say that the patients are 'totally unconscious', but he appears to have some sort of monitoring consciousness in mind, not phenomenal consciousness. In another publication, Searle (1990) criticizes the idea that there is any access-sense of consciousness, saying that the idea that there is such a thing confuses 'what I would call peripheral consciousness or inattentiveness with total unconsciousness. It is true, for example, that when I am driving my car "on automatic pilot", I am not paying much attention to the details of the road and the traffic. But it is simply not true that I am totally unconscious of these phenomena. If I were, there would be a car crash' (p. 635). Note the contradiction. In one place, he says that a 'totally unconscious' epileptic can drive home, and in another place he says that if a driver were 'totally unconscious' the car would crash. In the first place, he is thinking of total lack of phenomenal consciousness (combined with some degree of access-consciousness), whereas in the second, he is thinking of a total lack of access-consciousness (or both types of consciousness).

A variant on this mistake is found in the writings of many authors, including Flanagan (1992), who argues that since a thirsty blindsight patient will make no move towards a water fountain in his blind field, and since phenomenal consciousness of the water fountain is missing, phenomenal consciousness must have a function in initiating action. But in the blindsight patient, access-consciousness and monitoring consciousness of events in the blind field are *also* missing. We can explain why the blindsight patient does not move towards the water fountain by noting that with the missing access-consciousness, the content of the perceptual state is not available for rational control of action. (I don't have the space to argue here that in general we need not appeal to the missing monitoring consciousness to explain this phenomenon.) There is no need to appeal to the missing phenomenal consciousness, even if Flanagan is right that phenomenal consciousness is missing. (And if phenomenal consciousness is not missing in blindsight, we have a different fallacy—like the Searle mistake just

pointed out.) The main error here is to transfer by conflation an obvious function of access-consciousness to phenomenal consciousness.

See also CONTENT; *An Essay on Mind* section 2.2; PAIN; SENSATIONS; SUBJECTIVITY.

BIBLIOGRAPHY

Akins, K. 1993. A bat without qualities. In Davies and Humphreys, 1993a.

Alston, W. 1967. Religion. In *The Encyclopedia of Philosophy*. New York: Macmillan.

Armstrong, D.M. 1968. *A Materialist Theory of Mind*. London: Humanity Press.

Armstrong, D.M. 1980 'What is consciousness?' In *The Nature of Mind*. Ithaca: Cornell University Press.

Baars, B.J. 1988. *A Cognitive Theory of Consciousness*. Cambridge University Press.

Block, N. 1990. The computer model of the mind. In *An Invitation to Cognitive Science: Thinking*, ed. D. Osherson and E. Smith, Cambridge, MA: MIT Press.

Block, N. 1993. Review of D. Dennett, *Consciousness Explained. The Journal of Philosophy*, XC, 4: 181–93.

Carruthers, P. 1989. Brute experience. *Journal of Philosophy*, 86, 258–69.

Chalmers, D.J. 1993. *Toward a Theory of Consciousness*. University of Indiana Ph.D. thesis.

Churchland, P.S. 1983. Consciousness: the transmutation of a concept. *Pacific Philosophical Quarterly*, 64, 80–93.

Crick, F. and Koch, C. 1990. Towards a neurobiological theory of consciousness. *Seminars in the Neurosciences*, 2, 263–75.

Davies, M. and Humphreys, G. 1993a. *Consciousness*. Oxford. Basil Blackwell.

Davies, M. and Humphreys, G. 1993b. Introduction. In Davies and Humphreys 1993a.

Davies, M. forthcoming. Externalism and experience.

Dennett, D. 1986. Julian Jaynes' software archaeology. *Canadian Psychology*, 27: 2, 149–54.

Dennett, D. 1988. Quining Qualia. In *Consciousness in Contemporary Society*, ed. A. Marcel and E. Bisiach. Oxford University Press.

Dennett, D. 1991. *Consciousness Explained*. New York: Little Brown.

Dretske, F. 1993. Conscious experience. *Mind*, 102: 406, 263–84.

Flanagan, O. 1992. *Consciousness Reconsidered*. Cambridge, MA.: MIT Press.

Goldman, A. 1993. The psychology of folk psychology. *The Behavioral and Brain Sciences*, 16:1, 15–28.

Goldman, A. forthcoming. Consciousness, folk psychology and cognitive science. *Consciousness and Cognition*.

Humphreys, N. 1992. *A History of the Mind*. New York: Simon & Schuster.

Huxley, T.H. 1866. *Lessons in Elementary Physiology*. Quoted in Humphrey (1992).

Jaynes, J. 1976. *The Origin of Consciousness in the Breakdown of the Bicameral Mind*. Boston: Houghton-Mifflin.

Kuhn, T. 1964. A function for thought experiments. In *Melanges Alexandre Koyre*, vol. 1. Hermann.

Levine, J. 1983. Materialism and qualia: the explanatory gap. *Pacific Philosophical Quarterly*, 64, 354–61.

Levine, J. 1993. On leaving out what it is like. In Davies and Humphreys, 1993a.

Loar, B. 1990. Phenomenal properties. In *Philosophical Perspectives: Action Theory and Philosophy of Mind*, ed. J. Tomberlin. Atascadero, CA.: Ridgeview.

Lycan, W. 1987. *Consciousness*. Cambridge, MA.: MIT Press.

McGinn, C. 1991. *The Problem of Consciousness*. Oxford: Basil Blackwell.

Nagel, T. 1974. What is it like to be a bat? *Philosophical Review*, 83, 435–50.

Peacocke, C. 1992. *A Study of Concepts*. Cambridge, MA.: MIT Press.

Pendlebury, M. 1992. Experience, theories of. In *A Companion to Epistemology*, ed. J. Dancy and E. Sosa. Oxford: Basil Blackwell.

Penfield, W. 1975. *The Mystery of the Mind: A Critical Study of Consciousness and the Human Brain*. Princeton University Press.

Rey, G. 1983. A reason for doubting the existence of consciousness. In *Consciousness and Self-Regulation*, Vol. 3, ed. R. Davidson, G. Schwartz, D. Shapiro. New York: Plenum.

Rosenthal, D. 1986. Two concepts of consciousness. *Philosophical Studies*, 49, 329–59.

Searle, J. 1990. Who is computing with the brain? *Behavioral and Brain Sciences*, 13:4, 632–42.

Searle, J. 1992. *The Rediscovery of the Mind*. Cambridge, MA.: MIT Press.

Shoemaker, S. 1975. Functionalism and qualia. *Philosophical Studies*, 27, 291–315.

Shoemaker, S. 1981. Absent qualia are impossible – a reply to Block. *The Philosophical Review*, 90: 4, 581–99.

Sperling, G. 1960. The information available in brief visual presentations. *Psychological Monographs*, 74, 11.

Tye, M. forthcoming a. Does pain lie within the domain of cognitive psychology? In *Philosophical Perspectives*, 8, ed. J. Tomberlin. Atascadero, CA.: Ridgeview.

Tye, M. forthcoming b. How to become puzzled about phenomenal consciousness?

Weiskrantz, L. 1986. *Blindsight*. Oxford University Press.

White, S. 1991. Transcendentalism and its discontents. In *The Unity of the Self*, Cambridge, MA.: MIT Press.

Young, A.W. 1994. Neuropsychology of awareness. In *Consciousness in philosophy and cognitive neuroscience*, ed. M. Kappinen and A. Revonsuo. New York: Erlbaum.

NED BLOCK

content (1) Mental events, states or processes with content include seeing the door is shut; believing you are being followed; and calculating the square root of 2. What centrally distinguishes states, events or processes – henceforth, simply states – with content is that they involve reference to objects, properties or relations. A mental state with content can fail to refer, but there always exists a specific condition for a state with content to refer to certain things. When the state has a correctness or fulfilment condition, its correctness is determined by whether its referents have the properties the content specifies for them.

This highly generic characterization of content permits many subdivisions. It does not in itself restrict contents to conceptualized content; and it permits contents built from Frege's senses as well as Russellian contents built from objects and properties. It leaves open the possibility that unconscious states, as well as conscious

219

states, have content. It equally allows the states identified by an empirical, computational psychology to have content. A correct philosophical understanding of this general notion of content is fundamental not only to the philosophy of mind and psychology, but also to the theory of knowledge and to metaphysics.

ASCRIBING CONTENTS

A widely discussed idea is that for a subject to be in a certain set of content-involving states is for attribution of those states to make the subject as rationally intelligible as possible, in the circumstances. In one form or another, this idea is found in the writings of Davidson (1984), Dennett (1987), McDowell (1986), Putnam (1988) and Sellars (1963). Perceptions make it rational for a person to form corresponding beliefs. Beliefs make it rational to draw certain inferences. Beliefs and desires make rational the formation of particular intentions, and the performance of the appropriate actions. People are frequently irrational of course, but a governing ideal of this approach is that for any family of contents, there is some minimal core of rational transitions to or from states involving them, a core that a person must respect if his states are to be attributed with those contents at all (*see* RATIONALITY).

This approach must deal with the point that it seems metaphysically possible for there to be something that in actual and counterfactual circumstances behaves as if it enjoys states with content, when in fact it does not. If the possibility is not denied, this approach must add at least that the states with content causally interact in various ways with one another, and also causally produce intentional action (*see* REASONS AND CAUSES). The existence of such causal links could well be written into the minimal core of rational transitions required for the ascription of the contents in question.

It is one thing to agree that the ascription of content involves a species of rational intelligibility; it is another to provide an explanation of this fact. There are compet-

ing explanations. One treatment regards rational intelligibility as ultimately dependent upon what *we* find intelligible, or on what we could come to find intelligible in suitable circumstances (McDowell, 1986). This is an analogue of classical treatments of secondary qualities, and as such is a form of subjectivism about content. An alternative position regards the particular conditions for correct ascription of given contents as more fundamental. This alternative states that interpretation must respect these particular conditions. In the case of conceptual contents, this alternative could be developed in tandem with the view that concepts are individuated by the conditions for possessing them (Peacocke, 1992). These possession conditions would then function as constraints upon correct interpretation. If such a theorist also assigns references to concepts in such a way that the minimal rational transitions are also always truth-preserving, he will also have succeeded in explaining why such transitions are correct. Under an approach that treats conditions for attribution as fundamental, intelligibility need not be treated as a subjective property. There may be concepts we could never grasp because of our intellectual limitations, as there will be concepts that members of other species could not grasp. Such concepts have their possession conditions, but some thinkers could not satisfy those conditions.

Ascribing states with content to an actual person has to proceed simultaneously with attribution of a wide range of non-rational states and capacities. In general, we cannot understand a person's reasons for acting as he does without knowing the array of emotions and sensations to which he is subject; what he remembers and what he forgets; and how he reasons beyond the confines of minimal rationality. Even the content-involving perceptual states, which play a fundamental role in individuating content, cannot be understood purely in terms relating to minimal rationality. A perception of the world as being a certain way is not (and could not be) under a subject's rational control. Though it is true and important that perceptions give reasons for forming beliefs, the beliefs for which they funda-mentally provide reasons – observational beliefs about the environment – have con-tents which can only be elucidated by refer-ring back to perceptual experience. In this respect (as in others), perceptual states differ from those beliefs and desires that are indi-viduated by mentioning what they provide reasons for judging or doing; for frequently these latter judgments and actions can be individuated without reference back to the states that provide reasons for them.

What is the significance for theories of content of the fact that it is almost certainly adaptive for members of a species to have a system of states with representational con-tents which are capable of influencing their actions appropriately? According to tele-ological theories of content, a constitutive account of content – one which says what it is for a state to have a given content – must make use of the notions of natural function and teleology. The intuitive idea is that for a belief state to have a given content p is for the belief-forming mechan-isms which produced it to have the function (perhaps derivatively) of producing that state only when it is the case that p (Milli-kan, 1986; Papineau, 1987). One issue this approach must tackle is whether it is really capable of associating with states the classi-cal, realistic, verification-transcendent con-tents which, pretheoretically, we attribute to them. It is not clear that a content's holding unknowably can influence the replication of belief-forming mechanisms. But even if content itself proves to resist elu-cidation in terms of natural function and selection, it is still a very attractive view (one also developed in Millikan, 1984) that selection must be mentioned in an account of what associates something – such as a sentence – with a particular content, even though that content itself may be individu-ated by other means.

Contents are normally specified by 'that . . .' clauses, and it is natural to suppose that a content has the same kind of sequential and hierarchical structure as the sentence that specifies it. This supposition would be widely accepted for conceptual content. It is, however, a substantive thesis that all content is conceptual. One way of treating one sort of PERCEPTUAL CONTENT is to regard the content as determined by a spatial type, the type under which the region of space around the perceiver must fall if the experience with that content is to represent the environment correctly. The type involves a specification of surfaces and features in the environment, and their dis-tances and directions from the perceiver's body as origin (Peacocke, 1992). Such con-tents *prima facie* lack any sentence-like structure at all. Supporters of the view that all content is conceptual will argue that the legitimacy of using these spatial types in giving the content of experience does not undermine the thesis that all content is conceptual. Such supporters will say that the spatial type is just a way of capturing what can equally be captured by conceptual components such as 'that distance', or 'that direction', where these demonstratives are made available by the perception in ques-tion. Friends of non-conceptual content will respond that these demonstratives them-selves cannot be elucidated without men-tioning the spatial types which lack sentence-like structure.

CONTENT AND EXTERNALISM

The actions made rational by content-involving states are actions individuated in part by reference to the agent's relations to things and properties in his environment. Wanting to see a particular movie and believing that that building over there is a cinema showing it makes rational the action of walking in the direction of that building. Similarly, for the fundamental case of a subject who has knowledge about his environment, a crucial factor in making rational the formation of particular attitudes is the way the world is around him. One may expect, then, that any theory that links the attribution of contents to states with rational intelligibility will be committed to the thesis that the content of a person's states depends in part upon his relations to the world outside him. We can call this thesis the thesis of externalism about content.

Externalism about content should steer a middle course. On the one hand, it should not ignore the truism that the relations of rational intelligibility involve not just things and properties in the world, but the way they are presented as being – an externalist should use some version of Frege's notion of a mode of presentation (*see* CONCEPTS). On the other hand, the externalist for whom considerations of rational intelligibility are pertinent to the individuation of content is likely to insist that we cannot dispense with the notion of something in the world – an object, property or relation – being presented in a certain way. If we dispense with the notion of something external being presented in a certain way, we are in danger of regarding attributions of content as having no consequences for how an individual relates to his environment, in a way that is quite contrary to our intuitive understanding of rational intelligibility.

Externalism comes in more and less extreme versions. Consider a thinker who sees a particular pear, and thinks a thought 'that pear is ripe', where the demonstrative way of thinking of the pear expressed by 'that pear' is made available to him by his perceiving the pear. Some philosophers, including Evans (1982) and McDowell (1984), have held that the thinker would be employing a different perceptually based way of thinking were he perceiving a different pear. But externalism need not be committed to this. In the perceptual state that makes available the way of thinking, the pear is presented as being in a particular direction from the thinker, at a particular distance, and as having certain properties. A position will still be externalist if it holds that what is involved in the pear's being so presented is the collective role of these components of content in making intelligible in various circumstances the subject's relations to environmental directions, distances and properties of objects. This can be held without commitment to the object-dependence of the way of thinking expressed by 'that pear'. This less strenuous form of

externalism must, though, address the epistemological arguments offered in favour of the more extreme versions, to the effect that only they are sufficiently world-involving.

Externalism about content is a claim about dependence, and dependence comes in various kinds. In the discussions of the 1970s, the writings of Kripke (1980), Putnam (1975) and Burge (1979) moved the contents of beliefs to the forefront of discussion. The apparent dependence of the content of beliefs on factors external to the subject can be formulated as a failure of supervenience of belief content upon facts about what is the case within the boundaries of the subject's body (*see* SUPERVENIENCE). To claim that such supervenience fails is to make a modal claim: that there can be two persons the same in respect of their internal physical states (and so in respect of those of their dispositions that are independent of content-involving states), who nevertheless differ in respect of which beliefs they have. Putnam's celebrated example of a community on TWIN EARTH, where the water-like substance in lakes and rain is not H_2O but some different chemical compound XYZ – twater – illustrates such failure of supervenience. A molecule-for-molecule replica of you on twin earth has beliefs to the effect that twater is thus-and-so. Those with no chemical beliefs on twin earth may well not have any beliefs to the effect that water is thus-and-so, even if they are replicas of persons on earth who do have such beliefs. Burge emphasized that this phenomenon extends far beyond beliefs about natural kinds.

In the case of content-involving perceptual states, it is a much more delicate matter to argue for the failure of supervenience. The fundamental reason for this is that attribution of perceptual content is answerable not only to factors on the input side – what in certain fundamental cases causes the subject to be in the perceptual state – but also to factors on the output side – what the perceptual state is capable of helping to explain amongst the subject's actions. If differences in perceptual content always involve differences in bodily-described actions in suitable counterfactual circumstances, and if these different actions always have distinct neural bases, perhaps there will after all be supervenience of content-involving perceptual states on internal states. But if this should turn out to be so, that is not a refutation of externalism for perceptual contents. A different reaction to this situation is that the elaboration of the relation of dependence as one of supervenience is in some cases too strong. A better characterization of the dependence in question is given by a constitutive claim: that what makes a state have the content it does is certain of its complex relations to external states of affairs. This can be held without commitment to the modal separability of certain internal states from content-involving perceptual states.

Attractive as externalism about content may be, it has been vigorously contested, notably by Jerry Fodor (1981). Fodor endorses the importance of explanation by content-involving states, but holds that content must be narrow, constituted by internal properties of an individual (Fodor, 1991). One influential motivation for narrow content is a doctrine about explanation, that molecule-for-molecule counterparts must have the same causal powers. Externalists have replied that the attributions of content-involving states presuppose some normal background or context for the subject of the states, and that content-involving explanations commonly take the presupposed background for granted. Molecular counterparts can have different presupposed backgrounds, and their content-involving states may correspondingly differ. Presupposition of a background of external relations in which something stands is found in other sciences outside those that employ the notions of content, including astronomy and geology, as Davies (1986) and Burge (1986) have respectively noted.

A more specific concern of those sympathetic to narrow content is that when content is externally individuated, the explanatory principles postulated in which content-involving states feature will be a priori in some way that is illegitimate. For instance, it appears to be a priori that behaviour is intentional under some description involving the concept *water* will be explained by mental states that have the externally individuated concept *water* in their content. The externalist about content will have a twofold response. First, explanations in which content-involving states are implicated will also include explanations of the subject's standing in a particular relation to the stuff water itself, and for many such relations, it is in no way a priori that the thinker's so standing has a psychological explanation at all. Some such cases will be fundamental to the ascription of externalist content on treatments that tie such content to the rational intelligibility of actions relationally characterized. Second, there are other cases in which the identification of a theoretically postulated state in terms of its relations generates a priori truths, quite consistently with that state playing a role in explanation. It arguably is a priori that if a gene exists for a certain phenotypical characteristic, then it plays a causal role in the production of that characteristic in members of the species in question. Far from being incompatible with a claim about explanation, the characterization of genes that would make this a priori also requires genes to have a certain causal-explanatory role.

If anything, it is the friend of narrow content who has difficulty accommodating the nature of content-involving explanation. States with narrow content are fit to explain bodily movements, provided they are not characterized in environment-involving terms. But we noted that the characteristic explananda of content-involving states, such as walking towards the cinema, are characterized in environment-involving terms. How is the theorist of narrow content to accommodate this fact? He may say that we merely need to add a description of the context of the bodily movement, which ensures that the movement is in fact a movement towards the cinema. But adding a specification of a new environmental property of an event to an explanation of that event does not give one an explanation of the event's having that environmental property, let alone a content-involving explanation of the fact. The bodily movement may also be a walking in the direction of Moscow, but it does not follow that we have a rationally intelligible explanation of the event as a walking in the direction of Moscow. Perhaps the theorist of narrow content would at this point add further relational properties of the internal states, of such a kind that when his explanation is fully supplemented, it sustains the same counterfactuals and predictions as does the explanation that mentions externally individuated contents. But such a fully supplemented explanation is not really in competition with the externalist's account. It begins to appear that if such extensive supplementation is adequate to capture the relational explananda, it is also sufficient to ensure that the subject is in states with externally individuated contents (Peacocke, 1993). This problem affects not only treatments of content as narrow, but any attempt to reduce explanation by content-involving states to explanation by neurophysiological states.

One of the tasks of a subpersonal computational psychology is to explain how individuals come to have beliefs, desires, perceptions and other personal-level content-involving properties. If the content of personal-level states is externally individuated, then the contents mentioned in a subpersonal psychology that is explanatory of those personal states must also be externally individuated. One cannot fully explain the presence of an externally individuated state by citing only states that are internally individuated. On an externalist conception of subpersonal psychology, a content-involving computation commonly consists in the explanation of some externally individuated states by other externally individuated states.

This view of subpersonal content has, though, to be reconciled with the fact that the first states in an organism involved in the explanation of a particular visual experience – retinal states in the case of humans – are not externally individuated.

The reconciliation is effected by the presupposed normal background, whose importance to the understanding of content we have already emphasized. An internally individuated state, when taken together with a presupposed external background, can explain the occurrence of an externally individuated state.

An externalist approach to subpersonal content also has the virtue of providing a satisfying explanation of why certain personal-level states are reliably correct in normal circumstances. If the subpersonal computations that cause the subject to be in such states are reliably correct, and the final computation is of the content of the personal-level state, then the personal-level state will be reliably correct. A similar point applies to reliable errors, too, of course. In either case, the attribution of correctness conditions to the subpersonal states is essential to the explanation.

Externalism generates its own set of issues that need resolution, notably in the epistemology of attributions. A content-involving state may be externally individuated, but a thinker does not need to check on his relations to his environment to know the content of his beliefs, desires and perceptions. How can this be? A thinker's judgments about his own beliefs are rationally responsive to his own conscious beliefs. It is a first step to note that a thinker's beliefs about his own beliefs will then inherit certain sensitivities to his environment that are present in his original (first-order) beliefs. But this is only the first step, for many important questions remain. How can there be conscious externally individuated states at all? Is it legitimate to infer from the content of one's states to certain general facts about one's environment, and if so how, and under what circumstances?

Ascription of attitudes to others also needs further work on the externalist treatment. In order knowledgeably to ascribe a particular content-involving attitude to another person, we certainly do not need to have explicit knowledge of the external relations required for correct attribution of the attitude. How then do we manage it? Do we have tacit knowledge of the relations on which content depends, or do we in some way take our own case as primary, and think of the relations as whatever underlies certain of our own content-involving states? If the latter, in what wider view of other-ascription should this point be embedded? Resolution of these issues, like so much else in the theory of content, should provide us with some understanding of the conception each one has of himself as one mind amongst many, interacting with a common world which provides the anchor for the ascription of contents.

See also ACTION; BELIEF; CONTENT (2); DAVIDSON; FOLK PSYCHOLOGY; INTENTION; INTENTIONALITY; PROPOSITIONAL ATTITUDES; REPRESENTATION; THOUGHT.

BIBLIOGRAPHY

Burge, T. 1979. Individualism and the Mental. *Midwest Studies in Philosophy, Vol. 4*, 73–121.

Burge, T. 1986. Individualism and Psychology. *Philosophical Review*, XCV(1), 3–45.

Davidson, D. 1984. *Inquiries into Truth and Interpretation*. Oxford: Clarendon Press.

Davies, M. 1986. Externality, Psychological Explanation and Narrow Content. *Proceedings of the Aristotelian Society Supplementary Volume*, 60, 263–83.

Dennett, D. 1987. *The Intentional Stance*. Cambridge, MA.: MIT Press.

Evans, G. 1982. *The Varieties of Reference*. Oxford University Press.

Fodor, J. 1981. Methodological Solipsism considered as a Research Strategy in Cognitive Psychology. In *Representations*. Hassocks: Harvester Press.

Fodor, J. 1991. A Modal Argument for Narrow Content. *Journal of Philosophy*, LXXXVIII(1), 5–26.

Kripke, S. (1980). *Naming and Necessity*. Oxford: Basil Blackwell.

McDowell, J. 1984. *De Re* Senses. *Philosophical Quarterly*, xxxiv, 283–94.

McDowell, J. 1986. Functionalism and Anomalous Monism. In *Actions and Events: Perspectives on the Philosophy of Donald Davidson*, ed. E. Lepore and B. McLaughlin. Oxford: Basil Blackwell.

Millikan, R. 1984. *Language, Thought and Other Biological Categories*. Cambridge, MA.: MIT Press.

Millikan, R. 1986. Thoughts without Laws: Cognitive Science with Content. *Philosophical Review*, 95, 47–80.

Papineau, D. 1987. *Reality and Representation*. Oxford: Basil Blackwell.

Peacocke, C. 1992. *A Study of Concepts*. Cambridge, MA.: MIT Press.

Peacocke, C. 1993. Externalist Explanation. *Proceedings of the Aristotelian Society*, XCIII, 203–30.

Putnam, H. 1975. The Meaning of 'Meaning'. In *Mind, Language and Reality*. Cambridge University Press.

Putnam, H. 1988. *Representation and Reality*. Cambridge, MA.: MIT Press.

Sellars, W. 1963. Empiricism and the Philosophy of Mind. In *Science, Perception and Reality*. London: Routledge & Kegan Paul.

CHRISTOPHER PEACOCKE

content (2) A central assumption in much current philosophy of mind is that PROPOSITIONAL ATTITUDES like BELIEFS and DESIRES play a causal or explanatory role in mediating between PERCEPTION and behaviour (*see* REASONS AND CAUSES). This causal-explanatory conception of propositional attitudes, however, casts little light on their representational aspect. The causal-explanatory roles of beliefs and desires depend on how they interact with each other and with subsequent actions. But the representational contents of such states can often involve referential relations to external entities with which thinkers are causally quite unconnected. These referential relations thus seem extraneous to the causal-explanatory roles of mental states. It follows that the causal-explanatory conception of mental states must somehow be amplified or supplemented if it is to account for representational content.

INTERPRETATIONAL SEMANTICS

Much research in ARTIFICIAL INTELLIGENCE aims to develop computational systems which can simulate the working of other systems. For example, in arithmetical calculators the causal relations between different calculator states simulate arithmetical relations between numbers; in weather-forecasting computers the causal relations between computer states simulate meteorological interactions between weather conditions; and so on (*see* COMPUTATIONAL THEORIES OF MIND).

This has led some philosophers to suggest that representation is a matter of *interpretational semantics*, by which they mean that the states in a computational system can be taken to represent any system of objects whose relations are isomorphic to the causal relations between the computational states (*see* Cummins, 1989, ch. 8).

However, while this is arguably a satisfactory account of the notion of representation used in artificial intelligence, it is inadequate as an account of mental representation. This is because, according to interpretational semantics, every cognitive system will represent an indefinite number of other systems in addition to its 'intended interpretation'. Thus, for example, an adding machine can be interpreted, not only as representing sums of integers, but also as representing sums of even integers, sums of multiples of three sums of money accumulated in a bank account, sums of distances travelled on train journeys, and so on, *ad infinitum*.

In practice, of course, the beliefs of the human users of the adding machine will determine one of these as the appropriate interpretation. But this only serves to bring out the point that something beyond interpretational semantics must determine the representational features of human beliefs. For if the beliefs of human users can fix determinate representational contents for computer states, then they will need to have determinate contents themselves. And this cannot be because some further interpreter fixes those contents – for this would only set us off on a regress – but because human beliefs have determinate representational contents in their own right.

CAUSAL SEMANTICS

A natural alternative suggestion is to explain the representational contents of human beliefs as those *external* conditions that *cause* those beliefs. This suggestion in effect adds an external dimension to the causal-explanatory conception of mental states. Instead of thinking of causal-explanatory roles purely in terms of those mental interactions that occur inside the agent, we also include interactions between mental states and conditions external to the agent.

However, there is an obvious problem facing this simple *causal* strategy. It has difficulty accounting for *misrepresentation*, that is, for false beliefs. Take the belief that there is a cow in front of you, say. This belief will on occasion be caused by things other than cows, such as gnus, plastic cows, holograms of cows, and so on. But this then means that, on the present suggestion, this belief should stand, not just for the presence of a cow, but rather for the disjunctive condition: cow-or-gnu-or-plastic-cow-or . . . and so on, for all the other possible causes of the belief. And this would then make it impossible for the belief to be falsely held, since anything that can cause the belief will thereby be counted as part of its disjunctive truth condition (*see* CONCEPTS).

This 'disjunction problem' would be soluble if we could somehow distinguish a privileged set of 'typical' or 'ideal' circumstances for the formation of beliefs. For then we could equate the truth conditions of beliefs specifically with their causes in such ideal circumstances, and thus leave room for beliefs to be false when they arise from other possible causes in non-ideal circumstances. It is doubtful, however, whether there is any non-question-begging way of picking out such ideal circumstances. For there seems no principled way of specifying such circumstances, except as those where people form *true* beliefs. But this last mention of representational truth will then make the causal account of representational content circular (*see* Cummins, 1989, ch. 4; Fodor, 1990, ch. 2).

DRETSKE (1981) aims to solve the disjunction problem by identifying truth conditions specifically with those conditions that cause beliefs during learning. That is, Dretske argues that truth conditions are those conditions with which beliefs are associated while we are acquiring the ability to form them: other causes which operate after learning is over are excluded from truth conditions, and can hence give rise to false beliefs. There are obvious difficulties facing this theory, however: first, there is no clear point at which learning stops; second, it does not seem that a child will be disqualified from learning the concept *cow* just because it is shown a few gnus in the learning process (or, for that matter, just because it is shown some *pictures* of cows); third, this suggestion will not apply to any types of beliefs that are innate (*see* INNATENESS).

FODOR (1987, 1990) suggests a different way of dealing with the disjunction problem. He argues that our concept *cow* stands for cows, and not cows-or-gnus, because cows would still cause *cow*-thoughts even if gnus didn't, but gnus wouldn't cause *cow*-thoughts if cows didn't. Fodor's idea is that the occurrence of cow-thoughts depends on cows in a way it doesn't depend on gnus. This suggestion has been subject to a number of detailed objections (*see* Fodor, 1990, ch. 4). A more general worry is that it implicitly presupposes what it ought to be explaining: while it is true that cow-thoughts depend asymmetrically on cows rather than gnus, this is more naturally seen as a consequence of the representational significance of cow-thoughts, rather than as the basis of it.

Causal theories of representation share an important corollary with both traditional verificationist theories of meaning and with Donald DAVIDSON's philosophical semantics. This is because causal theories imply that in general believers will tend to have true beliefs. For if the truth conditions of beliefs are those conditions that (typically) cause those beliefs, then it follows that the beliefs that humans are (typically) caused to have will be true.

Verificationism and Davidson arrive at similar conclusions by different routes.

Verificationism analyses representation in terms of the rules governing judgments, rather than their causes. And Davidson argues that interpretation should be governed by a 'principle of charity'. But all three approaches take it that the truth conditions of beliefs should be equated, roughly speaking, with the conditions under which those beliefs are held.

Because of this, they all agree that there are principled reasons, flowing from the nature of representation, why true beliefs are the norm, and false beliefs the exception.

Some philosophers regard this as an attractive consequence, since it reduces the space available for sceptical arguments to challenge our claims to knowledge. However, other philosophers regard such verificationist consequences as intrinsically implausible, notwithstanding any desirable epistemological consequences they may have, and would prefer an analysis of representation that avoids them.

TELEOLOGICAL SEMANTICS

As we have seen, causal theories of content are stymied by the 'disjunction problem': they find it difficult to distinguish, among all the possible causes of a given belief, those that are part of its truth condition from those that are not. A number of philosophers have sought to remedy this defect by introducing *teleological* considerations (Millikan, 1984; Papineau, 1984). This account views beliefs as states with biological purposes, and analyses their truth conditions specifically as those conditions that they are biologically *supposed* to covary with. Our cow-beliefs stand for cows, and not gnus, according to this teleological account, because it is their purpose to be held when cows, but not gnus, are present.

This teleological theory of representation needs to be supplemented with a philosophical account of biological teleology. Defenders of the teleological theory of representation generally favour a natural selectionist account of biological purpose, according to which item F has purpose G if and only if it is now present as a result of past selection by some process which favoured items with G. So a given belief type will have the purpose of covarying with p say, if and only if some mechanism has selected it because it has covaried with p in the past.

On this account of biological purposes, the paradigm purposive traits are genes whose effects have led to increases in their frequency over generations. But such inter-generational selection of genes is not the only selection process that can give rise to biological purposes. For learning is also a natural selection process, namely a process that favours items that give rise to reward-ing results. So an item that has been learned will for that reason have a biologi-cal purpose. Most types of beliefs are learned rather than innate, and the teleological theory will therefore take their purposes to derive from processes of learning rather than inter-generational genetic selection.

When combined with the natural selec-tion account of teleology, the teleological theory of representation does have a counterintuitive consequence. Imagine that I suddenly acquire an 'accidental replica', which coagulates out of passing atoms by cosmic happenstance, but which is mol-ecule-for-molecule identical to myself. Since this being has no past, its states are not the result of any selection processes, and so, according to the teleological theory, will not have any representational contents. Despite its physical identity to myself, it won't share my thoughts.

Though this consequence is unquestion-ably counterintuitive, a number of re-sponses are open to defenders of the teleological theory. First, they can observe that recent debates about 'broad contents' provide independent grounds for doubting that representational contents are always fixed by ('supervene on') internal physical make-up (see EXTERNALISM/INTERNALISM). However, this is only part of an answer, for the accidental replica implies a far more radical failure of SUPERVENIENCE than the familiar examples of broad contents. Second, defenders of the teleological theory

can seek some alternative account of bio-logical purpose, which does not depend on past histories of natural selection, and which would thereby detach the teleological theory of representation from the natural selection account of teleology. This would allow them to argue that the accidental replica's states do have biological purposes, and hence representational contents, despite their lack of selectional history. However, prospects for a non-selectional account of biological purposes seem poor. Third, defen-ders of the teleological theory can argue that their theory is intended as a theoret-ical, rather than a conceptual, reduction of the everyday notion of representation. As such it is no objection that their theory has counterintuitive consequences, any more than it is an objection to the atomic theory of matter that water's being made of hydro-gen and oxygen runs counter to common sense.

A more substantial objection to the tele-ological theory is that it fails to solve the disjunction problem. Consider the state in a frog's brain which registers that a fly is crossing its field of vision. This state also responds to any small black dots. The tele-ological theory holds that this state rep-resents flies, rather than small black dots, because it is the *biological purpose* of this state to covary with flies. But, as Fodor has asked (1990, ch. 3), what shows that the biological purpose of this state is to covary with flies, rather than with flies-or-any-small-black-dots? After all, the frog's cog-nitive system is not *malfunctioning* when it responds to a black dot rather than a fly. So why not say that state's purpose is to respond to any small black dots (noting in addition that this is a useful purpose in environments where most small black dots are flies)?

However, Fodor's thinking is here overly influenced by the causal theory of repres-entation. The purpose of a belief, like the purpose of any other biological item, is primarily a matter of the *results* produced by the belief, not its causes. We need to ask what benefit the belief provides, once it is present, not what leads to the presence of the belief in the first place. More specifically, we need to focus on those conditions that enable the belief to produce the advantageous results which led to its selection. For the frog-state, these conditions specifically involve the presence of flies, not just any black dots, since it is specifically when flies are present that the frog-state leads the frog to behave in ways that have advantageous results.

Note that when the teleological theory is interpreted in this way, the verificationist thesis that beliefs generally tend to be true no longer follows. Truth conditions are now a matter of output – when will the belief lead to advantageous results? – rather than input – what conditions give rise to the belief? – and there is no reason to suppose that beliefs will normally, or even often, be present in those conditions where they lead to advantageous results. True, they must *sometimes* have led to advantageous results in the past, in order to have been favoured by natural selection. But selection does not require that advantageous results have a high frequency, provided that sufficient advantage accrues when they do occur. In addition, the environment may have changed since the initial selection in such a way as to further reduce the frequency with which advantageous results occur.

For example, if the frog-belief represents flies, then it is true that, according to the teleological theory, it must sometimes have been co-present with flies in the past, otherwise it could not have been selected for the advantageous results it then produced. But this still allows that the frog-belief may nearly always occur in the absence of flies, and so nearly always be false. Non-fly black dots may always have triggered the belief more often than flies, for even if the normal outcome of the belief was a mouthful of leaf or grit, rather than a fly, the state would still have been selected if sufficient nutrition accrued on those few occasions when a fly was caught. And maybe the environmental frequency of flies has fallen even further since the state was selected, with the result that the frog-belief is now triggered by non-fly black dots even more often. To have the

truth condition *fly*, the belief must have advantageous results when it is copresent with flies. But there is no reason why it should usually have advantageous results, and so no reason why it should usually be true.

SUCCESS SEMANTICS

Some beliefs have biological purposes that do not require them to be true, thus casting doubt on the teleological theory's equation of truth conditions with the conditions under which beliefs serve their biological purposes. Consider the not uncommon belief, found among those facing some imminent trial of violence, that they will not be injured in the ensuing conflict. It is arguable that humans are biologically prone to form this belief, in order to ensure that they will not flinch in battle. But this purpose, of stopping them flinching, will be fulfilled even in cases where they *do* get injured, in apparent conflict with the teleological theory of representation, which equates the truth condition of the belief – that they *won't* get injured – with the condition required for it to fulfil its purpose.

This objection requires that we look more closely at the different ways in which beliefs can give rise to advantageous results. It will turn out that the teleological theory of representation needs to be supplemented by a 'success semantics', which equates the truth conditions of beliefs specifically with the conditions under which beliefs will lead to the *satisfaction of desires*.

The *primary* way in which a belief can lead to advantageous results is by combining with a desire to generate an ACTION that succeeds in satisfying that desire because the belief is true. But some beliefs also have *secondary* purposes, apart from their primary purpose of enabling the satisfaction of desires, to which their truth is irrelevant. The belief about injury is a case in point: it has the secondary purpose of getting people to fight effectively, whether or not they desire to, and it will do this independently of whether it is true. (The reason that some beliefs have two biological purposes is that there are some circumstances in which normal human desires, like the desire to avoid injury at all costs, are biologically inappropriate. So natural selection has compensated by inclining us to form beliefs in those circumstances that will make us act in ways which won't satisfy those desires, but will satisfy our biological needs. Cf. Papineau, 1993, ch. 3, §4.)

So, in response to the objection that some beliefs have purposes that don't require truth, defenders of the teleological theory can say they are concerned specifically with primary purposes, and can correspondingly equate truth conditions specifically with those conditions under which beliefs enable the satisfaction of desires. That some beliefs have other secondary purposes, to which truth is irrelevant, does not discredit this equation of truth conditions with conditions that ensure desire satisfaction.

Some philosophers maintain that such a 'success semantics' offers a theory of representation that is independent of the teleological theory (cf. Whyte, 1990). Why not simply analyse truth conditions, they ask, as those conditions that ensure the satisfaction of desires, without bringing in biological purposes?

The difficulty facing this position, however, is to give some account of the notion of *satisfaction* for desires. For satisfaction is itself a representational notion, which stands to desires as truth stands to beliefs. So an account of representation that simply helps itself to the notion of satisfaction will to that extent be incomplete.

The teleological theory fills this gap by saying that the satisfaction condition of a desire is that result that it is the biological purpose of the desire to produce. However, it may be possible to fill this gap in other, non-teleological ways. One possibility would be to analyse the satisfaction conditions of desires as those results that extinguish the desire when they are known to obtain (cf. Whyte, 1991). Another would be to analyse satisfaction conditions as those results that reinforce the performance of actions prompted by the desire (cf. Dretske, 1988).

These alternatives all agree that truth conditions should be analysed as those conditions that ensure that actions will succeed in satisfying desires, and differ only in their accounts of desire satisfaction. This common commitment to 'success semantics' raises a number of issues which call for more detailed discussion (*see* Papineau, 1993, ch. 3, §6). In favour of this approach, it should be noted that 'success semantics' yields a natural explanation of the existence of 'broad contents'. For which conditions will satisfy an agent's desire will, according to all the above suggestions, often depend on the agent's environment and history as well as the agent's physical make-up; and so it follows that the truth conditions of beliefs – that is, the conditions under which actions issuing from those beliefs will succeed in satisfying desires – will similarly often depend on the agent's environment and history.

See also CONTENT (1); *An Essay on Mind* section 2.1; FOLK PSYCHOLOGY; REPRESENTATION.

BIBLIOGRAPHY

Cummins, R. 1989. *Meaning and Mental Representation*. Cambridge, MA. MIT Press.
Dretske, F. 1981. *Knowledge and the Flow of Information*. Cambridge, MA: MIT Press.
Dretske, F. 1988. *Explaining Behaviour*. Cambridge, MA.: MIT Press.
Fodor, J. 1987. *Psychosemantics*. Cambridge, MA. MIT Press.
Fodor, J. 1990. *A Theory of Content*. Cambridge, MA.: MIT Press.
Millikan, R. 1984. *Language, Thought and Other Biological Categories*. Cambridge, MA.: MIT Press.
Papineau, D. 1984. Representation and explanation. *Philosophy of Science*, 51, 550–72.
Papineau, D. 1993. *Philosophical naturalism* Oxford: Basil Blackwell.
Whyte, J. 1990. Success semantics. *Analysis*, 50, 149–57.
Whyte, J. 1991. The normal rewards of success. *Analysis*, 51, 65–73.

DAVID PAPINEAU

D

Davidson, Donald There are no such things as minds, but people have mental properties, which is to say that certain psychological predicates are true of them. These properties are constantly changing, and such changes are mental events. Examples are: noticing that it is time for lunch, seeing that the wind is rising, remembering the new name of Cambodia, deciding to spend next Christmas in Botswana, or developing a taste for Trollope. Mental events are, in my view, physical (which is not, of course, to say that they are not mental). This is a thesis that follows from certain premises, all of which I think are true. The main premises are:

(1) All mental events are causally related to physical events. For example, BELIEFS and DESIRES cause agents to act, and ACTIONS cause changes in the physical world. Events in the physical world often cause us to alter our beliefs, INTENTIONS and desires.

(2) If two events are related as cause and effect, there is a strict law under which they may be subsumed. This means: cause and effect have descriptions which instantiate a strict law. A 'strict' law is one which makes no use of open-ended escape clauses such as 'other things being equal'. Thus such laws must belong to a closed system: whatever can affect the system must be included in it.

(3) There are no strict psychophysical laws (laws connecting mental events under their mental descriptions with physical events under their physical descriptions).

Take an arbitrary mental event M. By (1), it is causally connected with some physical event P. By (2), there must be a strict law connecting M and P; but by (3), that law cannot be a psychophysical law. Since only physics aims to provide a closed system governed by strict laws, the law connecting M and P must be a physical law. But then M must have a physical description – it must be a physical event.

The three premises are not equally plausible. (1) is obvious. (2) has seemed true to many philosophers; Hume and Kant are examples, though their reasons for holding it were very different. It has been questioned by others. A detailed defence would be out of place here, but the defence of (2) would begin by observing that physics is defined by the aim of discovering or devising a vocabulary (which among other things determines what counts as an event) which allows the formulation of a closed system of laws. I shall offer considerations in favour of (3) below. It should be noted that (3) rules out two forms of reductionism: reduction of the mental to the physical by explicit definition of mental predicates in physical terms (some forms of BEHAVIOURISM suggest such a programme), and reduction by way of strict bridging laws – laws which connect mental with physical properties.

(1)–(3) do, however, imply ontological reduction, since they imply that mental entities do not add to the physical furniture of the world. The result is ontological monism coupled with conceptual dualism: this is in many ways like Spinoza's metaphysics. (However, Spinoza apparently rejected (1).) Because I deny that there are strict psychophysical laws, I call my position ANOMALOUS MONISM (Davidson, 1970).

What is the reason for the irreducibility of mental concepts? Why can't there be strict psychophysical laws? In trying to answer these questions I first call attention to the HOLISM of the mental. PROPOSITIONAL ATTITUDES, in terms of which mental events are characterized, cannot exist in isolation. Individual beliefs, intentions, doubts and desires owe their identities in part to their position in a large network of further attitudes: the character of a given belief depends on endless other beliefs; beliefs have the role they do because of their relations to desires and intentions and perceptions. These relations among the attitudes are essentially logical: the content of an attitude cannot be divorced from what it entails and what is entailed by it. This places a normative constraint on the correct attribution of attitudes: since an attitude is in part identified by its logical relations, the pattern of attitudes in an individual must exhibit a large degree of coherence. This does not, of course, mean that people may not be irrational. But the possibility of irrationality depends on a background of rationality; to imagine a totally irrational animal is to imagine an animal without thoughts (Davidson, 1975, 1982).

We typically identify attitudes by using sentences like 'Gertrude Stein thinks that Ezra Pound is a village explainer', or 'Allen Alker Read claimed that native speakers of a language cannot make linguistic mistakes'. An utterance of such a sentence must, for semantical reasons, be analysed as relational: it relates a person to an entity that is specified by uttering a contained sentence ('Ezra Pound is a village explainer', etc.). This entity is often unhelpfully called a proposition. It is unhelpful, that is, until it is explained exactly how the words in the contained sentence manage to name or describe a proposition, and here the proffered explanations (including Frege's) lack conviction. The reason for choosing a proposition as the appropriate entity is that propositions sound like the sort of things that can be 'before the mind', 'entertained', or 'grasped'.

Aside from misleading grammar, there is, however, no good reason to suppose that having a propositional attitude requires an entity which the mind entertains or grasps. Having an attitude is just being in a certain state; it is a modification of a person. There need not be any 'object' in or before the mind for the person to be thinking, doubting, intending or calculating. The object to

which an attitude attribution relates the holder of the attitude must, of course, be known, but it is only the attributor who must know it. Such objects serve much the same function as numbers serve in keeping track of temperature or weight. There are no such things as weights or temperatures; 'This box weighs 9 pounds' relates the box to a number on the pound scale, but the number is an abstract object unknown to the box (Davidson, 1986, 1989a).

Anyone capable of attributing an attitude has at his or her command an infinite set of abstract objects suited to keeping track of the attitudes of others: the sentences of his or her language. (An alternative is to take the relevant objects as the actual utterances of sentences rather than the sentences; there are advantages and disadvantages either way. I explore the utterance option in Davidson (1968). Success in interpretation is always a matter of degree: the resources of thought or expression available to an interpreter can never perfectly match the resources of the interpreted. We do the best we can. It is always possible, of course, to improve one's understanding of another, by enlarging the data base, by adding another dose of sympathy or imagination, or by learning more about the things the subject knows about. This is the process of radical interpretation. There is no further court of appeal, no impersonal objective standard against which to measure our own best judgments of the rational and the true.

Here lies the source of the ultimate difference between the concepts we use to describe mental events and the concepts we use to describe physical events, the difference that rules out the existence of strict psychophysical laws. The physical world and the numbers we use to calibrate it are common property, the material and abstract objects and events that we can agree on and share. But it makes no sense to speak of comparing, or coming to agree on, ultimate common standards of rationality, since it is our own standards in each case to which we must turn in interpreting others. This should not be thought of as a failure of objectivity, but rather as the point at which 'questions come to an end'. Understanding the mental states of others and understanding nature are cases where questions come to an end at different stages. How we measure physical quantities is decided intersubjectively. We cannot in the same way go behind our own ultimate norms of rationality in interpreting others. Priority is not an issue. We would have no full-fledged thoughts if we were not in communication with others, and therefore no thoughts about nature; communication requires that we succeed in finding something like our own patterns of thought in others (Davidson, 1991b).

I have been stressing rationality as coherence, the fitting of one thought to another. The need to find the thoughts of others more or less coherent (by our own standards, it goes without saying) in order to acknowledge and identify them as thoughts is sometimes called a principle of charity. The term is misleading, since there is no alternative if we want to make sense of the attitudes and actions of the agents around us. The principle of charity has another application, again with no implication of goodness of heart. It is plain that we learn what many simple sentences, and the terms in them, mean through ostension. 'This is green', 'That is thyme', 'It's raining', are often learned in this way (perhaps first as one-word sentences). It is my view that such situations establish what the learner correctly takes to be the meaning of these sentences as spoken by the teacher. It is irrelevant whether the teacher is speaking as he was taught, or as others in the neighbourhood or profession or family speak; as long as the learner comes to associate sentence with situation as the teacher does, he is on the way to understanding that much of what the teacher says. Similarly, communication between teacher and learner does not depend on the learner speaking as the teacher does; if the learner comes consistently to utter his own same sentence in situations in which the teacher utters his own same sentence, communication has taken hold (Davidson, 1986a).

I question, then, two familiar claims. One is that what someone means by what he says depends only on what is in or on his mind, and that the situations in which words are learned merely constitute evidence of what those words mean, rather than conferring meaning on them. (To hold that the situations in which words are learned confers meaning on them is to embrace a form of externalism (*see* EXTERNALISM/INTERNALISM).) The other is that what someone means depends, at least in part, on what others in his linguistic community mean by the same words, even if the speaker is ignorant of current or 'correct' usage. In this matter I am with Allen Alker Read.

If everyone spoke in his or her own way (as in fact they do to some degree), does this suggest that there is no answer to Wittgenstein's question how there can be a difference between following a rule and thinking one is following a rule? How can there be a rule if only one person follows it? I'm not sure the concept of a rule is idoneous, but there certainly must be a way of distinguishing between correct and incorrect uses of a sentence, cases where it is true and where it is false. What is required, I think, is not that people speak alike, though that would serve. What is required, the basis on which the concepts of truth and objectivity depend for application, is a community of understanding, agreements among speakers on how each is to be understood. Such 'agreements' are nothing more than shared expectations: the hearer expects the speaker to go on as he did before; the speaker expects the hearer to go on as before. The frustration of these expectations means that someone has not gone on as before, that is, as the other expected. Given such a divergence there is no saying who is wrong; this must depend on further developments or additional observers. But the joint expectations, and the possibility of their frustration, do give substance to the idea of the difference between being right and being wrong, and to the concept of objective truth. They therefore provide an answer to Wittgenstein's problem about 'following a rule' (Davidson, 1992).

For a speaker to follow a rule is, as I am interpreting it, for the speaker to go on as before; and this in turn means for the speaker to go on as his audience expects, and as the speaker intends his audience to expect. (A finer analysis must allow for cases in which the speaker goes on in a way the audience does not anticipate, but in which the audience nevertheless detects the anomaly as intended by the speaker.) How, though, can shared expectations be the basis of the concept of objective truth?

All creatures are born making distinctions. An infant from the start reacts differentially to loud noises, the breast, and soon to individual people and to certain facial expressions. Similarities are not marked by nature; it is we who find loud noises relevantly similar, and who classify the responses of the infant as similar. If we ask what, exactly, the infant is responding to, the answer is that it is those objects or events we naturally class together that are best correlated with the responses of the infant that we naturally class together. In the end, we must ask this notion of what comes naturally to do serious work. For how do we decide whether the infant is responding to the noise, or rather to the vibrations of its eardrum, or to the signals from the inner ear to the brain? It hardly matters when we are in a position to specify an appropriate stimulus at any of various points along the causal chain from noise source to brain. But if we think of responses to the mother, most of us have no idea what class of neural stimuli touch off the relevantly similar responses; the best we can do is to say it is the class of stimuli (sense data, appearances, etc.) caused by the mother. This is why, when we have taught the child to say 'Mama' when stimulated by the mother, we conclude that the child means that its mother is present (rather than that it is receiving a certain neural input).

The learning which confers meaning on the most basic sentences necessarily involves, then, three elements: the 'teacher' (which may be a community of speakers with no pedagogical intentions), the 'learner' (who may be entering a first language, or consciously trying to decipher another), and a shared world. Without the external world shared through ostension, there is no way a learner could discover how speech connects with the world. Without a 'teacher', nothing would give content to the idea that there is a difference between getting things right and getting them wrong. Only those who thus share a common world can communicate; only those who communicate can have the concept of an intersubjective, objective world.

A number of things follow. If only those who communicate have the concept of an objective world, only those who communicate can doubt whether an external world exists. Yet it is impossible seriously (consistently) to doubt the existence of other people with thoughts, or the existence of an external world, since to communicate is to recognize the existence of other people in a common world. Language, that is, communication with others, is thus essential to propositional thought. This is not because it is necessary to have the words to express a thought (for it is not); it is because the ground of the sense of objectivity is intersubjectivity, and without the sense of objectivity, of the distinction between true and false, between what is thought to be and what is the case, there can be nothing rightly called thought (Davidson, 1990a, 1991a).

It is characteristic of mental states that people usually know, without appeal to evidence or inference, that they are in them. (Let us call this characteristic 'FIRST-PERSON AUTHORITY'.) The existence of first-person authority is not an empirical discovery, but rather a criterion, among others, of what a mental state is. Among others; so it can happen that we concede error on occasion. But exceptions do not throw in doubt the presumption that we know our own minds. What accounts for this presumption? INTROSPECTION offers no solution, since it fails to explain why one's perceptions of one's own mental states should be any more reliable than one's perceptions of anything else. The suggestion, perhaps derived from Wittgenstein, that mental predicates just have the property that they are applied to oneself without benefit of evidence, but are applied to others on the basis of evidence, merely deepens the mystery: for why should what we believe without evidence be more certain than what we believe on the basis of evidence? And given that the grounds for attributing a mental state to others are so different from the grounds for attributing a mental state to ourselves, why should we think they are the same sort of state? I think the answer to this conundrum is simple: we must interpret the thoughts of others on the basis of evidence; interpreting ourselves does not (aside from special cases) make sense. It is, in theory, a difficult empirical question how I know that your sentence (and the thought it may express) 'Snow is white' is true if and only if snow is white. But if I am right about how anyone comes to be interpretable, then I must in general be right in thinking things like this: my sentence 'Snow is white' is true if and only if snow is white. The difference between the two cases is that when I interpret you, two languages are involved, yours and mine (the same words may mean different things in your language and mine). In the second case, only one language is involved, my own; interpretation is therefore not (exceptional instances aside) in the picture (Davidson, 1984b).

The explanation of first-person authority also shows why the external determinants of meaning do not threaten our knowledge of the character of our own thoughts. What we mean by what we say is, if my account of the role of learning in conferring meaning is right, partly fixed by events of which we may be ignorant. It does not follow that we do not know what we mean, for the content of what we think we mean is determined by exactly the same circumstances that determine what we mean (Davidson, 1987).

The topics I have discussed above are, in my view, inseparable from many further subjects. These include:

the philosophy of language, which includes the concepts of truth and refer-

ence, and has strong implications for ontology (Davidson, 1986b).

the theory of action, which belongs with the study of the mental because what makes an event an action is that it is intentional under some description, and intentionality is defined and explained by its relations to beliefs, affects, and intentions (Davidson, 1980);

irrationality, for example WEAKNESS OF THE WILL, wishful thinking, SELF-DECEPTION. The existence of irrationality creates puzzles for the account of practical reasoning and intention (Davidson, 1974, 1986b);

radical interpretation: the study of how it is possible, given the interdependence of mental states, for one person to come to understand another (Davidson, 1990b).

See also An Essay on Mind section 3.6.2; IDENTITY THEORIES; INTENTIONALITY; PHYSICALISM; QUINE; NATURALISM; REASONS AND CAUSES; SUPERVENIENCE; THOUGHT; THOUGHT AND LANGUAGE.

BIBLIOGRAPHY

Davidson, D. 1968. On saying that. *Synthese*, 19, 130–46.
—— 1970. Mental events. In *Experience and Theory*, ed. L. Foster and J. W. Swanson. The University of Massachussetts Press and Duckworth. Reprinted in Davidson, 1980.
—— 1974. Paradoxes of irrationality. In *Freud: A Collection of Essays*, ed. R. Wollheim. New York: Doubleday Press.
—— 1975. Thought and talk. In *Mind and Language*, ed. S. Guttenplan. Oxford University Press. Reprinted in Davidson, 1984.
—— 1980. *Essays on Actions and Events*. Oxford University Press.
—— 1982. Rational animals. *Dialectica*, 36, 317–27.
—— 1984a. First person authority. *Dialectica*, 38, 101–111.
—— 1984b. *Inquiries into Truth and Interpretation*. Oxford University Press.
—— 1986a. A nice derangement of epitaphs. In *Philosophical Grounds of Rationality*, ed. R.

Grandy and R. Warner. Oxford University Press.

—— 1986b. Deception and division. In *The Multiple Self*, ed. J. Elster. Cambridge University Press.

—— 1987. Knowing one's own mind. *Proceedings and Addresses of the American Philosophical Association*, 441–58.

—— 1989a. The myth of the subjective. In *Relativism: Interpretation and Confrontation*, ed. M. Krausz. University of Notre Dame Press.

—— 1989b. What is present to the mind? In *The Mind of Donald Davidson*, ed. J. Brandl and W. Gombocz. *Grazer Philosophische Studien Band*, 36, 3–18.

—— 1990a. A coherence theory of truth and knowledge. In *Reading Rorty*, ed. A. Malichowski. Oxford: Basil Blackwell.

—— 1990b. The structure and content of truth. *Journal of Philosophy*, 87, 279–328.

—— 1991a. Epistemology externalized. *Dialectica*, 45, 191–202.

—— 1991b. Three varieties of knowledge. In *A. J. Ayer Memorial Essays*, ed. A. P. Griffiths. Cambridge University Press.

—— 1992. The second person. *Midwest Studies in Philosophy*, Vol 17.

DONALD DAVIDSON

Dennett, Daniel C. In my opinion, the two main topics in the philosophy of mind are CONTENT and CONSCIOUSNESS. As the title of my first book, *Content and Consciousness* (1969) suggested, that is the order in which they must be addressed: first, a theory of content or INTENTIONALITY – a phenomenon more fundamental than consciousness – and then, building on that foundation, a theory of consciousness. Over the years I have found myself recapitulating this basic structure twice, partly in order to respond to various philosophical objections, but more importantly, because my research on foundational issues in cognitive science led me into different aspects of the problems. The articles in the first half of *Brainstorms* (1978a) composed in effect a more detailed theory of content, and the articles in the second half were concerned with specific problems of consciousness. The second recapitulation has just been completed, with a separate volume devoted to each half: *The Intentional Stance* (1987a) is all and only about content; *Consciousness Explained* (1991a) presupposes the theory of content in that volume and builds an expanded theory of consciousness.

BEGINNINGS AND SOURCES

Although quite a few philosophers agree that content and consciousness are the two main issues confronting the philosophy of mind, many – perhaps most – follow tradition in favouring the opposite order: consciousness, they think, is the fundamental phenomenon, upon which all intentionality ultimately depends. This difference of perspective is fundamental, infecting the intuitions with which all theorizing must begin, and it is thus the source of some of the deepest and most persistent disagreements in the field. It is clear to me how I came by my renegade vision of the order of dependence: as a graduate student at Oxford, I developed a deep distrust of the methods I saw other philosophers employing, and decided that before I could trust any of my intuitions about the mind, I had to figure out how the brain could possibly accomplish the mind's work. I knew next to nothing about the relevant science, but I had always been fascinated with how things worked – clocks, engines, magic tricks. (In fact, had I not been raised in a dyed-in-the-wool 'arts and humanities' academic family, I probably would have become an engineer, but this option would never have occurred to anyone in our family.) So I began educating myself, always with an eye to the curious question of how the mechanical responses of 'stupid' neurons could be knit into a fabric of activity that actually discriminated meanings. Somehow it had to be possible, I assumed, since it was obvious to me that DUALISM was a last resort, to be postponed indefinitely.

So from the outset I worked from the 'third-person point of view' of science, and took my task to be building – or rather sketching the outlines of – a physical structure that could be seen to accomplish the puzzling legerdemain of the mind. At the time – the mid-60s – no one else in philosophy was attempting to build that structure, so it was a rather lonely enterprise, and most of the illumination and encouragement I could find came from the work of a few visionaries in science and engineering: Warren McCulloch, Donald MacKay, Donald Hebb, Ross Ashby, Allen Newell, Herbert Simon, and J. Z. Young come to mind. Miller, Galanter and Pribram's 1960 classic, *Plans and the Structure of Behaviour*, was a dimly understood but much appreciated beacon, and Michael Arbib's 1964 primer, *Brains, Machines and Mathematics*, was very helpful in clearing away some of the fog.

Given my lack of formal training in any science, this was a dubious enterprise, but I was usually forgiven my naïveté by those who helped me into their disciplines, and although at the time I considered myself driven by (indeed defined by) my disagreements with my philosophical mentors, QUINE and RYLE, in retrospect it is clear that my deep agreement with both of them about the nature of philosophy – so deep as to be utterly unexamined and tacit – was the primary source of such intellectual security as I had.

The first stable conclusion I reached, after I discovered that my speculative forays always wandered to the same place, was that the only thing brains could do was to *approximate* the responsivity to meanings that we *presuppose* in our everyday mentalistic discourse. When mechanical push came to shove, a brain was always going to do what it was caused to do by current, local, mechanical circumstances, whatever it *ought* to do, whatever a God's-eye view might reveal about the actual meanings of its current states. But over the long haul, brains could be designed – by evolutionary processes – to do the right thing (from the point of view of meaning) with high reliability. This found its first published expression in *Content and Consciousness* (1969, §9, 'Function and Content') and it remains the

foundation of everything I have done since then. As I put it in *Brainstorms* (1978a), brains are *syntactic engines* that can mimic the competence of *semantic engines*. (*See also* the thought experiment – a forerunner of Searle's Chinese Room – about being locked in the control room of a giant robot, in 1978b.) Note how this point forces the order of dependence of consciousness on intentionality. The appreciation of meanings – their discrimination and delectation – is central to our vision of consciousness, but this conviction that *I*, on the inside, deal directly with meanings turns out to be something rather like a benign 'user illusion'. What Descartes thought was most certain – his immediate introspective grasp of the items of consciousness – turns out to be not even quite true, but rather a metaphorical by-product of the way our brains do their approximating work. This vision tied in beautifully with a doctrine of Quine's that I had actually vehemently resisted as an undergraduate: the indeterminacy of radical translation. I could now see why, as Quine famously insisted, indeterminacy was 'of a piece with' Brentano's thesis of the irreducibility of the intentional, and why those irreducible intentional contexts were unavoidably a 'dramatic idiom' rather than an expression of unvarnished truth. I could also see how to re-interpret the two philosophical works on intentionality that had had the most influence on me, Anscombe's *Intention* (1957) and Taylor's *The Explanation of Behaviour* (1964).

If your initial allegiance is to the physical sciences and the third-person point of view, this disposition of the issues can seem not just intuitively acceptable, but inevitable, satisfying, natural. If on the other hand your starting point is the traditional philosophical allegiance to the mind and the deliverances of introspection, this vision can seem outrageous. Perhaps the clearest view of this watershed of intuitions can be obtained from an evolutionary perspective. There was a time, before life on earth, when there was neither intentionality nor consciousness, but eventually replication got under way and simple organisms emerged.

Suppose we ask of them: Were they conscious? Did their states exhibit intentionality? It all depends on what these key terms are taken to mean, of course, but underneath the strategic decisions one might make about pre-emptive definition of terms lies a fundamental difference of outlook. One family of intuitions is comfortable declaring that while these earliest ancestors were unconscious automata, not metaphysically different from thermostats or simple robotic toys, some of their states were nevertheless semantically evaluable. These organisms were, in my terms, rudimentary intentional systems, and somewhere in the intervening ascent of complexity, a special subset of intentional systems has emerged: the subset of conscious beings. According to this vision, then, the intentionality of our unconscious ancestors was as real as intentionality ever gets; it was just rudimentary. It is on this foundation of unconscious intentionality that the higher-order complexities developed that have culminated in what we call consciousness. The other family of intuitions declares that *if* these early organisms were mere unconscious automata, then their so-called intentionality was not the real thing. Some philosophers of this persuasion are tempted to insist that the earliest living organisms were conscious – they were alive, after all – and hence their rudimentary intentionality was genuine, while others suppose that somewhere higher on the scale of complexity, real consciousness, and hence real intentionality, emerges. There is widespread agreement in this camp, in any case, that although a robot might be what I have called an intentional system, and even a higher-order intentional system, it could not be conscious, *and so* it could have no genuine intentionality at all.

In my first book, I attempted to cut through this difference in intuitions by proposing a division of the concept of consciousness into awareness$_1$, the fancy sort of consciousness that we human beings enjoy, and awareness$_2$, the mere capacity for appropriate responsivity to stimuli, a capacity enjoyed by honey bees and thermostats

alike. The tactic did not work for many thinkers, who continued to harbour the hunch that I was leaving something out; there was, they thought, a special sort of sensitivity – we might call it animal consciousness – that no thermostat or fancy robot could enjoy, but that all mammals and birds (and perhaps all fish, reptiles, insects, molluscs, . . .) shared. Since robotic devices of considerably greater behavioural and perceptual complexity than the simplest of these organisms are deemed unconscious by this school of thought, it amounts to some sort of latter-day vitalism. The more one learns about how simple organisms actually work, the more dubious this hunch about a special, organic sort of sensation becomes, but to those who refuse to look at the science, it is a traditional idea that is about as comfortable today as it was in the seventeenth century, when many were horrified by Descartes's claims about the mechanicity of (non-human) animals. In any event, definitional gambits are ineffective against it, so in later work I dropped the tactic and the nomenclature of 'aware$_1$' and 'aware$_2$' – but not the underlying intuitions.

My accounts of content and consciousness have subsequently been revised in rather minor ways and elaborated in rather major ways. Some themes that figured heavily in *Content and Consciousness* lay dormant in my work through the 70s and early 80s, but were never abandoned, and are now re-emerging, in particular the theme of learning as evolution in the brain and the theme of content being anchored in distributed patterns of individually ambiguous nodes in networks of neurons. The truth is that while I can fairly claim to have seen the beauty, and indeed the inevitability, of these ideas in *Content and Conciousness* (*see also* Dennett, 1974), and to have sketched out their philosophical implications quite accurately, I simply couldn't see how to push them further in the scientific domain, and had to wait for others – not philosophers – to discover these ideas for themselves and push them in the new directions that have so properly captured recent philosophical attention. My own recent discussions of these two themes are to be found in Dennett (1986, 1987b, 1991a, 1991b, 1991c, 1992a).

CONTENT: PATTERNS VISIBLE FROM THE INTENTIONAL STANCE

My theory of content is functionalist (see FUNCTIONALISM): all attributions of content are founded on an appreciation of the *functional roles* of the items in question in the biological economy of the organism (or the engineering of the robot). This is a specifically 'teleological' notion of function (not the notion of a mathematical function or of a mere 'causal role', as suggested by David LEWIS and others). It is the concept of function that is ubiquitous in engineering, in the design of artefacts, but also in biology. (It is only slowly dawning on philosophers of science that biology is not a science like physics, in which one should strive to find 'laws of nature', but a species of engineering: the analysis, by 'reverse engineering', of the found artefacts of nature – which are composed of thousands of deliciously complicated gadgets, yoked together opportunistically but elegantly into robust, self-protective systems.) These themes were all present in *Content and Consciousness*, but they were clarified in 'Intentional Systems' (1971) when I introduced the idea that an intentional system was, by definition, anything that was amenable to analysis by a certain tactic, which I called the intentional stance. This is the tactic of interpreting an entity by adopting the presupposition that it is an approximation of the ideal of an optimally designed (i.e. rational) self-regarding agent. No attempt is made to confirm or disconfirm this presupposition, nor is it necessary to try to specify, in advance of specific analyses, wherein consists RATIONALITY. Rather, the presupposition provides leverage for generating specific predictions of behaviour, via defeasible hypotheses about the content of the control states of the entity.

My initial analysis of the intentional stance and its relation to the design stance and physical stance was addressed to a traditional philosophical issue – the problem of free will and the task of reconciling mechanism and responsibility (1973). The details, however, grew out of my reflections on practices and attitudes I observed to be ubiquitous in ARTIFICIAL INTELLIGENCE. Both Allen Newell (1982) and David Marr (1982) arrived at essentially the same breakdown of stances in their own reflections on the foundations of cognitive science. The concept of intentional systems (and particularly, higher-order intentional systems) has been successfully exploited in clinical and developmental psychology, ethology, and other domains of cognitive science, but philosophers have been reluctant to endorse the main metaphysical implications of the theory (see COGNITIVE PSYCHOLOGY; DEVELOPMENTAL PSYCHOLOGY).

In particular, I have held that since *any* attributions of function necessarily invoke optimality or rationality assumptions, the attributions of intentionality that depend on them are *interpretations* of the phenomena – a 'heuristic overlay' (1969), describing an inescapably idealized 'real pattern' (1991d). Like such *abstracta* as centres of gravity and parallelograms of force, the BELIEFS and DESIRES posited by the highest stance have no independent and concrete existence, and since this is the case, there would be no deeper facts that could settle the issue if – most improbably – rival intentional interpretations arose that did equally well at rationalizing the history of behaviour of an entity. Quine's thesis of the indeterminacy of radical translation carries all the way in, as the thesis of the indeterminacy of radical interpretation of mental states and processes.

The fact that cases of radical indeterminacy, though possible in principle, are vanishingly unlikely ever to confront us is small solace, apparently. This idea is deeply counterintuitive to many philosophers, who have hankered for more 'realistic' doctrines. There are two different strands of 'realism' that I have tried to undermine:

(1) realism about the entities purportedly described by our everyday mentalistic

discourse – what I dubbed FOLK-PSYCHOLOGY (1981) – such as beliefs, desires, pains, the self;

(2) realism about content itself – the idea that there have to be events or entities that *really* have intentionality (as opposed to the events and entities that only behave *as if* they had intentionality).

Against (1), I have wielded various arguments, analogies, parables. Consider what we should tell the benighted community of people who speak of 'having fatigues' where we speak of being tired, exhausted, etc. (1978a). They want us to tell them what fatigues *are*, what bodily states or events they are identical with, and so forth. This is a confusion that calls for diplomacy, not philosophical discovery; the choice between an 'eliminative materialism' (*see* ELIMINATIVISM) and an 'IDENTITY THEORY' of fatigues is not a matter of which 'ism' is right, but of which way of speaking is most apt to wean these people of a misbegotten feature of their conceptual scheme.

Against (2), my attack has been more indirect. I view the philosophers' demand for content realism as an instance of a common philosophical mistake: philosophers often manoeuvre themselves into a position from which they can see only two alternatives: infinite regress versus some sort of 'intrinsic' foundation – a prime mover of one sort or another. For instance, it has seemed obvious that for some things to be valuable as means, other things must be intrinsically valuable – ends in themselves – otherwise we'd be stuck with a vicious regress (or circle) of things valuable only as means. It has seemed similarly obvious that although some intentionality is 'derived' (the aboutness of the pencil marks composing a shopping list is derived from the intentions of the person whose list it is), unless some intentionality is *original* and underived, there could be no derived intentionality.

There is always another alternative, which naturalistic philosophers should look on with favour: a *finite* regress that peters out without marked foundations or thresholds or essences. Here is an easily avoided paradox: every mammal has a mammal for a mother – but this implies an infinite genealogy of mammals, which cannot be the case. The solution is not to search for an essence of mammalhood that would permit us in principle to identify the Prime Mammal, but rather to tolerate a finite regress that connects mammals to their non-mammalian ancestors by a sequence that can only be partitioned arbitrarily. The reality of today's mammals is secure without foundations.

The best known instance of this theme in my work is the idea that the way to explain the miraculous-seeming powers of an intelligent intentional system is to decompose it into hierarchically structured teams of ever more stupid intentional systems, ultimately discharging all intelligence-debts in a fabric of stupid mechanisms (1971, 1974, 1978a, 1991a). Lycan (1981) has called this view homuncular functionalism. One may be tempted to ask: are the subpersonal components *real* intentional systems? At what point in the diminution of prowess as we descend to simple neurons does *real* intentionality disappear? Don't ask. The reasons for regarding an individual neuron (or a thermostat) as an intentional system are unimpressive, but not zero, and the security of our intentional attributions at the highest levels does not depend on our identifying a lowest-level of real intentionality. Another exploitation of the same idea is found in *Elbow Room* (1984): at what point in evolutionary history did real reason-appreciators, real selves, make their appearance? Don't ask – for the same reason. Here is yet another, more fundamental, version: at what point in the early days of evolution can we speak of *genuine* function, genuine *selection-for* and not mere fortuitous preservation of entities that happen to have some self-replicative capacity? Don't ask. Many of the most interesting and important features of our world have emerged, gradually, from a world that initially lacked them – function, intentionality, consciousness, morality, value – and it is a fool's errand to try to identify a first or most-simple instance of the 'real' thing. It is for the same reason a mistake to suppose that real differences in the world must exist to answer all the questions our systems of content attribution permit us to ask. Tom says he has an older brother living in Cleveland *and* that he is an only child (1975b). What does he *really* believe? Could he really believe that he had a brother if he also believed he was an only child? What is the *real* content of his mental state? There is no reason to suppose there is a principled answer.

The most sweeping conclusion I have drawn from this theory of content is that the large and well-regarded literature on PROPOSITIONAL ATTITUDES (especially the debates over wide versus narrow content, '*de re* versus *de dicto*' attributions, and what Pierre believes about London) is largely a disciplinary artefact of no long-term importance whatever, except perhaps as history's most slowly unwinding unintended *reductio ad absurdum*. By and large the disagreements explored in that literature cannot even be given an initial expression unless one takes on the assumptions I have argued are fundamentally unsound (*see* especially 1975b, 1978a, 1982, 1987b, 1991d): strong realism about content, and its constant companion, the idea of a LANGUAGE OF THOUGHT, a system of mental *representation* that is decomposable into elements rather like terms, and larger elements rather like sentences. The illusion that this is plausible, or even inevitable, is particularly fostered by the philosophers' normal tactic of working from examples of 'believing-that-*p*' that focus attention on mental states that are directly or indirectly language-infected, such as believing that the shortest spy is a spy, or believing that snow is white. (Do polar bears believe that snow is white? In the way we do?) There are such states – in language-using human beings – but they are not exemplary or foundational states of belief; needing a term for them, I call them *opinions* ('How to Change your Mind', in 1978a; *see also* 1991c). Opinions play a large, perhaps even decisive, role in our concept of a person, but

they are not paradigms of the sort of cognitive element to which one can assign content in the first instance. If one starts, as one should, with the cognitive states and events occurring in non-human animals, and uses these as the foundation on which to build theories of human cognition, the language-infected states are more readily seen to be derived, less directly implicated in the explanation of behaviour, and the chief but illicit source of plausibility of the doctrine of a language of thought. Postulating a language of thought is in any event a postponement of the central problems of content ascription, not a necessary first step. (Although a few philosophers – especially Millikan, Robert STALNAKER, Stephen White – have agreed with me about large parts of this sweeping criticism, they have sought less radical accommodations with the prevailing literature.)

CONSCIOUSNESS AS A VIRTUAL MACHINE

My theory of consciousness has undergone more revisions over the years than my theory of content. In *Content and Consciousness* the theory concentrated on the role of language in constituting the peculiar but definitive characteristics of human consciousness, and while I continue to argue for a crucial role of natural language in generating the central features of consciousness (our kind), my first version overstated the case in several regards. For instance, I went slightly too far in my dismissal of mental imagery (see the corrections in 1978a, 1991a), and I went slightly too fast – but not too far! – in my treatment of colour vision, which was unconvincing at the time, even though it made all the right moves, as recent philosophical work on colour has confirmed, in my opinion. But my biggest mistake in *Content and Consciousness* was positing a watershed somewhere in the brain, the 'awareness line', with the following property: revisions of content that occurred prior to crossing the awareness line *changed the content* of consciousness; later revisions (or errors) counted as post-experiential tamperings; all adjustments of content, veridical or not, could be located, in principle, on one side or the other of this postulated line. The first breach of this intuitive but ultimately indefensible doctrine occurred in 'Are Dreams Experiences?' (1975a), in which I argued that the distinction between proper and improper entry into memory (and thence into introspective report, for instance) could not be sustained in close quarters. Related arguments appeared in 'Two Approaches to Mental Imagery' (in 1978a) and 'Quining Qualia' (1988), but only in *Consciousness Explained* (1991a) and 'Time and the Observer' (Dennett and Kinsbourne, 1992) was an alternative positive model of consciousness sketched in any detail, the Multiple Drafts model.

The best way to understand this model is in contrast to the traditional model, which I call the Cartesian Theatre. The fundamental work done by any observer can be characterized as confronting something 'given' and *taking* it – responding to it with one interpretive judgment or another. This corner must be turned somehow and somewhere in any model of consciousness. On the traditional view, all the taking is deferred until the raw given, the raw materials of stimulation, have been processed in various ways and sent to central headquarters. Once each bit is 'finished' it can enter consciousness and be appreciated for the first time. As C. S. Sherrington (1934) put it:

> The mental action lies buried in the brain, and in that part most deeply recessed from outside world that is furthest from input and output.

In the Multiple Drafts model, this single unified taking is broken up in cerebral space and real time; the judgmental tasks are fragmented into many distributed moments of micro-taking (Dennett and Kinsbourne, 1992). Since there is no place where 'it all comes together', no line the crossing of which is definitive of the end of pre-conscious processing and the beginning of conscious appreciation, many of the familiar philosophical assumptions about the denizens of human phenomenology turn out to be simply wrong, in spite of their traditional obviousness.

For instance, from the perspective provided by this model one can see more clearly the incoherence of the absolutist assumptions that make QUALIA seem like a good theoretical idea. It follows from the Multiple Drafts model that 'inverted spectrum' and 'absent qualia' thought experiments, like the thought experiments encountered in the propositional attitude literature (Twin Earth, what Pierre believes, beliefs about the shortest spy), are fundamentally misbegotten, and for a similar reason: the 'common sense' assumption of 'realism' with regard to the mental items in question – beliefs, in the first instance, qualia, in the second – is too strong.

OVERVIEW

The intermediate ontological position I recommend – I call it 'mild realism' – might be viewed as my attempt at a friendly amendment to Ryle's (1949) tantalizing but unpersuasive claims about category mistakes and different senses of 'exist' (see especially 1969, ch. 1; 1991d). What do you get when you cross a Quine with a Ryle? A Dennett, apparently. But there is a novel texture to my work, and an attitude, which grows primarily, I think, from my paying attention to the actual details of the sciences of the mind – and asking philosophical questions about those details. This base camp in the sciences has permitted me to launch a host of differently posed arguments, drawing on overlooked considerations. These arguments do not simply add another round to the cycle of debate, but have some hope of dislodging the traditional intuitions with which philosophers previously had to start. For instance, from this vantage point one can see the importance of evolutionary models (1969, 1974, 1978a, 1983, 1984a, 1990b, 1991f) and, concomitantly, the perspective of cognitive science as reverse engineering (1989, 1991, 1992a), which goes a long way to overcoming the conservative mindset of pure philosophy. The idea that a mind could be a contraption composed of hundreds or thousands of gadgets takes us a big step away from the overly familiar mind presupposed by essentially all philosophers from Descartes to the present.

Something else of mine that owes a debt to Quine and Ryle is my philosophical style. No sentence from Quine or Ryle is ever dull, and their work always exhibits the importance of *addressing* an audience of non-philosophers, even when they know that philosophers will be perhaps 95% of their actual and sought-for audience. They also both embody a healthy scepticism about the traditional methods and presuppositions of our so-called discipline, an attitude to which I have always resonated. I have amplified these points, attempting to follow their example in my own writing. But I have also been self-conscious about philosophical methods and their fruits, and presented my reflections in various meta-level digressions, in particular about the role of intuition pumps in philosophy (1980, 1984a, 1991a), and about the besetting foible of philosophers: mistaking failures of imagination for insights into necessity.

My insistence on the need for philosophers to stoke up on the relevant science before holding forth, and my refusal to conduct my investigations by the traditional method of definition and formal argument, have made me a distinctly impure philosopher of mind. Moreover, on both main topics, content and consciousness, I maintain a 'radical' position, which in a rather lonely and implausible fashion declares that much of the work at the presumed cutting edge is beyond salvage. I thus cut myself off from some of the controversies that capture the imaginations of others in the field, but the philosophical problems that arise directly in non-philosophical research in cognitive science strike me as much more interesting, challenging, and substantive. So I concentrate on them: the frame problem (1984b, 1991e), problems about mental imagery and 'filling in' (1992b), the binding problem and the problem of temporal anomalies (1991a; Dennett and Kinsbourne, 1992). I take these to be the real, as opposed to artefactual, problems of mental representation, and I encourage philosophers of mind to contribute to their solution.

BIBLIOGRAPHY

Anscombe, G.E.M. 1957. *Intention*. Oxford: Basil Blackwell.
Dennett, D.C. 1969. *Content and Consciousness*. London: Routledge & Kegan Paul.
—— 1971. Intentional systems. *Journal of Philosophy*, 8, 87–106.
—— 1973. Mechanism and responsibility. In *Essays on Freedom of Action*, ed. T. Honderick. London: Routledge & Kegan Paul.
—— 1974. Why the law of effect will not go away. *Journal of the Theory of Social Behaviour*, 5, 169–87.
—— 1975. Are dreams experiences? *Philosophical Review*, 73, 151–71.
—— 1975b. Brain writing and mind reading. In *Language, Mind, and Meaning, Minnesota Studies in Philosophy of Science*, Vol. 7, ed. K. Gunderson. Minneapolis: University of Minnesota Press.
—— 1978a. *Brainstorms: Philosophical Essays on Mind and Psychology*. Montgomery, VT: Bradford.
—— 1978b. Current issues in the philosophy of mind. *American Philosophical Quarterly*, 15, 249–61.
—— 1980. The milk of human intentionality. *Behavioral and Brain Sciences*, 3, 428–30.
—— 1982. Beyond belief. In *Thought and Object*, ed. A. Woodfield. Oxford University Press.
—— 1983. Intentional systems in cognitive ethology: the 'Panglossian paradigm' defended. *Behavioral and Brain Sciences*, 6, 343–90.
—— 1984a. *Elbow Room: The Varieties of Free Will Worth Wanting*. Cambridge, MA: MIT Press.
—— 1984b. Cognitive wheels: the frame problem of AI. In *Minds, Machines and Evolution*, ed. C. Hookway. Cambridge University Press.
—— 1986. The logical geography of computational approaches: A view from the East Pole. In *The Representation of Knowledge and Belief*, ed. R. Harnish and M. Brand. Tucson: University of Arizona Press.

—— 1987a. *The Intentional Stance*. Cambridge, MA.: MIT Press.

—— 1987b. Evolution, Error and Intentionality. In 1987a.

—— 1988. Quining qualia. In *Consciousness in Contemporary Science*, ed. A. Marcel and E. Bisiach. Oxford University Press.

—— 1990a. Memes and the exploitation of imagination. *Journal of Aesthetics and Art Criticism*, 48, 127–35.

—— 1990b. The interpretation of texts, people and other artifacts. *Philosophy and Phenomenological Research*, 50, 177–94.

—— 1991a. *Consciousness Explained*. Boston: Little Brown.

—— 1991b. Mother Nature versus the walking encyclopedia. In *Philosophy and Connectionst Theory*, ed. W. Ramsey, S. Stich and D. Rumelhart. Hillsdale, NJ: Erlbaum.

—— 1991c. Two contrasts: folk craft versus folk science and belief versus opinion. in *The Future of Folk Psychology: Intentionality and Cognitive Science*, ed. J. Greenwood. Cambridge University Press.

—— 1991d. Real patterns. *Journal of Philosophy*, 89, 27–51.

—— 1991e. Producing future by telling stories. In *The Robot's Dilemma Revisited: The Frame Problem in Artificial Intelligence*, ed. K. M. Ford and Z. Pylyshyn. Norwood, NJ: Ablex.

—— 1991f. Ways of establishing harmony. In *Dretske and his Critics*, ed. B. McLaughlin. Oxford: Basil Blackwell.

—— 1992a. Cognitive science as reverse engineering: Several senses of 'top-down' and 'bottom-up'. In *Proc. of the 9th International Congress of Logic, Methodology and Philosophy of Science*, ed. D. Prawitz, B. Skyrms, and D. Westerstahl. North-Holland.

—— 1992b. Filling in versus finding out: A ubiquitous confusion in cognitive science. In *Cognition*, ed. H. Pick *et al.*, Washington DC: American Psychological Association.

Dennett, D.C., and Kinsbourne, M. 1992. Time and the observer: The where and when of consciousness in the brain. *Behavioral and Brain Sciences*, 15, 183–201.

Lycan, W.G. 1981. Form, function, and feel. *Journal of Philosophy*, 78, 24–49.

Marr, D. 1982. *Vision*. San Francisco: Freeman.

Miller, G., Galanter, E., and Pribram, K. 1960. *Plans and the Structure of Behavior*. New York: Holt, Rinehart and Winston.

Newell, A., 1982. The knowledge level. *Artificial Intelligence*, 18, 81–132.

Quine, W.V.O. 1960. *Word and Object*. Cambridge, MA.: MIT Press.

Ryle, G. 1949. *The Concept of Mind*. London: Hutchinson.

Sherrington, C.S. 1934. *The Brain and Its Mechanism*. London: Hamilton.

Taylor, C. 1964. *The Explanation of Behaviour*. London: Routledge & Kegan Paul.

DANIEL C. DENNETT

desire We contrast what we want to do, to begin with, with what we *must* do – whether for reasons of morality or duty, or even for reasons of practical necessity (to get what we wanted in the first place). Accordingly our own desires have seemed to be the principal source of the ACTIONS that most fully express our own individual natures and will, and those for which we are personally most responsible. But desire has also seemed to be a principle of action contrary to and at war with our better natures, as rational and moral agents. For it is principally from our own differing perspectives upon what would be good, that each of us wants what he does, each point of view being defined by one's own interests and pleasures. In this, the representations of desire are like those of sensory PERCEPTION, similarly shaped by the perspective of the perceiver and the idiosyncrasies of the perceptual, or appetitive, apparatus. So the philosophical dialectic about desire and its object recapitulates that of perception and sensible qualities. The strength of desire, for instance, varies with the state of the subject more or less independently of the character, and the actual utility, of the object wanted. Such facts cast doubt on the 'objectivity' of desire, and on the existence of a correlative property of *goodness*, inherent in the objects of our desires, and independent of them. Perhaps, as Spinoza put it, it is not that we want what we think good, but that we think good what we happen to want – the 'good' in what we want being a mere shadow cast by the desire for it (Spinoza, 1677, III, prop. 9, *scholium*). (There is a parallel Protagorean view of belief, similarly sceptical of truth.) The serious defence of such a view, however, would require a systematic reduction of apparent facts about goodness to facts about desires, and an analysis of desire which in turn makes no reference to goodness. While that is yet to be provided, moral psychologists have sought to vindicate an idea of objective goodness, for example as what would be good from all points of view, or none; or, in the manner of Kant, to establish another principle (THE WILL, or PRACTICAL REASON) conceived as an autonomous source of action, independent of desire or its object; and this tradition has tended to minimize the role of desire in the genesis of action.

In the general philosophy of mind, and more recently, desire has received new attention from those who would understand mental states in terms of their causal or functional role in the determination of rational behaviour, and in particular from philosophers trying to understand the semantic content or intentional character of mental states in those terms (*see* FUNCTIONALISM; CONCEPTIONAL ROLE SEMANTICS). The RATIONALITY of an action is determined by the contents of the BELIEFS and desires that explain why the agent does it: if something is done because the agent wants something that he believes he can get by doing that thing, the action is *prima facie* reasonable. This is a truism; but perhaps an account of the INTENTIONALITY of these mental states can be extracted from it, answering such questions as these: What *is* it for a desire to be *for* the particular object it's for? What *determines* that its object is the particular thing it is? Does a desire have some sense or CONTENT that determines what its object is, rather as the meaning of an expression determines its referent?

Of course, the *object* of the desire, i.e. *what* one wants, is the thing the possession of which (or the state of affairs the obtaining of which) would *satisfy* that desire. The object of the desire is referred to by the grammatical object of a sentence that attri-

butes the desire to some subject – a sentence of the form 'She wants a cow'. Generally, that phrase ('a cow') does not, on the face of it, express a proposition – as the grammatical object of 'She believes cows give milk' ('cows give milk') does do. But in fact the grammatical object of the desire sentence is also a clause or sentence: she wants it to be that *she has* a cow, as it might be put. (An ambiguity introduced by adverbs superficially modifying 'desire' provides grammatical evidence of this underlying subordinate clause with the unexpressed verb 'have', which on one reading of the sentence the adverb must be taken to modify: 'She wants a cow today' might mean that her desire today is for a cow, whereas yesterday it was a goat she wanted, or it might mean that she wants to *have* it today. And of course if she wants a cow her desire is that *she* should have one.)

The fact that sentences ascribing desires have *grammatical* objects that express propositions does not entail that the states themselves are 'PROPOSITIONAL ATTITUDES', which have those propositions as their INTENSIONAL objects. That conclusion is drawn instead from the fact that the truth of that proposition is what *satisfies* the desire, and that the desire that P makes it reasonable for the agent to act so as to bring it about that P – specifically *that* state of affairs, but not necessarily other, for example *coextensive*, states of affairs that the action also brings about. In any case, we may distinguish (1) the grammatical object of 'desire', from (2) the propositional object of the desire, or its 'objective', and that again, from (3) the representational content of the desire, and (4) the object or state the desire represents.

Now, what makes it the case that a given desire has the object that it does? Here 'logical behaviourism' made a suggestive, if flawed, beginning (*see* BEHAVIOURISM): mental states are dispositions to behave in appropriate ways, and they may be identified and distinguished by specifications of the way an agent in a given state is therein disposed to behave, with respect to something '*external*'. A desire might be a desire, specifically, *for an apple* – that might be its object – because a desire is a disposition to behave in such a way as to get one: to *try to get* an apple. (Anscombe 1957, p. 67: 'The primitive sign of wanting is *trying to get*'.) A real behaviourist might have thought this *trying to get* something was behaviour recognizable as such without assumptions about other inner states, but that idea has long since been given up. Someone's shaking a tree qualifies as an attempt to get an apple, and as behaviour 'appropriate' to the desire for one, only if he *believes* what he's doing might get him an apple (Geach, 1957, p. 8). And that belief is a disposition to do such things, but only assuming he wants an apple.

Beliefs and desires make an essentially coordinate contribution to the production of rational behaviour, and the behavioural effects of states of either kind can be identified by (though *only* by) reference to states of the other kind; more precisely, to the semantic character – the truth or the satisfaction-condition – of causally operative states of the other kind. Thus the actions a desire is a disposition to perform are those that would satisfy that desire provided the agent's operative beliefs were true – those being the beliefs (whatever they may be) which, together with those desires, cause the action in question, or comprise the reasons for which he does it. And a belief, in turn, is a state which, together with a relevant desire, would dispose the agent to do what would tend to satisfy that desire in case the belief is true (Stalnaker, 1984, ch. 1). Thus the characterization of desire depends essentially upon an interlocking definition of belief. It may seem that this approach to the object of desire is objectionably 'circular'. Be that as it may, the characterization of the desire in terms of its *effects* must be completed by a reference to its typical *causes* – and this will acknowledge factors that determine the objects of desire independently of the beliefs referred to in the definition. This reference to causes is required, arguably, to do justice to the status of desires as reasons (*see* REASONS AND CAUSES).

For a desire isn't merely a disposition to do certain things, it is a *reason* to do those things. Irritability is also a disposition, to react irritably – or solubility, a disposition to dissolve – but it is not a reason to do so. The desire is a reason for which we do what it causes us to do. It must be explained how this is so. A belief (that P) also comprises a reason to act accordingly, and there, to state *what* is believed, its 'propositional content' (P), is to specify that reason. The desire for an apple is likewise a reason to act accordingly, but here, to cite what is *wanted* – an apple; *or* that one have an apple – is *not* to cite a reason for doing anything. It is not to cite a *fact*, or an apparent fact, that might figure as a reason to act. It is not clear *why* wanting that object is a reason to behave accordingly, until (beyond its propositional object, or objective) the *representational* content of the desire is made clear. The belief that P contains a reason to act accordingly because, in belief, it is represented as being the case that P. The desire that P is also a reason to act accordingly, but what does it represent as being the case? It does not, certainly, represent it as being the case that P (*see* RE-PRESENTATION).

Some philosophers have denied that there *is* any representational content in desire. If no such representational content is found, it may still be possible to identify the object of the desire with the state which tends (through action) to result from the desire, specified more closely as a result which in turn has the effect of reinforcing the tendency of that desire to produce the behaviour that produced that result. (cf. Dretske, 1984, ch. 5.) This view yields an account of the causal efficacy of the desire's intentional character. If the desire's *having* an object O is identified with its being such that getting O will reinforce the desire's tendency to cause the behaviour that got O, then it is its being a desire *for* O that explains such behaviour. But is the object of the desire defined by the properties of O that reinforce that desire's capacity to cause behaviour, or instead by the properties of O that would apparently benefit the agent, and thus rationalize the behaviour it would cause? (See below on the intensionality of the context 'S wants O' read 'opaquely'.) It may be questioned, then, whether this does justice to the status of desires as reasons for behaving in ways that would satisfy them.

It was Hume who most famously denied that a desire (or any such 'passion') contains '. . . any representative quality, which renders it a copy of any other existence or modification' (Hume, 1739). When I want something, as when I am angry, 'I am actually possest with the passion, and in that emotion have no more a reference to any other object, than when I am thirsty, or sick, or more than five foot high'. Thus while a desire based on some unreasonable beliefs may be described, metonymically, as 'unreasonable', strictly, and in its own right, no desire can be contrary to reason, or conformable to it. The premise from which these dramatic pronouncements were derived is that desire represents nothing as being the case, and thus 'has no reference to' truth. Whereas the belief that there's a pot of gold at the end of the rainbow is true, in case what is believed is true, the desire for the pot of gold is not 'true' in case what is wanted (that one gets that pot of gold) is true.

But if one comes to have the pot of gold, the desire will *come* true; it will be satisfied, and the desire's being *satisfied* (which it is if and only if the propositional complement of 'desire' is true) is plainly parallel to the belief's being 'true', in case the propositional complement of 'believes' is true. That's one sort of 'reference' the desire has to truth, though it is truth by the name 'satisfaction'. (The paradigm causal relation between a desire and its satisfaction condition differs, of course, from that between a belief and its truth condition; while the belief tends to result *from* states in which its truth condition holds, for example through the medium of perception, a desire tends to result *in* states in which its satisfaction condition holds, through the medium of action.)

It is true that the desired pot of gold needn't be an 'existing reality' and neither is the envisioned possession of it an existing state of affairs; nor are they represented as such in the desire to have a pot of gold. But the claim that desire is not a representation of any *existing* reality, or state of affairs, in the way that a perceptual belief may be, is irrelevant to the question whether a desire might be reasonable. A belief is reasonable, roughly, if one has reason to believe that things are as they are believed to be, or therein represented as being. And a *desire* is reasonable if one has reason to *want* the thing wanted, that is, to want the desired state of affairs (wherein one has a pot of gold) to *be* 'an existing reality'. A reason to want the thing would be that *it would be good* to have it. Then why should *that* not be what a desire represents as being the case? If so, then there *is* something the desire represents, or misrepresents – namely, the benefit or *utility*, if you like, of having a pot of gold. And we may say that the object of a desire (whether *it* exists or not) is therein represented as *something the possession of which would be good*. In the desire that P, it is represented as being the case that it would be good were it the case that P. ('Good' drops out as redundant in the context 'S wants [= mentally represents it as good that] P', as 'true' drops out as redundant in 'S believes [mentally represents it as true that] P'.) Of course it needn't be true that it *would* be good if P were the case, in order for someone to want it to be so. If desires are, in effect, utility indicators, they need not be, and they are not, entirely reliable ones. (There are other views of the representational content of desire, including the important Socratic view: the desire that P represents its being the case that P as what would be *best*. Cf. Plato's *Gorgias*, 467c–468e; *Lysis*, 279d–282a.)

Nor is it obvious that such representational content can belong to desire only *via* some belief. A desire might result 'directly' from its being the case that it would be good to have the thing wanted (or its being such as to make it *seem* good), rather in the way a perception may have representational content without intervening belief. Something can *look* green to someone without the perceiver's believing it is green or even that it looks green. Further, that perception is in itself a reason to believe the thing is green, regardless of one's contrary beliefs. Similarly, perhaps, in the desire for sleep, it *seems* as if it would be good to sleep, and that, in itself, is a reason to sleep, regardless what one believes or even knows about the merits of sleeping, and even if one has better reason to stay awake (Stampe, 1987). This argues for a certain 'modularity' in the generation of desires.

The treatment of desire as a kind of perceptual state may be pressed further, identifying some state of the subject – for example, some state of deprivation or need – as the object of consciousness which causes it to seem as if the thing wanted would be good, as the object that is seen causes it to look to one as if such and such is the case. Here, then, through its connection with its causes, desire gains an infusion of semantic content independent of belief, breaking the circle in which the contents of one are defined in terms of contents of the other. And at this point, finally, we may deny what Hume asserts: the desire that it be the case that P *does* represent an actually 'existing reality', *sc.* some state of the subject that makes it seem to him as if it would be good if it were the case that P.

In his contention that 'Reason is and ought only to be the slave of the passions . . .' – desire being a passion – Hume meant to tweak an orthodox rationalism that pitted reason against desire, as if reason were an autonomous principle of action. A more egalitarian view is Aristotelian. Reason is not something on the side of judgment (or belief), but is rather a principle operative alike as beliefs give rise to further beliefs, or when desires give rise to intention and thus to action. In either case, the rational inference secures some relevant semantic value to its product: it guarantees the truth of beliefs validly derived from true beliefs, i.e. provided things are as they were therein represented as being; and it guarantees similarly that the action deriving from a desire will be *good* if what one would thereby get is as it was

represented as being, in that desire: as something that it would be good to have. A desire, like a belief, is itself a reason for the person to do things that would satisfy that desire. Of course, that desire apart, it may be madness to do such things, and that's why the desire, while it is a reason, may not be a *good* reason, to act accordingly. A representational view of desire accounts for that fact. It is reasonable to act in accordance with the belief that P because in that belief it is represented as being the case that P; by parity of reasoning, if it is reasonable to do what would make it the case that P, as one wants, that might likewise be owing to the way the object of desire is represented, in that state of mind. If, in a desire, its object (or one's having the thing wanted), is represented as something good, this falls into place.

(But there are apparent differences between the principles of sound practical reasoning and those of 'theoretical' (deductive or inductive) reasoning. Kenny (1966) suggested that the decision to do something believed merely *sufficient* (and not necessary) to satisfy some desire is, relative to that desire, a logically valid decision. Thus, unlike a valid deductive inference, a valid practical inference need not draw a conclusion that is necessary if its premises are true; instead, the conclusion must be *sufficient* for the truth of a premise representing some desire – that is, expressing the desire's propositional object. This turns on differences between the semantic values conferred on the conclusion by valid inferences of one kind or the other – that is, between truth on the one hand, and goodness or satisfactoriness on the other.)

Further support for a representational view of desire concerns the 'intensionality' of the terms designating what is wanted in sentences used to describe desires. '(Œdipus wanted to marry the Queen' says something true, but while the Queen was one and the same person as his own mother, we cannot substitute the phrase 'his own mother' for the term 'the Queen'. Why should this be so? Evidently, the term designating the object of this desire is doing something other than, or more than, referring to the thing wanted. Frege held that the phrase instead refers, here, to the meaning or sense the phrase would ordinarily have, but this leaves the question how a reference to the sense of a phrase might serve to characterize the desire. An alternative view is that the phrase here serves, as usual, to refer to the person herself (thus to say who (Œdipus wanted to marry) but in addition it *may* be used, in this context, to provide a further specification of the desire; and it may do this by specifying the reason the desire comprises for acting so as to satisfy it. (It makes sense that a desire should be identified in this way if a desire *is* a reason for acting so as to satisfy it.) Thus 'the Queen' identifies or refers to the woman by mentioning *properties* of her the possession of which comprises a reason the subject would therein have to act so as to satisfy the desire ascribed to him. While her being the Queen comprises such a reason, other properties that distinguish her, such as her being his own mother, are reasons for *not* marrying the woman. Accordingly the substitution of that phrase, though it refers to the same woman, may change the statement from true to false.

(We may ask, however, whether in identifying desires, co-referential expressions may be freely substituted when they refer to the object in terms of those of its properties that reinforce the state's merely *causal* efficacy, in the production of action – or must they describe it in terms of properties of the object that also make those actions *reasonable?* Consider someone who likes to experience the heights of euphoria, and therefore periodically wants to inject the most euphoric drug there is, and does so. Suppose that drug happens also to be the most powerfully addictive of drugs, so *that* property of it has reinforced the tendency of this desire to cause the action that satisfies it. Now, he wants to take the drug because – as a result of the fact that – it is addictive *and* because – i.e. for the *reason* that – it is so euphoric. But, narrowly specified, *what is it* that he wants? Is it to take the drug that will most powerfully addict him to its use? Or instead

to take the drug that will produce the greatest euphoria? The issue is aired in Stampe (1990) where Dretske responds.)

It seems that the causal power of a desire may outrun its capacity to rationalize actions done to satisfy it. There is a notion of the strength of a desire, which is something not determined solely by the quality of the reason the desire affords, so that there may be such a thing as a desire that is excessively powerful or insufficiently strong. I want to smoke, which is a reason to smoke, and I want not to offend my non-smoking companion, which is a reason not to smoke. The comparative *quality* of my reasons to smoke and not to smoke depends partly on how badly I want to do the one thing or the other, but largely, also, on factors external to those desires: on what other desires I have, and beliefs about how *their* satisfaction will be affected by my satisfying the desires in question. I have a better reason not to smoke, than to smoke, if I also want a job, and my companion is interviewing me for that job. Even so, the desire to light up may overwhelm 'my better judgment', if it is the more powerful or forceful of the two desires.

It may be questioned whether such references to the 'force' of a desire are genuinely explanatory, and thus whether there really *is* such a thing. Such doubts may be provoked by the dogmatic assertion of 'the law of preponderant desire', which says that the more powerful desire will necessarily prevail (J. S. Mill, 1867, ch. 26.) This, it is objected, is no law of psychology, but an empty tautology, for the 'stronger' desire is being merely *defined* as the one that actually prevails.

It would be a mistake to infer that the idea of the strength of desire cannot be given explanatory content. Other definitions of such a magnitude are possible, which would make the proposition that the stronger desire must prevail synthetic, in principle falsifiable, and, apparently, in fact false. For instance, the desire's power, relative to other desires, might be measured by the relative probability of each producing actions intended to satisfy it, *ceteris paribus* –

that is, where other factors are the same, such as the relative cost or difficulty of the acts, the relative probability of their success, their incidental benefits or drawbacks, etc. The stronger desire is the one that will more probably produce action, *ceteris paribus*, but where other factors are not the same, the weaker desire, thus defined, may prevail. If they cost the same, the desire to eat lobster would prevail over the desire to eat cod; it's the stronger desire. Since they don't cost the same, the weaker desire ordinarily prevails. This is principally because other desires (regarding money) come into play. (The strongest navy is the one that is stronger than any other *single* navy; it needn't be stronger than two others in alliance.)

The *excessively* powerful desire is one, intuitively, which may prevail though other desires could be satisfied with greater benefit. Acting upon that desire is unreasonable, since the reasonable action would maximize the satisfaction of *all* one's desires. It is an effect of rational deliberation that the power of any relevant desire is brought to bear on the decision, lending its power to the efficacy of the resulting intention. Ideally, the power of a desire would be proportional to the benefits of its satisfaction, and there is another mechanism (other than reason) which tends, if imperfectly, to produce that correlation: for the satisfaction of a desire provides positive reinforcement, augmenting the tendency of states of that type to produce behaviour of that type. But the principal cause of excessive strength in a desire also lies here. For the probability of a desire's being acted upon may be raised when its satisfaction coincides with the satisfaction of some second desire, with the result that the first desire's power is thereafter stronger, disproportionately to the benefits that would regularly, and in other contexts, attend its satisfaction. Thus the child's desire to please, when it causes compliant behaviour, is rewarded, so it incidentally yields satisfaction of the desire for candy, with the effect that the desire to please becomes so strong that it is effective, even when there is no candy in the offing, and even when the benefits of compliant

behaviour are smaller than the benefits of defiant behaviour that would satisfy other desires.

See also FOLK PSYCHOLOGY; PRACTICAL REASON; PSYCHOANALYTIC EXPLANATION; REPRESENTATION; WEAKNESS OF WILL.

BIBLIOGRAPHY

Anscombe, G.E.M. 1957. *Intention*. Oxford: Basil Blackwell.

Dretske, F. 1984. *Explaining Behavior*. Cambridge, MA.: MIT Press.

Geach, P. 1957. *Mental Acts*. London: Routledge & Kegan Paul.

Hume, D. (1739) 1960. *A Treatise of Human Nature*, Book II, Section iii; *Hume's Treatise*, ed. L. A. Selby-Bigge: Oxford University Press.

Jowett, B.A., trans. 1937. *The Dialogues of Plato*. New York: Random House.

Kenny, A. 1966. Practical inference. *Analysis*.

Marks, J. 1986. *The Ways of Desire*. Chicago: Precedent.

Mill, J.S. 1867. *An Examination of Sir William Hamilton's Philosophy*, ch. XXVI. London.

Spinoza, B. 1677. *Ethics demonstrated in geometrical order*; *The Ethics and Selected Letters*, trans. S. Shirley, ed. S. Feldman. Indianapolis: Hackett.

Stalnaker, Robert C. 1984. *Inquiry*. Cambridge, MA.: MIT Press.

Stampe, Dennis W. 1987. The authority of desire. *The Philosophical Review*, XCVI, 3, 335–81.

Stampe, Dennis W. 1990. Reasons and desires – discussion notes on Dretske's *Explaining Behavior*: *Philosophy and Phenomenological Research*, vol. L.

DENNIS W. STAMPE

developmental psychology This entry is about the developmental origins of natural philosophical ideas about the mind. Although there is some intriguing work on children's explicit philosophizing – most of it by the philosopher Gareth Matthews (1984) – we will be concerned here with children's philosophies of mind 'in action' (e.g. to explain another's behaviour) rather than their ability to construct philosophical arguments. Indeed, in order to engage in human interaction, to predict others' behaviour, to understand their INTENTIONS/BELIEFS/ DESIRES, to interpret their STATEMENTS/ GESTURES/ACTIONS, to understand irony/ metaphor, to interpret utterances or facial expressions which are discrepant from actual feelings, to understand how point of view and perception can influence belief formation, and so forth, children have to learn to become natural philosophers of mind. We will focus on two essential questions: (a) what do human beings bring into the world to make the development of successful social interaction possible?, and (b) what course does the development take?

DOMAIN-GENERAL VERSUS DOMAIN-SPECIFIC THEORIES OF MIND

We first need to introduce a distinction which underpins two fundamentally different ways of thinking about the child's conceptions of mind. It will become our chapter's *motif*. FODOR (1983) distinguished between 'input systems' in the mental architecture and 'central systems'. A simple way to capture their difference is by thinking of the first as being rather like reflexes and the second as being like thoughts, or of the first as bottom-up/data-driven and the second as top-down/hypothesis-driven.

The input systems are 'domain-specific' modules insofar as they perform *sui generis* kinds of computations for each domain. They are relatively unaffected by higher-level, knowledge-based systems and by current states of CONSCIOUSNESS. They operate swiftly, mandatorily and independently from other modules. They have fixed neural architectures and a fixed timetable of development. The central systems, by contrast, are domain-general and global. Indeed, to use Fodor's metaphor, one can see them as spreading horizontally above and across the many vertical input systems which package information from the external world. Colour vision, face-processing, movement perception, syntactic parsing are examples of input systems. The central systems cannot be listed so easily because

they do not naturally reduce to sets of computational tasks. 'Belief fixation' (how we acquire beliefs) and analogical reasoning are central, because they are both domain-general processes *par excellence*. That is to say, there is no limit on the number of ways we can come to hold a belief (no limit on the input systems we recruit and how) and no constraint on how we draw analogies.

In the light of the input system/central distinction, what can we immediately say about the development of children's philosophies of mind – about what it is now customary to call children's 'theory of mind'? Is such a theory best regarded as a domain-specific input system or as a domain-general central system? The advantage of the first option is that it allows us more easily to assume that the theory is innately specified (*see* INNATENESS). As Fodor aptly puts it, 'Here is what I would have done if I had been faced with this problem in designing Homo Sapiens. I would have made commonsense psychology innate; that way nobody would have to spend time learning it' (Fodor, 1987, p. 132). This certainly would be an advantage because it is difficult to see how the evidence could force upon us the theory that there are beliefs and desires which interact to cause behaviour. On the other hand, can our conception of mind be so neatly pre-packaged into an input module? Do we not call on many domain-general processes in our view of ourselves and others as conscious fallible agents who know some things and believe others?

The first modern account of theory of mind development was given by Jean Piaget (e.g. 1929, 1932). And it was the epitome of a domain-general view. One way of regarding Piaget's work is as an attempt to explain how the child comes to forge a division between subjectivity and objectivity, between what is true of my mind and what is true of reality. Piaget held that the basic lineaments of thought (substance, causality, space, time) evolved through sensorimotor experience in infancy; that between about 2 and about 6 years these early sensorimotor acquisitions gradually came to underpin concrete verbal judgments; and that it was

251

not until adolescence that children's thought could move beyond coordinating concrete judgments to coordinating hypotheses and possibilities. One of the main theoretical tools Piaget used for describing childish thought was *egocentrism*, by which he meant the failure to distinguish a subjective perspective (how it is to my mind) from objective reality.

For Piaget, egocentrism was pervasive in the thought of the child, in the sense that the child's judgments of reality were supposed to be infused with – and thus distorted by – egocentric information about the self's own physical, intellectual and social perspective. Thus the failure of infants to search for completely occluded objects was explained in terms of their rule 'what I see is what exists'; children's failure to judge that a quantity is conserved across perceptual transformations (e.g. pouring it from a short, fat to a tall, thin container) was explained in terms of their egocentric fixation upon a single, striking unidimensional change; children when asked to pick out the view of three mountains that a person sitting opposite them would actually see, tend to pick out the view that they see themselves. In other words, at different ages, depending on the task, children tend to overvalue the immediate evidence of their own senses. According to this theory, egocentrism appears, fades and re-emerges throughout development and *across the mental board*, with the domain-specific content of particular tasks having only a minor role to play.

What had to evolve in the mental journey towards a non-egocentric conception of reality? According to Piaget, the child had to acquire a capacity for self-regulation through mental action. She had to regulate and thereby structure (Piaget described this structuring by mathematical group theory) the representations which had been acquired in infancy. Restructuring caused thinking to move to progressively higher representational planes (from sensorimotor, to imagist, to verbal to hypothetical). Egocentrism is overcome through a central executive (not Piaget's term) reg-

ulating mental attention away from the salient-to-self information, to objective reality; and this regulation was supposed to spread across all domains of knowledge. Piaget was nothing if not a philosopher-psychologist of the central systems.

What does a theory like this imply about the young child's conception of mind? It implies an overly pessimistic view. Indeed, some of the claims that Piaget made about failures to distinguish, say, speaking from acting and dreaming from thinking till age 7 (Piaget, 1929) were certainly misguided. In any event, the theoretical pendulum has swung the other way, towards a domain-specific conception of children's mental philosophies. We will, in the next section, describe this alternative view, followed by some modern domain-general but non-Piagetian views, before giving a brief reconsideration of the Piagetian conceptions at the end.

THE PREREQUISITES TO THEORY OF MIND IN INFANCY

If we adopt a domain-specific view of theory of mind development, then we can expect to find precursors in early infancy. What might these be?

The first thing to say about them is that they are essentially perceptual, as befits input systems. Without the early perception of the basic characteristics of humans (gait, voice, face, etc.), it is difficult to see how basic mental systems which support theory-of-mind computations could ever get off the ground (Karmiloff-Smith, 1992). Neonates appear to be innately tuned to the gross features of the primate face (Johnson and Morton, 1991; Sargent and Nelson, 1992), are capable of imitating facial gestures (Meltzoff and Moore, 1977; Meltzoff, 1993) and attending to changes in their emotional expression (Field et al., 1983). Similarly for the human voice. At birth infants distinguish speech from other auditory input and at 4 days they attend preferentially to their native tongue, having already picked up something about its prosodic structure (Mehler et al., 1986).

But there is nothing specifically *mental* about human faces and voices. What about infants' perception of the quintessentially mental quality of agency? Leslie (1984) has shown that 7-month-olds can select out a manual pick-up event as being different from a non-manual means of raising objects. Moreover, Premack (1990; *see also* Dasser, Ulbaeck, and Premack, 1989), the theorist who coined the phrase 'theory of mind', has made the provocative claim that in the earliest months of life we operate with a purpose-built module for detecting agency. This is done on the basis of the distinction between non self-propelled objects and the self-propelling motion of biological beings. This may be an automatic, somewhat mindless pick-up of information; but without it, so the domain-specific theorist argues, the child is unlikely to acquire a conception of mental life – no matter how well-regulated her 'mental actions'.

Beyond these initial attention-perception biases, what aspects of very early interaction could play a role in the development of theory of mind? What kinds of behaviour suggest that young children have some inchoate conception of other minds? Communication can plausibly be said to require some form of 'mind reading', so perhaps we should look towards prelinguistic communication. Mutual eye-gaze or pointing to a specific referent at about 9–10 months act as a form of non-linguistic communication by directing the attention of the addressee to something of interest. It has been shown that young infants become progressively capable of joint attention via eye contact. Note that we are talking of 'joint *attention*', because eye contact alone can be much like attending to inanimate objects. Increasingly, infants make use of gaze alternation (between the caretaker's eyes and a coveted object or goal), to signal to the caretaker that they wish to obtain a particular object. It is the coordination between eye-contact and pointing gesture that leads to ostensive communication. Interestingly, several studies indicate that autistic children – who often fail to develop a theory of mind – are deficient in such joint attention co-ordinations of eye contact and gesture (Baron-Cohen, 1989; Dawson, Hill, Spencer, Gal-pert, and Watson, 1990; Sigman, Mundy, Sherman and Ungerer, 1986), suggesting that this is a fundamental aspect of the development of a theory of mind in normal children. We will return to the case of autism throughout the chapter.

What are the functions of these early ostensive communications in the human infant? They are of two types: so-called 'proto-imperatives' and 'proto-declaratives' (Baron-Cohen, 1989). Proto-imperatives involve the use of pointing or eye-gaze as the infant's means of trying to obtain an object by a non-verbal request directed at the interlocutor who can reach the object for the child. If the human infant were mobile at birth as many species are, then s/he would get the object herself or push the adult towards it. But human immobility is such that it forces the young infant into finding other, *interactional* means of reaching certain goals. The pointing gestures therefore start out as instrumental requests.

These proto-imperatives rapidly become proto-declaratives, i.e., a point becomes the infant's means of making a non-verbal comment about the state of the world (the equivalent of, say, 'look, that's a nice dog') rather than a request to obtain something. Again, the difference between normal and autistic children's proto-declarative pointing to affect another's *mental state* is striking. Autistic children neither use nor understand proto-declarative pointing (Baron-Cohen, 1989); their competence is limited to proto-imperative pointing to affect another's *behaviour*. They also rarely engage in so-called 'social referencing' (Hobson, 1989) in which the child gauges how she should respond to a novel event (is this danger or is it OK?) from the mother's facial expression. Normal children do this at around 12 months of age.

THE TODDLER'S THEORY OF MIND: A DOMAIN-SPECIFIC MODULE FOR MENTALIZING?

Here is a typical conundrum in cognitive development. By the time children reach the end of their third year of life, they not only use the language of mental states (*think, know, want, afraid,* and so forth), but they use these terms in a genuinely mentalistic way (Bretherton and Beeghly, 1982; Shatz et al., 1983). Surely this ability cannot arise out of language itself: the terms must be gaining some cognitive foothold in a pre-linguistic understanding of mental states. Leslie (1987, 1990) has suggested that it is an innately-specified module for computing mental representations which provides this foothold, a domain-specific module which matures at around 18 months of age in normal children. (*see* COMPUTATIONAL MODELS; MODULARITY; REPRESENTATION.)

This theory situates propositional attitude competence in the realm of *pretend play.* Leslie argues that children's pretend play involves the same distinction between propo-sitional CONTENT and PROPOSITIONAL ATTITUDE as that found in the subsequent use of mental state verbs. Because the psy-chological structures of pretence are deemed to be innately specified, the child can imme-diately understand pretend acts when she is first exposed to them. Leslie suggests that the structure of young children's pretend play should be understood as the computa-tion of a 3-term relation between an agent (usually the child herself), a primary repre-sentation (the actual objects being played with) and a decoupled, secondary repre-sentation which represents the content of the pretence. This contrasts sharply with Piaget's arguments that young children represent events as 'schemes' in which agent, event and object form an undiffer-entiated amalgam. For Leslie, it is the notion of a decoupled representation that is specific to theory of mind. The decoupling allows the child to treat the pretend content separately from the normal relations that the representation of the real object/event entertains. Thus, when a 3-year-old picks up a block of wood and declares: '*Vroom, vroom, vroom, toot, toot!*', the pretend com-putation involves: PRETEND [(Agent = child)(Primary Representation = a mental structure representing the fact that the object on the table is a block of wood)

(Decoupled Representation = a copy of the previous mental structure but cordonned off from veridical descriptions and standing for 'the car')]. The primary and decoupled representations involve different and sepa-rate levels of processing and obey distinct causal and logical inferential constraints. Thus, pretending that a simple block of wood has a steering wheel, a horn and four wheels in no way detracts from toddlers' understanding of the real properties of the block of wood and of real cars, nor does it change their representations of such proper-ties. It is the decoupled (temporary) repre-sentation that is 'tampered' with, not the primary representations which continue to entertain their normal representational rela-tionships. And the decoupled representa-tion, *not necessarily linguistically encoded,* involves a distinction between a proposi-tional attitude and the propositional content on which it operates:

[*I pretend that*] [*this block of wood*] [*it is a car*].

It is irrelevant to the truth value of the pro-positional attitude PRETEND (and of BELIEVE/THINK/CLAIM, etc.) that the block of wood is not actually a car. Some proposi-tional attitudes (e.g. KNOW/REMEMBER) do, of course, entail the truth of their propo-sitional contents.

DEVELOPING AN EXPLICIT BELIEF-DESIRE PSYCHOLOGY

The claim we have just considered about what pretence tells us about a child's understanding of the mental realm is a con-troversial one. Some would argue that there is no real warrant for assuming that a pre-tending (or pretence-observing) child is mentally erecting a proposition (e.g. [it is a car]) in relation to a mental attitude. All that we can infer, the objection goes, is that the child knows what it is to do something *pretendingly* rather than for real. Pretending may require fewer cognitive demands than belief, but it seems to require more mental insight than understanding what it means to do something in earnest. However, that does not force the conclusion that the child has mentally separated attitudes from contents – any more than understanding what it means to do something in earnest forces that reading of the child's behaviour. It may therefore be preferable to be more cautious and to suggest that the early conception of pretence is sub-propositional, though it may well ground the later understanding of the relation between attitudes and contents.

In any event, *if* the pretending child has some conception of what it means for a propositional attitude to have a content, then it is reasonable to expect that she also understands the attitude of belief. Mental contents are contents *in the running for truth*, with the difference between pretending and believing being that in the former case the individual knows the content is false whereas in the latter case the individual is committed to its truth. But how are we to assess the understanding of believing other than by linguistic means?

At this point, then, we encounter another developmental conundrum: how is one to test for the pre-linguistic presence of an ability which is – if what has just been said is true – essentially propositional? What is a non-verbal expression of belief? Are beliefs only available to language-users, as some philosophers would argue (DAVIDSON, 1974), or should we attribute beliefs promiscuously? Whatever the answer to this question, the assessment of the concept of belief by developmental psychologists has hitherto been only through verbal tests. In general, the assumption is that a conception of how *false beliefs* drive behaviour is a good diagnostic test, because this captures both the commitment to the truth of the proposition believed and the fact that it can be false.

Take the following experimental set-up for testing false belief, based on seminal work by Heinz Wimmer and Josef Perner (Wimmer and Perner, 1983). The child watches a scene in which the experimenter and a boy called Maxi are in a room together. The experimenter hides a piece of chocolate under a box in front of Maxi. Maxi then leaves the room momentarily and, while he is absent, the experimenter moves the chocolate to another hiding place. The child is then asked where the chocolate really is and, crucially for the task, where Maxi will look for it upon her return. In other words, the child has to distinguish between what she knows to be true of the current state of the world (cf. Piaget's 'egocentrism') and what she knows to be Maxi's current mental state. She also has to know that Maxi's behaviour will be a function of his mental representations, not of the physical reality.

This and other similar tasks (e.g. Perner, Leekam and Wimmer, 1987) are simple, yet stringent tests of the child's ability to impute mental states with content to others. Three-year-olds fail many false belief tasks (at least when presented in this form) and think that the protagonist will behave in accordance with the real-world situation. They do not seem to understand that he will behave on the basis of his false belief. Four-year-olds are successful. The minimal criteria for possessing a theory of mind are, according to DENNETT (1978), successfully dealing with circumstances in which an individual cannot rely on her own knowledge in order to assess another's mental state. But in many tasks 3-year-olds do rely solely on their own knowledge.

There are a number of theory-of-mind tasks in addition to false belief, and they share more than a family resemblance. They all require a grasp of the representational nature of thought, they are typically failed by 3-year-old children, and they correlate well together (Moore and Furrow, 1991). So it does look – to some developmentalists at least (Leslie, 1987, 1990) – that what we are seeing here is a special-purpose, mental-state computing device coming into operation. Taking a different but related tack, Fodor (1992) has recently argued that there is an innate belief-desire theory but that it is not always accessed by 3-years-olds due to computational capacity limitations that expand by age 4. But perhaps the strongest reason for believing in such a thing as an innate and specific theory of mind module is the case of autism.

Recall that autistic children fail to show the early markers of mentalizing ability such as joint attention and proto-declarative pointing. They are also very unlikely to engage spontaneously in pretend play; and they are dramatically impaired on the false-belief and other theory-of-mind tasks that normal children pass at age 4 (Frith, 1989). All this is consistent with the view first proposed by Baron-Cohen, Leslie and Frith (1985) that autism is the disorder which arises in children who are born without the theory of mind module, or with a module whose triggering is delayed or deviant.

ALTERNATIVES TO DOMAIN-SPECIFIC ACCOUNTS

The hypothesis that a theory of mind is not a domain-general system but one similar to syntactic parsing – formal, domain-specific and circumscribed from 'general intelligence' – is not only provocative but plausible. But does the autistic deficit prove that theory of mind computations are modular, i.e. encapsulated in a theory of mind module as Leslie (1990) and Fodor (1983) have argued? Frith (1989), for example, locates autistic people's perceptual and communicative difficulties in their domain-general central processing. What we find in autism, argues Frith, is lack of 'central cohesion' – the ability to synthesize fragments of information into meaningful wholes.

Looking upon the human theory of mind as a Fodorian module also presents us with a form of dilemma familiar to students of syntax development – a 'bootstrapping problem'. As Pinker has argued (e.g. 1984), knowing innately that there are (say) nouns still leaves the learner with the problem of determining what words in her native language actually *are* nouns: the learner must bootstrap herself from innate formal knowledge to a particular language. For Pinker, the solution is to recruit some rough-and-ready semantic generalizations (e.g. nouns tend to be thing words). A similar problem faces the novice philosopher of mind. It is all very well to have the concept of belief,

desire, and so forth in one's native armoury; but how is one to determine that *this* is a case of believing, that *this* is a case of desiring? Take pretence: a cognitive bridge of some kind has to be built between the innate representation of the pretending attitude and the visual input of mother putting a banana to her head and saying 'Oh Hi! How nice of you to ring!' In a similar vein, how could one recruit an innate representation of agency unless one had first-hand experience of being an agent? (This is the kind of point a Piagetian might make and, indeed, Meltzoff has recently argued that the pervasive human tendency to imitate other agents from birth onwards is the child's first entry into building up a theory of mind (Meltzoff, 1993).)

There is, in fact, no shortage of alternatives to modular nativism about the child's theory of mind (Astington, Harris and Olson, 1988; *see* Russell, 1992, for a review). Some draw an analogy between child and scientist in that domain-general theory development involves inferences on the basis of unobservables (mental states like belief), a coherent set of explanations of causal links between mental states and behaviour which are predictive of future actions, and a growing distinction between evidence and theory (Carey, 1985; Gopnik, 1993; Karmiloff-Smith, 1988; Perner, 1991; Wellman, 1990). Others reject entirely the claim that our knowledge of other minds has any theoretical structure, arguing that we make judgments about the beliefs of others by running a simulation of our own beliefs, and attempt to explain 3-year-olds' difficulties with the false belief task in these terms (Harris, 1991; and *see* special issue of *Mind and Language*, 1992). Others, notably Perner (1991), maintain that there is indeed a fundamental theoretical shift at 4 years but that it is a domain-general one in which a more adequate conception of representation *per se* is developing, a conception that applies to pictures, photographs, and words as well as to the mind. Note, however, that autistic subjects who fail theory of mind tasks have no difficulties with equivalent tasks involving photographs rather than other minds (Leslie and Thaiss, 1992). This would clearly argue against going all the way back to the domain-generality of Piagetian theory.

'THE MIND ITSELF', COMPARED TO CHILDREN'S THEORIES OF IT

Developmental psychologists are fairly unanimous that we should not return to classic Piagetian theory which fails to give modular mechanisms their due. But what Piagetian theory can tackle is a different question: How might a developing organism set itself apart from reality and thus *become* a mind? Piaget's answer, recall, was that it does so by virtue of agency, by gaining control over its perceptual (input-system?) representations, by becoming progressively less egocentric. It is by adapting to the contours of reality that the mind emerges; and such an entity exists over and above any theories that the mind might have about itself.

In a sense, then, the Piagetian student of the central systems and the modular theorist have somewhat different agendas when they talk about development. But there *is* an inevitable clash over empirical territory. For Piagetians will have to say that competence in mental agency (*qua* the ability to suppress egocentrism) will determine the child's efficient use of or access to the theory. They might argue, for example, that the child fails the false belief task when she cannot suppress the mental salience of her *own* knowledge that the object is no longer where it was. In support of this conjecture, 3-year-olds have a similar kind of difficulty with answering questions about which of two objects a protagonist needs, referring instead to the object which the child *herself* needs (Russell, Jarrold and Moore, 1994). With regard to autism, indeed, the Piagetian can even suggest a serious alternative to the theory-of-mind deficit view. We know that people with autism have clear difficulties with so-called 'executive function tasks' (tasks that require the instigation, control and monitoring of mental actions). They have, for example, problems

in planning, shifting their attention to new categories and performing means-end tasks (e.g. Hughes and Russell, 1993, Ozonoff, Pennington and Rogers, 1991). If this difficulty exists from the outset, if there is a profound impairment in determining which experiences are generated by one's mental action and which are generated by reality, the sense of self will fail to develop adequately – and thus the sense of others.

As in much of cognitive developmental psychology, there is no elegant denouement to the story of how the child's theory of mind develops. Theoretical disputes are intense, and the cognitive developmentalist certainly needs the philosopher's help in addressing the deeper questions. The child, by contrast, needs only the minimum of help to become a philosopher of mind. It's natural.

See also COGNITIVE PSYCHOLOGY; LANGUAGE OF THOUGHT.

BIBLIOGRAPHY

Astington, J.W., Harris, P.L., and Olson, D.R., eds. 1988. *Developing Theories of Mind*. Cambridge: Cambridge University Press.

Baron-Cohen, S. 1989. Perceptual role-taking and proto-declarative pointing in autism. *British Journal of Developmental Psychology*, 7, 113–27.

Baron-Cohen, S., Leslie, A.M. and Frith, U. 1985. Does the autistic child have a 'theory of mind'? *Cognition*, 21, 37–46.

Bretherton, I., and Beeghly, M. 1982. Talking about internal states: the acquisition of an explicit theory of mind. *Developmental Psychology*, 18, 906–21.

Carey, S. 1985. *Conceptual Change in Childhood*. Cambridge, MA.: MIT Press.

Chandler, M.J., and Boyes, M. 1982. Social-cognitive development. In *Handbook of Development Psychology*, ed. B. B. Wolman. Englewood Cliffs, NJ: Prentice-Hall.

Dasser, V., Ulbaeck, L, and Premack, D. 1989. The perception of intention. *Science*, 243, 365–7.

Davidson, D. 1974. Belief and the basis of meaning. *Synthese*, 27, 309–29.

Dawson, G., Hill, D., Spencer, A., Galpert, L., and Watson, L. 1990. Affective exchanges between young autistic children and their mothers. *Journal of Abnormal Child Psychology*, 18, 335–45.

Dennett, D.C. 1978. *Brainstorms: Philosophical Essays on Mind and Psychology*. Montgomery, VT: Bradford Books.

Field, T., Woodson, R., Greenberg, R., and Cohen, D. 1983. Discrimination and imitation of facial expression by neonates. *Science*, 218, 179–81.

Fodor, J.A. 1983. *The Modularity of Mind*. Cambridge, MA.: MIT Press.

Fodor, J.A. 1987. *Psychosemantics: The Problem of Meaning in the Philosophy of Mind*. Cambridge, MA.: MIT Press/Bradford Books.

Fodor, J.A. 1992. A theory of the child's theory of mind. *Cognition*, 44, 283–96.

Frith, U. 1989. *Autism: Explaining the enigma*: Oxford: Basil Blackwell.

Gopnik, A. 1993. How we know our minds: The illusion of first-person knowledge of intentionality. *Behavioral and Brain Sciences*, 16: 1, 1–14.

Harris, P. 1991. The work of imagination. In *Natural Theories of Mind*, ed. A. Whiten. Oxford: Basil Blackwell.

Hobson, P. 1989. On acquiring knowledge about people and the capacity for pretense. *Psychological Review*, 97, 114–21.

Hughes, C., and Russell, J. 1993. Autistic children's difficulty with mental disengagement from an object: Its implications for theories of autism. *Developmental Psychology*, 29, 498–510.

Johnson, M.H., and Morton, J. 1991. *Biology and Cognitive Development: The Case of Face Recognition*. Oxford: Basil Blackwell.

Karmiloff-Smith, A. 1988. The child is a theoretician, not an inductivist. *Mind and Language*, 3: 3, 183–95.

Karmiloff-Smith, A. 1992. *Beyond Modularity: A Developmental Perspective on Cognitive Science*. Cambridge, MA.: MIT Press/Bradford Books.

Leslie, A.M. 1984. Infant perception of a manual pickup event. *British Journal of Developmental Psychology*, 2, 19–32.

Leslie, A.M. 1987. Pretense and representation: The origins of 'Theory of Mind'. *Psychological Review*, 94, 412–26.

Leslie, A.M. 1990. Pretense, autism and the basis of 'Theory of mind'. *The Psychologist*, 3, 120–3.

Leslie, A.M., and Thaiss, L. 1992. Domain specificity in conceptual development: neuropsychological evidence from autism. *Cognition*, 43, 225–51.

Matthews, G.B. 1984. *Dialogues with Children*. Cambridge, MA.: Harvard University Press.

Mehler, J., Lambertz, G., Jusczyk, P., and Amiel-Tison, C. 1986. Discrimination de la langue maternelle par le nouveau-né. *C.R. Academie des Sciences*, 303, S. III, 637–40.

Meltzoff, A.N. 1993. Imitation as a tool for exploring the infant mind. Paper presented at the *Society for Research in Child Development*, New Orleans, March 1993.

Meltzoff, A., and Moore, M. 1977. Imitation of facial and manual gestures by human neonates. *Science*, 198, 75–8.

Moore, C., and Furrow, D. 1991. The development of the language of belief: The expression of relative certainty. In *Children's Theories of Mind*, ed. D. Frye and C. Moore. Hillsdale, NJ: Lawrence Erlbaum.

Ozonoff, S., Pennington, B.F., and Rogers, S.J. 1991. Executive function deficits in high-functioning autistic individuals: Relationship to theory of mind. *Journal of Child Psychology and Child Psychiatry*, 32, 1081–105.

Perner, J. 1991. *Understanding the Representational Mind*. Cambridge, MA.: MIT Press/Bradford Books.

Perner, J., Leekam, S., and Wimmer, H. 1987. Three year olds' difficulty with false belief: The case for a conceptual deficit. *British Journal of Developmental Psychology*, 5, 125–37.

Piaget, J. 1929. *The Child's Conception of the World*. London: Routledge & Kegan Paul.

Piaget, J. 1932. *The Moral Judgement of the Child*. London: Kegan Paul, Trench Trubner.

Pinker, S. 1984. *Language, Learnability and Language development*. Cambridge, MA.: Harvard University Press.

Premack, D. 1990. Words: What are they, and do animals have them? *Cognition*, 37, 197–212.

Russell, J. 1992. The theory theory: So good they named it twice? *Cognitive Development*, 7, 485–519.

Russell, J., Jarrold, C. and Moore, C. 1994. The 'false need' task: evidence for an executive transition between 3 and 4 years. Ms submitted for publication.

Sargent, P.L., and Nelson, C.A. 1992. Cross-species recognition in infant and adult humans: ERP and behavioral measures. Poster presented at the International Conference on Infant Studies, Miami Beach.

Shatz, M., Wellman, H.M., and Silber, S. 1983. The acquisition of mental verbs: A systematic investigation of the child's first reference to mental state. *Cognition*, 14, 301–21.

Sigman, M., Mundy, P., Sherman, T., and Ungerer, J. 1986. Social interactions of autistic, mentally retarded, and normal children and their caregivers. *Journal of Child Psychology and Psychiatry*, 27, 647–56.

Wellman, H.M. 1990. *The Child's Theory of Mind*. Cambridge MA.: MIT Press.

Wimmer, H., and Perner, J. 1983. Beliefs about beliefs. Representation and constraining function of wrong beliefs in young children's understanding of deception. *Cognition*, 13, 103–28.

ANNETTE KARMILOFF-SMITH
JAMES RUSSELL

Dretske, Fred An early interest in knowledge and PERCEPTION shaped my thinking about BELIEF and experience. One cannot think long about the relations, causal and otherwise, underlying our perceptual awareness of the world without reaching definite – indeed, I would say irresistible – conclusions about the nature of those internal states required for such awareness. If perception of, and knowledge about, physical objects is possible, then, or so it seemed to me, our experience of, and our beliefs about, these objects *must* have a certain character.

It is, I think, this epistemological perspective that most clearly distinguishes my own work in the philosophy of mind from others. In Dretske (1969, 1979), for example, I argued for a distinction between what I called epistemic and non-epistemic forms of perception. To describe someone (or some animal) as seeing a bug, for example, is to describe a relationship between the person and a bug which, like stepping on a bug, does not require (though it is compatible with) knowledge or belief about the bug. The relationship is non-epistemic in the sense that it does not involve any conceptual understanding of what is seen. Seeing (of objects and events) is not, not necessarily anyway, believing. This way of seeing is to be contrasted with epistemic forms: seeing *that* the bug is a bug or seeing the bug *as* a bug (i.e. recognizing it). This idea, obvious though I (still) think it is, is fundamental to understanding the basic difference between perception and conception and, hence, the nature of, and differences between, our experience of, and our beliefs about, the world. A theory of the mind that identifies all mental states, including experiences, with some form of belief or judgment (whether conscious or unconscious) has to be wrong. If seeing is not believing in a theory of knowledge, neither is it in the philosophy of mind.

I have, as a result, always regarded naturalistic theories in the philosophy of mind (*see* NATURALISM) as confronting at least two fundamentally different problems: (1) those associated with the propositional attitudes (belief and judgment) and related processes (inference and thought); and (2) those related to feelings and experiences, the qualitative states constituting our sensory life. No theory of the mind can be complete unless it has a story to tell about both aspects of our mental life. We need a theory that tells us, not only what .. is to believe, think, or know that Judith is playing the piano, but what the difference is between seeing her play it and hearing her play it.

Even more basic to my view of the mind is the externalism I brought from my work in epistemology (*see* EXTERNALISM/ INTERNALISM). Knowledge, or so I argued in Dretske (1969, 1971), is not a matter of justification, not a matter of getting your beliefs secured by an evidential chain to a foundational rock. It is, rather, a matter of such beliefs being connected to the facts in the right way, a relationship whose existence, because external or extrinsic to the total system of beliefs, might be quite unknown (perhaps even unknowable) to the knowing mind. Sense perception is one way, the most direct and reliable way, of getting oneself so connected. The widespread use of measuring instruments in science and elsewhere is merely a way of extending this connection to more inaccessible affairs. It later seemed to me that 'information' was a useful word to describe this external relation, and in Dretske (1981) I tried to articulate an externalist theory of knowledge by developing an account of informational content. The conclusive reasons of 1971 became the information of 1981. Since the notion of informational content I developed was an intentional idea (a signal could carry the information that something was F without carrying the information that it was G even though every F was in fact G) I also hoped that this general notion of information would be useful in the philosophy of mind and in semantics.

The naturalistic picture of knowledge and perception that emerged from this study had an obvious gap. Both perception and knowledge were identified with various mental states (experiences and beliefs) standing in appropriate external relations to objects and facts, but until the nature of experience and belief themselves were understood, the account was incomplete. Without a naturalistic theory of experience I had no naturalistic theory of perception, and without a naturalistic theory of belief I had no naturalistic theory of knowledge. My own research took a turn away from epistemology and toward the philosophy of mind when I started worrying more about what made something a belief than what made a belief knowledge, more about what made something an experience than how experiences figured in perception.

Nonetheless, the externalism remained. If one assumes that every belief aspires to be knowledge and every experience aspires to veridicality – assumes, that is, that the function or purpose of experience and belief is to inform and direct – then it is a short step to supposing that what makes some brain states into mental states (experiences or beliefs, as the case may be) is related to their information-carrying function. Just as information can convert a belief into knowledge and an experience into perception, the function of providing (in the case of perception) and using (in the case of belief) such information can convert physical states into mental states: an experience or a belief.

From both an evolutionary and a developmental standpoint, from both phylogeny and ontogeny, it is reasonable to suppose that sense experience and the beliefs normally consequent upon it have the job of supplying and organizing the information needed to coordinate behaviour with conditions, both external and internal, on which success in satisfying needs and desires depends. This being so, mental states (at least these mental states) might plausibly be identified with whatever brain states have (or service) the relevant functions. Experiences and beliefs are merely those internal, presumably physical, states of a system having the function of providing information (in the case of experience) and mobilizing it (in the case of belief) for use in the control of behaviour. When they do their job, the results are called perception and knowledge; when they fail, we speak of illusion, hallucination, false belief, and opinion. On this picture, then, the mind is merely the externalist face of the brain, that aspect of biological activity having to do with the provision, handling and use of information. Just as externalism in epistemology says that what converts a mental state – a belief, say – into knowledge is outside the mind, so externalism in the philosophy of mind says that what converts a physical state – some condition of the brain – into a belief is outside the head.

This general picture of the mind (or that part of it given over to cognitive affairs) began to emerge in the final three chapters of Dretske (1981). It was here that I began to think of concepts as physical structure types that acquired, in a process of learning, a specific information-carrying function. In speaking of a certain type of state as having an information-carrying function I mean (and meant) more than that these structures carry information, more than that they, in fact, function this way. There are many things (e.g. cloud formations) that carry information (about weather) that do not have this as their function. Not everything that holds papers down is a paperweight – has this as its function.

If concepts of the simple (observational) sort were internal physical structures that had, in this sense, an information-carrying function, a function they acquired during learning, then instances of these structure types would have a content that (like a belief) could be either true or false. After learning, tokens of these structure types, when caused by some sensory stimulation, would 'say' (i.e. mean) what it was their function to 'tell' (inform about). They would, therefore, qualify as beliefs – at least of the simple (observational) sort.

Any information-carrying structure carries all kinds of information. If, for example, it carries information A, it must also carry the information that A or B. As I conceived of it, learning was supposed to be a process in which a single piece of this information is selected for special treatment, thereby becoming the semantic content – the meaning – of subsequent tokens of that structure type. Just as we conventionally give artefacts and instruments information-providing functions, thereby making their activities and states – pointer readings, flashing lights, and so on – representations of the conditions in the world in which we are interested, so learning converts neural states that carry information – 'pointer readings' in the head, so to speak – into structures that have the function of providing some vital piece of the information they carry (see REPRESENTATION). When this process occurs in the ordinary course of learning, the functions in question develop naturally. They do not, as do the functions of instruments and artefacts, depend on the intentions, beliefs, and attitudes of users. We do not *give* brain structures these functions. They get it by themselves, in some natural way, either (in the case of the senses) from their selectional history or (in the case of thought) from individual learning. The result is a network of internal representations that have (in different ways) the power to represent: experiences and beliefs.

It is important, incidentally, to understand that this approach to THOUGHT and belief, the approach that conceives of them as forms of internal representation, is not a version of FUNCTIONALISM – at least not if this widely held theory is understood, as it often is, as a theory that identifies mental properties with functional properties. For functional properties have to do with the way something, in fact, behaves, with its syndrome of typical causes and effects. But, as pointed out above, not everything that functions as, say, a deterrent has deterrence as its function. An informational model of belief, in order to account for misrepresentation, a problem I struggled with in a preliminary way in both (1981) and (1986), needs something more than a structure that provides information. It needs something having that as its function. It needs something that is *supposed* to provide information. As Sober (1985) so nicely puts it, for an account of the mind we need functionalism with the function, the TELEOLOGY, put back in it.

As I conceived of it in 1981, concept learning of the simple (observational) sort was supposed to be the process by means of which certain neural states acquired an information-providing function appropriate to the classification of later tokens of that type as beliefs. If, during learning, a state acquired the function of indicating that some perceptual object was F, then later instances of that state, caused by some perceptual object X, were beliefs (representations), possibly false beliefs (misrepre-sentations), that X was F.

My (1981) account of this process was, admittedly, sketchy. Nonetheless, though short on details, the account was motivated by a basic idea, one that has remained with me up to the present and which formed the basis of the (1988) theory. It is this: the sort of conceptual states we invoke to explain behaviour (belief and desire) really only find a place in the world with animals capable of learning. Even with these, beliefs only put in an appearance with those of their behaviours that are in some way learned or, at least capable of being modified by learning.

We don't need beliefs, nor do we in fact appeal to them, to explain reflexes and other genetically determined behaviours. Even if I have reasons to blink when someone pokes at my eye, I do not blink for these reasons. Even if I think I can protect my eye by blinking, that isn't why I blink. Instead, some story about my genes will explain why I blink, and some story about evolution will presumably explain why I have such genes. Natural selection may, in this way, explain a lot about the behaviour of animals, including humans, but the behaviours it helps explain are not the behaviours that beliefs and desires explain. This, indeed, is why we have less and less use for the mind as we go down the phylogenetic scale, why it seems so pointless to credit paramecia and sea slugs with thoughts and intentions. Even when we speak of them this way, the attribution has a metaphoric, a stance-like, quality to it, as long as the behaviour being explained is neither the product of, nor modifiable by, learning. This being so, what is more natural than to suppose that beliefs (or, better, the concepts needed to form beliefs) are created in the very process in which are created the behavioural dispositions (and, thus, the behaviours) that beliefs are called upon to explain. It is, so to speak, a package deal: we get beliefs – at least the concepts needed to have beliefs – in the very process, the learning process, wherein is developed the neural basis for those behaviours that such beliefs are available to explain. This, in turn, means that the content of beliefs and desires, of fears and intentions, the representational content that is featured in every explanation of behaviour by reasons, must derive from the development in learning of those circuits that constrain and structure voluntary action (see DEVELOPMENTAL PSYCHOLOGY).

That, at least, was the guiding motivation behind my 1981 effort to install the informational processes underlying concept learning as the source of meaning and content. The effort was, as I say, short on details and it was criticized for this neglect. Besides this, though, there was a criticism by Jerry FODOR (1984) that stuck. This problem, the so-called disjunction problem, a problem for almost all extant naturalistic theories, is that, according to Fodor, I was making false belief possible only by an 'unprincipled' stipulation of what is relevant to the learning situation. Only by artificially restricting the circumstances, by ignoring relevant counterfactuals, could I give an internal structure one information-carrying function (the content P, say) rather than another (the content P or Q).

This criticism stuck because although I had thought about this kind of problem, and discussed similar sorts of examples at great length (see 1981, pp. 222–31), I really did not (as I did in 1988) have a developed theory of representation. All I had were robust intuitions that meaning, the concepts required to hold beliefs, *had* to develop there. Where else? My concept of a *martini*, and hence my capacity for holding beliefs about, and having desires for, martinis, beliefs and desires that sometimes help explain why, just before the dinner hour, I go into the kitchen, surely cannot be innate. Despite a tendency on the part of some philosophers to classify everything whose origin they do not understand as innate or non-existent, *that*, surely, cannot be the answer.

What I did not appreciate at the time, and what only became clear to me later when my interest shifted from epistemology to the philosophy of mind, was that I did not really understand the causal or explanatory role of information. The lacuna was not serious as long as I was interested in knowledge, but when (as in the final three chapters of Dretske (1981), I turned to belief itself, this problem became acute.

The problem became acute because if information has to do with the nomic dependencies between events, then for information to do any real causal or explanatory work in the world these dependencies have to do some causal or explanatory work in the world. But how could they? And of what? It is particular events, not the correlations or dependencies between them – hence, not information – that activate the receptors and trigger belief. These particular events may be correlated and dependent events; they may, as a result, carry information. Nonetheless, they are particular events whose causal efficacy is confined to, and hence explained by, their intrinsic properties. It is not, therefore, information itself that is causing belief, but, rather, the events that carry information. I acknowledged this point in 1981 but took it (I still do) to be unimportant to epistemological applications of information theory. What is important for knowledge is that the properties of the signal in virtue of which it carries information be the same as those that are causally responsible for the belief. I can come to know something by consulting a gauge if the pointer position (which carries the relevant information) causes the relevant belief. It is not necessary that the information itself (the relationship between the pointer and what it carries information about) cause the belief. It is information that is necessary for knowledge, not the causal efficacy of information.

Whether or not this is true, it appears to leave information itself (as opposed to the events and structures that carry it) in a metaphysically precarious position. If it does not cause or explain anything, who needs it? The causal impotence of information may be tolerable in epistemology where it is generally conceded that knowledge does not explain anything more about the behaviour of a person who has it than does a true belief. But in the philosophy of mind such causal irrelevance smacks, ominously, of EPIPHENOMENALISM. This threat is especially relevant when one is trying to erect, as I was, a theory of psychological content, a theory of belief, on an informational basis. In Dretske (1980, 1981) I traced the INTENTIONALITY of cognitive states, including belief, to the intentionality of information, to the modality inherent in the dependency relations constituting information. But if information had no causal or explanatory clout, what, then, was the purpose or point of intentionality? How could beliefs and desires be important in the natural scheme of things if what we

believed and desired, the intentional content of these states, was explanatorily irrelevant to everything we do? There is, I know, a small industry dedicated to making FOLK PSYCHOLOGY a convenient myth, but I have always taken such sceptical results, as I have taken scepticism in epistemology, as a *reductio* of the views that lead to it.

Explaining Behavior (1988) was an attempt to deal with this cluster of interlocking problems. Information had to be put to work. If my intuitions were right, the place for it to find useful employment was in learning. And if it did, indeed, do some useful work in learning, perhaps the work it actually did could be described in a way that illuminated the nature of mental content and, thereby, the character of belief and desire, those mental states that figure most prominently in the determination of behaviour. Experience was a tougher nut. That, as we like to say, could wait until later. (Note: Later has now arrived; this is a current research project.)

I found that I could not begin to think in any productive way about these issues without first getting clear, or clearer, about behaviour itself. Behaviour, after all, is what beliefs and desires are supposed to explain. Unless we understand what it is we are asking X to explain, we cannot expect to understand how it is that X explains it. And if we do not understand how beliefs and desires explain, we cannot hope to understand what it is about them, their meaning or content, that gives them their explanatory punch. One could as well try to understand force and mass, the explanatory ideas of Newtonian mechanics, without troubling to understand weight and acceleration.

This investigation took me down unexpected paths. Behaviour, I concluded, could not be identified with bodily movements. Nor could it be identified with any other event, state, or condition in which behaviour typically culminates. Instead, behaviour is a causal process having bodily movement as a part. The difference between a person moving her arm and her arm's movement is that the latter is a part of the former in the same way B is a part of A's causing B. Once this is accepted, the explanation of behaviour takes on a new look. Intentional action is no longer, *à la* Davidson, a bodily movement caused by reasons. It is, rather, the caus*ing* of bodily movements by reasons. This is not, at least not merely, grammatical hair-splitting. It is the metaphysically important difference between a process and its product, between a caused event and the causing of it. Once the product, bodily movement, is distinguished from the process, the behaviour, the moving of your body, reasons explain behaviour, not by causing it, but, rather, by having their content – what one believes and desires – explain the causing.

This fundamental change in the explanatory relation between reasons and behaviour forces a basic revision in one's picture of the role of learning in the explanation of behaviour. Learning of the relevant kind is a process in which the dependencies, the correlations defining information, play the role of what I call structuring causes: they help reconstitute effector circuits and thereby contribute, causally, to any future behaviour that depends on these reconstituted circuits. Information thereby gets a real job to do. Since concepts crystallize out of the learning process (this is where states acquire their information-carrying functions) at the same time as the connections are being created that underlie all future behaviour, later instantiations of these concepts become causally relevant to such behaviour.

I have always liked Ramsey's (1931) image of beliefs as maps by means of which we steer. As I now see it, beliefs become maps, acquire representational powers, in the same process, the learning process, as that in which the information from which they derive their content gets its hand on the steering wheel. I see no other way for content to become explanatorily relevant to what we do. If the content of thought is, as it seems it must be, an extrinsic fact about the brain, if it is a relational affair, then the only way to make content explanatorily relevant to what we do is to make these extrinsic facts, these relationships, active in the process in which is formed the neural

substrate of the behaviour they will eventually explain. This, then, means that the ultimate source of mental content, the sort of content associated with thought, must be learning.

This does, however, leave a question about the role of the senses in this total cognitive enterprise. If it is learning that, by way of concepts, is the source of the representational powers of thought, from whence comes the representational powers of experience? Or should we even think of experience in representational terms? We can have false beliefs, but are there false experiences?

My current research is focused on a representational account of sense experience. If beliefs are maps by means of which we steer – representations that help guide the ship – experience provides the information needed to construct these maps. The senses have the function, the *biological* function, of providing this information, and experience, as the vehicle of this information, thereby constitutes a representation of the objects about which it carries information. Experiences are not false, but they can misrepresent. On this account, then, experience and thought are both representational. The difference resides in the source of their representational powers: learning in the case of thought, evolution in the case of experience. Or so I hope to show.

See also CONTENT; DAVIDSON; DENNETT.

BIBLIOGRAPHY

Dretske, F. 1969. *Seeing and Knowing*. University of Chicago Press.
—— 1971. Conclusive reasons. *Australasian Journal of Philosophy*, 49, 1–22.
—— 1979. Simple seeing. In *Body, Mind and Method: Essays in Honor of Virgil Aldrich*, ed. D. F. Gustafson and B. L. Tapscott. Dordrecht, Holland: D. Reidel.
—— 1980. The intentionality of cognitive states. In *Midwest Studies in Philosophy*, Vol. 5. University of Minnesota Press, pp. 281–94.
—— 1981. *Knowledge and the Flow of Informa-*

tion. Cambridge, MA.: MIT Press/Bradford Books.

—— 1986. Misrepresentation. In *Belief*, ed. R. Bogdan. Oxford University Press.

—— 1988. *Explaining Behavior*. Cambridge, MA.: MIT Press, Bradford Books.

Fodor, J. 1984. Semantics, Wisconsin style. *Synthese*, 59, 231–50.

Ramsey, F.P. 1931. *The Foundations of Mathematics and Other Logical Essays*. London: Routledge & Kegan Paul.

Sober, E. 1985. Panglossian functionalism and the philosophy of mind. *Synthèse*, 64: 2, 165–93.

FRED DRETSKE

dualism The mind–body problem is the question how the mind is attached to the body. The materialist answer is that because the mind is the body, or perhaps, because of dead bodies, the body ticking over in ways yet to be specified in the glorious future of neuropsychology, each person's mind is necessarily embodied. In contrast, the dualist answer, as its name suggests, is that each person's mind is at least not identical with his body, so these are two different things.

Plato and Descartes are probably the two acknowledged philosophical masters who were most explicitly dualists, and Descartes' arguments for dualism remain live issues. One such argument which some detect in his text draws on central features of his system. That system begins with the method of systematic doubt; to begin with, we are to count ourselves as knowing only what we cannot doubt. The argument from dreaming, that all our sense experience could be hallucination because we have been asleep and dreaming all our lives, and the evil demon argument, that (in contemporary terms) a mad scientist could have extracted our brains at birth and wired them up to computers programmed to simulate in us the hallucinatory sense experience we have had, show that our beliefs in the existence of matter can be doubted. So we are not to begin with to count ourselves as knowing that there is matter. Since, in particular, our bodies

would be material, our bodies are at least initially dubious. But a doubt that we doubt is self-refuting, so we may be certain from the start that we are thinking and thus that we exist; this argument is called the *cogito*. So our bodies are at least initially dubious, but our minds are not, and thus by LEIBNIZ'S LAW (things not sharing all their properties are different) our minds are not identical with our bodies.

Whether Descartes intended this argument or not, it is inadequate. In the first place, psychological predicates do not express properties sufficient to establish differences by Leibniz's Law; some masked man could be your father even though you know who your father is but do not know who the masked man is. So, since 'is at least initially dubious' is a psychological predicate, the present argument makes a fallacious use of Leibniz's Law.

The second objection goes to the heart of dualism. Look at your left fist and open your left hand. Your left hand is still there but your left fist no longer is. So your left hand and your left fist exist at different times, and thus, by Leibniz's Law, are different things. Yet surely a hand–fist dualism would be preposterous, perhaps because your left fist being your left hand clenched, the fist could not exist without the hand. What the mind–body dualist like Descartes means is stronger than mere difference. He wants to say that his mind is no less basic a thing than his body (or, in the older terms of art, that his mind is no less a substance than his body). He means that his mind does not depend for its existence on his body. This notion of dependence is modal. That is, the dualist means that he (his mind, the person or self he is) *could* exist even if his body did not. For short, dualism is a claim to possibility, the claim that you could be disembodied. So taken, dualism yields difference but, as the hand–fist example shows, requires more. Since the argument from dreaming and the *cogito* would at most establish mere difference, it is too weak for dualism. But note that since dualism asserts only the possibility of disembodiment, Descartes need not claim that there actually are

265

any disembodied people about; he need not enlist in the lunatic fringe. Similarly, mares do not depend in any relevant way on stallions for their existence, since there could be mares (for a while) after stallions had been killed off. This independence holds despite the fact that mares are sired by stallions, so the sort of independence of mind from body that dualism requires is compatible with causal commerce between the minds and bodies there actually are.

But granted that dualism is a claim to possibility, how might such a claim be established? It seems plausible that mere (non-actual) possibilities neither act on, nor are acted on by actualities, so if knowledge is to be understood naturally in terms of interaction between knower and known, then perhaps there is no knowledge of objective possibility (that is, possibility whose existence and nature is independent of knowledge of it). In that case, the mind–body problem might be ineluctably moot, not because it misconceives mind or body, but simply because it is modal. Such a conclusion seems so extreme, or even extraneous to the problem, as to be a conclusion of, at best, later resort. If we do allow modal epistemology a run for its money, then we might do well to start from the natural history of modal belief. It seems likely that anyone willing to take modality seriously will grant that there could have been one more pigeon than there actually is. What so eases this conviction seems to be the ease with which we imagine an extra pigeon flapping about. With an eye to this example, we might then follow Hume in saying '. . . nothing we imagine is absolutely impossible', or that what you can imagine is possible.

If possibility is to remain objective, then Hume's principle should be taken not metaphysically but epistemologically. That is, it is not that possibilities are, for example, the images we form when we visualize. The idea is rather that imagination is to knowledge of (mere) possibility as perception is to knowledge of actuality. An empiricist can accept that perception is basic to knowledge of actuality without accepting Berkeley's

subjective idealist doctrine that to be is to be perceived; and Hume's principle can be taken as a way empiricism might try to accommodate knowledge of possibility without going idealist. (But doing so makes the problem of naturalizing knowledge of possibility more acute.) Note the analogy claims only that imagination is sufficient for knowledge of possibility, not that it is necessary. For some of the arcana of, say, contemporary physics may be too arcane to have been seen or even imagined, and yet for all that may be actual and so possible.

Many contemporary analytical philosophers deny Hume's principle, perhaps because of some of the possibilities to which it would commit them. But a principled objection to Hume's principle, a serious counterexample, should be a sentence to be substituted for 'p' such that one can imagine that p (and tell less-imaginative folk a story that enables them to imagine that p) plus a good argument that it is impossible that p. No such counterexamples have been forthcoming, which is evidence for Hume's principle. Not that such a counterexample would require for its second component an epistemology for possibility alternative to Hume's. It is that those who object to his principle refuse to provide, bluster about meaning or logic notwithstanding.

Much more could be said here, but our space is limited, so how could one get from Hume's principle to dualism. The major premise, Hume's principle, says that what you can imagine is possible. The conclusion, dualism, says that you could be disembodied. So the obvious minor premise in an argument for dualism says that you can imagine being disembodied. This argument is preferable to the one from dreaming and the *cogito* because it is valid and it is for the required conclusion.

To show how to imagine being disembodied, begin by dividing mental functions into three sorts: input, inside and output. Input from the world includes the five senses: sight, hearing, taste, touch and smell (*see* PERCEPTIONS). Output to the world includes ACTION, like moving oneself about the world. Inside the mind lies the rest of the mind, like THOUGHT and EMOTION. Neither input nor output are essential to the mind; disembodiment could blind and paralyse. But the interest of dualism is proportional to the extent of the mind that could be disembodied, so since input and output can be preserved, they should. (On the other hand, Descartes, who was after the essence of mind, may have shrunk it to its inside, thus exposing himself to charges of, say, intellectualism.)

Starting then with sight, can one imagine seeing while disembodied? Suppose that, still embodied, you awaken one morning but, before raising your eyelids, you stumble over to your mirror. Then, facing your mirror, you raise your eyelids, and see in the mirror that your eye sockets are empty; you can imagine how your face would look in the mirror if you had no eyes. Interested, you probe the sockets with a finger; you can imagine how it would look in the mirror and feel to probe the empty socket and channel where your optic nerve used to be. Even more curious, you take your surgical saw and cut off the top of your skull. In the mirror you see that your brain pan is empty; you can imagine how your empty brain pan would look in the mirror and feel. You've now imagined seeing without the two body-parts, eyes and a brain, most people think crucial to seeing. You don't need your legs to see, so imagine them away, and similarly for your arms, trunk and the rest of your head. Now of course what you see in the mirror is no longer your face, for that is gone; what you see now is the wall behind you opposite the mirror.

Have we really imagined seeing without a body? (Imagination is no more incorrigible than sight.) This is partly a matter of what sight is (and part of the interest of arguing for the minor premise is the light it casts on our faculties). Sight requires visual experience, and we have imagined having visual experience while disembodied. But visual experience is common to sight, visualizing and dreaming, and thus does not suffice for sight. At this point the tradition adds veridicality. Veridicality is to experience as truth

is to thought; a thought is true when the world is as the thinker thinks it to be, and a visual experience is veridical when the world is as it looks to the one with the experience. The tradition distinguishes sight from visualizing and dreaming by veridicality. But veridicality is a bare conjunctive property; all it requires is that it look to one as if *p, and p*. It is easy to add veridicality to our story about visual experience while disembodied.

But Grice showed that veridical visual experience is not sufficient for sight, since the world could be as one visualizes it to be, but only by accident. So, Grice inferred, veridical visual experience is sight only if it is caused by what makes it veridical. (Grice did not think that veridical visual experience caused by what makes it veridical suffices for sight, but that is another story.) So if our disembodied person with veridical visual experience is to see what makes his visual experience veridical, that experience should be caused by what makes it veridical. But how could there be causal commerce between immaterial disembodied people and the physical objects they see?

Here we come up against what has seemed since Descartes the most difficult problem confronting dualism, the interaction problem, the problem of how, if immaterial mind is as different from material body as Descartes claims, mind and body can interact causally (*see* REASONS AND CAUSES). (It is plain that they do so interact, since a kick in the shins, which is physical, hurts, which is mental, and fear, which is mental, makes one's heart beat faster, which is physical.) Not that the interaction problem is as much a problem about the nature of causation as it is a problem about the natures of mind and matter. Hume, for example, explains causation in terms of temporal priority, spatial contiguity and constant conjunction. Contiguity requires location. Suppose we could locate a disembodied person's visual experience. (As a subjective preliminary, note that visual experience is always along lines of sight. In visualizing fantasies, these subjective lines of sight need not coincide with real lines in space, but when visual experience is veridical, they will, and the point, or small region of their convergence is a subjectively described preliminary place where the disembodied person's visual experience lies.) The crux of causation for Hume is constant conjunction, by which he intended bare conjunction: this and then that. But bare constant conjunction between physical and mental (or vice versa) event types is no more problematic than such conjunction between physical and physical event types. Here judgment seems called for: either Hume is right about causation and there is no interaction problem, or else there is an interaction problem and we need a better view of causation to make sense of it. The second seems the better option.

Quine argues that causation is the flow of energy. Could any quantity pass between things as different as mind and matter are according to dualism? This formulation seems to do better justice to the interaction problem. But it also suggests a treatment of that problem. Energy (or mass-energy) is conserved, and conservation is a quantitative principle. So we need intrinsically psychological quantities. To cut a long story very short, we can give a general account of quantity (satisfied by temperature, mass, length and so on) that is pretty well satisfied by desire, belief, how much it looks to one as if such and such, and other psychological phenomena. Once we have such psychological quantities, we may imagine that as light from objects seen reaches the region of convergence along the disembodied person's lines of sight, it passes straight through but loses some electromagnetic energy and, at a fixed rate of conversion, that person acquires or is sustained in visual experience of those objects seen. Here is a way to imagine that the disembodied person's veridical visual experience be caused by that in virtue of which it is veridical, and thus far, that he sees. So we have solved the interaction problem. To be sure, we have not imagined exactly *how* light energy con-

verts into the psychic energy implicit in visual experience. But then neither do physicists tell us how mass turns into energy when an atom bomb goes off, and if their lacuna does not embarrass them, neither need ours embarrass us. (Now we can better locate visual experience where the conversion from electromagnetic energy to psychic energy occurs.)

A good deal more could, and should, be said, especially about action, but our space is limited, and it is already clear that our version of dualism differs from that of Descartes. His interaction problem was about how an embodied person's mind is, for example, acted on by objects he sees. It is difficult to take Descartes seriously about the pineal gland. For that would at best tell us only where interaction occurs, not what it is like. More deeply, Descartes takes extension to be the essence of matter. Under extension, Descartes seems to put all geometrical properties including location. So to keep mind immaterial, he must deny it location; his view of the mind is not so much other-wordly as a-wordly. We post-Newtonians accept geometrical objects in regions of space innocent of matter, so for us location does not require physicality, and thus disembodied minds can be somewhere in space without being thereby embodied. Note too that when disembodied people see on our model, light loses energy where their visual experience occurs, and if this loss were large enough, we could see where a disembodied person is. From one angle, it might look like a dimming where a part of the disembodied person is. So disembodied people could look like the hazy holograms in the haunted house at Disneyland. In other words, when we think and imagine disembodiment through, we rediscover the possibility of the folklore of ghosts. Therefore, scientistic propaganda from materialists notwithstanding, dualism is the commonsense solution to the mind–body problem.

See also An Essay on Mind section 3.5; HISTORY; IDENTITY THEORY; INTROSPECTION; PHYSICALISM; SUBJECTIVITY.

BIBLIOGRAPHY

Descartes, *Meditations*. In *Philosophical Works of Descartes*, trans. S. Haldene and G. R. T. Ross, 2 vols. New York: Dover, 1955.

Hart, W.D. 1988. *The Engines of the Soul.* Cambridge University Press.

Kripke, S. 1971. Identity and necessity. In *Identity and Individuation*, ed. M. K. Munitz. New York University Press.

Penelhum, T. 1970. *Survival and Disembodied Existence.* Atlantic Highlands, N.J: Humanities Press.

Williams, B. 1978. *Descartes: The Project of Pure Enquiry.* Penguin.

WILLIAM D. HART

E

eliminativism Eliminativists believe there to be something fundamentally mistaken about the common-sense (sometimes called 'folk psychological') conception of the mind, and they suggest that the way forward is to drop part or all of this conception in favour of one which does not use notions such as belief, experience, sensation and the like. The rationale for this suggestion is, in the main, because these notions are fraught with conceptual difficulties as well as being recalcitrant to any REDUCTION to natural science. Since the conception with which they propose to replace the common-sense conception is invariably physicalist or materialist, one finds eliminativism also called 'eliminative materialism'. (See CONNECTION-ISM; DENNETT; *An Essay on Mind* section 3.7; FOLK PSYCHOLOGY; LEWIS; SUPERVENIENCE.)

SAMUEL GUTTENPLAN

emotion In recent philosophy of mind, emotion has been treated as a poor relation. One reason for this is that emotions seem to overstep a threshold of messiness beyond which even the most masochistic of theoreticians tend to lose heart. The sheer variety of phenomena covered by the word 'emotion' and its close neighbours seems to discourage theory. Confusion about the nature of emotions is reflected in the historical vicissitudes of the words used to speak of it. Baier (1990) has noted, for example, that while 'emotion' used to mean 'violent passion', we now seem to use 'passion' to mean 'violent emotion'. Much of these shifts in emphasis through time are no doubt merely the outcome of random linguistic drift. We should expect that some of them, however, reflect real differences between different implicit background models of the architecture of the mind.

Such models differ in two different ways. One concerns the place of emotion within the general economy of mind. For Plato in the *Republic*, there seemed to have been three basic components of the human mind: the reasoning, the desiring, and the emotive parts. In subsequent theories, however, emotions as a category are apt be sucked into either of two other areas, of which emotions are then treated as a mere satrapy: a peculiar kind of BELIEF, or a vague kind of DESIRE or WILL, or even mere apprehension of bodily condition (James, 1884). For reasons that will be sketched below, Plato's side of this debate now seems the stronger.

A second set of alternative models relate to the taxonomy of emotions themselves. One model, advocated by Descartes as well as by many contemporary psychologists, posits a few basic emotions out of which all others are compounded. An alternative model views every emotion as consisting in, or at least including, some irreducibly specific component not compounded of anything simpler. Again, emotions might form, like colour, an indefinitely broad continuum comprising a small number of finite dimensions, like the sensitivity ranges of retinal cones corresponding roughly to primary hues. We might then hope for relatively simple biological explanations for the rich variety of emotions, though rigid boundaries between them would be logically arbitrary.

To date cognitive science does not seem to have provided any crucial tests to decide the second sort of question. Cross-cultural research strongly suggests that a number of emotions have intertranslatable names and

270

universally recognizable expressions. According to Paul Ekman (1989) these are happiness, sadness, fear, anger, surprise, and disgust (which some researchers, however, account too simple to be called an emotion (Panksepp, 1982)). Other emotions are not so easily recognizable cross-culturally, and some expressions are almost as local as dialects. But then this is an issue on which cognitive science alone should not, perhaps, be accorded the last word: what to a neurologist might be classed as two tokens of the same emotion type might seem to have little in common under the magnifying lens of a Proust. (*See* COGNITIVE PSYCHOLOGY; PSYCHOLOGY AND PHILOSOPHY.)

These complications do not suffice to explain philosophy's neglect of the emotions. (Philosophers, after all, tend rather to be fond of complications.) Indeed, this neglect is both relatively recent and already out of fashion. Most of the great classical philosophers – Plato, Aristotle, Spinoza, Descartes, Hobbes, Hume – have had recognizable theories of emotion. Yet in twentieth-century Anglo-American philosophy and psychology, the increasing attention recently devoted to emotion has had an air of innovation. Under the influence of a 'tough-minded' ideology committed to BEHAVIOURISM, theories of ACTION or THE WILL, and theories belief or knowledge, had seemed more readily achievable than theories of emotion. The recently dominant Bayesian-derived economic models of rational decision and agency are essentially assimilative models – two-factor theories, which view emotion either as a species of belief, or as species of desire.

That enviably resilient Bayesian model has been cracked, in the eyes of many philosophers, by such refractory phenomena as *akrasia* or 'WEAKNESS OF WILL'. In cases of akrasia, traditional descriptive rationality seems to be violated, insofar as the 'strongest' desire does not win, even when paired with the appropriate belief (DAVIDSON, 1980). Emotion is ready to pick up the slack – if only we had a theory of that.

It is one thing, however, to recognize the need for a theory of mind that finds a place for the unique role of emotions, and quite another to construct one. Emotions vary so much in various dimensions – transparency, intensity, object-directedness, or susceptibility to rational assessment – as to cast doubt on the assumption that they have anything in common.

What is distinctive about emotions is perhaps precisely what made them a theoretical embarrassment: that they have a number of apparently contradictory properties. In what follows, we shall sketch five areas in which emotions pose specific philosophical puzzles: emotion's relation to cognition; emotions and self-knowledge; the relation of emotions to their objects; the nature of emotional intensity; and the relation of emotions to rationality.

EMOTION AND COGNITION

It is a commonplace (whether true or false) that emotions are in some sense 'subjective'. Some have taken this to mean that they reflect nothing but the peculiar consciousness of the subject. But that conclusion follows only if one adopts a fallacious equation of point of view and SUBJECTIVITY. The existence of perspective does not invalidate cognition: that emotional states are perspectival, therefore, need not bar them from being cognitive or playing a role in cognition.

There are at least three ways in which emotions have been thought to relate to cognition.

(1) As stimulants of cognition: philosophers have been interested in learning from psycho-physiologists that you won't learn anything unless the limbic system – the part of the brain most actively implicated in emotional states – is stimulated at the time of learning (Scheffler, 1991).

(2) Many emotions are specified in terms of propositions: one can't be angry with someone unless one believes that person guilty of some offence; one can't be jealous unless one believes that one's

emotional property is being poached on by another. From this, it has been inferred that emotions are (always? sometimes?) cognitive in the sense that they involve PROPOSITIONAL ATTITUDES. This claim is relatively weak, however, since the existence of a propositional attitude is at best a necessary, but not a sufficient condition of the existence of an emotion.

(3) The most literal interpretation of cognitivism about emotions would be committed to ascribing to emotions a 'mind-to-world direction of fit'. The expression 'direction of fit', which is due to SEARLE (1983), distinguishes between an essentially cognitive orientation of the mind, in which success is defined in terms of whether the mind fits the world (a mind-to-world direction of fit) and an essentially conative orientation, in which success is defined in terms of the opposite, world-to-mind, direction of fit. We will what does not yet exist, and deem ourselves successful if the world is brought into line with the mind's plan.

A view ascribing to emotions a true mind-to-world direction of fit would involve a criterion of success that depended on correctness with respect to some objective property. Such a view was first defended by Scheler (1954), and has in general had more currency as a variant of an objectivist theory of aesthetics than as a theory of emotions as a whole.

To take seriously cognitivism in this sense, is to give a particular answer to the question posed long ago in Plato's *Euthyphro*: *Do we love X – mutatis mutandis* for the other emotions – *because X is lovable, or do we declare X to be lovable merely because we love it?* One way to defend a modest objectivism, in the sense of the first alternative, is to explore certain analogies between emotion and PERCEPTION. It requires first that we define clearly what is to count as 'objectivity' in the relevant sense. Second, it requires that we show that there is a valid analogy between some of the ways in which we can speak of perception as aspiring to objectivity and ways in which we can say the same of emotion.

Emotions are sometimes said to be subjective in this sense: that they merely reflect something that belongs exclusively and contingently to the mind of the subject of experience, and therefore do not covary with any property that could be independently identified. This charge presupposes a sense of 'objective' that contrasts with 'projective', in something like the psychoanalytic sense (*see* PSYCHOANALYTIC EXPLANATION). In terms of the analogy of perception, to say that emotions are universally subjective in this sense would be to claim that they resemble hallucinations more than veridical perceptions. The perceptual system is capable of the sort of vacuous functioning that leads to perceptual mistakes. Similarly, emotions may mislead us into 'hasty' or 'emotional' judgments (Solomon, 1984). On the other hand, the lack of perceptual capacities can be a crippling handicap in one's attempt to negotiate the world: similarly a lack of adequate emotional responses can hinder our attempts to view the world correctly and act correctly in it (Nussbaum, 1990; Thomas, 1989). This explains why we are so often tempted to take seriously ascription of reasonableness or unreasonableness, fittingness or inappropriateness, for common emotions. The big drawback of this view is that it is quite unclear how independently to identify the alleged objective property.

Closely related to the question of the cognitive aspect of emotion is the question of its passivity. Passivity has an ambiguous relation to subjectivity. In one vein, impressed by the bad reputation of the 'passions' as taking over our consciousness against our will, philosophers have been tempted to take the passivity of emotions as evidence of their subjectivity. In another vein, however, represented especially in the last few years by Robert Gordon (1987), philosophers have noted that the passivity of emotions is sometimes precisely analogous to the passivity of perception. How the world is, is not in our power. So it is only to be expected that our emotions, if they actually represent something genuinely and objectively in the world, should not be in our power either. To this extent, the cognitive model holds out rather well, while at the same time suggesting that our common notion of what cognition amounts to may be excessively narrow.

One more angle needs to be canvassed on the cognitive role of the emotions. This is their role not as specific cognitions, but as providing the framework for cognition. This we shall consider in the final section, about the rationality of emotion. First, however, let us look at a very specific sort of knowledge which emotions can either enhance or distort.

EMOTIONS AND SELF-KNOWLEDGE

We often make the 'Cartesian' assumption that if anyone can know our emotions it is ourselves. Descartes said it thus: 'it is impossible for the soul to feel a passion without that passion being truly as one feels it'. (*See* FIRST-PERSON AUTHORITY; INTROSPECTION; THE SELF.) Barely a page later, however, he noted that 'those that are most agitated by their passions are not those who know them best' (Descartes, 1984, §§26, 28). In fact, emotions are one of our avenues to self-knowledge, since few kinds of self-knowledge could matter more than knowing one's own repertoire of emotional responses. At the same time, emotions are both the cause and the subject of many failures of self-knowledge. Their complexity entails several sources for their potential to mislead or be misled. Insofar as most emotions involve belief, they inherit the susceptibility of the latter to SELF-DECEPTION. Recent literature on self-deception has dissolved the air of paradox to which this once gave rise (Fingarette, 1969). But there are also three distinct problems that are specific to emotions.

The first arises from the connection of emotion with bodily changes. There is something right in William James's notorious claim that the emotion follows on, rather than causing the voluntary and involuntary bodily changes which express it (James, 1884). Because some of these

changes are either directly or indirectly subject to our choices, we are able to pretend or dissimulate emotion. That implies that we can sometimes be caught in our own pretence. Sometimes we identify our emotions *by* what we feel: and if what we feel has been distorted by a project of deception, then we will misidentify our own emotions.

A second source of self-deception arises from the role of emotions in determining *salience* among potential objects of attention or concern. Poets have always known that the main effect of love is to redirect attention: when I love, I notice nothing but my beloved, and nothing of his faults. When my love turns to anger I still focus on him, but now attend to a very different set of properties. This suggests one way of controlling or dominating my emotion: *think about something else*, or think differently about this object. But this carries a risk. It is easier to think of something than to avoid thinking about it; and to many cases of emotional distress only the latter could bring adequate relief. Besides, one is not always able to predict, and therefore to control, the effect that redirected attention might produce. The best explanation for this familiar observation requires us to take seriously the hypothesis of the UNCONSCIOUS: if among the associations that are evoked by a given scene are some that I can react to without being aware of what they are, then I will not always be able to predict my own reactions, even if I have mastered the not altogether trivial task of attending to whatever I choose. Where the unconscious is, self-deception necessarily threatens. (*See* PSYCHOANALYTIC EXPLANATION.)

This brings us to the third source of emotional self-deception: the involvement of social norms in the determination of our emotions. This possibility arises in two stages from the admission that there are unconscious motivations for emotions. First, if I am experiencing an emotion that seems altogether inappropriate to its occasion, I will naturally confabulate an explanation for it. A neurotic who is unreasonably angry with his wife because he unconsciously identifies her with his mother will not rest content with having no reason for his anger. Instead, he will make one up. Moreover, the reason he makes up will typically be one that is *socially approved* (Averill, 1982).

When we are self-deceived in our emotional response, or when some emotional state induces self-deception, there are various aspects of the situation about which self-deception can take place. These relate to the different kinds of *intentional objects* of emotions.

INTENTIONAL OBJECTS

What does a mood, such as free-floating depression or euphoria, have in common with a precisely articulable indignation? The first seems to have as its object nothing and everything, and often admits of no particular justification; the second has a long story to tell typically involving other people and what they have done or said. Not only those people, but the relevant facts about the situations involved, as well as some of the special facts about those situations, aspects of those facts, the causal role played by these aspects, and even the typical aims of the actions motivated by the emotions, can all in some context or other be labelled *objects* of emotion. Objects are what we emote at, with, to, because of, in virtue of, or that (*see* INTENTIONALITY). This variety has led to a great deal of confusion and debate. A big question, for example, has been the extent to which the objects of emotions are to be identified with their causes. This identification seems plausible; yet it is easy to construct examples in which being the cause of an emotion is intuitively neither a necessary nor a sufficient condition for being its object: if A gets annoyed at B for some entirely trivial matter, drunkenness may have caused A's annoyance, yet it is in no sense its object. Its object may be some innocent remark of B's, which while it occasioned the annoyance cannot rightly be said to be its cause. More precisely, it may be a certain insulting quality in B's remark which is, as a matter of fact, entirely imaginary and therefore could not possibly be its true cause.

The right way to deal with these complexities is to embrace them. We need a taxonomy of the different sorts of possible emotional objects. One might then distinguish different types of emotions according to the different complex structures of their object relations. Many emotions, such as love, necessarily involve a *target*, or actual particular at which they are directed. Others, such as sadness, do not. On the other hand, although there may be a number of *motivating aspects* of the loved one on which our love is focused, love lacks a *propositional* object. Sadness, on the contrary, cannot be fully described without specifying such a propositional object. Depression or elation can lack all three kinds of object. And so on.

Special puzzles arise for those emotions that take propositional objects, such as being sad that *p*, pleased that *p*, or embarrassed that *p*. Does *p* actually have to be true for the emotion to be correctly attributed? It seems in general that they need not, since a mistake about the relevant facts seems to be one of the ways in which one can be mistaken while experiencing an emotion. Robert Gordon (1987), however, has defended the interesting thesis that all emotions taking propositional objects are either 'factive', or 'epistemic'. Factive emotions require for their correct ascription not only that the proposition in question be believed or thought probable, but that it actually be true. Epistemic emotions, on the other hand, require that the propositional object be neither definitely believed nor definitely disbelieved. Thus one cannot be sad that *p* unless it is true that *p* (although if it is false one can be sad *because* one mistakenly believe that *p*); and one can fear that *p* only if one is unsure whether *p*. Whatever its merits, this controversial thesis has an illuminating corollary: namely that in most attributions of emotion, speaker, hearer and subject share a common world. Unless the uncertainty of the situation is specifically in question, as in the epistemic emotions, or unless the assumption is explicitly defeated by the rider that the subject doesn't quite live in our shared world, we assume that we can all take the same facts for granted. This would give the emotions a kind of intrinsically realist bias, and would help to explain why arguments about emotions so often break down. They break down because each participant assumes a shared world which, in fact, consists only of the set of scenarios that define his or her own private emotional idiolect, or repertoire of intelligible emotions.

INTENSITY

It seems to be an irreducible differentia of emotions that they can be measured along a dimension of intensity. This corresponds neither to the strength of desire nor to a belief's degree of confidence. What does mild distaste have in common with the most murderous rage? Is it *just* a matter of degree? Or does intensity necessarily bring with it differences in kind? Two different sorts of considerations favour endorsing the latter view. The difference between them illustrates a characteristic methodological dilemma faced by emotions research. The first approaches taxonomy through social significance: mild distaste is one thing, rage quite another, in the sense that the circumstances in which the first or the second is generally appropriate and acceptable are radically disjoint. From this point of view, then, they must obviously be classed as entirely different phenomena. But a similar response might be derived from an entirely different approach: one might look at the brain's involvement in the two cases and find (perhaps) the first to be an essentially cortical response, while the second involves activity of the limbic system or even the brain stem – what Paul Maclean (1975) has dubbed the 'mammalian' or the 'crocodile' brain. In this case the classification of the two as entirely separate phenomena might have a strictly physiological basis. How are the two related?

The very notion of intensity is problematic exactly to the extent that the emotions call for disparate principles of explanation. Might a physiological criterion settle the question? One could stipulate that the most intense emotion is the one that involves the greatest quantity of physiological 'disturbance' (Lyons, 1980). But this approach must implicitly posit a state of 'normal' quietude hard to pin down among the myriad different measures of physiological activity one might devise. To select a measure that will count as relevant, one will inevitably have to resort to another level of more functional criteria: what are the types and levels of physiological activity that are relevant to the social functions subserved by those emotions? And what are the mental functions that should be deemed most important in the context of the relevant demands of social life? At that point, while physiological *explanations* may be of great interest, there is no hope from their quarter of any interesting *criteria* for emotional intensity.

RATIONALITY

There is a common prejudice that 'feelings', a word now sometimes vulgarly used interchangeably with 'emotions', neither owe nor can give any rational account of themselves. Yet we equally commonly blame others or ourselves for feeling 'not wisely, but too well', or for targeting inappropriate objects. As we have seen, the norms appropriate to both these types of judgment are inseparable from social norms, whether or not these are endorsed. Ultimately they are inseparable from conceptions of normality and human nature. Judgments of reasonableness therefore tend to be endorsed or rejected in accordance with one's ideological commitments to this or that conception of human nature. It follows that whether these judgments can be viewed as objective or not will depend on whether there are objective facts to be sought about human nature. On this question we fortunately do not need to pronounce. It is enough to note that there is no logical reason why judgments of reasonableness or irrationality in relation to emotions need be regarded as any more subjective than any other judgments of RATIONALITY in human affairs.

275

There is a further contribution that the study of emotions can make to our understanding of rationality. The clearest notions associated with rationality are coherence and consistency in the sphere of belief, and maximizing expected utility in the sphere of action. But these notions are purely critical ones. By themselves, they would be quite incapable of guiding an organism towards any particular course of action. For the number of goals that it is logically possible to posit at any particular time is virtually infinite, and the number of possible strategies that might be employed in pursuit of them is orders of magnitude larger. Moreover, in considering possible strategies, the number of consequences of any one strategy is again infinite, so that unless some drastic preselection can be effected among the alternatives their evaluation could never be completed. This gives rise to what is known among cognitive scientists as the 'Frame Problem': in deciding among any range of possible actions, most of the consequences of each must be eliminated from consideration a priori, i.e. *without any time being wasted on their consideration*. That this is not as much of a problem for people as it is for machines may well be due to our capacity for emotions. Emotions frame our decisions in two important ways. First, they define the parameters taken into account in any particular deliberation. Second, in the process of rational deliberation itself, they render salient only a tiny proportion of the available alternatives and of the conceivably relevant facts. In these ways, then, emotions would be all-important to rationality even if they could not themselves be deemed rational or irrational. For they winnow down to manageable size the number of considerations relevant to rational deliberation, and provide the indispensable framework without which the question of rationality could not even be raised.

BIBLIOGRAPHY

Averill, J. 1982. *Anger and Aggression: An Essay on Emotion*. New York: Springer-Verlag.

Baier, A. 1990. What emotions are about. *Philosophical Perspectives*, 4, 1–29.

Davidson, D. 1980. How is weakness of the will possible? In *Essays on Actions and Events*. Oxford University Press.

Descartes, R. 1984. *The Passions of the Soul*. Vol. 1 of *The Philosophical Writings of Descartes*, Trans. J. Cottingham, R. Stoothoff and D. Murdoch. Cambridge University Press.

de Sousa, R. 1987. *The Rationality of Emotion*. Cambridge, MA. MIT Press.

Ekman, P., and Friesen, W.V. 1989. The argument and evidence about universals in facial expressions of emotion. In *Handbook of Social Psychophysiology*. New York: John Wiley & Sons Ltd.

Fingarette, H. 1969. *Self Deception*. London: Routledge & Kegan Paul.

Gordon, R.M. 1987. *The Structure of Emotions*. Cambridge University Press.

James, W. 1984. What is an emotion? *Mind*, 19, 188–204.

Lyons, W. 1980. *Emotion*. Cambridge University Press.

MacLean, P.D. 1975. Sensory and perceptive factors in emotional functions of the triune brain. In *Emotions: Their Parameters and Measurement*, ed. L. Lev. New York: Raven Press.

Nussbaum, M. 1990. *Love's Knowledge*. Oxford University Press.

Panksepp, J. 1982. Toward a general psychobiological theory of emotions. *Behavioral and Brain Sciences*, 5, 407–76.

Scheffler, I. 1991. *In Praise of the Cognitive Emotions*. London: Routledge & Kegan Paul.

Scheler, M. 1954. *The Nature of Sympathy*. Trans. P. Heath, introduction by W. Stark. Hamden, CT: Archon.

Searle, J.R. 1983. *Intentionality*. Cambridge University Press.

Solomon, R.C. 1984. *The Passions: The Myth and Nature of Human Emotions*. New York: Doubleday.

Thalberg, I. 1977. *Perception, Emotion and Action*. New Haven: Yale University Press.

Thomas, L. 1989. *Living Morally: A Psychology of Moral Character*. Philadelphia: Temple University Press.

RONALD DE SOUSA

emergence   *see* SUPERVENIENCE.

epiphenomenalism   Mental phenomena – bodily sensations, sense experiences, emotions, memories, beliefs, desires, intentions, and the like – seem to have causal effects. For example, the sharp pain in my toe might make me wince. The wall's looking red to me might make me think that it is red. As I gaze over the edge of the cliff, my fear of heights might make my breath quicken and my heart beat faster. Remembering an embarrassing situation might make me blush. My desire to ring the alarm and belief that I can do so by pressing the button might result in my pressing the button. Despite my fatigue, I might keep grading papers, my intention to finish the grading before I go to sleep sustaining my effort. And as I reason through a problem, one thought leads to another. Or so it seems.

However, according to the traditional doctrine of epiphenomenalism, things are not as they seem: in reality, mental phenomena can have no causal effects; they are causally inert, causally impotent. Only physical phenomena are causally efficacious. Mental phenomena are caused by physical phenomena, but they cannot cause anything. In short, mental phenomena are epiphenomena.

The epiphenomenalist claims that mental phenomena seem to be causes only because there are regularities that involve types (or kinds) of mental phenomena, and regularities that involve types of mental and physical phenomena. For example, instances of a certain mental type M (e.g. trying to raise one's arm) might tend to be followed by instances of a physical type P (e.g. one's arm's rising). To infer that instances of M tend to cause instances of P would be, however, to commit the fallacy of *post hoc, ergo propter hoc*. Instances of M cannot cause instances of P; such causal transactions are *causally* impossible. P-type events tend to be followed by M-type events because instances of such events are dual-effects of common physical causes, not because such instances causally interact.

Mental events and states can figure in the web of causal relations only as effects, never as causes.

SOME APPARENT CONSEQUENCES OF THE DOCTRINE

Epiphenomenalism is a truly stunning doctrine. If it is true, then no pain could ever be a cause of our wincing, nor could something's looking red to us ever be a cause of our thinking that it is red. A nagging headache could never be a cause of a bad mood. Moreover, *if* the causal theory of memory is correct, then, given epiphenomenalism, we could never remember our prior thoughts, or an emotion we once felt, or a toothache we once had, or having heard someone say something, or having seen something; for such mental states and events could not be causes of memories. Furthermore, epiphenomenalism is arguably incompatible with the possibility of intentional action. For if, as the causal theory of action implies, intentional action requires that a desire for something and a belief about how to obtain what one desires play a causal role in producing behaviour, then, if epiphenomenalism is true, we cannot perform intentional actions. (*See* ACTION; INTENTION; REASONS AND CAUSES.) Notice that we cannot, then, *assert* that epiphenomenalism is true, if it is, since an assertion is an intentional speech act (cf. Malcolm, 1968). Still further, if epiphenomenalism is true, then our sense that we are agents who can act on our intentions and carry out our purposes is illusory. We are actually passive bystanders, never agents; in no relevant sense is what happens up to us. Our sense of partial causal control over our limb movements is illusory. Indeed, we exert no causal control over even the direction of our attention! Finally, suppose that reasoning is a causal process. Then, if epiphenomenalism is true, we never reason; for there are no mental causal processes. While one thought may follow another, one thought never *leads to* another. Indeed, while thoughts may occur, we do not engage in the *activity* of thinking. How, then, could we make inferences that commit the fallacy of *post hoc, ergo propter hoc*, or make any inferences at all for that matter?

One might try to dispute whether epiphenomenalism has some of these consequences by disputing, for example, the causal theory of memory, or the causal theory of action, or the claim that reasoning is a causal process. But rather than pursuing such issues, let us instead ask what considerations led to the doctrine of epiphenomenalism.

THE NEUROPHYSIOLOGICAL NO-GAP ARGUMENT

As neurophysiological research began to develop in earnest during the latter half of the nineteenth century, it seemed to find no mental influence on what happens in the brain. While it was recognized that neurophysiological events do not by themselves causally determine other neurophysiological events, there seemed to be no 'gaps' in neurophysiological causal mechanisms that could be filled by mental occurrences. Neurophysiology appeared to have no need of the hypothesis that there are mental events. (Here and hereafter, unless indicated otherwise, I follow the common philosophical practice of using 'events' in a broad sense to include states as well as changes.) This 'no gap' line of argument led some theorists to deny that mental events have any causal effects (Huxley, 1874). They reasoned as follows: if mental events have any effects, among their effects would be neurophysiological ones; mental events have no neurophysiological effects; thus, mental events have no effects at all. The relationship between mental phenomena and neurophysiological mechanisms was likened to that between the steam-whistle which accompanies the working of a locomotive engine and the mechanisms of the engine: just as the steam-whistle is an effect of the operations of the mechanisms but has no causal influence on those operations, so too mental phenomena are effects of the workings of neurophysiological mechanisms, but have no causal influence on their operations. (The analogy quickly breaks down, of course: steam-whistles have causal effects, but the epiphenomenalist alleges that mental phenomena have no causal effects at all.)

An early response to this 'no gap' line of argument was that mental events (and states) are not changes in (and states of) an immaterial Cartesian substance (*see* DUALISM), they are, rather, changes in (and states of) the brain. While mental properties or kinds are not neurophysiological properties or kinds, nevertheless, particular mental events are neurophysiological events (see Lewes, 1875; Alexander, 1920). According to the view in question, a given event can be an instance of both a neurophysiological type and a mental type, and thus be both a mental event and a neurophysiological event. (Compare the fact that an object might be an instance of more than one kind of object; for example, an object might be both a stone and a paper-weight.) It was held, moreover, that mental events have causal effects because they *are* neurophysiological events with causal effects. This response presupposes that causation is an *extensional* relation between particular events, that if two events are causally related, they are so related however they are typed (or described) (*see* ANOMALOUS MONISM; DAVIDSON). But that assumption is today widely held. We will accept it throughout this essay. Given that the causal relation is extensional, if particular mental events are indeed neurophysiological events with causal effects, then mental events are causes, and epiphenomenalism is thus false.

TYPE (PROPERTY) EPIPHENOMENALISM

This response to the 'no gap' argument, however, prompts a concern about the relevance of mental properties or kinds to causal relations. And in 1925, C. D. Broad tells us that the view that mental events are epiphenomena is the view 'that mental events either (a) do not function at all as causal-factors; or that (b) if they do, they do so in virtue of their physiological characteristics and not in virtue of their mental characteristics' (1925, p. 473). If particular mental events are physiological events with causal effects, then mental events function as cause-factors: they are causes. However, the question still remains whether mental events are causes *in virtue of* their mental characteristics. As we noted, neurophysiology appears to be able to explain neurophysiological occurrences without postulating mental characteristics. This prompts the concern that even if mental events are causes, they may be causes in virtue of their physiological characteristics, but not in virtue of their mental characteristics.

This concern presupposes, of course, that events are causes in virtue of certain of their characteristics or PROPERTIES. But it is today fairly widely held that when two events are causally related, they are so related in virtue of something about each. Indeed, theories of causation assume that if two events x and y are causally related, and two other events a and b are not, then there must be some difference between x and y and a and b in virtue of which x and y are, but a and b are not, causally related. And they attempt to say what that difference is; that is, they attempt to say what it is about causally related events in virtue of which they are so related. For example, according to so-called nomic subsumption views of causation, causally related events will be so related in virtue of falling under types (or in virtue of having properties) that figure in a 'causal law'. It should be noted that the assumption that causally related events are so related in virtue of something about each is compatible with the assumption that the causal relation is an *extensional* relationship between particular events (cf. McLaughlin, 1993). The weighs-less-than relation is an extensional relation between particular objects: if O weighs less than O*, then O and O* are so related however they are typed (or characterized, or described). Nevertheless, if O weighs less than O*, then that is so in virtue of something about each, namely their weights and the fact that the weight of one is less than the weight of the other. Examples are readily multiplied. Extensional relations between particulars typically hold

in virtue of something about the particulars. In what follows, we will remain neutral concerning the competing theories of causation. But we will grant that when two events are causally related, they are so related in virtue of something about each.

Invoking the distinction between event types and event tokens, and using the term 'physical', rather than the more specific term 'physiological', we can, following Broad, distinguish two kinds of epiphenomenalism (cf. McLaughlin, 1989):

TOKEN EPIPHENOMENALISM Mental events cannot cause anything.

TYPE EPIPHENOMENALISM No event can cause anything in virtue of falling under a mental type.

(*Property epiphenomenalism* is the thesis that no event can cause anything in virtue of having a mental property.) The conjunction of token epiphenomenalism and the claim that physical events cause mental events is, of course, the traditional doctrine of epiphenomenalism, as characterized earlier. Token epiphenomenalism implies type epiphenomenalism: for if an event could cause something in virtue of falling under a mental type, then an event could be both a mental event and a cause, and so token epiphenomenalism would be false. Thus if mental events cannot be causes, then events cannot be causes in virtue of falling under mental types. The denial of token epiphenomenalism does not, however, imply the denial of type epiphenomenalism, *if* a mental event can be a physical event that has causal effects. For, if so, then token epiphenomenalism is false. But type epiphenomenalism may still be true. For it may be that events cannot be causes in virtue of falling under mental types. Mental events may be causes in virtue of falling under physical types, but not in virtue of falling under mental types. Thus, even if token epiphenomenalism is false, the question remains whether type epiphenomenalism is.

(It should be noted, parenthetically, that much of the current literature on epiphenomenalism focuses on type (or property) epiphenomenalism, rather than on token epiphenomenalism. Keith Cambell's 'new' epiphenomenalism (1970, ch. 6) is a version of type (property) epiphenomenalism for 'phenomenal' mental types (properties). Moreover, many of the discussions of type epiphenomenalism in the current literature have focused on views espoused by Donald Davidson. Davidson (1970) holds that (i) causally related events must fall under a strict law, that (ii) all strict laws are physical laws, and that (iii) no mental type (or property) either is or 'reduces to' a physical type (or property). Commitment to (i)–(iii), it has been claimed, commits him as well to type (property) epiphenomenalism. (The literature is vast, but see, especially, Honderich (1982), Kim (1984), Sosa (1984), LePore and Loewer (1987), and Antony (1989).) Davidson (1993), however, denies that he is so committed; and McLaughlin (1989) argues that (i)–(iii), at least, would not commit Davidson to type epiphenomenalism. (For discussions of Davidson (1993), see McLaughlin (1993), Kim (1993), and Sosa (1993).)

SOME APPARENT CONSEQUENCES OF TYPE EPIPHENOMENALISM

Suppose, for the sake of argument, that type epiphenomenalism is true. Why would that be a concern if mental events are physical events with causal effects? On our assumption that the causal relation is extensional, it could be true, consistent with type epiphenomenalism, that pains cause winces, that desires cause behaviour, that perceptual experiences cause beliefs, that mental states cause memories, and that reasoning processes are causal processes. Nevertheless, while perhaps not as disturbing a doctrine as token epiphenomenalism, type epiphenomenalism can, upon reflection, seem disturbing enough.

Notice to begin with that 'in virtue of' expresses an explanatory relationship. Indeed, 'in virtue of' is arguably a near synonym of the more common locution 'because of' (cf. McLaughlin, 1989). But, in any case, the following seems to be true: an event causes a G-event in virtue of being an F-event if and only if it causes a G-event because of being an F-event. 'In virtue of' implies 'because of', and in the case in question at least the implication seems to go in the other direction as well. Suffice it to note that were type epiphenomenalism *consistent* with its being the case that an event could have a certain effect because of falling under a certain mental type, then we would indeed be owed an explanation of why it should be of any concern if type epiphenomenalism is true. We will, however, assume that type epiphenomenalism is *inconsistent* with that. We will assume that type epiphenomenalism could be reformulated as follows: no event can cause anything because of falling under a mental type. (And we will assume that property epiphenomenalism can be reformulated thus: no event can cause anything because of having a mental property.) To say that c causes e in virtue of being F is to say that c causes e because of being F; that is, it is to say that it is because c is F that it causes e. So understood, type epiphenomenalism is a disturbing doctrine indeed.

If type epiphenomenalism is true, then it could never be the case that circumstances are such that it is because some event or state is a sharp pain, or a desire to flee, or a belief that danger is near, that it has a certain sort of effect. It could never be the case that it is because some state is a desire to X (impress someone) and another is a belief that one can X by doing Y (standing on one's head) that the states jointly result in one's doing Y (standing on one's head). If type (property) epiphenomenalism is true, then nothing has any causal powers whatsoever in virtue of (because of) being an instance of a mental type (or having a mental property). For it could, then, never be the case that it is in virtue of being an instance of a certain mental type that a state has the causal power in certain circumstances to produce some effect. For example, it could never be the case that it is in virtue of being an urge to scratch (or a belief that danger is near) that a state has the causal power in certain circumstances to produce scratching behaviour (or fleeing behaviour). If type-epiphenomenalism is true, then the mental *qua* mental, so to speak, is causally impotent. That may very well seem disturbing enough.

What reason is there, however, for holding type epiphenomenalism? Even if neurophysiology does not need to postulate types of mental events, perhaps the science of psychology does. Note that physics has no need to postulate types of neurophysiological events; but that may well not lead one to doubt that an event can have effects in virtue of being (say) a neuron firing. Moreover, mental types figure in our everyday causal explanations of behaviour, intentional action, memory, and reasoning. What reason is there, then, for holding that events cannot have effects in virtue of being instances of mental types? This question naturally leads to the more general question of which event types are such that events have effects in virtue of falling under them. This more general question is best addressed after considering a 'no gap' line of argument that has emerged in recent years.

THE NO-GAP ARGUMENT FROM PHYSICS

Current physics includes quantum mechanics, a theory which appears able, in principle, to explain how chemical processes unfold in terms of the mechanics of subatomic particles. Molecular biology seems able, in principle, to explain how the physiological operations of systems in living things occur in terms of biochemical pathways, long chains of chemical reactions. On the evidence, biological organisms are complex physical objects, made up of molecules, atoms, and more fundamental physical particles (there are no entelechies or élan vital). Since we are biological organisms, the movements of our bodies and of their minute parts, including the chemicals in our brains, are, like the movements of all physical entities, causally determined, to whatever extent they are so, by events involving subatomic particles and fields. Such considerations have inspired a line of argument that only events within the domain of physics are causes.

Before presenting the argument, let us make some terminological stipulations: let us henceforth use 'physical event (state)' and 'physical property' in a *strict* and *narrow* sense to mean, respectively, a type of event (state) and a property postulated by (current) physics (*or* by some improved version of current physics). Event types and properties are postulated by physics if they figure in laws of physics. Finally, by 'a physical event (state)' we will mean an event (state) that falls under a physical type. Only events within the domain of (current) physics (or some improved version of current physics) count as physical in this strict and narrow sense.

Consider, then

The Token-Exclusion Thesis Only physical events can have causal effects (i.e. as a matter of causal necessity, only physical events have causal effects).

The premises of the basic argument for the token-exclusion thesis are:

Physical Causal Closure Only physical events can cause physical events.
Causation via Physical Effects As a matter of at least causal necessity, an event is a cause of another event if and only if it is a cause of some physical event.

These principles jointly imply the exclusion thesis. The principle of causation via physical effects is supported on the empirical grounds that every event occurs within space-time, and by the principle that an event is a cause of an event that occurs within a given region of space-time if and only if it is a cause of some physical event that occurs within that region of space-time. The following claim is offered in support of physical closure:

Physical Causal Determination For any (caused) physical event, P, there is a chain of entirely physical events leading to P, each link of which causally determines its successor.

(A qualification: if strict causal determinism is not true, then each link will determine the objective probability of its successor.) Physics is such that there is compelling empirical reason to believe that physical causal determination holds. Every physical event will have a sufficient physical cause. More precisely, there will be a deterministic causal chain of physical events leading to any physical event, P. Each link of the chain will be an occurrence involving all the particles and fields within some cross-section of the backward lightcone of P, but such links there will be. Such physical causal chains are entirely 'gapless'. Now, to be sure, physical causal determination does not imply physical causal closure; the former, but not the latter, is consistent with non-physical events causing physical events. However, a standard epiphenomenalist response to this is that such non-physical events would be, without exception, overdetermining causes of physical events, and it is *ad hoc* to maintain that non-physical events are overdetermining causes of physical events (*see An Essay on Mind* section 3.4)

Are mental events within the domain of physics? Perhaps, like objects, events can fall under many different types or kinds. We noted earlier that a given object might, for instance, be both a stone and a paperweight. However, we understand how a stone could be a paperweight. But how, for instance, could an event of subatomic particles and fields be a mental event? Suffice it to note for the moment that if mental events are not within the domain of physics, then, if the token-exclusion thesis is true, no mental event can ever cause anything: token epiphenomenalism is true.

THREE RESPONSES TO THE NO-GAP
ARGUMENT FROM PHYSICS

One might reject the token-exclusion thesis, however, on the grounds that, typical events within the domains of the special sciences – chemistry, the life sciences, etc. – are not within the domain of physics, but nevertheless have causal effects. One might maintain that neuron firings, for instance, cause other neuron firings, even though neurophysiological events are not within the domain of physics. Rejecting the token-exclusion principle, however, requires arguing either that physical causal closure is false or that the principle of causation via physical effects is.

But one response to the 'no gap' argument from physics is to reject physical causal closure. Recall that physical causal determination is consistent with non-physical events being overdetermining causes of physical events. One might concede that it would be *ad hoc* to maintain that a non-physical event, N, is an overdetermining cause of a physical event P, *and* that N causes P in a way that is independent of the causation of P by other physical events. However, perhaps N can cause a physical event P in a way that is dependent upon P's being caused by physical events. One might argue that physical events 'underlie' non-physical events, and that a non-physical event N can be a cause of another event, X (physical or non-physical), in virtue of the physical event that 'underlies' N being a cause of X. (This sort of response is developed in Kim, 1984 and Sosa, 1984.)

Another response is to deny the principle of causation via physical effects. Physical causal closure is consistent with non-physical events causing other non-physical events. One might concede physical causal closure but deny the principle of causation via physical effects, and argue that non-physical events cause other non-physical events without causing physical events. This would not require denying either that (1) physical events invariably 'underlie' non-physical events or that (2) whenever a non-physical event causes another non-physical event, some physical event that underlies the first event causes a physical event that underlies the second. Claims (1) and (2) do not imply the principle of causation via physical effects. Moreover, from the fact that a physical event, P, causes another physical event, P*, it may not follow that P causes every non-physical event that P* underlies. That may not follow even if the physical events that underlie non-physical events causally suffice for those non-physical events. It would follow from that that for every non-physical event, there is a causally sufficient physical event. But it may be denied that causal sufficiency suffices for causation; it may be argued that there are further constraints on causation that can fail to be met by an event that causally suffices for another. Moreover, it may be argued that given the further constraints, non-physical events are the causes of non-physical events. (This sort of response is developed in Yablo, 1992a, 1992b.)

However, the most common response to the 'no-gap' argument from physics is to concede it, and thus to embrace its conclusion, the token-exclusion thesis, but to maintain the doctrine of *token physicalism*, the doctrine that every event (state) is within the domain of physics. If special science events and mental events are within the domain of physics, then they can be causes consistent with the token-exclusion thesis (*see* Davidson, 1970; Fodor, 1975).

Now whether special science events and mental events are within the domain of physics depends, in part, on the nature of events; and that is a highly controversial topic about which there is nothing approaching a received view (*see* Bennett, 1988). The topic raises deep issues that are beyond the scope of this essay, issues concerning the 'essences' of events, and the relationship between causation and causal explanation. In any case, suffice it to note here that I believe that the same fundamental issues concerning the causal efficacy of the mental arise for all the leading theories of events, indeed for all the leading theories of the *relata* of the causal relation. The issues just 'pop up' in different places. However, that cannot be argued here, and it won't be assumed.

Since the token physicalist response to the no-gap argument from physics is the most popular response, we shall focus on it. Moreover, we will assume, just for the sake of argument, that special science events, and even mental events, are within the domain of physics. Of course, if mental events are within the domain of physics, then, token epiphenomenalism can be false even if the token-exclusion thesis is true: for mental events may be physical events which have causal effects.

THE TYPE EXCLUSION THESIS

However, concerns about the causal relevance of mental properties and event types would remain. Indeed, token physicalism, together with a fairly uncontroversial assumption, naturally leads to the question of whether events can be causes only in virtue of falling under types postulated by physics. The assumption is that physics postulates a system of event types that has the following features.

Physical Causal Comprehensiveness Whenever two physical events are causally related, they are so related in virtue of falling under physical types.

This, together with token physicalism, implies:

Universal Physical Causal Comprehensiveness Whenever two events are causally related, they are so related in virtue of falling under physical types.

That thesis naturally invites the question of whether the following is true:

The Type-Exclusion Thesis An event can cause something *only* in virtue of falling under a physical type (i.e. a type postulated by physics).

The type-exclusion thesis offers one would-be answer to our earlier question of which event types are such that events have effects in virtue of falling under them. If the answer is the correct one, however, then the fact (if it is one) that special science events and mental events are within the domain of physics will be cold comfort. For *type physicalism*, the thesis that every event type is a physical type, seems false. Mental types seem not to be physical types in our strict and narrow sense. No mental type, it seems, is necessarily coextensive (i.e. coextensive in every 'POSSIBLE WORLD') with any type postulated by physics. Given that, and given the type-exclusion thesis, type epiphenomenalism is true. However, typical special science types also fail to be necessarily coextensive with any physical types, and thus typical special science types fail to be physical types. Indeed, we individuate the sciences in part by the event (state) types they postulate. Given that typical special science types are not physical types (in our strict sense), if the type-exclusion thesis is true, then typical special science types are not such that events can have causal effects in virtue of falling under them.

SOME APPARENT CONSEQUENCES OF THE TYPE EXCLUSION THESIS

We see, then, that, given that type physicalism is false for the reasons discussed above, the type-exclusion thesis has truly incredible consequences, in addition to implying type epiphenomenalism. Since a neuron firing is not a type of event postulated by physics, given the type exclusion thesis, no event could ever have any causal effects in virtue of being a firing of a neuron! The neurophysiological *qua* neurophysiological is causally impotent! Moreover, if things have causal powers *only* in virtue of their physical properties, then an HIV virus, *qua* HIV virus, does not have the causal power to contribute to depressing the immune system; for being an HIV virus is not a physical property (in our strict sense). Similarly, for the same reason, the SALK vaccine, *qua* SALK vaccine, would not have the causal power to contribute to producing an immunity to polio. Furthermore, if, as it seems, phenotypic properties are not physical properties, phenotypic properties do not endow organisms with causal powers conducive to survival! Having hands, for instance, could never endow anything with causal powers conducive to survival since it could never endow anything with any causal powers whatsoever. But how, then, could pheno-

typic properties be units of natural selection? And if, as it seems, genotypes are not physical types, then, given the type exclusion thesis, genes do not have the causal power, *qua* genotypes, to transmit the genetic bases for phenotypes! How, then, could the role of genotypes as units of heredity be a *causal* role? There seem to be ample grounds for scepticism that any reason for holding the type-exclusion thesis could outweigh our reasons for rejecting it.

We noted that the thesis of universal physical causal comprehensiveness (hereafter, 'upc-comprehensiveness' for short) *invites* the question of whether the type-exclusion thesis is true. But does upc-comprehensiveness imply the type-exclusion thesis? Could one rationally accept upc-comprehensiveness while rejecting the type-exclusion thesis?

'IN VIRTUE OF' DOES NOT IMPLY 'ONLY IN VIRTUE OF'

Notice that there is a crucial one-word difference between the two theses: the exclusion thesis contains the word 'only' in front of 'in virtue of', while thesis of upc-comprehensiveness does not. This difference is relevant because 'in virtue of' does not imply 'only in virtue of'. I am a brother in virtue of being a male with a sister, but I am also a brother in virtue of being a male with a brother; and, of course, one can be a male with a sister without being a male with a brother, and conversely. Likewise, I live in the state of New Jersey in virtue of living in the city of New Brunswick, but it is also true that I live in New Jersey in virtue of living in the County of Middlesex; and one can live in the County of Middlesex without living in New Brunswick. Moreover, in the general case, if something, x, bears a relation, R, to something y in virtue of x's being F and y's being G, it does not follow that x bears R to y *only* in virtue of x's being F and y's being G. Suppose that x weighs less than y in virtue of x's weighing 10 lbs and y's weighing 15 lbs. Then, it is *also* true that x weighs less than y in virtue of x's weighing under 12 lbs and y's weighing over 12 lbs.

And something can, of course, weigh under 12 lbs without weighing 10 lbs. To repeat: 'in virtue of' does not imply 'only in virtue of'.

Why, then, think that upc-comprehensiveness implies the type-exclusion thesis? The fact that two events are causally related in virtue of falling under physical types does not seem to exclude the possibility that they are also causally related in virtue of falling under non-physical types, in virtue of the one being (say) a firing of a certain neuron and the other being a firing of a certain other neuron, or in virtue of one being a secretion of enzymes and the other being a breakdown of amino acids. Notice that the thesis of upc-comprehensiveness implies that whenever an event is an *effect* of another, it is so in virtue of falling under a physical type. But the thesis does not seem to imply that whenever an event is an effect of another, it is so *only* in virtue of falling under a physical type. Upc-comprehensiveness seems consistent with events being *effects* in virtue of falling under non-physical types. Similarly, the thesis seems consistent with events being *causes* in virtue of falling under non-physical types.

Nevertheless, an explanation is called for of *how* events could be causes in virtue of falling under non-physical types if upc-comprehensiveness is true. The most common strategy for offering such an explanation involves maintaining there is a dependence-determination relationship between non-physical types and physical types. Upc-comprehensiveness, together with the claim that instances of non-physical event types are causes or effects, implies that, as a matter of causal necessity, whenever an event falls under a non-physical event type, it falls under some physical type or other. The instantiation of non-physical types by an event thus depends, as a matter of causal necessity, on the instantiation of some or other physical event type by the event. It is held that non-physical types are, moreover, 'realized by' physical types in physical contexts; although, a given non-physical type might be 'realizable' by more than one physical type. The occurrence of a physical type in a physical context in some sense determines the occurrence of any non-physical type that it 'realizes.'

Recall the considerations that inspired the 'no gap' argument from physics: quantum mechanics seems able, in principle, to *explain how* chemical processes unfold in terms of the mechanics of subatomic particles; molecular biology seems able, in principle, to *explain how* the physiological operations of systems in living things occur in terms of biochemical pathways, long chains of chemical reactions. Types of subatomic causal processes 'implement' types of chemical processes; and certain types of chemical processes implement types of physiological processes. Many in the cognitive science community hold that computational processes implement mental processes; and that computational processes are implemented, in turn, by neurophysiological processes (*see* COGNITIVE PSYCHOLOGY; COMPUTATIONAL MODELS OF THE MIND). On this view, the sciences form a hierarchy with physics at the base, and which includes in ascending order chemistry, biology, and psychology. Types of 'lower-level' causal processes implement types of 'higher-level' processes. The types of lower-level causal processes that implement a higher-level causal transaction between A-type events and B-type events will contain a realization of A as their first stage and a realization of B as their final stage. Since A and B may be 'multiply realizable', that is, realizable by more than one lower-level type, there may be many distinct lower-level processes that could implement a given higher-level process. Every type of higher-level causal transaction is, however, implemented by at least one type of physical causal process.

It should be stressed, however, that there is no received view about the exact nature of the realization relation, and thus, no received view about the exact nature of the implementation relation. (But for discussions of such matters, *see* Putnam, 1975a; Hooker, 1981, pp. 496–506; McLaughlin, 1983; Jackson and Pettit, 1988; LePore and Loewer, 1989; Block, 1990; Yablo, 1992a,

1992b; Van Gulick, 1993.) Let us set aside the general issues of the nature of the realization relationship, and of how, in part, by virtue of being realized by physical types in physical contexts, non-physical types can be such that events have effects in virtue of falling under them. Let us assume, however, that a *causally necessary* condition for a non-physical type to be such that events can be causes in virtue of falling under it is that the non-physical type be realizable by physical types in physical contexts. Turn, then, to the case of mental types, in particular.

THE CAUSAL RELEVANCE OF CONTENT AND CONSCIOUSNESS

Some terminology will prove useful: let us stipulate that an event type, T, is a causal type if and only if there is at least one type, T*, such that something can cause a T* in virtue of being a T. And by saying that an event type is realizable by physical event types or physical properties, let us mean that it is at least causally possible for the event type to be realized by a physical event type. Given that non-physical causal types must be realizable by physical types, and given that mental types are non-physical types, there are two ways that mental types might fail to be causal. First, mental types may fail to be realizable by physical types. Second, mental types might be realizable by physical types but fail to meet some further condition for being causal types. Reasons of both sorts can be found in the literature on mental causation for denying that any mental types are causal. However, there has been much attention paid to reasons of the first sort in the case of phenomenal mental types (pain states, visual states, etc.). And there has been much attention to reasons of the second sort in the case of intentional mental types (i.e. beliefs that P, desires that Q, intentions that R, etc.). In what remains, we will very briefly consider these reasons in reverse order.

But first one preliminary: notice that intentional states figure in explanations of intentional actions not only in virtue of their intentional mode (whether they are beliefs, or desires, etc.), but also in virtue of their contents (i.e. what is believed, or desired, etc.). For example, what causally explains someone's doing A (standing on his head) is that the person wants to X (impress someone) and believes that by doing A he will X. The contents of the belief and desire (what is believed and what is desired) seem essential to the causal explanation of the agent's doing A. Similarly, we often causally explain why someone came to believe that P by citing the fact that the individual came to believe that Q and inferred P from Q. In such cases, the contents of the states in question are essential to the explanation. This is not, of course, to say that contents themselves are causally efficacious; contents are not among the *relata* of causal relations. The point is, rather, that we characterize states when giving such explanations not only as being in certain intentional modes, but also as having certain contents; we type states for the purposes of such explanations in terms of their intentional modes and their contents. We might call intentional state types that include content properties 'contentful intentional state types'; but, to avoid prolixity, let us call them 'intentional state types' for short; thus, for present purposes, by 'intentional state types' we will mean types such as the belief that P, the desire that Q, and so on, and *not* types such as belief, desire, and the like (*see* INTENTIONALITY).

Although it was no part of Putnam's or Burge's purpose to raise concerns about whether intentional state types are causal, their well-known 'TWIN EARTH' thought-experiments have prompted such concerns (Putnam, 1975b; Burge, 1979). These thought-experiments are fairly widely held to show that two individuals who are exactly alike in every intrinsic physical respect can have intentional states with different contents. If they show that, then intentional state types fail to *supervene* on intrinsic physical state types. The reason is that what contents an individual's beliefs, desires, etc. have, depends, in part, on *extrinsic, contextual* factors. Given that, the concern has been raised that states cannot have effects in virtue of falling under intentional state types.

One concern seems to be that states cannot have effects in virtue of falling under intentional state types because individuals who are in all and only the same intrinsic states must have all and only the same causal powers. In response to that concern, it might be pointed out that causal powers often depend on context. Consider weight. The weights of objects do not supervene on their intrinsic properties: two objects can be exactly alike in every intrinsic respect (and thus have the same mass) yet have different weights. Weight depends, in part, on extrinsic, contextual factors. Nonetheless, it seems true that an object can make a scale read 10 lbs in virtue of weighing 10 lbs. Thus, objects which are in exactly the same types of intrinsic states may have different causal powers due to differences in their circumstances.

It should be noted, however, that on some leading EXTERNALIST theories of content, content, unlike weight, depends on a historical context (see CONTENT. Call such theories of content 'historical-externalist theories'. On one leading historical-externalist theory, the content of a state depends on the learning history of the individual (DRETSKE, 1988, 1993); on another, it depends on the selection history of the species of which the individual is a member (Millikan, 1993). Historical-externalist theories prompt a concern that states cannot have causal effects in virtue of falling under intentional state types. Causal state types, it might be claimed, are *never* such that their tokens must have a certain causal ancestry. But, if so, then, if the right account of content is a historical-externalist account, then intentional types are not causal types. Some historical-externalists appear to concede this line of argument, and thus to concede that states do not have causal effects in virtue of falling under intentional state types (see Millikan, 1993). However, other historical-externalists attempt to explain *how* intentional types can be causal, even though their tokens must have appro-

priate causal ancestries (see Dretske, 1993). This issue is hotly debated, and remains unresolved.

I shall conclude by noting why it is controversial whether phenomenal state types can be realized by physical state types. Phenomenal state types are such that it is like something for a subject to be in them; it is, for instance, like something to have a throbbing pain (see CONSCIOUSNESS; QUALIA). It has been argued that phenomenal state types are, for that reason, *subjective* (see SUBJECTIVITY): to fully understand what it is to be in them, one must be able to take up a certain experiential point of view (Jackson, 1982; Nagel, 1986). For, it is claimed, an essential aspect of what it is to be in a phenomenal state is what it is like to be in the state; only by taking up a certain experiential point of view can one understand that aspect of a phenomenal state. Physical state types (in our strict and narrow sense) are paradigm objective states, i.e. non-subjective states. The issue arises, then, as to whether phenomenal state types can be realized by physical state types. How could an objective state realize a subjective one? This issue too is hotly debated, and remains unresolved. Suffice it to note that if only physical types and types realizable by physical types are causal, and if phenomenal types are neither, then nothing can have any causal effects in virtue of falling under a phenomenal type. Thus, it could never be the case, for example, that a state causally results in a bad mood in virtue of being a throbbing pain.

See also An Essay on Mind section 3.6; IDENTITY THEORY; PHYSICALISM; SUPERVENIENCE.

REFERENCES

Alexander, S. 1920. *Space, Time, and Deity.* 2 vols. London: Macmillan.
Antony, L. 1989. Anomalous monism and the problem of explanatory force. *Philosophical Review*, 2, 153–87.
Bennett, J. 1988. *Events and Their Names.* Indianapolis: Hackett.
Block, N. 1990. Can the mind change the

world? In *Meaning and Method: Essays in Honor of Hilary Putnam*. ed. G. Boolos. Cambridge University Press.

Broad, C.D. 1925. *The Mind and Its Place in Nature*. London: Routledge & Kegan Paul.

Burge, T. 1979. Individualism and the mental. *Midwest Studies in Philosophy*, Vol. 4, 73–121.

Cambell, K. 1970. *Body and Mind*. New York: Anchor Books.

Davidson, D. 1970. Mental events. In *Experience and Theory*. ed. L. Foster and J. W. Swanson. The University of Massachusetts Press and Duckworth.

Davidson, D. 1993. Thinking causes. In Heil and Mele 1993.

Dretske, F. 1988. *Explaining Behavior: Reasons in a World of Causes*. Cambridge MA: MIT Press/Bradford Books.

Dretske, F. 1993. Mental events as structuring causes of behavior. In Heil and Mele 1993

Fodor, J. 1975. *The Language of Thought*. New York: Thomas Y. Crowell.

Heil, J. and Mele, A. eds. 1993. *Mental Causation*. Oxford University Press.

Honderich, T. 1983. The argument for anomalous monism. *Analysis*, 42, 59–64.

Hooker, C.A. 1981. Toward a general theory of reduction. Part III. *Dialogue*, 20, 496–529.

Huxley, 1874. Of the hypothesis that animals are automata. Reprinted in *Science and Culture*, 1882.

Jackson, F. 1982. Epiphenomenal qualia. *Philosophical Quarterly*, 32, 127–36.

Jackson, F., and Pettit, P. 1988. Broad contents and functionalism. *Mind*, 47, 381–400.

Kim, J. 1984. Epiphenomenal and supervenient causation. *Midwest Studies in Philosophy*, Vol. 9, 257–70.

Kim, J. 1993. Can supervenience and 'nonstrict laws' save anomalous monism? In Heil and Mele 1993.

LePore, E., and Loewer, B. 1987. Mind Matters. *Journal of Philosophy*, 84, 630–42.

LePore, E., and Loewer, B. 1989. More on making mind matter. *Philosophical Topics*, 17, 175–91.

Lewes, G.H. 1875. *Problems of Life and Mind*, vol. 2. London: Kegan Paul, Trench, Turbner, & Co.

Malcolm, N. 1968. The conceivability of mechanism. *Philosophical Review*, 77, 45–72.

McLaughlin, B.P. 1983. Event supervenience and supervenient causation. *Southern Journal of Philosophy, Supplementary Volume on Supervenience*, 22, 71–92.

McLaughlin, B.P. 1989. Type dualism, type epiphenomenalism, and the causal priority of the physical. *Philosophical Perspectives*, 3, 109–35.

McLaughlin, B.P. 1993. On Davidson's response to the charge of epiphenomenalism. In Heil and Mele 1993, 27–40.

Millikan, R., 1993. Explanation in biopsychology. In Heil and Mele 1993, 211–32.

Nagel, T. 1986. *The View From Nowhere*. Oxford: Clarendon.

Putnam, H. 1975a. Philosophy and our mental life. In *Philosophical Papers*, vol. 2, ed. H. Putnam. Cambridge University Press.

Putnam, H. 1975b. The meaning of 'meaning'. In *Language, Mind, and Knowledge*, ed. K. Gunderson. *Minnesota Studies in Philosophy of Science*, 7. Minneapolis: University of Minnesota Press, pp. 131–93.

Sosa, E. 1984. Mind–body interaction and supervenient causation. *Midwest Studies in Philosophy*, 9, 271–81.

Sosa, E. 1993. Davidson's thinking causes. In Heil and Mele 1993,

Van Gulick, R. 1993, Who's in charge here? and who's doing all the work? In Heil and Mele 1993.

Yablo, S. 1992a. Mental causation. *Philosophical Review*, 101, 245–80.

Yablo, S. 1992b. Cause and essence. *Synthese*, 93, 403–449.

BRIAN P. McLAUGHLIN

explanans/explanandum This pair of terms has had a wide currency in philosophical discussions because it allows a certain succinctness which is unobtainable in ordinary English. Whether in science, philosophy or in everyday life, one often offers explanations. The particular statements, laws, theories or facts that are used *to explain* something are collectively called the *explanans*; and the target of the explanans – the thing *to be explained* – is called the *explanandum*. Thus, one might explain why ice forms on the surface of lakes (the explanandum) in terms of the special property of water to expand as it approaches freezing point together with the fact that materials less dense than liquid water float in it (the explanans). The terms come from two different Latin grammatical forms: 'explanans' is the present participle of the verb which means explain; and 'explanandum' is a direct object noun derived from that same verb.

SAMUEL GUTTENPLAN

extension   *see* INTENSION.

externalism/internalism In giving an account of what someone believes, does essential reference have to be made to how things are in the environment of the believer? And, if so, exactly what relation does the environment have to the belief? Answering these questions involves taking sides in the externalism/internalism debate. To a first approximation, the externalist holds that one's propositional attitudes cannot be characterized without reference to the disposition of objects and properties in the world – the environment – in which one is situated. The internalist thinks that propositional attitudes (especially belief) must be characterizable without such reference. (The motivation for internalism will be discussed below.) The reason that this is only a first approximation of the contrast is that there can be different sorts of externalism. Thus, one sort of externalist might insist that you could not have, say, a belief that grass is green unless it could be shown that there was some relation between you, the believer, and grass. Had you never come across the plant which makes up lawns and meadows, beliefs about grass would not be available to you. This does not mean that you have to be in the presence of grass in order to entertain a belief about it, nor does it even mean that there was necessarily a time when you were in its presence. For example, it might have been the case that, though you have never seen grass, it has been described to you. Or, at the extreme, perhaps grass no longer exists anywhere in

the environment, but your ancestors' contact with it left some sort of genetic trace in you, and that trace is sufficient to give rise to a mental state that could be characterized as about grass.

Clearly, these forms of externalism entail only the weakest kind of commitment to the existence of things in the environment. However, some externalists hold that propositional attitudes require something stronger. Thus, it might be said that in order to believe that grass is green, you must have had some direct experience – some causal contact – with it during your lifetime. Or an even stronger version might hold that there are beliefs that require that you be in direct contact with the subject matter of these beliefs in order to so much as have them. Obviously, such a strong form of externalism is implausible in connection with a general belief about grass, for example, that it is green. But when it comes to what are called singular beliefs, matters are not so clear. For example, on seeing something bird-like outside the window of my study, I may say: 'that bird was a greenfinch', thereby expressing what I believe. Suppose, however, that I never did see a bird on that occasion – it was only a movement of a leaf which I had mistaken for one. In this case, one sort of externalist would insist that, since nothing in my environment answers to the expression 'that bird' that I used, then I simply do not have the belief that that bird was a greenfinch. And this is true even if I myself am convinced that I have the belief. On this strong externalist stance, propositional attitudes become opaque to their possessors. We can think we believe and desire various things – that our attitudes have certain contents – though we might well just be wrong.

In contrast, the internalist would insist that the contents of our attitudes can be described in ways that do not require the existence of any particular objects or properties in the environment, and this is so even in the case of singular beliefs. There are several motivating factors here. First, there is the intuition that we do know the contents of our own minds. I may be wrong about there being a bird, but how can I be wrong about my believing that there is one? One way the internalist might try to embarrass the externalist into agreeing here is to ask how to explain our intuition that we have some sort of first-person authority with respect to the contents of our thoughts. For, on the strong form of externalism, what we actually think is dependent on the environment, and this is something that is as accessible to others as it is to oneself. The second motivation comes from the demands of action explanation. Suppose that I reach for my binoculars just after insisting that I saw the bird in the tree. The obvious explanation for my action would seem to mention, among other things, my belief that there is such a bird. However, since if the externalist is right, then I just do not have any such belief, it is unclear how to explain my reaching for the binoculars. Finally, internalism can seem the obvious way to deal with the otherwise puzzling consequences of versions of the TWIN EARTH thought experiment. Briefly, suppose this time that I really do see the bird, but suppose that my twin – someone who is a molecular duplicate of me on a duplicate planet called 'twin earth' – does not. (We can stipulate that the only difference between earth and twin earth at that very time is that there really is a bird in the tree on earth, but there is none on twin earth.) As would generally be agreed, my twin would *say* 'that bird is a greenfinch', whilst pointing in the direction of the tree. After all, being a molecular duplicate of me, one would expect his behaviour to resemble mine as closely as can be imagined. Moreover, it is difficult to deny that his saying this is good evidence that he actually believes it. The fact that my twin and I are molecule-for-molecule the same is often reckoned to imply that my twin and I are

psychological, as well as physical, duplicates. Yet the strong externalist position would be committed to saying that my twin has no such belief, whilst I do, and this because of the way things are in our respective environments. Yet, if I were suddenly to be in my twin's shoes – if I were instantaneously transported to twin earth without any knowledge of the move – there could be no doubt that I would say 'that bird is a greenfinch'. And what reason could be given for saying that my mental state had changed during the transportation? Why, if my saying something counted as evidence for my belief in the one case, doesn't it count in the other?

Given these factors, the internalist is apt to insist that beliefs and other attitudes must be characterizable 'from the inside', so to speak. What I share with my twin is a content, though we obviously do not share an environment that answers to that content in the same way. In not being answerable to how things are in the environment, it has been suggested that what I and my twin share is a *narrow* content. The *broad* or *wide* content does take the environment into consideration, and it is therefore true that my twin and I do not share broad content in the case imagined. However, what the internalist insists is that only the notion of narrow content is up to the task of explaining the intuitions we have about twin earth cases, explanation of action and first-person authority. To be sure, there are rejoinders available to the externalist in respect of each of these intuitions, and only the beginnings of the debate have been sketched here. (*See* BELIEF; CONTENT; *An Essay on Mind* section 2.1.3; PROPOSITIONAL ATTITUDES; THOUGHT; THOUGHT AND LANGUAGE.)

SAMUEL GUTTENPLAN

F

first-person authority Descartes (1596–1650) insisted that the mind was as a special kind of substance, one which contrasts sharply with material substance (*see* HISTORY). Hence, the label 'Cartesian' tends to be applied to any view that is DUALIST in thinking of the mind as fundamentally different from matter. Accompanying this Cartesian dualism of substances is a dualism of ways of knowing about minds and about matter. The Cartesian conception has it that we have access to the contents of our own minds in a way denied us in respect of matter. That is, we can know what we think, feel and want, and know this with a special kind of certainty that contrasts with our knowledge of the physical world. Indeed, Descartes thought that we could be mistaken about even the existence of our own bodies, whilst we could not be in error about what passes in our minds.

The doctrine that there is something special about our knowledge of our own minds goes naturally with Cartesian dualism, but it is by no means necessary to be a dualist to think this. Nor need one be committed to anything as strong as the Cartesian view that self-knowledge is certain. For whatever one's conception of mind and matter, there does seem to be an asymmetry between our knowledge of our own mind and our knowledge of the external world (including here our knowledge of other person's minds). One way to put it, without any specific commitment to dualism, is to say that a subject (or self) has *first-person authority* with respect to the contents of his or her mind, whereas others (third persons) can only get at these contents indirectly. You count as an authority about your own mind because you can know about it directly or immediately and this is very different from the type of knowledge others can have.

The notion of 'authority' is vague, but it can be sharpened in a number of different ways. First, one may say that first-person authority consists in the *infallibility* of your judgments about your own mental states; if you claim sincerely to be in pain, then you cannot be wrong. This is certainly the view held by Descartes himself. A little less radically, one might think that such authority only confers *incorrigibility*: your judgments about your pains might be wrong, but you cannot be corrected by others, you count as the highest authority. Finally, one might think that what counted most for first-person authority was that your mental states were transparently available to you: if you are in pain, then you know it. This is known as *self-intimation*. And it should be noted that this does not by itself require that we are either infallible or incorrigible about our pains or other mental contents.

The Cartesian conception of first-person authority encourages the idea that the mind is like a theatre whose show can only be witnessed by the subject whose theatre it is. This view of the mental as something like a private performance is a highly metaphorical way of motivating the idea of first-person authority, though it is a metaphor that comes naturally to us. Nonetheless, since it is possible to accept some form of first-person authority without any commitment to dualism, much effort has been expended in trying to explain the asymmetry between first- and third-person knowledge of the mind in a way that does not depend on the so-called 'Cartesian theatre'. (*See* CONSCIOUSNESS; *An Essay on Mind* section 2.2.3; INTROSPECTION, THE SELF).

SAMUEL GUTTENPLAN

291

Fodor, Jerry A. 'Hey, what do you think you're doing?' Fair question. When I was a boy in graduate school, the philosophy of mind had two main divisions: the mind/body problem and the problem of other minds. The project was to solve these problems by doing conceptual analysis. Nobody knew what conceptual analysis was, exactly; but it seemed clear that lots of what had once been considered the philosophy of mind (lots of Hume and Kant, for example) didn't qualify and was not, in fact, philosophy at all. Instead, it was a misguided sort of armchair psychology, best read by flashlight beneath the covers.

Philosophical fashions change. It's gotten harder to believe that there is a *special* problem about the knowledge of other minds (as opposed to other anything elses); and these days we're all materialists for much the reason that Churchill gave for being a democrat: the alternatives seem even worse. Correspondingly, there's a new research agenda: to reconcile our materialism with the psychological facts; to explain how minds qua material objects could have the properties they do.

It is, however, reasonable to wonder whether this is a research agenda in *philosophy*. If, after all, you wanted to know how rocks, trees, and spiral nebulas, qua material objects, could have the properties that they do, you would be well advised to consult *not* a philosopher but a geologist, a botanist, and an astrophysicist respectively. To explain how photosynthesis works is to explain how a plant qua material object could photosynthesize; so reconciling materialism with the facts about plants isn't a project distinct from the one that botanists are already engaged on. Parity of argument suggests that reconciling the facts about minds with materialism is not a project distinct from the one that *psychologists* are already engaged on, hence that psychology needs a philosophy of minds about as much as botany needs a philosophy of plants. This is a line of thought about which few philosophers of mind are enthusiastic.

On the other hand, some of the most pervasive properties of minds seem so mysterious as to raise the Kantian-sounding question how a materialistic psychology is *even possible*. Lots of mental states are *conscious*, lots of mental states are *intentional*, and lots of mental processes are *rational*, and the question does rather suggest itself how anything that is material could be any of these. This question is without a botanical counterpart since, though there is plenty that's puzzling about plants, their materiality seems not to be much in doubt.

'How is a materialistic psychology possible?' is, moreover, a question that may belong to philosophers by default; it's not one that psychologists have had a lot to say about. While behaviourism was in style, psychologists assumed, in effect, that psychology *isn't* possible. Now their research strategy is largely to assume, without much argument, that the conceptual apparatus of commonsense folk-psychological explanation can be adapted to scientific requirements. *De facto*, the status of this assumption has become the main topic in the philosophy of mind.

My philosophical concerns are mostly with this question, so what follows is mostly a discussion of its current status. For these purposes, 'FOLK PSYCHOLOGY' is primarily *intentional explanation*; it's the idea that people's behaviour can be explained by reference to the contents of their beliefs and desires. Correspondingly, the methodological issue is whether intentional explanations can be co-opted to make science out of. Similar questions might be asked about the scientific potential of other folk-psychological concepts (CONSCIOUSNESS, for example), but I won't discuss them here for want of space and lack of progress to report.

What makes intentional explanations problematic is that they presuppose that there are intentional states. What makes intentional states problematic is that they exhibit a pair of properties which (with one exception; see below) are never found together elsewhere (*see* INTENTIONALITY).

(1) *Intentional states have causal powers.* Thoughts (more precisely, havings of thoughts) *make things happen*; typically,

thoughts make behaviour happen. Self-pity can make one weep, as can onions.

(2) Intentional states are *semantically evaluable*. BELIEFS, for example, are *about how things are* and are therefore true or false depending on whether things are the way that they're believed to be. Consider, by contrast: tables, chairs, onions, and the cat's being on the mat. Though they all have causal powers, they are *not* about anything and are therefore not evaluable as true or false.

If there is to be an intentional science, there must be semantically evaluable things that have causal powers. Moreover, there must be *laws* about such things, including, in particular, laws that relate beliefs and desires to one another and to actions. If there are no intentional laws, then there is no intentional science. This claim is tendentious, but I think we had better assume that it's true. Perhaps scientific explanation isn't *always* explanation by law subsumption, but surely it often is, and there's no obvious reason why an intentional science should be exceptional in this respect. Moreover, one of the best reasons for supposing that common sense is right about there being intentional states is precisely that there seem to be many reliable intentional generalizations for such states to fall under. I assume that many of the truisms of folk psychology either articulate intentional laws or come pretty close to doing so.

So, for example, it's a truism of folk psychology that rote repetition facilitates recall. (More generally, repetition improves performance; 'How do you get to Carnegie Hall?' 'Practice, practice.') This generalization relates the content of what you learn to the content of what you say to yourself while you're learning it; so what it expresses is, *prima facie*, a lawful causal relation between types of intentional states. Real psychology has lots more to say on this topic, but it is, from the present point of view, mostly much more of the same. To a first approximation, repetition does causally facilitate recall, and that it does is lawful.

There are, to put it mildly, many other cases of such reliable intentional causal generalizations. There are also many, many kinds of folk psychological generalizations about *correlations* among intentional states, and these too are plausible candidates for fleshing out as intentional laws. For example, that anyone who knows what $7 + 5$ is also knows what $7 + 6$ is; that anyone who knows what 'John loves Mary' means also knows what 'Mary loves John' means; and so forth.

Philosophical opinion about folk psychological intentional generalizations runs the gamut from 'there aren't any that are *really* reliable' to 'they are all platitudinously true, hence not empirical at all'. I won't argue about this here. Suffice it, on the one hand, that the *necessity* of 'if $7 + 5 = 12$ then $7 + 6 = 13$' is quite compatible with the *contingency* of 'if someone knows that $7 + 5 = 12$, then he knows that $7 + 6 = 13$'; and, on the other hand, that I'd be rich if I could only find people prepared to bet against the reliability of such folk psychological truths.

So, then, part of the question 'how can there be an intentional science' is 'how can there be intentional laws?' I'll return to this presently. First, a bit about laws *per se*.

LAWS *PER SE*

I assume that laws are true generalizations that support counterfactuals and are confirmed by their instances. I suppose that every law is either basic or not. Basic laws are either exceptionless or intractably statistical. The only basic laws are laws of basic physics.

All non-basic laws, including the laws of all the non-basic sciences, including, in particular, the intentional laws of psychology, are 'c[eteris] p[aribus] laws;' they hold only 'all else being equal'. There is – anyhow there ought to be – a whole department of the philosophy of science devoted to the construal of cp laws; to making clear, for instance, how they can be explanatory, how they can support counterfactuals, how they can subsume the singularly causal truths that instance them . . ., etc. I omit

293

these issues in what follows because they don't belong to philosophical psychology as such. If the laws of intentional psychology are cp laws, that is because intentional psychology is a special (i.e. non-basic) science, not because it is an intentional science.

IMPLEMENTATION

There is a further quite general property that distinguishes cp laws from basic ones: non-basic laws want mechanisms for their implementation. Suppose, for a working example, that some special science says that being F causes xs to be G. (Being irradiated by sunlight causes plants to photosynthesize; being freely suspended near the earth's surface causes bodies to fall with uniform acceleration; and so forth.) Then it is a constraint on this generalization's being lawful that *How does being F cause xs to be G?* must have an answer. This is, I suppose one of the ways special science laws are different from basic laws. A basic law says that Fs cause (or are) Gs, punkt. If there were any explaining how, or why, or by what means Fs cause Gs, the law would *ipso facto* be not basic but derived.

Typically – though not invariably – the mechanism that implements a special science law is defined over the microstructure of the things that satisfy the law. The answer to 'how does sunlight make plants photosynthesize?' implicates the chemical structure of plants; the answer to 'how does freezing make water solid?' implicates the molecular structure of water; and so forth. In consequence, theories about how a law is implemented usually draw upon the vocabularies of two (or more) levels of explanation.

If you are specially interested in the peculiarities of aggregates of matter at the Lth level (in plants, or minds, or mountains, as it might be) then you are likely to be specially interested in implementing mechanisms at the L−1th level (the 'immediately' implementing mechanisms); this is because the characteristics of L-level laws can often be explained by the characteristics of their L−1th level implementations. You can

learn quite a lot about plants qua plants by studying their chemical constitution. You learn correspondingly less by studying their subatomic constitution though, no doubt, laws about plants are implemented, eventually, subatomically. The question thus arises what mechanisms might immediately implement the intentional laws of psychology, thereby accounting for *their* characteristic features. (We are, appearances to the contrary notwithstanding, rapidly arriving at a question that may actually have an answer.)

Intentional laws subsume causal interactions among mental processes; that much is truistic. But here's something substantive, something that a theory of the *implementation* of intentional laws ought to account for: The causal processes that intentional states enter into tend to *preserve* their semantic properties. For example, thinking true thoughts tends to cause one to think more thoughts that are also true. This is no small matter; the very rationality of thought depends on such facts as that true thoughts that $((P{\rightarrow}Q)$ and $(P))$ tend to cause true thoughts that Q.

A lot of what has happened in psychology – notably since Freud – has consisted of finding new and surprising cases where mental processes are semantically coherent under intentional characterization. Freud made his reputation by showing that this was true even for much of the detritus of behaviour: dreams, verbal slips and the like. But, as it turns out, the psychology of normal mental processes is largely grist for the same mill. For example, it turns out to be theoretically revealing to construe perceptual processes as inferences that take specifications of proximal stimulations as premises and yield specifications of their distal causes as conclusions, and that are reliably truth preserving in ecologically normal circumstances. The psychology of learning cries out for analogous treatment (e.g. for treatment as a process of hypothesis formation and confirmation).

Here's how things have gone so far in this discussion. We started with the question: 'How is intentional psychology possible?' and this led us to 'how can there be intentional laws?' which in turn raised 'how could intentional laws have implementing mechanisms?' A mark of a good answer to this last question is that it should explain why mental processes are generally coherent under semantic representation (roughly, why they tend to preserve semantic properties like truth). This is where cognitive science starts.

THOUGHTS AS SYMBOLS

I remarked that intentional states, as common sense understands them, have both causal and semantic properties and that the combination appears to be unprecedented: propositions are semantically evaluable, but they are abstract objects and have no causal powers. Onions are concrete particulars and have causal powers, but they aren't semantically evaluable. Intentional states seem to be unique in combining the two; that indeed, is what so many philosophers have against them.

Well, *almost* unique. Suppose I write 'the cat is on the mat'. On the one hand, the thing I've written is a concrete particular in good standing and it has, qua material object, an open-ended galaxy of causal powers. (It reflects light in ways that are essential to its legibility; it exerts a small but in principle detectable gravitational effect upon the moon; etc.) And, on the other hand, what I've written is about something and is therefore semantically evaluable; it's true if and only if there's a cat where it says that there is. So, my inscription of 'the cat is on the mat' has both content and causal powers; as does my thought that the cat is so mat. (I'm playing fast and loose with the TYPE/TOKEN distinction for both inscriptions and thoughts. Though it may seem to, the point I'm making doesn't depend on doing so; and it simplifies the exposition.)

What are we to make of this analogy between thoughts and symbols? The history of philosophical and psychological theorizing about the mind consists largely of attempts to exploit it by deriving the causal/semantic properties of thoughts from the causal/semantic properties of symbols; in effect, by supposing that thinking is a kind of talking to oneself. (Or of making pictures to oneself; for our purposes the difference doesn't matter since pictures are a kind of symbol too.) Correspondingly, according to this tradition, the laws that govern intentional processes are supposed to be implemented by causal relations among these mental symbols. Cognitive science, with its 'mental representations' and 'languages of thought' is merely the most recent avatar of this ancient idea. I'm inclined to take it very seriously if only for lack of alternative candidates.

(NB From the present lofty perspective, one can barely distinguish behaviourists from mentalists. Both assimilate thinking to talking to yourself, the major disagreement being over whether what you talk to yourself in when you think is English or Mentalese. It is pretty close to a literal truth that the tradition of theorizing about the mind offers only two options: either thinking is talking to yourself, or there is no such thing as thinking.)

Inclinations aside, however, it would tend to prove this traditional pudding if the hypothesis that intentional mental processes are causal interactions among mental symbols could somehow be made to explain why intentional mental processes are generally semantically coherent.

(NB 'If mental processes weren't generally semantically coherent, they wouldn't *be* intentional. This is a *conceptual* truth.' (Compare, among many others, Clark, 1989.) But assuming that the rationality of intentional processes is conceptually necessary makes no progress with the problem in hand; it just puts the pea under a different shell. The operative question now becomes: 'how can merely material processes meet the rationality conditions on intentionality?' Generally speaking, if a philosopher offers to 'dissolve' the problem that you're working on, tell him to go climb a tree.)

The hypothesis that mental processes are causal interactions was, in fact, the constraint that Empiricist psychology foundered on. Empiricists assumed that trains of thought consist of causally connected sequences of 'Ideas' (the Empiricist's term of art for mental representations). The semantic coherence of intentional processes was to be explicated by laws of association which, in effect, adjust the causal relations among Ideas to reflect corresponding relations among the things that they're ideas of. (Salt comes with pepper; so pepper-Ideas become associated to salt-Ideas; so thinking of salt makes you think of pepper.) According to the more advanced ('brain-like') Empiricist models, the associative laws are themselves supposed to be implemented by neurological mechanisms. For example, variations in the strength of associative relations between ideas might be achieved by varying the corresponding synaptic resistances. You can find this doctrine already pretty mature in books like Donald Hebb's *The Organization of Behavior*.

Not a word of it was true, of course. As everyone has known since Kant – but somehow forgets every thirty years or so – semantically coherent processes are not, in general, associative; and associative processes are not, in general, semantically coherent. Associationism died of this (CONNECTIONISTS have recently been trying to revive it, with predictably dismal unsuccess) and, when it did, nobody then had the slightest idea how merely material processes could implement the intentional laws that govern a semantically coherent mind. Or how merely immaterial ones could either. There the problem stood until Alan Turing had what I suppose is the best thought about how the mind works that anyone has had so far.

What TURING did was to take the traditional analogy between minds and symbols absolutely seriously. Symbols have both semantic and material properties. (*See above*: inscriptions of 'the cat is on the mat' both mean that the cat is on the mat and gravitationally attract the Moon.) 'Very well, then,' Turing (more or less) said, 'perhaps one could build a *symbol manipulating machine* whose changes of state are driven by the material properties of the symbols on which they operate (for example, by their weight, or their shape, or their electrical

conductivity). And perhaps one could so arrange things that these state changes are semantically coherent in, for example, the following sense: Given a true symbol to play with, the machine will reliably convert it into other symbols that are also true.'

TURING was right about its being possible to build such machines ('computers' as one now says). It's a fundamental idea of current theorizing that minds are machines of this kind, and that it is *because* they are that mental processes are, by and large, reliably rational. If intentional states are relations to mental symbols and mental processes are implemented by causal relations among these symbols, then we can begin to understand how the laws that subsume mental states could preserve their semantic coherence. So we see how an implementation theory for intentional laws might be possible.

Summary so far: An implementation theory for the law *Fs cause Gs* answers the question: '*How* do Fs cause Gs?' It does so by specifying a mechanism that the instantiation of F is sufficient to set in motion, the operation of which reliably produces some state of affairs that is sufficient for the instantiation of G. Postulating a computational level of psychological explanation provides for an implementation theory for intentional laws; one which promises to account for (some? much? all?) of their semantic coherence. Since computational mechanisms really are *mechanisms*, we are some way towards understanding how something rational could be material through and through, hence how an intentional psychology might be possibly compatible with materialist ontological scruples. So far, so good. In fact, so far very good indeed.

If you'll grant me this general framework, I will soon be able to tell you what it is that I think I'm doing.

PROPERTY THEORIES FOR AN INTENTIONAL PSYCHOLOGY

Remember that, in the typical case, the vocabulary that specifies an implementing

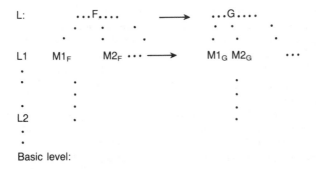

Figure 1. A typical relation between implemented laws (Fs cause Gs) and implementing mechanisms. Laws at any level are implemented by mechanisms whose behaviour is controlled by laws at the next level down. For example, the law that Fs cause Gs is implemented by mechanisms that obey the law that ($M1_F$s cause $M1_G$s). This law is itself implemented by mechanisms at the next lower level, and so on down to basic mechanisms. The present case assumes that both property F and property G are multiply realized at level L1.

mechanism is different from the vocabulary that specifies the law that it implements. In consequence, implementing state M_F's bringing about implementing state M_G explains how Fs cause Gs *only modulo a theory that explains how something's being F could be sufficient for something's being M_F* and how something's being M_G could be sufficient for something's being G. Figure 1 gives the general idea. I'll borrow a term from Robert Cummins (1983) and call any explanation of this kind a *property theory*. (Apparently Cummins assumes, as I should not wish to do, that property theories are *ipso facto* theories of property *identity*. I think that solving some of the problems to be discussed below may turn on rejecting this assumption (*see* Fodor, 1994).) Where I think we now are in the philosophical discussion of cognitive science is this: thanks to Turing's efforts (and despite those of connectionists) we can now see how there might be implementation theories for intentional laws on the assumption that mental processes are computational. But we are not at all clear how, on that assumption, there can be property theories for intentional laws. If we knew how there can be property theories for intentional laws, we would know how an intentional psychology is possible, and this part of the philosophy of

mind could justifiably opt for early retirement. (*See* COGNITIVE PSYCHOLOGY, COMPUTATIONAL MODELS.)

The problem is this: two kinds of relations between laws and mechanisms are recognized by property theories in cases outside psychology: *reduction* and *multiple realization*; and the relation between intentional laws and computational processes seems to be of neither of these kinds. So somebody needs to worry about what kind of relation it is.

You get reduction whenever some L-level property F is *identifiable* with some $L-1$ level property M_F. So, for example, being water is identical to being H_2O according to the usual understanding. You get multiple realization whenever there is a disjunction of $L-1$ level properties, such that the instantiation of F is sufficient for the instantiation of the disjunction but not for the instantiation of any of its disjuncts (see figure 1). In the classic case of multiple realization, a higher-level property is 'functionally defined', and the realizing disjunction includes all and only the mechanisms that can perform the defining function. (So, for example, there is presumably some disjunction of mechanisms any of which might serve as a carburettor, and such that every carburettor is an instance of one of the disjuncts or other.) These days, most philosophers of mind suppose that most psychological properties are multiply realized.

Now, it is built into both the notions of reduction and of multiple realization that the instantiation of an L−1 level property can be a sufficient condition for the instantiation of the corresponding L-level property and vice versa. If, for example, F in figure 1 is the same property as M1$_F$, then, of course, every instantiation of the latter is *ipso facto* an instantiation of the former. Similarly, if (M1$_F$ vs. M2$_F$ . . .) is the disjunction that realizes F, then the tokening of any of the disjuncts is sufficient for F. It is no accident that both of the concepts typically deployed by property theories should have this feature. As we've seen, the existence of a mechanism that eventuates in M$_G$ will not explain how Fs bring about Gs unless the instantiation of M$_G$ is sufficient for the instantiation of G and the instantiation of F is sufficient to set the mechanism in motion.

The upshot is that if the immediately implementing mechanisms for intentional laws are computational, then we need a property theory that provides computationally sufficient conditions for the instantiation of intentional properties. This, however, implies a nasty dilemma. On the one hand, we've seen that the computational account of the implementation of intentional laws is extremely well motivated; it's the only explanation of the semantic coherence of mental processes that looks like having a chance to work. But, on the other hand, there are well-known and persuasive reasons to doubt that there *could* be computationally sufficient conditions for the instantiation of intentional properties. If this dilemma can't be broken, it looks as though the usual constraints on property theories aren't satisfiable in the case of intentional laws. So maybe the answer to *how is an intentional psychology even possible?* is that it's not.

The force of this dilemma depends, of course, on the status of the claim that there can't be computationally sufficient conditions for instantiating intentional properties,

and this claim is not universally granted, either in cognitive science or in the philosophy of mind. For example, lots of people in cognitive science hold computational versions of the theory that the intentional content of a thought is determined by its 'inferential role' (roughly, by its causal role in mental processes). Readers familiar with the ARTIFICIAL INTELLIGENCE literature will recognize 'procedural' semantics as a version of this idea. Structuralism in linguistics and functionalism in the philosophy of language are among its other incarnations. It would be nice to be able to believe that inferential role views of content are right since, if the intentional properties of thoughts are determined by their inferential roles, it gets a lot easier to see how intentional laws could be computationally implemented. Inference is precisely what computers do best.

But inferential accounts of content don't work; there can't be computationally sufficient conditions for the instantiation of intentional properties. (More precisely, there can't be *metaphysically* sufficient computational conditions for the instantiation of intentional properties. This does not rule it out that there might be *nomologically* sufficient computational conditions for instantiation of intentional properties; indeed, I think that this possibility deserves *very* serious consideration. Here too, *see* Fodor, 1994.) That there can't be computationally sufficient conditions is because, as 'externalists' in the philosophy of language are forever reminding us, *the content of one's thoughts depends, at least in part, on their relations to things in the external world*. It is, for example, something about the way that they are *related to dogs* that makes some of one's thoughts dog-thoughts (rather than, say, cat-thoughts); and it is something about the way that they are *related to cats* that makes others of one's thoughts cat-thoughts (rather than, say, dog-thoughts). Inferential role theories of content were offered, in the first instance, as a corrective to the ' "Fido"–Fido Fallacy'; which, however, increasingly appears not to have been fallacious. (A further problem about inferential role semantics is that it is, almost invariably, suicidally holistic. For recent discussion, *see* Fodor, 1991; and Fodor and Lepore, 1992.)

If externalism is right, then (some of) the intentional properties of thoughts are essentially *extrinsic*; they essentially involve mind-to-world relations. But we are still following Turing in assuming that the computational role of a mental representation is determined entirely by its *intrinsic* properties (its weight, shape, or electrical conductivity, as it might be). The puzzle is that it is, to put it mildly, hard to see how the extrinsic properties of thoughts could supervene on their intrinsic properties; which is to say that it's hard to see how there could be computationally sufficient conditions for being in an intentional state; which is to say that it's hard to see how the immediate implementation of intentional laws could be computational.

So semantics and methodology join forces to make trouble for cognitive science: methodology requires property theories for special science laws, and semantics suggests that intentional properties can't be computational. But the idea that the implementation of intentional laws *is* computational is the only serious cognitive science we've got; without it, the semantic coherence of the intentional is completely a mystery. It would be nice to find a way out of this, and much of the discussion that is now taking place between philosophers of science, semanticists and philosophers of mind is concerned with how to do so.

AT LAST: WHAT I THINK I'M DOING

Folk psychology supposes that we act out of our beliefs and our desires; it is both relentlessly causal and relentlessly intentional. The analogy between thoughts and symbols – discovered, I suppose, by Plato, and refined by the likes of Descartes, Hume, Mill and Freud – helps us to see how thoughts could have both sorts of properties: we have only to assume that there are *mental* symbols. Turing's idea that mental processes are computational helps us see how thinking could take one from truths to truths: we have only to assume that mental processes are driven by the intrinsic properties of mental symbols. Put the two ideas together and one begins to have a glimmer how something that is merely material can nonetheless be rational. Thus far has the representational theory of the mind effected the transmutation of folk psychology into science.

But both Plato's idea and Turing's depend on there being *something that fixes the relation between a mental symbol and its content* and keeps this relation fixed as the symbol's causal role in computation unfolds. It's no use having a mechanism in virtue of which 'All men are bald and Socrates is a man' representations cause 'Socrates is bald' representations if 'bald' has stopped meaning *bald* in the course of the transaction. What could this content-fixing something be? If contents just *were* causal roles in computation, this property identity would be the glue. But they aren't, and it isn't, and some other story needs to be told.

I'm working on telling some other story. Doing so is part of a general project to which, in my view, most sensible psychologists and philosophers of mind have always been more or less wittingly devoted: the construction of a representational theory of mind; the reduction of minds to symbols. I sort of like the work. The pay is no good, and the progress is *very* slow. But you do get to meet interesting people.

See also CONCEPTUAL ROLE SEMANTICS; CONTENT; FUNCTIONALISM; LANGUAGE OF THOUGHT; MODULARITY; PSYCHOLOGY AND PHILOSOPHY; THOUGHT; THOUGHT AND LANGUAGE.

BIBLIOGRAPHY

Clark, A. 1989. *Microcognition*. Cambridge, MA: MIT Press.

Cummins, R. 1983. *The Nature of Psychological Explanation*. Cambridge, MA: MIT Press.

Fodor, J. 1991. *A Theory of Content and Other Essays*. Cambridge, MA: MIT Press.

Fodor, J., and Lepore, E. 1992. *Holism, A Shopper's Guide*. Oxford: Basil Blackwell.

Fodor, J. 1994. *The Elm and the Expert*. Cambridge, MA: MIT Press..

Hebb, D. 1949. *The Organization Of Behavior: A Neuropsychological Theory*. New York: Wiley.

JERRY. A. FODOR

folk psychology (1) What is folk psychology? Until recently, many philosophers would have answered something like this: folk psychology (henceforth 'FP') is a 'conceptual framework' and/or 'network of principles' (perhaps, largely implicit) used by ordinary people to understand, explain, and predict their own and other people's behaviour and mental states. Since these ways of characterizing FP are often associated with the claim that FP is a *theory* and that claim is now controversial, a more neutral formulation is called for.

Human beings are social creatures. And they are reflective creatures. As such, they continually engage in a host of cognitive practices that help them get along in their social world. In particular, they attempt to understand, explain, and predict their own and others' psychological states and overt behaviour; and they do so by making use of an array of ordinary psychological notions concerning various internal mental states, both occurrent and dispositional. Let us then consider FP to consist, *at a minimum*, of (a) a set of attributive, explanatory, and predictive practices, and (b) a set of notions or concepts used in those practices. Whether it also consists of a set of laws, generalizations, principles, or rules that are implicated in (a) or that help to define (b) I shall, for the moment, leave an open question.

OVERVIEW OF THE LITERATURE

Broadly speaking, contemporary philosophical discussion of FP has been primarily concerned with the question of FP's *status vis-à-vis* a future scientific theory of mind–brain. There have been two relatively distinct strands to the discussion. The first has identified the relevant scientific theory as a theory deriving from neuroscience and has fairly single-mindedly focused on the claim that FP will eventually be eliminated in favour of this theory. Churchland (1981) has been the major proponent of this eliminativist claim. There is also a sizeable literature which takes on the eliminativist challenge and tries to respond to it in various ways. (*See* e.g. Kitcher, 1984; Horgan and Woodward, 1985; Baker, 1987, unpublished; Boghossian, 1990.)

In contrast, the second strand takes the relevant mind–brain theory to be a theory derived from scientific psychology and the major question to be whether FP will be vindicated by scientific psychology. Suggested answers have ranged from 'definitely yes' (Fodor, 1975, 1987) to 'sort of, partly' (Dennett, 1987) to 'possibly not' (Stich, 1983).

The question of the status of FP *vis-à-vis* the ultimate future scientific theory of the mind–brain has been conducted under the assumption that FP is also something like a theory, consisting of a variety of generalizations or laws connecting mental states with other mental states and mental states with behaviour. A number of papers (Gordon, 1986, 1992; Goldman, 1989, 1992) have recently challenged this assumption. Although the question of whether FP is a theory (I shall call this the question of FP's *form*) has taken on a life of its own, it is also generally perceived as being closely tied to the question of its status. The reason is that it is generally assumed that if FP is *not* a theory, then it can't be a radically false theory (Stich and Nichols, 1992); hence, there will be no reason to want to eliminate it.

Although findings from and speculation about scientific psychology have increasingly been brought to bear on discussions about FP, there is still a surprising amount of dispute, especially of the eliminability question, which operates as if scientific psychology did not exist. I take this to be a serious mistake and in what follows I will attempt to redress the balance somewhat by focusing on what scientific psychology can tell us about FP. My view is that because a scientific theory exists (namely, scientific psychology) which is conceptually closer to FP and 'higher level' than neuroscientific theory, the question of whether FP will be eliminated in favour of neuroscientific theory can only be meaningfully asked as a two-step question: will FP eventually be eliminated in favour of scientific psychology? And will scientific psychology eventually be eliminated in favour of neuroscientific theory? (*see* COGNITIVE PSYCHOLOGY). In what follows I will address only the former question.

THE CONTENT OF FOLK PSYCHOLOGY

Given how we have defined FP, the 'content' of FP can be regarded as the *particular* concepts and practices (and if there are generalizations or rules – the *particular* generalizations or rules) employed by an ordinary person in understanding, explaining, and predicting human psychology, whether his or her own or someone else's.

The dominant philosophical picture of the content of FP is that it consists, first and foremost, of concepts pertaining to our various PROPOSITIONAL ATTITUDE states (especially, the attitudes of BELIEF and DESIRE) and, second, of practices (or principles) connecting these mental attitudes to each other, to perceptual stimuli, and to ACTIONS. This content is sometimes described by articulating a sample list of 'laws' which either analytically or synthetically, depending on your view, govern the concepts or states in question. (*See*, for example, Churchland, 1970, 1979, and FOLK PSYCHOLOGY (2), this volume.) There is also a vast literature that attempts to describe specific aspects of mind, as we ordinarily conceive it (e.g. belief, EMOTION, PRACTICAL REASON, etc.) based primarily on various 'armchair' methodologies such as conceptual analysis, INTROSPECTION, insight, and speculation. (For particularly good examples of this sort of approach, *see* Audi, 1973a, b.)

Philosophers are not the only ones that have concerned themselves with the content of FP, however. Systematic descriptions similar to the standard philosophical conception have recently been attempted by

Wellman (1990, ch. 4), a developmental psychologist, and d'Andrade (1987), an anthropologist. A somewhat different picture of FP emerges if we turn to social psychology, a field that has been investigating FP for nearly 50 years under the labels 'self perception', 'person perception', and, more recently, 'social cognition'. (For an introduction to this body of research, *see* Tedeschi, Lindskold, and Rosenfeld, 1985, chs 2, 4, and 5.)

Two general points emerge from a study of this literature. First, although there seem to be aspects of adult folk psychology that all humans beings share (at least at a certain developmental age), there is also considerable variation: historical, gender, and individual. (Recent work by anthropologists also provides evidence of significant cultural variation. See d'Andrade, 1987; Lutz, 1985, 1987). Second, the conceptual apparatus of folk psychology encompasses not only concepts of mental states such as the propositional attitudes but also a vast array of concepts pertaining to a person's personality traits and dispositions.

A classical example of social psychology research will make the latter point clear and give a sense of how social psychologists investigate FP. According to social psychologists, people not only make inferences about the immediate psychological causes of behaviour; they also, typically, go on to make inferences about other people's personality characteristics. We consider each other to be unhappy, vain, boring, unimaginative, humourless, moody, critical, shrewd, reserved, artistic, cautious, practical, reliable, modest, tolerant, helpful, sincere, sociable, and so on (Rosenberg, Nelson, and Vivekananthan (1969) list 60 such characteristics). In particular, once a person has assigned a few traits to another individual, he or she has little hesitation in assigning others. From the folk psychological perspective, certain traits just seem to 'go together'. Such 'trait implications' have been extensively studied by social psychologists beginning with a classic study by Asch in 1946. Several findings have emerged.

One is that in making trait–trait inferences, some traits matter more than others. For example, when Asch gave subjects a short list of traits describing a person and asked them to generate a more elaborate description of the person, he found that traits like 'warm' versus 'cold' generated bigger differences than traits like 'polite' versus 'blunt'. He suggested that the first group is *central* to impression formation whereas the second group is *peripheral*.

A second finding has been dubbed the 'halo effect' (Wegener and Vallacher, 1977). Once an observer has decided that another person has some positive characteristics, he or she tends to attribute other positive characteristics. Similarly, once a negative attribution has been made, other negative attributions will typically follow. Warm people tend to be seen as generous, good-natured, popular, wise, happy, and imaginative, for example, whereas cold people are seen as unsociable, humourless, stern, and critical.

In sum, there is good reason to believe that folk psychology is both more heterogeneous and richer than philosophers have typically taken it to be.

THE FORM OF FOLK PSYCHOLOGY

A key ingredient in Churchland's (1981) case for the eliminability of FP has been the assumption that FP is a theory. This is also an assumption embraced by many developmental and social psychologists (Wellman, 1990; Astington, Harris, and Olson, 1988; Bruner and Tagiuri, 1954; Heider, 1958; Wegener and Vallacher, 1977; to name but a few). In the past few years, the so-called 'theory-theory' (Morton, 1980) has been challenged by Gordon (1986, 1992) and Goldman (1989, 1992) who maintain that we explain and predict our own and other's behaviour not by adverting to a folk psychological theory but by engaging in a form of mental *simulation*. This view is called 'the simulation view'.

The theory-theory attempts to explain our FP practices by claiming that folk psychological theory is a theory not merely in some abstract, Platonic sense, but in the sense that people engage in the FP practices they do at least partly in virtue of *having* such a theory. In cognitivist terms, the clearest way to *have* a theory of some domain X is to employ a set of representations or a complex representational structure whose CONTENT constitutes a theory of X. Two features of such representational structures bear on the theory vs. simulation dispute. First, the content of a representational structure need not be consciously accessible. Second, representational structures can have many different kinds of representation 'bearers' (Von Eckardt, 1993). In particular, a mental representation can be 'borne' by a 'propositional' data structure (on the assumption that the mind–brain is a conventional computational device) or by a pattern of connections or a node (*see* CONNECTIONISM) (on the assumption that the mind–brain is a connectionist device). (The latter is the sort of view that Churchland (1989, and FOLK PSYCHOLOGY (2), this volume) currently has in mind.)

In contrast, the simulation view rejects the idea that people have a folk psychological theory in this sense. Instead, it claims that our FP practices are largely based upon a capacity to utilize our normal decision-making capability in simulation mode. Following Stich and Nichols (1992), let us assume that this capability rests, at least in part, on a Practical Reasoning System ('PRS'). What Gordon and Goldman hypothesize is that we predict and explain behaviour by running this system 'off-line', that is, decoupled from our 'action control system'. To *predict* another person's behaviour, we imagine ourselves in the other person's situation and then decide what we would do. Or in cognitivist terms, we input a set of 'pretend' or 'simulated' beliefs and desires (those we believe are held by the other person) into PRS and see what decision it comes up with. To *explain* why someone acted the way he or she did, we use our PRS in an 'analysis-by-synthesis' mode and ask: what beliefs and desires, when input into PRS, could have resulted in an INTENTION to perform the action in question?

Although the theory vs. simulation debate has produced a considerable amount of both a priori and empirical argumentation, the question of what underlies our FP practices is, at this point, still an open question. None of the a priori arguments that have been given are compelling, and there is serious disagreement regarding the theoretical import of the various experimental findings that have been brought to bear on the issue. On my view, the principal reason for the stalemate is that, to date, neither theory has been articulated in sufficient detail so that the opposing parties can *agree* on what sort of findings would count for or against each of the theories.

There are numerous points of insufficient articulation. I will comment on only two. According to the simulation theory, a person simulates another person's situation by running either his or her own PRS with 'pretend' inputs. But how do these systems work? We are not given a clue. The omission is an important one because *one* of the ways these systems might work is by exploiting a theory or set of rules. That is, as Goldman (1989, 1992) puts it: such systems may be 'theory-driven' rather than 'process-driven' (i.e. not involving a theory). But, of course, if the simulation theory is to constitute a *competitor* to the theory-theory, it must be articulated in such a way that the 'theory-driven' option is ruled out. The difficulty is that it is by no means clear how to do this. First, there is the conceptual problem of saying when a system does or does not involve a theory. Solving this problem will, in part, involve coming to grips with such ancillary questions as whether it is possible to have simulation without mental concepts (Gordon, 1992b, says 'yes'; Churchland, 1989, says 'no'), and if not, whether mental state concepts can have content without being embedded in a theory (again Churchland, 1989, says 'no'). And, assuming this first problem can be solved, there is the theoretical problem of devising a process-driven PRS that can account for all the features our capacity for reasoning actually has, including the notoriously troublesome feature of productivity (*see* Von Eckardt, 1993, pp. 81–2).

If we distinguish between the 'theoretical models' or systems being invoked in the theory-theory and simulation view and the claims ('theoretical hypotheses') *vis-à-vis* the real world being made for those models, the lack of clarity we have dealt with thus far concerns only the theoretical models. Unclarity also exists with respect to the respective theoretical hypotheses. In particular it is unclear what the *scope* of the two theoretical hypotheses is supposed to be. Is the claim that theory/simulation is used *every time* we engage in FP practices or only *some* of the time? And if the latter, under what circumstances? This question becomes particularly acute if one adopts the eminently sensible view that when people engage in their FP practices, they can and do sometimes use simulation and they can and do sometimes use theory.

THE STATUS OF FOLK PSYCHOLOGY

Philosophers have asked about the status of FP in various ways. Some have asked whether it is likely that FP will be elimin*ated* in favour of our ultimate future scientific theory of the mind–brain (ST); some have asked whether FP is elimin*able*; others, whether FP *should* be eliminated. Still others speak of vindication by ST or simply of the truth or falsity of FP.

Under what conditions would we expect that FP would actually be *eliminated* in favour of ST? There are four: (1) FP would have to be the sort of thing that is suitable for elimination; (2) ST would have to be able to do the explanatory, predictive, and descriptive job FP now does; (3) FP would have to be considered false to a significant degree (otherwise we would have no motivation for replacing it); and (4) various practical conditions would have to be satisfied (e.g. a change in first-language learning practices, government intervention, etc.) so that replacement would actually occur. (*See An Essay on Mind* section 3.7; ELIMINATIVISM.)

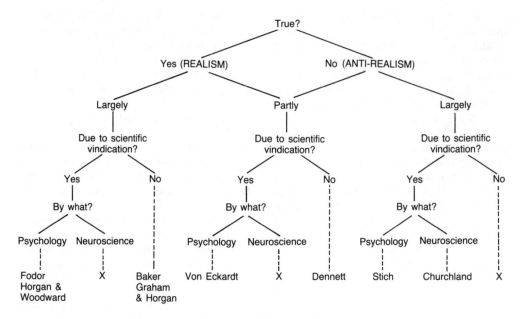

Figure 1. Taxonomy of positions on the truth of folk psychology.

For purposes of discussion I will follow most philosophers in assuming that condition (1) is satisfied. In other words, I will assume that either FP is a theory or, if it is not, it is nevertheless, replaceable by ST. I will also follow standard practice in ignoring condition (4). Thus, the focus of attention will be on whether, using our best current estimates about the nature of ST, ST could take over FP's explanatory and predictive functions and whether there is reason to believe that FP will eventually prove to be false. My discussion will, however, be somewhat idiosyncratic in that I will take ST to be identical to the mind–brain theory that eventually issues from scientific psychology rather than the theory that eventually issues from neuroscience.

Is there any reason to believe that ST could not eventually serve the explanatory, descriptive, and predictive functions of FP? To my knowledge, this question has not been directly addressed in the literature. My own view is that the answer is 'no'. In fact, there is every reason to believe that ST *will* serve these cognitive functions and will serve them better than FP can.

In the first place, the domain of scientific psychology (that is, the phenomena it is interested in explaining, predicting, and describing) includes the domain of FP. (It also encompasses a lot else besides, including all but one of Churchland's (1981, this volume) list of FP explanatory failures – mental illness, creativity, memory, intelligence differences, and the many forms of learning. Sleep will probably turn out to be a physiological rather than psychological phenomenon.) Second, there is no reason to believe that ST won't have the cognitive resources to do the requisite describing, explaining, and predicting. A negative case of this sort *can* be made *vis-à-vis* neuroscientific theory. That is, it can be argued that neuroscientific theory will never be able to explain our actions and capacities because it won't 'capture the generalizations' (Fodor, 1981) or because it won't posit states or entities with intentional properties (Von Eckardt, 1993). But neither of these failures is shared by scientific psychology which (despite the claims of Stich (1983)) shows every sign of retaining intentional modes of description (*see* INTENTIONALITY).

Even if ST could replace FP, it is not likely that we would actually seek to eliminate FP in favour of ST unless we thought that FP was largely false. Is there any reason to believe that FP will eventually prove to be false to a significant degree? This question has attracted a lot of philosophical attention. In fact, philosophers have taken just about every conceivable position on the truth of FP. A tree taxonomizing the major positions is depicted in figure 1. In sorting out this debate, it is important to note that there are a number of sources of disagreement.

First, there is disagreement regarding the role of vindication in establishing the truth or falsity of FP. Roughly speaking, one theory is said to be vindicated by another if the ontological commitments and claims of the first are somehow reflected in the second. Precisely what this 'reflection' comes to is a matter of controversy. See Horgan and Woodward (1985). Many philosophers, including leading proponents both of realism (Fodor, 1975, 1987; Horgan and Woodward, 1985) and anti-realism (Stich, 1983; Churchland, 1981), share the assumption that the ultimate arbiter of the reality of FP entities and the truth of FP generalizations is science. There are others, however (Baker, 1987 unpublished; Graham and Horgan, 1988; Horgan and Graham, 1991) who strongly object to this view, arguing that the probative and/or epistemic situation in favour of FP is so strong that scientific vindication or lack thereof is irrelevant to assessing its ontological and truth claims.

Second, philosophers who are committed to vindication sometimes disagree about what scientific psychology will be like. Fodor (1975), for example, speculates that cognitive psychology will continue to posit a representational system which is significantly language-like (in the sense of being evaluable, having constituent structure, and being compositional). In contrast, Ramsey, Stich, and Garon (1991) predicate their discussion of vindication on the serious possibility that the mind is a connectionist device in which the encoding of information is widely distributed and the most appropriate interpretation is 'subsymbolic' rather than symbolic.

Finally, there is often disagreement about what FP includes. There are those (like myself) who adopt a very 'thick' conception of FP maintaining that any concept or generalization ordinary people use in their FP practices is fair game for inclusion in FP. In contrast, others (like Baker, unpublished) adopt an extremely 'thin' conception according to which FP includes only the assumption that there are persons with attitudes identified by propositional content. And then, of course, there is the typical 'middle-size' conception according to which FP includes concepts of the propositional attitudes and various qualitative mental states but not concepts of traits or personality characteristics.

The stand one takes on each of these questions – on the role of vindication, on the nature of our future scientific psychology, and on the content of FP – makes a big difference with respect to one's stance on elimination. For example, philosophers who downplay the importance of vindication or who adopt a very 'thin' conception of FP tend to regard FP as clearly true. In contrast, those who opt for vindication but adopt a stringent criterion for vindication or envisage ST as quite dissimilar to FP tend to regard FP as most probably false.

My own view is this. If we take vindication to be relevant, ST to be conceptually similar to present-day scientific psychology, and FP to be 'thickly' conceived, then FP is likely to be partly false and partly true. The judgment that FP is likely to be partly false need not rest on educated guesses regarding future vindication. There are numerous findings from scientific psychology (including neuropsychology) which call various aspects of FP into question. Both Dennett (1987) and Stich (1983) describe phenomena that, at a minimum, put stress on our folk psychological modes of explanation. These phenomena include blindsight (Weiskrantz, 1983), the behaviour of split-brain patients (Gazzaniga, 1985), blindness denial and hemi-neglect (Churchland,

1986), and the fact that the explanations people give of their own behaviour often do not correspond with its true causes (Nisbett and Wilson, 1977).

Even more telling are the many social psychology studies indicating that the ways in which we form impressions of other people and the ways in which we typically explain their behaviour are 'biased' in various ways. Tedeschi, Lindskold, and Rosenfeld (1985) summarize their chapter 'Perceiving Persons and Explaining Behaviors' as follows:

> People make characteristic errors in assigning causes for behavior. In general, actors perceive the environment as the cause of their behavior, while observers attribute the same behavior to the actor. There is a universal self-serving bias associated with the outcomes of behavior. Actors tend to attribute success to something about themselves, usually ability, while they attribute failure to external circumstances, often task difficulty or bad luck.
>
> A number of factors are involved when we form overall impressions of strangers. . . . We are influenced by both the type of information presented and the order of presentation. Central traits, such as warm and cold, have been shown to highly influence people in determining their impression of an actor's behavior. A primacy effect occurs when early information has more impact on impressions than later information (p. 123).

Clearly there is reason to believe that FP is at least partly false. Why think that it is partly true? Here the argument does rest on a guess about what form a future theory of the mind–brain will take. Fodor (1987, p. 10) proposes that we take scientific psychology to vindicate propositional attitude FP just in case 'it postulates states (entities, events, whatever) satisfying the following conditions: (1) They are semantically evaluable. (2) They have causal powers. (3) The implicit generalizations of commonsense belief/desire psychology are largely true of them.' It is far too early to tell whether condition (3) will be true of ST. However, there is excellent reason to suppose that (1) and (2) will be. The project of cognitive psychology (and, more broadly, cognitive science) is, in part, to explain in virtue of what we have the cognitive capacities we do and in virtue of what these capacities have the basic properties they do, including such properties as intentionality, pragmatic evaluability, and productivity (Von Eckardt, 1993). Currently cognitive theorizing, including connectionist theorizing, attempts to explain our cognitive capacities and their basic properties by positing mental states that are both representational and causal. Unless our conception of what we want psychology to explain undergoes radical revision, it is difficult to imagine any successful theory getting by without such posits. Thus, although it may turn out that ST does not precisely vindicate the existence of beliefs, desires, and so forth, it will surely vindicate the existence of causally efficacious mental states with content. Hence, in that respect at least, FP will turn out to be true.

See also DENNETT; FODOR; LANGUAGE OF THOUGHT; LEWIS; PSYCHOLOGY AND PHILOSOPHY; REASONS AND CAUSES; STALNAKER; THOUGHT; THOUGHT AND LANGUAGE.

BIBLIOGRAPHY

Asch, S.E. 1946. Forming impressions of personality. *Journal of Abnormal and Social Psychology*, 41, 258–90.

Astington, J.W., Harris, P.L., and Olson, D.R., eds. 1988. *Developing Theories of Mind*. Cambridge University Press.

Audi, R. 1973a. The concept of wanting. *Philosophical Studies*, 24, 1–21.

Audi, R. 1973b. Intending. *Journal of Philosophy*, 70, 387–403.

Baker, L.R. 1970. *Saving Belief*. Princeton University Press.

Baker, L.R. 1987 unpublished. The cognitive status of common sense.

Boghossian, P. 1990. The status of content. *Philosophical Review*, 99, 157–84.

Bruner, J.S., and Tagiuri, R. 1954. The perception of people. In *Handbook of Social Psychology*, ed. G. Lindzey Cambridge, MA.: Addison-Wesley.

Churchland, P.M. 1970. The logical character of action explanations. *Philosophical Review*, 79, 214–36.

Churchland, P.M. 1979. *Scientific Realism and the Plasticity of Mind*. Cambridge University Press.

Churchland, P.M. 1981. Eliminative materialism and the propositional attitudes. *Journal of Philosophy*, 78, 67–90.

Churchland, P.M. 1989. *A Neurocomputational Perspective*. Cambridge, MA: MIT Press.

Churchland, P.S. 1986. *Neurophilosophy: Toward a Unified Science of the Mind/Brain*. Cambridge, MA.: MIT Press.

d'Andrade, R. 1987. A folk model of the mind. In *Cultural Models in Language and Thought*, ed. D. Holland and N. Quinn. Cambridge University Press.

Dennett, D. 1987. *The Intentional Stance*. Cambridge, MA.: MIT Press.

Fodor, J. 1975. *The Language of Thought*. Cambridge MA.: MIT Press.

Fodor, J. 1981. Computation and reduction. In *Representations*, ed. J. Fodor. Cambridge MA.: MIT Press.

Fodor, J. 1987. *Psychosemantics*. Cambridge MA.: MIT Press.

Gazzaniga, M. 1985. *The Social Brain: Discovering the Networks of the Mind*. New York: Basic Books.

Goldman, A. 1989. Interpretation psychologized. *Mind and Language*, 4, 161–85.

Goldman, A. 1992. In defense of the simulation theory. *Mind and Language*, 7, 104–19.

Gordon, R. 1986. Folk psychology as simulation. *Mind and Language*, 1, 158–71.

Gordon, R. 1992 The simulation theory: Objections and misconceptions. *Mind and Language*, 7, 11–34.

Graham, G.L., and Horgan, T. 1988. How to be realistic about folk psychology. *Philosophical Psychology*, 1, 69–81.

Heider, F. 1958. *The Psychology of Interpersonal Relations*. New York: Wiley.

Horgan, T., and Graham, G. 1991. In defense of southern fundamentalism. *Philosophical Studies*. 62, 107–34.

Horgan, T., and Woodward, J. 1985. Folk psychology is here to stay. *Philosophical Review*, 94, 197–225.

Kitcher, P. 1984. In defense of intentional psychology. *Journal of Philosophy*, 71, 89–106.

Lutz, C. 1985. Ethnopsychology compared to what?: Explaining behavior and consciousness among the Ifaluk. In *Person, Self, and Experience: Exploring Pacific Ethnopsychologies*, ed. G. White and J. Kirkpatrick. Berkeley: University of California Press.

Lutz. C. 1987. Goals and understanding in Ifaluk emotion theory. In *Cultural Models in Language and Thought*, ed. D. Holland and N. Quinn. Cambridge University Press.

Morton, A. 1980. *Frames of Mind*. Oxford University Press.

Nisbett, R., and Wilson, T. 1977. Telling more than we can know: Verbal reports on mental processes. *Psychological Review*, 84, 231–59.

Ramsey, W., Stich, S.P., and Garon, J. 1991. Connectionism, eliminativism, and the future of folk psychology. In *Philosophy and Connectionist Theory*, ed. W. Ramsey, S. P. Stich and D. E. Rumelhart. Hillsdale, NJ: Erlḫaum.

Rosenberg, S., Nelson, C., and Vivekananthan, P.S. 1969. A multidimensional approach to the structure of personality impressions. *Journal of Personality and Social Psychology*, 9, 293–94.

Stich, S.P. 1983. *From Folk Psychology to Cognitive Science: The Case Against Belief*. Cambridge, MA.: MIT Press.

Stich, S.P., and Nichols, S. 1992. Folk psychology: simulation or tacit theory?. *Mind and Language*, 7, 35–71.

Tedeschi, J.T., Lindskold, S., and Rosenfeld, P. 1985. *Introduction to Social Psychology*. St Paul, MN: West Publishing Co.

Von Eckardt, B. 1993. *What is Cognitive Science?* Cambridge, MA.: MIT Press.

Wegener, D.M., and Vallacher, R.R. 1977. *Implicit Psychology: An Introduction to Social Cognition*. Oxford University Press.

Weiskrantz, J. 1983. Evidence and scotomata. *Behavioral and Brain Sciences*, 6, 464–7.

Wellman, H. 1990. *The Child's Theory of Mind*. Cambridge, MA.: MIT Press.

BARBARA VON ECKARDT

307

folk psychology (2) 'Folk psychology' denotes the prescientific, common-sense conceptual framework that all normally socialized humans deploy in order to comprehend, predict, explain, and manipulate the behaviour of humans and the higher animals. This framework includes concepts such as *belief, desire, pain, pleasure, love, hate, joy, fear, suspicion, memory, recognition, anger, sympathy, intention,* and so forth. It embodies our baseline understanding of the cognitive, affective, and purposive nature of persons. Considered as a whole, it constitutes our conception of what a person is.

The term 'folk psychology' is also intended to portray a parallel with what might be called 'folk physics', 'folk chemistry', 'folk biology', and so forth. The term involves the deliberate implication that there is something *theory*-like about our commonsense understanding in all of these domains. The implication is that the relevant framework is speculative, systematic, and corrigible, that it embodies generalized information, and that it permits explanation and prediction in the fashion of any theoretical framework.

There is little disagreement about the existence of this shared conceptual framework, but there are important disagreements about its nature, its functions, its epistemology, and its future. In particular, the claim that our common-sense conception of human nature is like an empirical *theory* has been strongly contested by a number of writers, as has the related claim that it might be empirically false. These issues are best addressed by rehearsing the history of this notion.

ORIGINS OF THE IDEA

The first explicit portrayal of our collective self-conception as importantly theory-like appears in a landmark paper by Wilfrid Sellars (1956). Sellars describes an imaginary stage of human pre-history in which people have acquired the use of language, but have not yet developed the vocabulary for, nor even any conception of, the complex mental states and processes rou-

tinely recognized by modern humans. Their explanatory resources for explaining human behaviour are limited to a few purely dispositional terms, all of which can be operationally defined (like 'is soluble') in terms of some observable circumstance (such as being put in water) that is sufficient for an observable behaviour (such as dissolving). For this reason, Sellars refers to these people, pejoratively, as 'our Rylean ancestors' (*see* RYLE). They can explain some human behaviours, but only very few. Being limited to a set of operationally defined dispositional concepts, they have no conception of the complex dance of occurrent internal states driving human behaviour, no conception of the internal economy that is just waiting to be characterized by a full-blown theory of human nature.

As Sellars develops the story, this deficit is repaired by a visionary theorist named Jones. Taking as his model the overt declarative utterances already current in his society, he postulates the existence, within all humans, of covert, utterance-like events called 'thoughts'. These internal events are postulated to have the same semantic and logical properties as their overt counterparts, and to play an internal role comparable to the ongoing discursive and argumentative role often performed by overt speech. A suitable sequence of such internal events – some rough chain of practical reasoning, for example – is thus fit to explain certain human behaviours as the natural outcome of hidden speech-like antecedents, despite the absence of any overtly voiced practical reasonings preceding the behaviour on that occasion.

A further postulation by Jones, this time exploiting the model of external perceptual objects, brings the range of qualitatively distinct SENSATIONS into the picture. These are said to be internal perceivables, covert objects that can provoke appropriate cognition and ACTION even in the absence of their external public counterparts. Related postulations bring INTENTIONS onto the scene, and also BELIEFS and DESIRES as relatively lasting states of any individual (they are dispositions to have occurrent thoughts and intentions, respectively). In sum, Jones postulates the basic ONTOLOGY of our current folk psychology, and assigns to its elements their now familiar causal roles, much to the explanatory and predictive advantage of everyone who gains a command of its concepts.

Once learned by everyone, Jones's theory gets a final boost when it turns out that each adept can further learn to make spontaneous *first*-person ascriptions of the new concepts, ascriptions which are strongly consistent with the ascriptions made on purely explanatory or third-person criteria.

Jones's society has now reached the same conceptual level that we moderns enjoy. And what has raised them to this position, on Sellars' account, is their acquisition of a novel explanatory framework with a novel internal ontology. Sellars's lesson is that our modern folk psychology has precisely the same epistemological status, logical functions, and modelling ancestry as the framework postulated by Jones in the heroic myth. It is, in short, an empirical theory.

DEVELOPMENT OF THE IDEA

Sellars made much of the fact that our conception of the semantic properties of thoughts is derivative upon an antecedent conception of the semantic properties of overt declarative utterances. Our accounts of semantic properties in general, therefore, should not take the semantic features of thoughts as explanatory primitives fit for illuminating the semantics of overt speech, as is the common impulse (cf. Grice, 1957; Searle, 1983). Instead, Sellars proposed a conceptual-inferential-role account that would provide an independent but parallel explanation for semantics in both domains.

A more salient development of Sellar's account is the novel solution it provides to an old sceptical problem: the Problem of Other Minds. The Behaviourist attempt to forge a 'logical' connection between inner states and overt behaviour (*see* BEHAVIOURISM), and the Argument from Analogy's attempt to forge an inductive

connection between them, can both be put aside in favour of the quite different hypothetico-deductive connection implied by Sellars's account. Third-person ascriptions of mental states are typically *singular explanatory hypotheses* from which we can draw, in the context of folk psychology as a whole, consequences concerning the subject's observable behaviour. As with explanatory hypotheses in general, these mentalistic hypotheses are believable exactly to the degree that they are successful in allowing us to explain and to anticipate behaviour. In the main, the ascription of mental states to others is explanatorily and predictively successful. So it is reasonable to believe that other humans have mental states. Indeed, on this account the same hypothesis would be similarly reasonable as applied to any creature, human or non-human, so long as its behaviour yielded to the same explanatory strategy.

If folk psychology (hereafter: FP) is a theory, then its concepts must be embedded in a framework of laws, laws at least tacitly appreciated by those adept in its use. In the 60s and 70s, this inference was imposed on everyone by the unquestioned logical empiricist assumption that any theory is a set of sentences or propositions, typically universal in their logical form. Accordingly, some writers set about to 'recover' the laws of FP from our common explanatory practices – from the factors ordinarily appealed to in explanations of human behaviour, and from the ways in which they are occasionally subjected to criticism and defence (Churchland, 1970, 1979).

Any search of this kind quickly turns up hundreds of putative laws, all of which have the familiar ring of the obvious. These range from the very simple to the quite complex. For example:

(1) People who suffer bodily damage generally feel pain.
(2) People who are angry are generally impatient.
(3) People who fear that P generally hope that not-P.
(4) People who desire that P, and believe

that Q is a means to P, and have no overriding desires or preferred strategies, will generally try to bring it about that Q.

These 'laws', and thousands more like them, were claimed to sustain common-sense explanations and predictions in the standard deductive-nomological or 'covering-law' fashion. And the specific content of those laws was claimed to account for the relevance of the explanatory factors standardly appealed to in our daily practice. Examination of the fine logical structure of the many FP laws involving the propositional attitudes also revealed deep parallels with the logical structure of laws in the various mathematical sciences (Churchland, 1979, 1981). Further, the portrait of FP as a network of causal laws dovetailed neatly with the emerging philosophy of mind called FUNCTIONALISM (Putnam, 1960; Fodor 1968; Lewis 1972).

Critics often objected that such 'causal laws' are either strictly speaking false, or else only vacuously true by reason of sheer analyticity or implicit *ceteris paribus* clauses (Wilkes, 1981, 1984; Haldane, 1988). But defenders replied that folk-theoretic laws should not be expected to be anything more than rough-and-ready truths, and that theoretical laws in every science are to some degree qualified by *ceteris paribus* clauses, or restricted in their application to standard or to idealized situations. All told, the developing case for FP's theoretical status was compelling.

CONSEQUENCES OF THE IDEA

These proved alarming, at least to the idea's many critics. First, Sellars' account yields a modern version of the Kantian claim that one can know oneself, in consciousness, only as one represents oneself with one's own concepts. On Sellars' view, one represents oneself with the concepts of FP, a speculative empirical theory. Introspective knowledge is thus denied any special epistemological status: one's spontaneous first-person psychological judgments are no

better (and no worse) than one's spontaneous observation judgments generally (*see* FIRST-PERSON AUTHORITY; INTROSPECTION). They are all hostage to the quality of the background conceptual scheme in which they are framed. This contingency did not trouble Sellars. He was entirely confident that FP was empirically true. But it does trouble some others who are less willing to roll the dice against future experience.

A second consequence is that the traditional mind–body problem emerges as a straightforward scientific question – as a question of how the theoretical framework of FP will turn out to be related to whatever neuropsychological theory might emerge to replace it. If FP reduces smoothly to a materialist successor theory, then the IDENTITY THEORY will be vindicated. If it proves disjunctively so 'reducible', then Functionalism will be vindicated. If it proves irreducible by reason of finding no adequate materialist successor at all, then some form of DUALISM will be vindicated. And if it proves irreducible by reason of failing utterly to map onto its successful materialist successor theory, then a position called Eliminative Materialism will be vindicated (*see An Essay on Mind* section 3.7; ELIMINATIVISM). The successor theory will then displace Jones's antique theory in our social and explanatory practices, and the ontology of FP will go the way of phlogiston, caloric fluid, and the crystal spheres of ancient astronomy.

This eliminative possibility was urged as real fairly early in the discussion (Feyerabend, 1963; Rorty, 1965). Later it was defended as empirically the most likely outcome (Churchland, 1981). The bare possibility of a wholesale rejection of FP is of course a simple consequence of FP's speculative theoretical status. The positive likelihood of its rejection requires more substantial empirical premises. To this end, Churchland cited three major empirical failings of FP.

First, FP fails utterly to explain a considerable variety of central psychological phenomena: mental illness, sleep, creativity, memory, intelligence differences, and the many forms of learning, to cite just a few. A true theory should not have such yawning explanatory gaps. Second, FP has not progressed significantly in at least 2500 years. The Greeks appear to have used essentially the same framework that we deploy. If anything, FP has been in steady retreat during this period, as intentional explanations have been withdrawn from yet one domain after another – from the heavenly bodies, from the wind and the sea, from a plethora of minor gods and spirits, from the visitation of disease, and so forth. FP has not shown the expansion and developmental fertility one expects from a true theory. Last, FP shows no sign of being smoothly integratable with the emerging synthesis of the several physical, chemical, biological, physiological, and neurocomputational sciences (*see* COMPUTATIONAL MODELS). Since active coherence with the rest of what we presume to know is a central measure of credibility for any theory, FP's emerging wallflower status bodes ill for its future.

That FP is fated to be judged empirically false is the most intriguing and alarming of the three major consequences of Sellars's original idea, but clearly it is not a direct consequence of that idea alone. It requires additional premises about the empirical failings of FP. These additional premises can and have been hotly contested (Kitcher, 1984; Dennett, 1981; Horgan and Woodward, 1985). Most of these authors are quite prepared to accept or even to urge the theoretical nature of FP; but they are unanimous in their defence of its empirical integrity and rough truth.

As these authors see it, FP is simply not responsible for explaining most of the puzzling phenomena listed in the preceding paragraph. Those problems are set aside as the burden of some other theory. To the second complaint, it is replied that folk psychology has indeed changed somewhat over the centuries, although its approximate truth has never required of it more than minor adjustments. And to the third complaint there are voiced a number of *tertiam quids* – proposed alternatives to the stark choice, 'either reduce FP, or eliminate it'. Here the varieties of non-reductive materialism – FUNCTIONALISM and ANOMALOUS MONISM, for example – play a prominent role (*see* esp. Fodor, 1975; Dennett, 1981; Davidson, 1970; Clark, 1989).

A more radical and purely a priori response to eliminative materialism dismisses it as simply incoherent, on the grounds that in embracing or stating its case it must presuppose the integrity of the very framework it proposes to eliminate (Baker, 1987; Boghossian, 1990). Consider, for example, the evident conflict between the eliminativist's apparent *belief* that FP is false, and his simultaneous claim that there *are no* beliefs.

A straightforward response concedes the real existence of this and many other conflicts, but denies that they signal anything wrong with the idea that FP might someday be replaced. Such conflicts signal only the depth and far-reaching nature of the conceptual change being proposed. Insofar, they are only to be expected, and they do nothing to mark FP as unreplaceable. Even if current FP were to permit no coherent denial of itself within its own theoretical vocabulary, a new psychological framework need have no such limitation where the denial of FP is concerned. So long as a coherent, comprehensive alternative to FP can be articulated and explored, then no argument a priori can rightly single out FP as uniquely true of cognitive creatures.

In this connection it is worth noting that a similar 'incoherence argument' could be deployed to permit the uncritically conservative defence of any framework for understanding cognition, no matter how inadequate it might be, so long as it happened to enjoy the irrelevant distinction of being currently in use by the people attempting to criticize it. In short, the incoherence argument covertly begs the question in favour of current FP, the very framework being called into question (Churchland, 1981; Devitt, 1990).

This response returns us to the empirical issues raised two paragraphs ago. Whether FP is false and whether it will fail to reduce are empirical issues whose decisive settlement must flow from experimental research and theoretical development, not from any arguments a priori. The empirical jury is still out and there is ample room for reasonable people to disagree.

However, it must be noted that, according to the most fertile theoretical accounts currently under exploration in computational neuroscience (Anderson and Rosenfeld, 1988; Churchland and Sejnowski, 1992), the basic unit of occurrent cognition is apparently not the sentence-like state, but rather the high-dimensional neuronal activation vector (that is, a pattern of excitation levels across a large population of neurons) (see CONNECTIONISM). And the basic unit of cognitive processing is apparently not the inference from sentence to sentence, but rather the synapse-induced transformation of large activation vectors into other such vectors. It is not certain that such accounts of cognition are true, nor that even if they are, FP will fail to find some reduction thereto. But recent science already suggests that Jones' lingua-formal theory – Folk Psychology – fails utterly to capture the basic kinematics and dynamics of human and animal cognition.

CRITICISM AND DEFENCE OF THE IDEA

Many philosophers resist entanglement in these empirical issues and reject the possibility of FP's demise by rejecting the idea that FP is an empirical theory in the first place. Some play down the predictive and explanatory role of FP, and focus attention instead on the many social activities conducted with its vocabulary, such as promising, greeting, joking, threatening, congratulating, insulting, reassuring, inviting, provoking, sympathizing, questioning, demanding, cajoling, sniping, offering, advising, directing, confiding, and so forth (Wilkes, 1981, 1984). On this view, FP is less an empirical theory than an intricate social *practice*, one in which all normal

humans learn to participate (*see also* Putnam, 1988). A supporting consideration is the clearly *normative* character of many of the so-called 'laws' of FP, a feature at odds with the presumably descriptive character of any empirical theory. And if FP is not a theory, then there is no danger that it might be false and hence no question of its being eliminated.

There is much to be said for the positive half of this portrayal of FP, and it is surely counter-productive to resist it. But its negative half betrays a shallow understanding of what theories are and what the command of one typically involves. Since Kuhn's 1962 book, *The Structure of Scientific Revolutions*, it has been evident that learning the theories peculiar to any discipline is not solely or even primarily a matter of learning a set of laws and principles: it is a matter of learning a complex social practice, of entering a specialized community with shared values and expectations, both of the world and of each other. One slowly acquires the right skills of recognition and categorization, the right skills of instrumental and symbolic manipulation, the right sorts of expectations and the right standards of communication and evaluation.

Moreover, during normal science the exemplars of achieved understanding play a strongly normative role, both in setting the standards for further understanding, and even in imposing a standard on nature itself. Such peripheral phenomena as may fail to conform to the current paradigm are regularly counted as deviant, abnormal, pathological, or at least non-ideal.

In sum, the claim that FP is an empirical theory is entirely consistent with – indeed it is explanatory of – the intricate practical life enjoyed by its adepts. It is typical of theoretical adepts that their practical activities, and their practical worlds, are transformed by the relevant acquisition of knowledge. So it is with children who master FP in the normal course of socialization.

As regards immunity to elimination, we should observe that practices can be displaced just as well as theories, and for closely related reasons. Becoming a medieval alchemist, for example, was a matter of learning an inseparable mix of theory and practice. But when modern chemistry began to flower, the medieval practice was displaced almost in its entirety. Current chemical practice would be unintelligible to an alchemist. And given the spectacular power of modern chemistry, no one defends or mourns the passing of the alchemist's comparatively impotent practice.

The positive idea behind the projected displacement of FP is the hope of a comparably superior social practice rooted in a comparably superior account of human cognition and mental activity. If better chemical theory can sustain better chemical practice, then better psychological theory can sustain better social practice. A deeper understanding of the springs of human behaviour may permit a deeper level of moral insight and mutual care. Accordingly, a genuinely worthy scientific replacement for FP need not be 'dehumanizing', as so many fear. More likely it will be just the reverse. Perversity of practice is a chronic feature of our social history. Think of trial by ordeal, purification by fire, absolution by ritual, and rehabilitation by exorcism or by long imprisonment with other sociopaths. Against such dark and impotent practices, any source of light should be welcomed.

The 'criticism from practice' may be easily turned aside, but a different line of criticism cuts more deeply against the original claim of theoretical status for FP. This complaint focuses attention on the large number of laws that presumably must be stored in any FP adept, and on the psychological unreality of the idea that one's running comprehension and anticipation of one's ongoing social situation involves the continual application of appropriate general sentences somehow retrieved from memory, and the repeated performance of complex deductions from these and other premises in order to achieve the desired comprehension and anticipation (Gordon, 1986; Churchland, 1988; Goldman, 1993). People are generally unable to articulate the 'laws' on which their running comprehension is

alleged to rest, and it is in any case mysterious how they could perform such prodigious feats of retrieval and deductive processing in the mere twinklings of time typically involved in our ongoing social commerce.

This wholly genuine difficulty moves Gordon and Goldman to defend a refurbished version of the Argument from Analogy, called the 'Simulation Theory', as an account of our knowledge of other minds. The problems with this venerable approach are familiar. The capacity for knowledge of one's own mind may already presuppose the general knowledge that FP embodies (Strawson, 1958), and a generalization from one's own case may be both logically too feeble and explanatorily too narrow in its scope to account for the full range and robustness of one's general knowledge of human nature (Churchland, 1984). But there is an alternative response to our difficulty about knowing and deploying law-like sentences, one that strikes at the legacy of logical empiricism itself.

The difficulties in claiming FP as an explanatory theory stem not from that claim itself, but rather from the logical empiricist's crudely linguaformal conception of theories as sets of sentences, and his correlative conception of explanation as the deduction of the explanandum from such sentences. The psychological unreality of this picture, noted above in connection with FP explanations, is in fact a chronic defect of the logical empiricist's account in *every* theoretical domain in which cognitive agents are adepts, including the established sciences. This defect, and others, provide compelling grounds for rejecting entirely the classical picture of what theoretical knowledge is and how it is deployed on specific occasions for recognition, explanation, or prediction (Van Fraassen, 1980; Churchland, 1989a, 1989b). This critical assessment coheres with the already existing positive epistemological traditions established by Kuhn in America, by Heidegger on the continent, and more recently by the Connectionists in the field of artificial intelligence and cognitive neurobiology. FP can thus continue to be counted an explanatory theory, but the claim that it has this status needs to be reformulated within a new and independently motivated story of what theoretical knowledge, explanatory understanding, and pragmatic skills really are.

TRANSFORMATION OF THE IDEA

As sketched in the last section but one, the emerging account of how brains embody information has nothing to do with sentences, or with states that are even remotely sentence-like. A familiar analogy may help introduce this alternative account.

A television screen embodies a sequence of REPRESENTATIONS which are non-sentential in nature, in their syntax as well as their semantics. A specific TV representation has no logical structure: rather, it is a specific pattern of activation or brightness levels across a large population of tiny screen pixels. A human retina embodies a representation in much the same sense: what matters is the *pattern of activations* across the photoreceptors. These two examples are overtly pictorial in their 'semantics', but this is an incidental feature of the examples chosen. Tastes are also coded as a pattern of activations across the several types of gustatory neurons on the tongue, sounds are coded as a pattern of activations across the auditory neurons in the cochlea, and smells are coded as a pattern of activations across the olfactory neurons, but none of these representations is 'pictorial' in the familar two-dimensional spatial sense. And yet such pattern coding – or *vector* coding, as it is commonly called – is extremely powerful. Since each vectorial representation is one permutation of the possible values of its elements, the number of distinct things representable explodes as a power function of the number of available elements. Think how many distinct pictures a TV screen can display, using only 200,000 pixels, and think how many more the retina can embody, using fully 100 million pixels.

The suggestion of the preceding is that the brain's basic mode of occurrent representation is the activation vector across a proprietary population of neurons – retinal neurons, olfactory neurons, auditory neurons, and so forth. Such activation vectors have a virtue beyond their combinatorially explosive powers of representation. They are ideally suited to participate in a powerful mode of *computation*, namely, vector-to-vector *transformation*. An activation pattern across one neural population (e.g. at the retina) can be transformed into a distinct activation pattern (e.g. at the visual cortex) by way of the axonal fibres projecting from the first population to the second, and by way of the millions of carefully tuned synaptic connections that those fibres make with the neurons at the second or target population.

That second population of neurons can project to a third, and those to a fourth, and so on. In this way, a sensory activation pattern can undergo many principled transformations before it finally finds itself, profoundly transformed by the many intervening synaptic encounters, reincarnated as a vector of activations in a population of *motor* neurons, neurons whose immediate effect is to direct the symphony of muscles that produce coherent bodily behaviour appropriate to the original input vector at the sensory periphery. The animal dodges a seen snowball, freezes at the sound of a predator, or moves forward at the smell of food, all as a result of its well-tuned synaptic connections and their repeated transformation of its representational vectors.

Those synaptic connections constitute a second domain of stored information in the brain, a domain beyond the occurrent domain of fleeting neuronal activations. The well-tuned synaptic connections embody all of the creature's general knowledge and *skills*: of interpretation, of recognition, of anticipation, and of coherent, interactive behaviour. Here also is where *learning* enters the picture. Learning is not a matter of assembling a vast mass of sentences, as on the classical account. Instead, learning is a matter of configuring the trillions of synaptic connections between neurons so that incoming sensory vectors are automatically and almost instanta-neously transformed into appropriate 'pro-totype' vectors at the higher populations of cortical neurons. Such prototype vectors constitute the brain's learned perceptual and explanatory categories. These proto-types typically involve more information than is strictly present in the sensory input on any given occasion, and they thus con-stitute ampliative interpretations of that input, interpretations that place the input into an antecedently prepared context and fund expectations of features so far unper-ceived.

Further transformations produce further activation vectors or vector sequences in downstream neuronal populations, and these lead quite quickly to appropriate motor responses, since activation vectors are also an ideal means to direct and co-ordinate large populations of muscles. All of this happens in milliseconds because the relevant transformations are achieved by massively parallel processing: the many ele-ments in any input pattern go through the matrix of synaptic connections simulta-neously.

This brief sketch indicates how neuro-computational ideas suggest a unified account of perceptual recognition, explana-tory understanding, prediction, and motor control – an account untroubled by problems of retrieval or speed of processing. The motivation for this account derives primarily from its apparent success in accounting for the functional significance of the brain's microstructure, and the striking cognitive behaviours displayed by artificial neural networks. A secondary motive derives from the illumination it brings to traditional issues in epistemology and the philosophy of science. To learn a theoretical framework is to configure one's synaptic connections in such a fashion as to parti-tion the space of possible neuronal activa-tion patterns into a system or hierarchy of prototypes. And to achieve explanatory understanding of an event is to have activated an appropriate prototype vector from the waiting hierarchy (Churchland, 1989b).

Finally, a much smaller motive derives from the relief this view provides to our earlier difficulty with the theoretical status of FP. No longer need FP labour under its archaic portrayal as a set of universally quantified sentences, and no longer need its functions be falsely cast in terms of laborious deductions. The claim that FP is a corrigible theory need not be hobbled by its initial logical positivist dress. Instead, we can claim that FP, like any other theory, is a family of learned vectorial pro-totypes, prototypes that sustain recognition of current reality, anticipation of future reality, and manipulation of ongoing reality.

As the heroic myth of Jones underscores, FP does indeed portray human cognition in terms of overtly sentential prototypes, viz. in terms of the many propositional attitudes. But there is no reason why it must be *correct* in so representing our cognition, nor in representing itself in particular. Perhaps the internal kinematics and dynamics of human and animal cognition is not at all like the sentential dance portrayed in FP. This recalls the position of eliminative materialism discussed earlier. Perhaps we harbour instead a kinematics of activation patterns and a dynamics of vector-to-vector transformations driven by learned config-urations of synaptic connections. Evidently it is not inconceivable that FP might someday be challenged by a better account of human nature. Evidently the process is already underway. Jones would surely approve.

See also CONCEPTS; CONTENT; COGNITIVE PSYCHOLOGY; FODOR; INTENTIONALITY; LANGUAGE OF THOUGHT; LEWIS; PROPOSI-TIONAL ATTITUDES; PSYCHOLOGY AND PHILOSOPHY; REASONS AND CAUSES; STAL-NAKER; THOUGHT; THOUGHT AND LAN-GUAGE.

BIBLIOGRAPHY

Anderson, J.A., and Rosenfeld, E., eds. 1988. *Neurocomputing: Foundations of Research.* Cambridge, MA.: MIT Press.

315

Baker, L.R. 1987. *Saving Belief*. Princeton University Press.

Boghossian, P. 1990. The status of content. *Philosophical Review*, 99, 157–84.

Clark, A. 1989. *Microcognition*. Cambridge, MA.: MIT Press.

Churchland, P.M. 1970. The logical character of action explanations. *Philosophical Review*. 79: 2.

—— 1979. *Scientific Realism and the Plasticity of Mind*. Cambridge University Press.

—— 1981. Eliminative materialism and the propositional attitudes. *Journal of Philosophy*, LXXVIII: 2.

—— 1984. *Matter and Consciousness*. Cambridge, MA.: MIT Press.

—— 1988. Folk psychology and the explanation of human behaviour. *Proceedings of the Aristotelian Society*, suppl. vol. 62, 209–21. Reprinted in Churchland, P.M. 1989.

—— 1989a. On the nature of theories: A neurocomputational perspective. In *Scientific Theories: Minnesota Studies in the Philosophy of Science, vol. XIV*, ed. W. Savage. Minneapolis: University of Minnesota Press.

—— 1989b. On the nature of explanation: A PDP approach. In Churchland, P.M. 1989.

—— 1989c. *A Neurocomputational Perspective*. Cambridge, MA.: MIT Press.

Churchland, P.S., and Sejnowski, T. 1992. *The Computational Brain*. Cambridge, MA.: MIT Press.

Davidson, D. 1970. Mental events. In *Experience and Theory*, ed. L. Foster and J. Swanson. Amherst: University of Massachusetts Press.

Dennett, D.C. 1981. Three kinds of intentional psychology. In *Reduction, Time and Reality*, ed. R. Healey. Cambridge University Press. Reprinted in Dennett, D.C., *The Intentional Stance* (Cambridge, MA.: MIT Press, 1987).

Devitt, M. 1990. Transcendentalism about content. *Pacific Philosophical Quarterly*, 71: 4, 247–63.

Feyerabend, P.K. 1963. Materialism and the mind-body problem. *Review of Metaphysics*, 17.

Fodor, J.A. 1968. *Psychological Explanation*. New York: Random House.

Fodor, J.A. 1975. *The Language of Thought*. Cambridge, MA.: MIT Press.

Goldman, A. 1992. The psychology of folk psychology. *Behavioral and Brain Sciences*, 16, 15–28.

Gordon, R. 1986. Folk psychology as simulation. *Mind and Language*, 1: 2.

Grice, H.P. 1957. Meaning. *Philosophical Review*, 66, 377–88.

Haldane, J. 1988. Understanding folk. *Proceedings of the Aristotelian Society*, suppl. vol. 62, 223–54.

Horgan, T., and Woodward, J. 1985. Folk psychology is here to stay. *Philosophical Review* XCIV: 2, 197–225.

Kitcher, P. 1984. In defense of intentional psychology. *Journal of Philosophy*, LXXI: 2, 89–106.

Kuhn, T.S. 1962. *The Structure of Scientific Revolutions*. University of Chicago Press.

Lewis, D. 1972. Psychophysical and Theoretical Identifications. *Australasian Journal of Philosophy* L: 3, 249–58.

Putnam, H. 1960. Minds and Machines. In *Dimensions of Mind*, ed. S. Hook. New York University Press.

Putnam, H. 1988. *Representation and Reality*. Cambridge, MA.: MIT Press.

Rorty, R. 1965. Mind-body identity, privacy, and categories. *Review of Metaphysics*, 1.

Searle, J.R. 1983. *Intentionality: An Essay in the Philosophy of Mind*. Cambridge University Press.

Sellars, W. 1956. Empiricism and the philosophy of mind. In *Minnesota Studies in the Philosophy of Science, Vol 1*, Minneapolis: University of Minnesota Press. Reprinted in Sellars, W. *Science, Perception and Reality* (London: Routledge & Keegan Paul, 1963).

Strawson, P.F. 1958. Persons. In *Concepts, Theories, and the Mind-Body Problem: Minnesota Studies in the Philosophy of Science, Vol. 2*, ed. Minneapolis: University of Minnesota Press.

Wilkes, K. 1981. Functionalism, psychology, and the philosophy of mind. *Philosophical Topics*, 12: 1.

Wilkes, K. 1984. Pragmatics in science and theory in common sense. *Inquiry*, 27: 4.

Van Fraassen, B. 1980. *The Scientific Image*. Oxford University Press.

PAUL M. CHURCHLAND

formal   *see* SYNTAX/SEMANTICS.

functionalism (1)   The functionalist thinks of MENTAL STATES and events as causally mediating between a subject's sensory inputs and that subject's ensuing behaviour. Functionalism itself is the stronger doctrine that *what makes* a mental state the type of state it is – a pain, a smell of violets, a belief that koalas are dangerous – is the functional relations it bears to the subject's perceptual stimuli, behavioural responses, and other mental states.

RECENT HISTORY

(Most of the works to be mentioned without citation are included in Block, 1980; Lycan, 1990; Rosenthal, 1991.)

Twentieth-century functionalism gained its credibility in an indirect way, by being perceived as affording the least objectionable solution to the mind–body problem.

Disaffected from Cartesian DUALISM and from the 'first-person' perspective of introspective psychology, the behaviourists had claimed that there is nothing to the mind but the subject's behaviour and dispositions to behave (*see* BEHAVIOURISM). For example, for Rudolf to be in pain is for Rudolf to be either behaving in a wincing-groaning-and-favouring way or disposed to do so (in that he would so behave were something not keeping him from doing so); it is nothing about Rudolf's putative inner life or any episode taking place within him.

Though behaviourism avoided a number of nasty objections to dualism (notably Descartes' admitted problem of mind–body interaction), some theorists were uneasy; they felt that in its total repudiation of the inner, behaviourism was leaving out something real and important. U. T. Place spoke of an 'intractable residue' of conscious mental items that bear no clear relations to behaviour of any particular sort. And it seems perfectly possible for two people to differ psychologically despite total similarity of their actual and counterfactual beha-

viour, as in a Lockean case of 'inverted spectrum'; for that matter, a creature *might* exhibit all the appropriate stimulus-response relations and lack mentation entirely.

For such reasons, Place and Smart proposed a middle way, the IDENTITY THEORY, which allowed that at least some mental states and events are genuinely inner and genuinely episodic after all; they are not to be identified with outward behaviour or even with hypothetical dispositions to behave. But, contrary to dualism, the episodic mental items are not ghostly or non-physical either. Rather, they are neurophysiological (*see* PAIN). They are identical with states or events occurring in their owners' central nervous systems. To be in pain is, for example, to have one's c-fibres, or possibly a-fibres, firing. A happy synthesis: The dualists were wrong in thinking that mental items are non-physical but right in thinking them inner and episodic; the behaviourists were right in their PHYSICALISM but wrong to repudiate inner mental episodes.

However, PUTNAM (1960) and FODOR (1968) pointed out a presumptuous implication of the identity theory understood as a theory of types or kinds of mental items: that a mental type such as pain has *always and everywhere* the neurophysiological characterization initially assigned to it. For example, if the identity theorist identified pain itself with the firings of c-fibres, it followed that a creature of any species (earthly or science-fiction) could be in pain only if that creature *had* c-fibres and they were firing. But such a constraint on the biology of any being capable of feeling pain is both gratuitous and indefensible; why should we suppose that any organism must be made of the same chemical materials as us in order to have what can be accurately recognized as pain? The identity theorist had overreacted to the behaviourists' difficulties and focused too narrowly on the specifics of biological humans' actual inner states, and in so doing they had fallen into species chauvinism.

Fodor and Putnam advocated the obvious correction: What was important was not its being c-fibres (*per se*) that were firing, but what the c-fibre firings were doing, what their firing contributed to the operation of the organism as a whole. The *role* of the c-fibres could have been performed by any mechanically suitable component; so long as that role was performed, the psychology of the containing organism would have been unaffected. Thus, to be in pain is not *per se* to have c-fibres that are firing, but merely to be in some state or other, of whatever biochemical description, that plays the same functional role as did the firings of c-fibres in the human beings we have investigated. We may continue to maintain that pain 'tokens', individual instances of pain occurring in particular subjects at particular times, are strictly identical with particular neurophysiological states of those subjects at those times, viz. with the states that happen to be playing the appropriate roles; this is the thesis of 'token identity' or 'token physicalism'. But pain itself (the kind, universal or type) can be identified only with something more abstract: the causal or functional role that c-fibre firings share with their potential replacements or surrogates. Mental state-types are identified not with neurophysiological types but with more abstract functional roles, as specified by state-tokens' relations to the organism's inputs, outputs, and other psychological states.

(Terminological note: In this article, the label 'functionalism' is reserved for what Block calls 'psychofunctionalism'; what Block calls 'conceptual functionalism' is not *per se* discussed here' (*see* FUNCTIONALISM (2)). The term was originally applied only to psychofunctionalism; Block has extended it to cover the conceptual analyses of Lewis and Armstrong.)

MACHINE FUNCTIONALISM

Putnam compared mental states to the functional or 'logical' states of a computer: Just as a computer program can be realized or instantiated by any of a number of physically different hardware configurations, so can a psychological 'program' be realized by different organisms of various physiochemical composition, and that is why different physiological states of organisms of different species can realize one and the same mental state-type. Where an identity theorist's type-identification would take the form, 'To be in mental state of type M is to be in the neurophysiological state of type N', Putnam's machine functionalism (as we may call it) has it that to be in M is to be merely in some physiological state or other that plays role R in the relevant computer program (i.e. the program that at a suitable level of abstraction mediates the creature's total outputs given total inputs and so serves as the creature's global psychology). The physiological state 'plays role R' in that it stands in a set of relations to physical inputs, outputs and other inner states that matches one-to-one the abstract input/output/logical-state relations codified in the computer program. (For the beginnings of a formalization of this idea, *see* FUNCTIONALISM (2).)

The functionalist, then, mobilizes three distinct levels of description but applies them all to the same fundamental reality. A physical state-token in someone's brain at a particular time has a neurophysiological description, but may also have a functional description relative to a machine program that the brain happens to be realizing, and it may further have a mental description if some everyday mental state is correctly type-identified with the functional category it exemplifies. And so there is after all a sense in which 'the mental' is distinct from 'the physical': Though presumably there are no non-physical substances or stuffs, and every mental token is itself entirely physical, mental characterization is not physical characterization, and the property of being a pain is not simply the property of being such-and-such a neural firing. Moreover, unlike behaviourism and the identity theory, functionalism does not strictly entail that minds are physical; it might be true of non-physical minds, so long as those minds realized the relevant programs.

COGNITIVE PSYCHOLOGY, ARTIFICIAL INTELLIGENCE, AND THE COMPUTER MODEL OF THE MIND

In a not accidentally similar vein, behaviourism in psychology has almost entirely given way to 'cognitivism'. Cognitivism is roughly the view that (i) psychologists may and must advert to inner states and episodes in explaining behaviour, so long as the states and episodes are construed throughout as physical, and (ii) human beings and other psychological organisms are best viewed as in some sense *information-processing* systems. As COGNITIVE PSYCHOLOGY sets the agenda, its questions take the form, 'How does this organism receive information through its sense-organs, process the information, store it, and then mobilize it in such a way as to result in intelligent behaviour?' The working language of cognitive psychology is highly congenial to the functionalist, for cognitivism thinks of human beings as systems of interconnected functional components, interacting with each other in an efficient and productive way.

Meanwhile, researchers in computer science have pursued fruitful research programmes based on the idea of intelligent behaviour as the output of skilful information-processing given input. ARTIFICIAL INTELLIGENCE (AI) is, roughly, the project of getting computing machines to perform tasks that would usually be taken to demand human intelligence and judgment; and computers have achieved some modest successes. But a computer *just is* a machine that receives, interprets, processes, stores, manipulates and uses information, and AI researchers think of it in just that way as they try to program intelligent behaviour; an AI problem takes the form, 'Given that the machine sees this as input, what must it already know and what must it accordingly do with that input in order to be able to . . . [recognize, identify, sort, put together, predict, tell us, etc.] . . . ? And how, then, can we start it off knowing that and get it to do those things?' So we may reasonably attribute such success as AI has had to self-conscious reliance on the information-processing paradigm. And that in turn mutually encourages the functionalist idea that *human* intelligence and cognition generally are matters of computational information-processing (*see* COMPUTATIONAL MODELS).

TELEOLOGICAL FUNCTIONALISM

Machine functionalism supposed that human brains may be described at each of three levels, the first two scientific and the third familiar to common sense: the biological, specifically neurophysiological; the machine-program or computational; and the everyday mental or folk-psychological (*see* FOLK PSYCHOLOGY). Psychologists would explain behaviour, characterized in everyday terms, by reference to stimuli and to intervening mental states such as beliefs and desires, type-identifying the mental states with functional or computational states as they went. Such explanations would themselves presuppose nothing about neuroanatomy, since the relevant psychological/computational generalizations would hold regardless of what particular biochemistry might happen to be realizing the abstract program in question.

Machine functionalism as described has more recently been challenged on each of a number of points, that together motivate a specifically teleological notion of 'function' (Sober speaks aptly of 'putting the function back into Functionalism').

(1) The machine functionalist still conceived psychological *explanation* in the Positivists' terms of subsumption of data under wider and wider universal laws. But FODOR, DENNETT and Cummins (1983) have defended a competing picture of psychological explanation, according to which behavioural data are to be seen as manifestations of subjects' psychological capacities, and those capacities are to be explained by understanding the subjects as systems of interconnected components. Each component is a 'homunculus', in that it is identified by reference to the function it performs, and the various homuncular components

319

cooperate with each other in such a way as to produce overall behavioural responses to stimuli. The 'homunculi' are themselves broken down into subcomponents whose functions and interactions are similarly used to explain the capacities of the subsystems they compose, and so again and again until the sub-sub- . . . components are seen to be neuroanatomical structures. (An automobile works – locomotes – by having a fuel reservoir, a fuel line, a carburettor, a combustion chamber, an ignition system, a transmission, and wheels that turn. If one wants to know how the carburettor works, one will be told what its parts are and how they work together to infuse oxygen into fuel, and so on.) Nothing in this pattern of explanation corresponds to the subsumption of data under wider and wider universal generalizations, or to the Positivists' Deductive-Nomological model of explanation as formally valid derivation from such generalizations.

(2) The machine functionalist treated functional 'realization', the relation between an individual physical organism and the abstract program it was said to instantiate, as a simple matter of one-to-one correspondence between the organism's repertoire of physical stimuli, structural states and behaviour, on the one hand, and the program's defining input/state/output function on the other. But this criterion of realization was seen to be too liberal, since virtually anything bears a one-to-one correlation of some sort to virtually anything else; 'realization' in the sense of mere one-to-one correspondence is far too easily come by (Block, 1978; Lycan, 1987, ch. 3); for example, the profusion of microscopic events occurring in a sunlit pond (convection currents, biotic activity, or just molecular motion) *undoubtedly* yield some one-to-one correspondence or other to any psychology you like, but this should not establish that the pond is, or has, a mind. Some theorists have proposed to remedy this defect by imposing a teleological requirement on realization: a physical state of an organism will count as realizing such-and-such a functional description only if the organism has

genuine organic integrity and the state plays its functional role properly *for* the organism, in the teleological sense of 'for' and in the teleological sense of 'function' (*see* DRETSKE; TELEOLOGY). The state must do what it does as a matter of, so to speak, its biological purpose. This rules out our pond, since the pond is not a single organism having convection currents or molecular motions as organs. (Machine functionalism took 'function' in its spare mathematical sense rather than in a genuinely *functional* sense. NB, as used here, the term 'machine functionalism' is tied to the original libertine conception of 'realizing'; so to impose a teleological restriction is to abandon machine functionalism.)

(3) Of the machine functionalist's three levels of description, one is commonsensical and two are scientific, so we are offered a two-levelled picture of human psychobiology. But that picture is unbiological in the extreme. Neither living things nor even computers themselves are split into a purely 'structural' level of biological/physiochemical description and any one 'abstract' computational level of machine/psychological description. Rather, they are all hierarchically organized at many levels, each level 'functional' with respect to those beneath it but 'structural' or concrete as it realizes those levels above it. This relativity of the 'functional'/'structural' or 'software'/ 'hardware' distinction to one's chosen level of organization has repercussions for functionalist solutions to problems in the philosophy of mind (Lycan, 1987, ch. 5), and for current controversies surrounding CONNECTIONISM and neural modelling.

(4) Millikan, Van Gulick, Fodor, Dretske and others have argued powerfully that teleology must enter into any adequate analysis of the INTENTIONALITY or aboutness of mental states such as beliefs and desires, by reference to the states' psychobiological functions. If teleology is needed to explicate intentionality and machine functionalism affords no teleology, then machine functionalism is not adequate to explicate intentionality.

It would have been nice to stick with

machine functionalism, for the teleologizing of functionalism comes at a price. Talk of teleology and biological function seems to presuppose that biological and other 'structural'/states of physical systems really have functions in the teleological sense. The latter claim is controversial, to say the least. And if it is not literally true, then mental states cannot be type-identified with teleological states. But fortunately for the teleological functionalist, there is now a small but vigorous industry whose purpose is to explicate biological teleology in naturalistic terms, typically in terms of aetiology.

PROBLEMS WITH INTENTIONALITY

Functionalism, and cognitive psychology considered as a complete theory of human thought, inherit some of the same difficulties that earlier beset behaviourism and the identity theory. These remaining obstacles fall into two main categories: intentionality problems and QUALIA problems.

PROPOSITIONAL ATTITUDES such as beliefs and desires are directed upon states of affairs which may or may not actually obtain (e.g. that the Republican candidate will win), and are *about* individuals who may or may not exist (e.g. King Arthur). Franz Brentano raised the question of how any purely physical entity or state could have the property of being 'directed upon' or about a non-existent state of affairs or object; that is not the sort of feature that ordinary, purely physical objects can have.

The standard functionalist reply is that propositional attitudes have Brentano's feature because the internal physical states and events that realize them *represent* actual or possible states of affairs. (*See* REPRESENTATION, LANGUAGE OF THOUGHT.) What they represent (*see* CONTENT) is determined at least in part by their functional roles.

There are two difficulties. One is that of saying exactly *how* a physical item's representational content is determined; in virtue of what does a neurophysiological state represent precisely *that the Republican candidate will win?* An answer to that general question is what Fodor has called a 'psychosemantics', and several attempts have been made.

The second difficulty is that ordinary propositional attitude contents do not SUPERVENE on the states of their subjects' nervous systems, but are underdetermined by even the total state of that subject's head. Putnam's (1975) TWIN EARTH and indexical examples show that, surprising as it may seem, two human beings could be molecule-for-molecule alike and still differ in their beliefs and desires, depending on various factors in their spatial and historical environments. Thus we can distinguish between 'narrow' properties, those that are determined by a subject's intrinsic physical composition, and 'wide' properties, those that are not so determined, and representational contents are wide (*see* EXTERNALISM/INTERNALISM). Yet functional roles are, ostensibly, narrow; how, then, can propositional attitudes be type-identified with functional roles?

Functionalists have responded in either of two ways: One is to understand 'function' widely as well, specifying functional roles historically and/or by reference to features of the subject's actual environment. The other is simply to abandon functionalism as an account of content in particular, giving some alternative psychosemantics for propositional attitudes, but preserving functionalism in regard to attitude types (thus what makes a state *a desire* that P is its functional role, even if something else makes the state a desire *that P*). For more on these issues, *see* FUNCTIONALISM (2).

PROBLEMS WITH QUALIA

The 'quale' of a mental state or event (particularly a SENSATION) is that state or event's *feel*, its introspectible 'phenomenal character'. Many philosophers have objected that neither functionalist metaphysics nor any of the allied doctrines aforementioned can explain, illuminate or even tolerate the notion of *what it feels like* to be in a mental state of such-and-such a sort. Yet, say these philosophers, the feels are quintessentially mental – it is the feels that make the mental states the mental states they are. Something, therefore, must be drastically wrong with functionalism.

There is no *single* problem of qualia (cf. CONSCIOUSNESS); there are a number of quite distinct objections that have been brought against functionalism (some of them apply to materialism generally). Space permits mention of just three.

(1) Block (1978) and others have urged various counterexample cases against functionalism – examples in which some entity seems to realize the right program but lacks one of mentality's crucial qualitative aspects. (Typically the 'entity' is a group, such as the entire population of China acting according to an elaborate set of instructions, but our pond would also serve. Neither, it seems, would be *feeling* anything on its own.) Predictably, functionalists have rejoined by arguing, for each example, either that the proposed entity does not in fact succeed in realizing the right program (e.g. because the requisite teleology is lacking) or that there is no good reason for denying that the entity does have the relevant qualitative states.

(2) Gunderson and Nagel have worried over first-person/third-person asymmetries and the perspectivalness or subjective point-of-view-iness of consciousness. I can know *what it is like to have* such-and-such a sensation only if I have had that sensation myself; no amount of objective, third-person scientific information would suffice. In reply, functionalists have offered analyses of 'perspectivalness', complete with accounts of 'what it is like' to have a sensation, that make those things compatible with functionalism. Nagel and Jackson have argued, further, for the existence of a special, intrinsically perspectival kind of *fact*, the fact of 'what it is like', which intractably and in principle cannot be captured or explained by physical science. Functionalists have responded that the arguments commit a LEIBNIZ'S-LAW fallacy (that of applying the law in an intensional context); some have added that in any case, to 'know what it is

like' is merely to have an ability, and involves no fact of any sort.

(3) Levine and others have complained that no functionalist theory can *explain why* such-and-such a sensation feels to its subject in just the way it does. The question, 'But why do such-and-such functional goings-on constitute or produce a sensation like *this?*' seems always open. Some functionalists contend that a functionalist psychology could indeed explain that; others try to show why it need not, consistently with the truth of functionalism.

In sum, functionalism's besetting difficulties are significant but not daunting. Functionalism is not merely alive and well, but still and rightly the reigning paradigm in philosophy of mind.

See also CONCEPTUAL ROLE SEMANTICS; *An Essay on Mind* section 3.6.3; LEWIS; TURING.

BIBLIOGRAPHY

Block, N.J. 1978. Troubles with functionalism. In *Perception and Cognition: Minnesota Studies in the Philosophy of Science, Vol. 9*, ed. W. Savage. Minneapolis: University of Minnesota Press. Excerpts reprinted in Lycan, 1990.

Block, N.J., ed. 1980. *Readings in Philosophy of Psychology, Vol. 1*. Cambridge, MA.: Harvard University Press.

Cummins, R. 1983. *The Nature of Psychological Explanation*. Cambridge, MA.: MIT Press/ Bradford Books.

Fodor, J.A. 1968. *Psychological Explanation*. New York: Random House.

Lycan, W. 1987. *Consciousness*. Cambridge, MA.: MIT Press/Bradford Books.

Lycan, W.G., ed. 1990. *Mind and Cognition: A Reader*. Oxford: Basil Blackwell.

Putnam, H. 1960. Minds and machines. In *Dimensions of Mind*, ed. S. Hook. New York: Collier Books.

Putnam, H. 1975. The meaning of 'meaning'. In *Language, Mind and Knowledge: Minnesota Studies in the Philosophy of Science, Vol. 7*, ed. K. Gunderson. Minneapolis: University of Minnesota Press.

Rosenthal, D., ed. 1991. *The Nature of Mind*. Oxford University Press.

Shoemaker, S. 1981. Some varieties of functionalism. *Philosophical Topics*, 12, 93–120.

WILLIAM G. LYCAN

functionalism (2) Functionalism is one of the great 'isms' that have been offered as solutions to the mind/body problem. The cluster of questions that all of these 'isms' promise to answer can be expressed as: What is the ultimate nature of the mental? At the most general level, what makes a mental state mental? At the more specific level that has been the focus in recent years: What do thoughts have in common in virtue of which they are thoughts? That is, what makes a thought a thought? What makes a pain a pain? Cartesian DUALISM said the ultimate nature of the mental was to be found in a special mental substance. BEHAVIOURISM identified mental states with behavioural dispositions; PHYSICALISM in its most influential version identifies mental states with brain states (*see* IDENTITY THEORY). Functionalism says that mental states are constituted by their causal relations to one another and to sensory inputs and behavioural outputs. Functionalism is one of the major theoretical developments of twentieth-century analytic philosophy, and provides the conceptual underpinnings of much work in cognitive science.

A range of papers about functionalism are to be found in five anthologies, Block (1980), Lycan (1990), Rosenthal (1991), Beakley and Ludlow (1992) and Goldman (1993). (I will refer to these without dates henceforth.) Expositions of one or another version of functionalism are to be found in the Introduction and the papers by Block, Lewis and Putnam in Part III of Block, sections II and VII of Lycan, Section IIIB of Rosenthal, Part I of Beakley and Ludlow and Part III of Goldman. See also Chapter 12 of Shoemaker (1984) and Schiffer (1987).

Functionalism has three distinct sources. First, PUTNAM and FODOR saw mental states in terms of an empirical computational theory of the mind. Second, Smart's 'topic neutral' analyses led Armstrong and Lewis to a functionalist analysis of mental concepts. Third, Wittgenstein's idea of meaning as use led to a version of functionalism as a theory of meaning, further developed by Sellars and later Harman. (See FUNCTIONALISM (1) in this book and the introduction to the functionalism section in Block (1980)).

One motivation behind functionalism can be appreciated by attention to artefact concepts like *carburettor* and biological concepts like *kidney*. What it is for something to be a carburettor is for it to mix fuel and air in an internal combustion engine – *carburettor* is a functional concept. In the case of *kidney*, the scientific concept is functional – defined in terms of a role in filtering the blood and maintaining certain chemical balances.

The kind of function relevant to the mind can be introduced via the parity-detecting automaton illustrated in the figure below, which tells us whether it has seen an odd or even number of '1's (though it counts zero as even). This automaton has two states, S_1 and S_2; two inputs, '1' and blank (–); and two outputs, it utters either the word 'Odd' or 'Even'. The table describes two functions, one from input and state to output, and another from input and state to next state. Each square encodes two conditionals specifying the output and next state given both the current state and input. For example, the top-left box yields the following two conditionals. (1) If the machine starts in S_1

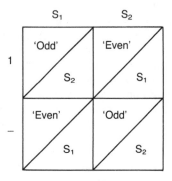

Figure 1.

and sees a '1', it says 'Odd' (indicating that it has seen an odd number of '1's) and (2) if the machine starts in S_1 and sees a '1', it goes to S_2. The entire machine is specified by eight such conditionals.

Now suppose we ask the question: 'What is S_1?' The answer is that the nature of S_1 is entirely relational, and entirely captured by the table. The nature of S_1 is given by the 8 conditionals, including that when in S_1 and having seen a '1' the machine goes into another state which is characterizable along the same lines as S_1.

Suppose we wanted to give an explicit characterization of 'S_1'. We could do it as follows.

Being in S_1 = being in the first of two states that are related to one another and to inputs and outputs as follows: being in one of the states and getting a '1' input results in going into the second state and emitting 'Odd'; being in the second of the two states and getting a '1' input results in going into the first and emitting 'Even'; and so on, for the remaining half of the table.

Here is a variant on this characterization in which the quantification is more explicit:

Being in S_1 = Being an x such that $\exists$ P $\exists$ Q[If x is in P and gets a '1' input, then it goes into Q and emits 'Odd'; if x is in Q and gets a '1' input it goes into P and emits 'Even'; and so on for the remaining half of the table; and x is in P] (Note: read '$\exists$ P' as *There is a property* P.)

This illustration can be used to make a number of points. (1) According to functionalism, the nature of a mental state is just like the nature of an automaton state: constituted by its relations to other states and to inputs and outputs. All there is to S_1 is having some property which, together with a '1' input results in a certain output and a certain state transition, etc. According to functionalism, all there is to being in pain is having some property that disposes you to say 'ouch', wonder whether you are ill, etc. (2) Because mental states are like automaton states in this regard, the illus-

trated method for defining automaton states is supposed to work for mental states as well. Mental states can be totally characterized in terms that involve only logico-mathematical language and terms for input signals and behavioural outputs. Thus functionalism satisfies one of the desiderata of behaviourism, characterizing the mental in entirely non-mental language. (3) S_1 is a second-order state in that it consists in having *other* properties, say mechanical or hydraulic or electronic properties that have certain relations to one another. These other properties, the ones quantified over in the definitions just given, are said to be the *realizations* of the functional properties. So, although functionalism characterizes the mental in non-mental terms, it does so only by quantifying over realizations of mental states, which would not have delighted behaviourists. (4) One functional state can be realized in different ways. For example, an actual metal and plastic machine satisfying the machine table might be made of gears, wheels, pulleys and the like, in which case the realization of S_1 would be a mechanical state; or the realization of S_1 might be an electronic state, and so forth. (5) Just as one functional state can be realized in different ways, one physical state can realize different functional states in different machines. This could happen, for example, if a single type of transistor were used to do different things in different machines. (6) Since S_1 can be realized in many ways, a claim that S_1 *is* a mechanical state would be false (at least arguably), as would a claim that S_1 is an electronic state. For this reason, there is a strong case that functionalism shows physicalism is false; if a creature without a brain can think, thinking can't be a brain state. (But see the section on functionalism and physicalism below.)

The notion of a realization deserves further discussion. In the early days of functionalism, a first-order property was often said to realize a functional property in virtue of a 1–1 correspondence between the two realms of properties. But such a definition of realization produces far too many realizations. Suppose, for example, that at t_1

we shout 'one' at a bucket of water, and then at t_2 we shout 'one' again. We can regard the bucket as a parity-detecting automaton by pairing the physical configuration of the bucket at t_1 with S_1 and the heat emitted or absorbed by the bucket at t_1 with 'Odd'; by pairing the physical configuration of the bucket at t_2 with S_2 and the heat exchanged with the environment at t_2 with 'Even'; and so on. What is left out by the *post hoc* correlation way of thinking of realization is that a true realization must satisfy the *counterfactuals* mentioned in the table. To be a realization of S_1, it is not enough to lead to a certain output and state given that the input is a '1'; it is also required that *had the input been a '0', the S_1 realization would have led to the other output and state*. Satisfaction of the relevant counterfactuals is built into the notion of realization mentioned in (3) above. (*See* Lycan, 1987.)

Suppose we have a theory of mental states that specifies all the causal relations among the states, sensory inputs and behavioural outputs. Focusing on pain as a sample mental state, it might say, among other things, that sitting on a tack causes pain and that pain causes anxiety and saying 'ouch'. Agreeing for the sake of the example, to go along with this moronic theory, functionalism would then say that we could define 'pain' as follows: being in pain = being in the first of two states, the first of which is caused by sitting on tacks, and which in turn causes the other state and emitting 'ouch'. More symbolicly

Being in pain = Being an x such that $\exists$ P $\exists$ Q[sitting on a tack causes P and P causes both Q and emitting 'ouch' and x is in P]

More generally, if T is a psychological theory with n mental terms of which the seventeenth is 'pain', we can define 'pain' relative to T as follows (the 'F_1' ... 'F_n' are variables that replace the n mental terms):

Being in pain = Being an x such that $\exists$ F_1 ... F_n[T(F_1 ... F_n) & x is in F_{17}]

(The existentially quantified part of the right-hand side before the '&' is the Ramsey sentence of the theory T.) In this way, functionalism characterizes the mental in nonmental terms, in terms that involve quantification over realizations of mental states but no explicit mention of them; thus functionalism characterizes the mental in terms of structures that are tacked down to reality only at the inputs and outputs.

The psychological theory T just mentioned can be either an empirical psychological theory or else a commonsense 'folk' theory, and the resulting functionalisms are very different. In the former case, which I named *psychofunctionalism*, the functional definitions are supposed to fix the extensions of mental terms. In the latter case, *conceptual functionalism*, the functional definitions are aimed at capturing our ordinary mental concepts. (This distinction shows an ambiguity in the original question of what the ultimate nature of the mental is – another ambiguity will be mentioned in the next section.) The idea of psychofunctionalism is that the scientific nature of the mental consists not in anything biological, but in something 'organizational', analogous to computational structure. Conceptual functionalism, by contrast, can be thought of as a development of logical behaviourism. Logical behaviourists thought that pain was a disposition to *pain behaviour*. But as Geach and Chisholm pointed out, what counts as pain behaviour depends on the agent's beliefs and desires. Conceptual functionalists avoid this problem by defining each mental state in terms of its contribution to dispositions to behave – and have other mental states. (See FUNCTIONALISM (1); the introduction to the functionalism section of Block, 1980, vol. 1.)

FUNCTIONALISM AND PHYSICALISM

Theories of the mind prior to functionalism have been concerned both with (1) *what there is* and (2) with what gives each type of mental state its own identity, for example what pains have in common in virtue of which they are pains. We might say

325

(stretching these terms a bit) that (1) is a matter of ONTOLOGY and (2) of metaphysics. Here are the ontological claims: dualism told us that there are both mental and physical substances, whereas behaviourism and physicalism are monistic, claiming that there are only physical substances. Here are the metaphysical claims: behaviourism told us that what pains, for example have in common in virtue of which they are pains is something behavioural; dualism gave a non-physical answer to this question, and physicalism gives a physical answer to this question.

Turning now to functionalism, *it answers the metaphysical question without answering the ontological question.* Functionalism tells us that what pains have in common – what makes them pains – is their function; but functionalism does not tell us whether the beings that have pains have any non-physical parts. This point can be seen in terms of the automaton described above. In order to be an automaton of the type described, an actual concrete machine need only have states related to one another and to inputs and outputs in the way described. The machine description does not tell us how the machine works or what it is made of, and in particular it does not rule out a machine that is operated by an immaterial soul, so long as the soul is willing to operate in the deterministic manner specified in the table. (*See* the papers by Putnam and by Fodor in Block, 1980, vol. 1.).

In thinking about the relation between functionalism and physicalism, it is useful to distinguish two categories of physicalist theses (*see* PHYSICALISM). One version of physicalism competes with functionalism, making a metaphysical claim about the physical nature of mental state properties or types (and is thus often called 'type' physicalism). As mentioned above, on one point of view, functionalism shows that type physicalism is false. (Another point of view, that of LEWIS will be mentioned later.)

However, there are more modest physicalisms whose thrusts are ontological rather than metaphysical. Such physicalistic claims are not at all incompatible with functionalism. Consider, for example, a physicalism that says that every actual thing is made up entirely of particles of the sort that compose inorganic matter. In this sense of physicalism, most functionalists have been physicalists. Further, functionalism can be modified in a physicalistic direction, for example, by requiring that all properties quantified over in a functional definition be physical properties. Type physicalism is often contrasted with *token* physicalism. (The word 'teeth' in this sentence has five letter tokens of three letter types.) Token physicalism says that each pain, for example, is a physical state, but token physicalism allows that there may be nothing physical that all pains share, nothing physical that makes a pain a pain.

It is a peculiarity of the literature on functionalism and physicalism that while some functionalists say functionalism shows physicalism is false (*see* the papers by Putnam, Fodor, and Block and Fodor in Block, 1980), others say functionalism shows physicalism is true. (*See* LEWIS and the papers by Lewis and by Armstrong in Block, 1980, and Rosenthal, 1991.) In Lewis's case, the issue is partly terminological. Lewis is a conceptual functionalist about *having pain*. 'Having pain' on Lewis's regimentation, could be said to be a rigid designator of a functional property. (A rigid designator names the same thing in each POSSIBLE WORLD. 'The colour of the sky' is non-rigid, since it names red in worlds in which the sky is red. 'Blue' is rigid, since it names blue even in worlds in which the sky is red.) 'Pain', by contrast, is a non-rigid designator conceptually equivalent to a definite description of the form 'the state with such and such a causal role'. The referent of this phrase in us, Lewis holds, is a certain brain state, though the referent of this phrase in a robot might be a circuit state, and the referent in an angel would be a non-physical state. Similarly, 'the winning number' picks out '17' in one lottery and '596' in another. So Lewis is a functionalist (indeed a conceptual functionalist) about having pain. In terms of the metaphysical issue described above – what do pains have in common in virtue of which they are pains – Lewis is a functionalist, not a physicalist. What my pains and the robot's pains share is a causal role, not anything physical. Just as there is no numerical similarity between 17 and 596 relevant to their being winning numbers, there is no physical similarity between human and Martian pain that makes them pains. And there is no physical similarity of any kind between human pains and angel pains. However, on the issue of the scientific nature of pain, Lewis is a physicalist. What is in common to human and Martian pain in his view is something conceptual, not something scientific.

The claim that functionalism shows type physicalism is false has received another (related) type of challenge repeatedly over the years, most effectively by Kim (1992). Kim notes that psychofunctionalists have taken the functional level to provide an autonomous level of description that is the right level for characterizing and explaining the mental because it lumps together all the different instantiations of the same mental structure, those made of silicon with those made of protoplasm. Kim argues that if functionalism is true, then mental terms are like 'jade' in not denoting natural kinds. A natural kind is nomic (suitable for framing laws) and projectible (see NATURAL KINDS). Jadeite and nephrite are natural kinds, but jade is not. If functionalism is true, then the natural kinds in the realm of the mental are physical rather than psychological – and thus as far as the scientific nature of the mental is concerned, physicalism is true, functionalism being a theory of mental *concepts* rather than mental kinds. So Kim ends up as a functionalist, but, importantly, a conceptual functionalist, not a psychofunctionalist. The upshot, if Kim and Lewis are right, is that the correct story about mental concepts is functional, but the correct story about the scientific nature of the mental is physicalistic.

The psychofunctionalist reply should be that the provinces of psychology and other special sciences are physically disparate entities that resemble one another functionally because they have been subjected to forces like evolution and conscious design. These forces have *created* a level of description – characterized by common properties – genuine natural kinds. Consider economics – lawlike generalizations about capital formation, inflation and the like are to a large degree independent of the physical nature of the economy. For example, one set of economic laws can govern systems in which the money is very different physically: gold, paper, beads, etc. Further, one set of economic laws could be expected to govern humans as well as silicon-based robots and Martians, if they approximate to rationality in roughly the way we do. But the existence of a level of economic science above the physical level presupposes aspects of a similar level for psychology. As with many areas of philosophy, the nub of the conflict between physicalists and functionalists comes down to a question of how sciences work.

White (1986) has further developed Smart's famous argument for topic-neutral analyses, the upshot of which is that anyone who accepts any empirical identity thesis, be it functionalist or physicalist, should also be a conceptual functionalist. Suppose that we accept an empirical identity thesis, say, that pain = state S_{17} where S_{17} can be either a psychofunctional state or a brain state. Since this is not an a priori truth (ex hypothesi), the terms flanking the '=' sign must pick out this common referent via different modes of presentation of the referent, in the manner of 'the evening star = the morning star'. After all, if the identity theorist believes both that he is in pain and that he is in S_{17}, these are distinct beliefs, as is shown by the fact that he could have believed that he was in pain but not in S_{17}. So the two terms must pick out the same entity in virtue of different properties of it. There is no mystery about how 'S_{17}' picks out the referent, but what is the mode of presentation associated with 'pain'? Presumably, this will be some mental property, say the phenomenal aspect of pain (see CONCEPTS; PROPERTY). But the identity theorist will have to see this phenomenal aspect as itself something functional or physical, so if he resists conceptual functionalism, he will suppose that there is *another* empirical identity, e.g. the phenomenal aspect = S_{134}. But now we are back where we started, for this identity raises the same issue as the original one. The only plausible way to escape an infinite regress, the argument concludes, is to accept an a priori identity between some mental property and a functional property, for only in the case of an a priori identity can the modes of presentation of terms flanking the identity sign be the same, and no physicalist or psychofunctionalist (or dualist) identities are plausibly a priori. Indeed, the only plausibly a priori identity is a functionalist conceptual analysis, so any identity theorist should be a conceptual functionalist.

One way of resisting this conclusion would be to adopt a holistic picture of how words get their reference (*see* HOLISM). The holistic psychofunctionalist can suggest that we arrive at psychofunctional identities in choosing among theoretical perspectives on the basis of evidence. If we want to know what the meanings of mental terms are, they should be given in terms of the entire theory, and those 'definitions' will not be happily classifiable as a priori or empirical. Another way out (Loar, 1990) is to regard the relation between 'pain' and its referent as unmediated by any mode of presentation, explaining how one can believe he is in pain without being in S_{17} by the different functional roles of 'pain' and 'S_{17}'. The idea is that to the extent that there is anything associated with 'pain' in the category of sense, it is a functional role, but this does not require any descriptional element in the background, taking 'pain' to its referent via a mediating property, so the Smart–White argument gets no purchase.

This sounds plausible as far as it goes, but it does not go far enough, for one wants to know more about the relation between 'pain' and its referent. Is 'pain' supposed to be a *name* for, say, a brain state? Loar supplies more detail, arguing that the concept of a phenomenal property is a recognitional disposition that is 'triggered' by its referent, a physical or functional state. But couldn't

a physical or functional state trigger a recognitional reaction without any phenomenal feel, in the manner of blindsight? To avoid such a possibility, it would seem that Loar would have to bring in a mode of presentation of the reference, a phenomenal mode, and that would get him back in the clutches of the Smart–White argument (*see* QUALIA).

FUNCTIONALISM AND PROPOSITIONAL ATTITUDES

The discussion of functional characterization given above assumes a psychological theory with a finite number of mental state terms. In the case of monadic states like pain, the sensation of red, etc., it does seem a theoretical option to simply list the states and their relations to other states, inputs and outputs. But for a number of reasons, this is not a sensible theoretical option for belief-states, desire-states, and other propositional-attitude states. For one thing, the list would be too long to be represented without combinatorial methods. Indeed, there is arguably no upper bound on the number of propositions any one of which could in principle be an object of thought. For another thing, there are systematic relations among beliefs: for example, the belief that John loves Mary and the belief that Mary loves John. These belief-states represent the same objects as related to each other in converse ways. But a theory of the nature of beliefs can hardly just leave out such an important feature of them. We cannot treat 'believes-that-grass-is-green', 'believes-that-grass-is-blue', etc. as unrelated primitive predicates. So we will need a more sophisticated theory, one that involves some sort of combinatorial apparatus. The most promising candidates are those that treat belief as a relation. But a relation to what? There are two distinct issues here. One issue is how to formulate the functional theory. *See* Loar (1981) and Schiffer (1987) for a suggestion in terms of a correspondence between the logical relations among sentences and the inferential relations among mental states. A second issue is what types of states could possibly realize the relational propositional attitude states. Field (1978) and Fodor (in Block, 1980, vol. 2, ch. 3) argue that to explain the productivity of propositional attitude states, there is no alternative to postulating a language of thought, a system of syntactically structured objects in the brain that express the propositions in propositional attitudes. (*See* Stalnaker (1984), chapters 1–3 for a critique of Field's approach.) In later work, Fodor (1987) has stressed the systematicity of propositional attitudes mentioned above. Fodor points out that the beliefs whose contents are systematically related exhibit the following sort of empirical relation: if one is capable of believing that Mary loves John, one is also capable of believing that John loves Mary. Fodor argues that only a language of thought in the brain could explain this fact. (*See* FODOR; LANGUAGE OF THOUGHTS; PROPOSITIONAL ATTITUDES.)

EXTERNALISM

The upshot of the famous 'TWIN EARTH' arguments has been that meaning and content are in part in the world and in the language community. Functionalists have responded in a variety of ways. One reaction is to think of the inputs and outputs of a functional theory as *long-arm*, as including the objects that one sees and manipulates. Another reaction is to stick with *short-arm* inputs and outputs that stop at the surfaces of the body, thinking of the intentional contents thereby characterized as *narrow* – supervening on the non-relational physical properties of the body. There has been no widely recognized account of what narrow content is, nor is there any agreement as to whether there is any burden of proof on the advocates of narrow content to characterize it (*see* CONTENT; EXTERNALISM/INTERNALISM; SUPERVENIENCE). (*See* the papers by Burge, Loar and Stalnaker in Rosenthal, 1991; *see also* Goldman, 1993.)

MEANING

Functionalism says that understanding the meaning of the word 'momentum' is a functional state. On one version of the view, the functional state can be seen in terms of the role of the word 'momentum' itself in thinking, problem solving, planning, etc. But if understanding the meaning of 'momentum' is this word's having a certain function, then there is a very close relation between the meaning of a word and its function, and a natural proposal is to regard the close relation as simply identity, that is, the meaning of the word just *is* that function (*see* Peacocke, 1992).

Thus functionalism about content leads to functionalism about meaning, a theory that purports to tell us the metaphysical nature of meaning. This theory is popular in cognitive science, where in one version it is often known as procedural semantics, as well as in philosophy where it is often known as CONCEPTUAL ROLE SEMANTICS. The theory has been criticized (along with other versions of functionalism) in Putnam (1988) and Fodor and LePore (1992).

HOLISM

Functionalism about content and meaning appears to lead to holism. In general, transitions among mental states and between mental states and behaviour depend on the contents of the mental states themselves. If I believe that sharks are dangerous, I will infer from sharks being in the water to the conclusion that people shouldn't be swimming. Suppose I first think that sharks are dangerous, but then change my mind, coming to think that sharks are not dangerous. However, the content that the first belief affirms can't be the same as the content that the second belief denies, because the transition relations (e.g. the inference from sharks being in the water to what people should do) that constitute the contents changed when I changed my mind (*see* Fodor and LePore, 1992). A natural functionalist reply is to say that some transitions are relevant to content individuation, whereas others are not. But functionalists have not told us how to do that. Appeal to a traditional analytic/synthetic distinction clearly won't do. For example, 'dog' and 'cat' would have the same content on such a view. It could not be analytic that dogs bark or that cats meow, since we can imagine a non-barking breed of dog and a non-meowing breed of cat. If 'Dogs are animals' is analytic, so is 'Cats are animals'. If 'Cats are adult kittens' is analytic, so is 'Dogs are adult puppies'. Dogs are not cats – but then cats are not dogs. So a functionalist account will not find traditional analytic inferential relations that will distinguish the meaning of 'dog' from the meaning of 'cat'. Other functionalists accept holism for 'narrow content', attempting to accommodate intuitions about the stability of content by appealing to wide content. (These issues are discussed in the 1993 volume of *Mind and Language*.)

QUALIA

Recall the parity-detecting automaton described at the beginning of this article. It could be instantiated by four people, each one of whom is in charge of the function as specified by a single box. Similarly, the much more complex functional organization of a human mind could 'in principle' be instantiated by a vast army of people. We would have to think of the army as connected to a robot body, acting as the brain of that body, and the body would be like a person in its reactions to inputs. But would such an army really instantiate a mind? More pointedly, could such an army have pain or the experience of red? If functionalism ascribes minds to things that don't have them, it is liberal. Lycan (1987) suggests that we include much of human physiology in our theory to be functionalized to avoid liberalism; that is, the theory T in the definition described earlier would be a psychological theory plus a physiological theory. But that makes the opposite problem, chauvinism, worse. The resulting functional description won't apply to intelligent Martians whose physiologies are different from ours. Further, it seems easy to imagine a simple pain-feeling organism that shares little in the way of functional organization

with us. The functionalized physiological theory of this organism will be hopelessly different from the corresponding theory of us. Indeed, even if one does not adopt Lycan's tactic, it is not clear how pain could be characterized functionally so as to be common to us and the simple organism. (*See* my 'Troubles with functionalism' which appears in all the anthologies mentioned.)

Much of the force of the problems just mentioned derives from attention to phenomenal states like the look of red. Phenomenal properties would seem to be intrinsic to (non-relational properties of) the states that have them, and thus phenomenal properties seem independent of the relations among states, inputs and outputs that define functional states. Consider, for example, the fact that lobotomy patients often say that they continue to have pains that feel the same as before, but that the pains don't bother them. If the concept of pain is a functional concept, what these patients say is contradictory or incoherent – but it seems to many of us that it is intelligible. (All the anthologies have papers on this topic; *see also* Lycan, 1987; chapters 8, 9, 14, and 15 of Shoemaker, 1984; Hill, 1991.)

The chauvinism/liberalism problem affects the characterization of inputs and outputs. If we characterize inputs and outputs in a way appropriate to our bodies, we chauvinistically exclude creatures whose interface with the world is very different from ours, e.g. creatures whose limbs end in wheels, or turning to a bigger difference, gaseous creatures who can manipulate and sense gases but for whom all solids and liquids are alike. The obvious alternative of characterizing inputs and outputs themselves functionally would appear to yield an abstract structure that might be satisfied by, e.g. the economy of Bolivia under manipulation by a wealthy eccentric, and would thus fall to the opposite problem of liberalism.

It is tempting to respond to the chauvinism problem by supposing that the same functional theory that applies to me also applies to the creatures with wheels. If they thought they had feet, they would try to act like us, and if we thought we had wheels, we would try to act like them. But notice that the functional definitions have to have some specifications of output organs in them. To be neutral among all the types of bodies that sentient beings could have would just be to adopt the liberal alternative of specifying the inputs and outputs themselves functionally.

Lewis allows imperfect realizers, and it might be thought that this device can avoid the chauvinism problem. If a weird alien believes that the sun is bigger than the moon, he will be prepared to make certain inferences and reject others, and these are examples of a host of psychological generalizations that have nothing to do with hands and feet. Perhaps most of the psychological generalizations about the aliens are the same as for us, and so they can be considered to be imperfect realizers of our functional organization. But this idea neglects the crucial difference between a theory (with all of its mental state terms) and its Ramsey sentence (with all those terms replaced by variables). If the alien's input and output organs are mostly different from ours, then the input/output constants in the Ramsey sentence will be mostly different from the constants in the Ramsey sentence for us. And given that difference, the only way the alien could count as a near-realization of our Ramsey sentence is if near isomorphism of the structure specified by the Ramsey sentence is what is taken to matter to realization – which makes inputs and outputs not very relevant. But now we are back to the economy of Bolivia problem mentioned above.

TELEOLOGY

Many philosophers (see the papers by Lycan and Sober in Lycan, 1990; FUNCTIONALISM (2); Lycan, 1987) propose that we avoid liberalism by characterizing functional roles teleologically. We exclude the armies and economies mentioned because their states aren't for the right things. A major problem for this point of view is the lack of an acceptable TELEOLOGICAL account. Accounts based on evolution smack up against the swamp-grandparents problem. Suppose you find out that your grandparents were formed from particles from the swamp that came together by chance. So, as it happens, you don't have any evolutionary history to speak of. If evolutionary accounts of the teleological underpinnings of content are right, your states don't have any content. A theory with such a consequence should be rejected.

CAUSATION

Functionalism dictates that mental properties are second-order properties that consist in having other properties that have certain relations to one another. But there is at least a *prima facie* problem about how such second-order properties could be causal and explanatory in a way appropriate to the mental. Consider, for example, provocativeness, the second-order property that consists in having some first-order property (say redness) that causes bulls to be angry. The cape's redness provokes the bull, but does the cape's provocativeness provoke the bull? The cape's provocativeness might provoke an animal protection society, but isn't the bull too stupid to be provoked by it? (*See* Block, 1990.)

Functionalism continues to be a lively and fluid point of view. Positive developments in recent years include enhanced prospects for conceptual functionalism and the articulation of the teleological point of view. Critical developments include problems with causality and holism, and continuing controversy over chauvinism and liberalism.

BIBLIOGRAPHY

Beakley, B., and Ludlow, P., eds. 1992. *Philosophy of Mind: Classical Problems/Contemporary Issues.* Cambridge, MA: MIT Press.
Block, N., ed. 1980. *Readings in Philosophy of Psychology, Vol. 1.* Cambridge, MA: Harvard University Press.

331

Block, N. 1990. Can the mind change the world? In *Meaning and method: Essays in honor of Hilary Putnam*, ed. G. Boolos. Cambridge University Press.

Field, H. 1978. Mental representation. *Erkentniss*, 13, 9–61.

Fodor, J. 1987. *Psychosemantics*. Cambridge, MA.: MIT Press.

Fodor, J., and Lepore, E. 1992. *Holism*. Oxford: Basil Blackwell.

Goldman, A. 1993. *Readings in Philosophy and Cognitive Science*. Cambridge, MA.: MIT Press.

Hill, C.S. 1991. *Sensations*. Cambridge University Press.

Kim, J. 1992. Multiple Realization and the metaphysics of reduction. *Philosophy and Phenomenological Research*, LII: 1.

Loar, B. 1981. *Mind and Meaning*. Cambridge University Press.

Loar, B. 1990. Phenomenal states. In *Philosophical perspectives 4: Action Theory and Philosophy of Mind*, ed. J. Tomberlin. Atascadero: Ridgeview.

Lycan, W.G. 1987. *Consciousness*. Cambridge, MA.: MIT Press.

Lycan, W.G., ed. 1990. *Mind and Cognition*. Oxford: Basil Blackwell.

Peacocke, C. 1992. *A Study of Concepts*. Cambridge, MA.: MIT Press.

Putnam, H. 1988. *Representation and Reality*. Cambridge, MA: MIT Press.

Rosenthal, D., ed. 1991. *The Nature of Mind*. Oxford University Press.

Schiffer, S. 1987. *Remnants of Meaning*. Cambridge, MA.: MIT Press.

Shoemaker, S. 1984. *Identity, Cause and Mind*. Ithaca: Cornell.

Stalnaker, R.C. 1984. *Inquiry* Cambridge, MA.: MIT Press.

White, S.L. 1986. Curse of the qualia. *Synthese*, 68, 333–68.

NED BLOCK

H

history: medieval and Renaissance philosophy of mind Since the late 1960s there has been a significant and fast-expanding interest in medieval philosophy, and though once largely confined to questions of logic and general ontology, the range of this interest has now extended to cover most aspects of normative enquiry such as ethics, politics and aesthetics (*see* Haldane, 1991, 1992). The philosophy of the Renaissance is far less widely studied, though in recent times there have been signs of a developing interest and no doubt in the coming years there will be an expansion and intensification of this. One may doubt, however, whether the renaissance is as likely as the medieval period to catch and hold the interests of philosophers, as distinct from cultural historians, for while the renaissance produced striking innovations in the style of speculative writing and saw the emergence of secular humanism it had relatively little to add to the philosophical systems developed in the middle ages. These systems were themselves related to earlier ways of thinking, in particular to those of Plato and Aristotle, but the medievals added much to what antiquity had produced. Here I shall mention authors of the early middle ages through whose work the ideas of antiquity were communicated to later periods, and writers of the early modern period who paved the way for Descartes; but I will focus upon the major figures of the high middle ages.

The expression 'philosophy of mind' is a modern one. In antiquity and in the medieval and renaissance periods writers discussed questions that are of central interest to present-day philosophers, such as the relation of persons to their bodies, the structure of intentional ACTION and the nature of IMAGINATION, MEMORY and mental reference, but these were taken to be aspects of psychology in an older sense of the term, connoting the description (*logos*) of the soul (*psuche*). The word 'psychology' itself probably first appears in the sixteenth century in writings by two German authors – Johannes Freigius and Goclenius of Marburg – published in 1575 and 1590, respectively. Like their medieval predecessors these authors considered the study of the soul to be part of natural philosophy and regarded the classic text on the subject to be Aristotle's *De Anima*. Indeed, it is barely an exaggeration to say that medieval and renaissance philosophy of mind consists of commentaries and reflections on that work.

A HISTORICAL OVERVIEW

The writings of Aristotle were received into the Latin West through two sources. First, through the work of early translators and commentators such as Boethius (480–524), Cassiodorus (490–585) and Isidore of Seville (570–636). However, these figures knew very little of Aristotle's authentic corpus and were themselves neo-Platonists subscribing to the dualistic world-view espoused by Plotinus (204–69) and, in Christianized form, by St Augustine (354–430). Isidore produced a work entitled *De Anima* but it was Augustinian, not Aristotelian, in inspiration. In it he argued for the immateriality and immortality of individual souls on the basis of the non-empirical nature of the objects of thought, i.e. transcendental essences and truths, and the ancient principle that activities and their objects are of like kind. From this period, however, two important and long-lasting definitions emerged: Augustine's account of the human soul as 'a rational substance suited for ruling a body' (*De Quantitate Animae*, 13) and Boethius' definition of a person as 'an individual substance of rational nature' (*Contra Eutychen*, 6). Both are dualistic in intent, though while Boethius' general account is worded so as to allow for unembodied persons its formulation permitted later non-dualists and even materialists to claim that their views were in accord with ancient tradition (*see* DUALISM). Indeed, this definition would be acceptable to a present-day philosopher such as DAVIDSON who advocates 'ANOMALOUS MONISM', a version of non-reductive PHYSICALISM.

The second and more fruitful source of Aristotelian writings was the Arab world. In the century prior to Boethius, Syrian Christians translated ancient Greek texts into Syriac, and several centuries later their successors arrived in Baghdad where they began to produce Arabic translations of these works. In due course Moslem philosophers became interested in these writings, making commentaries on them and appropriating some of their ideas. The most important of these Islamic figures were Alfarabi (890–950), Avicenna (980–1037) and Averroes (1126–98) – the last of whom was to be a source of major disputes, in both the medieval and renaissance periods, about the human soul. During the twelfth and thirteenth centuries, editions of Aristotle in Greek and Arabic, and supporting commentaries, began to appear in the West where they were rapidly translated into Latin. A mark of the significance of their reception is that St Thomas Aquinas (1225–74), undisputedly the greatest medieval philosopher, seems to have composed his discussions of human nature and the soul (*Summa Theologiae*, I, 75–89; *Quaestiones Disputatae De Anima*) and commentary on Aristotle's text (*Sententia super De Anima*) within a year or so of his Dominican associate William of Moerbeke (1215–86) having translated Aristotle into Latin in about 1268.

Such developments in psychology as were initiated during the renaissance were also coincident with the production of new translations of the *De Anima*. In the fifteenth century philosophers were still using Moerbeke's translation together with editions of Greek, Arab and Latin commentaries; but as the new humanism developed, inspired by the antiquarian rediscovery of the classical ages, writers became increasingly critical of what they regarded as 'corrupt' medieval Latin texts and they produced new Greek and 'refined' Latin editions in Ciceronian style. As important as the text of *De Anima* itself were the early Greek commentaries, for they provided secular authors with pre-scholastic, pre-Arabic perspectives on the Aristotelian idea of the soul. Furthermore, the rediscovery of antiquity brought Platonic and neo-Platonist views back onto the scene. During the fifteenth and early sixteenth centuries psychology was no longer pursued in a unitary scholastic fashion, and by about 1550 the tradition of medieval thought was more or less at an end. There were scholastic authors writing after that date – as there are even today. Francisco Suarez (1548–1617) and John of St Thomas (1589–1644) both took their inspiration from Aristotle and Aquinas; but by that point a new agenda was developing in psychology as Hobbes (1588–1679) and Descartes (1596–1650) tried in their very different ways (materialist and dualist, respectively) to relate the existence and nature of the mind, conceived largely in terms of CONSCIOUSNESS, to the human body, by then thought of as a machine composed out of material elements whose intrinsic nature is geometrical – in effect, atoms in the void.

MEDIEVAL SCHOLASTICISM

Descartes rejected many aspects of traditional Aristotelian psychology and introduced new ways of thinking. Most importantly, perhaps, he replaced the idea of the soul as a single source of life and reason with the notion that the latter is an attribute of a distinct element, viz. the *mind*. It is also worth observing, however, that much of what is regarded as definitive of Cartesianism is to be found in earlier writings, in particular in the work of Augustine and those scholastics whom he influenced such as St Bonaventure (1217–74). It is commonly assumed, for example, that Descartes is the author of the proof that even if one is deceived in believing one has a body, nonetheless it is certain that one exists as a thinking thing: '*Cogito ergo sum*', 'I think, therefore I am'. However, as contemporaries of Descartes, such as Antoine Arnauld (1612–94) and Andreas Colvius observed, this argument (or a close relative of it) is anticipated by Augustine in *De Civitate Dei* XI, 26, where he insists '*Si fallor sum*' ([Even] if I err, I am). Descartes' response to these observations was either to set them aside, as in his rejoinder to Arnauld (Reply to the Fourth Set of Objections, in Haldane and Ross, 1912), or else to claim, as in his reply to Colvius, that Augustine was making a different point (Letter to Colvius, 14 November 1640, in Kenny, 1970).

Similarly, it is common to credit Descartes with the idea that a thinker is infallible with respect to his own subjective psychology. But again this is to be found in Augustine: '[I]t could not possibly happen that the soul should think about what is itself in the same way that it thinks about what is not' (*De Trinitate*, X, 10; *see also De Vera Religione* 39, 73). Equally, while finding dualism compelling, Augustine is puzzled by the relationship between the soul and the body and the manner of their causal interaction in the same ways as would trouble Descartes. Augustine writes: 'The manner in which spirits are united to bodies is altogether wonderful and transcends the understanding of men (*De Civitate Dei*, XXI, 10); and *twelve hundred* years later Descartes comments: 'It does not seem to me that the human mind is capable of conceiving quite distinctly and at the same time both the distinction between mind and body, and their union' (Kenny, 1970, p. 142).

However, the reception of Aristotelianism in the thirteenth century brought with it a more naturalistic perspective on the central philosophical question of psychology; the ontological nature of human persons (*see* THE SELF). Clearly, in this context, NATURALISM is not to be identified with physicalism – though in succeeding centuries quasi-materialist views began to emerge. For the Latin authors of the high middle ages, however, materialism was unthinkable. For one thing they were religious believers, usually members of monastic religious orders (Albert the Great (1206–80) and Aquinas were Dominicans; Bonaventure, Duns Scotus (1266–1308) and William of Ockham (1285–1349) were Franciscans) and were committed to upholding theological doctrines concerning the human soul, such as that it is a spiritual entity specially created by God, which survives bodily death and may exist for eternity. In addition, many of them believed that reason alone is capable of demonstrating the immateriality and immortality of the soul. (The drift towards philosophical scepticism is marked by Scotus' doubting that the latter is provable (*Opus Oxoniense*, 4, 43) and Ockham's denying that it is (*Quodlibet*, I, 12).) There is not space here to consider these proofs, but given the present-day interest in the 'aboutness' of thought, it is worth noting that several of them (such as that offered by Aquinas in the *Summa Theologiae*, I, 75) turn upon the nature of INTENTIONALITY and its difference from physical relations. (Indeed, the very term and concept originate in the medieval notion of *esse intentionale*, the 'intentional being' of thoughts.)

While medieval philosophy remained anti-materialist, the availability of the *De Anima* together with sophisticated Arab commentaries led to a new and important phase in Western thinking about the nature of the mind. The two central issues concerned *the ontological category of the soul*, whether it is a particular thing in its own right (*hoc aliquid*) or a supervenient quality of something, namely a living human body (*see* SUPERVENIENCE); and *the identity of the soul*, whether each person possesses one or many souls, and indeed whether there is but a single transcendent soul which animates the plurality of human beings. In order to see how these questions arise, it is necessary to say something about the ideas of the *De Anima* and how they differ from the sorts of dualism espoused by Plato, Augustine and Descartes.

As was noted, St Augustine thought of persons as souls using bodies. That is to say he conceived of human beings as composites of two distinct elements, the one animating ('*anima*' being the Latin equivalent of '*psuche*') and expressing itself through the other. For Aristotle, by contrast, the soul is thought of in terms of the general scheme of *form* and *matter*. Matter is that out of which something is made, form is the organizing principle which makes it to be the thing it is. If I cut out a paper circle what then lies on the desk is, in Aristotelian vocabulary, a 'particular substance'. Although there is but one *thing* present, nonetheless two *aspects* of it can be identified: its *matter* (paper) and its *form* (circularity). Similarly, Aristotle claims that the organizing principle of a living human being, its form, is the soul (*De Anima*, II, 1). So here again we can say there is one thing possessed of two aspects, its matter and its form, the latter being in this case a certain kind of animality.

This is an attractive view for several reasons. One is that it offers the promise of avoiding some of the problems of dualism without lapsing into materialist reductionism. Another is that it provides a way of viewing reality as an ordered system of substances distinguished in point of various 'hylomorphic' (*hyle* = matter, *morphe* = form) relationships. This is part of what appealed to the medievals, but it was also to prove a source of problems and disagreements, and even contributed to the decline of scholasticism in the renaissance. One set of problems concerns the compatibility of the Aristotelian view with the theological doctrines listed above. If the soul stands to the body as the shape stands to the paper, then it seems to make no sense to say that the soul is a something in itself which can survive the body. Bonaventure's view is interesting in this respect since he tries unsuccessfully to combine the hylomorphism of the *De Anima* with the dualism of

Augustine's *De Quantitate Animae*. He claims that a living human being is indeed a composite of form (soul) and matter (flesh): 'The rational soul is the principle and form of the human body' (*Super Libros Sententiarum*, 18); but he insists that the soul is *itself* a hylomorphic union, in this case of *spiritual form* and *spiritual matter*. The effort to combine dualistic and hylomorphic perspectives is to some degree present in almost all medieval writers of the thirteenth century and is sometimes spoken of as the 'Augustinian/Aristotelian synthesis'.

Aquinas, who explicitly criticizes the notion of spiritual matter, goes further in the direction of Aristotle and away from dualism; yet he also claims that the soul, though the form of the body, is nonetheless a subsistent, if incomplete, entity (a *hoc aliquid*). Although it is difficult to make sense of, his view merits greater consideration than it has so far received from non-scholastic philosophers. Such consideration would do well to begin with the idea that as a separable subject the soul is no more than the locus of non-sensory mental acts; it is not a *subject* in the post-Cartesian sense of being a person. As Aquinas has it, '*Anima mea non est ego*' – 'my soul is not I' (*Commentarium Super Epistolas Pauli Apostoli* (1 Cor.: 15)). On the one hand Aquinas is appreciative of the difficulties with dualism and the empirical and philosophical considerations supporting a monistic view of persons. On the other hand he believes that persons are essentially psychological beings and that thought is a non-organic activity. Like his predecessors he associates the nature of human beings as living thinking individuals with their possession of rational souls, but he takes from Aristotle the idea that the soul is a form. Hence even if, unlike other forms, it is a subsistent entity it is incomplete in itself. In short, a human person is a psychophysical substance, and a separable soul is not a person but a minimal subject.

In working out his views, Aquinas was steering a course between a number of opposing positions. Set against Augustinian dualism was a form of radical Aristotelianism known, after the Arab commentator, as *Averroism*. The main medieval proponent of this was Siger of Brabant (1224–82), a contemporary of Aquinas. The Averroists were concerned with remarks in *De Anima* where Aristotle appears to suggest that the aspects of the soul that empower human beings with thought (the active and passive intellects) are a single universal principle, that, in effect, there is but one mind distributed through many bodies. Aquinas attacks this idea ('Monopsychism') in his *De Unitate Intellectus Contra Averroistas*, insisting that since reason belongs to the soul and the soul is the form of the human body there are as many intellects as there are human beings.

While the Averroists sought to posit a *single* universal soul others argued that each human being has *several* souls, i.e. several organizing forms: the vegetative, the sentient and the rational. Versions of this view were held by the Jewish philosopher Avicebron (1020–70) and later by Ockham (*Quodlibet* 2). Again Aquinas argues against it on the grounds that it is at odds with what common sense and philosophy teach, i.e. that each human being is a unity, neither an instance of a universal intellect nor a collection of individuals. Relatedly he takes issue with those who view the rational soul as something added to an existing living being, and with those who believe that it emerges naturally out of matter having been transmitted through sexual reproduction. The former position might be termed 'dualist creationism', the latter is known as 'traducianism'. What Aquinas himself offers is a version of creationism – rational souls are not naturally generated – but one in which of the act of creation is the imposition by God of a single soul possessed of vegetative, sentient and rational powers upon embryonic matter (*Summa Contra Gentiles*, II, 86).

RENAISSANCE HUMANISM

One may wonder about the philosophical stability of Aquinas's moderate Aristotelianism. Certainly in subsequent centuries writers tended to move away from it in the directions of either less, or more naturalistic views. In the renaissance period the former tendency was associated with the revival of neo-Platonism and in particular with the main figures of the Florentine Academy such as Marsilius Ficinus (1433–99) who translated Plato and Plotinus and whose philosophical psychology involves a deliberate return to the Christian dualism of St Augustine (*Theologia Platonica*).

During the lifetime of Ficinus, Aristotle's *De Anima* was re-translated at least twice and this prompted renewed interest in the views of pre-medieval commentators with the result that there was a revival of Averroism, particularly at the University of Padua, and of Alexandrism. The latter view takes its name from Alexander of Aphrodisias (*f.* 200) a commentator whose account of *De Anima* is free of the dualistic aspects associated with the Augustinian/ Aristotelian synthesis. The main renaissance Alexandrist was Pietro Pomponazzi (1462–1525) who argued for a position not unlike that of some present-day property dualists. For while he accepted that thought is a non-physical process he denied that this implied that the subject of thought is anything other than a living and mortal human being (*De Immortalitate Animae*). This view put him at odds with the declarations of the Church which, during the Fifth Lateran Council (1513), denounced Averroism and Alexandrism and proclaimed that individual immortality is philosophically demonstrable – just the issue which in the medieval period had divided Aquinas, Scotus and Ockham.

The renaissance trend towards naturalism led in due course to the kind of empirical approach that laid the basis both for materialism and for Descartes' separation of the philosophy of mind from the natural science of living bodies. Equally, though, as was seen earlier, one can view Cartesianism as a revival of the Platonic-Augustinean tradition. Either way it emerges out of a rich and complex past, the study of which promises to yield historical and philosophical insights.

BIBLIOGRAPHY

Adams, M. 1987. *William of Ockham*. Notre Dame, IN: University of Notre Dame Press.

Cassirer, E., Kristeller, P., and Randall Jr., J. eds. 1948. *The Renaissance Philosophy of Man*. University of Chicago Press.

Copleston, F.C. 1972. *A History of Medieval Philosophy*. London: Methuen.

Haldane, E., and Ross, G., eds. 1912. *The Philosophical Works of Descartes, Vol II*. Cambridge University Press.

Haldane, J. 1991. Medieval and renaissance ethics. In *A Companion to Ethics*, ed. P. Singer. Oxford: Basil Blackwell.

Haldane, J. 1992. Medieval and renaissance aesthetics. In *A Companion to Aesthetics*, ed. D. Cooper. Oxford: Basil Blackwell.

Hyman, A., and Walsh, J., eds. 1973. *Philosophy in the Middle Ages*. Indianapolis: Hackett Publishing Company.

Kenny, A., ed. 1970: *Descartes: Philosophical Letters*. Oxford: Clarendon Press.

—— 1980. *Aquinas*. Oxford University Press.

—— 1993. *Aquinas on Mind*. London: Routledge.

Kirwan C. 1989. *Augustine*. London: Routledge & Kegan Paul.

Kretzman, N., Kenny, A., and Pinborg, J., eds. 1982. *The Cambridge History of Later Medieval Philosophy*, Cambridge University Press.

Schmitt, C., and Skinner, Q. eds. 1988: *The Cambridge History of Renaissance Philosophy*. Cambridge University Press.

JOHN HALDANE

history: philosophy of mind in the seventeenth and eighteenth centuries   There was no such field of philosophical enquiry as the philosophy of mind in the seventeenth and eighteenth centuries. Nevertheless, the problems that are today regarded as the central problems in the philosophy of mind were first given something like their current formulations in the works of the major seventeenth- and eighteenth-century philosophers, as were the basic positions to be taken on these issues and some of the familiar lines of argument. These problems and the various leading responses to them came up chiefly as side issues incidental to larger controversies which have long since receded from active philosophical interest. What I will try to do here, accordingly, in giving a brief sketch of the treatment of some key issues by philosophers in the period, is to sketch also the larger context of the philosophers concern with these issues; this often changes our appreciation of the philosopher's arguments and their purport. The goal is not simply to point up anachronism in the common pictures of these positions and arguments, which are so frequently invoked in contemporary discussions in philosophy of mind, but rather to deepen our appreciation of the issues themselves. It is worth remarking, though, that there is more than a little bit of anachronism to be found in the understanding many contemporary writers have of positions and arguments drawn from the early Modern period, and that anachronism is not always entirely benign.

As I've already noted, many of the issues we take to be the central issues in philosophy of mind were first formulated in the seventeenth and eighteenth centuries. Among these are: the so-called mind–body problem, that is, the problem of the ontological status of the mind and/or mental or psychological states *vis-à-vis* the body and/or the physical states of material systems; the nature of personal identity; the nature of mental representation (incarnated in our period as the theory of ideas), and the closely related question of whether there are any innate ideas; the nature and content of the emotions or passions; and others. In this short essay I will give a brief overview of the treatment of two large issues which are a central part of the legacy left to contemporary philosophy of mind by the philosophers of the seventeenth and eighteenth centuries: the mind–body problem, and the problem of personal identity.

THE MIND–BODY PROBLEM

Dualism

The mind–body problem, as we think of it today, originated with Descartes. In his extremely influential (to put it mildly) 1641 work, *Meditations on First Philosophy*,

Descartes argued for a view that has been known ever since as Cartesian dualism: the view that the mind and the body are distinct substances, each of which could exist apart from the other. (We will arrive at a somewhat more precise formulation of the view a little later on.) The argument he gives for this thesis has several stages:

First, Descartes gives a battery of sceptical arguments that call into doubt most if not all of his preconceived beliefs and notions; chief among these sceptical arguments are the argument from dreaming, which calls into question not only all of his particular beliefs about external material objects, but even the global belief that there are any external material objects at all, and the evil genius argument which calls into question even those beliefs that are most certain, such as that $2 + 3 = 5$ or that a square has four sides. (These arguments take up most of the first of the six meditations.)

Next, at the beginning of the Second Meditation Descartes delivers (almost) what is one of the most famous philosophical dicta of all time: *Cogito ergo sum*; I think, therefore I am. (The classical formulation is actually given in the *Discourse on the Method*.) This is Descartes's Archimedean point of certainty, which is to provide the foundation for shoring up the whole edifice of scientific knowledge, and it is crucially important for understanding his later argument for dualism to understand how it works. The basic idea is that even if we accept the most radical sceptical thesis, the evil genius hypothesis, which holds that we are being deceived by an omnipotent being who thus has the power to make us go wrong even in those beliefs we hold most firmly to be true, and think we know best, we are committed by the acceptance of the hypothesis itself to hold that it is certain that we exist. For if the hypothesis is correct, we are deceived by the evil genius; but (a) it is impossible for there to be deceit unless there is belief (false belief, but belief nonetheless), and since belief is a mode of thinking, there must be thought or thinking; and (b) since thought or thinking cannot exist except in a thinking thing or

substance, there must be a thinking thing or substance. Thus even the most radical sceptical arguments possible cannot call into question the belief that I exist as a thinking thing; indeed, on the basis of these arguments we can show that belief to be certainly true.

The next stage, which takes up most of the rest of the Second Meditation, has two parts. First, on the basis of a lengthy analysis of the Cogito argument Descartes establishes that the mind, i.e. what 'I' refers to as it occurs in 'I think' or 'I am', must be (a) a thinking thing, i.e. a thing which has, among its states, states of thought or consciousness; and (b) it must be *essentially* a thinking thing, that is to say, it cannot have any states which are not states of thought or consciousness. The reason for (a) is that the premiss of the Cogito argument, 'I think' (or 'I am thinking') cannot be true unless there currently exists a thought (and as we have seen, thoughts cannot exist unless they are thought by some thinker); and the reason for (b) is that, since at this point in the *Meditations* the dreaming argument is still in force, so that the meditator must doubt that any external material objects exist, to attribute any material or physical states (which are the only kind of states there are besides states of thought or consciousness) to the thing referred to by 'I' would be to consider it a material thing, and thus call its existence into question, thus losing the certainty of the knowledge that I exist. It is on this basis that Descartes concludes that he has a clear and distinct conception of himself as *res cogitans* as a thing that thinks and whose whole essence it is to be a thinking thing. The second part of this stage of the argument establishes the complementary thesis about the conception of body: the notorious wax example is meant to show that body can be clearly and distinctly conceived as a substance whose whole essence is extension, i.e. having spatial dimension or any of the qualities or states (such as being in motion, or resistance to being put into motion by contact action, etc.) which presuppose the having of spatial dimension. So by the end of the

Second Meditation Descartes has shown that the mind (what 'I' refers to) is clearly and distinctly conceived as a substance which has no states except states of thought, and the body is clearly and distinctly conceived as a substance which has no states except states of extension.

In the closing stage of the argument, given in Meditation VI, Descartes goes from conceivability to (real) possibility. Having argued in Meditations III, IV and V that God exists and is no deceiver, and thus having now a rational basis for rejecting the evil genius hypothesis, Descartes takes himself to have established that whatever we clearly and distinctly conceive to be true must be as we conceive it. We are now in a position to say not merely that we conceive the mind to be a substance whose essence is thought, and body to be a substance whose essence is extension, but we can positively assert that those *are* their natures. It follows in turn from this that it is possible for the mind to exist even if no bodies or states of bodies exist, and for the body to exist even if no minds or states of minds exist. Mind and body are thus really distinct substances.

I've set out Descartes' argument at some length not only because it is the argument that initiates the modern philosophers' (and our) preoccupation with the mind–body problem but also because it exemplifies the gulf between the seventeenth-century take on these issues and our own. In the first place, and on the grossest level, it should be evident how inappropriate it is to characterize Cartesian dualism as consisting in the claim that there is some mysterious or incomprehensible 'soul-stuff' or 'mind-stuff' that is the substance in which mental states inhere. For Descartes, the substance of the mind is eminently intelligible, since the whole essence of the mind is captured in the attribute of thought, and we have a clear and distinct idea of this attribute. (There is, of course, room to question how well Descartes could do by way of providing a full explication of this supposedly clear idea – Locke, for one, argues that the notion of thought is not at all clear – but right now the issue has to do with Descartes's thesis as

he put it forward, not with how well he could defend it.) If Cartesian dualism is in this respect less silly a view than it is sometimes made out to be, in other respects it is less well off than might be gathered from current discussions. As the reconstruction of the argument given above makes clear, an ineliminable element of Descartes' a priori argument for dualism is its invocation of an omnipotent God to guarantee the truth of our clear and distinct perceptions. Without this, Descartes' argument is exposed to the charge that at most it can show that we must think of the mind as a substance that is distinct from the body, given our conception of the mind; but this doesn't reach the question of what the mind's nature actually is. Descartes' argument for the ontological conclusion thus becomes an *ignoratio elenchus*. Even more disturbing to the modern sensibility is the absolutely ineliminable use Descartes makes of the traditional Aristotelian-Scholastic categories of substance and mode or accident. A crucial step in his argument is the inference from the existence of a thought or belief to the existence of a substance thinking that thought, or in the technical lingo, in which that thought inheres; and equally crucial is his analysis of the attributes of thought and extension, which turn out to be essential or defining principal attributes sufficing for the existence and individuation of an individual substance. Once these commitments are given up, it is hard to see that anything is left of the theory; yet modern writers blithely invoke Cartesian dualism as at least a possible position on the mind–body problem, without troubling to clean up these problems (if indeed they can be cleaned up). (*See* DUALISM.)

I want now to connect up this discussion of Descartes' arguments with the general point with which I began, namely that whatever it was Descartes took himself to be doing when he argued for his dualism, he did not take himself to be carving out a position in the philosophy of mind. Why then did he argue so prominently for dualism? The most obvious suggestion is that he might really be interested in laying the basis for a proof of the immortality of the soul, just as he says he is. But the basic motivation for dualism in his case stems from the basic goal of his philosophical enterprise: to lay the foundations for the new mechanistic philosophy of nature demanded by the new science of the seventeenth century. According to the New Philosophy, as it was called, all changes of state of physical bodies are explicable by adverting only to the mechanical affections of material things: the sizes, shapes, and motions of their parts. (This is the payoff of the Cartesian claim that the essence of body is extension.) Crucial to the enterprise of establishing the New Philosophy is disestablishing the old one, viz. Aristotelian Scholasticism, which was committed to immaterial principles of organization and causation in bodies–forms. Descartes' radical break with traditional views of the soul is thus really part of his attack on the Scholastic doctrine of substantial forms. The Scholastics of Descartes' time maintained the Aristotelian–Thomist view of the soul, according to which the rational soul is, like the souls of plants and animals, the form of the living creature. ('Form' here is used in the technical sense it had in the context of hylomorphic theory, where the form is the essence or, as the lingo had it, the first actuality of the individual substance, which organizes the matter of the individual into a living thing which has the essential characteristics and functions typical of its species; form, in short, 'makes a thing to be what it is'.) Two crucial points about Aristotelian forms, are (1) that these forms are themselves immaterial principles of unity and causal action, and (2) they are intimately bound up with formal causes, i.e. with teleological causation in terms of final principles. Descartes, who has claimed to have established that the mind can have no connection whatever with any states of extension (or it would have to have some such states itself, contrary to the conception of mind yielded by the analysis of the Cogito argument, must reject the traditional conception of the rational soul as being both the proper subject of states of THOUGHT or

CONSCIOUSNESS and the form of the living human body; and reject it he does. (This was one of the bases for the formal condemnation of Descartes' works.)

If the doctrine of the soul as the form of the living body, which was the central case for the doctrine of substantial forms, were to be discarded, the hylomorphic theory as a whole would go as well, paving the way for the acceptance of the Mechanical Philosophy. A further benefit in this regard is that by getting rid of the soul in favour of the Cartesian mind, a substance not only ontologically distinct from body but also causally independent of it in its basic functions and operations (those, namely, having to do with pure intellect), Descartes delivers a version of the Mechanical Philosophy free of the suspicion of materialism and atheism that attached to mechanistic atomism by virtue of its origin in the works of ancient atomists such as Democritus and Lucretius.

Pre-established Harmony

If we survey some of the leading positions on the mind–body problem held by Descartes' successors we'll find a similar degree of obliquity to the current problem-situation in philosophy of mind as we found in Descartes, although the obliquities lie in different directions. Leibniz is a good case in point. His official stand on the mind–body problem stems from the doctrine he called the 'pre-established harmony.' The common view amongst philosophers of mind is that this view is basically just Cartesian dualism without the causal interaction Descartes allowed between mind and body. The regularities that Descartes put down to causal interaction are produced instead by God's having set up the events in the (separate, and causally isolated) mental and physical orders in synchronization; and the motivation for this view is widely supposed to have been Leibniz's recognition of the problems with conservation laws that attend dualistic interaction. Some of this is right: Leibniz was of course aware of the problems with conservation, and he did hold that the regularities between the order of mental events and the order of physical events was due to

341

God's having set up correspondences between the orders. But there's at least as much that is wrong in this picture of Leibniz's view as there is that is right. Leibniz is not a dualist: for him there are no physical substances, as such. The ultimate substances are monads, which are individual substances that have as their states only perceptions and appetitions; physical objects are just appearances. The basis of Leibniz's argument for this view, as well as for his denial that there is causal interaction between mind and body (the latter now conceived in terms of a phenomenalist reductionism, which makes bodies ontologically dependent upon perceptions or more exactly on the contents of perceptions) lies in his analysis of the notion of substance. Leibniz does not, as Descartes did, accept virtually whole and unrevised the Aristotelian-Scholastic categories of substance and accident; he thinks the notion of substance to be in need of explication, and he provides this explication by way of a concept-containment theory of truth and a related theory of individual concepts. Leibniz derives a number of metaphysical results from this analysis, most notably his doctrines about the nature of necessity and contingency, the causal isolation of substances, the unity and simplicity of substance, the principle of identity of indiscernibles, and the doctrine of pre-established harmony. Thus Leibniz arrives at his position on the mind–body problem as a consequence of claims he staked on these more general issues, and not simply as a response to the problem of conservation laws; and in any case his version of pre-established harmony is not straightforwardly dualistic.

Dual Aspect Theory

Another position on the mind–body problem tossed around by contemporary philosophers of mind (the most notable recent example is Brian O'Shaughnessy in his work *The Will: A Dual Aspect Theory*) and originating in our period is the dual aspect theory, associated with Spinoza. On this theory, neither mind nor body is a substance in its own right; instead, each is an aspect (or mode – for Spinoza, each is an infinite mode) of a single underlying substance. Some of the problems associated with dual aspect theories, such as that the underlying substance itself either has no nature (i.e. is a bare particular) or has a mysterious nature, are not problems for Spinoza, as he identifies the underlying substance as God. (Of course, to the modern philosopher of mind this 'solution' to the problems has all the advantages of theft over honest toil (to swipe a phrase from Bertrand Russell).) But here again the theory is a consequence of more basic commitments stemming from an analysis of the notion of substance, although one quite different from Leibniz's. Spinoza faults Descartes for not taking seriously (or perhaps one should say literally) his own definition of substance. If to be a substance is to be able to exist on one's own, depending on no other thing for existence, then Descartes's *res cogitans* (mind) and *res exstensa* (body) are not substances, since, as Descartes acknowledged, mind and body depend upon God for their existence. (Descartes' distinction between finite and infinite substances is then treated as just a dodge.) The only entity that can satisfy the traditional definition of substance, taken strictly, is God; so God is the only substance, with mind and body being just modes of this substance: different ways of expressing the essence of this substance. From this analysis Spinoza draws the conclusion that events in the mental order must parallel events in the physical order, as they express the same essence of the same substance. While this conclusion has some broad structural similarities to Leibniz's pre-established harmony, there are important differences: the regularities or parallelism between the mental and physical orders are not the result of creating intentions on God's part, and there is no hint of the phenomenalist reductionism that provides the context for Leibniz's doctrine.

Materialism

This view, which had its lease on life renewed in the seventeenth century, is perhaps the one position that is most conformable to its current incarnations (*see* IDENTITY THEORIES; PHYSICALISM). Roughly, the doctrine is that all that exists is matter in motion, and that mental states are ontologically dependent on states of bodies. Probably the most forceful and notorious early expression of materialism in this period is due to Hobbes. His motivation for embracing materialism stems from his commitment to mechanistic science, but he does not base an argument for materialism on its scientific credentials. Instead, he argues for materialism on the basis of his logical theory, wherein he replaces Aristotle's central category of substance with the category of body, on the grounds that the only clear idea we can attach to the notion of something that exists on its own is the idea of body. Hobbes devotes much energy and ingenuity to providing detailed accounts of how sensation, appetition, and even higher-order cognitive faculties ('reason', 'reasoning') can be reduced to material processes. This stance was more of an embarrassment to the champions of the new mechanistic science than it was a help; Boyle, Charleton, Locke, and other promoters of the New Philosophy in England had to distance themselves from the out-and-out materialism of Hobbes, which seemed to confirm the common complaint that mechanistic atomism was just the old materialistic, atheistic philosophy of Democritus and Lucretius in somewhat misleading new garb.

Locke is a particularly interesting case. He was accused of being a materialist or at least a fellow-traveller of materialism by Leibniz and by many contemporary critics in England; more recently, he has been seen as a dualist. He was neither; as usual, he preferred to remain agnostic in an area where human reason could make no reliable pronouncements. Thus in a famous passage in the *Essay* (Book IV, ch 3, §6) he argued that both doctrinaire materialism and doctrinaire dualism are misguided, since our ideas of matter and thinking are so impoverished. He did go on from this to argue that we can find no inconsistency in the suggestion that God superadded the

power of thought to merely material things, so that we cannot rule it out that a purely material substance might also be the subject of mental states, and hence that a thinking thing may be nothing but body. Once again, Locke's interest in arguing for the possibility of thinking systems of matter derived at least as much from his enterprise of laying the foundations for (Gassendi–Boyle style) mechanistic atomism as from any other motive; he took the superaddition of thought to matter as a model for God-ordained lawlike connections between primary and secondary qualities, thus securing the possibility of explanatory connections between secondary qualities and primary qualities even if these connections are unintelligible to us.

PERSONAL IDENTITY

Locke

Locke's most important legacy to current philosophers of mind lies in his formulation and treatment of the problem of personal identity. The pattern we've turned up in connection with the mind–body problem repeats itself here: Locke's treatment of the issue looks primarily to larger framing questions which are no longer current, and his actual position is somewhat different than the common view has it. First, a brief description of Locke's theory. Locke distinguishes between identity as determined by unity of substance and identity as determined by the idea of the kind to which an individual belongs. (Note that according to his theory of real and nominal essences, the idea of the kind, and consequently the kind itself, is framed by us, or as Locke puts it, it is 'the workmanship of the understanding'.) So the identity of a mass or parcel of matter is determined by unity of substance: as long as the same atoms are united together, we have the same parcel of matter. The identity of an oak-tree or horse, on the other hand, is determined by the idea of the kind: numerically distinct (and differently sized and shaped) parcels of matter may count as the same oak-tree or the same horse (now a sapling, later a mature tree; now a colt,

343

later an adult horse) as long as the change in constituent matter is gradual and a certain requisite organization of parts is preserved. Locke then suggests that the identity of a person is of the latter sort: it is determined by our idea of a person, which is, Locke says, that of 'a thinking intelligent Being, that has reason and reflection, and considers itself as itself, the same thinking thing in different times and places'; and since consciousness is thus the core defining quality of persons, sameness of consciousness constitutes personal identity. Locke is often described as having put forward a memory theory of personal identity, according to which the criterion of personal identity is the ability to remember having done a particular action or having had a particular experience, making one the same person as the one who did that action or had that experience. But this is not quite right; the psychological continuity required for memory is just an example of the sorts of continuity which constitute sameness of consciousness.

Perhaps Locke's most lasting contribution to the topic was the method he used in arguing for his theory. He introduced the method that is still the main vehicle of argument on this topic, the method of 'puzzle-cases' (as J. L. Mackie called it). To show, for example, that the identity of a person is not constituted by the identity of a particular human body, he asks us to imagine that a prince and a cobbler should suddenly switch bodies, where the body of the prince should now give voice to memories which only the cobbler could have had, but can remember nothing of the prince's life, and the same in reverse for the body of the cobbler. If we can imagine this as a genuine case of persons switching bodies, we see that the conditions for being the same person are distinct from those for being the same human being. Similarly, Locke argues against the immaterial substance theory of personal identity by asking us to imagine that the soul, or immaterial substance, that is the subject of our mental states may in earlier times have been that of Socrates' mental states; as long as we can

remember nothing of Socrates' experiences, we are not the same person with Socrates. On the other side, we can imagine that the soul or immaterial substance that is the subject of my states today might be a numerically distinct soul from the one I had yesterday (maybe the one I have today is the one you had yesterday), but that the memories had by the soul I had yesterday were passed on to its successor; in spite of the switch, I would still be the same person, or so Locke thinks we would judge. Locke concludes that the identity of a person does not consist in the identity of a human being (where that identity would be constituted by sameness of a living human body), nor in the identity of a soul or immaterial substance; as Locke's discussion of these and many other examples is meant to show, our intuitive judgments about when we have the same person and when we don't suggest an implicit commitment to the view that identity of person is constituted by sameness of consciousness and not by unity of substance, whether that substance is material or immaterial.

As before, Locke's theory of personal identity is motivated by larger issues. One set of issues is theological; there was much concern in seventeenth-century England with soteriology, and especially with the doctrine of the resurrection of the dead. Locke's theory makes consciousness the bearer of moral responsibility, so that one's moral accountability extends to any action to which one's consciousness extends, whether or not one is in the same body or has the same soul as when one did the action. This theory thus cuts through all the problems about which body it is that is resurrected – the body as it was at death? as it was in the prime of life? All particles of matter that were ever a part of it? And the toughest problem of all – what happens to cannibals and their victims? Locke can say that God simply attaches the consciousness, with its awareness of past actions, to any body, fashioned from any matter, and that body thereby becomes the person's body (so that the person can be said to live again).

Probably the major goal of Locke's discussion of personal identity is, however, to establish that we have no need of souls, considered as substantial forms of the living human animal, to provide for the identity of persons. Locke was at least as much interested as was Descartes in jettisoning the Scholastic doctrine of forms and paving the way for the mechanistic philosophy of nature. Accordingly, he presents the discussion of personal identity as an illustration of his general thesis about identity: except in those very limited cases in which identity is determined by unity of substance, identity is determined by the idea of the kind to which the individual belongs. So plants, animals, and persons, which were the Scholastics' prime examples of things whose souls, or substantial forms, determined their identity, are now seen to have their identity determined by our ideas of the kinds. There is no reason, on this account, to postulate substantial forms to account for the identity of persons, or of any other natural object.

Hume

Hume's treatment of personal identity, like Locke's, is presented as an illustration of a general theory of identity. But where Locke took himself to be explicating something real – the identity of individual things, persons – Hume instead is exposing the operations of mind that produce the *fiction* of a person as an individual thing. The famous 'bundle theory' of personal identity is thus not a theory setting out the conditions under which persons have their identity as real individual things, but instead provides an account of the mistakes of thought that make it seem as if there were such things. Hume calls on his general principles of association of ideas to account for the mind's propensity confusedly to telescope resembling perceptions into a (fictional) numerically identical perception, and thus mistake a train of distinct but highly resembling perceptions for a single enduring one. It is this fictional identity that gives rise to the conviction of real personal identity. (It bears noting that Hume himself, in the Appendix to the *Treatise of Human Nature*, expressed deep reservations about his

account, and did not return to the topic in his later reworking of the *Treatise*, the *Inquiry concerning Human Understanding*.)

Kant

The last great philosopher of our period was Kant; and in his work both of the large issues we have traced, the mind–body problem and the problem of personal identity, come together. Kant's most direct and extended treatment of these issues is contained in the charmingly titled section 'The Paralogisms of Pure Reason' in the *Critique of Pure Reason*. This section, like the other sections in this part of the *Critique* (the Transcendental Dialectic), is designed to show that human reason will inevitably go wrong if it tries to come to demonstrative certainty regarding the metaphysical status of the soul. The four paralogisms – concerning the soul as substance, the simplicity of the soul, the soul as personality (i.e. as the metaphysical basis of personal identity) and the soul as related to external objects via perception – all involve the same mistake, that of taking a merely formal unity for a property of empirical things. Kant's analysis is quite complex, but it can be sketched as follows. The basic principle that 'It must be possible for the "I think" to accompany all of my representations' (*CPR* B 131) correctly sets out the condition for being a thinking thing, but it does so only in a wholly general way: all thinking things as such must satisfy the condition, so it cannot provide for the individuation of any one thinking thing as opposed to any or all others. For that, we need to consider the particular causal relations that tie perceptions and other states of consciousness to particular material objects in space and time – in short, we need to consider the SELF (what 'I' refers to) as an empirical self. But then we find that the metaphysical attributes of the self (substancehood, simplicity, personality) that we derived from the pure concept of a self (defined only by the formal 'I think') cannot with any confidence be asserted of the empirical self, because the empirical emptiness of the pure concept was exploited in the derivations. Any attempt to establish a priori metaphysical conclusions about the self must therefore come to naught. As a result of Kant's work, issues in the philosophy of mind became almost inextricably connected with general epistemological issues, and it is only relatively recently that they have been pulled apart.

This brief overview of the high points of the seventeenth- and eighteenth-century treatments of these issues has, I hope, suggested two things: first, that there might be some value to contemporary philosophers of mind in looking more closely than is perhaps usually done at the historical roots of the problems that they deal with; and second, that if one does look back in this way, it is important to pay attention to the context of the discussion; otherwise we may just be projecting current preoccupations, not to say prejudices, back in time.

BIBLIOGRAPHY

Primary sources

René Descartes, *The Philosophical Writings of Descartes, Vols. 1 and 2*, trans. J. Cottingham, R. Stoothoff and D. Murdoch. Cambridge University Press, 1985.

David Hume, *A Treatise of Human Nature*, ed. L. A. Selby-Bigge, rev. P. H. Nidditch. Oxford. Clarendon Press, 1978.

Immanuel Kant, *Critique of Pure Reason*, trans. Norman Kemp Smith. London: Macmillan & Co, Ltd., 1929.

Gottfried Wilhelm Leibniz, *Leibniz: Philosophical Essays*, trans. R. Ariew and D. Garber. Indianapolis, Indiana, and Cambridge, MA: Hackett Publishing Company, 1989.

John Locke, *An Essay Concerning Human Understanding*, ed. P. H. Nidditch. Oxford University Press, 1975.

Baruch Benedictus Spinoza, *Ethics I and Descartes's Principles of Philosophy*, in *The Collected Works of Spinoza*, ed. and trans. E. M. Curley. Princeton University Press, 1985.

Secondary sources

On Descartes

Curley, E. 1978. *Descartes against the Skeptics.* Cambridge, MA.: Harvard University Press.

Mathews, G. 1992. *Thought's Ego: Augustine and Descartes.* Ithaca: Cornell University Press.

Williams, B. 1978. *Descartes: The Project of Pure Enquiry.* Atlantic Highlands, N.J. Humanities Press.

Wilson, M. 1978. *Descartes.* London: Routledge & Kegan Paul.

On Leibniz

Adams, R.M. 1983. Phenomenalism and corporeal substance in Leibniz. In *Midwest Studies in Philosophy*, Vol. 8 ed. P. French, T. Uehling and H. Wettstein. Minneapolis: University of Minnesota Press.

Mates, B. 1986. *The Philosophy of Leibniz.* Oxford University Press.

Sleigh, R.C. 1990. *Leibniz and Arnauld: A Commentary on their Correspondence.* New Haven: Yale University Press.

On Spinoza

Bennett J. 1984. *A Study of Spinoza's Ethics.* Indianapolis: Hackett Publishing Co.

Curley, E. 1969. *Spinoza's Metaphysics: An Essay in Interpretation.* Cambridge, MA.: Harvard University Press.

Curley, E. 1988. *Behind the Geometrical Method: A Reading of Spinoza's Ethics.* Princeton University Press.

On Locke

Atherton, M. 1983. Locke's theory of personal identity. In *Midwest Studies in Philosophy, Vol. 8*, ed. P. French, T. Uehling, and H. Wettstein. Minneapolis: University of Minnesota Press.

Ayers, M. 1991. *Locke*, 2 vols. London and New York: Routledge & Kegan Paul.

Winkler K. 1991. Locke on personal identity. *Journal of the History of Philosophy*, 29, 201–26.

On Hume

Flage, D.E. 1990. *David Hume's Theory of Mind.* London and New York: Routledge & Kegan Paul.

Stroud, B. 1977. *Hume* London and Boston: Routledge & Kegan Paul.

On Kant

Allison, H. 1983. *Kant's Transcendental Idealism.* New Haven: Yale University Press.

Ameriks, K. 1982. *Kant's Theory of Mind: An Analysis of the Paralogisms of Pure Reason.* Oxford: Clarendon Press.

Kitcher, P. 1990. *Kant's Transcendental Psychology*. New York: Oxford University Press.

General

Buchdahl, G. 1969. *Metaphysics and the Philosophy of Science*. Cambridge, MA.: MIT Press.

Loeb, L. 1981. *From Descartes to Hume: Continental Metaphysics and the Development of Modern Philosophy*. Ithaca: Cornell University Press.

Yolton, J. 1983. *Thinking Matter: Materialism in Eighteenth Century Britain*. Minneapolis: University of Minnesota Press.

Yolton, J. 1984. *Perceptual Acquaintance from Descartes to Reid*. Minneapolis: University of Minnesota Press.

EDWIN McCANN

holism Holism is the idea that the elements of a system have significance in virtue of their interrelations with each other. Of course, this definition is so general that it could be relevant to virtually any subject matter, and this threatens to rob the notion of interest. For holism to be worth discussing – for it to have any grip on our view of some subject matter – we require a more precise specification of the system and type of significance that is at issue.

In the philosophy of mind, holism has been most widely discussed in connection with both the contents of propositional attitudes and the meanings of linguistic constructions. For example, insofar as you think that the meaning of a given sentence in a language depends on its inferential or evidential connections to other sentences in that language, you are a holist about meaning. Or, insofar as you think that, in a given case, the content of someone's belief depends on the inferential or evidential connections to other beliefs that the person holds, you are a holist about content. Moreover, even these formulations are too imprecise. Sharpening them would require that we go into detail about the notions of 'inferential' or 'evidential' connections, and we would also have to say just how extensive these connections must be. A very moderate holism about language might maintain that the meanings of certain words depends on connections to a fairly restricted range of other words. Thus, if one argued that 'there are tigers' as used by a given speaker could only mean that there were tigers if that speaker was prepared to infer from this sentence such things as 'there are animals' and 'there are mammals', then this holism need not be seen as having drastic consequences. But if you insisted that the meaning of 'there are tigers' depended on the epistemic attitudes of the speaker (his tendency to voice dissent or assent) to every other sentence of his language, then the holism would seem to have very drastic consequences indeed. For it suggests that no two speakers could ever mean the same thing by some given sentence, since it is almost certainly true that any two speakers will differ somewhere in their epistemic attitudes. My thinking that it is very unlikely that tigers make good pets and your thinking it less unlikely, would make the sentence 'there are tigers' mean something different in my mouth than in yours.

Most recently, holism about linguistic meaning has tended to trade under the label 'CONCEPTUAL ROLE SEMANTICS', though this phrase can also be pressed into service to describe a holism about propositional attitude contents.

See also FODOR; FUNCTIONALISM.

SAMUEL GUTTENPLAN

I

identity theories What is the relation between mind and physical reality? Well-established schools of thought give starkly opposing answers to this question. Descartes insisted that mental phenomena are non-physical in nature. This view seems inviting because mental phenomena are indisputably different from everything else. Moreover, it's safe to assume that all phenomena that aren't mental have some physical nature. So it may seem that the best way to explain how the mental differs from everything else is to hypothesize that mind is non-physical in nature.

But that hypothesis is not the only way to explain how mind differs from everything else. It's also possible that mental phenomena are instead just a special case of physical phenomena; they would then have properties that no other physical phenomena have, but would still themselves be physical. This explanation requires that we specify what is special about mental phenomena which makes them different from everything else. But we must specify that in any case, just in order to understand the nature of the mental. Characterizing mental phenomena negatively, simply as not being physical, does little to help us understand what it is for something to be mental.

The claim that mental phenomena are a special kind of physical phenomenon is the root idea of mind–body materialism (also called PHYSICALISM). And the version of that thesis that's been most widely defended over the last three decades is the identity theory of mind.

In Descartes' time the issue between materialists and their opponents was framed in terms of substances. Materialists such as Thomas Hobbes and Pierre Gassendi maintained that people are physical systems with abilities that no other physical systems have; people, therefore, are special kinds of physical substance. Descartes' DUALISM, by contrast, claimed that people consist of two distinct substances that interact causally: a physical body and a non-physical unextended substance. The traditional conception of substance, however, introduces extraneous issues, which have no bearing on whether mental phenomena are physical or non-physical. And in any case, even those who agree with Descartes that the mental is non-physical have today given up the idea that there are non-physical substances. It's now widely accepted on all sides that people are physical organisms with two distinctive kinds of states: physical states such as standing and walking, and mental states such as thinking and feeling.

Accordingly, the issue of whether the mental is physical or non-physical is no longer cast in terms of whether people, and other creatures that have the ability to think and sense, are physical or non-physical substances. Rather, that question is put in terms of whether the distinctively mental states of thinking, sensing, and feeling are physical states or non-physical states. The identity theory is the materialist thesis that every mental state is physical, that is, that every mental state is identical with some physical state.

PROPERTIES OF MENTAL STATES

If mental states are identical with physical states, presumably the relevant physical states are various sorts of neural states. Our concepts of mental states such as thinking, sensing, and feeling are of course different from our concepts of neural states, of whatever sort. But that's no problem for the identity theory. As J. J. C. Smart (1962), who first argued for the identity theory, emphasized, the requisite identities don't depend on our concepts of mental states or the meanings of mental terms. For *a* to be identical with *b*, *a* and *b* must have exactly the same properties, but the terms '*a*' and '*b*' need not mean the same (*see* LEIBNIZ'S LAW).

But a problem does seem to arise about the properties of mental states. Suppose pain is identical with a certain firing of c-fibres. Although a particular pain is the very same state as a neural firing, we identify that state in two different ways: as a pain and as a neural firing. The state will therefore have certain properties in virtue of which we identify it as a pain and others in virtue of which we identify it as a neural firing. The properties in virtue of which we identify it as a pain will be mental properties, whereas those in virtue of which we identify it as a neural firing will be physical properties. This has seemed to many to lead to a kind of dualism at the level of the properties of mental states. Even if we reject a dualism of substances and take people simply to be physical organisms, those organisms still have both mental and physical states. Similarly, even if we identify those mental states with certain physical states, those states will nonetheless have both mental and physical properties. So disallowing dualism with respect to substances and their states simply leads to its reappearance at the level of the properties of those states.

There are two broad categories of mental property. Mental states such as thoughts and desires, often called PROPOSITIONAL ATTITUDES, have CONTENT that can be described by 'that' clauses. For example, one can have a thought, or desire, that it will rain. These states are said to have intentional properties, or INTENTIONALITY. SENSATIONS, such as pains and sense impressions, lack intentional content, and have instead qualitative properties of various sorts.

The problem just sketched about mental properties is widely thought to be most pressing for sensations, since the painful quality of pains and the red quality of visual sensations seem to be irretrievably non-physical. So even if mental states are all identical with physical states, these states appear to have properties that aren't physical. And if mental states do actually have non-physical properties, the identity of mental with physical states won't sustain a thoroughgoing mind–body materialism.

Smart's reply to this challenge is that, despite initial appearances, the distinctive properties of sensations are neutral as between being mental or physical; in the term Smart borrowed from Gilbert RYLE, they are topic neutral. My having a sensation of red consists in my being in a state that's similar, in respects that we need not specify, to something that occurs in me when I'm in the presence of certain stimuli. Because the respect of similarity isn't specified, the property is neither distinctively mental nor distinctively physical. But everything is similar to everything else in some respect or other. So leaving the respect of similarity unspecified makes this account too weak to capture the distinguishing properties of sensations.

A more sophisticated reply to the difficulty about mental properties is due independently to D. M. Armstrong (1968) and David LEWIS (1972), who argue that for a state to be a particular sort of intentional state or sensation is for that state to bear characteristic causal relations to other particular occurrences. The properties in virtue of which we identify states as thoughts or sensations will still be neutral as between being mental or physical, since anything can bear a causal relation to anything else. But causal connections have a better chance than similarity in some unspecified respect of capturing the distinguishing properties of sensations and thoughts.

This causal theory is appealing (see the following section). Still, it's misguided to try to construe the distinctive properties of mental states as being neutral as between being mental or physical. To be neutral as regards being mental or physical is to be neither distinctively mental nor distinctively physical. But since thoughts and sensations are distinctively mental states, for a state to be a thought or a sensation is perforce for it to have some characteristically mental property. We inevitably lose the distinctively mental if we construe these properties as being neither mental nor physical.

Not only is the topic-neutral construal misguided; the problem it was designed to solve is equally so. That problem stemmed from the idea that the mental must have some non-physical aspect, if not at the level of people or their mental states, then at the level of the distinctively mental properties of those states (*see* PROPERTY).

But the idea that the mental is in some respect non-physical cannot be assumed without argument. Plainly, the distinctively mental properties of mental states are unlike any other properties we know about. Only mental states have properties that are at all like the qualitative properties of sensations. And arguably nothing but mental states have properties that are anything like the intentional properties of THOUGHTS and DESIRES. But this doesn't show that these mental properties are not physical properties. Not all physical properties are like the standard cases; so mental properties might still be special kinds of physical properties. Indeed, it's question begging to assume otherwise. The doctrine that the mental properties of mental states are non-physical properties is simply an expression of the CARTESIAN doctrine that the mental is automatically non-physical.

To settle whether or not those mental properties are non-physical, we would need a positive account of what those properties are. Proposals are available that would account for intentional properties wholly in physical terms (*see* DENNETT, DRETSKE, and FODOR), and perhaps one of these will prove correct. It's been more difficult to give a positive account of the qualitative properties of sensations, and that's led some to conclude that such properties will inevitably turn out to be non-physical. But it's plainly unfounded to infer from the difficulty in explaining something to its being non-physical.

It's sometimes held that properties should count as physical properties only if they can be defined using the terms of physics. This is far too restrictive. Nobody would hold that to reduce biology to physics, for example, we must define all biological properties using only terms that occur in physics. And even putting REDUCTION aside, if certain biological properties couldn't be so defined, that wouldn't mean that those properties were in any way non-physical. The sense of 'physical' that's relevant here must be broad enough to include not only biological properties, but also most commonsense, macroscopic properties. Bodily states are uncontroversially physical in the relevant way. So we can recast the identity theory as asserting that mental states are identical with bodily states.

TYPES AND TOKENS

There are two ways to take the claim that every mental state is identical with some bodily state. It might mean identity at the level of types, that is, that every mental-state type is identical with some physical-state type. Such type identity would hold if all the instances of a particular type of mental state are also instances of a particular type of bodily state. This is called the type identity theory.

But the identity claim might instead mean only that every instance of a mental state is identical with an instance of a bodily state, of some type or other. On this construal, the various types of mental state wouldn't have to correspond to types of bodily state; instances of a single mental type might be identical with tokens of distinct bodily types. This weaker claim is known as the token identity theory.

There's reason to doubt that the type identity theory is true. It's plausible that organisms of different species may share at least some types of mental state – say, pain – even if their anatomical and physiological differences are so great that they can't share the relevant types of bodily state. No single bodily-state type would then correspond to these mental-state types. This possibility is called the multiple realizability of mental states. It's conceivable, of course, that biology will someday type physiological states in a way that corresponds tolerably well with types of mental state, but we can have no guarantee that this will happen.

Even if no physiological types correspond to types of mental state, the causal theory of Lewis and Armstrong would allow us to identify types of mental state with types described in other terms. On Lewis's version of the theory, mental states are whatever states occupy the causal roles specified by all our commonsense psychological platitudes, taken together. The various types of mental state correspond to the various causal roles thus specified; mental-state tokens are of a particular mental type if they occupy the causal role that defines that type. These causal roles involve causal ties to behaviour and stimuli and to other states that occupy these causal roles. Such a theory, which defines mental-state types in terms of causal roles, is often called FUNC-TIONALISM.

One could imagine that the individual states that occupy the relevant causal roles turn out not to be bodily states; for example they might instead be states of an Cartesian unextended substance. But it's over-whelmingly likely that the states that do occupy those causal roles are all tokens of bodily-state types. So the causal theory, together with this empirical likelihood, sus-tains at least the token identity theory. Moreover, this version of the causal theory bypasses the problematic idea that the mental properties of those states are neutral as between being mental or physical, since mental-state types are determined by our psychological platitudes.

To defend the type identity theory as well, however, would require showing that all mental-state tokens that occupy a particular causal role also fall under a single physio-logical type. Lewis (1980) expects sub-stantial uniformity of physiological type across the tokens of each mental-state type, at least within particular populations of creatures. But if tokens of different physiolo-gical types do occupy the same causal role, that would undermine the type identity theory, or at least make it relative to certain populations.

Multiple realizability is the possibility that mental-state types are instantiated by states of distinct physiological types. It's an empirical matter whether that's actually the case. If it is, physical-state types don't corre-spond to mental-state types, and the type identity theory is false.

But one might, with Hilary PUTNAM (1975), construe the type identity theory more strongly, as claiming that the mental properties that define the various types of mental state are identical with physical properties. And that's false even if the tokens of each mental-state type fall under a single physiological type; the property of occupying a particular causal role is plainly not identical with the property of belonging to a particular physiological type. On this construal, no empirical findings are needed to refute the type identity theory. But it's more reasonable to construe the type iden-tity theory less strongly, as requiring the claim only that all tokens of a particular mental-state type fall under a single physio-logical type.

Donald DAVIDSON (1970) has used differ-ent considerations to argue that mental-state types correspond to no physiological types, but that the token identity theory is nonetheless correct. Plainly, mental and bodily events cause each other. Moreover, as Davidson reasonably holds, one event token can cause another only if that causal connection instantiates some explanatory law. But Davidson also insists that an event token belongs to a particular mental type only relative to certain background assump-tions about meaning and RATIONALITY. Tokens of physical events, by contrast, belong to whatever physical type they do independently of any such background assumptions. Davidson infers that there can be no strict laws connecting physical and mental events. But if so, how can mental and bodily events cause each other? (*See* REASONS AND CAUSES.)

Davidson's solution relies on the fact that explanatory laws describe events in parti-cular ways and a different description of the same events might not sustain the explanatory connection. So the impossibility of laws connecting mental and physical events means only that no laws can connect physical events, described as such, with mental events, described as such. To interact causally, events must figure in explanatory laws. So each mental-event token that interacts causally with a bodily event can figure in a law only if that mental-event token can also be described in purely physical terms. The considerations that preclude laws connecting mental with physical events presumably show also that no physical types correspond to any mental-state types. But since we can describe every mental-event token in physical terms, that token will be identical with some physical-event token. This intriguing argument is difficult to evaluate, mainly because it's unclear exactly why background assumptions about meaning and rationality should preclude laws connecting events described in mental terms with those described physically.

In order for causal interactions between mental and bodily events to fall under laws that describe events solely in physical terms, physically indistinguishable events must be mentally indistinguishable, though not necessarily the other way around. That relationship is known as SUPERVENIENCE; in this case, mental properties would be said to *supervene* on physical properties. Jaegwon Kim (1984) has usefully explored such supervenience as a way to capture the relation between mental and physical.

ELIMINATIVE MATERIALISM

The Cartesian doctrine that the mental is in some way non-physical is so pervasive that even advocates of the identity theory have sometimes accepted it, at least tacitly. The idea that the mental is non-physical underlies, for example, the insistence by some identity theorists that mental properties are really neutral as between being mental or physical. To be neutral in this way, a property would have to be neutral as to whether it's mental at all. Only if one thought that being mental meant being non-physical

would one hold that defending materialism required showing that ostensibly mental properties are neutral as regards whether or not they're mental.

But holding that mental properties are non-physical has a cost that is usually not noticed. A phenomenon is mental only if it has some distinctively mental property. So, strictly speaking, a materialist who claims that mental properties are non-physical would have to conclude that no mental phenomena exist. This is the ELIMINATIVE-MATERIALIST position advanced by Richard Rorty (1979). (*See An Essay on Mind* section 3.7; ELIMINATIVISM.)

According to Rorty, 'mental' and 'physical' are incompatible terms. Nothing can be both mental and physical; so mental states cannot be identical with bodily states. Rorty traces this incompatibly to our views about incorrigibility; 'mental' and 'physical' are incompatible terms because we regard as incorrigible reports of one's own mental states, but not reports of physical occurrences. But he also argues that we can imagine a people who describe themselves and each other using terms just like our mental vocabulary, except that those people don't take the reports made with that vocabulary to be incorrigible. Since Rorty takes a state to be a mental state only if one's reports about it are taken to be incorrigible, his imaginary people don't ascribe mental states to themselves or each other. But the only difference between their language and ours is that we take as incorrigible certain reports which they don't. So their language has no less descriptive or explanatory power than ours. Rorty concludes that our mental vocabulary is idle, and that there are no distinctively mental phenomena.

This argument hinges on building incorrigibility into the meaning of the term 'mental'. If we don't, the way is open to interpret Rorty's imaginary people as simply having a different theory of mind from ours, on which reports of one's own mental states aren't incorrigible. Their reports would thus be about mental states, as construed by their theory. Rorty's thought experiment would then provide reason to conclude not that our mental terminology is idle, but only that this alternative theory of mental phenomena is correct. His thought experiment would thus sustain the non-eliminativist view that mental states are bodily states. Whether Rorty's argument supports his eliminativist conclusion or the standard identity theory, therefore, depends solely on whether or not one holds that the mental is in some way non-physical.

Paul M. Churchland (1981) advances a different argument for eliminative materialism. According to Churchland, the commonsense conceptions of mental states contained in our present FOLK PSYCHOLOGY are, from a scientific point of view, radically defective. But we can expect that eventually a more sophisticated theoretical account will replace those folk-psychological conceptions, showing that mental phenomena, as described by current folk psychology, don't exist. Since that account would be integrated into the rest of science, we'd have a thoroughgoing materialist treatment of all phenomena. So this version of eliminativist materialism, unlike Rorty's, does not rely on assuming that the mental is non-physical.

But even if current folk psychology is mistaken, that doesn't show that mental phenomena don't exist, but only that they aren't the way folk psychology describes them as being. We could conclude they don't exist only if the folk-psychological claims that turn out to be mistaken actually define what it is for a phenomenon to be mental. Otherwise, the new theory would still be about mental phenomena, and indeed would help show that they're identical with physical phenomena. Churchland's argument, like Rorty's, depends on a special way of defining the mental, which we needn't adopt. It's likely that any argument for eliminative materialism will require some such definition, without which the argument would instead support the identity theory.

NECESSARY IDENTITY

Early identity theorists insisted that the identity between mental and bodily events was contingent, meaning simply that the relevant identity statements were not conceptual truths. That leaves open the question of whether such identities would be necessarily true on other construals of necessity.

Saul A. Kripke (1980) has argued that such identities would have to be necessarily true if they were true at all. Some terms refer to things contingently, in that those terms would have referred to different things had circumstances been relevantly different. Kripke's example is 'The first Postmaster General of the U.S.', which, in a different situation, would have referred to somebody other than Benjamin Franklin. Kripke calls these terms non-rigid designators. Other terms refer to things necessarily, since no circumstances are possible in which they would refer to anything else; these terms are rigid designators.

If the terms 'a' and 'b' refer to the same thing and both determine that thing necessarily, the identity statement 'a = b' is necessarily true. Kripke maintains that the term 'pain' and the terms for the various brain states all determine the states they refer to necessarily; no circumstances are possible in which these terms would refer to different things. So if pain were identical with some particular brain state, it would be necessarily identical with that state. But Kripke argues that pain can't be necessarily identical with any brain state, since the tie between PAINS and brain states plainly seems contingent. He concludes that they cannot be identical at all.

This argument applies equally to the identity of types and tokens. Whenever the term 'pain' refers to a state, it refers to that state rigidly; similarly with the various terms for brain states. So if an individual occurrence of pain were identical with an individual brain state, it would be necessarily identical with it. Since they can't be necessarily identical, they can't be identical at all.

Kripke notes that our intuitions about whether an identity is contingent can mislead us. Heat is necessarily identical with mean molecular kinetic energy; no circumstances are possible in which they aren't identical. Still, it may at first sight appear that heat could have been identical with some other phenomenon. But it appears this way, Kripke argues, only because we pick out heat by our sensation of heat, which bears only a contingent tie to mean molecular kinetic energy. It's the sensation of heat that actually seems to be connected contingently with mean molecular kinetic energy, not the physical heat itself.

Kripke insists, however, that such reasoning cannot disarm our intuitive sense that pain is connected only contingently with brain states. That's because for a state to be pain is necessarily for it to be felt as pain. Unlike heat, in the case of pain there's no difference between the state itself and how that state is felt, and intuitions about the one are perforce intuitions about the other.

Kripke's assumption about the term 'pain' is open to question. As Lewis notes, one need not hold that 'pain' determines the same state in all possible situations; indeed, the causal theory explicitly allows that it may not. And if it doesn't, it may be that pains and brain states are contingently identical. But there's also a problem about a substantive assumption Kripke makes about the nature of pains, namely, that pains are necessarily felt as pains. First impressions notwithstanding, there is reason to think not. There are times when we are not aware of our pains, for example when we're suitably distracted. So the relationship between pains and our being aware of them may be contingent after all, just as the relationship between physical heat and our sensation of heat is. And that would disarm the intuition that pain is connected only contingently with brain states.

SUBJECTIVE FEATURES

Kripke's argument focuses on pains and other sensations, which, because they have qualitative properties, are frequently held to cause the greatest problems for the identity theory. Thomas Nagel (1974) traces the general difficulty for the identity theory to the CONSCIOUSNESS of mental states. A

mental state's being conscious, he urges, means that there's something it's like to be in that state. And to understand that, we must adopt the point of view of the kind of creature that's in the state. But an account of something is objective, he insists, only insofar as it's independent of any particular type of point of view. Since consciousness is inextricably tied to points of view, no objective account of it is possible. And that means conscious states cannot be identical with bodily states.

The viewpoint of a creature is central to what that creature's conscious states are like because different kinds of creatures have conscious states with different kinds of qualitative property. But the qualitative properties of a creature's conscious states depend, in an objective way, on that creature's perceptual apparatus. We can't always predict what another creature's conscious states are like, just as we can't always extrapolate from microscopic to macroscopic properties, at least without having a suitable theory that covers those properties. But what a creature's conscious states are like depends in an objective way on its bodily endowment, which is itself objective. So these considerations give us no reason to think that what those conscious states are like is not also an objective matter.

If a sensation isn't conscious, there's nothing it's like to have it. So Nagel's idea that what it's like to have sensations is central to their nature suggests that sensations cannot occur without being conscious. And that in turn seems to threaten their objectivity. If sensations must be conscious, perhaps they have no nature independently of how we're aware of them, and thus no objective nature. Indeed, it's only conscious sensations that seem to cause problems for the identity theory (see SUBJECTIVITY).

The assumption that mental states are invariably conscious, like the supposition that they're non-physical, is basic to the Cartesian view. But sensations do occur that aren't conscious. A mental state's being conscious consists in one's being conscious of it in a way that's intuitively direct and unmediated. But as already noted, distractions often make us wholly unaware of our sensations. Sensations that aren't conscious also occur in both subliminal perception and peripheral vision, as well as in more esoteric contexts. (*See* Weiskrantz, 1986.)

Sensations can, moreover, have qualitative properties without being conscious. Qualitative properties are sometimes called QUALIA, with the implication that we must be conscious of them; but we needn't be bound by that term's implications. Qualitative properties are simply those properties by means of which we distinguish among the various kinds of sensations when they're conscious. But a sensation's being conscious makes no difference to what its distinguishing properties are; its being conscious consists simply in one's being conscious of those properties in a suitable way. When a sensation isn't conscious its distinguishing properties seem to cause no difficulty for the identity theory. And since those properties are the same whether or not the sensation is conscious, there's nothing about those properties that undermines the identity theory. We would assume otherwise only if we held, with Nagel and Kripke, that sensations must all be conscious. (*See* Rosenthal, 1986.)

Perhaps multiple realizability refutes the type identity theory; but there are ample arguments that support the token identity theory. Moreover, the arguments against the token theory seem all to rely on unfounded Cartesian assumptions about the nature of mental states. The doctrine that the mental is in some way non-physical is straightforwardly question begging, and it's simply not the case that all sensory states are conscious. It is likely, therefore, that the identity theory, at least in the token version, is correct.

See also An Essay in Mind section 3.6.2.

BIBLIOGRAPHY

Armstrong, D.M. 1968. *A Materialist Theory of the Mind*. New York: Humanities Press.

Churchland, P.M. 1981. Eliminative materialism and the propositional attitudes. *Journal of Philosophy*, LXXVIII: 2, 67–90.

Davidson, D. 1970. Mental events. In *Experience and Theory*, ed. L. Foster and J. W. Swanson: Amherst, MA.: University of Massachusetts Press.

Kim, J. 1984. Epiphenomenal and supervenient causation. In *Midwest Studies in Philosophy, Vol 9*: Minneapolis: University of Minnesota Press.

Kripke, S.A. 1980. *Naming and Necessity*. Cambridge, MA.: Harvard University Press. Originally published in *Semantics of Natural Language*, ed. D. Davidson and G. Harman. Dordrecht: D. Reidel Publishing Company, 1972.

Lewis, D. 1980. Mad pain and Martian pain. In *Readings in Philosophy of Psychology, Vol. I*, ed. N. Block. Cambridge, MA.: Harvard University Press.

Lewis, D. 1972. Psychophysical and theoretical identification. *Australasian Journal of Philosophy*, L: 3, 247–58.

Nagel, T. 1974. What is it like to be a bat? *The Philosophical Review*, LXXXIII: 4, 435–50.

Putnam, H. 1975. The nature of mental states. *Mind Language and Reality: Philosophical Papers, Vol. 2*. Cambridge University Press.

Rorty, R. 1979. *Philosophy and the Mirror of Nature*. Princeton University Press.

Rosenthal, D.M., ed. 1991. *The Nature of Mind*. New York: Oxford University Press.

Rosenthal, D.M. 1986. Two concepts of consciousness. *Philosophical Studies*, XLIX: 3, 329–59.

Smart, J.J.C. 1962. Sensations and brain processes. In *The Philosophy of Mind*, ed. V. C. Chappell. Englewood Cliffs, N.J.: Prentice-Hall, Inc.

Weiskrantz, L. 1986. *Blindsight*. Oxford University Press.

DAVID M. ROSENTHAL

imagery Imagery has played an enormously important role in philosophical conceptions of the mind. The most popular view of images prior to this century has been what we might call 'the picture theory'. According to this view, held by such diverse philosophers as Aristotle,

Descartes, and Locke, mental images – specifically, visual images – are significantly picture-like in the way they represent objects in the world. Despite its widespread acceptance, the picture theory of mental images was left largely unexplained in the traditional philosophical literature. Admittedly most of those who accepted the theory held that mental images copy or resemble what they represent. But little more was said.

This century the pictorial view of images has come under heavy philosophical attack. Three basic sorts of objections have been raised. First, there have been challenges to the sense of the view: mental images are not seen with real eyes; they cannot be hung on real walls; they have no objective weight or colour. What, then, can it mean to say that images are pictorial? Secondly, there have been arguments that purport to show that the view is false. Perhaps the best known of these is founded on the charge that the picture theory cannot satisfactorily explain the indeterminacy of many mental images. Finally, there have been attacks on the evidential underpinnings of the theory. Historically, the philosophical claim that images are picture-like rested primarily on an appeal to INTROSPECTION. And today introspection is taken to reveal a good deal less about the mind than was traditionally supposed. This attitude towards introspection has manifested itself in the case of imagery in the view that what introspection really shows about visual images is not that they are pictorial but only that what goes on in imagery is experientially much like what goes on in seeing.

So, the picture theory has been variously dismissed by many philosophers this century as nonsensical, or false, or without support. Perhaps the most influential alternative has been a view that is now commonly known as descriptionalism. This view has some similarity with the claim made by the behaviourist, J. B. Watson, that imaging is talking to one's self beneath one's breath; for the basic thesis of descriptionalism is that mental images represent in the manner of linguistic descriptions. This thesis, however, should not be taken to imply that during imagery there must be present inner tokens of the imager's spoken language either in any movements of the imager's larynx or in the imager's brain. Rather the thought is that mental images represent objects in some neural code which is, in important respects, language-like.

Descriptionalism remains popular in philosophy today (*see* e.g. Dennett, 1981), and it also has significant support in contemporary psychology. Nevertheless the tide has begun to turn again back towards the pictorial view, and I think it is fair to say that the picture theory is now quite widely regarded as intelligible, perhaps true, and certainly not a theory in search of facts to explain. What has been responsible for this change in attitude more than anything else is the work of some cognitive psychologists, notably Stephen Kosslyn. In response to a large body of experimental data on imagery, Kosslyn and his co-workers have developed an empirical version of the pictorial view that seems much more promising than any of its philosophical predecessors.

In the following section of this entry, I present a brief sketch of Kosslyn's theory. In the section after, I turn to recent descriptional theories of imagery, and I make some observations of my own about imagistic representation. In the final section I lay out three further issues concerning imagery that are of interest to philosophers.

KOSSLYN'S THEORY

According to Kosslyn, mental images are to be conceived of on the model of displays on a cathode-ray tube screen attached to a computer. Such displays are generated on the screen by the computer from information that is stored in the computer's memory. Since there are obvious differences between mental images and screen displays, a question arises as to just what the respects are in which the former are supposed to be like the latter.

Kosslyn suggests that before we answer this question, we reflect upon how a picture is formed on a monitor screen and what makes *it* pictorial. We may think of the screen itself as being covered by a matrix in which there are a large number of tiny squares or cells. The pattern formed by placing dots in these cells is pictorial, Kosslyn asserts, at least in part because it has spatial features which correspond to spatial features of the represented object. In particular, dots in the matrix represent points on the surface of the object and relative distance and geometrical relations among dots match the same relations among object points. Thus if dots A, B, and C in the matrix stand respectively for points P_1, P_2, and P_3 on the object surface, then if P_1 is below P_2 and to P_3's left (as the object is seen from a particular point of view) then likewise A is below B and to C's left (as the screen is seen from a corresponding point of view). Similarly, if P_1 is further from P_2 than from P_3 then A is further from B than from C.

Kosslyn's reasoning now becomes more opaque. The main strand of thought which is to be found in Kosslyn's writings seems to be that although mental images lack the above spatial characteristics, they nonetheless function *as if* they had those characteristics. Thus, in Kosslyn's view, it is not literally true that mental images are pictures. Rather the truth in the picture theory is that mental images are *functional* pictures.

This claim itself is in dire need of clarification, of course. But before I try to clarify its meaning, I want briefly to sketch certain other aspects of Kosslyn's position. Consider again a cathode-ray tube screen on which a picture is displayed. The screen may be thought of as the medium in which the picture is presented. This medium is spatial and it is made up of a large number of basic units or cells some of which are illuminated to form a picture. Analogously, according to Kosslyn, there is a functional spatial medium for imagery made up of a number of basic units or cells. Mental images, on Kosslyn's view, are functional pictures in this medium,

Kosslyn hypothesizes that the imagery medium, which he calls 'the visual buffer', is shared with visual perception. In veridical

perception, any given unit in the medium, by being active, represents the presence of a just-noticeable object part at a particular two-dimensional spatial location within the field of view. In imagery, the same unit, by being active, represents the very same thing. Thus, imaged object parts are represented within an image as having certain viewpoint-relative locations they do not in fact occupy, namely those locations they would have occupied in the field of view had the same object parts produced the same active units during normal vision.

We are now in a position to see what Kosslyn means by the thesis that mental images are functional pictures. The basic idea is that a mental image of an object O (and nothing else) functions like a picture of O in two respects: (1) every part of the image that represents anything (i.e. any active cell in the buffer) represents a part of O; (2) two-dimensional relative distance relations among parts of O are represented in the image via distance relations among corresponding image parts (active cells). Distance in the imagery medium is not a matter of actual physical distance, however. Instead it is to be explicated in terms of number of intervening cells – the greater the distance represented, the greater the number of active cells representing adjacent portions of the object. Thus, Kosslyn's proposal does not require that cells representing adjacent object parts themselves be physically adjacent (as in a real picture). Rather, like the cells in an array in a computer, they may be widely scattered. What matters to the representation of adjacency is that the processes operating on such cells treat them *as if* they were adjacent.

The remaining elements of Kosslyn's theory concern the processes that operate on images in the visual buffer. Kosslyn postulates that there are three sets of processes, namely those that 'generate', 'inspect', and 'transform' the images. The generation process is decomposable, in Kosslyn's view, into further processes that combine together information about object parts and relations. The inspection process is also really a number of different processes that examine patterns of activated cells in the buffer thereby enabling us to recognize shapes, spatial configurations and other characteristics of the imaged objects. For example, if I form an image of a racehorse, it is the inspection process that allows me to decide if the tip of its tail extends below its rear knees. Similarly, if I image two equilateral triangles of the same size, one upright and one inverted with its tip touching the middle of the base of the upright one, the inspection process is what enables me to recognize the diamond-shaped parallelogram in the middle. Finally, there are transformation processes. These processes 'rotate', 'scale in size', or 'translate' the patterns of activated cells in the buffer.

That, then, in crude outline is Kosslyn's theory (for further discussion, see Block 1983; Tye, 1988, 1991). Why should we believe such a view? I cannot possibly go into all the relevant experimental evidence here. Instead I shall simply mention one important experiment. In this experiment, Kosslyn required subjects to study the map shown in figure 1.

When the subjects had become familiar enough with the map to be able to draw it,

Figure 1.

they were asked to form a mental image of it and then to focus in on one particular object in the image, and this request was repeated for different objects. It was found that the farther away an object was from the place on the image presently being focused on, the longer it took to focus on that new object. So, for example, shifting attention from the 'tree part' of the image to the 'hut part' took longer than shifting attention from the 'tree part' to the 'lake part'.

Kosslyn claims that this experiment shows that mental images can be scanned at fixed speeds. How exactly does this hypothesis explain the results? After all, images, on the pictorial view, are not so constituted that their parts bear the same relative distance relations to one another as the object parts they represent. The answer goes as follows. Scanning across a mental image involves accessing the appropriate image parts serially (either by shifting the locus of attention across a stationary image or by translating the imaged pattern across the visual buffer so that different aspects of the pattern fall under a fixed central focus of attention). More specifically, in the map case, scanning across the image involves accessing one after another the members of a sequence of representationally simple image parts, each of which represents a different, just-noticeable location on the map situated on a line connecting the figures represented at the beginning and end of scanning. Thus, if the image has parts A, B, and C which represent respectively map parts X, Y, and Z, and X is nearer to Y than to Z, then scanning across the image from A to B will involve accessing one after another fewer image parts than scanning from A to C. Thus, assuming a fixed scanning speed, Kosslyn's view predicts that the time it takes to scan from A to B will be shorter than the time it takes to scan from A to C. And this is indeed the result we get.

I want now to mention one serious difficulty for Kosslyn's view. It concerns the representation of the third dimension. How is this to be accomplished, if mental images are functional pictures? On Kosslyn's view, the visual buffer is arranged like a two-dimensional monitor screen in that the cells in the buffer themselves only represent surface patches in two dimensions. The third dimension gets represented via processes that inspect the contents of the buffer and interpret depth cues much as we do when viewing the display on a (real) monitor screen. The major problem with this view is that it conflicts with the results of an experiment conducted by Steven Pinker. In this experiment, subjects examined an open box, in which five toys were suspended at different heights, until they were able to form an accurate image of the display with their eyes closed. The subjects then scanned across their images by imagining a dot moving in a straight line between the imaged objects. It was found that scanning times increased linearly with increasing three-dimensional distance between the objects. What this result strongly suggests is that mental images cannot simply represent in the manner of two-dimensional screen displays.

Let us now take a quick look at the view of some influential cognitive scientists that images represent in the manner of structural descriptions.

DESCRIPTIONAL THEORIES

A structural description of an object is simply a complex linguistic representation whose basic non-logical semantic parts represent object parts, properties, and spatial relationships. The explicit representation of properties and spatial relations is one key difference between structural descriptions and functional pictures. Consider, for example, the representation of relative distance relations in functional pictures. We saw earlier that this is achieved indirectly via the number of image parts: more parts, more distance. No explicit representation is possible here, since every part of a functional picture that represents anything represents an object part. In a structural description this is not the case, however. The fact that A is further from B than from C can be represented by some such proposition as 'F(abc)', where 'F' is a symbol for the

relation, and 'a', 'b', and 'c' are symbols for the object parts. Since 'F' is as much a part of 'F(abc)' as 'a', 'b', and 'c', there is in this proposition a representational part that doesn't represent an object part.

Another key difference between structural descriptions and functional pictures arises with respect to syntax. Structural descriptions have syntactic parts, the contents of which, together with their syntactic combinations, determine the overall representational content. In 'F(abc)', for example, 'F' belongs to a different syntactic category than 'a', 'b', and 'c'. Moreover the content of 'F(abc)' is different from the content of 'F(bac)' even though the parts are the same. For a functional picture there are no syntactically distinguishable parts; and there is no syntactic order (so that two functional pictures that differ in what they represent must differ in what some of their parts represent).

Zenon Pylyshyn maintains that mental images are structural descriptions no different in kind from the representations involved in other areas of cognition. In Pylyshyn's view there is an inner language within which mental representation whatever its stripe is confined. This inner language is largely unconscious and is not itself a natural public language, although it is translated into such a language when we talk. According to Pylyshyn, Kosslyn's experiments on imagery can be explained by reference to the task demands placed on subjects by the experimenter's instructions together with facts the subjects already know. Consider, for example, the map scanning experiment. When subjects are told to scan across their images to an object they are not presently focusing on, they interpret the instructions as requiring them to construct inner representations something like the representations they would undergo were they actually scanning across the map with their eyes. The subjects know that it takes longer for their eyes to scan greater distances. So they set a mental clock ticking for a length of time that permits them to mimic the response they would give in the real scanning case.

It is important to realize that although this account is compatible with Kosslyn's claim that subjects are accessing serially image parts that represent adjacent just-noticeable map parts situated on a line connecting the appropriate figures, it does not presuppose that Kosslyn's claim is true. This is because the representations the subjects construct in response to the instructions may well not represent any just-noticeable map parts, and even if some such parts are represented, not all of those lying on the appropriate line need be. Perhaps, for example, there is a sequence of representations like the following: 'The hut is in the centre of the field of view', 'The hut is a little to the left and below the centre of the field of view', 'The hut is as far below and to the left of the centre of the field of view as the lake is above and to the right', 'The lake is in the centre of the field of view'. And perhaps there is also a further symbolic representation of the distance on the map between the lake and the hut. On this conception of what is going on, for different distances scanned there may be no corresponding difference in the number of representations or parts thereof. So, Pylyshyn claims, the map-scanning experiment does not demonstrate that subjects are transforming a special picture-like image. And what is true in this one case is true, Pylyshyn thinks, for Kosslyn's other experiments on imagery. Subjects, in responding to the demands placed on them by the tasks they are set (demands built into the instructions), draw upon their (frequently tacit) knowledge of the world and their own visual systems. So, the data Kosslyn has collected give us no information about images as they really are.

It is far from clear that the appeal to tacit knowledge can explain all the imagery data, contrary to Pylyshyn's claim (see Kosslyn, 1981). There are, however, other descriptional theories of imagery that have no need of the doctrine of tacit knowledge (e.g. Hinton, 1979). So, descriptionalism cannot be refuted simply by attacking the doctrine of tacit knowledge.

Who, then, is on the right track about image representation? My own view is that, given the plentiful evidence of shared mechanisms and representations in imagery and vision, images are best modelled on certain representations called '2½-D sketches', which are posited in the most promising theory of vision we have, namely the theory of David Marr. 2½-D sketches are arrays very like Kosslyn's functional pictures except that their cells contain symbols for the features of any tiny patch of surface lying on its associated line of sight (e.g. depth, orientation, presence of edge). Mental images, I believe, represent in something like the manner of 2½-D sketches to which global sentential interpretations have been affixed, for example 'This represents a horse' (see Tye, 1991). So, mental images are, in some respects, like pictures but in others they are like descriptions. The truth about images, I maintain, is that they are a mixed breed.

I want now to mention some additional matters of dispute.

FURTHER PHILOSOPHICAL ISSUES

One issue discussed historically by philosophers and still of interest today concerns the nature and origins of the vagueness that infects many mental images. As I noted at the beginning of this entry, image indeterminacy has often been considered a problem for the picture theory. Is this really the case? Moreover, just how much indeterminacy is possible in images?

Another topic much discussed of late is the subjective character of mental images (and visual percepts). It is widely held in philosophy that mental images have, over and above their representational contents, intrinsic, introspectively accessible qualities partly in virtue of which they have those contents (see INTROSPECTION; SUBJECTIVITY). On this view, a mental image of a zebra, for example, has certain intrinsic qualities accessible to consciousness partly in virtue of which it represents a zebra. This is supposedly why imaging a zebra 'feels' different to one from merely thinking of a zebra without forming any image: in the latter case, one's MENTAL REPRESENTATION lacks the phenomenal qualities or visual QUALIA, as they are sometimes called, that are present in the former. Several philosophers have recently argued that this whole conception of the phenomenal or subjective character of mental images is mistaken.

A third issue of interest is the causal role of image content. This issue may be illustrated as follows. Suppose you form an image of a snake and suppose you have a snake phobia. Your image may cause you to perspire. In the event that this happens, it is the fact that your image has the content that it does (the fact that it is of a snake and not of a bird, say) that is responsible for its causing you to perspire. If, as seems likely, a complete neurophysiological accont may be given of the origins of your perspiring, how is it possible for the content of your image (apparently not a neurophysiological property) to make any difference to your behaviour? And what reason is there to suppose that the content of your image is causally efficacious in this instance, given that the contents of things elsewhere are sometimes causally inert, as, for example, when the pitch, but not the content, of the sounds produced by a soprano causes a glass to shatter?

There is no general agreement among philosophers about how to settle the above issues any more than there is among cognitive scientists about how to understand the nature of imagistic representation. Nevertheless, it is hard to come away from a reading of recent work in cognitive science or philosophy on imagery without the feeling that real progress is being made.

See also COGNITIVE PSYCHOLOGY; COMPUTATIONAL MODELS; CONSCIOUSNESS; FUNCTIONALISM; IMAGINATION; LANGUAGE OF THOUGHT; PERCEPTUAL CONTENT; REASONS AND CAUSES; REPRESENTATION.

BIBLIOGRAPHY

Block, N., ed. 1981. *Imagery*. Cambridge, MA.: MIT Press.

Block, N. 1983. Mental pictures and cognitive science. *Philosophical Review*, 92, 499–542.

Dennett, D. 1981. The nature of images and the introspective trap. In Block, 1981.

Hinton, G. 1979. Some demonstrations of the effects of structural descriptions in mental imagery. *Behavioral and Brain Sciences*, 3, 231–50.

Kosslyn, S. 1980. *Image and Mind*. Cambridge, MA.: Harvard University Press.

Kosslyn, S. 1981. The medium and the message in mental imagery. In Block, 1981.

Pinker, S. 1980. Mental imagery and the third dimension. *Journal of Experimental Psychology: General*, 109, 354–71.

Pylyshyn, Z. 1981. The imagery debate: analog media versus tacit knowledge. *Psychological Review*, 88, 16–45. Reprinted in Block, 1981.

Tye, M. 1988. The picture theory of mental images. *Philosophical Review*, 97, 497–520.

Tye, M. 1991. *The Imagery Debate*. Cambridge, MA.: MIT Press.

Watson, J.B. 1928. *The Ways of Behaviorism*. New York: Harper.

MICHAEL TYE

imagination It is probably true that philosophers have shown much less interest in the subject of the imagination during the last fifteen years or so than in the period just before that. It is certainly true that more books about the imagination have been written by those concerned with literature and the arts than have been written by philosophers in general and by those concerned with the philosophy of mind in particular. This is understandable in that the imagination and imaginativeness figure prominently in artistic processes, especially in romantic art. Indeed, those two high priests of romanticism, Wordsworth and Coleridge, made large claims for the role played by the imagination in views of reality, although Coleridge's thinking on this was influenced by his reading of the German philosophy of the late eighteenth and early nineteenth centuries, particularly Kant and Schelling. Coleridge distinguished between primary and secondary imagination, both of them in some sense productive, as opposed to merely reproductive. Primary imagination is involved in all perception of the world in accordance with a theory which, as we shall see, Coleridge derived from Kant, while secondary imagination, the poetic imagination, is creative from the materials that perception provides. It is this poetic imagination which exemplifies imaginativeness in the most obvious way.

Being imaginative is a function of THOUGHT, but to use one's imagination in this way is not just a matter of thinking in novel ways. Someone who, like Einstein for example, presents a new way of thinking about the world need not be by reason of this supremely imaginative (though of course he may be). The use of new CONCEPTS or a new way of using already existing concepts is not in itself an exemplification of the imagination. What seems crucial to the imagination is that it involves a series of perspectives, new ways of seeing things, in a sense of 'seeing' that need not be literal. It thus involves, whether directly or indirectly, some connection with perception, but in different ways, some of which will become evident later. The aim of subsequent discussion here will indeed be to make clear the similarities and differences between seeing proper and seeing with the mind's eye, as it is sometimes put. This will involve some consideration of the nature and role of images.

IMAGINATION AND PERCEPTION

Connections between the imagination and PERCEPTION are evident in the ways that many classical philosophers have dealt with the imagination. One of the earliest examples of this, the treatment of *phantasia* (usually translated as 'imagination') in Aristotle's *De Anima* III.3, seems to regard the imagination as a sort of half-way house between perception and thought, but in a way which makes it cover appearances in general, so that the chapter in question has as much to do with perceptual appearances, including illusions, as it has to do with, say, imagery. Yet Aristotle also emphasizes that imagining is in some sense voluntary, and

that when we imagine a terrifying scene we are not necessarily terrified, any more than we need be when we see terrible things in a picture. How that fits in with the idea that an illusion is or can be a function of the imagination is less than clear. Yet some subsequent philosophers, Kant in particular, followed in recent times by P. F. Strawson, have maintained that all perception involves the imagination, in some sense of that term, in that some bridge is required between abstract thoughts and their perceptual instances. This comes out in Kant's treatment of what he calls the 'schematism', where he rightly argues that someone might have an abstract understanding of the concept of a dog without being able to recognize or identify any dogs. It is also clear that someone might be able to classify all dogs together without any understanding of what a dog is. The bridge that needs to be provided to link these two abilities Kant attributes to the imagination.

In so arguing Kant goes, as he so often does, beyond Hume who thought of the imagination in two connected ways. First, there is the fact that there exist, Hume thinks, ideas which are either copies of impressions provided by the senses or are derived from these. Ideas of imagination are distinguished from those of memory, and both of these from impressions of sense, by their lesser vivacity. Second, the imagination is involved in the processes, mainly association of ideas, which take one from one idea to another, and which Hume uses to explain, for example, our tendency to think of objects as having a continuing existence, even when we have no impressions of them. Ideas, one might suggest, are for Hume more or less images, and imagination in the second, wider, sense is the mental process which takes one from one idea to another and thereby explains our tendency to believe things which go beyond what the senses immediately justify. The role which Kant gives to the imagination in relation to perception in general is obviously a wider and fundamental role than Hume allows. Indeed one might take Kant to be saying that were there not the role that he, Kant, insists on there would be no place for the role which Hume gives it. Kant also allows for a free use of the imagination in connection with the arts and the perception of beauty, and this is a more specific role than that involved in perception in general.

SEEING-AS AND IMAGES

In seeing things we normally see them as such and suches (*see* PERCEPTION). But there are also special, imaginative, ways of seeing things, which WITTGENSTEIN emphasized in his treatment of 'seeing-as' in his *Philosophical Investigations* II. xi and elsewhere. To see a simple triangle drawn on a piece of paper as standing up, lying down, hanging from its apex and so on is a form of seeing-as which is both more special and more sophisticated than simply seeing it as a triangle. Both involve the application of concepts to the objects of perception, but the way in which this is done in the two cases is quite different. One might say that in the second case one has to adopt a certain perspective, a certain point of view, and if that is right it links up with what I said earlier about the relation and difference between thinking imaginatively and thinking in novel ways.

Wittgenstein (1953, p. 212e) used the phrase 'an echo of a thought in sight' in relation to these special ways of seeing things, which he called 'seeing aspects'. Roger Scruton has spoken of the part played in it all by 'unasserted thought' (Scruton, 1974, chs 7 and 8), but the phrase used by Wittgenstein brings out more clearly one connection between thought and a form of sense-perception which is characteristic of the imagination. Wittgenstein (1953, p. 213e) also compares the concept of an aspect and that of seeing-as with the concept of an image, and this brings out a point about the imagination that has not been much evident in what has been said so far – that imagining something is typically a matter of picturing it in the mind and that this involves images in some way (*see* IMAGERY). This aspect of the imagination is crucial for the philosophy of mind, since it

raises the question of the status of images, and in particular whether they constitute private objects or states in some way. Sartre, in his early work on the imagination (Sartre, 1940), emphasized, following Husserl, that images are forms of consciousness of an object, but in such a way that they 'present' the object as not being; hence, he said, the image 'posits its object as nothingness'. Such a characterization brings out something about the role of the form of consciousness of which the having of imagery may be a part; in picturing something the images are not themselves the object of consciousness. The account does less, however, to bring out clearly just what images are or how they function.

PICTURING AND SEEING WITH THE MIND'S EYE

As part of an attempt to grapple with this question, RYLE too has argued that in picturing, say, Helvellyn (the mountain in the English Lake District), in having it before the mind's eye, we are not confronted with a mental picture of Helvellyn; images are not seen. We nevertheless can 'see' Helvellyn, and the question is what this 'seeing' is, if it is not seeing in any direct sense. One of the things that may make this question difficult to answer is the fact that people's images and their capacity for imagery vary, and this variation is not directly related to their capacity for imaginativeness. While an image may function in some way as a REPRESENTATION in a train of imaginative thought, such thought does not always depend on that; on the other hand, images may occur in thought which are not really representational at all, are not, strictly speaking, 'of' anything. If the images *are* representational, can one discover things from one's images that one would not know otherwise? Many people would answer 'No', especially if their images are generally fragmentary, but it is not clear that this is true for everyone. On the other hand, and this affects the second point, fragmentary imagery which is at best ancillary to the process of thought in which it occurs may not be in any obvious sense representational, even if the thought itself is 'of' something.

Another problem with the question what it is to 'see' Helvellyn with the mind's eye is that the 'seeing' in question may or may not be a direct function of MEMORY. For one who has seen Helvellyn, imagining it may be simply a matter of reproducing in some form the original vision, and the vision may be reproduced unintentionally and without any recollection of what it is a 'vision' of. For one who has never seen it the task of imagining it depends most obviously on the knowledge of what sort of thing Helvellyn is and perhaps on experiences which are relevant to that knowledge. It would be surprising, to say the least, if imaginative power could produce a 'seeing' that was not constructed from any previous seeings. But that the 'seeing' is not itself a seeing in the straightforward sense is clear, and on this negative point what Ryle says, and others have said, seems clearly right. As to what 'seeing' is in a positive way, Ryle answers that it involves fancying something and that this can be assimilated to pretending. Fancying that one is seeing Helvellyn is thus at least like pretending that one is doing that thing. But is it?

IMAGINING AND PRETENDING

There is in fact a great difference between, say, imagining that one is a tree and pretending to be a tree. Pretending normally involves doing something, and even when there is no explicit action on the part of the pretender, as when he or she pretends that something or other is the case, there is at all events an implication of possible action. Pretending to be a tree may involve little more than standing stock-still with one's arms spread out like branches. To imagine being a tree (something that I have found that some people deny to be possible, which is to my mind a failure of imagination) need imply no action whatever. (Imagining being a tree is different in this respect from imagining that one is a tree, where this means believing falsely that one is a tree; one can

imagine being a tree without this committing one to any beliefs on that score.) On the other hand, to imagine being a tree does seem to involve adopting the hypothetical perspective of a tree, contemplating perhaps what it is like to be a fixture in the ground with roots growing downwards and with branches (somewhat like arms) blown by the wind and with birds perching on them.

Imagining something seems in general to involve contemplating some change or partial change of identity on the part of something or other, and in imagining being something else, such as a tree, the partial change of identity contemplated is in oneself. The fact that the change of identity contemplated cannot be complete does not gainsay the point that it is a change of identity which is being contemplated. One might raise the question whether something about the SELF is involved in all imagining (see e.g. Bernard Williams, 1973, ch. 3). Berkeley even suggested that imagining a solitary unperceived tree involves a contradiction, in that to imagine that is to imagine oneself perceiving it. (There is a similar argument in Schopenhauer's The World as Will and Representation, II, 1.) In fact there is a difference between imagining an object, solitary or not, and imagining oneself seeing that object. The latter certainly involves putting oneself imaginatively in the situation pictured; the former involves contemplating the object from a point of view, indeed from that point of view which one would oneself have if one were viewing it. Picturing something thus involves that point of view to which reference has already been made, in a way that clearly distinguishes picturing something from merely thinking of it.

MUST IMAGES BE PICTORIAL?

Imagining a scene need not involve having mental images which are for the person concerned anything like pictures of the scene. Certainly, to revert to a point already made in connection with Ryle, to picture a scene is not to regard inwardly a picture of the scene. This does not rule out the possibility that an image might come into one's mind which one recognizes as some kind of depiction of a scene. But when actually picturing a scene, it would not be right to say that one imagines the scene *via* a contemplation of an image which plays the part of a picture of it. Moreover, it is possible to imagine a scene without any images occurring, the natural interpretation of which would be that they are pictures of that scene. It is not impossible for one imagining, say, Helvellyn to report on request the occurrence of images which are not in any sense pictures of Helvellyn – not of that particular mountain and perhaps not even of a mountain at all. That would not entail that he or she was not imagining Helvellyn; a report of what was imagined might still be relevant to or associated with Helvellyn, even if the images reported would not be thought by others to be of Helvellyn.

This raises a question which is asked by Wittgenstein (1953, p. 177e) – 'What makes my image of him into an image of *him?*' To which Wittgenstein replies 'Not its looking like him', and he goes on to suggest that a person's account of what his imagery represents is decisive. Certainly it is so when the process of imagination which involves the imagery is one that the person engages in intentionally. The same is not true, as Wittgenstein implicitly acknowledges in the same context, if the imagery simply comes to mind without there being any intention; in that case one might not even know what the image is an image of.

THE ROLE AND NATURE OF IMAGES

All this complicates the question what the status of mental images is. It might seem that they stand in relation to imagining as SENSATIONS stand to perception, except that the occurrence of sensations is a passive business, while the occurrence of an image can be intentional, and in the context of an active flight of imagination is likely to be so. Sensations give perceptions a certain phenomenal character, providing their sensuous, as opposed to conceptual, content (*see* CONTENT; PERCEPTUAL CONTENT). In thinking, where operation

with concepts looms largest and has perhaps the overriding role, it still seems necessary for our thought to be given a focus in thought-occurrences such as images. These have sometimes been characterized as symbols which are the material of thought, but the reference to symbols is not really illuminating. Nevertheless, while a period of thought in which nothing of this kind occurs is possible, the general direction of thought seems to depend on such things occurring from time to time. (*See* Hamlyn, 1976.) In the case of the imagination images seem even more crucial, in that without them it would be difficult, to say the least, for the point of view or perspective which is important for the imagination to be given a focus.

I say that it would be difficult for this to be so, rather than impossible, since it is clear that entertaining a description of a scene, without there being anything like a vision of it, could sometimes give that perspective. The question still arises whether a description could always do quite what an image can do in this respect. This point is connected with an issue over which there has been some argument among psychologists, such as S. M. Kosslyn and Z. W. Pylyshyn, concerning what are termed 'analogue' versus 'propositional' theories of representation. This is an argument concerning whether the process of imagery is what Pylyshyn (1986) calls 'cognitively penetrable', i.e. such that its function is affected by beliefs or other intellectual processes expressible in propositions, or whether, on the other hand, it can be independent of cognitive processes although capable itself of affecting the mental life because of the pictorial nature of images (what Pylyshyn calls their 'analogue medium'). One example, which has loomed large in that argument, is that in which people are asked whether two asymmetrically presented figures can be made to coincide, the decision on which may entail some kind of mental rotation of one or more of the figures. Those defending the 'analogue' theory point to the fact that there is some relation between the time taken and

365

the degree of the rotation required, this suggesting that some process involving changing images is entailed. For one who has little or no imagery this suggestion may seem unintelligible. Is it not enough for one to go through an intellectual working out of the possibilities, based on features of the figures that are judged relevant? This could not be said to be unimaginative as long as the intellectual process involved reference to perspectives or points of view in relation to the figures, the possibility of which the thinker might be able to appreciate. Such an account of the process of imagination cannot be ruled out, although there are conceivable situations in which the 'analogue' process of using images might be easier. Or at least it might be easier for those who have imagery most like the actual perception of a scene; for others the situation might be different.

The extreme of the former position is probably provided by those who have so-called 'eidetic' imagery, where having an image of a scene is just like seeing it, and where, if it is a function of memory as it most likely is, it is clearly possible to find out details of the scene imagined by introspection of the image. The opposite extreme is typified by those for whom imagery, to the extent it occurs at all, is at best ancillary to propositionally styled thought. But, to repeat the point made repeatedly before, that thought, even when unasserted, will not count as imagination unless it provides a series of perspectives on its object. Because images are or can be perceptual analogues and have a phenomenal character analogous to what sensations provide in perception they are most obviously suited, in the workings of the mind, to the provision of those perspectives. But in a wider sense, imagination enters the picture wherever some link between thought and perception is required, as well as making possible imaginative forms of seeing-as. It may thus justifiably be regarded as a bridge between perception and thought.

See also IMAGERY; PERCEPTION; REPRESENTATION; THOUGHT.

BIBLIOGRAPHY

Hamlyn, D.W. 1976. Thinking. In *Contemporary British Philosophy, Fourth Series*, ed. H. D. Lewis. London: Allen & Unwin.

Ishiguro, H. 1966. Imagination. In *British Analytical Philosophy*, ed. B. A. O. Williams and A. Montefiore. London: Routledge & Kegan Paul.

Ishiguro, H. 1967. 'Imagination', *PASS*, XLI, 37–56.

Pylyshyn, Z. 1986. *Computation and Cognition*. Cambridge, MA.: MIT Press/Bradford Books.

Ryle, G. 1949. *The Concept of Mind*. London: Hutchinson.

Sartre, J.-P. 1972. *The Psychology of Imagination*. London: Methuen. First published as *L'imaginaire*, 1940.

Scruton, R. 1974. *Art and Imagination*. London: Methuen.

Strawson, P.F. 1974. *Freedom and Resentment*. London: Methuen.

Warnock, M. 1976. *Imagination*. London: Faber & Faber.

Williams, B.A.O. 1973. *Problems of the Self*. Cambridge University Press.

Wittgenstein, L. 1953. *Philosophical Investigations*. Oxford: Basil Blackwell.

Wittgenstein, L. 1967. *Zettel*, esp. §§621 ff. Oxford: Basil Blackwell.

D. W. HAMLYN

incorrigibility *see* FIRST-PERSON AUTHORITY.

infallibility *see* FIRST-PERSON AUTHORITY.

innateness The debate about whether there are innate ideas is very old. Plato in the *Meno* famously argues that all of our knowledge is innate. Descartes and Leibniz defended the view that the mind contains innate ideas; Berkeley, Hume and Locke attacked it. In fact, as we now conceive the great debate between European Rationalism and British Empiricism in the seventeenth and eighteenth centuries, the doctrine of innate ideas is a central bone of contention: rationalists typically claim that knowledge is impossible without a significant stock of general innate *concepts* or judgments; empiricists argued that all ideas are acquired from experience. This debate is replayed with more empirical content and with considerably greater conceptual complexity in contemporary cognitive science, most particularly within the domains of psycholinguistic theory and cognitive developmental theory (*see* COGNITIVE PSYCHOLOGY; DEVELOPMENTAL PSYCHOLOGY).

One must be careful not to caricature the debate. It is too easy to see the debate as one pitting innatists, who argue that all concepts, or all of linguistic knowledge is innate (and certain remarks of Fodor (1975, 1987) and of Chomsky (1966, 1975) lend themselves to this interpretation) against empiricists who argue that there is no innate cognitive structure to which one need appeal in explaining the acquisition of language or the facts of cognitive development (an extreme reading of Putnam (1975, 1992), Harman (1969, 1975), or Nelson (1987) might give this impression). But this debate would be a silly and a sterile debate indeed. For obviously, *something* is innate. Brains are innate. And the structure of the brain must constrain the nature of cognitive and linguistic development to *some* degree. Equally obviously, *something* is learned, and is learned as opposed to merely *grown* as limbs or hair grow. For not all of the world's citizens end up speaking English, or knowing the Special Theory of Relativity. The interesting questions then all concern exactly *what* is innate, to what degree it counts as *knowledge*, and what is learned, and to what degree its content and structure are determined by innately specified cognitive structures. And that is plenty to debate about.

The arena in which the innateness debate has been prosecuted with the greatest vigour is that of language acquisition, and so it is appropriate to begin there. But it will be important to see how this debate has more recently been extended to the domain of general knowledge and reasoning abilities through the investigation of the development of *object constancy* – the disposition to conceive of physical objects as persistent when unobserved, and to reason about

their properties and locations when they are not perceptible. To this we will turn after an initial discussion of the innateness controversy in psycholinguistics.

The most prominent exponent of the innateness hypothesis in the domain of language acquisition is CHOMSKY (1966, 1975). His research and that of his colleagues and students is responsible for developing the influential and powerful framework of transformational grammar that dominates current linguistic and psycholinguistic theory. This body of research has amply demonstrated that the grammar of any human language is a highly systematic, abstract structure and that there are certain basic structural features shared by the grammars of all human languages, collectively called *universal grammar*. Variations among the specific grammars of the world's languages can be seen as reflecting different settings of a small number of parameters that can, within the constraints of universal grammar, take any of several different values. All of the principal arguments for the innateness hypothesis in linguistic theory rely on this central insight about grammars. The principal arguments are these: (1) the argument from the existence of linguistic universals; (2) the argument from patterns of grammatical errors in early language learners; (3) the poverty of the stimulus argument; (4) the argument from the ease of first language learning; (5) the argument from the relative independence of language learning and general intelligence; (6) the argument from the modularity of linguistic processing. We will consider each of these arguments and the plausible replies in turn.

Innatists argue (Chomsky 1966, 1975) that the very presence of linguistic universals argues for the innateness of linguistic knowledge, but more importantly and more compellingly that the fact that these universals are, from the standpoint of communicative efficiency, or from the standpoint of any plausible simplicity criterion, adventitious. There are many conceivable grammars, and those determined by Universal Grammar are not *ipso facto* the most efficient or the simplest. Nonetheless all human languages satisfy the constraints of Universal Grammar. Since neither the communicative environment nor the communicative task can explain this phenomenon, it is reasonable to suppose that it is explained by the structure of the mind – and therefore by the fact that the principles of Universal Grammar lie innate in the mind and constrain the language that a human can acquire.

Linguistic empiricists, on the other hand, reply that there are alternative possible explanations of the existence of such adventitious universal properties of human languages. For one thing, such universals could be explained, Putnam (1975, 1992) argues, by appeal to a common ancestral language, and the inheritance of features of that language by its descendants. Or it might turn out (Harman, 1969, 1975) that despite the lack of direct evidence at present the features of Universal Grammar in fact do serve either the goals of communicative efficacy or simplicity according to a metric of psychological importance. Finally, empiricists point out, the very existence of Universal Grammar might be a trivial logical artefact (Quine, 1968): for one thing, any finite set of structures will have some features in common. Since there are a finite number of languages, it follows trivially that there are features they all share. Moreover, it is argued, many features of Universal Grammar are interdependent. So in fact the set of fundamental principles shared by the world's languages may be rather small. Hence even if these are innately determined, the amount of innate knowledge thereby required may be quite small as compared with the total corpus of general linguistic knowledge acquired by the first language learner.

These replies are rendered less plausible, innatists argue, when one considers the fact that the errors language learners make in acquiring their first language seem to be driven far more by abstract features of grammar than by any available input data (Marcus et al., 1992). So, despite receiving correct examples of irregular plurals or past tense forms for verbs, and despite having correctly formed the irregular forms for those words, children will often incorrectly regularize irregular verbs once acquiring mastery of the rule governing regulars in their language. And in general, not only the correct inductions of linguistic rules by young language learners, but more importantly, given the absence of confirmatory data and the presence of refuting data, children's erroneous inductions are always consistent with Universal Grammar, often simply representing the incorrect setting of a parameter in the grammar. More generally, innatists argue (Chomsky 1966, 1975; Crain, 1991) all grammatical rules that have ever been observed satisfy the structure-dependence constraint. That is, many linguists and psycholinguists argue that all known grammatical rules of all of the world's languages, including the fragmentary languages of young children must be stated as rules governing hierarchical sentence structures, and not governing, say, sequences of words. Many of these, such as the constituent-command constraint governing anaphor, are highly abstract indeed, and appear to be respected by even very young children (Solan, 1983; Crain, 1991). Such constraints may, innatists argue, be necessary conditions of learning natural language in the absence of specific instruction, modelling and correction, conditions in which all first language learners acquire their native languages.

An important empiricist reply to these observations derives from recent studies of CONNECTIONIST models of first language acquisition (Rummelhart and McClelland, 1986, 1987). Connectionist systems, not previously trained to represent any subset of Universal Grammar that induce grammars which include a large set of regular forms and a few irregulars also tend to overregularize, exhibiting the same U-shaped learning curve seen in human language acquirers. It is also noteworthy that connectionist learning systems that induce grammatical systems acquire 'accidentally' rules on which they are not explicitly trained, but which are consistent with those upon which they are trained, suggesting that as children acquire portions of their grammar, they may accidentally 'learn' other consistent rules, which may be correct in other human languages, but which then must be 'unlearned' in their home language. On the other hand, such 'empiricist' language acquisition systems have yet to demonstrate their ability to induce a sufficiently wide range of the rules hypothesized to be comprised by Universal Grammar to constitute a definitive empirical argument for the possibility of natural language acquisition in the absence of a powerful set of innate constraints.

The poverty of the stimulus argument has been of enormous influence in innateness debates, though its soundness is hotly contested. Chomsky (1966, 1975) notes that (1) the examples of the target language to which the language learner is exposed are always jointly compatible with an infinite number of alternative grammars, and so vastly underdetermine the grammar of the language; and (2) the corpus always contains many examples of ungrammatical sentences, which should in fact serve as falsifiers of any empirically induced correct grammar of the language; and (3) there is, in general, no explicit reinforcement of correct utterances or correction of incorrect utterances, either by the learner or by those in the immediate training environment. Therefore, he argues, since it is impossible to explain the learning of the correct grammar – a task accomplished by all normal children within a very few years – on the basis of any available data or known learning algorithms, it must be that the grammar is innately specified, and is merely 'triggered' by relevant environmental cues.

Opponents of the linguistic innateness hypothesis, however, point out that the circumstance that Chomsky notes in this argument is hardly specific to language. As is well known from arguments due to Hume (1978), Wittgenstein (1953), Goodman (1972), and Kripke (1982), in all cases of empirical abduction, and of training in the use of a word, data underdetermine theories. This moral is emphasized by Quine

(1954, 1960) as the principle of the underdetermination of theory by data. But we nonetheless do abduce adequate theories in science, and we do learn the meanings of words. And it would be bizarre to suggest that all correct scientific theories or the facts of lexical semantics are innate.

But, innatists reply, when the empiricist relies on the underdetermination of theory by data as a counterexample, a significant disanalogy with language acquisition is ignored: the abduction of scientific theories is a difficult, laborious process, taking a sophisticated theorist a great deal of time and deliberate effort. First language acquisition, by contrast, is accomplished effortlessly and very quickly by a small child. The enormous relative ease with which such a complex and abstract domain is mastered by such a naïve 'theorist' is evidence for the innateness of the knowledge achieved.

Empiricists such as PUTNAM (1975, 1992) have rejoined that innatists underestimate the amount of time that language learning actually takes, focusing only on the number of years from the apparent onset of acquisition to the achievement of relative mastery over the grammar. Instead of noting how short this interval, they argue, one should count the total number of hours spent listening to language and speaking during this time. That number is in fact quite large, and is comparable to the number of hours of study and practice required in the acquisition of skills that are not argued to derive from innate structures, such as chess playing or musical composition (see Simon, 1981). Hence, they argue, once the correct temporal parameters are taken into consideration, language learning looks like one more case of human skill acquisition than like a special unfolding of innate knowledge.

Innatists, however, note that while the ease with which most such skills are acquired depends on general intelligence, language is learned with roughly equal speed, and to roughly the same level of general syntactic mastery regardless of general intelligence. In fact even significantly retarded individuals, assuming no special language deficit, acquire their native language on a time-scale and to a degree comparable to that of normally intelligent children. The language acquisition faculty hence appears to allow access to a sophisticated body of knowledge independent of the sophistication of the general knowledge of the language learner.

Empiricists reply that this argument ignores the centrality of language to a wide range of human activities, and consequently the enormous attention paid to language acquisition by retarded youngsters and their parents or caretakers. They argue as well that innatists overstate the parity in linguistic competence between retarded children and children of normal intelligence.

Innatists point out that the MODULARITY of language processing is a powerful argument for the innateness of the language faculty. There is a large body of evidence, innatists argue, for the claim that the processes that subserve the acquisition, understanding and production of language are quite distinct and independent of those that subserve general cognition and learning. (*See* Fodor, 1975; Garfield, 1989; Chomsky, 1966, 1975 for more on modularity theory.) That is, language learning and language processing mechanisms and the knowledge they embody are domain specific – grammars and grammatical learning and utilizations mechanisms are not used outside of language processing. They are informationally encapsulated – only linguistic information is relevant to language acquisition and processing. They are mandatory – language learning and language processing are automatic. Moreover, language is subserved by specific dedicated neural structures, damage to which predictably and systematically impairs linguistic functioning, and not general cognitive functioning. All of this suggests a specific 'mental organ', to use Chomsky's phrase, that has evolved in the human cognitive system specifically in order to make language possible. The specific structure of this organ simultaneously constrains the range of possible human languages and guides the learning of the child's target language, later making rapid on-line language processing possible. The principles represented in this organ constitute the innate linguistic knowledge of the human being. Additional evidence for the early operation of such an innate language acquisition module is derived from the many infant studies that show that infants selectively attend to soundstreams that are prosodically appropriate, that have pauses at clausal boundaries, and that contain linguistically permissible phonological sequences. (*See* the literature reviewed in Karmiloff-Smith, 1991.)

This argument, of course, depends on the modularity thesis, which is highly contentious in contemporary cognitive science. Critics of the innateness hypothesis argue that the processes involved in language acquisition and processing are merely instances of general learning strategy (Putnam, op. cit.; Rummelhart and McClelland, op. cit., that language learning and processing requires semantic information, access to which violates modularity (Marslen-Wilson and Tyler, 1987; Jackendoff, 1983; Putnam, op. cit.) and that much highly skilled behaviour that is not innate is nonetheless automated.

A particularly strong form of the innateness hypothesis in the psycholinguistic domain is FODOR's (1975, 1987) LANGUAGE OF THOUGHT hypothesis. Fodor argues not only that the language learning and processing faculty is innate, but that the human representational system exploits an innate language of thought which has all of the expressive power of any learnable human language. Hence, he argues, all concepts are in fact innate, in virtue of the representational power of the language of thought. This remarkable doctrine is hence even stronger than classical rationalist doctrines of innate ideas: whereas Chomsky echoes Descartes in arguing that the most general concepts required for language learning are innate, while allowing that more specific concepts are acquired, Fodor echoes Plato in arguing that every concept we ever 'learn' is in fact innate.

Fodor defends this view by arguing that

the process of language learning is a process of hypothesis formation and testing, where among the hypotheses that must be formulated are meaning postulates for each term in the language being acquired. But in order to formulate and test a hypothesis of the form 'X' means Y, where 'X' denotes a term in the target language, prior to the acquisition of that language, the language learner, Fodor argues, must have the resources necessary to express 'Y'. Therefore there must be, in the language of thought, a predicate available co-extensive with each predicate in any language that a human can learn. Fodor also argues for the language of thought thesis by noting that the language in which the human information processing system represents information cannot be a human spoken language, since that would, contrary to fact, privilege one of the world's languages as the most easily acquired. Moreover, it cannot be, he argues, that each of us thinks in our own native language since that would (a) predict that we could not think prior to acquiring a language, contrary to the original argument, and (b) would mean that psychology would be radically different for speakers of different languages, which does not appear to be the case. Hence, Fodor argues, there must be a non-conventional language of thought, and the facts that the mind is 'wired' in mastery of its predicates together with its expressive completeness entail that all concepts are innate.

This argument has been criticized (Garfield, 1989a; Putnam, 1975, 1992) for relying on a misleading and unsubstantiated model of language learning – the hypothesis formation and testing model. Rather, it is argued by these critics, following Ryle (1949), Sellars (1963), and Wittgenstein (1953), that language acquisition – in particular the acquisition of the meanings of words, which is what is at issue in this argument – is first and foremost the acquisition of a set of skills, a species of 'knowing-how'. So, when we learn the meaning of the word 'green' in English, on this view, we learn how to use that word correctly, and not a new fact of the form

'green' means the same as 'X' where 'X' is an expression in the language of thought. And, it is argued, the abilities that permit the acquisition of these skills are quite possibly of the same kind as those that enable the acquisition of a wide range of cognitive skills. On this view, no innate language of thought is needed to explain first language acquisition, and hence no corresponding set of innate ideas is demanded to explain the acquisition of the concepts we employ when we use natural language.

It is important to emphasize once again that in reviewing these arguments and counter-arguments, what is at stake is not whether anything at all is innate. Even the most extreme empiricist with regard to language learning must agree that there are innately specified cognitive mechanisms that attune human infants to language and that predispose humans to learning languages. Even the most extreme nativist must agree that without an environment sufficient to support language development, including prominently adults speaking the target language and interacting in a supportive way with the child, no child learns its first language. The debate concerns just how much of what is eventually learned is constrained by what is innate, and how much is determined by the environment. And it must be emphasized that though some of the arguments are primarily conceptual, the most significant arguments are empirical in character, and the resolution of the innateness debate in the domain of language acquisition is a thoroughly empirical matter.

It is also important to ask to what degree extra-linguistic knowledge about the world is innate. A fertile field for clarifying this debate has been that body of research devoted to examining the development of object constancy in infants. Piaget (1930, 1952, 1954, 1969, 1974) argued that object constancy – the recognition that objects remain existent when they pass out of sight and the ability to take into account in reasoning and acting the existence of unseen objects – does not emerge until about 9 months of age, and emerges as a consequence of cognitive development involving both simple neurobiological maturation and cognitive development conditioned by learning. The results of Baillargeon (1987a, 1987b), Baillargeon and Graber (1988), Baillargeon, Spelke and Wasserman (1985), Baillargeon and Hanko-Summes (1990) and Spelke (1982, 1988, 1990) cast doubt on this timetable, however. They demonstrate that infants as young as three months of age respond differentially to 'possible' and 'impossible' trajectories for objects behind screens, even when what renders those trajectories possible or impossible are the positions of other hidden objects that the infants have been shown prior to the fixing of the screen. Infants seem at very early ages to be aware of constraints on objects' support as well. These results are noteworthy because they are achieved at ages at which infants could be expected to have very little if any empirical familiarity with the constraints on object motion and permanence to which they are evidently responding.

One plausible interpretation of these results is that infants come to the world with innate knowledge – or at least the innately determined propensity to acquire such knowledge as a consequence of maturation – of certain physical or metaphysical properties of physical objects. How else could they respond differentially to these situations at such an early age? These data certainly make a strong case for this interpretation. On the other hand one must move cautiously in inferring innateness from precocity. For one thing there may be learning by observation between birth and the age at which object constancy is observed that accounts for the phenomenon. For another, the differential response that is observed at these early ages (differential looking time is the dependent measure in these studies) does not indicate with any certainty the presence of a full-fledged concept of an object, let alone that of constancy, and may be reckoned an innate but non-epistemic precursor of that concept, even if we grant the innate basis for the observed phenomena.

Again, the issues at stake in the debate concerning the innateness of such general concepts pertaining to the physical world cannot be as stark as a dispute between a position according to which nothing is innate and one according to which all empirical knowledge is innate. Rather the important – and again, always empirical questions concern just *what* is innate, and just *what* is acquired, and how innate equipment interacts with the world to produce experience. 'There can be no doubt that all our knowledge begins with experience. . . . But though all our knowledge begins with experience it does not follow that it all arises out of experience' (Kant, 1929, p. 1).

See also PSYCHOLOGICAL EXPLANATION.

BIBLIOGRAPHY

Baillargeon, R. 1987a. Object permanence in 3.5- and 4.5-month-old-infants. *Developmental Psychology*, 23, 655–64.

Baillargeon, R. 1987b. Young infants' reasoning about the physical and spatial characteristics of hidden objects. *Cognitive Development*, 2, 178–200.

Baillargeon, R. In press. Reasoning about the height and location of a hidden object in 4.5- and 6.5-month-old-infants. *Cognition*.

Baillargeon, R., and Graber, M. 1988. Evidence of location memory in 8-month-old-infants in a non-search AB task. *Developmental Psychology*, 24, 502–11.

Baillargeon, R., and Hanko-Summes, S. 1990. Is the top object adequately supported by the bottom object? Young infants' understanding of support relations. *Cognitive Development*, 5, 29–54.

Baillargeon, R., Spelke, E.S., and Wasserman, S. 1985. Object permanence in five-month-old infants. *Cognition*, 20, 191–208.

Chomsky, Noam. 1966. Cartesian linguistics. In *Acquisition and Use of Language*. New York: Harper and Row. In Stich, 1975.

Chomsky, Noam. 1975. *Reflection of Language*. New York: Pantheon.

Crain, S. 1991. Language Learning. *Behavioral and Brain Sciences*, 14: 4, 597–649.

Fodor, J. 1975. *The Language of Thought*. New York: Thomas Y. Crowell, Co. Reprinted by Harvard University Press, 1979.

Fodor, J. 1987. *Psychosemantics: The Problem of Meaning in the Philosophy of Mind*. Cambridge, MA.: MIT Press.

Garfield, J.L. 1989a. Mentalese and mental se: keeping language and thought distinct. Conference on Mind, Meaning and Nature, Wesleyan University.

Garfield, J.L., ed. 1989b. *Modularity in Knowledge Representation and Natural Language Understanding*. Cambridge, MA.: MIT Press.

Goodman, N. 1972. The new riddle of induction. In *Problems and Projects*. Indianapolis: Hackett.

Harman, G. 1969. Linguistic competence and empiricism. In *Language and Philosophy*, ed. S. Hook. New York: NYU Press.

Harman, G. 1975. Psychological aspects of the theory of syntax. In Stich. 1975.

Hume, D. 1978. *A Treatise of Human Nature*. Ed. Selby-Bigge and Niditch. Oxford University Press.

Jackendoff, R. 1983. *Semantics and Cognition*. Cambridge, MA: MIT Press.

Kant, I. 1929. *Critique of Pure Reason*. Trans. N. Kemp Smith. London: Macmillan. Original work published in 1787.

Karmiloff-Smith, A. 1991. Beyond modularity: Innate constraints and developmental change. In *The Epigenesis of Mind: Essays on Biology and Cognition*, ed. S. Carey and R. Gelman. Hillsdale, NJ: Lawrence Erlbaum Associates, Publishers.

Kripke, S. 1982. *Wittgenstein on Rules and Private Language*. Cambridge: Harvard University Press.

Marcus, G., S. Pinker, M. Ullman, M. Hollander, T.J. Rosen, and F. Xu, 1992. *Overregularization in Language Acquisition*. Chicago. Monographs of the Society for Research in Child Development.

Marslen-Wilson, W.D., and L.K. Tyler. 1987. Against modularity. In *The Modularity of Mind* ed. J. L. Garfield. Cambridge, MA: MIT Press.

Nelson, K. 1987. Nativist and functionalist views of cognitive development; reflection on Keil's review of making sense: The acquisition of shared meaning. In *Cognitive Development*. Norwood, New Jersey: Ablex Publishing Corporation.

Piaget, J. 1929. *The Child's Conception of the World*. London: Routledge & Kegan Paul.

Piaget, J. 1930. *The Child's Conception of Physical Causality*. London: Routledge & Kegan Paul.

Piaget, J. 1952. *The Origins of Intelligence in Childhood*. New York: International Universities Press.

Piaget, J. 1954. *The Construction of Reality in the World*. New York: Basic Books.

Piaget, J. 1969. *The Child's Conception of Movement and Speed*. New York: Basic Books.

Piaget, J. 1974. *Understanding Causality*. New York: Norton.

Plunkett, K., and Marchman, V. 1990. Regular and irregular morphology and the psychological status of rules of grammar. In *Proceedings of the 17th Annual Meeting of the Berkeley Linguistics Society*. Berkeley, CA: Berkeley Linguistics Society.

Plunkett, K., and Marchman, V. 1991. U-shaped learning and frequency effects in a multilayered perception: implications for child language acquisition. *Cognition*, 38, 43–102.

Putnam, H. 1975. The 'innateness hypothesis' and explanatory models in linguistics. In Stich, 1975.

Putnam, Hilary. 1992. What is innate and why: comments on the debate. In *The Philosophy of Mind*, ed. B. Beakley and P. Ludlow, Cambridge, MA.: MIT Press.

Quine, W.V. 1954. The scope and language of science. Bicentennial Conference at Columbia University. Reprinted in *The Ways of Paradox and Other Essays*, 1975. Cambridge, MA.: Harvard University Press.

Quine, W.V. 1960. *Word and Object*. Cambridge MA.: MIT Press.

Quine, W.V. 1968. Linguistics and philosophy. Lecture. Reprinted in Stich, 1975.

Rummelhart, D.E., and McClelland, J.L. 1986. On learning the past tenses of English verbs. In *Parallel Distributed Processing: Explorations in the Microstructure of Cognition: Vol. 2. Psychological and Biological Models*, J.L. McClelland, D.E. Rummelhart, and the PDP Research Group. Cambridge, MA.: MIT Press/Bradford Books.

Rummelhart, D.E., and McClelland, J.L. 1987. Learning the past tenses of English verbs: implicit rules or parallel distributed processing? In *Mechanisms of Language Acquisition*, ed. B. MacWhinney. Hillsdale, N.J. Erlbaum.

Ryle, G. 1949. *The Concept of Mind*. New York: Barnes and Noble.

Sellars, W. 1963. Empiricism and the philosophy of mind. In *Science, Perception and Reality*. New York: Routledge & Kegan Paul.

Simon, H.A. 1981. *The Sciences of the Artificial, 2nd edition*. Cambridge MA.: MIT Press.

Solan, L. 1983. *Pronominal Reference: Child Language and the Theory of Grammar*. Reidel.

Spelke, E.S. 1982. Perceptual knowledge of objects in infancy. In *Perspectives on Mental Representation*, ed. J. Mehler, M. Garrett, and E. Walker. Hillsdale, N.J. Lawrence Erlbaum Associates.

Spelke, E.S. 1988. Where perceiving ends and thinking begins: The apprehension of objects in infancy. In *Perceptual Development in Infancy*, ed. A Yonas. Minnesota Symposium on Child Psychology, vol. 20, 191–234. Hillsdale, N.J. Lawrence Erlbaum Associates.

Spelke, E.S. 1990. Principles of object perception. *Cognitive Science* 14, 29–56.

Stich, P. 1975. *Innate Ideas*. University of California Press.

Wittgenstein, L. 1958. *Philosophical Investigation*. Oxford: Basil Blackwell.

JAY L. GARFIELD

intensional The word 'intensional' was coined as the converse of 'extensional' and both notions figure prominently in semantics and logic. When logicians speak of the extension of a predicate such as, for example, 'is a horse', they have in mind the set of creatures that this predicate picks out. But in addition to its extension, a predicate can be understood to have an intension, some feature – grasped by anyone who has linguistic mastery of the predicate – that determines the extension. There are various proposals in the literature for more specific accounts of intensions in respect of predicates. For example, some think of the intension as something like the meaning of the predicate, whilst others prefer to think of it in more formal terms as the principle ('function') that would determine the set of things which are horses in any POSSIBLE WORLD.

Predicates are not the only linguistic constructions which have extensions as well as intensions. Most importantly, and due mainly to the work of the logician and philosopher Frege, it is usual to describe sentences as having them. Thus, the extension of a sentence is taken to be a truth value (either true or false, or, in multi-valued logics, some further value). And the intension of a sentence could be variously understood as the thought expressed by it, its meaning, or the function from the sentence to a truth value in any possible world. Additionally, one can think of proper names as having both intension and extension. The extension of the name 'Mark Twain' is the human being who wrote various well-known books. Its intension is less easy to describe in everyday terms: some think of it as the individual concept that determines the author; others prefer to stick with the possible-world definition and say that the intension of – 'Mark Twain' is the function that picks out that author in any possible world. In logic and the philosophy of language, the whole question of how to understand intensions is fraught with difficulties, but the outlines of the notion are clear enough.

Of special importance in the philosophy of mind is the use of this pair of terms in connection with sentences attributing propositional attitudes. Consider the sentence: 'John believes that Mark Twain wrote Huckleberry Finn.' The sentence *contained* within this attitude report, 'Mark Twain wrote Huckleberry Finn' happens to be true. In the terminology introduced above, one would say that its extension was the truth value *true*. Moreover, since Mark Twain was Samuel Clemens, one could replace the author's name in this sentence without changing its extension. For 'Samuel Clemens wrote Huckleberry Finn' is also true. When such replacement or substitution does not change the truth value, the sentence within which the substitutions are made is said to constitute an 'extensional context'. Returning now to the attitude report that contains the sentence about Mark Twain, one can see problems for substitution. The believer, John, may not know that 'Mark Twain' was the name adopted by Samuel Clemens and many feel that, in this event, it is just false to say: 'John believes that Samuel Clemens wrote Huckleberry Finn.' The fact that substitution fails in this way to preserve extension (truth value) is captured by saying that the belief report constitutes an *intensional context*. That is, it is a context where one can preserve truth value only by substituting expressions with the same *intension*. (It should be noted here that it is controversial whether one ought to appeal to intensions in saying what is going on in this case.)

Though the word 'intension' has a technical sense in semantics deriving from its opposite number 'extension', there is what can be an initially confusing similarity between 'intensional' and 'intentional'. The second of this pair – the one spelled with a 't' in place of 's' – has been widely used to describe the feature of propositional attitudes by which they are said to be about or directed to something. Thus, with the earlier example in mind, one would say that John's belief is about or directed to Mark Twain and his authorship of Huckleberry Finn. Propositional attitudes have what philosophers call 'INTENTIONALITY'. And confusion can arise because, as was noted above, propositional attitude *reports*, constitute intensional (with an 's') contexts.

See also BELIEF; CONCEPTS; PROPOSITIONAL ATTITUDES.

SAMUEL GUTTENPLAN

intention Our concept of *intention* is a central part of a web of concepts at the heart of our commonsense conceptions of intelligent agency. Included also in this web are concepts of various attitudes, like belief, knowledge, and desire; general notions of meaning; and concepts that classify actions – for example, concepts of intentional action and of free action. (*See* FOLK PSYCHOLOGY.)

We use our concept of intention both to classify ACTIONS and to characterize minds. We do the former when we describe an action as *intentional* or done *with a certain intention*; we do the latter when we say whether someone *intends to* do something,

now or later (Anscombe, 1963). A common approach is to begin with action. We ask: what is it to act intentionally, or with a certain intention? A natural answer is that for me to act intentionally is for my action to be explainable, in an appropriate way, by what I want (desire) and what I believe (Anscombe, 1963; Davidson, 1980, essay 1). (*See* BELIEF, DESIRE.) My walking towards the telephone is intentional, for example, because it is explainable by my desire to contact my friend and my belief that I can do so by using the phone. Given my desire and belief I have a reason to walk towards the phone and I act because of that reason; that is why my walking towards the phone is *intentional*; and that is why I so walk *with the intention of* contacting my friend. To classify an action as intentional, or as done with a certain intention, is, then, to say it has the appropriate *relation* to the agent's desires and beliefs. One acts intentionally, or with a certain intention, just in case one's action stands in the appropriate relation to one's desires and beliefs; no distinct state or event of intending is involved (DAVIDSON, 1980, essay 1).

We not only act intentionally and with certain intentions. We also form intentions concerning the future. What can such a relational conception say about intending to do something later? As Davidson himself later noted (1980, essay 5), future-directed intending cannot in general be simply a relation between belief, desire, and action; for though I now intend (for example) to go swimming tomorrow there may never be a relevant action. Nevertheless, many theorists in this tradition try to extend to the case of intending to do something later, the machinery already introduced in the account of intention in action. This leads naturally to a *reductive* conception, one that tries to analyse future-directed intending in terms of the agent's relevant desires and beliefs.

We can call this collection of views – the methodological decision to begin with intentional action, the relational conception of intentional action and of action done with an intention, and the reduction of

future-directed intending to desire and belief
– the *desire–belief model* of intention. Along
with this view has gone a certain (roughly,
Humean) conception of PRACTICAL REA-
SONING – reasoning about what to do. In
practical reasoning we weigh our relevant
desire-belief reasons for and against our
different alternative options. Such reasoning
typically issues in action. There is no clear
place in the model for a decision or
intention which can then function as a distinctive input into further practical reasoning; for decision and intention about the
future are understood solely in terms of
desire and belief, and intention in action is
simply implicit in the relation between
desire, belief, and action.

The desire-belief model of intention has
been, at least until recently, the standard
view in a wide range of philosophical
discussions of action. It is, for example, typically assumed in debates about whether
reasons are causes, including the large,
recent literature on the role of CONTENT in
psychological explanation (*see* REASONS
AND CAUSES). But recent years have
seen a re-examination of the desire-belief
model of intention. This has lead to the
development both of some more elaborate
versions of the desire-belief model and of
competing models according to which
intending is a distinctive kind of psychological attitude.

A main theme in this re-examination of
the desire-belief model has been the idea of
commitment to action. Consider my intention now to go to Boston next week. In
intending so to act later I seem to be in
some sense *committed to* or *settled on* so
acting. In some important sense, the issue of
whether so to act is *no longer a live issue* for
me: the issue is settled. In being settled on
so acting I seem to go beyond merely
having desire-belief reasons for and/or
against this option and its alternatives. Yet
there is as yet no action.

What is this commitment to action that
seems characteristic of intention? My commitment now to going to Boston next week
does not reach its ghostly hand over time
and control my action next week; that

would be action at a distance. Nor should
such commitment mean that I am irrevocably settled on so acting. Such irrevocability
would clearly be irrational; after all, things
change and we do not always correctly
anticipate the future. But if my commitment
now does not itself control my action, and is
subject to review and change later, why
bother? Why not just cross my bridges
when I come to them? So, on the one hand,
it may seem that an account of intention
really must provide for a distinctive kind of
commitment to action. Yet, on the other
hand, the very idea of this commitment
leads to puzzles of its own.

One might try to come to terms with
commitment while staying within the
desire-belief framework by emphasizing the
relation between an intention to A and a
belief that one will. In particular, one might
try to see intention as itself a special kind of
belief about one's own conduct. In intending now to A later I see the question of
whether so to act as settled in the sense that
I now am confident that I will so act. My
intention to A is not simply some desire-
belief reason in favour of my A-ing, or even
the fact that such a reason is in some sense
the strongest of my relevant, competing
reasons. In intending to A I go beyond such
reasons and believe I will in fact A. But
though I go beyond my desire-belief reasons
for A-ing, my intention is not a fundamentally new kind of attitude. In this way one
can try to accommodate the special commitment involved in intention without
going beyond the resources of the desire-
belief framework.

Of course, many beliefs about one's future
conduct are not intentions. I might believe I
will miss a shot in a basketball game and
yet not intend to miss, and in a race I might
believe I will wear down my sneakers but
not intend to wear them down. (In the terminology of Bentham (1789) I might be
said 'obliquely' to intend to wear down my
sneakers, whereas I 'directly' intend to run.
But our concern here is with so-called
'direct' intention.) A defender of a belief-
conception of intention will need to specify
further the type of belief about my own

conduct in which my intention consists. Velleman (1989), for example, argues that my intention to A is my belief, adopted out of my desire for its truth, that I will A as a result of this very belief. This introduces two further ideas. The idea that intentions involve a kind of self-referentiality is developed in a number of recent studies, many of which reject the identification of intention and belief. (*See* Donagan, 1987; Harman 1986; SEARLE, 1983.) The idea that intentions are beliefs that are adopted out of relevant desires raises issues that had been discussed earlier by Grice (1971).

Grice had argued that my intention to A does indeed require a belief on my part that I will A. In this respect Velleman's account follows Grice's. But Grice went on to argue that my intention cannot just be identified with some such belief. Suppose I intend to go to London tomorrow. If this is a belief of mine that I will go, we may ask what my justification is for that belief. Grice worried, roughly, that if my justification for my belief were my desire to go, that would make my case one of wishful thinking. But if my justification were instead some form of inductive evidence (as when I expect I will sneeze when I am exposed to your cat) then my belief would be an ordinary prediction and not an intention. Grice concluded that my intention to go, while it involved my belief that I will go, could not be identified simply with my belief. Instead, my intention also involves a special attitude of *willing* that I go. Willing that I go does not itself require that I believe I will; but it does involve something like wishing wholeheartedly that I go – so willing is not merely desiring. To intend to go is to will that I go and to believe that, as a result of such willing, I will go. My intention involves the belief that I will go; but this belief is based on evidence that includes my knowledge that that is what I will. (*See* THE WILL.)

Grice and Velleman agree that an intention to A at least involves a belief that one will A. But this may be challenged. In a later paper (1980, essay 5) Davidson gave up on his earlier claim that talk of intention was never talk about some state or event of intending. But he also argued that an intention to A does not require a belief that one will A (though it does require that one not think it impossible that one will A). I might intend to achieve some goal and yet be doubtful about my ultimate success. Rather than understand intention as consisting, at least in part, in a belief that one will so act, Davidson argued that we could see intention as a special kind of *evaluation* of conduct. Davidson treats a desire to act in a certain way as a *prima facie* judgment that so acting would be, in some respect, desirable. An intention to act is also an evaluative judgment; but it is not merely a *prima facie* judgment. It is what Davidson calls an 'all-out judgment'. My intention to go to London, for example, is my 'all-out judgment' that my so acting would be best. In reaching such an all-out evaluative judgment I am settled on so acting. And Davidson took great pains to argue that, contrary to initial appearances, this view is compatible with the possibility of weak-willed intentions – intentions that are contrary to one's best judgment about what to do (*see* WEAKNESS OF WILL).

Return now to practical reasoning. As noted, it is common to see such reasoning as consisting in the weighing of desire-belief reasons for and against conflicting alternatives. But we also sometimes decide to act in a certain way and then reason about how. I can decide – and so form an intention – to go to London next week. Given this new intention I will need to reason about how I am going to get there. In such reasoning my intention to go to London provides an end, and my reasoning aims at settling on appropriate means. A general conception of practical reasoning should make room for, and explain the interrelations between, both kinds of practical reasoning – the weighing of desire-belief reasons, and reasoning about how to do what one already intends to do.

These observations suggest yet another way of approaching intention. We try to say how intentions function in practical reasoning, not only as outputs of such reasoning, but also as characteristic inputs to further reasoning. Castañeda (1975) has developed a version of this approach. He sees intention as the acceptance of a distinctive kind of content – what he calls a 'first-person practition'. A practition is, roughly, the content normally involved in commands and prescriptions. If, for example, I order you to open the window my command has the content: *You to open the window*. Typical commands are addressed to others. But intentions are analogous to self-addressed commands – to intend is to accept a *first-person* practition. To intend to open the window is to endorse the practition: *I to open the window*. This is not to say that for me so to intend I must literally perform a speech act of commanding myself so to act. It is only to say that the contents of intendings have a structure and logic analogous to that of the contents of ordinary commands and prescriptions.

Castañeda tries to develop an account of the special logical relations between such practitions and ordinary propositions, the contents of beliefs. At the heart of this special logic is the idea that a practition, *S to* A, neither implies nor is implied by its corresponding proposition *that S* A's. The underlying motivation for trying to develop such a special logic includes two ideas. (a) We understand intention in large part in terms of its roles in practical reasoning; (b) We understand those roles by articulating a special logic of the contents that are distinctive of intention.

But we can accept (a) without following Castañeda in also accepting (b). We can try to lay out the roles of intention in practical reasoning – including its roles as a distinctive input to such reasoning – without supposing that we need some special logic of the contents of intendings. For we can distinguish a theory of reasoning from a theory of logical implication (Harman, 1986).

The idea is to say what intentions are in part by saying how they function in practical reasoning, without assuming that to do this we must articulate a special logic of the distinctive contents of intentions. In particular, we try to articulate the roles of future-directed intentions in practical reasoning, and we try to say how these roles differ from those played by desires and beliefs (Harman, 1986; Bratman, 1987).

An account of the roles of intentions in practical reasoning should support, and be supported by, answers to our earlier question: why bother with intentions for the future anyway? Here one may argue (Bratman, 1987) that there are two main answers. First, we are not frictionless deliberators. Deliberation is a process that takes time and uses other resources, so there are limits to the extent of deliberation at the time of action. By settling on future-directed intentions we allow present deliberation to shape later conduct, thereby extending the influence of Reason on our lives. Second, we have pressing needs for coordination, both intra-personal and social; and future-directed intentions play a central role in our efforts at achieving such coordination.

Future-directed intentions typically play these roles as elements of larger, partial plans. My intention to go to London this Sunday helps coordinate my various activities for this weekend, and my activities with the activities of others, by entering into a larger plan of action. Such plans will typically be partial and will need to be filled in as time goes by with appropriate specifications of means, preliminary steps, and the like. In filling in such partial plans in stages we engage in a kind of practical reasoning that is distinctive of planning agents like us and that is, on the view being considered, central to our understanding of intention. Such approaches seek to articulate the basic principles involved in such planning. In this way they try to shed light on the nature of intention and on its relations to other psychological attitudes, like belief and desire (Harman, 1986; Bratman, 1987).

Such planning conceptions of intention focus on intention as a state of mind, and pay special attention to future-directed intentions and plans. But it can be asked whether the structures that are thereby revealed are peculiar to the special case of sophisticated agents engaged in planning for the future, and not generally applicable to all cases of intentional action (*see* Wilson, 1989). Are there agents capable of intentional action but not capable of such future-directed planning? Even for planning agents, are there some intentional activities (e.g. relatively spontaneous and yet intentional conduct) that do not plausibly involve the kinds of psychological structures highlighted by a focus on future-directed intention?

These queries return us to Anscombe's (1963) general question of how to understand the relation between intention as a state of mind and the characterization of action as intentional or done with a certain intention. According to what has been called 'the Simple View' intentional *A*-ing always involves intending to *A*. But some argue that there are cases in which one intentionally *A*s and yet, though one does intend *something* one does not, strictly speaking, intend *to A* (Harman, 1986; Bratman, 1987). The concerns raised in the previous paragraph suggest that planning conceptions of intention may drive an even greater wedge between intention as a state of mind and the characterization of action as intentional. If so, we need to ask whether that is an acceptable conclusion. Anscombe (1963, p. 1) had urged that it is implausible that 'intention' is equivocal in these different contexts. In contrast, Velleman (1989, pp. 112–13) argues that we should give up on the search for a unitary meaning of 'intention'.

These debates about intention interact with a wide range of issues. For example, it is common to suppose that an agent's desires and beliefs give her reasons for action. If we see intention as a distinctive attitude, over and above an agent's desires and beliefs, we will want to know how this attitude affects what reasons the agent has to act in various ways and what it is rational of the agent to do (*see* RATIONALITY). Again, we frequently talk about the intentions of groups of agents. Speaking for you and me, I might say that *we* intend to sing a duet together. We are social creatures: shared intentions and shared intentional activities pervade our lives together.

A theoretical approach to intention should help us understand these important phenomena.

BIBLIOGRAPHY

Anscombe, G.E.M. 1963. *Intention*, 2nd edn. Ithaca: Cornell University Press.

Bentham, J. 1789. *An Introduction to the Principles of Morals and Legislation*. London: Methuen, 1982.

Bratman, M.E. 1987. *Intention, Plans, and Practical Reason*. Cambridge MA.: Harvard University Press.

Castanĕda, H.N. 1975. *Thinking and Doing*. Dordrecht: Reidel.

Davidson, D. 1980. *Essays on Actions and Events*. Oxford University Press.

Donagan, A. 1987. *Choice: The Essential Element in Human Action*. London: Routledge & Kegan Paul.

Grice, H.P. 1971. Intention and uncertainty. *Proceedings of the British Academy*, 57, 263–79.

Harman, G. 1986. *Change in View*. Cambridge MA.: MIT Press.

Searle, J. 1983. *Intentionality*. Cambridge University Press.

Velleman, J.D. 1989. *Practical Reflection*. Princeton University Press.

Wllson, G.M. 1989. *The Intentionality of Human Action: Revised and Enlarged Edition*. Stanford University Press.

MICHAEL E. BRATMAN

intentionality (1) The concept of intentionality was originally used by medieval scholastic philosophers. It was reintroduced into European philosophy by Franz Brentano in the nineteenth century. In its current usage the expression 'intentionality' refers to that property of the mind by which it is *directed at, about,* or *of* objects and states of affairs in the world. Intentionality, so defined, includes such mental phenomena as BELIEF, DESIRE, INTENTION, hope, fear, love, hate, lust, disgust (*see* EMOTION), and MEMORY as well as PERCEPTION and intentional ACTION.

The concept of intentionality is a source of at least two sorts of confusion. First there is a temptation to confuse intentionality-with-a-t, the capacity of the mind to represent objects and states of affairs in the world, with intensionality-with-an-s, the property of certain sentences by which they fail certain sorts of tests for extensionality (more of this latter distinction later). A second sort of confusion for English speakers is to suppose mistakenly that 'intentionality' as a technical notion in philosophy has some special connection with 'intending' in the ordinary sense, in which, for example, one intends to go to the movies tonight. Intending in the ordinary sense is just one form of intentionality along with belief, desire, hope, fear, etc.

INTENTIONALITY AND CONSCIOUSNESS

Some intentional states are conscious, some not. The belief that George Washington was the first president can be consciously entertained, but a person can have that belief while he or she is sound asleep. In such a case, the intentional state is unconscious (see CONSCIOUSNESS; THE UNCONSCIOUS). Furthermore, many forms of consciousness are intentional, but many are not. Thus, a conscious desire to drink a cold glass of beer or a conscious fear of snakes are both intentional, but a feeling of pain or a sudden sense of anxiety, where there is no object of the anxiety, are not intentional. In short, there is an overlap between consciousness and intentionality but they are by no means coextensive.

THE IRREDUCIBILITY OF INTENTIONALITY

Many attempts have been made to eliminate intentionality or analyse it away in terms of some simpler notions. Thus, in the *behaviourist* period of the philosophy of mind, many philosophers felt that having a state of belief or desire was simply a matter of being disposed to behave in certain ways, given certain stimuli (see BEHAVIOURISM). Subsequent *functional* theories try to analyse intentionality in terms of causal relations (see FUNCTIONALISM). For example, on function-

alist accounts, a belief is analysed as a certain functional state which is caused by external stimuli, and which, in conjuction with other states such as desires, causes certain sorts of external behaviour. More recent versions of functionalism try to identify intentional states with computational states. The idea is that being in a mental state is just being in a certain state of a computer program, and the mind is construed as a computer program running in the wetware of the brain. On this view, called 'strong artificial intelligence' or 'computer functionalism' the mind is to the brain as the program is to the hardware (see ARTIFICIAL INTELLIGENCE; COMPUTATIONAL MODELS).

All of these attempts to analyse intentionality fail for the reason that they try to reduce intentionality to something else (see REDUCTION). As soon as one recognizes the existence of intentionality as a genuine phenomenon, one is committed to rejecting any reductive or eliminative account of intentionality; for such accounts implicitly deny that the phenomenon exists as a genuine feature of the world.

This discussion will not attempt to establish the existence of intentional states, such as beliefs and desires, but will simply take their existence for granted and explore their logical properties.

THE STRUCTURE OF INTENTIONAL STATES

I have characterized intentionality as that feature of the mind by which it is directed at or about or of objects or states of affairs in the world, but that only raises the further question, what is meant by 'directed at', 'about', or 'of'? This question becomes more pressing when one realizes that an intentional state can be about something even though the thing it is about does not exist. Thus a child can have a belief that Santa Claus will come on Christmas Eve even though Santa Claus does not exist. The simplest way to explain the structure of intentional states is to compare them with speech acts. It is not surprising that intentional states and speech acts have parallel structures since every speech act is the expression of a corresponding intentional state. For example, every statement is an expression of a belief. Every promise is the expression of an intention, etc. Notice that this point holds even when the speaker is insincere, even when he does not have the belief, intention, etc., which he expresses.

There are several structural similarities between speech acts and intentional states, among them the following three:

(1) *The distinction familiar in the theory of speech acts between the force or type of the speech act and the propositional content of the speech act carries over exactly into the distinction in intentional states between the type of the intentional state and its propositional content.*

In the theory of speech acts, there is a familiar distinction between illocutionary force and propositional content. A speaker can perform three different types of speech act in uttering the three different sentences:

Leave the room!

You will leave the room.

Will you leave the room?

even though there is something common to all three utterances. In each utterance, the propositional content, that you will leave the room, is expressed, but it is expressed in speech acts with different illocutionary forces. The first has the force of an order or request; the second has the force of the prediction; and the third has the force of a question. The general structure of the speech act as exemplified by these three cases is F(p), where the 'F' marks the illocutionary force of an order, question, statement, etc.; and the 'p' marks the propositional content, that you will leave the room. These distinctions carry over exactly to intentional states. Just as one can assert, query, or order that you leave the room, so one can hope that you will leave the room, fear you will leave the room, believe you

will leave the room, wish you would leave the room, etc. In each case, the same propositional content – that you will leave the room – is presented in a different psychological mode – the psychological mode of hope, fear, belief, etc. The structure of such intentional states is S(p).

(2) *The distinction between different directions of fit, also familiar from the theory of speech acts, carries over to intentional states.*

Statements, for example, are supposed to represent an independently existing reality, and insofar as they succeed or fail in representing it accurately, they are said to be true or false. Thus, for example, if one makes the statement that John has left the room, one's statement will be true or false depending on whether or not John has left the room. But orders, commands, promises are not like statements in that they are not supposed to match an independently existing reality, but rather, they are supposed to bring about changes in reality so that the world comes to match the propositional content of the order, command, or promise. Thus, if an order is given to John, 'John, please leave the room!', then the order is not said to be true or false, but is said to be obeyed or disobeyed, depending on whether or not John's subsequent behaviour comes to match the propositional content of the order.

In the first sort of case – statements, assertions, descriptions, etc. – the utterance has the word-to-world direction of fit; it is true or false depending on whether or not the words match the world. But in the second sort of case – orders, commands, promises, etc. – the utterance has the world-to-word direction of fit; and the utterance is said to be obeyed, fulfilled, kept, etc., depending on whether or not the world comes to match the propositional content of the utterance. 'Truth' and 'falsity' are names for success and failure in the word-to-world direction of fit.

Some utterances with a propositional content do not have a direction of fit of either word-to-world or world-to-word.

These are cases where the propositional content is simply taken for granted as a presupposition. Thus, for example, if I apologize for stepping on your foot, or congratulate you on winning the race, in each case there is a propositional content – that I stepped on your foot, that you won the race – but the aim of the utterance is neither to assert that propositional content nor to try to change the world by getting the world to match the propositional content. In all three cases, the propositional content is simply taken for granted, and we can say therefore that such speech acts have the null direction of fit. Similarly there are intentional states with a propositional content where the truth of the propositional content is taken for granted. Feeling glad that you won the race or feeling sorry that I stepped on your foot have propositional contents, but like the corresponding speech acts, they have the null direction of fit.

In summary, there are certain exact parallels in the way that the notion of direction of fit applies to both speech acts and intentional states. Beliefs, like statements, have the word (or mind)-to-world direction of fit, and like statements, they can be said to be true or false. Desires and intentions have the world-to-word (or mind) direction of fit, and like orders and promises, they can be said to be carried out or fulfilled, but cannot be said to be true or false. Joy and sadness, sorrow and gladness like apologies and thanks have no direction of fit.

(3) *The notion of conditions of satisfaction applies generally to both speech acts and to intentional states.*

Statements are said to be true or false; orders are said to be obeyed or disobeyed; promises are said to be kept or broken. What stands to the statement being true is what stands to the order being obeyed is what stands to the promise being kept. In each case we can say quite generally that the speech act will be satisfied or not satisfied depending on whether or not the propositional content comes to match the world with the appropriate direction of fit.

For all such cases we can say that the speech act represents its conditions of satisfaction, and the illocutionary force determines the direction of fit with which it represents its conditions of satisfaction.

Exactly analogously in the structure of intentional states, what stands to the belief's being true is what stands to the desire's being fulfilled is what stands to the intention's being carried out. In each case the intentional state with a direction of fit has conditions of satisfaction, and we can say that the intentional state is a representation of its conditions of satisfaction, and the psychological mode determines the direction of fit with which the intentional state represents its conditions of satisfaction.

On this account, then, the key to understanding intentionality is representation in a special sense of that word that we can explain from our theory of speech acts. Every intentional state with a direction of fit is a representation of its conditions of satisfaction. Intentional states in general have both a propositional content and a psychological mode, and the psychological mode will determine the direction of fit with which the intentional state represents its conditions of satisfaction.

This account of intentionality is quite general, but it still does not account for two sorts of phenomena. First, what about those intentional states that have the null direction of fit. In what sense do they have conditions of satisfaction? And secondly, what about those intentional states that do not have an entire propositional content, such as admiring Einstein or hating Hitler?

If we consider such intentional states which do not have a direction of fit – as being glad that the Republicans won the election, or feeling sorry that the value of the dollar has declined – we find that each of these contains both beliefs and desires, and these component beliefs and desires have a direction of fit. In general one can say, for example, that in order to be glad that p, one must believe it to be the case that p and to want it to be the case that p. In order to be sorry that p, one must believe it to be the case that p and want it to be the case that not p. This phenomenon is characteristic of all of those intentional states with a propositional content which do not have a mind-to-world or world-to-mind direction of fit: all of these contain beliefs and desires, and the component beliefs and desires do have a direction of fit.

This suggests a pattern of analysis for the EMOTIONS which in the space of this article I can only sketch. Emotions such as love and hate, jealousy, anger, and lust all have certain features which are somewhat unusual among intentional states. They all matter to us in ways that many of our beliefs and desires are regarded with relative indifference. For example, I believe it is raining somewhere in the world right now, but I don't care much about it. When it comes to our emotions, however, of love and hatred, jealousy, and lust etc., we do care desperately about these. Why? In general, emotions are very strong agitated forms of desire. It is because the emotion is itself a form of strong desire, typically a desire caused by a belief which is also a component of the emotion, that one cares so strongly about one's emotions. A typical strong emotion will contain a whole package of desires. Lovers, for example, notoriously have varied and complex desires toward the beloved. For most of what philosophers have called 'the emotions' – love, hate, anger, jealousy, envy, etc. – an essential component of the emotion is an agitated form of desire.

How do we analyse those intentional states which only make reference to a single object and do not contain an entire propositional content, such as loving Sally or admiring Mother Theresa? Though none of these can be completely analysed into propositional contents that have directions of fit, in general, they require the presence of beliefs and desires, and the beliefs and desires do have a direction of fit.

THE INTENTIONALITY OF PERCEPTION AND ACTION

It is characteristic of discussions of intentionality that the paradigm cases discussed are usually beliefs or sometimes beliefs and desires. However, the biologically most basic forms of intentionality are in perception and in intentional action. These also have certain formal features which are not common to beliefs and desires. Consider a case of perception. Suppose I see my hand in front of my face. What are the conditions of satisfaction? First, the perceptual experience of the hand in front of my face has as its condition of satisfaction that there be a hand in front of my face. Thus far the condition of satisfaction is the same as the belief that there is a hand in front of my face. But with perceptual experience there is this difference: in order that the intentional content be satisfied, the fact that there is a hand in front of my face must cause the very experience whose intentional content is that there is a hand in front of my face. This has the consequence that perception has a special kind of condition of satisfaction that we might describe as 'causally self-referential'. The full conditions of satisfaction of the perceptual experience are, first that there be a hand in front of my face, and second, that there is a hand in front of my face caused the very experience of whose conditions of satisfaction it forms a part. We can represent this in our canonical form, S(p), as follows:

Visual experience (that there is a hand in front of my face and the fact that there is a hand in front of my face is causing this very experience.)

Furthermore, visual experiences have a kind of conscious immediacy not characteristic of beliefs and desires. A person can literally be said to have beliefs and desires while sound asleep. But one can only have visual experiences of a non-pathological kind when one is fully awake and conscious because the visual experiences are themselves forms of consciousness.

Event memory is a kind of halfway house between the perceptual experience and the belief. Memory, like perceptual experience, has the causally self-referential feature. Unless the memory is caused by the event of which it is the memory, it is not a case of a satisfied memory. But unlike the visual experience, it need not be conscious. One can literally be said to remember something while sound asleep. Belief, memory and perception all have the mind-to-world direction of fit, and memory and perception have the world-to-mind direction of causation. (*See* MEMORY; PERCEPTION; PERCEPTUAL CONTENT.)

Intentional action has interesting symmetries and asymmetries to perception. Like perceptual experiences, the experiential component of intentional action is causally self-referential. If, for example, I am now walking to my car, then the condition of satisfaction of the present experience is that there be certain bodily movements, and that this very experience of acting cause those bodily movements. Furthermore, like perceptual experience, the experience of acting is typically a conscious mental event. However, unlike the case of perception and memory, the direction of fit of the experience of acting is world-to-mind, and the direction of causation is mind-to-world. My intention will only be fully carried out if the world changes so as to match the content of the intention (hence world-to-mind direction of fit) and the intention will only be fully satisfied if the intention itself causes the rest of the conditions of satisfaction (hence, mind-to-world direction of causation).

Furthermore, just as in the case of the cognitive faculties, we needed to distinguish between perception and memory, so in the case of the volitional faculties, we need to distinguish between the actual experience of acting which we have while carrying out an intentional action and a prior intention that we sometimes form prior to the carrying out of the action. We may dub these two forms of intentionality as the intention-in-action and the prior intention. Both intentions-in-action and prior intentions are causally self-referential, but the prior intention, unlike the intention-in-action, need not be a conscious experience. As with memory, a man who is sound asleep can be said to have prior intentions.

THE NETWORK AND THE BACKGROUND

All intentional states only function in relation to other intentional states, and thus, in any case of intentionality, the intentional state only functions within a network of intentionality. For example, if I form the intention to go to Europe, I can only have that intention within a network of other beliefs, desires, and intentions. I must believe that Europe is a certain distance away, that it can be reached by airplane, that the cities I wish to visit are located within Europe, etc. I must desire that the plane I am on will go to Europe and not to Asia, that it will be able to take off, etc. I must intend to buy a plane ticket, to pack my bags, to go to the airport, to get on the plane, etc. One intentional state only functions in connection with an indefinite number of other intentional states. This phenomenon is called the 'Network' of intentionality.

If we follow out the threads in the Network, we soon reach a series of mental capacities that are not themselves further intentional states. There is a large bedrock of capacities, abilities, tendencies, etc., that are simply taken for granted or presupposed, but do not themselves form the structure of the intentional network. Thus, for example, in my dealings with the world, I presuppose the solidity of objects and the traversability of three-dimensional space. I presuppose the persistence of continents such as Europe and America, and that most of human life goes on at or near the surface of the earth. All of this forms a pre-intentional Background to my forming the intention to go to Europe, but it is not itself a matter of further intentional contents. This Background of intentionality consists in the various abilities, skills, and competences that I have for engaging in various physical and social activities. I know how to walk across the room, to buy a plane ticket, to get on an airplane, to sit in a seat, etc. In general, where intentional action is concerned, one may say that an agent's abilities rise to the level of the Background skill, but for that very reason, they reach to the bottom of the physical exercise of that skill. Let us consider each of these points in turn.

The man who has the ability to walk from his home to his office does not have to form a separate intention for each leg movement. He simply forms the intention to walk to his office, and then he simply does it. His intentionality rises to the level of his Background abilities. Nonetheless, each of the subsidiary voluntary movements within the execution of his intention is performed intentionally. Thus, each leg movement is intentional, though there is no separate intention determining the leg movements. How can this be? The answer is simply that the top-level intention, by invoking the Background ability, by deriving its conditions of satisfaction from the Background ability, governs each of the voluntary movements within the execution of the skill determined by the Background ability. The only intention is the intention to walk to his office. But the foot and leg movements are not thereby rendered unintentional. They are intentionally performed as part of the higher-level intentional act. (*See* ACTION; THE WILL.)

INTENTIONALITY-WITH-A-T AND
INTENSIONALITY-WITH-AN-S

A standard confusion in the philosophical literature is to suppose that there is some special connection between intentionality-with-a-t and intensionality-with-an-s. Some authors even allege that these are identical. But in fact, the two notions are quite distinct. Intentionality-with-a-t is that property of the mind by which it is directed at, or is about objects and states of affairs in the world. Intensionality-with-an-s is that phenonemon by which sentences fail to satisfy certain tests for extensionality. Let us now consider the relations between them.

There are many standard test for extensionality, but the two most common in the literature are substitutability of identicals (LEIBNIZ'S LAW) and existential inference. The principle of substitutability states that co-referring expressions can be substituted for each other without changing the truth value of the statement in which the sub-

stitution is made. The principle of existential inference states that any statement which contains a referring expression implies the existence of the object referred to by that expression. But there are statements that do not satisfy these principles and such statements are said to be intensional with respect to these tests for extensionality. An example of each is as follows.

From the statement that

(1) The sheriff believes that Mr Howard is an honest man

and

(2) Mr Howard is identical with the notorious outlaw, Jesse James

it does not follow that

(3) The sheriff believes that the notorious outlaw, Jesse James, is an honest man.

This is a failure of the substitutability of identicals.

From the fact that

(4) Billy believes that Santa Claus will come on Christmas Eve

it does not follow that

(5) There is some x such that Billy believes x will come on Christmas Eve.

This is a failure of existential inference. Thus, statements (1) and (4) fail tests for extensionality and hence are said to be intensional with respect to these tests.

What, then, exactly is the relation between intentionality-with-a-t and intensionality-with-an-s? Notice that the sentences that are intensional-with-an-s are about states that are intentional-with-a-t. The truth conditions of these intensional-with-an-s sentences do not require that the world be as represented by the original intentional states, but only that the content

385

of the intentional state be as represented in the sentences about those intentional states. Since intentional-with-a-t states are representations, and since the content of the representation can be reported independently of whether or not it is satisfied, or even independently of whether or not the objects purportedly referred to by the representation even exist, the report of the intentional state does not commit the person making the report to the existence of the objects referred to by the original representation (existential generalization); nor does the report necessarily remain true under substitution of co-referring expressions in the report (substitutability).

The explanation for the failure of the tests is that the ground floor intentional states in the minds of the sheriff and Billy are representations, but their reports in sentences such as (1) and (4) are representations of representations. The truth of the representation of the representation depends *not* on how things are in the real world represented by the original intentional representation (the original intentional state), but rather, how they are in the mental world of that intentional representation. And that mental representation can be reported accurately even though the objects purportedly referred to by that representation do not exist. This accounts for the failure of existential generalization. And the expressions occurring in the report, since they are not used to refer to any such objects, but only express the content of a representation, are not subject to the law of the substitutability of co-referring expressions. The substitution of any such expression may fail to preserve the mental content of the original intentional state being reported, and thus such substitutions cannot guarantee sameness of truth value. This accounts for the failure of the substitutability test.

On this account, intentionality-with-a-t and intensionality-with-an-s are quite distinct phenomena. The only connection is that characteristically reports of intentional-with-a-t states are intensional-with-an-s reports, for the reasons I have just given. Other sorts of sentences such as

modals, for example, also are intensional-with-an-s.

THE INTENTIONALITY OF MEANING

So far I have defined intentionality in such a way that it applies only to mental phenomena. Such states as beliefs and desires are intrinsically intentional. But just as beliefs and desires can represent states of affairs in the world, so can sentences, pictures, symbols and a host of other non-mental phenomena. In all such cases the intentionality of the mind is imposed on some non-mental phenomena. Mental states have *intrinsic* intentionality, material objects in the world that are used to represent something have *derived* intentionality. The most important form of derived intentionality is in language and there is a special name in English for this form of intentionality. It is called 'meaning' in one of the many senses of that word.

See also An Essay on Mind section 2.1.
CONTENT; FOLK PSYCHOLOGY; PRO-POSITIONAL ATTITUDES; REPRESENTATION; THOUGHT AND LANGUAGE

JOHN R. SEARLE

intentionality (2) Many mental states and activities exhibit the feature of intentionality: being directed at objects. Two related things are meant by this. First, when one desires or believes or hopes, one always desires or believes or hopes something. Let's assume that belief report (1) is true:

(1) Dan Quayle believes that George Bush is a Republican.

(1) tells us that a *subject*, Quayle, has a certain *attitude*, belief, to something, designated by the nominal phrase *that George Bush is a Republican* and identified by its *content-sentence*,

(2) George Bush is a Republican.

Following Russell and contemporary usage I'll call the object referred to by the that-clause in (1) and expressed by (2) a *proposition*. Notice that this sentence might also serve as Quayle's *belief-text*, a sentence he could utter to express the belief that (1) reports him to have. Such an utterance of (2) by itself would assert the truth of the proposition it expresses, but as a part of (1) its role is not to assert anything, but to identify *what the subject believes*. This same proposition can be the object of other attitudes and of attitudes of other people. Dole may regret that Bush is a Republican, Reagan may remember that he is, Buchanan may doubt that he is.

The second way in which mental states and activities are directed at objects has to do with more familiar sorts of objects: spatiotemporal objects like persons and things, abstract particulars like numbers, and universals like the property of being a Republican or the relation of standing next to. The truth of a proposition requires that certain objects will have or come to have certain properties or stand in certain relations. The attitude is about these objects, properties, and relations. Quayle's belief, for example, is *about* George Bush and the property of being a Republican. While we can have attitudes about ourselves and even our own mental states, we have an enormous number of attitudes about other things (*see* PROPOSITIONAL ATTITUDES). These things may be quite remote from us. I have never seen Bill Clinton in person, never talked to him. But I have many beliefs, hopes, desires, doubts, and fears about him. We all have attitudes about people who are long dead, like Aristotle and Caesar, and things that are millions of miles away, like the planet Pluto. This can seem rather puzzling. What exactly is the relation between a subject, and the objects about which they have attitudes?

The concept of intentionality was introduced into modern philosophy by Franz Brentano, who took what he called 'intentional inexistence' to be a feature that distinguished the mental from the physical (Brentano, 1960). In this article, we focus on two puzzles about the structure of intentional states and activities, an area in which the philosophy of mind meets the philoso-phy of language, logic, and ontology. We need to note that the term *intentionality* should not be confused with the terms *intention* and *intension*. Intentions, such as Bush's intention to run for re-election, are one kind of intentional state. Intensions are properties or concepts, as opposed to extensions: objects and sets of objects. To use Russell's imperfect but memorable example, *featherless biped that is not a plucked chicken* has the same extension as *human being*, but a different intension. There is an important connection between intensions and intentionality, for semantical systems, like extensional model theory, that are limited to extensions, cannot provide plausible accounts of the language of intentionality (*see* INTENSIONAL).

TWO PUZZLES

The attitudes are philosophically puzzling because it is not easy to see how the intentionality of the attitudes fits with another conception of them, as *local mental phenomena*.

Beliefs, desires, hopes, and fears seem to be located in the heads or minds of the people that have them. Our attitudes are accessible to us through INTROSPECTION. Quayle can tell that he believes Bush to be a Republican just by examining the 'contents of his own mind'; he doesn't need to investigate the world around him. We think of attitudes as being caused at certain times by events that impinge on the subject's body, specifically by perceptual events, such as reading a newspaper or seeing a picture of an ice-cream cone (*see* REASONS AND CAUSES). These attitudes can in turn cause changes in other mental phenomena, and eventually in the observable behaviour of the subject. Seeing the picture of an ice-cream cone leads to a desire for one, which leads me to forget the meeting I am supposed to attend and walk to the ice-cream shop instead. All of this seems to require that attitudes be states and activities that are localized in the subject.

But the phenomenon of intentionality suggests that the attitudes are essentially relational in nature; they involve relations to the propositions at which they are directed and at the objects they are about. These objects may be quite remote from the minds of subjects. An attitude seems to be individuated by the agent, the type of attitude (belief, desire, etc.), and the proposition at which it is directed. It seems essential to the attitude reported by (1), for example, that it is directed towards the proposition that Bush is a Republican. And it seems essential to this proposition that it is about Bush. But how can a mental state or activity of a person essentially involve some other individual? The difficulty is brought out by two classical problems, which I will call *no-reference* and *co-reference*.

Consider,

(3) Elwood believes the King of France is bald.

It seems that if France were a monarchy, and had a king, that king would be a constituent of the proposition that Elwood believed; his belief would be about him. Since there is no king, there must be no such proposition; what then does Elwood believe? This is the no-reference problem.

Compare (1) and (4),

(4) Quayle believes that the person who will come in second in the election is a Republican.

In September 1992, (1) was surely true and (4) was probably false. And yet Bush was the person who was going to come in second; that is, *Bush* and *the person who will come in second in the election* co-referred. But then it seems that the propositions Quayle is said to believe by (1) and (4) are the same. But then how can (1) be true and (4) be false? This is the *co-reference* problem.

THE CLASSICAL SOLUTION

The classical solution to these problems is to suppose that intentional states are only indirectly related to concrete particulars, like George Bush, whose existence is con-

tingent, and that can be thought about in a variety of ways. The attitudes directly involve abstract objects of some sort, whose existence is necessary, and whose nature the mind can directly grasp. These abstract objects provide concepts or ways of thinking of concrete particulars. On this view the propositions:

that George Bush is a Republican,

that the person who will come in second in the election is a Republican

are quite different, involving different concepts. These concepts correspond to different inferential/practical roles in that different PERCEPTIONS and MEMORIES give rise to these BELIEFS, and they serve as reasons for different ACTIONS. If we individuate propositions by concepts rather than individuals, the co-reference problem disappears.

This proposal has the bonus of also taking care of the no-reference problem. Some propositions will contain concepts that are not, in fact, of anything. These propositions can still be believed, desired, and the like.

This basic idea has been worked out in different ways by a number of authors. The Austrian philosopher Ernst Mally thought that propositions involved abstract particulars that *encoded* properties, like being the loser of the 1992 election, rather than concrete particulars, like Bush, who *exemplify* them. There are abstract particulars that encode clusters of properties that nothing exemplifies, and two abstract objects can encode different clusters of properties that are exemplified by a single thing (*see* Zalta, 1988). The German philosopher Gottlob Frege distinguished between the *sense* and the *reference* of expressions. The senses of *George Bush* and *the person who will come in second in the election* are different, even though the references are the same. Senses are grasped by the mind, are directly involved in propositions, and incorporate *modes of presentation* of objects (*see An Essay on Mind* section 2.1.3; CONCEPTS).

For most of the twentieth century, the

most influential approach was that of the British philosopher Bertrand Russell. Russell (1905, 1929) in effect recognized two kinds of propositions. *Singular propositions* consist of particulars and properties or relations. An example is a proposition consisting of Bush and the property of being a Republican. *General propositions* involve only universals. The general proposition corresponding to *someone is a Republican* would be a complex consisting of the property of being a Republican and the higher-order property of being instantiated. (The terms *singular proposition* and *general proposition* are from Kaplan (1989).)

Russell's *theory of descriptions* gives us general propositions where we might have thought we were getting singular ones. Consider (5),

(5) The person who will come in second in the election is a Republican.

Since Bush will lose the election, one might suppose that this expresses the singular proposition we mentioned above. But, in fact, it expresses the same general proposition expressed by (6),

(6) There is a unique person that will come in second in the election, and he or she is a Republican.

Even (2) turns out not to express a singular proposition on Russell's theory. Ordinary proper names like *Bush* are *hidden descriptions*. Where ψ is some crucial set of Bush's properties, (1) reports that Quayle believes that the ψ is a Republican.

Similarly, (3) tells us that Elwood has a belief about a number of universals, such as being a King of France and being bald. All of these universals can exist, even though there is no King of France, so the fact that Elwood has the belief he has does not imply that there is such a person.

DIRECT REFERENCE

Over the past twenty-five years, the hidden descriptions treatment of proper names has come in for a lot of criticism (see Donnellan, 1970; Kripke, 1972). According to this critique, the classical solution provides at best a partial solution to the no-reference and co-reference problems, and at worst rests on a mistaken conception of intentionality.

To make the hidden descriptions treatment of proper names work, we need a description that (i) denotes the bearer of the proper name, (ii) provides the correct content for the proposition expressed by the sentence in which the proper name occurs. There seem to be two places to look for such a description, in the mind of the subject, and in the rules of language.

Someone like Quayle, who knows Bush well, would associate a rich set of descriptions or conditions with his name. Let's assume that our description, *the ψ* incorporates all the facts that Quayle believes most firmly about Bush. Then, on the hidden descriptions view, it seems that (2) expresses the same proposition as (7):

(7) The ψ is a Republican.

But is this right? Suppose, as seems likely, that one of the properties Quayle is most sure about, with respect to Bush, is that he is a Republican. Then this property will be incorporated into ψ and (7) will be a trivial proposition. But (2) is not trivial. Even Quayle could probably imagine circumstances in which George Bush might not have become a Republican.

Or consider Clinton, who also believes that George Bush is a Republican. Intuitively, Clinton and Quayle believe the same thing, that George Bush is a Republican. But, on the hidden descriptions view, they really do not, since the complex of things Clinton associates most firmly with Bush will not be exactly the same as ψ, the complex that Quayle associates with him. If Clinton uses sentence (1) to describe Quayle, which proposition is at issue? The one based on Clinton's conception of Bush or the one based on Quayle's?

Finally, suppose that Elwood has heard of Bush, like virtually everyone in the world. But Elwood's beliefs about Bush, like his beliefs about many things, are confused and fragmentary. He is not sure what party Bush belongs to, or whether he is King or President. All the true things he believes about Bush don't amount to enough to pick Bush out uniquely. Still, it seems that as long as Elwood has heard about Bush – careless as he may be reading the newspaper articles, inattentive as he may be listening to the radio, inept as he may be in remembering the little he manages to understand – he can have beliefs about Bush, even if they are mostly wrong.

The second place to look for the appropriate description is the linguistic conditions of reference. It seems there must be some relation π that obtains between a name and the object to which it refers. It has been suggested, for example, that the relation is basically causal: a is the bearer of N iff a stands at the beginning of a certain sort of causal chain that leads to the use of N. This may be more or less independent of the speaker's belief, since many speakers do not have the foggiest idea what π might be.

It does not seem, however, that the associated description, *the x such that $\pi(N,x)$* meets our second condition. For, whatever π might turn out to be, it does not seem that (2) expresses the same proposition as (8),

(8) The x such that $\pi(George\ Bush,\ x)$ is a Republican.

Intuitively, (2) doesn't tell us anything about the name *George Bush*, and (8) doesn't tell us anything about the person George Bush. What (2) says could be true, even if no one were named *George Bush* (although we couldn't express it this way), and what (8) says could be true even if George Bush were a Democrat, so long as someone else was named *George Bush*, and that person were a Republican.

The conclusion to which these considerations seem to point is, in Russellian terms, that a statement like (2) expresses a singular proposition after all, and (1) attributes to Quayle a belief in a singular proposition. In David Kaplan's terminology, names are *directly referential* (Kaplan, 1989). This does

not mean (as it might seem to) that the link between a name and the object to which it refers is unmediated. It means that the object a name refers to is directly involved in the propositions expressed by sentences in which the name occurs.

But then the classical solutions to the co-reference and no-reference problems are at least very incomplete. We'll focus on the first. Recall that Bill Clinton's original name was *Bill Blythe* – he took *Clinton*, his step-father's name, while a teenager. Suppose that at one point Elwood is willing to assert (9) but not (10):

(9) Bill Clinton is a Democrat.

(10) Bill Blythe is a Democrat.

Then he learns about Clinton having two names, and becomes willing to assert (10). It seems that there was an important change in Elwood's beliefs. And yet it seems that the belief he expressed earlier with (9) and the one he expressed later with (10) express exactly the same singular proposition, with Clinton and the property of being a Democrat as constituents.

Things are still more complicated, for there are strong arguments that indexicals (*I, you, now*) and demonstratives (*this* ϕ, *that* ϕ) are also directly referential. Let u be a use by Clinton of:

(11) I am a Democrat.

What proposition does this express? Since uses of the word *I* refer to the speaker, one can associate the following condition with the *I* in use u of (11),

(12) Being the speaker of u.

One might then be tempted to suppose that (11) expresses the same proposition as

(13) The speaker of u is a Democrat.

But this isn't plausible. The proposition expressed by u, Clinton's utterance of (11), will be true in circumstances in which

Clinton is a Democrat, but doesn't utter u. In uttering u, he says that he is a Democrat. This was no doubt true before he uttered u, and would have been true even if he had not uttered u. The utterance u says nothing about itself. In uttering (11), Clinton would be confirming Elwood's belief that he is a Democrat, a belief Elwood would express with (9). It seems that u expresses a singular proposition.

Now suppose that Clinton himself was ignorant of, or has forgotten, his original name. Imagine that someone trustworthy tells him that Bill Blythe is a Democrat but doesn't reveal that Bill Blythe is Clinton himself. Clinton is willing to assert both (9) and (10). Given that names and indexicals are directly referential, by doing this he expresses his beliefs in exactly the same singular proposition. But Clinton clearly has two beliefs in the same proposition: yet another version of the co-reference problem.

MENTAL REPRESENTATIONS

Russell considered his theory to be a version of realism, in the sense that the objects of the attitudes were taken to be objective entities, external to the mind of the subject. Realists in this sense suppose that the mind can directly grasp such objects as Frege's senses, Mally's abstract objects, or Russell's universals. Cognition of concrete particulars is indirect, mediated by cognition of abstract objects.

An equally natural response to the puzzles is to reject realism in this sense, in favour of the alternative that intentionality basically involves having mental representations: ideas, thoughts, or mental terms and sentences in the subject's mind. Cognition of external objects, both abstract and concrete, is mediated by concrete particulars in the mind. There are as many varieties of this approach as there are theories of mental representations. According to a very straightforward theory patterned after the enthusiastic FODOR (1981) and the sceptical Stich (1983), the representations are best thought of as terms, predicates, and sentences of a 'LANGUAGE OF THOUGHT'.

This approach inherits both the traditional empiricist distinction between simple and complex ideas, and the theme of compositionality from the philosophy of language. One supposes that the basic expressions of the language of thought gain their meaning from their role in perception, cognition, and action, and the meaning of complex expressions is determined by the meanings of their parts.

An advocate of this view can adapt Russell's theory of descriptions to the language of thought, and adopt his partial solutions to the no-reference and co-reference problems. A mental description may be denotationless, and different mental descriptions may denote the same object. But there is no need to adopt the hidden descriptions view of basic expressions like names and indexicals. One can suppose that the reference of these basic terms is determined by their cognitive role and their links with perception and action, rather than by any hidden descriptive content.

Consider the mental equivalents of (9), (10), and (11). We can imagine Elwood to have formed two mental names (opened two mental 'files') for Clinton that are not internally connected, based on different causal interactions with Clinton, as childhood friend and as candidate. When Elwood reads about Clinton in the newspapers, new predicates become associated with the second name but not with the first. We can suppose that the mental analogue of I is that term in the language of thought that a person uses to keep track of information gained in the special ways one can gain information about oneself. The mental sentences corresponding to (9), (10), and (11) will have different causal and cognitive roles, even though it is the political affiliation of the same person that makes them each true.

So far, so good, but the story is very incomplete. To flesh out this sort of account, one needs to understand the relation of the internal mental representations involved in the attitude to the texts that express them and the content sentences of reports that describe them. With respect to texts, the most natural view is that the mental representation involved in an attitude is synonymous with the text that expresses it.

The question of content sentences is more complicated. Let's return to (1). What exactly does this tell us about Quayle's mental representations on this theory?

The natural hypothesis is that Quayle's mental representation should have the same meaning as (2), which is both the content sentence of the belief report and Quayle's belief text. However, things are not so simple. Again, it is proper names and indexicals that provide problems. Suppose Clinton has a mental sentence with the same meaning as (10) in the belief structure of his mind. How would a knowledgeable person, Quayle, say, report this belief of Clinton's? He would *not* use the English translation of the sentence in Clinton's head and say (14),

(14) Clinton believes that I am a Democrat.

This would be to say that Clinton believes the false proposition that Quayle is a Democrat, not the true one that Clinton is. He would say, instead,

(15) Clinton believes that he is a Democrat.

The connection between the content sentences in accurate attitude reports and mental sentences in the mind then is looser than having the same meaning. Clinton's mental version of *I* and Quayle's use of the pronoun *he* have the same reference, but not the same meaning. It seems that Quayle is not characterizing Clinton's belief in terms of the meaning of the mental words in Clinton's head, but rather in terms of the objects to which those words refer.

TWO-TIERED VIEWS

With these last considerations, propositions sneak back into the mental representations account, albeit with a somewhat diminished status. Propositions are not directly grasped by the mind, but are tools we use to describe something important that different attitudes, involving different subjects and different ways of thinking about objects, may have in common.

On the family of views I shall call *two-tiered*, our original notion of the object of the attitudes assimilates two different levels of comparison among attitudes (see Barwise and Perry, 1983; Crimmins, 1992; Crimmins and Perry, 1989; Kaplan, 1989; Perry, 1993; Richard, 1990; Salmon, 1986; Salmon and Soames, 1988; Schiffer, 1978, 1990). Consider the hopes of Clinton, Bush, and Perot as the election draws near. They each might say,

(16) I hope that I win the election.

Their hopes are similar at the level of mental representations, but different, indeed incompatible, at the level of the proposition hoped for. On the other hand, Hillary Clinton would not say (16), although she hopes for the same thing that Clinton does:

(17) Bill Clinton hopes that he wins the election, and so does Hillary Clinton.

On a typical view of this sort, for an attitude report to be true, the subject must have a mental sentence $\phi(\alpha)$ in the appropriate structure, which expresses *the same proposition* as the content sentence of the report. For (1) to be true, Quayle must have some sentence that expresses the singular proposition that Bush is a Republican. This sentence need not be a translation of the content sentence; the terms in it need not have the same meaning as those in the content sentence, only the same reference.

Indeed, as our reflections above about Quayle, Clinton, and (14) and (15) showed, sometimes the content sentences *cannot* be translations of the mental sentences. The job of the attitude reporter is to express from his or her perspective the same proposition that the subject's mental sentence expresses from the subject's perspective. Propositions are not directly grasped by minds, but are artefacts of our method of keeping track of truth conditions across differences in subject and mode of identification.

On this view, the language we use to

report the attitudes is basically incomplete and bound to be misleading at times. An attitude involves an agent having a certain sort of mental representation, which, given the agent's identity and circumstances, determines a certain proposition (which is usually thought of as a structured proposition of the sort Russell provides, although other approaches are possible). It is the subject and mental representation that are crucial to the occurrence of the attitude; if circumstances are wrong, no proposition may be determined, or the same proposition may be determined by quite different attitudes. But the attitude report focuses on the agent and proposition, only providing indirect information about the mental representation. It is this incompleteness that accounts for the no-reference and co-reference problems.

Consider our example involving three ways of referring to Clinton. *Bill Clinton* and *Bill Blythe* correspond to two ways anyone can think of Clinton, and *I* corresponds to another, the 'self-thinking' way of thinking about Clinton, which is a way of thinking we can each use to think about ourselves. Now if Quayle utters (15), we will naturally suppose that Clinton's mental sentence is *I am a Democrat*. But the content sentence of (15) identifies only the proposition Clinton believes, not *how* he believes it. For all (15) tells us, Clinton's mental sentence might be *Bill Blythe is a Democrat* or (looking at himself in a mirror, noticing the moderately liberal demeanor, but not recognizing himself), *that man is a Democrat*. Basically, attitude reports explicitly identify only two parameters of the three that are involved in the attitudes.

Among philosophers who offer two-tiered accounts, there is agreement that our attitude reports are looser than is envisaged on the other accounts, and rely more on pragmatic factors to communicate facts about the mental representations involved in the attitudes. For example, unless we are told otherwise, we naturally expect that people believe things about themselves in the first-person way, and not only by an abandoned name from their youth. Hence we would

normally infer from Quayle's utterance of (15) that Clinton has a belief he would express with *I am a Democrat* and not just one he would express with *Bill Blythe is a Democrat*.

When we get to details, however, two-tiered theorists disagree not only about the mechanisms involved, but even about the basic facts about which attitude reports are true and false in problematic situations. Recall Elwood, who a few pages back was willing to assert (9) but not (10):

(9) Bill Clinton is a Democrat.

(10) Bill Blythe is a Democrat.

Now consider (18), (19) and (20):

(18) Elwood believes that Bill Clinton is a Democrat.

(19) Elwood believes that Bill Blythe is a Democrat.

(20) Elwood doesn't believe that Bill Blythe is a Democrat.

On one approach, each report has an implicit quantifier that ranges over the hidden parameter (see Barwise and Perry, 1983; Salmon, 1986). So (18) and (19) are true and (20) is false because Elwood does believe the proposition that Clinton is a Democrat *in some way or another* – namely, thinking of him as *Bill Clinton*. (20) suggests that he believes the proposition when he thinks of Clinton as *Bill Clinton*, while (19) suggests that he believes it when he thinks of Clinton as *Bill Blythe*. On the present approach, this is conceived as merely a matter of pragmatics. In the case of Elwood, we would be reluctant to assert (19), since it suggests that Elwood is in a state that would lead him to assert (10). This reluctance to assert (19) may be mistaken for an intuition of the falsity of (19). But on the present approach, it is literally true. Similarly, we might be willing to assert (20), since it suggests, correctly, that Elwood would not assert (10). And this willingness might be mistaken for an intuition of the truth of (20). But, on the present approach, (20) is literally false.

Another approach takes it that the ways of thinking about Clinton are inexplicit or unarticulated parts of what (18), (19), and (20) are about (see Crimmins, 1992; Crimmins and Perry, 1989; Schiffer, 1978). For a belief report to be true, the subject has to believe the proposition identified by the content sentence in virtue of thinking about the objects *in the way provided by the context*. The report is about certain ways, however, and doesn't merely quantify over them. The words *Bill Clinton* in (18) suggest that it is thinking of Bill Clinton as *Bill Clinton* that is at issue; given this, (18) says that Elwood believes the proposition in this way. For the truth of (19) and (20), however, the other way of thinking about Clinton, as *Bill Blythe*, is relevant. On this view, (18) and (19) are true, and (20) is false, given the facts about Elwood.

On the two-tiered view, the attitudes are local mental phenomena, involving subjects and mental representations. But the cognitive role of these mental representations has to be understood in terms of the interactions of the agent with external objects, abstract and concrete, for we use these objects to classify and describe the attitudes.

Earlier we noted a tension between two conceptions of the attitudes, the intentional or object-directed conception, and the natural conception of them as local mental phenomena. Each tier of the two-tiered view corresponds to one of these conceptions. Mental representations are local phenomena, located in the heads or minds of the people that have them. When we describe these representations in terms of the objects they are representations of, however, our descriptions involve not only what goes on in the mind, but also the circumstances that link representations with various parts of an external reality.

Quayle's belief that Bush was a Republican was no doubt acquired on the basis of perception, and involved a change in the system of representations in his mind. This change is a local mental phenomenon, which can be cited in explanations of Quayle's actions, since it no doubt altered the ways in which he was disposed to behave in various circumstances.

This change is linked, by the circumstances of the perception that caused it, to George Bush. In certain circumstances, it is useful and convenient to describe the mental representation in terms of the object that gave rise to it. We think that Quayle will be good at recognizing Bush on subsequent occasions, so that the knowledge of his party affiliation will flow along these identifications and guide his actions towards Bush, however described or encountered. Our two-tiered system works best in such circumstances. When knowledge of a single object is not integrated in this way – as in the case of Elwood, who did not recognize Clinton as the boy he once knew as Bill Blythe – the two-tiered approach can be confusing and misleading. This is even more true in the case in which an internal representation has come into play with no proper external referent. The co-reference and no-reference problems call our attention to these limitations of the two-tiered system. In practice, however, we seldom have a problem in making the details of the case clear. Where singular propositions do not readily make clear what is believed and not believed, general propositions come quickly to the rescue. Elwood believed that there was a kid he once knew named 'Bill Blythe', and there is a man running for President named 'Bill Clinton' and they are not the same and the latter is a Democrat.

See also An Essay on Mind section 2.1; CONTENT; INTENTIONALITY (1); THOUGHTS; THOUGHT AND LANGUAGE.

BIBLIOGRAPHY

Brentano, F. 1960. The distinction between mental and physical phenomena. In *Realism and the Background of Phenomenology*, ed. R. M. Chisholm. Atascadero, CA: Ridgeview Publishing.

Barwise, J., and J. Perry. 1983. *Situations and Attitudes*. Cambridge, MA.: MIT Press, Bradford Books.

Castañeda, H. 1990. *Thinking and the Structure of the World*. Berlin: W. de Gruyter.

Crimmins, M. 1992. *Talk About Beliefs*. Cambridge, MA: MIT Press/Bradford Books.

Crimmins, M., and Perry, J. 1989. The prince and the phone booth: reporting puzzling beliefs. *The Journal of Philosophy*, LXXXVI, 685–711.

Donnellan, K. 1970. Proper names and identifying descriptions. *Synthèse*, 21 3–31.

Evans, G. 1982. *Varieties of Reference*. Oxford University Press.

Fodor, J. 1981. Propositional Attitudes. In *Representations*. Brighton: Harvester Press.

Frege, G. 1970. On sense and reference. In *Translations from the Philosophical Writings of Gottlob Frege*, ed. and trans. P. Geach and M. Black. Oxford: Basil Blackwell.

Hintikka, J. 1975. *The Intentions of Intentionality*. Dordrecht: D. Reidel.

Kaplan, D. 1989. Demonstratives. In *Themes From Kaplan*, ed. I. Almog, J. Perry and H. Wettstein. Oxford University Press.

Kripke, S. 1972. Naming and Necessity. In *Semantics of Natural Language*. Dordrecht: D. Reidel, 253–354.

Peacoke, C. 1986. *Thoughts: an Essay on Content*. Oxford: Basil Blackwell.

Perry, J. 1993. *The Problem of the Essential Indexical*. Oxford University Press.

Richard, M. 1990. *Propositional Attitudes*. Cambridge University Press.

Russell, B. 1905. On denoting. *Mind* 14, 479–93.

Russell, B. 1929. Knowledge by acquaintance and knowledge by description. In *Mysticism and Logic*. New York: W. W. Norton.

Salmon, N. 1986. *Frege's Puzzle*. Cambridge, MA.: MIT Press/Bradford Books.

Salmon, N., and S. Soames, eds. 1988. *Propositional Attitudes*. Oxford University Press.

Searle, J. 1983. *Intentionality*. Cambridge University Press.

Schiffer, S. 1978. The basis of reference. *Erkenntnis*, 13, 171–206.

Schiffer, S. 1990. The mode-of-presentation problem. In *Propositions and Attitudes*, ed. C. A. Anderson and J. Owens. Stanford, CA.: CSLI.

Stalnaker, R. 1985. *Inquiry*. Cambridge, MA.: MIT Press/Bradford Books.

Stich, S. 1983. *From Folk Psychology to Cognitive Science*. Cambridge, MA.: MIT Press/Bradford Books.

Zalta, E. 1988. *Intensional Logic and the Metaphysics of Intentionality*. Cambridge, MA.: MIT Press/Bradford Books.

JOHN PERRY

introspection The term 'introspection' derives from the Latin words *spicere* ('to look') and *intra* (within), and is believed to have first made its appearance in the second half of the seventeenth century. It has been used by philosophers and psychologists in a number of different though related senses. In its broadest sense it refers to the non-inferential access each person has to a variety of current mental states and events – SENSATIONS, feelings, THOUGHTS, etc. – occurring in that person. When the term is used in this broad sense it is an open question whether introspection is appropriately thought of as a kind of PERCEPTION or observation, involving an 'inner sense'. But sometimes the use of the term is tied to the view (suggested by its etymology) that our introspective access to our mental states is perceptual or quasi-perceptual. Some writers distinguish introspection from a pre-introspective awareness of mental phenomena, saying that one is not properly speaking introspecting unless one is not only aware of some mental phenomenon but aware that one is aware of it. And some have suggested that introspection should be thought of as a kind of low-level theorizing about what is going on in one's mind, the data for this theorizing presumably being, at least in part, the knowledge gained from 'pre-introspective' awareness. It is perhaps introspection in this last sense that 'introspective' people are given to.

In this essay 'introspection' will be used in its broadest sense, i.e to include what some would classify as pre-introspective awareness. We are concerned, then, with something allowed to exist by all except behaviourist philosophers – a special, non-inferential, access which each person has to (some of) his or her own mental states, and, going with this, a special authority that attaches to (some) first-person mental state ascriptions (*see* FIRST-PERSON AUTHORITY). Whether this special access and authority deserve the name 'privileged access' is a further question.

An influential tradition in modern philosophy, often associated with Descartes, claims that CONSCIOUSNESS is the essence of mentality, that each mind is 'transparent' to itself, and that the awareness each mind has of its current states and processes yields knowledge having the highest possible degree of certainty. Such a view has often gone with a version of foundationalist epistemology which takes all empirical knowledge to be grounded, ultimately, in the knowledge (here called 'introspective') each mind has of its own states, including its sensations and perceptual experiences. To single out two important components of this view, it holds first that the judgments a person makes about his or her current mental states are 'incorrigible', or 'infallible', and it holds that the mental states are, by their very nature, 'self-intimating'. To say that a judgment is incorrigible is to say that it is impossible that it could be *shown* to be mistaken, while to say that a judgment is infallible is to say that it is impossible that it could *be* mistaken. Incorrigibility doesn't straightforwardly entail infallibility, but it is not easy to see how a kind of judgment could be incorrigible without being infallible. To say that a mental state is necessarily self-intimating means that it follows from someone's having the state that the person is aware of having it, or, on a weaker version of the notion, that the person would be aware of having the state if he or she considered the matter.

One source of the infallibility doctrine is Descartes' *Cogito* (*see* HISTORY). The propositional content 'I am thinking' (and likewise such contents as 'I am conscious' and 'I have some beliefs') is such that, necessarily, if it is judged to be true, or even considered, it must be true. The same is true more generally of contents of the form 'I am having a thought that P'. Judgments with such contents are necessarily self-verifying. But where a judgment is self-verifying, its infallibility can be explained on purely logical grounds and provides no evidence of the existence of a perceptual or quasi-perceptual access to mental states which is immune to error. And most judgments thought to be infallible are not self-verifying, as is shown by the fact that their negations, e.g. 'I am not in pain', are not self-falsifying. If they are infallible, it must be for another reason.

For a variety of reasons, 'CARTESIAN' views about our access to our own minds, including claims about infallibility and self-intimation, have fallen out of favour. Freud persuaded many that beliefs, wishes, and feelings (e.g. of hostility, or jealousy) are sometimes unconscious, and even sceptics about Freudian theory acknowledge that there is a such a thing as SELF-DECEPTION about one's motives and attitudes. Recent work in psychology has revealed that in certain circumstances people are regularly wrong in the claims they make about their reasons for action, and that such claims are sometimes the result of 'confabulation'. Psychologists have also discovered such phenomena as 'blindsight', in which a patient cortically blind in some portion of the visual field sincerely denies seeing anything there but, when forced to make 'guesses' about what is there, guesses correctly well above chance. Cartesian views about introspective access have also been challenged on more purely philosophical grounds. The alleged impossibility of imagining cases in which someone is mistaken about whether he or she is in PAIN has been challenged on the basis of a variety of examples. For example, there is the 'fraternity initiation' example, in which the blindfolded subject is told that a knife is about to be applied to his throat, and takes himself to feel pain when a piece of ice is applied.

Lying behind many of these challenges is what has been called the 'distinct existences' argument, advanced by (among others) David Armstrong. This takes it as given that introspective awareness of a mental state involves having a belief that one has that mental state. And it takes it as obvious that where one has a mental state and the belief that one has it, the state and the belief are 'distinct existences', i.e. such that it is at least logically possible that either of them should exist without the other. If one's toothache could, logically, exist without one's believing that one has a toothache (even if one considers the matter), that shows that toothaches are not self-intimating. If the belief that one has a toothache could, logically, exist without being accompanied by a toothache, that shows that such beliefs are not infallible. Sometimes the claim that the first-order mental state (e.g. the toothache) and the introspective belief are distinct existences is supported by the claim that if the belief constitutes *knowledge* of the first-order state, this must be because it is *caused* by it via a reliable mechanism, and that, as Hume taught us, causes and effects are always distinct existences.

Implicit here is a simple yet compelling account of the nature of introspective self-knowledge. On this view, our special access to our mental states consists simply in the fact that each of us is so constituted that, under certain conditions, being in a mental state produces, via some mechanism in the mind or brain, a belief that one is in a mental state of that sort. The belief counts as knowledge because the mechanism is by and large reliable, i.e. by and large produces true beliefs.

Many who take this view present it as a version of the perceptual, or 'inner sense', model of introspective self-knowledge. Many others have denied that introspective self-knowledge should be thought of on the model of sense-perception. But it is not altogether clear what is at stake when it is affirmed or denied that introspection is a kind of perception. One probably should not think of the issue as that of whether introspection shares a 'real essence' of perception which unites the various 'outer' senses. There may be no such thing. It is better to think of the question as whether introspection fits one or another stereotype of perception. And different stereotypes need to be distinguished.

John Locke said that we perceive our ideas and the operations of our minds, and so might be held to conceive of introspection (what he called 'reflection') as inner sense. But Locke clearly did not think of introspection on the model of sense-perception *as he thought it actually is* – for he thought that our perceptual access to external things is mediated by their production in us of 'ideas' of them, and he certainly did not think of our introspective access to our ideas as mediated in this way. If he thought of introspection on the model of perception, the operative stereotype of perception was not sense-perception as it actually is but rather sense-perception as we naïvely take it to be. This is not the stereotype modern advocates of the inner sense model have in mind, for, unlike Locke, they think of the deliverances of introspection as being subject to error in the same way those of sense-perception are.

One stereotype of perception, of which Locke's was perhaps a special case, is what I shall call the object-perception stereotype. This takes visual perception as its paradigm of perception, and takes it that perception is in the first instance perception of (non-factual) objects, and only derivatively perception of facts. The central idea is that we perceive facts by perceiving the objects involved in them and identifying those objects as being of certain kinds, or as being certain particular things, by perceiving their intrinsic features and their relations to other objects.

Introspection differs in obvious ways from visual perception. There is no organ of introspection whose disposition is under our voluntary control in the way the orientation of our eyes is. And while visual perception involves our having visual experiences of the object, which constitute its appearing to us in certain ways (ways in which it may or may not be), no one supposes that introspecting a pain, say, involves one's having an experience of the pain, distinct from the pain itself, which constitutes its appearing to one in some way. Introspective awareness of a sensation does not involve having yet another sensation that is 'of' the first one. For some this is enough to show that introspection is not inner sense. But there are other parts of the object-perception stereotype that are independent of this, to which some kinds of introspective awareness have been thought to conform.

It is primarily the introspective awareness of sensations and sensory states that philosophers have found it plausible to think of in terms of the object-perception model. For it is here that it is natural to think of there being non-factual objects that we are aware of, such that it is *by* being aware of these, and of their intrinsic features, that we are aware of whatever facts we are aware of. It is not natural to think of our awareness of beliefs, for example, in this way. Nothing seems to answer to the description: becoming aware of something in oneself, and identifying it as the belief that the cold war ended in 1991. While we speak of being aware of beliefs, it would seem inappropriate to say that one is aware that one believes that so-and-so *by* being aware of the belief that so-and-so. Being aware of the belief just *is* being aware of the fact that one believes a certain thing – so here we do not have object-awareness in the appropriate sense. By contrast, it is very natural to say that one is aware that one has a pain or an itch *by* being aware of the pain or itch. And it is natural to say that one is aware that one is seeing a yellow after-image *by* being aware of the after-image and seeing that it is yellow.

But here the question of whether a perceptual model of introspection is appropriate becomes inextricably bound out with questions about the nature of the mental phenomena to which we have introspective access. What makes the inner sense model irresistible in the case of sensory phenomena is the acceptance of what has been called the 'act-object' conception of sensation. Applied to the case of after-imaging, this says that the phenomenon we describe by saying 'I see a red after-image' involves the existence somewhere in the mind of an entity that is actually red. It is questionable whether one can accept this view about after-imaging without being committed to full-scale acceptance of the sense-datum

theory of perceptual experience – the view that every case of perceiving or seeming to perceive involves 'sensing' or 'immediately perceiving' a phenomenal object, a sense-datum, distinct from the external object (if any) that is perceived, and having whatever sensory features one's experience represents the external object as having. This theory is almost universally rejected. And in the opinion of many, its rejection requires the rejection of the act-object conception across the board. Some who reject the act-object conception favour an 'adverbial' account of sensory experience, according to which what the act-object theorist describes as seeing a red image is more appropriately described as 'being appeared to redly'. Others hold that the mistake of the act-object conception is to misconstrue the *intentional* object of a sensory state as an actually existing object (*see* INTENTIONALITY). Thus, just as Ponce de Leon could think of and look for the fountain of youth, even though there is no such thing, so the person experiencing a red after-image can be seeing something red even though in fact there is nothing red, either outside his mind or inside it, that he is seeing. If any such view is adopted, it is not clear that any of the entities we are left with in the sensory realm qualify as 'objects' in the sense required for the applicability of the object-perception model of introspection. What we are left with are states of being appeared to redly, or experiencings with certain representational contents. And just as being aware of a belief does not seem something distinct from being aware that one has such and such a belief, it is not clear that being aware of such an experiencing, or state, is distinct from being aware that one is undergoing such an experiencing.

When philosophers attack the idea that introspection is perception, what they are often attacking is what I am calling the object-perception model of perception. But it is far from clear that recent philosophers who have endorsed a perceptual model of introspection have meant to be endorsing the object-perception model. Some of them explicitly reject the act-object conception of sensation. And some of them clearly want their account of introspection as perception to apply as much to the case of awareness of beliefs and desires as to the case of awareness of sensations, and give no indication that they think that the former conforms to the object-perception model. Nor does it seem that someone who speaks of introspection as perception is thereby committed to endorsing the object-perception model – for there is a good deal of paradigmatic sense perception, e.g. perception by smell, that does not conform to this model (if I say that I 'smell a skunk', I do not mean that there is a particular skunk I smell). It seems plausible that these philosophers are operating with a broader conception of perception than this. The key elements of this broad conception are, first, that perception involves the production by the object or state of affairs perceived, via a reliable belief-producing mechanism, of a belief about that object or state of affairs, and, second, that the existence of the object or state of affairs perceived is logically independent of its being perceived and of there being the belief-producing mechanisms that would be required for its perception. Call these, respectively, the causal condition and the independence condition. It seems plausible that these conditions are satisfied in ordinary cases of sense perception. Is it also plausible to suppose that they are satisfied in cases of introspective awareness of one's own mental states?

This brings us back to the issue of whether mental phenomena or states of affairs are, in any good sense, 'self-intimating'. If they are, our awareness of them fails the independence condition, and is not perceptual even in the broad sense. The Cartesian idea that the mind is completely transparent to itself has been thoroughly discredited. But one needn't accept that idea in order to question the view that all mental phenomena and states of affairs satisfy the independence condition. The latter view implies that for every sort of mental state, there could be creatures that have states of that sort but are totally devoid of introspective access to those states – as we might

put it, creatures who are introspectively self-blind with respect to that sort of state. Since such self-blindness is supposed to be a perceptual disability, not a cognitive one, it would seem that if it is possible at all it should be possible for it to occur in creatures who are cognitively and conceptually on a par with us. Could such creatures be self-blind with respect to their own beliefs? Such a creature would have to have an appreciable degree of RATIONALITY. And such rationality would require a sensitivity on the part of the creature to what the contents of its belief-desire system are, since only so could it make the revisions of its belief-desire system, in the light of new experience, that rationality requires. It is arguable that such sensitivity would require some introspective access to its beliefs and desires. Also, it is questionable whether it is coherent to suppose that there could be a creature, possessed of the concepts of belief and desire, who has the ability to express beliefs and desires linguistically but not the ability to report beliefs. Or consider the case of sensations. Could there be a creature with normal human intelligence and conceptual capacity who has pains but is totally without introspective access to its pains? Or who has a persistent ringing in its ears, but is incapable of becoming introspectively aware of it? If not, it would seem that even the broad perceptual model for introspection should be rejected.

If one takes the view that mental states are defined or constituted by their causal or functional roles, then one possible view is that it is essential to the functional roles of some kinds of mental states that under certain conditions these mental states produce in their subjects' introspective awarenesses of them, these awarenesses consisting of 'higher-order beliefs', or 'higher-order thoughts', about the states that produce them. This would be a functionalist version of the view that certain kinds of mental states are self-intimating (see FUNCTIONALISM). Among the problems faced by such a view is that of explaining how, if at all, we can allow for the apparent fact that we share many kinds of mental states with creatures who lack the capacity for introspective awareness.

See also An Essay on Mind section 2.2; EMOTION; IMAGERY; IMAGINATION; PERCEPTUAL CONTENT; QUALIA; THE SELF; SUBJECTIVITY.

BIBLIOGRAPHY

Alston, W.P. 1971. Varieties of privileged access. *American Philosophical Quarterly*, 8, 223–41.

Armstrong, D.M. 1968. *A Materialist Theory of the Mind*. London: Routledge & Kegan Paul.

Descartes, R. 1985. Meditations on first philosophy. In *The Philosophical Writings of Descartes*, ed. J. Cottingham, R. Stoothhoff, and D. Murdoch. Cambridge University Press.

Hill, C.S. 1991. *Sensations: A Defense of Type Materialism*. Cambridge University Press.

Locke, J. 1975. *An Essay Concerning Human Understanding*, ed. P. H. Nidditch. Oxford: Clarendon Press.

Lyons, W.E. 1986. *The Disappearance of Introspection*. Cambridge, MA: MIT Press/Bradford Books.

Myers, G.E. 1986. Introspection and self-knowledge. *American Philosophical Quarterly*, 23, 199–207.

Nisbett, R., and Wilson, T. de C. 1977. Telling more than we know: verbal reports on mental processes. *Psychological Review*, 84, 231–59.

Shoemaker, S.S. 1988. On Knowing One's Own Mind. *Philosophical Perspectives*, 2, 183–209.

SYDNEY SHOEMAKER

inverted spectrum *see* FUNCTIONALISM; QUALIA.

L

Language of Thought (1) The Representational Theory of the Mind arises with the recognition that thoughts have contents carried by mental representations. For Abelard to think, for example, that Pegasus is winged is for Abelard to be related to a MENTAL REPRESENTATION whose content is that Pegasus is winged. Now, there are different kinds of representations: pictures, maps, models, and words – to name only some. Exactly what sort of REPRESENTATION is mental representation? (*See* IMAGERY; CONNECTIONISM.) Sententialism distinguishes itself as a version of representationalism by positing that mental representations are themselves linguistic expressions within a 'language of thought' (FODOR, 1975, 1987; Field, 1978; Maloney, 1989). While some sententialists conjecture that the language of thought is just the thinker's spoken language internalized (Harman, 1982), others identify the language of thought with Mentalese, an unarticulated, internal language in which the computations supposedly definitive of cognition occur. Sententialism is certainly a bold and provocative thesis, and so we turn to the reasons that might be offered on its behalf.

SEMANTICS AND REASONING

THOUGHTS, in having contents, possess semantic properties (*see* CONTENT; SEMANTIC/SYNTACTIC). Thinking that Pegasus is winged, Abelard somehow both thinks *about* Pegasus, despite the horse's non-existence, and thinks of the horse *as* winged. Thoughts appear, then, to denote and attribute, denotation and attribution thus being among the semantic properties of thoughts. What kind of mental representation might

support denotation and attribution if not linguistic representation? Perhaps, when thinking of Pegasus, Abelard deploys an actual Mentalese name for that actually non-existent horse. After all, names evidently can denote even what wants existence. And if Abelard's thinking of Pegasus is his mentally naming Pegasus, then Abelard's thinking of Pegasus as winged would be Abelard's concatenating the Mentalese adjective meaning winged with Pegasus's Mentalese name. The Mentalese sentence 'PEGASUS IS WINGED' would then serve to bring Pegasus to mind and to portray him as winged. Also, in thinking of Pegasus simply as winged, Abelard might well ignore other of Pegasus's characteristics, including his colour. In this sense, thoughts are surgically precise in just the way that sentences are and, say, pictures are not. 'PEGASUS IS WINGED' predicates only wingedness of Pegasus while remaining silent on his colour. However, a picture of Pegasus that depicts his wings will struggle to conceal his colour. If, then, thoughts denote and precisely attribute, sententialism may be best positioned to explain how this is possible.

Beliefs are true or false. If, as representationalism would have it, beliefs are relations to mental representations, then beliefs must be relations to representations that have truth values among their semantic properties. Sentences, at least declaratives, are exactly the kind of representations that have truth values, this in virtue of denoting and attributing. So, if mental representations are as sententialism says, we could readily account for the truth valuation of mental representations.

Beliefs serve a function within the mental economy. They play a central part in reasoning and, thereby, contribute to the control of behaviour (*see* BELIEF; RATIONALITY). Reason capitalizes on various semantic and evidential relations among antecedently held beliefs (and perhaps other attitudes) to generate new beliefs to which subsequent behaviour might be tuned. Apparently, reasoning is a process that attempts to secure new true beliefs by exploiting old (true) beliefs. By the lights of representationalism, reasoning must be a process defined over mental representations. Sentialism tells us that the type of representation in play in reasoning is most likely sentential – even if mental – representation. (*See* ARTIFICIAL INTELLIGENCE; COGNITIVE PSYCHOLOGY; COMPUTATIONAL MODELS.) Abelard believes both that Eloise is ashen and that if she is ashen, then she is ill. Remarkably, he concludes that Eloise is ill. How does this happen? Suppose that both the beliefs he exploits and the one he produces in concluding that Eloise is ill all essentially involve mental sentences. If that were the case, then we would have a route, even if largely uncharted, to understanding how reasoning unfolds in Abelard. Possibly, in reasoning mental representations stand to one another just as do public sentences in valid *formal derivations*. Reasoning would then preserve truth of belief by being the manipulation of truth-valued sentential representations according to rules so selectively sensitive to the syntactic properties of the representations as to respect and preserve their semantic properties. The sentialist hypothesis is thus that reasoning is formal inference; it is a process tuned primarily to the structures of mental sentences. Reasoners, then, are things very much like classically programmed computers (Fodor, 1980; Searle, 1980).

Would that the story could be so tidily told! Arguably we have infinitely many beliefs. Yet certainly the finitude of the brain or relevant representational device defies an infinity or corresponding representations. So preserving sentialism requires disavowing the apparent infinitude of beliefs in favour of something like a distinction between (finitely many) actual beliefs – these being relations to actual Mentalese sentences – and (infinitely many) dispositional beliefs – these being the unactualized but potential consequences of their actual counterparts. But, this distinction in hand, we will now need to know how the mind – as a sentential processor – is able so elegantly to manage and manipulate its actual beliefs so as regularly to produce the new beliefs rationally demanded of it in response to detectable environmental fluctuations. This and other related matters lead to notoriously difficult research problems whose solution certainly bears upon the plausibility of the language of thought. The sentialist must admit that if these problems finally prove intractable, then whatever warrant sentialism might otherwise have had will have evaporated (Fodor, 1983). But this aside, there are additional reasons in abductive support of sentialism.

SYSTEMATICITY AND PRODUCTIVITY

Thinking is also *systematic* and *productive* (Fodor and Pylyshyn, 1988; Dennett, 1987). Abelard wonders whether William is taller than Roscelin. This implies that Abelard is capable of considering that Roscelin is taller than William. More generally, the fact that Abelard can have some thoughts entails that he can have certain other semantically related thoughts. How is this systematicity possible?

Suppose that Abelard's thought that William is taller than Roscelin involves the registration of 'WILLIAM IS TALLER THAN ROSCELIN'. This Mentalese sentence is itself a complex representation containing simpler representations, mental words in the most rudimentary case. As complex mental representations, mental sentences result from processes ultimately defined on Mentalese words and expressions. So, if Abelard can produce 'WILLIAM IS TALLER THAN ROSCELIN', he must have access to 'WILLIAM', 'ROSCELIN' and 'IS TALLER THAN'. And if he has these mental representations, he is capable of producing 'ROSCELIN IS TALLER THAN WILLIAM' and, thereby, considering that Roscelin is taller than William. Sententialism posits that mental representations are linguistically complex representations whose semantic properties are determined by the semantic properties of their constituents. If this should prove correct, then we would be poised to explain the systematicity of thought (Schiffer, 1987).

Closely related to thought's systematicity is its productivity. Thought is productive in that we appear to have a virtually unbounded competence to think ever more complex novel thoughts having certain clear semantic ties to their less complex predecessors. Abelard's thinking that Eloise is ashen suffices for his being able to think that Eloise is *not* ashen, which in turn secures his ability to think that Eloise is *not* not ashen. And so on, until the brain's physical resources are exhausted. Systems of mental representation apparently exhibit the sort of productivity distinctive of spoken languages. Sententialism accommodates this fact by identifying the productive system of mental representation with a language of thought, the basic terms of which are subject to a productive grammar.

Opacity

The opacity of thought also legislates in favour of sententialism. While thought respects some semantic relations among mental representations, it can be utterly blind to others. Abelard believes that Eloise is ashen. Eloise is, in fact, the most literate woman in Paris, though Abelard is ignorant of that. He fails, then, to believe that the most literate woman in Paris is ashen. How is this opacity possible? (*See* INTENTIONALITY.) Sententialism answers: To believe that Eloise is ashen is distinctively to be related to 'ELOISE IS ASHEN'. To believe that the most literate woman in Paris is ashen is to be related to the different mental sentence, 'THE MOST LITERATE WOMAN IN PARIS IS ASHEN'. The sheer fact that Abelard is related to the first does not suffice for his being similarly related to the second, even though the two mental sentences happen to agree in truth value in virtue of

denoting the same woman and attributing to her the same property. Thinking, according to sententialism, may then be like quoting. To quote an English sentence is to issue, in a certain way, a token of a given English sentence type; it is certainly not similarly to issue a token of every semantically equivalent type. Perhaps thought is much the same. If to think is to token a sentence in the language of thought, the sheer tokening of one mental sentence need not insure the tokening of another formally distinct equivalent. Hence, thought's opacity.

OBJECTIONS TO THE LANGUAGE OF THOUGHT

Objections to the language of thought come from various quarters. Some will not tolerate any edition of representationalism, including sententialism; others endorse representationalism while denying that mental representations could involve anything like a language. We first remark on general objections to representationalism and then glance at complaints specific to sententialism. This done, we conclude with a peek at the naturalization of the semantics of the language of thought.

Adverbialism

Representationalism is launched by the assumption that psychological states are relational, that being in a psychological state minimally involves being related to something. But perhaps psychological states are not at all relational (Churchland, P.M., 1981). Might not the logical form of 'Abelard thinks that Eloise is ashen' be the same as 'Abelard argues with eloquence' rather than 'Abelard argues with William'? 'Abelard argues with eloquence' is equivalent to 'Abelard argues eloquently', a monadic predication assigning the monadic property of arguing eloquently. Similarly, 'Abelard thinks that Eloise is ashen' may attribute to Abelard not a relation to anything but simply the monadic property of thinking in a certain way, namely 'Eloise-is-ashen-ly'. *Adverbialism* begins by denying that expressions of psychological states are relational, infers that psychological states themselves are monadic and, thereby, opposes classical versions of representationalism, including sententialism.

Adverbialism aspires to ontological simplicity in eschewing the existence of entities as theoretically recondite as mental representations. Nevertheless, it is hard pressed plausibly and simply to explain what is intuitively semantically common to Abelard's thoughts that Eloise is ashen and that Roscelin is ashen. The supposed monadic properties of thinking Eloise-is-ashen-ly and thinking Roscelin-is-ashen-ly are, apparently, no more mutually similar than either is to the property of thinking William-is-tall-ily. It is, after all, only an orthographic accident and totally without significance that the predicates for the first two properties have portions of their spelling in common. Thus, unless adverbialism allows for internally complex properties – in which case it seems to have no metaphysical advantage over its relational rival – it seems unable to meet the psychological facts.

Instrumentalism

Others urge that talk of mental representations not be construed realistically but only as a sort of useful, predictive psychological calculus (Dennett, 1987). Possibly ascriptions of thoughts are simply attempts to explain behaviour in the face of massive ignorance of the relevant internal dynamics. A small child may speak grammatically correct English, and we may say of her that she knows that 'corn' is a noun. However, from this it would be quite a long leap to infer that the child actually deploys a specific mental representation that itself literally means that 'corn' is a noun. No, better to say that installed in the child is some unspecified cognitive architecture that warrants our saying only that she implicitly knows 'corn' to be a noun and not that she manipulates any representation explicitly representing that 'corn' is a noun. The child's knowledge is perhaps best viewed as simply a state supervenient on any of many quite disparate cognitive architectures (see SUPERVENIENCE).

A representationalist will reply that, yes, not all thought ascriptions do point to specific mental representations, but those that do not nevertheless do ride piggy-back on those that do. Strictly, the child does not think that 'corn' is a noun. Rather, she literally thinks, say, that it is permissible to utter 'Please pass the corn' but not 'Please corn the plate'. When we ascribe to the child the thought that 'corn' is a noun, we do not speak literally but only acknowledge that she is disposed to use 'corn' in certain ways. And if we are representationalists, we will hold that the child's way with 'corn' is the result of her processing specific mental representations in certain ways. As casual observers of ourselves and others, we cannot cavalierly suppose that our psychological attributions correctly capture the targeted internal dynamics. Nonetheless, when scientists of the mind finally manage to isolate the states over which psychological processes are defined, the isolated states will prove to be relations to mental representations, indeed mental sentences.

Attitudes and Conceptual Roles

Other anti-representationalists, for the sake of *reductio*, begin from the hypothesis of representationalism and suppose that Abelard's (propositional attitude of) believing Mars to be a planet consists in his being related in a certain way to a particular mental representation, R, meaning that Mars is a planet. If it is just such an occurrence of R in Abelard that constitutes his believing Mars to be a planet, then if R were to be copied in, say, Roscelin, Roscelin would thereby believe Mars to be a planet. But this is absurd. For Roscelin need not, simply by registering R, have any attitude that must be said to be about Mars. He might, despite the copying, know nothing at all about Mars. He might have never seen it. He might not know that it is to be found in the night sky or have any notion whatsoever of what distinguishes planets from stars. Deprived of this information, Roscelin could hardly be said to believe anything about Mars, much less that it is a planet, despite the fact that he happens, by artifice, to register R. Thus, *belief* is not just a relation to a representation and, *a fortiori*, not a relation to a mental sentence (Dennett, 1987).

This objection to representationalism generally and sententialism particularly shows at most that belief cannot simply be a relation to an isolated mental representation. Believing that Mars is a planet may typically require that a certain mental representation play a designated conceptual role in a production involving a cast of attitudes and a chorus of representations. Yet so much is consistent with representations – mental sentences – figuring prominently in holistic doxastic systems (*see* HOLISM). Perhaps to believe anything one must be disposed to deploy many representations in lots of ways. It may well be that the example at hand simply shows that the belief relation is itself to be functionally construed (*see* FUNCTIONALISM). That is, Roscelin's being related by belief to R may entail that Roscelin be disposed to issue R in certain contexts and, in other contexts, to use R in the production of other representations and behaviour. Nevertheless, this is consistent with Roscelin's mentally *representing* – as opposed to *believing* – that Mars is a planet sheerly by tokening, and not otherwise using, R.

Non-verbal Thinkers

Still, some representationalists want nothing of sententialism. Most simply put, their complaint is this: sententialism puts the cart before the horse. First comes the ability to think, then the ability to use language. Non-linguistic animals and neonates can think, but neither can speak. Therefore, thinking must involve some form of non-linguistic mental representation (Churchland, P.S., 1980).

Put so baldly, the complaint is plainly a non sequitur. Yes, some thinking creatures do not speak; some do not have a public language. Still, that does not imply that they lack an unspoken, internal, mental language. Sententialism need not insist that the

language of thought be any natural spoken language like Chinese or English. Rather, it simply proposes that psychological states that admit of the sort of semantic properties scouted above are likely relations to the sort of structured representations commonly found in, but not isolated to, public languages. This is certainly not to say that all psychological states in all sorts of psychological agents must be relations to mental sentences. Rather the idea is that thinking – at least the kind Abelard exemplifies – involves the processing of internally complex representations. Their semantic properties are sensitive to those of their parts much in the manner in which the meanings and truth conditions of complex public sentences are dependent upon the semantic features of their components. Abelard might also exploit various kinds of mental representations and associated processes. A sententialist may allow that in some of his cognitive adventures Abelard rotates mental images or recalibrates weights on connections among internally undifferentiated networked nodes. Sententialism is simply the thesis that some kinds of cognitive phenomena are best explained by the hypothesis of a mental language. There is, then, no principled reason to suppose that the cognitive prowess of non-verbal creatures precludes the language of thought.

NATURALISTIC SEMANTICS AND SENTENTIALISM

Such are among sententialism's replies to some classical objections. Nonetheless, while sententialism may be able to withstand these objections, if it hopes to triumph it must finally march on the fundamental semantic question: How do expressions in the language of thought take on meaning (Field, 1978)? Minimally, it is necessary to specify sufficient conditions for Mentalese expressions coinciding in meaning or content. Here sententialism might dragoon its structured representations and conjecture that Mentalese expressions with the same structure are the same in content (Fodor, 1980). This hypothesis is radically *individualistic*; it asserts that sameness of mental meaning is determined by non-relational properties intrinsic to Mentalese expressions (*see* SUPERVENIENCE). Individualism asserts that mental sentences that are physically, formally or functionally the same are semantically the same.

Certainly, individualism is disconfirmed if Mentalese should include indexicals. 'I AM THE WINNER' in the minds of both Abelard and Eloise cannot be true in each case. But if the truth value of this mental sentence can vary with its tokening, then copies of the same need not mean the same. However, consideration of mental indexicals to one side, individualism is subject to another, now classic, challenge (Putnam, 1975; Burge, 1979). Might not an extrinsic difference in physical, social or historical setting establish a semantic difference in intrinsically identical mental representations? Assume that Twin-Abelard is a synchronized molecular duplicate of Abelard. So, all and only the mental sentences in Abelard occur in Twin-Abelard. The Abelards inhabit numerically distinct but otherwise similar worlds, with the only difference between the worlds residing in a non-evident, deep theoretical difference in the phenomenally identical stuffs called 'water' in both worlds. Strictly, then, whereas Abelard's world contains water, Twin-Abelard's world does not. Both Abelards happen to token the Mentalese sentence 'WATER IS WET'. They therefore satisfy the condition individualism takes to suffice for sameness of thought content. Yet do they really think the same? Abelard thinks of water; Twin-Abelard does not (*see* TWIN EARTH).

BROAD AND NARROW CONTENT

It is universally agreed that, since the truth conditions of the Abelards' thoughts differ, there is a sense in which the mental sentences of the Abelards do indeed differ in content – *broad* content. Still, there is another sense, one oblivious to differences in truth conditions, in which the Abelards' mental representations are the same in content – *narrow* content. From the viewpoint of Abelard – from the inside, as it were – his thought is semantically indistinguishable from that of his twin. If, by some artifice, Abelard should be instantaneously put in the situation of Twin-Abelard but otherwise unaltered, Abelard's thinking would continue just as it otherwise would have. But then there must be a sense in which contextual differences do not determine semantic differences. Thus, duplicate mental sentences have the same narrow content even if they should have different broad content.

How, then, do broad and narrow contents mesh? Minimally, what secures water's being wet as the truth condition for Abelard's, but not Twin-Abelard's, token of 'WATER IS WET'? An answer here certainly would serve to sanction the notion of narrow mental content. For narrow content is evidently a function from the context in which a mental representation occurs to its truth (or satisfaction) conditions. That is, mental representations are the same in narrow content just in case they have the same broad content or truth conditions in all the same contexts (Fodor, 1990). Thus, what contextually determines the truth conditions of Abelard's token of 'WATER IS WET'? Since this mental representation is itself complex, it is natural to suppose that its truth conditions are somehow influenced by the semantic properties of its constituents. Accordingly, what – if anything – naturalistically determines that, in Abelard's actual context, his 'WATER' denotes water (Field, 1978; Schiffer, 1987)?

HOLISM AND ATOMISM

Holism (Harman, 1982; Field, 1978); and *atomism* (Dretske, 1988; Fodor, 1990; Millikan, 1984) compete as strategies for answering this last question. Holists hold that 'WATER' denotes as it does because it plays the specific inferential (or causal) role it does in Abelard's cognitive economy. This role must be construed in terms embracing facts extrinsic to Abelard's skin under pain of preserving the broad semantic distinction between the Abelards' mental representations (Block, 1986).

Holistic theories of mental content are terribly brittle. They entail that agents in the same environment cannot have thoughts with the same content unless they have perfectly isomorphic representational systems. This brittleness mocks the fact that mental content can remain constant over variation in conceptual organization, including learning. Also, one wonders whether holists, in relying on the inferential connections among representations in order to specify their meanings, will find it necessary to distinguish between those inferences that are central to a representation's meaning and those that are not (Fodor and LePore, 1992). For in that case holists appear to be required to resurrect the distinction between the analytic and synthetic long ago buried by QUINE.

Atomists hope to pin the denotation of a mental representation on the manner in which it nomically depends on its environment. Here too there is competition. Some atomists are satisfied to fuss with the naturalized notions of information (Dretske, 1988). Others want to complement that with attention to the asymmetric dependencies among relations between mental representations and their various external causes (Fodor, 1990). Others still look to the historical or evolutionary niche a mental representation occupies (Millikan, 1984). In any case, it yet remains on the research agenda of representationalists generally and sentientialists particularly to explain how, exactly, mental symbols accrue content.

See also An Essay on Mind section 2.1.3; CONCEPTS; CONCEPTUAL ROLE SEMANTICS; CONTENT; DENNETT; DRETSKE; FODOR; FOLK PSYCHOLOGY; PROPOSITIONAL ATTITUDES; THOUGHT AND LANGUAGE.

BIBLIOGRAPHY

Block, N. 1986. Advertisement for a semantics for psychology. *Midwest Studies in Philosophy: Studies in the Philosophy of Mind, Vol. 10,* 615–78.

Burge, T. 1979. Individualism and the mental. *Midwest Studies in Philosophy: Studies in Metaphysics, Vol. 4,* 73–122.

Churchland, P.M. 1981. Eliminative materialism and the propositional attitudes. *Journal of Philosophy,* 78, 67–90.

Churchland, P.S. 1980. Language, thought and information processing. *Noûs,* 14, 147–70.

Dennett, D. 1987. *The Intentional Stance.* Cambridge, MA.: MIT Press/Bradford Books.

Dretske, F. I. 1988. *Explaining Behavior.* Cambridge, MA.: MIT Press/Bradford Books.

Field, H. 1978. Mental representation. *Erkenntnis,* 13, 9–61.

Fodor, J. 1975. *The Language of Thought.* New York: Thomas Y. Crowell.

Fodor, J. 1980. Methodological solipsism considered as a research strategy in cognitive psychology. *Behavioral and Brain Sciences,* 3, 63–110.

Fodor, J. 1983. *Modularity of Mind.* Cambridge, MA.: MIT Press/Bradford Books.

Fodor, J. 1987. *Psychosemantics.* Cambridge, MA.: MIT Press/Bradford Books.

Fodor, J. 1990. *A Theory of Content.* Cambridge, MA.: MIT Press/Bradford Books.

Fodor, J., and LePore, E. 1992. *Holism: A Shopper's Guide.* Oxford: Basil Blackwell.

Fodor, J., and Z. Pylyshyn. 1988. Connectionism and cognitive architecture: A critical analysis. *Cognition,* 28, 3–71.

Harman, G. 1982. Conceptual role semantics. *Notre Dame Journal of Formal Logic,* 23, 432–3.

Maloney, J.C. 1989. *The Mundane Matter of the Mental Language.* Cambridge: Cambridge University Press.

Millikan, R.G. 1984. *Language, Thought and Other Biological Categories.* Cambridge, MA: MIT Press/Bradford Books.

Putnam, H. 1975. The meaning of 'Meaning'. In *Mind, Language and Reality.* Cambridge: Cambridge University Press.

Schiffer, S. 1987. *Remnants of Meaning.* Cambridge, MA.: MIT Press/Bradford Books.

Searle, J. 1980. Minds, brains and programs *Behavioral and Brain Sciences,* 3, 417–24.

Stich, S. 1983. *From Folk Psychology to Cognitive Science: The Case Against Belief.* Cambridge, MA.: MIT Press/Bradford Books.

J. CHRISTOPHER MALONEY

language of thought (2) There is no denying it: the Language of Thought (LOT) hypothesis has a compelling neatness about it. A thought is depicted as a structure of internal representational elements, combined in a lawful way, and playing a certain functional role in an internal processing economy (*see* FUNCTIONALISM; REPRESENTATION). Relations between thoughts (e.g. the semantic overlap between the thought that John loves wine and the thought that John loves food) consist in the recurrence of some of the inner representational elements. Novel thoughts and the much-vaunted systematicity of thought (the fact that beings who can think 'John loves wine' and 'Mary loves food' can always think 'John loves food' and 'Mary loves wine' – *see* Fodor and Pylyshyn, 1988) are accounted for in the same way. Once the representational elements and combinatoric rules are in place, of course such interanimations of potential contents will occur. The predictive success of propositional attitude talk (the ascription of e.g. beliefs and desires such as 'John believes that the wine is good') is likewise explained, on the hypothesis that the public language words pick out real inner representational complexes which are causally potent and thus capable of bringing about actions. And finally, what distinguishes an intentional action from a mere reflex is, on this model the fact that intervening between input and action there is, in the intentional case, an episode of actual tokening of an appropriate symbol string. 'No intentional causation without explicit representation', as the rallying cry (*see* Fodor, 1987, p. 25) goes. A pretty package indeed. And all for the price of a language of thought. My advice to the consumer, however, is 'beware': all that neatness masks some hidden costs.

COST A: CONSERVATIVE ATTITUDE
TOWARDS REPRESENTATIONAL CHANGE

It is fair to ask where we get the powerful inner code whose representational elements need only systematic construction to express, for example, the thought that cyclotrons are bigger than black holes (*see* INNATENESS). But on this matter, the Language of Thought theorist has little to say. All that CONCEPT learning could be (assuming it is to be some kind of rational process and not due to mere physical maturation or a bump on the head), according to the LOT theorist, is the trying out of combinations of existing representational elements to see if a given combination captures the sense (as evidenced in its use) of some new concept. The consequence is that concept learning, conceived as the expansion of our representational resources, simply does not happen. What happens instead is that we work with a fixed, innate repertoire of elements whose combination and construction must express any content we can ever learn to understand (*see* e.g. Fodor, 1975). And note that this is not the (trivial) claim that in some sense the resources a system starts with must set limits on what knowledge it can acquire. For these are limits which flow not, for example, from sheer physical size, number of neurons, connectivity of neurons, etc., but from a base class of genuinely representational elements. They are more like the limits that being restricted to the propositional calculus would place on the expressive power of a system than, say, the limits that having a certain amount of available memory storage would place on one.

But this picture of representational stasis, in which all change consists in the redeployment of existing representational resources, is one that is fundamentally alien to much influential theorizing in DEVELOPMENTAL PSYCHOLOGY. The prime example of a developmentalist who believed in much stronger forms of representational change is probably Piaget (*see* e.g. Piaget, 1955). But much contemporary work is likewise committed to studying kinds of change which a staunchly nativist Fodorian must deem impossible. One example is work by Annette Karmiloff-Smith (e.g. Karmiloff-Smith, 1992) which places episodes in which there occurs a genuine expansion of representational power at the very heart of a model of human development. In a similar vein, recent work in the field of connectionism (*see* CONNECTIONISM, and below) seems to open up the possibility of putting well-specified models of strong representational change back at the centre of the cognitive scientific endeavour (*see* e.g. Bates and Elman, 1992; Plunkett and Sinha, 1991).

Someone might, of course, adopt the Language of Thought hypothesis as a model of the structure of adult human cognition yet reject the strong nativist version of its origins. The combinatorial inner code would then be treated as a product of an extended developmental process. The question that would then arise is: how deep is the role of this product, and how are we to explain its development? For example, it might be (*see* e.g. DENNETT, 1991) that the kind of combinatorial inner code thus isolated is developed only (at best) by language-users and that much of (non-human) animal cognition, as well as much of what goes on in other kinds of human problem solving, requires understanding in very different terms. To the extent that this was so, the Language of Thought would not play quite the central role in cognitive science that Fodor imagines (*see* cognitive psychology). Instead such a quasi-linguistic code would be one developmental product among many, whose explanatory role was limited to a particular sub-area of human cognition. Such a sub-area might be so small as to include only those episodes of reasoning and planning which involve the conscious rehearsal of sentences (as in Dennett's (1987) idea of 'linguistically infected cognition') or it may be large enough to include many other kinds of cognitive episode (such as musical thought). But either way, the understanding of how the underlying combinatoric code *develops* might actually be more crucial, in terms of the deep understanding of cognitive process, than understanding the structure and use of the code itself (though, doubtless, the two projects would need to be pursued hand-in-hand).

COST B: REPRESENTATIONAL ATOMISM

The Language of Thought story depicts thoughts as structures of CONCEPTS, which in turn exist as elements (for any basic concepts) or concatenations of elements (for the rest) in the inner code (*see* Fodor, 1986). One upshot of this is that little can be said about intrinsic relations *between* basic representational items. Even bracketing the (difficult) question of which, if any words in our public language may express contents which have as their vehicles atomic items in the Language of Thought (an empirical question on which I assume Fodor to be officially agnostic), the question of semantic relations between atomic items in the Language of Thought remains. Are there any such relations? And if so, in what do they consist? Two thoughts are depicted (we saw) as semantically related just in case they share elements from the language of thought. But the elements themselves (like the words of public language on which they are modelled) seem to stand in splendid isolation from one another. An advantage of some connectionist approaches (*see* CONNECTIONISM) lies precisely in their ability to address questions of the interrelation of basic representational elements (in fact, activation vectors) by representing such items as locations in a kind of semantic space. In such a space related contents are always expressed by related representational elements. The connectionist's conception of significant structure thus goes much deeper than the Fodorian's. For the connectionists representations need never be arbitrary. Even the most basic representational items will bear non-accidental relations of similarity and difference to one another. The Fodorian, having reached representational bedrock, must explicitly *construct* any such further relations. They do not come for free as a consequence of using an integrated representational space. Whether this is a bad thing or a good one will depend, of course, on what kind of facts we need to explain. But my suspicion is that representational atomism may turn out to be a conceptual economy that a science of the mind cannot afford.

COST C: NO MODEL OF GLOBAL PROCESSES

Consider FODOR (1983). Fodor (1983) is, surprisingly, a compact and (to my mind) decisive demonstration of the ultimate inadequacy of the LOT story. For the LOT story, as Fodor often reminds us, gets its clearest computational expression in so-called classical ARTIFICIAL INTELLIGENCE (AI) approaches. Specifically, in such classical AI approaches as posit a fixed set of representational primitives and a kind of grammar defined over them, and which go on to model mental processes as involving sequences of legal transitions among the stored representational complexes. Yet the argument in Fodor (1983) is that this kind of model faces its greatest challenge in trying to account for the nature of so-called Central Processing. Central Processing, in this usage, means the system or systems involved in belief-fixation and rational thought and inference (*see* RATIONALITY), viz. the very systems which would be the locus of what, in his (1987) were called 'episodes of mental causation'. The claim, in 1983, was that classical, symbolic AI had made great progress in the understanding of non-central systems – these were largely domain-specific input systems (*see* e.g. Fodor, 1983, p. 103). But two properties distinguished the processing achieved by such systems from that achieved by the central systems, and these properties were shown to be highly resistant to any classical treatment. These were the properties of being Quinean and being isotropic. A Quinean system is one in which 'the degree of confirmation assigned to any given hypothesis is sensitive to properties of the entire belief system' (Fodor, 1983, p. 107).

An isotropic system is one in which any part of the knowledge encoded can turn out to be relevant to the system's decisions about what to believe (*see* Fodor, 1983, p. 105). The two properties are obviously closely bound up. Together, they characterize systems in which information processing is profoundly global. And much of what goes on in Central Processing, according to Fodor, has just this global character. When we choose whether or not to accept a new belief, we do so by allowing both that any other belief we hold could in principle be relevant to the decision (isotropic) and by allowing the decision to turn also on the collective impact of the sum of our other beliefs (Quinean; *see* QUINE). Moreover all forms of analogical reasoning, by effecting the 'transfer of information among cognitive domains previously assumed to be mutually irrelevant' (Fodor, 1983, p. 107), are themselves evidence of the fundamentally isotropic nature of Central Processing. These kinds of global information processing, Fodor believes, are distinctive of 'higher cognition'. Yet they have not succumbed to the advances of classical AI and cognitive science. And for a very good reason. It is that such globally sensitive processing runs classical systems very quickly into well-known problems of combinatorial explosion. For there are no fixed sets of beliefs, markable out in advance, amongst which the relevant ones can be assumed to hide. But the problem of searching amongst the contents of the entire belief set is simply intractable in classical models; the amount of time and/or computation required increases exponentially with the number of items to be taken into account. One instance of this, noted by Fodor, is the so-called frame problem in AI, viz. how to update the right sub-set of a system's beliefs as new information is received. The frame problem, Fodor claims, is just one instance of the general inability of classical AI to model globally sensitive information processing. Indeed, so pessimistic does Fodor become about the whole situation that he proclaims his infamous 'First law of the non-existence of Cognitive Science', viz.: 'The more global . . . a cognitive process is, the less anybody understands it' (Fodor, 1983, p. 107).

Classical AI, to sum this all up, is depicted by Fodor (1983) as a research programme which has done well in helping us model a variety of input systems and peripheral, modular processing. But one which has failed to illuminate the domain of real thought, i.e. belief-fixation and central processing. How strange, then, that the upshot of Fodor and Pylyshyn (1988) seems to be that although connectionist models might (perhaps) help us understand various peripheral, perceptual processing devices, the classical approach must be preferred in the domain of 'real' thought, since real thoughts (like the thought that Mary loves John) form a systematic set and the best explanation of such systematicity lies in our supposing them to be underpinned by classical processing strategies. Strange too, that Fodor (1987, pp. 143–7) stresses the commitments of actual cognitive models to symbol-manipulating approaches (using examples drawn from the processing of language parsing input devices) as part of an argument in favour of a symbolic model of real thought, i.e. central processing. There is no mention of the fact that all the successful models, it seems, are targeted on the fundamentally different class of non-global computational processes. Strangeness is not, of course, to be confused with inconsistency. It is quite consistent to hold that

(1) classical AI faces fundamental problems in dealing with the global processes characteristic of Central Processing,

and

(2) classical AI is especially well placed to deal with the systematicity of contents characteristic of Central Processing.

Still, to completely reject connectionism for its alleged failure to explain systematicity whilst simultaneously believing that the classical alternative fails to explain an equally deep feature of central processing seems a trifle partisan. The more so since (to a degree) the acknowledged strengths of the connectionist approach lie in its ability to make computationally tractable the task of globally sensitive information processing. The fixation of belief, insofar as it is to be sensitive to both the individual and the collective properties of a large set of simultaneously held beliefs, is surely a prime case for a connectionist treatment. Such systems excel at simultaneously satisfying large bodies of constraints, and the time taken to perform such a task does not increase exponentially with the number of constraints to be respected (for a nice discussion, *see* Oaksford and Chater, 1991).

To sum up, then, I am not convinced that the benefits of the LOT story outweigh its costs. The key benefit is, I suppose, the neat account of systematic and productive thought. The key costs are: the association with a strong nativist model of our representational resources (and the associated antipathy towards the idea of strong representational change); the commitment to representational atomism and consequent inability to pursue the question of semantic structure beyond a given (and all-too-rapidly reached) point; and the self-acknowledged intractability of globally sensitive information processing to (at least the classical AI incarnation of) the LOT approach.

My own belief, as the reader will surely have guessed, is that something a bit like a language of thought may well exist. But it is the symbolic problem-solving tip of a large and developmentally extended iceberg. Beneath the symbolic waters, and reaching back across our individual developmental history, lie the larger, less well-defined shapes of our basic cognitive processes. To understand these, and the episodes of genuine representational change in which they figure, is to address the fundamentals of cognition.

See also COMPUTATIONAL MODELS; CONCEPTUAL ROLE SEMANTICS; MODULARITY; PSYCHOLOGY AND PHILOSOPHY; THOUGHTS; THOUGHT AND LANGUAGE.

BIBLIOGRAPHY

Bates, E., and Elman, J. 1992. Connectionism and the study of change. *Technical Report 9202*, Center for Research and Language, University of California, San Diego.

Dennett, D. 1987. *The Intentional Stance*. Cambridge, MA: MIT Press/Bradford Books.

Dennett, D. 1991. Mother Nature versus the walking encyclopedia. In *Philosophy and Connectionist Theory*, ed. W. Ramsey, S. Stich, and D. Rumelhart. Hillsdale, N.J.: Erlbaum.

Fodor, J. 1975. *The Language of Thought*. New York: Crowell.

Fodor, J. 1983. *The Modularity of Mind*. Cambridge, MA: MIT Press/Bradford Books.

Fodor, J. 1986. The present status of the innateness controversy. In *Representations*. Sussex: Harvester.

Fodor, J. 1987. *Psychosemantics: The Problem of Meaning in the Philosophy of Mind*. Cambridge, MA: MIT Press/Bradford Books.

Fodor, J., and Pylyshyn, Z. 1988. Connectionism and cognitive architecture. A critical analysis. *Cognition*, 28, 3–71.

Karmiloff-Smith, A. 1992. *Beyond Modularity: A Developmental Perspective on Cognitive Science*. Cambridge, MA: MIT Press/Bradford Books.

Oaksford, M., and Chater, C. 1991. Against logicist cognitive science. *Mind and Language*, 6: 1, 1–38.

Plunkett, K., and Sinha, C. 1991. Connectionism and developmental theory. *Psykologisk Skriftserie Aarhus*, 16: 1, 1–34.

Piaget, J. 1955. *The Child's Construction of Reality*. Routledge & Kegan Paul.

ANDY CLARK

Lewis, David: Reduction of Mind I am a realist and a reductive materialist about mind. I hold that mental states are contingently identical to physical – in particular, neural – states. My position is very like the 'Australian materialism' of Place, Smart, and especially Armstrong. Like Smart and Armstrong, I am an ex-Rylean, and I retain some part of the Rylean legacy. In view of how the term is contested, I do not know whether I am a 'functionalist'. (*See* FUNCTIONALISM; IDENTITY THEORIES; PHYSICALISM; RYLE.)

SUPERVENIENCE AND ANALYSIS

My reductionism about mind begins as part of an a priori reductionism about everything. This world, or any possible world, consists of things which instantiate fundamental properties and which, in pairs or triples or . . ., instantiate fundamental relations. Few properties are fundamental: the property of being a club or a tub or a pub, for instance, is an unnatural gerrymander, a condition satisfied by miscellaneous things in miscellaneous ways. A fundamental, or 'perfectly natural', property is the extreme opposite. Its instances share exactly some aspect of their intrinsic nature. Likewise for relations (*see* Lewis, 1983a and 1986a, pp. 59–69). I hold, as an a priori principle, that every contingent truth must be made true, somehow, by the pattern of coinstantiation of fundamental properties and relations. The whole truth about the world, including the mental part of the world, supervenes on this pattern. If two POSSIBLE WORLDS were exactly isomorphic in their patterns of coinstantiation of fundamental properties and relations, they would thereby be exactly alike *simpliciter* (Lewis, 1992, p. 218). (*See* SUPERVENIENCE.)

It is a task of physics to provide an inventory of all the fundamental properties and relations that occur in the world. (That's because it is also a task of physics to discover the fundamental laws of nature, and only the fundamental properties and relations may appear in the fundamental laws; *see* Lewis, 1983a, pp. 365–70). We have no a priori guarantee of it, but we may reasonably think that present-day physics goes a long way toward a complete and correct inventory. Remember that the physical nature of ordinary matter under mild conditions is very well understood (Feinberg, 1966). And we may reasonably hope that future physics can finish the job in the same distinctive style. We may think, for instance, that mass and charge are among the fundamental properties; and that whatever fundamental properties remain as yet undiscovered are likewise instantiated by very small things that come in very large classes of exact duplicates. We may further think that the very same fundamental properties and relations, governed by the very same laws, occur in the living and the dead parts of the world, and in the sentient and the insentient parts, and in the clever and the stupid parts. In short: if we optimistically extrapolate the triumph of physics hitherto, we may provisionally accept that all fundamental properties and relations that actually occur are physical. This is the thesis of materialism.

(It was so named when the best physics of the day was the physics of matter alone. Now our best physics acknowledges other bearers of fundamental properties: parts of pervasive fields, parts of causally active spacetime. But it would be pedantry to change the name on that account, and disown our intellectual ancestors. Or worse, it would be a tacky marketing ploy, akin to British Rail's decree that second class passengers shall now be called 'standard class customers'.)

If materialism is true, as I believe it is, then the a priori supervenience of everything upon the pattern of coinstantiation of *fundamental* properties and relations yields an a posteriori supervenience of everything upon the pattern of coinstantiation of fundamental *physical* properties and relations. Materialist supervenience should be a contingent matter. To make it so, we supply a restriction that makes reference to actuality. Thus: if two worlds were physically isomorphic, and if no fundamental properties or relations alien to actuality occurred in either world, then these worlds would be exactly alike *simpliciter*. Disregarding alien worlds, the whole truth supervenes upon the physical truth. In particular, the whole mental truth supervenes. So here we have the common core of all materialist theories of the mind (Lewis, 1983a, pp. 361–5).

A materialist who stops here has already said enough to come under formidable attack. An especially well-focused version of the attack comes from Frank Jackson (1982). Mary, confined in a room where all she can see is black or white, studies the physics of colour and colour vision and colour experience (and any other physics you might think relevant) until she knows it all. Then she herself sees colour for the first time, and at last she knows what it's like to see colour. What is this knowledge that Mary has gained? It may seem that she has eliminated some possibilities left open by all her previous knowledge; she has distinguished the actual world from other possible worlds that are exactly like it in all relevant physical respects. But if materialist supervenience is true, this cannot be what happened. (*See* CONSCIOUSNESS; QUALIA.)

Materialists have said many things about what does happen in such a case. I myself, following Nemirow (1990), call it a case of know-how: Mary gains new imaginative abilities (Lewis, 1990). Others have said that Mary gains new relations of acquaintance, or new means of mental representation: or that the change in her is just that she has now seen colour. These suggestions need not be taken as rival alternatives. And much ink has been spent on the question whether these various happenings could in any sense be called the gaining of 'new knowledge', 'new belief', or 'new information'. But for a materialist, the heart of the matter is not what *does* happen but what *doesn't*: Mary does not distinguish the actual world from other worlds that are its physical duplicates but not its duplicates *simpliciter*.

Imagine a grid of a million tiny spots – pixels – each of which can be made light or dark. When some are light and some are dark, they form a picture, replete with interesting intrinsic gestalt properties. The case evokes reductionist comments. Yes, the picture really does exist. Yes, it really does have those gestalt properties. However the picture and the properties reduce to the arrangement of light and dark pixels. They are nothing over and above the pixels. They make nothing true that is not made true already by the pixels. They could go unmentioned in an inventory of what there is without thereby rendering that inventory incomplete. And so on.

Such comments seem to me obviously right. The picture reduces to the pixels. And that is because the picture supervenes on the pixels: there could be no difference in the picture and its properties without some difference in the arrangement of light and dark pixels. Further, the supervenience is asymmetric: not just any difference in the pixels would matter to the gestalt properties of the picture. And it is supervenience of the large upon the small and many. In such a case, say I, supervenience is reduction. And the materialist supervenience of mind and all else upon the arrangement of atoms in the void – or whatever replaces atoms in the void in true physics – is another such case.

Yet thousands say that what's good about stating materialism in terms of supervenience is that this avoids reductionism! There's no hope of settling this disagreement by appeal to some uncontested definition of the term 'reductionism'. Because the term *is* contested, and the aim of some contestants is to see to it that whatever position they may hold, 'reductionism' shall be the name for something else.

At any rate, materialist supervenience means that for anything mental, there are physical conditions that would be sufficient for its presence, and physical conditions that would be sufficient for its absence. (These conditions will include conditions saying that certain inventories are complete: an electron has only so-and-so quantum numbers, for instance, and it responds only to such-and-such forces. But it's fair to call such a condition 'physical', since it answers a kind of question that physics does indeed address.) And no matter how the world may be, provided it is free of fundamental properties or relations alien to actuality, a condition of the one sort or the other will obtain. For all we know so far, the conditions associated with a given mental item might be complicated and miscellaneous – even infinitely complicated and miscellaneous. But so long as we limit ourselves just to the question of how this mental item can find a place in the world of fundamental physics, it is irrelevant how complicated and miscellaneous the conditions might be.

It may seem unsatisfactory that physical conditions should always settle whether the mental item is present or absent. For mightn't that sometimes be a vague question with no determinate answer? A short reply to this objection from vagueness is that if it did show that the mental was irreducible to fundamental physics despite supervenience, it would likewise show that boiling was irreducible to fundamental physics – which is absurd. For it is a vague matter just where simmering leaves off and boiling begins.

A longer reply has three parts. (1) If the physical settles the mental insofar as anything does, we still have materialist supervenience. Part of what it means for two physically isomorphic worlds to be just alike mentally is that any mental indeterminacy in one is exactly matched by mental indeterminacy in the other. (2) Whenever it is a vague question whether some simplistic mental classification applies, it will be determinate that some more subtle classification applies. What's determinate may be not that you do love him or that you don't, but rather that you're in a certain equivocal state of mind that defies easy description. (3) If all indeterminacy is a matter of semantic indecision (Lewis, 1986a, pp. 212–13), then there is no indeterminacy in the things themselves. How could we conjure up some irreducible mental item just by failing to decide exactly which reducible item we're referring to?

It may seem that when supervenience guarantees that there are physical conditions sufficient for the presence or absence of a given mental item, the sufficiency is of the wrong sort. The implication is necessary but not a priori. You might want to say, for instance, that black-and-white Mary really did gain new knowledge when she first saw colour; although what she learned followed necessarily from all the physics she knew beforehand, she had remained ignorant because it didn't follow a priori.

A short reply to this objection from necessity a posteriori is that if it did show that the mental was irreducible to fundamental physics, it would likewise show that boiling was irreducible to fundamental physics – which is absurd. For the identity between boiling and a certain process described in fundamental physical terms is necessary a posteriori if anything is.

(A longer reply, following Jackson (1992), is founded upon the 'two-dimensional' analysis of necessity a posteriori put forward by Stalnaker (1978), Davies and Humberstone (1980), and Tichý (1983). Two-dimensionalism says that there is no such thing as a necessary *a posteriori* proposition. However, one single sentence θ may be associated in two different ways with two different propositions, one of them necessary and the other one contingent; and the contingent one can be known only *a posteriori*. Suppose we choose to adopt a conception of meaning under which our conventions of language sometimes fix meanings only as a function of matters of contingent fact – for example, a conception on which the meaning of 'boils' is left dependent on which physical phenomenon turns out to occupy the boiling-role. Then if we interpret a sentence θ using the meanings of its words as fixed in world W_1, we get proposition H_1; using the meanings as fixed in W_2, we get H_2; and so on. Call these the propositions *horizontally expressed* by θ at the various worlds: and let H be the proposition horizontally expressed by Θ at the actual world. The proposition *diagonally expressed* by θ is the proposition D that holds at any world W iff the proposition horizontally expressed by θ at W is true at W. So if we know D, we know that θ horizontally expresses some truth or other, but we may not know which truth. Sentence θ is necessary a posteriori iff H is necessary but D is knowable only a posteriori. Likewise, a proposition P *necessarily* implies that θ iff P implies H; but P a priori implies that θ iff P implies D. Our worry was that when θ was about the mind, and P was a premise made true by fundamental physics, P might imply that θ necessarily but not a priori. But if so, and if you think it matters, just take another proposition Q; let Q be true at exactly those worlds where θ horizontally expresses the same proposition H that it actually does. Q is true. Given the materialist supervenience of everything, Q as well as P is made true by fundamental physics. P and Q together imply a priori that θ. So the gap between physical premises and mental

conclusion is closed. Anyone who wants to reopen it – for instance, in order to square materialist supervenience with Mary's supposed ignorance – must somehow show that the two-dimensional analysis of necessity a posteriori is inadequate.)

If we limit ourselves to the question how mind finds a place in the world of physics, our work is done. Materialist supervenience offers a full answer. But if we expand our interests a little, we'll see that among the supervenient features of the world, mind must be very exceptional. There are countless such features. In our little toy example of the picture and the pixels, the supervenient properties number 2 to the power: 2 to the millionth power. In the case of materialist supervenience, the number will be far greater. The infinite cardinal beth-3 is a conservative estimate. The vast majority of supervenient features of the world are given only by miscellaneously infinite disjunctions of infinitely complex physical conditions. Therefore they are beyond our power to detect, to name, or to think about one at a time. Mental features of the world, however, are not at all beyond our ken. Finite assemblies of particles – us – can track them. Therefore there must be some sort of simplicity to them. Maybe it will be a subtle sort of simplicity, visible only if you look in just the right way. (Think of the Mandelbrot set: its overwhelming complexity, its short and simple recipe.) But somehow it must be there. Revealing this simplicity is a job for conceptual analysis.

Arbiters of fashion proclaim that analysis is out of date. Yet without it, I see no possible way to establish that any feature of the world does or does not deserve a name drawn from our traditional mental vocabulary. We should repudiate not analysis itself, but only some simplistic goals for it. We should allow for semantic indecision: any interesting analysandum is likely to turn out vague and ambiguous. Often the best that any one analysis can do is to fall safely within the range of indecision. And we should allow for semantic satisficing: analysis may reveal what it would take to

415

deserve a name perfectly, but imperfect deservers of the name may yet deserve it well enough. (And sometimes the perfect case may be impossible.) If so, there is bound to be semantic indecision about how well is well enough.

I offer not analyses, but a recipe for analyses. We have a very extensive shared understanding of how we work mentally. Think of it as a theory: FOLK PSYCHOLOGY. It is common knowledge among us; but it is tacit, as our grammatical knowledge is. We can tell which particular predictions and explanations conform to its principles, but we cannot expound those principles systematically. (*Pace* Lewis, 1972, p. 256, eliciting the general principles of folk psychology is no mere matter of gathering platitudes.) Folk psychology is a powerful instrument of prediction. We are capable of all sorts of behaviour that would seem bizarre and unintelligible, and this is exactly the behaviour that folk psychology predicts, rightly, will seldom occur. (But we take a special interest in questions that lie beyond the predictive power of folk psychology: wherefore ingrates may fairly complain of a lack of *interesting* predictions!) Folk psychology has evolved through thousands of years of close observation of one another. It is not the last word in psychology, but we should be confident that so far as it goes – and it does go far – it is largely right.

Folk psychology concerns the causal relations of mental states, perceptual stimuli, and behavioural responses. It says how mental states, singly or in combination, are apt for causing behaviour; and it says how mental states are apt to change under the impact of perceptual stimuli and other mental states. Thus it associates with each mental state a typical causal role. Now we have our recipe for analyses. Suppose we've managed to elicit all the tacitly known general principles of folk psychology. Whenever M is a folk-psychological name for a mental state, folk psychology will say that the state M typically occupies a certain causal role: call this the M-role. Then we analyse M as meaning 'the state that typically occupies the M-role'. Folk psychology

implicitly defines the term M, and we have only to make that definition explicit.

Since the causal roles of mental states involve other mental states, we might fear circularity. The remedy is due in its essentials to Ramsey (1931a, pp. 212–236) and Carnap (1963, pp. 958–66); see also Lewis (1970, 1972). Suppose, for instance, that folk psychology had only three names for mental states: L, M, N. We associate with this triplet of names a complex causal role for a triplet of states, including causal relations within the triplet: call this the LMN-role. Folk psychology says that the states L, M, N jointly occupy the LMN-role. That implies that M occupies the derivative role: coming second in a triplet of states that jointly occupy the LMN-role. Taking this as our M-role, we proceed as before. Say that the names L, M, N are *interdefined*. The defining of all three via the LMN-role is a package deal.

We might fear circularity for another reason. The causal roles of mental states involve responses to perceptual stimuli. But the relevant feature of the stimulus will often be some secondary quality – for instance, a colour. We cannot replace the secondary quality with a specification of the stimulus in purely physical terms, on pain of going beyond what is known to folk psychology. But if we analyse the secondary quality in terms of the distinctive mental states its presence is apt to evoke, we close a definitional circle. So we should take interdefinition further. Let folk psychology include folk psychophysics. This will say, for instance, that the pair of a certain colour and the corresponding sensation jointly occupy a complex causal role that consists in part, but only in part, of the former being apt to cause the latter. Now we have a derivative role associated with the name of the colour, and another associated with the name of the sensation: the role of coming first or coming second, respectively, in a pair that jointly occupies this complex role.

We might worry also about the behaviour that mental states are apt for causing. Often we describe behaviour in a mentally loaded way: as action. To say that you kicked the ball to your team-mate is to describe your behaviour. But such a description presupposes a great deal about how your behaviour was meant to serve your desires according to your beliefs; and also about the presence of the ball and the playing surface and the other player, and about social facts that unite players into teams. More threat of circularity? More need for interdefinition? I don't know how such further interdefinition would work; and anyway, it would be well to call a halt before folk psychology expands into a folk theory of the entire *Lebenswelt*!

Describing the behaviour in purely physical terms – the angle of the knee, the velocity of the foot – would get rid of those presuppositions. But, just as in the case of the stimuli, it would go beyond what is known to folk psychology. Further, these descriptions would never fit the behaviour of space aliens not of humanoid shape; and yet we should not dismiss out of hand the speculation that folk psychology might apply to aliens as well as to ourselves.

Fortunately there is a third way to describe behaviour. When you kicked the ball, your body moved in such a way that *if* you had been on a flat surface in Earth-normal gravity with a suitably placed ball in front of you and a suitably placed team-mate some distance away, *then* the impact of your foot upon the ball would have propelled the ball onto a trajectory bringing it within the team-mate's reach. That description is available to the folk. They wouldn't give it spontaneously, but they can recognize it as correct. It presupposes nothing about your mental states, not even that you have any; nothing about whether the ball and the playing field and the gravity and the team-mate are really there; nothing about your humanoid shape, except that you have some sort of foot. It could just as well describe the behaviour of a mindless mechanical contraption, in the shape of a space alien (with a foot), thrashing about in free fall.

(I don't say that we should really use these 'if-then' descriptions of behaviour. Rather, my point is that their availability shows how to unload the presuppositions from our ordinary descriptions.)

If M means 'the state that typically occupies the M-role' and if that role is only imperfectly occupied, what are we to do? – Satisfice: let the name M go to a state that deserves it imperfectly. And if nothing comes anywhere near occupying the M-role? – Then the name M has no referent. The boundary between the cases is vague. To take an example from a different term-inducing theory, I suppose it to be indeterminate whether 'dephlogisticated air' refers to oxygen or to nothing. But folk psychology is in far better shape than the phlogiston theory, despite scare stories to the contrary. We can happily grant that there are no perfect deservers of folk-psychological names, but we shouldn't doubt that there are states that deserve those names well enough.

What to do if the M-role, or the LMN-role, turns out to be doubly occupied? I used to think (Lewis, 1970, 1972) that in this case too the name M had no referent. But now I think it might be better, sometimes or always, to say that the name turns out to be ambiguous in reference. That follows the lead of Field (1973): and it is consistent with, though not required by, the treatment of Carnap (1963). Note that we face the same choice with phrases like 'the moon of Mars'; and in that case too I'd now lean toward ambiguity of reference rather than lack of it.

My recipe for analyses, like Rylean analytic BEHAVIOURISM, posits analytic truths that constrain the causal relations of mental states to behaviour. (We have no necessary connections between distinct existences, of course; the necessity is verbal. The state itself could have failed to occupy its causal role, but would thereby have failed to deserve its mental name.) But the constraints are weak enough to be credible. Because the state that typically occupies a role need not occupy it invariably, and also because a state may deserve a name well enough in virtue of a role that it occupies imperfectly, we are safe from the behaviourist's bugbears. We have a place for the resolute deceiver, disposed come what may to behave as if his mental states were other than they really are. We have a place for the total and incurable paralytic with a rich mental life and no behavioural dispositions whatever. We even have a place for a madman whose mental states are causally related to behaviour and stimuli and one another in a totally haywire fashion (Lewis, 1980). And yet not anything goes. At some point – and just where that point comes is a matter of semantic indecision – weird tales of mental states that habitually offend against the principles of folk psychology stop making sense; because at some point the offending states lose all claim to their folk-psychological names. To that extent, analytic behaviourism was right. To quote my closest ally in these matters, '. . . outward physical behaviour and tendencies to behave do in some way enter into our ordinary concept of mind. Whatever theory of mind is true, it has a debt to pay, and a peace to be made, with behaviourism' (Armstrong, 1968, p. 68).

When we describe mental state M as the occupant of the M-role, that is what Smart (1959) calls a topic-neutral description. It says nothing about what sort of state it is that occupies the role. It might be a non-physical or a physical state, and if it is physical it might be a state of neural activity in the brain, or a pattern of currents and charges on a silicon chip, or the jangling of an enormous assemblage of beer cans. What state occupies the M-role and thereby deserves the name M is an a posteriori matter. But if materialist supervenience is true, and every feature of the world supervenes upon fundamental physics, then the occupant of the role is some physical state or other – because there's nothing else for it to be. We know enough to rule out the chip and the cans, and to support the hypothesis that what occupies the role is some pattern of neural activity. When we know more, we shall know what pattern of neural activity it is. Then we shall have the premises of an argument for psychophysical identification:

mental state M = the occupant of the M-role (by analysis),

physical state P = the occupant of the M-role (by science),

therefore M = P.

(*See* Lewis, 1966, 1972; *and see* Armstrong, 1968, for an independent and simultaneous presentation of the same position, with a much fuller discussion of what the definitive causal roles might be.)

That's how conceptual analysis can reveal the simple formula – or anyway, the much less than infinitely complicated formula – whereby, when we know enough, we can pick out a mental feature of the world from all the countless other features of the world that likewise supervene on fundamental physics.

The causal-role analyses would still hold even if materialist supervenience failed. They might even still yield psychophysical identifications. Even if we lived in a spook-infested world, it might be physical states that occupied the causal roles (in us, if not in the spooks) and thereby deserved the folk-psychological names. Or it might be non-physical states that occupied the roles. Then, if we knew enough parapsychology, we would have the premises of an argument for psycho-*non*-physical identification.

When our argument delivers an identification M = P, the identity is contingent. How so? – All identity is self-identity, and nothing could possibly have failed to be self-identical. But that is not required. It's contingent, and it can only be known a posteriori, which physical (or other) states occupy which causal roles. So if M means 'the occupant of the M-role' it's contingent which state is the referent of M: it's contingent whether some one state is the common referent of M and P: so it's contingent whether M = P is true.

Kripke (1972) vigorously intuits that some names for mental states, in particular 'pain', are rigid designators: that is, it's not contingent what their referents are. I myself intuit no such thing, so the non-rigidity imputed by causal-role analyses troubles me not at all.

Here is an argument that 'pain' is not a rigid designator. Think of some occasion when you were in severe pain, unmistakable and unignorable. All will agree, except for some philosophers and faith healers, that there is a state that actually occupies the pain role (or near enough); that it is called 'pain'; and that you were in it on that occasion. For now, I assume nothing about the nature of this state, or about how it deserves its name. Now consider an unactualized situation in which it is some different state that occupies the pain role in place of the actual occupant; and in which you were in that different state; and which is otherwise as much like the actual situation as possible. Can you distinguish the actual situation from this unactualized alternative? I say not, or not without laborious investigation. But if 'pain' is a rigid designator, then the alternative situation is one in which you were not in pain, so you could distinguish the two very easily. So 'pain' is not a rigid designator.

Philosophical arguments are never incontrovertible – well, hardly ever. Their purpose is to help expound a position, not to coerce agreement. In this case, the controverter might say that if the actual occupant of the pain role is not a physical state, but rather is a special sort of non-physical state, then indeed you can distinguish the two situations. He might join me in saying that this would not be so if the actual occupant of the role were a physical state – else neurophysiology would be easier than it is – and take this together with intuitions of rigidity to yield a *reductio* against materialism. Myself, I don't see how the physical or non-physical nature of the actual occupant of the role has anything to do with whether the two situations can be distinguished. Talk of 'phenomenal character' and the like doesn't help. Either it is loaded with question-begging philosophical doctrine, or else it just reiterates the undisputed fact that pain is a kind of experience.

(The controverter just imagined would agree with the discussion in Kripke, 1972, pp. 344–42. But I don't mean to suggest that Kripke would agree with him. At any rate, the words I have put into his mouth are not Kripke's.)

If there is variation across worlds with respect to which states occupy the folk-psychological roles and deserve the folk-psychological names (and if this variation doesn't always require differences in the laws of nature, as presumably it doesn't) then also there can be variations within a single world. For possibility obeys a principle of recombination: roughly, any possible kind of thing can coexist with any other (Lewis, 1986a, pp. 86–92). For all we know, there may be variation even within this world. Maybe there are space aliens, and maybe there will soon be artificial intelligences, in whom the folk-psychological roles are occupied (or near enough) by states very different from any states of a human nervous system. Presumably, at least some folk-psychological roles are occupied in at least some animals, and maybe there is variation across species. There might even be variation within humanity. It depends on the extent to which we are hard-wired, and on the extent of genetic variation in our wiring.

We should beware, however, of finding spurious variation by overlooking common descriptions. Imagine two mechanical calculators that are just alike in design. When they add columns of numbers, the amount carried goes into a register, and the register used for this purpose is selected by throwing a switch. Don't say that the carry-seventeen role is occupied in one machine by a state of register A and in the other by a state of register B. Say instead that in both machines alike the role is occupied by a state of the register selected by the switch. (Equivalently, by a state of a part of the calculator large enough to include the switch and both registers.) If there is a kind of thinking that some of us do in the left side of the brain and others do in the right side, that might be a parallel case.

If M means 'the occupant of the M-role' and there is variation in what occupies the

M-role, then our psychophysical identities need to be restricted: not plain M = P, but M-in-K = P, where K is a kind within which P occupies the M-role. Human pain might be one thing, Martian pain might be something else (Lewis, 1980). As with contingency, which is variation across worlds, so likewise with variation in a single world: the variability in no way infects the identity relation, but rather concerns the reference of the mental name.

The threat of variation has led many to retreat from 'type-type' to 'token-token' identity. They will not say that M = P, where M and P are names for a state that can be common to different things at different times – that is, for a property had by things at times. But they will say that m = p, where m and p are mental and physical names for a particular, unrepeatable event. Token-token identities are all very well, in their derivative way, but the flight from type-type identities was quite unnecessary. For our restricted identities, of the form M-in-K = P, are still type-type.

But don't we at least have a choice? Couldn't our causal role analyses be recast in terms of the causal roles of tokens, and if they were, would they not then yield token-token identities? After all, the only way for a type to occupy a causal role is through the causes and effects of its tokens. The effects of pain are the effects of pain-events. – I think, following Jackson, Pargetter, and Prior (1982), that this recasting of the analyses would not be easy. There are more causal relations than one. Besides causing, there is preventing. It too may figure in folk-psychological causal roles; for instance, pain tends to prevent undivided attention to anything else. Prevention cannot straightforwardly be treated as a causal relation of tokens, because the prevented tokens do not exist – not in this world, anyway. It is better taken as a relation of types.

If a retreat had been needed, a better retreat would have been to 'subtype-subtype' identity. Let MK name the conjunctive property of being in state M and being of kind K; and likewise for PK. Do we really want psychophysical identities of the form MK = PK? – close, but I think not quite right. For one thing, M-in-K is not the same thing as MK. The former but not the latter can occur also in something that isn't of kind K. For another thing, it is P itself, not PK, that occupies the M-role in things of kind K.

Non-rigidity means that M is different states in different possible cases; variation would mean that M was different states in different actual cases. But don't we think that there is *one* property of being in the state M – one property that is common to all, actual or possible, of whatever kind, who can truly be said to be in state M? – There is. It is the property such that, for any possible X, X has it just in case X is in the state that occupies the M-role for X's kind at X's world. (In Lewis, 1970, I called it the 'diagonalized sense' of M.) The gerund 'being in M' can be taken, at least on one good disambiguation, as a rigid designator of this property. However, this property is not the occupant of the M-role. It cannot occupy that or any other causal role because it is excessively disjunctive, and therefore no events are essentially havings of it (Lewis, 1986c). To admit it as causally efficacious would lead to absurd double-counting of causes. It would be like saying that the meat fried in Footscray cooked because it had the property of being either fried in Footscray or boiled in Bundoora – only worse, because the disjunction would be much longer and more miscellaneous.

Since the highly disjunctive property of being in M does not occupy the M-role, I say it cannot be the referent of M. Many disagree. They would like it if M turned out to be a rigid designator of a property common to all who are in M. So the property I call 'being in M', they call simply M; and the property that I call M, the occupant of the M-role, they call 'the realization of M'. They have made the wrong choice, since it is absurd to deny that M itself is causally efficacious. Still, their mistake is superficial. They have the right properties in mind, even if they give them the wrong names.

It is unfortunate that this superficial

question has sometimes been taken to mark the boundary of 'functionalism'. Sometimes so and sometimes not – and that's why I have no idea whether I am a fuctionalist.

Those who take 'pain' to be a rigid designator of the highly disjunctive property will need to controvert my argument that 'pain' is not rigid, and they will not wish to claim that one can distinguish situations in which the pain-role is differently occupied. Instead, they should controvert the first step, and deny that the actual occupant of the pain-role is called 'pain'. I call that denial a *reductio*.

CONTENT

A mind is an organ of REPRESENTATION. Many things are true according to it; that is, they are believed. Or better, they are more or less probable according to it; that is, they are believed or disbelieved to varying degrees. Likewise, many things are desired to varying positive or negative degrees. What is believed, or what is desired, we call the CONTENT of BELIEF or DESIRE.

(I think it an open question to what extent other states with content – doubting, wondering, fearing, pretending, . . . – require separate treatment, and to what extent they can be reduced to patterns in belief and desire and contentless feeling. Be that as it may, I shall ignore them here (*see* EMOTION).)

What determines the content of belief and desire? – The occupation of folk-psychological roles by physical states, presumably neural states; and ultimately the pattern of coinstantiation of fundamental physical properties and relations. But to say just that is to say not much. Those who agree with it can, and do, approach the problem of content in very different ways.

I can best present the approach I favour by opposing it to an alternative. A crude sketch will suffice, so in fairness I name my opponent *Strawman*. I doubt there is anyone real who takes exactly the position that Strawman does – but very many are to be found in his near vicinity.

Strawman says that folk psychology says – and truly – that there is a LANGUAGE OF THOUGHT. It has words, and it has syntactic constructions whereby those words can be combined into sentences. Some of these sentences have a special status. Strawman says they are 'written in the belief box' or 'in the desire box', but even Strawman doesn't take that altogether literally. There are folk-psychological causal roles for the words, for the syntactic constructions, and for the belief and desire boxes. It is by occupying these roles that the occupants deserve their folk-psychological names.

The question what determines content then becomes the question: what determines the semantics of the language of thought? Strawman says that folk psychology specifies the semantic operations that correspond to syntactic constructions such as predication. As for the words, Strawman says that folk psychology includes, in its usual tacit and unsystematic way, a causal theory of reference (more or less as in Kripke, 1972). There are many relations of acquaintance that connect the mind to things, including properties and relations, in the external world. Some are relations of perceptual acquaintance. Others are less direct: you are acquainted with the thing by being acquainted with its traces. Often, you are acquainted with the thing by way of its *linguistic* traces that is, you have heard of it by name. Somehow, in virtue of the different causal roles of different words of the language of thought, different words are associated with different relations of acquaintance, which connect them to different external things. Whatever a word is thus connected to is the referent of that word.

Once the words of the language of thought have their referents, the sentences have their meanings. These are structures built up from the referents of the words in a way that mirrors the syntactic construction of the sentences from the words. Take predication – Strawman's favourite example. A word F of your language of thought is connected by one relation of acquaintance to the property of being French. Another word A is connected by another relation of acquaintance to the man André. (The first relation might be linguistic, for instance, and the second perceptual.) The syntactic construction of predication builds a sentence F(A). Its meaning is the ordered pair of the property of being French and André. Such a pair is a 'singular proposition', true just in case its second element instantiates its first. (Other singular propositions are triples, quadruples, . . ., with relations in the first place.) If you have F(A) written in your belief box, you thereby believe that André is French.

Strawman's account of content is sketchy, as I said it would be. Even with help from all his allies, I doubt he will find it easy to fill the gaps. I especially wonder what he can say about how the words get hooked up to the right relations of acquaintance. A causal theory of reference for public language might usefully mention mutual expectations among language-users, intentions to instill beliefs, semantic intentions, or other such instances of mental content. But even if we had corresponding expectations or intentions about our own language of thought, Strawman could not without circularity use them in a general account of mental content.

Suppose, all the same, that Strawman's account could be completed successfully by its own lights. I would still have four objections.

First, I don't believe that folk psychology says there is a language of thought. Rather, I think it is agnostic about how MENTAL REPRESENTATION works – and wisely so.

What is the issue? Of course everybody should agree that the medium of mental representation is somehow analogous to language. A raven is like a writing-desk. Anything can be analogized to anything. And of course nobody thinks the head is full of tiny writing.

A serious issue, and one on which I take folk psychology to be agnostic, concerns the relation between the whole and the parts of a representation. Suppose I have a piece of paper according to which, *inter alia*, Collingwood is east of Fitzroy. Can I tear the paper up so that I get one snippet that has exactly the content that Collingwood is east of Fitzroy, nothing more and nothing less? If the paper is covered with writing, maybe I can; for maybe 'Collingwood is east of Fitzroy' is one of the sentences written there. But if the paper is a map, any snippet according to which Collingwood is east of Fitzroy will be a snippet according to which more is true besides. For instance, I see no way to lose the information that they are adjacent, and that a street runs along the border. And I see no way to lose all information about their size and shape.

(A hologram, or famously a connectionist network (see CONNECTIONISM), differs even more from a paper covered with writing. If we make a hologram of the map and break it into snippets, detail will be lost in blur. But the arrangement of *all* the suburbs, provided it was shown with sufficient prominence on the original map, will remain to the last.)

Mental representation is language-like to the extent that parts of the content are the content of parts of the representation. If our beliefs are 'a map . . . by which we steer', as Ramsey said (1931b, p. 238), then they are to that extent not language-like. And to that extent, also, it is misleading to speak in the plural of beliefs. What is one belief? No snippet of a map is big enough that, determinately, something is true according to it, and also small enough that, determinately, nothing is true according to any smaller part of it. If mental representation is map-like (let alone if it is hologram-like) then 'beliefs' is a bogus plural. You have beliefs the way you have the blues, or the mumps, or the shivers.

But if mental representation is language-like, one belief is one sentence written in the belief box, so 'beliefs' is a genuine plural. Whether the plural is bogus or genuine is not settled by rules of grammar. Rather, it is an empirical question, and a question that folk psychology leaves open. 'The shivers' might be a parallel case. Is there such a thing as one shiver? – Maybe and maybe not. I don't think one cycle of vibration should be called 'one shiver', but there might be a better candidate. What if one firing of a control neuron would set you shivering for four seconds, and prolonged shivering is caused by this neuron firing every two seconds? If so, I think the shivering set off by one firing could well be called 'one shiver', and then it is right to say that shivering consists of a sequence of overlapping shivers. Under this hypothesis, the plural is genuine. Under other hypotheses, the plural is bogus.

Of course you might say, under the hypothesis that mental representation is map-like, that any proposition true according to the mental map is one belief. Or you might say that the one belief that Collingwood is east of Fitzroy is the highly disjunctive state of having some mental map or other according to which that *inter alia* is true. Say so if you like. But I only insist that if you say either thing, then you may not also assume that 'one belief' is the sort of thing that can occupy a causal role. You may still say '. . . because he believes that Collingwood is east of Fitzroy', but only if you mean by it '. . . because he has beliefs' – bogus plural! – 'according to which *inter alia* Collingwood is east of Fitzroy'.

If Strawman heeds the advice of some of his allies, he will respond by changing his position. He will give away conceptual analysis and folk psychology, and market his wares as 'cognitive science' (see COGNITIVE PSYCHOLOGY). No problem, then, if the folk are agnostic about the language of thought. Let it be a new hypothesis, advanced because it best explains . . . What? Well-known facts about belief? – But 'belief' is a folk-psychological name for a kind of state posited by folk psychology. If Strawman leaves all that behind him, where shall he find his evidence? He can never again set up thought experiments and ask us what we want to say about them. That would only elicit our folk-psychological preconceptions. He can make a fresh start if he really wants to – I assume he will not want to – but he cannot have his cake and eat it too. (*See* Jackson, 1992.)

If Strawman stands his ground, on the other hand, he will insist that folk psychology is far from agnostic about the language

of thought. It has plenty to say, after all, about our 'concepts' (or 'ideas') of things. Our concept of a concept, says Strawman, is just our concept of a word of the language of thought. – I doubt it. I haven't much of any concept of Elsternwick. I have little idea what the place looks like, what sort of people live there, . . . All I know is that there is a place of that name, and roughly where it is. But I *do* have the word. (At least, I have the word 'Elsternwick' of our public language. *If* I have a language of thought, presumably this word has been borrowed into it.) My lack of a concept isn't lack of a word; rather, I lack any very rich cluster of associated descriptions.

Strawman can reply that even if I haven't *much* concept of Elsternwick, still I have enough of one that I can think about Elsternwick (for instance, when I think how little I know about it). It is this minimal concept of a concept, he says, that is our folk-psychological concept of a word of the language of thought. – Yes, I have a concept of Elsternwick in the minimal sense that I have *whatever it takes* to be able to think about it. But must the basis of such an ability, in general or even in this case, be the possession of a word? On that question, the folk and I remain agnostic.

My second objection to Strawman's account is that it delivers only wide content. Which singular propositions you believe depends upon which external things are suitably connected by relations of acquaintance to the words of your language of thought.

Strawman holds that all content is wide because he has learned the lesson of TWIN EARTH. Recall the example (Putnam, 1975, pp. 139–42). Oscar the Earthling believes that water often falls from clouds. Twoscar on Twin Earth is in no way acquainted with water, that is, with H_2O. Rather, Twoscar is acquainted with XYZ, a superficially similar liquid that is abundant on Twin Earth, in exactly the way that Oscar is acquainted with H_2O. There is no other relevant difference between Twoscar and Oscar. We are invited to agree that Twoscar does not believe that water falls from clouds, and

423

believes instead that XYZ falls from clouds. Strawman does agree.

And so do I, but with many reservations. For one thing, I think agreement is not compulsory. Like any up-to-date philosopher of 1955, I think that 'water' is a cluster concept. Among the conditions in the cluster are: it is liquid, it is colourless, it is odourless, it supports life. But, *pace* the philosopher of 1955, there is more to the cluster than that. Another condition in the cluster is: it is a natural kind. Another condition is indexical: it is abundant hereabouts. Another is metalinguistic: many call it 'water'. Another is both metalinguistic and indexical: *I* have heard of it under the name 'water'. When we hear that XYZ off on Twin Earth fits many of the conditions in the cluster but not all, we are in a state of semantic indecision about whether it deserves the name 'water'. (*See* Unger, 1984, pp. 79–104. But while I agree with Unger about what happens in various cases, I don't endorse all the morals he draws.) When in a state of semantic indecision, we are often glad to go either way, and accommodate our own usage temporarily to the whims of our conversational partners (Lewis, 1979b). So if some philosopher, call him Schmutnam, invites us to join him in saying that the water on Twin Earth differs in chemical composition from the water here, we will happily follow his lead. And if another philosopher, Putnam (1975), invites us to say that the stuff on Twin Earth is not water – and hence that Twoscar does not believe that water falls from clouds – we will just as happily follow his lead. We should have followed Putnam's lead only for the duration of that conversation, then lapsed back into our accommodating state of indecision. But, sad to say, we thought that instead of playing along with a whim, we were settling a question once and for all. And so we came away lastingly misled.

The example half suceeds. It is not compulsory, but certainly it is permissible, to say that Oscar does believe that water falls from clouds and differently acquainted Twoscar does not. Therefore wide content does serve a purpose. It enters into the ana-

lysis of some sentences that are about belief, or at least partly about belief; or at least it does so under some permissible disambiguations of these sentences.

Other examples are similar. Twoscar is acquainted with molybdenum as Oscar is with aluminium; with a disease of bone as Oscar is with a disease of joints; with spy robots as Oscar is with cats; and so on. It seems to matter little whether Twoscar is our neighbour, or whether he lives on a remote planet, or whether he lives in a different possible world. In each case we find that the difference in what Twoscar and Oscar are acquainted with makes a difference to the truth value, under some disambiguation, of some sentences that are at least partly about belief. But that is all we find. There is nothing here to support Strawman's thesis that wide content is the only kind of content; or that it is in any way pre-eminent or basic.

We should not jump to the conclusion that just any belief sentence is susceptible to Twin Earth examples. Oscar thinks that square pegs don't fit round holes; I don't think you can tell an even halfway convincing story of how Twoscar, just by being differently acquainted, fails to think so too. Oscar believes there's a famous seaside place called 'Blackpool'; so does differently acquainted Twoscar, though of course it may not be Blackpool – not *our* Blackpool – that he has in mind. Oscar believes that the stuff he has heard of under the name 'water' falls from clouds. So does Twoscar – and so does Twoscar even if you alter not only his acquaintance with water but his relations of acquaintance to other things as well. You know the recipe for Twin Earth examples. You can follow it in these cases too. But what you get falls flat even as an example of how content is sometimes wide, let alone as evidence that content is always wide.

The famous brain in a bottle is your exact duplicate with respect to brain states and their typical causal roles; but is acquainted only with aspects of the computer that fabricates its virtual reality. You and the brain share no objects of acquaintance. So, according to Strawman, you and the brain share no common beliefs whatever.

Newborn Swampman, just this moment formed by an unlikely chance assembly of atoms, also is your exact duplicate with respect *inter alia* to brain states and their typical causal roles (Davidson, 1987). But so far, he hasn't had time to become acquainted with much of anything. Therefore, according to Strawman, he believes not much of anything.

Strawman and his allies may think that we have here two remarkable philosophical discoveries. I think, rather, that Strawman's thesis that all content is wide has here met with a twofold *reductio ad absurdum*. Granted, the brain in a bottle shares no wide content of belief with you. Granted, Swampman has no wide content of belief at all. Yet there must be some good sense in which both the brain and Swampman are your mental twins; some good sense in which they believe just what you do. (And in our less extreme cases, there must be some good sense in which Twoscar believes just what Oscar does.) Strawman's position is unacceptable. Not because it posits wide content; but because it omits narrow content, content independent of what one is acquainted with. It omits the sort of content that you and the brain and Swampman, and likewise Oscar and Twoscar, have in common.

(Narrow content is independent of what you are acquainted with, but that does not mean that it is altogether intrinsic to you. For it still depends on the causal roles of your brain states; causation depends on the laws of nature; and if some sort of regularity theory of lawhood is true, living under such-and-such laws is not intrinsic to you. Further, it is the typical causal roles of your brain states that matter. But you may be an atypical member of your kind; hence what is typical of your kind is not intrinsic to you. So I can say only this: if X and Y are intrinsic duplicates, and if they live under the same laws of nature, and if they are the same in kind, then they must be exactly alike in narrow content.)

In insisting on the existence of narrow content, I am not guided by any preconception about what sort of properties may figure in causal explanation, or in truly scientific explanation. I dare say the fundamental laws of physics must concern perfectly natural, intrinsic properties. But that's irrelevant, since causal and scientific explanation seldom consists in subsumption under these fundamental laws. Rather, it is a matter of giving information about how things are caused (Lewis, 1986b). Such information can come in many forms, both within science and without, and there is no reason to proscribe extrinsic classifications. (Lynne Baker told me a nice example: the science of economics is all about extrinsic properties like poverty and debt. Yet there is nothing wrong, and nothing unscientific, in saying that Fred stays poor because of his burden of debt.)

I am guided, rather, by my tacit mastery of the principles of folk psychology. I said: Oscar believes that the stuff he has heard of under the name 'water' falls from clouds; and so does Twoscar. (And so do you, and so does the brain in a bottle, and so does Swampman.) These are ordinary folk-psychological belief sentences; but narrow ones, as witness the fact that they are not susceptible to Twin Earth examples.

This narrow content is content, rightly so-called: something is true according to the belief-system in question. The content is true on condition that the stuff the believer has heard of under the name 'water' does indeed fall from clouds; otherwise false. It is not 'purely syntactic content' – something I take to be a contradiction in terms. Nor is it a mere function that delivers genuine content as output when given circumstances of acquaintance as input. Nor is it merely phenomenalistic content, restricted in subject matter to the believer's experience.

However, it is not content that can be given by a singular proposition, and that leads to my third objection against Strawman's account.

Strawman's singular propositions suffice to specify which things have which properties. If all else supervenes upon the pattern of coinstantiation of fundamental properties, that in turn will suffice to specify the way the world is. But much of the content of our knowledge and belief is *de se*: it concerns not the world but oneself. (*See* Perry, 1977; Lewis, 1979a; Chisholm, 1979.) However much I may know about the things that make up the world, their properties and their arrangement, it is something extra to know which one of all these things is *me*. This is *de se* knowledge, whereby I locate myself in the world and self-ascribe the properties I think myself to possess, but is not knowledge of how the world is. Its content cannot be captured by singular propositions. What singular proposition is expressed when I say, or I think, 'I am DL'? – Just the proposition that DL = DL. And when I self-ascribe the property F? – Just the proposition that DL is F. But I can know these propositions without knowing who I am, or whether I am F. (And you can know them too.) Strawman's only recourse is to say that *de se* knowledge is characterized not by its *de se* content but some other way – and if he says that, he confesses that his account of content is inadequate. Belief that falls short of knowledge can likewise have *de se* content. If you take *your*self to be DL, your false belief and my true belief have their *de se* content in common. Desire also has *de se* content. If you desire to be F and I believe myself to be F, again the two attitudes have their *de se* content in common.

There is also tensed content. The world is spread out over many times; but we can have knowledge, or belief or desire, about which of these times is now. Again, this is not knowledge of how the whole spread-out world is. It is something extra. Some would speak of content *de se et nunc*, but I would subsume *de nunc* under *de se*. For I think we persist through time by consisting of many time-slices, or momentary selves; and in the last analysis, it is these momentary selves that do our thinking. So when I think 'It's now time for lunch', that's one of my momentary selves self-ascribing *de se* the property of being located at lunchtime.

The 'propositions', if we may call them that, which make up *de se* content are true

or false not absolutely, as singular propositions are, but relative to a subject. (Or to a subject at a time, if you don't believe in momentary selves.) The content of my knowledge *de se* that I am DL is something that is true for me but not for you. Its linguistic expression requires a first-person pronoun, or some equivalent device. We could call it an 'egocentric proposition' (or 'egocentric and tensed'). Or we can simply identify it with the property that I self-ascribe: the property of being DL. Likewise the *de se* content of my belief that I have F is just the property of F itself; the *de se* content of my belief that it's lunchtime is the property (possessed not by the whole of me but by some of my momentary selves) of being located at lunchtime; and so on. A *de se* self-ascription of a property is true just on condition that the self-ascriber possesses the self-ascribed property.

(May I say, then, that *de se* belief has 'truth conditions'? Not if Strawman has his way. He goes in for terminological piracy. He transforms one term after another into a mere synonym for 'singular proposition'. He has taken 'object of thought'. He has taken 'content'. He has taken 'proposition'. He is well on the way to taking 'truth condition'. When he has taken all the terms for his own, dissident thoughts will be unsayable.)

Since Strawman has no place for *de se* content, it makes sense that he overlooks narrow content as well. For narrow content is very often *de se*. To revisit our previous example: Oscar self-ascribes having heard, under the name of 'water', of a liquid that falls from clouds. He also self-ascribes the property of being at a place (and time) in the vicinity of which the most abundant liquid is one that falls from clouds. Differently acquainted Twoscar self-ascribes these same two properties, and in this way Oscar and Twoscar share the same *de se* narrow content of belief.

On my own view, it is just such *de se* narrow content that underlies wide content. The semantics of the alleged language of thought needn't enter into it. To the extent that language enters my story at all, it is not by way of the language of thought, but rather by way of thought about language – about the ordinary public language, whereby, for instance, Oscar heard of something under the name 'water'.

Here is one recipe (Lewis, 1979a, pp. 538 –43): if R is a relation of acquaintance, and subject S self-ascribes being R-acquainted uniquely with something that has property F (the narrow part), and if S is R-acquainted uniquely with A (the wide part), S thereby widely believes the singular proposition that A has F. There are variants on the recipe. Our example of French André was a case in which property F as well as individual A enters indirectly as an object of acquaintance; we must of course let in cases where the property F gives way to a relation with two or more *relata*; maybe sometimes we should drop the qualification 'uniquely'; and maybe sometimes the relation R is not, or not entirely, a matter of acquaintance. But in every case, wide belief in a singular proposition derives from narrow *de se* self-ascription plus facts about what the subject is related to.

Often we know a lot about which singular propositions someone believes in this wide and derivative way; but we know less about *how* – in virtue of just which self-ascriptions and relations of acquaintance – he believes those singular propositions. So it's no surprise to find that our ordinary-language belief sentences often seem to be ascriptions of wide content. Often; but not always. In these last few paragraphs I've been talking about *de se* narrow content, and I've been talking about it in plain English. (Such bits of jargon as I used were first explained in plain English.)

There are still other dimensions to the semantic complexity and the multifarious ambiguity of ordinary-language belief sentences. Think of the belief sentences that show up as test cases in articles advocating one semantic analysis or another. I *always* want to say: 'in a sense that's true, in a sense false'. One complication is that we get direct-quotational effects even in what is ostensibly indirect quotation (*see* Rieber, 1992). An example: Fred knows perfectly well that the house he lives in is made of

wood, but Fred also thinks that 'abode' is the English word for a house made of mud-brick. 'Fred believes that he has an abode – yes or no?' In at least some contexts (this isn't one of them) I'd be prepared to insist on 'no'. Wouldn't you? Moral: if you hope to understand the folk psychology of belief by studying the linguistic phenomenology of ordinary belief sentences, you're in for big trouble.

I've said that narrow content is very often *de se*, but by resorting to a cheap trick I can change 'often' to 'always'. Take an apparent exception: the narrow belief that square pegs won't fit in round holes. Take this to be the *de se* self-ascription of the property of inhabiting a world wherein square pegs won't fit in round holes. A peculiar property, since either all the inhabitants of the world share it or else none do; and, like many other self-ascribed properties, very far from fundamental: but in a broad enough sense of the word, a property all the same. Likewise you can self-ascribe the property of inhabiting a world where there's a famous seaside place called 'Blackpool'. And so on, until all narrow content has been included as *de se*. Hoky, but maybe worthwhile for the sake of uniform treatment.

My final objection is that Strawman ignores large parts of the folk psychology of belief and desire: the parts that characterize aspects of our RATIONALITY. Folk psychology says that a system of beliefs and desires tends to cause behaviour that serves the subject's desires according to his beliefs. Folk psychology says that beliefs change constantly under the impact of perceptual evidence: we keep picking up new beliefs, mostly true, about our perceptual surroundings; whereupon our other beliefs (and our instrumental desires) change to cohere with these new beliefs. Folk psychology sets presumptive limits to what basic desires we can have or lack: *de gustibus non disputandum*, but still a bedrock craving for a saucer of mud would be unintelligible (Anscombe, 1958, pp. 69–71). Likewise it sets limits to our sense of plausibility: which hypotheses we find credible prior to evidence, hence which hypotheses are easily confirmed when their predictions come true. And it sets presumptive limits on what our contents of belief and desire can be. Self-ascribed properties may be 'far from fundamental', I said – but not *too* far. Especially gruesome gerrymanders are *prima facie* ineligible to be contents of belief and desire. (See Lewis, 1983a, pp. 370–7; Lewis, 1986a, pp. 38–9 and 105–8.) In short, folk psychology says that we make sense. It credits us with a modicum of rationality in our acting, believing, and desiring.

(Beware. 'Rationality' is an elastic word, and here I've stretched it to cover a lot. If you'd rather use it more narrowly – just for the serving of desires according to beliefs, say – no harm done. So long as you don't just ignore the several other departments of rationality that I listed, it doesn't matter what you call them.)

If mental states are to be analysed as occupants of folk-psychological roles, and if the folk psychology of belief and desire has a lot to say about rationality, and if what it says is framed in terms of content, then it seems that constraints of rationality are constitutive of content. Yet Strawman's account of content makes no place for constitutive rationality. Why not?

Perhaps Strawman thought, wisely, that it would be better to say too little than too much. It wouldn't do to conclude that, as a matter of analytic necessity, anyone who can be said to have beliefs and desires at all must be an ideally rational *homo economicus*! Our rationality is very imperfect, Strawman knows it, and he knows that the folk know it too. Of course we overlook options and hypotheses, we practice inference to the third-best explanation, we engage in double think, and so on, and on, and on.

But there is no cause for alarm. Folk psychology can be taken as a theory of imperfect, near-enough rationality, yet such rationality as it does affirm can still be constitutive. And even if folk psychology did set too high a standard – even if, to take the worst case, it were a theory of ideal rationality – still an imperfect but near-enough occupant of a folk-psychological role could

thereby be an imperfect but near-enough deserver of a folk-psychological name. Remember also that the *typical* occupant of a role needn't occupy it in every case. In short, constitutive rationality leaves plenty of room for human folly.

(I think that systematic theories of ideal rationality – decision theory, for instance, and the theory of learning from experience by conditionalizing a subjective probability distribution – are severely idealized versions of parts of folk psychology. They are founded upon our tacit knowledge of folk psychology, elicited in the guise of 'intuition'. But folk psychology also supplies the grains of salt to be applied to these idealizations. Sometimes it supplies complementary pairs of opposite idealizations: a quantitative theory of subjective probabilities and utilities precise to however many decimal places, and alongside it a non-quantitative theory of beliefs and desires that don't admit of degree at all.)

Constitutive rationality is part of the legacy of behaviourism, and that is a second reason why Strawman mistrusts it. A behaviourist analysis might say, roughly, that a subject's beliefs and desires are those beliefs and desires, attribution of which would best make sense of how the subject is disposed to behave, and of how his changing behavioural dispositions depend on the changing perceptible features of his surroundings. But Strawman is a robust realist about beliefs and desires. He takes them to be genuine inner states, and causes of behaviour. He won't like an analysis that dispenses with efficacious inner states in favour of mere patterns of dispositions. Still less would he like it if the behaviourist went on to say that attributions of belief and desire governed by constitutive rationality were instrumentally useful, or warranted by rules of assertability, but not straightforwardly true.

I applaud these misgivings. I too am a robust realist about beliefs and desires. (About whole systems of beliefs and desires, anyway, though maybe not about all the little snippets – the sentences written in the belief and desire boxes – of which these systems may or may not be composed.) But

I say the proper remedy is not to shun constitutive rationality, but to apply it differently. The behaviourist applies it directly to the subject; I say we should apply it to the subject's inner state. The behaviourist says that the subject *has* that system of beliefs and desires that best makes sense of how the subject is disposed to behave. Whereas I'd say that the inner state *is* that system of beliefs and desires that best makes sense of the behaviour which that state is apt for causing in subjects. Thus I'd use constitutive rationality not to dispense with causally efficacious inner states, but rather to define their content.

A third reason why Strawman shuns constitutive rationality is that sometimes it needs to be applied not to the singular propositions that are the wide content of belief and desire, but instead to the underlying *de se* narrow content. The furniture of the *Lebenswelt* which presents us with our problems of decision and learning consists, in the first instance, of objects given *qua* objects of acquaintance, and individuated by acquaintance. (*See* Hintikka, 1972; Lewis, 1983b.) That is a matter of narrow content. If you are lucky, and you're never wrong or uncertain about whether you're really R-acquainted with something, and you're never wrong or uncertain about whether the thing you're R_1-acquainted with is or isn't the same as the thing you're R_2-acquainted with, then we can talk about your beliefs and desires entirely in terms of wide content. We can safely let things *simpliciter* stand in for things-*qua*-objects-of-acquaintance. But if you're not so lucky, that won't work. Take unlucky Pierre (Kripke, 1979). He self-ascribes being R_1-acquainted with a pretty city and being R_2-acquainted with an ugly city. But in fact he is R_1-acquainted and R_2-acquainted with the same city, London. Thereby he believes both that London is pretty and that London is ugly. (Kripke derives this conclusion from certain premises, but I find the conclusion at least as obvious as the premises.) I take this to be a conflict in wide content: Pierre widely believes two singular propositions that predicate conflicting properties of the same thing. Folk psychology says that by careful attention we can detect and eliminate conflicts in our beliefs – especially if we're good at logic, as Pierre is. But plainly that was never meant to apply to Pierre's conflict of singular propositions. Mere thought can't save him. What he needs is the information *de se* that he is R_1-acquainted and R_2-acquainted with the very same thing. (*See* Lewis, 1981.)

And suppose Pierre believes that by boarding the bus before him, he can be taken to London for a week of sight-seeing. Would boarding that bus serve his desires according to his beliefs? It helps not at all to know that he widely believes both that London is pretty and that London is ugly. What does help is the information already given about his narrow self-ascriptions, plus one further thing: he also self-ascribes having a bus before him that would take him to the place he is R_1-acquainted with. (*See* Lewis, 1986a, p. 58.)

(On constitutive rationality, *see* Stalnaker, 1984, pp. 1–42; Lewis, 1974, 1986a, pp. 27–40. But see Lewis, 1974, with caution: it began as a conversation with Donald Davidson, and I went rather too far in granting undisputed common ground. (1) I gave an important place to the subject Karl's beliefs as expressed in Karl's own language; that certainly suggests language-of-thoughtism, though I hope I committed myself to nothing more than the safe thesis that Karl's medium of mental representation is *somehow* analogous to language. (2) I was too individualistic: I ignored the possibility that deviant Karl might believe something in virtue of the causal role of his inner state not in Karl himself but in others who are more typical members of Karl's kind. (3) I had not yet come to appreciate the role of *de se* content. *Also see* Lewis, 1986a, pp. 27–40, with caution: besides endorsing constitutive rationality, I also stated it within a controversial framework of realism about unactualized *possibilia*. I still think that's a good way to state it; but I never said it was the only way. Constitutive rationality and realism about *possibilia* needn't be a package deal!)

This completes my list of objections against Strawman's program for explaining content. Doubtless you can think of ever so many ways of amending Strawman's theses to get around my objections. Some lists of amendments would take us to the positions really held by real people. Of course I can't show that no version of Strawman-amended can work. But for myself, I pin my hopes on a more radical reversal of Strawman's position.

With Strawman for a foil, my own approach can be summed up quickly. The contentful unit is the entire system of beliefs and desires. (Maybe it divides up into contentful snippets, maybe not.) That system is an inner state that typically causes behaviour, and changes under the impact of perception (and also spontaneously). Its content is defined, insofar as it is defined at all, by constitutive rationality on the basis of its typical causal role. This content is in the first instance narrow and *de se* (or *de se et nunc* if you'd rather steer clear of momentary selves). Wide content is derivative, a product of narrow content and relationships of acquaintance with external things.

See also DAVIDSON; DENNETT; FODOR; PHILOSOPHY AND PSYCHOLOGY; PROPOSITIONAL ATTITUDES; REASONS AND CAUSES; THOUGHTS; THOUGHT AND LANGUAGE.

BIBLIOGRAPHY

Anscombe, G.E.M. 1958. *Intention*. Oxford: Blackwell.

Armstrong, D.M. 1968. *A Materialist Theory of Mind*. London: Routledge & Kegan Paul.

Carnap, R. 1963. Replies and expositions. In *The Philosophy of Rudolf Carnap*, ed. P. A. Schilpp. Cambridge University Press, 859–1013.

Chisholm, R.M. 1979. The indirect reflexive. In *Intention and Intentionality: Essays in Honour of G. E. M. Anscombe*, ed. C. Diamond and J. Teichman. Brighton: Harvester.

Davidson, D. 1987. Knowing one's own mind. *Proceedings and Address of the American Philosophical Association*, 60, 441–58.

Davies, M.K., and Humberstone, I.L. 1980. Two notions of necessity. *Philosophical Studies*, 38, 1–30.

Feinberg, G. 1966. Physics and the Thales problem. *Journal of Philosophy*, 66, 5–13.

Field, H. 1973. Theory change and the indeterminacy of reference. *Journal of Philosophy*, 70, 462–481.

Hintikka, J. 1972. Knowledge by acquaintance – individuation by acquaintance. In *Bertrand Russell: A Collection of Critical Essays*, ed. D. Pears. Garden City, N.J.: Doubleday.

Jackson, F.C. 1982. Epiphenomenal qualia. *Philosophical Quarterly*, 32, 127–36.

Jackson, F.C. 1992. Armchair metaphysics. Presented at a conference on the place of philosophy in the study of the mind, University of New South Wales.

Jackson, F.C., Pargetter, R., and Prior, E.W. 1982. Functionalism and type-type identity theories. *Philosophical Studies*, 42, 209–25.

Kripke, S. 1972. Naming and necessity. In *Semantics of Natural Language*, ed. D. Davidson and G. Harman. Dordrecht: Reidel.

Kripke, S., 1979. A puzzle about belief. In *Meaning and Use*, ed. Avishai Margalit.

Lewis, D. 1966. An argument for the identity theory. *Journal of Philosophy*, 63, 17–25. Reprinted with additions in Lewis, 1983c.

—— 1970. How to define theoretical terms. *Journal of Philosophy*, 67, 427–46. Reprinted in Lewis, 1983c.

—— 1972. Psychophysical and theoretical identifications. *Australasian Journal of Philosophy*, 50, 249–58.

—— 1974. Radical interpretation. *Synthèse*, 23, 331–44. Reprinted with postscripts in Lewis, 1983c.

—— 1979a. Attitudes *de dicto* and *de se*. *Philosophical Review*, 88, 513–43. Reprinted with postscripts in Lewis, 1983c.

—— 1979b. Scorekeeping in a language game. *Journal of Philosophical Logic*, 8, 339–59. Reprinted in Lewis, 1983c.

—— 1980. Mad pain and Martian pain. In *Readings in Philosophy of Psychology. Vol. 1*, ed. N. Block. Cambridge, MA: Harvard University Press. Reprinted with postscript in Lewis, 1983c.

—— 1981. What puzzling Pierre does not believe. *Australasian Journal of Philosophy*, 59, 283–89.

—— 1983a. New work for a theory of universals. *Australasian Journal of Philosophy*, 61, 343–77.

—— 1983b. Individuation by acquaintance and by stipulation. *Philosophical Review*, 92, 3–12.

—— 1983c. *Philosophical Papers, Vol. 1*. Oxford University Press.

—— 1986a. *On the Plurality of Worlds*. Oxford: Basil Blackwell.

—— 1986b. Causal explanation. In Lewis, *Philosophical Papers, Vol. 2*. Oxford University Press.

—— 1986c. Events. In Lewis, *Philosophical Papers, Vol. 2*. Oxford University Press.

—— 1990. What experience teaches. In *Mind and Cognition: A Reader*, ed. W. G. Lycan. Oxford: Basil Blackwell.

—— 1992. Critical notice of D. M. Armstrong, *A Combinatorial Theory of Possibility*. *Australasian Journal of Philosophy*, 70, 211–24.

Nemirow, L. 1990. Physicalism and the cognitive role of acquaintance. *In Mind and Cognition: A Reader*, ed. W.G. Lycan. Oxford: Basil Blackwell.

Perry, J. 1977. Frege on demonstratives. *Philosophical Review*, 86, 474–97.

Putnam, H. 1975. The meaning of 'meaning'. In *Language, Mind and Knowledge*, ed. K. Gunderson. Minneapolis, MN: University of Minnesota Press.

Ramsey, F.P. 1931a. Theories. In Ramsey, *The Foundations of Mathematics*. London: Routledge & Kegan Paul.

Ramsey, F.P. 1931b. General propositions and causality. In Ramsey, *The Foundations of Mathematics*. London: Routledge & Kegan Paul.

Rieber, S. 1992. A test for quotation. *Philosophical Studies*, 68, 83–94.

Smart, J.J.C. 1959. Sensations and brain processes. *Philosophical Review*, 68, 141–156.

Stalnaker, R. 1978. Assertion. *Syntax and Semantics*, 9, 315–32.

Stalnaker, R. 1984. *Inquiry*. Cambridge, MA.: M.I.T. Press.

Tichý, P. 1983. Kripke on necessity a posteriori. *Philosophical Studies*, 43, 225–41.

Unger, P. 1984. *Philosophical Relativity*. Minneapolis, MN: University of Minnesota Press.

Thanks to the Boyce Gibson Memorial Library and the philosophy department of Birkbeck College; and to the editors, Ned Block, Alex Byrne, Mark Crimmins, Allen Hazen, Ned Hall, Elijah Millgram, Thomas Nagel, and especially Frank Jackson.

DAVID LEWIS

Leibniz's Law Named after the seventeenth-century philosopher and logician G. W. von Leibniz, this so-called 'law' is better thought of as a logical principle which governs our use of the identity relation. Perhaps more than other such principles, it has been subject to various challenges, but many regard it as fundamental to the explanation of identity. The law is most easily stated against the background of some dispute about identity. For example, suppose that you have lost your treasured fountain pen, and notice, some weeks later, someone who works in your office sporting a pen just like yours in his pocket. Being of a suspicious character, you wonder to yourself whether the pen in his pocket is the pen you lost. What you wonder of course is not whether the pen is the same *type* as yours, but whether it is *the very same* pen. Using '*a*' as a name for the pen that has gone missing, and '*b*' for the one seen in the pocket, what you wonder is whether the following statement (expressed in logical symbols) is true:

$$a = b$$

In it the equality sign is read as: 'is one and the same as'. What Leibniz's Law says is that if this identity is true, then any property of *a* is also a property of *b* (and vice versa). And many think this is virtually a truism about identity, since if the above identity is true, there is really only one pen, and things cannot have and lack the same property at the same time. In somewhat more formal terms, Leibniz's Law is usually stated this way:

For any x, any y and any property $\varnothing$,
IF x = y THEN $\varnothing$x if and only if $\varnothing$y

The importance of this principle for the philosophy of mind comes from its role in discussions of IDENTITY THEORIES of the mind. For, using this principle, one can at least attempt to refute specific versions of the identity theory by finding some property of a mental item not shared by the physical, or vice versa. If some such property can be found then the part of the principle following the 'THEN' will be false, and, by contraposition, the identity itself will be false. However, two things make this strategy less than straightforward: first, as was mentioned earlier, not everyone thinks that Leibniz's Law is true (e.g. that it doesn't apply in modal contexts), even though it has the air of a truism; and, secondly, versions of the identity theory in the philosophy of mind are PROPERTY identity theories, whereas the above formulation is appropriate to individual things like pens.

This is important because it seems possible to formulate Leibniz's Law for properties in ways that make it less of a weapon against the type identity theory.

See also DAVIDSON; LEWIS.

SAMUEL GUTTENPLAN

M

---

materialism *see* LEWIS; PHYSICALISM.

memory We are acutely aware of the effects of our own memory, its successes and its failures, so that we have the impression that we know something about how it works. But, with memory, as with most mental functions, what we are aware of is the outcome of its operation and not the operation itself. To our introspections, the essence of memory is language based and intentional. When we appear as a witness in court then the truth as we are seen to report it is what we say about what we intentionally retrieve. This is, however, a very restricted view of memory albeit with a distinguished history. William James (1890) said 'Memory proper is the knowledge of a former state of mind after it has already once dropped from consciousness; or rather it is the knowledge of an event, or fact, of which meantime we have not been thinking, with the additional consciousness that we have thought or experienced it before' (p. 648).

One clue to the underlying structure of our memory system might be its evolutionary history. We have no reason to suppose that a special memory system evolved recently or to consider linguistic aspects of memory and intentional recall as primary. Instead, we might assume that such features are later additions to a much more primitive filing system. From this perspective one would view memory as having the primary functions of enabling us (the organism as a whole, that is, not the conscious self) to interpret the perceptual world and helping us to organize our responses to changes that take place in that world.

SOME USES OF THE TERM 'MEMORY'

Before continuing, it is necessary to refer to certain distinctions made concerning memory so that it will be clear what I am not talking about. The first distinction is that between Short Term Memory (STM) and Long Term Memory (LTM). These are highly misleading terms, in that they imply that there are two, and just two such entities, separate and integral with STM characterized as having limited capacity and being available for limited amounts of time only, in contrast with LTM where capacity is unlimited and memories are permanent. In practice, STM and LTM are operationalized in terms of particular tasks. Experiments supposedly testing the properties of these two mental entities, in fact, initially distinguished them solely on the basis of the time interval between presentation of the stimulus and the recall. Subsequently, there has been much research aimed at establishing the distinction between the two – other than, that is, in terms of long and short – that has tested such propositions as STM is subject to phonological interference and LTM to semantic interference. The straightforward memory span task was taken as being equivalent to STM. Finding that this task was subject to semantic influences, and that tasks indexing LTM could be subject to phonological influences, led some writers to abandon the distinction on the grounds of economy. Unfortunately, most theories of memory tend to say nothing about the processes required for speech, language and meaning although most memory experiments involve words. All theories of language processing, however, require processors that have the ability to integrate over a number of items

433

and, thus, information must be preserved over short amounts of time specifically for the purpose of language-oriented computations. The structures within which this takes place are called buffer memories. While we are performing tasks involving the recall of information over short intervals, the contents of these buffer memories will be available. Notions of economy in the theory of memory do not apply. Thus a contentious claim such as *STM is the route of entry to LTM for new memories* could be reformulated as the non-contentious *prior to the creation of a permanent memory, the relevant material will be found in one or more structures having the function of acting as buffers.*

The second distinction commonly made is that between implicit memory and explicit memory. Implicit memory is revealed when performance on a task is facilitated in the absence of conscious recollection. Alternatively, the abilities of densely amnesic patients to learn while having no conscious recollection at all of the episodes during which the learning took place (or, indeed, of anything else since the onset of the amnesia) are seen as evidence of the distinction. A typical experimental paradigm is that of repetition priming, where previous study of a list of words will help in a following task to make a word/non-word judgment of a letter string or to complete word fragments such as A–A–IN or U–V–SE. Such priming is quite generally found with amnesic subjects and also for normal subjects in the case that they do not remember having seen the words in the study period. Now, nearly all theories of word recognition require there to be structures responsible for decoding the stimulus at a low level (which may or may not be related to the buffer memories already referred to). These structures are termed *input lexicons* – or some such name. From studies of the effects of priming in word recognition it is reasonable to suppose that input lexicons carry traces of their activity over time. There is also good reason to believe that we have no conscious control over the activity of the input lexicons and are unaware of activity in

them. Much of the evidence for implicit memory can be accounted for on the basis of the operation of such structures or those required to organize verbal or other output. Note that the implicit/explicit distinction has nothing to do with the usual conscious/unconscious distinction. Implicit memory could be seen as non-conscious rather than unconscious. More important is that influences on performance in experiments testing implicit memory will derive from different sources than those involved in other memory performance.

MEMORY PROPER

The memory we will focus on was defined above as that enabling us to interpret the perceptual world and helping us to organize our responses to changes that take place in that world. For both of these functions we have to accumulate experience in a memory system in such a way as to enable the productive access of that experience at the appropriate times. The memory we are interested in here, then, can be seen as the repository of experience. Of course, beyond a certain age, we are able to use our memories in different ways, both to store information and to retrieve it. Language is vital in this respect and it might be argued that much of socialization and the whole of schooling are devoted to just such an extension of an evolutionary (relatively) straightforward system. It will follow that most of the operation of our memory system is preconscious. That is to say, consciousness only has access to the product of the memory processes and not to the processes themselves. The aspects of memory that we are conscious of can be seen as the final state in a complex and hidden set of operations.

How should we think about the structure of memory? The dominant metaphor is that of association. Words, ideas, and, indeed, emotions are seen as being linked together in an endless, amorphous net. That is, indeed, the way our memory can seem to us if we attempt to reflect on it directly. But, as already indicated, it would be a mistake to dwell too much on the products of consciousness and imagine that they represent the inner structure. For a cognitive psychologist interested in natural memory phenomena there were a number of reasons for being deeply dissatisfied with theories based on associative nets. One ubiquitous class of memory failure seemed particularly troublesome. This is the experience of being able to recall a great deal of what we know about an individual, other than their name. On one such occasion, I was discussing someone's research with a colleague. The main results were familiar to us both. We knew where the man worked, where he lived, what his wife was called and the last time we had heard him talk. We felt certain we would instantly recognize his name if it were produced by someone else and that if we had started with his name we would have been able to retrieve the rest of the information.

How might various theories of memory account for this phenomenon? First we can take an associative network approach (e.g. Anderson, 1976, 1983; Anderson and Bower, 1973; Raajmaker and Shiffrin, 1980). In the idealized associative network, concepts, such as the concept of a person, are represented as nodes, with associated nodes being connected through links. Generally speaking, the links define the nature of the relationship between nodes, e.g. the subject–predicate distinction (Anderson, 1976; Anderson and Bower, 1973). Let us suppose that the name of the person we are trying to recall is Bill Smith. We would have a BILL SMITH node (or a node corresponding to Bill Smith) with all the available information concerning Bill Smith being linked to form some kind of propositional representation. Now, failure to retrieve Bill Smith's name, while at the same time being able to recall all other information concerning Bill Smith, would have to be due to an inability to traverse the links to the BILL SMITH node. However, this seems contradictory to one principle of associative networks: content addressability (e.g. Anderson and Bower, 1973; Anderson, 1976). That is to say, given that any one constituent of a propositional representation can be

accessed, the propositional node, and consequently all the other nodes linked to it, should also be accessible. Thus, if we are able to recall where Bill Smith lives, where he works, whom he is married to, then, we should, in principle, be able to access the node representing his name. To account for the inability to do so, some sort of temporary 'blocking' of content addressability would seem to be needed. Alternatively, directionality of links would have to be specified (Anderson, 1976, 1983), though this would have to be done on an *ad hoc* basis.

Next we can consider schema approaches (Bartlett, 1932; Rumelhart, 1980; Schank, 1980; Schank and Abelson, 1977). Schema models stipulate that there are abstract representations, i.e. schemata, in which all invariant information concerning any particular thing are represented. So we would have a person schema for Bill Smith that would contain all the invariant information about him. This would include his name, personality traits, attitudes, where he lived, whether he had a family, etc. It is not clear how one would deal with our example within a schema framework. Since someone's name is the quintessentially invariant property, then, given that it was known, it would have to be represented in the schema for that person. From our example, we knew that other invariant information, as well as variant, non-schematic information (e.g. the last talk he had given) were available for recall. This must be taken as evidence that the schema for Bill Smith was accessed. Why, then, were we unable to recall one particular piece of information that would have to be represented in the schema we clearly had access to? We would have to assume that within the person-schema for Bill Smith are sub-schemata (*see* e.g. Schank, 1980) one of which contained Bill Smith's name, another containing the name of his wife, and so on. We would further have to assume that access to the sub-schemata was independent and that, at the time in question, the one containing information about Bill Smith's name was temporarily inaccessible. Unfortunately the concept of temporary inaccessibility is without precedent in schema theory and does not seem to be independently motivated.

There are two other classes of memory problem that do not fit comfortably into the conventional frameworks. One is that of not being able to recall an event in spite of most detailed cues. This is commonly found when one partner is attempting to remind the other of a shared experience. Finally, we all have the experience of a memory being triggered spontaneously by something that was just an irrelevant part of the background for an event. Common triggers of such experiences are specific locales in town or country, scents and certain pieces of music.

What we learn from these three kinds of event are that we need a model which readily allows the following three properties:

(1) not all knowledge is directly retrievable;
(2) the central parts of an episode do not necessarily cue recall of that episode;
(3) peripheral cues, which are non-essential parts of the context, can cue recall.

In response to these requirements, we proposed the Headed Records model of memory (Morton, Hammersley and Bekerian, 1985; Morton and Bekerian, 1986; Morton, 1990, 1991). The framework within which the model is couched is that of information processing. In trying to solve the problems, we first supposed, following Norman and Bobrow (1979), that memory consists of discrete units, or *Records*, each containing information relevant to an 'event', an event being, for example, a person or a personal experience. Information contained in a Record could take any number of forms, with no restrictions being placed on the way information is represented, on the amount being represented or on the number of Records that could contain the same nominal information. Attached to each of these Records would be some kind of access key. The function of this access key, we suggested, is singular: it enables the retrieval of the Record and nothing more. Only when the particular access key is used can the Record, and the information contained

therein, be retrieved. As with the Record, we felt that any *type* of information could be contained in the access key. However, two features would distinguish it from the Record. First, the contents of the access key would be in a different *form* to that of the Record, e.g. represented in a phonological or other sensory code rather than a semantic or other central code. Second, the contents of the access key would not be retrievable. The access key was termed the *Heading*, and the framework became *Headed Records* (henceforth HR).

Following Norman and Bobrow (1979), the first thing that happens when memory is interrogated is that a *Description* is formed. This is the information used in the search. What is needed is something which is suitable as a memory probe. To give an example, if I asked you the question 'Could you give me the name of your best friend's wife?', it would not make much sense for you to interrogate your memory for ⟨*best friend's wife*⟩. What you have to do is to split the task up into its component parts. The first part is ⟨*best friend*⟩. Once that has been decided then ⟨*X's wife*⟩ can be found. The Description is formed from currently available information from external sources (such as an explicit question), internal sources (a Record that has just been retrieved) and a Task Specification. The Task Specification contains a list of the current goals. A Description can comprise a number of independent fields. These will include some environmental information and some internal state variables as well as lexical, propositional or other content.

The nature of the match required between the Description and a Heading will be a function of the type of information in the Description. If the task is to find the definition of a word or information on a named individual then a precise match may be required at least for the verbal part of the Description. We assume that the Headings are searched in parallel. On many occasions there will be more than one Heading that matches the Description. However, we require that only one Record be retrieved at a time (*see also* Anderson, 1976; Anderson and Bower, 1973; Rumelhart, 1980; Schank, 1980). Evidence in support of this assumption is summarized in Morton, Hammersley and Bekerian (1985). The data indicate that the more recent of two possible Records is retrieved. We conclude first that once a match is made the search process terminates and secondly that the matching process is biased in favour of the more recent Heading (*see also* Hasher et al., 1981; Martin, 1971; Postman and Underwood, 1973). There is, of course, no guarantee that the retrieved Record will contain the information that is sought. The Record may be incomplete or wrong. In such cases, or in the case that no Record had been retrieved, there are two options: either the search is continued or it is abandoned. If the search is to be continued then a new Description will have to be formed since searching again with the same Description would result in the same outcome as before. Thus, there has to be a list of criteria upon which a new Description can be based.

Retrieval depends upon a match between the Description and the Heading. The relationship between the given cue and the Description is open. It is clear that there needs to be a process of Description formation which will pick out the most likely descriptors from the given cue. Clearly, for the search process to be rational the set of descriptors and the set of Headings should overlap. Indeed, the only reasonable state of affairs would be that the creation of Headings and the creation of Descriptions is the responsibility of the same mechanism.

ACCOUNTING FOR PHENOMENA

The model contrasts with most other models of memory in that it is explicitly *not* freely content addressable. In the model, search only occurs on Headings. Information that is central to an event memory will serve as a cue for the recall of that memory only if it is found in the Heading. If such information is only present in the Record, it cannot be used as a retrieval cue. The converse of this is that information in the Heading need not be present in the linked Record. Thus, something which would be a reliable cue for a set of knowledge might be unretrievable if that set of knowledge were accessed by other means. Not being able to retrieve people's names is a common example of such a principle operating in practice.

The account of this phenomenon in HR terms is that the name forms a part of a Heading. Since the Headings have a number of components, and it is not necessary for the match between Heading and Description to be complete, it would be possible for the Record to be accessed by some other cue, such as the place where the subject of the Record, Bill Smith in the previous analysis, had last been encountered. The information in the Record would be retrieved, but there would be no way of retrieving the contents of the Headings. For another individual, of course, the name could be in the Record and the situation would not arise. Such variability in memory organization is as much a burden to the theorist as it is to the owner of the memory.

An experimental way of determining the components of Headings is through a comparison of the relative effectiveness of variables on recognition memory compared with recall. The reason for this lies in the difference between the way these two tasks map onto the HR framework. Recognition memory involves the subject's judging whether or not the presented material had previously been experienced. This requires that the material forms a Description which matches a Heading and that the Record that is retrieved contains information which enables the evaluation system to decide whether or not the task demands have been satisfied. In recall, on the other hand, the subject is given only some notion of the topic and the circumstances of the previous encounter. The material itself has to be found in a Record.

The data indicate that the literal form of the stimulus serves as a cue in recognition memory. In recognition memory for text, high- and low-level propositions (defined by their centrality to the theme of the passage) are equally well recognized (Yekovitch and

437

Thorndyke, 1981). In free recall, the higher-level propositions are better reported in spite of instructions for literal recall (Kintsch, 1974). The HR interpretation of this would be that the literal form of each sentence is directly addressable – i.e. constitutes a Heading, whereas only what is evaluated as most important finds its way into the Record. Equally, the sensitivity of recall to state and context variables contrasted with the relative insensitivity of recognition memory also indicates that such variables are to be found in Headings. There are other experimental ways of determining what kind of information gets into the Headings. Thus, an experiment by Godden and Baddeley (1975, 1980) showed that the context is important. They asked deep-sea divers to learn material on the sea bed, and showed that subsequent recall was worse on land compared with back under water. Further data of interest to us here indicate that state variables such as mood and drug state affect recall and not recognition (Bower, 1981; Eich, 1980), which in HR terms means that they are to be found in Headings.

In the course of our development we will have built up a large number of routines to guide our behaviour in different circumstances. When such a Record is accessed it serves as a *referent Record*. The basic cycle involves first of all the default retrieval of the control Record used to select a salient feature of the environment as a suitable descriptor. Next a Description is formed and the search process leads to the retrieval of a referent Record which is used to interpret the environment and guide our actions. An evaluation process must be operating continuously during the last of these stages to ensure that the referent Record continues to be appropriate. Such a process is not peculiar to the present model but would also be required in some forms of schema theory.

An important question is how we move from one record to another, i.e. how the whole system operates in interpreting situational experience; being in a restaurant, for example. A switch of referent Record may be necessitated by a change in the environ-ment (if, for example, someone starts a brawl in the restaurant), a change in the demands imposed in the same environment (e.g. starting to discuss business with one's dinner companions after having ordered dinner), or some change requiring a general problem-solving routine to be retrieved (as when one's spouse arrives unexpectedly in the same restaurant). In all these cases the sequence of events would be:

(1) detection of the inadequacy of the refer-ent Record by the evaluation routine;
(2) formation of a new Description;
(3) retrieval of a different referent Record.

We have assumed that only one referent Record can be used at a time. This is the simplest assumption. In any case we could not expect a very direct relationship between the dynamics of behaviour and the underlying representation. The processes that mediate between the representations in the Records and actual behaviour will have the effect of smoothing over the underlying joints, much as the underlying multi-layered structure of an utterance is disguised by the time it becomes speech.

One consequence of a Headed Records system is that there will be multiple repre-sentations both of knowledge and of skills. This will occur for a number of reasons. First of all, procedures corresponding to mental or physical skills will be represented in Records. Whenever such a developing skill is used and is changed as a result of this practice then there will be a new Record of the improved form of the proce-dure. However, the old form will remain, since there is no overwriting in the system. The new form will be used next time the procedure is called, following the recency principle, but the old form would be re-used if, for example, the context of use of the two forms had been different and the context for the old form were reinstated. This may seem to go against a body of evidence that has accumulated over the last 20 years con-cerning the unreliability and changeability of memory especially in the work of Loftus (1979) and Loftus and Ketcham (1991).

438

Loftus and her colleagues have demonstrated quite conclusively that memory performance is subject to change following false or misleading information. However, Bekerian and Bowers (1983) showed that at least one of Loftus's results could be reversed by a change in the testing conditions. The reconciliation is that, under questioning or testing, new Records are set up. To the extent to which the Heading on the new Record is the same as that on the old one, the more recent will be retrieved. Functionally, then, in many cases it will be as if the old memory is inaccessible.

AMNESIA

The most common cause of amnesia in adults is Korsakoff's syndrome. It is characterized by loss of ability to recall incidents from the past (retrograde amnesia), inability to recall current activities after intervals sometimes as short as a minute (anterograde amnesia) and often an almost normal performance in short-term memory tasks. Learning can take place for a variety of materials in spite of the patient denying that they have ever been in the situation before. My assumption is that the breakdown in organic amnesia is multifaceted and variable.

Baddeley (1984) has come the nearest to a characterization of amnesia that I have seen that approaches the complexity of its target. The starting point was what amnesics *can* learn. He points out that a wide range of amnesic patients show apparently normal learning both on verbal tasks and on complex and apparently semantically based perceptual tasks. What the tasks have in common is that they allow the patient to reflect learning without having to consider the provenance of the information that was used.

In an attempt to give this characterization of amnesic learning some theoretical force, Baddeley invokes a distinction between relatively automatic retrieval processes and the active problem-solving aspect of recall that he terms 'recollection'. Suppose, then, that amnesic patients lack the ability to recollect, although they can still build up and run off 'procedures'. The consequences of the disability would include:

(1) an inability to use incidental detail as confirmation of the correctness of something retrieved;
(2) an inability to reject incorrect associations produced by automatic procedures;
(3) an inability to iterate a retrieval cycle to follow clues and check them through memories with episodic characteristics.

Baddeley points out that the concept of recollection only goes a little way towards accounting for amnesia. Nonetheless it has the outstanding advantage that it is dynamic and makes contact with real memory phenomena.

Within an HR model there are a number of ways that apparent forgetting can take place. First, the material may not be laid down in either Headings or in Records. These problems would affect recognition and recall respectively. Secondly, particular kinds of information may not be represented in new Records. This could have the effect of the Record being rejected by the evaluation process on the basis of particular task specifications. This could also account for the massive increase in proactive interference in list learning with amnesics except where the contexts are exaggeratedly distinct (Winocur and Kinsbourne, 1978).

The third possibility is that Heading formation or Description formation might be altered. If both are altered then there would be no anterograde amnesia but there would be retrograde amnesia. This is the principle I have used to account for infantile amnesia (Morton, 1990). If Heading formation alone is changed then there could be no retrograde amnesia but there would be anterograde amnesia. Then, of course, these factors, together with others, could co-occur in ways which are unique, and we will find the need to define a number of subtypes.

Amnesia characterizes certain non-organic states such as multiple personality disorder (MPD). The manifestation of MPD is variable, but it seems possible to characterize the condition as one where part of the memory system is divided up into a number of mutually exclusive sets. Each personality can be seen as being able to access only one such set plus a common set of linguistic and other general information. In HR terms, this would be achieved by having a *self* marker in the Headings that had to be matched by a component of the Description during memory search. Whichever personality dominated the processing systems, the corresponding *self* marker would automatically be part of the Description, and Records lacking a matching component in the Heading could not be retrieved.

The opposite of forgetting is the creation of false memories. Loftus (1993) has described an ingenious method of inducing such memories under experimental conditions. Specifically, she and her colleagues showed that it was quite easy to make people believe that they had been lost on a particular occasion when they were five years old. Their technique involves getting a relative to recall a number of events that occurred in the subject's past, including the fictitious event. Sometimes after a few days, the subject comes to believe in the event, even retrieving confirmatory visual images and other of the indices we use in assessing our own recollection of real events.

There is other evidence to suggest that some of our recall of the past is reconstructive, without any awareness on our part, as Bartlett (1932) demonstrated. However, it is also clear that the demands of the questioning are quite crucial and that under some circumstances people can assess the reliability of their recall.

In sum, memory can be seen as a phenomenon that results from the interpretation of material selected from a retrieved Record which contains a selection of an individual's sensory experience of an external event in the past plus such bits of prior, related memories and default values that happened to get attached in the original process of Record formation or filled in at the time of recall. If it is a conceptual truth that no one can remember that p when p is false, it is a psychological truth that you can never remember.

See also ARTIFICIAL INTELLIGENCE; COGNITIVE PSYCHOLOGY; COMPUTATIONAL MODELS; CONSCIOUSNESS; REPRESENTATION.

BIBLIOGRAPHY

Anderson, J.R. 1976. *Language, Memory and Thought*. Hillsdale, NJ: Erlbaum.

Anderson, J.R. 1983. *Architecture of Cognition*. Cambridge, MA.: Harvard University Press.

Anderson, J.R., and Bower, G. 1973. *Human Associative Memory*, Washington, D.C.: Winston.

Baddeley, A.D. 1984. Neuropsychological evidence and the semantic/episodic distinction. *Behavioral and Brain Sciences*, 7, 238–9.

Bartlett, F.C. 1932. *Remembering*. Cambridge University Press.

Bekerian, D.A., and Bowers, J.M. 1983. Eyewitness testimony: Were we misled? *Journal of Experimental Psychology: Learning Memory and Cognition*, 9, 139–45.

Bower, G.H. 1981. Mood and memory. *American Psychologist*, 36, 129–48.

Eich, J.E. 1980. The cue-dependent nature of state-dependent retrieval. *Memory and Cognition*, 8, 157–73.

Godden, D.R., and Baddeley, A.D. 1975. Context-dependent memory in two natural environments: On land and under water. *British Journal of Psychology*, 66, 325–32.

Godden, D.R., and Baddeley, A.D. 1980. When does context influence recognition memory? *British Journal of Psychology*, 71, 99–104.

Hasher, L., Attig, M., and Alba, J. 1981. I knew it all along: Or did I? *Journal of Verbal Learning and Verbal Behavior*, 20, 86–96.

James, W. 1890. *Principles of Psychology*, vol. 1. New York: Holt.

Kintsch, W. 1974. *The representation of meaning in memory*. Hillsdale, N.J.: Lawrence Erlbaum.

Loftus, E.F. 1979. *Eyewitness Testimony*. Cambridge, MA.: Harvard University Press.

Loftus, E.F. 1993. The reality of repressed memories. *American Psychologist*, 48, 518–37.

Loftus, E.F., and Ketcham, K. 1991. *Witness for the Defence*. New York: St Martin's Press.

Martin, E. 1971. Verbal learning theory and independent retrieval phenomena. *Psychological Review*, 78, 314–32.

Morton, J. 1990. The development of event memory. *The Psychologist*, 3, 3–10.

Morton, J. 1991. Cognitive pathologies of memory: a headed records analysis. In *Memories, Thoughts, and Emotions: Essays in Honor of George Mandler*, ed. W. Kessen, A. Ortony, and F. Craik. Hillsdale, NJ: Erlbaum.

Morton, J., and Bekerian, D.A. 1986. Three ways of looking at memory. In *Advances in Cognitive Science 1*, ed. N. E. Sharkey. Chichester: Ellis Horwood.

Morton, J., Hammersley, R.H., and Bekerian, D.A. 1985. Headed records: A model for memory and its failures. *Cognition*, 20, 1–23.

Norman D.A. and Bobrow, D.G. 1979. Descriptions: an intermediate stage in memory retrieval. *Cognitive Psychology*, 11, 107–23.

Postman, L., and Underwood, B. 1973. Critical issues in interference theory. *Memory and Cognition*, 1, 19–40.

Raajmakers, J., and Shiffrin, R. 1980. SAM: A theory of probabilistic search of associative memory. In *The Psychology of Learning and Motivation*, vol. 14, ed. G. Bowes. New York: Academic Press.

Rumelhart, D. 1980. The building of blocks of cognition. In *Theoretical Issues in Reading Comprehension*, ed. R. Spiro, B. Bruce and W. Brewer. Hillsdale, NJ: Erlbaum.

Schank, R.C. 1980. Language and memory. *Cognitive Science*, 4, 243–84.

Schank, R.C., and Abelson, R.P. 1977. *Scripts Plans, Goals and Understanding: An Inquiry into Human Knowledge Structures*. Hillsdale, NJ: Erlbaum.

Winocur, G., and Kinsbourne, M. 1978. Contextual cuing as an aid to Korsakoff amnesics. *Neuropsychologia*, 16, 671–82.

Yekovitch, F.R., and Thorndyke, P. 1981. An evaluation of alternative functional models of narrative schemata. *Journal of Verbal Learning and Verbal Behavior*, 20, 454–69.

JOHN MORTON

mental representation When we think about the Eiffel Tower we can be said to represent it in our thought. In slightly different terminology, we can be said to possess a mental representation of the Eiffel Tower, and to differ in this from someone who lacks the means to think about that famous iron structure. So understood, a mental representation is simply a species of REPRESENTATION. However, deep and vexing problems arise when one tries to go beyond this minimal description and say more fully what kind of thing a mental representation is. Are thoughts somehow made up of mental presentations? Do mental representations have a causal and/or functional presence in the individual human mind or brain? And if they do have some such presence, are they like images, or more like linguistic signs? These questions set the agenda for a large part of contemporary philosophy of mind. *See* CONCEPTS; DENNETT; DRETSKE; FODOR; FUNCTIONALISM; IMAGERY; LANGUAGE OF THOUGHT.

SAMUEL GUTTENPLAN

mind–body problem *see An Essay on Mind* section 3; DAVIDSON; DUALISM; FODOR; FUNCTIONALISM; IDENTITY THEORIES; LEWIS; PHYSICALISM; RYLE; SEARLE; SUPERVENIENCE.

modality *see* POSSIBLE WORLD.

modularity One could stretch the use of the term 'modularity', and argue that even Plato held a doctrine of the modularity of mind (in the *Republic*) or that he explicitly rejected the modularity of long-term MEMORY (in the *Thaeatetus*). FODOR himself (1983) credits nineteenth-century phrenologist Gall with the idea of the modularity of mind. But in fact the modularity debate as it is currently framed in Cognitive Science derives straightforwardly from the argument advanced in Fodor's book *The Modularity of Mind* (1983) and the literature it inspired. Subsequent to the appearance of this influential volume, scholars and scientists in philosophy, COGNITIVE PSYCHOLOGY, ARTIFICIAL INTELLIGENCE and linguistics have all actively pursued research aimed at discovering which of the mind's subsystems are modular, and the respects and degrees to which they are so.

Broadly speaking, a module is a relatively autonomous component of the mind – one which, while it interacts with, receives input from and sends output to, other cognitive processes or structures, performs its own internal information processing unperturbed by external systems. The theory of a single module and its operation could hence, with the exception of mentioning its input and output interfaces, in the ideal case, be developed without ever mentioning the remainder of the mind. Following Fodor, for a process to be modular is for it to satisfy these eight conditions, the first four of which played the greatest role in the empirical assessment of the modularity hypothesis: (1) domain specificity; (2) mandatoriness; (3) informational encapsulation; (4) speed; (5) shallow output; (6) lack of access of other processes to intermediate representations; (7) neural localization; (8) succeptibility to characteristic breakdown.

Typically, input and output modules – those responsible for PERCEPTION and ACTION – are candidates for modularity. It is much less plausible to argue that central processes such as those recruited in inductive reasoning or interpreting Platonic dialogues are subserved by modules. For one thing, such central processes demand broad access to a wide range of knowledge. For another, it would be bizarre to suggest that evolutionary processes would issue in the existence of special neural structures devoted to these tasks. Perception and motor control, on the other hand, are typically highly data-driven, and the processes subserving them plausibly respond fairly directly to selection pressure. Debates in contemporary cognitive science concerning the modularity hypothesis typically focus on one or more of the following questions. (1) Which cognitive faculties, if any, exhibit all or most of these characteristics? (2) Does this list of characteristics in fact cluster and determine a cognitive 'natural kind', or is there a more felicitous characterization of what are intuitively modular systems?

(3) Are cognitive modules part of the innate cognitive architecture of the human mind or is modularity, to the extent that it is present, an artefact of learning or other developmental processes? (See DEVELOPMENTAL PSYCHOLOGY.)

Let us consider each of these characteristics and the way they figure in current debates concerning modularity in cognitive science. When we ask of a cognitive capacity whether it is *domain specific*, we are asking whether it has as its object a unique and idiosyncratic domain. So, for instance, the claim that the phonological analysis system is modular would be the claim that there are specific auditory processes or capabilities that are brought into play for speech analysis that are not recruited for any other kind of hearing – for instance for listening to music, and that these processes are triggered by and exploit unique features of human speech. Domains that have been argued by modularists to have such unique features and for the analysis of which dedicated modules have evolved include human language, human speech, medium-sized visual objects, depth relations, and motor control.

Critics of general modularity claims or of claims to the domain specificity of a particular candidate module typically argue that the processes to which modularists advert are in fact instances of more general cognitive processes that are recruited across domains, or that even plausibly central processes can be highly domain specific. For instance Fodor and others argue that on-line language processing recruits domain-specific processes, since the mechanisms called upon to transduce speech sounds into linguistic representations – whether these outputs are characterized as phonological or syntactic representations – do not operate on, say, automobile noise or bird songs. Arbib (1972, 1979, 1989), Arbib and Hanson (1987), Arbib, Boylls and Deb (1974) and Stillings (1989) among others point out, on the other hand, that the fact that the sighted can learn to read type, that the blind can learn to read braille and that the deaf can learn to use sign suggests that the parsing mechanism can hardly be specialized to the domain of speech signals. Moreover, contemporary connectionist models of language learning (Rumelhart and McClelland, 1986; Rumelhart, Hinton and Williams, 1986) challenge the idea that even phonological and syntactic parsing are idiosyncratic processes 'wired in' to the cognitive architecture for the purposes of linguistic processing (*see* CONNECTIONISM). These models suggest that they may only be specific instances of general learning and perceptual processing strategies fine-tuned by training to linguistic processing. This line of argument gains further support from the observation that skill acquisition results in performance having exactly the characteristics Fodor and others ascribe to modules: speed, mandatory operation, encapsulation, and perhaps even localization. This is a quite general feature of models of skill acquisition, despite other architectural differences, and so is apparent in production systems as well as connectionist systems. (*see* Stillings (1989a, 1989b). Karmiloff-Smith (1979, 1985, 1986, 1990, 1993) however, points out that much of this may be accounted for by the propensity of the mind to acquire modules that are not innately specified.

Modularists argue that modules are *mandatory* in operation. We don't have a choice regarding whether to bring our scene recognition mechanisms to bear on incoming visual data. Objects emerge from the optic array whether we would prefer a 'bloomin, buzzin confusion' or not. Similarly, we have no choice about whether to regard a sequence of words uttered in our native language as a linguistic expression or a non-linguistic soundstream. But we can choose what to think about – modularity or cricket, for instance. Mandatoriness makes good sense as Fodor (1989) notes for systems that are designed to detect features of the immediate environment that have significant implications for survival, and for systems designed to act on that environment when speed makes a difference. Where it is important to act quickly, it is an advantage to have a system that acts automatically. On the other hand, central cognitive processes

must, if they are to be flexible enough to serve their function – presumably that of allowing us to adapt our behaviour to the variable demands of our physical and social environments – be subject to voluntary control. Modularists point to the phenomena to which we have just adverted to argue that perceptual and motor processes typically are mandatory. (The mandatory character of motor processes is actually a bit delicate to spell out: we certainly have the ability to decide to act, say, to type, to walk, or to speak, and motor action is voluntary in that sense. But we don't have the ability, unless we really work at it, to determine via conscious control the trajectories of our fingers over the keyboard, the precise movements of our legs, or the positions our tongues and lips adopt as we speak. To place these under conscious control, we cease to simply move, and begin to act, in the theatrical sense of that term, at least according to modularity theory.)

Critics of modular claims, on the other hand, point out that many central processes seem to be mandatory in the same sense that modularists claim that modular peripheral processes must be. Marslen-Wilson and Tyler (1989), for instance, point out that mapping linguistic input onto discourse representation is as mandatory as speech recognition or syntactic parsing. But inasmuch as discourse representation recruits central processes, this observation would seem to undermine the modularity thesis. Moreover, many obviously central processes seem to be mandatory. While we have a great deal of voluntary control over what we think about, we often find what we think about is forced upon us, and we have no reason to believe that we have any more control over the microprocesses of abstract thought than over those involved in locomotion or speech.

When modularists argue that modular processes are *informationally encapsulated* they mean that cognitive modules have no access to information from elsewhere in the cognitive system (except of course for the initial input into an output system). All of the information available to a module comes directly from its own subsystems or from their dedicated input devices. So, according to modularists, when processing incoming speech, my parser has access only to its internally represented grammar and to the acoustic properties of the speech signal; when viewing the Müller–Lyer illusion, my visual system has access only to the visible properties of the drawing, and not, importantly, to my own knowledge that the main lines are in fact of equal length. Central processes, on the other hand, share knowledge freely. When I reason about cognitive science, for instance, it is important that my knowledge about the history of philosophy is able to interact with my ability to reason deductively and my knowledge of cognitive psychology. But none of this knowledge helps me a bit, according to the modularist, when my visual recognition system or my parser is called upon to interpret incoming data. After all, the assignment of a semantic value to a sentence requires first determining its syntactic structure and logical form, and the information needed to do this is entirely represented in the phonological and syntactic portion of the grammar. Informational encapsulation is at the very heart of the modularity thesis. For this characteristic of a system is what ensures that it is really autonomous in operation from the remainder of the mind.

Anti-modularists cite a variety of phenomena as putative counterexamples to the claim that input and output modules are in fact encapsulated. Altmann (1986), Marslen-Wilson (1975, 1980) and Marslen-Wilson and Tyler (1989), for instance, argue that general knowledge and context penetrate the syntactic parsing of sentences. Miller (1977, 1981) presents evidence that syntactic information can drive phonological processing. And even plausibly encapsulated movements can be penetrated by intentions to act differently. Arbib (1989) suggests as well that much visual computation, even at fairly low levels, is influenced by representations that penetrate the visual system from more central cognitive processes.

Modular processes are, according to modularity theory, very fast. In fact speed is one good diagnostic characteristic of a system in determining whether it is modular, and the speed of input analysis and output execution is often used as a premise in arguments for modularity. Fodor (1983, 1987) for instance, argues that since perceptual processes are fast, and since it takes time to decide which of a vast store of general knowledge to bring to bear on problem solving, modular processes must be encapsulated. He also argues that the speed of modular processes derives in part from their mandatoriness: the fact that there is no need to decide whether to bring a modular process into play or how to do so eliminates planning time from total response time. And of course speed is achieved by the evolutionary tailoring of the modular system to its particular domain. Whereas a general-purpose system achieves its generality at the expense of efficiency in any one domain, modular systems are useless in domains other than their proper ones precisely because they have evolved to be optimal in their particular domains. And indeed the contrasts between on-line sentence processing in one's native tongue and deliberate parsing of a sentence in an unfamiliar language using explicit grammatical knowledge, or between walking naturally and imitating someone else's walk are dramatic.

The argument from the speed with which allegedly modular systems operate to their modularity is, however, non-demonstrative. It relies on the important premise that speed in perceptual and motor processing is achieved by serial computations utilizing efficient algorithms that operate on a constrained range of data. That is indeed one way to achieve speed. But there are others. As Fodor acknowledges, Bruner argued – and more recent connectionist work on perception has supported this view – that speed can also be bought by the efficient exploitation of a wide range of relevant knowledge if that knowledge is felicitously represented. Connectionist perceptual networks accomplish highly efficient and plausibly psychologically realistic recognition and categorization using distributed representation systems that make all of the system's knowledge relevant to each discrimination. These systems violate encapsulation, and, when suitably integrated or generalized, may turn out to violate domain specificity as well (McClelland, 1988; McClelland and Rumelhart, 1981; Jacobs et al., 1991).

There is another line of criticism against the argument from speed to other modular properties. Highly skilled behaviour becomes quite rapid. The classic work of de Groot (1966) and Chase and Simon (1973) on chess perception, as well as the phenomenon of athletic or musical skill development show that it is possible to develop highly rapid processing of phenomena to which it is highly implausible that there is a domain-specific module dedicated. These phenomena raise the possibility that such phenomena as sentence parsing or visual scene analysis may be so fast simply because they are so well-practised.

It is essential to the view of the mind as comprising a non-modular central processing system together with a set of modular input/output faculties that the input faculties deliver relatively shallow representations – that is, that this information be given in a rather 'raw' state. For if the input presented by the perceptual faculties were to be too highly processed, those faculties would require far more knowledge than is permitted by encapsulation. Correspondingly, the instructions delivered to output modules must be highly processed motor programs, requiring no interpretation on the part of those modules that would demand the use of central processes or more general data structures.

Arguments concerning the interface between the centre and the periphery are vexed, and are hard to assess independently of the fate of the remainder of the modularity hypothesis. For if the modular view of the mind is accepted, then the shallow output condition follows simply from the fact that so much of language understanding – in particular discourse representation – is driven by background knowledge and reasoning, and from the fact that we can

plan our movements. On the other hand, arguments such as those of Marslen-Wilson and Tyler (1989), Forster (1980, 1981) and others suggest that discourse representation, or other forms of semantic evaluation, are as fast and mandatory as any 'purely' perceptual or syntactic processes, and even casual observation of athletic performance suggests that very complex movements can be planned by a skilled actor. These considerations tend to push the boundaries of candidate modules towards the centre to a degree that must make modularists uncomfortable. For then the boundary between non-modular central processes and modules becomes theoretically insignificant, and the distinction becomes one of degree rather than of kind.

Another important consequence of the modular view is that central processes will have no access to the intermediate representations produced or utilized by the modules. For the modules by definition interact with central processes, including attentional processes, only at their proper interfaces. This is a happy consequence for the modularity view, since it accords both with naïve intuition and with the striking disparity between the deliverances of psychological and psycholinguistic research on the one hand and our introspective awareness on the other: It seems overwhelmingly plausible that underlying even the simplest cognitive operations, to which we have only the vaguest introspective access, there are countless cognitive processes running automatically. As you read this sentence, for instance, there are stages of visual analysis, lexical access, syntactic representation, logical form analysis and semantic evaluation which we can only hypothesize based upon our best theories, but which we can never observe. The modularity hypothesis gives us a tidy explanation of the lack of introspective awareness of these stages of processing (see INTROSPECTION): they occur inside modules, and central processes have access only to the outputs of modules, and awareness is a central process.

On the other hand, critics of modularity

will point out that we lack introspective awareness of many of our cognitive processes, prominently including many that the modularity theory would regard as central. As Kahneman and Tversky and their associates have demonstrated, our own views about the processes we use in logical and statistical inference are often far off the mark, and we have no reliable introspective access to the processes we in fact use. So while it is true that modularity correctly predicts our inability to introspect too far into our perceptual and motor processes, the fact that we also need an explanation of our inability to introspect our central processes, in the view of critics of modularity, diminishes the confirmatory virtues of this consequence.

The final two characteristics of modular system are tightly connected, and may best be discussed together: modular systems are, according to standard modularity theory, neurally localized and are subject to characteristic and isolated patterns of breakdown. This second characteristic is, of course, a straightforward consequence of the first. If each cognitive module is subserved by a specific local neural structure then it should be possible to selectively impair the function of a single module through injury to the specific structure in which it is realized. This is an important empirical prediction for modularity theory, and represents an area of research that has been on balance highly favourable to the modularist viewpoint. For a wealth of recent neurophysiological evidence supports the view that such systems as vision, audition, olfaction, language perception, proprioception, motor control and speech production are largely localized in specific areas of the brain, and that, *modulo* some neural plasticity that allows variable recovery of function, injury to these specific areas causes significant degradation in the function of the corresponding cognitive modules.

The fact that the brain has evolved in such a way as to incorporate specific 'dedicated processors' supports the general viewpoint of modularity theory: it suggests that there are anatomical structures that are domain-specific in their function, at least with respect to some specification of domain. The verifiable fact that these structures are active whenever their appropriate stimulus conditions are present supports the mandatoriness thesis. The presence of such dedicated structures explains the speed of modular processes in a way harmonious with that in which modularism seeks to explain such speed for independent reasons. The satisfaction by the candidate modules of the remaining conditions – encapsulation, shallowness of output, and lack of access of central processes to intermediate representations – are neither directly confirmed nor disconfirmed by these data. But the fact of localization suggests that further neuroanatomical study of the connectivity of these modular sections of the brain to those sections subserving general cognition and the other modules might shed light on these questions.

Neuroanatomical data however do not at this stage settle the modularity question. For one thing, localization is not as neat as this picture suggests. Many areas of the brain are activated in the course of, for example, visual perception or language understanding, including areas thought to be involved with memory and reasoning. Such phenomena may lend comfort to anti-modularists. Moreover, on some partition of the brain, even semantic memory is going to turn out to be local. The choice of what to consider a theoretically relevant boundary in the brain depends to some degree on what one is looking for. And no modularist would want such a localization to count in favour of such a central process as semantic memory counting as modular. In that case *everything* would be a module, and the theory would collapse. Finally, even if there is relative localization of function, and even if these locales should be modular in many senses, the patterns of connectivity in the brain might be such that so much information passes between so many levels of so many modules that their distinctively modular character is lost. All of these, of course, are empirical matters, and all remain to be settled.

Before closing it is worth considering the relationship between connectionism and modularity. For connectionist models of cognitive processes are becoming increasingly prominent in cognitive science, and it is often claimed (Churchland, 1986, 1989) that these models are incompatible with 'classical' views of cognitive processes including, presumably, modularist views. Connectionism might seem especially threatening to modularity theory in that connectionist models typically emphasize the broad connectivity of their networks and the distributed character of their representations, whereas modular models typically emphasize the insular character of peripheral processing and the localized character of representations and the processes operating thereon. But though the general outlooks that motivate connectionism and modularity may be at odds, it would be incorrect to conclude that connectionist models are inherently non-modular. As Tannenhaus, Dell and Carlson (1989) have shown, it is quite possible to construct modular connectionist networks. And it could well turn out that the arguments and programmes of modularists and connectionists could converge in a model of a connectionist but modular cognitive architecture in which distinct regions of a vast network are dedicated to specific cognitive tasks and are only weakly connected to other regions, save for strong local 'output' or 'input' connections.

This survey in no way exhausts the literature or debates concerning modularity, and should suggest no correct answer to any specific modularity debate, let alone to the debate as a whole. Most if not all of the interesting questions are empirical, and the current state of our understanding of human cognition leaves all of them unsettled.

See also COMPUTATIONAL MODELS.

BIBLIOGRAPHY

Altmann, G.T. 1986. Reference and the resolution of local syntactic ambiguity: The effect of context during human sentences processing. Ph.D. Dissertation, University of Edinburgh.

Arbib, M.A. 1972. *The Metaphorical Brain: An Introduction to Cybernetics as Artificial Intelligence and Brain Theory.* Wiley-Interscience.

Arbib, M.A. 1989. Modularity and interaction of brain regions underlying visoumotor coordination. In J.L. Garfield 1989.

Arbib, M.A., and A.R. Hanson, eds. 1987. *Vision, Brain, and Cooperative Computation.* Cambridge, MA.: MIT Press.

Arbib, M.A., C.C. Boylls, and P. Dev. 1974. Neural models of spatial perception and the control of movement. In Keidel et al.

Chase, W.G., and H.A. Simon. 1973. The Mind's eye in chess. In Chase 1973.

Churchland, Paul M. 1989. *A Neurocomputational Perspective: The Nature of Mind and the Structure of Science.* Cambridge, MA. MIT Press.

Churchland, P.S. 1986. *Neurophilosophy Toward a Unified Science of the Mind–Brain.* Cambridge, MA.: MIT Press.

de Groot, Andriaan D. 1966. Perception and memory versus thought: Some old ideas and recent findings. In *Problem Solving*, ed. B. Kleinmuntz.

Fodor, J.A. 1975. *The Language of Thought.* Crowell.

Fodor, J.A. 1979. Superstrategy. In Cooper and Walker.

Fodor, J.A. 1981. Methodological solipsism considered as a research strategy in psychology. In *Representation: Philosophical Essays on the Foundations of Cognitive Science*, ed. J. A. Fodor. Cambridge, MA. MIT Press.

Fodor, J.A. 1983. *The Modularity of Mind.* Cambridge, MA.: MIT Press.

Fodor, J.A. 1989. Modules, frames, fridgeons, sleeping dogs, and the music of the spheres. In J. L. Garfield 1989.

Fodor, J.A., T.G. Bever. 1965. The psychological reality of linguistic segments. *Journal of Verbal Learning and Verbal Behavior*, 4, 414–20.

Fodor, J.A., and I. Sag. 1982. Referential and quantificational indefinites. *Linguistics and Philosophy*, 5, 344–89.

Fodor, J.A., T.G. Bever, and M.F. Garret. 1974. *The Psychology of Language: An Introduction to Psycholinguistics and Generative Grammar*, McGraw-Hill.

Forster, K.I. 1980. Absence of lexical and orthographic effects in a same-different task. *Memory and Cognition*, 8, 210–15.

Forster, K.I. 1981. Priming and the effects of sentence and lexical contexts on naming time: Evidence for autonomous lexical processing. *Quarterly Journal of Experimental Psychology*, 33, 465–95.

Garfield, J.L. 1989. *The Modularity of Mind*. Cambridge, MA.: MIT Press.

Jacobs, R.A., Jordan, M.I., and Barton, A.G. 1991. Task decomposition through competition in a modular connectionist architecture: The what and where vision tasks. *Cognition*, 15, 195–212.

Karmiloff-Smith, A. 1979. *A functional approach to child language*. Cambridge University Press.

Karmiloff-Smith, A. 1985. Language and cognitive processes from a developmental perspective. *Language and Cognitive Processes*, 1, 61–85.

Karmiloff-Smith, A. 1986. From meta-processes to conscious access: evidence from children's drawing. *Cognition*, 23, 95–147.

Karmiloff-Smith, A. 1990. Constraints on representational change: evidence from children's drawing. *Cognition*, 34, 57–83.

Karmiloff-Smith, A. 1993. *Beyond modularity: A developmental perspective on cognitive science*. Cambridge, MA.: MIT Press.

Marslen-Wilson, W.D. 1975. The Limited compatibility of linguistics and perceptual explanations. In *CLS Papers from the Parasession on Functionalism*.

Marslen-Wilson, W.D. 1980. Sentence perception as an interactive parallel process. *Science*, 198, 226–8.

Marslen-Wilson, W.D., and A. Welsh. Processing interactions and lexical access during world recognition in continuous speech. *Cognitive Psychology*, 10, 29–63.

Marslen-Wilson, W.D., and L.K. Tyler. 1975. Processing structure of sentence perception, *Nature*, 257, 784–6.

Marslen-Wilson, W.D., and L.K. Tyler. 1980. The temporal structure of spoken language understanding. *Cognition*, 8, 1–71.

Marslen-Wilson, W.D., and L.K. Tyler. 1989. Against modularity. In J.L. Garfield 1989.

McClelland, J.L. 1988. Connectionist models and psychological evidence. *Journal of Memory and Language*, 27, 429–39.

McClelland, J.L., and Rumelhart, D.E. 1981. An interactive activation model of context effects. In letter perception. I: An account of basic findings. *Psychological Review*, 88, 357–407.

Miller, J.L., ed. 1977. *Systems Neuroscience*. Academic Press.

Miller, J.L. 1981. Effects of speaking late on segmental distinctions. In Ellis, 1985.

Plunkett, K., and Marchman, V. 1990. Regular and irregular morphology and the psychological status of rules of grammar. In *Proceedings of the 17th Annual Meeting of the Berkeley Linguistics Society*. Berkeley, CA.: Berkeley Linguistics Society.

Plunkett, K., and Marchman, V. 1991. U-shaped learning and frequency effects in a multilayered perception: implications for child language acquisition. *Cognition*, 38, 43–102.

Rumelhart, D.E., and McClelland, J.L. 1986. On learning the past tenses of English verbs. In *Parallel distributed Processing: Explorations in the Microstructure of Cognition. Vol. 2: Psychological and Biological Models*, ed. J. L. McClelland, D. E. Rumelhart, and the PDP Research Group. Cambridge MA.: MIT Press/Bradford Books.

Rumelhart, D.E., Hinton, G.E., and Williams, D. 1986. Learning internal representations by error propagation. In *Parallel Distributed Processing: Explorations in the Microstructure of Cognition. Vol. 1: Foundations*, ed. D.E. Rumelhart, J.L. McClelland, and the PDP Research Group. Cambridge, MA.: MIT Press/Bradford Books.

Stillings, N. 1989a. Introduction. In J.L. Garfield 1989.

Stillings, N. 1989b. Modularity and naturalism in theory of vision. In J.L. Garfield 1989.

Tanenhaus, M.A., Gary, S. Dell., and Greg Carlson. 1989. Context effects and lexical processing: A connectionist approach to modularity. In J.L. Garfield 1989.

Tversky, A. 1982. *Judgement Under Uncertainty: Heuristics and biases*. Cambridge University Press.

JAY L. GARFIELD

monadic *see* PROPERTY.

multiple realization *see* FUNCTIONALISM; IDENTITY THEORIES; SUPERVENIENCE.

N

---

narrow/broad content *see An Essay on Mind* section 2.1.3; CONTENT; EXTERNAL-ISM/INTERNALISM.

naturalism Naturalism with respect to some realm is the view that everything that exists in that realm, and all those events that take place in it, are empirically accessible features of the world. Sometimes naturalism is taken to imply that some realm can be in principle understood by appeal to the laws and theories of the natural sciences, but one must be careful here since naturalism does not by itself imply anything about reduction. Historically, 'natural' contrasts with 'supernatural', but in the context of contemporary philosophy of mind where debate centres around the possibility of explaining mental phenomena as part of the natural order, it is the *non-natural* rather than the supernatural that is the contrasting notion. The naturalist holds that they can be so explained, whilst the opponent of naturalism thinks otherwise, though it is not intended that opposition to naturalism commits one to anything supernatural.

'Naturalism' is often used interchangeably with 'PHYSICALISM' and 'materialism', though each of these hints at more specific doctrines. Thus, 'physicalism' suggests that, among the natural sciences, there is something especially fundamental about physics. And 'materialism' has connotations going back to eighteenth- and nineteenth-century views of the world as essentially made of material particles whose behaviour is fundamental for explaining everything else. Moreover, as noted above, one should not take naturalism in regard to some realm as committing one to any sort of reductive explanation of that realm, and

there are such commitments in the use of 'physicalism' and 'materialism'.

See also DENNETT; FODOR; LEWIS.

SAMUEL GUTTENPLAN

natural kind The collection or set of things that are, have been, or will be in someone's briefcase is a heterogeneous one; there is probably nothing which the members of this set have in common except their presence in the briefcase. In contrast, there are sets of things that have a more unified or homogeneous membership, e.g. the set of typewriters and the set of tigers. The members of each of these have features or PROPERTIES in common (or at least overlapping) that give the sets their unity and make it appropriate to call them 'kinds'. To understand the concept of a natural kind, one must focus on the difference between kinds as represented by the set of typewriters and those as represented by the set of tigers.

Typewriters and tigers are certainly kinds of thing, but there is an important difference. Tigers have evolved to become a species whose offspring are caused genetically to resemble one another. In contrast, typewriters, being an invention of ours, do not by nature come to share properties. If anything it is the other way around: we use our knowledge of nature to turn bits of metal and plastic into devices that perform the typewriting function of making our words visible. Tigers thus form a *natural kind*, whereas typewriters form an *artificial kind*.

Though *tiger* is a central case, there are features of this example which could mislead someone into thinking of natural

449

kinds too restrictively. For one thing, philosophers have spoken of natural kinds where evolution and genetics have no role: gold is often cited as a natural kind and the members of this kind – atoms of gold – certainly do not have a common biological background, though they do share certain physical properties. Yet it is not merely the sharing of properties – whether biological or physical – that makes the idea of a natural kind philosophically important. What is crucial to the notion is that the shared properties have an independence from any particular human way of conceiving of the members of the kind. Thus, we think of tigers as having stripes and living in jungles, and we think of gold as yellow, malleable and used in making jewellery. But insofar as each is a natural kind, we must allow that our usual ways of thinking of these things might be wrong. For example, it is intelligible that something belong to the kind *tiger* though it lacked stripes – perhaps we just haven't yet come across tigers like that; or that gold might be found which was not yellow and malleable. This is because what makes something a tiger or gold is a matter of what is sometimes called its 'real essence' – that set of properties shared by members of the kind, whether we have discovered them or not. Gold is a particularly good example here because we have only recently discovered that what is crucial to this kind is that its members are atoms with atomic number 79. Before the atomic theory had been worked out, people knew that this or that substance was gold, but they didn't properly know what made something a member of the kind.

It is this feature of natural kinds that gives the concept a certain prominence in philosophy of mind. For example, a common way of discussing the status of beliefs is to ask: do beliefs form a natural kind? Those who answer 'yes' think that there are discoverable, though not yet discovered, features of beliefs which give them the required unity. Among the possibilities here are that beliefs are a certain type of brain state, a certain type of functional state, or a state that has evolved to play a

certain role in human endeavour. (*See* CONTENT; FUNCTIONALISM; IDENTITY THEORIES.) But however one spells it out, the idea is that, in being a natural kind, belief has a real essence which could be revealed by the right kind of research. Those who demur tend to think of belief more as something that human beings have invented for certain purposes, but that does not have anything like an elusive real essence.

SAMUEL GUTTENPLAN

neurophysiology   *see* PAIN.

normative   As a rule, satellites follow elliptical orbits, and, also as a rule, drivers in the UK keep to the left side of the road. But there is a big difference between these two sorts of rule-guided behaviours: satellites are *governed* by the rules or laws of motion; whereas drivers *choose to follow* the rules of the road. In this second case, one speaks of the rules as norms. Moreover, though this is more controversial, it has been maintained that one can speak of normativity even when there is no exercise of explicit choice in the relevant behaviour. Thus, many linguists, following CHOMSKY, think of our use of language as a case of rule-following even though speakers are not usually aware of the relevant norms.

The notion of normativity, in a slightly different guise, figures in other areas of the philosophy of mind. Firstly, it is often said that the attribution of propositional attitudes is normative, though it may not be immediately apparent what rules or norms are at issue in this case. What is meant is roughly this: there are standards of RATIONALITY that govern our attribution of attitudes to each other even though it may well be impossible to spell these standards out in terms of specific rules or norms. For example, it seems plausible that we cannot attribute beliefs about atoms and electrons to a child of three. The 'cannot' here marks the fact that it would not be rationally explicable or intelligible that such a young child could have acquired the concepts necessary to have such beliefs. (*See* DAVIDSON.)

Secondly, it has been maintained that the very possession of CONCEPTS is a normative matter. The computerized robot which can sort nuts and bolts by size and shape operates according to rules. But these rules are those the programmers have built in – the robot itself no more aims to conform to rules than do satellites in earth orbit. For this reason, though the robot has a discriminative ability in respect of nuts and bolts, one might well resist the idea that the robot has the concepts of a nut or a bolt. To have a concept one has to have the idea that one is *justified* in making the relevant discriminations, and such talk of justification is of a piece with talk of rationality and intelligibility – it is a matter of being guided by rules in a fully normative sense.

The above brief discussion may make it seem as if there is a clear line between rule-governed and rule-guided behaviour, but in fact it is a matter of great controversy how one is to spell out this difference (*see* WITTGENSTEIN). And it is also a matter of great importance for our understanding of such things such as language use, concept possession and the attribution of propositional attitudes.

SAMUEL GUTTENPLAN

O, P

ontology Ontology is the branch of metaphysics centrally concerned with determining what there is. (The name comes from the present participle of the Greek verb corresponding to the English verb 'to be'.) Thus, if one asks whether there are numbers and other abstract objects, or whether there are PROPERTIES, one is asking ontological questions. Given the fundamental nature of these questions, ontology plays a part in virtually all areas of philosophical investigation, but it has a specific importance to certain debates within the philosophy of mind. For example, suppose one agrees that, besides particular things such as books and tables, there are also properties of these things (such as being made of wood or paper) and relations among them (such as the book's lying on the table). Allowing properties and relations the same sort of reality or existence as particular things is by no means uncontroversial. Many philosophers think that one should keep one's ontological commitments to the minimum, and these philosophers – known as 'nominalists' – would count only particular physical objects as ontologically suitable. But even if you are willing to accept properties and relations into your ontology, it is still a further question whether you would count, e.g. beliefs as properties of persons and/or as relations between persons and belief contents. This sort of question about belief is ontological, and such questions figure widely in most areas of philosophy of mind. Discussions of consciousness and action are often cast as debates about the ontological status of such things as pains, sensations of colour, qualia and particular instances of action. (*See An Essay on Mind* section 2.1; DENNETT; FODOR; LEWIS.)

SAMUEL GUTTENPLAN

pain (perceptual properties and neural mechanisms) Pain is an unpleasant sensory experience that is typically associated with bodily injury and/or is described by people using terms that imply bodily injury or damage. Pain is virtually universal amongst humans and probably all other mammalian species. Though common, the experience is personal. Furthermore, the language used to communicate the experience to others encompasses an enormous variety of words, phrases, and metaphors. Despite its subjective nature and complexities, neural and psychological studies have provided insights into the mechanisms of pain. In this chapter we will focus upon what is known of the nature of bodily pain and the neural mechanisms that are considered to subserve it.

THE NATURE OF PAIN

Although pain has the general properties of a sensory experience, it has, in addition, features beyond sensation that make it both more complex and of interest to a range of people other than sensory physiologists. The most important distinguishing feature of pain is its affective-motivational aspect. In contrast to most other sensations, the pain experience necessarily includes a quality of unpleasantness and the wish for its immediate termination. Thus pain is one of the major forces, along with pleasure, that can shape behaviour.

THE SUBJECTIVE EXPERIENCE OF BODILY PAIN

(1) 'Pain' refers to a subjective experience (*see* SUBJECTIVITY), an unpleasant sensation, that is felt in a particular location

452

within the body. In addition to location, the other simple sensory properties of pain include intensity and duration. Location and intensity may vary with time.

(2) In common with all somatic sensations, pain has the property of sensory quality (*see* QUALIA). Quality is a compound property that distinguishes a specific type of pain from non-painful sensations and from different types of pain. For example, aching and burning are different qualities. The quality of a pain is often described in terms of a stimulus that might elicit it (i.e. burning, pricking or tearing). These terms often convey the sense of penetration, intrusion and assault upon the body. The quality of a pain is in part determined by the temporal and spatial variation of its primary properties (e.g. a brief sharp throbbing pain that radiates into the wrist).

(3) In addition to the intensity of the stimulus that elicits it, the intensity of perceived pain is influenced by powerful modifying factors. These factors include the attention, expectation and state of arousal of the subject. For example, when two stimuli are applied simultaneously at different sites on the body, one stimulus may enhance or suppress the sensation resulting from the other stimulus. The effect of one stimulus on the sensation evoked by a second stimulus depends on the proximity of the two stimuli and their relative intensities (e.g. biting one's lip may ease the pain of a sprained ankle). Another example is that identical noxious stimuli, when repeatedly applied at the same site, evoke pain sensations that progressively increase in intensity and area.

(4) The experience of pain characteristically includes a negative EMOTION. This emotion is experienced by human subjects as the desire to escape, to terminate the sensation. When the sensation is intense and/or prolonged or its duration uncertain, the experience includes anxiety and/or depression. This negative emotional component is called the affective-motivational dimension of pain to distinguish it from the sensory-discriminative dimensions described in (1) and (2) above.

(5) The negative effect of pain confers upon it the power, along with pleasure, to shape behaviour. This motivational power assures pain a place of great and unique importance relative to other sensations. Obviously, better understanding of learning, MEMORY and the human personality requires a fuller understanding of pain. The reverse is also true. Thus pain is a fascinating object of study not only for neuroscientists but for medical scientists, psychologists, philosophers and theologians.

(6) As with all other sensory phenomena, pain has a cognitive-evaluative component. This component represents both an abstraction and synthesis of the sensory and affective dimensions. Thus you might be aware of a severe pain in your heel which forces you to stop walking. The cognitive-evaluative aspect of pain may involve remembering how far you will have to walk and weighing the decision to endure the unpleasant sensations against not getting to work on time.

This dimension of pain includes its meaning. In some situations the meaning of a pain is by far its most important dimension to the individual. For example, the development of even mild pain in a patient being treated for cancer may be terrifying and depressing if it is believed 'o signify recurrence of a malignant tumour.

(7) The sensory, affective and evaluative dimensions of pain have lawful inter-relationships. The examples cited in (6) illustrate how affect can be closely tied to meaning. In humans, psychological studies confirm that the affective dimension of pain can be powerfully reduced or increased by factors such as psychological set and personality traits or by manipulations such as hypnosis or distraction.

(8) Duration is a critical factor that influences pain. Clinically, the persistence of pain is associated with profound changes in the affective and evaluative dimensions of pain. Whereas acute pain (minutes to hours and days) is associated with restlessness, arousal and fear, chronic pain (weeks to months and years) is associated with resignation, depression, reduced activ-

ity, and preoccupation with all bodily sensations.

The nervous system can be envisaged as the organ of CONSCIOUSNESS, and its properties constrain what is accessible to the conscious mind. When certain noxious stimuli are applied to appropriately innervated parts of the body, a coded message is 'delivered' to the brain. The result is a series of tissue-protective responses plus the subjective experience of pain. In this section we will briefly outline what is known of the neural elements involved in generating the different dimensions of pain: their location, connectivity and coding properties.

Since a major goal of pain research is to explain the experience of pain in terms of the activity of neurons, parallel psychophysical and neurophysiological studies have been very informative. This approach makes it possible to compare subjective responses reported by human subjects with neuronal responses using identical stimuli. Such an approach allows neuroscientists to determine how neural information related to pain is processed and transformed at various levels of the nervous system.

It is important to point out that pain is the subjective accompaniment of activity in specific nervous system pathways. A major function of activity in these pathways is to protect the tissues of the body from damage. Thus, stimuli which elicit the sensation of pain characteristically produce tissue-protective responses including withdrawal or escape from the offending stimulus, increased blood flow to the affected area and increased vigilance. Furthermore, such stimuli produce changes that lead to our learning to avoid situations similar to those previously associated with pain.

Primary Afferent Nociceptors, Adequate Stimuli, Access to the Nervous System
(1) There are nerve endings in most bodily tissues that selectively respond to stimuli (e.g. pinching, burning) that usually cause pain. These nerve endings are called nociceptors. They respond to mechanical distortion, damage, deformation, or intense thermal stimulation of the tissues they innervate. Nociceptors also respond to local increases in the concentration of chemicals that are produced by tissue damage.

(2) Nociceptors are transducers, which means that they transform one form of energy of (i.e. thermal, mechanical or chemical stimuli) to another form, electrochemical impulses, which can be transmitted and interpreted by the central nervous system.

(3) Each nociceptor is connected to a cell process called the axon through which it communicates to the central nervous system. Together, the nerve ending, its axon and the cell body that supports it are called the primary afferent nociceptor (*see* figure 1). In the usual course of events, a noxious stimulus leads to a transduction event that produces electrochemical impulses in primary afferent nociceptors. The electrochemical impulses (called spikes), propagate along the axon of the primary afferent nociceptor from the site of the stimulus to the central nervous system. In the central nervous system, the primary afferent nociceptor activates other neurons that are part of a network whose activity eventuates in the sensation of pain.

The Criteria for Identification of Neurons and Pathways Involved in Pain
Neuroscientists studying pain have used a variety of criteria to identify particular neurons as candidates for a role in pain transmission:

(1) They have compared the response of the neurons to reproducible noxious stimuli with the response of human subjects to the same stimulus. For example, one can apply thermal stimuli of increasing intensity to the skin of human subjects and have them report their perceived pain intensity using a quantifiable rating scale. With this approach subjects report that perceived pain intensity increases exponentially with temperatures above a threshold value of about

THE PRIMARY AFFERENT NOCICEPTOR

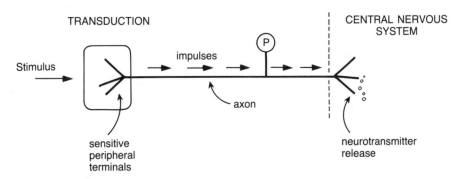

Figure 1. *The primary afferent nociceptor*. These nerve cells have three major components. The cell body, P, which provides all the requisite energy and structural components of the nerve cell. The axon is a narrow tube which bifurcates, sending one branch into the central nervous system and another into the bodily tissues. A noxious stimulus activates the nociceptor by a transduction process (see text) resulting in impulses which propagate along the axon to the central nervous system where they communicate with second-order neurons by release of neurotransmitter.

45°C. In parallel electrophysiological experiments, primary afferent nociceptor impulse frequency has been shown to increase with stimulus intensity in a manner that parallels the human psychophysical intensity function. This neural–psychological parallel is a major criterion by which to identify a neuron that could be involved in pain transmission.

(2) Imposed (e.g. artificial electrical) activation of that type of neuron evokes a sensation identified as painful by human subjects. For example, electrical stimulation of the axons of primary afferent nociceptors in a peripheral nerve reliably elicits reports of pain in human subjects. Conversely, blocking primary afferent nociceptors blocks pain (for example, when a dentist blocks a nerve with a local anaesthetic).

(3) The neurons in question have appropriate anatomical connections for a role in pain. In other words, given our understanding of the anatomy of pain pathways, a neuron should fulfil criteria (1) and (2) above and send its axon to a region that has been implicated in pain transmission.

(4) Manipulations that reduce perceived pain intensity also reduce the response of these neurons to a constant noxious stimulus. For example, morphine, which is a powerful pain reliever, reliably inhibits the activity of central nervous system neurons that fulfil criteria (1)–(3). Thus the inhibition of a neuron by an analgesic dose of morphine can be used as a criterion to implicate the neuron in pain transmission.

Central Nervous System Pathways for Pain

The sensory neurons that innervate bodily tissues, that is, the primary afferent nociceptors, have been described above. Under typical conditions, tissue injury sufficient to cause pain will produce activity in a population of primary afferent nociceptors. The particular population of active nociceptors will be determined by the stimulus type (e.g. a burn), its intensity, duration and location. The coding properties will be discussed in more detail below; however, it is obvious that this population of primary afferent nociceptors will generate a wave of impulses that is conducted through the peripheral nerves to the central nervous system.

Each primary afferent nociceptor is connected to many neurons in the central nervous system at structures called

455

SYNAPTIC TRANSMISSION

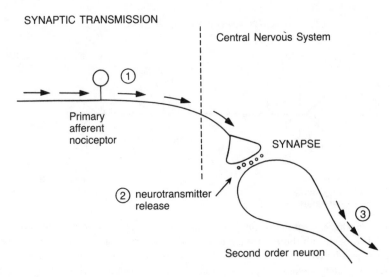

Figure 2. *Synaptic transmission*. Impulses invading the central nervous system terminals of primary afferent nociceptors cause release of neurotransmitter which diffuses across the synaptic cleft to activate the second-order neuron.

synapses. At each synapse, the axon of the primary afferent nociceptor terminates on a secondary neuron. As the electrochemical impulse in the afferent reaches the termination of the axon, it causes the release of molecules called neurotransmitters from the terminal. These neurotransmitters diffuse across the narrow synaptic gap to activate the neuron contacted by the terminal (*see* figure 2).

Each central neuron receives multiple contacts from a variety of primary afferents, including, but not limited to, nociceptors. Furthermore, the neurons that receive input from primary afferents also receive significant input from other cells in the central nervous system. Some of these inputs cause an excitatory response, other inputs cause inhibitory responses. The major point is that the second-order neuron contacted by the primary afferent nociceptor does not simply relay the message it receives. The second-order neuron performs an integrative transformation of inputs from multiple primary afferent nociceptors and from other central nervous system neurons (*see* figure 3).

When the balance between its excitatory and inhibitory inputs is positive the central

neuron is activated and begins to generate impulses that propagate along its axon to its terminals, which contact other central neurons both locally and in other regions of the central nervous system.

Clearly, the barrage of primary afferent impulses entering the central nervous system initiates a cascade of activity in successive neuronal relays. Shortly after a noxious stimulus, there is a distinct spatio-temporal pattern of activated (and inhibited) neurons throughout the nervous system. Somehow, this pattern of activity gives rise to the subjective experience of pain.

Although the pattern of activity elicited by a noxious stimulus is widespread in the central nervous system, the distribution is discrete and has important regularities. For example, the axons of primary afferent nociceptors activated by a noxious stimulus to the leg enter the central nervous system at the part of the spinal cord that lies in the lower part of the spinal canal. In human beings, this part of the spinal cord lies in a canal within the vertebral column of the lower back. The axons of the spinal cord neurons which conduct the information about noxious stimuli to particular destina-

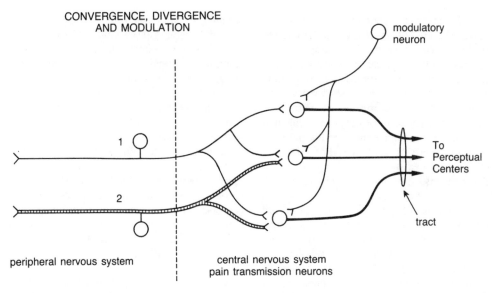

CONVERGENCE, DIVERGENCE AND MODULATION

modulatory neuron

To Perceptual Centers

tract

peripheral nervous system

central nervous system
pain transmission neurons

Figure 3. *Convergence, divergence and modulation.* Primary afferent nociceptor 1 branches to supply several second-order neurons. This is *divergence*. Primary afferents 1 and 2 *converge* on two of the three second-order cells. The axons of second-order cells are gathered in a fascicle called a tract which ascends to perceptual centres. Second-order neurons are subject to input from *modulatory* neurons which control their response to primary afferent nociceptors.

tions in the brain are gathered together in a circumscribed bundle (figure 3). Such a spatially discrete bundle of axons of common origin and destination within the central nervous system is called a *tract*. Most of the axons in this 'pain' tract ascend to terminate in a restricted region deep in the cerebral hemisphere called the *thalamus*. The regions of the thalamus that receive these terminals are each reciprocally connected to a discrete region of the cerebral cortex. Damage to this pathway anywhere between the spinal cord and the thalamus can impair a person's ability to detect stimuli that produce pain. Furthermore, artifically imposed electrical stimulation of the pathway can induce pain-like sensations that the subject reports to be located in a particular body part (*see* the following section, para. (2) for a discussion of projected sensation).

There are limits to what objective measurement can tell us about the pain experience. Thus, although we can determine by experiment which parts of the nervous system are necessary for a subject to identify a stimulus as painful and to gauge its intensity, it is not clear that it is possible to determine the site or sites in the brain where the subjective experience actually 'occurs'. In fact it is arguable whether a subjective experience has a spatial location. What we can determine is how neural networks identify stimuli as noxious and communicate this information to other neurons.

How Neurons Encode Information Related to Pain Sensation

As discussed above, neuronal communication has two major components, impulses and synaptic transmission. In the central nervous system neurons are chemically activated by synaptic input, the information is then encoded in impulses which propagate along the axon of the neuron to a synapse upon the next neuron in the pathway. Neurons have limited possibilities for encoding information; these include frequency and duration of discharge, the number of neurons activated and the particular subset of neurons activated.

457

(1) Coding of pain intensity. The simplest neuronal code is that of impulse frequency. As illustrated above in the example of the primary afferent nociceptor, stimulus intensity is clearly encoded by impulse frequency. In fact, many studies have shown that frequency coding of stimulus intensity is a general characteristic of neurons implicated in transmitting information about pain. In addition, there is evidence that intensity may be encoded by the number of nociceptive neurons activated at each successive level along the pain pathway.

(2) Coding of pain location, projected sensation. The location of a noxious stimulus is encoded by the location of the neurons that it activates. At each level of the pain pathway, neurons are arranged in an orderly topographical representation (map) of the body. Thus noxious stimuli to adjacent body areas activate neurons in adjacent regions of each representation.

There is direct evidence that these maps encode information relevant to the subjectively experienced location of the sensation. Thus, in awake human subjects, artificial electrical stimulation at a brain site corresponding to the neural representation of a body region (e.g. the hand area of the cerebral cortex) elicits a sensation that is reported by the subject to be located in that body region. These experiments illustrate quite clearly the phenomenon of projected sensation. They demonstrate that activity in a specific brain location is sufficient to produce a sensation that is perceived as occurring at a specific location in the body. No actual stimulus (or injury) to the body part is required. In fact, the presence of the body part itself is not required. Following amputation of a limb, virtually all amputees report having the sensation that the limb is still present, even though they can see that it is no longer present. Frequently, patients with pain in a limb before amputation continue to experience pain after the limb is amputated. This 'phantom limb' pain is notoriously difficult to relieve.

(3) Coding of pain quality. The quality of a somatic sensation is a complex function related to stimulus intensity and location and the temporal variation of these parameters. Pain quality will be encoded by the temporal pattern of activity produced in the relevant set of neurons by the stimulus. It is important to emphasize that it is not just the nociceptors that contribute to the quality of pain. An intense stimulus will activate receptors that respond to light stimuli (e.g. touch receptors) in addition to receptors that only respond to noxious stimuli (e.g. nociceptors). Thus, stimuli that produce pain activate neurons that in themselves do not encode 'painfulness' but that do contribute an aspect of the quality of the sensory experience that is labelled 'pain' by the subject.

The Modulation of Pain Transmission

The experience of pain is characteristically variable. Thus, stimuli that are virtually identical may be reported as painful in one situation and innocuous in another situation. We now know that a significant part of this variability is due to activity in specific neuronal networks that can selectively control pain transmission neurons. The activity of these pain modulating networks partly depends on the subject's expectation, focus of attention and level of arousal. Thus fear, anger or heightened awareness may change the perceived intensity of pain produced by an injury. The point is that the brain does not respond passively to information about stimuli, it actively controls its own input through these modulatory networks (*see* figure 3).

One of the best known of the modulatory networks controls neurons that receive direct connections from primary afferent nociceptors. This modulating network is activated by a certain class of pain-relieving drugs, the narcotics (e.g. morphine and codeine). It has also been shown that endogenous morphine-like compounds (e.g. endorphins) are present in many of the neurons of this pain-modulating network. It seems likely that narcotics relieve pain at least partly by mimicking the action of endogenous opioids. Interestingly, one of the most reliable activators for this endorphin-mediated pain-modulating network is prolonged, inescapable pain.

It is also important to point out that there is good evidence that modulating networks can enhance pain perception under some circumstances. It is thus possible in theory for modulating networks to generate a pain signal in the absence of an intense stimulus to the body.

SUMMARY

In this chapter we have discussed the nature of pain from the neurobiological and psychophysical perspective with an emphasis on the neural mechanisms underlying pain perception. For the sake of clarity and brevity we have focused on the sensory aspects of pain because this is what is subject to the most straightforward mechanistic analysis. We have said very little about the neurological basis of the affective-motivational aspect of pain, which is an essential feature. Even less is known about those distinctively human evaluative aspects of pain that deal with its meanings and the suffering associated with them. These are all crucial and characteristic parts of the pain experience, however, and their study requires an experiential approach that is distinctly different from the methods currently used to study the purely sensory aspects of pain. As our conceptual framework and methodological sophistication grow, so will our understanding of these complex phenomena.

BIBLIOGRAPHY

Fields, H.L. 1987. *Pain*. New York: McGraw-Hill.
Price, D.D. 1988. *Psychological and neural mechanisms of pain*. New York: Raven Press.
Wall, P.D., and Melzack, R. 1994. *Textbook of Pain*, 2nd Edn. Churchill Livingstone.

HOWARD L. FIELDS
DONALD D. PRICE

perception Philosophical issues about perception tend to be issues specifically about *sense*-perception. In English (and the same is true of comparable terms in many other languages) the term 'perception' has a wider connotation than anything that has to do with the senses and sense-organs, though it generally involves the idea of what may imply, if only in a metaphorical sense, a point of view. Thus it is now increasingly common for news-commentators, for example, to speak of people's perception of a certain set of events, even though those people have not been witnesses of them. In one sense, however, there is nothing new about this; in seventeenth- and eighteenth-century philosophical usage, words for perception were used with a much wider coverage than sense-perception alone. It is, however, sense-perception that has typically raised the largest and most obvious philosophical problems.

Such problems may be said to fall into two categories. There are, first, the epistemological problems about the role of sense-perception in connection with the acquisition and possession of knowledge of the world around us. These problems – does perception give us knowledge of the so-called 'external world'?, how and to what extent? – have become dominant in epistemology since Descartes because of his invocation of the method of doubt, although they undoubtedly existed in philosophers' minds in one way or another before that. In early and middle twentieth-century Anglo-Saxon philosophy such problems centred on the question whether there are firm data provided by the senses – so-called sense-data – and if so what is the relation of such sense-data to so-called material objects. Such problems are not essentially problems for the philosophy of mind, although certain answers to questions about perception which undoubtedly belong to the philosophy of mind can certainly add to epistemological difficulties. If perception is assimilated, for example, to SENSATION, there is an obvious temptation to think that in perception we are restricted, at any rate initially, to the contents of our own minds.

The second category of problems about perception – those that fall directly under

459

the heading of the philosophy of mind – are thus in a sense prior to the problems that exercised many empiricists in the first half of this century. They are problems about how perception is to be construed and how it relates to a number of other aspects of the mind's functioning – sensation, concepts and other things involved in our understanding of things, BELIEF and judgment, the IMAGINATION, our ACTION in relation to the world around us, and the causal processes involved in the physics, biology and psychology of perception. Some of the last were central to the considerations that Aristotle raised about perception in his *De Anima*.

CONSCIOUSNESS

It is obvious enough that sense-perception involves some kind of stimulation of sense-organs by stimuli that are themselves the product of physical processes, and that subsequent processes which are biological in character are then initiated. Moreover, only if the organism in which this takes place is adapted to such stimulation can perception ensue. Aristotle had something to say about such matters, but it was evident to him that such an account was insufficient to explain what perception itself is. It might be thought that the most obvious thing that is missing in such an account is some reference to CONSCIOUSNESS. But while it may be the case that perception can take place only in creatures that have consciousness in some sense, it is not clear that *every* case of perception directly involves consciousness. There is such a thing as unconscious perception and psychologists have recently drawn attention to the phenomenon which is described as 'blindsight' – an ability, generally manifested in patients with certain kinds of brain-damage, to discriminate sources of light, even when the people concerned have no consciousness of the lights and think that they are guessing about them. It is important, then, not to confuse the plausible claim that perception can take place only in conscious beings with the less plausible claim that perception always

involves consciousness of objects. A similar point may apply to the relation of perception to some of the other items I mentioned earlier, e.g. concept-possession.

SENSATION

Historically, it has been most common to assimilate perception to sensation on the one hand and judgment on the other. The temptation to assimilate it to sensation arises from the fact that perception involves the stimulation of an organ and seems to that extent passive in nature. The temptation to assimilate it to judgment on the other hand arises from the fact that we can be said to perceive not just objects but *that* certain things hold good of them, so that the findings, so to speak, of perception may have a propositional character (Dretske, 1969, ch. 2). But to have a sensation, such as that of a pain, by no means entails perceiving anything or indeed having awareness of anything apart from itself. Moreover, while in looking out of the window we may perceive (see) that the sun is shining, this may involve no explicit judgment on our part, even if it gives rise to a belief, and sometimes knowledge. (Indeed, if 'see that' is taken literally, seeing-that *always* implies knowledge; to see that something is the case is already to apprehend, and thus know, that it is so.)

The point about sensation was made admirably clear by Thomas Reid in the eighteenth century (Reid, 1941, Essays 1 and 2). Reid said that sensation involved an act of mind 'that hath no object distinct from the act itself'. Perception, by contrast, involved according to Reid a 'conception or notion of the object perceived', and a 'strong and irresistible conviction and belief of its present existence', which, moreover, are 'immediate, and not the effect of reasoning'. Reid also thought that perceptions are generally accompanied by sensations and offered a complex account of the relations between the two. Whether all this is correct in every detail need not worry us at present, although it is fairly clear that perceiving need not be believing. Certain illusions, such as the Müller–Lyer illusion, are such that we may see them in a certain way, no matter what our beliefs may be about them or whether we have any beliefs about them. Once again, however, it is arguable that such (mis)perceptions could only take place in believers, whether or not beliefs about the objects in question occur in the actual perception.

CONCEPTS AND ACTIVITY

Similar considerations apply to concept-possession (Reid's 'conception or notion'). (*See* CONCEPTS.) It is certainly not the case that in order to perceive a cyclotron I must have the (or a) concept of a cyclotron; I may have no idea of what I am perceiving, except of course that it is something. But to be something it must have some distinguishable characteristics and must stand in some relation to other objects, including whatever it is that constitutes the background against which it is perceived. In order to perceive it I must therefore have some understanding of the world in which such objects are to be found. That will, in the case of most if not all of our senses, be a spatial world in which things persist or change over time. Hence, perception of objects presupposes forms of awareness that are spatiotemporal. It is at least arguable that that framework would not be available were we not active creatures who are capable of moving about in the world in which we live (Hamlyn, 1990, ch. 5). Once again, it is not that every perception involves some activity on our part, although some may do so, but that perception can take place only in active creatures, and is to that extent, if only that extent, not a purely passive process.

It must be evident in all this how far we are getting from the idea that perception is simply a matter of the stimulation of our sense-organs. It may be replied that it has long been clear that there must be some interaction between what is brought about by stimulation of sense-organs and subsequent neural, including cortical, processes. That, however, does not end the

problem, since we are now left with the question of the relation between all that and the story about sensations, beliefs, concepts and activity that I have mentioned. Some of that issue is part of the general MIND–BODY PROBLEM, but there is also the more specific problem of how these 'mental' items are to be construed in such a way as to have any kind of relation to what are apparently the purely passive causal processes involved in and set up by the stimulation of sense-organs.

INFORMATION-PROCESSING AND REPRESENTATIONS

One idea that has in recent times been thought by many philosophers and psychologists alike to offer promise in that connection is the idea that perception can be thought of as a species of information-processing, in which the stimulation of the sense-organs constitutes an input to subsequent processing, presumably of a computational form. The psychologist J. J. Gibson suggested that the senses should be construed as systems the function of which is to derive information from the stimulus-array, indeed to 'hunt for' such information (Gibson, 1966). He thought, however, that it was enough for a satisfactory psychological theory of perception that his account should be restricted to the details of such information pick-up, without reference to other 'inner' processes such as concept-use. Although Gibson has been very influential in turning psychology away from the previously dominant sensation-based framework of ideas (of which gestalt psychology was really a special case), his claim that reliance on his notion of information is enough has seemed incredible to many. Moreover, his notion of 'information' is sufficiently close to the ordinary one to warrant the accusation that it presupposes the very ideas of, for example, concept-possession and belief that he claimed to exclude. The idea of information espoused by him (though it has to be said that this claim has been disputed) is that of 'information about', not the technical one involved in information theory or that presupposed by the theory of computation.

The most influential psychological theory of perception has in consequence been that of David Marr, who has explicitly adopted the 'computational metaphor' in a fairly literal way (Marr, 1982). He distinguished three levels of analysis: (1) the description of the abstract computational theory involved, (2) the account of the implementation of that theory in terms of its appropriate algorithm, and (3) the account of the physical realization of the theory and its algorithm. All this is based on the idea that the senses when stimulated provide representations on which the computational processes can work (*see* COMPUTATIONAL MODELS; REPRESENTATION). Other theorists have offered analogous accounts, if differing in detail. Perhaps the most crucial idea in all this is the one about representations. There is perhaps a sense in which what happens at, say, the level of the retina constitutes, as a result of the processes occurring in the process of stimulation, some kind of representation of what produces that stimulation, and thus some kind of representation of the objects of perception. Or so it may seem if one attempts to describe the relation between the structure and character of the objects of perception and the structure and nature of the retinal processes. One might indeed say that the nature of that relation is such as to provide information about the part of the world perceived, in the sense of 'information' presupposed when one says that the rings in the sectioning of a tree's trunk provide information of its age. This is because there is an appropriate causal relation between the two things, which makes it impossible for it to be a matter of chance. Subsequent processing can then be thought to be one carried out on what is provided in the representations in question.

One needs to be careful here, however. If there are such representations, they are not representations *for* the perceiver. Indeed it is the thought that perception involves representations of *that* kind which produced the old, and now largely discredited,

philosophical theories of perception which suggested that perception is a matter, primarily, of an apprehension of mental states of some kind (e.g. sense-data) which are representatives of perceptual objects, either by being caused by them or in being in some way constitutive of them. Also, if it be said that the idea of information so invoked indicates that there is a sense in which the processes of stimulation can be said to have content, but a non-conceptual content (Evans, 1982, chs 5 and 6; Peacocke, 1983, ch. 1), distinct from the content provided by the subsumption of what is perceived under concepts, it must be emphasized that that content is not one *for* the perceiver. What the information-processing story provides is, at best, a more adequate categorization than previously available of the causal processes involved. That may be important but more should not be claimed for it than there is. If in perception in a given case one can be said to have an experience as of an object of a certain shape and kind related to another object it is only because there is presupposed in that perception the possession of concepts of objects, and more particularly, a concept of space and how objects occupy space.

THE REQUISITES OF PERCEPTION AND THE NATURE OF EXPERIENCE

Perception is always concept-dependent at least in the sense that perceivers must be concept possessors and users, and almost certainly in the sense that perception entails concept-use in its application to objects. It is at least arguable that those organisms that react in a biologically useful way to something but that are such that the attribution of concepts to them is implausible, should not be said to perceive those objects, however much the objects figure causally in their behaviour. Moreover, in spite of what was said earlier about unconscious perception and blindsight, perception normally involves consciousness of objects. Moreover, that consciousness presents the objects in such a way that the experience has a certain phenomenal character, which is derived from the sensations which the causal processes involved set up. This is most evident in the case of touch (which being a 'contact sense' provides a more obvious occasion for speaking of sensations than do 'distance senses' such as sight). Our tactual awareness of the texture of a surface is, to use a metaphor, 'coloured' by the nature of the sensations that the surface produces in our skin, and which we can be explicitly aware of if our attention is drawn to them (something that gives one indication of how attention too is involved in perception).

It has been argued (Millar, 1991b) that the phenomenal character of an experience is detachable from its conceptual content in the sense that an experience of the same phenomenal character could occur even if the appropriate concepts were not available. Certainly the reverse is true – that a concept-mediated awareness of an object could occur without any sensation-mediated experiences – as in an awareness of something absent from us. It is also the case, however, that the look of something can be completely changed by the realization that it can be thought of in a certain way, so that it is to be seen as X rather than Y. To the extent that that is so, the phenomenal character of a perceptual experience should be viewed as the result of the way in which sensations produced in us by objects blend with our ways of thinking of and understanding those objects (which, it should be noted, are things in the world and should not be confused with the sensations which they produce).

Seeing things in certain ways also sometimes involves the imagination (Wittgenstein, 1953, II, xi) (and in what is perhaps a special sense of 'imagination' (Strawson, 1974, ch. 3) it perhaps always does). In imagination we may bring to bear a way of thinking about an object which may not be the immediately obvious one, and being visually imaginative, as an artist may have to be, is at least a special case of our general ability to see things as such and suches. But that general ability is central to the faculty of visual perception and, *mutatis mutandis* of

the faculty of perception in general. What has been said may be enough to indicate the complexities of the notion of perception and how many different phenomena have to be taken into consideration in elucidating that notion within the philosophy of mind. But the crucial issue, perhaps, is how they are all to be fitted together within what may still be called the 'workings of the mind'.

See also COGNITIVE PSYCHOLOGY; CONTENT; INTENTIONALITY; PERCEPTUAL CONTENT; PSYCHOLOGY AND PHILOSOPHY.

BIBLIOGRAPHY

Dretske, F. 1969. *Seeing and Knowing* London: Routledge & Kegan Paul.
Evans, G. 1982. *Varieties of Reference*. Oxford: Clarendon Press.
Gibson, J.J. 1966. *The Senses Considered as Perceptual Systems*. Boston, MA.: Houghton Mifflin.
Hamlyn, D.W. 1990. *In and Out of the Black Box*. Oxford: Basil Blackwell.
Marr, D. 1982. *Vision*. San Francisco: W. H. Freeman.
Millar, A. 1991a. Concepts, experience and inference. *Mind*, C. 4, 495–505.
Millar, A. 1991b. *Reasons and Experience*. Oxford: Clarendon Press.
Peacocke, C. 1983. *Sense and Content*. Oxford: Clarendon Press.
Strawson, P.F. 1974. *Freedom and Resentment*. London: Methuen.
Reid, T. 1941. *Essays on the Intellectual Powers of Man*, ed. A. D. Woozley. London: Macmillan. Originally published 1785.
Wittgenstein, L. 1953. *Philosophical Investigations*. Oxford: Basil Blackwell.

D. W. HAMLYN

perceptual content Where the term 'content' was once associated with the phrase 'content of consciousness' to pick out the subjective aspects of mental states, its use in the phrase 'perceptual content' is intended to pick out something more closely akin to its old dual 'form', the objective and publicly expressible aspects of mental states.

There are nevertheless important links between these diverse uses. We might call a theory which attributes to perceptual states a content in the new sense, 'an intentional theory' of perception. On such a view, perceptual states represent to the subject how her environment and body are. The content of perceptual experiences is how the world is represented to be. Perceptual experiences are then counted as illusory or veridical depending on whether the content is correct and the world is as represented. In as much as such a theory of perception can be taken to be answering the more traditional problems of perception, it will be addressing the same issues as led earlier writers to discuss the content of consciousness. In the first part of this essay, I raise the question of how a theory of perceptual content may be seen to answer the traditional problems; in the second, I look to some of the debates about the nature of content in the light of this answer.

APPEARANCE AND CONTENT

Why attribute an intentional content to perceptual states at all? To see perceptual states as intentional is to assimilate them to other mental phenomena which are paradigm examples of INTENTIONALITY: BELIEFS and DESIRES, and also occurrent mental episodes, such as acts of judgment and consciously entertaining a thought. The basic justification for thinking of perceptual states as intentional will be the same as that for these other mental states: their general functional role within our mental economies – that is, how they interact with other mental states, in particular in the fixation of belief and control of ACTION – can only be understood in terms of attributing to them such content. A subject gains information about the state of her body and her immediate environment through perception. We can explain why the subject's perceptual beliefs have the content that they do, and why her intentional actions are performed in the way that they are, by positing a corresponding content to the perceptual states which give rise to those beliefs and control those actions.

This idea contrasts with the once dominant sense-datum theory of perception. This is often defined solely in terms of the objects of perception: as the claim that there are certain mental entities, sense data, whose existence and qualitative nature depend upon a subject's awareness of them, and which are the only immediate objects of perception (cf. Jackson, 1977; Perkins, 1983). Yet this traditional view has implications not only for an account of the objects of perceptual states, but also for that of their nature and how they relate to other mental states. A sense-datum theory explains the phenomenological character of perceptual states in terms of the properties that these mental entities have: on this view, how things appear to the subject will correspond to how these entities are. If the view seeks to give an account of perceptual experience purely in terms of the immediate awareness of sense data, it must hold that the phenomenological character of perceptual experience can be completely described, if at all, in terms independent of the subject's immediate, physical environment.

That consequence seems at odds with the introspectible evidence of what it is like for us to perceive (see INTROSPECTION), as has been noted by many critics of sense-datum theories (cf. Strawson, 1979). When you look at the page of the book in front of you, the scene before your eyes looks some way to you. The most natural way to describe what it is like to be looking at the book, introspecting one's current experience, is to employ the very same vocabulary as one would use to describe the scene perceived. One might put this point by saying that the experience strikes one as being of the book in front of one or, allowing for the fact that one may be deluded as to the nature of what is there, that it is at least as if such a book is there – as of a book, in shorthand – but certainly not of any mental surrogate of that book. Not only is this the most natural way to describe the experience, no adequate description of what the experience is like for one could leave this out.

In turn, it is difficult to see how, on a purely sense-datum theory of perception, the immediate awareness of mental entities alone could explain the fixation of beliefs about the environment or actions upon that environment (*see* CONTENT; EXTERNALISM/ INTERNALISM). Such experiences could only figure in the rational production of such beliefs and actions against a background of beliefs of the subject which link the presence to her of a mental entity with the presence in her environment of some object, such as beliefs about what normally causes such mental states. It is questionable whether all perceivers do have such beliefs, or that such beliefs are operative in the fixation of their perceptual beliefs.

In contrast, an intentional theory of perception does not conflict with the introspective claims of common sense and is able to attribute to perceptual experience an explanatory role in the fixation of belief and control of action without appeal to such sophisticated background beliefs. On such a view, one's current visual experience may represent the presence of a book in one's immediate environment. One's visual experience will then have a certain phenomenological character in virtue of how it represents the immediate environment to be. Where the sense-datum theory claims that one is immediately aware of mental entities, the intentional theory can simply claim that one is aware of the objects in one's environment, and aware of them in virtue of the content of one's experience. In normal circumstances, where perceptual experience fixes belief, the content of the experience, which will be how things appear to the subject, will be matched, in part, by the content of the belief formed.

While the above expresses a disagreement between sense-datum theories and intentional theories, there is a further matter on which they agree. It is common to assume that the mental state one is in when perceiving, the perceptual experience, is of a kind which could occur even if one has an illusion or hallucination. This assumption is often appealed to in the so-called argument from illusion. If you could have had the same state of mind as you now do while looking at this page even though you were suffering an hallucination, then it cannot be essential to your being in such a state of mind that any object independent of you should have certain qualities or be perceived by you. A sense-datum theory assumes, nevertheless, that there must be some object with the requisite qualities perceived by you and hence concludes that the object in question is a mental one, dependent for its existence entirely on one's awareness of it. Commonly intentional theories accept the same claim about the commonality of perceptual experience, but respond to it in a radically different way, drawing an analogy between experience and belief. It is possible to believe that Tucson is north of Boston even though that is not so. No one supposes that because there is no appropriate objective fact in the world for one's belief to correspond to, it must instead be a relation to some subjective fact. Instead it is in the nature of beliefs that they can be true or false, and the intentional content of the belief specifies how the world would have to be for the belief to be true. Similarly, if perceptual experience has an intentional content, that experience can be of some physical state of affairs, even if the state of affairs in question is not actual.

An alternative response to the problem of illusion is to reject the assumption shared by both views above that experience forms a common kind among perception, illusion and hallucination. On this view, a report of one's experience such as 'It looks to me as if there is a book before me' does not describe a single kind of state of mind present whether or not I am perceiving, but would be made true by a disjunction of distinct types of mental state – either a state of veridical perception or one which although not veridical perception is nevertheless indistinguishable from it (cf. McDowell, 1982). Where the negative component of this view is to deny that there is a common account of how things appear to a perceiver across the three cases – veridical perception, perceptual illusions and hallucinations – the positive element is to allow an alternative

465

account of the one case, veridical perception. In contrast to the sense-datum theory's claim that we are only immediately aware of mental objects, this view will claim that we immediately perceive physical objects. To this extent the position will be in accord with the intentional theory and the introspective support for it. But it will arguably be at odds with the intentional theory on another ground. The sense-datum theory assumes that the objects and qualities in virtue of which perceptual experience has its character must exist or be realized in order for the experience to be so, and this assumption will likewise be made on this view: the kinds of physical object and qualities that one's experience is of, or as of, must exist or be realized in order for one to have an experience of the kind one does when veridically perceiving. One's perceptual experience having the PHENOMEN-OLOGICAL character it does is constituted, according to this view, by one's physical environment being so. In contrast to this the intentional theory claims that the phenomenological character of experience is constituted by the experience having a certain intentional content, which content it could have were the environment not so. The intentional theory denies that there are any intermediary objects between us and the external world of which we are aware, but it may yet not accommodate the thought that we are immediately aware of the external world, if that thought is best expressed in terms of this third view – 'naïve realism', as we may label it.

Naïve realism is a form of extreme externalism and consequently comes with a high price. The thought that perceptual experiences form a common kind among the three cases is seemingly supported by appearances – what better evidence could there be for the common nature of the three kinds of case than that they are indistinguishable to the subject of those mental states? It is also supported by facts about the possible immediate causes and behavioural effects of perceptual states, since it is plausible that the same immediate stimulation of the retina could in one case produce a visual

perception of an apple and in another the hallucination as of such an apple; and plausible to suppose that each state could produce the same kind of physical movement. Since many philosophers are prepared to endorse some form of externalism about the mind, the consequence that the same physiological causes and effects correspond to distinct mental states may not be too high a price for them. But the phenomenological considerations mark the perceptual case out from other areas and may be thought to give specific reasons for resisting externalism. The issue may then turn on whether naïve realism can make good its claims concerning the common-sense thought that we are immediately aware of the external world. For if one can only make sense of the immediacy of experience in naïve realist terms, then any perceptual experience which genuinely gives one immediate access to the external world will be constituted by the world being so. In as much as illusions and hallucinations are indistinguishable from perceptions, they too will, on this view appear to possess this property even though they lack it. If naïve realism is correct about the nature of perceptual experience, at least some perceptual experiences will be genuinely immediate while others will merely appear to be so. However, even if naïve realism is wrong about the actual nature of experience, its claims about common sense might still be correct. It would then be the best account not of the nature of experience but what that nature appears to us to be.

The above discussion presents the debate as one between three contrasting theories. But it is best to see the fundamental divisions here as concerning the different types of aspects or features that the conscious character of perceptual experience can have. For the intentional theory and the naïve realist both suppose that experience has features that are as of objects in the subject's physical environment which can exist independently of her, while the sense-datum theory claims that there are features of experience individuated by reference to sense data and their qualities which exist only in as much as the subject is aware of them. On the other hand, the sense-datum theory and the naïve realist both claim that experience has features that require that the objects or qualities in virtue of which it is individuated should exist or be realized; while the intentional theory allows that experience may have a feature as of some object or quality, without that existing or being realized. These differences can be seen in terms of the answers to two questions about the relation between features of experience and the objects or qualities in terms of which those features are individuated. Can that object or quality exist or be realized independently of the experience having that feature? Can the experience have that feature independently of the object or quality existing or being realized? We can represent this on a matrix:

commitment to sense data but still claim that there are subjective features of experience, often called QUALIA, where they take these to be modifications of the experiential act itself rather than any object of that act. An intentional theory of perception, which ascribes perceptual content to sensory states, attributes intentional properties to experience. The naïve realist, on the other hand, supposes that veridical perception possesses naïve realist features. There is a fourth option on the matrix here left unfilled. This is not to claim that there are no such properties of experience, but if we assume that the argument from illusion motivates the positing of either intentional or subjective features, it is not surprising that no theory would appeal to such qualities. Note also that on some views of intentional content, the view here labelled

Can the object/quality exist/be realized independently of the experiential feature?

	Yes	No		
	Intentional Feature	?	Yes	Can the experience have this feature without the object/ quality existing/ being realized?
	Naïve Realist Feature	Subjective Feature	No	

There are three types of feature that the theories of perception are appealing to. However, an experience possessing one of these features is not precluded from possessing either of the others. Rather the debate between the different theories concerns whether the phenomenological character of experience can be explained without positing one or other of these features. Theories of perception differ according to which attributes they claim perceptual experience to have. A sense-datum theory claims that they have at least some subjective features; there are other views which seek to avoid

'naïve realist' will be taken to be a variety of the intentional theory, and the debate between them seen as one internal to that theory.

Intentional theories of perception have come to be accepted where it is agreed that we must posit intentional properties of experience; and alternative approaches have been rejected either where they are thought unnecessary or inadequate. The main focus of debate among intentional theorists has been over the nature of perceptual content and the nature of the mental state that has that content.

467

VARIETIES OF CONTENT

Content and Consciousness

What relation is there between the content of a perceptual state and conscious experience? One proponent of an intentional approach to perception notoriously claims that it is 'nothing but the acquiring of true or false beliefs concerning the current state of the organism's body or environment' (Armstrong 1968, p. 209). Many critics of Armstrong have supposed that it is a defect of Armstrong's own account and even of any intentional theory that it cannot give an adequate account of what conscious experience is like. Beliefs need not be conscious states of mind, and there is no reason to think that the acquiring of beliefs need be conscious either. Armstrong claims, not implausibly, that there can be unconscious perception, but the complaint remains that he cannot give an adequate account of conscious perception, given the 'nothing but' element of his account. However, an intentional theory of perception need not be allied with any general theory of CONSCIOUSNESS, one which explains what the difference is between conscious and unconscious states. If it is to provide an alternative to a sense-datum theory, the theory need only claim that where experience is conscious, its content is constitutive, at least in part, of the phenomenological character of that experience. This claim is consistent with a wide variety of theories of consciousness, even the view that no account can be given.

An intentional theory is also consistent with either affirming or denying the presence of subjective features in experience. Among traditional sense-datum theorists of experience, H. H. Price (1932) attributed in addition an intentional content to perceptual consciousness. Among recent accounts, Peacocke (1983, ch. 1) and Shoemaker (1990) both attribute subjective properties to experience – in the former case labelled sensational properties, in the latter qualia – as well as intentional content. One might call a theory of perception that insisted that all features of what an experience is like are determined by its intentional content, a purely intentional theory of perception. Harman (1990) is an example of one who holds such a view.

Experience and Belief

Armstrong not only sought to explain perception without recourse to sense-data or subjective qualities but also sought to equate the intentionality of perception with that of belief. There are two aspects to this: the first is to suggest that the only attitude towards a content involved in perceiving is that of believing, and the second is to claim that the only content involved in perceiving is that which a belief may have. The former suggestion faces an immediate problem, recognized by Armstrong, of the possibility of having a perceptual experience without acquiring the corresponding belief. One such case is where the subject already possesses the requisite belief – here Armstrong talks of perception maintaining, rather than leading to the acquisition of, belief. The more problematic case is that of disbelief in perception, where a subject has a perceptual experience but refrains from acquiring the corresponding belief. For example, someone familiar with the Müller–Lyer illusion, in which lines of equal length appear unequal, is unlikely to acquire the belief that the lines are unequal on encountering a recognizable example of the illusion. Despite that, the lines may still appear unequal to them.

Armstrong seeks to encompass such cases by talk of dispositions to acquire beliefs and talk of potentially acquiring beliefs. On his account this is all we need say of the psychological state enjoyed. However, once we admit that the disbelieving perceiver still enjoys a conscious occurrent experience, characterizing it in terms of a disposition to acquire a belief seems inadequate. There are two further worries. One may object that the content of perceptual experiences may play a role in explaining why a subject disbelieves in the first place: someone may fail to acquire a perceptual belief precisely because how things appear to her is inconsistent with her prior beliefs about the world. Secondly some philosophers have claimed that there can be perception without any corresponding belief. Cases of disbelief in perception are still examples of perceptual experience that impinge on belief; where a sophisticated perceiver does not acquire the belief that the Müller–Lyer lines are unequal, she will still acquire a belief about how things look to her. Dretske (1969) argues for a notion of non-epistemic seeing, on which it is possible for a subject to be perceiving something while lacking any belief about it because she has failed to notice what is apparent to her. If we assume that such non-epistemic seeing nevertheless involves conscious experience it would seem to provide another reason to reject Armstrong's view and admit that if perceptual experiences are intentional states then they are a distinct attitude-type from that of belief. However, even if one rejects Armstrong's equation of perceiving with acquiring beliefs or dispositions to believe, one may still accept that he is right about the functional links between experience and belief, and the authority that experience has over belief, an authority which can nevertheless be overcome.

CONCEPTUAL AND NON-CONCEPTUAL CONTENT

Increasingly, proponents of the intentional theory of perception argue that perceptual experience is to be differentiated from belief not only in terms of attitude, but also in terms of the kind of content that experience is an attitude towards (*see* CONTENT). According to them we need to accept that there are varieties of content, that we need to distinguish between what has been called 'conceptual' and 'non-conceptual' content. It is claimed that one cannot accommodate the nature of perceptual experience solely in terms of conceptual content, the only kind of content that beliefs and other PROPOSITIONAL ATTITUDES possess, but must ascribe to it a non-conceptual content.

If thought is structured, having a thought is to exercise the conceptual abilities corresponding to the concepts that compose that thought (*see* CONCEPTS). An individual's possession of a given concept is revealed in the range of thoughts that she is able to have that contain that concept (cf. Evans, 1982, ch. 4). The conditions on any of her conceptual mental states possessing a content will then derive from the conditions of her possessing the concepts that compose that content. If perceptual experiences possess certain contents where the corresponding conditions on concept-possession are not met, they thereby possess a non-conceptual content. The various arguments used to support the claim that experience has a non-conceptual content tend to include two components: the first is to argue that a given condition on possessing a concept has not been met by a given individual; the second is to give grounds for nevertheless attributing a given content to the experience.

For example, it may be argued that only relatively sophisticated creatures such as ourselves, who employ language and are able to think about our own states of mind genuinely possess concepts, and so have conceptual thought. On the other hand, it may be claimed, other animals and infants, although not sapient, are sentient; and their experiences, no less than ours, purvey information to them and control their behaviour. It is not implausible to claim that there are some ways in which we experience the world in which they can too. If that is so, then there is a common content between some of their mental states and ours, even though only we are concept-possessors. It cannot be a constraint on that content that one possess the requisite concepts, hence that content is non-conceptual (Evans, 1982, ch. 5; Dretske, 1982, ch. 6).

Another argument derives from the phenomenological character of experience. It is often claimed that the character of a perceptual experience is much richer and more fine-grained than is the corresponding propositional attitude to which it may give rise. Confronted by a beech tree, a subject may be unable to put into words the specific outline that she sees the tree to have, or the various shades its leaves possess. Furthermore, outside of the context of actually viewing the tree, she may be unable to recognize the same shape again, or to think about it. Nevertheless she may be able to discriminate between that particular outline of the tree or shade of leaf and others that it could have had. Here it is tempting to claim that how things look to her outrun the conceptual capacities that she then possesses, as evidenced by her verbal descriptions of what is before her, or her later ability to think about it.

One response to this line of reasoning is to point out that she is at least able to attend to and indicate the outline when presented with it, and think, 'That outline is particularly striking' – so it is not true that how things appear to her cannot have a bearing on her thoughts. This is a nice issue, and it is not clear that the response answers the full force of the original intuition. The fact that a perceiver may, through attending to features of her experience, come to be able to demonstrate that feature, or even acquire a recognitional capacity for it, certainly supports the claim that each aspect could be matched by a corresponding concept. That does not yet show that in order for the perceiver to have an experience with that content, she must thereby possess the relevant concept. Rather it seems more plausible to say that we can explain the demonstrative concept she possesses in that context, or the recognitional capacity she acquires, in terms of the content of the experience. This would require us to suppose that the experience has the content independently of the conceptual capacities she actually possesses.

What forces us, an opponent of this view might press, to view the extra element as intentional but non-conceptual, rather than non-intentional and possibly subjective? Subjectivists have commonly argued for the need for some subjective features to experience on precisely the ground that we need to recognize the phenomenological differences between sensing and mere thinking. Likewise they have often treated this subjective aspect as the 'given' in experience which plays a part in explaining the acquisition and application of empirical concepts. Within the present context, the non-conceptual content appealed to by intentional theories seems to have taken over both roles.

In defence, the proponent of a plurality of contents may seek support in two directions. On the one hand, she may insist that introspection supports the view that even those aspects of experience that outrun the subject's current conceptual capacities seem to be as of the objective world, and do not seem to be subjective. On the other, the theorist may appeal outside of philosophical debates, to the notions of content at play within psychological theories of perception to show the need for notions of content which are not obviously tied to the subject's conceptual powers.

Whether this response is finally sufficient is perhaps undecided. What is clear is that where the problems of perception are themselves ancient, debates about perceptual content are as yet in their infancy.

BIBLIOGRAPHY

D.M. Armstrong 1968. *A Materialist Theory of the Mind*. London: Routledge & Kegan Paul.

T.M. Crane, ed. 1992. *The Contents of Experience*. Cambridge University Press.

F. Dretske, 1969. *Seeing and Knowing*. London: Routledge & Kegan Paul.

F. Dretske, 1982 *Knowledge and the Flow of Information*: Oxford: Basil Blackwell.

G. Evans 1982. *The Varieties of Reference*. Oxford: Clarendon Press.

G. Harman, 1990. The intrinsic quality of experience. *Philosophical Perspectives*, 4, 31–52.

F. Jackson, 1977, *Perception: A Representative Theory*. Cambridge University Press.

J. McDowell, 1982. Criteria, defeasibility and knowledge. *Proceedings of the British Academy*, 68, 455–79.

C.A.B. Peacocke, 1983. *Sense and Content*. Oxford: Clarendon Press.

C.A.B. Peacocke, 1989. Perceptual content. In *Themes from Kaplan*, ed J. Almog et al. New York: Oxford University Press.

C.A.B. Peacocke, 1992. *A Study of Concepts*. Cambridge MA: MIT Press.

Perkins, M. 1983. *Sensing the World*. Indianapolis: Hackett Publishing Co.

H.H. Price, 1932. *Perception*. London: Methuen.

S. Shoemaker, 1990. Qualities and qualia: what's in the mind?' *Philosophy and Phenomenological Research*, 50, 109–31.

P.F. Strawson, 1979. Perception and its objects. In *Perception and Identity*, ed. G. F. McDonald. London: Macmillan.

M. G. F. MARTIN

phenomenal/phenomenological Strictly speaking, a phenomenon is that which is present to the mind when we exercise our senses. Put in a slightly different way, it is whatever is in consciousness when something is seen, touched, heard, etc. When one hears it said that scientists have 'observed some phenomenon such as the passage of a comet', this is a deviation from the strict usage: the phenomenon is the *appearance to us* of the comet and not the 'external' fact of the comet's passage.

In the philosophy of mind, the adjectival form 'phenomenal' tends to be used in the strict sense to describe that which passes in our consciousness in PERCEPTION, but there is a no consensus at all about whether there really are such things as phenomenal states or events. (Philosophers, like most current English speakers, are not so strict with the nominal form 'phenomenon'.) Phenomenal states or events often trade under other names: 'SENSATIONS', 'sense-data', 'QUALIA' (though many think of qualia as properties of phenomenal states and not the states themselves).

As is typical of 'ology' forms, 'phenomenology' is the *study* of phenomena understood in the strict sense. Thus, if you investigate what appears to us when we perceive the world rather than the world that so appears, you are engaged in phenomenology. Through the writings of Edmund Husserl (1859–1938), phenomenology came to be regarded as a branch of philosophy, though as such it has a complexity not revealed by the above-mentioned simple perceptual example. As with 'phenomenon', there tends to be a certain carelessness in the use of 'phenomenological'.

One often hears reference to 'phenomenological' states when what is at issue are phenomenal states. This use of the 'study of' form has probably arisen because of the felt need to have a word not likely to be confused with the now more outward looking 'phenomenon'. (*See also* CONSCIOUSNESS; SUBJECTIVITY.)

SAMUEL GUTTENPLAN

physicalism (1) The term 'physicalism' has been used in a variety of family-resemblance related ways in recent philosophy of mind. The same is true of 'materialism'. Often the two terms are used interchangeably, although there has also been some tendency to employ 'materialism' more generically than 'physicalism' – in particular, to use 'physicalism' for psychophysical IDENTITY THEORIES, while employing 'materialism' in a more inclusive way (as in 'eliminative materialism' and 'non-reductive materialism'). Here I will survey the range of philosophical doctrines that have been placed under the rubrics 'physicalism' and 'materialism' from the late 1950s to the present, in an effort to give a sense for the differences among these doctrines, the underlying similarities, and some of the reasons why there has been disagreement about what should count as a physicalist or materialist conception of mentality.

On this topic, as with many topics in philosophy, there is a distinction to be made between (i) certain vague, partially inchoate, pre-theoretic ideas and beliefs about the matter at hand; and (ii) certain more precise, more explicit, doctrines or theses that are taken to articulate or explicate those pre-theoretic ideas and beliefs. There are various potential ways of precisifying our pre-theoretic conception of a physicalist or materialist account of mentality, and the question of how best to do so is itself a matter for ongoing, dialectical, philosophical inquiry. (In order to emphasize this conceptual slack, I will hereafter use 'materialism' for the body of pre-theoretic ideas, and will treat the various potential precisifications as alternative referents of 'physicalism'.)

471

I begin by formulating, as generically and neutrally as possible, some central ideas constitutive of a materialist conception of human nature:

(1) Humans are, or are fully constituted by, entities of the kind posited in (an ideally completed) physics. There are no incorporeal Cartesian souls, or vital spirits, or entelechies (*see* DUALISM; HISTORY).
(2) The human body is a causally complete physico-chemical system: although the body is highly susceptible to external causal influence, all physical events in the body, and all bodily movements, are in principle fully explainable in physico-chemical terms.
(3) Any instantiation of any property by, or within, a human being is ultimately explainable in physico-chemical terms.

These first three assertions are typically viewed as highly confirmed empirical hypotheses, not as a priori assumptions. They do not yet mention mentality, and in fact are compatible with the contention that humans never undergo any mental events or states, and never instantiate any mental properties, at all. (Here and henceforth, the terms 'event' and 'state' are used for concrete, spatiotemporally located, occurrences and conditions – i.e. *token* events and states.) Standardly, however, materialism takes mentality seriously:

(4) Mentality is real; humans undergo mental events and states, and instantiate mental properties.
(5) Much of human behaviour is describable as ACTION, not merely as raw motion; and action is mentalistically explainable.
(6) Much of human mental life is mentalistically explainable.

And standardly, though not invariably, mentalistic explanation is taken to be causal:

(7) Mentalistic explanation is a species of causal explanation; mentality is caus-

ally efficacious, both intra-mentally and in the aetiology of behaviour.

In embracing claims (4)–(7) in addition to (1)–(3), materialism embodies the idea that mentality can be *accommodated* within a conception of human beings as complex physico-chemical systems whose behaviour, whose internal events and states, and whose properties are all explainable in physico-chemical terms.

The various candidate precisifications of these generic materialist ideas – i.e. the various versions of physicalism – differ largely with respect to what they say about the status of mental properties. I turn now to typology.

REDUCTIVE PHYSICALISM

The simplest, most straightforward, versions of physicalism approach theses (1)–(7) in the context of discussions of inter-theoretic reduction in philosophy of science. Human psychology is construed as a theory, or perhaps a body of theories; and materialism is explicated by way of the contention that human psychology is 'micro-reducible' to neuroscience, in much the same manner that classical thermodynamics was micro-reduced to statistical molecular mechanics.

The Type/Type Identity Theory

According to traditional accounts in philosophy of science, micro-reduction is a form of explanation: the higher-level theory is shown to be derivable from the lower-level theory together with 'bridge laws' asserting the nomic coextensiveness of higher-level theoretical properties of structurally complex entities (e.g. temperature, a property of a gas), and lower-level theoretical properties involving micro-components (e.g. mean kinetic energy, a property involving the gas's component molecules). But in addition, the received view is that these so-called bridgelaws, although empirically established, actually reveal the *identity* of the properties they cite. A gas's temperature, for instance, just *is* its mean molecular kinetic energy. Bridge laws that did not reflect underlying property identities, it is claimed, would be insufficient for full-fledged reduction: they would be fundamental, unexplainable, theoretical principles over and above the theoretical principles of the reducing science.

The type/type identity theory thus explicates claims (3) and (4) of materialism in the simplest possible way: mental properties are real, and mental property-instantiations in humans are physico-chemically explainable, because mental properties just *are* physico-chemical properties. Likewise, *mutatis mutandis*, for mental events and states.

Early papers defending the identity theory stressed both the ever-mounting evidence for systematic micro-explainability of the phenomena described in the various special sciences on the basis of more basic sciences (ultimately physics), and the ontological queerness that would attend unexplainable correlations between physical and non-physical properties. Smart (1962) put it this way:

> That everything should be explicable in terms of physics . . . except the occurrence of sensations seems to be frankly unbelievable. Such sensations would be 'nomological danglers,' to use Feigl's expression. . . . I cannot believe that ultimate laws of nature could relate simple constituents to configurations consisting of perhaps billions of neurons. . . . Such laws would be like nothing so far known in science. They have a queer 'smell' to them. (pp. 161–2)

Some defenders of the type/type identity theory also invoke a causal account of mental terms and concepts. As Lewis (1966) summarizes the reasoning:

> The definitive characteristic of any (sort of) experience as such is its causal role, its syndrome of most typical causes and effects. But we materialists believe that these causal roles which belong by analytic necessity to experiences, belong in fact to certain physical states.

Since those physical states possess the definitive characteristics of experience, they must be the experiences. (p. 17)

Lewis (1980) has refined the causal account of mental notions by claiming that our terms for mental state-types denote in a population-relative way. Thus, Martians could have mentality even if they are drastically different, physico-chemically, from humans: mental-state terms would denote different physical properties relative to the Martian population than they do relative to the human population (*see* LEWIS).

Reduction without Identity

A few philosophers reject the type/type identity theory while still espousing, or at least allowing the possibility of, the micro-reducibility of psychology to natural science. Shaffer (1963), for instance, argues that even if concrete mental events are identical to physical events, nevertheless the properties of mental events by which we introspectively notice them and categorize them are non-physical:

> Let us take the case where a person reports the having of some mental event, the having of an after-image, a thought, or a sensation of pain. Now such a person has surely noticed that *something* has occurred, and he has surely noticed that this something has *some* features. . . . Now it seems to me obvious that, in many cases at least, the person does not notice any *physical* features. . . . Yet he does notice *some* feature. . . . The noticing of some non-physical feature is the only way to explain how anything is noticed at all. (p. 163)

Shaffer maintains, as does Kim (1966), that genuine micro-reduction can be underwritten by universally quantified biconditional bridge laws, even if these bridge laws express nomic correlations between distinct properties. In effect, they hold that this brand of property dualism still does justice

473

to materialism, since it is still a reductionist conception of mentality.

However, if the bridge laws are themselves unexplainable, hence metaphysically fundamental, then a serious *prima facie* doubt arises whether this brand of property dualism really comports with tenet (3) of materialism – and whether it really counts as a reductionist position. In genuine reductive explanation, presumably, any unexplained laws should either be part of the reducing theory or else should reside at a still more fundamental explanatory level. This judgment, I take it, is one principal reason for the received view that the socalled 'bridge laws' in classic models of intertheoretic reduction really must reflect intertheoretic *property identities* in order to effect a genuine reduction.

ELIMINATIVE PHYSICALISM

Eliminative physicalism embraces claims (1)–(3) of materialism, while arguing that claims (4)–(7) are very likely false (*see* ELIMINATIVISM). Eliminative physicalists typically share reductive physicalism's conception of how theses (4)–(7) of materialism are to be construed. That is, the eliminativists too maintain that in order for mentality to be accommodatable within a materialist metaphysics, psychology would have to be reducible to physical theory; and, in accordance with the received view of inter-theoretic reduction, they maintain that such reduction would involve systematic type/type psychophysical identities. But they then point out the serious empirical possibility that this reducibility requirement cannot be met – that our mental categories will turn out not to correlate neatly with the properties and natural kinds of natural science. They argue that such type/type matchups are rather unlikely – among other reasons, because commonsense mentalistic psychology (so-called FOLK PSYCHOLOGY) predates modern science. As Churchland (1981) puts it:

If we approach *homo sapiens* from the perspective of natural history and the physical sciences, we can tell a coherent story of his constitution, development, and behavioral capacities which encompasses particle physics, atomic and molecular theory, organic chemistry, evolutionary theory, biology, physiology, and materialistic neurotheory. That story, though still radically incomplete, is already extremely powerful. . . . And it is deliberately and self-consciously coherent with the rest of our developing world picture. . . . But FP [folk psychology] is no part of this growing synthesis. Its intentional categories stand magnificently alone, without visible prospect of reduction to that larger corpus. (p. 75)

Eliminative physicalists sometimes offer further reasons in support of the falsity of folk psychology, in addition to its likely irreducibility to natural science. For instance, they sometimes argue (i) that folk psychology is committed to the existence of language-like mental representations in *homo sapiens*; and (ii) that in light of recent theoretical developments in cognitive science and neuroscience, this LANGUAGE OF THOUGHT hypothesis is probably false.

NON-REDUCTIVE PHYSICALISM

Much recent philosophy of mind, while still remaining true to materialism, has questioned in one way or another the contention that in order for theses (4)–(7) to be true, mentalistic psychology must be reducible to physical science via type/type psychophysical bridge laws expressing either property identities or nomic coextensiveness of distinct properties. The rubric 'non-reductive physicalism' covers a range of philosophical positions that meet this description. I will give a broad typology of these views. Let me remark at the outset, though, that for the term 'reduction' (just as for 'physicalism'), one should really distinguish between (i) a vague, pre-theoretic meaning, and (ii) proposed precisifications or explications of the pre-theoretic notion. Although the positions to be described are 'non-reductive' relative to the traditional, received, standard explication of reduction in philosophy of science, they also can be – and often are – called 'reductive' anyway. As the traditional explications of materialism get replaced by less-restrictive conceptions, there is a natural tendency for the received explication of reduction to begin undergoing the same fate.

Anomalous Monism

DAVIDSON (1970) adopts a position that explicitly repudiates reductive physicalism, yet purports to be a version of materialism nonetheless. Davidson holds that although *token* mental events and states are identical to token physical events and states, mental *types* – i.e. kinds, and/or properties – are neither identical to, nor nomically coextensive with, physical types. His argument for this position relies largely on the contention that the correct assignment of mental and actional properties to a person is always a holistic matter, involving a global, temporally diachronic, 'intentional interpretation' of the person.

Davidson's reasoning suggests that the demand for psychophysical type/type identities, or for nomic coextensions, is an excessive demand for a materialist to make – that even though mental properties do not conform to this demand, there is nothing inherently objectionable or mysterious, from a materialistic perspective, about the fact that humans are susceptible to intentional interpretation, and hence that mental kinds and attributes can be accommodated within a materialistic metaphysics in some other way. As regards claims (4)–(7) of materialism, he is sometimes interpreted as maintaining that the psychophysical identity theory suffices, by itself, to underwrite these claims: mental events are physical, hence are part of the physico-chemical causal nexus, hence are causally explanatory.

But as many philosophers have in effect pointed out, accommodating claims (4)–(7) of materialism evidently requires more than just token mental/physical identities. Mentalistic explanation presupposes not merely that mental events *are* causes, but

also that they have causal/explanatory relevance *as* mental – i.e. relevance insofar as they fall under mental kinds or types. Thus a *prima facie* question arises whether Davidson's position, which denies there are strict psychophysical or psychological laws, can accommodate the causal/explanatory relevance of the mental *qua* mental. If not, then his view would amount, in effect, to EPIPHENOMENALISM with respect to mental properties.

Apart from anomalism *per se*, the problem of causal/explanatory relevance evidently arises for any form of non-reductive physicalism (and, indeed, for non-identity versions of reductive physicalism too). For, if mental properties are not identical to physical properties, and if claims (1)–(3) of materialism are true, then there is a *prima facie* worry that physico-chemical properties 'do all the real causal/explanatory work', and that mental properties are epiphenomenal. Non-reductive physicalists of all stripes, whether or not they espouse Davidson's anomalism, thus bear the burden of arguing that mental properties, despite being irreducible to physical ones, nevertheless have genuine causal/explanatory relevance even though the human body is a causally complete physico-chemical system. The task is to explain why, and how, there can be genuine causal explanation at higher levels of description (the mental level in particular), rather than 'explanatory exclusion' of higher levels by lower levels. Substantial recent attention in philosophy of mind has been devoted to this task (*see* REASONS AND CAUSES).

Although Davidson himself said rather little by way of a positive, non-reductive, account of the interrelations between physical and mental properties, he did make these suggestive remarks:

Although the position I describe denies there are psychophysical laws, it is consistent with the view that mental characteristics are in some sense dependent, or supervenient, on physical characteristics. Such supervenience might be taken to mean that there

475

cannot be two events alike in all physical respects but different in some mental respect, or that an object cannot alter in some mental respect without altering in some physical respect. Dependence or supervenience of this kind does not entail reducibility through law or definition. (Davidson, 1970, p. 88)

This passage has inspired a substantial amount of philosophical effort, in philosophy of mind and also elsewhere in metaphysics, seeking to harness the notion of SUPERVENIENCE to undergird claims (4)–(7) of materialism. Supervenience has been invoked, for instance, in efforts to account for the causal/explanatory efficacy of mental properties *qua* mental (e.g. Kim, 1984). And it has often been regarded in the manner intimated by Davidson in the above-quoted passage: as a relation that makes mental properties dependent on the physical, and hence 'materialistically respectable', without reducing them to physical properties.

Functionalism

FUNCTIONALISM denies that mental properties are identical to specific physicochemical properties, and asserts instead that they are multiply realizable properties whose essence is their typical causal role within creatures that instantiate them. Mental properties are like the properties *being locked* and *being unlocked*, instantiable by those physical devices that are locks. These properties are not narrowly physical (since there are innumerably many kinds of locks, physically quite different from one another), but rather are causal/functional. To be locked (unlocked) is to be in a state which prevents the lock from opening (causes the lock to open) when subjected to the appropriate opening-action. Likewise, the functionalist claims, the essence of each mental property is its syndrome of typical causal connections to sensory properties, behavioural properties, and other such mental properties. Although mental properties are not narrowly physical, on this view,

they are materialistically kosher even so. For, on any occasion when a mental property is instantiated, there is an explanation available for *why* it is being instantiated: viz. a physical property is instantiated whose causal role, in the given creature, qualifies this property as a realizer of the higher-order, mental, property.

Functionalists typically invoke the physical possibility of multiple realization as a reason to reject reductive physicalism and instead identify mental properties with functional properties. Yet as I remarked earlier, some reductive physicalists also advocate a causal account of mental terms and concepts, and employ this account in arguing *in favour* of psychophysical property identities. The reductionists propose to accommodate the physical possibility of Martian mentality not by allowing that mental properties are differently realized in Martians than in humans, but instead by treating mental property-terms as species-relative non-rigid designators: these terms denote physical properties, all right, but different ones relative to Martians than relative to humans.

But the appropriate functionalist rejoinder is to point out the apparent physical possibility of a *single* species of creatures whose individual members are so constituted physically that mental properties are realizable, *within a single creature*, by a radical multiplicity of distinct physical properties. (For all we now know, humans themselves might be like this.) Thus, once one appreciates the full extent of the possibilities concerning multiple realization, reductive physicalism comes to look excessively strong. This point applies not just to psychology, but to the special sciences generally (cf. FODOR, 1974).

'Naturalizing' Projects

Functionalism has begun to wane in popularity in philosophy of mind, in part because of the relevance of TWIN EARTH thought experiments: it seems that an Earthling and his Twin Earth duplicate could be in identical functional states but distinct mental states. (The Earthling is thinking about water; the duplicate is thinking about XYZ.)

(*See* EXTERNALISM INTERNALISM; INTER-
NATIONALITY.) Nevertheless, there is still
widespread acceptance of the contention
that mental properties are multiply realizable physically, rather than being identical
to physical properties or nomically coextensive with them. So in the wake of functionalism there have arisen a variety of
philosophical positions and projects which
seek to accommodate theses (1)–(7) in some
way other than via traditional reductive
physicalism. Typically these projects get
placed together under the rubric 'naturalization'. The project of naturalization
involves giving a tractable specification, in
non-intentional and non-semantic terms –
though not necessarily in narrowly *physical*
terms – for the instantiation of any mental
property with specific intentional CONTENT.
'Tractability' is my own term; and the
demand for it is usually implicit in recent
philosophical work, rather than being on
the surface. Roughly, a tractable specification is a relatively compact, relatively non-
baroque, non-disjunctive, cognitively surveyable, formulation of *sufficient conditions*
(for some philosophers, sufficient *and necessary* conditions). Recent philosophical proposals for 'naturalizing' intentional mental
properties have centred, for instance, on
systematic *correlation* between MENTAL
REPRESENTATIONS and what they represent
(e.g. Fodor, 1990); on the biological notion
of *relational proper function* (e.g. Millikan,
1984; DRETSKE, 1988); or on the computer
scientist's notion of simulation (e.g.
Cummins, 1989).

Post-Analytic Physicalism

A number of philosophers (e.g. Baker,
1987; Stich, 1992; Tye, 1992) have
recently argued that projects for 'naturalizing' mentality probably cannot succeed. For
one thing, counterexamples keep surfacing,
and the accumulating inductive evidence
suggests that they always will. For another,
it looks increasingly likely that our mental
concepts (indeed, most of our concepts) are
essentially vague, and have some kind of
'prototype' structure – rather than having
sharply delimited applicability conditions,

expressible via 'conceptual analyses' of the
kind traditionally sought during the heyday
of High Church analytic philosophy. So
there are reasons to seek out some new
way of explicating claims (4)–(7) of materialism still further removed from the traditional type/type psychophysical identity
theory. Let me now sketch such a post-
analytic physicalism (cf. Horgan, 1992,
1993).

One key tenet is that mental properties
and facts are supervenient on physical properties and facts. It is important to appreciate
that this supervenience thesis could well be
true even if there is no way to *tractably*
specify the non-mental conditions that
suffice for mental phenomena. Perhaps, for
instance, the physical supervenience base
for an intentional mental property, on a
given occasion of instantiation, generally
involves a good-sized chunk of spacetime
extending well beyond the cognizer's own
body and well beyond the time at which the
mental event occurs; perhaps it involves
a rather gargantuan number of physico-
chemical goings-on within that extended
spatiotemporal region; and perhaps there
isn't any simple way to describe, in non-
intentional vocabulary, all the *relevant*
aspects of this hugely complex supervenience base. Perhaps, in addition, the
supervenience of the mental is largely a
holistic matter – with mental properties
supervening collectively, as part of the
correct global intentional interpretation
of a cognizer – or perhaps the cognizer's
whole community or whole species. In
short, it might be that the search for tractably specifiable, cognitively surveyable, non-
intentional sufficient conditions for mentality is utterly hopeless – and yet that the
mental supervenes on the physical nonetheless.

A second tenet of post-analytic physicalism, as with other versions of non-
reductive physicalism, is that mental
properties have genuine causal/explanatory
relevance even though the human body is a
causally complete physico-chemical system.
Although mental properties always have
their efficacy via the physical properties

477

that realize them on particular occasions of instantiation – rather than being fundamental force-generating properties, on a par with the force-generating properties of physics – nevertheless they are causally and explanatorily efficacious anyway. (A physical property that realizes a mental property, on a given occasion of the mental property's instantiation, does not necessarily constitute the full *supervenience base* for that mental property.)

A third tenet is that inter-level supervenience facts are in principle *explainable*, rather than being fundamental and *sui generis*. This tenet is evidently dictated by contention (3) of materialism. For, unless psychophysical supervenience facts are themselves explainable, then the instantiation of mental properties is not explainable on the basis of physico-chemical facts, but only on the basis of such facts *plus metaphysically fundamental inter-level, supervenience facts*.

Even if there are no *tractably specifiable* non-semantic and non-intentional sufficient conditions for intentional mental states, the supervenience of the mental on the physical may well be susceptible, in principle, to explanation anyway. Exploring what kinds of criteria these explanations should meet, and making a case that psychophysical supervenience relations are indeed susceptible to such explanations (cf. Horgan and Timmons, 1992), are thus important projects for post-analytic physicalism. To be sure, a position that asserts the explainability of psychophysical supervenience relations, but does not offer any tractable specification of non-intentional sufficient conditions for mentality, would differ from the versions of physicalism that have dominated the recent philosophical landscape. But this would be yet another phase in the ongoing dialectical interplay between philosophers' pre-theoretic understanding of materialism and their attempts to give that understanding an adequate theoretical articulation.

See also An Essay on Mind section 3; PHYSICALISM (2).

BIBLIOGRAPHY

Baker, L.R. 1987. *Saving Belief: A Critique of Physicalism*. Princeton University Press.

Churchland, P.M. 1981. Eliminative materialism and propositional attitudes. *Journal of Philosophy*, 78, 67–90.

Cummins, R. 1989. *Meaning and Mental Representation*. Cambridge, MA.: MIT Press/ Bradford Books.

Davidson, D. 1970. Mental events. In *Experience and Theory*, ed. L. Foster and J. W. Swanson. Amherst: University of Massachusetts Press.

Dretske, F. 1988. *Explaining Behavior: Reasons in a World of Causes*. Cambridge, MA.: MIT Press/Bradford Books.

Fodor, J. 1974. Special sciences (or: the disunity of science as a working hypothesis). *Synthèse*, 28, 97–115.

Fodor, J. 1990. *A Theory of Content and Other Essays*. Cambridge, MA.: MIT Press/Bradford Books.

Horgan, T. 1992. From cognitive science to folk psychology: computation, mental representation, and belief. *Philosophy and Phenomenological Research*, 52, 447–84.

Horgan, T. 1993. Nonreductive materialism and the explanatory autonomy of psychology. In *Naturalism: A Critical Appraisal*, ed. S. J. Wagner and R. Warner. Notre Dame: University of Notre Dame Press.

Horgan, T., and Timmons, M. 1992. Troubles on moral twin earth: moral queerness revived. *Synthèse*, 92, 221–60.

Kim, J. 1966. On the psycho-physical identity theory. *American Philosophical Quarterly*, 3, 227–35.

Kim, J. 1984. Epiphenomenal and supervenient causation. *Midwest Studies in Philosophy*, Vol. 9, Minneapolis: University of Minnesota Press.

Lewis, D. 1966. An argument for the identity theory. *Journal of Philosophy*, 63, 17–25.

Lewis, D. 1980. Mad pain and Martian pain. *Readings in the Philosophy of Psychology, Vol. 1*, ed. N. Block. Cambridge, MA.: Harvard University Press.

Millikan, R. 1984. *Language, Thought, and Other Biological Categories*. Cambridge, MA.: MIT Press/Bradford Books.

Shaffer, J. 1963. Mental events and the brain. *Journal of Philosophy*, 60, 160–66.

Smart, J.J.C. 1962. Sensations and brain processes. In *Philosophy of Mind*, ed. V. C. Chappell. Englewood Cliffs: Prentice-Hall.

Stich, S. 1992. What is a theory of mental representation? *Mind*, 101, 243–61.

Tye, M. 1992. Naturalism and the mental. *Mind*, 101, 421–41.

TERENCE E. HORGAN

physicalism (2): against physicalism 'How the purer spirit is united to this clod' said Joseph Glanvill, 'is a knot too hard for fallen humanity to untie'. Although some contemporary philosophers share this pessimism about the MIND–BODY PROBLEM, there is in general a consensus that some form of *physicalism* is the solution to the problem. Physicalism is the thesis that all entities – whether objects, events, properties, relations or facts – are, or are reducible to, or are ontologically dependent on, physical entities. Physicalists might differ in their other metaphysical commitments: they may deny that there are any events, properties or facts at all, for example. But common to all forms of physicalism is the view that whatever exists is in some sense physical. My aim here is to outline the main physicalist positions, and express some scepticism about the physicalist consensus.

Opposition to physicalism standardly arises from reflection on the irreducible nature of the conscious properties of the mind (*see* CONSCIOUSNESS; QUALIA). These properties are claimed to be essentially subjective, something that a purely physical world must lack, because knowledge of these properties is supposed to essentially involve subjective experience in a way that knowledge of the physical does not (see the celebrated 'knowledge argument' of Jackson, 1986).

However, this sort of argument is more properly directed against *naturalism* – the thesis that the empirical world can be entirely accounted for by the natural sciences, including empirical psychology – rather than physicalism as such. (So naturalism is distinct from physicalism if there

are 'natural' features of the world that are not physical.) The knowledge argument, if successful, would refute any view that claims that everything in the world is objective, and thus the potential subject-matter of a natural science. Such a view need not be physicalism. In this essay I shall be concerned only with arguments specifically against physicalism proper, not those against the weaker thesis of naturalism.

THE DEFINITION OF 'PHYSICALISM'

Before assessing physicalism, we need to know what it is. But the definition of 'physicalism' gives rise to a problem even before we consider the difficulties posed, for example, by consciousness. The problem is how to formulate a conception of the *physical* that is not so strong as to collapse into an implausible ELIMINATIVISM – the outright denial of mental phenomena – but not so weak as to let in the mental as physical by definition. In defining the physical, physicalists must steer a path between the two horns of this dilemma: the physical must not be defined in such a way as to make physicalism obviously false, nor trivially true.

I shall have to assume here without argument that the first horn of this dilemma – eliminative physicalism – is unacceptable. The second horn is a problem because physicalism needs a principled distinction between the mental and the physical if it is not to be vacuous. It needs a characterization of the essential marks of the mental, such as consciousness and INTENTIONALITY. But it also needs a characterization of the essential marks of the physical. And many attempts to give such a characterization either fail to include obviously physical phenomena, or fail to exclude obviously mental phenomena.

As an example, consider the claim made by a number of philosophers that the physical is the *spatial* (*see* Charles, 1992). This captures many things that are obviously physical: as well as the medium-sized dry goods of everyday experience, the atoms, electrons and quarks of microphysics come out as physical on this definition. But does the definition rule out the mental? Surely nothing is more natural than the idea that my thoughts and sensations occur where my body is. So how can this definition of the physical fail to count the mental as being trivially physical? There is of course a philosophical conception of the mental on which mental phenomena are not spatial – this is what some dualists believe (*see* DUALISM). But this conception is part of a specific and contentious *theory* of the mental, not a constraint on any such theory.

In any case, not every dualist is committed to the non-spatiality of the mental (*see* Hart, 1988). A dualist could coherently hold that I am not the same thing as my body or brain, even though I occupy the same space as it. The physicalist could respond that even if the mental were spatial, on this dualist conception it would fail to be physical if it could occupy the same space as a physical thing without sharing that thing's parts (*see* Charles, 1992, p. 281). So a 'ghostly' conception of the mental would be ruled out by this definition of the physical. But now the definition rules out too much, since rainbows and clouds will turn out not to be physical objects: a bird can pass through a cloud without sharing any of its parts.

The proper response for a physicalist is to give up the attempt to define the physical in a a priori terms, and to define it instead in terms of the entities postulated by physical science. After all, physicalism is standardly supposed to be an empirical conjecture, not an a priori truth. Understood in this way, physicalism is the claim that physical science has a certain ontological authority. Different kinds of physicalism say different things about this authority: some say that the only entities there are are those physical science talks about. Others say that if there are entities other than those physical science talks about, these will be ultimately dependent on physical entities.

I shall discuss a couple of these different options below. But the prior question is: what is physical science? Obviously physical science includes all the many branches of physics as now conceived: mechanics, electromagnetism, thermodynamics, gravity, particle physics, etc. But no physicalist thinks that this is the full extent of physical science. For one thing, chemistry and molecular biology are normally considered unproblematically physical. For another, no one believes that physics proper is now finished: physics may discover many new entities and laws in order to adequately account for reality.

But why are chemistry and molecular biology thought to be *physical* sciences? One possibility is that these sciences *reduce* to physics in some sense (*see* REDUCTION). But this is not based on the fact that reductions between (say) all theories in chemistry and physics have actually been achieved; the idea is rather that they reduce to physics 'in principle'. But what is the principle? It cannot be physicalism itself, if reducibility to the physical is supposed to tell us the boundaries of physical science. Yet if some physical theories are not reducible to physics proper, then what prevents an irreducible psychology from being a physical science in this sense?

What about the development of future physics? If current physics develops in certain unforseeable ways, then how can physicalism be defined *now* in such a way as to rule out the mental? Perhaps physical science can be defined as the final theory of everything. But if it turns out that irreducible psychological properties are appealed to in the final theory of everything, then the mental will once again count as physical by mere definition.

There are therefore real difficulties in defining the physical which the physicalist must address (*see* Crane and Mellor, 1990). For the purposes of this article, however, we need to fix on a rough definition of physical science, in order to assess current physicalist proposals. Let this (admittedly vague) notion of the physical be: the entities appealed to by the true completed science whose explananda are uncontroversially physical (*see* Papineau, 1990).

ARGUMENTS FOR PHYSICALISM

So what do physicalists claim to be the relation between the mental and the physical, so conceived? Physicalist answers can be divided into two kinds: those that say that mental phenomena are strictly identical to certain physical phenomena (*see* IDENTITY THEORIES), and those that say mental phenomena are not identical with, but *dependent* or *supervenient upon* certain physical phenomena (*see* SUPERVENIENCE). These two views can be seen as two ways of reading the claim that the mental is physical: the first view says that the 'is' in question is the 'is' of identity, the second that it is the 'is' of constitution.

There are a number of arguments for the various forms of identity theory that have a common structure. First a claim is made about the causal nature of the physical world: every physical effect has a complete physical cause. Purely physical causes suffice to fix (or to fix the chances of) every physical effect. For brevity, call this claim 'Completeness'. Then a claim is made about mental causation: some or all mental states have some physical effects. We then have a conflict: if physical effects are not massively overdetermined by distinct physical and mental causes, then how is mental causation possible, given Completeness (*see* REASONS AND CAUSES)? The physicalist solution is to identify the mental cause with some physical state of the brain. (For the argument in this form, *see* Papineau, 1990; for other arguments that derive an identity theory from versions of such a conflict – in very different ways – *see* LEWIS, 1966 and DAVIDSON, 1980.)

Notice that if there is to be a conflict between mental causation and Completeness, the notion of causation as applied to the mental must be the same as that applied to the physical. For if mental causation were utterly different from physical causation, then mental and physical causes would not be competitors, and there would be no motivation for the identity claim. I shall call this assumption the 'Homogeneity' of mental and physical causation. According-

ing to this Homogeneity claim, the terms 'physical' and 'mental' in 'physical/mental causation' are really transferred epithets: what is physical or mental are the relata of causation, not the causation itself.

The general argument from reconciling Completeness with mental causation is an argument for the identity of mental phenomena with certain physical phenomena. There are two kinds of identity theory: the reductive type identity theory which says that mental properties are physical properties (Lewis, 1966); and the token identity theory which says merely that mental particulars are physical particulars (Davidson, 1980).

What can be said for this general argument? It might be thought that someone looking for a reason for believing in physicalism as a solution to the mind–body problem would not be impressed by the appeal to Completeness. For Completeness seems just too close to the physicalist conclusion to be persuasive. Why should someone unpersuaded of the truth of physicalism about the mind be swayed by the claim that all physical effects have complete physical causes?

The response will be that Completeness, while not a law of physics itself, is a high-level empirical generalization about the practice and content of physical science. David Lewis formulates a version of Completeness in terms of the idea of *explanation*:

> there is some unified body of scientific theories of the sort we now accept, which together provide a true and exhaustive account of all physical phenomena. They are unified in that they are cumulative: the theory governing any physical phenomenon is explained by theories governing phenomena out of which that phenomenon is composed and by the way it is composed out of them. The same is true of the latter phenomena, and so on down to fundamental particles or fields governed by a few simple laws, more or less as conceived in present-day theoretical physics. (Lewis, 1966, p. 105)

481

Lewis here appeals to two ideas: first, that entities are exhaustively composed out of physical parts; and second, that the theories that explain the whole are themselves explained by theories that explain the parts out of which the whole is composed.

Can Completeness be derived from these ideas? I think not: non-physicalists can accept these ideas without accepting Completeness. So for one thing, certain non-physicalists can accept that non-physical objects have physical parts, since they will want to formulate their thesis in terms of non-physical *properties*, not parts. So the idea that macroscopic objects are composed out of physical parts will not trouble this kind of non-physicalist, so long as these objects have properties that are non-physical. And if properties are implicated in causation, it is therefore open for this non-physicalist to deny that all effects have complete physical causes.

In any case, the thesis about explanation is questionable. What it implies is that all macro-phenomena can be explained by the laws governing their micro-parts. But many physicalists are happy to accept that psychological *explanations* have a degree of autonomy from physical explanations – this is why I framed Completeness as a claim about *causation*, rather than explanation. And even in physics, it is not always true that all explanations are micro-reductive in the above way. For example: consider a gas sample at a constant temperature whose voume is suddenly halved. If the gas is ideal, then according to Boyle's law, it will reach an equilibrium pressure that is twice its initial pressure. The law does not explain what all the gas's molecules must do before it reaches equilibrium, *except* that they must be such as to double the sample's pressure. The law thus explains the molecules' behaviour in terms of the behaviour of the whole sample (*see* Crane and Mellor, 1990, p. 190).

To respond to this that macro-laws like these are ultimately reducible to micro-laws only raises the question-begging assumptions about reducibility 'in principle' mentioned above. And this move also introduces a stronger physicalist commitment than that involved in Completeness; so it would be unwise to employ it in a defence of Completeness.

Nor does Completeness follow from philosophical claims about causation, even if the 'real essence' of causation is the flow of energy (*see* Crane and Mellor, 1990, pp. 191–192; Hart, 1988, ch. 9). So with 'physical' understood in a non-trivial way, Completeness is a substantial empirical conjecture that seems at least to lack decisive support. In the face of this, it is not absurd for a non-physicalist to deny Completeness, and hold that some physical effects have irreducible mental causes. The non-physicalist does not thereby have to hold that actions break the laws of physics – if there are laws linking mental and physical phenomena, these will have to be consistent with the laws of physics. But this is just a special case of the truism that all truths must be consistent.

A less extreme non-physicalist response is to allow Completeness but hold that actions are overdetermined by mental and physical causes. Physicalists cannot, and usually do not, deny that overdetermination is possible; their standard objection is rather to the *extent* of the overdetermination involved in the psychophysical case. As Stephen Schiffer puts it, 'it is hard to believe that God is such a bad engineer' (Schiffer, 1987, p. 148). But non-physicalism can make its position more palatable by emphasizing the nomic links between the mental and physical causes. Massive overdetermination of action will thus be shown to be explicable, and not a mere coincidence.

NON-REDUCTIVE PHYSICALISM

So far, I have discussed only the identity theories. However, many physicalists think that identity theories are not essential to physicalism, and are objectionable even on physicalist grounds. Type identity is thought to be too strong to be plausible, because of the well-known 'variable realization' objection: it seems empirically unlikely that every instance of a mental property is an instance of the same physical property (*see* TYPE/TOKEN).

Token identity, on the other hand, is considered too weak to *explain* the relation between the mental and the physical. To say that every mental particular (object or event) is a physical particular does not tell us what it is about the physical nature of the particular that makes it the mental particular it is. An analogy: it is hardly an explanation of why all US presidents have been white males to simply assert the token identity claim that each particular US president is identical with some particular white male.

For this reason, no physicalist holds a token identity theory without supplementing it with some claim about the relation between mental and physical properties. The claim is standardly that the physical properties of a mental particular *determine* its mental properties: physical type identity guarantees mental type identity, but not vice versa. To put it another way, the mental *supervenes* upon the physical (*see* SUPERVENIENCE). So all mental particulars are physical, without mental properties being identical with physical properties: this is *non-reductive* physicalism.

However, supervenience alone does not give you physicalism, since any theory that asserts a nomic dependence of the mental on the physical (e.g. epiphenomenalist dualism) can accept supervenience (*see also* Charles, 1992). To get physicalism, what has to be added to supervenience is the claim that the mental is 'nothing over and above' its supervenience base. If you take away the physical base, you take away the mental too, since the mental is in some sense 'composed' out of or 'realized' by the physical. For some philosophers, this claim is the essence of physicalism (*see* Snowdon, 1989).

The non-reductive physicalist now owes us an account of composition or realization. But whatever the account, I think that a serious problem will nonetheless arise for non-reductive physicalism. Again the issue turns on Completeness. If Completeness is true, and massive overdetermination is false, what happens to mental causation? Non-reductive physicalism faces a dilemma: either mental states or events are genuine causes, in which case it has to embrace massive overdetermination or deny Completeness – since the mental and the physical causes are not identical. Or the mental is causally impotent, in which case non-reductive physicalism embraces EPIPHENOMENALISM.

Physicalists typically respond to this dilemma in one of two ways. The first is to say that supervenience allows mental properties to inherit the causal efficacy of their subvening physical bases (*see* Segal and Sober, 1991). Completeness is preserved at the physical level, and given supervenience, mental properties 'ride on top' of the fundamental physical causes. The second response distinguishes between the notions of causal explanation as applied to the mental and as applied to the physical (*see* Jackson and Pettit, 1990). Again, Completeness is preserved at the level of microphysical particles, but some sort of causal role for the mental is preserved by the fact that mental explanations have a different structure than physical explanations.

Neither of these responses, it seems to me, avoids epiphenomenalism. The first response must deprive the mental – and indeed, any supervening features – of genuine causal efficacy, on pain of violating Completeness. (Some physicalists agree: *see* Schiffer, 1987, p. 154.) The second response is epiphenomenalist in a somewhat different sense: in distinguishing between the kinds of causation applied to the mental and the physical, it is committed to the denial of Homogeneity. But if this is abandoned, we no longer have the problem to which physicalism was supposed to be the solution.

And this is the reason why the physicalist should be worried by epiphenomenalism: it deprives physicalism of its only plausible motivation. The physicalist assumption that was driving the arguments for the Identity Theories was Completeness. The mind has to be physical because otherwise we could not account for its effects in the physical world. But now if we deny that the mind has effects, then we have no reason for saying it is physical (*see* Lewis, 1966, esp. pp. 105–6). For what exactly would be the content of insisting that the epiphenomenal mental properties were 'really' or 'fundamentally' physical, once it is admitted that they are not the same as physical properties, nor reducible to them? Once mental causation is out of the picture, it seems a mere terminological issue whether we call ourselves epiphenomenalist dualists or epiphenomenalist physicalists. Calling these epiphenomena 'physical' would be to relegate the term 'physical' once again to a merely honorific label.

Certainly many physicalists would feel the need to insist on the physical nature of these epiphenomena, just to rule out anything that looks, by their lights, too peculiar or weird. But if there is no conflict with Completeness, this requirement seems unmotivated. This objection to non-physical epiphenomena is reminiscent of J. L. Mackie's well-known 'argument from queerness' against the existence of objective moral values. And the reaction to both arguments should be the same: the world might turn out to be stranger than we think. Which is, after all, something that we have learned from physics itself.

See also An Essay on Mind section 3; PHYSICALISM (1).

BIBLIOGRAPHY

Charles, D. 1992. Supervenience, composition and physicalism. In *Reduction, Explanation and Realism*, ed. D. Charles and K. Lennon. Oxford: Clarendon Press. pp. 265–296.

Crane, T., and Mellor, D.H. 1990. There is no question of physicalism. *Mind*, 99, 185–206.

Davidson, D. 1980. Mental events. In *Essays on Actions and Events*. Oxford University Press.

Hart, W.D. 1988. *The Engines of the Soul*. Cambridge University Press.

Jackson, F. 1986. What Mary did not know. *Journal of Philosophy*, 83, 291–95.

Jackson, F., and Pettit, P. 1990. Causation in the philosophy of mind. *Philosophy and Phenomenological Research*, 50, 195–214.

Lewis, D. 1966. An argument for the identity theory. *Journal of Philosophy*, 63, 17–25. Reprinted in Lewis, D., *Philosophical Papers Volume I*, Oxford University Press, 1983.

Papineau, D. 1990. Why supervenience?. *Analysis*, 50, 66–71.

Schiffer, S. 1987. *Remnants of Meaning*. Cambridge, MA.: MIT Press.

Segal, G., and Sober, E. 1991. The causal efficacy of content. *Philosophical Studies*, 63, 1–30.

Snowdon, P. 1989. On formulating materialism and dualism. In *Cause, Mind and Reality*. Dordrecht: Kluwer, pp. 137–58.

TIM CRANE

possible world 'England might win the next test match in cricket.' This sentence says something about the fortunes of the English team, but it certainly does not assert that they will win. Instead, it makes what is called a 'modal' claim, where the specific mode is that of possibility. The sentence would mean just the same if it took this more explicit modal form: 'It is possible that England will win the next test match.' In addition to the mode *possibility*, there is the correlative mode of *impossibility*. One could have said: 'It is not impossible that England will win the next test match', and, though this has an undeniably pessimistic flavour, it strictly and literally says the same thing as the sentence cast in terms of possibility. Impossibility is a form of the mode *necessity*: a claim is said to be impossible when it is necessarily false. An example of an affirmative claim of necessity would be: 'Bachelors must be unmarried'. This last could also be rendered in the more explicit modal idiom as: 'It is necessary that bachelors are unmarried.'

Modal claims are fundamental to the ways we characterize the world, but, since they are not claims about how things actually are or will be, it is far from obvious what makes them true. And it is here that the notion of a possible world has a part to play. If you think of the totality of how things are as one world – the actual world – then one could conceive of lots of other worlds simply by imagining different one or more features of the actual world. Thus, there will be worlds almost exactly like ours, but containing one more grain of sand on a certain beach, or lacking one mole hill on a certain lawn. And of course there will be many worlds much more radically different from the actual world.

The complete set of these worlds (including the actual world) make up the infinite set of *possible worlds*. Depending on your ontological leanings (*see* ONTOLOGY), you can think of this set as genuinely existing, or existing only as an experiment in thought. But in either case they have a real use in providing straightforward truth conditions for modal claims. Take the earlier example: 'It is possible that England will win the next test match.' We can understand this as the following claim about the set of possible worlds:

There is at least one possible world in which it is true that England will win the test match.

Notice that, in this construal, we have traded the explicit use of modality for language that is directly assertoric. As one says, we are 'quantifying' over possible worlds ('there is at least one possible world . . .') and the claim made about these worlds does not employ the language of modality ('it is true that . . .'). Correlatively, we can use the set of possible worlds to give us a direct characterization of the truth conditions for claims of necessity:

In all possible worlds bachelors are unmarried.

The usefulness of possible worlds in providing truth conditions for modal claims is undeniable, though the examples given are only the beginning of the story. Moreover, since modality is integral to notions such as SUPERVENIENCE and identity (*see* IDENTITY THEORIES), there is a widespread use of possible worlds talk in the philosophy of mind.

SAMUEL GUTTENPLAN

practical reasoning   From the premises:

Socrates is a man,
All men are mortal,

one can justifiably draw the conclusion that:

Socrates is mortal.

This typical example of what is called 'theoretical' reasoning consists in moving from one set of things which are thought true to another, and a great deal of human enterprise depends upon correctly making such transitions in thought. However, there is another kind of reasoning which is no less important, but whose object is not merely transition from one set of thoughts to another. Following Aristotle, who first described it, this kind of reasoning is called (a little misleadingly) 'practical'; it is reasoning whose conclusion is not some further thought but the undertaking of some action. For example, if one thinks:

I am thirsty,
The water in front of me will quench my thirst,

then the conclusion likely to be drawn is not some further thought, but the action of reaching for the water.

Whilst it is easy to characterize practical reasoning as in this way parallel to theoretical reasoning, real difficulties emerge when one tries to exploit the parallel further. The canons of theoretical reasoning one finds in branches of logic are not obviously matched by practical reasoning, not least because actions, unlike thoughts, are neither true nor false. One cannot thus say that a good piece of practical reasoning preserves truth or even a high probability of truth. Yet, there is no doubt that some sort of standards apply. (*See* INTENTION; RATIONALITY; REASONS AND CAUSES.)

SAMUEL GUTTENPLAN

privacy (of the mental)   *see* FIRST-PERSON AUTHORITY.

private language argument *see An Essay on Mind* section 2.2.4; WITTGENSTEIN.

property A thorough discussion would take one deep into metaphysical and ontological issues, but, in the context of philosophy of mind, it is important to have some grasp of this notion. The best way to appreciate what is meant by a property is by contrast with two others: predicate and concept. Consider first the sentence: 'John is bearded.' The word 'John' in this sentence is a bit of language – a name of some individual human being – and no one would be tempted to confuse the word with what it names. Consider now the expression 'is bald'. This too is a bit of language – philosophers call it a 'predicate' – and it brings to our attention some property or feature which, if the sentence is true, is possessed by John. Understood in this way, a property is not itself linguistic though it is expressed, or conveyed, by something that is, namely a predicate. What might be said is that a property is a real feature of the world, and that it should be contrasted just as sharply with any predicates we use to express it as the name 'John' is contrasted with the person himself. However, it is a matter of great controversy just what sort of ontological status should be accorded to properties (*see* ONTOLOGY), so one should treat this particular formulation of the contrast with caution. What is important, though, is to recognize that, in terms of the natural divide between language and what language is about, predicates fall on the language side and properties on the other.

It should be mentioned here that properties (and predicates) can be more complicated than the above example allows. For instance, in the sentence, 'John is married to Mary', we are attributing to John the property of being married, and, unlike the property of being bald, this property of John is essentially relational. The predicate ('is married to') which expresses this property requires two names (for example, 'John' and 'Mary') in order to make up a complete sen-

tence, whilst 'is bald' only requires a single name. (Predicates like 'is bald' are called *monadic*, and those like 'is married to' *dyadic*. Moreover, it is commonly said that 'is married to' expresses a relation, rather than a property, though the terminology is not fixed here. Some authors speak of relations as different from properties in being more complex but like them in being non-linguistic, though it is more common to treat relations as a sub-class of properties.)

The second notion to contrast with property is CONCEPT, but one must be very careful here, since 'concept' has been used by philosophers and psychologists to serve many different purposes. One use has it that a concept is something mental, it is a certain way of conceiving of some aspect of the world. As such, concepts have a kind of subjectivity: two different individuals might, for example, have different concepts of birds, one thinking of them primarily as flying creatures and the other as feathered. Concepts in this sense are often described as a species of MENTAL REPRESENTATION, and as such they stand in sharp contrast to the notion of a property, since a property is something existing in the world. Also, given what was said above about the non-linguistic nature of properties, any understanding of concepts as linguistic would make it impossible to identify concepts and properties. However, it is possible to think of a concept as neither mental nor linguistic, and this would allow, though it doesn't dictate, that concepts and properties are the same kind of thing.

SAMUEL GUTTENPLAN

proposition When an English speaker says 'it is raining', and a French speaker says 'il pleut', it is natural to claim that they are saying the same *thing*, but it is not all that clear what that 'thing' is. It can scarcely be the sentence that each utters, for these are markedly different. Also, whilst it is true that these sentences mean the same, it is odd to say that they are 'saying the same meanings'. Indeed, aside from oddness, any appeal to meaning here seems to put the cart before the horse. For one would think that two sentences mean the same when they are used to say the same thing, and this brings us back to the question of what thing it is that is said.

Almost universally, the first step in clearing up the problem is to use the word 'proposition': we can say that the speakers in the above example used sentences in their own languages to *express the same proposition*. But now we need to be told what a proposition is, and this is no simple matter. Two ways of going about it can be found in the philosophical literature. The first is based on the notion of a POSSIBLE WORLD. The actual world consists of all actual things, properties and relations. But one can imagine other worlds which differ from the actual world in respect of the things they contain and/or in respect of properties and relations characterizing those things. Thus, there are possible worlds in which I am sitting with both feet on the floor now instead of with legs crossed, as well as others in which I don't exist at all. Indeed, it is obvious that once you think of possible worlds in this way, there will be an infinite number of them, each slightly or greatly different from the others and from the actual world. Consider now the sentence: 'Grass is green.' In some worlds – including the actual world – this will be true. In others, it will be false – either grass will be some other colour, or, perhaps, there will be no such thing as grass. Thus, the sentence *partitions* all possible worlds into two sorts: those in which the sentence is true, and those in which it is false. And we can define the proposition expressed by the sentence 'grass is green' as the set of possible worlds in which the sentence is true.

The second way to deal with propositions is to regard them as having a structure that mirrors the structure of sentences. On this conception, a proposition is an ordered set of things and their properties and/or relations. Moreover, the specific constituents of a given proposition structurally correspond to the sentence expressing the proposition. Thus the proposition expressed by 'grass is green' is a special sort of abstract entity consisting of grass, the property of being green, and the relation between these that makes it true that grass is green. It is felt by some writers that a notion of proposition that allows such structure has advantages in certain cases over the possible-worlds conception. For example, consider the sentence 'The number three is odd.' Numbers are plausibly regarded as having their properties *essentially*, i.e. as keeping them in all possible worlds. After all, how could something be the number three without being odd? For this sort of reason, the sentence 'The number three is odd' will be true in exactly the same worlds as the sentence: 'The number three is prime', and thus, on the possible worlds conception these two sentences will express the same proposition. But this seems unacceptable: someone could surely assert one and not the other – the sentences just don't seem to express the same thing. However, on the structured-entity conception of, proposition, this is easily handled: 'odd' and 'prime' pick out different properties, so the constituents of each relevant proposition will be different.

In the philosophy of mind, propositions understood in one way or another have figured centrally in attempts to understand INTENTIONALITY. As described above, a proposition, on one or another construal, is what a sentence expresses. However, attitudes have CONTENTS and it is natural to regard these contents as propositions. Indeed, attitudes are often simply called PROPOSITIONAL ATTITUDES. Of course, when someone believes or desires something, there need be no sentence uttered, and one cannot therefore say that a proposition is what a belief or a desire expresses. Instead it is usual to regard the attitudes as mental states directed either toward a sentence that expresses a proposition, or toward a proposition itself. Of course, establishing the relations between attitudes and propositions is only the first step in attempting to describe intentionality and this whole area is fraught with intricate difficulties.

SAMUEL GUTTENPLAN

487

propositional attitudes Our everyday conception of mentality bristles with notions like BELIEF, DESIRE, INTENTION, hope, fear, wish. Philosophers group these together and call them 'propositional attitudes'. What links these attitudes is the fact that they are identified by their propositional contents: a belief that snow is white is identified by the proposition that snow is white. Since propositional contents are attributed in English by 'that'-clauses, two people's beliefs, say, are counted as different if they are correctly identified by non-equivalent 'that'-clauses.

Propositional attitudes are woven into almost all aspects of ordinary life. Legal, social, political and economic practices would be unthinkable without the attitudes (*see* Baker, 1987). For example, nothing would be a contract if the parties to it lacked attitudes – such as belief that they were incurring certain obligations. No one could be held responsible for anything in the absence of attitudes about, among other things, what one is doing. In general, we make sense of behaviour in terms of attitudes: Smith turned up at 4 o'clock, because she thought that the meeting had been scheduled for that time. Reasons for action are intimately tied to attitudes (*see* ACTION). Indeed, some philosophers (such as Donald Davidson) take the attitudes to be definitive of the mental.

On the one hand, propositional attitudes are pervasive in our descriptive, explanatory, and justificatory practices. On the other hand, as mental states, they seem problematic to contemporary philosophers seeking insurance against DUALISM. Such philosophers, perhaps a majority, think that propositional attitudes stand in need of 'vindication' either by materialistic metaphysics or by science. In pursuit of such vindication, they have raised a number of questions about propositional attitudes, of which I shall discuss three that remain unresolved after intense investigation. (1) How are attitudes identified by content related to presumably less problematic physical states? (2) Given that brain states cause bodily movements, can propositional attitudes also have a causal role in behaviour? (3) In what way, if at all, will propositional attitudes figure in a comprehensive scientific psychology?

THE NATURALIZATION PROJECT

The first question – How are attitudes identified by content related to physical states? – has given rise to efforts to provide conditions, in naturalistic terms, for an internal state to have propositional content. Roughly, to require that the conditions be given in naturalistic terms is to require that they be statable without the use of 'that'-clauses and without the use of semantic terms like 'denotes', 'refers to', or 'means that'. Those engaged in naturalization are investigating a special case of the general question: how can one physical state represent another? Under what physical conditions does a state have a certain content? How can a state be 'directed upon' a state of affairs – one that may not even obtain? (*See* CONTENT; INTENTIONALITY.)

Not only are contents intentional-with-a-'t' (i.e. directed upon a state of affairs that may or may not obtain), but also attributions of contents are intensional-with-an-'s': substitution of co-referring terms may change the truth value of the attribution. For example, from the attribution to Smith of a belief that the robber fled the scene, and the fact that the robber is the mayor, we cannot infer that Smith believes that the mayor fled the scene. If Smith is unaware that the robber is the mayor, she may have the first belief, but lack the second. Contents (and hence beliefs) are thus sensitive to the way things are described.

The naturalizer ties propositional attitudes to types or tokens of internal states. (A type is a kind of state; a token is a particular spatiotemporal instance of a kind of state.) (*See* IDENTITY THEORIES; SUPERVENIENCE.) The idea is that people token internal states that have certain 'shapes' or other non-semantic properties, and these states have content in virtue of correlations of one sort or another between their tokenings and external conditions. The naturalization project is to spell out the kind of correlation that confers content. There are several versions, of which I shall describe three. Each traces content back to what causes tokens of a certain type (aetiological theories) and/or to what is the function of tokens of a certain type (teleological theories).

On Ruth Millikan's (1984) 'teleofunctional' evolutionary account, contents of attitudes derive from the functions of mechanisms designed by natural selection to make and to use abstract 'maps' or 'diagrams' or 'mental sentence' pictures of the world in order to produce actions appropriate to that world. These mechanisms have biologically normal ways of accomplishing the abstract map-making and map-using tasks, but may also fail quite often, just as the mouse-tracking abilities of the house-cat may fail in particular cases. Then maps are produced that are 'wrong', given how the system is designed to use them. A question for this approach is whether the psychological mechanisms of concept- and belief-formation in humans, as designed by evolution, are determinate enough, as regards their historical biologically normal ways of functioning, to yield the determinacy we find in belief content. (For a different kind of teleological functionalism, see Lycan, 1988.)

A second approach to naturalizing the attitudes looks to lawful covariation of tokenings of certain states and certain external conditions. Certain states are natural indicators of other states: for example, the number of tree rings indicates the age of the tree. There is a general causal dependency of the indicator on what it indicates. Another way to put the point is to say that the number of tree rings carries information about the age of the tree: under optimal or ideal conditions, the number of tree rings covaries with the age in years of the tree. DRETSKE and others have used the notions of carrying information and of indicating something (Dretske, 1988) to show how physical states could have content or meaning.

A difficulty for this approach to naturalization is to account for the possibility of error. Suppose that tokens of a certain type have regularly been caused by the presence of dogs; but on some occasion, a token of that type is caused by a cat. Then, if the content of a token is determined by what information it carries (i.e. by what caused it), there is no way for the token to misrepresent a dog as a cat. Here are two ways in which 'indicator' theories may try to meet the problem of error. (i) Specify ideal conditions. Identify the content of a token by its cause in ideal conditions; then construe misrepresentation in terms of what causes tokens of the type in non-ideal conditions. (ii) Specify a learning period, during which tokens of a certain type acquire a given content. Identify the content with the causes of the tokens during the learning period; then construe misrepresentation in terms of post-learning-period causes that differ from learning-period causes of tokens of the given type. A central difficulty for the 'indicator' theories is to specify non-circularly either ideal conditions or conditions that define a learning period. Neither non-circular specification has been forthcoming.

The deepest difficulty for the naturalization project is what FODOR has called the 'disjunction problem'. The disjunction problem is a generalization of the problem of error: roughly, if the content of a token is determined by what causes it, then why is not the content of tokens of a certain type a disjunction of the indefinitely many kinds of causes that produce tokens of that type? For example, if tokens of type T are caused at different times by cows, horses and thoughts about cowboys, then why doesn't T have the content cow-or-horse-or-thoughts-about-cowboys?

Fodor's solution – and this is the third approach to naturalizing the attitudes – is to specify content in terms of asymmetric dependence. Fodor (1987, 1990), develops this approach in conjunction with his postulation of a LANGUAGE OF THOUGHT. The general idea is that a symbol in the language of thought – say, 'C' – expresses the property of being a cow if and only if (i) it is a law that cows cause tokens of 'C', (ii) some tokens of 'C' are caused by non-cows (horses, say); and (iii) if cows did not cause 'C's, then neither would non-cows; but cows would still cause 'C's even if non-cows did not cause 'C's.

None of these reductive accounts of the attitudes has found full acceptance. Many philosophers simply assume that the attitudes supervene on some physical states or other, whether or not anybody can specify any supervenience base for any propositional attitude, and move on to other issues (*see* SUPERVENIENCE).

THE PROBLEM OF MENTAL CAUSATION

One of the issues to which philosophers have recently turned is the second of the questions: Given that brain states cause bodily movements, can propositional attitudes also have a causal role in behaviour? The problem of mental causation (Kim, 1988) is to find a causal role for propositional attitudes in the aetiology of behaviour.

One way to see the problem is to consider DAVIDSON's view of mental events as physical events described in the vocabulary of propositional attitudes. This is a kind of non-reductive materialism, since each mental token is a physical token, but mental types are not identified with physical types. On Davidson's view of causation, propositional attitudes are causes of behaviour, even though (i) all causal transactions are governed by strict laws, and (ii) there are no strict laws between propositional attitudes and the physical events that constitute the behaviour. The strict laws that subsume the mental causes and the physical effects are wholly physical.

This view has suggested to some a problem of mental causation. For, on this view, propositional attitudes (mental events) have effects in virtue of their physical properties but not in virtue of their having content or of their being propositional attitudes. The fact that neural events are describable as propositional attitudes is irrelevant to what they cause, or to the fact that they cause anything at all; for the physical properties of a mental event preempt or 'screen off' the mental properties.

Mental events, so the charge goes, are causally impotent.

This line of argument has elicited the following response. First, one may appeal to non-strict, or hedged, laws (laws with open-ended *ceteris paribus* clauses), and take properties mentioned in the antecedents of such laws to be causally relevant to producing instances of properties mentioned in the consequents. Hedged laws are common throughout the special sciences (Fodor, 1987). The existence of laws of the form 'If S believes that doing A will bring it about that p, and S wants to bring it about that p, and . . ., then, *ceteris paribus*, S will do A' would suffice to secure a causal role for propositional attitudes, on this Fodorean view. Those worried about mental causation will point out that even if propositional attitudes are causes, citing '*ceteris paribus*' laws does not show that they bring about their effects in virtue of having their contents. (*See* REASON AND CAUSES.)

For example, Jaegwon Kim has argued for a principle of explanatory exclusion, according to which there cannot be two or more complete and independent explanations of a single event. If there seem to be two complete and independent explanations of an event (e.g. one physical and one mental), then either at least one is not complete, or they are not independent. On the basis of certain metaphysical assumptions – such as that every physical event has a complete physical cause, and that every event is (or supervenes on) a physical event – Kim argues that every event has a completely sufficient physical cause, and hence a complete explanation in terms exclusively of physical properties. If any 'other' properties (such as propositional attitudes) seem also to explain an event, Kim concludes, they must be identical with, or reducible to, physical properties. If Kim is right, there is no 'logical space' for non-reductive materialism of either the Davidsonian or Fodorean variety.

There are difficult metaphysical issues here about supervenience and reducibility (*see* REDUCTION). For example, Kim's position seems to have unwanted consequences.

For the grounds that he gives to show that there is a problem of mental causation are equally good grounds to show that there is a problem of macrocausation generally (*see* PHYSICALISM (2)). Suffice it to say that the verdict is not yet in on the problem of mental causation.

THE SCIENTIFIC STATUS OF PROPOSITIONAL ATTITUDES

The third and final question – In what way, if at all, will propositional attitudes figure in a comprehensive scientific psychology? – concerns the scientific status of the propositional attitudes. Many philosophers hold that the fate of the propositional attitudes turns on the outcome of scientific psychology (*see* FOLK PSYCHOLOGY). If the explanatory kinds of scientific psychology turn out to be radically different from the attitudes, such philosophers hold, then the attitudes should go the way of phlogiston and witches.

Although a conclusive answer to the third question must await the outcome of scientific psychology, there has been important philosophical work done already on the issue of individuation. Say that a scheme of individuation is relational or wide if it classifies propositional attitudes in part by reference to the cognizer's environment, so that cognizers in different environments may have different attitudes even if they are molecule-for-molecule duplicates. (*see* EXTERNALISM/INTERNALISM; PUTNAM; TWIN EARTH). Say that a scheme of individuation is non-relational or narrow if it classifies propositional attitudes so that molecule-for-molecule duplicates necessarily have the same attitudes, regardless of differences in their environments.

Are propositional attitudes classified or individuated in a way that would put them at odds with entities countenanced by a scientific psychology? Here are four prominent views on the amenability of attitudes for incorporation into scientific psychology. (i) Propositional attitudes are individuated relationally, and are, therefore, ill-suited for science (Stich, 1983). (ii) Propositional attitudes are individuated relationally, but still are suitable for science (Burge, 1986). (iii) Propositional attitudes are individuated relationally, but they have narrow contents ('in the head') that are suitable for science (Fodor, 1987). (iv) Propositional attitudes are individuated non-relationally and are not, therefore, ill-suited for science (Lewis, 1983). Each of these positions remains controversial.

Consider the 'worst case'. Suppose that we had a comprehensive theory of human behaviour – say, one based on ARTIFICIAL INTELLIGENCE models known as 'parallel distributed processing' (*see* CONNECTIONISM). Suppose further that not only does the scientific theory fail to postulate internal states that have propositional or narrow content, but also that the states that it does postulate do not even loosely correlate with attitudes. Although this is extremely vague, the point is to suppose that 'mature scientific psychology' turns out in such a way that even under the loosest interpretation of 'vindication', we would all agree that mature scientific psychology failed to vindicate the attitudes.

The reason that vindication of the attitudes by science is so desired is that, failing vindication, only two alternatives are envisaged: we must either take propositional attitudes to resist incorporation into the physical world of science, and embrace dualism (widely considered untenable), or we must give up propositional attitudes as fictions, and embrace eliminative materialism.

ELIMINATIVE MATERIALISM AND BEYOND

Eliminative materialists, who deny the reality of propositional attitudes altogether, take a variety of positions. For example, QUINE (1960) takes the language of propositional attitudes to be a 'dramatic idiom'. Churchland (1989) envisages a new kind of everyday language that lacks commitment to propositional attitudes. Typically, eliminative materialists hold the view that the natural sciences are the exclusive arbiter of what there is, and that propositional attitudes fail to measure up to the standards of science.

An eliminative materialist whose position rests upon the assumed fact that scientific psychology will not show how attitudes 'fit' into the physical world, it would seem, ought to be an eliminativist about properties of middle-sized objects (like pillows and predators) as well. If by 'the physical world' one means the world described by fundamental physics, then we have no idea how predators fit into the physical world either: could a characterization of predators be given in the language of microphysics? If by 'the physical world' one means the world described non-intentionally and non-semantically, then pillows and other artefacts fail to fit into the physical world: there is no physically specifiable fact in virtue of which something is a pillow; what makes something a pillow depends in part on facts about its design and use – facts that we do not know how to specify in a non-intentional vocabulary. But these are not great philosophical discoveries that should motivate eliminativism about pillows or predators.

DENNETT used to be an 'instrumentalist', who appreciated the usefulness of belief-attributions while denying the reality of beliefs and desires. Such a position has seemed to many to be unstable, and Dennett himself has backed away from it (Dennett, 1991). Now he grants to the attitudes a kind of reality – the reality that patterns of dots may have – and we may look forward to further elaborations of his views in the future.

On the reigning pretheoretical conception of the propositional attitudes, there are beliefs only if there are internal states that satisfy the open sentences of the form 'x is a belief that p'. Putting aside Cartesian dualism, the idea is that if an attribution of an attitude is true, there is some particular neural state (at least partly) in virtue of which it is true. This conception, call it 'the standard view', is held by those who take attitudes (if there are any) to covary in a systematic way with neural states of believers. Eliminative materialists endorse the standard view when they infer that there are no attitudes from the supposed fact that the best scientific theories do not postulate internal states that correspond to attributions of attitudes.

The standard view is responsible, I believe, not only for eliminative materialism but also for the three intractable questions that I have discussed – questions that would lose their urgency in the absence of the standard view. The standard view, however, is neither metaphysically innocent, nor is it embedded in our ordinary attributions of attitudes. Perhaps it is time for philosophers to attend to the standard view itself, and to rethink what we are doing when we attribute to each other propositional attitudes. Shifting focus to the explanatory (and other) uses to which we put attributions of propositional attitudes may circumvent the metaphysical conundrums just surveyed.

See also An Essay on Mind section 2.1; FUNCTIONALISM; THOUGHTS.

BIBLIOGRAPHY

Baker, L.R. 1987. *Saving Belief: A Critique of Physicalism*. Princeton University Press.

Burge, T. 1986. Individualism and psychology. *Philosophical Review*, 95, 3–45.

Churchland, P.M. 1989. *A Neurocomputational Perspective: The Nature of Mind and the Structure of Science*. Cambridge, MA.: MIT Press/Bradford Books.

Davidson, D. 1980. *Essays on Actions and Events*. Oxford: Clarendon Press.

Dennett, D.C. 1991. Real patterns. *Journal of Philosophy*, 88, 27–51.

Dretske, F. *Explaining Behavior: Reasons in a World of Causes*. Cambridge, MA.: MIT Press/Bradford Books.

Fodor, J.A. 1987. *Psychosemantics: The Problem of Meaning in the Philosophy of Mind*. Cambridge, MA.: MIT Press/Bradford Books.

Fodor, J.A. 1990. *A Theory of Content and Other Essays*. Cambridge, MA: MIT Press/Bradford Books.

Kim, J. 1988. Explanatory realism, causal realism and explanatory exclusion. *Midwest Studies in Philosophy*, vol. 12, Minneapolis: University of Minnesota Press. pp. 225–40.

Lewis, D. 1983. *Philosophical Papers, Vol. 1.* Oxford University Press.

Lycan, W.G. 1988. *Judgement and Justification.* Cambridge University Press.

Millikan, R.G. 1984. *Language, Thought and Other Biological Categories: New Foundations for Realism.* Cambridge, MA.: MIT Press/ Bradford Books.

Quine, W.V.O. 1960. *Word and Object.* Cambridge, MA.: MIT Press.

Stich, S.F. 1983. *From Folk Psychology to Cognitive Science: The Case Against Belief.* Cambridge, MA.: MIT Press/Bradford Books.

LYNNE RUDDER BAKER

psychoanalytic explanation The task of analysing psychoanalytic explanation is complicated initially in several ways. One concerns the relation of theory to practice. There are various perspectives on the relation of psychoanalysis, the therapeutic practice, to the theoretical apparatus built around it, and these lead to different views of psychoanalysis' claim to cognitive status. The second concerns psychoanalysis' legitimation. The way that psychoanalytic explanation is understood has immediate implications for one's view of its truth or acceptability, and this is of course a notoriously controversial matter. The third is exegetical. Any philosophical account of psychoanalysis must of course start with Freud himself, but it will inevitably privilege some strands in his thought at the expense of others, and in so doing favour particular post-Freudian developments over others.

A plausible view of these issues is as follows. Freud clearly regarded psychoanalysis as engaged principally in the task of explanation, and held fast to his claims for its truth in the course of alterations in his view of the efficacy of psychoanalytic treatment. Some of psychoanalysis' advocates have, under pressure, retreated to the view that psychoanalytic theory has merely instrumental value, as facilitating psychoanalytic therapy; but this is not the natural view, which is that explanation is the autonomous goal of psychoanalysis, and that its propositions are truth-evaluable.

Accordingly, it seems that preference should be given to whatever reconstruction of psychoanalytic theory does most to advance its claim to truth; within, of course, exegetical constraints (what a reconstruction offers must be visibly present in Freud's writings).

PSYCHOANALYTIC EXPLANANDA

The explananda of psychoanalysis require some comment. They may be divided, first, into primary and secondary explananda. The latter include art, morality, religion and other cultural phenomena for which Freud offered explanations. They are secondary because psychoanalytic explanation in these areas depends for its plausibility on the theory's success in dealing with the psychological phenomena of individuals which are psychoanalysis' primary explananda.

Ultimately, the object of psychoanalytic explanation is nothing less than the entire shape of a person's life (*see* Wollheim, 1984), but the theory is formulated initially in its application to the phenomena that Freud described as 'gaps' in CONSCIOUSNESS. By this phrase Freud meant to indicate those psychological phenomena that present ordinary psychology with puzzles of explanation – actions and experiences with an irrational, or at least non-rational character.

This last distinction is important. Dreams and parapraxes (slips of the tongue, bungled actions such as accidentally dropping an object, exceptional lapses of memory) are phenomena about whose explanation ordinary psychology has nothing very helpful to say, and which provide essential material for the formulation of psychoanalytic theory. But such phenomena do not strictly evince irrationality on the part of the subject, for they do not stand out in commonsense psychology as violating norms of rationality (*see* FOLK PSYCHOLOGY). In this respect they are merely *non*-rational, and may be compared with such phenomena as individual character or change of mood, which commonsense psychology also tends to recognize without endeavouring to explain.

Non-rational gaps in commonsense psychology contrast sharply with the *irr*ational, intrusive symptoms of hysterics and neurotics, whose inappropriate emotions and disorders of thought fill Freud's case histories (Dora's ailments, Little Hans' phobia, the obsessions of the Ratman and Wolfman). Here it is clear that the subject is not just in error or incompetent, or undergoing an unusual experience supplementary to ordinary rational self-consciousness, like dream: rather, she violates rational norms and encounters opacity in her own, fully self-conscious experience of herself. Symptomatic conditions contrast, moreover, with the familiar, common-or-garden irrationality of SELF-DECEPTION and akrasia (*see* WEAKNESS OF WILL), for which failures of reason ordinary psychology is by and large able to propose adequate explanations.

Because irrational phenomena of the symptomatic kind allow us to see psychoanalytic explanation as motivated by problems internal to ordinary psychology, there is reason to conclude that it is irrational phenomena which provide the principal warrant for psychoanalytic explanation. From this starting-point, psychoanalytic theory may be seen as at once growing in scope and gaining evidential support: the theory, developed in one context, is recruited to other contexts, which in turn suggest its development in certain directions, and provide data that enable its attributions to be cross-checked from several angles, as any interpretative procedure ideally permits (*see* Wollheim, 1991, Preface; Hopkins, 1991, 1992). Such a process of expansion and consolidation may plausibly be claimed to fit the actual trajectory of Freud's theoretical development.

CAUSAL MECHANISMS OR CONNECTIONS OF MEANING?

It will now help to take a historical route, and focus on the terms in which analytical philosophers of mind began to discuss seriously psychoanalytic explanation. These were provided by the long-standing, and presently unconcluded, debate over cause and meaning in psychology (the debate over psychoanalysis' scientificity is held over for comment at the end).

It is not hard to see why psychoanalysis should be viewed in terms of cause and meaning. On the one hand, Freud's theories introduce a panoply of concepts which appear to characterize mental processes as mechanical and non-meaningful. Included here are Freud's neurological model of the mind, outlined in his 'Project for a scientific psychology'; more broadly, his 'economic' description of the mental, as having properties of force or energy (e.g. as 'cathexing' objects); and his accounts of the mechanism of repression. So it would seem that psychoanalytic explanation employs terms logically at variance with those of ordinary, commonsense psychology, where mechanisms do not play a central role. But on the other hand, and equally strikingly, there is the fact that psychoanalysis proceeds through interpretation, and engages on a relentless search for meaningful connections in mental life – something that even a superficial examination of *The Interpretation of Dreams*, or *The Psychopathology of Everyday Life*, cannot fail to impress upon one. Psychoanalytic interpretation adduces meaningful connections between disparate and often apparently dissociated mental and behavioural phenomena, directed by the goal of 'thematic coherence', of giving mental life the sort of unity that we find in a work of art or cogent narrative. In this respect, psychoanalysis would seem to adopt as its central plank the most salient feature of ordinary psychology, its insistence on relating actions to reasons for them through contentful characterizations of each that make their connection seem rational, or intelligible; a goal that seems remote from anything found in the physical sciences (*see* CONTENT; RATIONALITY; REASONS AND CAUSES.)

The application to psychoanalysis of the perspective afforded by the cause-meaning debate can also be seen as a natural consequence of another factor, namely the semi-paradoxical nature of psychoanalysis' explananda. With respect to all irrational phenomena, something like a paradox arises (*see* Davidson, 1982). Irrationality involves a failure of rational connectedness and hence of meaningfulness, and so, if it is to have an explanation of any kind, relations that are non-meaningful and causal appear to be needed. And yet, as observed above, it would seem that, in offering explanations for irrationality – plugging the 'gaps' in consciousness – what psychoanalytic explanation hinges on is precisely the postulation of further, albeit non-apparent, connections of meaning.

For these two reasons, then – the logical heterogeneity of its explanations and the ambiguous status of its explananda – it may seem that an examination in terms of the concepts of cause and meaning will provide the key to a philosophical elucidation of psychoanalysis. The possible views of psychoanalytic explanation that may result from such an examination can be arranged along two dimensions. (1) Psychoanalytic explanation may then be viewed, after reconstruction, as either causal and non-meaningful; or meaningful and non-causal; or as comprising both meaningful and causal elements, in various combinations. Psychoanalytic explanation then may be viewed, on each of these reconstructions, as either licensed or invalidated, depending on one's view of the logical nature of psychology.

So, for instance, some philosophical discussions infer that psychoanalytic explanation is void, simply on the grounds that it is committed to causality in psychology. On another, opposed view, it is the virtue of psychoanalytic explanation that it imputes causal relations, since only causal relations can be relevant to explaining the failure of meaningful psychological connections. On yet another view, it is psychoanalysis' commitment to meaning which is its great fault: it is held that the stories that psychoanalysis tries to tell do not really, on examination, add up to coherent wholes, and so do not explain successfully. And so on.

It is fair to say that the debates between these various positions fail to establish anything definite about psychoanalytic explanation. There are two reasons for this. First, there are several different strands in Freud's writings, each of which may be drawn on, apparently conclusively, in support of each alternative reconstruction. Second, preoccupation with a wholly general problem in the philosophy of mind, that of cause and meaning, distracts attention from the distinguishing features of psychoanalytic explanation. At this point, and in order to prepare the way for a plausible reconstruction of psychoanalytic explanation, it is appropriate to take a step back, and take a fresh look at the cause-meaning issue in the philosophy of psychoanalysis.

Suppose, first, that some sort of cause-meaning compatibilism – such as that of Donald DAVIDSON – holds for ordinary psychology. On this view, psychological explanation requires some sort of parallelism of causal and meaningful connections, grounded in the idea that psychological properties play causal roles determined by their content. Nothing in psychoanalytic explanation is inconsistent with this picture: after his abandonment of the early 'Project', Freud exceptionlessly viewed psychology as autonomous relative to neurophysiology, and at the same time as congruent with a broadly naturalistic world-view (*see* NATURALISM). If psychoanalytic explanation gives the impression that it imputes bare, meaning-free causality, this results from attending to only half the story, and misunderstanding what psychoanalysis means when it talks of psychological mechanisms. The economic descriptions of mental processes that psychoanalysis provides are never replacements for, but rather themselves always presuppose, characterizations of mental processes in terms of meaning. Mechanisms in psychoanalytic contexts are simply processes whose operation cannot be reconstructed as instances of rational functioning (they are what we might by preference call mental activities, by contrast with actions; *see* Wollheim, 1991, Preface). Psychoanalytic explanation's postulation of mechanisms should not therefore be regarded as a regrettable and expungable incursion of scientism into Freud's thought, as is often claimed.

Suppose, alternatively, that hermeneuticists such as Habermas – who follow Dilthey in regarding the understanding of human beings as an interpretative practice to which the concepts of the physical sciences, such as cause, are alien – are correct in thinking that connections of meaning are misrepresented through being described as causal. Again, this does not impact negatively on psychoanalytic explanation since, as just argued, psychoanalytic explanation nowhere imputes meaning-free causation. Nothing is lost for psychoanalytic explanation if causation is excised from the psychological picture.

The conclusion must be that psychoanalytic explanation is at bottom indifferent to the general meaning-cause issue. The core of psychoanalysis consists in its tracing of meaningful connections with no greater or lesser commitment to causality than is involved in ordinary psychology, (which helps to set the stage – pending appropriate clinical validation – for psychoanalysis to claim as much truth for its explanations as ordinary psychology). But the discussion also brings to light what is, surely, the true key to psychoanalytic explanation: its attribution of *special kinds* of mental states, not recognized in ordinary psychology, whose relations to one another *do not have the form of patterns of inference or practical reasoning.*

In the light of this, it is easy to understand why some compatibilists and hermeneuticists assert that their own view of psychology is uniquely consistent with psychoanalytic explanation. Compatibilists are right to think that, in order to provide for psychoanalytic explanation, it is necessary to allow mental connections that are unlike the connections of reasons to the actions that they rationalize, or to the beliefs that they support; and that, in outlining such connections, psychoanalytic explanation must outstrip the resources of ordinary psychology, which does attempt to force as much as possible into the mould of PRACTICAL REASONING. Hermeneuticists, for their part, are right to think that it would be futile to postulate connections which were nominally psychological but

not characterized in terms of meaning, and that psychoanalytic explanation does not respond to the 'paradox' of irrationality by abandoning the search for meaningful connections.

Compatibilists are, however, wrong to think that non-rational but meaningful connections require the psychological order to be conceived as a causal order. The hermeneuticist is free to postulate psychological connections that are determined by meaning but not by rationality: it is coherent to suppose that there are connections of meaning that are not bona fide rational connections, without these being causal. Meaningfulness is a broader concept than rationality. (Sometimes this thought has been expressed, though not helpfully, by saying that Freud discovered the existence of 'neurotic rationality'.) Although an assumption of rationality is doubtless necessary to make sense of behaviour in general, it does not need to be brought into play in making sense of each instance of behaviour. Hermeneuticists, in turn, are wrong to think that the compatibilist's view of psychology as causal signals a confusion of meaning with causality, or that it must lead the compatibilist to deny that there is any qualitative difference between rational and irrational psychological connections.

THE FORM OF PSYCHOANALYTIC EXPLANATION: WISH AND PHANTASY

The next task must evidently be to describe more fully the nature of the non-rational meaningful connections that figure in psychoanalytic explanation.

The naïve view of psychoanalysis' restoration of meaningful connections in mental life refuses to acknowledge its distance from ordinary psychology: it sees psychoanalysis as attributing unconscious practical syllogisms, in the premises of which unconscious beliefs and desires are put to work. In this spirit one might try to view phobias, for example, as explained by a false belief about the danger constituted by an external object, which is falsely believed to be identical with some (e.g.

oedipal) threat to one's physical safety, and consequently a proper object of fear and avoidance. Or, one might view hysterical symptoms as explained by false beliefs to the effect that sexual desires may be satisfied by, or traumatic experiences undone by, the physical incarnation of those desires or experiences.

There are some explanatory purposes which may well be served by the attribution of unavowed pieces of practical reasoning (as in 'revealed preference' theory), and such attributions may indeed have a subordinate place in the architecture of psychoanalytic explanation. But the examples above show lucidly that the *core* of psychoanalytic explanation cannot be viewed as taking this form. The reason for this is simply that the proposed syllogistic reconstructions do no more than highlight, without making any more intelligible, the real explananda: where do such irrational desires and beliefs come from, and why are they not integrated into, and so dissolved away by rational mental functioning?

(Note that the practical syllogism model cannot be saved by saying that what figure as minor premises in psychoanalytic explanations are phantasies instead of beliefs, for we have no more understanding of how phantasy, in any ordinary sense of the term, may combine with DESIRE to produce a reason for action, than we have of how something that one merely imagines may do so.)

The lesson to draw is, once again, that the true form of psychoanalytic explanation makes a clean break with practical reasoning, and can only be understood in terms of Freud's complex account of unconscious mental functioning (*see* THE UNCONSCIOUS). There are many, equally cogent ways of organizing Freud's theories of the unconscious, but they all revolve around a single fundamental supposition, to the effect that MENTAL REPRESENTATIONS in the unconscious are formed in direct response to the person's basic sources of motivation, and without an interest in truth. Unconscious processing registers reality only obliquely, principally insofar as reality fails to allow

the satisfaction of desire or occasions mental conflict. In response to this awareness of desire as unsatisfied, or of the self as anxiously conflicted, self and world are pictured *wishfully* in the unconscious: as though the mind were able to remake the world immediately and without action, through mere force of wish, in such a way that the world is portrayed as meeting one's needs and one's mental conflict is resolved (a manner of functioning that shows the mind to operate unconsciously as if it took itself to be omnipotent). The mental representations formed in this way are manifested in conscious mental life through various routes and encountered, in unrecognizable and symbol-laden forms, as symptoms, dreams, parapraxes and so on; and take concrete form in the bizarre, gratifying, but otherwise futile forms of symbolic behaviour that psychoanalysis calls 'acting-out'.

All of this comprises the functional aspect of unconscious processing. It has also a formal aspect, which has to do with the way in which unconscious mental representations interact, described by Freud as primary process. Primary process thinking is characterized by its sensory and concrete character, its lack of a firm grasp of identity, its exaggerated sensitivity to conceptually irrelevant connections between ideas, and the consequently associative, metaphoric routes that it takes. Primary process is not constrained by the logical conditions of discursive thought.

It may seem as if these characterizations of the unconscious leave entirely undecided its specific contents. These, it may be thought, ought to be filled in purely a posteriori, as clinical material dictates. So it may be argued that Freud's stress on infantile experience and the role of biological and instinctual factors in psychoanalytic explanation is really optional (Jung alleges that here Freud betrays arbitrariness and reductionist prejudices). But there are strong reasons for thinking that the connection of psychoanalytic explanation with motivation whose content has an infantile and instinctual character is not just contingent. The functional and formal aspects of unconscious processing are hypothesized with reference to the facts of adult psychopathology encountered in clinical work, but Freud also embeds them in a developmental theory of the mind. The developmental theory, which observation of children's mental life does a great deal to corroborate (as witnessed in Freud's *Three Essays on Sexuality*, and later in Melanie Klein's child analyses), allows the pre-verbal, unrealistic, egoistic, and pleasure-directed features of unconscious processing to be explained in a deep sense, though the supposition that the unconscious is an active repository of infantile experience and the medium through which instinctual forces enter into motivation. Without the developmental story, the unconscious's functional and formal aspects would be left hanging. Equally, without its developmental dimension, psychoanalytic explanation would be stuck for determinate directions in which to interpret. It is part of the logic of interpretation that diverse phenomena should be shown to derive from unifying and simplifying sources. Ordinary psychology's inventory of human motives is not a resource which psychoanalytic explanation can draw on, for ordinary kinds of motive are fitted out to explain rational interactions with the world. From within any broadly naturalistic conception of human beings, this leaves a theory which seeks to extend ordinary psychology's picture of motivation with effectively no alternative but to refer itself to infantile experience and biological givens. A commitment to an infantile-instinctual picture of the sources of human motivation is needed for psychoanalytic explanation to avail itself of causes apt for the production of the symptoms and other irrational phenomena which are its principal target.

Freud's own conceptualization of the unconscious' dynamism centres on the concepts of wish-fulfilment, repression and the opposition between the reality and pleasure principles. The family of Kleinian concepts constituted by phantasy, the inner world, and internal objects deepens, and to some extent subsumes Freud's con-

ceptualizations. Klein's concepts have a simple and powerful rationale. The attribution of PROPOSITIONAL ATTITUDES in ordinary psychology may be viewed as casting a net over the phenomena of overt behaviour in a way that aims to reproduce the schemes of classification and object-individuation adopted by the subject interpreted. Roughly, where behaviour reveals a constant in the subject's apprehension of the world, interpretation attributes a single object of thought. Now, exactly the same strategy can be seen to underlie psychoanalysis, with the difference that here it is the spread of propositional attitudes itself, rather than behaviour, which is the object of interpretation. Psychoanalysis can be viewed as embarking on a second wave of interpretation, based on and giving reapplication to one of the fundamental principles of ordinary psychology. Just as behaviour becomes intelligible when set against a background of propositional attitudes, so a person's propositional network gains in intelligibility when it is set against the kind of unconscious, partly constitutional background defined by psychoanalytic attributions. It is essential for this enterprise that a different set of objects from those taken by propositional attitudes be supposed. For this reason, analysts take clinical material to reveal thoughts about internal objects, whose relation to external objects, onto which they are mapped, is fluid and elastic. Kleinian theory identifies the earliest internal objects, which provide templates for those of later life, with bodies, or parts of bodies such as the mother's breast, which the unconscious represents itself as containing. The conjunction of ordinary and psychoanalytic explanation enables us to understand people as characterizing external objects in a double fashion: both as real, and as bearing the significance of phantasized objects. The phantastic characterization helps to determine the way in which external objects are responded to, desired and so on. In this way, psychoanalysis functions as a crucial supplement to ordinary psychology: the latter's shortfallings –

the explanation of irrational phenomena, and the 'giving out' that we inevitably find when we press our questions (about, for example, why people desire what they do) beyond a certain point – are compensated for when psychoanalytic explanation is appended.

If it is thought necessary to identify a deeper philosophical supposition in support of the idea that our minds are really such as to be capable of engaging in the kinds of processes just described – something that ordinary wakeful self-consciousness might lead one to doubt – then the answer must be this: mental states have the sort of autonomy which disposes them to, simply, *find expression*, in whatever form. Expression is by its nature a function that does not require rationally appropriate vehicles, in the sense of actions which have instrumental value (*see* Wollheim, 1991, Preface). This is something that one is likely to overlook if one concentrates on the role of practical reasoning in generating intentional ACTION, although it is in fact a supposition that may fairly be said to permeate ordinary psychology, albeit in an inexplicit form; it is shown in our understanding of EMOTION, and underpins our registration of one another's mental life at the level of physiognomy. The irrational wish-fulfilling character of unconscious processes results from the mind's natural tendency to leak into outward forms – a tendency more primitive than its role in producing instrumental action.

THE LEGITIMATION OF PSYCHOANALYTIC EXPLANATION

Viewed in these terms, psychoanalytic explanation is an *extension* of ordinary psychology, one that is warranted by demands for explanation generated from within ordinary psychology itself. This has several crucial ramifications. It eliminates, as ill-conceived, the question of psychoanalysis' scientific status (*see* Hopkins, 1988, 1992) – an issue much discussed, as proponents of different philosophies of science have argued for and against psychoanalysis' agreement

with the canons of scientific method, and its degree or lack of corroboration. Demands that psychoanalytic explanation should be demonstrated to receive inductive support, commit itself to testable psychological laws, and contribute effectively to the prediction of action, have then no more pertinence than the same demands pressed on ordinary psychology – which is not very great. When the conditions for legitimacy are appropriately scaled down, it is extremely likely that psychoanalysis succeeds in meeting them: for psychoanalysis does deepen our understanding of psychological laws, improve the predictability of action in principle, and receive inductive support in the special sense which is appropriate to interpretative practices (*see* Hopkins, 1991, 1992).

Furthermore, to the extent that psychoanalysis may be seen as structured by and serving well-defined needs for explanation, there is proportionately diminished reason for thinking that its legitimation turns on the analysand's assent to psychoanalytic interpretations, or the transformative power (whatever it may be) of these. Certainly it is true that psychoanalytic explanation has a reflexive dimension lacked by explanations in the physical sciences: psychoanalysis understands its object, the mind, in the very terms that the mind employs in its unconscious workings (such as its belief in its own omnipotence). But this point does not in any way count against the objectivity of psychoanalytic explanation. It does not imply that what it is for a psychoanalytic explanation to be true should be identified, pragmatically, with the fact that an interpretation may, for the analysand who gains self-knowledge, have the function of translating their semi-inchoate unconscious mentality into a properly conceptual form. Nor does it imply that psychoanalysis' attribution of unconscious content needs to be understood in anything less than full-bloodedly realistic terms. Truth in psychoanalysis may be taken to consist in correspondence with an independent mental reality, a reality that is both endowed with SUB-

JECTIVITY and in many respects opaque to its owner.

See also PSYCHOLOGY AND PHILOSOPHY.

BIBLIOGRAPHY

Cavell, M. 1993. *The Psychoanalytic Mind: From Freud to Philosophy.* Cambridge, MA.: Harvard University Press.

Davidson, D. 1982. Paradoxes of irrationality. In *Philosophical Essays on Freud,* ed. R. Wollheim and J. Hopkins. Cambridge University Press.

Freud, S. 1953–74. *Standard Edition of the Complete Psychological Works of Sigmund Freud,* 24 vols, trans. under the general editorship of J. Strachey, in collaboration with A. Freud, assisted by A. Strachey and A. Tyson. London: Hogarth Press and the Institute of Psycho-Analysis.

Gardner, S. 1993. *Irrationality and the Philosophy of Psychoanalysis.* Cambridge University Press.

Hopkins, J. 1988. Epistemology and depth psychology: critical notes on *The Foundations of Psychoanalysis. Mind, Psychoanalysis and Science,* ed. P. Clark and C. Wright. Oxford: Basil Blackwell.

Hopkins, J. 1991. The interpretation of dreams. In *The Cambridge Companion to Freud,* ed. J. Neu. Cambridge University Press.

Hopkins, J. 1992. Psychoanalysis, interpretation, and science. In *Psychoanalysis, Mind and Art: Perspectives on Richard Wollheim,* ed. J. Hopkins and A. Savile. Oxford: Basil Blackwell.

Klein, M. 1951, 1975. *The Writings of Melanie Klein,* 4 vols, ed. R. E. Money-Kyrle. London: Hogarth Press and the Institute of Psycho-Analysis.

Wollheim, R. 1984. *The Thread of Life.* Cambridge University Press.

Wollheim, R. 1991. *Freud,* 2nd edn. London: Harper Collins.

Wollheim, R., ed. 1974. *Freud: a Collection of Critical Essays.* New York: Anchor Doubleday. Reprinted as *Philosophers on Freud: New Evaluations.* New York: Aronson (1977).

Wollheim, R., and Hopkins, J. eds. 1982. *Philosophical Essays on Freud.* Cambridge University Press.

SEBASTIAN GARDNER

psychology and philosophy The last two decades have been a period of extraordinary change in psychology. COGNITIVE PSYCHOLOGY, which focuses on higher mental processes like reasoning, decision making, problem solving, language processing and higher-level visual processing, has become a – perhaps *the* – dominant paradigm among experimental psychologists, while behaviouristically oriented approaches have gradually fallen into disfavour (*see* BEHAVIOURISM). Largely as a result of this paradigm shift, the level of interaction between the disciplines of philosophy and psychology has increased dramatically. The goal of this article is to sketch some of the areas in which these interactions have been most productive, or at least most provocative. The interactions I will discuss fall into three categories, though the boundary between the first two is sometimes rather fuzzy.

COGNITIVE PSYCHOLOGY AS A SUBJECT FOR 'DESCRIPTIVE' PHILOSOPHY OF SCIENCE

One of the central goals of the philosophy of science is to provide explicit and systematic accounts of the theories and explanatory strategies exploited in the sciences. Another common goal is to construct philosophically illuminating analyses or explications of central theoretical concepts invoked in one or another science. In the philosophy of biology, for example, there is a rich literature aimed at understanding teleological explanations, and there has been a great deal of work on the structure of evolutionary theory and on such crucial concepts as fitness and biological function (*see* DRETSKE; TELEOLOGY). The philosophy of physics is another area in which studies of this sort have been actively pursued. (For an excellent example in the philosophy of biology, *see* Sober, 1984; in the philosophy of physics, *see* Sklar, 1974). In undertaking this work, philosophers need not (and typically do not) assume that there is anything wrong with the science they are studying. Their goal is simply to provide accounts of the theories, concepts and explanatory strategies that scientists are using – accounts that are more explicit, systematic and philosophically sophisticated than the often rather rough-and-ready accounts offered by the scientists themselves.

Cognitive psychology is in many ways a curious and puzzling science. Many of the theories put forward by cognitive psychologists make use of a family of 'intentional' concepts – like *believing* that p, *desiring* that q, and *representing* r – which don't appear in the physical or biological sciences, and these intentional concepts play a crucial role in many of the explanations offered by these theories (*see* INTENTIONALITY; PROPOSITIONAL ATTITUDES). People's decisions and actions are explained by appeal to their beliefs and desires. Perceptual processes, some of which may themselves be representational, are said to result in mental states which represent (or sometimes *mis*represent) one or another aspect of the cognitive agent's environment (*see* PERCEPTION; REPRESENTATION). While cognitive psychologists occasionally say a bit about the nature of intentional concepts and the explanations that exploit them, their comments are rarely systematic or philosophically illuminating. Thus it is hardly surprising that many philosophers have seen cognitive psychology as fertile ground for the sort of careful descriptive work that is done in the philosophy of biology and the philosophy of physics. Jerry FODOR's *The Language of Thought* (1975) was a pioneering study in this genre, one that continues to have a major impact on the field. Robert Cummins (1983, 1989), Daniel DENNETT (1978a, 1987) and John Haugeland (1978) have also done important and widely discussed work in the what might be called the 'descriptive' philosophy of cognitive psychology.

PHILOSOPHY AS A SOURCE OF PROPOSALS FOR IMPROVING COGNITIVE PSYCHOLOGY

The goal of the projects discussed in the previous section is to provide accurate, illuminating descriptions of what is going on in cognitive psychology. These philosophical accounts of cognitive theories and the concepts they invoke are generally much more explicit than the accounts provided by psychologists, and they inevitably smooth over some of the rough edges of scientists' actual practice. But if the account they give of cognitive theories diverges significantly from the theories that psychologists actually produce, then the philosophers have just gotten it wrong. There is, however, a very different way in which philosophers have approached cognitive psychology. Rather than merely trying to characterize what cognitive psychology is actually doing, some philosophers try to say what it *should* and *should not* be doing. Their goal is not to explicate scientific practice, but to criticize and improve it. The most common target of this critical approach is the use of intentional concepts in cognitive psychology. Intentional notions have been criticized on various grounds. The two that I will consider here are that they fail to supervene on the physiology of the cognitive agent, and that they cannot be 'naturalized'.

Perhaps the easiest way to make the point about SUPERVENIENCE is to use a thought experiment of the sort originally proposed by Hilary PUTNAM (1975). Suppose that in some distant corner of the universe there is a planet, Twin Earth, which is very similar to our own. On Twin Earth there is a person who is an atom for atom replica of President Clinton. Now the President Clinton who lives on Earth believes that Vice President Gore was born in Tennessee. If you asked him, 'Was Gore born in Tennessee?' he'd say, 'Yes'. Twin-Clinton would respond in the same way. But it is not because he believes that our Gore was born in Tennessee. Twin-Clinton has no beliefs at all about our Gore. His beliefs are about Twin-Gore, and Twin-Gore was certainly *not* born in Tennessee. Indeed, we may even suppose that Twin-Gore was not born in Twin-Tennessee, and thus that Clinton's belief is true while Twin-Clinton's is false. What all this is supposed to show is that two people can share all their physio-

501

logical properties without sharing all their intentional properties. To turn this into a problem for cognitive psychology, two additional premises are needed. The first is that cognitive psychology attempts to explain behaviour by appeal to people's intentional properties. The second is that psychological explanations should not appeal to properties that fail to supervene on an organism's physiology. (Variations on this theme can be found in Stich (1978, 1983) and in Fodor (1987, ch. 2).)

Reactions to this argument have taken a variety of forms. Perhaps the most radical is the proposal that cognitive psychology should recast its theories and explanations in a way that does not appeal to intentional properties of mental states but only to their formal or 'syntactic' properties (Stich, 1983). Somewhat less radical is the suggestion that we can define a species of representation or CONTENT – often called 'narrow content' (see EXTERNALISM/INTERNALISM) – which *does* supervene an organism's physiology, and that psychological explanations that appeal to ordinary ('wide') intentional properties can be replaced by explanations that invoke only their narrow counterparts (Fodor, 1987). Both of these proposals accept the conclusion of the argument sketched in the previous paragraph, and they go on to propose ways in which cognitive psychology might be modified. But many philosophers have urged that the problem lies in the argument, not in the way that cognitive psychology goes about its business. The most common critique of the argument focuses on the normative premise – the one that insists that psychological explanations ought not to appeal to 'wide' properties that fail to supervene on physiology. Why shouldn't psychological explanations appeal to wide properties, the critics ask? What, exactly, is wrong with psychological explanations invoking properties that don't supervene on physiology? (*See* Burge, 1979, 1986.) Various answers have been proposed in the literature, though they typically end up invoking metaphysical principles that are less clear and less plausible than the normative thesis

they are supposed to support. (*See*, for example, Fodor, 1987, 1991.)

My own view is that the extensive literature in this area is mostly a tempest in a teapot, though I'm afraid I bear some of the responsibility for provoking it. I know of no clear or persuasive argument for excluding wide properties from psychological theories and explanations. But if you are inclined to demand that psychology invoke only properties that supervene on physiology, the demand is easy enough to satisfy. Given any psychological property that fails to supervene on physiology, it is trivial to characterize a narrow correlate property that does supervene. The extension of the correlate property includes all actual and possible objects in the extension of the original property, plus all actual and possible physiological duplicates of those objects. Theories originally stated in terms of wide psychological properties can be recast in terms of their narrow correlates with no obvious loss in their descriptive or explanatory power. It might be protested that when characterized in this way, narrow belief and narrow content are not really species of belief and content at all. But it is far from clear how this claim could be defended, or why we should care if it turns out to be right. (For more details see Stich (1991) and Stich and Laurence (forthcoming).)

The worry about the 'naturalizability' of intentional properties is much harder to pin down (*see* NATURALISM). According to Fodor, the worry derives from 'a certain ontological intuition: that there is no place for intentional categories in a physicalistic view of the world,' (1987, p. 97) and thus that 'the semantic (and/or the intentional) will prove permanently recalcitrant to integration in the natural order' (Fodor, 1984, p. 32). If intentional properties can't be integrated into the natural order, then presumably they ought to be banished from serious scientific theorizing. Psychology should have no truck with them. Indeed, if intentional properties have no place in the natural order, then nothing in the natural world has intentional properties, and intentional states do not exist at all. So goes the worry. Unfortunately, neither Fodor nor anyone else has said anything very helpful about what is required to 'integrate' intentional properties into the natural order. There are, to be sure, various proposals to be found in the literature. But all of them seem to suffer from a fatal defect. On each account of what is required to naturalize a property or integrate it into the natural order, there are lots of perfectly respectable non-intentional scientific or commonsense properties that fail to meet the standard. Thus all the proposals that have been made so far end up throwing out the baby with the bath water. (For the details, *see* Stich and Laurence (forthcoming).)

Now, of course, the fact that no one has been able to give a plausible account of what is required to 'naturalize' the intentional may indicate nothing more than that the project is a difficult one. Perhaps with further work a more plausible account will be forthcoming. But one might also offer a very different diagnosis of the failure of all accounts of 'naturalizing' that have so far been offered. Perhaps the 'ontological intuition' that underlies the worry about integrating the intentional into the natural order is simply muddled. Perhaps there is no coherent criterion of naturalizability that all properties invoked in respectable science must meet. My own guess is that this diagnosis is the right one. Until those who are worried about the naturalizability of the intentional provide us with some plausible account of what is required of intentional categories if they are to find a place in 'a physicalistic view of the world' I think we are justified in refusing to take their worry seriously.

Recently, John SEARLE (1992) has offered a new set of philosophical arguments aimed at showing that certain theories in cognitive psychology are profoundly wrong-headed. The theories that are the targets of Searle's critique offer purely formal or computational explanations of various psychological capacities – like the capacity to recognize grammatical sentences, or the capacity to judge which of two objects in one's visual field is further away. Typically these theories are set out in the form of a computer program – a set of rules for manipulating symbols – and the explanation offered for the exercise of the capacity in question is that people's brains are executing the program. The central claim in Searle's critique is that being a symbol or a computational state is not an 'intrinsic' physical feature of a computer state or a brain state. Rather, being a symbol is an 'observer relative' feature. But, Searle maintains, only intrinsic properties of a system can play a role in causal explanations of how they work. Thus appeal to symbolic or computational states of the brain could not possibly play a role in a 'causal account of cognition'.

There is something quite paradoxical about Searle's argument. To see the point, imagine that we find an unfamiliar object lying on the beach. After playing with it for a while, we discover that it has some remarkable capacities. If you ask it mathematical questions like, 'How much is 345 times 678?' or 'What is the square root of 1492?' the correct answer appears on a video display screen. How does the object do it? In order to find out, we turn it over to a group of scientists and engineers. After studying it for a while, they report that the object is a remarkable computer whose program includes a sophisticated algorithm for processing English along with a set of algorithms for various mathematical tasks. The report from the research team includes a detailed specification of the program they believe the object is using. Now most of us would be inclined to think that this report provides deep insight into how the object manages to produce answers to the questions we ask it. But if Searle is right, the program couldn't possibly explain how the object works. Obviously something has gone wrong somewhere. As I see it, the problem with Searle's argument lies in his assumption that cognitive theories of the sort he is criticizing aim at providing a 'causal account of cognition'. One of the important lessons of what I earlier called the 'descriptive' philosophy of science is that there are lots of different strategies of explanation in science. One of the most useful explanatory strategies is functional decomposition, in which a complicated capacity is explained by showing how it can be accomplished by assembling a number of simpler capacities in an appropriate way. This strategy is widely used in biology. And, as Fodor (1968), Dennett (1978b), Cummins (1983) and others have argued, it is also central to the explanatory approach in cognitive psychology. Thus, even if we grant Searle's claim that being a computational state is not an intrinsic property of a state, and that only intrinsic properties can play a role in causal explanations, we will have no reason to conclude that the sort of computational explanations that Searle is criticizing are in any way problematic.

COGNITIVE PSYCHOLOGY SUGGESTS WAYS TO RESOLVE PHILOSOPHICAL PROBLEMS

The last section surveyed some of the philosophical arguments aimed at showing that cognitive psychology is confused and in need of reform. My reaction to those arguments was none too sympathetic. In each case, I maintained, it is the philosophical argument that is problematic, not the psychology it is criticizing. In this section I want to turn the tables and consider some of the proposals that have been made for using psychological findings to criticize philosophical theories and to resolve traditional philosophical problems. The tone in this section will be much more optimistic than in the previous section, since in this area I think there is some real progress to report.

Perhaps the most impressive example of the way in which psychological research can contribute to the resolution of philosophical disputes is to be found in the venerable debate between empiricist and rationalist accounts of knowledge. Though this debate is complex and multifaceted, one central issue has been the extent to which our knowledge in various domains is derived from experience, and the extent to which it is innate (*see* INNATENESS). Empiricists typically claim that most or all of our knowl-

edge is derived from experience, while rationalists maintain that important aspects of what we know are innate. Rationalists generally recognize that some input from experience may be needed to activate our innate knowledge and make it useable. Without appropriate environmental 'triggers' our innate knowledge may lie dormant. To make this point, Leibniz uses the analogy of a deeply grained block of marble. The block may have the shape of a man or a horse within it, though a fair amount of hammering and chiselling may be necessary to turn the block into a statue.

In the mid-1960s, Noam CHOMSKY began developing a set of arguments aimed at showing how considerations from linguistics and psycholinguistics might be used to resolve the dispute between the rationalists and the empiricists. (*See*, for example, Chomsky 1965, 1980.) The basic strategy in Chomsky's argument is obvious enough. What we should do, he urged, is look at the input to the process of language acquisition and the output of that process. If there is a significant amount of information in the output that cannot be found in the input, then the only plausible hypothesis is that the excess information is innate. What was novel and striking in Chomsky's argument was the empirical evidence he offered about the richness and complexity of the information that competent speakers of a language possess. Chomsky and his followers argued that there are lots of examples of grammatical rules that people acquire quite reliably, though the evidence available to them is not adequate to select the rule actually acquired over various alternatives that are not acquired. (For details, *see* Hornstein and Lightfoot, 1981.) In the years since Chomsky first advanced this argument, a number of other lines of evidence have been developed that underscore the extent to which human knowledge is strongly influenced by information-rich, domain-specific innate mental capacities. Some of the most impressive studies have demonstrated that very young children recognize phoneme boundaries and other subtle features that are essential for language mastery (Mehler and Fox, 1984). Studies of visual perception in young children have also revealed a great deal of innate structure (Spelke, 1990). Though the details about what is innate and what is acquired in many domains remains to be determined, I think it is now quite clear that the sort of radical empiricist view often associated with Locke and with behaviourism is simply untenable.

Another area in which psychological studies have made important contributions to philosophy is in the branch of epistemology that attempts to characterize the notion of RATIONALITY and the related notion of justified inference. Here there are two quite different lines of influence to report. Some philosophers have offered accounts of rationality that build upon the actual inferences that people make and endorse. The best-known account of this sort is the one developed by Nelson Goodman (1965). According to Goodman, the justified inferences are the ones that would be sanctioned by a certain process. That process begins with the inferences we are actually inclined to accept, and it attempts to provide the simplest and most satisfying set of rules that will capture those inferences. As the process proceeds, certain inferences that we are initially inclined to accept may have to be thrown out, and certain rules that we initially find appealing may have to be amended or rejected entirely. Obviously, the sort of rules that will ultimately be sanctioned by this process will depend to a significant extent on the sorts of inferences that those using the process are initially inclined to make. And, while they rarely stress the point, it is clear that Goodman and others who are attracted to this account of justification typically assume that people's untutored inclinations are generally pretty good. But during the last twenty years or so, psychologists studying inference have accumulated a substantial body of data that casts serious doubt on this assumption. In many studies of both deductive and probabilistic reasoning it has been shown that normal subjects regularly draw inferences that would be classified as invalid (or worse) by the prevailing normative theory. (*See*, for example, Nisbett and Ross, 1980; Kahneman et al., 1982.) Moreover, there is good reason to think that at least some of these patterns of inference are quite robust enough to survive the pruning process that Goodman describes. If this is right, it would not constitute a knock-down argument against Goodmanian accounts of justified inference. But the psychological findings do indicate that resolute Goodmanians are going to have some unpleasant bullets to bite. If they want to hang on to their account of justification, they are going to have to classify some pretty weird inferences as 'justified'. (For further details, *see* Stich, 1990, ch. 4; for a defence of the Goodmanian strategy, *see* Cohen, 1981.)

Quite a different approach to the assessment of reasoning is one that grows out of the pragmatist tradition. On this approach, reasoning is viewed as a tool for achieving various ends, and good strategies of reasoning are those that do a good job in enabling people to achieve their ends. Which strategies will facilitate which goals is an empirical question, not a matter to be determined by philosophical argument. So if we want to know what good reasoning in a given domain is like, the best way to find out is to locate people who have been particularly successful in that domain, and study the way in which they reason. In recent years, this strategy has been pursued in a particularly sophisticated way by Herbert Simon and his co-workers (Langley, Simon, Bradshaw and Zytkow, 1987.) Simon and his colleagues are interested in characterizing good scientific reasoning. They proceed by locating clear examples of people who have been successful in science (the people whose pictures appear in the science textbooks, as Simon sometimes puts it) and then trying to construct computer models that will simulate the reasoning of these successful scientists. There is, of course, no guarantee that this strategy will work, since it might turn out that the reasoning patterns of successful scientists have little or nothing in common – that successful scientific reasoning is not a 'natural kind' in psychology. However, Simon's work so far suggests that there are important patterns to be discovered in the thinking of successful scientists. To the extent that Simon's project succeeds, it will constitute a particularly exciting sort of 'naturalized epistemology'.

Before closing I want to mention one other domain in which psychological research promises to have an important impact on philosophical theorizing. In ethics there are a number of views that presuppose substantive theses about human psychology. Often these psychological theses are taken to be part of received common sense about the mind, and thus no defence is offered. In psychology, however, received common sense has a distressing tendency to be mistaken. Consider, for example, those versions of utilitarian theory that rank actions on the basis of how well they do in satisfying people's preferences. These proposals make little sense unless we make the commonsensical assumption that people have determinate and reasonably stable preferences which may be elicited in a variety of ways. However, much recent work on the psychology of choice and preference suggests that this seemingly innocuous assumption may well be mistaken (Fischhoff et al., 1980; Slovic, 1990.) As Goldman has noted in a recent discussion of this literature, 'subtle aspects of how problems are posed, questions are phrased, and responses are elicited can have a substantial effect on people's expressed judgements and preferences. This leads some researchers to doubt whether, in general, there are stable and precise values or preferences antecedent to an elicitation procedure' (Goldman, 1993). If these doubts turn out to be justified, then a great deal of work in moral theory may well turn out to be indefensible, perhaps even incoherent.

See also ARTIFICIAL INTELLIGENCE; COMPUTATIONAL MODELS; DEVELOPMENTAL PSYCHOLOGY.

BIBLIOGRAPHY

Burge, T. 1979. Individualism and the mental. *Midwest Studies in Philosophy, Vol. 4*, 73–121.

Burge, T. 1986. Individualism and psychology. *Philosophical Review*, 95, 3–46.

Chomsky, N. 1965. *Aspects of the Theory of Syntax*. Cambridge, MA.: MIT Press.

Chomsky, N. 1980. *Rules and Representations*. New York: Columbia University Press.

Cohen, J. 1981. Can human irrationality be experimentally demonstrated? *Behavioral and Brain Sciences*, 4.

Cummins, R. 1983. *The Nature of Psychological Explanation*. Cambridge, MA.: MIT Press Bradford Books.

Cummins, R. 1989. *Meaning and Mental Representation*. Cambridge, MA.: MIT Press/Bradford Books.

Dennett, D. 1978a. *Brainstorms*. Cambridge, MA.: MIT Press/Bradford Books.

Dennett, D. 1978b. Artificial intelligence as philosophy and as psychology. In Dennett, 1978a.

Dennett, D. 1987. *The Intentional Stance*. Cambridge, MA.: MIT Press/Bradford Books.

Fischhoff, P., Slovic, P., and Lichtenstein, S. 1980. Knowing what you want: Measuring labile values. In *Cognitive Processes in Choice and Decision Behavior*, ed. T. Wallsten. Hillsdale, N.J.: Erlbaum.

Fodor, J. 1968. The appeal to tacit knowledge in psychological explanation. *Journal of Philosophy*, 65.

Fodor, J. 1975. *The Language of Thought*. New York: Thomas Y. Crowell.

Fodor, J. 1984. Semantics, wisconsin style. *Synthèse*, 59. Reprinted in Fodor, 1990; page reference is to the latter.

Fodor, J. 1987. *Psychosemantics*. Cambridge, MA.: MIT Press/Bradford Books.

Fodor, J. 1990. *A Theory of Content and Other Essays*. Cambridge, MA.: MIT Press/Bradford Books.

Fodor, J. 1991. A modal argument for narrow content. *Journal of Philosophy*, 88.

Goldman, A. 1993. Ethics and cognitive science. In *Philosophical Applications of Cognitive Science*. Boulder, CO: Westview Press.

Goodman, N. 1965. *Fact, Fiction and Forecast*. Indianapolis: Bobbs-Merrill.

Haugeland, J. 1978. The Nature and plausibility of cognitivism. *Behavioral and Brain Sciences*, 1.

Hornstein, N., and Lightfoot, D. 1981. *Explanation in Linguistics*. London: Longman.

Kahneman, D., Slovic, P., and Tversky, A., eds

1982. *Judgment Under Uncertainty: Heuristics and Biases*. Cambridge University Press.

Langley, P., Simon, H., Bradshaw, G., and Zytkow, J. 1987. *Scientific Discovery: Computational Explorations of the Creative Processes*. Cambridge, MA.: MIT Press.

Mehler, J., and Fox, R., eds. 1984. *Neonate Cognition: Beyond the Blooming, Buzzing Confusion*. Hillsdale, N.J.: L. Erlbaum Associates.

Nisbett, R., and Ross, L. 1980. *Human Inference: Strategies and Shortcomings of Social Judgment*. Englewood Cliffs, N.J.: Prentice-Hall.

Putnam, H. 1975. The meaning of 'Meaning'. In *Language, Mind and Knowledge: Minnesota Studies in the Philosophy of Science, Vol. 7*, ed. K. Gunderson. Minneapolis: University of Minnesota Press.

Searle, J. 1992. *The Rediscovery of the Mind*. Cambridge, MA.: MIT Press/Bradford Books.

Sklar, L. 1974. *Space, Time and Spacetime*. Berkeley, CA: University of California Press.

Slovic, P. 1990. Choice. In *Thinking*, ed. D. Osherson and E. Smith. Cambridge, MA.: MIT Press/Bradford Books.

Sober, E. 1984. *The Nature of Selection*. Cambridge, MA.: MIT Press/Bradford Books.

Spelke, E. 1990. Origins of visual knowledge. In *An Invitation to Cognitive Science: Visual Cognition and Action*, ed. Hollerbach. D. Osherson, S. Kosslyn and J. Cambridge, MA.: MIT Press/Bradford Books.

Stich, S. 1978. Autonomous psychology and the belief-desire thesis. *Monist*, 61.

Stich, S. 1983. *From Folk Psychology to Cognitive Science*. Cambridge, MA.: MIT Press/Bradford Books.

Stich, S. 1990. *The Fragmentation of Reason*. Cambridge, MA.: MIT Press/Bradford Books.

Stich, S. 1991. Narrow content meets fat syntax. In *Meaning in Mind: Fodor and His Critics*, ed. B. Loewer and G. Rey. Oxford: Basil Blackwell.

Stich, S., and Laurence, S. Forthcoming. Intentionality and Naturalism.

STEPHEN STICH

Putnam, Hilary In 1960 I published a paper titled 'Minds and Machines' (1975, ch. 18), which suggested a possible new option in the philosophy of mind, and in 1967 I published two papers (1975, ch. 20 and 21) which became, for a time, the manifestos of the 'functionalist' current. FUNCTIONALISM (as many of my readers doubtless already know) holds that we are analogous to computers, and that our psychological states are simply our 'functional states', that is, they are the states that would figure in an ideal description of our 'program'. In the present 'self-portrait' of myself as a philosopher of mind I shall review the reasons that led me to propose functionalism and the reasons that subsequently led me to abandon it.

ROBOT CONSCIOUSNESS AND THE PROBLEM OF MAKING FUNCTIONALISM PRECISE

'Functionalism' views us as *automata*; that is as computers that happen to be made of flesh and blood. According to the functionalist view, a robot with the same program as a human being would *ipso facto* be conscious (*see* CONSCIOUSNESS). Although in a talk to the American Philosophical Association in 1964 (1975, ch. 19), I had drawn back from that view, arguing that the question whether any automaton was *conscious* was not really a question of fact but called for a 'decision' on our part, a decision 'to treat robots as fellow members of our linguistic community', when I came to write the two papers I described as 'functionalist manifestos'. I considered both the question as to whether psychological states are really 'functional' (i.e. computational) in nature and the question as to whether an automaton could be conscious to be factual questions. The earlier talk, I had come to see, contained an error.

In the 1964 paper, I assumed that if an 'IDENTITY THEORY' (a theory to the effect that psychological states are identical either with brain states or with functional states) were true, then it would have to be true as a consequence of (1) the meanings of psychological words, and (2) empirical facts that do not themselves beg the question as to whether a robot could be conscious. But the same line of reasoning, I saw in the 1967 papers, if applied to the question

507

whether light is electromagnetic radiation of such-and-such wavelengths, would lead to the conclusion that this too was not a question of fact but called for a 'decision' on our part, a decision to treat electromagnetic radiation as light! For persons who, knowing what we do about the causes and effects of electromagnetic radiation, still insisted that light is not *identical* with electromagnetic radiation (of such-and-such wavelengths), but only *correlated* with the presence of such radiation would not be contradicting themselves. That light is electromagnetic radiation does not follow *analytically* from 'non-question-begging' facts about electromagnetic radiation and about light.

It is wrong, I now realized, to insist that statements that make theoretical identifications of phenomena originally described in different vocabularies must follow *analytically* from 'non-question-begging facts' in order to be true. If we wish to claim that light is electromagnetic radiation, we need only maintain that it is *rational to believe* that it is, given what we now know; the question of analyticity is a red herring. Thus, I was led to drop my concern with analyticity entirely, and to return to my earlier concern (in 1975, ch. 18) with *theoretical identification* and with a notion that I now introduced to go with it, the notion of synthetic identity of properties. (I spoke of synthetic identity of properties because, in the papers published in 1967 and subsequently, I said that not only is light passing through an aperture the same *event* as electromagnetic radiation passing through the aperture, but that the *property of being light* is the very same property as *the property of being electromagnetic radiation of such-and-such wavelengths*.) I rejected the traditional view that predicates P and Q correspond to the same property only if P and Q are analytically coextensive, or if in some way the necessary coextensiveness of the predicates is a matter of 'conceptual analysis'. (*See* PROPERTY.) In short, I held (and still hold) that properties can be synthetically identical, and the way in which we establish that properties are synthetically identical is by showing that identifying them simplifies our explanatory endeavours in certain familiar ways (For a detailed discussion, *see* Putnam, 1979, ch.9).

In my earliest paper on the issue of minds and machines (1975, ch. 18), the theoretical identification I predicted we might come to make in two hundred years was an identification of human psychological states with the assumed 'corresponding' brain states. Although I also suggested in that paper that we might think of psychological states as more analogous to what I there called 'logical states' of machines (states defined at the 'programming' level) than to 'structural states' of machines (states defined at the hardware level), thereby introducing functionalism as an option, I did not follow up the option at the time. I now, however, took up the option with a vengeance, and suggested (particularly in 1975, ch. 21) that just as light is empirically identical with electromagnetic radiation, so (I proposed as a hypothesis) psychological states are empirically identical with functional states. Here is the hypothesis as I stated it (1975, p. 434) (for simplicity I stated it only for the case of pain, but I made clear that it was intended to hold for psychological states in general):

(1) All organisms capable of feeling pain are Probabilistic Automata

A Probabilistic Automaton is a device similar to a TURING Machine, except that (1) its memory capacity has a fixed finite limit, whereas a Turing Machine has a potentially infinite external memory; and (2) state transitions may be probabilistic rather that than deterministic. I assumed that the Probabilistic Automata in question were equipped with motor organs and with sensory organs and that certain states corresponded to possible 'inputs' and 'outputs'.

(2) Every organism capable of feeling pain posseses at least one Probabilistic Automaton Description (specifying the functional states of the Automaton and the transition probabilities between them)

of a certain kind (i.e. being capable of feeling pain *is* possessing an appropriate kind of functional organization).

(3) No organism capable of feeling pain possesses a decomposition into parts that separately possess Probabilistic Automaton Descriptions of the kind referred to in (2). (This rules out a society of organisms, or a person in a room running a program.)

(4) For every Probabilistic Automaton Description of the kind referred to in (2), there exists a subset of the sensory inputs such that an organism with that Description is in pain when and only when some of its sensory inputs are in that subset.

I admitted (p. 435), that the hypothesis was very vague, but I argued that 'in spite of its admitted vagueness, [it] is far *less* vague than the "physical-chemical state" hypothesis is today, and far more susceptible to investigation of both a mathematical and an empirical kind.' And then I added (and this reveals the extent of my 'scientism' at that time), 'Indeed, to investigate this hypothesis is just to attempt to produce "mechanical" models of organisms – and isn't this, in a sense, just what psychology is all about? The difficult step, of course, will be to pass from models of *specific* organisms (sic) to a *normal form* for the psychological description of organisms – for this is what is required to make (2) and (4) precise. But this too seems to be an inevitable part of the program of psychology.'

A paper that ended up being published in the same year (1975, ch. 20) closes by allowing that while the functional organization of a Turing Machine or a Probabilistic Automaton is given by the machine table, the description of the functional organization of a human being 'might well be something different and more complicated'. But like the paper from which I just quoted, it does not doubt, that the very *raison d'être* of psychology is to produce mechanical models of organisms. Nor does it express any reservations about the idea that it is an 'inevitable part of the program of psychology' to provide a *normal form for the psychological description of organisms*: not just for the psychological description of human beings, please note (as if that were not Utopian enough!), but a normal form for the psychological description of an arbitrary organism! Once psychology has progressed far enough in the pursuit of this 'inevitable program' to make the hypothesis that mental states are just functional states precise, it will possible – or so I claimed – to confirm the hypothesis in a way analogous to the way in which we have confirmed theoretical identifications in physics: the laws of unreduced psychology, to the extent that they are true, will be explained by the fact that the psychological states they speak of are really these functional states, just as the laws of unreduced optics, to the extent that they were true, were explained by the fact that the 'light rays' and 'light waves' they spoke of were really electromagnetic radiation of certain wavelengths.

FUNCTIONALISM WITHOUT TURING MACHINES, AND A PROBLEM FOR FUNCTIONALISM

At the beginning of 'Philosophy and Our Mental Life' (1975, ch. 14, p. 292), I expanded on my qualm about supposing that psychological states of human beings are *literally* Turing Machine states (in these papers I frequently spoke generally of Turing Machines, rather than, more precisely, of Probabilistic Automata). I recognized (1975, ch. 14) that 'the difficulty with the notion of psychological isomorphism is that it presupposes the notion of something's being a functional or psychological description.' And I went on to say that it is for that reason that in my previous papers I explained the notion in terms of Turing Machines, and I remarked that 'I felt constrained, therefore, to defend the idea that we are Turing Machines.' Turing Machines, I explained, come with a normal form for their functional description, the Machine Table, a standard style of program. 'But it does not seem fatally sloppy to me, although it is sloppy,' I wrote, 'if we apply the notion

509

to systems for which we have no detailed idea at present what the normal form description would look like – systems like ourselves.' I claimed that even if we don't have any idea what a 'comprehensive psychological theory' would look like, we know enough to point out illuminating differences between any possible psychological theory, or even a functional description of an automaton, and a physical description. The most important of those differences is this: that systems that are models of the same psychological theory, systems that are 'psychologically isomorphic', to use the terminology I developed in this series of papers, do not have to be in the same physical state in order to count as being in the same functional state. States that play the same psychological/functional role are *identified* at this level of description. A human being, a robot with the 'positronic brain' imagined in Isaac Asimov's science fiction, and a disembodied spirit might be psychologically isomorphic, and if they were, they could be in the same psychological states without ever being in the same physical state.

At this point, although I was still a functionalist, I had begun to be aware of a very serious problem for the position. Originally the thesis of functionalism was that our mental states are identical with (a subset of) our functional states, where the notion of a functional state was made clear by identifying it with the notion of a Turing Machine (or Probabilistic Automaton) State. But in this paper (1975, ch. 14), I pointed out that our mental states cannot literally be Turing Machine States (Turing Machine States don't have the right sorts of properties; for details, *see* 1975, pp. 298–9), and I replaced the notion of a Turing Machine Description with the notion of *the sort of description that will be provided by an ideal psychological theory*. What is an ideal psychological theory? We will know what that is when we have the 'normal form' for psychological theories that I had earlier claimed it must be 'an inevitable part of the programme of psychology' to provide.

But is it really any part of the programme of psychology to provide such a thing?

THE UTOPIAN CHARACTER OF FUNCTIONALISM

A psychological theory, in the ordinary sense, does not pretend to give a complete description of *all* of a human being's, or even of a rat's, psychological states (even if we assume that we know what we mean by talking about *all* of an organism's psychological states). Nor does it pretend to give all of the causal relations between psychological states. And this is so whether we think of Chomskian theories, behaviourist theories, Freudian theories, or whatever. No one has ever claimed to provide a theory in which so much information about the state of believing, say, that there are cows in Romania, and about the connections between that state and other psychological states, and between all of these states and 'sensory inputs' and 'behavioural outputs', is provided as to *individuate* the state of believing that there are cows in Romania. A Machine Table does distinguish a functional state of a Turing Machine from all other functional states of that Turing Machine: it *individuates* that state, in the sense of providing a necessary and sufficient condition for being that state. Even if we are charitable, we shall have to admit that the 'ideal psychological theory' that I envisaged in my functionalist papers, the kind of theory that could provide as complete a description of our psychological states as a Turing Machine Table provides of the functional states of a computer, is an utterly Utopian project (and if we are uncharitable we will simply say it is a 'we know not what').

This sort of utopianism is also an excellent illustration of what is called 'scientism'. Scientism is, of course, not the same thing as a respect for science, or a desire to learn the results of science, or a conviction that those results are relevant to philosophical investigation. But when one is in a frame of mind (as I was) in which one fails to distinguish between science in the sense in which science is actually done in today's laboratories and the most Utopian sort of speculation, then one is indeed in the grip of scientism. What is wrong with this sort of

Utopianism is not that there is something wrong with speculating about possibilities that we are not presently able to realize when we are able to make clear just what the hypothetical 'possibilities' *are*: such speculation is as old as philosophy itself. The problem is that it is completely unclear just *what* possibility is being envisaged when one speaks of a 'normal form description of the psychology of an arbitrary organism'; and the talk about 'the program of psychology' and about what is 'an inevitable part of the program of psychology' was, I blush to admit, a way of hiding this sorry state of affairs (in the first instance, from myself).

The degree of utopianism required to be a functionalist becomes all the greater when one recognizes something that I had emphasized in my writings on the philosophy of language from 1970 on (1970; 1975, ch. 12; 1988), namely that the meanings of our words (and, I argued, the content of our thoughts as well) are not determined simply by our functional organization in the sense that I talked about in my functionalist papers, that is, the sense in which our functional organization is simply a matter of 'sensory inputs', transitions from one 'state' to another, and 'motor outputs'. According to the semantic externalism that I defended (and still defend), the content of our words and thoughts is partly determined by our relations with things in our environment (including other people). The fact that what causes us to speak of *water* is water and not some other liquid has everything to do with the fact that the word *water* refers to water, for example (*see* EXTERNALISM/INTERNALISM).

Although I did not discuss this in 'Philosophy and Our Mental Life' (1975, ch. 14), I was, of course, aware of it, and what I would have said if someone had asked 'Isn't your functionalism incompatible with your semantic externalism?' is that strictly speaking an 'ideal psychological theory' has to be not a theory of one organism in isolation, but a theory of a group of organisms, and has to include a description of their interactions with one another and with their environment, and of the nature of the relevant parts of that environment. (In conversation, Richard Boyd suggested the name 'sociofunctionalism' for this position.) But the stipulation that the ideal psychological theory must include, properly speaking, also an ideal *sociolinguistic* theory makes the idea of such a theory, if possible, even *more* Utopian. Thus it is not surprising that by the middle 1980s I began seriously to ask myself '*How* meaningful, even as a regulative ideal, is the idea of an ideal psychological (cum socio-linguistic) theory that individuates all possible psychological states?'

Let us go back to the robot who was supposed to be 'psychologically isomorphic' to a human being (call it 'Leslie'). Suppose we observe that Leslie (or, for that matter, a human) produces the sound 'sheleg' when it snows. Especially when the snow is unexpected, and Leslie exhibits a 'startled reaction' at the onset of snow, he is likely to exclaim 'Sheleg!' (At least it seems to us like an exclamation.) It might well be part of the ideal psychological theory we postulated that 'under normal conditions an organism who has the belief that it is snowing in its conceptual repertoire will be caused to have that belief by the onset of snow'. It is compatible with that piece of 'the ideal psychological theory' that Leslie may believe that it is snowing on these occasions, and that Leslie may be expressing that belief by saying (or thinking) 'sheleg'. Unfortunately, there are a host of other possibilities. Suppose, for example, Leslie and his fellow robots have a religion of a rather primitive kind (remember, Leslie's sort of robot is psychologically isomorphic to human beings), and it is a peculiarity of this religion that snow is a sure sign that the gods are angry. In such a case, 'sheleg' might well mean 'The gods are angry'.

The reply of the functionalist, of course, will be that still Leslie's *total* internal goings-on will be different in some way from the internal goings-on of a robot that thinks 'it's snowing' when it says 'Sheleg'. If we knew the totality of the robot's internal goings-on and knew the ideal psychological theory we would be able to determine that the content of 'sheleg' thoughts is 'The gods are angry' and not 'It's snowing'. What does this require of the ideal psychological theory?

It requires that the ideal psychological theory be rich enough to describe *the beliefs of a believer of any possible religion.* Or Leslie may not be a believer in a primitive religion; the robot may be a superscientist. It may be saying 'quantum state such-and-such' when it snows, or making a comment in a physical theory we don't have yet. In short, it looks as if an ideal psychological theory, a theory that would be able to determine the content of an arbitrary thought, would have to be able to describe every belief of every possible kind, or at least every human belief of every possible kind, even of kinds that are not yet invented, or that go with institutions that have not yet come into existence. More and more, the suspicion grows that such a theory is a pure 'we know not what'.

What I think finally pushed me over the anti-functionalist edge was a conversation I had one day with Noam CHOMSKY. Chomsky suggested that the difference between a rational or a well-confirmed belief and a belief that is not rational or not well-confirmed might be determined by rules that are innate in the human brain (*see* INNATENESS). It struck me at once that it ought to be fairly easy to show, using the techniques one uses to prove the Gödel theorem, that if Chomsky is right then we could never discover that he is right; that is to say, that if what it is rational and not-rational to believe is determined by a recursive procedure which is specified in our ideal competence description D, then it could never be rational to believe that D *is* our ideal competence description. And I was able to show that this indeed is the case without too much trouble (1985).

I do not want to claim that this argument applies directly to our present discussion, since what we are talking about is not determining what is well confirmed but with determining what the content of thoughts is. What did occur to me is this: what the Gödel theorem shows is that

human reason is unable to survey itself well enough to see its own limits. That is to say that any description of our capacities that we are able to formalize is a description of a set of capacities that we are able to go beyond. But this suggests to me, not that we can *prove* that functionalism can't be made less vague than it presently is, but that we have no reason to believe that it could be. In short, it suggests to me that, first of all, if there *is* an 'ideal psychological theory', that is, a theory that does everything that the functionalist wants a 'description of human functional organization' to do (*let alone* a 'normal form for the description of the functional organization of an arbitrary organism'), then there is no reason to believe that it would be within the capacity of human beings to discover it. But, secondly, the *property* of being a 'description of human functional organization' is itself such an unclear property that the idea that *there is such a description even if we cannot recognize it* surely goes beyond the bounds of sense.

POST-FUNCTIONALIST PROGRAMMES

Of course, those who are sympathetic to functionalism have not given up as a result of my recantation; there are a number of what we might call 'post-functionalist' programmes on the market. One kind of post-functionalist programme seeks to deal with the problem which, in my opinion, is fatal for the 'implicit definition by a theory' idea which was at the heart of classic functionalism – an idea that was central not only to my version of functionalism but also to the somewhat different version proposed by David LEWIS (1983). (In Lewis's view we already *have* the ideal psychological theory required to implicity define the content of an arbitrary thought: it is just folk psychology!) That programme is the one of fixing the content of thoughts, by relying *entirely* on external factors to do that. DRETSKE (1981) and STALNAKER (1984) for example try to define the content of thoughts as well as of expressions in a language by simply looking for *probabilistic relations* between the occurrences of thoughts and expressions and external states of affairs. However, I believe that Putnam (1983) and Loewer (1987) have shown that the information theoretic concepts upon which Dretske and Stalnaker rely cannot individuate contents finely enough. FODOR (1990) proposes to rely not on information theoretic notions, but rather on the notion of causality. In *Renewing Philosophy* (1992, ch. 3) I show the following. (i) The notion of causality Fodor employs presupposes intentional notions; in particular, Fodor needs to assume a distinction between contributory causal factors and *the* cause of an event; I regard this as an intentional notion because which is *the* cause of an event depends on the interests we have in the context; it is not something that is inscribed in the phenomena themselves. (ii) The assignments of contents that result if we look only at the causes of utterances are the wrong ones. Block (1986) proposes a 'dual aspect' semantics in which the content of thoughts is determined by two factors: one factor, called 'narrow content' is determined, as in my functionalist theories, by the relations involved in the internal cognitive processing, in particular by 'inferential roles', and the other factor, the reference relation, is determined by causal connections. A difficulty with the first factor (Putnam, 1988, ch. 3) is that the inferential roles of concepts change enormously as the result of changes in belief as well as on account of changes in the meanings of words, and that there is no reason to suppose that one can distinguish between changes in inferential roles that represent only changes in beliefs from changes that represent changes in meaning without explicitly invoking some such notion as 'meaning'. In addition, the failures of causal theories of reference and of information-theoretic accounts of reference suggest that the other aspect of the 'dual aspect theory' is in no better shape.

I do not have space here to explain where I think we should go next. But – and this will be the subject of my next work on philosophy of mind (my Dewey Lectures (to be delivered in the spring of 1994) will deal with the philosophy of mind) – I am struck by the ways in which key elements of functionalism – in particular, both the causal theory of perception and the picture of *conception* as manipulation of symbols – operate within a seventeenth-century picture of the mind. I believe that a very different way of looking at the problems is possible (one suggested, in different ways, by the writings of Austin and Wittgenstein, as well as certain earlier philosophers); I hope to develop that way in future writing.

See also CONTENT; COMPUTATIONAL MODELS; CONCEPTS; CONCEPTUAL ROLE SEMANTICS; INTENTIONALITY; RATIONALITY; REPRESENTATION.

BIBLIOGRAPHY

Block, N. 1986. An advertisement of a semantics for psychology. *Midwest Studies in Philosophy, Vol. 10*, 615–78.

Churchland P. 1984. *Matter and Consciousness*. Cambridge, MA: MIT Press.

Dretske, F. 1981. *Knowledge and the Flow of Information*. Cambridge, MA: MIT Press.

Fodor, J. 1990. *A Theory of Content*. Cambridge, MA: MIT Press.

Lewis, D. 1983. *Philosophical Papers, Vol. 1*. Oxford University Press.

Loewer, B. 1987. From information to intentionality. *Synthèse*, 70: 2, 287–316.

Putnam, H. 1975: *Philosophical Papers, Vol. 2, Mind, Language and Reality*. Cambridge University Press.

—— 1979. *Philosophical Papers, Vol. 1. Mathematics, Matter and Method*, 2nd edn. Cambridge University Press.

—— 1985. Reflexive reflections. *Erkenntnis*, 22, 143–153.

—— 1988. *Representation and Reality*. Cambridge, MA: MIT Press.

—— 1992. *Renewing Philosophy*. Cambridge, MA: Harvard University Press.

Stalnaker, R. 1984. *Inquiry*. Cambridge, MA: MIT Press.

HILARY PUTNAM

Q

qualia Qualia include the ways it feels to see, hear and smell, the way it feels to have a pain; more generally, what it's like to have mental states. Qualia are experiential properties of sensations, feelings, perceptions and, in my view, thoughts and desires as well. But, so defined, who could deny that qualia exist? Yet, the existence of qualia is controversial. Here is what is controversial: whether qualia, so defined, can be characterized in intentional, functional or purely cognitive terms. Opponents of qualia think that the content of experience is intentional content (like the content of thought), or that experiences are functionally definable, or that to have a qualitative state is to have a state that is monitored in a certain way or accompanied by a thought to the effect that I have that state (*see* CONTENT FUNCTIONALISM; INTENTIONALITY). If we include the idea that experiential properties are not intentional or functional or purely cognitive in the definition of 'qualia', then it is controversial whether there are qualia.

This definition of 'qualia' is controversial in a respect familiar in philosophy. A technical term is often a locus of disagreement, and the warring parties will often disagree about what the important parameters of disagreement are. DENNETT, for example, has supposed in some of his writings that it is of the essence of qualia to be non-relational, incorrigible (to believe one has one is to have one) and to have no scientific nature (*see* Flanagan, 1992, p. 61). This is what you get when you let an opponent of qualia define the term. A proponent of qualia ought to allow that categorizations of them (beliefs about them) can be mistaken, and that science can investigate qualia. I think that we ought to allow that qualia

might be physiological states, and that their scientific nature might even turn out to be relational. Friends of qualia differ on whether or not they are physical. In my view, the most powerful arguments in favour of qualia actually presuppose a physicalistic doctrine, the supervenience of qualia on the brain. (*See* PHYSICALISM; SUPERVENIENCE.)

Perhaps the most puzzling thing about qualia is how they relate to the physical world. Sometimes this is put in terms of the explanatory gap, the idea that nothing we know or can conceive of knowing about the brain can explain why qualia feel the way they do. The explanatory gap is closely related to the thought experiments that dominate the literature on qualia.

THE KNOWLEDGE ARGUMENT

One of these thought experiments is the case of Jackson's (1986) Mary, who is raised in a black and white environment in which she learns all the functional and physical facts about colour vision. Nonetheless, when she ventures outside for the first time, she learns a new fact: what it is like to see red. So, the argument goes, what it is like to see red cannot be a functional or physical fact. Dennett (1991) objects that perhaps she could have figured out which things are red; but that is beside the point for two reasons. The question is: does she know what it is like to see red, not which things are red? And does she know it simply in virtue of knowing all the functional and physical facts about colour vision, whether or not she is clever enough to figure it out on the basis of what she knows?

LEWIS denies that Mary acquires any new knowledge-that, insisting that she only acquires knowledge-how, abilities to imagine and recognize. But as Loar points out, the knowledge she acquires can appear in embedded contexts. For example, she may reason that *if* this is what it is like to see red, *then* this is similar to what it is like to see orange. Lewis's ability analysis of Mary's knowledge has the same problem here that non-cognitive analyses of ethical language have in explaining the logical behaviour of ethical predicates.

Here is a different (and in my view more successful) objection to Jackson (Horgan, 1984b; Peacocke, 1989; Loar, 1990; Papineau, 1993; van Gulick, 1993). What Mary acquires when she sees red is a new PHENOMENAL concept, a recognitional disposition that allows her to pick out a certain type of phenomenal feel. This new phenomenal concept is a constituent of genuinely new knowledge – knowledge of what it is like to see red. But the new phenomenal concept picks out old properties, properties picked out by physical or functional concepts that she already had. So the new knowledge is just a new way of knowing old facts. Before leaving the room, she knew what it is like to see red in a third-person way; after leaving the room, she acquires a new way of knowing the same fact. If so, what she acquires does not rule out any POSSIBLE WORLDS that were not already ruled out by the facts that she already knew, and the thought-experiment poses no danger to physicalistic doctrines. Incidentally, the recognitional disposition account indicates how qualia could turn out to be relational; perhaps the recognitional disposition picks out a relational physical state of the brain or even a functional state. (But see the criticism of Loar in FUNCTIONALISM(2).)

ABSENT QUALIA

Another familiar conundrum is the absent qualia hypothesis. If human beings can be described computationally, as is assumed by the research programme of cognitive science, a robot could in principle be built that was computationally identical to a human. But would there be anything it was like to be that robot? Would it have qualia? (*See* Shoemaker, 1975, 1981, and White, 1986.) Some thought experiments have appealed to oddball realizations of our functional organization, e.g. by the economy of a country. If an economy can share our functional organization, then our functional organization cannot be sufficient for qualia. Many critics simply bite the bullet at this point, saying that the oddball realizations do have qualia. Lycan (1987) responds by making two additions to functionalism as spelled out in FUNCTIONALISM (2). The additions are designed to rule out oddball realizations of our functional organization of the ilk of the aforementioned economy. He suggests thinking of the functional roles in teleological terms and thinking of these roles as involving the details of human physiology (*see* TELEOLOGY). Economies don't have the states with the right sort of evolutionary 'purpose', and their states are not physiological. On the first move, *see* FUNCTIONALISM (2). On the second, note that including physiology in our functional definitions of mental states will make them so specific to humans that they won't apply to other creatures that have mental states. Further, this idea violates the spirit of the functionalist proposal, which, being based on the computer analogy, abstracts from hardware realization. Functionalism without multiple hardware realizations is functionalism in name only.

THE INVERTED SPECTRUM

One familiar conundrum that uses a physicalistic idea of qualia against functionalist and intentionalist ideas is the famous inverted spectrum hypothesis, the hypothesis that things we both call 'red' look to you the way things we both call 'green' look to me, even though we are functionally (and therefore behaviourally) identical. A first step in motivating the inverted spectrum hypothesis is the possibility that the brain state that I have when I see red things is the same as the brain state that you have when you see green things, and conversely.

(Nida-Rumelin, forthcoming, presents evidence that this is a naturally occurring phenomenon.) Therefore, it might be said, our experiences are inverted. What is assumed here is a supervenience doctrine, that the qualitative content of a state supervenes on physiological properties of the brain.

There is a natural functionalist reply. Notice that it is not possible that the brain state that I get when I see things we both call 'red' is *exactly* the same as the brain state that you get when you see things we both call 'green'. At least, the *total* brain states can't be the same, since mine causes me to say 'It's red', and to classify what I'm seeing as the same colour as blood and fire hydrants, whereas yours causes you to say 'It's green', and to classify what you are seeing with grass and Granny Smith apples. Suppose that the brain state that I get when I see red and that you get when you see green is X-oscillations in area V4, whereas what I get when I see green and you get when you see red are Y-oscillations in area V4. The functionalist says that phenomenal properties should not be identified with brain states quite so 'localized' as X-oscillations or Y-oscillations, but rather with more holistic brain states that include tendencies to classify objects together as the same colour (*see* HOLISM). Thus the functionalist will want to say that my holistic brain state that includes X-oscillations and your holistic brain state that includes Y-oscillations are just alternative realizations of the same experiential state (Harman, 1990). So the fact that red things give me X-oscillations but they give you Y-oscillations doesn't show that our experiences are inverted. The defender of the claim that inverted spectra are possible can point out that when something looks red to me, I get X-oscillations, whereas when something looks green to me, I get Y-oscillations, and so the difference in the phenomenal aspect of experience corresponds to a local brain state difference. But the functionalist can parry by pointing out that this difference has only been demonstrated intra-personally, keeping the larger brain state that specifies the roles of X-oscillations in classifying things con-

stant. He can insist on typing brain states for inter-personal comparisons holistically. And most friends of the inverted spectrum are in a poor position to insist on typing experiential states locally rather than holistically, given that they normally emphasize the 'explanatory gap', the fact that there is nothing known about the brain that can adequately explain the facts of experience (*see* CONSCIOUSNESS). So the friend of the inverted spectrum is in no position to insist on local physiological individuation of qualia. At this stage, the defender of the inverted spectrum is stymied.

One move the defender of the possibility of the inverted spectrum can make is to move to an intra-personal inverted spectrum example. Think of this as a four-stage process. (1) You have normal colour vision. (2) You have colour inverting devices inserted in your retinas or in the lateral geniculate nucleus, the first way-station behind the retina, and red things look the way green things used to look, blue things look the way yellow things used to look, etc. (3) You have adapted, so that you naturally and spontaneously call red things 'red', etc., but when reminded, you recall the days long ago when ripe tomatoes looked to you, colourwise, the way Granny Smith apples do now. (4) You get amnesia about the days before the lenses were inserted. Stage 1 is functionally equivalent to stage 4 in the relevant respects, but they are arguably qualia-inverted. So we have an inverted spectrum over time. The advantages of this thought experiment are twofold. First, the argument profits from the force of the subject's testimony at stages 2 and 3 for qualia inversion. Second, the four-stage setup forces the opponents to say what stage is the one where my description goes wrong. (*See* Shoemaker, 1981; Block, 1990.) Rey (1993) attacks (3), Dennett (1991) attacks (2) and (3), and White (1993) attacks (4). In my view, the most vulnerable stage is (3) because the functionalist can raise doubts about whether what it's like to see red things *could* remain the same during the changes in responses that have to go on in the process of adaptation.

Why, an opponent might ask, is the inverted qualia argument against functionalism any more powerful than the inverted qualia argument against physicalism? After all, it might be said, one can imagine particle-for-particle duplicates who have spectra that are inverted with respect to one another. But though physical duplicates with inverted spectra may be imaginable, they are ruled out by a highly plausible principle that any materialist should accept: that qualia supervene on physical constitution. The thought experiments that I have been going through argue that even materialists should accept the possibility of an inverted spectrum, and further, that for all we know, such cases are feasible via robotics or genetic engineering, or even actual. And in so doing, they make the case for conceptual possibility stronger, for one is surer that something is genuinely conceptually possible if one can see how one might go about making it actual.

INVERTED EARTH

An interesting variant of the inverted spectrum thought-experiment is Inverted Earth (Block, 1990). Inverted Earth is a planet that differs from Earth in two relevant ways. First, everything is the complementary colour of the corresponding earth object. The sky is yellow, the grass-like stuff is red, etc. (To avoid impossibility, we could imagine, instead, two people raised in rooms in which everything in one room is the complementary colour of the corresponding item in the other room.) Second, people on Inverted Earth speak an inverted language. They use 'red' to mean green, 'blue' to mean yellow, etc. If you order paint from Inverted Earth, and you want yellow paint, you fax an order for 'Blue paint'. The effect of both inversions is that if you are drugged and kidnapped in the middle of the night, and inverters are inserted behind your eyes (and your body pigments are changed), you will *notice no difference* if you are placed in the bed of your counterpart on Inverted Earth. (Let's assume that the victim does not know anything about the science of colour.)

Now consider the comparison between you and your counterpart on Inverted Earth. The counterpart could be your identical twin who was fitted with inverting lenses at birth and put up for adoption on Inverted Earth, or the counterpart could be you after you've been switched with your twin and have been living there for a long while. Looking at blue things gives you Z-oscillations in the brain, yellow things give you W-oscillations; your twin gets the opposite. Now notice the interesting difference between this twin case and the one mentioned earlier: there can be perfect inversion in the *holistic* brain states as well as the local ones. At this moment, you both are looking at your respective skies. You get Z-oscillations because your sky is blue, he gets Z-oscillations because his sky is yellow. Your Z-oscillations make you say 'How blue!', and his Z-oscillations make him say 'How blue!' too. Indeed, we can take your brains to be molecular duplicates of one another. Then the principle of the supervenience of qualia on holistic brain state dictates that experientially, at the moment of looking at the skies, you and your twin have the same qualia.

But though you and your twin have the same qualia, you are functionally and intentionally inverted. If you are asked to match the colour of the sky with a Munsell colour chip, you will pick a blue one, but if your twin is shown the same (earth-made) Munsell chips, he will pick a yellow one. Further, when he says 'How blue!' he *means* 'How yellow!' Recall that the Inverted Earth dialect, of which he is a loyal member, has colour words whose meanings are inverted with respect to ours. You and your twin are at that moment functionally and intentionally inverted, but qualitatively identical. So we have the converse of the inverted spectrum. And there is no problem about local versus holistic brain states as in the intersubjective inverted spectrum; and no problem about whether qualia could persist unchanged through adaptation as in the intra-subjective inverted spectrum.

The argument that you and your twin are qualitatively the same can work either of two ways. We can assume the principle of supervenience of qualia on the brain, building the brain-identity of the twins into the story. Or we can run the story in terms of your being kidnapped, drugged, and placed in your twin's niche on Inverted Earth. What justifies the idea that your qualia are the same is that you notice no difference when you wake up in your Twin's bed after the switch; no appeal to supervenience is required.

Notice that the functional differences between these qualia-identical twins are long-arm functional differences (*see* FUNC-TIONALISM) and the intentional differences are external intentional differences. Perhaps, you might say, the twins are not inverted in short-arm functional roles and narrow intentional content. The cure for this idea is to ask the question of what the purely internal functional or intentional differences could be that would define the difference between an experience as of red and an experience as of green. The natural answer would be to appeal to the internal aspects of beliefs and desires. We believe, for example, that blood is red but not that it is green. However, someone could have colour experience despite having no standing beliefs or desires that differentiated colours. Imagine a person raised in a room where the colour of everything is controlled by a computer, and nothing retains its colour for more than 10 seconds. Or imagine a person whose colour perception is normal but who has forgotten all colour-facts.

There is no shortage of objections to these lines of reasoning. I will very briefly mention two closely related objections. It has been objected (Hardin, 1988) that red is intrinsically warm, whereas green is intrinsically cool, and thus inversion will either violate functional identity or yield an incoherent cool-red state. (Note, incidentally, that this isn't an objection to the inverted earth thought experiment; since that is a case of qualitative identity and functional *difference*, no functional identity is involved.) But the natural reply (Block, 1990) is that warm and cool can be inverted too. So long as there is no intrinsic connection between colour qualia and behaviour, the inverted spectrum is safe. But is there such an intrinsic connection? Dennett (1991) says there is. Blue calms, red excites. But perhaps this is due to culture and experience; perhaps people with very different cultures and experiences would have colour experiences without this asymmetry. The research on this topic is equivocal; Dennett's sole reference, Humphrey (1992), describes it as 'relatively second-rate', and that is also my impression. The fact that we don't know is itself interesting, however, for what it shows is that this asymmetry is no part of our colour concepts. As Shoemaker (1981) points out, even if human colour experience is genetically asymmetrical, there could nonetheless be people much like us whose colour experience is not asymmetrical. So an inversion of the sort mentioned in the thought experiments is conceptually possible, even if it is not possible for the human species. But then colour inversion may be possible for a closely related species whose colour qualia are not in doubt, one which could perhaps be produced by genetic engineering. Functionalism would not be a very palatable doctrine if it were said to apply to some people's colour experiences but not to others.

THE EXPLANATORY GAP AGAIN

At the outset, I mentioned the 'explanatory gap', the idea that nothing now known about the brain, nor anything anyone has been able to imagine finding out would explain qualia. We can distinguish inflationary and deflationary attitudes towards this gap among those who agree that the gap is unclosable. McGinn (1991) argues that the gap is unclosable because the fundamental nature of consciousness is inaccessible to us, though it might be accessible to creatures with very different sorts of minds. But a number of authors have favoured a deflationary approach, arguing that the unclosability of the explanatory gap has to do with our concepts, not with nature itself. Horgan (1984), Levine (1993), Jackson (1993), Chalmers (1993) (and interestingly, McGinn, 1991, too) have contributed to working out the idea that reductive explanation in science depends on a priori analyses of the phenomena to be explained, usually in functional terms. (A version of this point was made in Nagel, 1974.) Consider Chalmers' example of the reductive explanation of life. Life can be roughly analysed in terms of such general notions as metabolism and adaptation, or perhaps more specific notions such as digestion, reproduction and locomotion, and these concepts can themselves be given a functional analysis. Once we have explained these functions, suppose someone says 'Oh yes, I see the explanation of those functions, but what about explaining *life?*' We can answer that, a priori, to explain these functions *is* to explain life itself.

In some cases, the a priori analysis of the item to be explained is more complicated. Consider water. We can't give an a priori analysis of water as the colourless, odourless liquid in rivers and lakes called 'water', because water might not have been colourless, it might have been called 'glue', there might not have been lakes, etc. But we can formulate an a priori reference fixing definition of the sort that Kripke has emphasized: water = R(the colourless, odourless liquid in rivers and lakes called 'water'), where the 'R' is a rigidification operator that turns a definite description into a rigid designator. (A rigid designator picks out the same thing in all possible worlds in which the thing exists; for example, 'Aristotle' is rigid. To rigidify a definite description is to treat it as a name for whatever the definite description *actually* picks out.) Thus, suppose we want to explain the fact that water dissolves salt. It suffices to explain that H_2O dissolves salt and that H_2O is the colourless, odourless liquid in rivers and lakes called 'water'. If someone objects that we have only explained how something colourless, odourless, etc. dissolves salt, not that water does, we can point out that it is a priori that water is the actual colourless, odourless, etc., substance. And if someone objects that we have only explained how H_2O dissolves salt, not how water does, we can answer

that from the fact that H_2O is the colourless, odourless, etc., stuff and that, a priori, water is the (actual) colourless, odourless, etc., stuff, we can derive that water *is* H_2O.

The upshot is that closing the explanatory gap requires an a priori functional analysis of qualia. If Kripke (1980) is right that we pick out qualia by their qualitative character and not by their functional role, then no a priori reference fixing definition can be given for qualitative concepts of the sort that can be given for 'water' and 'life'. Of course, if there is a *true* functional analysis that picks out a quale, it can be rigidified, but it still won't be an a priori characterization. Pain = R(Aunt Irma's favourite sensation) can be true and necessary without being a priori. And if the arguments about qualia inversion just sketched are right, there is no a priori conceptual analysis of qualitative concepts either, and so the explanatory gap is unclosable. As Chalmers points out, with a physical or a functional account, we can explain the functions associated with qualia, the capacity to classify things as red, for example. But once we have explained these functions, there will be a further question: why are these functions accompanied by qualia? Such a further question does not arise in the case of life and water precisely because of the availability of an a priori functional analysis.

It would be natural to suppose that the explanatory gap derives from the fact that neuroscientists have not yet come up with the required concepts to explain qualia. Nagel (1974) gives an analogy that suggests this idea. We are in the situation, he suggests, of a caveman who is told that matter is energy. But he does not have the concepts to appreciate how this could be so. These concepts, however, are ones that some of us do have now, and it is a natural thought that a few hundred years from now, the concepts might be available to explain qualia physically. But the deflationary account of reductive explanation denies this, blaming the explanatory gap on our ordinary concepts, not on science.

See also An Essay on Mind section 2.2.

519

BIBLIOGRAPHY

Block, N. 1990. Inverted earth. In *Philosophical Perspectives*, Vol. 4, ed. J. Tomberlin. Ridgeview.

Chalmers, D.J. 1993. *Toward a Theory of Consciousness*. University of Indiana Ph.D. thesis.

Davies, M., and Humphreys, G. 1993. *Consciousness*. Oxford: Basil Blackwell.

Dennett, D. 1988. Quining qualia. In *Consciousness in Contemporary Society* ed. A. Marcel and E. Bisiach. Oxford University Press.

Dennett, D. 1991. *Consciousness Explained*. New York: Little, Brown.

Flanagan, O. 1992. *Consciousness Reconsidered*. Cambridge, MA.: MIT Press.

Hardin, C. 1988. *Color for Philosophers*. Indianapolis: Hackett.

Harman, G. 1990. The intrinsic quality of experience. In *Philosophical Perspectives*, Vol. 4, ed. J. Tomberlin. Atascadero, CA: Ridgeview.

Horgan, T. 1984a. Supervenience and cosmic hermeneutics. *Southern Journal of Philosophy, Supplement 22*, 19–38.

Horgan, T. 1984b. Jackson on physical information and qualia. *Philosophical Quarterly*, 34, 147–53.

Humphrey, N. 1992. *A History of the Mind*. New York: Simon & Schuster.

Jackson, F. 1986. What Mary didn't know. *Journal of Philosophy*, 83, 291–95

Jackson, F. 1993. Armchair metaphysics. In *Philosophy in Mind* ed. J. O'Leary-Hawthorne and M. Michael. Kluwer.

Kripke, S. 1980. *Naming and Necessity*. Cambridge, MA.: Harvard University Press.

Levine, J. 1993. On leaving out what it is like. In Davies and Humphreys, 1993.

Loar, B. 1990. Phenomenal properties. In *Philosophical Perspectives, Vol. 4*, ed. J. Tomberlin. Atascadero, CA: Ridgeview.

Lycan, W. 1987. *Consciousness*. Cambridge, MA.: MIT Press.

McGinn, C. 1991. *The Problem of Consciousness*. Oxford: Basil Blackwell.

Nagel, T. 1974. What is it like to be a bat? *Philosophical Review*, 83, 435–50.

Nida-Rumelin, M. Forthcoming. Pseudonormal vision. An actual case of qualia inversion? *Philosophical Studies*.

Papineau, D. 1993. Physicalism, Consciousness and the Antipathetic Fallacy. *Australasian Journal of Philosophy*, 71: 2, 169–184

Peacocke, C. 1989. No resting place: a critical notice of *The View from Nowhere*. *Philosophical Review*, 98, 65–82.

Rey, G. 1993. Sensational sentences switched. *Philosophical Studies*, 70, 1.

Shoemaker, S. 1975. Functionalism and qualia. *Philosophical Studies*, 27, 291–315.

Shoemaker, S. 1981. Absent qualia are impossible – a reply to Block. *Philosophical Review*, 90: 4, 581–99.

Van Gulick, R. 1993. Understanding the phenomenal mind: Are we all just armadillos? In Davies and Humphreys, 1993.

White, S.L. 1986. Curse of the qualia. *Synthèse*, 68, 333–68.

White, S.L. 1993. Color and the narrow contents of experience. Paper delivered at the Eastern Division of the American Philosophical Association.

NED BLOCK

Quine, Willard Van Orman Although few of his writings directly address traditional issues in the philosophy of mind, Quine's work has been a major influence upon the area since the 1950s. His contributions to the philosophy of language shook the prejudices underlying much 'traditional' philosophical analysis, forcing philosophers to adopt new models and approaches in thinking about the mind. By defending 'naturalism', the idea that philosophy is continuous with the sciences and has no privileged source of knowledge, he contributed to the growth of cognitive science and the idea that an adequate philosophical understanding of mind should take into account developments in psychology and biology (*see* COGNITIVE PSYCHOLOGY). And his uncompromising defence of physicalism since the 1950s has shaped our understanding of what this position commits us to.

Quine's earliest discussions of mind attack 'mentalism', the claim that there are irreducibly mental entities or events. Since his aim was normally to show that such theories have no role in the explanation of linguistic meaning, his underlying philosophy of mind was rarely explicitly presented. Fortunately, some of Quine's more recent work remedies this lack (Quine, 1975, and especially 1985, and 1990, ch. IV).

NATURALISM: MIND AND BODY

Quine's naturalism affirms that there can be no 'philosophical' study of mind outside psychology: progress in philosophical understanding of the mind is inseparable from progress in psychology. Furthermore, psychology is a 'natural science' studying a 'natural phenomenon, viz. a physical human subject' (1969, p. 82): Brentano was wrong to advocate an autonomous discipline studying its own distinctively mental objects. 'Unless a case can be made for disembodied spirits', Quine argued, 'a dualism of mind and body is an idle redundancy.' (1985, p. 5)

'States of mind' (1985, p. 5) offers the following brief argument:

Corresponding to every mental state, however fleeting or however remotely intellectual, the dualist is bound to admit the existence of a bodily state that obtains when and only when the mental one obtains. The bodily state is trivially specifiable in the dualist's own terms, simply as the state accompanying a mind that is in the mental state. Instead of ascribing the one state to the mind, then, we may equivalently ascribe the other to the body. The mind goes by the board, and will not be missed.

(The relevance of 'disembodied spirits', whose states would not be correlated with bodily ones, is clear.) This 'effortless physicalism' encourages us to retain the traditional mentalistic terms (we speak of pains, beliefs, sudden thoughts and so on), but 'we reckon mental states as states of the body rather than as states of another substance, the mind' (ibid). The target here appears to be substance dualism, the idea that our ontology should contain non-physical mental *objects* (*see* DUALISM; PHYSICALISM). But Quine may be making the stronger

claim that all of our explanatory and descriptive needs are met by talk of the 'bodily states' of physical objects. This would exclude property dualism, the idea that psychological terms express irreducibly mental properties of physical objects. As we shall see, his position is more complex than this: there *are* irreducible psychological properties, but all *explanation* is ultimately physical.

His account of our mental concepts emerges as he examines how we acquire them, how we learn 'to call our anxieties anxieties, and our dull aches dull aches, our joys joys and our awareness awareness'. He explains that:

such terms are applied in the light of publicly observable symptoms: bodily symptoms strictly of bodily states, and the mind is as may be. Someone observes my joyful or anxious expression, or perhaps observes my gratifying or threatening situation itself, or hears me tell about it. She then applies the word 'joy' or 'anxiety'. After another such lesson or two I find myself applying those words to some of my subsequent states in cases where no outward signs are to be observed beyond my report itself. Without the outward signs, to begin with, mentalistic terms could not be learned at all. (1985, p. 6)

He is no crude behaviourist: mental states are inner states which may (but need not) be manifested in behaviour (*see* BEHAVIOURISM). Nor is he a dualist: a mental state is a bodily state, 'a state of nerves'. Exploiting their links with behaviour, mentalistic language enables us to refer to inner neurological states and use them in explanation, while ignorant of the neural mechanisms involved. In effect, we identify mental states as the bodily states (whatever they may be) which occupy various specifiable causal roles in the determination of behaviour: the position is close to FUNCTIONALISM. Patterns in behaviour enable us to identify states which occupy distinctive

521

causal roles; further research may help us to construct neurophysiological descriptions of them. This may accord with the apparent rejection of property dualism: the apparent ineliminability of psychological concepts is a reflection of our ignorance of the neurophysiological underpinning of our thoughts and actions. But the position is more complex than that.

SOME COMPARISONS: BEHAVIOURISM, ELIMINATIVISM, IDENTITY THEORIES

Quine is sometimes misdescribed as a behaviourist, and was certainly influenced by writers such as B. F. Skinner. The passages just cited show that he is closer to the IDENTITY THEORY than to behaviourism: mental states are physical states, usually of the brain. But they are identified as the neurophysiological grounds of behavioural dispositions: behaviour is fundamental to the development of our psychological concepts. Moreover, although behaviourism is not compulsory in psychology, it is 'mandatory' in linguistics:

> Each of us learns his language by observing other people's verbal and other behaviour and having his own faltering verbal behaviour observed and reinforced or corrected by others. We depend strictly on overt behaviour in observable situations. As long as our command of our language fits all external checkpoints, where our utterance or our reaction to someone's utterance can be appraised in the light of some shared situation, so long all is well. Our mental life between checkpoints is indifferent to our rating as a master of the language. There is nothing in linguistic meaning beyond what is to be gleaned from overt behaviour in observable circumstances. (1990, pp. 37–8)

Since many of Quine's remarks about mentalism and the mind occur when his real interest is in understanding and linguistic representation, it is unsurprising that his writings often give an impression of an adherence to behaviourism which reflects his philosophy of language rather than his philosophy of mind.

Materialist philosophers are often classified according to whether they hold that ordinary psychological terms denote physical or bodily states, or whether they hold that traditional mentalistic language ('FOLK PSYCHOLOGY') will eventually be repudiated, eliminated from the language as part of a discredited theory. Quine occasionally allies himself with each of these opposed tendencies. In 'Mind and verbal dispositions' (1975, p. 94) he emphasizes the advantages of dispensing with mental states, doing our theorizing in physiological terms. The more recent 'States of mind' advocates 'an identification of mental states with bodily ones, neural ones: a construing of the mental as neural' (1985, p. 6).

In fact, as Quine sees, his philosophy of language robs this debate of its point. A philosopher who is realist about properties, viewing the world as containing objectively natural kinds of properties, and who believes that the notion of reference is a fundamental explanatory notion within an account of how language works, might address this question of whether two disparate expressions generally *refer* to the *same property*. But since Quine rejects realism about properties and believes that reference is radically inscrutable, no sense attaches to the question whether 'pain' expresses the property of being in a particular brain state. Quine consistently denies that a distinction can be drawn between 'identifying the mental states with the states of nerves . . . and repudiating them in favor of the states of nerves' (1985, p. 6). Hence he is content to talk of identity and identification; but one misunderstands his position if one looks for a considered refutation of elimination (*see* ELIMINATIVISM).

IDENTITY: TYPE, TOKEN, ANOMALOUS MONISM

For Quine, expressions like 'Tom's toothache' or 'an itch behind the left ear' collect together heterogeneous classes of neural states and events. A 'type identity' theorist expects that such classes will be unified by some common neurophysiological trait: the mental kind will correspond to a physical kind. Those who expect only 'token identities' do not anticipate that such classes of physical events will form physical kinds, that they can be seen to 'belong together' except by reference to the corresponding mental properties. Quine has recently declared that we should expect no more than token identities: no neurophysiological kinds correspond to our systems of psychological description (*see An Essay on Mind* section 3.6; TYPE/TOKEN). Indeed, he has declared his adherence to a position associated with Donald DAVIDSON, 'ANOMALOUS MONISM' (Quine, 1985, p. 7; 1990, pp. 70–3; Davidson, 1980, pp. 214–25).

In *Pursuit of Truth*, he explains that *Tom's perceptions of rain* can differ 'because there are different indicators of rain'. Although these perceptions may form a class that is too complex and heterogeneous for us to give it a satisfying general description in neurophysiological terms, we can be confident that there is a 'neural trait that unifies these neural events as a class; for it was by stimulus generalization, or subjective similarity, that Tom eventually learned to make the observation sentence "It's raining" do for all of them' (1990, p. 62). Thus far, type identity. But if we move to the more general mental property *perceiving that it is raining* (which can be shared by many different people) the position is different: 'a neurological rendering of "perceives that it is raining", applicable to all comers, would be out of the question' (1990, p. 70). This is because people's 'nerve nets' differ in consequence of their genetic endowments and their educational histories. The expression 'cuts through all that hopeless neurological complexity' (1990, p. 62) unifying such states by reference to a symptom rather than by a common neural mechanism: token identity seems to be the order of the day.

Once we turn from perceptions to beliefs and other propositional attitudes, the complexities grow. The evidence upon which we rely in ascribing beliefs to people is enormously varied: we note what they say, the wagers they are prepared to accept, such behaviour as searching and fleeing, information about past experience and training, etc. (1985, pp. 6–7). Quine writes: 'The empirical content of ascriptions of belief is thus heterogeneous in the extreme, and the physiological mechanisms involved are no less so'. We group states together as cases of 'perceiving that p' and 'believing that p': they are unified not by any common physiological feature but rather by the 'that clause' or CONTENT clause. Thus, for Quine, although mental events are all physical events, their occurrence being explicable by reference to physical law, there are 'irreducibly mental . . . ways of grouping them: grouping a lot of respectably physical perceptions as perceptions that *p*, and grouping a lot of respectably physical belief instances as the belief that *p*' (p. 71). This is the view that Quine calls 'anomalous monism': it signals his acceptance of a form of property dualism.

EMPATHY AND THE PROPOSITIONAL ATTITUDES

How are we to understand our use of 'irreducibly mental' ways of classifying physical events? The behavioural manifestations of BELIEFS, DESIRES and INTENTIONS are enormously varied, as we have suggested. When we move away from perceptual beliefs, the links with behaviour are intractable and indirect: the expectations I form on the basis of a particular belief reflect the influence of numerous other opinions; my ACTIONS are formed by the totality of my preferences and all those opinions which have a bearing upon them. The causal processes that produce my beliefs reflect my opinions about those processes, about their reliability and the interferences to which they are subject. Thus behaviour justifies the ascription of a particular belief only by helping to warrant a more inclusive interpretation of the overall cognitive position of the individual in question. Psychological description, like translation, is a HOLISTIC business. And once this is taken into account, it is all the less likely that a common physical trait will be found which grounds all instances of the same belief. The ways in which all of our PROPOSITIONAL ATTITUDES interact in the production of behaviour reinforce the anomalous character of the mental and render any sort of reduction of the mental to the physical impossible (*see* RATIONALITY; REDUCTION).

Quine's hints concerning how we arrive at an acceptable set of belief ascriptions are vague. Clearly, we are to ascribe perceptual beliefs only when the opinion in question is appropriately linked to sensory input; and we are required to ascribe sets of beliefs and desires which are (broadly) logically coherent. In *Pursuit of Truth*, Quine (1990) gestures towards a role for 'empathy': 'Empathy is why we ascribe a propositional attitude by a content clause' (p. 68). Parents train children in their home languages by evaluating 'the appropriateness of the child's observation sentences by noting the child's orientation and how the scene would look from there' (p. 42). This 'uncanny knack for empathizing another's perceptual situation, however ignorant of the physiological or optical mechanism of his perception' (p. 42) underlies all translation and understanding of other people. Quine's remark that it is comparable to 'our ability to recognize faces while unable to sketch or describe them' suggests that the basis of psychological interpretation is not reducible to a set of rules or principles. 'Practical psychology' employs the method of 'empathy': we are to imagine ourselves in our subject's position as well as we can (p. 46) – we expect our imagined responses to provide a clue to how they have responded.

One of Quine's most famous theses emerges here: feeling our way into another's language and into their beliefs and desires, we rely upon our empathetic understanding of their position and try to make sense of their projects and their cognitive position. Since the behavioural clues upon which we rely reflect the complex interactions of innumerable beliefs and desires, there is no reason to expect that only one

set of ascriptions will enable us to understand their behaviour and enter into dialogue with them. In talking of translation, Quine remarks that 'What is utterly factual is just the fluency of conversation and the effectiveness of negotiation that one or another manual of translation serves to induce' (1990, p. 43). In parallel vein, we might say of psychological ascription that what is utterly factual is the fact that a set of interpretations enables us to empathize with someone, conversing, negotiating, cooperating and so on. We have no reason to suppose that only one set of interpretations will enable us to do this. Since propositional attitudes do not identify neurophysiological states which embody any kind of physical unity, we should not be surprised if a variety of sets of interpretations made psychological sense of this enormous variety of physical events. Translation and psychological description are both indeterminate: there is no fact of the matter which translation or description is correct. Fortunately this indeterminacy rarely intrudes to block understanding in practice.

SCIENCE AND THE MIND

Quine employs an analogy between psychological terms and terms for diseases: each identifies an initially unknown bodily state by reference to its symptoms (1985, p. 6). But there is a disanalogy: while we may eventually hope to identify the kind of bodily disorder associated with a particular disease, Quine sees no reason to expect such associations to be possible for propositional attitudes. We cannot expect to show that psychological generalizations are explicable by reference to neurological laws; at best we can hope for physical explanations of particular instances of psychological states. Mentalistic psychology is not to be integrated with natural science as chemistry is to be integrated with physics.

As Quine sees it, this has given succour to dualism: Brentano and his followers have sought an autonomous science of content, exploring further the properties of intentional states or propositional attitudes

(1985, p. 7; 1960, p. 221). Agreeing with Brentano about the irreducibility of mental discourse to physical, he enjoins us not to try to 'weave [intensional discourse] into our scientific theory of the world to make a more comprehensive system' (1990, p. 71). The events referred to as beliefs and perceptions also receive physical descriptions, and so described, they receive properly scientific explanations. This is all the integration of psychology and physical science that is required. If, contrary to the indeterminacy of translation, the evidence was sufficient to determine one set of propositional attitudes, the prospects for an autonomous science of propositional attitudes may seem more attractive. Since this is not the position, there is no reason to follow Brentano (*see* INTENTIONALITY).

Moreover, it is Quine's opinion that natural science is extensional: its claims can be regimented employing the familiar first-order logic of quantifiers and relations. Much work on the logic of propositional attitudes has been prompted by Quine's demonstration that such discourse is not extensional. Quine's refusal to incorporate mentalistic talk in science enables the latter to enjoy 'the crystalline purity of *extensionality*' (1990, p. 71):

As long as extensional science can proceed autonomously and self-contained, with no gaps of causality that intensional intrusions could serve to close, the sound strategy is the linguistic dualism of anomalous monism. (p. 72)

So we find at least two reasons convincing Quine that scientific explanation of mental phenomena should be physiological and, ultimately, physical. However valuable it may be, talk of propositional attitudes has no place in science.

This is not to suggest, as some have, that intensional discourse could one day be abandoned, replaced by a respectably scientific vocabulary to characterize our mental states: 'The stubborn idioms of propositional attitude are as deeply rooted as the overtly physical ones' (1985, p. 7). For example, language learning is only possible because our teachers empathize with us, estimating what we perceive and correcting our utterances accordingly. Rather propositional attitude talk is a practically indispensable habit (1960, pp. 216–221), irreducible to physical discourse, guided by empathy, wholly rational and answerable to evidence; but it is a way of talking about physical states and events, grouping them in ways that do not serve directly the needs of scientific explanation but which do serve other needs.

BIBLIOGRAPHY

Davidson, D. 1980. *Essays on Actions and Events*. Oxford University Press.

Quine, W.V. 1960. *Word and Object*. Cambridge, MA.: MIT Press.

—— 1969. *Ontological Relativity and Other Essays*. New York: Columbia University Press.

—— 1975. Mind and verbal dispositions. In *Mind and Language*, ed. S. Guttenplan. Oxford University Press.

—— 1976. *The Ways of Paradox*. Revised and Enlarged Edition, Cambridge, MA.: Harvard University Press. First published, 1966.

—— 1981. *Theories and Things*. Cambridge, MA.: Harvard University Press.

Quine, W.V. 1985. States of mind. *Journal of Philosophy*, LXXXII, 5–8.

Quine, W.V. 1990. *Pursuit of Truth*. Cambridge, MA.: Harvard University Press.

CHRISTOPHER HOOKWAY

R

radical interpretation   Though not meant as a practical procedure, it can help our thinking about language and the mind if we ask what would be involved in interpreting someone's words and actions. Moreover, if we imagine ourselves beginning this interpretative process without any prior knowledge of what the person means by her words or what PROPOSITIONAL ATTITUDES she has, then we are engaged in what is called 'radical interpretation'. QUINE originally discussed the idea of radical translation in respect of another's language and DAVIDSON, generalizing on this so that interpretation and not merely translation is at issue, has made this notion central to his account of the mind. (*See also* RATIONALITY.)

SAMUEL GUTTENPLAN

rationality   To be rational, a set of BELIEFS, DESIRES, and ACTIONS (also PERCEPTIONS, INTENTIONS, decisions) must fit together in various ways. If they do not, in the extreme case they fail to constitute a mind at all – no rationality, no agent. This core notion of rationality in philosophy of mind thus concerns a cluster of personal identity conditions, that is, holistic coherence requirements upon the system of elements comprising a person's mind (*see* HOLISM). A person's putative beliefs must mesh with the person's desires and decisions, or else they cannot qualify as the individual's beliefs; similarly, *mutatis mutandis*, for desires, decisions, etc. This is 'agent-constitutive rationality' – that agents possess it is more than an empirical hypothesis. A related conception is epistemic or 'normative rationality': To be rational (that is, reasonable, well-founded, not subject to

epistemic criticism), a belief or decision at least must cohere with the rest of a person's cognitive system – for instance, in terms of logical consistency and application of valid inference procedures. Rationality constraints therefore are key linkages among the cognitive, as distinct from qualitative, mental states. The main issue is characterizing these types of mental coherence. The discussion below concentrates on agent-constitutive rationality, proceeding through a spectrum of accounts, from most to least stringent.

STANDARD IDEALIZATIONS

Current philosophical conceptions of rationality inherit central features of models of the rational agent propounded in microeconomic, game, and decision theory of the last half-century (e.g. Von Neumann and Morgenstern, 1944; Hempel, 1965). These standard rationality models tie an agent's beliefs (or knowledge representation) and desires (or goal structure) to its actions (or decisions). The underlying idea is approximated by a necessary condition on the cognitive system of an agent A: 'If A has belief-set B and desire-set D, then A would decide upon all and only actions that are (the most) apparently appropriate.' Roughly, an action is apparently appropriate for A if, according to B, it would tend to satisfy D.

To guarantee unfailing choice of the best of all possible acts, such rationality conceptions require an ideal agent of great inferential insight. The agent must possess deductive, perhaps also inductive, competencies at least along the lines of: 'If A has belief-set B, then A would make all and only sound inferences from B that are apparently appropriate.' Otherwise, A might fail to identify some unobvious actions most desirable according to B. In addition, the belief-set must perfectly cohere not only over time, but also at any given time; such agents must always maintain belief consistency. That is, 'If A has belief-set B then if any inconsistency arose in B, A would eliminate it.'

Some familiar philosophical positions not explicitly under a rationality rubric are now discernible. In standard epistemic logic (Hintikka, 1962), the deductive closure requirement on the agent's belief-set is even stronger than the above ideal inference condition: A actually believes (or infers) all logical consequences of B. The principle of charity of translation of QUINE entails the above ideal consistency condition; in our making sense of another agent's utterances, the ruling maxim is, 'Fair translation preserves logical laws', that is, the attributor is obliged to construe the speaker's beliefs so that the latter does not 'accept contradiction', explicit or tacit. (1960, p. 59) However, one may then begin to worry whether, from our present viewpoint, we are implausibly supposed to 'translate' away, for example, Frege's apparent affirmations of his set theory axiomatization in *The Basic Laws of Arithmetic* – which is now conventionally construed to be subject to Russell's Paradox, i.e. inconsistent. Similarly, the principles of charity of interpretation of DAVIDSON, broadening the holistic Quinian paradigm to include, in making behaviour intelligible, consideration of the agent's desires as well as beliefs and meanings, sometimes amount to ideal rationality requirements. As an instance again of an ideal consistency condition, in keeping with the traditional decision-theoretic postulate that the agent always maintains perfect preference transitivity, Davidson states, 'I do not think we can clearly say what should convince us that a man at a given time . . . preferred a to b, b to c, and c to a.' (1980, p. 237) However, so perfectionistic an interpretation methodology seems *prima facie* at odds with a wide range of psychological studies (e.g. Kahneman, Slovic, and Tversky, 1982) of apparent preference transitivity failures in real-world human decision-making.

More generally, from the perspective of computational accounts of mind, ideal rationality requires vast capacities indeed (*see* COMPUTATIONAL MODELS). The idealization is committed to abstracting from a fundamental fact of the human condition, our finitude. If one assumes the ideal agent's deductive ability is represented as some finite algorithm for always deciding whether or not any given sentence is a first-order consequence of its belief-set, then the creature must violate Church's Undecidability Theorem for first-order predicate calculus. Otherwise, there will have to be some deductive questions that the creature's inference algorithm cannot settle in any finite runtime, yet that the creature could believe to be high-priority (say, life or death) matters; hence the creature would be paralysed on these and so not satisfy the earlier ideal inference condition. Similarly, it should be observed that for this ideal agent, a significant portion of the deductive sciences would be trivial. For instance, such an agent must have (e.g. for when it ranks the task as highly desirable) a capacity to determine whether Goldbach's Conjecture or its negation follows from the axioms of arithmetic, an important open question – for human beings – in number theory for over a century. In effect, the standard rationality models deny that our inquiries even have a history, where we prove a theorem, then in turn use it as a lemma in subsequent proofs of other theorems. Indeed, characterizations of the agent's deductive ability in standard epistemic logic axiomatizations recall depictions of some of the omniscience of God under conventional conceptions of His perfection.

Debate about the role of idealizations thus takes a central position in recent theorizing about rationality. Certainly idealizations have indispensable functions in mature scientific theory in general (cf. the familiar ideal gas law example, representation of the complex structure of molecules as perfectly elastic, dimensionless spheres). Witness also the success stories of the agent-idealizations in economic, game, and decision theory; such perfection may be profoundly impossible, but it is simple, that is, manageable for the purposes of useful formalization. Part of the key to effective use of an idealization consists in recognition – often only at the level of unarticulated lore or practice – of the degree of approximation and the limits of applicability of the idealization to reality. A sense that we tend uncritically to reify the rationality idealizations, combined with an awareness of how deeply they cannot in fact apply to human beings, may in turn motivate anti-realist or instrumentalist accounts of all cognitive theory. The cognitive system attributed to an individual then attenuates to little more than a convenient but impossible fiction to aid the attributor in predicting the agent's behaviour (such a tendency seems evident in some earlier accounts of DENNETT (1978)).

The above conception of rationality conditions that are *sine qua non* for agenthood in the first place ought to be distinguished from another type of even more stringent norm of rationality in terms of which an agent's reasoning is evaluated. A belief or inference of mine may be criticized as irrational while I still manage, by the rest of my epistemic track record, to continue to qualify as an agent or person. Failure to distinguish such normative rationality from the above weaker agent-constitutive rationality will tend to reinforce the high levels demanded for the latter. In general, a sense of the limited applicability of the ideal rationality models has tended to fuel doubts about the very possibility of a cognitive science.

PSYCHOLOGICALLY REALISTIC ACCOUNTS

After recognizing that nothing could count as an agent for which there are no rationality constraints, one can stop to wonder whether one has to jump to a conclusion that the agent must therefore be ideally rational. Is rationality all or nothing, or is there some cognitive *via media* between perfect, Cartesian unity of mind and utter, anarchic disintegration of personhood?

Such an approach attempts to deal with the *aperçu* that human beings – indeed, all physically realizable intelligences – must have limited cognitive resources. A cognitivist, post-behaviourist paradigm permits modellers to abandon empty-organism approaches and attempt to represent the agent's internal psychological reality.

This latter type of option traces back at least to the research programme of Simon (1982) on normative and empirically descriptive models of 'bounded rationality'. Simon's account begins as a critique of traditional idealizations. Actual human beings generally have neither perfect information about their world of alternative choices nor a capacity to use such knowledge. Therefore, in place of the conventional postulate, '*A* always acts so as to maximize its expected utility' (i.e. *A* does, or ought to, choose the apparently most appropriate actions), Simon proposed a principle to the effect that '*A* "satisfices" its expected utility'. Rational agents do, and ought only to, try to 'satisfice' rather than maximize, in that they should not be required to do the impossible, to identify decisions that perfectly optimize their expected utility; they need only choose options that in this respect are 'good enough'.

An approach for real-world agent-constitutive rationality similar to Simon's for normative and empirically hypothesized rationality can be found in Cherniak (1986). Weakening the ideal rationality requirement, while still recognizing that nothing could qualify as a person without 'some' internal coherence, yields psychologically more realistic rationality conditions of the type, 'If *A* has belief-desire set $B \cup D$, then *A* would decide upon some (but not necessarily all) of the apparently appropriate actions for that set.' In turn, such moderate rationality only requires the agent to be a fair logician in order to choose enough of the right actions: 'If *A* has belief set *B*, then *A* would make some (not necessarily all) sound inferences from *B* that are apparently appropriate.' – Namely, *A* must accomplish enough of the inferences that are useful in identifying apparently appropriate actions.

Unlike ideal inference capacity, such a moderate capacity itself requires a non-trivial ability to select apparently appropriate inferential tasks to undertake so that the limited cognitive resources are not wasted. For this type of minimal agent, computation no longer need be virtually costless. These 'some, but not all' conditions are conceived as embedded in ancillary cognitive theory that helps to fill in *which* inferences are most likely to be made, including modules concerning the reasoning psychology and the memory structure of the agent.

Such a resource-realistic rationality framework possesses systematicity in that it links together recent independent research programmes in COGNITIVE PSYCHOLOGY and in computer science. The psychological studies focused on the strikingly ubiquitous human use of reasoning procedures that are formally incorrect and/or incomplete 'heuristics'. An example studied by Kahneman and Tversky (Kahneman, Slovic, and Tversky, 1982) is the 'availability heuristic' – the strategy, widespread in intuitive assessment of probability of a type of event – of judging how easy to recall or imagine such an event is, instead of its actual objective frequency. (Hence, e.g. rare but vividly recollectable disaster scenarios are consistently overestimated as risks.) Another field that developed contemporaneously with, but separately from, non-ideal rationality accounts and experimental studies of reasoning heuristics is computational complexity theory in computer science (Cherniak, 1986, ch. 4); the basic insight is that formally correct and complete inference procedures (e.g. even for propositional calculus) appear to be intrinsically intractable, that is, with quite small problem instances requiring literally cosmic-scale resources of time and memory. From a minimal rationality perspective, use of the heuristics need not be viewed as mere uninteresting exceptions to a rule of perfect rationality, or even as irrationality. For, if formally adequate procedures mean practical paralysis, then the heuristics may represent a trade-off of perfection – formal correctness/completeness – for speed and usability.

This approach in turn suggests an optimistic reinterpretation of the semantic and set-theoretic paradoxes, the response to which has so shaped the rise of modern logic. Instead of, for instance, the Liar or Russell's Paradoxes being *par excellence* symptoms of disease at the core of our conceptual scheme, they may be manifestations of our use of inconsistent procedures as another type of 'quick but dirty heuristic' in a rational speed-reliability trade-off. These heuristics may work well in the ordinary contexts where they developed, and break down in the new situations into which recent metamathematical enquiries have led us.

ALTERNATIVE VIEWS

Ideal and more realistic rationality models may well be able to coexist peacefully, where simplicity of an approximation can be progressively exchanged for real-world applicability as necessary. Another ideal-agent type of response to account for the phenomenon of apparently widespread human use of incorrect reasoning procedures employs a 'competence/performance' distinction along lines promoted by CHOMSKY. In linguistic theory, a competence model of, say, a speaker's underlying knowledge of syntax is represented as a set of formally adequate rules the speaker accepts and uses; however, the speaker's performance – actual linguistic behaviour – often does not conform simply to the postulated syntactic competence. For example, limitations on the speaker's language processing memory, time pressures, other demands on attention, and even fatigue will disrupt the speaker's observed judgments of grammaticality. Cohen (1981) similarly proposed to explain away people's reasoning fallacies in terms of a perfect underlying inferential competence that is to be represented as a formally correct rule set they accept. When a person's ideal competence is manifested in actual inferential performance, it is degraded just like linguistic performance by the inevitable limitations of memory, time, and so on, yielding the observed errors.

529

The underlying inferential competence is thus still very like the inference capacity of the earlier standard ideally rational agent. One concern about this competence account focuses on how satisfying is an explanation of the widespread heuristics as so to speak mere 'noise' – is it too *ad hoc*, does it acquire too many epicycles? The concern can parallel questions about extremely 'abstract' competence accounts for syntax, as well as for semantics (e.g. as in FODOR). Formally adequate rules – for reasoning, syntax, or meaning-representation – are supposed to be possessed and used by agents to the degree that they approximate 'ideal speaker-hearers'. However, even for moderate nativists, as eliciting conditions for the tacit knowledge grow more elaborate, the genuineness of this acceptance seems to fade (a problem already evident for Plato's claims in the *Meno* that the unlettered slave really 'knew' the Pythagorean Theorem even before Socrates' brilliant coaching). The psychological reality of actual human beings' internal representations of the inference rules thereby seems to dissipate; what does it mean to say that a person really now is using so abstract a rule, as opposed to, for instance, one of the messy heuristics? Once again, it becomes hard to tell whether the subject's acceptance of the ideal rules is a convenient fiction of the theoretician or cognitive reality of the subject.

There is a connection here in turn to accounts of FOLK PSYCHOLOGY, the practical, pre-philosophical theory that human beings possess (perhaps in part innately) concerning their own and others' minds, and use in everyday dealings. In particular, a doctrinal symbiosis may operate between a sense of the unreality of ideal competence models of our psychology, and eliminativist impulses against folk psychology (*see* ELIMINATIVISM). That is, to the extent that the competence idealizations become of problematic psychological reality, so also can the entire nexus of intentional psychology become a candidate for future extirpation as unscientific lore. The concept of rationality will of course be embedded centrally within folk psychology, and so a prime eliminativist target.

Against this background appears the most minimalist type of rationality account, the pluralistic theory of Stich (1990). On the spectrum of rationality constraints ranging from maximal for the idealizations, through moderate for so-called 'minimal' theories, Stich's relativism most closely approaches the true minimalist pole. The relevant thesis here is that we can place no a priori conditions on rationality for all possible agents. For, along pragmatist lines, Stich views reasoning procedures as tools, the effectiveness of which varies for different purposes and circumstances, hence there is no single inferential canon all people ought to obey. Correspondingly, the rationality constitutive of agenthood becomes wide open; for example, possibilities for radical cognitive diversity extend without limit.

One 'No rationality, no agent' response begins by insisting that rationality is a metaphysical matter of part of the *essential* nature of a particular type of object – a mind, person, or agent. Hence, with the identity of rationality itself also fixed (e.g. including some logical consistency), some rationality constraints are just true of anything that can count as an agent. Latitude for diversity still remains; interpretation methodology can now be reconstructed in terms of a principle of 'moderate charity', where the agent's behaviour need only be so construed that the attributed cognitive system comes out moderately, instead of perfectly, rational. However, one must immediately, and uneasily, add a 'Neurath's Boat' qualification; our conceptual scheme, like a boat at sea which even as we reconstruct we must still keep afloat, cannot just be set aside wholesale. That is, the required moderate rationality has to be evaluated in terms of the only standards available to us, our own current ones. And so one may yet retain a feeling that any constitutive rationality constraints, however unavoidable, just amount to a Procrustean Bed into which genuine cognitive differences are unwarrantedly forced.

Perhaps such dialectical tug of war is a sign that the nature of rationality remains one of those pieces of unfinished business so distinctive of the philosophical enterprise.

See also CONCEPTUAL ROLE SEMANTICS; INNATENESS; INTENTIONALITY; LANGUAGE OF THOUGHT; MEMORY; REPRESENTATION.

BIBLIOGRAPHY

Cherniak, C. 1986. *Minimal Rationality.* Cambridge, MA.: MIT Press.
Cohen, L. 1981. Can human irrationality be experimentally demonstrated? *Behavioral and Brain Sciences,* 4, 317–31.
Davidson, D. 1980. *Essays on Action and Events.* Oxford University Press.
Dennett, D. 1978. *Brainstorms.* Cambridge, MA.: MIT Press.
Hempel, C. 1965. Aspects of scientific explanation. In *Aspects of Scientific Explanation,* §10. New York: Free Press.
Hintikka, J. 1962. *Knowledge and Belief.* Ithaca, N.Y.: Cornell University Press.
Kahneman, D., Slovic, P., and Tversky, A., eds. 1982. *Judgment Under Uncertainty: Heuristics and Biases.* Cambridge University Press.
Quine, W. 1960. *Word and Object.* Cambridge, MA.: MIT Press.
Simon, H. 1982. *Models of Bounded Rationality,* 2 vols, Vol. 2. Cambridge, MA.: MIT Press.
Stich, S. 1990. *The Fragmentation of Reason: Preface to a Pragmatic Theory of Cognitive Evaluation.* Cambridge, MA.: MIT Press.
Von Neumann, J., and Morgenstern, O. 1944. *Theory of Games and Economic Behavior.* New York: Wiley.

CHRISTOPHER CHERNIAK

reasons and causes The psychological level of description carries with it a mode of explanation which 'has no echo in physical theory' (Davidson, 1980, pp. 207–25); explanation in terms of reasons. We regard ourselves and each other as 'rational purposive creatures, fitting our BELIEFS to the world as we perceive it and seeking to obtain what we desire in the light of them'. (Hopkins, 1982, pp. vii–xix). Reason-giving

explanations can be offered not only for ACTIONS and beliefs, which will gain most attention in this entry; but also for DESIRES, INTENTIONS, hopes, fears, angers and affections, etc. Indeed, their positioning within a network of rationalizing links is part of the individuating characteristics of this range of psychological states and the intentional acts they explain (*see* INTENTIONALITY).

THE REASON-GIVING RELATION

At the heart of the reason-giving relation is a normative claim. An agent has a reason for believing, acting, etc., if, given her other psychological states, this belief/action is justified or appropriate. Displaying someone's reasons consists in making clear this justificatory link. Paradigmatically, the psychological states that provide an agent with reasons are intentional states individuated in terms of their propositional content (*see* CONTENT; PROPOSITIONAL ATTITUDES). There is a long tradition that emphasizes that the reason-giving relation is a logical or conceptual one. One way of bringing out the nature of this conceptual link is by the construction of reasoning, linking the agent's reason-providing states with the states for which they provide reasons. This reasoning is easiest to reconstruct in the case of reasons for belief where the contents of the reason-providing beliefs inductively or deductively support the content of the rationalized belief. For example, I believe my colleague is in her room now, and my reasons are (1) she usually has a meeting in her room at 9.30 on Mondays and (2) it is 9.30 on Monday. To believe a proposition is to accept it as true: and it is relative to the objective of reaching truth that the rationalizing relations between contents are set for belief. They must be such that the truth of the premises makes likely the truth of the conclusion.

In the case of reasons for actions the premises of any reasoning are provided by intentional states other than beliefs. Classically, an agent has a reason to perform a certain kind of action when she has (a) a pro-attitude towards some end or objective, and (b) a belief that an action of that kind will promote this end. The term pro-attitude derives from Donald DAVIDSON. It includes 'desires, wantings, urges, promptings and a great variety of moral views, aesthetic principles . . .' (Davidson, 1980, pp. 3–19). It is common to use 'desire' as a generic term for such pro-attitudes. It is relative to the constitutive objectives of desire that the rationalizing links are established in the practical case. We might say that the objective of desires is their own satisfaction. In the case of reasons for acting therefore we are looking for a relationship between the contents of the agent's intentional states and the description of the action which show that performing an action of that kind has some chance of promoting the desired goals. I find it desirable to own a Burmese kitten. I believe that putting an advertisement in the paper will help bring it about that I own a Burmese kitten; so putting an advertisement in the paper is a thing to be done. (There are a number of suggestions for formalizing practical reasoning; *see* Von Wright, 1971; Davidson, 1980; Kim, 1984; Lennon, 1990.)

The presence of a reason for believing or acting doesn't necessarily make it rational for an agent to believe or act in that way. From the agent's point of view overall she may have other beliefs which provide conflicting evidence, or conflicting desires. To establish what is rational to believe or do overall we would need to take into account principles for weighing competing beliefs and desires. Of course, we do not always believe what is rational, or act in the light of what we judge best (cases of SELF-DECEPTION and WEAKNESS OF WILL show this). However, a minimum of RATIONALITY must be present in the pattern of a person's beliefs, desires, intentions and actions before they can be regarded as an agent with intentional states at all. (Davidson, 1980, pp. 207–25)

When the reason-giving relation is articulated as a piece of reasoning, or calculation, it is not being suggested that whenever we have a reason we go through a process of conscious or unconscious deliberation. Rather the reasoning is a device to spell out the kind of conceptual links between intentional contents which frequently constitute the reason-giving relation. One of the things such a mode of articulation serves to make clear is the dependency of the reason-giving links on the intentional descriptions of our psychological states and our actions. This makes any project of reducing such states to extensionally characterizable phenomena highly problematic. Such a reduction, it is argued, cannot capture the rationalizing relations constitutive of the intentional realm (Davidson, 1980, pp. 207–25; Lennon, 1990, pp. 85–104).

Calculative presentation, however, does not seem essential to all reason-giving links. If providing reasons consists in displaying the appropriateness of an agent's response, given her other perceptions and attitudes, then this may not always be capturable in propositional form (e.g. what reasons do you have for believing she took the money? I saw her). This may be particularly the case when we are considering reasons for emotions (for an illuminating discussion of this point, *see* Taylor, 1985, pp. 1–16). If we accept that reasons are not always presentable in the form of calculations, this also opens the door for psychological states with phenomenal or qualitative content to play a rationalizing role (Gilbert, 1992).

For some writers the justificatory and normative character of reason-giving relations renders such relations perspectival or subjective in character (*see* SUBJECTIVITY). Appreciating the rationality of a belief or an action requires appreciating it *from the perspective* of an agent evaluating beliefs and deciding how to act (McDowell, 1985). The subjective or perspectival quality which is here being claimed of reason-giving links and consequently for the intentional kinds which find their anchorage within them, parallels that are commonly claimed to attach to psychological states with phenomenal content (*see* PERCEPTUAL CONTENT; QUALIA).

EXPLAINING WITH REASONS

What is the explanatory role of providing reasons for our psychological states and intentional acts? Clearly part of this role comes from the justificatory nature of the reason-giving relation: 'things are made intelligible by being revealed to be, or to approximate to being, as they rationally ought to be' (McDowell, 1985). For some writers the justificatory and explanatory tasks of reason-giving simply coincide. The manifestation of rationality is seen as sufficient to explain states or acts quite independently of questions regarding causal origin. Within this model the greater the degree of rationality we can detect, the more intelligible the sequence will be. Where there is a breakdown in rationality, as in cases of weakness of will or self-deception, there is a corresponding breakdown in our ability to make the action/belief intelligible.

The equation of the justificatory and explanatory role of rationalizing links can be found within two quite distinct pictures. One account views the attribute of rationality from a third-person perspective. Attributing intentional states to others, and by analogy to ourselves, is a matter of applying to them a certain pattern of interpretation. We ascribe whatever states enable us to make sense of their behaviour as conforming to a rational pattern. Such a mode of interpretation is commonly an *ex post facto* affair, although such a mode of interpretation can also aid prediction. Our interpretations are never definitive or closed. They are always open to revision and modification in the light of future behaviour, if such revisions enable the person as a whole to appear more rational. Where we fail to detect a rational pattern then we give up the project of seeing a system as rational and instead seek explanations of a mechanistic kind (DENNETT, 1979).

The other picture is resolutely first-personal, linked to the claimed perspectivity of rationalizing claims. When we provide rationalizing explanations we make an action, for example, intelligible by adopting the agent's perspective on it. Understanding is a reconstruction of actual or possible decision making. It is from such a first-person perspective that goals are detected as desirable and the courses of action appropriate to the situation. The standpoint of an agent deciding how to act is not that of an observer predicting the next move. When I find something desirable and judge an act an appropriate route for achieving it, I conclude that a certain course of action should be taken. This is different from my reflecting on my past behaviour and concluding that I will do X in the future (*see* Kim, 1984; McDowell, 1985).

For many writers, however, the justificatory and explanatory role of reasons cannot simply be equated. To do so fails to distinguish cases where I have reasons from cases where I believe or act *because* of these reasons. I may have beliefs from which your innocence would be deduced but nonetheless come to believe you are innocent because you have blue eyes. I may have intentional states that give me altruistic reasons for giving to charity but nonetheless contribute out of a desire to earn someone's good opinion. In both these cases, although my belief could be shown to be rational in the light of other beliefs, and my actions in the light of my altruistic states, neither of these rationalizing links would form part of a valid explanation of the phenomena concerned. Moreover, cases of weakness of will show that I can have sufficient reason for acting and yet fail to act, e.g. I continue to smoke although I judge it would be better to abstain. This suggests that the mere availability of reasoning, however good, in favour of an action cannot, in itself, be sufficient to explain why it occurred.

If we resist the equation of the justificatory and explanatory work of reason-giving, we must look for a connection between reasons and action/belief in cases where these reasons genuinely explain, which is absent in cases of mere rationalizations (a connection that is present when I act on my best judgment and not when I fail). Classically, of course, the connection that has been suggested here is that of causality. In cases of genuine explanation, the reason-providing intentional states cause the belief/actions for which they also provide reasons. This position also seems to find support from considering the conditionals and counterfactuals that our reason-providing explanations sustain, which parallel those in cases of other causal explanations. Imagine I am approaching the Arts Building looking for the caféteria. If I believe the café is to the left, I turn to the left; if I believe it is to the right, I will turn to the right. If my approach to the building is explained simply by my desire to find the café, then in the absence of such a desire I would not have walked in that direction. In general terms, where my reasons explain my action, then the presence of such reasons was, in those circumstances, necessary for the action and at least made probable its occurrence. These conditional links can be explained if we accept that the reason-giving link is also a causal one. Any alternative account would therefore also need to accommodate them (Lennon, 1990, pp. 42–55).

The most famous defence of the view that reasons are causes is found in Davidson's article 'Actions, Reasons and Causes' (Davidson, 1980, pp. 3–20). However, within the Davidsonian picture reason-giving explanations perform two quite *disconnected* tasks; namely showing an action/belief to be rational and pointing to its cause. For Davidson the fact that events are of a kind to make an action rational is irrelevant to their causal role in the production of that action. This position is a result of his claim that there can be no empirical causal laws employing intentional vocabulary (Davidson, 1980, pp. 207–24). The causal generalizations required to support the singular causal links between reasons and actions must therefore rest on the nonintentional characteristics of these events. Intentional states therefore cause actions in virtue of their neurophysiological characteristics.

For most causal theorists, however, the radical separation of the causal and rationalizing role of reason-giving explanations is unsatisfactory. For such theorists, where we can legitimately point to an agent's reasons to explain a certain belief or action, then those features of the agent's intentional states that render the belief or action reasonable must be causally relevant in explaining how the agent came to believe or act in a way which they rationalize. One way of putting this requirement is that reason-giving states not only cause but also causally explain their explananda.

On most accounts of causation an acceptance of the causal explanatory role of reason-giving connections requires empirical causal laws employing intentional vocabulary. It is arguments against the possibility of such laws that have, however, been fundamental for those opposing a causal explanatory view of reasons. What is centrally at issue in these debates is the status of the generalizations linking intentional states to each other, and to ensuing intentional acts. An example of such a generalization would be 'If a person desires X, believes A would be a way of promoting X, is able to A and has no conflicting desires then (*ceteris paribus*) she will do A'. For many theorists such generalizations are grounded in the constitutive relationships between desire, belief and action. Grasping the truth of such a generalization is required to grasp the nature of the intentional states concerned. For some theorists the a priori elements within such generalizations are sufficient to exclude them from consideration as empirical laws. That, however, seems too quick, for it would similarly rule out any generalizations in the physical sciences that contain a priori elements, as a consequence of the implicit definition of their theoretical kinds in a causal explanatory theory. Causal theorists, including functionalists in philosophy of mind (*see* FUNCTIONALISM), can claim that it is just such implicit definition that accounts for the a priori status of our intentional generalizations.

In the hands of Davidson, the a priori status of intentional generalizations is used to a somewhat different end. Such generalizations provide the constitutive principles of rationality which govern our attribution of intentional states to ourselves and others. He argues that such attributions are open to constant revision and retain a residual indeterminacy which render our intentional notions quite unsuitable for inclusion in strict causal laws (Davidson, 1980, pp. 207–225). The Davidsonian argument, however, requires us to anchor our intentional classifications in a necessarily indeterminate process of interpretation. For the causal theorist, in contrast, they are akin to natural kind terms, generating causal explanatory generalizations, and subject to no more than the epistemic indeterminancy of other such terms (Lennon, 1990, pp. 99–104).

The causal explanatory approach to reason-giving explanations also requires an account of the intentional content of our psychological states, which makes it possible for such content to be doing such work (Dretske 1989). It also provides a motivation for the reduction of intentional characteristics to extensional ones, in an attempt to fit such intentional causality into a fundamentally materialist world picture. The very nature of the reason-giving relation, however, can be seen to render such reductive projects unrealizable (Davidson, 1980; Lennon, 1990). This, therefore, leaves causal theorists with the task of linking intentional and non-intentional levels of description in such a way as to accommodate intentional causality, without either overdetermination or a miraculous coincidence of prediction from within distinct causally explanatory frameworks.

See also An Essay on Mind section 3.2; CONTENT; DRETSKE; EPIPHENOMENALISM; FODOR; IDENTITY THEORIES; PHYSICALISM.

BIBLIOGRAPHY

Davidson, D. 1980. *Essays on Actions and Events*, Oxford University Press.
Dennett, D. 1979. Intentional systems. In *Brainstorms*, Brighton; Harvester.
Dretske, F. 1991. Reasons and causes. In *Philosophical Perspectives, 3: Philosophy of Mind and Action Theory*, ed. J. Tomberlin. California, Ridgeview.
Gilbert, P. 1992. Immediate experience, *Proceedings of the Aristotelian Society*, XCII, 233–250.
Hopkins, J. 1982. Introduction. In *Philosophical Essays on Freud*, ed. J. Hopkins and R. Wollheim. Cambridge University Press.
Kim, J. 1984. Self understanding and rationalising explanations. *Philosophia Naturalis*, 21.
Lennon, K. 1990. *Explaining Human Action*. London: Duckworth.
McDowell, J. 1985. Functionalism and anomalous monism. In *Action and Events: Perspectives on the Philosophy of Donald Davidson*, ed. E. Lepore and B. McLaughlin. Oxford: Basil Blackwell.
Taylor, G. 1985. Emotions and beliefs. In *Pride, Shame and Guilt*. Oxford: Clarendon Press.
Von Wright, G. 1971. *Explanation and Understanding*. Ithaca: Cornell University Press.

KATHLEEN LENNON

reduction This notion is best approached in its most natural setting: the philosophical understanding of science. The standard, text-book example here is that of the relation between thermodynamics and mechanics. Up until the nineteenth century, these two theories played an important part in our understanding of the physical world. On the one hand, thermodynamics described the behaviour of what was thought of as a substance, heat; its principles accounted for such facts as that heat moved from hotter to colder bodies, and that the amount of heat so transferred depended on the material constitution of the relevant bodies. On the other hand, the principles of mechanics – largely due to the work of Newton – accounted for the ways in which bodies, either in motion or at rest, affected one another.

Due to theoretical and experimental work in the nineteenth century, it became possible to unify these two theories, and it is in this unification that the notion of reduction comes into play. Once we recognize that all matter is made up of smaller 'particles' (atoms or molecules) and that the motion of these particles is governed by the principles of mechanics, it becomes possible to identify heat as the degree to which these particles move or vibrate. But once this is done, then the explanations offered in thermodynamics can be subsumed under the broader explanations of mechanics. For example, transfer of heat is explained by the laws governing the transmission of motion among atoms and molecules. In this case, one can say that thermodynamics has been reduced to mechanics. However, in contrast to thermodynamics, the account of combustion which made central use of the notion of phlogiston has proven to be irreducible to the laws of chemistry and physics, and, being thus irreducible, phlogiston is now treated as chimerical – as not being the name of any genuine existent. So, reduction is often a way of preserving the ontological security of some item.

Outside of the scientific context, the notion of reduction is used, but it is not always obvious that the conditions for its proper application are fulfilled. In philosophy of mind, the type IDENTITY THEORY is often thought of as reductionist. The identification of various mental items with types of physical phenomena seems to be analogous to the above-mentioned identification of heat with molecular motion, and this then promises the reduction of our understanding of the mind to our understanding of the brain and related physical systems. Moreover, such reduction promises to secure the ontological *bona fides* of the mental, since, as was seen above, a reduced realm is guaranteed a certain reality. However, it is not clear that one can think of our understanding of the mind as theoretical, as genuinely analogous to something like thermodynamics. And if our everyday, 'folk psychological' conception of the mind is not like an explanatory theory, then the idea of reduction might well just be inappropriate. Indeed, there are a number of writers who insist, for various reasons, that the mind is not reducible to anything physical, even though mental phenomena have a material substrate. The notion that they appeal to here is supervenience: the mental is said to supervene on the physical without

being reducible to it. However, the relations between supervenience and reduction are controversial. (*See* BELIEF; DAVIDSON; FODOR; FOLK PSYCHOLOGY; LEWIS; SUPERVENIENCE.)

SAMUEL GUTTENPLAN

representation Although linguistic and pictorial representations are undoubtedly the most prominent symbolic forms we employ, the range of representational systems humans understand and regularly use is surprisingly large. Sculpture, maps, diagrams, graphs, gestures, music notation, traffic signs, gauges, scale models, and tailors' swatches are but a few of the representational systems that play a role in communication, thought, and the guidance of behaviour. Indeed, the importance and prevalence of our symbolic activities has been taken as a hallmark of being human.

What is it that distinguishes items that serve as representations from other objects or events? And what distinguishes the various kinds of symbols from each other? As for the first question, there has been general agreement that the basic notion of a *representation* involves one thing's 'standing for', 'being about', 'referring to or denoting' something else. The major debates here have been over the nature of this connection between a representation and that which it represents. (See below.) As for the second question, perhaps the most famous and extensive attempt to organize and differentiate among alternative forms of representation is found in the works of C. S. Peirce (1931–1935). Peirce's theory of signs is complex, involving a number of concepts and distinctions that are no longer paid much heed. The aspect of his theory that remains influential and is widely cited is his division of signs into Icons, Indices and Symbols. Icons are signs that are said to be like or resemble the things they represent (e.g. portrait paintings). Indices are signs that are connected to their objects by some causal dependency (e.g. smoke as a sign of fire). Symbols are those signs that are related to their object by virtue of use or association; they are arbitrary labels (e.g. the word 'table'). This tripartite division among signs, or variants of this division, is routinely put forth to explain differences in the way representational systems are thought to establish their links to the world. Further, placing a representation in one of the three divisions has been used to account for the supposed differences between conventional and non-conventional representations, between representations that do and do not require learning to understand, and between representations, like language, that need to be read, and those which do not require interpretation. Some theorists, moreover, have maintained that it is only the use of Symbols that exhibits or indicates the presence of mind and mental states.

Over the years this tripartite division of signs, although often challenged, has retained its influence. More recently, an alternative approach to representational systems (or as he calls them 'symbolic systems') has been put forth by N. Goodman (1976). Goodman has proposed a set of syntactic and semantic features for categorizing representational systems. His theory provides for a finer discrimination among types of systems than Peirce's, and the categorizations he elaborates cut across many of the boundaries of the Peircian format. What also emerges clearly is that many rich and useful systems of representation lack a number of features taken to be essential to linguistic or sentential forms of representation (e.g. discrete alphabets and vocabularies, syntax, logical structure, inference rules, compositional semantics, and recursive compounding devices). As a consequence, although these representations can be appraised for accuracy or correctness, it does not seem possible to analyse such evaluative notions along the lines of standard truth theories, geared as they are to the structures found in sentential systems.

In light of this newer work, serious questions have been raised about the soundness of the tripartite division and about whether various of the psychological and philosophical claims concerning conventionality,

learning, interpretation, etc., that have been based on this traditional analysis, can be sustained. It is of special significance that Goodman has joined a number of theorists in rejecting accounts of Iconic representation in terms of resemblance (similarity or 1–1 correspondence). (*See* Gombrich, 1960.) The rejection has been twofold. First, as Peirce himself recognized, resemblance is not sufficient to establish the appropriate referential relations. The numerous prints of a lithograph do not represent one another, any more than an identical twin represents his or her sibling. Something more than resemblance is needed to establish the connection between an Icon or picture and what it represents. Second, since Iconic representations lack as many properties as they share with their referents, and certain non-Iconic symbols can be put in 1–1 correspondence with their referents, it is difficult to provide a non-circular account of what the similarity is that distinguishes Icons from other forms of representation. What's more, even if these two difficulties could be resolved, it would not show that the representational function of pictures can be understood independently of an associated system of interpretation. The design, $\boxed{\diagdown}$, may be a picture of a mountain. Alternatively, it could be a graph of the economy, a circuit diagram, or a letter or word in a foreign language. Or it may have no representational significance at all. Whether it is a representation and what kind of representation it is, is relative to a system of interpretation.

REPRESENTATION AND INTENTIONALITY

Representations, along with mental states, especially beliefs and thoughts, are said to exhibit INTENTIONALITY in that they refer to or stand for something else. The nature of this special property, however, has seemed puzzling. Not only is intentionality often assumed to be limited to humans, and possibly a few other species, but the property itself appears to resist characterization in physicalist terms. The problem is most obvious in the case of 'arbitrary' signs, like words, where it is clear that there is no connection between the physical properties of a word and what it denotes. (As noted above, the problem also remains for Iconic representations.)

Early attempts tried to establish the link between sign and object via the mental states of the sign user. A symbol # stands for * for S, if it triggers a *-idea in S. On one account, the reference of # is the *-idea itself. On the other major account, the denotation of # is whatever the *-idea denotes. The first account is problematic in that it fails to explain the link between symbols and the world. The second is problematic in that it just shifts the puzzle inward. For example, if the word 'table' triggers the image '☐' or 'TABLE' what gives this mental picture or word any reference at all, let alone the denotation normally associated with the word 'table'?

An alternative to these mentalistic theories has been to adopt a behaviouristic analysis (see BEHAVIOURISM). On this account, # denotes * for S is explained along the lines of either: (i) S is disposed to behave to # as to *; or (ii) S is disposed to behave in ways appropriate to * when presented #. Both versions prove faulty in that the very notions of the behaviour associated with or appropriate to * are obscure. In addition, once one gets beyond a few trivial cases there seems to be no reasonable correlations between behaviour towards signs and behavior towards their objects that is capable of accounting for the referential relations.

A currently influential attempt to 'naturalize' the representation relation takes its cue from Indices. The crucial link between sign and object is established by some causal connection between * and #. (See Dretske, 1986.) It is allowed, however, that such a causal relation is not sufficient for full-blown intentional representation. An increase in temperature causes the mercury to rise in the thermometer, but the mercury level is not a representation for the thermometer. In order for # to represent * to S, #, it is said, must play an appropriate role in the functional economy of S's activities. The notion of 'function', in turn, is to be spelled

out along biological or other lines so as to remain within 'naturalistic' constraints (see NATURALISM). This approach runs into problems in specifying a suitable notion of 'function' and in accounting for the possibility of misrepresentation. Also, it is not obvious how to extend the analysis to encompass the semantical force of more abstract or theoretical symbols. These difficulties are further compounded when one takes into account the social factors that seem to play a role in determining the denotative properties of our symbols.

The problems faced in providing a reductive naturalistic analysis of representation has led many to doubt that this task is achievable or necessary. Although a story can be told about how some words or signs are learned via association or other causal connections with their referents, there is no reason to believe that the 'stand-for' relation, or semantic notions in general, can be reduced to or eliminated in favour of nonsemantic terms.

DIGITAL AND ANALOGUE

Spurred by the work of CHOMSKY and advances in computer science, the 1960s saw a rebirth of 'mentalistic' or cognitivist approachs to psychology and the study of mind (see COGNITIVE PSYCHOLOGY). Two features have loomed large in these developments. One is the extensive use of the notion of a representation in characterizing mental states and activities. (See Fodor, 1975; Mandler, 1983. See also CONNECTIONISM for an alternative approach.) The other is the adoption of computer models of mind and cognitive processing (see COMPUTATIONAL MODELS). In turn, two questions have become the centre of much debate and discussion: (i) What kinds of representational systems are employed in cognition? (ii) What type of computer, if any, is a cognitive being? Not surprisingly, in philosophy, with its 20th-century focus on language, logic and formal systems, the answers to these two questions tended to be respectively (i) language-like systems of representation and (ii) a digital computer.

The two answers fit together nicely in that language is assumed to be a digital form of representation and, therefore, readily suited for use by a digital computer. To give these assumptions some bite and generality, though, it is important to provide a clear specification of the difference between digital and non-digital (analogue) representations and processing.

There appears to be wide agreement that digitalness has to do with things that are discrete and analogue involves the continuous. Beyond this the issues get fuzzy. Not only is there no consensus about the correct definitions of 'digital' and 'analogue', but there is much confusion over whether the distinction applies to representational systems, to the person or machine using the system, to a combination of system and user, or to the nature of the physical laws and physical stuff the symbols or the symbol user are made of. Those following Goodman propose that a distinction be drawn between digital and analogue symbol systems based on the syntactic and semantic density of the elements of the system. Others have taken the crucial distinction between digital and analogue symbols to depend on whether the representation is an *analogue* of that which it represents. (*See* Pylyshyn, 1986.) The notion of an 'analogue' being appealed to here varies. Some stress a 1–1 correspondence between sign and object, assuming pictures and maps (i.e. Icons) to be paradigm cases of analogue representation. Others think that representation is analogical if there is some law-like connection between the referents and signs. For them, an example of an analogue system would be the representation of temperature by the level of mercury in a thermometer. This last analysis allies analogue representation with Indices that reflect (continuously valued) law-like relations between sign and object.

The digital/analogue distinction has taken on metaphysical importance in that many theorists assume that analogue signs are not 'real' representations. They are not the sorts of representations that exhibit intentionality or implicate mind. Only Symbols, free as they are from physical constraints, do this. If the digital/analogue distinction is treated in terms of the syntactic and semantic features of the system, however, metaphysical claims of this sort would seem to be unfounded. They result from running together claims about the structural properties of the representational system with claims about how the system is used. We tend to reject attributions of intentionality when production and/or response to a sign is 'triggered' by present stimuli, hence our reluctance to consider the doings of the thermometer or the bee dances as 'truly' symbolic activities, indicating the presence of mind. (*See* Bennett, 1964.) But the question whether *use* of a representational system is, in Chomsky's (1968) terms, creative and free from the control of stimuli is separate from whether the system is syntactically or semantically dense. We can program a bank-teller machine to communicate and respond in a totally fixed or unfree manner, while using a digital symbol system, like English. Alternatively, we humans could come to understand the symbolically dense bee language without the sight of a dance or the sighting of nectar triggering any behaviour on our part. We could, that is, employ the bee language in the same stimulus-free ways we use English.

The idea that analogue *processing* is somehow non-mental or non-cognitive also seems peculiar from the syntactic/semantic density perspective taken above. The pocket calulator that computes on discrete representations for each number is usually considered to operate digitally, while computation by slide-rule seems to involve continuous or analogue processing. Human mathematical competence would appear to be a paradigm case of cognitive activity. It is hard to see, however, why it should lose this status if it turned out that our computations are carried out by a neuronal device that operates like a slide-rule rather than like a calculator.

IMAGERY

The ascendancy of cognitive approaches to mind has brought with it a renewed interest in imagery. (*See* IMAGERY. *See also* Block, 1981.) Two problems concerning representation have held centre stage in these discussions. The first problem is of a piece with older ontological worries over the status of so-called 'pictures in the mind'. Proponents of imagistic theories often talk in ways that seem to presuppose that images are objects, like physical objects, that can be rotated, scanned, approached, enlarged, etc. Yet it is hard to make sense of such reification, given that mental images have no mass, physical size, shape, or location. The second problem concerning imagery has close ties to debates over the adequacy of the (digital) computer model of mind. The reason for this is that images are typically identified with pictures and thus allied with analogue representation. So it is held that if we employ images in cognition, it shows that claims that all mental representation is propositional or sentential (i.e. digital) is false. In turn, if mental processing involves the use of non-digital, pictorial representations, our minds and cognitive activities cannot be understood within the constraints of the standard computer model. Although seemingly separate matters, the issue of ontological reification and the issue of analogue representation come together for those who assume that analogue representations function via their sharing or having features *analogous* to those they represent. Most proponents of imagistic explanations allow that their theories would be unsustainable if they did require that there literally be items in the mind that possessed spatial dimensions and other physical properties. They have offered various proposals attempting to show how it is possible to cash in on talk of using or manipulating images without falling into the trap of reification. In any case, it should be clear that questions of reification also pose a problem for proponents of sentential models of mind, who claim that we think in words. For the ontological quandary of giving a satisfactory account of how there can be pictures or maps in the head is at root no different than the problem of how there can be words and sentences in the head. And if a satisfactory answer is available to the latter, it should be adaptable to the former.

A good deal of the debate over imagery has been obscured by problematic accounts of the basis of the 'stand for' relation and by unsupported assumptions about the nature, function and distinction between and among linguistic and non-linguistic forms of representation. For example, it is common for both proponents and critics of imagery to identify images with pictures or picture-like items, and then take it for granted that pictorial representation can be explained in terms of resemblance or some other notion of 1–1 correspondence, or assume that since pictures are like their referents they require no interpretation. But it is highly questionable whether such accounts are adequate for dealing with our everyday use of pictures (maps, diagrams, etc.) in cognition. The difficulties involved with this older understanding of Iconic representation become more acute when applied to imagistic or mental pictures.

EXPANDING THE REPRESENTATIONAL DOMAIN

There is something problematic in the very way the imagery controversy, along with other debates over mind and cognition, have been set up as a choice between whether humans employ one or two kinds of representational systems. As mentioned at the start, we know that humans make use of an enormous number of different types of (external) representational systems. These systems differ in form and structure along a variety of syntactic, semantic and other dimensions. It would appear there is no useful sense in which these various and diverse systems can be divided into two well-specified kinds. Nor does it seem possible to reduce, decode, or capture the cognitive content of all of these forms of representation into sentential symbols. Any adequate theory of mind is going to have to deal with the fact that many more than two types of representation are employed in our cognitive activities. It would seem all the more premature, then, to assume that yet-to-be discovered modes of internal representation must fit neatly into one or two pre-ordained categories.

Appeals to representations play a prominent role in contemporary work in the study of mind. With some justification, most attention has been focused on language or language-like symbol systems. Even when some non-linguistic systems are countenanced, they tend to be given second-class status. This practice, however, has had a rather constricting affect on our understanding of human cognitive activities. It has, for example, resulted in a lack of serious examination of the function of the arts in organizing and reorganizing our world. And the cognitive uses of metaphor, expression, exemplification, and the like are typically ignored. Moreover, recognizing that a much broader range of representational systems plays a role in our cognitive activities should throw a number of philosophical presuppositions and doctrines in the study of mind into question. Among these are: (1) claims about the unique significance of language or syntactic systems of representation as the mark of the mental; (2) the identification of contentful or informational states with the sentential or PROPOSITIONAL ATTITUDES; (3) the idea that all thought can be expressed in language; (4) the assumption that compositional accounts of the structure of language provide the only model we have for the creative or productive nature of representational systems in general; and (5) the tendency to construe all cognitive transitions among representations as cases of INFERENCE (based on syntactic or logical form.)

See also CONTENT; DEVELOPMENTAL PSYCHOLOGY; DRETSKE; FODOR; LANGUAGE OF THOUGHT; PERCEPTION; RATIONALITY.

BIBLIOGRAPHY

Bennett, J. 1964. *Rationality*. London: Routledge & Kegan Paul.
Block, N., ed. 1981. *Imagery*. Cambridge, MA.: MIT Press.
Chomsky, N. 1968. *Language and Mind*. New York: Harcourt Brace Jovanovich.
Dretske, F. 1986. Misrepresentation. In *Belief*, ed. R. Bogdan. Oxford University Press.
Fodor, J. 1975. *Language of Thought*. New York: T. Crowell.
Gombrich, E. 1960. *Art and Illusion*. New York: Pantheon Books.
Goodman, N. 1976. *Languages of Art*, 2nd edn. Indianapolis: Hackett Publishing.
Mandler, J.M. 1983. Representation. In *Handbook of Child Psychology, Vol. III: Cognitive Development*, ed. J. Flavell and E. Markman. New York: John Wiley and Sons.
Peirce, C.S. 1931–5. *Collected Papers*, vol. II. Cambridge, MA.: Harvard University Press.
Pylyshyn, Z. 1986. *Computation and Cognition*. Cambridge, MA.: MIT Press.

ROBERT SCHWARTZ

Ryle, Gilbert (1900–1982) Gilbert Ryle's *The Concept of Mind* (1949) had for a considerable time an enormous influence, but, despite its open and direct style, it was never easy to characterize. One reason for this can be found in its origins. Ryle tells us in his Autobiographical Sketch (1970) that his main interest was in the metaphilosophical question: 'what constitutes a philosophical problem and what is the way to solve it?' Questions specifically to do with the mind were not in the forefront of his thinking when he embarked on *The Concept of Mind*. Instead, he was looking around for, as he wrote, 'some notorious and large-size Gordian Knot' upon which to 'exhibit a sustained piece of analytical hatchet-work'.

Leaving aside the fact that Ryle was more interested in philosophical method than in the philosophy of mind itself, there is a second reason for the difficulty one has in interpreting the book. The Gordian knot Ryle chose was the product of a conception of mind that is generally attributed to Descartes. On that conception, there is, in addition to material substance, a kind of mind substance, and we have a more direct – indeed privileged – access to what passes in the mind than to what takes place in the material world. Thus, for example, I can know for certain and immediately that I have a pain, though I could doubt that

I have a damaged hand which I take to be the cause of my pain. The notorious Cartesian possibility of there being an evil demon who could deceive me about my body and about the external world does not extend to what I am currently thinking or experiencing, and this makes the mental substance knowable in a way nothing else can be. Now one may feel that there is a kind of authority we each have about the contents of our minds – that we know these contents in a way unavailable to anyone else – but it is possible to say things about this kind of authority which do not go so far as to commit one to the Cartesian conception (*see* CONSCIOUSNESS; FIRST-PERSON AUTHORITY; INTROSPECTION). One can separate certain problematic features of the mind from the particular dualistic Cartesian account of those features. However, in Ryle, it is not easy to tell whether the target is the Cartesian conception or, more radically, the intuitions it seeks to explain. Officially, it is the 'Ghost in the Machine' – a Cartesian ghost if ever there was one – which is to be exorcized. Yet, when it comes to giving detailed arguments, Ryle can sound as if he is denying that we have any kind of introspective knowledge of our own mental states. And this leads to the third elusive aspect of the *Concept of Mind* – its degree of commitment to BEHAVIOURISM.

Some behaviourists, most notably psychologists such as Skinner and Watson, seem to have flirted with the idea that there simply are no phenomena of mind, that the mind is a kind of fiction superimposed on the complex movements of human bodies. Such an extreme eliminativist behaviourism was certainly never part of Ryle's project. However, less radically, there is a kind of behaviourism which treats the mind, not as a fiction, but as itself consisting in, or definable in terms of, behaviour. And there is a real question just how far Ryle can be understood as advocating this sort of view.

On the one hand, it is not easy to see what Ryle is getting at when he speaks of the 'category mistakes' we make in speaking about mental phenomena unless there is some kind of behaviourism lurking in the background. According to Ryle, a category mistake consists in taking one kind of thing for another as when, to use his example, the confused tourist says that he has seen all the college buildings in Oxford, but has yet to find the University. What the tourist has failed to appreciate is that the University is a different kind of thing from an assortment of colleges and buildings. Applied to the mind, the idea seems to be this: it is easy to be misled into thinking it is a special kind of thing, different from, but belonging to, the same general category as the matter that makes up the physical world. (This would be like thinking that the University, being different from, but in the same category as, the colleges and buildings, was itself something one could see by being in the right place in Oxford.) But Ryle insists: 'the hallowed contrast between Mind and Matter will be dissipated, but dissipated not by either of the equally hallowed absorptions of Mind by Matter or of Matter by Mind (p. 23).' So, for example, he suggests that when one tries to find the difference between intelligence and lack of it, one should not look for some special mind-stuff, the operation of which makes someone intelligent. Instead, one should be 'asking by what criteria intelligent behaviour is actually distinguished from non-intelligent behaviour.' In this and in numerous other examples Ryle suggests that the mind consists in patterns of behaviour – that it can be reductively identified with behaviour – and that to think otherwise about it is precisely to categorize it wrongly.

Yet, on the other hand, Ryle never gave the kind of analysis of behaviour that would be necessary to support a fully reductive account. In his examples, behaviour is always treated as fully intentional; there is no attempt to characterize it in non-mental, physicalistic terms. So, it remains simply unclear how thoroughgoing a behaviourism one ought to find in *The Concept of Mind*. Some of the things he says might even encourage one to think of Ryle as suggesting an early form of FUNCTIONALISM. On this view (roughly) each mental phenomenon is thought of as a state dispositionally located in a network of behaviour and other mental states. But here again Ryle's text would seem to confound such an interpretation, for he offers an account of dispositions that is both highly idiosyncratic and inconsistent with the functional account.

In spite of the difficulties of interpretation and the fact that *The Concept of Mind* is less often cited in present work in the philosophy of mind, it contains a wealth of highly specific, important insights into mental concepts. And no account of Ryle's masterwork should neglect to mention the exquisite style and subtle humour it contains, which was characteristic of the man himself.

See also DENNETT; WITTGENSTEIN.

BIBLIOGRAPHY

Ryle, G. 1949. *The Concept of Mind*. London: Hutchinson.
Woods, O., and Pitcher, G. eds. 1970. *Ryle: Critical Essays*. New York: Doubleday.

SAMUEL GUTTENPLAN

S

Searle, John R. My work in the philosophy of mind developed out of my early work in the philosophy of language, especially the theory of speech acts. Most of my work in the philosophy of mind has been concerned with the topics of INTENTIONALITY and its structure, particularly the intentionality of PERCEPTION and ACTION and the relation of the intentionality of the mind to the intentionality of language. I have also written extensively on cognitive science (*see* COGNITIVE PSYCHOLOGY), especially on the limitations of the COMPUTATIONAL MODEL of the mind. Other work has concerned the MIND-BODY PROBLEM, the nature and structure of CONSCIOUSNESS, the relation of consciousness to UNCONSCIOUSNESS, the proper form of explanation in the social sciences and in the explanation of human behaviour generally, and the background of intentionality. I can only discuss a small number of these topics in this article, so I will confine myself to four of the most controversial areas.

THE MIND–BODY PROBLEM

The traditional mind–body problem arises out of the Cartesian assumption that 'mental' and 'physical' name two different *metaphysical categories* of phenomena. Given that assumption, the problem is what are the relations between the two, and, specifically, how can there be causal relations? Many contemporary philosophers of mind, though they are not always aware of it, still accept the basic assumption that 'mental', construed naïvely in terms of consciousness, subjectivity, privacy, qualia, etc., implies 'non-physical'; and 'physical' implies non-mental. Those who think of themselves as materialists typically deny the existence of any special, irreducible mental phenomena;

and those who think of themselves as property dualists or dual aspect theorists think that we must recognize the existence of some non-physical phenomena in the world. I reject these assumptions and I think both sides are mistaken. I think that this is one of those rare questions in philosophy where you can have your cake and eat it too. The materialists are right to think that the world consists entirely of physical phenomena; the dualists are right to think that it contains irreducible mental phenomena, such as my present state of consciousness. My claim is that these are not inconsistent. Given that they are both true, we need to redefine the notions of the 'mental' and the 'physical'.

The solution to the apparent paradox is what I call biological naturalism. Mental phenomena are part of our natural biological history, as much a part of biology as growth, digestion, enzyme secretion or reproduction. So construed, the general form of the relations between the mental and the physical can be stated as follows.

All mental states, from the profoundest philosophical thoughts to the most trivial itches and tickles are caused by neurobiological processes in the brain. As far as we know anything at all about how the world works, this point is well established. Neuronal processes cause mental states and events. But what, then, are these mental states and events? Does the causal relation between the two not commit us to some kind of dualism? No! Mental phenomena, such as my present state of conscious awareness of the table in front of me, are higher-level features of the brain. But how can that be? How can there be causal relations without two distinct events, hence two different phenomena, the mental and the physical? Actually this sort of relation is quite common in nature. Consider the liquidity of the water in the glass in front of me or the solidity of the table on which I am working. In both cases a higher-level feature of a system is caused by the behaviour of lower-level elements, molecules, even though the entire system is composed of those lower-level elements. Similarly in the brain a higher-level feature of a system, consciousness, is caused by the behaviour of lower-level elements – synapses, neurons, modules, etc., even though the entire system is composed of those (and other) lower-level elements. And, just as the liquidity and solidity of systems of molecules is not a property of any molecule, so the consciousness in the brain is not a feature of any single neuron. And, just as liquidity and solidity are not separate substances, so to speak, squirted out by the molecules, so consciousness and intentionality are not separate juices squirted out by the neurons, they are simply states that the whole neuronal system is in at certain times and under certain conditions.

We can summarize biological naturalism rather crudely in two propositions:

(1) Brains cause minds.
(2) Minds are higher-level features of brains.

Two caveats. First, like all analogies, the ones I have used only go so far. There are many disanalogies between the relations of solidity and liquidity to molecular behaviour on the one hand, and that of consciousness and intentionality to neuronal behaviour, on the other. Most importantly, consciousness is by its very nature subjective and, in some sense at least, 'private' and 'inner', not equally accessible to all competent observers.

Second, I am not suggesting that all our problems about mind–body relations are now solved. On the contrary, neurobiologically speaking we are just getting started. Once we see, however, that there is no philosophical or metaphysical mystery to mind–brain relations we can kick the problem of specifying the exact details of

mind–body relations out of philosophy, where it does not belong, and into neurobiology, where it does. The questions of how exactly which brain processes cause which mental phenomena and how they are realized in neuroanatomy are empirical scientific issues, not problems for philosophical analysis.

The 'solution' to the mind–body problem enables us to deal with several other traditional problems:

The Other Minds Problem

The standard view is that:

(1) we know of the existence of consciousness in other people by *inference*;
(2) the inference is based on observation of their behaviour, especially their verbal behaviour;
(3) the principle of the inference is analogy. Because their behaviour is similar to ours in similar circumstances we infer that their mental states are like ours.

I believe that (1)–(3) are all false. Our relations to other people, and to the world generally, are not epistemic except in odd circumstances. I do not infer that other people are conscious, except in very special circumstances. My confidence that other people are conscious is not based on their behaviour. If it were a matter of behaviour I would have to infer that my radio is conscious because it engages in more varied and more coherent verbal behaviour than any human I ever met. The basis of my total confidence that other people are conscious is that I can see that their causal structure is like mine. They have eyes, nose, skin, mouth and all the rest, and the behaviour is relevant to the question of their conscious states only because we see it as situated in an overall causal order. The principle that warrants my complete confidence in the existence of other minds is not: similar-behaviour-ergo-similar-mental-states. Rather the principle is: similar-causal-structures-ergo-similar-cause-and-effect-relations.

545

Epiphenomenalism

It is obvious to any conscious agent that consciousness enters crucially into his or her causal relations with the world. I decide to raise my arm, and lo and behold it goes up. No philosopher or neurobiologist is going to convince us that there is no causal relation. But how is such a thing possible? Does consciousness secrete acetylcholene (the neurotransmitter most responsible for muscle movements), does it shake the axons and dendrites? On the account given by biological naturalism, consciousness is causally efficacious in a way that is typical of higher-level system features. For example the solidity of the piston in the car engine is entirely caused by and realized in the system made up of the microelements, but the solidity does not thereby become epiphenomenal. The solidity of the piston is causally essential to the functioning of the engine. Similarly consciousness is entirely caused by and realized in the system made up of neurons, but consciousness does not thereby become epiphenomenal. It is causally essential to the functioning of the organism. The fact that it is grounded in the system of neurons, far from showing it to be epiphenomenal, precisely explains how it can, like other higher-level causal features of systems, be causally efficacious. (*See* EPI-PHENOMENALISM)

THE CRITIQUE OF COGNITIVE SCIENCE

Cognitive Science is currently one of the most exciting areas in the study of the mind, but it unfortunately was founded on a mistake. This need not be fatal, many other successful sciences have been founded on mistakes. In cognitive science the mistake is: the mind is a computer program; and the mind is to the brain as the program is to the hardware. Minds, in short, are computer programs implemented in brains.

This view, which I have baptized 'Strong ARTIFICIAL INTELLIGENCE' (Strong AI for short), can be refuted in one sentence. Minds cannot be identical with computer programs, because programs are defined syntactically in terms of the manipulation of formal symbols, such as 0s and 1s, whereas minds have mental or semantic CONTENTS; they have more than a syntax, they have a semantics. This refutation came to be known as *The Chinese Room Argument*, because I originally illustrated it with the following parable.

Imagine that I, a non-Chinese speaker, am locked in a room with a lot of Chinese symbols in boxes. I am given an instruction book in English for matching Chinese symbols with other Chinese symbols and for giving back bunches of Chinese symbols in response to bunches of Chinese symbols put into the room through a small window. Unknown to me, the symbols put in through the window are called questions. The symbols I give back are called answers to the questions. The boxes of symbols I have are called a database, and the instruction book in English is called a program. The people who give me questions and designed the instruction book are called the programmers, and I am called the computer. We imagine that I get so good at shuffling the symbols, and the programmers get so good at writing the program, that eventually my 'answers' to the 'questions' are indistinguishable from those of a native Chinese speaker. I pass the TURING test for understanding Chinese. But all the same, I don't understand a word of Chinese and – this is the point of the parable – if I don't understand Chinese on the basis of implementing the program for understanding Chinese, then neither does any digital computer solely on that basis because no digital computer has anything that I do not have.

This is a simple refutation of Strong AI. Like all arguments it has a logical structure. It is a derivation of a conclusion from three premises:

premise 1: programs are formal (syntactical),
premise 2: minds have contents (semantics),
premise 3: syntax is not sufficient for semantics.

The story about The Chinese Room illustrates the truth of premise 3. (*See* SYNTAX/

SEMANTICS.) From these three propositions the conclusion logically follows:

programs are not minds.

And this conclusion refutes Strong AI.

Of all the arguments that I have ever published I regard this one as among the most obviously sound and valid, but I have to say that nothing has aroused more debate than this. I am constantly amazed to see the implausibility of the various replies that for over a decade have been given to the Chinese Room Argument.

There are several common misunderstandings of the Chinese Room Argument and of its significance. Many people suppose that it proves that 'computers cannot think'. But that is a misstatement. The original meaning of 'computer' was 'person who computes'. On this definition, we are all computers whenever we compute anything and we can certainly think. The definition of 'computer' and 'computation' has since evolved to mean anything to which we can attach a computational interpretation. This has the consequence that everything is a computer because you can always attach zeros and ones to anything. For example, consider the door: let door open = 0, door closed = 1. So the door is a primitive computer. Neither the original narrow nor the new expanded definition of computation has the consequence that computers cannot think. On the contrary, on the narrow definition all computers are thinkers. On the wide definition, everything is a computer, so a fortiori, all thinkers are computers.

Another misunderstanding of the Chinese Room Argument is to suppose that I am arguing that as a matter of logic, as an a priori necessity, only brains can have consciousness and intentionality. But I make no such claim. The point is that we know in fact that brains do it causally. And from this it follows as a logical consequence that any other system that does it causally, i.e. that produces consciousness and intentionality, must have causal powers to do it at least equal to those of human and animal brains.

But it does not follow that other systems have to have neurons to do it. (Compare: airplanes do not have to have feathers in order to fly, but they do have to share with birds the causal powers to overcome the force of gravity in the earth's atmosphere.) The question of which systems are causally capable of producing consciousness and intentionality is an empirical factual issue, not to be settled by a priori theorizing. Since we do not know exactly how brains do it we are in a poor position to figure out how other sorts of systems, natural or artificial might do it. But there is no logical or metaphysical obstacle to consciousness and intentionality being caused in some other sorts of system, whether natural or artificial.

There is an even more powerful argument against the computational model of the mind which I did not publish until after 1990. A basic distinction fundamental to all the sciences is between those intrinsic features of the world whose existence is independent of us and those features of the world whose existence is relative to observers, users, makers and to intentionality in general. That an object is made of cellulose fibres is *intrinsic*, that it is a chair is *observer-relative*, even though the same object is both made of cellulose fibres and is a chair. In general the natural sciences deal with intrinsic features of nature; the social sciences deal with observer-relative features. I am using the expression 'observer-relative' to include the notions of user/maker/designer/intentionality-relative, etc.

Now what is the status of computation? Is it intrinsic or observer-relative? Well, on the narrow definition considered above, where conscious agents actually do, e.g. arithmetic, it is intrinsic. It is not a matter of what any outside observer says. If I am adding 2 + 2 to get 4, that is an intrinsic fact about me. But what about the electronic circuit on which I am now writing this? Such cases of computation are observer-relative. Intrinsically the object is an electronic circuit with state transitions between voltage levels. But that it is a 'computer', like the fact that the illuminated shapes on the screen in front of me are words and sentences, is observer-relative. The simple fact that computation is observer-relative is devastating to the claim that the brain is a digital computer. The question, 'Is the brain a digital computer?' lacks a clear sense. If it asks, 'Is the brain intrinsically a digital computer?', the answer is: Nothing is intrinsically a digital computer. A process is computational only relative to some observer or user who assigns a computational interpretation to it. If it asks, 'Could we assign a computational interpretation to the brain?', the answer is: We can assign a computational interpretation to anything.

This is a separate argument from the Chinese Room. That argument showed that semantics is not intrinsic to syntax, this one shows that syntax is not intrinsic to physics. The upshot is that the computational theory of the mind is incoherent. It is untestable because it lacks a clear sense. There is no answer to the question: what intrinsic physical facts about the system make it computational?

THE CENTRALITY OF CONSCIOUSNESS

Until recently there were few discussions of consciousness in philosophy, psychology or cognitive science. There are historical reasons for this neglect, but it has had unfortunate consequences because consciousness is the central mental notion. All of the other crucial mental notions, such as subjectivity, intentionality and mental causation can only be understood in terms of conscious mental states and processes.

It may seem strange to say that consciousness is the central mental notion when at any given moment most of our mental states, our beliefs, desires, memories, etc., are unconscious. But the crucial connection between consciousness and the unconscious can be stated as follows: There is a logical connection between the notion of consciousness and the notion of the unconscious such that in order for a state to be an unconscious *mental* state it must be the sort of thing that could be conscious in principle. I call this 'The Connection Principle'.

There are many arguments for the Connection Principle but perhaps the simplest is this. There is no way to make intelligible the notion of an aspectual shape of an intentional state except in terms of consciousness or accessibility to consciousness. Every intentional state has what I call an 'aspectual shape'. This just means that it represents its conditions of satisfaction under some aspects and not others. Thus, for example, the desire for water is a different desire from the desire for H_2O even though water and H_2O are identical. If I represent what I desire under the aspect 'water', that is a different aspectual shape from representing the same substance under the aspect 'H_2O'. What is true of this example is true generally. All intentional states represent their conditions of satisfaction under some aspects and not others; and this has the consequence that every intentional state, conscious or unconscious, has an aspectual shape.

For conscious intentional states, such as the conscious desire for water, there is no problem about specifying the aspectual shape. It is determined by how one thinks about whatever it is that the state is about. But what about unconscious intentional states? When a mental state is entirely unconscious, the only occurrent reality of that state is in the form of neurophysiological states and processes. Therefore, the only sense that we can give to the claim that an unconscious intentional state has a determinate aspectual shape, is that it is the sort of thing that could be brought to consciousness in the form of conscious thoughts, actions, etc.

What then, is the ontology of the unconscious when unconscious? Strictly speaking, the only occurrent ontology of the unconscious is that of neurobiological states and processes. As far as the occurrent reality is concerned, all of my mental life consists of two and only two features: consciousness and neurobiological processes. When we talk of unconscious intentional states, we are talking about the capacity of the brain to produce conscious thoughts, actions, etc.

Attributions of unconscious mental states, then, are in a sense 'dispositional'. To say of the man who is sound asleep that he believes that Clinton is president is like saying of a bottle of fluid on the shelf that it is poison or bleach. It does not imply that the substance is poisoning or bleaching anyone or anything right then and there, but it describes the substance in terms of its causal capacity, not in terms of its occurrent realization of that capacity. Now, similarly with attributions of unconscious mental states, when we say of someone that he has an unconscious mental state, we are describing his brain not in terms of its structural features, but in terms of its causal capacities, such as the causal capacity to think the appropriate thoughts on waking.

The Connection Principle gives us a further basis for the criticism of cognitive science. Much of the cognitive science literature postulates mental states that are not only unconscious in fact, but unconscious in principle. They are not the sort of thing that could be brought to consciousness. If my account is correct, this view is incoherent. There are no such states. The only unconscious mental states are those features of the brain that are capable of causing the state in a conscious form.

THE BACKGROUND OF INTENTIONALITY

A large part of my work in the philosophy of mind has dealt with intentionality. Since I present some of my views on this subject in another article in this volume, INTENTIONALITY, I will confine this part of the discussion to an aspect where my views are different from those which are common in the field.

On my view, all intentional states can function, that is they only determine their conditions of satisfaction, such as truth conditions in the case of beliefs, or fulfilment in the case of desires and intentions, against a Background of capacities, abilities, tendencies, dispositions and other causal structures that are not and could not be analysed in terms of other intentional states. This point

differs from the current orthodoxy in the following respect: the currently accepted view recognizes that intentional states are not atomistic but function within holistic networks of other intentional states. For example, in order to believe that dinner is ready, I have to have a network of other beliefs. But the point I am making is that in addition to all of these other beliefs, the beliefs themselves only function against a Background of abilities, capacities, knowhow, etc., which are not and could not be analysable into further sets of beliefs.

The simplest argument for the thesis of the Background is that if you try to follow out the threads in the network, the task is endless. This is not simply because you do not know where to stop, but because each further intentional state allows for an indefinitely large range of interpretations unless the correct interpretation is fixed by something not itself an intentional state. Thus, if I understand the sentence 'dinner is ready', I have to understand that dinner is something you eat. Further, I have to know that it is eaten through the mouth and not through the ear or the toe. I have to know that dinner is made of edible material objects as opposed to prime numbers or car factories. This list of beliefs goes on indefinitely, but – and this is the crucial point – each of these other beliefs is itself subject to an indefinitely large range of different interpretations, and that has the consequence that there has to be some point at which the series comes to a stop. It comes to a stop with my simple ability to cope with the world. As WITTGENSTEIN, who presents a similar argument, maintains, understanding is fixed by an ungrounded way of acting – we just know what to do – and on my view, what to do includes how to understand, interpret and apply intentional states.

The thesis of the Background together with the critique of cognitive science has significant implications for the understanding of human cognition. Instead of saying that human beings in the exercise of their cognitive capacities are everywhere following rules that are inaccessible in principle to consciousness, we should say,

549

rather, that they have a Background structure which enables them to cope in certain ways with their environment, and that structure is what it is because the environment is what it is and their relations to that environment are what they are.

CONCLUSION

My work in the philosophy of mind is by no means complete. I am currently working on the social character of many mental phenomena and the role of the mind in constructing a social reality, a reality of money, property, marriage, professions, government and other institutions. In this article I have only discussed a few of the topics that interest me. But even in this narrow scope I hope to have sketched the main features of my overall vision. Mental phenomena are above all biological phenomena and they are as real as any other biological phenomena, such as growth, digestion, photosynthesis or the secretion of bile. They cannot be reduced to something else, such as behaviour or computer programs. There are exactly two sorts of processes that go on in the brain, first-person subjective consciousness and third-person neurobiological phenomena. Talk of unconscious mental states and processes is always dispositional. Talk of unconscious mental phenomena that are in principle inaccessible to consciousness is incoherent. There is no intermediate level of computation between the level of the mental and the level of the neurobiological. And the problem is not that we lack evidence for such a level, rather the claim is untestable because it is incoherent. A genuine science of cognition would allow for at least three levels of explanation – a neurobiological level, a level of intentionality, and a functional level where we identify the operation of Background capacities in terms of their functional role in the life of the organism.

See also BELIEF; FUNCTIONALISM; IDENTITY THEORIES; THOUGHT; THOUGHT AND LANGUAGE.

BIBLIOGRAPHY

Lepore, E., and van Gulick, R., eds. 1991. *John Searle and His Critics*. Oxford: Basil Blackwell.
Searle, J.R. 1979. *Expression and Meaning*. Cambridge University Press.
—— 1983. *Intentionality: An Essay in the Philosophy of Mind*. Cambridge University Press.
—— 1980. Minds, brains and programs. *Behavioral and Brain Sciences*, 3, 417–24.
—— 1984. *Minds, Brains and Science: The 1984 Reith Lectures*. Cambridge, MA.: Harvard University Press.
—— 1992. *The Rediscovery of the Mind*. Cambridge, MA.: MIT Press.

JOHN R. SEARLE

the self The individuals to which we attribute thoughts, beliefs, desires, emotions, intentions, memories, sensations, and intentional actions – together with responsibility for those actions, are persons. Human beings are the obvious bearers of these attributes, sharing with other physical objects those properties that accrue to them by virtue of their location in space and time. But two particularly problematic features of the attribution of the mental properties to persons may be isolated that give rise to the idea that a person is something 'over and above' a material body.

The first feature is that of self-consciousness: experiences require a subject, at least potentially aware of it*self* as the subject of those experiences. But how can the thing that *has* the experiences itself be an item *within* these experiences? As will emerge in the next section, when we consider the differences between self-awareness and the awareness of the objects of experience that enters into the content of experience, it is tempting to posit a 'pure' experiencing consciousness that is identifiable only from the first-person perspective – an entity of a quite different sort from the physical body by which, as things are, third-person identification is available of the experiencing subject.

The second feature is the capacity of persons for intentional action (*see* THE WILL). Although much of what happens to persons is accountable for in the same way as that which happens to material bodies – for instance the ways in which the world impacts on them are conditioned by where they happen to be located at particular times – many of their interactions with the world are conditioned not by that world impersonally conceived, but by how they themselves represent the world to be. Persons are self-motivated beings with a considerable degree of autonomy over what happens to them and the world they inhabit. Again it is tempting to view the author of action as something over and above a material body. An apparently unbridgeable gulf opens between the subjective and the objective, with subjectivity here conceived as an extra-worldy *source* of a unique perspective on what is available from the third-person view.

Such considerations can make it seem that a person is an individual that, in addition to a body, *has* a self. Perhaps a person is a composite of a self – in some sense requiring explication – and a body. There has been much debate in the literature about the role the conception of the self should play in arriving at the identity conditions for persons over time.

SELF-CONSCIOUSNESS

Philosophical problems about self-consciousness are best approached by consideration of the reference of the 'I' of the 'I think' that, as Kant insisted, is in principle appendable to all *my* conscious experiences (*see* CONSCIOUSNESS). A peculiarity of self-reference is what Evans (1982) calls its 'immunity to error through misidentification' (but also see Evans, 1982, for arguments that self-reference is not unique in this respect). Thus I employ no criterion of identity in order to know which entity I am thinking about in thoughts about myself as experiencing subject, nor is there is any question of my needing to keep track of some entity – at least in the way that I must in the case of reindentification of material objects – in order for my thoughts about myself at different times to latch on to

the correct object of such thoughts. If as noted above the 'I' considered merely with respect to its role as the owner of experiences cannot itself be encountered in experience, it cannot be mistakenly encountered in experience. Famously, such considerations led Descartes to reason that the only thing that was immune to doubt was his own existence as a 'thinking thing' – a substantial, but non-material, self or soul, that had infallible access to an interior mental realm, however fallible that realm might be in its purported representation of an external world. (*See* HISTORY; INTROSPECTION.)

Hume by contrast took the unencounterability of the self in experience to impugn its very existence. He argued:

> For my part, when I enter most intimately into what I call *myself*, I always stumble on some perception or other ... I never catch *myself* at anytime without a perception, and never can observe anything but the perception ... nor do I conceive what is further requisite to make me a perfect nonentity. (1978, p. 254)

He concluded that the idea of the self as an entity that owns experiences should be replaced with the idea of the sum of those experiences themselves – 'I' am nothing but a 'bundle of perceptions' – a conclusion that left him highly dissatisfied, for his own philosophical framework lacked the resources to individuate such bundles. Hume's insistence that no a priori conclusions about the self are derivable from an idea that lacks experiential content marked an important development in thought about self-consciousness, which was expanded upon by Kant (see the next section). But Hume's conclusions were flawed by his inheritance of the Cartesian view of mind according to which it is mental items, or 'perceptions', that are themselves the objects of thought and perception in an independent interior realm – a view that invites the postulation of an elusive inner observer to witness such items (*see*, further, McDowell, 1986).

A more recent 'no-ownership' view of the self, or at least the view that a certain class of 'I' statements fail to refer, may be attributed to Wittgenstein (1958) who contrasted statements such as 'I have grown six inches' with those such as 'I have a toothache'. In the latter case he writes 'It is as impossible that in making the statement . . . I should have mistaken another person for myself, as it is to moan with pain by mistake, having mistaken someone else for me. To say "I have pain" is no more a statement *about* a particular person than moaning is.' And Anscombe (1975) concludes, from considerations about the feature of immunity to reference-failure of 'I'-thoughts when 'I' is taken to be a referring expression, that self-conscious thought is not about an object at all.

An alternative approach to establishing what selfhood consists in is to abandon the quest for an entity answering to the peculiarities of the logical grammar of 'I'-thought sentences, and focus instead on the *criteria* of identity for persons overtime. This is in effect Locke's strategy, who invokes as crucial a memory criterion:

> in this alone consists personal identity, i.e., the sameness of a rational being: . . . as far as . . . consciousness can be extended backwards to any past action or thought, so far reaches the identity of that person. (1959, p. 333)

Many objections have been raised against Locke's criterion, and many refinements that meet them proposed. Indeed Locke's own elaborations of his criterion suggest that it is a more general criterion of continuity of consciousness that he has in mind. I shall be considering some accounts that might be called Lockean in flavour in the next section but one. But for now the important point to note is that Locke's criterion is, essentially, detachable from a bodily criterion. He is himself explicit about this, arguing that were a prince to exchange his soul, 'carrying with it the consciousness of the prince's past life' with a cobbler, then 'everyone would see' that

the cobbler would then be the same person as the prince. (But see Williams, 1956, for doubts about the coherence of such thought-experiments.) As such, Locke's account of the self shares with that of Descartes and Hume an underlying assumption that considerations about what is constitutive of the subjective are detachable from considerations about that which is available to the objective view. It is time to examine that assumption.

SUBJECTIVITY AND THE OBJECTIVE WORLD

How, then, is the subject of experience to be conceived as situated in the objective world? A first step is to look to Kant, who argued for a crucial interdependence between the notions of subjectivity and objectivity.

In his famous Transcendental Deduction of the Categories Kant attempts to prove that there are certain concepts – the categories – whose application within experience is presupposed by the very possibility of experience. Kant uncontroversially assumes that judgments are the vehicles of knowledge claims, and so of experience itself. He begins by arguing that all judgments – requiring as they do a judge, and so their (at least potential) accompaniment by 'I think' – must conform to the requirements of what he calls the 'necessary unity of apperception [or self-consciousness]'. This requirement is expressed by the analytic principle 'All my representations in any given intuition must be subject to that condition under which alone I can ascribe them to the identical self as *my* representations' [B138]. Although no substantive a priori truths about the self are derivable from the analytic principle that is Kant's starting point, he nevertheless derives some important 'synthetic a priori' claims about the nature experience must have in order to conform to the condition of being the experience of a self-conscious subject. He proceeds to 'deduce' the categories by establishing a reciprocal relation between judgments, and the judge's representation of the content judged as belonging to a unitary consciousness. It emerges that it is only if the data presented to sensibility are conceived of – via the categories employed in judgments – as constituting relatively permanent items, enjoying law-governed causal relations, that the experiencing subject would be able to distinguish itself as judge distinct from them, the order of whose subjective representational states is distinguishable from the order of the represented items, thus allowing room for the thought that they are *my* representations. And this, famously, amounts to the thought of my series of representations jointly constituting a course of experience through an objective realm. As Strawson (1966) puts it: 'its members collectively build up or yield, though not all of them contribute to, a picture of a unified objective world through which the experiences themselves constitute a single, subjective, experiential route, one among other possible subjective routes through the same objective world.' The provision for, at the very least, what Strawson terms the 'self-reflexivity' of experience – the room within experience for the *thought* of experience – must be made if a requirement on making judgments at all is to be met: the ability to discriminate between 'this is how things are', and 'this is how things seem'. But once that minimal self-conception within experience has been provided for, so have the conditions for the conception of the world as independent from the judging subject's experience of it. Subjectivity and objectivity from this perspective are not opposed but interdependent.

In the Paralogisms, which deal explicitly with the problem of the self, Kant stresses that the necessity of the unity of apperception is a necessity of *thought*. Although we must *conceive* of ourselves as unitary consciousnesses, it does not follow from this that we know ourselves as unitary consciousnesses; nor even may we conclude that we know ourselves to be unitary consciousnesses. The identity of the 'I' of the 'I think' that is a 'permanent element' accompanying my judgments as a mere logical form is a purely logical identity, and no 'permanent element in appearance' should

be postulated to answer to it. That we do conceive ourselves as unitary consciousnesses is indeed inevitable, given that we must so conceive ourselves in order to conceive – in judgment – anything at all. Hence the fallacious reasoning engaged in deriving a priori truths about the self – its simplicity, immortality, spirituality and so forth – is 'paralogistic', 'without intent to deceive'. But the reflective, second-order thought about the nature of experience, that we *must* so conceive ourselves, is not a thought that we ought to try to render 'objectively valid'. That is to say, in recognizing a necessity of experience we should not take ourselves to have supplied ourselves with an intuition – an item *within* experience – to which the idea of a unitary consciousness corresponds. Rather, all we have is an *explanation* of why, groundlessly, we consider ourselves to know ourselves as unitary consciousnesses.

We are still some way from a conception of the self as itself an element of the objective world, and so a candidate for knowledge. But if we could show that the subjects of experience must further conceive of themselves as physical entities in order to instantiate the attributes about whose ownership they have such direct awareness, then we could reinstate the common-sense view that the proper bearers of those attributes are ordinary, physical, human beings. And the Kantian conception of the 'I' as a pure logical form may be considered to be an *abstraction* from the common-sense conception rather than a component of it, requiring an entity or some sort of construction to answer to it.

This is roughly Strawson's (1959) strategy. He starts with two questions: '(1) why are states of consciousness ascribed to anything at all? and (2) why are they ascribed to the very same thing as certain corporeal characteristics?' Strawson acknowledges that experiential attributes and states owe their existence to the identity of the individual whose states they are: they are 'logically non-transferable'. He argues that a necessary condition of ascribing states of consciousness to oneself is that one be able to make sense of their ascription to others. And a necessary condition of ascribing states of consciousness to others is that one be able to identify them as individuals of the same type as oneself. If the owners of states of consciousness were Cartesian egos, then there would be no means of identifying them, and so no means of ascribing states of consciousness at all. On the other hand, a no-ownership theorist who is prepared to allow that all *my* experiences contingently depend on a certain body either illegitimately presupposes a referent for the '*my*' of a sort that he has disallowed, or ends up stating a necessary truth. Rather, Stawson concludes, 'person' is a logically *primitive* concept of an entity to which both states of consciousness *and* corporeal characteristics are ascribable. Furthermore the logical character of predicates denoting states of consciousness requires that they have third-personal – constitutive behavioural – and first-personal attributional conditions. Mastery of such predicates requires an understanding of both such conditions of attribution. Thus questions (1) and (2) are answered by noting that (2) is a necessary condition for (1).

Where Strawson stresses the importance of the ascribability of different types of predicate to the same type of individual, Evans (1980) emphasizes the other aspect of what he calls the 'Generality Constraint' on knowledge of which object one is thinking about. Namely, that self-knowledge requires an understanding of what it would be to ascribe predicates of the same type to different individuals of the same type as oneself. Indeed self-knowledge requires a sensitivity to certain ways of gaining information (for instance knowledge of what must be the case for 'I am in pain' to be true rests upon my ability to decide whether or not I am in pain merely on the basis of how I feel), as well as a capacity to manifest 'I' – thoughts in action. But equally self-knowledge requires the capacity to understand propositions about ourselves whose truth is not so grounded on these distinctive ways of gaining information, or manifesting our grasp of them (for

instance propositions about our infancy, or future events involving ourselves). And this type of self-knowledge requires that one know what it would be for an identity statement of the form 'I = x' to be true, where 'x' is 'an identification of a person which – unlike one's "I" – identification – is of a kind which could be available to someone else'.

This, crucially, requires a conception of persons as physical things, locatable in space and time, and so the practical ability to know how to locate oneself in space and time (Evans, 1980, p. 209).

Evans shows that there is a mistaken tendency to assume that the immunity to error through misidentification of 'I'-thoughts arises only with respect to thoughts about oneself as the subject of *mental* self-ascriptions. But this phenomenon attaches equally to bodily self-ascriptions such as 'my legs are crossed', 'I am moving', 'I am in front of a house', where – at least in ordinary circumstances – no knowledge of anything would be gained if the ways in which such thoughts were arrived at involved the application of some identity criterion that left room for error about *who* such thoughts concerned.

In the case of mental self-ascriptions it cannot be overemphasized that it is the world, and not some inner informational state, to which the subject looks in thinking those thoughts that grant him an infallible awareness of himself as their owner. Indeed an 'I think', as Kant claims, accompanies all my 'representations'; but as Kant insists, as such it is purely formal. Self-*knowledge* requires in addition the range of capacities that Evans describes. But such knowledge is, on Evans account, achievable, for '[t]he very idea of a perceivable, objective, spatial world brings with it the idea of the subject as being in the world, with the course of his perceptions due to his changing position in the world and the more or less stable way the world is' (Evans, 1980, p. 222). On this view the concept of the self involved in self-reflection is the concept of the same entity as a person, objectively conceived, and not a component of it.

PERSONAL IDENTITY

Even if it can be argued that selves are necessarily embodied, it does not follow that bodily identity is a necessary condition of personal identity. Considerations about dead bodies would seem to show that it is clearly not a sufficient condition. But various thought experiments have been devised to show that it is not a necessary condition either; and others devised that seem to allow the concepts of self and person once again to diverge.

The underlying intuition driving such thought experiments is an elaboration of the Lockean thought that what matters in questions about personal identity is the fulfilment of some sort of psychological-continuity criterion (underwritten by a plausible causal condition). Thus, Shoemaker (1963) asks us to consider a case where Brown's brain is successfully transplanted into Robinson's head. Intuition seems to argue in favour of allowing that Brown survives as the resulting man, 'Brownson'. After all, he will, it is to be assumed, retain Brown's memories, dispositions, character traits and so forth (see again, Williams, 1956b, for doubts about this). Such a case could, of course, be considered a case of bodily continuity, with the brain taken to be a vital enough bodily component for brain-identity to be sufficient for bodily identity. But more tendentious examples, involving 'brain state transfer devices', that are intended to elicit the same intuitions suggest that it is merely the brain's (contingent) casual role as realizer of a particular set of psychological states that grants it the privileged status as identity criterion. 'Psychological continuity' is essentially abstractable from it, and the self may be viewed not as an entity at all, but as a construction of casually related states, or perhaps (see Lewis, 1976) as a sum of person-stages. (But see Williams (1970), for an argument to show that the intuitions elicited by thought-experiments of this latter sort are merely the result of the way such examples are described.)

Perhaps the most perplexing case is of the sort discussed by Wiggins (1967) and Parfit (1971), where the brain of a man, let us call him S, is divided, and each half – retaining S's memories, character traits, etc., – transplanted in a new body. Both resulting people, S_1 and S_2, would seem to be psychologically continuous with S in the way that it is proposed 'matters' for personal identity. But we surely do not have here a case of *identity*, for identity is a transitive relation. And while the appropriate conditions seem to exist for S's identity with both S_1 and S_2, it seems clear that S_1 and S_2 are not identical: they have different spatial locations, for instance, and proceed to enjoy entirely separate lives. It seems clear that S 'survives' in some sense – after all, were half his brain to be destroyed in the process and the other half to leave him with his memories and character traits intact, his survival would be indisputable. Why should the existence of a second person resulting from the success of the operation cast doubt upon his survival?

Parfit's own conclusion is that what matters about survival is not identity at all, but psychological continuity, which only contingently coincides with identity. Psychological continuity differs from identity not only in its intransitivity, but also in being a matter of degree. S_1 and S_2 may themselves divide, and subdivide, and the more remote 'branches' will eventually fail to retain S's memories, still less character traits. Still, a relation Parfit characterizes as 'connectedness' will be retained between S and such branches, by virtue of the stronger, direct relation of continuity that obtains between the intervening stages. And a vagueness attending the issue of at which stage we should allow that S himself survives is inevitable.

The example has been much discussed (*see* especially Lewis, 1976; Perry, 1972, 1976; Parfit, 1976; Wiggins, 1976, 1980). But for now let us note that the chief difficulty it gives rise to is how a person – individuated in any of the ways the imagined circumstances allow as a matter of arbitration – is to conceive of him*self*. If it

555

were I who were to be divided in this way tomorrow, and I were to learn that some piece of good fortune I now covet were to befall my left-half survivor rather than the right-half survivor, I am unable to avoid hoping that I will turn out to be left-half rather than right. But in so doing I am adopting the Cartesian conception, derided by Kant, assuming that 'I' refers to a pure consciousness that I will, at some future date, *know* to be identical with that that expresses the hope now. Left-half, I hope, will somehow house this consciousness, and right-half merely mimic it. But it is unclear what alternative conception of my future self – the fulfiller of *my* hopes – is available to me. Further difficulties attend thoughts about the past on this conception. For instance, as Wiggins (1980) asks, how is S later to represent to himself some past achievement (to use Wiggins's example, sailing single-handed between Scylla and Charybdis)? Let us say there are three paths psychologically continuous with S and so three equally good claimants for remembering the feat. But such claimants will have differing attitudes towards the feat, attitudes that, on the conception driving the claim that psychological continuity is what matters, are partly constitutive of their own self-conceptions. But unless we are to claim that all three at one time were in the same place, the only plausible notion of a person available to each is that of being a fusion of person-stages. But as Wiggins notes, the properties of fusions are derivative from those attributable to its constituent stages. And too many of the predicates ascribable to persons are not so derivable: Wiggins offers, amongst others, 'weak, strong, clever, stupid, a good goalkeeper, a fair weather friend'. Wiggins argues that the concept of a person is the concept of a member of a NATURAL KIND – an organism, with clear principles of individuation. An illusion of technical omnipotence encourages the mistaken idea that thought-experiments of the sort under consideration, which violate those principles, are genuine conceptual possibilities.

THE SELF AND ACTION

I omitted from the discussion of Kant's account of the self (above) a feature of his framework that ultimately renders that account untenable. It was noted that the conception of an objective world is interdependent with one's own self-conception – a conclusion also reached by Evans. Kant's insight was to show that the ordinary world of experience is, necessarily, a world *conceived* in certain ways. There is no unconceptualized experience: that which is represented – what experiential states are about – is the world as experienced, which is the empirical world. But Kant also warns against our claim to knowledge of 'things in themselves', unnervingly characterized as inhabiting a 'supersensible' realm. A relatively innocuous construal of 'things in themselves' might simply be that they are unconceptualized things, or things considered in abstraction from the necessary conditions for our thinking about them, where the implication is that such things may not be considered as 'things' – in any sense that carries ontological commitments – at all. Individuation of objects requires concepts, and so a judging subject. And the supersensible is merely the empirical realm considered in abstraction from the conditions for experiencing it. But Kant unambiguously consigns the *self* to the realm of the supersensible: there are no empirical conditions of application for selfhood. But *we* are the conceptualizers, and if it is 'we' as we are in ourselves, from a supersensible realm, that do the conceptualizing, then it seems there is after all a perspective from which the ordinary world of experience is a mere *appearance* of things in themselves. And it surely undermines Kant's insight if the conceptualized world – the world of experience – turns out to be only *qualifiedly* real.

Why should Kant have refused to allow that as conceptualizing beings we are elements of the empirical world? The most likely answer is the link Kant insisted upon between rationality and freedom. And he held that it is only in our capacity as moral agents that we are genuinely free. Kant argued for causality as a crucial objective feature of the world, but he equated causality with the causally determined – the province of the events of the natural sciences *as opposed to* exercises of rationality. In order to exercise our moral capacities we must escape the deterministic net.

But if we reinstate the self in the empirical world, then taking Kant's point that the world of experience is one represented by the subject presents no obvious obstacle to our allowing that our causal interactions with the world that involve our believing it to be a certain way, or desiring it to be some other way – in other words our intentions – are exercises of our rational capacities, and so manifestations of freedom. But if this is the conception of the self we want to vindicate, it is surely an important project in the philosophy of mind to show how such causation is possible within a world governed by physical law (*see* IDENTITY THEORIES; PHYSICALISM; SUPERVENIENCE). For let us assume that intentional concepts and the common-sense, lawlike generalizations in which they figure are in some sense incommensurate with physical concepts and physical laws (*see* DAVIDSON). Then without some account of the relation instantiations of intentional properties by persons bear to instantiations of physical properties, it will seem mysterious, if not miraculous, how instances of the laws at the physical level harmonize so happily with the generalizations of the other. If we just insist on the disparate nature of the two explanatory schemes, and take their explanatory success to underwrite their status as *causally* explanatory schemes without saying more, then the picture of the mental realm that we are likely to be left with is of a superimposed pattern that – from a perspective that is coloured by our own concerns – *we* discern in what is independently there. But how then are 'we' as pattern-discerners to conceive of ourselves? What are we doing in imposing our patterns if there is a perspective from which particular exercises of our pattern-discerning capacities are abstractable from the

pattern discerned? It is difficult to see how such a picture allows for intentional properties making a genuine difference to what happens – to what is there on which to impose our interpretations.

The problem of establishing a plausible conception of the *subject* of experience, or the self, as an element of the objective world, turns out to be inseparable from a major problem in the philosophy of mind: how to vindicate the causal efficacy of the mental properties distinctive of subjects of *experience* (*see* EPIPHENOMENALISM).

See also An Essay on Mind section 1; CONSCIOUSNESS; REASONS AND CAUSES; SUBJECTIVITY.

BIBLIOGRAPHY

Anscombe, E. 1975. The First Person. In *Mind and Language*, ed. S. Guttenplan. Oxford: Basil Blackwell.
Evans, G. 1982. *The Varieties of Reference*. Oxford University Press.
Hume, D. 1978. *A Treatise of Human Nature*, ed. L. A. Selby-Bigge, 2nd edn rev. P. H. Nidditch. Oxford: Clarendon Press.
Kant, I. 1929. *Critique of Pure Reason*, trans. N. Kemp Smith. London: Macmillan & Co. Ltd.
Lewis, D. 1976. Survival and Identity. In Rorty, ed., 1976.
Locke, J. 1975. *An Essay Concerning Human Understanding*, ed. P. H. Nidditch. Oxford University Press.
McDowell, J. 1986. Singular thought and the extent of inner space. In *Subject, Thought, and Context*, ed. P. Pettit and J. McDowell. Oxford: Clarendon Press.
Nagel, T. 1970. *The Possibility of Altruism*. Oxford: Clarendon Press.
Parfit, D. 1971. Personal identity. *Philosophical Review*, LXXX: 1, 3–27.
Parfit, D. 1976. Lewis, Perry, and what matters. In Rorty, ed., 1976.
Perry, J. 1972. Can the self divide? *Journal of Philosophy*, LXIX, 463–88.
Perry, J. 1976. The importance of being identical. In Rorty, ed., 1976.
Rorty, A., ed. 1976. *The Identities of Persons*. University of California Press.
Shoemaker, S. 1963. *Self-Knowledge and Self-Identity*, Ithaca: Cornell University Press.

Strawson, P.F. 1959, *Individuals: An Essay in Descriptive Metaphysics*. London: Methuen.

Strawson, P.F. 1966. *The Bounds of Sense: An Essay on Kant's Critique of Pure Reason*. London: Methuen.

Wiggins, D. 1967. *Identity and Spatio-Temporal Continuity*. Oxford: Basil Blackwell.

Wiggins, D. 1976. Locke, Butler and the stream of consciousness: And men as a natural kind. In Rorty, ed., 1976.

Wiggins, D. 1980. *Sameness and Substance*. Oxford: Basil Blackwell.

Williams, B. 1956. Personal identity and individuation. *Proceedings of the Aristotelian Society*, LVII.

Williams, B. 1970. The self and the future. *Philosophical Review*, LXXIX.

KIRSTIE MORRISON

self-deception The idea of self-deception is problematic on two levels. First, there seems to be something superficially paradoxical about it from an analytical point of view. But, secondly, given that it seems to be a fundamental and pervasive feature of human life, there are much deeper questions about its rationality and its connection with agency and action.

The paradoxical nature of self-deception shows itself as soon as one thinks about the conditions necessary for deception in general. If I set about to deceive Smith – say, by lying – then I would typically try to get him to believe something true, which I know (or believe) to be false. Thus, if I know there to be a train to Oxford at 11 p.m., then I deceive Smith if I can get him to believe that there is no such train. How or why I would do this is not of immediate relevance, but what is crucial to deception is that there is a certain deliberateness about it. If I myself believe there to be no such train – if I have made a mistake – then telling Smith this does not count as attempted deception. To be sure, Smith may come to believe something false, but, insofar as my assertion was sincere, I have not deceived him; my assertion was not a lying one. Now, as one presumes from the label, what one must do to be 'self-deceived' is to fulfil the conditions of deception in respect of oneself. For example, lying to oneself would count as a central case. But how could one possibly try to convince oneself of something believing it false? If I do believe that some proposition p is false, then it would seem to be impossible for me to also believe that p is true. So, it would seem that self-deception consists in bringing about something which is impossible.

Of course in less schematically characterized cases, there seems to be a bit more room to manoeuvre. Suppose that Jones's husband is having an affair, and suppose also that he is not very good at hiding this. All Jones's friends are aware of what is going on and they see in her behaviour evidence that she too knows. For example, though she does not normally like to spend a night away at her sister's, she does so often enough to make it seem as if she is somehow getting out of the way. This and other examples add up to a pattern of behaviour that only makes sense if she knows what is happening, but, when confronted by the inevitable busybody, she seems wholly surprised that anyone would have thought such a thing. Additionally, she makes it clear how incapable she would be of tolerating any infidelity on the part of her husband. Her surprise and revulsion at the idea seem so genuine that it would be very difficult to think she was feigning ignorance. Yet she takes no steps to find out the truth, whilst all the while continuing to do things consistent with her really knowing it. In the end, her friends come to think that she is deceiving herself about her husband's affair.

What this sort of example introduces is the important connection between how one acts and what one believes. This makes it possible to think that self-deception is not the paradoxical believing that p and not-p, so much as acting as if one believed that p, whilst also acting as if p was false. Much of Jones's non-verbal behaviour showed her to believe that the affair was going on. But her verbal behaviour, when confronted with the unpleasant fact, was unequivocally on the other side.

Whilst the complex interaction between action and belief might seem to get us out of logical trouble, its ultimate success is doubtful. For it seems reasonable, given the nature of propositional attitudes, to ask whether someone does or does not believe something: acting *as if* one believed p is not yet believing. But, as the general conditions for deception revealed, you are only really deceived when you are intentionally led to believe something true which is believed by your informant to be false. So, to be self-deceived, Jones, believing the affair was going on, would have had to convince herself quite intentionally that it wasn't. If in some way she merely acted as if she believed it – perhaps in some unconscious way – this wouldn't be enough: her denial would not have been the result of any intention on her part.

One way it might be tempting to take matters further is by appealing to the notion mentioned above in passing: THE UNCONSCIOUS. The thought might be that our minds are composed of at least two elements: a conscious and an unconscious self. In cases of self-deception, the one would be the engineer of the deception of the other. Or, less psycholanalytically, one might go in for talk of the mind as inherently compartmental. Given the right circumstances, it can happen that a single agent is able to harbour the beliefs and propensities to act of two or more distinct individuals. In the case of Jones, as described above, her revulsion at the thought of her husband's infidelity was strong enough to push the belief that he was indeed having an affair into a compartment of her mind insulated from her otherwise positive picture of him.

Of course, talk of unconscious and multiple selves needs much more filling out before it can be taken seriously. And in the case of self-deception there is a particularly important constraint on any such background story. For as we have seen, the self-deceiver seems to go in for the deception deliberately – it is motivated – and the very idea of motivation presupposes that there is an agent at work. Now consider how we would view a compartmentalized mind if what we were discussing were the overt actions of some agent. Suppose that Peter were to do two things which appeared to be in tension, say buying a particularly extravagant car and yet going miles out of his way to save a small amount on washing powder. Our feeling that these are in tension comes from the fact that we have trouble imagining the motivational background in a single agent that would explain two such different ways of dispensing money. Of course, it may be that Peter, loving expensive cars, believes that any little savings on other things will make ownership of such a car possible. But, supposing that we could dismiss this sort of circumstance, what could be said about Peter's behaviour? Surely, we would say that it is in some sense irrational. However, if we went in for the compartment view of Peter's mind, then we seem free to say that one part of Peter did the one thing and another part, the other. And this would seem to rule out the judgment that Peter's actions were irrational; indeed it would remove the basis for saying that they were even in tension with one another. For if we treat Peter as somehow harbouring two different agents, then we can do no more than remark on the very different kinds of money-directed behaviour these two agents display. But of course that is not how we would treat such a case: for agency is not so easily divisible when it comes to things people do.

This is not to say that we would never compartmentalize agency. In cases of multiple personality and schizophrenia we may well do just that. But this makes rather than challenges the point. For cases of behaviour like Peter's are not usually taken as evidence of multiple personality, and yet that is what one form of the compartment theory requires of us. Of course, nothing said here about how we understand agency is meant to tell finally against the compartment view. It is simply that such a view must be spelled out in a way that makes it clear how *one and the same agent* can have what we might call a divided mind.

Trying to soften the paradoxical hard edges of the idea of self-deception has led us to consider the intricate connection of attitude and action, as well as the possibility of less-than-integrated selves. Still another way to complicate matters so as to avoid paradox is to bring in the notion of time. Unlike ordinary cases of deception which can, as it were, happen in an instant, when the deceived victim takes in and accepts the falsehood deliberately provided, cases of self-deception are typically more spread out in time. Jones's friends were happy enough to describe her as self-deceived about the faithfulness of her husband, but they came to this conclusion only after a fairly protracted examination of Jones's behaviour and only after dismissing a number of initially more plausible alternatives. Moreover, accepting for the argument's sake the idea that Jones deceived herself because she could find no other way to reconcile her love of her husband with her detestation of infidelity, it should be clear that deceiving oneself, if it can happen, is more in the nature of a project. It takes time and a degree of careful, if devious, planning to get oneself to ignore what would otherwise be plainly admitted. And perhaps it is in the temporal extendedness of the feat that one can defuse the paradoxical air of self-deception. Nonetheless, however the feat is managed, it is undeniable that self-deception is something ordinarily accepted as fairly commonplace, as well as often beneficial. For there is no denying that, however irrational the state of mind that comes with self-deception, there are circumstances when, in a broader sense, it is rational to go in for it. When what one believes is just too painful to acknowledge, the alchemical transformation of belief characteristic of self-deception can come to the rescue. In such cases, the deceiving of oneself may well be a project whose goal is in one's own best interests, and is thus wholly intelligible as well as rational.

BIBLIOGRAPHY

Pears, D. 1975. The paradoxes of self-deception. In his collection *Questions in the Philosophy of Mind*. London: Duckworth.

Fingarette, H. 1969. *Self-Deception*. London: Routledge & Kegan Paul.

Davidson, D. 1982. Paradoxes of irrationality. In *Philosophical Essays on Freud*, ed. R. Wollheim and J. Hopkins. Cambridge University Press.

SAMUEL GUTTENPLAN

self-intimation *see* FIRST-PERSON AUTHORITY.

sensation What one experiences when touching a radiator or diving into a cold mountain stream are sensations of heat and cold. Thus understood, a sensation is some experience or feeling that arises from the way the world affects certain of our senses. However, it is not obvious either that sensations require a specific sensory modality or that all sensory modalities have associated sensations. For example, we are said to have sensations arising from our awareness of the internal states of our bodies and these are not the result of touch or any other 'external' sense. Of course, one might simply maintain that we have a non-external bodily sensory system which gives rise to sensations of pain, upsets in the stomach, etc. In this way, one would be able to say that a sensation was an experience brought about either by some mechanism for sensing the world *or* by one which tells us about the states of our bodies.

However, the most difficult problem in this area comes from considering the question of whether sensations – as just described – are typical of all the sensory modalities. Many feel that touch, smell and taste are unproblematically accompanied by sensations, but hearing, and especially sight, give rise to lots of problems. For example, when we see something blue, do we have a sensation, and, if so, how can we characterize it? Moreover, what, if any, role does such a sensation play in the accounts we might give of PERCEPTION? Answers to these questions range surprisingly widely. At one extreme is the view that the very idea of seeing something blue is to be analysed as the having of a particular kind of sensation (sometimes called a 'sense-datum') which itself has properties (qualia) that resemble the seen object. Thus, we see something as blue because we have a 'blue-ish' sensation and infer from that that the object of our seeing is blue. (Of course, it would be odd to describe the sensation itself as blue, so one is forced to talk about these sensational properties in quotation marks, or in some other way.)

At the other extreme, is the view that visual perception does not involve sensation – that it is simply a mistake to assimilate the case of seeing something blue to the kind of thing we experience when we touch something hot. This kind of view is often called the 'intentional' theory of perception, because what is attempted is an account of perception as wholly consisting in content-ful intentional states on a par with the propositional attitudes (see QUALIA; PERCEPTUAL CONTENT).

See also CONSCIOUSNESS; FUNCTIONALISM; IDENTITY THEORIES.

SAMUEL GUTTENPLAN

simulation theory and theory theory These are two, many think competing, views of the nature of our commonsense, proposi-tional attitude explanations of action. For example, when we say that our neighbour cut down his mulberry tree because he believed that it was ruining his patio and didn't want it ruined, we are offering a typi-cally commonsense explanation of his action in terms of his beliefs and desires. But, even though wholly familiar, it is not clear what *kind* of explanation is at issue. On one view, the attribution of beliefs and desires is taken as the application to actions of a *theory* which, in its informal way, func-tions very much like theoretical explanation in science. This is known as the 'theory theory' of everyday psychological explana-tion. In contrast, it has been argued that our propositional attributions are not theor-etical claims so much as reports of a kind of *simulation*. On such a 'simulation theory'

of the matter, we decide what our neigh-bour will do (and thereby why he did it) by imagining ourselves in his position and deciding what we would do. For fuller accounts of these two views and further examples, see BELIEF (2) and FOLK PSY-CHOLOGY.

SAMUEL GUTTENPLAN

Stalnaker, Robert In this sketch of my own philosophical views and approach I will focus on the problem of INTENTION-ALITY, a problem that has held my atten-tion since I first started thinking about the philosophy of mind. I will say what I take the problem to be, what strategies for responding to it I advocate, and what some of the remaining puzzles about intention-ality are.

Like most fat philosophical problems with such labels (the problem of free will, the MIND–BODY PROBLEM) the problem of intentionality does not pose a single well-defined question, but is a cluster of inter-related questions and puzzles that seem to derive from what is, in some sense, a common underlying philosophical problem. As with those other problems, there is philosophical work to be done to turn the puzzles and vague feelings of conceptual dis-comfort into well-defined questions and pro-jects – to articulate what needs to be done to solve the problem. As with the other problems, one cannot even begin the task of formulating a well-focused project without making controversial philosophical commit-ments. A large part of the task is to defend claims about what questions should be asked, and about what would count as an answer. I will begin by trying to say, in general and impressionistic terms, what the intentional phenomena are, what is puz-zling and problematic about them, and what needs to be done to clarify them.

Some things – for example, names and utterances, memories, mental images and feelings of anger, pictures, charts and graphs – are said to represent, or be about, or be directed at other things (see REPRE-SENTATION). Intentional relations are relations that hold between such things and what they represent, or are directed at. Intentional relations seem to be distinctively mental; to the extent that inanimate objects such as names or maps have intentional properties, these properties seem to derive from the intentional properties of the thinkers and agents who create or use the objects. And intentional relations seem to have peculiarities not shared by relations found to hold more widely between things in the natural order – causal relations, spatiotemporal relations, and relations of similarity and difference – and these peculiarities seem not only to make it difficult to understand how rational agents could be a part of the natural order, they also are puzzling in themselves. How is it possible to stand in a relation of any kind to a thing, such as Zeus or the planet Vulcan, that does not exist? How can one admire the man on the beach while having a low opinion of the man in a brown hat when they are one and the same man? A satisfactory clarification of intentional relations must begin by responding to these traditional puzzles (*see An Essay on Mind* section 2.1).

The first move in this direction that I and many others make is to propose that intentional relations generally are to be explained in terms of relations to *propositions*. Intentional relations between agents and other persons or physical object (x wants, loves, admires, worships, or fears y, for example) are to be explained in terms of PROPOSITIONAL ATTITUDES that the agent x has toward propositions that involve or are defined in terms of the object y. There will be work to be done saying how individual objects and concepts of them are involved in defining or identifying propositions, but the prior tasks, according to this way of approaching the problem, are to clarify, first, what propositions are, and second, what it is for speakers, thinkers and agents to be in intentional states or to perform intentional acts such as asserting, believing, hoping and fearing that take propositional objects. One of my central concerns has been to connect the two questions: what is a proposition? and what is it to stand in an

intentional relation to one? The strategy for connecting and clarifying these questions is to use assumptions about the answer to the second in order to motivate an answer to the first. That is, one begins with a certain kind of account of how we are related to propositions, and asks what propositions must be in order for us to be related to them in that way.

One cannot begin without saying something about what propositions are, but the idea is to make only tentative and relatively neutral assumptions about these abstract objects: they are what is said or thought, whatever is the content of a BELIEF or a DESIRE, whatever is the referent of a clause of the form *that P* when it is the direct object of an attribution of speech or thought. Then the first question is this: what is it to stand in a relation such as belief or desire to such an object? But more needs to be said about what kind of answer to this rather vague question we are looking for, and this requires that we say more about what is problematic about intentional relations: what puzzlement about them we expect an explanation of intentional relations to resolve.

Even before committing ourselves to any specific account of propositions, it does seem reasonable to assume that they are abstract objects of some kind, and one may be puzzled about how human agents, if they are a part of the natural order, manage to get themselves into relationships with abstract objects. The metaphors with which we characterize our relations to propositions are metaphors of causal interaction: we 'grasp' the propositions we understand; in communication, we receive and convey information. But how is it possible to stand in something like a causal relation to an abstract object? And more specifically, how is it possible for intentional relations to the abstract objects, propositions, to exhibit the peculiar and distinctive features such as referential opacity, and the apparent capacity to be related, by way of propositions 'about' them, to things that do not exist?

The strategy for solving this problem that I adopted (*see* 1984, ch. 1) was a modest one, but one that I would argue suffices to solve the problem, at least in its initial form. Rather than attempting to provide analyses or definitions of the problematic intentional relations – propositional attitudes such as belief, desire and INTENTION – I aimed only to exhibit some simple relations between persons or physical objects and propositions, relations that were manifestly unmysterious, intelligible in themselves, and obviously compatible with a naturalistic understanding of the things that stood in the relation, but that had the features that were said to be problematic about intentional relations (*see* NATURALISM). The simple and artificial relations that I used to make this point were relations defined in terms of causal and counterfactual constructions. Let me give a purely abstract example, just to make the strategy clear: suppose we define a relation R between a person and a proposition in terms of a counterfactual in something like the following way: $R(x, \text{ that } P) =_{df}$ if it were the case that P, then x would be F. ('x' and 'that P' are here variables for persons or physical objects and propositions, respectively, while 'F' stands in for some particular predicate of things of the kind that the 'x' ranges over.) Such a definition might, of course, be much more complex. All that is required to show how persons or other things can be related to propositions is that the relation be defined in terms of some open expression that contains two variables, one taking an individual as value, and the other a proposition. Now if such examples succeed in making their point – that is, if the relations defined are unmysterious, but also manifest the features that were said to be what was puzzling about intentional relations – then they show that there is nothing mysterious or problematic about an empirical relation between a person and a proposition, or about the features that were said to distinguish intentional relations from relations that hold between things in the natural order. This may not solve the underlying problem, but it at least sharpens the issue by challenging the poser of the problem of intentionality to say what features distinguish real intentional relations from the simple relations exhibited.

The particular relations that I defined to make this point – specifically a 'tendency to bring about' relation, and a relation of 'indication' – were intended also to suggest a slightly more ambitious claim: that intentional relations might actually be explained in terms of relations of the kind I defined. 'Indication' as I defined it was a kind of tendency to carry information, where carrying information is understood in terms of relations of counterfactual dependency between the thing carrying the information and its environment. It does not seem implausible to suggest that belief is a kind of indication, one that plays a certain role, in interaction with motivational states, in the determination of rational action. Even if some such claim is right, this is a long way from an analysis of belief. At best, it puts belief into a category that includes many kinds of states of persons and systems that are clearly not belief states, or intentional states in any ordinary sense, for example states of the immune system, of hard disks, of thermostats. But even if the work of distinguishing full-blooded rational agents and their intentional mental states from simpler systems and simpler representational states remains to be done, it may be that much of the puzzlement about representation is removed by getting clear about how simple representation is possible. And it may be that the puzzlement that remains is more easily articulated in the context of a more general account of representation.

Now if we assume that the way intentional states such as belief, desire and intention relate us to propositions is to be explained in terms of the kinds of causal and counterfactual constructions used to define the simple example relations, then we can draw some conclusions about what propositions must be. Specifically, we can conclude that propositions should be individuated by truth conditions; necessarily equivalent propositions – propositions true under the same conditions – will behave identically in causal and counterfactual constructions, and so should behave

563

identically in contexts explained in terms of those constructions.

The original version that I gave of this argument (in Stalnaker, 1976) made more specific assumptions about the way in which the intentional states, belief and desire, should be analysed – assumptions that I later came to think left out an essential dimension of intentionality (a historical, or backward-looking dimension that is exhibited by the relation of indication). But the argument depended only on very abstract and general features of the kind of analysis proposed, features that are shared by a wide range of different kinds of hypotheses about the nature of the relations that give intentional states their content. Intentional states of agents may have the content they have partly because of facts about the way they came to be, and partly because of the way they dispose the agent to behave, and one need assume nothing about the particular way in which content depends on such facts about the way agents are situated and disposed.

The conception of CONTENT motivated by this argument is one that individuates propositions by their truth conditions. The POSSIBLE WORLDS analysis of proposition – propositions are sets of possible worlds, or functions from possible worlds into truth values – is no more than a way of representing a conception of propositional content that is individuated in this way. In saying this, I am advocating a metaphysically deflationary conception of possible worlds: possible worlds should be understood simply as the elements of the conceptual space used to characterize intentional states and acts. The intuitive idea is this: to form a conception of the world – to have beliefs, or to make suppositions about the world – is to locate it in a space of alternative possibilities; to understand a thought or a statement is to see how that thought or statement locates the world in the relevant space of possibilities.

The possible worlds representation of content provides a conceptual distinction between truth conditions themselves and the statements we use to say what the truth conditions are. The advantage of this conceptual separation is that it gives us the resources to make sense of intentional states that are not expressed in speech, or represented in linguistic form, and to clarify questions about the relation between language and thought (see THOUGHT AND LANGUAGE). Many philosophers in this century have argued or assumed that the order of explanation of intentional phenomena should go from language to thought: first solve the problem of intentionality for language and then explain the intentionality of thought in terms of the intentionality of the language with which thoughts are expressed. This seems to me to get things backwards, but even if one thinks that in some sense speech precedes and is presupposed by thought – it is useful, and begs no questions, to begin with a conceptual distinction between content and the means by which it is expressed, and to have a neutral characterization of content. An explanation of content in terms of speech could take the form of an explanation of the possibilities used to define content in terms of patterns of linguistic behaviour.

While I think the truth-conditional conception of propositional content has considerable intuitive appeal, it was recognized from the beginning that the conclusion of the argument sketched above – that the contents of ordinary mental states are propositions of this kind – has consequences that are strongly counterintuitive, even paradoxical. It seems that if we really believe all necessary equivalents of our beliefs, then we must be essentially logically omniscient, but obviously we are not. Some take the argument as a *reductio ad absurdum* of its assumption. I prefer to take it as the next step in the dialectical discussion of the problem of intentionality: the initial puzzles about intentionality are dissolved by exhibiting unmysterious relations between persons and propositions, including simple relations that are plausibly described as relations of representation. The challenge then is to say what problems about the full-blooded intentional states are not solved by seeing them as states of the same kind as simple representational states that can be shown to be unproblematic. The argument that if intentional content is explained in the way proposed, then propositions must be coarse-grained contents individuated by their truth conditions can be interpreted as an attempt to sharpen the problem in this way.

Whatever further things need to be said about intentional states in order to solve the further problems about them, I think it should not be controversial to conclude that one thing about us that is essentially connected with the fact that we are intentional agents is that we absorb and use information, that intentional states are states involved in such processes, and that seeing them as such is an important part of understanding intentionality. If this is right, then it is reasonable to conclude that the conception of informational content – content individuated by truth conditions – is at least one important aspect of content, one that must play a role in a full story about intentionality. And it is reasonable to conclude that the causal or information-theoretic conception of representation is at least a step on the way to an adequate account of intentionality, a step that provides a context for formulation of further problems. Whether this step is progress or a dead-end depends on whether the further problems that this step leaves us with are problems that it is fruitful to try to solve, and whether the problems that we all share are clarified by being seen in this context. (Some may be inclined to think of the further problems raised by a philosophical account as costs in the cost-benefit analysis used to evaluate such an account. But sometimes the problems faced by an account should be placed on the benefit side. It is the job of a philosophical project to raise problems as well as to solve them, and it may be a limitation of, for example, an analysis of propositions, that it fails to raise certain problems. Of course there is no neutral or easy way to distinguish cases where a real problem has been swept under the rug from cases where a pseudo-problem has been successfully dissolved. To make this distinction, we need to look at the details.)

In conclusion, I will sketch very briefly four clusters of problems about intentional phenomena that arise in the context of the strategy I have advocated for solving the problem of intentionality, and that I think the information theoretic story about intentional relations and the possible worlds conception of propositions that it motivates help to clarify. Then I will comment in a little more detail about the last and most difficult of the problems.

First, there are problems raised by externalism: how to come to terms with the fact, or apparent fact, that meanings, and even beliefs, 'ain't in the head'. (*See* EXTERNALISM/INTERNALISM; PUTNAM.) The thesis that the contents of speech and thought are determined in part by facts about the physical and social environment of the speaker or thinker was given a compelling defence with intuitive examples and thought experiments, but the thesis itself was thought to be paradoxical (*see* TWIN EARTH). How can the contents of my thoughts – the way the world seems to me – depend on facts about my environment that are, in some sense, inaccessible to me? The possible worlds conception of propositions and the information-theoretic conception of intentionality helps to provide the externalist thesis with a theoretical context, to clarify what is paradoxical about it, and to respond at least to some of the reasons for resisting it. (*See* 1989, 1990, 1993.)

Second, there are problems about self-locating, or indexical attitudes. Can my belief that today is Tuesday, my realization that I am late for the meeting, or my wish that my dentist appointment were not tomorrow be understood as attitudes toward impersonal and timeless propositions? I have argued that we can reconcile this phenomenon with the assumption that the contents of belief are propositions, and clarify the status of indexical attitudes and expressions of them, if we define propositions in terms of possible worlds (or at least in terms of relevant alternative possibilities). (*See* 1981.)

Third, there are problems about the relation between intentional states themselves and the semantic devices we use to attribute and describe intentional states. It is widely recognized that attitude ascriptions are highly context dependent, and that some of the problems and puzzles about propositional attitudes arise from the complexities of the way we talk about attitudes rather from complexities in the attitudes being talked about, but it is controversial and unclear exactly how these should be distinguished. If we have a representation of a belief state that is conceptually distinguishable from the language used to describe it, then we can more easily separate questions such as, 'what is the world like according to Pierre?' from questions about the truth or falsity of specific belief attributions. ('Does Pierre believe that London is pretty or not?'). Separating the questions does not by itself resolve the puzzles, but it does help to bring them into focus. (*See* 1987, 1988.)

Fourth, there is the recalcitrant problem alluded to above, the problem of deduction, or of logical omniscience. If the contents of intentional states are individuated by their truth conditions, and if the contents of belief states are explained in terms of the information they tend to carry, then how is it possible to explain the fact that we don't believe all the consequences of our beliefs? To try to reconcile the facts about belief attribution with the thesis that propositions are individuated by truth conditions, I have argued, first, that one should recognize more complexity in the relation between sentences and the propositions they express: even if P and Q, as usually construed, are necessarily equivalent, perhaps they should be construed differently in the relevant belief attribution contexts. Second, it must be recognized that beliefs may be fragmented: one may be in separate belief states that are not integrated into a single conception of the world, and so one may fail to believe conjunctions of propositions that one believes. (*See* Stalnaker, 1984. ch. 5.) I think these strategies show some promise of throwing light on deductive ignorance and enquiry, but it is obvious that there is no quick fix; solving this problem in the terms that are set by the assumptions about inten-

tionality that it makes is a large and daunting project. One might ask, why bother trying to jump over the hurdles that this conception of intentionality and content puts in our way when there are alternative accounts of the contents of intentional states that bypass these problems? Since it is obvious that we take different attitudes toward necessarily equivalent propositions and that we are often ignorant of deductive relationships, why accept an account of intentionality that seems to imply that we are not, or that at least raises the question how it is possible for us to do something that we obviously do? Even if such manœuvres succeed, for the moment, in evading decisive refutation of the hypothesis that the objects of attitudes are coarse-grained propositions, wouldn't it be better to respond more directly to the problem by trying to find a fine-grained conception of proposition that gets the examples right? I concede that some kind of fine-grained object may play a role in the solution to the problem, but simply accepting the thesis that such an object is the content of attitudes is not responsive to the problem. It is clear that the problem of deduction is a genuine problem, and not just an artefact of certain philosophical assumptions; it is a problem that raises its head in theoretical contexts that have no stake in any philosophical account of intentionality, or of the content of intentional states. In accounts of reasoning and knowledge representation studied by theoretical computer scientists, and in accounts of deliberative reasoning in economics, decision theory and game theory, all of the well-understood models of representation, reasoning and decision-making involve the kind of idealization that abstracts away from deductive ignorance, and the fact that they do so is regarded as a major conceptual problem (*see* RATION-ALITY). It is no help with the problem as it arises in those non-philosophical contexts simply to choose a more fine-grained object – for example a structured meaning or a Russellian proposition – as the object of knowledge, belief and partial belief, preference and desire.

The assumption that I started with – that an account of what the objects of belief are must be motivated by an account of what belief is – provides a challenge to the defender of the thesis that the object of belief is some kind of fine-grained object. Suppose we grant that the object denoted by a clause of the form *that P* in an attribution of attitude is a structured meaning containing individuals or individual concepts, truth functions, properties and relations, and so forth. According to this conception, the object of belief is a kind of recipe for determining a coarse-grained informational content; the object is more fine-grained because the same informational content may be determined in different ways – as the values of different functions applied to different things, or to things in a different order. Suppose we grant further that where M and N are two such recipes that determine the same truth-conditional content, an agent might stand in the belief relation to M, but not to N. The challenge is to explain the role of the structure that distinguishes M from N in distinguishing a state of believing M from a state of believing N. Is it, for example, that a claim about what one believes makes a claim, not only about the informational content, but also about the form in which that information is stored in the brain? Or alternatively, is it that a belief attribution makes a claim about the structure of the sentences that a believer is disposed to use to express his belief in speech? I have argued (in Stalnaker, 1990) that neither of these answers is defensible, but even if I am wrong about this, I think that the move to structured propositions is not responsive to the real problem of deduction, or more generally to the problem of intentionality.

One reason that the problem of intentionality is of central philosophical concern is that our conception of a proposition constrains our conception of the distinctions there are to be made in describing the world. The propositions we express in saying how the world is – in doing physics, sociology and metaphysics – must be the propositions that our account of intention-ality says are the objects of speech and thought. If, in our metaphysics, we claim that there is a distinction to be made between the world being such that P and being such that Q, and a fact of the matter about which way it is, then our account of intentionality must allow that there is a distinction between believing or supposing or expressing the thought that P and believing, supposing, or expressing the thought that Q. This is an obvious point, but in the light of it, at least some of the disputes between proponents of coarse-grained informational contents and fine-grained structured meanings or Russellian propositions can be seen as a side issue for the following reason. Whatever view of propositions one takes, one may distinguish two questions about anything (for example, an utterance or an intentional mental state) that expresses a proposition: (1) what information does it convey (where this is understood to mean, what is the informational content – the coarse-grained proposition expressed), and (2) by what means does it convey that information? A fine-grained account of the object of belief is an account that says that the object referred to in the that-clause of an attitude attribution is an object that answers a part of question (2) as well as question (1), whereas the coarse-grained account says that the referent of a that-clause answers question (1), but says nothing about question (2). But whatever view one takes about this issue, if one of the things at stake in an account of intention-ality is the range of possibilities that we have the capacity to represent, then it is important to distinguish the question of informational content from the question of the means by which that content is expressed, and it is only the first that is relevant to this concern.

If we rely on an intuitive distinction between content and form – between what is said or thought and how it is said or thought – then everyone will of course agree that to say what a person says or thinks is to say only what that person says or thinks, and not to say how it was said or thought. The problem is that distinctions

567

between fine-grained propositions seem, from an intuitive point of view, to be distinctions of content. If I am ignorant of the fact that 343 is 7 cubed, then it seems intuitively that I lack a piece of information, and not just that I fail to use a certain means to represent the necessary proposition. This is indeed a problem – it is, I think, the most pressing remaining part of the problem of intentionality. But the problem is evaded rather than solved by a conception of content that simply builds a part of the means by which content is represented into the object that is called 'content'. The real problem is to understand the nature of the information that is conveyed, expressed or stored when one conveys, expresses or stores information that does not seem, on the face of it, to be explainable in terms of distinctions between possibilities. The account of intentionality that I have been promoting does not offer an easy solution to this problem, but I think it does help to bring it into focus.

See also DENNETT; DRETSKE; FODOR; THOUGHT.

BIBLIOGRAPHY

Stalnaker, R. 1976. Propositions. In *Issues in the Philosophy of Language*, ed. A. MacKay and D. Merrill. New Haven and London: Yale University Press.
—— 1981. Indexical belief. *Synthèse*, 49, 129–51.
—— 1984. *Inquiry*. Cambridge, MA.: MIT Press/Bradford Books.
—— 1987. Semantics for belief. *Philosophical Topics*, 15, 177–90.
—— 1988. Belief attribution and context. In *Contents of Thought*, ed. R. Grimm and D. Merrill. Tucson: University of Arizona Press.
—— 1989. On what's in the head. In *Philosophical Perspectives, 3: Philosophy of Mind and Action Theory*; reprinted in *The Nature of Mind*, ed. D. M. Rosenthal. Oxford University Press.
—1990a. Mental content and linguistic form. *Philosophical Studies*, 58, 129–46.
—1990b. Narrow content. In *Propositional Attitudes: The Role of Content in Logic, Language and Mind*, ed. C. A. Anderson and J. Owens. Stanford: CSLI.
—— 1991. The problem of logical omniscience, I. *Synthèse*, 89, 425–40.
—— 1993. Twin Earth revisited. *Proceedings of the Aristotelian Society*, XCIII, 297–311.

ROBERT STALNAKER

subjectivity With a fair amount of irony, and a goodly amount of truth, one may say that 'subjectivity' means different things to different people. This entry will discuss three notions of subjectivity. There is, first, the subjectivity of phenomenal experience. By 'phenomenality', I mean the 'feel' of certain of our experiences. Because a great deal has been said about phenomenality elsewhere in this volume (*see* CONSCIOUSNESS; QUALIA), only a little will be said here. Second, there is a notion of subjectivity associated with THE WILL. This notion is central to developmental psychologists, like Piaget; and the greatest part of the present entry will focus on it. This notion of subjectivity underlies one's concept of oneself as a *subject* of experience, distinguished, in the first place, from the objects of experience, and, latterly, from other subjects of experience as well. The third idea of subjectivity, tied in a deep way to a notion of a point of view, is the realization that one is not only a different subject of experience from other subjects of experience but also that the world is *experienced differently* by different subjects of experience. This third idea of subjectivity is also prominent among DEVELOPMENTAL PSYCHOLOGISTS and is closely tied to the previous one: that of a subject of experience.

PHENOMENALITY

People experience phenomenal states. Perceptual and other sensory experiences, especially, seem to possess phenomenal qualities (qualia). It is very difficult to say exactly what phenomenal states or properties are; but, in experiencing them, we somehow distinguish them from other sorts of states, and from each other. An ice-cube just feels different from a warm compress; a blue cube just looks different from a red square; a mental image of a blue circle just 'looks' different from an image of a red square; and a toothache just feels different from the SENSATION of relief that occurs when the tooth stops hurting.

Although there is no way to capture it completely, the idea of phenomenality is perhaps best expressed in Nagel's (1974, 1979a) well-known claim (I will call it 'Nagel's slogan') that when an organism experiences phenomenality, there is *something it is like to be* that organism. Nagel points out that we could know the physiology of a bat's 'sonar' sense and still not know what it is like to *be* a bat. We would not know what the bat's sonar experience feels like *for the bat*. In a similar way, a congenitally blind person is unable to grasp what the quality of a sighted person's colour experience is like.

Closely related to Nagel's slogan is the *privacy* of phenomenal states. Phenomenal states are individuated by the person whose states they are, as are broken arms; but while both Sarah and Benjamin can observe Sarah's broken arm, only Sarah can feel the pain caused by it. If Benjamin feels pain on observing Sarah's broken arm, that is Benjamin's pain, not Sarah's. Benjamin cannot observe or experience Sarah's pain – at least not in the direct way Sarah can. The same is true for all other phenomenal states.

Besides this ontological privacy of phenomenal states, various forms of epistemological privacy are claimed for them. (i) Only the person experiencing a phenomenal state can *know* he or she is experiencing it and what it is like; others can have, at best, only probable beliefs about it. (ii) One knows one is experiencing some phenomenal state – pain, for instance – simply by experiencing it; no other criteria are required. (iii) If one is in a given phenomenal state, then one knows oneself to be in that state. (iv) If one believes oneself to be in that state, then one *knows* oneself to be in that state.

While ontological privacy and epistemological privacy have often been thought to go hand in hand, they are distinct (as are the epistemological forms from each other). Furthermore, the privacy claims might be questioned. (1) How do we know that only a single person can experience a given phenomenal state? Is this a deep fact about phenomenal states, or only a convention of our use of words like 'pain', 'after-image', and so forth? (2) If only the person undergoing a phenomenal experience – say, pain – can know it, and knows it only on the basis of experiencing it, how did that person ever come to have a concept of that sort of experience? Call the person P. Surely, one may argue, the person would at best have a concept of P-pain, not of pain itself. If so, one could never ascribe this state to *others*, for others cannot have P-pains. So, if the privacy claims were correct, solipsism would follow. (3) Worse, could the person even acquire the concept of P-pain? What would be the criteria for whether instances fell under the concept? What would be the criteria of relevant similarity among instances? Wouldn't it be a case of whatever one says goes? If so, such a 'criterion' is inadequate for concept possession. (*See An Essay on Mind* section 2.2.)

Such questions and objections, only mentioned here, have at times been backed by extensive use of argument and example. The most famous of these discussions is WITTGENSTEIN'S (1953) 'Private-language Argument'. But exactly what the argument is, and what its intended target is, are in dispute. Wittgenstein has been read variously as saying that there are no phenomenal states that are private, even ontologically; as saying that phenomenal states are not sufficient determiners of *pain* (and other sensations) – an interpretation supported by the first part of the 'beetle in the box' paragraph: 'Here it would be quite possible for everyone to have something different in his box' (1953, §293, 100e); or as saying that phenomenal states are not even necessary to pains (and other sensations) – as suggested by the second claim of the 'beetle in the box' paragraph: 'The box might even be empty'. No modern discussion of phenomenal subjectivity can avoid considering the issues raised by Wittgenstein.

One last set of remarks on phenomenality. It is often claimed that Nagel's slogan applies to another sort of experience, which is not quite like phenomenal experience. It might be agreed, for instance, that there is no phenomenal experience required for thinking that a 1000-sided figure is larger than a 999-sided one – phenomenal experiences (mental images and the like) at most *accompany* such thoughts. But one might go on to claim that such thoughts are 'felt', even if not *felt*, and that we are aware of these 'feelings' when we introspect our thinking. 'How else *could* we be conscious of our thoughts?' seems to be the motivating question. For we usually are conscious that we are thinking such thoughts. If so, there must be a *basis* for our awareness. Surely, the claim runs, it just 'feels' different when we are thinking this thought from when we are not. And these 'feelings' are the basis of our consciousness of the thought. Thoughts (and other experiences like them) have *phenomenological* properties, even if not phenomenal ones; and it is these properties that constitute the *experience* of those thoughts.

My own view is to be sceptical about the existence of such properties. Like Hume, when he looked inside himself but could not find his *self*, when I look inside myself, I find no such states. I don't mean to deny that I am able to introspect my thoughts; but thoughts, and the introspecting of them, have *no* phenomenal, or phenomenal-like, properties. And Nagel's slogan does not apply to mental states like thought, belief, hope, and so forth (*see* Nelkin, 1993, for a fuller argument).

For similar reasons, it is a mistake to treat all notions of subjectivity on the paradigm of phenomenal states. Other notions of subjectivity can be usefully discussed without even mentioning phenomenal states.

SUBJECTIVITY AND THE WILL

Nagel (1979a, 1986) has spent a good deal of time discussing two ways of viewing the world: the objective and the subjective. An objective point of view involves viewing the world from an 'impartial', third-person aspect, while the subjective point of view involves viewing the world as it appears to *oneself* from a 'partial', first-person aspect. Nagel conflates this 'first-personness' with his slogan that there is something it is like to be that person, but these are different notions of subjectivity. As we will see, the notion of a *subject of experience*, the quintessential notion of subjectivity, need make no reference to any sort of phenomenal feeling (or phenomenological 'feeling', for that matter).

Nagel argues that, on many questions of life, whether descriptive or normative, the subjective and objective views are incompatible and that there is no way to resolve disputes between them. Before investigating this claim, we will consider a prior question. How do we separate the subjective and the objective in the first place? And for answering this question, the most interesting set of views to turn to are those that might broadly be called Piagetian (*see* Piaget, 1954; Piaget and Inhelder, 1969).

We have good reason to believe that human beings have no simple relation of apprehension and belief to the world they inhabit. PERCEPTION involves large amounts of processing; and whether one believes perception is representational (as do most psychologists) or non-representational (as do followers of J. J. Gibson), all would agree that the perceptual story is a highly complex one (*see* REPRESENTATION, IMAGERY). And if concepts and beliefs based on perception are prior to any of our other concepts and beliefs, then certain difficult questions need answers. For instance, if we are in a sense being bombarded by information from the external world, but in a fashion such that the information needs to be filtered, processed, subtracted from, added to, attended to, recognized, and so on in order to be useful, how does our perceptual experience ever lead us to conceive our SELF, as a *subject* of that experience, and the world of spatiotemporal things that make up the notself, as the *object* of that experience?

Piagetians believe that we are able to make these distinctions because there is, *given as a primitive in our experience*, a recognition of a distinction between doing things and having things happen to us. Because we can sometimes manipulate the world, we come to distinguish our self (the subjective), from the out-there (the objective). The story to follow is brief and oversimplified (and not every Piagetian would agree to every part of the story), but it gives the flavour of a Piagetian view (a view with which I am broadly in sympathy).

As newborn infants (though there is evidence that the process begins before we are born – fetuses seem to *initiate* movements in the womb), we are presented with an unbroken stream of experience (where 'experience' includes more than phenomenal states – *see* Nelkin, 1989). This stream, as such, displays neither its types nor its tokens on its surface. The neonate's experience is a 'buzzing, blooming confusion'. However, two factors allow the infant to begin sorting this undifferentiated stream into tokens and types.

The first factor is INTROSPECTION: the infant is aware of its awareness of at least some of this unbroken stream. The second factor is that in some cases the infant is able to affect and effect its own experiences, while in others it is not. Putting these two factors together, Piagetians maintain that the infant finds itself apparently in control of some of its experiences, while finding that other experiences are apparently not in its control. There is evidence that infants are already aware of this distinction as early as eight weeks of age. Piagetians claim that infants are aware of this distinction right from the beginning. The words, 'finds itself' are somewhat misleading, because at this point the infant has no awareness of itself *as itself*, i.e. no concept of a self.

It may be objected that infants cannot *do* anything, so they cannot be in control of any of their experiences. But experiments show that newborn infants can do quite a bit. They can turn their heads, move their eyes, fix them on an object, track an object as it moves, kick their legs, and wave their arms – among other things. When they do these things, their experiences alter.

The basic distinction neonates are able to make, then, is that of in-control/not-in-control. The dichotomy is an either-or one: either *this* (kind of) cause of experience (an in-control experience – an action) or *that* (kind of) cause of experience (a not-in-control experience – not an action). This primitive distinction allows the infant to begin dividing the stream at first into tokens. (These parts of the stream were in-control; those parts, not-in-control.) Equally important, the in-control/not-in-control distinction is also the basis for the first *type* distinction, which I will call the me/not-me (or self/not-self) distinction, though the name is somewhat misleading, because at this point the 'me' is not exactly conceived of as an individual thing, a self. We can think of it as a kind of *proto-self* (and there is evidence in the developmental literature for this proto-self). The not-me is also not yet individualized, but it can be thought of as the proto-external-world (the proto-out-there). It is crucial to emphasize that the in-control/not-in-control distinction underlies both one's primitive concepts of one's very self and of an external world. It is only because one takes oneself to successfully *will* certain behaviours, but not others, that this primitive (and primary) distinction of self and other can be made. All concept formation begins with this in-control/not-in-control distinction and our introspective awareness of *it*.

To continue the story, we need to focus on the not-self. The not-self, as cause of those experiences that are not-in-control, gets broken up, by whatever mechanisms, into objects: *bodies*. And those bodies are categorized into *types* of objects. Only after bodies are differentiated do we come to recognize our *self* as an individual thing: a *body* inhabiting the same world as all other bodies, yet different, as a token, from all other bodies. Perception itself also leads to this same notion of a bodily self (*see* Gibson, 1979). We first identify our individual *self* as a *body*, one that not only has shape, size, and so forth, but also is a subject of experi-

571

ence: one that *thinks* – especially one that wills. We then come to perceive that our self, this particular body, is a member of a type: human being. So we come thereby to ascribe subjectivity to all members of the type, to all human beings (and also to many other animals, though to human beings first and foremost).

There is much evidence for this account in the development literature. For instance, infants seem to grasp at least a crude idea of bodies very early in the first year of life, but the idea of the mental is not evidenced until the middle of the second year. When an infant does grasp the mental as divisible into types, it ascribes those states to itself first, only later to others (and, then, first to human beings; later, to other animals). Although we ascribe the mental features of human beings to our self first, we apparently learn human body parts first of others, and only later as ascribable to our self. That is, only when we conceive of our self as the *same* type as other human beings do we begin to ascribe subjectivity to others.

On this account, underlying all concept formation is an essential subjectivity: that *experiential* distinction of the in-control from the not-in-control, and an introspective capacity that makes one aware of this distinction in one's own experience. But the underlying, essential subjectivity is one of will and introspection, not of phenomenal states.

With this brief, Piagetian account as background, there is a road that appears to be open, one which leads swiftly to the fundamental tension that Nagel (1979a) finds between the subjective and the objective (though the 'road' represents only one way of interpreting the Piagetian account). An important feature of the above account of concept formation is that we first understand subjects of experience (thinking, willing beings) – our own self and others – as *physical* objects: objects in space and time. The mind/body division comes only later. As we come to realize that the body is often outside our control – as in disease, or when a bodily part is asleep, or when we are frozen with fear, and so on – we are

tempted to identify the self only with our mental activities, especially with our will. Inherent in these loss-of-control experiences is an increased recognition of how much is out of our control, of how even what we believed to be in our control is instead at the mercy of external forces.

Finally, we come to realize that our very mind is often out of our control. Despite our best efforts, we cannot stop thinking about someone or something; despite our strong wishes not to, we cannot help eating a second pastry; and so forth. At this point we begin to suspect that our very self, however we identify it, is not in our control, that we are always in subjection to the not-self, that our sense of being in control is only an illusion. When we view ourselves from the objective, impartial world of science, we seem to be influenced, both in action and thought, by external causes as much as is anything we label an object.

In initially identifying our self, we relied on a sense of control that made it appear that our actions originate entirely within ourselves. This sense was not one of omnipotence (as Freud thought): without a recognition of the not-in-control, we would not have had a concept of self at all. Rather it was a sense of total freedom in those actions over which we took ourselves to have control. But at some point we discover that we are not, and never have been, the sole and unfettered origin of our own behaviours. The external world hinders/helps our actions, it affects our very thoughts, and it influences or thwarts our very will itself. The sense of control, of autonomy, looks to be mere illusion.

But if the key ingredient – the in-control – is illusory, what can be said of all the crucial distinctions based on it? If we can be so wrong about that very foundation for making all distinctions, if our sense of control is not itself based in fact, then how can we be certain – how can we be anything but uncertain – about the resulting distinctions themselves? Why shouldn't illusion just give rise to further illusion? It all begins to slide away. All the distinctions dependent on our sense of control – *all* our distinctions – seem threatened: that there is a community we are part of; our very self; our very world. No wonder the problem of free will is so disturbing.

This *essential subjectivity* – the sense of control – underlies our 'discovery' not only of self but also of the objective. Moreover, and ironically, objective science – in this case, developmental psychology – provides a basis for believing that this essential subjectivity itself exists. Yet, at the same time, objective science seems to tell us that such a subjectivity is an illusion. Science tells us that no causes can be autonomous in the sense required for the in-control/not-in-control distinction to be genuine. But if the subjectivity that underlies all our distinctions is itself called into question, then our hold on both the subjective *and the objective* is loosened, for the path to the objective is by way of the subjective. It is only because of the in-control (the subjective) that we ever come to recognize the not-in-control (the objective world), but then 'objectively' we come to doubt the subjective altogether. There appears to be no resting place. Our only basis for believing in the objective is the subjective, and the objective tells us the subjective is illusory. It is this tension that Nagel, perhaps more than anyone else since Kant, has realized and called to our attention.

If there is no solution to these problems, then it appears that there really is a fundamental tension in our lives: the subjective leading inevitably to the objective, and the objective casting doubt on the autonomy of the essential subjectivity that made distinguishing the objective possible.

Is there any solution to this problem? Certainly attempts have been made to solve it (Nagel just recognizes it, but makes no real attempt to solve it). Kant tried to solve the problem by putting the *real* subject of experience in a different world altogether: the transcendent, non-empirical world. For Kant, the empirical self is an *object* like all other objects. It is not the subject whose subjectivity underlies all distinctions, the one that makes experience of *things* possible.

Buddhism may be seen as another sort of attempt to resolve the problem. The aim of meditation is to 'escape' into that pure subjectivity that precedes all distinction, that precedes any notion of the objective, but also precedes any notion of the subjective, of the self. The aim of Buddhist meditation is to eliminate the self, to eliminate the subjective/objective distinction itself.

Another, more familiar, solution to the problem is to defend some sort of soft determinism (compatibilism). Compatibilists argue that the problem is a spurious one, the result of identifying the crucial notion of 'in-control' with a not-understandable notion of 'autonomy'. Compatibilists claim that a more realistic notion of 'in-control' will do the Piagetian job of making concept formation explainable, without getting us into all the apparent metaphysical entanglements that Nagel, Kant, and Buddhism each claims to see.

Whether Kant, Buddhists, or compatibilists actually resolve the paradox seen by Nagel (who doesn't put the paradox in quite the way I have), is beyond the scope of this entry to evaluate. But the notion of subjectivity discussed in this section, the gist of which remains whether Nagel or one of the others is right, puts much of the history of philosophy into clear relief – in addition to providing an apparently coherent and evidence-sensitive theory of concept formation.

One's realization of oneself as a subject of experience, based on the idea of the in-control, also makes understandable why many philosophers have identified persons with their subjectivity. Persons, whatever else they are, seem to be enduring things. If the essential subjectivity that makes a distinction of self possible is rooted in the will, then that subject of experience must endure in time. To be *in-control* is to have one's plans (and intentions) for the future result as one planned (or intended), for one to remember – when the actions do result as planned (or intended) – that one had planned (or intended) these results, and so on. The notion of 'in-control' is a time-encompassing notion. The person *in-control* must be a *thing* which persists through the relevant time-span (or be a construction of things which participate in this process – as suggested by Locke, and defended by Parfit (1984), who claims that persons are constructions out of person-stages). Since one's subjectivity persists, it is natural to make the identification of self and subjectivity.

Yet, even if subjectivity makes possible our conceiving of our self in the first place, it may still be a mistake to *identify* persons with that subjectivity rather than as bodily things (I think it *is* a mistake). While this topic has been widely investigated, like most philosophical questions, it bears considerably more investigation.

POINTS OF VIEW

The third notion of subjectivity, as Nagel again sees, is the notion of a *point of view*, what psychologists call a constructivist theory of mind (Chandler, 1988). Undoubtedly, this notion is closely tied to the notion of essential subjectivity, but it is worth discussing in its own right. This kind of subjectivity is constituted by an awareness of the world's being experienced differently by different subjects of experience. (It is thus possible to see how the privacy of phenomenal experience might be easily confused with the kind of privacy inherent in a point of view.)

Point-of-view subjectivity (PVS) seems to take time to develop. The developmental evidence suggests that even toddlers are able to understand others as being subjects of experience. For instance, at a very early age, we begin ascribing mental states to other things – generally to those same things to which we ascribe 'eating' (Carey, 1985). And at quite an early age we can say what others would see from where they are standing, i.e. we early on demonstrate an understanding that the information available is different from different perceptual points of view, and so to different perceivers. It is in these perceptual senses that we first ascribe PVS to others.

However, some experiments seem to show that the PVS then ascribed to others is limited. A well-known and influential series of experiments by Wimmer and Perner (1983) is usually taken to illustrate these limitations (though there are disagreements about the interpretation of these and the other experiments to be mentioned). Two children – Dick and Jane, say – watch as an experimenter puts a box of candy somewhere, such as in a cookie jar, which is opaque. Jane leaves the room. Dick is asked where Jane will look for the candies, and he correctly answers, 'In the cookie jar'. The experimenter, in Dick's view, then takes the candy out of the cookie jar and puts it in another opaque place, a drawer, say. When Dick is asked where to look for the candy, he says quite correctly, 'In the drawer'. When asked where Jane will look for the candy when she returns, Dick answers, 'In the drawer'. Dick ascribes to Jane, not the PVS she is likely to have, but the one that fits the facts. Dick is unable to ascribe to Jane *false* beliefs – his ascription is 'reality driven' – and his inability demonstrates that Dick does not yet have a fully developed PVS.

At around the age of four, children in Dick's position do ascribe the likely PVS to children in Jane's position (i.e. 'Jane will look in the cookie jar'); but, even so, a fully developed notion of a PVS is not yet attained. Suppose that Dick and Jane are shown a dog under a tree, but only Dick is shown the dog's arriving there by chasing a boy up the tree. If Dick is asked to describe what Jane, who he knows not to have seen the chase, will describe when seeing the dog under the tree, Dick will display a more fully developed PVS only if his description will not entail the preliminaries that only he witnessed. It turns out that four-year-olds, despite passing the Wimmer-Perner test, are unable to pass role-playing tests such as this one. Only when children are six to seven do they succeed.

Yet, even when successful in these cases, children's PVS is reality-driven. Ascribing a PVS to others is still in terms relative to information available. Only in our teens do we seem capable of understanding that others can view the world differently from ourselves, even when given access to the same information. Only then do we seem to become aware of the subjectivity of the knowing procedure itself: interpreting the 'facts' can be coloured by one's knowing procedure and history. There are no 'merely' objective facts.

Thus, there is evidence that we ascribe a more and more subjective point of view to others: from the PVSs we ascribe being completely reality-driven, to the possibility that others have insufficient information, to their having merely different information, and, finally, to their understanding the same information differently. This developmental picture seems insufficiently familiar to philosophers – and yet well worth our thinking about and critically evaluating.

The following questions all need answering. Does the apparent fact that our PVS ascriptions to others develop over time, becoming more and more of a 'private' notion, shed any light on the sort of subjectivity we ascribe even to our own self? Do our self-ascriptions of subjectivity themselves become more and more 'private', more and more removed both from the subjectivity of others and from the objective world? If so, what is the philosophical importance of these facts? At the least, this developmental history shows that disentangling our self from the world we live in is a complicated matter.

CONCLUSION

Even this brief survey makes clear that 'subjectivity' is not the name of a single concept, but names a set of intertwining and overlapping concepts. I have discussed three notions: phenomenality, will, and point of view. And three claims are worth re-emphasizing. (1) Nagel's slogan – that there is something it is like to be in a subjective state – applies only to phenomenality. (2) The subjectivity associated with a sense of control is the deepest sort of subjectivity, underlying all concept formation, including one's concept of one's very self. (3) Finally, experimentation seems to show that the PVS we ascribe to others becomes more and more sophisticated, more and more *subjective*.

BIBLIOGRAPHY

Carey, S. 1985. *Conceptual Change in Childhood*. Cambridge, MA: MIT Press/Bradford Books.

Chandler, M. 1988. Doubt and developing theories of mind. *Developing Theories of Mind*, ed. J. W. Astington, P. L. Harris, and D. R. Olson. Cambridge University Press.

Gibson, J.J. 1979. *The Ecological Approach to Vision*. Boston: Houghton-Mifflin; reprinted 1986, Hillsdale, N.J.: Lawrence Erlbaum.

Nagel, T. 1974. What is it like to be a bat? *Philosophical Review*, 83, 435–50.

Nagel, T. 1979a. *Mortal Questions*. Cambridge University Press.

Nagel, T. 1979b. Moral luck. In Nagel, 1979, pp. 24–38.

Nagel, T. 1986. *The View from Nowhere*. Oxford University Press.

Nelkin, N. 1989. Propositional attitudes and consciousness. *Philosophy and Phenomenological Research*, 49, 413–30.

Nelkin, N. 1993. What is consciousness? *Philosophy of Science*, 60, 419–34.

Parfit, D. 1984. *Reasons and Persons*. Oxford: Clarendon Press.

Piaget, J. 1954. *The Construction of Reality in the Child*, trans. Margaret Cook. New York: Basic Books.

Piaget, J., and Inhelder, B. 1969. *The Psychology of the Child*, trans. H. Weaver. New York: Basic Books.

Wimmer, H., and Perner, J. 1983. Beliefs about beliefs: representation and constraining the function of wrong beliefs in young children's understanding of deception. *Cognition*, 13, 103–28.

Wittgenstein, L. 1953. *Philosophical Investigations*. Oxford: Basil Blackwell.

I would like to thank Edward Johnson, Carolyn Morillo, and Samuel Guttenplan for comments made on earlier drafts of this entry.

NORTON NELKIN

supervenience During the past two decades or so, the concept of supervenience has seen increasing service in philosophy of mind. The thesis that the mental is supervenient on the physical – roughly, the claim that the mental character of a thing is wholly determined by its physical nature –

575

has played a key role in the formulation of some influential positions on the MIND–BODY PROBLEM, in particular versions of non-reductive PHYSICALISM. Mind–body supervenience has also been invoked in arguments for or against certain specific claims about the mental, and has been used to devise solutions to some central problems about the mind – for example, the problem of mental causation (see PROPOSITIONAL ATTITUDES; REASONS AND CAUSES). There are also questions about mind–body supervenience itself, such as exactly how it ought to be formulated, what its relationship is to mind–body reduction, whether certain types of mental states, such as 'QUALIA' and intentional states, are plausibly regarded as physically supervenient, and what the implications are for physicalism if they fail to supervene.

The idea of supervenience is usually thought to have originated in moral theory, in the works of such philosophers as G. E. Moore and R. M. Hare (see below, however, on emergentism). Hare, for example, claimed that ethical predicates are 'supervenient predicates' in the sense that no two things (persons, acts, states of affairs) could be exactly alike in all descriptive or naturalistic respects but unlike in that some ethical predicate ('good', 'right', etc.) truly applies to one but not to the other. That is, there could be no difference in a moral respect without a difference in some descriptive, or non-moral, respect. Evidently the idea is generalizable so as to apply to any two sets of properties (to secure greater generality it is more convenient to speak of PROPERTIES than predicates). Donald DAVIDSON (1970) was perhaps first to introduce supervenience into discussions of the mind–body problem, when he wrote: '. . . mental characteristics are in some sense dependent, or supervenient, on physical characteristics. Such supervenience might be taken to mean that there cannot be two events alike in all physical respects but differing in some mental respect, or that an object cannot alter in some mental respect without altering in some physical respect.' Following Moore and Hare, from

whom he avowedly borrowed the idea of supervenience, Davidson went on to assert that supervenience in this sense is consistent with the irreducibility of the supervenient to their 'subvenient', or 'base', properties: 'Dependence or supervenience of this kind does not entail reducibility through law or definition . . .'

Thus, three ideas have come to be closely associated with supervenience: (1) *property covariation* (if two things are indiscernible in base properties, they must be indiscernible in supervenient properties); (2) *Dependence* (supervenient properties are dependent on, or determined by, their subvenient bases); and (3) *non-reducibility* (property covariation and dependence involved in supervenience can obtain even if supervenient properties are not reducible to their base properties).

Hellman and Thompson (1975), apparently independently of earlier writers, proposed a model-theoretic analysis of *determination*, in terms of which they formulated a version of physicalism free of reductionist commitments. The central thesis of their physicalism is the claim that the physical facts of the world 'determine' all the facts, including facts concerning the mental. Interestingly, their concept of determination turns out to be a form of what is now known as 'global supervenience' (see below), although they did not use the terminology of 'supervenience' and seem not to have been aware of the historical antecedents of their approach.

These writers, however, were not the first to use the idea of supervenience, or the term 'supervenience', in connection with the mind–body problem. The emergentists, who were active during the first half of this century, especially in Britain, sometimes used 'supervenient' as a stylistic variant of 'emergent' (especially Lloyd Morgan, 1923), and there is a striking similarity between emergence and supervenience. According to emergentism, higher-level properties, notably CONSCIOUSNESS and other mental properties, emerge when, and only when, an appropriate set of lower-level 'basal conditions' are present, and this means that the occurrence of the higher properties is determined by, and dependent on, the instantiation of appropriate lower-level properties and relations. In spite of this, emergent properties were held to be 'genuinely novel' characteristics irreducible to the lower-level processes from which they emerge. Clearly, then, the concept of emergence combines the three components of supervenience delineated above, namely property covariance, dependence, and non-reducibility. In fact, emergentism can be regarded as the first systematic formulation of non-reductive physicalism.

TYPES OF PROPERTY COVARIATION

The idea that mentality supervenes on physical-biological nature arises quite intuitively. Suppose that we could build an exact physical replica of you, a creature who is molecule-for-molecule, cell-for-cell, indistinguishable from you. (It would make no difference if your replica had been naturally created.) Would this creature, who is physically indiscernible from you, be also psychologically indiscernible? To put it another way: are *physical duplicates* necessarily *psychological duplicates* as well? If you are inclined to answer yes, that means that you are disposed to accept mind–body supervenience: no two things (organisms, events, etc.) could differ in a mental respect unless they differed in some physical respect – that is, indiscernibility with respect to physical properties entails indiscernibility with respect to mental properties. That is the core idea of mind–body supervenience.

Recent work has shown, however, that this core idea can be explicated in various non-equivalent, but interestingly related, ways, yielding supervenience claims of varying strengths (Kim, 1984, 1987). In what follows, we will assume that our domain consists of organisms and other structures of interest from the psychological point of view (which could include electromechanical systems, parts of whole organisms, etc.), and that two sets of properties are defined over this domain, one, M, consisting of mental properties and the other, P, consisting of physical properties (in the

broad sense that includes biological as well as physicochemical properties). If we wish, we could think of 'states' and 'events' as an organism's (or structure's) instantiating, or changing in respect of, one or more of these properties at a time. Thus, the supervenience of events and states can be explained in terms of property supervenience. In any case, what is it *for M to supervene on P over our domain* (henceforth we will often delete reference to the domain)?

We may begin with the following:

Weak supervenience: Necessarily (that is, in every possible world), if any x and y (in the domain) are indiscernible in P ('P-indiscernible' for short), x and y are M-indiscernible.

On weak mind–body supervenience, then, no possible world contains two individuals which are alike in respect of properties in P but unlike in some mental property in M. It is clear that if P were so comprehensive (e.g. it includes spatiotemporal locations as physical properties) that no two individuals in the domain could have exactly the same P-properties, weak supervenience would hold trivially, no matter what the supervenient properties are. To generate a meaningful thesis of weak supervenience, therefore, P may be appropriately circumscribed (e.g. to biological properties, computational properties, etc.).

Suppose you are creating worlds: weak supervenience prohibits you from placing in the same world physical duplicates that are not mental duplicates. But it does not prohibit you from creating two physical duplicates that are not mental duplicates *as long as you put them in different worlds*. The distinctive feature of weak supervenience is that its constraint applies only *intra-world*, not *cross-world*; that is, the way in which mental and physical properties are distributed in one world places no restriction whatever on how they may be distributed in another world. In fact, weak mind–body supervenience permits: (1) a world which is exactly like the actual world in all physical

577

respects but which is totally devoid of mentality; (2) worlds that are physically just like our world but in which everything is conscious in exactly the same way; and (3) worlds that, again, are physically indistinguishable from our world but in which unicellular organisms, but no humans or other higher animals, are conscious. The conclusion seems unavoidable, then, that weak supervenience is not strong enough to support the kind of mind–body *dependence* demanded by robust physicalism. Physicalism must require at least this much: physical facts of a world *determine* all the facts of that world. This means that once physical properties have been distributed over the individuals in a certain way, that leaves but one way to distribute psychological properties. But that is precisely what is not required by weak supervenience.

Consider then the following two theses of mind–body supervenience:

Global supervenience: Any two worlds that are indiscernible with respect to *P* (i.e. worlds in which physical properties are distributed over the individuals in the same way) are indiscernible with respect to *M* (that is, they cannot differ in how mental properties are distributed).

Strong supervenience: For any individuals x and y, and any worlds w_j and w_k, if x in w_j is *P*-indiscernible from y in w_k (that is, x has in w_j exactly the same properties in *P* that y has in w_k), then x in w_j is *M*-indiscernible from y in w_k.

Global supervenience applies indiscernibility considerations globally, to whole worlds taken as units rather than to individuals within worlds, and requires that worlds that are indistinguishable from the physical point of view do not differ from the mental point of view, although of course worlds that are alike mentally could differ in physical respects. This evidently explicates one clear sense in which the mental character of a world can be said to depend on, or be determined by, its physical character.

Strong supervenience, unlike global supervenience, applies indiscernibility considerations 'locally', to individuals, not directly to whole worlds. It says of any individuals from anywhere in the panoply of all possible worlds that they cannot differ psychologically without differing physically. Strong supervenience, therefore, differs from weak supervenience in that individuals compared for indiscernibility may be recruited from different worlds, whereas on weak supervenience individuals are compared only as they are within the same world. This is why the constraint of strong supervenience, unlike that of weak supervenience, applies cross-world as well as intra-world.

It is easily seen that strong supervenience entails both global and weak supervenience, and that weak supervenience entails neither strong nor global supervenience (Kim, 1984, 1987). Does global supervenience entail strong or weak supervenience? It *formally* implies neither (Kim, 1987; Paull and Sider, 1992), but this does not fully settle the issue, since there may be plausible metaphysical premises which together with global supervenience yield strong supervenience (Paull and Sider, 1992; Kim, 1993). Moreover, it has been shown (Paull and Sider, 1992) that when restricted to 'intrinsic properties', strong and global supervenience are fully equivalent.

SUPERVENIENCE AND NON-REDUCTIVE PHYSICALISM

For various reasons, psychophysical reductionism, or type physicalism, had lost favour with philosophers by the early 1970s, and many physicalists looked for a way of characterizing the primacy and priority of the physical that is free from reductionist implications. As we saw with Davidson and Hellman and Thompson, the key attraction of supervenience to physicalists has been its promise to deliver *dependence without reduction*. Here, the example of moral theory has seemed encouraging: Moore and Hare, who made much of the supervenience of the moral on the naturalistic, were, at the same time, strong critics of ethical naturalism, the principal reductionist position in ethical theory. And there has been a broad consensus among ethical theorists that Moore and Hare were right, that the moral, or more broadly the normative, is supervenient on the non-moral without being reducible to it.

The issue is complicated, however. For one thing, it is possible that Moore and Hare were just wrong about the relationship between supervenience and reducibility. For another, the issue surely depends on the kind of supervenience involved and what one understands by 'reduction'. It may well be that the sense of reduction appropriate for the mind–body case differs crucially from the kind of a priori definitional reduction Moore and other ethical theorists apparently had in mind; and the supervenience relations involved in the two cases may be dissimilar in some respect that makes a difference to the question of reduction.

Most anti-reductionist arguments concerning the mental focus on the availability of type-type correlations between the mental and the physical – that is, correlations between mental and physical properties. The heart of these arguments is that psychophysical reduction requires such correlations, but that they are unavailable. But what sorts of correlations are required for reduction? Logical BEHAVIOURISM tried to provide each mental predicate with an analytically equivalent definition framed exclusively in terms of physical-behavioural expressions; so the behaviouristic reduction was to be implemented by providing every mental property with an analytically equivalent physical property, a project abandoned as entirely hopeless several decades ago. The demise of logical behaviourism has led would-be reductionists to look to the model of *nomological reduction*, which was thought to characterize inter-theoretic reductions in empirical science (e.g. thermodynamics to statistical mechanics, optics to electromagnetic theory). Mind–body reduction, on this model, would consist in the derivation of psychological laws from those of some underlying physical theory (presumably, neurobiology) taken together with

'bridge laws', empirical laws correlating mental kinds with physical-neural kinds. The idea was that reduction could be carried out by finding for each mental property a nomologically coextensive physical property, rather than an analytically coextensive one. In any case, the idea that mind–body reduction must be underwritten by a pervasive system of type-type correlations between the mental and the physical has been a tacit but widely shared presupposition of the recent debate on reductionism. This requirement can be stated as follows:

The requirement of strong connectibility: For each mental property M there is a physical property P such that *necessarily*, M is instantiated by a system at t if and only if P is instantiated by it at t.

Definitional reduction and nomological reduction differ from each other only in that different senses of 'necessarily' are involved, analytic or logical necessity in the former and nomological necessity in the latter.

This means that the question whether supervenience is consistent with the irreducibility of the mental amounts to the question whether it is consistent with the failure of strong connectibility between the mental and the physical. But which superve..ience relation do we have in mind? It is clear that weak supervenience is not a candidate, for it is unable to generate psychophysical type-type correlations with an appropriate modal force of necessity. This leaves strong and global supervenience. It will be convenient to make use of the following alternative formulation of strong supervenience:

Strong supervenience (alternative version): Necessarily, for each property M in *M*, if anything x has M, then there is a property P in *P* such that x has P, and *necessarily* if anything has P it has M.

When a thing has a mental property, M, strong supervenience calls for a subvenient physical base, P, for M, and the relationship between P and M carries over into other possible worlds, as indicated by the italicized inner modal operator 'necessarily'. This stability of psychophysical type-type correlations across possible worlds is, as may be recalled, precisely what was lacking in weak supervenience. The exact force of 'necessarily' is open to further specification: some might want only nomological necessity, but others might insist on metaphysical necessity or even analytic necessity. (This version of strong supervenience is sometimes called 'the operator formulation', to contrast it with the earlier 'possible-world formulation'. The two formulations are provably equivalent under certain assumptions concerning property composition (Kim, 1987).

Under strong psychophysical supervenience, therefore, every mental property M has a (possibly infinite) series of physical properties P_1, P_2, . . ., each of which is sufficient for M. Consider then the union (disjunction) of these Ps, $\cup P_i$. It is easily seen that $\cup P_i$ is a necessary coextension of M. Does this mean that strong supervenience entails the satisfaction of the strong connectibility requirement? Could $\cup P_i$ serve as a reduction base for M?

It can scarcely be denied that strong supervenience, at least in its alternate version, entails the strong connectibility of the mental with the physical. The anti-reductionist physicalist can, however, respond in one of the following two ways: first, she might argue that the strong connectibility is not sufficient for reduction, and, in particular, that properties like $\cup P_i$, because of their complexity and artificiality, are unsuited as a reduction base for mental properties; second, she might look to global supervenience to secure psychophysical dependence without the threat of reductionism.

Neither of these moves is entirely unproblematic, however. Consider the first move: it has never been convincingly argued why 'complexity' and 'artificiality' of $\cup P_i$ should count against it as a reduction base. The point is often made to the effect that the complexity and open-ended heterogeneity of $\cup P_i$ makes it entirely unusable in scientific theory reduction; it may not even be possible to state, in a finite way, bridge laws

involving such properties. It may be replied, though, that the alleged complexity and heterogeneity are primarily characteristic of how $\cup P$ is represented or specified, not necessarily of the property $\cup P_i$ itself, and that as long as this property is there, there is always the possibility of its being represented by a perspicuous description in an appropriate scientific theory. Even if this never happens and, indeed, cannot happen given our cognitive capacities or inclinations, why isn't the demonstrated existence of $\cup P_i$ for M, and similar physical coextensions for all other mental properties, sufficient to show the *metaphysical reducibility* of mental properties? Obviously, it is not the business of a philosophical argument to generate actual reductions of scientific theories or properties, but only to show their metaphysical possibility.

Could global supervenience then help the non-reductivist? Some non-reductive physicalists find this form of supervenience particularly attractive because, unlike strong supervenience, it does not posit, at least not directly, type-type relationships between the mental and the physical (Post, 1987). But, as we saw, the question whether global supervenience entails strong supervenience has not been fully settled. When restricted to intrinsic properties, global and strong supervenience turn out to be equivalent, and it appears that global supervenience fails to entail strong supervenience only if mental properties, but not the subvenient physical properties, are allowed to include non-intrinsic properties. Moreover, it should be noted that in the sense in which global supervenience does not imply strong supervenience, it does not imply weak supervenience either (Kim, 1987). And we may very well doubt whether a supervenience relation which permits the violation of weak supervenience could yield a robust enough dependence relation adequate for physicalism.

DOES MIND–BODY SUPERVENIENCE HOLD?

Much of our evidence for mind–body supervenience seems to consist in our knowledge of specific correlations between mental states and physical (in particular, neural) processes in humans and other organisms. Such knowledge, although extensive and in some ways impressive, is still quite rudimentary and far from complete (what do we know, or can we expect to know, about the exact neural substrate for, say, the sudden thought that you are late with your rent payment this month?). It may well be that our willingness to accept mind–body supervenience, although based in part on specific psychophysical dependencies, has to be supported by a deeper metaphysical commitment to the primacy of the physical; it may in fact be an expression of such a commitment.

But there are kinds of mental states that raise special issues for mind–body supervenience. One such kind is 'wide content' states, i.e. contentful mental states that seem to be individuated essentially by reference to objects and events outside the subject (see CONTENT; PROPOSITIONAL ATTITUDES; TWIN EARTH). You believe that water is wet, but your physical duplicate on Twin Earth (where a substance, XYZ, observationally indistinguishable from H_2O, fills the lakes and oceans, comes out of the tap, etc.) believes that XYZ is wet, not that water is wet. It would seem then that the belief that water is wet does not supervene on the physical states of organisms. The same considerations evidently apply to all wide-content states.

However, what this shows is only the failure of 'local supervenience', i.e. the supervenience of wide-content states on the local, intrinsic physical-neural properties of a given subject. It does not show that these states fail to supervene physically *tout court*; in order to secure supervenience we need to broaden the supervenience base, to include the relational, or extrinsic, physical properties of the subject, including historical-causal properties (e.g. having matured in an environment including XYZ but no water). What this implies about the causal powers of wide-content states is a question that has been intensely debated in recent years.

Another type of mental states that has raised doubts about mind–body supervenience are 'phenomenological' or 'qualitative' states or events ('QUALIA' for short). These are mental states with sensory qualities, like pains and itches, seeing of green, etc. Many philosophers believe that 'qualia inversion' is perfectly conceivable – that is, it is conceivable and perfectly intelligible that when you look at a ripe tomato, the colour you sense is the colour your physical duplicate senses when she looks at a fresh cucumber, and vice versa (see CONSCIOUSNESS). Now, if such a possibility is coherently conceivable, as it seems to be, that could defeat supervenience, both strong and global. (The details here will depend on the specific type of supervenience claim involved – in particular, its modal force.) If you take the view that not only is qualia inversion coherently conceivable, but there is no way to know that it doesn't occur all around us (even if we knew all about human neurophysiology), you are taking the position that there is no good evidence for weak supervenience either.

Many physicalists take mental properties to be 'physically realized' – in fact, realized by a multiple set of physical properties. The idea that mental properties are multiply realized physically is very closely related to the idea that they are physically supervenient. There seems to be no single concept of 'realization'; however, those who use the idiom of 'realization' will agree that physical duplicates realize exactly the same set of mental properties – except possibly wide-content properties noted above. The idea that mentality is physically realized is integral to the FUNCTIONALIST conception of mentality, and this commits most functionalists to mind–body supervenience in one form or another.

PSYCHOPHYSICAL SUPERVENIENCE AS A THEORY OF MIND

Supervenience of the mental – in the form of strong supervenience, or at least global supervenience – is arguably a minimum commitment of physicalism. But can we think of the thesis of mind–body supervenience itself as a *theory* of the mind–body relation – that is, as a solution to the mind–body problem?

As we saw, a supervenience claim consists of a claim of covariance and a claim of dependence (leaving aside the controversial claim of non-reducibility). This means that the thesis that the mental supervenes on the physical amounts to the conjunction of the two claims: (1) the mental covaries with the physical (*à la* strong or global supervenience), and (2) the mental depends on the physical. Notice, however, the fact that *the thesis says nothing about just what kind of dependence is involved in mind–body supervenience*. When you compare the supervenience thesis with the standard positions on the mind–body problem, you are struck by what the supervenience thesis doesn't say. For each of the classic mind–body theories has something to say, not necessarily anything very plausible, about the kind of dependence that characterizes the mind–body relationship. According to epiphenomenalism, for example, the dependence is one of causal dependence; on logical behaviourism, dependence is rooted in meaning dependence, or definability; on the standard type physicalism, the dependence is one that is involved in the dependence of macroproperties on micro-structural properties; etc. Even Leibniz and Malebranche had something to say about this: the observed property covariation is due not to a direct dependency relation between mind and body but rather to divine plans and interventions. That is, mind–body covariation was explained in terms of their dependence on a third factor – a sort of 'common cause' explanation.

It would seem that any serious theory addressing the mind–body problem must say something illuminating about the nature of psychophysical dependence, or why, contrary to common belief, there is no dependence here either way. However, there is reason to think that 'supervenient dependence' does not signify a special *type* of dependence relation. This is evident when we reflect on the varieties of ways in which we could explain why the supervenience

relation holds in a given case. For example, consider the supervenience of the moral on the descriptive: the ethical naturalist will explain this on the basis of definability; the ethical intuitionist will say that the supervenience, and also the dependence, here is a brute fact you discern through moral intuition; and the prescriptivist will attribute the supervenience to some form of consistency requirement on the language of evaluation and prescription. And distinct from all of these is mereological supervenience, namely the supervenience of properties of a whole on properties and relations of its parts. What all this shows is that there is no single type of dependence relation common to all cases of supervenience; supervenience holds in different cases for different reasons, and does not represent a type of dependence that can be put alongside causal dependence, meaning dependence, mereological dependence, etc.

If this is right, the supervenience thesis concerning the mental does not constitute an explanatory account of the mind–body relation, on a par with the classic alternatives on the mind–body problem. It is merely the claim that the mental covaries in a systematic way with the physical, and that this is due to a certain dependence relation yet to be specified and explained. In this sense, the supervenience thesis states the mind–body problem rather than offers a solution to it.

There seems to be a promising strategy for turning the supervenience thesis into a more substantive theory of mind, and it is this: to explicate mind–body supervenience as a special case of mereological supervenience – that is, the dependence of the properties of a whole on the properties and relations characterizing its proper parts. Mereological dependence does seem to be a special form of dependence that is metaphysically *sui generis* and highly important. If one takes this approach, one would have to explain psychological properties as macroproperties of a whole organism that covary, in appropriate ways, with its microproperties, i.e. the way its constituent organs, tissues, etc. are organized and function. This more specific supervenience thesis may well be a serious theory of the mind–body relation that can vie with the classic options in the field.

See also; CONTENT; IDENTITY THEORIES; PHYSICALISM.

BIBLIOGRAPHY

Davidson, D. 1970. Mental events. In *Experience and Theory*, ed. L. Foster and J. W. Swanson. Amherst: University of Massachusetts Press.

Hellman, G., and Thompson, F. 1975. Physicalism: ontology, determination, and reduction. *Journal of Philosophy*, 72, 551–64.

Horgan, T. 1982. Supervenience and microphysics. *Pacific Philosophical Quarterly*, 63, 29–43.

Kim, J. 1984. Concepts of supervenience. *Philosophy and Phenomenological Research*, 65, 153–76.

Kim, J. 1987. 'Strong' and 'global' supervenience revisited. *Philosophy and Phenomenological Research*, 68, 315–26.

Kim, 1990. Supervenience as a philosophical concept. *Metaphilosophy*, 21, 1–27.

Kim, J. 1993. *Supervenience and Mind*. Cambridge University Press.

Lloyd Morgan, C. 1923. *Emergent Evolution*. London: Williams and Norgate.

Paull, R.C., and Sider, T.R. 1992. In defense of global supervenience. *Philosophy and Phenomenological Research*, 52, 833–54.

Post, J. 1987. *The Faces of Existence*. Ithaca: Cornell University Press.

Teller, P. 1984. Poor man's guide to supervenience and determination. *Southern Journal of Philosophy*, 22 (The Spindel Conference Supplement), 137–62.

JAEGWON KIM

syntax/semantics Consider the sentence, 'The cat is on the mat.' It is constructed from six words, it has a subject and a predicate, two of its words are nouns, there is a preposition and two definite articles as well as the copula 'is'. All these are remarks about the syntax of this sentence – its form. One could know all of them and still not know what the sentence expresses, what it means. The latter sort of knowledge is semantical.

The syntax/semantics distinction seems straightforward, but there are deep issues in linguistics and the philosophy of language lying in wait to make things more complex. First of all, though syntax is a matter of form, there are many possible levels of such form. Thus, knowing that a sentence is of the subject-predicate sort is a fairly sophisticated level of formal description; one must know something about grammatical categories to appreciate it. Whereas saying of the original sentence that it contains 16 letters and 5 spaces, or that it is composed of certain kinds of black-on-white shapes are descriptively no less formal, though they can be appreciated without any background grammatical knowledge.

However, the complications really multiply in respect of semantics. It is one thing to say that the semantics of a sentence is its meaning, it is another to say what meaning is, or even to say how one would go about describing the meaning of words or sentences. Is it enough to say that the sentence 'The cat is on the mat' expresses the fact that the cat is on the mat? On the one hand, this seems uninformative – imagine it was the sole explanation of the meaning of this sentence. On the other hand, it is not clear how to understand 'expresses the fact that'.

Exactly what form a theory of meaning should take, and what level of syntactical description is most appropriate to understanding language, are problems for linguists and philosophers of language. But the notions of syntax and semantics also play an important part in philosophy of mind. This arises because it is widely maintained that words and sentences are not the only kinds of thing that have syntax and semantics; in one way or another these features have been claimed for mental phenomena such as beliefs and other propositional attitudes (*see* REPRESENTATIONS). Thus, there is a view known as the 'LANGUAGE OF THOUGHT' theory which maintains that beliefs are syntactically characterizable items in the mind/brain and that they are semantically evaluable. According to this account, we can best explain, for example, Smith's belief that snow is white as his having in his mind/brain a token of a language of thought sentence – a sentence with some kind of syntax – which has as a semantical value the appropriate relation to snow and whiteness. Also, many not committed to the idea of a language of thought would still believe there to be a semantics of attitude states. So, the very difficult issue of how to describe the semantical relation carries over from the philosophy of language to the philosophy of mind. It is often called the 'problem of intentionality', though this label covers other issues as well. (*See* CONTENT; DRETSKE; FODOR; INTENTIONALITY; PROPOSITIONAL ATTITUDES; THOUGHTS.)

SAMUEL GUTTENPLAN

T

teleology Derived from the Greek word 'telos' meaning purpose or goal, 'teleology', as it is most often used in the philosophy of mind, is thought of as the study of the purposes, goals or, more broadly, biological functions of various elements of the mental realm. For example, it has been suggested that we can better understand the PROPOSITIONAL ATTITUDES when we have discerned their evolutionary function. It has even been suggested that one can begin to understand specific propositional attitude contents in this way. (*See* CONTENT.)

SAMUEL GUTTENPLAN

thought The most significant feature of thought is its INTENTIONALITY or CONTENT: in thinking, one thinks *about* certain things, and one thinks certain things *of* those things – one entertains propositions that stand for states of affairs. Nearly all the interesting properties of thoughts depend upon their content: their being coherent or incoherent, disturbing or reassuring, revolutionary or banal, connected logically or illogically to other thoughts. It is thus hard to see why we would bother to talk of thought at all unless we were also prepared to recognize the intentionality of thought. So we are naturally curious about the nature of content: we want to understand what makes it possible, what constitutes it, what it stems from. To have a theory of thought is to have a theory of its content.

Four issues have dominated recent thinking about the content of thought; each may be construed as a question about what thought depends on, and about the consequences of its so depending (or not depending). These potential dependencies

concern: (i) the world outside of the thinker himself, (ii) language, (iii) logical truth, (iv) CONSCIOUSNESS. In each case the question is whether intentionality is essentially or accidentally related to the items mentioned: does it exist, that is, only by courtesy of the dependence of thought on the said items? And this question determines what the intrinsic nature of thought is. Let us consider each question in turn.

THOUGHT AND THE WORLD

Thoughts are obviously about things in the world, but it is a further question whether they could exist and have the content they do whether or not their putative objects themselves exist. Is *what* I think intrinsically dependent upon the world in which I happen to think it? This question was given impetus and definition by a thought experiment due to Hilary PUTNAM, concerning a planet called TWIN EARTH. On Twin Earth there live thinkers who are duplicates of us in all internal respects but whose surrounding environment contains different kinds of natural object. The suggestion then is that what these thinkers refer to and think about is individuatively dependent upon their actual environment, so that where we think about cats when we say 'cat' they think about some other species when they use that word – the different species that actually sits on their mats and so on. The key point is that since it is not possible to individuate natural kinds like cats solely by reference to the way they strike the people who think about them, thinking about *them* cannot be a function simply of internal properties of the thinker. Thought content, here, is relational in nature; it is fixed by external facts as they bear upon the thinker.

585

Much the same point can be made by considering repeated demonstrative reference to distinct particular objects: what I refer to when I say 'that bomb', of different bombs, depends upon the particular bomb in front of me and cannot be deduced from what is going on inside me. Context contributes to content.

Inspired by such examples, many philosophers have adopted an 'externalist' view of thought content: thoughts are not autonomous states of the individual, capable of transcending the contingent facts of the surrounding world. One is therefore not free to think whatever one likes, as it were, whether or not the world beyond cooperates in containing suitable referents for those thoughts. And this conclusion has generated a number of consequential questions. Can we know our thoughts with special authority, given that they are thus hostage to external circumstances? How do thoughts cause other thoughts and behaviour, given that they are not identical with any internal states we are in (*see* PRO-POSITIONAL ATTITUDES; REASONS AND CAUSES)? What kind of explanation are we giving when we cite thoughts? Can there be a science of thought if content does not generalize across environments? These questions have received many different answers, and of course not everyone agrees that thought has the kind of world-dependence claimed. What has not been considered carefully enough, however, is the scope of the externalist thesis – whether it applies to all forms of thought, all concepts. For unless this question can be answered affirmatively we cannot rule out the possibility that thought in general depends on there being *some* thought that is purely internally determined, so that the externally fixed thoughts are a secondary phenomenon. What about thoughts concerning one's present sensory experience, or logical thoughts, or ethical thoughts? Could there, indeed, be a thinker for whom internalism was generally correct? Is external individuation the rule or the exception? And might it take different forms in different cases?

THOUGHT AND LANGUAGE

Since words are also about things, it is natural to ask how their intentionality is connected to that of thoughts. Two views have been advocated: one view takes thought content to be self-subsistent relative to linguistic content, with the latter dependent upon the former; the other view takes thought content to be derivative upon linguistic content, so that there can be no thought without a bedrock of language (*see* THOUGHT AND LANGUAGE). Thus arise controversies about whether animals really think, being non-speakers, or computers really use language, being non-thinkers. All such questions depend critically upon what one is to mean by 'language'. Some hold that spoken language is unnecessary for thought but that there must be an inner language in order for thought to be possible; while others reject the very idea of an inner language, preferring to suspend thought from outer speech. However, it is not entirely clear what it amounts to to assert (or deny) that there is an inner LANGUAGE OF THOUGHT. If it means merely that concepts (thought-constituents) are structured in such a way as to be isomorphic with spoken language, then the claim is trivially true, given some natural assumptions. But if it means that concepts just are 'syntactic' items orchestrated into strings of the same, then the claim is acceptable only in so far as syntax is an adequate basis for meaning – which, on the face of it, it is not. Concepts no doubt have combinatorial powers comparable to those of words, but the question is whether anything else can plausibly be meant by the hypothesis of an inner language.

On the other hand, it appears undeniable that spoken language does not have autonomous intentionality, but instead derives its meaning from the thoughts of speakers – though language may augment one's conceptual capacities. So thought cannot postdate spoken language. The truth seems to be that in human psychology speech and thought are interdependent in many ways, but that there is no conceptual necessity about this. The only 'language' on which thought essentially depends is that of the structured system of concepts itself: thought indeed depends upon there being isolable concepts that can join with others to produce complete propositions. But this is merely to draw attention to a property any system of concepts must have; it is not to say what concepts are or how they succeed in moving between thoughts as they do. Appeals to language at this point are apt to founder on circularity, since words take on the powers of concepts only insofar as they express them. Thus there seems little philosophical illumination to be got from making thought depend upon language.

THOUGHT AND LOGIC

This third dependency question is prompted by the reflection that, while people are no doubt often irrational, woefully so, there seems to be some kind of intrinsic limit to their unreason. Even the sloppiest thinker will not infer anything from anything. To do so is a sign of madness. The question then is what grounds this apparent concession to logical prescription. Whence the hold of logic over thought? For the dependence here can seem puzzling: why should the natural causal processes of thought mirror the normative abstract relations of logic? I am free to flout the moral law to any degree I desire, but my freedom to think unreasonably appears to encounter an obstacle in the requirements of logic. My thoughts are sensitive to logical truth in somewhat the way they are sensitive to the world surrounding me; they have not the independence of what lies outside my will or self that I fondly imagined. I may try to reason contrary to *modus ponens*, but my efforts will be systematically frustrated. Pure logic takes possession of my reasoning processes and steers them according to its own dictates; not invariably, of course, but in a systematic way that seems perplexing (*see* RATIONALITY).

One view of this is that ascriptions of thought are not attempts to map a realm of independent causal relations, which might then conceivably come apart from logical relations, but are rather just a useful method of summing up people's behaviour. Another view insists that we must acknowledge that thought is not a natural phenomenon in the way merely physical facts are: thoughts are inherently normative in their nature, so that logical relations constitute their inner essence (*see* DAVIDSON). Thought incorporates logic in somewhat the way externalists say it incorporates the world. Accordingly, the study of thought cannot be a natural science in the way the study of (say) chemical compounds is. Whether this view is acceptable depends upon whether we can make sense of the idea that transitions in nature, such as reasonings appear to be, can also be transitions in logical space, i.e. be confined by the structure of that space. What must thought be such that this combination of features is possible? Put differently, what is it for logical truth to be self-evident?

THOUGHT AND CONSCIOUSNESS

This dependency question has been studied less intensively than the previous three. The question is whether intentionality is dependent upon CONSCIOUSNESS for its very existence, and if so why. Could our thoughts have the very content they now have if we were not to be conscious beings at all? Unfortunately, it is difficult to see how to mount an argument in either direction. On the one hand, it can hardly be an accident that our thoughts are conscious and that their content is reflected in the intrinsic condition of our state of consciousness; it is not as if consciousness leaves off where thought content begins – as it does with, say, the neural basis of thought. Yet, on the other hand, it is by no means clear what it is about consciousness that links it to intentionality in this way. Much of the trouble here stems from our exceedingly poor understanding of the nature of consciousness in general. Just as we cannot see how consciousness could arise from brain tissue (the mind–body problem), so we fail to grasp the manner in which conscious states bear meaning. Perhaps content is fixed by extra-conscious properties and relations and only subsequently shows up in consciousness, as various naturalistic reductive accounts would suggest; or perhaps consciousness itself plays a more enabling role, allowing meaning to come into the world, hard as this may be to penetrate. In some ways the question is analogous to, say, the properties of PAIN: is the aversive property of pain, causing avoidance behaviour and so on, essentially independent of the conscious state of feeling pain, being possibly present without the feeling; or is it that pain could only have its aversive function in virtue of the conscious feeling? This is part of the more general question of the epiphenomenal character of consciousness (*see* EPIPHENOMENALISM): is conscious awareness just a dispensable accompaniment of some mental feature – such as content or causal power – or is it that consciousness is structurally involved in the very determination of the feature? It is only too easy to feel pulled in both directions on this question, neither alternative being utterly felicitous. Some theorists, indeed, suspect that our uncertainty over such questions stems from a constitutional limitation to human understanding. We just cannot develop the necessary theoretical tools with which to provide answers to these questions; so we may not in principle be able to make any progress with the issue of whether thought depends upon consciousness and why. Certainly our present understanding falls far short of providing us with any clear route into the question.

It is extremely tempting to picture thought as some kind of inscription in a mental medium, and of reasoning as a temporal sequence of such inscriptions. The model here is language and its spoken and written expression (hence the appeal of the second dependency thesis above). On this picture all that a particular thought requires in order to exist is that the medium in question should be impressed with the right inscription. This makes thought independent of anything else. On some views the medium is conceived as consciousness itself, so that thought depends on consciousness as writing depends on paper and ink. But ever since WITTGENSTEIN wrote, we have seen that this conception of thought has to be mistaken; in particular, it cannot provide an acceptable account of intentionality. The definitive characteristics of thoughts cannot be captured within this model. Thus, it cannot make room for the idea of intrinsic world-dependence, since any inner inscription would be individuatively independent of items outside the putative medium of thought. Nor can it be made to square with the dependence of thought on logical patterns, since the medium could be configured in any way permitted by its intrinsic nature, without regard for logical truth – as sentences can be written down in any old order one likes. And it misconstrues the relation between thought and consciousness, since content cannot consist in marks on the surface of consciousness, so to speak. States of consciousness do contain particular meanings but not as a page contains sentences: the medium conception of the relation between content and consciousness is thus deeply mistaken. The only way to make meaning enter internally into consciousness is to deny that it acts as a medium for meaning to be expressed. However, as remarked above, it is devilishly difficult to form an adequate conception of how consciousness *does* carry content – one puzzle being how the external determinants of content find their way into the fabric of consciousness.

Only the alleged dependence of thought upon language fits the naïve tempting inscriptional picture, but as we have seen this idea tends to crumble under examination. The indicated conclusion seems to be that we simply do not possess a conception of thought that makes its real nature theoretically comprehensible; which is to say that we have no adequate conception of mind. Once we form a conception of thought that makes it seem unmysterious, as with the inscriptional picture, it turns out to have no room for content as it presents itself; while building in content as it is leaves us with no clear picture of what could have such content. Thought is real, then, if and only if it is mysterious.

See also BELIEF; FODOR; IDENTITY THEORIES; PHYSICALISM.

BIBLIOGRAPHY

Fodor, J. 1975. *The Language of Thought*. New York: Crowell.
McGinn, C. 1989. *Mental Content*. Oxford: Basil Blackwell.
McGinn, C. 1991. *The Problem of Consciousness*. Oxford: Basil Blackwell.
Putnam, H. 1981. The meaning of 'Meaning'. In *Mind, Language and Reality*. Cambridge University Press.
Wittgenstein, L. 1953. *Philosophical Investigations*. Oxford: Basil Blackwell.

COLIN McGINN

thought and language The relation between language and thought is philosophy's chicken-or-egg problem. Language and thought are evidently importantly related, but how exactly are they related? Does language come first and make thought possible, or vice versa? Or are they on a par, each making the other possible?

When the question is stated this generally, however, no unqualified answer is possible. In some respects language is prior, in other respects thought is prior, and in still other respects neither is prior. For example, it is arguable that a language is an abstract pairing of expressions and meanings, a function, in the set-theoretic sense, from expressions onto meanings (*see* LEWIS, 1983). This makes sense of the fact that Esperanto is a language no one speaks, and it explains why it is that, while it is a contingent fact that 'La neige est blanche' means that snow is white *among the French*, it is a necessary truth that it means that *in French*. But if natural languages such as French and English are abstract objects in this sense, then they exist whether or not anyone speaks them; they even exist in POSSIBLE WORLDS in which there are no thinkers. In this respect, then, language, as well

as such notions as meaning and truth in a language, is prior to thought.

THE DEPENDENCE OF LANGUAGE ON THOUGHT

But even if languages are construed as abstract expression-meaning pairings, they are construed that way as abstractions from actual linguistic practice – from the use of language in communicative behaviour – and there remains a clear sense in which language is dependent on thought. The sequence of marks 'Naples is south of Rome' means among us that Naples is south of Rome. This is a contingent fact, dependent on the way we use 'Naples', 'Rome' and the other parts of that sentence. Had our linguistic practices been different, 'Naples is south of Rome' might have meant something entirely different or nothing at all among us. Plainly, the fact that 'Naples is south of Rome' means among us that Naples is south of Rome has *something* to do with the BELIEFS and INTENTIONS underlying our use of the words and structures that compose the sentence. More generally, it is a platitude that the semantic features that marks and sounds have in a population of speakers are at least partly determined by the PROPOSITIONAL ATTITUDES those speakers have in using those marks and sounds, or in using the parts and structures that compose them. This is the same platitude, of course, which says that meaning depends at least partly on use; for the use in question is intentional use in communicative behaviour. So here is one clear sense in which language is dependent on thought: thought is required to imbue marks and sounds with the semantic features they have in populations of speakers.

The sense in which language does depend on thought can be wedded to the sense in which language does not depend on thought in the following way. We can say that a sequence of marks or sounds (or whatever) σ means q in a language L, construed as a function from expressions onto meanings, iff $L(\sigma) = q$. This notion of meaning-in-a-language, like the notion of a language, is a mere set-theoretic notion that is independent of thought in that it presupposes nothing about the propositional attitudes of language users: σ can mean *q* in *L* even if *L* has never been used. But then we can say that σ also means *q* in a population *P* just in case members of *P* use some language in which σ means *q*; that is, just in case some such language is a language of *P*. The question of moment then becomes: What relation must a population *P* bear to a language *L* in order for it to be the case that *L* is a language of *P*, a language members of *P* actually speak? (*see* Lewis, 1983, 1992). Whatever the answer to this question is, this much seems right: in order for a language to be a language of a population of speakers, those speakers must produce sentences of the language in their communicative behaviour. Since such behaviour is intentional, we know that the notion of a language's being the language of a population of speakers presupposes the notion of thought. And since that notion presupposes the notion of thought, we also know that the same is true of the correct account of the semantic features expressions have in populations of speakers.

This is a pretty thin result, not one likely to be disputed, and the difficult questions remain. We know that there is some relation *R* such that a language *L* is used by a population *P* iff *L* bears *R* to *P*. Let us call this relation, whatever it turns out to be, *the actual-language relation*. We know that to explain the actual-language relation is to explain the semantic features expressions have among those who are apt to produce those expressions, and we know that any account of the relation must require language users to have certain propositional attitudes. But how exactly is the actual-language relation to be explained in terms of the propositional attitudes of language users? And what sort of dependence might those propositional attitudes in turn have on language or on the semantic features that are fixed by the actual-language relation? Let us continue for a while with the first question, about the relation of lan-

guage to thought, before turning to the relation of thought to language.

All must agree that the actual-language relation, and with it the semantic features linguistic items have among speakers, is at least partly determined by the propositional attitudes of language users. This still leaves plenty of room for philosophers to disagree both about the extent of the determination and the nature of the determining propositional attitudes. At one end of the determination spectrum, we have those who hold that the actual-language relation is wholly definable in terms of non-semantic propositional attitudes. This position in logical space is most famously occupied by the programme, sometimes called *intention-based semantics* (IBS), of the late Paul Grice and others. The foundational notion in this enterprise is a certain notion of *speaker meaning*. It is the species of communicative behaviour reported when we say, for example, that in uttering 'Il pleut', Pierre meant that it was raining, or that in waving her hand, the Queen meant that you were to leave the room. IBS seeks to define this notion of speaker meaning wholly in terms of communicators' audience-directed intentions and without recourse to any semantic notions. Then it seeks to define the actual-language relation in terms of the now-defined notion of speaker meaning, together with certain ancillary notions such as that of a conventional regularity or practice, themselves defined wholly in terms of non-semantic propositional attitudes. The definition of the actual-language relation in terms of speaker meaning will require the prior definition in terms of speaker meaning of other agent-semantic notions, such as the notions of speaker reference and Austin's notion of an illocutionary act, and this, too, is part of the IBS programme.

Some philosophers object to IBS because they think it precludes a dependence of thought on the communicative use of language. This is a mistake. Even if IBS definitions are given a strong reductionist reading, as saying that public-language semantic properties (i.e. those semantic properties that supervene on use in communicative behaviour) *just are* psychological properties, it might still be that one could not have propositional attitudes unless one had mastery of a public language. (*See* REDUCTION; SUPERVENIENCE.) Whether or not this is plausible (that is a separate question), it would be no more logically puzzling than the idea that one could not have any propositional attitudes unless one had ones with certain sorts of contents. Tyler Burge's insight, to be discussed later, that the contents of one's thoughts is partly determined by the meanings of one's words in one's linguistic community (*see* Burge, 1979), is perfectly consistent with any IBS reduction of the semantic to the psychological. Nevertheless, there is reason to be sceptical of the IBS programme. First, no IBS theorist has succeeded in stating a *sufficient* condition for speaker meaning, let alone succeeded at the much more difficult task of stating a *necessary*-and-sufficient condition. And a plausible explanation of this failure is that what typically makes an utterance an act of speaker meaning is the speaker's intention to be *meaning* or *saying* something, where the concept of meaning or saying used in the content of the intention is irreducibly semantic. Second, whether or not an IBS account of speaker meaning can be achieved, there are difficulties with the IBS way of accounting for the actual-language relation in terms of speaker meaning. The essence of the IBS approach is that sentences are used as conventional devices for making known a speaker's communicative intentions, and on this view language understanding is an inferential process wherein a hearer perceives an utterance and, thanks to being party to relevant conventions or practices, infers the speaker's communicative intentions. Yet it appears that this inferential model is subject to insuperable epistemological difficulties (*see* Schiffer, 1987, ch. 7). Third, there is no pressing reason to think that the semantic *needs* to be definable in terms of the psychological. Many IBS theorists have been motivated by a strong version of PHYSICALISM,

which requires the reduction of all intentional properties (i.e. all semantic and propositional-attitude properties) to physical or at least topic-neutral, or functional, properties; for it is plausible that there could be no reduction of the semantic and the psychological to the physical without a prior reduction of the semantic to the psychological (*see* Loar, 1981; Schiffer, 1982). But it is arguable that such a strong version of physicalism is not what is required in order to fit the intentional into the natural order.

So the most reasonable view about the actual-language relation is that it requires language users to have certain propositional attitudes, but there is no prospect of defining the relation wholly in terms of non-semantic propositional attitudes. It is further plausible, I submit, that any account of the actual-language relation must appeal to speech acts such as speaker meaning, where the correct account of these speech acts is irreducibly semantic (they will fail to supervene on the non-semantic propositional attitudes of speakers in the way that intentions fail to supervene on an agent's beliefs and desires). If this is right, it would still leave a further issue about the *definability* of the actual-language relation. Is it possible to define the actual-language relation, and if so, will any irreducibly semantic notions enter into that definition other than the sorts of speech act notions already alluded to? These questions have not been much discussed in the literature; there is neither an established answer nor competing schools of thought. My own view is that the actual-language relation is one of the few things in philosophy that can be defined, and that speech act notions are the only irreducibly semantic notions the definition must appeal to (*see* Schiffer, 1993).

THE DEPENDENCE OF THOUGHT ON LANGUAGE

This brings us to the dependence of thought on language. A useful starting point is a claimed dependence I think does *not* obtain. This is the claim that propositional attitudes are relations to linguistic items which obtain at least partly by virtue of the CONTENT those items have among language users. This position does not imply that believers have to be language users, but it does make language an essential ingredient in the concept of belief. The position is motivated by two considerations: (a) the supposition that believing is a relation to things believed, which things have truth values and stand in logical relations to one another; and (b) the desire not to take things believed to be propositions – abstract, mind- and language-independent objects that have essentially the truth conditions they have. Now (a) is well motivated: the relational construal of propositional attitudes is probably the best way to account for the quantification in 'Harvey believes something nasty about you'. But there are problems with taking linguistic items, rather than propositions, as the objects of belief. In the first place, if 'Harvey believes that flounders snore' is represented along the lines of 'B(Harvey, "flounders snore")', then one could know the truth expressed by the sentence about Harvey without knowing the content of his belief; for one could know that he stands in the belief relation to 'flounders snore' without knowing *its* content. This is unacceptable (*see* Schiffer, 1987, ch. 5). In the second place, if Harvey believes that flounders snore, then what he believes – the reference of 'that flounders snore' – is that flounders snore. But what is this thing, *that flounders snore?* Well, it is abstract, in that it has no spatial location; it is mind and language independent, in that it exists in possible worlds in which there are neither thinkers nor speakers; and, necessarily, it is true iff flounders snore. In short, it is a proposition – an abstract, mind- and language-independent thing that has a truth condition and has essentially the truth condition it has.

A more plausible way that thought depends on language is suggested by the topical thesis that we think in a 'LANGUAGE OF THOUGHT'. On one reading, this is nothing more than the vague idea that the neural states that realize our thoughts 'have elements and structure in a way that is analogous to the way in which sentences have elements and structure' (Harman, 1978, p. 58). But we can get a more literal rendering by relating it to the abstract conception of languages already recommended. On this conception, a language is a function from 'expressions' – sequences of marks or sounds or neural states or whatever – onto meanings, which meanings will include the propositions our propositional-attitude relations relate us to. We could then read the language of thought hypothesis as the claim that having propositional attitudes requires standing in a certain relation to a language whose expressions are neural states. There would now be more than one 'actual-language relation'. The one discussed earlier might be better called *the public-language relation*, since it makes a language the instrument of communication of a population of speakers. Another relation might be called *the language-of-thought relation*, because standing in that relation to a language makes it one's *lingua mentis*. Since the abstract notion of a language has been so weakly construed, it is hard to see how the minimal language-of-thought proposal just sketched could fail to be true. At the same time, it has been given no interesting work to do. In trying to give it more interesting work, further dependencies of thought on language might come into play. For example, it has been claimed that the language of thought of a public-language user is the public language she uses: her neural sentences are related to her spoken and written sentences in something like the way her written sentences are related to her spoken sentences. For another example, it might be claimed that even if one's language of thought is distinct from one's public language, the language-of-thought relation makes presuppositions about the public-language relation in ways that make the content of one's thoughts dependent on the meanings of one's words in one's public-language community.

Tyler Burge has in fact shown that there is a sense in which thought content is dependent on the meanings of words in one's linguistic community (Burge, 1979).

Alfred's use of 'arthritis' is fairly standard, except that he is under the misconception that arthritis is not confined to the joints; he also applies the word to rheumatoid ailments not in the joints. Noticing an ailment in his thigh that is symptomatically like the disease in his hands and ankles, he says to his doctor, 'I have arthritis in the thigh'. Here Alfred is expressing his false belief that he has arthritis in the thigh. But now consider a counterfactual situation that differs in just one respect (and whatever it entails): Alfred's use of 'arthritis' is the *correct* use in his linguistic community. In this situation, Alfred would be expressing a true belief when he says 'I have arthritis in the thigh'. Since the proposition he believes is true while the proposition that he has arthritis in the thigh is false, he believes some other proposition. This shows that standing in the belief relation to a proposition can be partly determined by the meanings of words in one's public language. The Burge phenomenon seems real, but it would be nice to have a deep explanation of why thought content should be dependent on language in this way.

Finally, there is the old question of whether, or to what extent, a creature who does not understand a natural language can have thoughts. Now it seems pretty compelling that higher mammals and humans raised without language have their behaviour controlled by mental states that are sufficiently like our beliefs, desires and intentions to share those labels. It also seems easy to imagine non-communicating creatures who have sophisticated mental lives (they build weapons, dams, bridges, have clever hunting devices, etc.). At the same time, ascriptions of particular contents to non-language-using creatures typically seem exercises in loose speaking (does the dog really believe that there is a *bone* in the yard?), and it is no accident that, as a matter of fact, creatures who do not understand a natural language have at best primitive mental lives. There is no accepted explanation of these facts. It is possible that the primitive mental lives of animals account for their failure to master natural

languages, but the better explanation may be CHOMSKY's, that animals lack a special language faculty unique to our species (see Chomsky 1968, 1975). As regards the inevitably primitive mental life of an otherwise normal human raised without language, this might simply be due to the ignorance and lack of intellectual stimulation such a person would be doomed to. On the other hand, it might also be that higher thought requires a neural language with a structure comparable to that of a natural language, and that such neural languages are somehow acquired *pari passu* as the child learns its native language. Finally, the ascription of content to the propositional-attitude states of languageless creatures is a difficult topic that needs more attention. It is possible that as we learn more about the logic of our ascriptions of propositional content, we will realize that these ascriptions are egocentrically based on a similarity to the language in which we express our beliefs. We might then learn that we have no principled basis for ascribing propositional content to a creature who does not speak something a lot like one of our natural languages, or who does not have internal states with natural-language-like structure. It is somewhat surprising how little we know about thought's dependence on language.

See also FODOR; PUTNAM; STALNAKER.

BIBLIOGRAPHY

Austin, J.L. 1962. *How to Do Things with Words*. Oxford University Press.
Avramides, A. 1989. *Meaning and Mind*, Cambridge, MA.: MIT Press.
Bennett, J. 1976. *Linguistic Behaviour*. Cambridge University Press.
Burge, T. 1979. Individualism and the mental. *Studies in Philosophy*, 4, 73–121.
Chomsky, N. 1968. *Language and Mind*. New York: Harcourt Brace.
Chomsky, N. 1975. *Reflections on Language*. New York: Pantheon Books.
Curtiss, S. 1977. *Genie: A Psycholinguistic Study of a Modern-Day 'Wild Child'*. New York: Academic Press.

Davidson, D. 1984a. *Truth and Interpretation.* Oxford University Press.

Davidson, D. 1984b. On saying that. In Davidson 1984a.

Davidson, D. 1984c. Thought and talk. In Davidson, 1984a.

Dummett, M. 1989. Language and communication. In *Reflections on Chomsky*, ed. A. George. Oxford: Basil Blackwell.

Field, H. 1978. Mental representation. *Erkenntnis*, 13, 9–61.

Fodor, J. 1975. *The Language of Thought.* New York: Crowell.

Grice, P. 1989. *Studies in the Way of Words.* Cambridge, MA.: Harvard University Press.

Harman, G. 1973. *Thought.* Princeton University Press.

Harman, G. 1978. Is there mental representation? In *Perception and Cognition: Issues in the Foundations of Psychology*, ed. C. Savage. Minneapolis: University of Minnesota Press.

Higgenbotham, J. 1986. Linguistic theory and Davidson's program in semantics. In *Truth and Interpretation: Perspectives on the Philosophy of Donald Davidson*, ed. E. LePore. Oxford: Basil Blackwell.

Lewis, D. 1969. *Convention.* Cambridge, MA.: Harvard University Press.

Lewis, D. 1983. Languages and language. In *Philosophical Papers*, vol. 1. Oxford University Press.

Lewis, D. 1992. Meaning without use: Reply to Hawthorne. *Australasian Journal of Philosophy*, 70, 106–110.

Loar, B. 1976. Two theories of meaning. In *Truth and Meaning*, ed. G. Evans and J. McDowell. Oxford University Press.

Loar, B. 1981. *Mind and Meaning.* Cambridge University Press.

Sacks, O. 1989. *Seeing Voices: A Journey into the World of the Deaf.* Berkeley: University of California Press.

Segal, G. 1989. A preference for sense and reference. *Journal of Philosophy*, 86, 73–89.

Schiffer, S. 1972. *Meaning.* Oxford University Press.

Schiffer, S. 1981. Indexicals and the theory of reference. *Synthèse*, 49, 43–100.

Schiffer, S. 1982. Intention-based semantics. *Notre Dame Journal of Formal Logic*, 23, 119–56.

Schiffer, S. 1987. *Remnants of Meaning.* Cambridge, MA.: MIT Press.

Schiffer, S. 1992. Belief ascription. *The Journal of Philosophy*, 89, 499–521.

Schiffer, S. 1993. Actual-language relations. *Philosophical Perspectives*, 7, 231–58.

Strawson, P. 1964. Intention and convention in speech acts. *Philosophical Review*, 73, 439–60.

Strawson, P. 1969. *Meaning and Truth.* Oxford University Press.

STEPHEN SCHIFFER

Turing, Alan (1912–54)   Alan Turing was a mathematical logician who played a crucial role in the development of the theory of computation. His most well-known contribution to this theory was cast in terms of what has come to be called a 'Turing machine', though for reasons that will be obvious, this was not a machine in any concrete sense. What is relevant in the present context is that the notion of a Turing machine has had a decisive influence on certain views about the nature of the mind, and, fittingly, Turing himself published a celebrated article in the philosophical journal *Mind* outlining some of the philosophical consequences of his 'machine'.

Ironically, given the fact that Turing's work underpins the ideas that gave birth to the digital computer, Turing used the term 'computer' – long before there were such devices – of a human being engaged in calculation. In fact, it was partly by thinking about such human 'computers' that he came to develop the idea of Turing machines. What he suggested was that one could simplify and mechanize the process by which a human computer did calculation, and then, by generalizing on this mechanized process, one could use it to define a special class of numbers. Turing called these 'computable' numbers. Finally, by reflecting on the way in which these numbers were mechanically generated, he showed that there were bound to be numbers that were not computable, though there was no mechanically describable way by which you could demonstrate this of a particular number. In essence, Turing had used his imagined device – the generalized mechanical calculator – to prove that there were what mathematicians call 'undecidable' problems.

Important as it has been in the sophisticated reaches of computational and logical theory, the idea of a Turing machine is very simple. Imagine that you have a typewriting device which can do a restricted range of things: it can type a symbol on a paper tape, it can remove such a symbol and it can move left or right one unit along the tape. Figure 1 shows the device poised over a section of an infinitely long paper tape which is divided into squares, some of which are empty and some of which contain an 's' (for 'symbol').

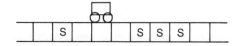

Figure 1

The whole of what is pictured in figure 1 is a Turing machine. By specifying more precisely what symbols the typewriter can use, and how it is disposed to react to them as it passes along the tape, we can get the Turing machine to transform one set of symbols and spaces (the 'input') into another (the 'output'). And despite its simplicity, it is enormously powerful. Turing showed that his device could take any input and transform it into any output so long as there is some computable relation between them. Of course, if the function relating input to output is very complex, the machine will take a long time to do the calculation. So no one would seriously contemplate building one as a practical way of doing computation, nor is it even possible to build a true Turing machine given the fact that it is essential to the machine's operation that the tape be infinite. As mentioned earlier, a Turing machine is essentially a machine in thought.

Despite the fact that a Turing machine is not intended to be a real device, and that its original field of application was the theory

of mathematical functions, it has had a major influence on thinking about the mind. To see why this is so, one must first accept – as most are prepared to do – that mental phenomena are dependent on the workings of the brain. Then one is invited to recognize that, at some level of description more general than the neurophysiological, the brain is a device that receives complex inputs from sensory systems and effects equally complex outputs to the motor systems. Moreover, as seems plausible, these relations between input and output are functionally well-behaved enough to be describable by various – albeit mind-bendingly complicated – mathematical relationships. This is plausible for many reasons, not least because our mental lives have a certain orderliness to them: we avoid obstacles we can see, we tend to pursue goals based on our needs and desires, we come to believe new things on the basis of those we already accept, etc. Finally, it should be noted that we do not have actually to know what the mathematical relationships are for the story to be interesting. For, so long as they exist, we know that some specific version of a Turing machine will be able to mimic them. There will be a Turing machine that perfectly simulates input-output structure of any specific brain.

What the above reasoning comes to is this: the brain is a computational device and when we talk about the mind, we are in effect, describing this device. Of course, when we speak about what persons want, believe, need, intend, etc. we are speaking at a much higher level of description than would be appropriate to a Turing machine. But the fact that we can depend on there being a Turing machine that captures the functional relations of the brain supports the idea that our talk about the mind is also a functional characterization. Or so many currently think. Turing (1950) himself was quite clear about this. Using his celebrated 'imitation' game, he suggested that one could envisage a computational device that would be indistinguishable from a human 'computer' (to revert to Turing's original use of this word). The game essentially consists of three 'players': a computer which responds uses a teletype to respond to various inputs it receives, a human being who also responds via a teletype, and a second human being who provides the input to the other two – who interrogates them. The object of the game is to see if the second human being can, by asking questions and examining the answers, tell which of the unseen 'devices' is human and which a machine. Turing was in no doubt that, if a computational device succeeded in fooling the human questioner, then that device would have all that is required for having a mind. And, as mentioned earlier, he thought that some such device would one day manage the task.

Much has been written about Turing's own interpretation of the imitation game, and not all those otherwise committed to COMPUTATIONAL MODELS OF MIND would accept Turing's conception of the mind. But, in the development of his 'machine', Turing managed to make a crucial contribution to logical and mathematical theory as well as to the philosophy of mind. The functionalist theory of the mind owes him a great debt, even if in some of its forms, it uses the idea of a Turing machine only in the background (see FUNCTIONALISM).

See also ARTIFICIAL INTELLIGENCE.

BIBLIOGRAPHY

Turing, A.M. 1950. Computing machinery and intelligence. *Mind*, 59, 433–60.
Hodges, A. 1983. *Alan Turing: The Enigma of Intelligence*. London: Hutchinson.

SAMUEL GUTTENPLAN

twin earth In a paper published in 1975, Hilary Putnam described a thought experiment in which one imagined a duplicate of of our planet, down to *almost* the last detail. However, what is crucial to the thought experiment is that there is one small difference between earth and twin earth: on twin earth the substance which looks and behaves just like water is not in fact water. Its chemical composition is imagined to be something called 'XYZ' rather than H_2O. The original purpose of this thought experiment was to show that the meanings of words in language couldn't be, as Putnam put it, 'in the head'. This consequence was held to follow from the fact that a thinker on earth and a thinker on twin earth – both of whom were ignorant of the chemical composition of things on their planets – would be exact duplicates as far as brain and behavioural organization went, and they would produce exactly the same sounds in the same circumstances. But a speaker on earth would be referring to water (that is, H_2O) when he spoke, whereas the speaker on twin earth would be referring to XYZ (twin water, or 'twater' as it is called when one tells the story).

The original thought experiment, and variations on it, have been used extensively in the philosophy of mind, though often with aims that go beyond any in Putnam's original paper. In this volume, the thought experiment is either described in detail or mentioned by many of the authors. (*See* CONCEPTUAL ROLE SEMANTICS; EPIPHENO- MENALISM; EXTERNALISM/INTERNALISM; THOUGHTS.)

BIBLIOGRAPHY

Putnam, H. 1975 The meaning of 'meaning'. In *Philosophical Papers, Vol. 2: Mind, Language and Reality*. Cambridge University Press.

SAMUEL GUTTENPLAN

type/token How many words are there in the sentence: 'The cat is on the mat'? There are of course at least two answers to this question, precisely because one can either count word *types*, of which there are five, or individual occurrences – known as *tokens* – of which there are six. Moreover, depending on how one chooses to think of word types, another answer is possible. Since the sentence contains definite articles, nouns, a preposition and a verb, there are four grammatically different types of word in the sentence.

The type/token distinction, understood as a distinction between sorts of thing and instances, is commonly applied to mental phenomena. For example, one can think of pain in the type way as when we say that we have experienced burning pain many times; or, in the token way, as when we speak of the burning pain currently being suffered. The type/token distinction for mental states and events becomes important in the context of attempts to describe the relationship between mental and physical phenomena. In particular, the IDENTITY THEORY asserts that mental states *are* physical states, and this raises the question whether the identity in question is of types or tokens. (*See also* DAVIDSON; LEWIS; SUPERVENIENCE.)

SAMUEL GUTTENPLAN

U

the unconscious Psychoanalytic theory describes a range of motives, mental states, and processes of which persons are ordinarily unaware, and which they can acknowledge, avow, and alter only with difficulty. Freud's collective term for these, and for the functional division of the mind to which he assigned them, was *the unconscious*. (For references and further discussion of italicized terms *see* Laplanche and Pointalais, 1973). The term has also been used to describe other mental states, such as hypothesized beliefs about language, taken to play a comparable role (Fodor, 1991, p. 278). In what follows, however, we shall concentrate on the psychoanalytic use.

Freud sometimes illustrated unconscious motivation by examples from hypnosis. Someone may, for example, comply with a post-hypnotic suggestion, while seeming to remember nothing about it, and citing some implausible motive of his or her own. Here, it seems, we do not accept the subject's own account, but rather suppose that the action is caused by a motive (e.g. a desire to do what the hypnotist said) of which the subject is unaware. Further hypnotic research has produced a variety of examples apparently fitting Freud's descriptions of the unconscious and its working (Erickson, 1939; Luria, 1976, ch. 4). While such phenomena seem genuinely illustrative, it remains unclear how far they should be assimilated to those encountered in psychoanalytic practice. So let us begin with the clinical work of Freud and his successors, and then turn to the more abstract *metapsychology* based on work of this kind.

CLINICAL

Early in his career Freud discovered that dreams and symptoms could be seen as related, causally and in their contents, to motives. In particular, both could be seen as *wishfulfilments*, that is, as representing the satisfaction of DESIRES or *wishes*, which had not been subjected to the rational thought requisite for INTENTIONAL action. This emerged when the dream or symptom was considered in the context of the patient's full and uncensored account of related thoughts and feelings, as obtained through the process of *free association*.

This can be illustrated by the example with which Freud begins *The Interpretation of Dreams* (Freud, 1974 vol. 4, ch. 2), his own dream of Irma's injection. In this dream Freud met Irma, a family friend and patient, whom he had diagnosed as hysterical, and treated by analysis. He told her that if she still felt pains, this was her own fault, for not accepting his solution. He became alarmed, however, that she was suffering from an organic illness which he had failed to diagnose, and this turned out to be true. His senior colleague M examined Irma, and confirmed that she was indeed organically ill; and it became manifest that her illness was caused by a toxic injection given by another of Freud's colleagues, his family doctor Otto. The dream ended with Freud censuring Otto's practice, saying 'Injections of that kind ought not to be made so thoughtlessly' and adding 'probably the syringe had not been clean'.

On the surface this dream dealt with topics that were not pleasant to Freud, such as the continued suffering of a friend and patient, and the possibility that he had misdiagnosed an organic illness, which he described as 'a constant anxiety' to someone offering psychological treatment. Freud's associations, however, enable us to see that the treatment of these topics in the dream was in fact thoroughly wishful. The day before the dream Otto – who had recently visited Irma and her family – had briefly discussed Irma with Freud. Otto had said that Irma was looking 'better, but not yet well'; Freud had thought he detected a reproof in this, and was vaguely annoyed. That night, in order to justify himself, Freud had started to write up Irma's case to show to M, who was respected by both himself and Otto, and who appeared in the dream as diagnosing Irma's illness and becoming aware that it was Otto's fault. Also, as it happened, Otto had been called on to give someone an injection while at Irma's (cf. the topic of the dream), and Freud had just had news indicating that another of his female patients had been given a careless injection by some other doctor, and had been contemplating his own careful practice in this respect.

In considering the dream Freud noted that his desire to justify himself in respect of Irma's case, and in particular not to be responsible for her suffering, was apparent from the beginning, in which he told Irma that her pains were now her own fault. Also, he felt that his alarm at her illness in the dream was not entirely genuine. So, Freud realized, it seemed that he was actually wishing that Irma be organically ill: for as he undertook to treat only psychological complaints, this also would mean that he could not be held responsible for her condition. This theme, indeed, seemed carried further in the rest of the dream, in which M found that Otto, not Freud, bore responsibility for Irma's illness. The whole dream, in fact, could be seen as a wishful response to Otto's remark. According to the dream, and contrary to what Freud had taken Otto to imply, Freud bore no responsibility whatever for Irma's condition. Rather, Otto was the sole cause of her suffering, and this was a result of Otto's bad practice with injections, a matter about which Freud himself was particularly careful.

To see the role of wishfulfilment here more clearly, let us consider Freud's desire that he be cleared of responsibility for Irma's suffering, as this operated, on the

one hand, in his intentional action, and on the other, in his dream. Very schematically, we hold that in rational action the causal role of a desire that P is to bring about (cause) a situation that P, which both satisfies the desire and pacifies it, that is, causes the desire to cease to operate. Acting on a desire that P (that one be cleared of culpable responsibility) should ideally bring it about that P (that one is cleared of culpable responsibility), that is, should bring about a situation which constitutes the satisfaction of the desire. This, in turn, should cause the belief that P (that one has been cleared . . .), and this, perhaps acting together with the satisfying situation, should pacify the desire that P, so that it ceases to govern action. This is approximately the sequence of results that Freud was seeking to produce, in accord with standard medical practice, in writing up Irma's case history on the night of the dream to discuss with M, his respected senior colleague. M would be able to offer an independent, authoritative opinion on Freud's treatment of Irma; so his judgment could partly serve to clear Freud, and, we may presume, Freud's conscience.

In Freud's dream the same motive was apparently also at work, but in a different way. There it produced no rational action, but rather gave rise directly to a (dreamt) representation of a situation in which Freud was cleared of responsibility, and by M. This representation, moreover, was extravagantly wishful – Irma was made physically ill, Freud was cleared in a great number of ways, Otto was elaborately blamed, and so on. Taking this example as typical, we can contrast the causal role of desire, as between action and wishfulfilment. In rational action a desire that P serves to bring about a situation that P, and this to cause a (justified and true) belief that P, so that the desire is pacified. In wishfulfilment, by contrast, this process is short-circuited, so as to leave a satisfying or justifying reality out. Here the desire that P causes a wishful and belief-*like* representation that P directly, and this serves to pacify the desire, regardless of reality, at least temporarily. In

rational action we find both the real satisfaction and also the pacification of desire,
with the latter a causal and rational consequence of the former. In wishfulfilment
we find only pacification, via a version of
wishful imagining or make-believe: that is,
imaginary pacification without real satisfaction. Although Freud did not describe
matters in these terms, he took this feature
to be characteristic of wishfulfilment
generally.

We can thus put part of Freud's conception by saying that wishfulfilment seems to
be the mind's (or brain's) way of pacifying
desires – and thus stabilizing or redirecting
its own functioning in a certain way –
without actually satisfying them. Still the
mode of pacification seems analogous in
both cases. In rational action pacification is
consequent on satisfaction and veridical
BELIEF, and in wishfulfilment on belief-like
representation. Belief itself, however, can be
regarded as the limiting case of belief-like
representation. So we can say that in
general pacification proceeds via representation of this kind.

Freud also found that a given dream,
symptom, or other wishfulfilment characteristically involved a range of wishes, connected in their contents. We have seen that
Freud's wish to avoid responsibility for Irma
went with one to blame Otto. But also his
associations make clear that the dream was
wishfulfilling on levels deeper than his
present concern with Irma. For example in
analysing his dream Freud realized that
Irma was linked in his mind with two
persons who had previously died as a result
of his medical interventions. One of his
friends had suffered from incurable nerve
pain, and was addicted to the morphia he
used for relief from it. Freud had suggested
that his friend use cocaine instead, not
grasping that it too was addictive. The
friend later died from injections of cocaine.
Also, Freud had himself once repeatedly
prescribed a woman patient a standard
medication, which, unpredictably, had
killed her; and he had consulted with M
about this case also.

These memories were integral to Freud's

associations, and connected with many
other details of the dream; so they can be
seen to have influenced the dream as well.
Hence the remark with which Freud ended
the dream – 'Injections of that kind ought
not to be made so thoughtlessly' – was
actually one with which he might well have
reproached himself, in respect of treatments
he associated with Irma's. But in the dream
this deeper reproach – regarding thought-
lessness, the misuse of toxic substances, and
damaging injections – was also wishfully
deflected on to Otto. In representing Otto
but not himself as responsible for Irma's suffering, Freud also represented Otto but not
himself as bearing precisely the kinds of
responsibility involved in the deaths of his
other friend and other patient. Hence this
dream can also be regarded as representing
the fulfilment of a wish on Freud's part not
to be responsible in these cases also. But
this wish, and indeed the whole topic of his
own responsibility for death, was entirely
kept from Freud's CONSCIOUSNESS in the
dream, and came to light only via his
associations.

This also illustrates further mechanisms
that Freud found to be common in dreams,
and characteristic of unconscious functioning generally. In the dream the figure of
Freud's friend and patient Irma also represented, or stood for, Freud's other friend and
other patient who had died as a result of his
therapeutic interventions. So this example
shows what Freud called the *condensation* of
several significant figures and topics from
the *latent content* of the dream – the
thoughts and feelings uncovered by association as related to the dream, which in this
case included the links between Irma and
these dead others – into one composite
figure and topic appearing in the *manifest
content* of which the dreamer was aware.
This went also with a *displacement* of Freud's
guilt, again in a way connected with all
three cases, on to the figure of Otto. These
processes contributed to the *distortion* of the
manifest mental CONTENT effected by what
Freud called the *dream work*. As noted
below, Freud later found MEMORY and conscious belief generally to be liable to similar

distortion; and some of this may be visible in the material connected with this analysis, for example in Freud's own conscious inclination to regard Otto as 'thoughtless' or 'jumping to a conclusion' about Irma's case.

In light of the above we can give the following preliminary and schematic characterization of Freud's clinical method and project. In commonsense psychology we interpret actions in accord with a basic generalization about desire: the role of a desire that P is to produce a situation that P, which in turn should produce a belief that P serving, together with the situation, to pacify the desire, and so to redirect action (*see* FOLK PSYCHOLOGY). In our everyday understanding of persons we both tacitly use this generalization, and also sustain it inductively, bearing it out through the successful interpretation of desire in action in case after case. This generalization includes the idea that a representation (belief) that P plays a role in pacifying a desire that P. Hence we also take it as an intelligible, and indeed common, phenomenon that a desire that P should play a role in causing a belief-like imaginative representation that P, which tends to pacify the desire. This is another generalization which we both use and sustain, in understanding many forms of wishful imagining, make-believe, and so forth, with which we are familiar.

Freud's work on dreams and symptoms uses, extends, and supports this latter generalization, by finding instance after instance, and in previously unsuspected cases, such as the dream above. Such interpretative work, as Freud claimed, enables one to see dreams and symptoms as pacifying deeper desires with the same sort of regularity as actions can be seen as satisfying them. This in turn serves also to extend and support the basic generalization about desires (above): for each interpretation of a wishfulfilment adds new values for P to the contents of the probable desires of an agent, and so gives rise to further and better interpretations of other of the agent's thoughts and actions as well. (Thus in the course of understanding Freud's interpretation of the Irma dream, we naturally frame further and

deeper explanations of his annoyance at Otto's remark, his desire to justify himself, his contemplation of his own conscientiousness about injections, etc.). Such further ascriptions of desires, in turn, may make it possible to detect further wishfulfilments; and so on.

We can thus say that Freud sought to extend commonsense psychology by means internal to it: namely, the supportive extension of basic causal generalizations concerning the satisfaction and pacification of desire already employed in commonsense interpretative practice. His extension is therefore potentially sound, cumulative, and radical. Sound, because the extending interpretations can gain support from the basic generalizations, and can also support them in turn, as in commonsense psychology itself. Cumulative, because each addition to the contents of probable wishes or desires can facilitate the discovery of others. And radical, because the extension offers significantly deeper and fuller explanations of actions and wishfulfilments generally, and by reference to motives which, in the main, had not previously been contemplated.

Freud found that the unconscious motives characteristically pacified in adult dreams and symptoms could be traced back into childhood, and included sensual love for one parent combined with rivalry and jealous hatred for the other, a constellation he called the *Oedipus Complex*. This, as it emerged, had one version in which the child's love was for the parent of the opposite sex, and another in which the love was for the parent of the same sex (and vice versa for the concomitant rivalry). It thus appeared that the feelings and phantasies of very young children showed remarkable *plasticity*, and, in particular, a degree of *bisexuality*. Little children were liable to intense psychic conflict, as between desires to harm or displace each parent, envied and hated as a rival for the love of the other, and desires to preserve and protect that same parent, loved sensually and also as a caretaker, helper, and model. In consequence, Freud thought, these conflicting motives were subjected to a process of *repression,* which removed them from thinking and planning of which the agent was aware; and concomitantly, in the course of normal development, they were both organized and modified by the child's formative *identification* with the parent of the same sex, that is, the child's taking that parent as a basic model for agency and the satisfaction of desire. Still, the repressed motives continued to exist in the unconscious, and to exercise their causal role in the production of dreams, symptoms, and *parapraxes*; and, in those cases in which conflict remained particularly extreme, in forms of neurotic or psychotic illness.

Following Freud's description of the role of belief-like representation in the pacification of desire, psychoanalysts now commonly describe the kind of representation which serves to pacify unconscious desire as *phantasy.* Particular phantasies, moreover, can be seen as constituting or implementing many of the unconscious mental processes, including those of both development and *defence,* which are described in psychoanalytic theory. Thus persons form lasting and life-shaping phantasies of themselves on the model of others, thereby establishing identifications with those others, as mentioned above. Again, persons represent others as having, and themselves as lacking, certain of their own impulses, aspects of mind, or traits of character, and thus accomplish the *projection* of these items onto or into others. The projection, or phantasied location, of parts of oneself in another may create a particular kind of mirror-image identification with that other, now often called *projective identification.* (*See also* Hinshelwood, 1991.) Such a process can also effect the *splitting* of the self, for example into good and bad, with the bad located elsewhere; and likewise (the representation of) the other may by the same means be split into good and bad, as with the image of the good mother and evil (step)mother in a fairy tale. (These processes are similar to those observed in dreams and symptoms; for example, the dream above might be taken as exemplifying a phantasy in which Freud represented motives connected with lack of professional care as in Otto rather than himself, and hence as an instance of splitting and projection on Freud's part.)

Although Freud's hypotheses about childhood were mainly based on data from adults, later analysts, and in particular Anna Freud (1946, 1974) and Melanie Klein (1932) were able to extend his techniques to children. Even very small children often have symptoms and difficulties analogous to those of adults; but they characteristically cannot produce such articulate thoughts and feelings connected with these, as Freud used in analysing their elders. They do, however, spontaneously and constantly represent things in play, with, e.g. dolls, toys, clay, paints, and games of make-believe. Child analysts have been able to understand these representations as Freud understood dreams, that is, as systematically reflecting motive and mental state, and in particular as embodying wishfulfilling phantasy. This has made it possible to analyse disturbed children, and hence to learn more about their mental life. Such work is now taken both as confirming and extending hypotheses based on the analysis of adults. So let us consider some material from the treatment of a little boy (Loeb, 1992), in order to illustrate some of the ideas sketched above.

This little boy suffered from nightmares – for example about 'red crayfish monsters' – and also behaved in an exaggeratedly feminine way. From the age of two he had wished to grow up to be a 'mommy', and as a toddler he would cover his chest with a towel after his bath, as if he had breasts. When he began therapy at four and a half he liked to pretend that he had breasts, and to dress as a 'fancy lady' in women's clothes, and to walk and talk accordingly. He took female parts in his play with other children, and by himself played with Barbie dolls; and in his daydreams he imagined himself to be Wonder Woman.

In part this behaviour showed an identification with his father's attractive and fashionable mother, his 'fancy grandmother', with whom he had spent a lot of time as a baby. This woman both behaved seductively towards the little boy and fostered his feminine ways. Thus she took off her clothes in front of him, and also would, for example, ask him to feel the soft leather pants she was wearing, as a result of which he got an erection and felt anxious. But also she let him wear her own high-heeled shoes, and dressed him in the make-up, jewellery, and other female finery he had come to make his own. We can see that from this seemingly contradictory behaviour one could extract a single coherent message, as to the overriding power and desirability of the grandmother's own feminine glamour; and it seems that the little boy had done so. In his first session of therapy he played with two Barbie dolls, one of which he dressed in plain clothing, the other in a 'fancy' low-cut gown. The plain doll he called 'mother', and the fancy doll 'queen grandmother'.

The little boy was thus able to express feelings about his parental figures – including here, perhaps, a sense of rivalry between his mother and grandmother, and also a division in his representation of women as between plain and 'fancy' – in terms of his play with dolls. At the same time he began the *transference* of these feelings on to his (female) analyst. He asked her, for example, to undress for him as his grandmother did; and when he was upset he would attack her, saying that it was the monsters that came in his nightmares who were doing it. In one such nightmare a 'half-lady, half-pinching lobster' chased him, and ran in and out of his mother's nose. It could thus be seen that in his mind an important sort of aggression was represented by pinching, and through phantasies involving pinching figures or creatures. Such aggression could be expressed in a dream, as related to himself and his mother, or in his behaviour, as related to the analyst; and he was liable to imagine the analyst as a fearful pinching figure as well.

Later in his analysis, as the little boy began to play out the marriage of the dolls Ken and Barbie, the role of such figures emerged more vividly. After the wedding, as the boy represented things, Ken would put

his penis in Barbie's vagina; and then Barbie would take the penis, leaving Ken with a vagina. The little boy would scream 'Ken lost his penis.' Often he said 'If you dress and act like a girl, nobody will think you have a penis. Then you don't have to worry that anyone will take it.' In time he was able to make one basis of these fears more clear. He talked about his (female) analyst having a 'hidden penis', and said it was 'the one that was taken from Ken – the one women get back.' Women, he said 'steal penises because they are jealous of men . . . Women come to the men at night and steal their penises. They have pinchers . . . the press-on nails are their pinchers . . . But no woman will ever get mine.' It thus appeared that he likened women in general, and his grandmother in particular, to the pinching monsters of his dreams, and also likened such women's pinching to *castration*, aimed at taking away men's penises so as to keep them for themselves.

This material can be seen both in light of Freud's general method, and also a number of particular claims about the unconscious, as sketched above. We can see, for example, how it might be that the little boy's wish to be a 'mommy' who had breasts (itself perhaps an indication of a natural bisexuality) was reflected even from the age of two in wishfulfilling identification with female behaviour, such as hiding his chest after a bath. Apparently such desires were later organized and represented as satisfied through identification with his 'fancy grandmother', and were expressed, elaborated, and pacified in a variety of representational activities, ranging from daydreams through play to dress, posture, and behaviour. Also we can see some of what Freud described as the sexual phantasies of children: e.g. that of the *phallic woman*, who has a hidden penis; or of the *primal scene* of parental intercourse, as one of violence and, in this particular case, danger to men.

The little boy's phantasy life thus seemed dominated by *imagos* – perhaps formed partly by projection – of fearful pinching figures, salient both in his nightmares and the underlying phantasies about women which emerged in his analysis. The material suggests that he was liable to identify himself with these phantasy figures, and that this served two connected functions, as specified by psychoanalytic theory. First, it enabled him wishfully to represent himself as the kind of powerful, glamorous, and castrating female figure he unconsciously imagined his grandmother, or again his analyst, to be. Secondly, it served to protect the masculinity that was threatened by figures of this same kind – if he represented himself as such a woman, he might escape the castration which such women dealt to men. Thus, it would seem, through projective identification, or again, *identification with the* (phantasied) *aggressor*, this little boy sought both to enjoy, and to escape, a form of aggression with which he was pre-occupied. It would seem that such deep projective and identificatory phantasies were constitutive of his unconscious mental life, and hence both of his character and the conflicts he suffered, until understood and thereby altered through analysis.

METAPSYCHOLOGICAL

In clinical work Freud described the unconscious in commonsense terms, as including wishes, beliefs, memories, and so forth. But he also sought to integrate his clinical findings with more abstract and theoretical concepts, as well as with physiological research, which was beginning to focus on the neurons composing the brain.

In his early *Project for a Scientific Psychology* Freud hypothesized that the working of the brain could be understood as the passage among neurons of some form of excitation, or *cathexis*, via connections which he called 'contact-barriers'. Information, on this hypothesis, would be stored in the brain in the form of alterations – facilitations or inhibitions – of these connections, and would be processed by the passage through the interconnected neurons themselves. Hence, as Freud put it, 'psychic acquisition generally', including memory, would be *'represented by the differences in the facilitations'* of neural connec-

tions (Freud, 1974, vol. I, p. 300). Freud thus anticipated the contemporary claim that the brain can be understood as a computational device whose 'knowledge is *in the connections'* among neuronal processing units (Rumelhart et al., 1988, p. 75), and also the associated view of mental processes as forms of neural activation, and mental states as dispositions to these, or structures determining them (*see* Glymour 1992; and also CONNECTIONISM). He sketched a model representing his early clinical findings in these terms, and seems to have framed his later discussions to be consistent with this.

On Freud's early physiological model the signalling of a bodily need, *instinct*, or *drive* – say for nutrition in an infant – causes a disequilbrium in neural excitation. This at first results in crying and uncoordinated bodily movements, which have at best a fleeting tendency to stabilize it. Better and more lasting equilibration requires satisfaction, e.g. by feeding; and this causes the facilitation of the neural connections involved in the satisfying events. The brain thus lays down neural records, or prototypes, of the sequences of perceptions, internal changes, bodily movements, and so on, involved in the restoration of equilibrium by satisfaction. Then when disequilibrium again occurs – e.g. when the infant is again hungry – the input signals engage previously facilitated pathways, so that the records of relevant past satisfactions are naturally reactivated. This, Freud hypothesized, constitutes early wishfulfilment.

Freud thus identified the wishfulfilling pacification of infantile proto-desire with what can be regarded as a form of neural prototype activation. (For a recent general account of this notion *see* Churchland, 1989, chs 9 and 10.) He took it that this provided more stability in disequilibrium than the random ennervations it replaced, and also that it served to organize the infant's responses, e.g. to hunger, by reproducing those previously associated with satisfaction. Then as the infant continued to lay down prototype upon prototype, the original wishful stabilizations evolved towards a system of thought, while also coming to govern a growing range of behaviour, increasingly coordinated to the securing of satisfaction. This, however, required the brain to learn to delay the wishfulfilment-governed neural behaviour associated with past satisfaction until present circumstances were perceptibly appropriate – that is, to come increasingly under the sway of what Freud called the *reality principle*.

This capacity for delay depended upon a tolerance of frustration, and of the absence of the satisfying object, which permitted *reality testing*, and hence the *binding* of the neural connections involved in the securing of satisfaction to perceptual information about the object, and later to rational thought. By this means what Freud regarded as a *primary process* leading to precipitate wishfulfilment was progressively overlaid and inhibited by a *secondary* one, which provided for the securing of satisfaction in realistic conditions. This benign development could, however, be blighted, if frustration (or intolerance of it) too much led to the overactivation of inappropriate prototypes, and this to greater frustration. Such a process could render the mind/brain increasingly vulnerable to disequilibrium and delusion, and hence increasingly reliant on earlier and more wishfulfilling modes of stabilization, in a vicious circle constitutive of mental disturbance and illness.

Freud allocated the task of fostering the sense of reality, and so providing for the satisfaction and reality-based pacification of desire, to a hypothetical neural structure, or functional part of the mind, which he called the *ego*. In later work Freud extended his account of the ego to include, among other things, the way it developed through identification with other persons. As noted above, the child's ego was partly formed through its identification with the parents in their role as agents, or satisfiers of their own desires. But the child also achieved self-regulation by laying down images of the parents as others in relation to the self, that is, in their role as satisfiers, or again frustrators or controllers, of its own bodily impulses and desires, and particularly the

early impulses connected with feeding, defecation, and the like. The child thus *introjected* helpful or controlling figures, and *internalized* its relations with them, as these were registered in the perspective of early experience, distorted both by projection and by the extremes of infantile emotion. The resulting distorted and controlling imagos formed the basis of a distinct, self-critical part of the ego, which Freud called the *super-ego*. This faculty tended to be far more aggressive, threatening, and punitive than the actual parents, and so could be a source of great anxiety or guilt, and even, in the extreme, suicide.

Freud also related the development of the ego and of conscious thought to language. The earliest prototypes, he assumed, were concerned with needs and actions bearing on objects in the immediate environment, and so with what he called *thing-presentations*. A limited relation of *symbolism* might obtain among thing-presentations, in the sense that one such presentation could become activated by, or in place of, another. In learning language, however, the brain laid down a further set of facilitations, constituting a network of *word-presentations*, including 'sound-images', 'word-images', and a system of 'speech associations' which linked these linguistic prototypes both with one another and with (those of) the things and situations associated with words and sentences. This system, Freud hypothesized, was responsible for 'cognition' and for 'conscious observing thought'. Cognition could partly be understood in terms of the activation of connections which were mediated by linguistic prototypes, and which, therefore, might be logical or rational. The consciousness of thought could be seen as resulting from the interactivation of linguistic and objectual representations; and in consequence the unconscious could be understood as that which was not properly linked with, or was somehow cut off from, the system of thought-facilitating connections laid down with the acquisition of language.

Freud elaborated these ideas on symbolism, language, and the unconscious in his later work (*see*, e.g. Freud, 1974, vol. I, p. 365, and vol. XIV, p. 209ff). He also attempted to describe how infantile sexual and aggressive motives could undergo *sublimation*, and thus be redirected towards ends which were benign, or socially valued. Subsequent psychoanalytic research, particularly with schizophrenic patients, has suggested that both the capacity for such emotional development, and that for rationally integrated thought and feeling, depend upon certain abilities to form and use symbols; and that these in turn depend upon a capacity to tolerate frustration, and in particular to bear the absence, distinctness, and separateness of the satisfying object, in ways related to Freud's original suppositions. (*See* Segal, 1986, ch. 4; Bion, 1967, ch. 4; Hinshelwood, 1991.)

CONCLUSION

As sketched above, Freud's early clinical work began a systematic and potentially cogent extension of commonsense psychology, providing deeper explanations for dreams, symptoms, and also many aspects of everyday thought, feeling, and action, by reference to unconscious motives. This provided the basis for a more general and theoretical account of normal and pathological functioning and development, which has been revised and extended by relation to data gained from the analysis both of children and psychotic patients. Much of this account can be cast in terms of the concept of unconscious phantasy, and associated processes such as projection and identification; and many of the constituent hypotheses were framed to accord with a conception of the working of the brain that has recently become an independent focus of research. Psychoanalytic hypotheses about the unconscious thus provide an explanatory and unifying account of a great range of mental and behavioural phenomena, many of which are commonsensically or clinically observable, and which are addressed by no other theory. Since these hypotheses are arguably cogent, and based on data gathered by many researchers over

years of systematic observation, they deserve serious philosophical attention.

See also CONSCIOUSNESS; PSYCHOANALYTIC EXPLANATION; PSYCHOLOGY AND PHILOSOPHY; RATIONALITY; SEARLE; SUBJECTIVITY.

BIBLIOGRAPHY

Bion, W. 1967. A theory of thinking. In *Second Thoughts*. London: Heinemann.
Churchland, P. 1989. *A Neurocomputational Perspective*. Cambridge, MA.: MIT Press.
Erickson, M. 1939. Experimental demonstrations of the psychopathology of everyday life. *Psychoanalytic Quarterly*, vol. 8, 1939; reprinted in *Freud and Psychology: Selected Readings*, ed. S. G. M. Lee and M. Herbert. Harmondsworth: Penguin Books, 1970.
Fodor J. 1991. Replies. In *Meaning in Mind: Fodor and his Critics*, ed. B. Loewer and G. Rey. Oxford: Basil Blackwell.
Freud, A. 1946. Introduction to the technique of the analysis of children. In *The Psychoanalytical Treatment of Children*. New York: International Universities Press.
Freud, A. 1974. Four lectures on child analysis. In *The Writings of Anna Freud*, vol. 1. New York: International Universities Press.
Freud, S. 1974. *The Standard Edition of the Complete Psychological Works of Sigmund Freud*. London: Hogarth.
Gardner, S. 1992. The unconscious. In *The Cambridge Companion to Freud*, ed. J. Neu. Cambridge University Press.
Glymour, C. 1992. Freud's androids. In *The Cambridge Companion to Freud*, ed. J. Neu. Cambridge University Press.
Hinshelwood, R., 1991. *A Dictionary of Kleinian Thought*. London: Free Associations Books.
Klein, M. 1932. *The Psychoanalysis of Children*. London: Hogarth; reprinted in *The Collected Works of Melanie Klein*, vol. 2. London: Hogarth, 1975.
Laplanche, J., and Pontalis, J.-B., eds. 1973. *The Language of Psycho-Analysis*. London: Hogarth.
Loeb, L. 1992. Transsexual symptoms in a child. *Journal of the American Psychoanalytic Association*, 40: 2.

Luria, A. 1976. The investigation of complexes produced during hypnosis by suggestion. In *The Nature of Human Conflicts*. New York: Liveright.

Segal, H. 1986. Notes on symbol formation. In *The Work of Hanna Segal*. London: Free Associations Press.

Rumelhart, D., Hinton, G., and McClelland, J. 1988. A general framework for parallel distributed processing. In *Parallel Distributed Processing, Vol. 1*, ed. D. Rumelhart et. al. Cambridge, MA.: MIT Press.

Wollheim, R. 1991. *Freud*. London: Fontana.

JIM HOPKINS

W

weakness of will   The notion of weakness of will or 'akrasia' (to use its Greek name) figures importantly in moral philosophy. Agents are said to be weak-willed when they have reached conclusions about their moral duties, but then fail to act on these conclusions. Since it is often difficult to be moral – to live up to one's moral principles – there would seem to be nothing particularly surprising or troubling about this notion, and certainly nothing especially pressing for the philosophy of mind. But this appearance is wrong on both counts.

First, there are certain conceptions of morality that make akratic action very puzzling indeed. Suppose, as did Plato and Aristotle, that an agent's opinion about what is morally required of him in some specific situation is an expression of what that agent thinks true about the situation – it is a cognitive state. One might here say that the agent *sees* the situation as morally requiring him to do some particular act. And suppose further that what leads an agent to act is precisely this view of how things are in respect of the relevant situation. That is, the *complete* motive or source of the action is the state of mind described above as 'seeing the situation as requiring a particular act'. Given these two things – that a moral opinion is a cognitive state and that this state provides the motivation for action – the very idea of an agent having such an opinion and not acting on it is problematic. For if an agent does genuinely have the moral view that, say action A, is morally required then there would seem to be no source of motivation that could explain why the agent does something else. Yet failing to do A, i.e. doing not-A, is plausibly describable as doing something else.

Of course, someone may form an opinion and then have a change of heart. Or the opinion may not be held in a fully sincere way. But in neither of these cases do we have the right conditions for akrasia. What is required is that the moral opinion be sincerely held, and continue to hold, whilst the agent does something other than what is dictated by that opinion. The usual view is that such weak-willed action is perfectly possible, but, given the cognitive account of morality described above, it would seem impossible.

This is not the place to consider the kinds of solution that Aristotle and others have offered to this problem; that investigation belongs to moral philosophy. And of course it might seem that the best thing to do in this case is simply to reject the moral account that makes akratic action so problematic. For example, one might insist that moral opinions are only *part* of our motivation – that various non-cognitive elements such as desires are equally necessary. If you regard moral opinions as requiring moral desires to be translated into action, then any particular case of weak-willed action might be ascribable to the effect of some non-moral desire lurking in the background. However, though there may be good reasons to reject the cognitive picture of morality, the problem of weakness of will by itself should not count as one. For, even in the brief sketch of this problem in moral philosophy, one can recognize the ingredients of a more generalized version of akrasia which is, if anything, more puzzling, and which cannot be solved by tinkering with one's conception of morality. Indeed, in its most general form, the problem of weakness of will is a problem for the very idea of rational action.

One can see the problem by juxtaposing certain apparently obvious principles of rational action with a description of akrasia that leaves behind all talk of morality and any wrangles about cognitive or non-cognitive motivation. First, we shall consider the principles of rational action, though it should be noted that 'rational action' does not mean action that deserves praise for its intelligence or logicality. It just means actions intelligible in the light of an agent's beliefs, desires and intentions – ingredients in what are thought of as an agent's reasons.

Suppose you think one course of action is much better for you than any other you can think of, where 'better' is to be understood as neutral in respect of morality. It would seem just obvious that in this state of mind you would want to undertake that course of action in preference to any other. Moreover, given that you have such a preference – that you want to do something more than you want to do anything else – it seems equally obvious that you will intentionally do it, so long of course as you count yourself able and free to do that thing. For example, suppose that I think it better for me to go to the cinema this evening – better than anything else I could do, and in absolutely no conflict with anything that I ought morally to do or not to do. From this it would seem to follow that I want to go to the cinema more than I want to do anything else. (There is a sense of 'better for me' which might not carry that implication, as when one speaks of something not all that pleasant but that would be better for me if I did it. A trip to the dentist might be described this way. However, in the principle above, one should not take the judgment that way: 'better for me' does not carry any sense of something undesirable but necessary. What you judge best for you is just that thing you put top of the list.) Finally, given that I want to go to the cinema more than I want to do anything else, it would seem equally to follow that I will intentionally go to the cinema when the time comes, assuming of course that I feel free to do so and have not changed my mind. These claims are straightforward considerations governing our conception of what it is to be an agent who makes judgments, has wants or preferences, and acts intentionally after deliberation. In short, they are claims about rational agency.

We turn next to a description of akratic action – one borrowed from Davidson (1980). To a first approximation, an agent is said to act in a weak-willed way when he or she does something at the same time as thinking that what is done is not the best thing. Thus, I may decide that it would be best if I did not stay up late, given that I have a lot to do the next day – things that I have been looking forward to doing and that I know can only be fully enjoyed if I am not exhausted by lack of sleep. But being weak-willed, I nonetheless do stay up. Generalizing on this example, and being careful about certain details, we can say an agent acts in a weak-willed way when: (i) the agent does something intentionally whilst (ii) believing there to be another available course of action which, all things considered, that agent regards as genuinely better. The word 'intentionally' is important here because we wouldn't count a piece of behaviour as weak-willed unless it was an action in the full sense. And it is equally important that the other course of action be both available and judged better by the agent's own lights.

Combining the discussions of the last two paragraphs, it is not too difficult to appreciate that we have trouble. For, according to the principles of rational action, insofar as an agent regards one of two courses of action as better, then that agent wants most to do that which is better and will in fact do it, unless for some reason neither of them is undertaken. But, as in the case of going to bed early, it seems possible for an agent to be akratic – to do intentionally something which is judged to be less good than something else, though both are thought possible. The principles of rational action seem to rule out akrasia, but not many examples are needed to show us that there is in fact such a thing. The combination of things we accept about action and weakness entails

the contradictory and thus paradoxical conclusion that there both can and cannot be
such a thing as akrasia.

As characterized, weakness of will creates
difficulties that go right to the heart of our
general conception of what it is to act for
reasons. Morality and moral theories just
don't come into it. Moreover, there is no
universally accepted way to deal with the
paradox. Yet, since the work expended on
akrasia, has also served to sharpen our
understanding of such things as desire,
intention, action, and judgment, there is
every reason to think that the problem of
weakness of will is genuine and quite deeply
embedded in our concept of action.

See also DESIRE; INTENTION; RATIONALITY;
REASONS AND CAUSES.

BIBLIOGRAPHY

Davidson, D. 1980. How is weakness of will
possible? In his *Essays on Actions and Events.*
Oxford University Press.
McDowell, J. 1981. The role of *eudaimonia* in
Aristotle's ethics. In *Essays on Aristotle's
Ethics*, ed. A. O. Rorty. University of Cali-
fornia Press.
Mortimore, G., ed. 1972. *Weakness of Will: A
Collection of Papers.* London: Macmillan &
Co.
Wiggins, D. 1987. Weakness of will, commen-
surability, and the objects of deliberation
and desire. In his *Needs, Values, Truth.*
Oxford: Basil Blackwell).

SAMUEL GUTTENPLAN

the will The word 'will' has been used in
at least two different ways by philosophers.
At the time of the German Romantics there
was a tendency to use it to designate a psychological phenomenon, force-like in character and linked in ways to traits like
determination, which was broadly of the
nature of desire or instinct – the main precursor of Freudian 'Libido' and 'Id'. The
connection with intentional action was
close, but no more than that: thus, we find
Schopenhauer speaking of 'acts of will', but
also of 'the will' itself with a broader sig-

nification. According to him the will constituted one great half of the mind, indeed
constituted its reality or essence. 'Will' here
signifies something to be opposed to the
cognitive and intellectual part of the mind,
close to 'heart' and remote from 'head', in
which our very being lay.

This usage is to be distinguished from a
different and more widespread usage in
which 'will' is exclusively linked with acting
and trying to act. Here 'will' stands for a
supposed psychological event which is
present of necessity and uniquely on such
active occasions. It is *this supposed phenomenon* that is the subject-matter of the
ensuing discussion. In short, I shall be
discussing 'the will' as the term is understood by Descartes, Locke, Hume, (later)
WITTGENSTEIN and RYLE; and not as
understood by Fichte, Schelling, and Schopenhauer.

Before I begin this discussion I would like
to make three preliminary points, (α), (β),
(γ). The first point (α) is that questions of
language are of particular relevance when
we debate the existence of contentious phenomena like 'willing' and 'sense-data'. This
is because we embark upon such discussions in ignorance of the necessary and sufficient marks of the phenomena in question.
In my opinion we are right to do so. Science
has taught us that this is a genuine possibility – in science: that it is possible to single
out a particular something in nature (e.g.
gold) by means of a designating expression,
which accordingly acquires the sense of
standing for that something, without our
knowing what the something is. A similar
situation can occur in philosophy; and in
particular in the case of those debatable
entities 'willing' and 'sense-data'. Thus, it
seems to me to be perfectly possible that
Descartes and others had truly divined the
presence of a psychological something
which they described as 'willing', even
though the characterization which they
gave of 'willing' was incorrect. We should
not judge the validity of their claim that
'willing' is a reality, by the veridicality of
their theories as to its nature. To be sure,
we can tolerate so much and no more

discrepancy between the actual nature of that item and what they take that nature to be; for we need reason in what they say to know what it is that they are talking of. Nonetheless the discerning of, and the correct characterizing of the truly discerned, are distinguishable phenomena. We should therefore note that we can approach the question of the reality of the will, without as yet being able to state criterial necessary and sufficient conditions for the use of 'will'. Designation can precede identification.

The second preliminary point (β) is, that the problem(s) of the Will is not the same as the problem(s) of ACTION. The first problem is, whether or not the will exists, and what is its nature. More exactly, whether or not there exists anything that is endowed with a set of properties that sufficiently resemble the set that philosophers (traditionally using the word 'will') took to be the identifying marks of 'willing', to justify crediting them with its detection; and the nature of that phenomenon. The problem of Action is different. Now the actual *existence* of such a type as 'action' – which is allowed to range over INTENTIONAL and unintentional examples, and which excludes mere causing 'actions' such as storms 'do' – is I think a matter concerning which there is widespread agreement. It is a consensus that extends far beyond Philosophy, and exists in most legal and moral systems. While non-rational animals act (e.g. walk) in precisely the sense we do, most crime and wickedness takes the form either of action or its neglect. Then the problems concerning action are at least two. What are the necessary and sufficient conditions for the occurrence of an act of given type; and what are the phenomenal constituents of such an act? Now it may well be the case that the necessary conditions of any action include the occurrence of an event we are entitled to describe as a 'willing'. If so, it may well be the case that such an event is *either* identical with *or* part of *or* necessary cause of the act in question. Evidently the problems arising over the phenomenon of action are intimately connected with those appertaining to the will. Indeed, a resolu-tion of the latter problems appears to be a pre-condition of a resolution of the former. Then I would like to emphasize that my concern here is exclusively with the problem of the will. It is not that of the conditions of, and the constitution of, actions.

The third and last preliminary point (γ) concerns the close relation between theories as to the existence and nature of the will, and mind–body theory. The identification-conditions employed by DUALISTS like Descartes and Locke show a tendency to include elements that betray the presence of that dualist standpoint. Are such beliefs essential to their belief in the reality of the will? I do not think so. After all, Hume and Berkeley cannot be described as dualists, yet unquestionably believed in the selfsame phenomenon mentioned by Locke. Indeed, Hume in the *Enquiries* (section vii, part I) impressively refutes Locke's attempt to trace the origin of our idea of Power to the will, by appeal to the mysteriousness of the relation between willing and its bodily effect, and could scarcely have done so had he and Locke had different phenomena in mind. Theories of the will's existence and nature almost wholly transcend theories of the mind–body relation. There is nothing to prevent a latter-day PHYSICALIST of all but the most destructively reductionist variety from believing in a theory of the will which is more or less in total agreement with seventeenth- and eighteenth-century dual-ists, eighteenth-century idealists, and the twentieth-century heirs of the theory.

In sum, we must distinguish (α) theories concerning the existence of the will, from theories as to its nature, (β) theories concerning the existence and nature of the will, from theories concerning the conditions of and constitution of actions, (γ) theories concerning the nature of the will, from mind–body theory.

IDENTIFYING CONDITIONS OF THE WILL

I pass now to a consideration of the identifying conditions of this supposed phenom-enon. The identifying conditions adopted by such traditional believers in the phenom-

611

enon as Descartes, Locke, Berkeley, Hume (et al.), include the following at least:

(i) the item in question is a mental event W,
(ii) which we 'do' in the very sense in which we do actings and tryings,
(iii) which occurs of necessity whenever we either act or try to act,
(iv) W is a distinct event from, and generally a regular causally sufficient condition of, the bodily event x which occurs when we engage in a bodily act x' of x-production (e.g. if x is arm-rise, x' is arm-raising).

A Cartesian might very well embellish this (existential) theory with the following additional features:

(v) W occurs in a purely mental substance,
(vi) W is non-physical in nature.

Since (v) and (vi) derive from more general metaphysical views on the person/mind/body relation, I think we have a right to disregard them, and say that those philosophers who endorsed (i)–(iv) and those who endorsed (i)–(vi) shared a belief in the existence of the will. More, they shared a belief as to its nature: namely, that it is a distinctive mental event that is 'done' and necessary to and unique to active situations (whether of success or failure, intentionalness or unintentionalness). And they shared in addition a belief concerning its causal explanatory power. These three beliefs – in the will's existence, nature, and explanatory power – will be held by anyone endorsing (i)–(iv); and might very well be held by a physicalist. They are not identical beliefs, but they are nonetheless very closely linked. Thus it is not possible to entertain a belief in the will's existence without holding at least some view as to its nature; though it may well be possible to hold beliefs on these latter two matters without endorsing any particular theory as to the will's causal explanatory properties.

The distinguishing of these three beliefs –

in the existence, nature, and power of will – as separate from one another, is a little more difficult when we come to consider philosophers like Schopenhauer (or Spinoza) who conceive of the mind–body relation in radically unified terms. Schopenhauer described 'acts of the body' as 'acts of the will objectified'; and what he meant was that physical actions like (say) walking were at once physical phenomena and identical with willings. In short, not only would Schopenhauer not endorse (v) and (vi), he would not endorse (iv) either! Now the causal explanatory properties of the will have generally been taken to be of the first importance – rightly, in my view. Ought we therefore to say that Schopenhauer cannot have believed in the existence of the phenomenon postulated by Descartes and Locke (etc.)? Or ought we instead to say that he believed in the existence of the selfsame phenomenon, yet held a different theory concerning its pivotal causal-explanatory properties, and conceivably also a different theory as to its nature? I have no doubt the latter is the correct interpretation of the situation. I have no doubt that Schopenhauer believed in 'acts of the will' in the received traditional sense. The considerations advanced earlier wherein we distinguished grounds for saying a phenomenon had been discerned, and grounds for attributing a particular theory concerning either the nature or pivotal causal properties of that phenomenon, are surely decisive. There can I think be no doubt that Descartes, Hume, Schopenhauer, and (say) Pritchard, are in agreement as to the existence of willing; and in disagreement with (say) RYLE and Anglo-American philosophers in the Wittgensteinian era.

So much for what it is to entertain a theory concerning the existence and character of the will. A word now about *disbelief* in this phenomenon. Belief in the existence of the will (and sense-data) became very unpopular between (say) 1935 and 1970. The main cause of this disbelief was I think verificationist and neo-behaviourist styles of thought, and in particular the influence of the earlier and the later philosophies of

WITTGENSTEIN. Both the will and sense-data smelled of 'bad metaphysics'. To many they seemed philosophical inventions, scarcely on a par with The Absolute or The Transcendental Ego, but suffering like them from the unforgivable sin of being postulated for reasons of an entirely philosophical kind. The very idea of phenomenal items, whose existence was a matter for philosophy to decide, ran against the entire verificationist spirit of the era (which extends into our own!) Now I think it is no exaggeration to say that the general attitude of the philosophical community to will (and sense-data) was (and to a degree still is) near-phobic in character and marked by a special form of *intolerance*. Lodged at the strategic points of interaction between mind and extra-mental physical nature, these entities were seen as threatening us with a domain of 'private objects' and a mind–body divide which would plunge us all back in 'reactionary' Cartesian dualistic individualism. I think this is superstitious. And if anything the boot is on the other foot! For such a view of will and sense-data evidences a somewhat flimsy commitment to a naturalistic-physicalistic account of the mind–body relation. Thus, it vastly overestimates the extent to which the admission of such entities could weaken such an account. Provided those entities are embedded in a law-governed psychophysical framework, they constitute no more of a threat to a unified account of mind and body than does the admission of mental phenomena into one's ontology. Indeed, I personally am persuaded that a particular account of willing manages to accomplish a vitally significant form of unification of mind and body which cannot be expressed in other terms. Inside many opponents of will and sense-data – indeed, inside some physicalists! – a closet or unconscious Cartesian is wildly signalling to be let out!

These are no more than speculations. And it has to be admitted that it is something of a paradox, if acts of the will and sense-data do indeed exist, that Philosophy should be called upon to demonstrate their existence. Surely it is an empirical issue whether or not these phenomena are realities? Surely observation, in these particular cases introspective observation, must be the ultimate court of appeal? And it has here and now to be acknowledged that in either case the findings of INTROSPECTIVE observation are precisely nil. Stare within as you act or visually perceive and you come across nothing but acting or seeing! And yet many philosophers have posited the existence of these entities. Why? What is the way out of this seeming impasse? It is, to begin with, at least facilitated with the assistance of a very little philosophy of language. The first thing to note is, that 'will' and 'sense-datum' are philosophical terms of art, which stand in need of explanation, an explanation which must take the form either of a paraphrase or a definite description. In short, we need to be able to say *what it is* that we are looking for if we are to come across these entities. Here we have one non-observational issue. And we need in addition to know *what is to count* as an introspective awareness of the phenomenon in question. And so on. It is through loopholes like these that the question as to whether or not these entities exist manages to escape the rigid ruling that the existence of phenomenal entities is as such purely and simply an observational issue. Whether or not it is a matter for observation, it is without doubt a matter for philosophy.

THE REALITY OF THE WILL: PRELIMINARY CONSIDERATIONS

Then what philosophical considerations support belief in the reality of the will? Before I advance an argument in the following section, a few preliminary considerations. One important preliminary to the argument is linguistic, the discovery of a name or description of the phenomenon that is cast in terms of ordinary established usage and eschews philosophical terminology. Once this has been settled, we should have a clearer idea of what is to count as evidence *pro* or *con* its existence. Now one such descriptive term is 'try' ('strive', 'attempt'), which in my opinion precisely singles out the phenomenon traditionally singled out by the word 'will'. However, this expression suffers from the disadvantage that pragmatic linguistic presumptions restrict its application in certain situations in which truth considerations alone would license its application. A tendency to confuse truthfulness of saying with pertinence of saying obscures the vital issue of *truth*. While there is absolutely nothing the matter with expressing the argument in terms of trying or attempting, it involves one in argumentative antics one could do without. For these reasons alone I shall instead appeal to the word 'do'. There can be no doubt that there is a sense of the word 'do' that is uniquely reserved for actings (whether intentional of unintentional) and tryings (whether successful or failing). 'What are you doing?' 'Fixing the lock', 'Daydreaming', 'Trying to fix the lock', are acceptable answers, as 'Reflecting the light', 'Imprinting my image on your retina', 'Generating knowledge of my presence in you', are not. These last are unacceptable responses to the above question, and acceptable answers instead to a different question, 'What are you doing?', which merely amounts to 'What are you causing?' However intimately linked, these are different varieties of 'doing': a fact that is simply demonstrated by their diverse space-time properties: the time and place of the action-doing being that generally of a bodily action, of the merely-causal-doing that of an effect. Thus, the act of killing someone by intentionally starting an avalanche occurred when and where the murderer (stood, and with unnerving slowness) did his repellent deed; but the killing by the avalanche, which the murderer intentionally engineered, occurred precisely when and where the victim expired. The agent act-killed in one place and cause-killed in another. 'Killed' is ambiguous.

I am trying to assemble an argument in favour of the reality of the will, expressed in words whose use is agreed, and I am appealing to the familiar active use of the word 'do' (as expounded above). The argument – which I shall set out in the next section – seeks to demonstrate a *particular complex proposition*, which is in my opinion equivalent to an affirmation of the reality of the will. Namely, that whenever we perform an action, whether it be intentional or unintentional, or a trying, whether it be successful or unsuccessful, then an item W comes into existence which is endowed with the following properties:

(a) W is an event,
(b) W is psychological in status,
(c) we 'do' W in a distinctive sense which is the sense in which we 'do' actings and tryings – as distinct from that in which we 'do' mere causings,
(d) the psychological type of W is a 'doing' in the above sense,
(e) the content of W is the doing of the intentional deed or trying.

To demonstrate the reality of the will, I think we need do no more than prove this complex claim. It will be noted that (a)–(e) include no mention of the causal powers of W – which accords with the position adopted earlier when I urged that Schopenhauer's unusual account of the will's causal properties did not disqualify him from believing in its existence. However, I can well believe that to some people such a theoretical position must verge upon absurdity. Is not the production of phenomena precisely what the will is all about? And does not the above theory threaten to *trivialize* will-theory? Thus, if one omits a causal differentia, and endorses (a)–(e) as necessary and sufficient conditions of the phenomenon of willing, it looks as if all one need believe to believe in the reality of the will is that actings and tryings exist and are psychological events. But this seems relatively uncontroversial – unlike the theory of the will. Many people might be ready to endorse this seeming truism, and at the same time firmly disavow belief in the existence of the 'volitional' phenomenon posited by Descartes and Hume (etc.). Surely we need to add a causal clause to (a)–(e) to block this trivialization of the claim, and to ensure that the W in question really is the will!

I do not find this objection cogent. It encapsulates two errors. In the first place it objects to the claim that (a)–(e) amounts to an affirmation of the will's existence, on the grounds that one must know the will's causal powers to know of its existence. But this is false. No doubt we must know that 'willing' *in some sense* explains 'willed' bodily movements; but one can be wholly ignorant as to whether the 'willing' encompasses or is distinct from these movements, wholly ignorant therefore as to its causal powers, and know nonetheless that whenever we act or try, a distinctive immediately-given active psychological event occurs (which seems enough to know the will exists). The second flaw in the above objection is this. The objection rests on the supposition that the psychologicality of actions is a *non-controversial* matter. But how could it be? Suppose that one believed – as many have believed – that the physical act (x′) of moving a limb was identical with the limb movement (x). In that case the claim that actions were psychological in status would imply that suitably originated finger-movements (say) could be psychological events. But *could* they? Could *any* causal history make of such a simple mechanical event something psychological? It would need to be a psychological event whose immediate origin is muscular, whose existence is discovered proprioceptively, which is wholly distinct from cerebral events! The suggestion is surely absurd. These considerations make it clear that a belief that bodily actions are psychological in status commits one to a position on the *constitution* of bodily actions – which is a highly controversial matter.

I think this disposes of the objection that the complex proposition (a)–(e) is trivially true, and cannot therefore amount to an affirmation of the existence of the will. Nevertheless *the question remains*: are (a)–(e) sufficient to demonstrate the reality of the phenomenon putatively designated by the traditional term 'will'? I am strongly inclined to say that they are, bearing in mind that (a)–(e) ensure the existence of an active psychological event of type 'doing'

whenever we act or try – which looks like enough to guarantee coincidence of reference. However, it must be emphasized that the issue, at least as stated above, is not in itself a matter of prime *philosophical* importance. What in effect we are asking is: what propositions would prove the traditionalists right concerning the existence of the will? This is undoubtedly of philosophical-*historical* importance, which is not a negligible consideration, but not I think of great philosophical moment in its own right. Now some may detect the unfolding of a sort of dialectical process in the preceding discussion. With the advent of Constitution-Theory, and theories as to the nature of the mental and/or psychological, it might seem that our concept of will must *develop*, closing off some possibilities and opening up others as it gathers in complexity. In a word, that it follows a line of development which it need not have followed. Then how can we be sure that we are contesting or endorsing the existence of what earlier simpler conceptual systems purported to identify? This counsels a *relativistic* reading of the situation – which I resist. Here I have to be dogmatic. I can merely reiterate that if (a) – (e) is demonstrable, then the reality of what Descartes and others had in mind when they spoke of 'the will' will have been demonstrated. What is at issue is the existence, and omnipresence in active situations, of an immediately given psychological event of purely active ('doing'-) type: a question that surely transcends philosophical-historical development. How can such a question be relative to era?

THE REALITY OF THE WILL

What is certainly not historical, and is a matter of prime philosophical importance, is the *truth* of (a)–(e). If this can be established, we will have established the existence in animal life of a purely active psychological event matching the above specifications. It is *at that point* that the causal properties of such a psychological event become a fit subject for investigation. Now I am myself of the opinion that good arguments exist in favour of (a)–(e). They are for the most part variants on the much despised – but absolutely invaluable – argument from illusion (error, failure, etc.). Certain intelligible situations in which (say) it erroneously seems to a wide-awake subject in his right mind, who is *in fact* busy obeying an order to move a finger (say), that he has just been and even now still is the victim of several perceptual illusions, can reveal that whenever we intentionally and confidently perform a bodily action we are mentalistically-immediately aware of a mentalistically-immediately-caused 'doing' of something or another. One has merely to imagine that the above person is brought perfectly rationally (but erroneously) to doubt that he is or has been moving his finger, let us say by his being convinced that scientifically induced neurological proprioceptor and ocular events are and have been generating proprioceptive and visual illusions. Such a person would *know*, and with the authority typical of first-person present-tense experience, that an immediately-mentally-caused event of an active kind (a 'doing') had occurred. He would know, not merely that he had *intended* to obey the order, but that he had in addition *done* all that he could to obey: he would know that *an event* had expressed his intention. These situations of apparent active failure combined with apparent epistemological error act as filters, whereby the common presence across a whole series of cases of a 'doing' endowed with all the appurtenances of psychologicality is exposed to view. Such a 'doing' is to be found in normal situations of confident and intentional success, as well as in situations of total and timorous failure. Along these lines we can I think establish the existence of a phenomenon that is the same as that traditionally singled out under the word 'will' and disbelieved in by so many twentieth-century philosophers.

The residual and very important question remains as to the causal properties of the aforementioned psychological event. Space will not permit me to discuss this question satisfactorily. It is undoubtedly true that seventeenth- and eighteenth-century philosophers understood the will to be both cause and causal explanation of the 'willed' bodily movement; and true in addition that their beliefs concerning the mind–body relation were a partial determinant of this theory. I myself do not in any way wish to play down the significance of the causal properties of the will, and am convinced that if the will is a reality it must in some sense constitute the causal explanation of the 'willed' bodily movement. Thus, if I had not willed it, the finger would not have moved – this, surely, is true. However, whether or not the will is a distinct cause of that movement is an additional and difficult question. The view that recommends itself to me, for a series of rather complicated reasons which I cannot here consider, is that willing is generally a causally sufficient condition of, but not a distinct cause of, such 'willed' bodily movement. The proof of this theory depends upon a contentious conjunctive proposition: namely, that bodily actions (like walking) are *non-distinct* from the 'willed' bodily movement (like leg motion) their occurrence necessitates; *and* that all succeeded-in attempts-to-do-act-X are *identical with* X-acts. The first half of this conjunction seems relatively obvious: considerations of visibility, locality, etc., strongly support the view that (say) walking does not occur *in the head alone*! It is the second half of the conjunction that is difficult to establish – though there seems little doubt that the claim or principle is true of absolutely all instrumental action. I shall not here try to demonstrate that 'the attempt to perform basic act X that *is* successful is the basic act X', though I am myself persuaded that it can be done. Once the conjunctive proposition is established, a particular theory of bodily actions seems natural. This theory involves the supposition that the bodily action *is* a willing, which is at once a psychological event *and* a physical event constituted out of nothing but motor-events, a phenomenon that spreads developmentally out from mind/brain to the bodily extremity involved. When we conjoin this theory with the theory affirming (a)–(e), we have a theory – now enriched with an account of the vitally important causal properties of the phenomenon in question – which continues to sufficiently well match the traditional specifications of willing, to count as a theory of the will. Whether or not the phenomenon has this latter historical property, pales in significance beside the truly philosophical question as to whether or not anything has the former complex array of features. This last is of the first importance in the understanding of the relation of mind and body.

See also ACTION; *An Essay on Mind* section 2.3.; HISTORY; INTENTION; REASONS AND CAUSES.

BIBLIOGRAPHY

O'Shaughnessy, B. 1980. *The Will.* (2 vols.) Cambridge: Cambridge University Press.

BRIAN O'SHAUGHNESSY

Wittgenstein, Ludwig Wittgenstein's philosophy of mind must be seen in the light of his conception of the nature of philosophical problems and what is necessary to resolve them. For he believed that philosophical problems are puzzles induced by misinterpretations of the use of words in our language and they are solved by paying attention to the ways in which the problematic words really are used. Hence it is wrong to think that the aim of philosophy is to provide an explanation of various phenomena by means of a theory. Rather, philosophy must eschew explanation and be purely descriptive. What it describes are the ways in which words are used in our language, or, as Wittgenstein often expresses it, the 'grammar' of words. Accordingly, Wittgenstein's work in the philosophy of mind does not issue in philosophical theses about the mind, but is directed towards dissipating philosophical puzzlement about the mind by the identification of misleading images and superficial similarities and by a description of the actual use of those words that lie at the heart of the problem. This makes his philosophy of mind unusually resistant to summary presentation, its force often deriving from its particularity. This should be borne in mind in reading what follows.

Three main themes in Wittgenstein's philosophy of mind are (i) the diversity or heterogeneity of mental concepts, (ii) the illusion of the essential privacy of states of consciousness, and (iii) the nature and basis of mental REPRESENTATION or INTENTIONALITY.

THE HETEROGENEITY OF MENTAL CONCEPTS

A fundamental feature of Wittgenstein's later philosophy is the insistence that superficial linguistic uniformity conceals 'grammatical' diversity, so that the variety of reality is hidden from our reflective understanding by similarities in our means of representation of that reality in language. Wittgenstein applies this insight to words in our mental vocabulary in two ways. First, there is the simple point that the grammars of words for SENSATIONS, EMOTIONS, THOUGHTS, IMAGES, INTENTIONS, and so on, are very different from one another, despite more or less superficial resemblances. Accordingly, Wittgenstein is at pains to spell out these differences and warn against the assimilation of one kind of mental state or occurrence to a different kind (for example, the feeling of how your arm is moving to the feelings you experience in your arm when it is so moving (Wittgenstein, 1953, II, §viii)). Second, there is the more subtle point that even an apparently uniform mental category can exhibit considerable diversity in the kinds of state that fall within it, so that a failure to recognize this diversity results in a mistaken assimilation of mental states. Perhaps Wittgenstein's best illustration of this is the variety of visual experiences. We can see colour, shape, a likeness between one face and another, what a picture depicts, a person's melancholy expression or hesitant posture, a sign as the mirror-image of an F, a person's glance, and endless other sorts of thing. All of these experiences fall under our concept of seeing (*see* PERCEPTION; IMAGERY; IMAGINATION). Yet, as Wittgenstein shows, there are subtle differences between the concept of one kind of visual experience and the concept of another. Consider the experience of suddenly seeing melancholy in someone's face – a face that does not change in any way at the moment you see the melancholy. This is one instance of what Wittgenstein calls 'seeing an aspect'. Wittgenstein rejects two opposed positions as false alternatives. One insists that this visual experience is on all fours with the paradigm of a genuine visual experience, namely the experience of seeing a colour or a shape. The other insists that it is not really a case of seeing, but instead something that is not a visual experience at all, namely an interpretation of what is seen. Both positions are mistaken, Wittgenstein argues, for the experience of seeing melancholy – like any experience of seeing an aspect – shares some, but only some, grammatical features with the alleged paradigm, and some, but not all, features with the suggested alternative. Whereas seeing an aspect resembles seeing a colour with respect to 'genuine duration' – that is, each is a continuous state the onset and end of which take place at precise moments – seeing an aspect, unlike seeing a colour, is 'subject to the WILL', that is, it is the kind of state which it makes sense to try to induce in oneself when seeing an object without distorting the object's visual appearance. This means not that the experience of seeing melancholy is in any way problematic, but that the concept of that kind of experience is not reducible to either of the proposed kinds: the concept of seeing melancholy exhibits a significant difference from that of seeing a colour or a shape and yet it is distinguishable from the concept of a mere adjunct of thought to what is allowed to be a genuine visual experience. To adapt the well-known remark of Bishop Butler that impressed Wittgenstein: the concept of *seeing* something *as* we interpret it 'is what it is and not another thing'. This is the moral that Wittgenstein emphasizes

time and time again in his examination of mental concepts.

THE ILLUSION OF ESSENTIAL PRIVACY

Wittgenstein's target in his investigation of the concept of a state of consciousness, such as the experience of pain, is the seductive idea that a state of CONSCIOUSNESS is essentially private, in the sense that, in virtue of the nature of a state of consciousness, it is such that only the subject of that state can know whether he is in that state. This conception is often thought to underlie the notable first-person/third-person asymmetry in the use of psychological words: whereas the third-person use is based on observation, the first-person singular present indicative is not based on observation. This way of thinking is usually supplemented by the claim that the nature of a state of consciousness guarantees not only essential privacy, but also the subject's immediate and infallible awareness of what his present state of consciousness is. Accordingly, a person's consciousness is thought of as an essentially private realm, and his assertions about his states of consciousness as infallible descriptions of what happens in this realm – descriptions that cannot be checked against the reality by any other person and about which the person himself cannot be mistaken. (*See* INTROSPECTION.)

Wittgenstein argues on a number of grounds that this is a misrepresentation of the concept of pain. First, it is false that, in the ordinary sense of the expression, one person cannot *know* that another person is in pain: on the contrary, one person often does know that another is in pain. (I return to this blunt rejection of the essential privacy of pain later.) Second, the idea that, in virtue of the nature of pain, the subject of pain knows ('with certainty') that he is in pain is a misconstruction of the grammar of the word 'pain'. It is true that it is senseless for the subject of pain, but not another person, to express doubt about whether he is in pain; but this is not a matter of the subject's being endowed by the nature of pain with a uniquely privileged epistemic authority about the current state of his consciousness. The grammatical rules governing the word 'pain' are no more derivable from the nature of pain than are any other grammatical rules derivable from the reality with which they deal; and the senselessness of uncertainty should not be represented as a peculiarly well-founded guarantee that whatever seems to the subject right about his state of consciousness is right. Rather, the senselessness of uncertainty is a feature of the 'language-game' we play with the word 'pain', and a person's assertion that he is in pain is an 'utterance' (*Äusserung*) of the pain, not a description of an essentially private and self-intimating event. Third, if pain were essentially private, then, in the first place, each person would know only what *he* calls 'pain', not what anyone else does. But then what each of us calls 'pain' would be irrelevant to the use of the word 'pain' in our language: the use of a word in a public language cannot be constrained by considerations about what is essentially private, and whether someone understands the word 'pain' and uses it correctly is determined by publicly accessible criteria. Hence it would not matter whether the supposed private reference of the word 'pain' were the same or different across people or in any individual's case: there would be neither an intersubjective nor an intrasubjective requirement of common reference to something essentially private – a requirement that would need to be met for the word 'pain' to have a constant meaning in the language. This is the force of Wittgenstein's remark that 'if we construe the grammar of the expression of sensation on the model of "object and name" the object drops out of consideration as irrelevant' – the moral of his famous 'beetle-in-the-box' analogy (Wittgenstein, 1953, § 293).

These considerations are buttressed by Wittgenstein's critique of so-called 'private ostensive definition'. If there were to be essentially private events or states that a subject of consciousness refers to in his own language, he would himself have to introduce the names of these events or states

into his language, rather than acquire an understanding of them from others. This would require him to introduce a word as a name of a kind of state – an essentially private state – solely on the basis of his apparent awareness of the occurrence of the state. But how would it be possible for him to do so? It would seem that all he could do would be to concentrate his attention on the state he is in on some occasion, as it were pointing to it in the privacy of his consciousness, and give himself a quasi-ostensive definition of some sign 'S' by saying to himself '*This* is called "S"'. But, as Wittgenstein demonstrates, this would be a pointless exercise: it could not serve as an introduction of the word 'S' into the person's language as a name of some kind of thing that happens to the person. The reason it could not do this is that a definition provides a rule for the use of a word and this act of quasi-pointing and 'stipulation' fails to specify a rule. But without a rule for the application of 'S' no sense has been given to the idea that some applications of the sign will be correct (i.e. the named item will be of the *same* kind as the original (*this*)) and some incorrect (i.e. the named item will not be of the same kind).

To appreciate the force of this consideration, ask yourself the question, What could the rule be? It could not be 'Call something "S" if it is the same as *this*', for since this in no way constrains the use of 'S', i.e. it fails to make some uses of 'S' correct and some incorrect, it is not a rule. The reason it does not provide a standard of correct application is that it is entirely indefinite, failing to indicate the *kind* that 'S' is supposed to be the name of. To be a rule it would need to be completed by an answer to the question, 'Same *what* as *this*?'. But what completion would be possible, given that 'S' is intended to be the name of something that is essentially private? The rule could not be 'Call something "S" if it is the same kind of *sensation* as *this*'. Apart from any other considerations, 'sensation' is a word of our common language, and so its use in the rule would be legitimate only if 'S' were to be used in accordance with the grammar of words of sensations, which is precluded by its being intended as the name of something essentially private. There are two questions that can be asked about a sign that is claimed to be the name of a sensation: Is the sign a word for a *sensation?* and Is the sign a word for *a* sensation (i.e. a sensation of some kind S, rather than T)? Wittgenstein rightly faults the attempt to give sense to the sign 'S' by 'private ostensive definition' on both grounds: 'S' is not used as a name of *a* sensation (Wittgenstein, 1953, §258), nor as a name of a *sensation* (Wittgenstein, 1953, §261). But he also rightly goes further. For it would be equally illegitimate to claim that 'S' is being used as a name of *something the subject has*, or as a name of . . ., where the gap is filled by any words of our common language.

So we reach the conclusion that the alleged essential privacy of states of consciousness implies not only that one person cannot impart his private 'knowledge' to others but that he cannot express it to himself. He will believe that he can express it to himself only if he illegitimately allows himself to use words of our common language as the vehicle of his soliloquy. But he has no right to use any of *our* words to refer to what he forever denies us access to.

Wittgenstein's blunt rejection of the thesis of the essential privacy of pain and his critique of philosophical scepticism about the minds of other people is closely connected with the failure of private ostensive definition. Both the other minds sceptic and the believer in private ostensive definition help themselves to a notion of sameness without being prepared to accept the requirement the use of the notion implies. Whereas the believer in private ostensive definition needs an intrasubjective notion of sameness but cannot specify a criterion of identity that would give content to the idea, the other minds sceptic needs an intersubjective notion of sameness, i.e. a notion of sameness to apply across people's sensations (or other mental states), but can maintain his scepticism – which is thereby rendered incoherent – only by failing to specify a criterion

of identity. These failings are, of course, two sides of the same coin: the idea of a kind of sensation has content only if it has *both* an intrasubjective and intersubjective application; and the criterion of sameness across persons is all-important, since your application of a name you understand to your present sensation is criterionless (Wittgenstein, 1953, §§374–82).

MENTAL REPRESENTATION

A major theme of Wittgenstein's later philosophy is his opposition to a 'mentalistic' conception of someone's meaning, understanding, or intending something by something he does or encounters; and the target he aims at is not restricted to these central instances but includes many other cases in which a person's state is directed towards an object or has an intentional content, as in propositional remembering, imagining, thinking, wishing or expecting. (*See* INTENTIONALITY.)

There are two principal propositions that Wittgenstein advances against the mentalistic conception, and these define the mentalistic view he opposes. First, the intentional CONTENT of a state is not an 'experience': meaning, understanding, intending, propositional remembering, thinking, and so on, do not have an experiential content (Wittgenstein, 1953, II, pp. 216–17, 231). The prime reason that this is so is that the intentional content of these mental states lacks the kind of duration characteristic of an experience: unlike a pain, which you can begin to experience at a certain moment, endure for a time, and which might suddenly cease, there is no question of your thought that p beginning at a moment, continuing and then coming to an end. An intentional state of one of these kinds does not consist in the continuous presence to consciousness of its intentional content, as a pain can remain present to consciousness. In fact, 'meaning', 'understanding' and 'thinking a thought' are not the names of processes of any kind, and so not the names of conscious processes. A thought is neither 'articulated' nor 'non-articulated': it is neither a series of distinguishable phases of a process occurring in a segment of time nor a uniform state lasting from one point of time to another. It follows that an individual's linguistic expressions of his thoughts, memories, intentions, or expectations are not infallible reports of essentially private processes that take place in him when he thinks, remembers, intends or expects. Second, whether a subject is in a state with a certain intentional content is not determined by the intrinsic, non-relational nature of anything that happens to the subject when in the state but is dependent upon what else is true of the subject, and the context in which the subject is located. The significance of any occurrence, even an occurrence in the individual's consciousness, is a matter of how it is embedded in the individual's life and the interpretation he gives it. If we consider in isolation anything that happens in someone when he thinks the thought that p – if we abstract it from the individual's past, his present capacities and dispositions, and the prevailing circumstances – we will fail to find anything to ground the attribution of that thought to the person. Even if the occurrence is one the subject is aware of, how he understands or intends it is not a state of consciousness but a matter of the use he makes of it. Moreover, it is not a condition of someone's thinking the thought that p that he should be aware of *anything* happening in him when he thinks the thought. We must therefore change our focus and look elsewhere, in particular at how the individual would represent his thought if he were to give it expression. For the subject's sincere expression of his state in words – what memory, understanding, intention or thought the subject would attribute to himself – is criterial of the state's content. The common conception of a person's accounts of his memories, intentions or thoughts needs to be turned upside down. Rather than looking at a subject's sincere assertion of what he means, remembers, intends, understands or expects as a report, somehow automatically guaranteed to be

correct, of an occurrence the nature of which he monitors at the moment it happens, his verbal expression should be seen as being definitive of the content of his mental state. His mental state does not have a nature that is logically independent of how he would express it: there is no state with an intrinsic nature specifiable independently of the subject's disposition to express it by an utterance of 'p' (or some synonymous sentence) which the subject reports when he confesses his thought that p. This might seem to render problematic an individual's ability to attribute thoughts to himself, a mystery that can be removed only by an explanation of this ability. But remember that Wittgenstein's aim is not to *explain* anything, in this case an individual's ability to attribute thoughts to himself. Rather, he wants to encourage a clear understanding of the language-game played with the word 'thought'. Hence he supplements the identification of a person's utterance of his thought as a criterion of the thought by drawing attention to the circumstances in which it would be appropriate to attribute a thought to someone and to the consequences of such an attribution; for at the level of a description of the language-game, there is nothing more to do. As he says, the significance of a truthful confession of a thought resides, not in its being a true description of a process hidden from all but the thinker, but in 'the special consequences which can be drawn from a confession whose truth is guaranteed by the special criteria of *truthfulness*' (Wittgenstein, 1953, II, p. 222).

Wittgenstein's approach to the philosophy of mind is rooted in and dictated by his philosophy of language (and hence his philosophy of philosophy). The meaning of a word is its use in the language, and understanding a word is mastery of the language-games in which it figures – not something that underlies and explains that mastery (such as an awareness of the nature of what the word refers to). Furthermore, language-games are heterogeneous and do not need to conform to or be reducible to some paradigm of language use (as was required by the so-called 'picture theory' of the *Tractatus*). Hence when we have described, compared and contrasted the various language-games played with psychological words, which often ramify in ways that preclude a simple description, there is nothing for philosophy to do except to expose false accounts and to diagnose the insidious seductiveness of such misconceptions.

Wittgenstein's philosophy of mind represents a radical break with the past. For his investigation of psychological concepts shows that the traditional philosophical picture of the mind is a fantasy. We have seen that the expression of our mental events in words is wrongly thought of as the report of essentially private occurrences that we observe within ourselves and that we can only conjecture in others. Furthermore, mental words are not such that we are able to understand them only in virtue of being directly acquainted in our own case with what they refer to – thus possessing exemplars that guide our use of the terms. Accordingly, the mind is not an internal microcosm, the contents of which are inevitably hidden from everyone but the subject, who, in contradistinction from others, has direct and infallible access to whatever takes place in his inner world.

See also BEHAVIOURISM; SUBJECTIVITY.

BIBLIOGRAPHY

Budd, M. 1989. *Wittgenstein's Philosophy of Psychology*. London: Routledge & Kegan Paul.

Geach, P.T., ed. 1988. *Wittgenstein's Lectures on Philosophical Psychology 1946–47* London: Harvester Wheatsheaf.

Wittgenstein, L. 1953. *Philosophical Investigations*, trans. G. E. M. Anscombe. Oxford: Basil Blackwell.

Wittgenstein, L. 1960. *The Blue and Brown Books*. Oxford: Basil Blackwell.

Wittgenstein, L. 1980. *Remarks on the Philosophy of Psychology*, 2 vols, trans. G. E. M. Anscombe. Oxford: Basil Blackwell.

Wittgenstein, L. 1982. *Last Writings on the Philosophy of Psychology*, vol. 1, trans. C. G. Luckhardt and M. A. E. Aue. Oxford: Basil Blackwell.

MALCOLM BUDD

Index

Note: Page references in **bold** type indicate chief discussions of major topics or persons. References in *italics* indicate figures. Where names of contributors to the *Companion* are indexed, the references are to citations in articles other than their own or to specific articles describing their own philosophy.